SEMANTIC DIFFERENTIAL TECHNIQUE

A SOURCEBOOK

edited by

JAMES G. SNIDER
INTERNATIONAL DIVISION,
AMERICAN INSTITUTES FOR RESEARCH

and

CHARLES E. OSGOOD
INSTITUTE OF COMMUNICATIONS RESEARCH,
UNIVERSITY OF ILLINOIS

ALDINE PUBLISHING COMPANY / *Chicago*

First published 1969 by
ALDINE Publishing Company
529 South Wabash Avenue
Chicago, Illinois 60605

Library of Congress Catalog Card Number 68-19874
Published in the United States of America

ABOUT THE EDITORS

James G. Snider received his Ph.D. from Stanford University and has taught at the University of Idaho, Foothills College, and the University of Calgary. He is Senior Research Scientist at the American Institutes for Research (International Division) and is now with the Test Development and Research Office of the West African Examinations Council in Lagos, Nigeria. He has contributed many articles to the literature.

A lifelong interest in words and meanings had almost convinced Charles E. Osgood to become a writer. However, at Dartmouth College he became interested in psychology and went on to receive a doctorate in the field at Yale University. After a short period of teaching at the University of Connecticut, he went to the University of Illinois and its then new Institute of Communications Research. It was at Illinois that Professor Osgood began working in earnest on what is now known as semantic differential technique. His research endeavors resulted in The Measurement of Meaning in 1957. This book had an enormous impact on the field of psychology and has since become important to all the behavioral sciences. Charles Osgood is Professor of Psychology and Research Professor of Communications at the University of Illinois.

SEMANTIC DIFFERENTIAL TECHNIQUE

Preface

Over the past sixteen years or more, the semantic differential technique has gradually captured the imagination of psychologists. During this time they have used the technique in a tremendous variety of studies, and, in recent years, hundreds of articles using the technique have appeared in professional journals. From a few scattered uses, the semantic differential technique has come to play an important role in almost all of the behavioral sciences and in many applied areas.

Because of the proliferation of literature in which the technique has been used, an understanding of it has become increasingly difficult to obtain. The quantity and diversity of its literature is today almost overwhelming. A comprehensive bibliography—as well as information on its methodology, validity, and uses is needed.

This book is intended as a sourcebook to meet these needs. It should be interesting and useful to sophisticated and beginning experimenters alike, since it brings together for the first time in one volume as many as possible of the materials that adequately and accurately illustrate the origins, history, criticism, methodology, validity, and specific uses of the semantic differential technique. Also included are a *Semantic Atlas for 550 Concepts* and an extensive bibliography.

The selection of materials was guided by several criteria. First, we included those references that have proved their enduring relevance, as shown by their repeated quotation in the literature. Following this, we considered materials according to their relevance to the semantic differential—if they investigated the technique directly or if they used it as the principal instrument. Finally, we considered articles that illustrated well the application of the technique to some particular area of psychology.

Part I contains writings on the origin and nature of the semantic differential technique, followed by materials from *The Measurement of Meaning*. The major reviews, pro and con, of that book are presented in Part II, followed by methodological and validity studies in Parts III and IV. Part V presents the generality checks—across concepts, across language groups and culture groups. Finally, the rest of the book is a delineation of the applications, in developmental and experimental psychology (Parts VI and VII), in social psychology (Part VIII), in personality and clinical psychology (Part IX), and in esthetics and communications research (Part X).

A *Semantic Atlas for 550 Concepts* is appended in the expectation that researchers in a variety of disciplines may find it useful, even though it is limited to American English speakers. A paper by Osgood (1964) in Part V describes the cross-cultural project within which these data were collected. The data are more extensive than those published by Jenkins, Russell, and Suci (1958) and are based on scales of pan-culturally general factorial composition. The present *Atlas* can be used directly to test hypotheses and also as a source of verbal materials having known affective loadings.

The bibliography also should be valuable to researchers. These references are the joint effort of the editors and Dr. Conrad R. Hill, of Rhode Island University, to whom we are very grateful. Every attempt has been made to be as thorough as possible in collection, but it is obviously not possible to be completely exhaustive or completely up-to-date. New studies using the semantic differential appear regularly. However, the present bibliography is almost certainly the most recent and most complete.

Any venture of this sort must end with compromise, a compromise with space. Of the hundreds of articles included in the appended bibliography, covering the broad span of the behavioral and social sciences, we could choose only about fifty to represent somehow the history, development, properties, and uses of the semantic differential technique. It was painful to have to choose among so many excellent alternatives for each Part, and many important contributions had to be excluded.

This book will be used primarily by research workers and students in the behavioral and social sciences, particularly those concerned with language and communication. For the researcher, it will be a useful reference work. For students, it will provide an introduction to the technique, an overview and sampling of its many uses, and sources for its utilization in research. Although the book is intended essentially as a sourcebook, it can also serve as a supplemental text for courses in psycholinguistics, communications, and related areas.

Since this is the first sourcebook of readings on the semantic differential technique, there is little evidence upon which to predict the needs of those using such a book. It may be found that the book does not meet these needs as well as was hoped. For the sake of possible future revision, the editors would be interested to learn the reactions and suggestions of readers.

Many techniques of measurement are proposed in psychology, but few are chosen for consistent use. The semantic differential has apparently been one of those chosen, probably because it was designed to get at a very important variable in human behavior —meaning—and because it is extremely flexible in application. In any case, the technique appears to have a future. We hope that this sourcebook will contribute to that future.

This co-editor owes his greatest debt of gratitude to Charles Osgood. Having been for many years an admirer of Charles Osgood and for several years a semantic differential user, it was a rare pleasure to work with the "grand-daddy" of the semantic differential on a sourcebook on the technique! It is to Charles Osgood that so many of us in the behavioral sciences who are interested in language and meaning owe a debt of gratitude, for the semantic differential and for many other things. It is my privilege to express some of that gratitude through the co-editorship of this volume.

JAMES G. SNIDER

Introduction

Both the co-editor of this sourcebook on the semantic differential technique, James G. Snider, and the publisher, Alexander J. Morin of Aldine Publishing Company, have asked me to write a personal introduction, saying some things about the technique's origin and development not likely to be found in the literature. I am happy to comply with this request to the best of my ability and recollection, but the reader must realize that there is much of it I have forgotten and that some probably was never available to me consciously.

At the conclusion of talks on the semantic differential, I am sometimes asked just how it was that the idea of measuring meaning this way occurred to me originally. Of course, it didn't "occur" to me; it sort of "grew" on me. My Grandfather Osgood was a successful dentist in Boston who was always frustrated because he had not become a college professor. As early as I can remember, he played all kinds of word games with me, teasing out subtle distinctions in meaning, giving me lists of relatively rare words to memorize, and rewarding me with penny candies when I used them spontaneously and correctly. Miss Grace Osgood, or Auntie Grae as I called her then (and do still), was a student at Wellesley College and soon to become a teacher at Thayer School in Braintree; she listened in on these games and on my tenth birthday (I believe it was) gave me Roget's *Thesaurus*—probably to even the odds a bit with Granpa O!

I remember spending hours and hours exploring the *Thesaurus*, not as a tool but as an object of esthetic pleasure. I also recall my visual representation of the *Thesaurus*— a vivid and colorful image of words as clusters of starlike points in an immense space. I have always been a visualizer, which may explain why I did well in geometry but miserably in algebra. Soon after

this, I began what I thought was to be a career as a writer, and then I did use the *Thesaurus* as a tool. Since I was already devouring all the fantasy, horror, and science fiction I could lay my hands on—an appetite acquired from my father—naturally my earliest efforts dealt with oozy monsters from the crypts of ancient castles, armies of giant ants sweeping the earth, and suchlike.

The notion of a semantic space, potentially quantifiable, lay dormant until I had been at Dartmouth College for a couple of years. I had gone with the vague idea that I would get experience on the college newspaper while studying English literature and creative writing, and then I would support myself by newspaper work while writing the Great American Novel. But as a sophomore I happened to take introductory psychology and then an advanced course with the late Professor Theodore F. Karwoski, affectionately known on campus as "The Count." I found what I had been looking for all the time, the right combination of demand for rigor and room for creativity, and I forgot about writing the Great American Novel.

Karwoski was a most remarkable person —quietly insightful, capable of thinking simultaneously on several levels and moving between them, warmly supportive (my own father had died when I was 13), and thoroughly disorderly. If one could dedicate a book of readings to anyone, this one would be to "The Count." At the point when I moved into his life, he was doing casual experiments on color-music synesthesia and, more importantly, thinking deeply about their implications for human thinking. He had the notion of "parallel polarity" among dimensions of experience (e.g., visual *bright-dark* and auditory *loud-soft*) and conceived of synesthesia as translation across equivalent portions of the dimensions thus made parallel. This, of course, is a complex and continuous case of what would be called "metaphor" in language. Karwoski's associate in this research was a younger man from Harvard, Henry Odbert, who had done his thesis research on the semantics of personality traits under Gordon Allport. Later Ross Stagner brought to Dartmouth his interests in attitude measurement and in the issues of peace and war—with World War II just over the horizon.

It would be hard to imagine an intellectual environment better suited to a youngster with visions of semantic space in his head. Out of my intimate apprenticeship with these men—more intimate and exciting than most graduate students are privileged to have in these crowded days—came studies of parallelism of visual and auditory dimensions, as observed both in complex synesthetes and in the descriptive adjectives of ordinary language, studies on the generality of such dimensional parallelisms across cultures, as derived from firsthand ethnographic studies (I was a minor in anthropology), and studies of the changing meanings of critical concepts as the United States moved closer to and then, with Pearl Harbor, into World War II. The latter studies, with Ross Stagner, employed the rating of concepts against 7-step scales defined by verbal opposites, which was to later become embodied in our semantic differential work—but the multidimensional conception was lacking, nearly all scales being attitudinal (evaluative) in nature.

After an extra year at Dartmouth beyond my degree—during which I served as everything from research associate to mimeograph operator and got used to being married—I went to Yale for graduate work. It could have been Harvard or Princeton (Yale merely offered me a better assistantship), and I have sometimes wondered what kind of a psychologist I would have been if I had made a different choice. Like nearly everyone else at Yale at the time, I was swept up into the monumental edifice of learning theory that Clark Hull was building,

and I had the heady feeling that here, with appropriate elaborations, lay the key to even the most complex of human behaviors, including language. Visions of semantic space receded, but the problem of dealing with meaning in learning theory terms came to the fore. My doctoral thesis, among other things, was a test of a theory of meaning based upon reciprocally antagonistic, mediating reaction systems. I owe a debt of gratitude to Donald G. Marquis for keeping my interest in language alive during this period, as well as to Charles Morris, who came to Yale as a visitor at the end of my stay there. It would have been so easy to become a ratpusher.

The next few years were spent teaching at the University of Connecticut and writing like mad on what I thought was to be an introductory text for Oxford University Press, *Method and Theory in Experimental Psychology*. Then came one of those bolts from the blue that young academics pray for: the possibility of becoming a tenured, associate professor (at a tenderer age than was then usually the case), engineered jointly by Ross Stagner, Hobart Mowrer, and Wilbur Schramm, then at the University of Illinois—the latter Director of a new Institute of Communications Research in which I might have half-time on pure research! These gentlemen, understandably enough, wanted to know what I would be doing with my research time, and this is when I brought my vision of semantic space out of wherever one stores such things.

It was just about this time that the possibilities in factor analysis were beginning to stir the minds of psychologists interested in things other than intellectual abilities. I could see factor analysis as a means of giving order and perhaps a bit of elegance to my vague and disorderly image of semantic space. At the core of my proposal for research on language and communication was a program of studies exploring the dimensionality of human meaning systems, using a general model that combined mediation learning theory with factor analytic technique. It also just so happened that Illinois was already a hotbed of multivariate statistics, including Lee Cronbach and Ray Cattell. Somehow, I got the job; somehow, also, I got support for research into what then was certainly considered a rather esoteric area—meaning. For this I must thank Wilbur Schramm (who was willing to gamble Institute funds on me), the University of Illinois Research Board (which regularly takes overhead funds from those who hath and delivers them to those who hath not), and to the Social Science Research Council (which offered me a two-year research fellowship).

With these supports—very modest by today's standards, I might say—I was able to gather around me a small but dedicated group of colleagues, including other young faculty, graduate students, and even some very bright undergraduates. Particularly I should mention George Suci and Percy Tannenbaum, my first two Ph.D. students, the former in psychology and the latter in communications. There were many others who in doctoral or master's theses and in service as research associates (called assistants and paid as such, of course) contributed to a gradually expanding program. I dare not mention some for fear that I might forget others. Some things I really get nostalgic about now, when I function more as research facilitator than research doer: the interminable and exciting debates about our work, over data tables, over coffee tables, and even over cocktail glasses—it was wonderfully never-ending; constructing our first solid model of a semantic space—for 40 emotion labels—out of dowels and little rubber balls with Al Heyer, and getting so tired that everything became incredibly funny; and George Suci's spending six months growling over a desk calculator computing our first factor analysis, while we tried to figure out mathematical shortcuts.

The results of these research endeavors are in *The Measurement of Meaning* (1957) —whose original clothboard version didn't have an index because Suci, Tannenbaum, and I never thought it would be anything more than a research monograph. For reasons that are not at all clear to me, the notion of a quantifiable semantic space caught the imaginations of others, and the past ten years have witnessed a minor explosion of studies about or using the technique—the appended bibliography records as much of it as we have been able to locate.

I must confess that sometimes I feel like the Geppetto of a wayward Pinocchio who has wandered off into the Big City, and Lord knows what mischief he is getting into. Some people think Pinocchio is a specific standardized test; he is not, of course, being subject to concept/scale interaction. Some think he is a measure of meaning-in-general; he is not, of course, reflecting primarily affective meaning by virtue of the metaphorical usage of his scales. And in recent years Pinocchio has been trotting around the world, introducing himself to people who speak different languages and enjoy different cultures; but in these travels, Geppetto has at least been able to keep a hand on the puppet's strings.

In reading over this little introduction, I realize it is not only quite personal but also just a bit maudlin. I let it go as is, however, because I suspect that any scientist's reminiscences are likely to have a similar tone. After all, science-in-process as contrasted with science-in-document *is* an intensely personal business. I am pleased and honored that Aldine Publishing Company saw fit to publish a book of readings on the semantic differential technique and that James Snider saw fit to include me in the editorial task. I regret that so many significant and intriguing studies, including some by my closest friends and associates, had to be omitted.

CHARLES E. OSGOOD

Contents

Part I

ORIGIN AND NATURE
OF THE SEMANTIC
DIFFERENTIAL TECHNIQUE

1. The Nature and Measurement of Meaning

Charles E. Osgood

The language process within an individual may be viewed as a more or less continuous interaction between two parallel systems of behavioral organization: sequences of central events ("ideas") and sequences of instrumental skills, vocalic, gestural, or orthographic, which constitute the communicative product. A communicator vocalizes, "It looks like rain today; I'd better not wash the car." This output is a sequence of skilled movements, complicated to be sure, but not different in kind from tying one's shoes. Even the smallest units of the product, phonetic elements like the initial "l"-sound of "looks," result from precisely patterned muscle movements. The organization of these movements into word-units represents skill sequences of relatively high predictability; certain longer period sequences involving syntactical order are also relatively predictable for a given language system. But execution of such sequences brings the communicator repeatedly to what may be called "choice-points"—points where the next skill sequence is not highly predictable from the objective communicative product itself. The dependence of "I'd better not wash the car" upon "looks like rain today," the *content* of the message, reflects determinants within the semantic system which effectively "load" the transitional probabilities at these choice-points.

It is the communicative product, the spoken or written words which follow one another in varying orders, that we typically observe. Since we are unable to specify the stimuli which evoke these communicating reactions—since it is "emitted" rather than "elicited" behavior in Skinner's terminology (97)—measurements in terms of rates of occurrence and transitional probabilities (dependence of one event in the stream upon others) are particularly appropriate (cf., Miller, 76). Interest may be restricted to the lawfulness of sequences in the observable communicative product itself, without regard to the semantic parallel. This is traditionally the field of the linguist, but even here it has proved necessary to make some assumptions about meaning (cf., Bloomfield, 4). On the other hand, one may be specifically interested in the semantic or ideational level. Since he is presently unable to observe this level of behavior directly, he must use observable characteristics of the com-

Reprinted from *Psychological Bulletin* (1952), 49: 197–237, by permission of the author and the American Psychological Association.

municative product as a basis for making inferences about what is going on at the semantic level. He may use sequential orderliness in the product to draw conclusions as to semantic orderliness in the speaker's or writer's mediation processes (i.e., which "ideas" tend to go together in his thinking with greater than chance probabilities). Or he may wish to study the ways in which central, semantic processes vary from concept to concept, from person to person, and so on. It is the problem of measuring meaning in this latter sense which will be discussed in the present paper.

Before inquiring into the measurement of the meaning of signs, for which there are no accepted, standardized techniques available, we may briefly mention certain fairly standard methods for measuring the comparative strength of verbal habits. Thorndike and his associates (102, 103) have made extensive *frequency-of-usage counts* of words in English; that this method gets at the comparative habit strengths of word skill sequences is shown by the fact that other measures of response strength, such as latency and probability within the individual (Thumb and Marbe, 106; Cason and Cason, 19), are correlated with frequency-of-usage. Zipf (117, 118, and elsewhere) has described innumerable instances of the lawfulness of such habit-strength measures. Whether samples be taken from Plautine Latin, newspaper English, or the English of James Joyce in his *Ulysses*, a fundamental regularity is found, such that frequency of occurrence of particular words bears a linear relation to their rank order in frequency, when plotted on double-log paper (Zipf's Law). Measurement of flexibility or diversity in communicative products is given by the *type-token ratio* (TTR): with each instance of any word counting as a token and each different word as a type, the greater the ratio of types to tokens the more varied is the content of a message. This measure can be applied comparatively to different forms of material, different kinds of individuals, and so forth (cf., Carroll, 16, 17; Johnson, 45; Chotlos, 20), provided the sizes of samples are constant. One may also count the ratios of adjectives to verbs (Boder, 5), the frequencies of different pronouns, intensives, and so forth (cf., Johnson, 45).

Although the above measures get at the comparative strengths of verbal skill sequences per se (i.e., without regard to meaning), this is not a necessary restriction. Frequency counts of this type can be applied to *semantic habit strengths* as well. Skinner (96) has shown that a similar lawfulness applies to the frequencies of "free" associations in the Kent-Rosanoff tests. When frequencies of particular associates to given stimulus words for a group of subjects are plotted against their rank order in frequency, a straight-line function on double-log paper results (Zipf's Law). In other words, associations at the semantic level appear to be organized in such a way that few have very high probability of occurrence and many have low probabilities of occurrence. Bousfield and his collaborators (**7, 8, 9, 10, 11**) have described a *sequential association method* for getting at comparative semantic habit strengths. When subjects associate successively from the same "pool," e. g.,"names of four-legged animals," (*a*) the rate of successive associates shows a negatively accelerated curve, (*b*) varying in its constants with certain characteristics of materials and subjects, (*c*) the order of appearance of particular associates in individuals being predictable from the frequency of usage in the group, and (*d*) distortions in the function being related to particular transitional probabilities among associates, i.e., clustering. Useful though these measures are for many purposes, they do not get at meaning. The fact that "dog" has a higher probability of occurrence in sequential association than "otter" says nothing whatsoever about the differences in meaning of these two signs.

An extensive survey of the literature fails to uncover any generally accepted, standardized method for measuring meaning. Perhaps it is because of the philosophical haziness of this concept, perhaps because of the general belief that "meanings" are infinitely and uniquely variable, or perhaps because the word "meaning" as a construct in our language connotes mental stuff, more akin to "thought" and "soul" than to anything observable—for some combination of reasons there has been little attempt to devise methods here. Nevertheless, whether looked at from the viewpoints of philosophy or linguistics, from economic or sociological theory, or—interestingly enough—from within the core of psychological theories of individual behavior, the nature of meaning and change in meaning are found to be central issues. The proposals to be made in the latter portion of this paper are part of a program aimed at the development of objective methods of measuring meaning. Beyond obvious social implications, it is felt that this direction of research is a logical extension of scientific inquiry into an area generally considered immune to its attack.

THEORIES OF MEANING

Not all stimuli are signs. The shock which galvanizes a rat into vigorous escape movements usually does not stand for anything other than itself, nor does the pellet of food found at the end of a maze, nor a hammer in one's hand or a shoe on one's foot. The problem for any meaning theorist is to differentiate the conditions under which a pattern of stimulation is a sign of something else from those conditions where it is not. This certainly seems simple enough, yet it has troubled philosophers for centuries. By stating the problem somewhat formally, the chief differences between several conceptions of the sign-process can be made evident: let

$\dot{S}$ = object = any pattern of stimulation which evokes reactions on the part of an organism, and

Ⓢ = sign = any pattern of stimulation which is not this S but yet evokes reactions relevant to $\dot{S}$—conditions under which this holds being the problem for theory.

The definition of $\dot{S}$ is broad enough to include any pattern of stimulation which elicits any reaction from an organism. Although one usually thinks of "objects" as those things denoted by signs, actually any pattern of stimulation—a gust of northerly wind against the face, the sensations we call "belly-ache," the sensations of being rained upon—is an "object" at this level of discourse. One sign may be the "object" represented by another sign, as when the picture of an apple is called "DAX" in certain experiments. The definition of Ⓢ is purposely left incomplete at this point, since it depends upon one's conception of the nature of the sign-process.

We may start a logical analysis of the problem with a self-evident fact: *the pattern of stimulation which is the sign is never identical with the pattern of stimulation which is the object.* The word "hammer" is not the same stimulus as is the object hammer. The former is a pattern of sound waves having characteristic oscillations in frequency and intensity; the latter, depending upon its mode of contact, may be a visual form having characteristic color and shape, a pattern of tactual and proprioceptive sensations, and so on. Similarly, the buzzer in a typical rat experiment is not identical as a form of stimulation with the shock which it comes to signify. Yet these signs—the word "hammer" and the buzzer—do elicit behaviors which are in some manner relevant to the objects they signify, a characteristic *not* shared with an infinite number of other stimulus patterns that are *not* signs of these objects. In simplest terms, therefore, the question is: *under what conditions does something which is not an object become a sign of that object?* According to the way in which this question is answered we may distinguish several theories of meaning.

Mentalistic View

The classic interpretation derives directly from the natural philosophy of Western culture, in which the dualistic connotations of language dictate a correlation between two classes of events, material and nonmaterial. Since meanings are obviously "mental" events and the stimuli representing objects and signs are obviously "physical" events, any satisfying theory of meaning must specify interrelation between these levels of discourse. At the core of all mentalistic views, therefore, we find an "idea" as the essence of meaning; it is this mental event which links or relates the two different physical events, sign and object. The word "hammer" gives rise to the idea of that object in the mind; conversely, perception of the object hammer gives rise to the same idea, which can then be "expressed" in appropriate signs. In other words, *something which is not the object becomes a sign of that object when it gives rise to the idea associated with that object.* Probably the most sophisticated expression of this view is given by Ogden and Richards (82) in their book, *The Meaning of Meaning.* Most readers will recall their triangular diagram of the sign-process: the relation between symbol and referent (the base of their triangle) is not direct but inferred, mediated through mental "thought" or "interpretation" (the third corner of their triangle).

Substitution View

Naive application of Pavlovian conditioning principles by early behaviorists like Watson led to the theory that signs achieve their meanings simply by being conditioned to the same reactions originally made to objects. This, in essence, is the view one encounters in many introductory texts in general psychology. An object evokes certain behavior in an organism; if another pattern of stimulation is consistently paired with the original object, it becomes conditioned to the same responses and thus gets its meaning. The object is the unconditioned stimulus and the sign is the conditioned stimulus, the latter merely being substituted for the former. The definition of the sign-process here is that *whenever something which is not the object evokes in an organism the same reactions evoked by the object, it is a sign of that object.* The very simplicity of this theory highlights its inadequacy. Signs almost never evoke the *same* overt responses as do the objects they represent. The word FIRE has meaning to the reader without sending him into headlong flight. Nevertheless, this represents a first step toward a behavioral interpretation of the sign-process.

Meaning as "Set" or "Disposition"

In a monograph entitled *Foundation of the Theory of Signs* (77), Charles Morris, a semiotician working in the tradition established by Peirce and other American pragmatists, proposed a formula for the sign-process which avoids the pitfalls of substitution theory but seems to step backward toward the mentalistic view. In essence he states that signs achieve their meanings by eliciting reactions which "take account of" the objects signified. The sign "hammer" may evoke quite different responses from those evoked by the object signified, but these responses must have the character of being relevant to the object. The response made to the sign is called the "interpretant" which mediately takes account of the object signified. But it would seem that this process of "taking account of" is precisely what needs elucidation.

During the period intervening between this monograph and his recent book, *Signs, Language and Behavior* (78), Morris studied with two prominent behavior theorists, Tolman and Hull. The effects of this immersion in learning theory are evident in his book, which is a pioneer attempt to reduce semiotic to an objective behavioral basis. He states that "if anything, A, is a preparatory stimulus which in the absence of stimulus-objects initiating response-sequences of a certain behavior-family causes a disposition in some organism to respond under certain conditions by response-sequences of this behavior-family, then *A* is a sign" (p. 10). Reduced to its essentials and translated into our terms, this becomes: *any pattern of stimulation which is not the object becomes a sign of that object if it produces in an organism a "disposition" to make any of the responses previously elicited by that object.* There is no requirement that the *overt* reactions originally elicited by the object also be made to the sign; the sign merely creates a disposition or set to make such reactions, actual occurrence depending upon the concurrence of supporting conditions.

Beyond the danger that "dispositions" may serve as mere surrogates for "ideas" in this theory, there are certain other difficulties with the view as stated. For one thing, Morris seems to have revived the substitution notion. The sign is said to dispose the organism to make overt response-sequences of the *same* behavior-family originally elicited by the object. But is this necessarily the case? Is my response to the word "apple" (e.g., free-associating the word "peach") any part of the behavior-family elicited by the object apple? For another thing, Morris' formulation fails to differentiate sign-behavior from many instinctive reactions and from ordinary conditioning. To appreciate this difficulty will require a brief digression.

When a breach is made in a termite nest, the workers set up a distinctive pounding upon the floor of the tunnel and the warriors come charging to the spot, where they take up defensive positions. Is this pounding sound a sign to the warrior-termites that there is a breach in the nest? It happens that this behavior is purely instinctive, and most students of sign-behavior believe that signs must achieve their signification through *learning*. But is learning a sufficient criterion? Are all stimuli that elicit learned reactions automatically signs? In developing any skill, such as tying the shoes, the proprioceptive stimuli produced by one response become conditioned to the succeeding response—but of what are these proprioceptive stimuli signs? With repeated experience on an electrified grill a rat will often learn to rear up on its hind legs and alternately lift them, this act apparently reducing the total intensity of pain—the painful stimulation is thus conditioned to a new response, but of what is the pain a sign?

If only some of the stimuli which elicit learned responses are signs, we must seek a reasonable distinction *within* the class of learned behaviors. We cannot draw a line between human and subhuman learning: the buzzer is operationally as much a sign of shock to the rat in avoidance-training experiments as are dark clouds a sign of rain to the professor—both stimuli elicit reactions appropriate, not to themselves, but to something other than themselves. Is voluntariness of response a criterion? Meaningful reactions may be just as involuntary as perceptions—try to observe a familiar word and avoid its meaning! Is it variability of response to the stimulus? Meaningful reactions may be just as stable and habitual as motor skills.

The Mediation Hypothesis

I shall try to show that the distinguishing condition of sign behavior is the presence or absence of *a representational mediation process* in association with the stimulus. This conception of sign behavior is based upon a general theory of learning rather than being concocted specifically to account for meaning as seen in human communication.[3] The essence of the viewpoint can be given as follows:

1. *Stimulus-objects* ($\dot{S}$) *elicit a complex pattern of reactions from the organism, these reactions varying in their dependence upon presence of the stimulus-object for their occurrence.* Electric shock galvanizes the rat into vigorous jumping, squeaking, and running activities, as well as autonomic "anxiety" reactions. Food objects elicit sequences of salivating, chewing, lip-smacking, and so forth. Components like salivating and "anxiety" are relatively independent of the food or shock stimulation respectively and hence can occur when such objects are not present.

2. *When stimuli other than the stimulus-object, but previously associated with it, are later presented without its support, they tend to elicit some reduced portion of the total behavior elicited by the stimulus-object.* This reduction process follows certain laws: (*a*) mediating reactions which interfere with goal-achievement tend to extinguish; (*b*) the more energy expenditure involved in making a particular reaction, the less likely it is to survive the reduction process; (*c*) there is evidence that certain reactions (e.g., autonomic) condition more readily than others (e.g., gross skeletal) and hence are more likely to become part of the mediation process—this may merely reflect factor (*b*) above.

3. *The fraction of the total object-elicited behavior which finally constitutes the stable mediation process elicited by a sign* ($\boxed{S}$) *will tend toward a minimum set by the discriminatory capacity of the organism.* This is because the sole function of such mediating reactions in behavior is to provide a distinctive pattern of self-stimulation (cf., Hull's conception of the "pure stimulus act").

4. *The self-stimulation produced by sign-elicited mediation processes becomes conditioned in varying strengths to the initial responses in hierarchies of instrumental skill sequences.* This mediated self-stimulation is assumed to provide the "way of perceiving" signs or their "meaning," as well as mediating instrumental skill sequences—behaviors to signs which take account of the objects represented.

Whereas Morris linked sign and object through partial identity of object-produced and disposition-*produced* behaviors, we have linked sign and object through partial identity of the "disposition" *itself* with the behavior elicited by the object. Words represent things because they produce some replica of the actual behavior toward these things, as a mediation process. This is the crucial identification, the mechanism that ties particular signs to particular stimulus-objects and not to others. Stating the proposition formally: *a pattern of stimulation which is not the object is a sign of the object if it evokes in an organism a mediating reaction, this* (a) *being some fractional part of the total behavior elicited by the object and* (b) *producing distinctive self-stimulation that mediates responses which*

---

[3] This hypothesis, as an elaboration from Hullian theory (43), is described in my forthcoming book, *Method and Theory in Experimental Psychology*.

would not occur without the previous association of nonobject and object patterns of stimulation. This definition may be cumbersome, but all the limiting conditions seem necessary. The mediation process must include some part of the same behavior made to the object if the sign is to have its particularistic representing property. What we have done here, in a sense, is to make explicit what may be implicit in Morris' term "disposition." The second stipulation (*b*) adds the learning requirement—the response of warrior-termites to pounding on the tunnel floor is ruled out since it does not depend upon prior association of pounding with discovery of a breach in the nest.

Paradigm *A* in Figure 1 gives an abbreviated symbolic account of the development of a *sign*, according to the mediation hypothesis. Take for illustration the connotative meaning of the word SPIDER. The stimulus-object ($\dot{S}$), the visual pattern of hairy-legged insect body often encountered in a threat context provided by other humans, elicits a complex pattern of behavior (R_T), which in this case includes a heavy loading of autonomic "fear" activity. Portions of this total behavior to the spider-object become conditioned to the heard word, SPIDER. With repetitions of the sign sequence, the mediation process becomes reduced to some minimally effortful and minimally interfering replica— but still includes those autonomic reactions which confer a threatening significance upon this sign. This mediating reaction (r_m) produces a distinctive pattern of self-stimulation (s_m) which may elicit a variety of overt behaviors (R_X)—shivering and saying "ugh," running out of a room where a spider is said to be lurking, and even refusing a job in the South, which is said to abound in spiders.

The vast majority of signs used in ordinary communication are what we may term *assigns*—their meanings are literally "assigned" to them via association with other signs rather than via direct association with the objects represented. The word ZEBRA is understood by most six-year-olds, yet few of them have ever encountered zebra-objects themselves. They have seen pictures of them, been told they have stripes, run like horses, and are usually found wild. As indicated in Figure 1 (*B*), this new stimulus pattern, ZEBRA, "picks up" by the mechanisms already described portions of the mediating reactions already elicited by the primary signs. In learning to read, for example, the "little black bugs" on the printed page are definitely assigns; these visual patterns are seldom directly associated with the objects signified, but rather with auditory signs (created by the child and teacher as they verbalize). Obviously, the more quickly the child can learn to make the right noises to these visual stimuli (the modern phonetic approach to reading), the more quickly these new, visual assigns will acquire significance. The child already has meanings for HOUSE, DOG, and even TYPEWRITER as *heard* stimulus patterns, but these mediation processes must be assigned to *seen* stimulus patterns.

It is apparent from the foregoing that the meanings which different individuals have for the same signs will vary with their behaviors toward the objects represented. This is because the composition of the mediation process, which *is* the meaning of a sign, is entirely dependent

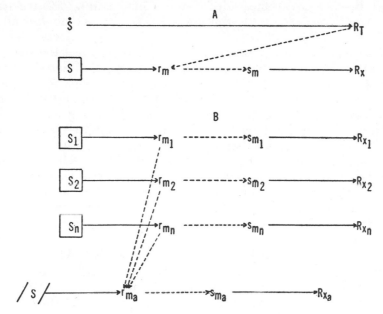

FIG. 1. SYMBOLIC ACCOUNT OF THE DEVELOPMENT OF SIGN PROCESSES:
A. DEVELOPMENT OF A SIGN; *B*. DEVELOPMENT OF AN ASSIGN.

upon the composition of the total behavior occurring while the sign-process is being established. This indicates that to change the meaning of signs we must change behavior with respect to objects (keeping in mind that the "objects" for assigns are other signs). On the other hand, meanings are quite independent of the stimulus characteristics of the signs themselves, a point repeatedly stressed by linguists. According to the present theory, there is nothing sacred about the particular mouth-noises we use in communication any more than there is about the buzzer that becomes a sign of shock to the rat—a flash of light or a blast of air would serve as well. Of course, in human communication (in contrast to sign-behavior in the rat) it is necessary that the users of signs be able to produce as well as receive them.

EVALUATION OF EXISTING TECHNIQUES OF MEASUREMENT

Physiological Methods

Meaning has been identified with representational mediation processes. Although no conclusive evidence as to the nature of these processes can be given at this time—whether they require participation of peripheral motor and glandular mechanisms or are sufficiently characterized as central phenomena—it is convenient to conceive of them as implicit response processes which produce self-stimulation. The meager evidence available certainly does not refute this view. In any case, the investigator is encouraged to see whether or not any physiological measures display covariance with changes in meaning. Correlates of this sort would be direct indices of meaning.

Action potentials in striate musculature. Working under the impetus given by the Würzburg School of imageless thought, introspective psychologists of another generation tried to tease out the sensory content of ideas. Students like Marbe (69), Clark (21), Washburn (110), Comstock (25) and Crosland (26) agreed in finding kinaesthetic sensations present as a residue when everything but "meaningful thought" was excluded. But here the limitations inherent in the introspective method made themselves apparent: pressed to the limits of critical self-analysis, the trained human observer reported vague muscular and organic sensations as being present during thought—but did these sensations constitute thoughts and meanings themselves or were they merely a background of bodily tonus? The method did not permit this kind of discrimination.

Experimentalists picked up the problem at precisely the point where the introspectionists had per force dropped it—was it possible that sufficiently sensitive apparatus could record the minimal motor events that eluded conscious analysis? Watson's (111) statement about thought being implicit speech was the "open sesame" for a small host of gadgeteers (Wyczoikowski, 116; Reed, 89; Clark, 22; Thorson, 104) who filled subjects' mouths with an astounding variety of mechanical devices and then had them both think and mumble unusual items like "psychology." That they found little or no correspondence between the movements made during thought and speech is not particularly surprising. The "thought" movements were results of irritation in all probability, and (contrary to Watson) there is no a priori reason to expect relevant mediation processes to be restricted to the organs of speech.

Apparatus of sufficient sensitivity came with the development of electrical methods of recording and amplifying action. Electrodes placed near the motor end-plates of efferent fibers pick up minute changes in potential which cause deflections in a sensitive string galvanometer. These signals are fed through a vacuum tube amplifier, magnified thousands of times, and recorded on photographic film. Using this method, Jacobsen (44) and Max (72, 73) obtained suggestive correlations between introspectively specifiable events and objectively recorded muscular events. Jacobsen showed, for example, that when a subject, trained in techniques of progressive relaxation, *imagines* lifting his right arm, distinctive potential changes are recorded from muscles in that member but not elsewhere. Max, using deaf-mutes as an ingenious control, was able to show that these individuals display more frequent and larger potential changes in the muscles controlling their fingers while solving mental problems and while dreaming than normal individuals; he also described a negative correlation between the magnitude of such implicit activity and intelligence scores, i.e., more intelligent subjects showed less overt activity.

Are these recordable motor events the mediating reactions (r_m) in the mediation processes we have specified as essential in sign behavior?

Does this technique provide an index for the presence or absence of meaning, its degree, and quality? This is an attractive possibility, but the index is a crude one. There is no way of "reading" the meaning of a sign to a subject from the recorded activity. The ultimate criterion of meaning is still introspection of the subject—he verbalizes meaning while the experimenter scurries about his periphery trying to pick it up on instruments, and when activity fails to appear at predicted locus *a* it is assumed it must be occurring at some other locus *b*. No satisfactory demonstration of the *necessity* of the motor component has been offered; meaning might be present without measurable motor activity which, when it does occur, is simply a specific overflow of excitation into motor pathways—an epiphenomenon. The same criticism applies with equal force to the other physiological correlates that have been studied.

Salivary reaction. Another pioneer investigation into the organic correlates of meaning was that by Razran (**87**), serving as his own subject. Meaningfulness of a series of signs was the independent variable, the stimuli being words for "saliva" in languages with which Razran had varying familiarity. Amount of salivary secretion was the dependent variable—following presentation of each stimulus, a dental cotton-roll was placed in his mouth for two minutes and its weight determined immediately afterward. As "meaningless" controls he used the Gaelic word for saliva, the nonsense syllables QER SUH, and periods of "blank consciousness." Salivation was greatest in his childhood tongue (Russian), next in his most proficient one (English), and less in three slightly known languages (French, Spanish, and Polish). The control conditions showed no differences among themselves, despite the fact that Razran "knew" the Gaelic word stood for saliva. This experiment demonstrates a relation between amount of salivation and degree of meaningfulness of signs to a sophisticated subject. We have here another feasible index of some aspect of meaning, albeit a very limited one.

The galvanic skin response. The GSR is one of several indices of autonomic activity, and to the extent that meanings include emotional components this measure should be useful. There are a large number of studies using the GSR that are remotely related to this problem: GSR is readily elicited by any warning or preparatory stimulus that precedes shock (Darrow and Heath, **28**; Switzer, **101**; Mowrer, **80**), and it, therefore, may serve as an indication that the preparatory stimulus has become a sign of shock. It has been used to index the intensity of pleasant or unpleasant connotations of words and experiences (Jones, **46**; Lynch, **63**). In connection with free association, GSR has been found to be a good indicator of the emotional effect of stimulus words (Jones and Wechsler, **47**). It is unfortunate, therefore, that the two most pertinent experiments in this area leave much to be desired in the way of methodological finesse.

Mason (**70**) asked this question: do changes in GSR accompany changes in meaning? What were called three types of change in meaning were studied: "certainty of meaning" (the expression of certainty by the subject as to the correctness of his recall in learning a list of nonsense syllables), "discovery of meaning" (the point in a series of readings of a trick sentence without punctuation at which the subject achieved insight), and "loss of meaning" (where the subject pressed a foot-pedal whenever the continuously vocalized word "tangerine" seemed to lose its meaning). Although the procedures and results of this experiment are reported in great detail, no tests of significance were employed and none of the necessary controls was introduced. In the first two experiments, for example, it is impossible to determine whether the deflections in GSR should be attributed to change in meaning or simply to vacillations in emotional stress (the latter seems quite likely). In the experiment on loss of meaning, no check was made to see what effect simply pressing the indicator pedal and seeing a signal light come on might have had upon GSR.

Bingham (3) measured psychogalvanic reaction to 72 words "selected from the educational and philosophical writings of John Dewey and Rabindranath Tagore as the most frequently occurring words in samples of 8,000 from each writer." After the galvanic measurements were made, the 50 undergraduate subjects rated the words on a three-point scale in terms of their personal meaningfulness, significance, and importance (combined into a single scale, MSI). These untrained subjects further introspected on the sensory content in the meaning of each of these words, being requested to report any visual, auditory, kinaesthetic, etc., imagery or sensations. Words having the highest MSI ratings yielded the greatest average change in skin resistance. High MSI words also had more "organic" sensory content, according to the introspections (the high "organic" content words were *intellectual*, *freedom*, *God*, *truth*, and *love*, in this order!). Much remains to be done in these directions.

Learning Methods

There are many learning studies employing meaningful materials, but rarely is meaning itself the experimental variable. Even where meaning has been deliberately varied, interest has generally centered on the effect upon learning rather than upon the use of learning as an index of meaning. Only the more relevant studies will be considered here.

Semantic generalization. When a reaction conditioned to one stimulus transfers to another, and the amount of transfer varies directly with the similarity between the two stimuli, we speak of stimulus generalization. The operations whereby semantic generalization is demonstrated are the same—except that the necessary similarities lie in meaning rather than in objective physical characteristics of the eliciting stimuli. There is no physical similarity between the *word* "blue" and light of 450 mμ yet generalization between such stimulations is easily demonstrated—we infer that the common overt reaction is mediated by some common implicit process. In the experiments to be summarized here, the precise nature of the overt reaction is unimportant—all the standard CR's have been used, salivation, GSR, finger retraction, pupillary reflex, and so on. Much of the research in this area is contributed by Russian investigators and, unfortunately, the available reports are mostly in the form of brief abstracts.

1. *From object to sign.* Kapustnik (**49**) set up conditioned salivary reactions to visual and auditory stimuli, transfer to verbal signs for the original cues being tested. Kotliarevsky (**59**) employed a cardio-vasomotor reflex: following conditioning to the sound of a bell, response to the word "bell" was tested. Metzner (**75**) reports a similar experiment with the pupillary reflex. In all these cases significant amounts of generalization were obtained. Traugott (**107**) was able to demonstrate the generalization of conditioned inhibition from blue light to the words, "blue, blue"—in fact, these words (quite different as physical stimuli) showed greater generalization than actual red light. This investigator was also able to show that the inhibitory effect of the words "blue, blue" transferred to *other* conditioned reactions more broadly than did the effect of blue light itself, a finding which fits well with our notions as to the abstractability of sign-processes. Traugott and Fadeyeva (**108**) combined conditioning and free association techniques: with excitatory CR's set up to a bell-whistle-light pattern and inhibitory CR's to a whistle-touch pattern, free associations to the verbal signs of these stimuli were recorded along with the latencies of these associations. Association to words representing conditioned excitors were made more rapidly than those to words representing conditioned inhibitors and, interestingly enough, after extinction of the excitatory CR's associations became slower and generically older, i.e., associations which had referred to the experimental situation now referred to pre-experimental situations.

2. *From sign to sign.* When a response is conditioned to one sign (e.g., the word TREE) and generalization to other signs (e.g., BUSH or the picture of a tree or bush) is measured, the essential role of meaningful mediation is merely more obvious than in the preceding situation. Razran (**88**) flashed single words and short sentences on a screen while six adults were eating—conditioned salivation developed rapidly. In a second session, different words and sentences were used to measure generalization. For the single words generalization was found to be greater for semantically related words (e.g., STYLE to FASHION) than for phonetically related words (e.g., STYLE to STILE), a result in keeping with Traugott's results discussed above and data more recently obtained by Riess (**90**) using the GSR as a measure. A slightly discordant note is contributed by Keller (**55**). After conditioning the GSR to a *picture* of a boy-scout hat, tests for generalization were made for a picture of a fireman's hat and the the printed word HAT, neutral control items being pictures of a duck and baseball and the words DUCK and BALL. While significant generalization to the picture of a fireman's hat occurred, no transfer to the word HAT was obtained. Keller argues reasonably that if the generalization between the two pictured hats was based on a common mediating response, thinking or subvocalizing "hat," the printed word should have shown the same effect. In one of the most interesting studies of this type, Riess (**91**) has related semantic generalization to stages in genetic development. Four groups of subjects, varying in mean age from 7:9 years to 18:6 years of age, were trained to give the GSR to selected verbal stimuli. Tests for transfer to synonyms, antonyms, and homonyms of the original words were run. The generalization results indicate that meaningful or semantic similarities (synonym and antonym relations) increase in importance as the individual matures while the importance of physical similarities (homonym relation) decreases.

3. There are other semantic relations that could be studied with similar

techniques, but there is little evidence available. Generalization between *hierarchial levels of signs*, e.g., between DOG and ANIMAL, has been studied by Goodwin, Long, and Welch (**36**), but there are certain difficulties with the research design (see below). Generalization would also be expected to occur *from sign to object*, even though this seems to reverse the sequence followed in the development of meaning. Kapustnik (**49**) found that salivary reactions conditioned to verbal signs transfer to the stimuli signified. This is the only directly relevant study I have uncovered, but observations on much of social behavior fit the paradigm. The prejudicial reactions associated with "Wop" and "Jap" on a verbal stereotype level certainly tend to transfer to the social objects represented, once they are encountered. Finally, mention should be made of generalization *from object to object via semantic mediation*. The reverential care with which the adolescent handles a certain handkerchief, a certain lock of hair, a certain lipstick-printed napkin has nothing to do with physical similarities among these objects themselves. Similarly, an "inferiority complex" may render a wide range of physically dissimilar social objects and situations equivalent in meaning and hence reaction to a particular individual (cf., G. W. Allport's [1] trait hypothesis).

Cofer and Foley have related the various studies of semantic generalization to the theoretical mediation process. They state that semantic generalization "thus presupposes and depends upon the preexperimental formation of conditioned responses or associations, i.e., *the gradient of generalization is a gradient along a dimension of conditioned stimulus functions*. The stimuli need be similar only in so far as they have previously been conditioned to the same (or similar) response" (**23**, p. 520). The pre-experimental formation of conditioned responses to which they refer is a special case of the formation of mediation processes, as discussed earlier in this paper. It is probably necessary to assume that primary generalization occurs both among mediating reactions and the stimuli they produce, in order to account for the fact that *gradients* of semantic generalization are correlated with *degrees* of meaningful similarity.

Transfer and interference in learning. The experiments contributed by Cofer and Foley in support of their hypotheses fit the standard transfer design. The general procedure was as follows: first a single repetition on a *buffer list* of numbers (spelled out) was given as warm-up; then an *equating list* of proper names was presented once and scored for recall immediately, subjects being assigned to various experimental conditions on this basis; each subject was then given four unscored repetitions on either a *reinforcement list* or a *control list;* finally, all subjects were tested for recall of a *test list* of words immediately after a single presentation. Experimental, control and test lists used in the first experiment (Foley and Cofer, **32**) are given in Table 1. All words on a given reinforcement list bear the same relation to the test list, either some degree of synonymity or some degree of homonymity.

Although all experimental conditions yielded better recall scores than the control condition, there are several curious points about these results. In the first place, the best homonym list shows more "generalization" to the test list than the best synonym list—this is in flat contradiction to most other findings (cf., Traugott, Razran, Riess above). Secondly, the difference in recall between the two homonym lists is clearly greater than that between the two synonym lists, yet the former are obviously equivalent (both being identical in sound to the test words) while the latter are definitely not equivalent (the words on I are close synonyms of the test words but those on II bear no relation whatever to the test words, viz., sent-killed, vein-help, pear-result, sow-factory). Fortunately, the difference between "Synonym II" and the control condition was not significant.

TABLE 1

MATERIALS FOR AN EXPERIMENT ON MEDIATED TRANSFER
(FOLEY AND COFER, 32)

Control List	Reinforcement Lists				Test List
	Homonym I	*Homonym II*	*Synonym I*	*Synonym II*	
palm	cent	scent	dispatched	killed	sent
set	vain	vane	vessel	ship	vein
reed	pare	pair	fruit	result	pear
very	sew	so	plant	factory	sōw
numb	rain	rein	rule	principle	reign
me	seas	seize	looks	appearance	sees
day	write	rite	just	barely	right
snap	noes	nose	apprehends	arrests	knows
rope	meat	mete	join	enlist	meet
spire	dō	doe	batter	bruise	dough

Mean Number of Words on Test List Recalled Following Above

| 4.80 | 6.72 | 5.64 | 5.88 | 5.24 | |

In searching for an explanation of these points, a flaw in design was discovered which renders this entire technique suspect. Since all the words on a given reinforcement list bore the same relation to those on the test list, all a subject had to do was to "catch on" to this abstract relation and then proceed to manufacture the test list rather than recall it. Given four trials on a list of only 10 meaningful words, the subject presumably masters most of it. If, on the single presentation of the test list, he now notes that the new words are homonyms of the old, by merely recalling *cent*, *vain*, and *pare* he can do a pretty good job of manufacturing (and checking by recognition) *sent*, *vein*, and *pear*. He can do the same thing with synonym lists, but here he will make more errors since there are more alternatives. The same loophole in design is even more apparent in later studies in this series. In a study on *antonym gradients*, for example, Cofer, Janis, and Rowell (24) themselves point out that 19 of 28 subjects reported that they recognized the opposition relation. Foley and Mathews (34) and Goodwin, Long and Welch (36) report experiments using the same method, and their results are of dubious value for the same reasons.

Two experiments on interference in verbal learning by Osgood (83, 84) were explicitly designed to test certain hypotheses regarding the nature of meaning. The following hypotheses were set up: (1) Words of opposed meaning are so because they elicit reciprocally antagonistic mediating processes. (2) Repeated reinforcements of the association between a new stimulus and a particular mediating reaction produce a negatively accelerated increase in the excitatory tendency associating this stimulus with this reaction *and simultaneously an equal inhibitory tendency associating this stimulus with the reciprocally antagonistic reaction.* In other words, in learning to make a reaction to a stimulus the organism is simultaneously learning *not* to make the directly antagonistic reaction to that stimulus. (3) Both excitatory and inhibitory tendencies generalize in the usual fashion among both mediating reactions and the stimuli they produce.

With nonsense letter-pairs as constant stimuli and meaningful adjectives as varied responses in the standard retroactive interference paradigm ($A–B$; $A–K$; $A–B$), it was predicted that for both transfer and retroaction tests interpolated responses *similar* in meaning to the original responses should show the least interference (generalization of excitatory tendency) and responses *opposed* in meaning should show the most interference (generalization of inhibitory tendency), as compared with an intermediary neutral condition. The total design was such that each subject learned an equal number of items in each meaningful relation, thus avoiding the type of set that troubled the Foley and Cofer studies. The results for both transfer and retroaction situations were essentially those predicted (**83**). The second study (**84**) offered further evidence that a special form of reciprocal inhibition is operating in the successive learning of opposed meanings for the same sign. Different groups of subjects were given varying degrees of learning on the interpolated materials (cf. the design used by Melton and Irwin, **74**) and only similar and opposed meaningful responses were compared. The learning of opposed responses was characterized by longer latencies of reaction and more frequent blanks (failures of response), both increasing with the degree of interpolated learning. Since both these phenomena are characteristic of weakened habit strength, they follow from the hypotheses.

These findings point to the following general conclusion: *when a sign or assign is conditioned to a mediator, it will also tend to elicit other mediators in proportion to their similarity to the original reaction; it will tend to inhibit other mediators in proportion to the directness of their antagonism to the original reaction.* In everyday language, this indicates that signs which develop a certain meaning through direct training will readily elicit similar meanings but resist being associated with opposed meanings. If the sign RUSSIAN means *bad* to the conservative college student he easily accepts substitution of *dirty, unfair,* and *cruel,* but it is difficult for him to think of Russians as *clean, fair,* and *kind* (cf., Stagner and Osgood, **100**).

Perception Methods

There is an intimate relation between perceptual and meaningful phenomena (**14, 105**). It is borne out by the confusions psychologists display in using these terms. In one of Maier's (**67**) ingenious insight situations, for example, the crux of the problem lay in whether or not the human subject could shift from utilizing the handle of an ordinary lab clamp as something to tighten (original use) to something to hang one's hat on (use which would solve the problem). We could say that this handle must be "perceived differently" or the "field restructured perceptually" (cf., Köhler, 58; Wertheimer, 112), or that it must be "given a new functional value" (cf., Duncker, 30), or that it must "acquire a new meaning or significance as a stimulus." The voluminous literature on memory for forms has been interpreted both as demonstrating perceptual dynamics (cf., Koffka, 57) and semantic dynamics (cf., Bartlett, 2)—witness particularly the experiment by by Carmichael, Hogan, and Walter (15) in which the deliberate introduction of different meaningful words in association with the same abstract forms markedly influenced the way they were recalled.

As was the case with the learning approach, there are few experiments in which meaning has been deliberately introduced as a variable. Remotely relevant are a group of studies in which the effect of hunger upon perception in ambiguous situations has been measured (Sanford, 93, 94; Levine, Chein, and Murphy, 62; McClelland and Atkinson, 64). The way of perceiving the ambiguous stimuli was clearly modulated by the presence or absence of this motive state. Postman and Bruner (86) have studied the effect of a different motive state, frustration, upon the perception of tachistoscopically presented sentences. Most significant from our present point of reference was the marked increase in "aggressive" and "escape" words as misperceptions following frustration. Generalizing, we might say that the internal *motive state* of the individual, as part of the total stimulus context, changes the probabilities of occurrence (availability) of alternate mediating processes for the same external stimulus. Whether the known *value* of an object, as one dimension of its meaning, can influence the way it is perceived is a moot question at this time. Bruner and Goodman (12), with apparent size of coins as the perceptual characteristic measured and rich or poor 10 year olds as subjects, obtained what may be interpreted as positive results; Carter and Schooler (18), under generally similar conditions, failed to substantiate the earlier conclusions. Mausner and Siegel (71), using recognition-time as a measure and stamps of varying value as stimuli, also report negative conclusions. Most relevant to the problem of measuring meaning are the following experiments.

Bruner and Postman (13) compared the apparent sizes of a dollar sign (positive symbol), swastika (negative symbol), and an abstract geometrical design (neutral control), as estimated by manipulating a spot of light when plastic discs of identical size bearing these symbols were held in the subject's hands. Both dollar sign and swastika showed significant *over*estimation. According to the investigators, two dynamic processes were operative: (a) perceptual enhancement due to the positive value of the dollar sign and (b) perceptual accentuation of apparent size due to the swastika alerting the organism to danger or threat—a single process of enhancement in size due to distinctiveness might be more parsimonious, and there are many other possible hypotheses.

Postman, Bruner, and McGinnies (**86**) hypothesized that personal values (as defined by scores on the Allport-Vernon test) are among the behavioral or attitudinal determinants of perception. Twenty-five subjects were shown 36 words, one at a time, in a modified Dodge tachistoscope, these words being presented in random orders and being chosen to represent the six Allport-Vernon values. The usual method for obtaining recognition thresholds was used—gradually increasing the flash exposure time until the subject correctly identifies the word. Take for illustration a subject with high social values and low theoretical: according to the investigators, his threshold for perceiving words like "loving" and "devoted" should be lowered by *selective sensitization;* in the presolution period he should misperceive words covaluant with the correct word because of *value resonance;* and his threshold for words like "verify" and "research" should be raised because of *perceptual defense.* The results were consistent with the general thesis, but the single principle of selective sensitization seems sufficient to explain them.

McGinnies (**65**) inquired more penetratingly into the matter of "perceptual defense," conjecturing that autonomic reactions are aroused prior to conscious awareness of the meaning of a threatening word and hinder its perception. A list of 11 neutral words and seven emotionally charged words were presented tachistoscopically and recognition thresholds determined in the usual manner; GSR was recorded as a measure of emotional disturbance. Taboo words were found to require longer exposures for recognition and their prerecognition presentations were accompanied by significantly stronger emotional reactions. When asked if they had reported their perceptions promptly and accurately, all undergraduate subjects said they had.

Both this study and the preceding one on values have come in for their share of criticism. Howes and Solomon (**40**) argue that it is unnecessary to appeal to "selective sensitization" in the former case and "perceptual defense" in the latter, since recognition thresholds for words have been shown to vary with their frequency of usage or familiarity (Howes and Solomon, **41**) and this would provide a parsimonious explanation of both sets of findings. In the case of Allport-Vernon value systems, it seems reasonable to suppose that people with high theoretical values (and hence presumably with more courses, books, etc., in scientific fields) will have had more frequent visual contact with words like "logical" and "research"; in the case of taboo words, it also seems reasonable to suppose that the frequency of visual contact with words like "whore," "penis," and "bitch" is much less than with such control words as "child," "clear," and "dance." McGinnies' argument that these taboo words are much more frequent in ordinary conversations seems to be largely beside the point, since the test conditions were visual. The other main point raised by Howes and Solomon is that the emotional reactions *accompanied* recognition of the taboo words, appearing to precede simply because subjects inhibited reporting them— particularly since a member of the opposite sex was always present.

These critics draw a delightful picture of what might have been going on in the subjects' minds during the McGinnies experiment. In an answer to these criticisms, McGinnies (**66**) draws a different picture. This is another issue yet to be resolved by further research. In this connection, a recent study by Lazarus and McCleary (**61**) reports that subjects may show heightened GSR to nonsense syllables previously associated with shock even when exposures are stopped prior to actual recognition. But here again one questions the validity of the demonstration—how can one react emotionally to the meaning of a sign before its significance has been appreciated? It may be that we will be forced to accept some conception of "unconscious" and "conscious" levels of perception or meaning.

Skinner (**95**) devised a "verbal summator" technique for studying language behavior which resembles these perception methods. Samples of meaningless speech sounds, obtained by permuting and combining elemental phonemes—a sort of verbal inkblot—are repeated until the subject himself perceives some meaningful form. According to Skinner, the verbal summator "evokes latent verbal responses through summation with imitative responses to skeletal samples of speech." That this method gets at the comparative strengths of verbal habits is indicated by the fact that the same double-log function of frequency to rank (Zipf's Law) appears when a large sample of such responses are analyzed. Estes (**31**) has described a visual form of summator which presents skeletonized verbal materials tachistoscopically.

Association Methods

Freud would have been the first to point out that the associations produced when a patient "allows one idea to lead to another" are in no sense "free" or random, but rather are semantically determined. Another analyst, Jung (**48**) used a more formal association method to get at the meanings of words to individuals. Lists of verbal stimuli calculated to touch off complexes were imbedded among neutral words. Among the indices of "unusual" responses was the rareness of the association itself. In order to judge the commonness or rareness of particular associations, it was necessary to know the comparative frequencies with which various responses to a given stimulus word occur in a representative sample of the population. Kent and Rosanoff (**56**) obtained responses to 100 common English nouns and adjectives from 1,000 subjects; their sample must have been fairly representative because the occasional re-checks that have been made show rather surprising agreement. Given norms like these, the unusualness of a subject's responses can be indexed by the frequency of occurrence of that response in the populations; *sharp* can be expected as a response to NEEDLE 152 times per 1,000 (15.2%), but *weapon* occurs only once (00.1%).

The gross majority of word associations are semantically determined, i.e., result from the mediation process set in motion by the verbal stimulus as a sign. All such associates are similar in some way to the stimulus word, either similar in meaning (NEEDLE–*pin*), which would include hierarchial relations (NEEDLE–*tool*), or in terms of commonness of context (NEEDLE–*thread*). The venerable associationistic principles of similarity and contiguity will be recognized here. After an intensive analysis of ways of classifying associates, Karwoski and Berthold (50) conclude that nearly all responses can be categorized as either some form of similarity or contrast. What about contrast responses? The single most frequent associate is often the direct opposite (LIGHT–*dark;* MAN–*woman*). For a number of reasons, this writer believes such contrast responses are *not* semantically determined at all, but rather reflect overlearning of verbal skill sequences, quite akin to FOOT–*ball*, APPLE–*cart*, and WASTE–*basket*. The tendency to free associate opposites increases with age, children readily giving similar and contextual responses but rarely opposites (cf., Woodworth, 114, p. 346). Furthermore, rather than being distributed among many varied but roughly equivalent words, as is the case with similar associates, the opposition tendency is largely restricted to a single word, the direct opposite (cf., Kent and Rosanoff tables). Karwoski and Schachter (54) report this same effect with opposites and add the fact that opposites are given with significantly shorter reaction-times than similars.

One of the more interesting applications of the association method has been in differentiating responses to sign, symbol, and object levels of stimulation. In an early study on this, Dorcus (29) compared associations to color words (signs) and actual bits of colored paper (objects). Whereas co-ordinate and contrast responses were most common to color signs (WHITE–*black*, RED–*blue*), the names of contextually related objects were most commonly given to color objects (BLUE PAPER–*ribbons;* RED PAPER–*fingernails*). More recently Karwoski, Gramlich, and Arnott (51) have obtained associations to visually perceived actual objects, pictures of these objects, and verbal labels for these objects. The stimulus materials were such everyday things as *pipe, leaf, dollar,* and *pistol*. Where differences appeared, the dividing line was typically between the verbal level and the other two modes. For example, the most common response to the *word* FORK was, of course, *knife*—on both picture and objects levels the most common response was *eat*. Reaction times for the verbal level were also shorter.

Related to associational procedures are the effects of *context* upon meaning. It is a matter of common observation that a man's moods, emotions, and motives influence the character of his verbalizations. Bousfield and Barry (9) and Bousfield (8) found that subjects' rated moods (on a scale from "feeling well as possible" to "feeling as badly as possible") correlated with their rates of production of pleasant vs. unpleasant associates. The relatively stable attitudes of an individual also exert a contextual effect upon associations. Foley and MacMillan (33) have shown that associates to 40 ambiguous words (like *binding, administer, discharge*) are clearly influenced by the occupational status of subjects, as law students, medical students, or nonprofessional students. Perhaps because of the obviousness of the matter, no research seems to have been done upon the effect of the external, situational context upon meaning. This context includes the facial expressions and gestures of speakers, the objects present, and the activities underway, and so on (cf., Malinowski's [68] enlightening discussion of this in relation to decoding the language of another culture). Many slips of the tongue completely escape notice, simply because the situational context "carries" the intended meaning.

Howes and Osgood[4] have given attention to the manner in which the meaning of a particular sign is affected by the pattern of verbal materials within which it is imbedded. A sequence of four spoken words made up each item, the first three serving as the context and the fourth, spoken with greater emphasis, serving as the actual stimulus for word-association by the subjects. One experiment was designed to get at the effect of varying the *density* of contextual items having a common semantic direction: Group A heard three contextual stimuli of very similar meaning (e.g., *sinister, devil, evil*–DARK), Group B had one neutral word added (*eat, devil, evil*–DARK), Group C two neutral words (*eat, basic, evil*–DARK), and Group D, as control, had all neutral words in the context. When the frequencies of response-words related to the particular context (e.g., *thief, mystery, dead*, etc.) were plotted as a function of the density of influence in the context, number of influenced associates turned out to be a simple multiple of the number of relevant words in the context. In a second experiment, three influencing words of relatively independent meaning were used as "context," and the question was how *temporal proximity* of contextual stimuli affects the meaning of the eliciting sign. With an item like *feminine, strong, young*–MAN, the responses clearly relevant to each contextual stimulus could be isolated (*woman, girl* vs. *hard, work* vs. *boy, child*, for examples). Then the frequency of occurrence of such related responses was plotted as a function of the order of presentation of their contextual stimuli (e.g., frequencies of *woman* as a response when "feminine" is in third position, nearest MAN, second position, and first position, most remote from MAN). The results indicate that degree of influence of a contextual stimulus upon the meaning of a sign is a sharply negatively accelerated function of the temporal interval between them. In other words, the influence of one word upon another falls off rapidly as the amount of intervening material increases.

Scaling Methods

Considering the number of traits, abilities, and attitudes that psychologists have attempted to measure by scaling methods, it is signifi-

---

[4] HOWES, D. H., & OSGOOD, C. E. Studies on the combination of associative probabilities in linguistic contexts (in preparation).

cant that there has been practically no attempt to measure meaning this way. Since many psychologists must have thought about the problem at one time or another, this probably reflects the general belief that meanings are too complicated or too unique, or both. The few timid steps that have been taken in this direction involved drastic limitations on the scope of measurement, being aimed at scaling one or two isolated dimensions of meaning rather than meaning-in-general.

One group interested in scaling meaning has been the researchers in human learning, who wanted to be able to select materials for their experiments which could be specified with respect to this variable. A number of studies have been reported on the meaningfulness or "association value" of nonsense syllables (Glaze, **35**; Hull, **42**; Witmer, **113**). The typical method was to use nonsense syllables as stimuli for word-associations, "meaningfulness" being indexed by proportions of subjects who could find any associations. One could then select equated lists for learning experiments, equated on this one basis at least.

Also motivated to provide learning experimenters with standardized materials, Haagen (**37**) scaled 400 pairs of common adjectives in terms of their synonymity, vividness, familiarity, and association value. The method used was to have 280 college undergraduates judge these words on defined scales: (a) *synonymity* of a given word was judged on a seven-point scale in terms of the degree to which it denoted the same actions, objects or conditions as a standard word; (b) *vividness*, also judged on a seven-point scale, was defined as the clarity of graphicness of the impressions which a given word aroused; (c) *familiarity* was judged on a five-point scale, defined as the degree to which the judge knew the meaning of the word; and (d) *association value*, judged on a seven-point scale, referred to the degree to which the given word and a standard were associated in thought (e.g., hungry-thirsty, big-large, would have high association value). Useful though synonymity and associative value may be for purposes of learning experiments, they do not offer anything in the way of a measure of meaning—these judgments were always relative to some particular standard word, varying from one set of test words to another. The familiarity measure has nothing to do with meaning, of course. The vividness scale, being applied to each word separately rather than comparatively, probably is tapping some generalizable dimension of meaning.

Mosier (**79**) made the most direct application of scaling methods to the study of meaning. College subjects rated some 296 adjectives on an 11-point scale in terms of their favorableness-unfavorableness, these adjectives being selected from Thorndike's word lists as words expressing some degree of general evaluation. Frequency distributions of the responses to each word were scaled according to the method of successive intervals and plotted on probability paper. Plots for approximately 200 of these words were linear, indicating normal distribution of the data, when treated in this manner. Most of the words showed the "precipice effect" at one side or the other of the midpoint of the scale, indicating a higher degree of agreement on the *direction* (favorable or unfavorable) of the evaluation than on the *intensity*. Mosier was able to demonstrate a reasonable ordering of evaluative words in terms of their mean locations (e.g., excellent, good, common, fair, poor, etc.), including such information as the fact that "better" is connotatively less favorable than "good" (grammarians to the contrary). The most significant point is that Mosier demonstrated the feasibility of scaling certain aspects of meaning.

Summary on Existing Methods

The purpose of the preceding review has been to see if there already exist adequate methods of measuring meaning. By "adequate" I mean already meeting most of the criteria of satisfactory measuring instruments. What are these criteria? (*a*) *Objectivity*. The method should yield quantitative and verifiable (reproducible) data. (*b*) *Reliability*. It should yield the same values within acceptable margins of error, when the same conditions are duplicated. (*c*) *Validity*. The data obtained should be demonstrably covariant with those obtained with some other, independent index of meaning. (*d*) *Sensitivity*. The method should yield differentiations commensurate with the natural units of the material studied, i.e., should be able to reflect as fine distinctions in meaning as are typically made in communicating. (*e*) *Comparability*. The method should be applicable to a wide range of phenomena in the field, making possible comparisons among different individuals and groups, among different concepts, and so on. (*d*) *Utility*. It should yield information relevant to contemporary theoretical and practical issues in an efficient manner, i.e., it should not be so cumbersome and laborious as to prohibit collection of data at a reasonable rate. While this is not an exhaustive listing of criteria, it is sufficient for our purposes.

1. The *physiological measures* (including action potential, GSR, and salivary records) are of somewhat dubious validity, since there has been no demonstration of the necessity of these peripheral components, and they are not sensitive measures in that we are unable to interpret details of the records in our present ignorance. Their chief drawback, however, is cumbersomeness—the subject has to be "rigged up" in considerable gadgetry to make such measurements. For this reason, even should validity and sensitivity problems be met satisfactorily, it seems likely that physiological indices will be mainly useful as criteria against which to evaluate more practicable techniques.

2. *Learning measures* (including semantic generalization and transfer/interference methods) are also somewhat cumbersome procedurally, but their main drawback as general measures of meaning is their lack of comparability. Any measure of generalization or interference is made with respect to the original learning of some standard which necessarily varies from case to case. The chief usefulness of learning measures, therefore, lies in the test of specific hypotheses.

3. The chief drawback with *perception measures* (e.g., what is perceived in ambiguous stimulus forms, the recognition-times for tachistoscopically presented words) is that they are not valid measures of *meaning*. They get at the availability or comparative habit strengths of alternate meanings or ways of perceiving. The fact that a religious person perceives VESPERS with a shorter presentation time than a theoretically oriented person says nothing about *how* the meaning of this term differs for them; the fact that the religious person perceives VESPERS more quickly than THEORY says nothing about the difference in meaning of these two words to this individual. The same statements apply to Skinner's "verbal summator" technique.

4. The selection of responses in *association methods* is partly dependent upon the meaning of the stimulus items (and hence indexes meaning) and partly dependent upon habit strength factors. The chief drawback, as a general measure of meaning, is lack of comparability. The responses of two individuals to the same stimulus, or of the same individual to two stimulus words, are essentially unique as bits of data. Comparability can be obtained with group data, but this limits the method.

5. *Scaling methods* can be viewed as forms of controlled association in which the nature of the association is specified by definition of the scales (favorable-unfavorable, vividness, etc.) but the direction and intensity of association is unspecified. By the very nature of the scaling method, the comparability criterion is usually satisfied (provided the subjects can be shown to agree upon the meaning of the scale and its divisions). As used by Mosier, however, the method can have only partial validity. This is because he tapped only one dimension of meaning, the admittedly important evaluative dimension, whereas we know that meanings vary multidimensionally.

The Semantic Differential

The method to be proposed here is a combination of associational and scaling procedures. It is an indirect method in the same sense that an intelligence test, while providing objective and useful information, does not directly measure this capacity. However, unlike the intelligence test which treats this ability *as if* it were distributed along a single continuum (e.g., IQ scores vary along a single scale), we accept at the outset that meanings vary in some unknown number of dimensions and frame our methodology accordingly.

Research Origins of the Method

This method had its origins in research on synesthesia, defined by Warren in his *Dictionary of Psychology* (**109**) as "a phenomenon characterizing the experiences of certain individuals, in which certain sensations belonging to one sense or mode attach to certain sensations of another group and appear regularly whenever a stimulus of the latter type occurs." This implies a sort of "neural short-circuiting" that is present in only a few freak individuals, and it is true that many of the classic case histories in this area gave credence to this view: a subject reported pressure sensations about his teeth and cheeks whenever cold spots on his arms were stimulated (Dallenbach, **27**); a girl displayed a rigid system of relations between specific notes on the musical scale and specific color experiences, consistent when tested over a period of seven and one-half years (Langfeld, **60**). But here, on the other hand, was a man who imagined the number "1" to be yellow, "2" to be blue, "3" to be red . . . and, of course, "8" to be black (anyone who has played pool will recognize the origin of this system); and here was a little girl who recalled her friends as having pink faces and her enemies as having purple faces. What modalities are crossed in these cases?

A more recent series of investigations by Karwoski, Odbert, and their associates related synesthesia to thinking and language in general (cf., also Wheeler and Cutsforth, **115**). Rather than being a rare phenomenon, Karwoski and Odbert (**52**) report that as many as 13 per cent of Dartmouth College students regularly indulged in color-music synesthesia, often as a means of enriching their enjoyment of music. These photistic visualizers varied among themselves as to the modes of translation employed and the vividness of their experiences, and their difference from the general population appeared to be one of degree rather than kind. Whereas fast, exciting music might be pictured by the synesthete as sharply etched, bright red forms, his less imaginative brethren would merely agree that terms like "red-hot," "bright," and "fiery," as verbal metaphors, adequately described the music; a slow and melancholic selection might be visualized as heavy, slow-moving "blobs" of sombre hue and described verbally as "heavy," "blue," and "dark." The relation of this phenomenon to ordinary verbal metaphor is evident: a happy man is said to feel "high," a sad man feels "low"; the pianist travels "up" and "down" the scale from treble to bass; souls travel "up" to the good place and "down" to the bad place; hope is "white" and despair is "black." The process of metaphor in language as well as in color-music synesthesia can be described as the parallel alignment of two or more dimensions of experience, defined verbally by pairs of polar opposites, with translations occurring between equivalent portions of the continua (Karwoski, Odbert, and Osgood, **53**, pp. 212–221).

Interrelationships among color, mood, and musical experiences were studied more analytically by Odbert, Karwoski, and Eckerson (**81**). Subjects first listened to 10 short excerpts from classical scores and indicated their dominant moods by checking descriptive adjectives arranged in a mood circle (cf., Hevner, **39**). Then, on a second hearing, they listed the colors appropriate to each score. Significant relations were shown; the color associations to musical scores followed the moods created. A portion of Delius' *On Hearing the First Cuckoo in Spring* was judged leisurely in mood and preponderantly green in color; a portion of Wagner's *Rienzi Overture* was judged exciting or vigorous in mood and preponderantly red in color. When another group of subjects was merely shown the mood adjectives (with no musical stimulation) and asked to select appropriate colors, even *more* consistent relations appeared, suggesting that the unique characteristics of the musical selections had, if anything, somewhat obscured the purely verbal or metaphorical relations between colors and moods. Almost identical findings have been reported by Ross (**92**) for relationships between the colors used in stage lighting and reported moods produced in the audience. Data are also available for the effects of color upon mood in mental institutions and in industrial plants.

Responses to complex selections of music such as used in the above studies are themselves too complex for analysis of specific relations between auditory-mood variables and color-form variables. In order to get closer to the mechanisms of translation, Karwoski, Odbert, and Osgood (**53**) used simple melodic lines recorded by a single instrument (clarinet) as stimuli. In a first experiment the subjects were typical photistic visualizers and they drew their photisms with colored pencils after hearing each short selection in a darkened room. The simplest

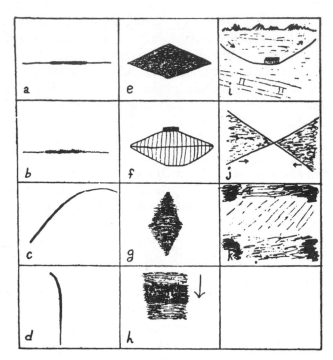

FIG. 2. SAMPLE OF PHOTISMS DRAWN BY COMPLEX SYNESTHETES TO REPRESENT A SIMPLE TONE WHICH GROWS LOUDER AND THEN SOFTER.

stimulus was a combination of crescendo and diminuendo on a single note—the sound merely grew louder, then softer—and this will serve to illustrate the results. As shown in Figure 2, subject *a* indicates increasing LOUDNESS by making the center of his line *heavier*, subject *b* by increasing *amplitude of vibration*, subjects *e*, *f*, and *g* by greater *thickness* of a solid form, subject *j* by more *concentrated focusing*, and subject *h* by more *saturated coloring* of the central portion. Subject *i* always created meaningful rather than abstract forms—here, a little car that comes *nearer* and then away again—yet the formal characteristics of his productions were generally like those of abstract synesthetes. These are functionally or meaningfully equivalent responses to the same auditory stimulus dimension—i.e., there are alternate visual continua that can be paralleled with the loud-soft auditory continuum—and the advantage of the method is that its simplicity allows these relationships to show up clearly.

Are these photistic visualizers exercising a "rare" capacity or are they merely expressing overtly modes of translation that are implicit in the language of our culture? A second experiment used subjects who had never even thought of "seeing things" when they heard music (if they reported any such tendencies, they were eliminated). The same simple melodic lines as above were played and the subjects were instructed to "force themselves to draw something to represent what they heard." They produce the same types of visual forms and in approximately the same relative frequencies as the experienced visualizers. Finally, a group of 100 unselected students was given a purely verbal *meaning-polarity test*, each item of which appeared in the following form: LARGE–small; SOFT–LOUD, with instructions to circle that word in the second pair which "seems most clearly related to" the capitalized word in the first pair. Here again, essentially the same relations between music-mood variables and color-form variables discovered among sensitive synesthetes were linked meaningfully on the polarity test. *Large* was linked to *loud* by 96 per cent of these subjects, *near* with *fast* by 86 per cent, *bright* with *happy* by 96 per cent, *treble* with *up* by 98 per cent, and so on. It seems clear from these studies that the imagery found in synesthesia is on a continuum with metaphor, and that both represent *semantic* relations.

Are such semantic relations entirely dependent upon culture or is it possible that they reflect more fundamental determinants common to the human species? In an attempt to get at this question, the writer studied anthropological field reports on five quite widely separated primitive cultures—Aztec and Pueblo Indian, Australian Bushman, Siberian Aborigine, Negro (Uganda Protectorate), and Malayan—with the view of obtaining evidence on semantic parallelism. Special emphasis was given to nonmaterial aspects of culture (mythology, religion, arts, medical beliefs, birth, marriage, death complexes, etc.). The numerous pitfalls in the way of such analysis are probably obvious. Particularly, there is the danger of attributing relations to a primitive group when they are actually projections on the part of the observer or borrowings from the dominant Western culture. Therefore the results should be considered merely suggestive.

Nevertheless, the generality of certain relationships was quite striking. For example, *good* gods, places, social positions, etc., were regularly *up* and *light* (*white*) in relation to *bad* things, which were *down* and *dark* (*black*). A prevalent myth tells of how the gods helped the original man to struggle "up" from the "dark," "cold," "wet," "sad" world below the ground to the "light," "warm," "dry," "happy" world on the surface of the earth. Among certain Siberian Aborigines, members of a privileged clan call themselves the "white" bones in contrast to all others who are referred to as "black" bones. And even among the Uganda Negroes we find some evidence for a white god at the apex of the hierarchy, and white cloth is clearly associated with purity, being used to ward off evil spirits and disease. Such data suggest the existence of a pervasive semantic frame of reference. Further study of the problem by more adequately trained investigators could be richly rewarding.

Stagner and Osgood (**100**) adapted this method and the logic underlying it to the study of social stereotypes. The notion of a continuum between the polar terms was made explicit by using such terms to define the ends of 7-step scales. Rather than studying the relations between continua, as above, a set of scales was used to measure the "meaning" of particular concepts, such as PACIFIST, RUSSIAN, DICTATOR, and NEUTRALITY. Successive samples of subjects were tested between April, 1940, and March, 1942 (including a sample obtained just prior to the Pearl Harbor incident). A single item on the tests appeared as follows:

PACIFIST: Kind ___:___:___:___:___:___:___ cruel

with the subject instructed to check that position on the scale which best represented the direction and intensity of his judgment. The concepts and scales related in successive items of the test were randomized to insure as much independence of judgment as possible. The feasibility and efficiency of using this method to record the changing structures of social stereotypes (e.g., the changing meanings of a set of social signs) were demonstrated. That a total shift from an essentially pacifistic to an essentially militaristic frame of reference had been accomplished, even before the Pearl Harbor incident provided the spark to overt expression, was clearly evident in the data.

More important from the point of view of methodology was the following observation: As used by our subjects in making their judgments, the various descriptive scales fell into highly intercorrelated clusters. Fair-unfair, high-low, kind-cruel, valuable-worthless, Christian-anti-Christian, and honest-dishonest were all found to correlate together .90 or better. This cluster represented, we assumed, a single, general factor in social judgments, the evaluative (good-bad) dimension of the frame of reference. Gradients like strong-weak, realistic-unrealistic, and happy-sad were independent of this evaluative group and pointed to the existence of other dimensions within the semantic framework. Enforced shifts in the apparent reference point of the observer (by having subjects judge the same concepts "as a German" or "as an Englishman") produced gross and appropriate changes in the evaluative dimension but did not disrupt the qualitative pattern of each stereotype—e.g., the stereotype GERMANS, when judged by students playing the role of Germans, was still seen as relatively more "strong" and "happy" (remember, this was during 1940–1942) than "noble" or "kind." This illustrates the kind of difficulty experienced when one tries to assume the point of view of another (cf., Stagner and Osgood, **99**).

Logic of the Proposed Method

The researches described above gave rise to the following hypotheses:

1. *The process of description or judgment can be conceived as the allocation of a concept to an experiential continuum, definable by a pair of polar terms.* An underlying notion in our research is that these "experiential continua" will turn out to be reflections (in language) of the sensory differentiations made possible by the human nervous system. In other words, it is assumed that discriminations in meaning, which is itself a state of awareness, cannot be any finer or involve any more variables than are made possible by the sensory nervous system (cf., Boring, *The Dimensions of Consciousness*, **6**). While failure to confirm this notion would not eliminate the proposed method as an index of meaning, its confirmation would greatly enhance the theoretical implications of this work.

2. *Many different experiential continua, or ways in which meanings vary, are essentially equivalent and hence may be represented by a single dimension.* This functional equivalence of many alternate continua was clearly evident in both the studies on synesthesia and those on the changing structure of social stereotypes. It is this fact about language and thinking that makes the development of a quantitative measuring instrument feasible. If the plethora of descriptive terms we utilize were in truth unique and independent of one another, as most philosophers of meaning seem to have assumed, then measurement would be impossible.

3. *A limited number of such continua can be used to define a semantic space within which the meaning of any concept can be specified.* From the viewpoint of experimental semantics, this both opens the possibility of measuring meaning in-general objectively and specifies factor analysis as the basic methodology. If it can be demonstrated that a limited number of dimensions or factors are sufficient to differentiate among the meanings of randomly selected concepts, and if the technique devised satisfies the criteria of measurement stated earlier, then such a "semantic differential," as I have termed it, *is* an objective index of meaning. From the viewpoint of psychological theory, we may look upon the procedures followed in obtaining this measure as an operational definition of meaning, in the same sense that the procedures followed in obtaining the IQ score provide an operational definition of intelligence.

The operations followed in the present instance are explicit. They involve the subject's allocation of a concept within a standard system of descriptive dimensions by means of a series of independent associative judgments.   The judgmental situation is designed to be maximally simple.   Presented with a pair of descriptive polar terms (e.g., *rough–smooth*) and a concept (e.g., LADY), the subject merely indicates the direction of this association (e.g., LADY–*smooth*).   We have developed two different methods for collecting data: In the *graphic method*, a pencil-and-paper technique which has the advantage that data can be collected from groups of subjects and hence very speedily, the subject indicates the intensity of his association by the extremeness of his checking on a 7-step scale.   In the *judgment-time method*, which has the advantage that the subject cannot anticipate what concept is to be judged on a particular scale and hence cannot rationalize his reaction, intensity of association is indicated by the latency of the individual subject's choice reaction toward one or the other of the polar terms.   In both methods each associative judgment of a particular concept against a particular descriptive scale constitutes one item.   In successive items, concepts and dimensions are paired in deliberately rotated orders until every concept has been associated with every scale by every subject.

A Factor Analysis of Meaning

The procedures and results of this factor analysis will be described in detail elsewhere.   A total of 50 descriptive scales, selected in terms of their frequency of usage, have been used in the judgment of 20 varied concepts, yielding a 1,000-item test.   One hundred college students served as subjects.   The graphic method was used.[5]   The purpose of this factor analysis is to isolate a limited number of general dimensions of meaning having a maximal differentiating power, to try to bring some order out of semantic chaos.   The larger the proportion of total variance in meaning accounted for by these factors, the more satisfactory will be the measuring instrument finally set up.   A preliminary estimation of factors in the 50×50 matrix (each scale correlated with every other scale) indicates the existence of several roughly independent dimensions.   An "evaluative factor" accounts for by far the largest portion of the variance.   There is also evidence for a "strength factor," an "activity factor," and several others not clearly defined in this rough approximation.   Given such factors, it will be possible to select those specific scales (e.g., good-bad, strong-weak, active-passive, smooth-rough, hot-cold, etc.) which best represent them.

We have done some exploratory work on the use of the semantic

---

[5] Apparatus for obtaining latency measurements from individual subjects has been constructed and will be standardized upon the reduced set of descriptive scales we hope to derive from this preliminary factor analysis.   While this apparatus has the advantage that materials are projected from a film-strip and responses (directions and latencies) are photographed by a single-frame camera—all automatically—it is still applicable only to a single subject at a time and hence is time-consuming.

differential as a practical measuring device. The two sets of profiles
in Figure 3 will serve to illustrate the method. Two groups of only 20

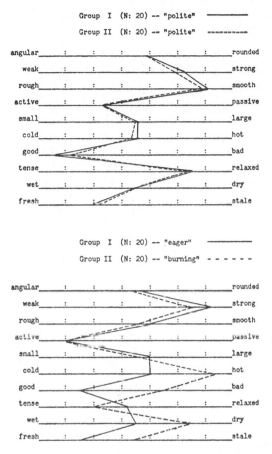

FIG. 3. ILLUSTRATION OF APPLICATION OF A PRELIMINARY FORM OF THE SEMANTIC
DIFFERENTIAL FOR MEASURING THE CONNOTATIVE MEANINGS OF ADJECTIVES: *A.*
UPPER PROFILES, MEDIANS FOR TWO GROUPS OF 20 SUBJECTS DIFFERENTIATING
"POLITE"; *B.* LOWER PROFILES, MEDIANS FOR SAME TWO GROUPS OF 20 SUBJECTS
DIFFERENTIATING "EAGER" AND "BURNING."

subjects each differentiated the meaning of the adjective "polite";
Group I also differentiated "eager" while Group II also differentiated
"burning" (as part of a larger study). Median judgments of the 20
subjects on each scale are plotted. There is high agreement on the differentiation of the same sign, "polite." The different, but somewhat
similar signs, "eager" and "burning," show significant points of discrimination: whereas they are equally *strong* and *active*, "burning"
is relatively *hot* and *dry* as compared with "eager," and "eager" is
relatively *good* and *fresh* as compared with "burning." These differences
are obviously what they would have to be if the method has any valid-

ity. It must be emphasized that the sample of scales shown here does *not* necessarily represent those to be finally derived from our factor analysis.

Evaluation of the Method

Evaluation of this instrument against the criteria of measurement listed earlier will be the subject of future reaserch, but some evidence can be presented now.

1. *Objectivity.* The semantic differential yields quantitative data which are presumably verifiable, in the sense that other investigators can apply the same sets of scales to equivalent subjects and obtain essentially the same result.

2. *Reliability.* In the test form from which data for the factor analysis were collected, 40 of the 1,000 items were selected at random and repeated. None of the subjects was aware that this had been done. The reliability coefficient was .85. The minimum variation in profile for the two groups of 20 subjects judging "polite" is another indication of the stability of the method.

3. *Validity.* All of the data collected so far on several problems display convincing face-validity and several direct experimental checks are planned. These include (a) correlation of attitudes toward various social objects as measured on standard tests with allocation of signs of these social objects within the semantic differential, and (b) the use of experimentally induced changes in meaning of signs (cf., Stagner and Britton, **98**). We are not concerned about the problem of "labeling" factors, a point where the precision gained by the factor analytic method is often lost in the obscurities of language. Selection of specific scales to match factors can proceed on a purely objective basis, in terms of the factor loadings for each scale. As a matter of fact, the polar terms which define the scales do not admit much in the way of misinterpretation.

4. The question of *sensitivity* of the method comes down to whether it is able to reflect as fine distinctions in meaning as are ordinarily made. We have incidental evidence that a semantic differential can tease out nuances in meaning which are clearly felt but hard to verbalize deliberately.[6] If there is a real difference in the meaning of two signs, such that they would not be used in precisely the same contexts, and if our measuring instrument includes a sufficient number of dimensions of the semantic space, then a significant difference should appear on at least one of the scales.

5. *Comparability.* It is here that the most serious questions arise. (a) *Is the method culture-bound?* If the tendency to dichotomize experiential continua is characteristic of Western culture but not necessarily elsewhere, then the method would not have generality. This is an empirical question requiring the skills of anthropologists and linguists for solution. (b) *Is the method limited to the differentiation of nouns against adjective scales?* The structure of our language is such that "adjectives" typically reflect abstracted qualities of

---

[6] By way of illustration, most English-speaking Americans feel that there is a difference, somehow, between "good" and "nice" but find it difficult to explain. We gave several people these words to differentiate and it turned out that wherever "male" and "female" show a significant divergence, there also were "good" and "nice" differentiated (e.g., "good," like "male," is somewhat stronger, rougher, more angular, and larger than is "nice," which like "female" shifts toward the weak, smooth, rounded, and small directions of the space). Thus "nice man" has a slightly effeminate tone whereas "good woman" (as compared with "nice woman") has a narrowly moral tone.

experience and "nouns" the concepts and things dealt with. We have found it possible to set up scales like giant–midget, fire–iceberg, god–devil and to judge "concepts like INSINUATE and AGITATED against them. This does not seem "natural" to members of our language community, however; it is probably the stem or root meaning of words that our method taps. (c) *Can different concepts be compared?* To the extent that judgments of different concepts involve the same factor structure, any concept may be compared with any other against a single, standardized semantic framework. (d) *Can different individuals be compared?* This also comes down to the generality of the semantic factor structure. It is quite conceivable that different classes of people (scientists, ministers, etc.) have somewhat varied semantic structures, differing in the emphasis upon certain factors and interrelationships among them. In fact, a significant source of individual differences may lie here.

Our method can be criticized on the ground that it only gets at *connotative* meaning, not *denotative* meaning. This is a limitation. Both SIMON LEGREE and WAR might be allocated to approximately the same point in semantic space by our method. This would indicate similar connotative meaning, to be sure, but it would not indicate that these signs refer to the same object. Our differential will draw out the *hard, heavy, cold, ugly, threatening* connotations of the sign HAMMER, but it will not indicate that HAMMER is "an instrument for driving nails, beating metals, and the like, consisting of a head, usually of steel, fixed crosswise to a handle" (Webster's *Collegiate Dictionary*). In part, this limitation stems from our method of selecting descriptive scales in terms of frequency of usage rather than in terms of a logically exhaustive coverage, as given in Roget's *Thesaurus*, for example.

6. *Utility.* In any area of science, the development of an adequate method of measuring something (be it the wave length of radiation, blood chemistry, intelligence, or meaning) opens up well-nigh inexhaustible possibilities for application. (a) *Semantic norms.* In much the same way that Thorndike has established his norms for frequency-of-usage of common words in the English language, the semantic differential could be used to compile a functional lexicon of connotative meanings, a quantized thesaurus. Similarly, the gradual drift of changing meanings, both temporally and geographically, could be charted. (b) *Individual differences in meaning.* It is a truism that the meanings of socially significant signs differ for different classes of people. Concepts like CHURCH, LABOR LEADER, STALIN, and TRUMAN have different connotative significance to different people, and the semantic differential can be used to quantify these differences. In this sense, it can be used as a generalized, multidimensional attitude test. For example, 10 people may have identical degrees of favorableness toward NEGRO (evaluative dimension) and yet vary markedly with respect to other dimensions of the meaning-space. (c) *Changes in meaning.* Under the pressure of events, the meanings of social signs change, e.g., the meaning of ITALIANS to Americans during the past half century. Similarly, under the "pressure" of psychotherapy, the meaning or emotional significance of certain critical concepts (e.g., FATHER, THERAPIST, ME, etc.) undergoes change. (d) *Quantification of subjective language data.* We have recently used the semantic differential as a means of scoring TAT reactions; not only is the testing process greatly speeded up, but the data are in easily manipulable form. Preliminary studies indicate that the essential individual differences in meaning of such projective materials, as teased out of complicated verbatim "stories," are sharply etched in the semantic differential data. (e) *Cross-cultural communication problems.* If the structure of the semantic space proves to be sufficiently general that the method can be translated into equivalent differentials in other languages, numerous possibilities are opened

up. Are the fundamental factors in meaning and their relationships independent of the language spoken? Can the significant points of deviation in meaning of critical concepts, as between Americans and Russians, for example, be discovered? Can the finer, subtler degrees of acculturation into a new society be traced? And there are other potential applications, to aesthetics, to studying the development of meaning in children, and so on.

SUMMARY

The first portion of this paper describes a behavioral conception of the sign-process as developed from a general mediation theory of learning. The remainder is concerned with the problem of measuring meaning. Various existing approaches to the problem—physiological, learning, perception, association, and scaling methods—have been evaluated against the usual criteria of measurement and have been found inadequate. The development of a semantic differential as a general method of measuring meaning is described. It involves (a) the use of factor analysis to determine the number and nature of factors entering into semantic description and judgment, and (b) the selection of a set of specific scales corresponding to these factors which can be standardized as a measure of meaning. Using this differential, the meaning of a particular concept to a particular individual can be specified quantitatively as a particular point in the multidimensional space defined by the instrument. Some of the possible uses of such a measuring instrument are briefly indicated.

BIBLIOGRAPHY

1. ALLPORT, G. W. *Personality: a psychological interpretation.* New York: Holt, 1937.

2. BARTLETT, F. C. *Remembering.* Cambridge, England: Cambridge Univer. Press, 1932.

3. BINGHAM, W. E., JR. A study of the relations which the galvanic skin response and sensory reference bear to judgments of the meaningfulness, significance, and importance of 72 words. *J. Psychol.*, 1943, **16**, 21–34.

4. BLOOMFIELD, L. *Language.* New York: Holt, 1933.

5. BODER, D. P. The adjective-verb-quotient: a contribution to the psychology of language. *Psychol. Rec.*, 1940, **3**, 310–343.

6. BORING, E. G. *The physical dimensions of consciousness.* New York: Appleton-Century, 1933.

7. BOUSFIELD, W. A. An empirical study of the production of affectively toned items. *J. gen. Psychol.*, 1944, **30**, 205–215.

8. BOUSFIELD, W. A. The relationship between mood and the production of affectively toned associates. *J. gen. Psychol.*, 1950, **42**, 67–85.

9. BOUSFIELD, W. A., & BARRY, H., JR. Quantitative correlates of euphoria. *J. exp. Psychol.*, 1937, **21**, 218–222.

10. BOUSFIELD, W. A., & SEDGWICK, C. H. W. An analysis of sequences of restricted associative responses. *J. gen. Psychol.*, 1944, **30**, 149–165.

11. BOUSFIELD, W. A., & BARCLAY, W. D. The relationship between order and frequency of occurrence of restricted associative responses.

J. exp. Psychol., 1950, **40**, 643–647.

12. BRUNER, J. S., & GOODMAN, C. C. Value and need as organizing factors in perception. *J. abnorm. soc. Psychol.*, 1947, **42**, 33–44.

13. BRUNER, J. S., & POSTMAN, L. Symbolic value as an organizing factor in perception. *J. soc. Psychol.*, 1948, **27**, 203–208.

14. BRUNSWIK, E. Die Zugänglichkeit von Gegenständen für die Wahrnehmung. *Arch. ges. Psychol.*, 1933, **88**, 377–418.

15. CARMICHAEL, L., HOGAN, H. P., & WALTER, A. A. An experimental study of the effect of language on the reproduction of visual perceived form. *J. exp. Psychol.*, 1932, **15**, 73–86.

16. CARROLL, J. B. Diversity of vocabulary and the harmonic series law of word-frequency distribution. *Psychol. Rec.*, 1938, **2**, 379–386.

17. CARROLL, J. B. The analysis of verbal behavior. *Psychol. Rev.*, 1944, **51**, 102–119.

18. CARTER, L. F., & SCHOOLER, K. Value, need and other factors in perception. *Psychol. Rev.*, 1949, **56**, 200–207.

19. CASON, H., & CASON, E. B. Association tendencies and learning ability. *J. exp. Psychol.*, 1925, **8**, 167–189.

20. CHOTLOS, J. W. Studies in language behavior: IV. A statistical and comparative analysis of individual written language samples. *Psychol. Monogr.*, 1944, **56**, No. 2 (Whole No. 255), 75–111.

21. CLARK, H. M. Conscious attitudes. *Amer. J. Psychol.*, 1911, **22**, 214–249.

22. CLARK, R. S. An experimental study of silent thinking. *Arch. Psychol.*, 1922, **7**, No. 48. Pp. 101.

23. COFER, C. N., & FOLEY, J. P., JR. Mediated generalization and the interpretation of verbal behavior. I. Prolegomena. *Psychol. Rev.*, 1942, **49**, 513 540.

24. COFER, C. N., JANIS, M. G., &

ROWELL, M. M. Mediated generalization and the interpretation of verbal behavior. III. Experimental study of antonym gradients. *J. exp. Psychol.*, 1943, **32**, 266–269.

25. COMSTOCK, C. On the relevancy of imagery to the processes of thought. *Amer. J. Psychol.*, 1921, **32**, 196–230.

26. CROSLAND, H. R. A qualitative analysis of the process of forgetting. *Psychol. Monogr.*, 1921, **29**, No. 1 (Whole No. 130).

27. DALLENBACH, K. M. Synaesthesis: "Pressury" cold. *Amer. J. Psychol.*, 1926, **37**, 571–577.

28. DARROW, C. W., & HEATH, L. L. Reaction tendencies relating to personality. In C. P. Stone, C. W. Darrow, C. Landis, and L. L. Heath. *Studies in the dynamics of behavior.* Chicago: Univer. Chicago Press, 1932.

29. DORCUS, R. M. Habitual word associations to colors as a possible factor in advertising. *J. appl. Psychol.*, 1932, **16**, 277–287.

30. DUNCKER, K. On problem-solving. (Trans. by L. S. Lees from 1935 original.) *Psychol. Monogr.*, 1945 **58**, No. 5 (Whole No. 270).

31. ESTES, W. K. A visual form of the verbal summator. *Psychol. Rec.*, 1940, **4**, 174–180.

32. FOLEY, J. P., JR., & COFER, C. N. Mediated generalization and the interpretation of verbal behavior: II. Experimental study of certain homophone and synonym gradients. *J. exp. Psychol.*, 1943, **32**, 169–175.

33. FOLEY, J. P., JR., & MACMILLAN, Z. L. Mediated generalization and the interpretation of verbal behavior: V. "Free association" as related to differences in professional training. *J. exp. Psychol.*, 1943, **33**, 299–310.

34. FOLEY, J. P., JR., & MATHEWS, M. Mediated generalization and the interpretation of verbal behavior:

IV. Experimental study of the development of interlinguistic synonym gradients. *J. exp. Psychol.*, 1943, **33**, 188–200.

35. GLAZE, J. A. The association value of non-sense syllables. *J. genet. Psychol.*, 1928, **35**, 255–269.

36. GOODWIN, J., LONG, L., & WELCH, L. Generalization in memory. *J. exp. Psychol.*, 1945, **35**, 71–75.

37. HAAGEN, C. H. Synonymity, vividness, familiarity, and association value ratings of 400 pairs of common adjectives. *J. Psychol.*, 1949, **27**, 453–463.

38. HEBB, D. O. *The organization of behavior.* New York: Wiley, 1949.

39. HEVNER, KATE. Experimental studies of the elements of expression in music. *Amer. J. Psychol.*, 1936, **48**, 246–268.

40. HOWES, D. H., & SOLOMON, R. L. A note on McGinnies' "Emotionality and perceptual defense." *Psychol. Rev.*, 1950, **57**, 229–234.

41. HOWES, D. H., & SOLOMON, R. L. Visual duration threshold as a function of word-probability. *J. exp. Psychol.*, 1951, **41**, 401–410.

42. HULL, C. L. The meaningfulness of 320 selected nonsense syllables. *Amer. J. Psychol.*, 1933, **45**, 730–734.

43. HULL, C. L. *Principles of behavior: An introduction to behavior theory.* New York: Appleton-Century, 1943.

44. JACOBSON, E. Electrophysiology of mental activities. *Amer. J. Psychol.*, 1932, **44**, 677–694.

45. JOHNSON, W. Studies in language behavior: I. A program of research. *Psychol. Monogr.*, 1944, **56**, No. 2 (Whole No. 255), 1–15.

46. JONES, H. E. Emotional factors in learning. *J. gen. Psychol.*, 1929, **2**, 263–272.

47. JONES, H. E., & WECHSLER, D. Galvanometric technique in studies of association. *Amer. J. Psychol.*, 1928, **40**, 607–612.

48. JUNG, C. G. *Studies in word-association.* (Trans. by M. D. Eder.) London: William Heinemann, 1918.

49. KAPUSTNIK, O. P. The interrelation between direct conditioned stimuli and their verbal symbols (trans. from Russian title), 1930. *Psychol. Abstracts*, 1934, **8**, No. 153.

50. KARWOSKI, T. F., & BERTHOLD, F., JR. Psychological studies in semantics: II. Reliability of free association tests. *J. soc. Psychol.*, 1945, **22**, 87–102.

51. KARWOSKI, T. F., GRAMLICH, F. W., & ARNOTT, P. Psychological studies in semantics: I. Free association reactions to words, drawings, and objects. *J. soc. Psychol.*, 1944, **20**, 233–247.

52. KARWOSKI, T. F., & ODBERT, H. S. Color-music. *Psychol. Monogr.*, 1938, **50**, No. 2 (Whole No. 222).

53. KARWOSKI, T. F., ODBERT, H. S., & OSGOOD, C. E. Studies in synesthetic thinking: II. The roles of form in visual responses to music. *J. gen. Psychol.*, 1942, **26**, 199–222.

54. KARWOSKI, T. F., & SCHACHTER, J. Psychological studies in semantics: III. Reaction times for similarity and difference. *J. soc. Psychol.*, 1948, **28**, 103–120.

55. KELLER, MARGARET. Mediated generalization: the generalization of a conditioned galvanic skin response established to a pictured object. *Amer. J. Psychol.*, 1943, **56**, 438–448.

56. KENT, GRACE H., & ROSANOFF, A. J. A study of association in insanity. *Amer. J. Insanity*, 1910, **67**, 37–96, 317–390.

57. KOFFKA, K. *Principles of gestalt psychology.* New York: Harcourt Brace, 1935.

58. KÖHLER, W. *The mentality of apes.* (Trans. by E. Winter.) New York: Harcourt Brace, 1925.

59. KOTLIAREVSKY, L. I. Cardio-vascular conditioned reflexes to direct and to verbal stimuli (trans. from Russian title), 1936. *Psychol. Abstracts*, 1939, **13**, No. 4046.

60. Langfeld, H. S. Note on a case of chromaesthesia. *Psychol. Bull.*, 1914, **11**, 113–114.

61. Lazarus, R. S., & McCleary, R. A. Autonomic discrimination without awareness: A study of subception. *Psychol. Rev.*, 1951, **58**, 113–122.

62. Levine, R., Chein, I., & Murphy, G. The relation of the intensity of a need to the amount of perceptual distortion: a preliminary report. *J. Psychol.*, 1942, **13**, 283–293.

63. Lynch, C. A. The memory values of certain alleged emotionally toned words. *J. exper. Psychol.*, 1932, **15**, 298–315.

64. McClelland, D. C., & Atkinson, J. W. The projective expression of needs: I. The effect of different intensities of the hunger drive on perception. *J. Psychol.*, 1948, **25**, 205–222.

65. McGinnies, E. Emotionality and perceptual defense. *Psychol. Rev.*, 1949, **56**, 244–251.

66. McGinnies, E. Discussion of Howes' and Solomon's note on "Emotionality and perceptual defense." *Psychol. Rev.*, 1950, **57**, 235–240.

67. Maier, N. R. F. Reasoning in humans. III. The mechanisms of equivalent stimuli and of reasoning. *J. exp. Psychol.*, 1945, **35**, 349–360.

68. Malinowski, B. The problem of learning in primitive languages. Supplement in C. K. Ogden, & I. A. Richards. *The meaning of meaning*. New York: Harcourt Brace, 1938.

69. Marbe, K. *Experimentell-psychologische Untersuchungen über das Urteil*. Leipzig: Engelmann, 1901.

70. Mason, M. Changes in the galvanic skin response accompanying reports of changes in meaning during oral repetition. *J. gen. Psychol.*, 1941, **25**, 353–401.

71. Mausner, B., & Siegel, A. The effect of variation in "value" on perceptual thresholds. *J. abnorm. soc. Psychol.*, 1950, **45**, 760–763.

72. Max, L. W. An experimental study of the motor theory of consciousness. III. Action-current responses in deaf-mutes during sleep, sensory stimulation, and dreams. *J. comp. Psychol.*, 1935, **19**, 469–486.

73. Max, L. W. An experimental study of the motor theory of consciousness. IV. Action-current responses in the deaf during awakening, kinaesthetic imagery, and abstract thinking. *J. comp. Psychol.*, 1937, **24**, 301–344.

74. Melton, A. W., & Irwin, J. McQ. The influence of degree of interpolated learning on retroactive inhibition and the overt transfer of specific response. *Amer. J. Psychol.*, 1940, **53**, 173–203.

75. Metzner, C. A. The influence of preliminary stimulation upon human eyelid responses during conditioning and during subsequent heteromodal generalization. *Summ. Doct. Diss. Univ. Wis.*, 1942, **7**, 152–154.

76. Miller, G. A. *Language and communication*. New York: McGraw-Hill, 1951.

77. Morris, C. *Foundations of the theory of signs*. Internat. Encycl. Unif. Sci., Vol. 1, No. 2. Chicago: University of Chicago Press, 1938.

78. Morris, C. *Signs, language and behavior*. New York: Prentice-Hall, 1946.

79. Mosier, C. I. A psychometric study of meaning. *J. soc. Psychol.*, 1941, **13**, 123–140.

80. Mowrer, O. H. Preparatory set (expectancy): Some methods of measurement. *Psychol. Monogr.*, 1940, **52**, No. 2 (Whole No. 233).

81. Odbert, H. S., Karwoski, T. F., & Eckerson, A. B. Studies in synesthetic thinking: I. Musical and verbal associations of color and mood. *J. gen. Psychol.*, 1942, **26**, 153–173.

82. Ogden, C. K., & Richards, I. A. *The meaning of meaning*. London:

Kegan Paul, 1923.

83. OSGOOD, C. E. Meaningful similarity and interference in learning. *J. exp. Psychol.*, 1946, **36**, 277–301.

84. OSGOOD, C. E. An investigation into the causes of retroactive interference. *J. exp. Psychol.*, 1948, **38**, 132–154.

85. POSTMAN, L., & BRUNER, J. S. Perception under stress. *Psychol. Rev.*, 1948, **55**, 314–324.

86. POSTMAN, L., BRUNER, J. S., & MC-GINNIES, E. Personal values as selective factors in perception. *J. abnorm. soc. Psychol.*, 1948, **43**, 142–154.

87. RAZRAN, G. H. S. Salivating and thinking in different languages. *J. Psychol.*, 1935–1936, **1**, 145–151.

88. RAZRAN, G. H. S. A quantitative study of meaning by a conditioned salivary technique (semantic conditioning). *Science*, 1939, **90**, 89–90.

89. REED, H. B. The existence and function of inner speech in thought processes. *J. exp. Psychol.*, 1916, **1**, 365–392.

90. RIESS, B. F. Semantic conditioning involving the galvanic skin reflex. *J. exp. Psychol.*, 1940, **26**, 238–240.

91. RIESS, B. F. Genetic changes in semantic conditioning. *J. exp. Psychol.*, 1946, **36**, 143–152.

92. ROSS, R. T. Studies in the psychology of the theater. *Psychol. Rec.*, 1938, **2**, 127–190.

93. SANFORD, R. N. The effects of abstinence from food upon imaginal processes: A preliminary experiment. *J. Psychol.*, 1936, **2**, 129–136.

94. SANFORD, R. N. The effects of abstinence from food upon imaginal processes: A further experiment. *J. Psychol.*, 1937, **3**, 145–159.

95. SKINNER, B. F. The verbal summator and a method for the study of latent speech. *J. Psychol.*, 1936, **2**, 71–107.

96. SKINNER, B. F. The distribution of associated words. *Psychol. Rec.*, 1937, **1**, 69–76.

97. SKINNER, B. F. *The behavior of organisms*. New York: Appleton-Century-Crofts, 1938.

98. STAGNER, R., & BRITTON, R. H., JR. The conditioning technique applied to a public opinion problem. *J. soc. Psychol.*, 1949, **29**, 103–111.

99. STAGNER, R., & OSGOOD, C. E. An experimental analysis of a nationalistic frame of reference. *J. soc. Psychol.*, 1941, **14**, 389–401.

100. STAGNER, R., & OSGOOD, C. E. Impact of war on a nationalistic frame of refefence: I. Changes in general approval and qualitative patterning of certain stereotypes. *J. soc. Psychol.*, 1946, **24**, 187–215.

101. SWITZER, S. C. A. Disinhibition of the conditioned galvanic skin response. *J. gen. Psychol.*, 1933, **9**, 77–100.

102. THORNDIKE, E. L. *The teacher's word book.* New York: Teachers College, Columbia Univ., 1921.

103. THORNDIKE, E. L., & LORGE, I. *The teacher's word book of 30,000 words.* New York: Bureau of Publications, Teachers College, Columbia Univ., 1944.

104. THORSON, A. M. The relation of tongue movements to internal speech. *J. exp. Psychol.*, 1925, **8**, 1–32.

105. THOULESS, R. H. Phenomenal regression to the real object. II. *Brit. J. Psychol.*, 1931, **22**, 1–30.

106. THUMB, A., & MARBE, K. *Experimentelle Untersuchungen über die psychologischen Grundlagen der sprachlichen Analogiebildung.* Leipzig: W. Engelmann, 1901.

107. TRAUGOTT, N. N. The interrelations of immediate and symbolic projections in the process of the formation of conditioned inhibition (trans. from Russian title), 1934. *Psychol. Abstracts*, 1935, **9**, No. 1166.

108. TRAUGOTT, N. N., & FADEYEVA, V. K. The effect of difficult extinction of food-procuring conditioned reflexes upon the general and speech behavior of children (trans. from Russian title), 1934. *Psychol. Abstracts*, 1935, **9**, No. 1167.

109. WARREN, H. C. (Ed.) *Dictionary of*

psychology. New York: Houghton Mifflin, 1934.

110. WASHBURN, M. *Movement and mental imagery.* Boston: Houghton Mifflin, 1916.

111. WATSON, J. B. *Behavior, an introduction to comparative psychology.* New York: Holt, 1914.

112. WERTHEIMER, M. *Productive thinking.* New York: Harper, 1945.

113. WITMER, L. R. The association value of three-place consonant syllables. *J. genet. Psychol.*, 1935, **47**, 337–360.

114. WOODWORTH, R. S. *Experimental*

psychology. New York: Holt, 1938.

115. WHEELER, R. H., & CUTSFORTH, T. D. Synaesthesia and meaning. *Amer. J. Psychol.*, 1922, **33**, 361–384.

116. WYCZOIKOWSKI, A. Theoretical and experimental studies in the mechanism of speech. *Psychol. Rev.*, 1913, **20**, 448–458.

117. ZIPF, G. K. *The psychobiology of language.* New York: Houghton Mifflin, 1935.

118. ZIPF, G. K. *Human behavior and the principle of least effort.* Cambridge, Mass.: Addison-Wesley, 1949.

2. Factor Analysis of Meaning

Charles E. Osgood and George J. Suci

Although there are objective methods for studying many aspects of language behavior, a survey of the literature (3) failed to uncover any standard ways of measuring meaning which meet the usual criteria of measurement. Perhaps because "meanings" are generally assumed to be uniquely and infinitely variable, or perhaps because of the philosophical haziness of this concept, there have been few attempts to devise methods here. Nevertheless, whether looked at from the viewpoints of philosophy or linguistics, from political or sociological theory, or—interestingly enough—from within the core of psychological theory itself, the nature of meaning and change in meaning are central issues.

This paper is one of a series describing research on the development of an objective method of measuring meaning. A previous report gave a review of this problem, describing attempts to establish physiological, learning, and associational indices, and also summarized several theoretical conceptions of the sign process. Subsequent papers will be concerned with evaluations of the validity, reliability, sensitivity, and generality of the method proposed here, and will describe some applications of the method. The present paper presents the results of two independent factor analyses of semantic judgments. The first used Thurstone's centroid method (5) and the second a method of analysis recently developed by the second author. Both of these analy-

Reprinted from *Journal of Experimental Psychology* (1955), 50: 325–338, by permission of the authors and the American Psychological Association.

ses, based on independent samples of subjects and different procedures of judgment, yield similar factor structures, indicating some degree of stability in the semantic factors uncovered so far.

LOGIC OF THE SEMANTIC DIFFERENTIAL

The purpose of our factor analytic work is to devise a scaling instrument which gives representation to the major dimensions along which meaningful reactions or judgments vary. In the course of several applications of preliminary forms of this measuring instrument, it has acquired the label, *semantic differential*. Since this label points quite accurately to the intended operation—a multivariate differentiation of concept meanings in terms of a limited number of semantic scales of known factor composition—we shall continue this usage. This term is not to be confused with the general semanticist's *structural differential* which involves logical operations of a very different order.

The semantic differential had its origin in research on synesthesia (2). In these studies it was found that the process of translating from musical stimulus to "visual" response, for example, could be described as the parallel alignment in thinking of two or more dimensions of experience, each defined in terms of polar opposites (*high–low, hot–cold, loud–soft, light–dark*, etc.), with translations occurring between equivalent portions of these related continua. It was shown that this process is not limited to rare synesthetic individuals, rather being quite general and consistent in the population and congruent with standard systems of metaphor in the culture. Subsequent studies on the changing meaning of social stereotypes during the involvement of this country in World War II (4) made the notion of scaled continua between these polar terms explicit in a graphic method of collecting data and also was our first attempt to measure the meaning of concepts against a system of semantic dimensions. This background has been described in more detail in the earlier paper in this series (3).

Deriving from this earlier work, the logical basis of the semantic differential is as follows:

1. *The process of description or judgment can be conceived as the allocation of a concept to an experiential continuum, definable by a pair of polar terms.* This process reveals itself in the behavior of synesthetic subjects and in ordinary language metaphor, as well as in the more refined judgments elicited in psychophysical experiments. The content of many complex linguistic assertions (e.g., "I don't think these Chinese Communists are to be trusted") can be reduced to the allocation of a concept to a scale, e.g.,

CHINESE COMMUNISTS:
trustworthy : : : : :X : untrustworthy.

The greater the intensity of particular assertions (e.g., "These Chinese Communists are completely untrustworthy"), the more extreme becomes the allocation toward one or the other of the polar terms. This relation of graphic extremeness to intensity or strength of association will be detailed in a subsequent report. The process of judgment here has much in common with the single-stimulus or absolute-judgment method in psychophysics. Subjects use the differential in ways suggesting that they "carry about" stabilizing frames of reference based upon a lifetime of

making such judgments, i.e., each "absolute" judgment of a particular concept on a particular scale is really a comparative judgment against a multitude of previous concept-scale allocations.

2. *Many different experiential continua, or ways in which meanings can vary, are essentially equivalent and hence may be represented by a single dimension.* In the example given above, the specific scale *trustworthy-untrustworthy* would presumably appear as an essentially evaluative judgment—the same speaker might well have said, "Chinese Communists are no good." This functional equivalence of many alternate modes of semantic judgment was clearly evident in both the studies on synesthesia and those on the changing structure of social stereotypes. In the latter case, for instance, six of eight scales used on one form intercorrelated .90 or better (*fair-unfair, high-low, kind-cruel, valuable-worthless, Christian-anti-Christian,* and *honest-dishonest*), clearly indicating the existence of a generalized evaluative factor. It is this characteristic of language and thinking that makes the development of a quantitative measuring instrument feasible.

3. *A limited number of such continua can be used to define a semantic space within which the meaning of any concept can be specified.* This statement specifies some variant of factor analysis as the basic methodology. If it can be demonstrated that some limited number of dimensions or factors is sufficient to differentiate among the meanings of randomly selected concepts, and if the scale system finally selected satisfies the usual criteria of measurement, then the data obtained with such a semantic differential become an operationally defined index of meaning. In the present instance, the operations can be made explicit and thereby repeatable (see under

"Procedure" below). It is, of course, true that one cannot define fundamental factors in any final form on the basis of a single factor-analytic study; it is necessary to demonstrate repeatedly, over independent samples of subjects, concepts, and descriptive continua, that essentially the same sets of factors appear and in approximately the same relations. In this paper we report the results of two such studies.

ANALYSIS I: CENTROID METHOD, GRAPHIC DATA

Since the purpose of our factor analysis of meaning is to discover the "natural" dimensionality of the semantic space, i.e., the system of factors which together account for variance in semantic judgments, it is important to obtain as representative a sampling of scales, concepts, and subjects as possible. The nature and number of factors obtained in any analysis is limited by the sources of variability in the original data, and we wished to avoid both the production of artificial factors and the omission of significant ones through biased sampling.

Sampling.—In obtaining a sample of *scales* of semantic judgment, it was decided to use a frequency-of-usage or availability criterion. Forty nouns were taken from the Kent-Rosanoff list of stimulus words for free association and these were read in fairly rapid succession to a group of approximately 200 undergraduate students. These subjects were instructed to write down after each stimulus noun the first descriptive adjective that occurred to them (e.g., TREE—*green*, HOUSE—*big*, PRIEST—*good*). These subjects were asked not to search for exotic qualifiers, but simply to give whatever occurred to them immediately, and the rapid rate of presentation further restricted the likelihood of getting rare associates. These data were then analyzed for frequency of occurrence of all adjectives, regardless of the stimulus words with which they had appeared. As might be expected, the adjectives *good* and *bad* occurred with frequencies more than double those of any other adjectives. Perhaps less expected was the fact that nearly half of the 50 most frequently ap-

pearing adjectives were also clearly evaluative in nature. Also among the frequently given adjectives were most of the common sensory discriminanda, however, such as *heavy–light*, *sweet–sour*, and *hot–cold*. These frequently used adjectives were made into sets of polar opposites and served as the sample of descriptive scales used in this study. For theoretical reasons, a few additional sensory continua were inserted in this set of 50; these scales were *pungent–bland*, *fragrant–foul*, and *bright–dark*. The kind of bias that this method of sampling has probably introduced will be considered later under "Discussion." The entire set of scales is given in Table 1.

The sampling of *concepts* presented a less critical problem, since our purpose was a factor analysis of scales of judgment rather than of concepts. It was important, however, that these concepts be others than those on which the adjective sample had been based (the 40 original stimulus words from the Kent-Rosanoff lists), that they be as diversified in meaning as possible so as to augment the total variability in judgments, and that they be familiar to the subjects we intended to use. On these bases the experimenters simply selected the following 20 concepts: LADY, BOULDER, SIN, FATHER, LAKE, SYMPHONY, RUSSIAN, FEATHER, ME, FIRE, BABY, FRAUD, GOD, PATRIOT, TORNADO, SWORD, MOTHER, STATUE, COP, AMERICA.

Ideally, the sample of subjects (Ss) for this type of analysis would be a representative cross section of the general population. As is so often the case, however, the availability and test sophistication of the college student population dictated our choice. A group of 100 students in introductory psychology served as Ss; they were well paid for their work, and internal evidence testifies to the care with which they did what was a long and not very exciting task.

Procedure.—The pairing of 50 descriptive scales with 20 concepts in all possible combinations generates a 1000-item test form. For checking reliability, 40 of these 1000 items, chosen at random but with the restriction that no concept should be used more than twice and no scale more than once, were repeated as a final page of the mimeographed test booklet. The ordering of concept-scale pairings was deliberately rotated rather than random; it was felt that this procedure would better guarantee independence of judgments, since the maximum of 19 items would intervene between successive judgments of the same concept and the maximum of 49 items would intervene between successive judgments on the same scale. Each item appeared as follows:

LADY:

rough___:___:___:___:___:___smooth

with *S* instructed to place a check mark in that position indicating both the direction and intensity of his association. The method is thus a combined scaling and controlled association procedure. The exact instructions were as follows:

"The purpose of this study is to measure the meanings of certain words to various people by having them judge each word against a series of descriptive scales. In taking this test, please judge the words on the basis of what they mean to *you*. Each numbered item presents a CONCEPT (such as DICTATOR), and a scale (such as *high–low*). You are to rate the concept on the 7-point scale indicated.

If you felt that the concept was *very closely associated* with one end of the scale, you might place your check mark as follows:

DICTATOR:

up____:____:____:____:____:__X__down.

"If you felt that the concept was *quite closely related* to one side of the scale, you might check as follows:

HOUSE:

straight____:_X_:____:____:____:____crooked.

"If the concept seemed *only slightly related* to one side as opposed to the other, you might check as follows:

CLOUD:

easy____:__:_X_:____:____:____difficult.

"If you considered the scale *completely irrelevant*, or *both sides equally associated*, you would check the middle space on the scale:

TREE:

idealistic____:__:__:_X_:__:__:__realistic.

Sometimes you may feel as though you have had the same item before on the test. This will not be the case; every item is different from every other item. *So do not look back and forth throughout the test.* Also, do not try to remember how you marked similar items earlier in the test. *Make each item a separate and independent judgment.* Work at fairly high speed, without worrying or puzzling over the individual items for long periods. It is your first impressions that we want.

"Of course, some of the items will seem highly irrelevant to you. It was necessary, in the design of this test, to match every concept with every scale at some place, and this is why some items seem irrelevant—so give the best judgment you can and move along.

"Do not try to complete the whole form in one sitting. As soon as you begin to feel a little

fatigued—as soon as the meanings of the concepts begin to get a little 'fuzzy' in your mind—put this test aside for a while and do something else."

Treatment of data.—The combination of scales, concepts, and *S*s used in this study generates a 50 × 20 × 100 cube of data, as shown by the model in Fig. 1. Each scale position was assigned a number, from 1 to 7, arbitrarily from left to right, and hence each cell in this cube contains a number representing the judgment of a particular concept, on a particular scale, by a particular subject. These data were punched into IBM cards in the order in which they appeared in the test forms. The first step in treatment of the data was to re-order them in such a way as to match the model, e.g., so that each subject would have a separate card for each of the 20 concepts judged, with the scales running in constant order from 1 through 50. These cards were then arranged into 20 blocks, one for each concept, each

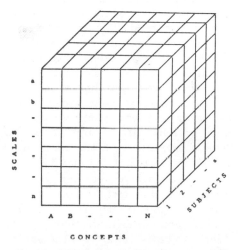

FIG. 1. Three-dimensional raw-score data matrix, obtained when a group of *S*s (1, 2, . . . s) judges a sample of concepts (A, B, . . . N) against a set of semantic scales (a, b, . . . n). Each cell contains a number from 1 to 7, representing the judgment of a particular concept on a particular scale by a single subject.

containing the complete ordered data for 100 subjects.

Reliability check.—The reliability with which semantic judgments are made with this 7-point graphic scale procedure was estimated by applying the retest method to the sample of 40 duplicated items. It will be recalled that the last page of the test form was made up of a randomly selected set of items from the 1000-item test form proper. In this connection it is interesting to note that, when questioned at the conclusion of their work, not a single S realized that these were repeat items. This was because, as they had been warned, there would be many similar items to judge (e.g., item 87 might be LAKE *tense–relaxed* and item 592 might be LAKE *calm–agitated*), and therefore the actual repeats were not recognized as such. The coefficient of reliability was calculated by correlating pairs of scores, original and repeat check positions, for the same items. The summation of cross products and the summations for means and variances were taken across both Ss and items. Since there were 40 duplicated items per subject, and 100 Ss, 4000 pairs contributed to the reliability coefficient. The resulting uncorrected coefficient was .85. This, it should be noted, is the reliability with which positions on these scales are checked, as estimated over a brief time period, not the reliability of any particular scale. Inspection of the data indicates that certain items may be more stable than others over the Ss as a group and that certain positions on the scale (particularly the extremes, 1 or 7) are more stable than others. This is to be expected from the nature of the task, where concepts of ambiguous or indefinite meaning will tend to be allocated to positions near the neutral point (Position 4). Considering the speed with which these responses are elicited from Ss—better than 10 items per minute on the average—this represents a reasonably high degree of stability.

Matrix of intercorrelations.—Referring back to Fig. 1, it can be seen that each S provides a complete set of 50 judgments on each concept—each vertical column is such a set. Since both Ss and concepts are replicated, it would be possible to obtain separate matrices of scale intercorrelations for individual Ss (summing over concepts) as well as for individual concepts (summing over subjects). However, since our long-run purpose was to set up a semantic measuring instrument which would be applicable to people and concepts in general, we wished to obtain that matrix of intercorrelations among scales which would be most representative or typical. We have therefore summed over both Ss and concepts, generating a single 50 × 50 intercorrelational matrix of every scale with every other scale to which the total data contribute. Another reason for summing over concepts was to avoid spuriously low correlations resulting from low variability of judgments on single concepts. If nearly all Ss call TORNADO extremely *cruel* and also agree in calling it extremely *unpleasant*, the correlation between *kind–cruel* and *pleasant–unpleasant* would approach indeterminacy, despite the fact that over concepts in general there is a high positive correlation between these scales.

Each of our 50 scales was responded to 2000 times, each of the 100 Ss responding once to each of 20 concepts. Thus, every scale can be paired with every other scale 2000 times, each S contributing 20 pairs to the total, and each concept contributing 100 pairs. In computing each correlation, the summations for cross products, means, and variances were taken across both

Ss and concepts. In symbolic form, if X_{ijv} is the score on the ith scale, for the jth concept, and the vth subject, and $\bar{X}_{i..}$ as is the mean for the ith scale found by summing over concepts and Ss and dividing by 20×100, then the cross products between scales i and k in deviations from the means were found from:

$$\sum_i \sum_v (X_{ijv} - \bar{X}_{i..})$$
$$(X_{kjv} - \bar{X}_{k..}) \quad (1)$$

The expression for the variance on scale i is then:

$$\frac{\sum_j \sum_v (X_{ijv} - \bar{X}_{i..})^2}{N} \quad (2)$$

These intercorrelations were calculated with IBM equipment. To make possible a later analysis of factor structures for individual concepts, subtotals were printed for each block of 100 cards representing the total data for each concept. The matrix of correlations whose factorization is reported here was based on summation over all concepts. Therefore the variance due to differences between concept means (the difference between $\bar{X}_{ij}$'s) is necessarily included in the correlation values. The possible effect of this on our results will be discussed in greater detail at a later point.

Factor analysis.—Thurstone's Centroid Factor Method (5) was applied to this matrix of correlations. Four factors were extracted and rotated into simple structure, maintaining orthogonality.[1] The rotated factor matrix appears as Table 1. Since orthogonal relations were maintained

in rotation, the matrix in this table represents uncorrelated factors. We stopped extracting factors after the fourth; this factor accounted for less than 2% of the variance and appeared by inspection to be a residual— the pattern of scales having noticeable loadings on it (between .20 and .27) made no sense semantically. It is to be expected that a larger sampling of scales, with less emphasis on the evaluative factor, would allow a number of additional factors of a denotative sort to appear.

The problem of labeling factors is somewhat simpler here than in the usual case. In a sense, our polar scales label themselves as to content. The first factor is clearly identifiable as *evaluative* by listing the scales which have high loadings on it: *good–bad, beautiful–ugly, sweet–sour, clean–dirty, tasty–distasteful, valuable–worthless, kind–cruel, pleasant–unpleasant, bitter–sweet, happy–sad, sacred–profane, nice–awful, fragrant–foul, honest–dishonest,* and *fair–unfair*. All of these loadings are .75 or better, and it will also be noted by referring to Table 1 that these scales are "purely" evaluative in the sense that the extracted variance is almost entirely in this first factor. Several other scales, *rich–poor, clear–hazy, fresh–stale,* and *healthy–sick,* while not as highly loaded as the first set on the evaluative factor, nevertheless restrict their loadings chiefly to this factor.

The second factor identifies itself fairly well as a *potency* variable (or, as one of our undergraduate statistical assistants puts it, a "football player" factor): *large–small, strong–weak, heavy–light,* and *thick–thin* serve to identify its general nature, these scales having the highest and most restricted loadings. The tendency for scales representing this factor to be contaminated, as it were, with the evaluative factor is apparent in Table

[1] Due to space limitations, the original 50×50 correlation matrix, the unrotated factor matrix, and the transformation matrix are not included in this paper. They may be obtained by writing to the authors.

The writers wish to thank Mr. Kellogg Wilson for the work he did for us on these rotations and also those involved in the second analysis.

TABLE 1

ROTATED FACTOR LOADINGS—ANALYSIS I

Adjective Pairs	Loadings				h^2
	I	II	III	IV	
1. good–bad	.88	.05	−.09	.09	.79
2. large–small	.06	.62	.34	.04	.51
3. beautiful–ugly	.86	.09	.01	.26	.82
4. yellow–blue	−.33	−.14	.12	.17	.17
5. hard–soft	−.48	.55	.16	.21	.60
6. sweet–sour	.83	−.14	−.09	.02	.72
7. strong–weak	.19	.62	.20	−.03	.46
8. clean–dirty	.82	−.05	.03	.02	.68
9. high–low	.59	.21	.08	.04	.40
10. calm–agitated	.61	.00	−.36	−.05	.50
11. tasty–distasteful	.77	.05	−.11	.00	.61
12. valuable–worthless	.79	.04	.13	.00	.64
13. red–green	−.33	−.08	.35	.22	.28
14. young–old	.31	−.30	.32	.01	.29
15. kind–cruel	.82	−.10	−.18	.13	.73
16. loud–soft	−.39	.44	.23	.22	.45
17. deep–shallow	.27	.46	.14	−.25	.37
18. pleasant–unpleasant	.82	−.05	.28	−.12	.77
19. black–white	−.64	.31	.01	−.03	.51
20. bitter–sweet	−.80	.11	.20	.03	.69
21. happy–sad	.76	−.11	.00	.03	.59
22. sharp–dull	.23	.07	.52	−.10	.34
23. empty–full	−.57	−.26	−.03	.18	.43
24. ferocious–peaceful	−.69	.17	.41	.02	.67
25. heavy–light	−.36	.62	−.11	.06	.53
26. wet–dry	.08	.07	−.03	−.14	.03
27. sacred–profane	.81	.02	−.10	.01	.67
28. relaxed–tense	.55	.12	−.37	−.11	.47
29. brave–cowardly	.66	.44	.12	.03	.64
30. long–short	.20	.34	.13	−.23	.23
31. rich–poor	.60	.10	.00	−.18	.40
32. clear–hazy	.59	.03	.10	−.16	.38
33. hot–cold	−.04	−.06	.46	.07	.22
34. thick–thin	−.06	.44	−.06	−.11	.21
35. nice–awful	.87	−.08	.19	.15	.82
36. bright–dark	.69	−.13	.26	.00	.56
37. treble–bass	.33	−.47	.06	−.02	.33
38. angular–rounded	−.17	.08	.43	.12	.23
39. fragrant–foul	.84	−.04	−.11	.05	.72
40. honest–dishonest	.85	.07	−.02	.16	.75
41. active–passive	.14	.04	.59	−.02	.37
42. rough–smooth	−.46	.36	.29	.10	.44
43. fresh–stale	.68	.01	.22	−.11	.52
44. fast–slow	.01	.00	.70	−.12	.50
45. fair–unfair	.83	.08	−.07	.11	.71
46. rugged–delicate	−.42	.60	.26	.27	.68
47. near–far	.41	.13	.11	−.05	.20
48. pungent–bland	−.30	.12	.26	.05	.17
49. healthy–sick	.69	.17	.09	.02	.59
50. wide–narrow	.26	.41	−.07	−.11	.25
% of total variance	33.78	7.62	6.24	1.52	.4916
% of common variance	68.55	15.46	12.66	3.08	.9975

1. The following scales are mainly potency continua, but reflect considerable evaluative meaning as well: *hard–soft, loud–soft, deep–shallow,* *brave–cowardly, bass–treble, rough–smooth, rugged–delicate,* and *wide–narrow.* It also should be noted from inspection of this table that in general

loadings on the evaluative factor are higher than those on potency, even where "pure" scales are involved.

The third factor appears to be mainly an *activity* variable in judgments, with some relation to physical sharpness or abruptness as well. The most distinctively loaded scales are *fast–slow* (.70), *active–passive* (.59), and *hot–cold* (.46); somewhat different in apparent meaning, but displaying similar factor loadings, are *sharp–dull* (.52) and *angular–rounded* (.43). The following scales have considerable loading on this activity factor, but also as much or more loading on evaluation: *red–green*, *young–old* (our *S*s were college undergraduates), *ferocious–peaceful*, and *tense–relaxed*. The noticeable tendency for both activity and power to be associated with positive evaluation (e.g., *good*, *strong*, *active* tend to go together rather than *good*, *weak*, *passive*) is probably a cultural semantic bias. All we can say is that there appear to be independent *factors* operating, even though it is difficult to find many specific *scales* which are orthogonal with respect to evaluation.

The percentages of total variance and common variance at the bottom of Table 1 confirm the dominant role of evaluation in semantic judgments and further indicate that the three factors we have isolated account for approximately 50% of the total variance in judgments. Of the common factor variance, about 70% is evaluative.

Analysis II: Forced–Choice Data[2]

The method for obtaining correlations described in the previous section, by summing over both concepts and subjects, necessarily in-

cludes the variance attributable to differences between concepts. Does this source of variance influence the factor results? To the extent that there are differences in factor structure as between concepts, and to the extent that our sampling of concepts was nonrepresentative, the factor-analytic results could be biased. One way to get at the contribution of particular concepts is to check the degree of correlation between specific scales within each of the 20 concepts separately. When this was done by using the *good–bad* scale as a reference and obtaining the correlations of all other scales with this reference, the sizes of correlations were found to vary considerably with the concept involved.

Rather than to reanalyze our entire data with statistical procedures which would eliminate concept variance, it was decided to do another analysis of the same scales with a new population of subjects, but to employ a method of collecting data which would itself eliminate specific concept differences. The method used involves a forced choice between pairs of descriptive scales as to the direction in which they should be aligned, with no concept being specified. This method had been used in an earlier study on synesthetic thinking (1) and referred to as a "parallel polarity" test. If a group of *S*s is given the following item,

sharp–dull; relaxed–tense,

and asked to encircle the one of the second pair which is closest in meaning to the capitalized word in the first pair, there is no restriction on the concept (if any) that may be used. Some *S*s might be thinking of "people" concepts, others of "object" concepts, and yet others of "aesthetic" concepts, and so forth. Introspectively (as judged by comments of individuals taking such a test), there is often no par-

[2] The writers wish to express their appreciation of the work done by Mrs. Joan Dodge in collecting and analyzing the data for this study.

ticular concept involved. If 100% of the subjects select *tense*, as might happen above, this would· indicate that *sharp–tense* vs. *dull–relaxed* is a generally appropriate parallelism, regardless of type of concept; if subjects divide randomly (e.g., 50% one way) on an item, for example,

FRESH–stale; long–short,

it would appear that either the multitude of conceptual contexts in which these qualities might be related are random as to direction or that subjects differ randomly in their absolute judgments of relation. In any case, no particular concept or set of concepts is forcing the direction of relation.

Procedure.—The pairing of each of 50 scales (the same as used in the first analysis) with every other scale generates a test comprising 1,225 items. Again, a rotational procedure was followed to maximize the separation of identical scales. A total of 40 subjects was used, of the same type used in the previous analysis but not including any of the same individuals. The exact instructions were as follows:

We want to find out what dimensions of meaning are related and what the basic factors in the system seem to be. This is a very important problem for building any measuring instrument and we ask your complete cooperation in carrying out the following instructions

Procedure to Follow:

a. Each item you see will be composed of two pairs of words. Your job is to encircle the word in the second pair which goes best with the capitalized word in the first pair.

STRAIGHT–crooked   noble–bestial

b. Don't look back over the judgments you have already completed. Judge each item by itself.
c. Be sure to look at *both* words in each pair, so as to be judging the relation of the scales as wholes.
d. Check back after you have made each judgment to be sure you answered the way you wanted to. Correct any judgment that you feel was not what you meant.
e. Try not to base your judgments on your likes or dislikes of particular individual words. It is the relation among scales as wholes that you are judging.

General Suggestions:

a. Some relations will be immediately obvious. With others it will be harder for you to make your decision. In some cases it might seem that both words could do equally well. Do not waste time worrying over any single item —we want your first impression. On the other hand, do a careful conscientious job. The results will be worthless if you do your work thoughtlessly.
b. Do not work so long at one stretch that you become fatigued. Distribute your work on this test as you see fit. We would like to have it returned within one week.
c. Be sure you do all the judging *yourself.* Forms filled out by more than one person would be *worse* than useless for our purpose.
d. Return the form *to this class* no later than one week from today.
e. If, for any reason, you feel that you cannot comply with the above instructions, please return the incomplete form to us. You may still keep your dollar, since no data at all is preferable to erroneous data.

Treatment of data.—The measure of relation used in this analysis was simply the percentage of agreement between scales, i.e., the percentage of persons who associated one of the right-hand terms with the capitalized adjective. In the example above, the number of Ss who circled *relaxed* as going with SHARP was divided by 40 (number of Ss) and the resulting percent was entered into a 50 × 50 matrix of percentages of relations[3] between descriptive terms. Since the number of persons circling one of the terms directly determines the number circling the other, calculations were necessary for only one term. The left-hand term was chosen since this corresponded to the original direction taken as positive in the first study. A perfect relation is inferred from 100%; 50% indicates no relation, since equal numbers of Ss choose both terms; less than 50% indicates that the terms are negatively related in

[3] The 50 × 50 matrix of percentages, the unrotated dimension matrix, and the transformation matrix are not included here because of space limitations. They may be obtained from the authors.

their given positions (e.g., as in the first illustration above). The resulting 50×50 matrix of percentages was factored by a technique described below and the results compared with those of the original centroid analysis.

Factor analysis.—Since the method of factoring applied to the matrix of percentages has only recently been developed and is as yet unpublished it is necessary to give the basic notion of the method here. The 50 variables are viewed as mutually orthogonal axes in k space, where $k = 50$. These axes intersect in an origin of zero where the origin corresponds to zero relation; in this study the origin corresponds to 50%. The percentages of relation obtained for each variable are considered coordinates fixing the variable as a point in k space. The higher the coordinate of a variable on any dimension, the higher the relation with that dimension. The aim is to find a minimum number of orthogonal dimensions which adequately describe the k-space structure in terms of a set of coordinates for each variable on the dimensions. These new coordinates are taken as indicating the degrees of relation of the variable to the minimum number of dimensions.

One method of deriving these coordinates is the following: If P, the matrix of percentages, is filled with 1.00 in the main diagonal (one would expect each variable to be chosen as going with itself 100% of the time), Thurstone's diagonal method (cf. **5**, pp. 101–105) can be applied to a new matrix generated by PP' and the resulting factor loadings will be the coordinates described above.

A mathematically identical method, but one which represents a considerable saving in time over the above process, was used in this study.[4] This technique is briefly described below. It can easily be shown that if a dimension passes

---

[4] The operations involved in this technique are presently described in mimeographed form.

through point j then the coordinate of variable i on this dimension is given by

$$c_{ij} = \frac{D_{ij}^2 - L_j^2 - L_i^2}{-2L_j},$$

where c_{ij} = the coordinate of i on a dimension passing through j, D_{ij} = the Euclidean distance between i and j in k space, L_j and L_i = the vector lengths from the origin to points j and i, respectively. For subsequent dimensions D and L are reduced to their values in the reduced space, and the reduced values are applied in the above formula. Each new dimension is selected to pass through one of the variables. This formula is applied repeatedly until some criterion for stopping is reached or until the vector lengths are reduced to zero. Unlike factor loadings, the coordinates may have absolute values greater than 1.00.

After the fifth dimension had been extracted, it became clear that only dimensions with single high coordinates ("specifics") would continue to emerge. Analysis was therefore discontinued. These dimensions were then rotated graphically in an attempt to maximize the similarity between this structure and that obtained with the centroid method.[5] The rotated dimension matrix appears as Table 2.

COMPARISON OF ANALYSES I AND II

The purpose of the rotation in the second analysis was to determine to what extent the factors isolated in the original centroid analysis, using concept-scale pairings, could also be demonstrated in the dimensional analysis, based on forced-choice judgments among scales themselves. We shall refer to "loadings" of variables on "factors" in speaking of results of the centroid method and to "coordinates" of variables on "dimensions" in speaking of results of the second method. Similarity between the results of the

---

[5] We thank Dr. C. F. Wrigley for bringing this measure to our attention. The measure, e_{ij}, is found from

$$e_{ij} = \frac{\sum_k f_{ki} \cdot g_{kj}}{\sqrt{\sum_k f_{ki}^2 \cdot \sum_k g_{kj}^2}}$$

where f_{ki}, g_{kj} represent the loadings for the kth variable on the ith and jth factors. References to the use of this index are found in (1) and (6).

TABLE 2

RotATED DIMENSION COORDINATES—ANALYSIS II

Adjective Pairs	Coordinates				
	I	II	III	IV	V
1. good–bad	2.29	.84	.07	1.54	0
2. large–small	.12	1.76	−.02	1.00	−.34
3. beautiful–ugly	2.40	.41	.38	1.48	−.01
4. yellow–blue	−.31	−.27	−.15	.73	−.44
5. hard–soft	−1.39	1.06	.68	.45	.39
6. sweet–sour	2.29	.71	.14	.98	−.26
7. strong–weak	.38	1.81	.67	1.36	−.53
8. clean–dirty	2.38	.46	.60	1.26	−.06
9. high–low	1.35	1.21	1.00	1.00	−.26
10. calm–agitated	2.25	.36	−.62	.48	−.14
11. tasty–distasteful	2.11	1.05	.21	1.21	−.33
12. valuable–worthless	1.87	1.12	.25	1.53	−.46
13. red–green	−.59	1.03	.78	.58	−.19
14. young–old	1.22	.83	1.26	.87	−.33
15. kind–cruel	2.40	.49	−.18	1.23	−.23
16. loud–soft	−1.71	1.03	.61	.69	.06
17. deep–shallow	.30	1.46	−.65	.72	.97
18. pleasant–unpleasant	2.38	.56	.24	1.38	−.29
19. black–white	−2.11	.18	−.64	−.53	.13
20. bitter–sweet	−2.22	−.30	.16	−.82	.43
21. happy–sad	2.09	.97	.61	1.50	−.22
22. sharp–dull	.51	1.31	1.88	.53	0
23. empty–full	−.62	−1.22	−.05	−.72	1.47
24. ferocious–peaceful	−2.25	.25	.44	.16	−.09
25. heavy–light	−1.60	1.68	−.92	.06	0
26. wet–dry	−.62	.35	−.46	.00	−.34
27. sacred–profane	2.29	.58	−.25	1.04	−.24
28. relaxed–tense	2.17	.24	−.63	.62	−.30
29. brave–cowardly	1.45	1.56	.40	1.66	−.50
30. long–short	.59	1.01	.02	.72	−.38
31. rich–poor	1.31	1.33	.22	1.19	−.36
32. clear–hazy	1.92	.69	.98	.93	−.09
33. hot–cold	.42	.83	.65	.57	−.50
34. thick–thin	−.35	1.48	−.37	.60	−.61
35. nice–awful	2.39	1.07	−.02	1.15	−.07
36. bright–dark	1.71	.78	1.32	1.07	−.21
37. treble–bass	1.15	−.18	1.42	.06	−.01
38. angular–rounded	−1.31	.30	.77	−.08	.42
39. fragrant–foul	2.32	.62	.23	1.12	−.31
40. honest–dishonest	1.99	.89	.10	1.50	−.37
41. active–passive	.30	1.64	1.39	.79	−.40
42. rough–smooth	−2.32	.28	.17	−.07	.31
43. fresh–stale	2.05	.82	.68	1.27	−.32
44. fast–slow	.42	1.10	1.50	.63	−.02
45. fair–unfair	2.22	.89	.37	1.33	−.29
46. rugged–delicate	−2.41	.60	.05	1.10	0
47. near–far	.85	1.09	.67	.74	−.17
48. pungent–bland	−1.41	.66	.48	.06	−.39
49. healthy–sick	1.79	1.38	.63	1.81	−.54
50. wide–narrow	.60	1.24	−.14	.99	−.60

two methods were gauged in three ways: (*a*) qualitatively, by the extent to which variables heavily loaded on factors have high coordinates on dimensions, (*b*) by the magnitude of correlation between factor loadings and dimension coordinates across variables, (*c*) by the magnitude of indices of factorial similarity, *e*.[5] "Heavily loaded" and "high coordinates" were defined by arbitrarily selected criterion values: the criteria for "heavily loaded" were that variables have loadings $> .80$, $> .50$, and $> .50$ for Factors I, II, and III, respectively; the criteria for "high coordinates" were that variables have coordinates > 2.25, > 1.30, and > 1.30 for Dimensions I, II, and III, respectively.

Table 3 presents a comparison

TABLE 3

RELATIONS BETWEEN FACTORS (METHOD I) AND DIMENSIONS (METHOD II)

Adjective Pairs	Factor I Criterion, .80 Dimension I Criterion, 2.25 ($r = .944$, $e = .952$)	
	Both	
good–bad	.88	2.29
nice–awful	.87	2.39
beautiful–ugly	.86	2.40
fragrant–foul	.84	2.32
sweet–sour	.83	2.29
clean–dirty	.82	2.38
pleasant–unpleasant	.82	2.38
sacred–profane	.81	2.29
	Factor Only	
honest–dishonest	.85	1.99
fair–unfair	.83	2.22
	Dimension Only	
rugged–delicate	−.42	−2.41
rough–smooth	−.46	−2.32
	Factor II Criterion, .50 Dimension II Criterion, 1.30 ($r = .421$, $e = .622$)	
	Both	
strong–weak	.62	1.81
large–small	.62	1.76
heavy–light	.62	1.68
	Factor Only	
rugged–delicate	.60	.60
hard–soft	.55	1.06
	Dimension Only	
active–passive	.04	1.64
brave–cowardly	.44	1.56
thick–thin	.44	1.48
deep–shallow	.46	1.46
healthy–sick	.17	1.38
	Factor III Criterion, .50 Dimension III Criterion, 1.30 ($r = .639$, $e = .722$)	
	Both	
fast–slow	.70	1.50
active–passive	.59	1.39
sharp–dull	.52	1.88
	Factor Only (none)	
	Dimension Only	
treble–bass	.06	1.42
bright–dark	.26	1.32

between factors and dimensions. The descriptive adjective pairs are placed in one of the following categories: variables with both heavy loadings and high coordinates, variables with heavy loadings but low coordinates, and variables with light loadings but high coordinates.

The values r and e between factors and dimensions are given at the top of each column.

I. Evaluation. The high similarity between Dimension I and Factor I is apparent from both e ($= .952$) and r ($= .944$) and the agreement between variables considered high on both. Even the variables that only meet the criterion on one method are actually close to the criterion on the other. This again testifies to the prominence and stability of the evaluative component in semantic judgment. That Dimension I is evaluative is obvious in a catalogue of the high-coordinate variables—*beautiful–ugly, nice–awful, clean–dirty, pleasant–unpleasant,* and so on. The evaluative "dimension" also draws in *delicate–rugged* and *smooth–rough,* which are not quite as prominent in the first analysis.

II. Potency. The potency variable displays the lowest correspondence between factors and dimensions, but even here the evidence is satisfactory. The correlation over all 50 variables is .421 with an e of .622. The three most heavily loaded variables on Factor II are also the three variables having the highest coordinates on Dimension II, *strong–weak, large–small,* and *heavy–light.* Of the two variables meeting the factor loading criterion only, *hard–soft* does have a sizable coordinate on Dimension II, but *rugged–delicate* clearly has become an evaluative variable in the forced-choice method. Of the variables meeting the high coordinate criterion only, three also have sizable loadings on Factor II (*brave–cowardly, thick–thin,* and *deep–shallow*). *Healthy–sick* has nearly as high a coordinate on the evaluative dimension (1.79), where it belongs according to the first analysis, and *active–passive* has nearly as high a coordinate on the activity dimension (1.39), where it belongs according to the first analysis.

III. Activity. Dimension III and Factor III correlate .639 with an *e* of .722. It is also clearly interpretable as an activity factor from both loadings and coordinates. The three most highly loaded variables, *sharp–dull, active–passive,* and *fast–slow,* are also among the four variables having the highest coordinates on Dimension III. There are no variables meeting the factor-loading criterion that do not also meet the coordinate criterion. Of the two variables meeting the co-ordinate criterion only, *bright–dark* is actually higher on the evaluative dimension, as it is also on the evaluative factor in Analysis I. *Treble–bass* does not correspond to the results of the first analysis, but its loading on the activity dimension does correspond to the findings of earlier studies on synesthesia.

DISCUSSION

The two factor analytic studies reported in this paper yield highly similar structures among the relations of 50 bipolar descriptive scales. The first factor to appear in both studies is clearly *evaluative* in nature and accounts for more than half of the extractable variance. The second and third factors to appear in both studies seem to represent *potency* and *activity* factors in semantic judgments, respectively, and again there is considerable correspondence between the two analyses. Since entirely different subjects and entirely different methods of collecting data (concepts rated on scales in the first analysis and

forced choice among scales themselves in the second analysis) were employed in the two analyses, this over-all correspondence of the first three factors to emerge in both studies increases our confidence that we are isolating something basic to the structuring of human judgments. What is perhaps remarkable is that such a large portion of the total variance in human judgment or meaning can be accounted for in terms of such a small number of basic variables. In the first study, for example, almost 50% of the total variance of judgments of 20 varied concepts against 50 varied scales by 100 *S*s is accountable for in terms of these three factors—and these were college student *S*s.

This is not taken to imply that these three, largely connotative factors represent an exhaustive description of the meaning space. There is evidence in our data for a large number of "specific" factors, quite possibly denotative in nature and representative of the ways in which our sensory nervous systems are capable of differentiating input signals (e.g., *hot–cold, black–white, wet–dry, treble–bass,* and so on). When used *connotatively*, such descriptive scales tend to rotate into one of the first three factors (e.g., *hot–cold* is activity connotatively, *white–black* is evaluation connotatively, and so forth), but when used *denotatively* in judging sensorily relevant concepts such scales represent independent factors (e.g., when ice cream and baked potatoes are compared on *hot–cold* and objects varying in brightness are judged on *white–black*). One of the reasons for the failure of our factor analytic work to date to bring out such denotative factors in sufficient magnitude to be isolated is the method of sampling scales employed —a frequency-of-usage method which overemphasized the readily available evaluative alternates. In research now being planned we intend to use Roget's *Thesaurus* as a source of scales, in other words, a logically exhaustive coverage rather than an availability sampling. Having already isolated three dominant connotative dimensions, these factors can be given merely token representation in subsequent factor analytic work.

Finally it should be noted that there is a tendency in both analyses for what might be called a convergence of scales toward a single, composite good-strong-active vs. bad-weak-passive factor. In other words, although we have evidence in both analyses for three independent connotative factors—evaluation, potency, and activity—specific scales representing the second two factors tend to be contaminated with a pervasive evalu-ativeness. Scales like *wide–narrow, brave–cowardly, rough–smooth* and *healthy–sick* (Factor II) and like *young–old, ferocious–peaceful, tense–relaxed,* and *bright–dark* (Factor III) also have as high or higher loadings or coordinates on evaluation. This is quite probably a characteristic of our culture—and possibly all human cultures—that both potency and activity (rather than weakness and passivity) are positive values. This means that it is difficult to discover specific connotative scales to represent purely our second and third factors even though these factors as such are demonstrable. The shift of such scales as those above from denota-tive to connotative usage is probably one of the reasons for differences between Factor Analyses I and II. When the concepts BOULDER and FEATHER, for example, are judged against *rugged–delicate* and later against evaluative scales, the former is clearly *rugged* and the latter clearly *delicate* denotatively, but both are judged near "4" on evalu-ation, i.e., irrelevant, and the correlation between this scale and evaluation is zero. But when no specific concepts are used, as in our second method, the pervasive evaluative connotation dominates the scale-pairing, *pleasant–unpleasant* vs. *delicate–rugged,* for example, and most *S*s encircle *delicate* as going with *pleasant,* e.g., we speak connotatively as having had a rugged (hard, unpleasant) time.

SUMMARY

Two factor analytic studies of meaningful judgments are reported in this paper, both based upon the same sample of 50 bipolar descriptive scales. The first analysis applied Thurstone's centroid method to correlations derived from 7-step graphic scale data obtained by having 100 *S*s judge 20 specific concepts against the 50 scales. The second analysis applied a new method developed by the second author to a matrix of percentages of agreement obtained by having 40 different *S*s make forced-choice pairings of the polar terms themselves, i.e., without any specific concepts being judged. The first three factors to appear in both analyses show considerable correspondence, both in order of appearance and magnitude and in the par-ticular scales which define them. The evidence as a whole points to the existence in meaningful judgments of three major connotative factors: evaluation, potency, and activity. The evalu-ative factor accounts for by far the largest portion of the extracted variance. These three factors are taken as independent dimensions of the semantic space within which the meanings of concepts may be specified.

REFERENCES

1. BURT, C. The factorial study of tempera-mental traits. *Brit. J. Psychol. Statist. Sect.,* 1948, **1,** 178–203.
2. KARWOSKI, T. F., ODBERT, H. S., & OSGOOD, C. E. Studies in synesthetic thinking: II. The role of form in visual responses to music. *J. gen. Psychol.,* 1942, **26,** 199–222.
3. OSGOOD, C. E. The nature and measurement of meaning. *Psychol. Bull.,* 1952, **49,** 197–237.
4. STAGNER, R., & OSGOOD, C. E. An experi-mental analysis of a nationalistic frame of reference. *J. soc. Psychol.,* 1941, **14,** 389–401.
5. Thurstone, L. L. *Multiple-factor analysis.* Chicago: Univ. of Chicago Press, 1947.
6. TUCKER, L. R. A method for synthesis of factor analysis studies. *Dep. of the Army, Personnel Res. Sec. Rep.,* 1951, No. 984, p. 43.

3. The Measurement of Meaning

Charles E. Osgood, George J. Suci, and Percy H. Tannenbaum

THE SEMANTIC DIFFERENTIAL

Let us glance back at the theoretical paradigm shown in Figure 1 again. What we shall call *encoding* is the selective evocation of overt instrumental acts (R_x) by the representational mediation process, ($r_m \rightarrow s_m$), presumably on the basis of differential reinforcement. These R_x's are responses to the *sign*, which are assumed to depend upon the prior association of sign and significate and which are therefore, presumably appropriate to the meaning of the sign. What types of overt responses may constitute R_x and hence serve as an index of r_m? Many intentionally encoded responses are *non-linguistic*. We often infer (rightly or wrongly) the meaning of a sign to an individual from his facial expressions, gestures, gross bodily movements, etc. — he smiles and stretches out his arms in welcome, he draws back his head and wrinkles up his nose in disgust, or he flees or strikes with his fists. But not only is such behavior difficult to quantify and cumbersome to record, it also does not yield comparable units and is probably insensitive to subtler meanings, at least in most of us.

Language as an Index of Meaning

What about *linguistic encoding*, ordinary intentional language? After all, the basic function of language is supposed to be the communication of meaning — it is often defined as "the expression of ideas." Ordinarily, if we want to find out what something *means* to a person, we ask him to tell us. What does a POLITICIAN mean to you? "Well, it is someone who campaigns and does or does not get elected. It's usually a hearty, husky, good-natured guy who's always on the 'go' — but also a 'glad-hander' and liable to be untrustworthy, a double-talker. Not as good as a statesman, of course. . . ." What does SOPHISTICATED mean? "Well . . . I know what it means, all right, but it's hard to put into words. It's being clever and wise about people and things — knowing the ropes, so

Excerpted from *The Measurement of Meaning* (Urbana: University of Illinois Press, 1957), pp. 18–30, 318–331, by permission of the authors and the publisher.

to speak. It's sort of smooth and polished, graceful but not awkward . . . poised, 'savvy,' you know. . . ." It might be noted in passing that the responses one gets when he asks what something *means* are usually quite different from those he gets when he asks for associations (e.g., what *other things* X makes him think of). POLITICIAN: Washington, smoke-filled room, insincere, laws, investigations, etc. SOPHISTICATED: lady, cocktails, music, educated, clever, smart, etc. There is some overlap, of course, because a common mediation process (elicited by the stimulus sign) is operating in both cases.

Unrestricted linguistic output of this sort has high presumptive validity, unless we question the honesty of the subject — and there is no more reason to expect malingering here than in other psychological test situations (a poorly instructed or motivated subject in a psychophysical experiment may say "heavier" when it actually feels lighter; he may take a wrong alternative in a finger-maze when he knows it is wrong). At least we can say it has as much validity as any other technique based upon requested introspection. For highly intelligent and verbally fluent subjects this method would be sufficiently sensitive, since it seems likely that a language will tend to include those discriminations which its users find necessary to communicate. Less fluent subjects, however, find it very difficult to encode meanings spontaneously (in a taste test on brands of ice cream, one of the authors found that most subjects could produce "creamy," "tasty," and a few other terms, but little more, yet given a form of the semantic differential these same individuals quickly and confidently indicated a large number of judgments). But what spontaneous linguistic output may gain in validity and sensitivity, it certainly loses on other grounds — casual introspections are hardly comparable and do not lend themselves to quantification. What sort of quantitative index of meaning could be applied to the two sample outputs above? How could we compare the outputs of two different subjects discussing their meanings of the same term and indicate the degree of similarity or difference in meaning?

It is apparent that if we are to use linguistic encoding as an index of meaning we need (a) a carefully devised *sample of alternative verbal responses* which can be standardized across subjects, (b) these alternatives to be *elicited from* subjects rather than emitted so that encoding fluency is eliminated as a variable, and (c) these alternatives to be *representative* of the major ways in which meanings vary. In other words, rather than relying on the spontaneous emission of words relating to a particular stimulating sign, we need to play a game of "Twenty Questions" with our subject: SOPHISTICATED — is it *hard* or *soft*? Is it *pleasant* or *unpleasant*? Is it *fast* or *slow*? Just as in "Twenty Questions" the selection of successive alternatives gradually eliminates uncertainty as to the object being thought about, so selection among successive pairs of common verbal opposites should gradually isolate the "meaning" of the stimulus sign. To increase the sensitivity of our instrument, we may insert a scale between each pair of terms, so that the subject can indicate both the *direction* and the *intensity* of each judgment.

The semantic differential is essentially a combination of controlled association and scaling procedures. We provide the subject with a concept to be differentiated and a set of bipolar adjectival scales against which to do it, his only task being to indicate, for each item (pairing of a concept with a scale), the direction of his association and its intensity on a seven-step scale. The crux of the method, of course, lies in selecting the sample of descriptive polar terms. Ideally, the sample should be as representative as possible of all the ways in which meaningful judgments can vary, and yet be small enough in size to be efficient in practice. In other words, from the myriad linguistic and non-linguistic behaviors mediated by symbolic processes, we select a small but carefully devised sample, a sample which we shall try to demonstrate is chiefly indicative of the ways that meanings vary, and largely insensitive to other sources of variation.

Research Background of the Semantic Differential

The semantic differential as a technique for measuring meaning was not developed directly out of the reasoning described above. As is so often the case, the actual measurement procedures developed more or less "Topsy-like" in the course of experimental research along other, though related, lines, and the reasonings leading to the measurement of meaning in general grew out of interpretations of the findings in this earlier research.

The notion of using polar adjectives to define the termini of semantic dimensions grew out of research on synesthesia with Theodore Karwoski and Henry Odbert at Dartmouth College. Synesthesia is defined by Warren in his *Dictionary of Psychology*

(1934) as "a phenomenon characterizing the experiences of certain individuals, in. which certain sensations belonging to one sense or mode attach to certain sensations of another group and appear regularly whenever a stimulus of the latter type occurs." This implies a sort of "neural cross-circuiting" that occurs in only a few freak individuals, and it is true that many of the classic case histories gave credence to this view. The series of researches by Karwoski, Odbert, and their associates, however, related synesthesia to thinking and language in general. Rather than being a freak phenomenon, color-music synesthesia was reported by Karwoski and Odbert (1938) as being regularly indulged in by as many as 13 per cent of Dartmouth College students, often as a means of enriching their enjoyment of music. A much larger number reported that they had such experiences occasionally.

The regular photistic visualizers varied among themselves as to the modes of translation between sound and vision and as to the vividness of their experiences, and their difference from the general population seemed to be one of degree rather than kind. Whereas fast, exciting music might be pictured by the synesthete as sharply etched, bright red forms, his less imaginative brethren would merely agree that *words* like "red-hot," "bright," and "fiery," as verbal metaphors, adequately described the music; a slow, melancholic selection might be visualized as heavy, slow-moving "blobs" of somber hue and be described verbally as "heavy," "blue," and "dark." The relation of this phenomenon to ordinary metaphor is evident: A happy man is said to feel "high," a sad man "low"; the pianist travels "up" and "down" the scale from treble to bass; souls travel "up" to the good place and "down" to the bad place; hope is "white" and despair is "black."

Interrelationships among color, mood, and musical experiences were studied more analytically by Odbert, Karwoski, and Eckerson (1942). Subjects first listened to ten short excerpts from classical selections and indicated their dominant moods by checking sets of adjectives arranged in a mood circle (see Hevner, 1936); on a second hearing they gave the names of colors that seemed appropriate to the music. The colors were found to follow the moods created by the music. Delius' *On Hearing the First Cuckoo in Spring* was judged leisurely in mood and predominantly green in color; a portion of Wagner's *Rienzi Overture* was judged exciting or vigorous in mood and predominantly red in color. When another group of subjects was merely shown the mood adjectives (with no musical stimulation) and asked to select appropriate colors, even more consistent relations appeared. There is a great deal of supporting evidence, of course, for consistent relations between colors and moods.

These results indicate that stimuli from several modalities, visual, auditory, emotional and verbal, may have shared significances or meanings — cross-modality stimulus equivalence. Further experiments with even simpler stimuli by Karwoski, Odbert, and Osgood

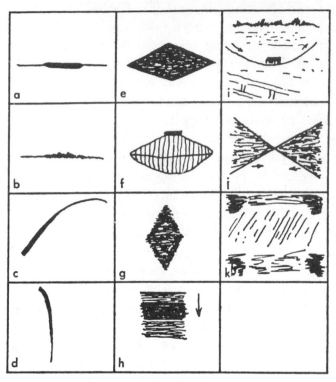

Fig. 2. Sample of photisms drawn by complex synesthetes to represent a simple tone which grows louder and then softer.

(1942) indicated that such equivalence across modalities shows continuity along dimensions of experience. In one study complex synesthetes drew pictures to represent what they visualized when simple melodic sequences were played by a single instrument. Figure 2 shows a sample of reactions to a tone which simply gets louder and then softer (*crescendo-diminuendo*). Subject *e*, for example, drew a solid form which grows continuously *thicker* and then thinner; subject *h* made a color continuously more and then less *saturated;* subject *i* (who always created meaningful rather than abstract forms) reported a little car that came continuously *nearer* and then farther away. These are functionally or meaningfully equivalent responses to the same auditory stimulus, and they display continuous translation between modalities. That these practiced synesthetes were not exercising a "rare" capacity was shown in two subsequent experiments: In one, subjects who had never even thought of "seeing things" when they heard music were played the same stimulus selections and told that they *had* to draw something to represent each one — exactly the same types of productions were obtained. In another experiment, 100 unselected college sophomores were given a purely verbal metaphor test in which the auditory-mood and visual-spatial characteristics, observed in synesthetes, translated into adjectives and presented as pairs (c.g., LOUD-soft; SMALL-LARGE), were combined in all possible ways and judged (by circling that member of the second pair which seemed to go best with the first, capitalized member of the first pair). Here again the relations utilized by complex synesthetes were regularly chosen by unselected subjects — 96 per cent, for example, linking LOUD with LARGE in the example above.

Are such relations entirely dependent upon culture or is it possible that they represent even more fundamental determinants operating in the human species? In an early attempt to get at this question, the senior author[1] studied anthropological field reports on five widely separated primitive cultures — Aztec and Pueblo Indian, Australian Bushman, Siberian Aborigine, Negro (Uganda Protectorate), and Malayan — with the purpose of obtaining evidence on semantic parallelism. The generality of certain relationships was quite striking: for example, *good* gods, places, social positions, etc., were almost always *up* and *light (white)*, whereas *bad* things were *down* and *dark (black)*. A prevalent myth tells how the gods helped the original man to struggle from the *dark, cold, wet, sad* world below the ground *up* to the *light, warm, dry, happy* world on the surface. Among certain Siberian Aborigines, members of a privileged clan call themselves the *white* bones in contrast to all others who are referred to as the *black* bones. Recently he has studied a small number of Southwest Indian subjects, playing simple tape-recorded melodic lines of the same type used earlier with synesthetes in our own culture and having the Indian subjects draw their visualizations. Although it was often difficult to secure

---

[1] C. E. Osgood, undergraduate thesis in psychology, Dartmouth College.

cooperation, in those cases where it was obtained essentially the same types of translations again appeared.

It seems clear from these studies that the imagery found in synesthesia is intimately tied up with language metaphor, and that both represent *semantic* relations. Karwoski, Odbert, and Osgood summarized this work with the statement that the process of metaphor in language as well as in color-music synesthesia can be described as the parallel alignment of two or more dimensions of experience, definable verbally by pairs of polar adjectives, with translations occurring between equivalent portions of the continua. This is translatable into our learning theory model as an instance — complex, to be sure — of *mediated generalization.* Take the case of parallelism between auditory pitch and visual size (synesthetes typically represent high tones as small and low tones as large): it is characteristic of the physical world that large-sized resonators produce low frequency tones and small-sized resonators, high frequency tones (think of a series of organ pipes, bells, or even hollow logs and sticks, and of the voices of men vs. boys, large dogs vs. little dogs, or lions vs. mice). This means that repeatedly the visual stimulus of large objects will be paired with the auditory stimulus of low-pitched tones, and so on consistently throughout the continuum. Any representational processes associated with one (e.g., danger significance of threatening big dog vs. play significance of little dog) will tend to be associated with the other as well (e.g., sounds produced). Thus will a hierarchy of equivalent signs come to be associated with a common mediation process. Any encoding responses associated with this mediator, such as "large" drawing movements and saying the word "large," will tend to transfer to any sign which elicits this mediator — thus "synesthesia" when a deep tone produces "large" drawing movements and "metaphor" when the word "deep" is associated with the word "large." Much learning of this type is carried in the culture, of course, as when the storyteller speaks of the BIG DADDY BEAR (bass), The Mother Bear (normal voice), and the little baby bear (soprano voice).

Stagner and Osgood (1946) adapted this method for measuring social stereotypes and also made explicit the notion of a continuum between the polar terms, by using such terms to define the ends of seven-step scales. Rather than studying the relations between continua, a set of scales was used to determine the "profiles" of various social stereotypes, such as PACIFIST, RUSSIAN, DICTATOR, and NEUTRALITY. Successive samples of subjects were tested throughout the period of the United States' gradual involvement in World War II. The feasibility of using this method to record the changing structures of social stereotypes (i.e., the changing meanings of a set of social signs) was demonstrated. More important from the point of view of methodology, it was found that, as used by our subjects in making their judgments, the semantic scales fell into highly intercorrelated clusters. For example, *fair-unfair, high-low, kind-cruel, valuable-worthless, Christian-antiChristian,* and *honest-dishonest* were all found to correlate together .90 or better. Such a cluster represents the operation of a single, general factor in social judgments, obviously here an *evaluative* factor. Scales like *strong-weak, realistic-unrealistic,* and *happy-sad* were independent of this evaluative group and pointed to the existence of other dimensions of the semantic framework.

Logic of Semantic Differentiation

Most of our work to date has been concentrated on developing the measuring instrument and applying it to a variety of practical problems. Little has been done in testing the various learning theory implications that may arise from the method; what evidence and experimental proposals we do have will be summarized in a later chapter. But this has been a major gap in our work so far. There has been no explicit statement of the relation between the theoretical conception of meaning as a representational mediation process, and the operations of measurement which constitute the semantic differential technique. The account to be given here is admittedly a highly speculative one — a sort of preliminary architect's sketch of what a bridge between these two levels of discourse might eventually resemble. To accomplish the building of such a bridge, it is necessary to analyze and express our operations of measurement in terms of the constructs of the theoretical model.

We begin by postulating a *semantic space,* a region of some unknown dimensionality and Euclidian in character. Each semantic scale, defined by a pair of polar (opposite-in-meaning) adjectives, is assumed to represent a straight line function that passes through the origin of this space, and a sample of such scales then represents a multidimensional space. The larger or more representative the sample, the better defined is the space as a whole. Now, as we have seen in both the synesthesia studies and in the measurement of social stereotypes, many of the "directions" established by particular scales are essentially the same (e.g., the evaluative cluster in the Stagner and Osgood study) and hence their replication adds little to the definition of the space. To define the semantic space with maximum efficiency, we would need to determine that minimum number of *orthogonal dimensions* or axes (again, assuming the space to be Euclidian) which exhausts the dimensionality of the space — in practice, we shall be satisfied with as many such independent dimensions as we can identify and measure reliably. The logical tool to uncover these dimensions is factor analysis, and in the following chapter we shall describe a number of such investigations.

What is meant by "differentiating" the meaning of a concept? When a subject judges a concept against a series of scales, e.g.,

FATHER

happy ____:____:__X__:____:____:____:____ sad
hard ____:__X__:____:____:____:____:____ soft
slow ____:____:____:____:__X__:____:____ fast, etc.,

each judgment represents a selection among a set of given alternatives and serves to localize the concept as a point in the semantic space. The larger the number of scales and the more representative the selection of these scales, the more validly does this point in the space represent the operational meaning of the concept. And conversely, of course: Given the location of such a point in the space, the original judgments are reproducible in that each point has an orthogonal projection onto any line that passes through the origin of the space, i.e., onto any scale. By semantic differentiation, then, we mean the successive allocation of a concept to a point in the multidimensional semantic space by selection from among a set of given scaled semantic alternatives. Difference in the meaning between two concepts is then merely a function of the differences in their respective allocations within the same space, i.e., it is a function of the multidimensional distance between the two points. It is apparent that some index of this generalized distance is a desideratum of the system, and such a measure is introduced in Chapter 3.

We now have two definitions of meaning. In learning-theory terms, the meaning of a sign in a particular context and to a particular person has been defined as the representational mediation process which it elicits; in terms of our measurement operations the meaning of a sign has been defined as that point in the semantic space specified by a series of differentiating judgments. We can draw a rough correspondence between these two levels as follows: The point in space which serves us as an operational definition of meaning has two essential properties — *direction* from the origin, and *distance* from the origin. We may identify these properties with the *quality* and *intensity* of meaning, respectively. The direction from the origin depends on the alternative polar terms selected, and the distance depends on the extremeness of the scale positions checked.

What properties of learned associations — here, associations of signs with mediating reactions — correspond to these two attributes of direction and intensity? At this point we must make a rather tenuous assumption, but a necessary one. Let us assume that there is some finite number of representational mediation reactions available to the organism and let us further assume that the number of these alternative reactions (excitatory or inhibitory) corresponds to the number of dimensions or factors in the semantic space. Direction of a point in the semantic space will then correspond to what reactions are elicited by the sign, and distance from the origin will correspond to the *intensity* of the reactions.

Let us try to clarify this assumed isomorphism somewhat. Corresponding to each major dimension of the semantic space, defined by a pair of polar terms, is a pair of reciprocally antagonistic mediating reactions, which we may symbolize as r_{mI} and $\bar{r}_{mI}$ for the first dimension, r_{mII} and $\bar{r}_{mII}$ for the second dimension, and so forth. Each successive act of judgment by the subject using the semantic differential, in which a sign is allocated to one or the other direction of a scale, corresponds to the acquired capacity of that sign to elicit either r_m or $\bar{r}_m$, and the extremeness of the subject's judgment corresponds to the intensity of reaction associating the sign with either r_m or $\bar{r}_m$. There is actually evidence that words of opposed meaning are mediated by such reciprocally antagonistic reactions. Osgood (1948) demonstrated that the successive pairing of words of opposed meaning with the same stimulus produced significant amounts of blocking (failure of response) and decreased speed of responding, as compared with words of similar meaning, both phenomena predictable from the reciprocal inhibition hypothesis. Evidence for a direct relation between extremeness of graphic judgment on the semantic differential and speed of associative judgment (an index of reaction intensity) will be offered later in this book.

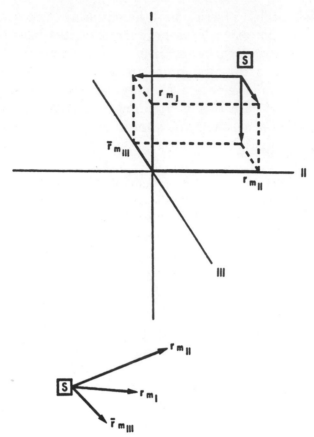

Fig. 3. Assumed relation between mediation and semantic space models.

Figure 3 represents an attempt to coordinate these models graphically. The sign is represented as a point in an n-dimensional space (here, three dimensions). As a point in space, the sign has projections onto each of the dimensions. The magnitude and direction of the coordinate on each dimension is, on the one hand, estimated from the direction and extremeness of the subject's judgment against those scales of the differential representing this dimension and, on the other hand, is assumed to be proportional to the intensity with which the sign elicits the r_m or $\bar{r}_m$ corresponding to this dimension. The lower portion of Figure 3 represents the meaning of this sign as a simultaneous hierarchy of representational reactions, the intensity of evocation varying for $r_{mII} > r_{mI} > \bar{r}_{mIII}$. It should be noted that whereas the reciprocal reactions *within* each dimension are assumed to be incompatible, those corresponding to independent dimensions are assumed to be compatible and hence capable of simultaneous excitation. What we have done, in other words, is to divide the total representational mediation process into a set of bipolar components, the meaning of a sign corresponding to the pattern and intensity with which these components are elicited.

It remains to express the actual behavior of subjects taking the semantic differential in terms of the learning theory model. Each item (pairing of a specific concept with a specific scale) presents the following situation:

(CONCEPT)

polar term X ____:____:____:____:____:____:____ polar term Y
$$\quad\quad\quad (1)\quad (2)\quad (3)\quad (4)\quad (5)\quad (6)\quad (7)$$

in which the scale positions have already been defined for the subject in the instructions (see Chapter 3) as:

(1) *extremely* X   (7) *extremely* Y
(2) *quite* X   (6) *quite* Y
(3) *slightly* X   (5) *slightly* Y
(4) *neither* X nor Y; *equally* X and Y

We shall assume that, on the basis of a great deal of prior experience in encoding, the terms "extremely," "quite," and "slightly" as linguistic quantifiers have been associated with more or less equal *degrees* of intensity of whatever representational process (X or Y) happens to be elicited, and therefore, that the sign combinations "extremely X," "quite X," and so forth will elicit an r_m of the quality X and of the intensity given by the quantifier. In a subsequent chapter, data will be offered to substantiate this scaling assumption. We shall also assume that, even though the instructions relating scale positions to quantifying terms are only given once at the beginning of the "test," they persist throughout.

Now, following our general analysis, any concept being judged is a sign eliciting a distinctive set of component r_m's and $\bar{r}_m$'s with differing intensities. Similarly, the polar terms defining the scales are signs eliciting their own characteristic patterns of r_m's and $\bar{r}_m$'s, and, when combined with quantifiers associated with scale positions, each scale position elicits an r_m pattern whose selection depends upon the polar term and whose intensity depends upon the quantifier. Two additional comments about the representational processes associated with the scales should be made: First, since the polar terms X and Y are meaningful opposites, we assume that the r_m pattern characteristic of X will be reciprocally antagonistic to that characteristic of Y (i.e., wherever a component of X is r_m, the same component of Y will be $\bar{r}_m$, and conversely). Second, since, as will be seen in subsequent chapters, scales are chosen which maximize one factor or component and minimize all others, the r_m pattern elicited by any X-Y set will tend to have one dominant component.

To summarize our theoretical analysis, it can be seen that what is operationally quite simple (the procedure of the subject in responding to the semantic differential) proves to be quite complex behaviorally. The location of a concept in the semantic space defined by a set of factors is equated with the evocation by the concept of a set of component mediating reactions, direction in space being equated to *what* mediators are evoked (from among reciprocally antagonistic pairs) and distance from the origin being equated to *how intensely* (with what habit strength) these are evoked. Each position on one of our semantic scales is also assumed to be associated with a complex mediating reaction, the dominant component depending on the polar terms, X and Y, and its intensity depending upon the qualifiers, "extremely," "quite," etc. These different mediators are associated, in encoding, with checking the various scale positions. Through the functioning of a generalization principle, the concept will elicit checking of that scale position whose dominant mediator component most closely matches in intensity the corresponding component in the process associated with the concept itself. Since the positions checked on the scales constitute the coordinates of the concept's location in semantic space, we assume that the coordinates in the measurement space are functionally equivalent with the components of the representational mediation process associated with this concept.

This, then, is one rationale by which the semantic differential, as a technique of measurement, can be considered as an index of meaning. One may well ask whether such an elaborate and speculative analysis — which perhaps impresses the reader as a *tour de force* — is necessary? It is true that many of the practical uses of the semantic differential, indeed its own empirical validity, depend little, if at all, on such a tie-in with learning theory. On the other hand, if we are to use the semantic differential as an hypothesis-testing instrument, and if the hypotheses regarding meanings and changes in meaning are to be drawn from learning-theory analyses, some such rationale as has been developed here is highly desirable.

Further, from the writers' point of view, it is an awkward and somewhat embarrassing state of affairs to entertain simultaneously a theoretical conception of the nature of meaning and a procedure for measuring it which have no relation to one another. Whether this attempt at resolving this state of affairs has reduced this awkwardness is another matter.

SUMMARY AND PROSPECTUS

It must be evident by now that this book is a progress report and not any final statement. We feel that we have come far enough along to be confident that there is some sort of path here, but just what may be its actual course and destination remains obscured. We believe that we are validly measuring at least certain aspects of a very important variable in human behavior, *meaning*, and that therefore our type of instrument has many valuable applications. But it has also become increasingly clear that our original conceptions were insufficient, that human semantic processes are very complex, and that problems of meaning are inextricably confounded with more general problems of human thinking or cognition. Certainly, when viewed from some future vantage point, our theoretical notions and measuring operations will seem very crude and inadequate — but we have come far enough along to think that we are more or less on the right track. In this final chapter we will try to define where we stand at present (as a kind of summary) and thereby be better able to say where we should go in the future (as a kind of prospectus of contemplated research).

The Semantic Differential as an Index of Meaning States

In Chapter 1 we identified the aspect of meaning in which we were interested as a strictly psychological one: those cognitive states of human language users which are necessary antecedent conditions for selective encoding of lexical signs and necessary subsequent conditions in selective decoding of lexical signs in messages. Within the general framework of learning theory, the meaning of a sign was identified as a representational mediation process — representational by virtue of comprising some portion of the total behavior elicited by the significate and mediating because this process, as a kind of self-stimulation, serves to elicit overt behaviors, both linguistic and non-linguistic, that are appropriate to the things signified. In semantic decoding, stimulus patterns (signs as stimuli) selectively elicit representational processes as reactions; in semantic encoding, vocal, orthographic, gestural, and other response patterns (signs as responses) are selectively elicited by representational processes as stimuli. Thus we have a two-stage, mediational mechanism.

To provide a coherent rationale for our proposed measuring technique, we have tried to show how such a theory of meaning as this could be coordinated with the actual operations of measurement with the semantic differential. To accomplish this it was necessary to assume that the representational mediation process is a complex affair, a compound reaction made up of some n bipolar reaction components. Within each such set of bipolar components we assume reciprocal antagonism — given some support by retroactive interference studies using verbal opposites — which corresponds to the bipolar character of our measurement dimensions; between each such set of components we assume functional independence, which corresponds to the statistical independence of the factors of the semantic space. When the subject decodes a given sign, we assume that a complex mediating reaction occurs, consisting of a pattern of these alternative bipolar reactions elicited with varying intensities; when the subject encodes this semantic state against the differential, we assume that his selection of directions in the semantic space (toward *good* vs. *bad*, toward *active* vs. *passive*, etc.) is coordinate with what reactions are elicited by the sign and that his degree of polarization or extremeness in the space (how far out along the scales he checks) is coordinate with how intensely these reactions are made.

Some readers will consider this rationale to be an unnecessary *tour de force*, quite arbitrary, and certainly not essential to the usefulness of the measuring instrument as such. They are quite correct in this, but there are other considerations. For one thing, the behavior of a subject reacting to the semantic differential is lawful and, somewhere along the line, must be coordinated with behavior theory — which may not be of the sort offered here, of course. For another thing, the authors find it awkward and uncomfortable to have on the one hand a fairly elaborate and rigorous theory of meaning and, on the other, a fairly elaborate and reasonably effective method of measuring it and yet have them proceeding on completely independent paths. Finally, it is possible to generate many hypotheses about sign behavior from learning theory; these can only be tested with measurements on the semantic differential to the extent that this instrument is coordinated with theory.

It therefore follows that one of the most challenging tasks facing us in the future is to make even more explicit this coordination of measurement with theory, and test various implications which can be derived. A few steps in this direction have already been taken: Using a judgmental latency device, we have been able to show that extremeness of judgment against the graphic form of the differential corresponds very closely to intensity of judgment as indexed by latency. Since this apparatus prevents the subject from rationalizing his judgments — or rather provides a record of such time-consuming rationalizations — more work with it should be done. For example, more consistent data on word mixture effects might be obtained in this way. Work by some of our colleagues (e.g., Solley and Messick) has shown that frequencies of input experiences with experimental concepts are reflected faithfully by the differential, which is another step in the coordination of learning theory with measurement. On the planning boards at the time of this writing are perhaps the most direct tests of the implied coordination: first, an experiment to determine if amounts of mediated generalization are predictable from the similarity of signs as measured with the semantic differential, and second, an experiment comparing mediated generalization in compound and coordinate bilinguals, again against predictions from the differential. Many other predictions about the meanings of signs (e.g., about the development of assign meanings, as in Dodge's study) can be derived from learning theory, and these can be tested with the semantic differential.

In What Sense Is the Semantic Differential a Measure of Meaning?

One of the most serious criticisms of this book probably could have been anticipated at the outset: "Although we understand pretty well what you are measuring and appreciate its value," many readers may say, "why do you call it *meaning?* Aren't you really measuring the emotive reaction to words rather than 'meaning' as I have understood the term?" In the first chapter we tried to indicate, at least roughly, that aspect of meaning in which we were interested. And at that time we promised to return to the question after our findings had been presented.

As psychologists we find it necessary to focus on that "state of" or "event in" a sign-using organism that is at once a necessary subsequent condition (r_m) in the decoding of signs and a necessary antecedent condition (s_m) in the encoding of signs. Note carefully that we do not say necessary *and sufficient*. Although it may be trivial in one sense to insist that all discriminable events in messages must ultimately be correlated with discriminable events in language users, this must be the case if we are to avoid mysticism in our interpretation of language behavior. When a language user comes out with sequences of linguistic responses which are ordered both as to structural and semantic characteristics, we must assume that there is some ordered, selective system operating within the organism. Ultimately it is the job of the psycholinguist to make a science out of the correlations between message events and states of the organism. In our work on what we have been calling "meaning," we have mapped only a small region of this complex set of correlations, and that rather sketchily.

But is it justifiable to use the term *meaning* for the kinds of correlations between signs and organismic states indexed by the semantic differential? We can best indicate the issue here, perhaps, by setting up two questions that have frequently been put to us. Both involve the distinction between what has variously been called denotative, designative, or referential "meaning" and what has been called connotative, emotive, or metaphorical "meaning."

1 *How can there be interpersonal communication despite connotative disagreement?* Many linguists and philosophers would say (and have, to us) that two people must first agree on the "meaning" of a sign before they can disagree on their diverse emotive and other reactions to it. For example, man A may find THUNDER (object) challenging and exciting while man B finds it extremely frightening, but before they can communicate about this state of affairs they must agree on the *referent* of the linguistic sign "thunder" in their common language. As a matter of fact, our data are replete with cases where individuals differ in their semantic differential profiles for the same sign-vehicles — one of the major uses of the instrument is to measure such differences between people. What, then, is the problem here? If we agree that the "meaning" of "thunder" for A and B must in some sense be the same because they are obviously referring to the same object or event, and if we were to claim that the representational mediation process as we have defined it is a *sufficient* antecedent condition for language encoding, then the semantic differential profiles we derive from A and

B should correspond in some way. A few moments' consideration shows that we can not make this claim: Men A and B will probably experience no more referential confusion on "thunder" (where their profiles disagree on most factors) than they do on "blueberry pie" (where their profiles agree closely, let us say). In other words, we must admit that distances in our semantic space as between individuals judging the same concepts are not indicative of degrees of *referential* agreement — if, indeed, one can speak of "degrees" of such agreement.

How can you have referential agreement despite lack of correspondence in the psychological states we index with the differential? A color-blind person may go through his whole life correctly labeling and referring to most colored objects and yet in a test case (e.g., choosing between particular orange vs. brown ties) show conclusively that he cannot be "seeing things" the way the rest of us do — what looks obviously different to us looks just the same to him! Let us postulate two hypothetical people: F (father) is normal; S (son) is not only red-green blind, but he is also allergic to what are commonly called "apples" — they make him deathly sick. We shall assume that F has an evaluatively favorable "meaning" of "apple": part of the gratifying reaction to APPLES-as-eaten has become associated with the perceptual and linguistic signs of this object. Now, on repeated occasions S is stimulated by APPLE visually (and necessarily has experiences different from F because he is color-blind); he also sees F point to this rounded patch of stimulation and say "apple" and point to this and other similar patches and say "red." Given human learning capacity and language facility, S rapidly learns to say "apple" to recurrent appearances of this object and to say "red" to radiant patches similar to the ones F calls "red" — even though, we must agree, the internal states of F and S cannot be identical. But even beyond this, F encourages S to bite into the APPLE object, saying it is "tasty" and "good" — to S it tastes horrible and makes him sick.

On the basis of a number of such experiences, and following the behavioral principles governing the formation of representational mediation processes discussed in Chapter 1, S must develop a "meaning" (in our sense) of "apple" which is quite different from that of F — and he would check it quite differently on many of the scales of the semantic differential as well as displaying different behavior in response to the object. Here, we have two users of the same language, F and S, who, despite their manifest differences in mediation processes, will point to the same things and say to each other, "Oh, I know what you mean," when they employ the noises "apple" and "red." Similarly, returning to our original example, it is clear that men A and B may agree on what "thunder" refers to *even though* the distinctive representational states in each may differ.

We may summarize our argument on Question 1 as follows: Agreement on the referents of signs implies nothing whatsoever about similarity of the representational states associated with these signs, but rather that these states have entered into the same sets of relations between situations and verbal responses. It therefore follows that agreement on the reference of signs despite lack of profile correspondence on the semantic differential is not evidence for insufficiency of the instrument as a psychological measuring device.

2 *How can there be discriminative encoding despite connotative indiscriminability?* This problem becomes apparent when one considers the lack of perfect reversibility of our measurement operations with the semantic differential. Given only the profile produced by a subject in judging a particular concept, or the point in the space specified by this profile, we are unable to work the system backwards and identify that concept. The force of the argument really is this: Many denotatively distinct concepts may occupy essentially the same region of our semantic space, i.e., may have highly similar profiles — "hero" and "success" and "nurse" and "sincere" would be examples. If the state of the speaker which the semantic differential presumably indexes were a *sufficient* condition for selective encoding, how could we account for discriminative selection of "nurse" rather than "sincere," of "hero" rather than "success," when the states in each case are essentially the same?

One possible answer to this problem would be to take the position that the factors or dimensions of the semantic space we have isolated so far are insufficient. Increase the number of factors, this argument goes, and any two concepts would have to be distinguished on at least one dimension. Although we admit the insufficiency of present factors even for our purposes, this solution seems to envisage an almost infinite proliferation of dimensions and becomes practically infeasible. Furthermore, it takes it for granted that variations among representational processes must be a sufficient condition for selective encoding.

A better answer, we think, takes off from the assumption that the representational state indexed by the semantic differential is not the only determinant operating in lexical encoding. It is a necessary but not a sufficient condition. In the simplest cases, this is obvious: given essentially the same semantic process, the speaker will encode "eats" in one linguistic context and "eat" in another, depending on whether the subject of the sentence is singular or plural. Here we have selection among two word alternatives on the basis of something other than semantic factors. Going a step further, it has been shown in word association experiments that the form class of the stimulus word markedly influences the form class of the response word from the subject, e.g., given MAN he'll say "woman" but given MEN he'll say "women," given COME he'll say "go" but given CAME he'll say "went." Again, we assume that the "meaning" (in the sense of our measurements) of the stimulus terms stays constant. Coming now to the examples given above, it seems likely that, even with near identical representational states of the sort we hypothesize and try to measure, a speaker will encode "hero" in the context, "The villain was vanquished by the . . . ," rather than "success"; conversely he will encode "success" in the context, "He is always striving for . . . ," rather than "hero."

In other words, we believe that *habits of usage and association* serve to refine the relatively gross differentiations of which the representational system is capable. Although lexical items *a, b, c,* and *d* may be associated with the same representational process, X, indiscriminately, context 1 plus X selects *a*, context 2 plus X selects *b*, and so forth. To summarize our argument on Question 2, then: Self-stimulation from the representational system ($r_m \rightarrow s_m$), as indexed by the semantic differential, provides a necessary but not sufficient condition for encoding lexical items; cues from both the linguistic and the situational context combine with those from the representational system to select more discriminatively among alternative responses. By way of analogy, there are some classic experiments in the psychology of the emotions in which the subject is given an injection of adrenalin in a completely neutral, non-arousing situation; the subject typically reports experiencing a vague, stirred-up feeling, a sort of objectless, nameless emotion, as if "something were about to happen." If we could get inside the speaker somehow and produce a particular $r_m \rightarrow s_m$ without any context, it is possible that he too would experience a kind of "reference-less," "denotation-less" meaning, referable to some

region of the semantic space but non-specific as to designation —
"something bad, strong, and active, but *what* I do not know."

In what sense, then, are we measuring meaning with the semantic
differential? It is certain that we are not providing an index of
what signs refer to, and if reference or designation is the *sine qua
non* of meaning, as some readers will insist, then they will conclude
that this book is badly mistitled. On the other hand, language users
do develop representation processes in association with signs and
these processes are intimately concerned with their behavior. The
psychologist quite naturally focuses his attention on processes that
are relevant to the prediction and interpretation of differential behaviors, and, as we have tried to demonstrate, agreement in the
reference of signs carries no necessary implication of relatedness of
representational states. As we also tried to show, however, the representational states indexed by the semantic differential are not the
only determinants operating in language production; linguistic and
situational variables also contribute to selective encoding. Perhaps
we should admit that the word "meaning" is used in several senses;
whether or not it is *meaning* that we are measuring, then, would
seem to be merely a matter of choice of terms.

The Dimensionality of the Semantic Space

We began our research on the measurement of meaning with the
simplest — and most naïve — conceptual model. We hoped that
most of the variance in human semantic judgments could be explained in terms of a relatively small number of orthogonal factors,
these factors being completely general over both subjects and concepts and always represented by the same set of scales — i.e., we
wanted to set up a perfectly general and simple measuring instrument. What is perhaps surprising is how close to the truth this
naïve model actually seems to be. The same three major factors
of *evaluation, potency,* and *activity* (which were empirically rather
than theoretically derived) have reappeared in a wide variety of
judgmental situations, particularly where the sampling of concepts
has been broad. The relative weights of these factors have been
fairly consistent: evaluation accounting for approximately double
the amount of variance due to either potency or activity, these two
in turn being approximately double the weight of any subsequent
factors. But since a large portion of the total variance remains unaccounted for, we assume that there must be other factors operating;

since their individual contributions to the total variance are small, we assume their number must be large — i.e., a large number of relatively specific semantic factors.

Just how general are the factors isolated so far? When we sample across sets of subjects with the concepts judged held constant, a very high degree of consistency in factor structure is revealed — essentially the same factors appearing in the judgments of such diverse groups as normals vs. schizophrenics or Americans vs. Japanese or Koreans. When we sample across sets of concepts, however, it becomes evident that the scales of judgment and the concepts being judged interact, this interaction influencing the relative weights and even appearance of identifiable factors and certainly determining what specific scales contribute to factors. Despite variation in scale composition, the factors which can be identified over most (though not all) concepts judged are *evaluation, potency, stability,* and *receptivity* (or *sensory adiency*); the *activity* factor, at least in the blind rotations of individual concept matrices we have used so far, seems to vary in alignment with other dimensions.

How are we to account for this instability of individual scales in relation to each other? There seems to be a general principle operating here: all scales of judgment, to the extent that they have correlation with the dominant attribute for a particular concept, tend to rotate toward this dominant attribute. It also seems that the greater the emotionality involved in the concept, the greater this rotational tendency, leading to a tight, single factor of judgment in some extreme cases. The scales representing the evaluative factor appear to be most susceptible to this rotational effect, i.e., what is "good," scale-wise, depends heavily upon the concept being judged. These explanations stand pretty much as hunches at present; there is much that we can do, both with our available data on single-concept correlational matrices and by means of more experimental procedures, to test the validity of these hunches. It should also be remarked that this is but one of the many points where our work on experimental semantics leads us into basic problems about the nature of human thought and judgment.

What do these findings have to say about the practical problems of semantic measurement? For one thing, it now seems less likely that we will be able to discover a single set of scales which represent an adequate set of factors and which are stable across whatever concepts may be judged. On the other hand, it may be possible to identify classes of concepts for which general instruments may be used, and perhaps, in course, the principles which operate in determining a common semantic frame of reference can be discovered. Here the work of Suci on determining the characteristic attributes of concept sets seems promising. Also on the agenda is further research directed at the isolation of additional factors; but rather than further general factorial studies with random samples of scales, it now seems better to deliberately put together sets of scales to represent potential factors and test them within a matrix of scales representing known factors; i.e., the new scales, or at least some of them, must maintain high correlations with each other and insignificant correlations with scales representing other factors. We have sufficient materials from the Thesaurus Study to begin this work.

Construction and Evaluation of Semantic Differentials

Among the "constants" in our work have been the use of *seven-step scales* having a *bipolar* (verbal opposites) form and defined by *adjectives*. Is this type of instrument necessarily the "natural" grid against which to differentiate the meanings of concepts? We have fairly satisfying evidence that our seven-step scales, defined by the linguistic quantifiers "extremely," "quite," and "slightly," in both directions from a neutral "meaningless" origin, do yield nearly equal psychological units in the process of judgment, and we intend to assemble additional evidence on this point. But what about the use of bipolar scales defined by verbal opposites? We have been following a more or less implicit assumption that thinking in terms of opposites *is* "natural" to the human species; data presently being collected on Indians in the Southwest seem to support this assumption, and the ethnolinguists we have talked to — after due consideration and checking with their own experiences — usually agree that semantic opposition is common to most, if not all, language systems. However, it still might be true that unidirectional scales would serve as well as those we now use. One of the difficult methodological problems we have faced — unsuccessfully so far — is to demonstrate that the polar terms we now use are true psychological opposites, i.e., fall at equal distances from the origin of the semantic space and in opposite directions along a single straight line passing through the origin. The use of unidirectional scales might eliminate this problem, but it would probably involve us in another: if there is a "natural" human tendency to think in terms of opposites, the so-called neutral point at one extreme of unidirectional scales would probably tend to take on the semantic properties of opposition.

And why the use of adjectives? We assume that it is the lexical (root) meanings of our polar terms that determine judgments; adjectives are merely the most general and natural qualifiers *in English*. We think that scales could be made up with polar terms defined by nouns (*good* vs. *evil*, *strength* vs. *weakness*, etc.) or verbs (*loving* vs. *hating*, *going* vs. *stopping*, etc.) and yield the same dimensionality, but this remains to be demonstrated.

Much of our energy to date has been spent on evaluation of the instrument. Evaluation and refinement of the measuring technique seems to be more our job than application. We have amassed a considerable amount of data on reliability. The evidence shows that for individual subjects a shift of more than two scale units probably represents a significant change or difference in meaning, and a shift of more than 1.00 to 1.50 scale units in factor score (depending on the particular factor) is probably significant. For group data ("cultural meanings"), changes or differences in measured meaning as small as one-half of a scale unit are significant at the 5 per cent level. These levels of reliability should be satisfactory for most applications of the instrument. Regarding validity, there seems to be little question about the general face validity of the differential, because it obviously differentiates among and clusters concepts much the way most of us do spontaneously. There are at least two validity issues on which we need more evidence. One of these concerns the use of the method of triads (where the subject determines his own dimensions of judgment) as a way of validating the dimensions arrived at through factor analysis: Does the semantic differential force the subject to use unnatural bases of judgment? The data we have show considerable correspondence, but more research of this type is needed. However, this method can probably only validate the major factors, i.e., the differential probably does force the subject to attend to some dimensions he would not use otherwise in addition to those used spontaneously. The second issue concerns behavioral validity: Does the semantic differential accurately predict meaningful behaviors in test situations? We have meager amounts of data here — on the prediction of voting behavior in the 1952 election and on certain phenomena of problem-solving — and again more evidence of this sort is needed.

The Congruity Principle

This is another instance where our work with experimental semantics has led us into problems of human thinking. The congruity principle deals with the interaction of cognitive events that occur more or less simultaneously. It states, in effect, that along each semantic dimension these events modify each other in proportion to their relative intensities, yielding changes in meaning or resolutions into new combined meanings that are predictable from the congruity formulae. There is no necessary dependence of this principle upon the semantic differential as a kind of measurement operation (witness the work of Leon Festinger with a very similar notion but very different measures), but to the extent that the differential provides an index of cognitive events, it provides a "natural" means of testing the principle. Thus, we have tested predictions about attitude change, about the effects of colors upon the meanings of advertised products and sculptured abstractions, about the development of assign meanings from association with signs, and about the semantic effects of combining adjectives and nouns into nominal phrases — all against measurements obtained with the semantic differential. The range of prediction situations covered testifies to the potential range of such a principle of human thinking. But it is very clear that congruity does not operate in a vacuum. We have evidence that its operation is conditioned by such variables as the relevance of the two or more concepts to each other, the intensity of the assertions made, and the psychological comparability of the concepts. These and other parameters affecting the operation of congruity in human thinking need to be further studied.

Applications of Semantic Measurement

A fairly representative sample of applications of semantic measurement has been reported in this book. It includes attitude assessment, the study of personality traits and dynamisms, measurement of the course of psychotherapy, studies in psycholinguistics, in aesthetics, in advertising, and in other mass communications. There is nothing surprising or remarkable about this. Meaning is one of the most significant pivotal variables in human behavior, and even a crude and very provisional measure of it, such as the semantic differential now is, readily finds uses. As a matter of fact, we are now more concerned that its applications — and claims for it —

will outstrip development and evaluation of the basic methodology, and this is one reason why our own staff has been concentrating more on these methodological matters.

There are, of course, many applications we intend to make ourselves. In the area of personality and psychotherapy, for example, we think that with sufficient trial and effort it should be possible to develop a semantic tool for use in psychotherapy that would sensitively and accurately gauge the course of treatment and differences between treatments. Also, our factor analysis of the single concept, MYSELF, revealed a number of dimensions of self-evaluation which could lead to a useful personality test. In the social area, the generalized character of our attitude index makes feasible the development of a standardized "social attitude index" which could be very useful to sociologists, political scientists, and the like. The field of experimental aesthetics begs for quantitative studies with an instrument like the differential — extension of factor analysis to other aesthetic modes than painting, color-music synesthesia, and color TV (which are closely related problems), development of tests of aesthetic appreciation and communication, to name only a few — but a great deal of preliminary digging around needs to be done first.

In psycholinguistics, the semantic differential finds its place in the tool bin quite naturally, for it is at base a psycholinguistic instrument. We think that our work on word mixture (which could be extended to larger units than the adjective-noun phrase) will lead to a method of identifying lexical units (e.g., the combination HOT DOG is functionally a new lexical unit because its meaning is not predictable from the meanings of the components HOT and DOG). The differential seems to open new ways of studying onomatopoeia, both within and across cultures. And the study of the cross-cultural generality of semantic factors, which is already under way, certainly deserves extension because of its potential contribution to international communication and understanding. One can also envisage the gradual construction of "a functional dictionary of connotative meanings" — a quantized Thesaurus — in which the writer would find nouns, adjectives, verbs, and adverbs (all lexical items) listed according to their locations in the semantic space, as determined from the judgments of representative samples of the population; wishing to find an adjective which would be like WARRIOR in meaning (21134XXX), but derogatory, he might search under the listing 71134XXX and find words like *vicious, savage,* and *barbaric.* A variety of potential uses of semantic measurement in advertising and other mass communications has been suggested in the last chapter.

But many of these applications must wait upon further refinement of the measuring instrument. It would, for example, be foolish to begin collecting data for a functional dictionary of connotative meanings when the factor structure remains unclear and obviously insufficient, and the nature of the concept-scale interaction is still obscure. Therefore we shall continue to concentrate on further development, evaluation, and refinement of the measuring technique itself. In this work, and in further extending the range of application, we welcome the help and advice of students and colleagues both at Illinois and at other institutions.

Part II
REVIEWS OF
THE MEASUREMENT
OF MEANING

4. Is A Boulder Sweet or Sour?

Roger W. Brown

THIS book is not the first we have heard of the Semantic Differential. Charles Osgood, who is associate director of the Institute of Communications Research at the University of Illinois, published his basic article on the subject in the *Psychological Bulletin* in 1952 (vol. 49, 197–237). About that same time I remember hearing Professor O. H. Mowrer describe the differential method at a meeting of the American Psychological Association. His topic was psychotherapy and he used a wonderful arrangement of colored balls and wooden dowels to demonstrate a Patient's Progress through semantic space. Since then, George Suci and Percy Tannenbaum, who are research assistant professors at the Illinois Institute, have applied the differential method to the study of social attitudes, and others have used it in experimental semantics, esthetics, advertising, and even for the analysis of a case of multiple personality. The appearance of the present book, summarizing all of this and more, provides a welcome opportunity to congratulate the authors on a distinguished contribution to psychology.

There are two kinds of research described in this book; the first uses factor analysis to discover the dimensions of meaning. An original group of 100 subjects was given a list of concepts, an odd lot including *lady, boulder, sin* and 17 others, and also a list of 50 bipolar,

7-point scales whose extremes were labeled with such familiar adjective antonyms as *good-bad, sweet-sour,* and *active-passive.* The job was to place each concept on each scale. A few of these 1,000 judgments (50 scales × 20 concepts) were quite prosaic; e.g., deciding whether *boulder* is *light* or *heavy.* In the majority of cases, however, the scales could not be said to have any 'literal' application to the concepts and subjects had to extend themselves to think in metaphors and difficult-to-explain associations. Does *sin* seem to be *red* or *green*? Is a *boulder sweet* or *sour*?

When the data were examined, it could be seen that some scales functioned as near synonyms, with judgments on one scale being highly predictable from judgments on another. Using Thurstone's Centroid Method, the authors analyzed the matrix of intercorrelations and extracted three identifiable factors. Such scales as *good-bad* and *beautiful-ugly* were heavily loaded with the first factor and so it was called *evaluation.* The second factor was named *potency,* since it was identified with such scales as *strong-weak* and *large-small.* The third factor was called *activity*; for it the most distinctively loaded scales included *fast-slow* and *active-passive.* There are many similar factor analyses described in this book. The most elaborate of these made use of 76 scales selected to represent the dimensions of meaning utilized in Roget's *Thesaurus.* In this case there were eight identifiable factors but the first three were the reliable trio—*evaluation, potency,* and *activity.*

Reprinted from *Contemporary Psychology* (1958), 3: 113–115, by permission of the author and the American Psychological Association.

The second kind of research described in this book builds on the factor analytic studies. Since the meanings of concepts appear usually to have three major dimensions, it should be possible to devise an instrument for the economical measurement of meaning by selecting a small number of scales to represent each factor. Such an instrument is called a *Semantic Differential*. Researchers have most commonly used four scales to represent evaluation, three for potency, and three for activity. Subjects have been asked to place concepts (or pictures from the Thematic Apperception Test, the names of political candidates, representational paintings, even sonar signals) on each of these ten scales. The data are usually summarized as a score for each scaled item on each of the three factors, a three-dimensional meaning score. The investigator is sometimes interested in differences of meaning from one concept to another, sometimes in differences between groups or persons and sometimes in differences over time. The reader comes to feel very much at home in this agreeable Euclidean semantic space.

While the 10-scale form of the differential has been used more than any other, it is important to understand that there is no one differential which can be considered a standard test to be used whenever meaning is to be measured. There are many reasons why this is so. The most important of these is the fact that the factor loadings of particular scales can change with a change in the items scaled; e.g., whereas *deep-shallow* is not heavily loaded with evaluation for a miscellany of concepts, it is so loaded when sonar signals are scaled. The authors give the potential researcher all possible guidance on the problem of selecting *a* Semantic Differential for his particular purpose.

F OR all their vital empiricism the authors have not neglected theory con-

struction. Osgood's original article on the logic of the measure was accompanied by a paper setting forth a behavioral interpretation of meaning as a mediating reaction (a near relative of Hull's pure-stimulus act). In the present book the authors elaborate their theoretical construct so as to improve its coordination with meaning as it is now measured. They suggest that the mediating process has bipolar components corresponding to the dimensions of semantic space. Mediating processes are conceived to vary, therefore, in the components activated and in the intensities of activation. Several experimental results are said to "validate" this coordination; e.g., extremity of placement of a concept on a scale is inversely related to the latency of the scaling response. While I find these results and all the others in the book *consistent* with the amended theory, I cannot see that they have been predicted by it. This conclusion does not, of course, exclude the possibility that the researches have been *inspired* by the theory for reasons that have to do with the personal psychology of the researchers.

D IFFERENTIAL research is much closer to the literature on synesthesia and metaphor than it is to the semantic analyses of logicians. The authors say that the meaning measured by the differential is "connotative," but, in terms of any standard semantic analysis, the differential must be considered a mixture and a mixture that changes with the problem at hand. Consider, for example, the concept called *boulder*. The *denotation* of this concept is the population of objects which may be so designated. According to some usage the *connotation* of the concept would be a listing of the attributes that define the class called *boulder*. Such scales as *large-small* and *hard-soft* might be considered connotative in this sense. There is, however, another way of using the term *connotation*. It is sometimes said to indicate any non-defining accidental associate of the concept; anything 'suggested' by the concept. There are many kinds of these. *Boulder,* for example, would probably be scaled as more *loud* than *soft*. This might be because (*a*) when boulders fall they make more noise than do pebbles; (*b*) among animal species the large adult specimens are generally able to make more noise than the smaller immature specimens and this rule is extended to stones; (*c*) *soft* means yielding as well as not-loud and boulders are not yielding; etc. In some cases differential research even involves something very like denotation. When *things* are scaled rather than words, the thing (a Rorschach blot or a sonar signal) may belong to a class denoted by one or another term in the scales. A blot may be more *dark* than *bright*; a signal may be more *loud* than *soft*. The reason why the meaning measured by the differential seems to be best designated *connotative* can only be because *connotation* is a very ambiguous term.

The differential solves none of the problems of meaning posed by philosophers and does not even observe the distinctions of which they feel most confident. This may be just the bold step needed to advance the empirical study of meaning whose movement until now has been glacier-like in its imperceptibility. However, the uncertainty about the sort of meaning measured by a differential sometimes causes uncertainty about the precise interpretation of a research result. Let me offer one example.

The book reports the fascinating discovery (made by Kumata and Schramm) that native speakers of Japanese working with a Japanese translation of 20 scales and 30 concepts made judgments which had the same factor structure as judgments made by American subjects with the scales and concepts in English. The Japanese terms for *clean-dirty,*

beautiful-ugly, and *brave-cowardly* are loaded with the evaluation factor as are their English equivalents. Even since the present book went to press, several similar studies using different language groups have been completed. Just over the horizon lurks the very important generalization—the various languages of the world operate with the same basic semantic dimensions, however much they disagree on the scaling of individual concepts like communism and capitalism. This conclusion would be a major disconfirmation of the "linguistic relativity" postulated by Benjamin Whorf.

These comparative linguistic studies begin with the mysterious process of translation. For each English scale and concept, translators must select the nearest 'equivalent' in a second language. What is equivalence? To what degree does the translator rely on equivalence of denotation or on one or another sort of connotation? If the translation is based on the aspects of meaning measured by the differential, then the similarity of factor structure is a foregone conclusion. In the study of Kumata and Schramm, for example, translators may have maximized equivalence of extended verbal associations and thereby *produced* the equivalence of structure in the two sets of judgments. It is, of course, something to know that such translations can be made between two unrelated languages, but the fact leaves us wondering about the relative familiarity to native speakers of the two equivalent vocabularies and also wondering whether the vocabularies are equivalent in unmeasured aspects of meaning. Which faces and costumes and landscapes would the Japanese *denote* with their word for *beautiful* and what kinds of conduct would they *denote* with their equivalent of *dirty*? Is there really no difference in the world-views of the two nationalities? What would happen, we wonder, if translators were required to produce denotatively equivalent expressions in a second language? It is possible that such expressions would not have similar factor loadings in a test of extended verbal associations. In general we must ask whether it is possible to make an exact interpretation of this sort of research so long as meaning remains unanalyzed.

The immense appeal of the Semantic Differential Method is evidenced by the large number of footnotes in this book describing researches in progress all over the country and on a great variety of problems. The appearance of the book itself will accelerate the rapid rate at which psychologists are finding uses for a measure of meaning. The authors have put a lot of their muscle into the explication of the measure and its coordination with theory. Certainly they will hope to see this work advance as rapidly as the discovery of promising new applications.

5. How To Make Meaning More Meaningful

Harold Gulliksen

THIS book surveys the research on measurement of meaning conducted by Osgood and his associates over the last ten years, including a dozen unpublished PhD theses from the University of Illinois.

The authors discuss various methods of measuring "meaning" and present the "semantic differential." Since the review by Roger Brown presents the results in considerable detail, it is necessary here only to describe the scaling method in a little greater detail as a basis for comments to follow.

Each semantic scale is defined by a pair of antonyms with seven possible locations between them. Each concept in the set to be scaled is assigned a location (1 to 7) on each of the scales utilized for differentiating that set of concepts. To illustrate this process concretely, the concept FATHER may be judged on three scales as follows:

FATHER

```
              X
happy — — — — — — — sad
        X
hard — — — — — — — soft
                X
slow — — — — — — — fast
```

The book presents an impressive series of studies showing both originality in developing the semantic differential as a measuring device, and ingenuity in applying this device to various problems in a broad range of psychological fields. These studies make a definite contribution in showing that one can obtain con-

Reprinted from *Contemporary Psychology* (1958), 3: 115–118, by permission of the author and the American Psychological Association.

sistent and stable results when investigating meaning by scaling methods.

I have been asked to review the methods used in this work with particular reference to desirable lines of further experimentation. It seems to me that the results so far reported indicate certain critical points that should be carefully explored in subsequent studies.

FINENESS OF MEASUREMENT

FOR any measuring instrument, and particularly for psychological measuring instruments, we need some definite statement of the difference to be expected in making two measurements of the same quantity. The problem is discussed on pages 129–132. A table of test-retest deviations is shown on page 132, with 54.0% of the responses having zero deviation. In other words, when the same semantic differential schedule was given twice to a group of subjects, 54% of the responses on the second administration were the same as the response on the first administration. An initial reaction to such a high percentage of perfect agreement might be pleasure. Once we recognize, however, the necessity for *independent* repeat judgments and the possibility of spurious agreement due to habits or memory, we can realize that 54% perfect agreement is undesirable. For any measurement, the *standard error of measurement* should be determined—particularly for new measurement techniques; but that is impossible unless measurement is fine enough to give a *distribution* of measurements of the same quantity into at least five or ten categories. Then, if one gets astonishingly high agreement in so-called independent repeats, he may have evidence that the replicates were not independent. Such unreasonably high agreement has, for example, been found in careful studies of measurement in biological and chemical fields and is taken to indicate that the supposedly independent replicates are in fact not independent.

In Osgood's data, 54.0% of complete agreements indicates extremely coarse grouping for determining the standard error of measurement. In terms of a normal curve this middle interval is at least 1.4 sigma in width. The problem is pointed out by Osgood himself on page 127. "On many individual items . . . the variance approaches zero." Clearly, it is not possible to determine accuracy of measurement when such coarse grouping is used. For any measurement one needs a unit so fine that a reasonable determination of error is possible. This point is discussed in detail by Tukey (7, 64), who says: "Many times scale makers and measurers stop far short of the limit [of fineness of measurement] set by the danger of non-cooperation [from the subjects]. . . . If more than 10% are exact checks, either the scale is too coarse, or the duplicates are not independent." Even if one sets a standard of 20% or 30% identical remeasurements, instead of only 10%, it is still clear that the 7-category scale results in far too coarse grouping.

It may prove feasible to introduce a finer unit in the semantic differential by simply using a 20-point or 30-point scale instead of the 7-point one. (In one recent unpublished scaling study it was found that subjects can make apparently reasonable judgments on a 30-point scale.) Or it may prove better to use some other scaling device that will give more accurate discrimination.

In view of the tendency mentioned in the book for some groups (for example, the American Legion) to use only categories 1 and 7 or categories 1, 4, and 7 (pp. 227, 229), it may prove inadequate in such cases to use more categories in the scale. It may be necessary to employ a paired-comparison procedure or a checking of each of a number of statements as in the Thurstone scaling procedure.

DIMENSIONALITY OF SEMANTIC SPACE

WHEN a set of concepts is judged on 50 different semantic scales, such as good-bad, high-low, cold-warm, it becomes necessary to determine the degree of overlap among these scales. Our authors have used the method of correlating the scales and factoring the resultant correlation matrix. They find three to eight factors in different studies. Several of the studies are found to agree in giving an Evaluative, a Potency, and an Activity factor.

In the material reported in Chapter 2 only the final factor matrices are given. Evaluation of the results would be facilitated if more information, such as the original correlation matrices and the residuals, were presented. Adequate reporting of factor studies requires at least this much information.

From the point of view of the general stability of the data, it is encouraging to find that several different factor studies give similar results. With regard to factor analysis, however, the authors mention (Chap. 4) a number of disturbing characteristics of the data, such as "concept-scale interaction" (p. 187), variation in scales contributing to a given factor (p. 180), variation in interscale correlation for different concepts (p. 177), and the possibility of metaphorical vs. denotative use of scales (p. 177), as noted by Roger Brown in the preceding review. In the same vein, Osgood states that "the vast majority of scales show significant variation in their correlations with other scales across concepts" (p. 178), that there is variation in the "relevance" of particular scales to particular concepts (p. 78), and that some scales shift in meaning with the concept being judged (p. 179).

The foregoing comments may be summarized by saying that there is a marked "concept-scale interaction." For data which exhibit this characteristic, a general factor analysis of a number of scales judged over a large number of concepts may give quite misleading results. Such interaction means that the emphasis throughout the book on correlational analysis is to be regretted. Other methods of analysis should be considered.

If, in considering the relation between, say, scales A and B, shown in Fig. 1, we find that the various concepts all fall fairly close to one regression line, and therefore show *no* concept-scale interaction, despite marked variations in correlations, then the conclusion that A and B are two parallel scales seems reasonable. It must, however, be emphasized again that the correlation of scale A with scale B may nevertheless be *high* for some concepts and *low* for others. In order to stress this point I have illustrated two concepts for which r_{AB} is high by the solid ellipses, and have also illustrated three concepts with low r_{AB} by the dotted circles (Fig. 1); that is, to say, it is perfectly possible for some concepts with high r_{AB} and others with very low r_{AB} to show a clustering about a single regression line.

If, however, the concepts fall about different regression lines when comparing (say) scales C and D, shown in Fig. 2, this means that these two scales give different information about these concepts so that, regardless of the correlations, these scales cannot be regarded as 'parallel.' In the case illustrated (Fig. 2), the dotted regression line for one concept is relatively flat, the dashed line

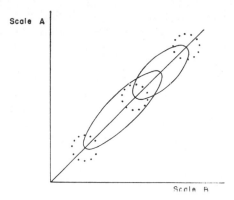

Fig. 1. PARALLEL SCALES
No concept-scale interaction

for another is relatively steep, while the solid line is intermediate. It should be noted that it is possible to have different regression lines for different concepts even if the correlations are fairly similar, as is illustrated in Fig. 2. Both C and D must then be retained in order not to lose information. The approach suggested by data of this type is a "covariance analysis" (2, 4).

Referring to the preceding section, we may note that variations of the type discussed by the authors in Chapter 4 can probably not be described and differentiated adequately with the 7-point scale used.

Another possible method of analysis is suggested by the results reported on

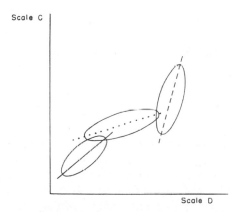

Fig. 2. NONPARALLEL SCALES
High concept-scale interaction

interindividual and intra-individual variance for various concepts. For example, FEATHER on light-heavy or MOTHER on kind-cruel show a very small intra-subject and intersubject variance (p. 127). Surely SENATOR MCCARTHY and ADLAI STEVENSON, on scales such as good-bad or honest-dishonest, show a large intersubject variance (as compared with the intra-subject variance). Using methods that are adequate for determining these variances, it might then be reasonable in scaling to use initially only a selected subset (x) of concepts and a related subset (y) of scales chosen so that each of the concepts in set x has a small intersubject variance on each of the scales in set y. It would then perhaps be possible to use this set of data to determine the basic dimensions in the domain represented by concepts x and scales y. Multidimensional scaling methods, as described by Torgerson (6), for example, would be a useful technique here. Concepts with high intersubject variance on these scales could then be scaled *for each individual* with reference to their position in relation to the stable concepts.

The studies reported in this book demonstrate a wealth of interesting and complex interrelationships between scales and concepts. These complexities may well preclude routine factor analyses for a general determination of the dimensionality of the semantic space for all concepts. Much more work using other analytical methods needs to be done on this basic problem.

PARALLEL SETS OF SCALES

IN discussing the problem of reliability, it is pointed out that we do not know the extent to which *"measured unreliability of an instrument [is] really an index of its sensitivity in recording real changes in the thing being measured"* (p. 133). This comment, and the extrapolation method of determining reliability

suggested on page 134, point to one lack in the present development. *No parallel sets of scales are presented.* The "test-retest (with the same test)" method of measuring reliability is defective in that, if the retest is given immediately, there may be spurious agreement due to responses being repeated from memory, while, if the retest is given a week or a month later, the agreement may be spuriously low because of a genuine change in opinion. A correct estimate of the reliability or of the error of measurement cannot be obtained either by the method of extrapolation to zero time, as suggested by Osgood (p. 134), or by taking the correlation between scores on test and retest with a short interval between.

If parallel tests are available, then one has a clean method of distinguishing reliability or error of measurement at a given time from possible real change over a period of time. Osgood has clearly recognized and stated this problem but has not adopted the necessary solution—developing parallel sets of scales.

It is not necessary to insist on unreasonably high correlations in order to have parallel scales. One needs only a reasonable approximation to the requirement, as in the Spearman-Brown formula, that the pattern of intercorrelations be reasonably similar for the two sets of parallel scales. Three or four scales with certain known intercorrelations are now used to represent a single factor. Other scales with a similar pattern of intercorrelations could also represent the same factor and would constitute an appropriate parallel scale. To insist that the parallel scales have distinctly higher correlations than those used to represent a single factor is *inappropriate.*

TESTS OF SIGNIFICANCE

THE effect of number of cases on the sensitivity of significance tests must be appropriately considered in interpreting the results. A difference so small as to be trivial for many purposes can be statistically significant with a large number of cases. On the other hand, with a small number of cases one will conclude that even large differences are "not statistically significant." For an excellent statement of this point, see Cochran (1).

Osgood and his colleagues conclude that "language used (e.g., English vs. Korean or Japanese) has little effect on the semantic judgments" (pp. 171–174). Yet the three groups studied contained only 22, 24, and 25 students each. Even with such a small number of cases some differences were found, as is pointed out in the discussion of Table 28 (p. 173). It would be expected that differences undetectable with 25 cases could be detected as significant with more cases. In another study the authors conclude that the meaning of a concept is not influenced by the other concepts contained in the test form. The experiment utilized comparisons between three groups of 15 subjects each (p. 84). It is concluded from another experiment that the factorial structure for normals and schizophrenics is the same, because no significant differences were found among two groups of 40 divided for purposes of analysis into four groups of 20 subjects each (p. 224).

It is concluded that there is no significant difference between the Thurstone scale and the semantic differential. The conclusion is based on the fact that for a *total* of 50 subjects the across-techniques correlation is never *significantly* lower than the reliability coefficient for the Thurstone scale (p. 194). Differences that are not statistically significant for 50 subjects may be statistically significant in a more thorough investigation. It is also pointed out that the semantic differential and the Thurstone scales are similar because their intercorrelation corrected for attenuation is about .90. A correlation (corrected for attenuation)

of .90, based on 100 cases, may, however, be detectably different from unity. For 600 cases, such a coefficient is clearly significantly different from unity (3).

CORRELATIONS BETWEEN SCALES VS. CURVILINEARITY

IT should be noted that a high correlation between two different scales (obtained possibly by different scaling methods) does not necessarily mean that the two scales are essentially equivalent for all purposes. A definite curvilinear relationship (even though the correlation is high) usually indicates important differences in the scales. For example, "length in inches" and "log length in inches" will show quite a good correlation over selected ranges of length, yet it would not be generally concluded that these two scales could be used interchangeably.

For similar reasons, studies of changes in attitude, undertaken to verify the "congruity hypothesis," require careful measurement and might well be sensitive to differential curvilinearity in the scales (p. 240).

Curvilinear relationships between scales are not to be dismissed on evidence of over-all correlations (5). All the curvilinearly related scales discussed in Stevens' paper are very highly correlated, yet it is important to compare the scales with respect to their relative sensitivity in different parts of the range. Fig. 3 illustrates scales x and y which are highly correlated but *not equivalent* since y gives more accurate measurement in the lower part of the range, while x gives more accurate measurement in the upper part of the range. (Points a, b, and c are spread out on the y scale but not on the x scale. Points e, f, and g are differentiated on the x scale but not on the y scale.) Scales z and w (Fig. 4), on the other hand, are

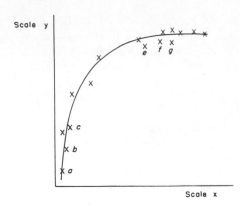

Fig. 3. HIGH CORRELATION
Different scales

not highly correlated, yet one may be substituted for the other, or, if one wishes more accurate measurement, the average of the two may be used. It may be noted that the curvilinearity represented between scales x and y does not imply that one of the scales is a *true* scale and that the other is curved with reference to this *true* scale. All that is demonstrated is that two measures have been found such that scale y makes finer differentiations than x at one end of the scales while the reverse is true at the other end.

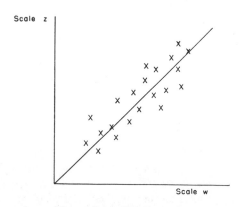

Fig. 4. LOW CORRELATION
Parallel scales

SUMMARY

IN the above discussion, five major points have been stressed.

1. It is desirable to use scaling methods that will give better discrimination, particularly for the more homogeneous concepts, than is furnished by the present 7-category scales. Repeat measures should give, let us say, not more than 20% identical results. It might be possible to achieve such a goal by using a 15-point or 25-point scale. Or it might prove necessary to use other scaling methods.

2. In view of the significant concept-scale interaction, the methods of factor analysis may give misleading conclusions regarding dimensionality of the semantic space. Other methods should be tried out, such as covariance analyses or a multidimensional scaling of concepts that show low intersubject variance.

3. The development of parallel sets of scales would help to solve the problem of differentiating between low reliability and a change in attitude.

4. Nonsignificant differences found with small numbers of cases should not be interpreted as a reliable indication of similarity of the groups or variables tested until the results have been duplicated with a reasonably large number of cases.

5. Scales which are significantly curvilinearly related to each other cannot be regarded as interchangeable for all purposes, even though there is a high correlation between them.

The studies reported in the book under review form an impressive demonstration of the potential value of the measurement of meaning from the point of view of both basic research and practical applications. The authors show how this method can be used to solve problems in a variety of fields, such as attitude measurement, research on personality and on communications. It is hoped that the evidence they have presented will stimulate further studies in this interesting area.

(The reviewer wishes to thank Carroll Pratt, Ledyard Tucker, and Samuel Messick for reading his review in MS and for suggesting certain revisions which he was glad to make. He remarks, however, that the sole responsibility for errors of fact or comment remains with him.)

REFERENCES

1. W. G. COCHRAN. The chi-square test of goodness of fit. *Ann. math. Statist.*, 1952, 23, 315–345.

2. HAROLD GULLIKSEN and S. S. WILKS. Regression tests for several samples. *Psychometrika,* 1950, 15, 91–114.

3. F. M. LORD. A significance test for the hypothesis that two variables measure the same trait except for errors of measurement. *Psychometrika,* 1957, 22, 207–220.

4. G. W. SNEDECOR. *Statistical methods.* Ames: Iowa State College Press, 1946. Chap. 12.

5. S. S. STEVENS. On the psychophysical law. *Psychol. Rev.,* 1957, 64, 153–181.

6. W. S. TORGERSON. Multidimensional scaling: I. Theory and method. *Psychometrika,* 1952, 17, 401–419.

7. Symposium on statistics for the clinician. *J. clin. Psychol.,* 1950, 6, 1–76.

6. Review of The Measurement of Meaning

John B. Carroll

The title of this book provides scant indication of the wide-angle view which the authors have given of a variety of subjects in psycholinguistics and the study of communication processes in both their theoretical and their practical aspects. One can find a little of everything, from pure psychological theory (in the tradition of Clark L. Hull), personality theory, and attitude research, to journalism and advertising. All this is by way of presenting the rationale and the uses of the measuring technique which Osgood has called the *semantic differential* (hereafter SD). Linguists will be most concerned to learn how the authors have dealt with what they call *meaning* and how the SD can aid in the development of the branch of linguistics which is covered by the widely used and misused term *semantics*.

Both in the introduction and towards the close of the book (318) the reader is warned that it represents largely a 'progress report'; he is asked therefore to discount the 'tone of assurance not actually felt'. Certainly he cannot but admire the energy and imagination with which the studies described in this volume have been pursued; he will take note of the fact that psychologists here, there, and everywhere have been quick to adopt the SD as a tool of broad usefulness.[1] But he will ponder. Indeed, the authors predict (320) that he will raise questions—about whether the SD is really a measure of 'meaning', about whether there are really only three main dimensions of the 'semantic space', and about how much the results of SD research can contribute to our understanding of the nature of meaning.

The meaning of meaning. An author of a treatise on meaning is under obligation to define what he means by 'meaning', and Osgood and his co-authors have not failed in this respect. One might have expected them to give us a 'measurement' of the meaning of 'meaning', but it will later be apparent why

Reprinted from *Language* (1959), 35: 58–77, by permission of the author and the Linguistic Society of America.

[1] For example, see Carolyn K. Staats and Arthur W. Staats, Meaning established by classical conditioning, *J. exper. psychol.* 54.74–80 (1957); W. E. Lambert, J. Havelka, and C. Crosby, The influence of language-acquisition contexts on bilingualism, *J. abn. soc. psychol.* 56.239–44 (1958).

this was not practicable. It is a commentary on the ambiguity of the term, however, that their concept of meaning is so very different from what we commonly understand by it—at least what we commonly understand to be its 'head' meaning. The common meaning of 'meaning' derives from its use in such contexts as these:

> *What does the word 'syllepsis' mean?*
> *German Pferd means horse.*

Osgood's meaning of 'meaning' derives from such contexts as:

> *What did you mean by that remark?*
> *I meant to tell him.*
> *Lucky Strike means fine tobacco.*

Yet it goes far beyond such contexts. We are told already on the first page of the first chapter that meaning 'certainly refers to some implicit process or state' (1), and soon after, that it is a 'distinctive mediational process or state which occurs in the organism whenever a sign is received (decoded) or produced (encoded).' This definition is consistently adhered to: a record of muscle potential during periods of sustained thought can be a 'crude index of meaning' (12); 'from the fact that two subjects differ in their associations to a given stimulus word we can probably infer at least momentary differences in their meanings of the stimulus word' (16); 'we often infer ... the meaning of a sign to an individual from his facial expressions, gestures, gross bodily movements, etc.' (18); and the unreliability of semantic judgments on the SD may be interpreted as due, among other things, to 'increasing unstability of the things being measured (meaning of concepts) through time' (133). Indeed, we read that 'it certainly seems likely that the meanings of concepts to people can change from time to time and that changes are more likely over long intervals than short—e.g. one's meaning of MY MOOD TODAY is likely to vary with today's experiences, and experiences are likely to vary more between one day and another than between one minute and the next' (135). Quotidian fluctuations in such 'meanings' are a far cry from the semantic changes with which linguists have traditionally been concerned.

A fuller understanding of Osgood's 'meaning' of 'meaning' can be achieved only if the reader will have the patience to take a short excursion into psychological theory. In the analysis of the classical Pavlovian conditioning experiment (in which the dog learns to salivate when there is the sound of a buzzer which has previously signaled the presentation of food) it turns out that the conditioned response (salivation in response to a buzzer) is never quite the same as the unconditioned response (salivation in direct response to food)—it is not as fast or complete, for example. Osgood and many other behavior theorists assume, therefore, that the conditioned response depends upon the occurrence of a self-stimulating 'mediating reaction' which can have partial identity with the unconditioned response and thus be associated with it. The mediating reaction is internal and 'representational' because it is a 'light-weight' PART of the behavior produced by the unconditioned stimulus (the food). Some will be tempted to propose that the mediating reaction is a sort of 'image' or 'idea' of the unconditioned stimulus, but Osgood and his co-authors make no such suggestion; they merely claim that they are forced to postulate some sort of intervening, internal process which arises in all conditioning of 'significates' to 'signs' (6). It is this process which they identify as 'meaning'. Thus, the meaning of the sign HOUSE[2] is identified with whatever representational process occurs in behavior when an individual has been conditioned to the word HOUSE in contiguity with stimulus patterns which can be characterized as houses.

This concept of meaning has the virtue of making it a matter of individual learning and experience. The 'meaning' which the individual attaches at any given moment to the sign HOUSE is the sum total of the processes which at that time represent his experiences with houses—their stimulus patterns and all their associative values for him. And since what an individual will say about houses can be assumed to depend upon the mediational processes occurring at the moment of utterance, our predictions of his utterances can reasonably be based upon whatever indices of the 'meaning' of house we can obtain for him.

Nevertheless, the treatment of 'meaning' offered in *The measurement of meaning* does not take full account of different kinds of meaning. Although there is mention in several places (2, 47, 79, 177) of a difference between denotative and connotative meaning, and even a fairly extensive discussion (320–5) of the implications of this difference, these terms are nowhere precisely defined, much less distinguished in the light of the psychological model which is offered in the first chapter. All the kinds of meaning elucidated by Ogden and Richards, by Charles Morris, or by many other writers on meaning are ignored or mentioned in the briefest possible manner. Concerning 'linguistic meaning', as exemplified by the fact that *the happy boy* in the utterance *the happy boy is playing in the pond* is 'nominative substantive form class', our authors say only that 'it is clear that these meanings of "meaning" serve to define the relationship of signs to other signs in the message matrix, but are independent operationally of both the sociological situation-behavior matrix and the psychological organismic-process matrix' (3). All of this is not necessarily a criticism of Osgood and company; I merely wish to point out that this book cannot claim and in fact does not pretend (325) to be a full-dress study of meaning (unless one generalizes too broadly from its title), for it fixes attention on a particular definition of meaning, namely (9),

The meaning of "meaning" for which we wish to establish an index is a psychological one— that process or state in the behavior of a sign-using organism which is assumed to be a necessary consequence of the reception of sign-stimuli and a necessary antecedent for the production of sign-processes.

By the authors' own admission, the theory of meaning which is presented here has a certain ad-hoc flavor about it—it is truer to say that it was built around the (prior) measuring device, the SD, than to say that the SD was a logical out-

---

[2] Following Osgood, I shall use SMALL CAPITALS for the 'concepts' which are rated on the SD, and *italics* for the adjectival scales (such as *good–bad*) on which the concepts are rated.

come of the theory. Osgood goes to considerable length (20–5) to show how the SD developed, almost by accident, in the course of research on synesthesia (the association of sense modalities, as in 'colored music'). Nevertheless, the theory of 'mediational processes' developed here is widely recognized as a very substantial contribution to psychological theory, and this fact will stand regardless of one's views on the relevance of the theory to 'meaning'.

The meaning of 'measurement'. The book gives an extensive treatment of the measurement of meaning by the specially developed technique known as the SD. Whether the SD actually 'measures' 'meanings' even if we accept the authors' own definition of 'meaning' is a subject for debate. The reader will have some difficulty appraising this question, owing to the fact that the book presents extremely few *measurements* of meaning. Except for a table (88) which gives one person's 'meanings' of ten 'concepts' including QUICKSAND, WHITE ROSE BUDS, and METHODOLOGY, the only 'meanings' presented anywhere in the book are those found for a series of 'concepts' (TAFT, UMT, STEVENSON, etc.) of interest to political scientists, obtained through analysis of SD ratings collected from groups of Taft Republicans, Eisenhower Republicans, and Stevenson Democrats in the 1952 presidential election. The reader who wishes to study SD 'meanings' of a fairly large sample of 'concepts' may be referred to a recent compilation of SD average ratings of 360 'concepts' on 20 SD adjectival scales.[3] Even though such a compilation is now available (though with limited distribution), it is to be regretted that Osgood, Suci, and Tannenbaum did not display more of the substantive (as distinct from the methodological) fruits of their labors.

It is implied in any instance of measurement that there is a universe of objects to be measured, that these objects vary in some specified character or characters, and that there is an appropriate set of procedures for securing an index of the *value* of a given object with respect to any specified character. Thus, if we wish to measure height, we assume that there is a universe of objects which vary in height (persons, bushes, trees, mountains, etc.) and we note that there are appropriate operations (use of foot rules, measuring tapes, theodolites, etc., in conjunction with the frame of reference provided by a plumb line) which yield quantitative values (62 inches, 72.43 feet, 2.31 kilometers). Subsidiary problems arise: reliability or accuracy (the extent to which errors of measurement are minimized), objectivity (lack of bias on the part of the observer), validity (the extent to which the desired characteristic, rather than some other, is measured), and the choice of a metric.

What is the universe of objects measured by the SD? Presumably it should be composed of those internal states or mediational processes which stand at the center of Osgood's theory. But these states are ephemeral and transient, any given state being only sporadically present in the stream of behavior. Osgood's problem is to bring them into the laboratory, as it were, and this means that they must be elicited by special stimulation. It is appropriate at this point to

[3] James J. Jenkins, Wallace A. Russell, and George J. Suci, *An atlas of semantic profiles for 360 words*, (37 pages mimeographed; University of Minnesota, Department of Psychology, 1957).

describe the SD technique in sufficient detail for the subsequent discussion. We shall omit consideration of a number of subsidiary measurement problems (reliability, equality of units of measurement, etc.) which are of interest to the psychometrician[4] but not especially to the linguist.

Description of the SD technique. Perhaps we should not speak of *the* SD lest we spread the impression that there is one and only one SD. It is a technique rather than a device. Typically, Osgood sets the stage for the mediating processes that he wants to measure by presenting the subject with a 'concept' (always identified here in SMALL CAPITALS) and with a series of bipolar scales with respect to which the subject is to judge the 'concept'. For example, the concept FATHER might be presented for 'semantic differentiation' on such scales as these:

$$happy\_\_\_:\_\_\_:\_\_\_:\_\_\_:\_\_\_:\_\_\_:\_\_\_sad$$
$$hard\_\_\_:\_\_\_:\_\_\_:\_\_\_:\_\_\_:\_\_\_:\_\_\_soft$$
$$slow\_\_\_:\_\_\_:\_\_\_:\_\_\_:\_\_\_:\_\_\_:\_\_\_fast$$

That is, the subject is asked to judge the 'concept' in terms of whether it is more associated with *happy* or *sad*, *hard* or *soft*, etc. After judging FATHER in this way on a number of scales, he may be asked to judge other 'concepts'. The rating task is preceded by complete instructions illustrating the type of ratings wanted, how the marks are to be made, and the like (82–4). A rating session typically might secure from a subject ratings of (say) 20 concepts on 50 scales, or 1000 separate judgments. The concepts to be rated and the scales to be used are sampled or otherwise selected in the light of the purposes of the investigation.

The underlying rating scale technique is of course not new. Psychologists have been obtaining ratings of all sorts of things—personality, musical selections, color patches, etc.—for a long time. Indeed, there have been elaborate studies of ratings of personality using a technique very similar to the SD and also using the kinds of statistical analysis employed by Osgood, Suci, and Tannenbaum.[5] What seems to be novel in the SD is the explicit application of rating techniques to word meanings.

Certain variations in procedure are possible. One is to present a different concept with every scale and to rotate concepts and scales with each other (81); a possible disadvantage of this is that it may be confusing to the subject to have to alter his set with every item presented. Another variant is possible only in testing subjects one by one: a scale is presented on a screen as a pair of polar terms, one at the right, one at the left. The concept is then presented and 'the time required for the subject to react by moving a lever toward one or the other of the polar terms is automatically recorded' (81). It is found in this case that the speed of the reaction is correlated with the extent to which the concept tends to be rated toward the extremes of the scale.

Still another variant is of special interest, for it eliminates altogether the need for presenting concepts. In this, the subject is asked to match the ends of two polar adjectival scales. 'Given the following item, for example:

SHARP–dull; relaxed–tense

[4] See the review by Harold Gulliksen, *Contemporary psychology* 3.115–9 (1958).

[5] Raymond B. Cattell, *Personality and motivation: Structure and measurement* (Yonkers-on-Hudson, 1957).

the subject is asked to simply encircle that one of the second pair which seems closest in meaning to the capitalized member of the first pair' (40). Unhappily, in order to investigate every possible pairing of n scales it is necessary to generate a test consisting of $n(n - 1)/2$ items. The measure of relationship is simply the percentage of agreement in direction of alignment.

We may now ask the question, in what sense does the SD 'measure' 'mediational processes'? Evidently Osgood Suci, and Tannenbaum believe that the presentation of a 'concept' in conjunction with a bipolar scale gives rise to some sort of mediational process which is stable enough to give reliable and useful results. With respect to what characteristics do these staged mediational processes vary? One might first suggest that they vary in speed and intensity, but although Osgood gives some attention to this type of variation he is much more concerned with their direction with respect to the bipolar scales. There is the implication that any mediational state can be fractionated into a number of distinct mediating reactions, each of which can take either a positive (excitatory) or negative (inhibitory) form. The task of research with the SD is to identify the independent dimensions along which mediating reactions may vary. The analytic instrument chosen for this task is the mathematical technique known as factor analysis.

Factor analysis and the 'semantic space'. Factor analysis has been widely used in the behavior sciences[6] (but also elsewhere, as in chemistry[7]) as a means of seeking a minimal number of independent dimensions which will allow the description of a body of data to a satisfactory degree of precision. The geometric model is that of an m-dimensional Euclidean hyperspace. The variables under study are regarded as vectors (directed lines of specified length starting at the origin) in this hyperspace, and the first object of the analysis is to specify the coordinates of the termini of the vectors, in some arbitrary reference frame, in such a way that the size of the angles between the vectors will be inversely related to the degree of their relationship or similarity.

From the standpoint of factor analysis, the variables under study in the SD are the adjectival scales (regardless of whether any 'concepts' are also involved); they constitute the dimensions along which the 'meanings' (mediational processes represented by the confrontation of scale with concept or scale with scale) are measured initially. The purpose of the factor analysis is to reduce these dimensions to a certain minimal set. Before any factor analysis can be done, it is necessary to measure all the relations between the scales, for example by computing a correlation matrix showing the correlation of each scale with every other scale. Consider again the rating task presented by the SD in its usual forms: one must rate 'concepts' like LADY, BOULDER, SIN, FATHER, LAKE, SYMPHONY, RUSSIAN, etc. on scales like *good–bad, large–small, beautiful–ugly, yellow–blue, hard–soft*, etc. To the extent that certain scales are similar in meaning (or, as I suppose Osgood would have it, evoke similar mediational processes), concepts will tend to be rated similarly. If one rates LADY as *good*, one is likely to rate LADY as

[6] Sten Henrysson, *Applicability of factor analysis in the behavioral sciences: A methodological study* (Stockholm, 1957).

[7] B. Higman, *Applied group-theoretic and matrix methods*, Chap. 11 (Oxford, 1955).

beautiful. If one rates SIN as *bad,* one is thereby likely to rate SIN as *ugly.* It comes to the same thing even if the sample contains a few perverse individuals who rate SIN as *good* and also *beautiful;* what would alter the case would be a datum in which a concept is rated as both *good* and also *ugly.* All that is necessary, actually, is that a sufficient variety of concepts be provided so that there is variation on each scale; it does not really matter how individuals rate concepts so long as they are to some degree consistent in their use of adjectives. For example, if the 'concept' presented is a political figure like EISENHOWER or STEVENSON, the underlying scale relationships will be preserved even if our sample of raters contains a mixture of Republicans and Democrats, as long as the raters consistently tend to use adjectives like *good, beautiful, sweet, kind, happy, sacred,* and *nice* for their preferred concept and adjectives like *bad, ugly, sour, cruel, sad, profane,* and *awful* for their nonpreferred concept. For under these conditions the statistical operations which Osgood uses in analyzing his data would yield high positive correlations among all the scales *good–bad, beautiful–ugly, sweet–sour, kind–cruel, happy–sad, sacred–profane,* and *nice–awful.* At the same time, the correlations of these scales with scales like *large–small, wet–dry, thick–thin,* and *fast–slow* might be found to be close to zero, reflecting the fact that 'concepts' judged *good* might in the long run tend to be judged equally often *large* or *small, wet* or *dry,* etc.

In order to illustrate certain factor-analytic operations more concretely, let us assume that the scales we have used for a small SD study consist of the following: *good–bad, kind–cruel, large–small, strong–weak,* and *brave–cowardly.* We find that there is a high correlation (.72) between the first two, a correlation of .40 between the next two, and correlations of .60, .50, .31, and .40, respectively, between the first four and the last; the remaining correlations are negligible. By resorting to the mathematical procedures of factor analysis, we can take three necessary initial steps: (1) determine the lengths of each of the vectors representing the several scales, (2) ascertain the minimum number of dimensions which can contain these vectors in view of their interrelations, and (3) compute the locations of the termini of the vectors with respect to some arbitrary set of coordinates. In the present case, we determine the lengths of the five vectors to be .88, .83, .62, .65, and .79, respectively; we find that the vectors span no less than two dimensions; and we can represent the positions of the vectors with respect to two arbitrary coordinates as in Figure 1. It now appears that *large* (naming the scales by one end) is very close to *strong,* that *good* is very close to *kind,* and that *brave* is about halfway between these. Indeed, the relative positions of the vectors represent the correlations between them; it is the function of factor analysis to locate the vectors in a minimal space such that their correlations will be adequately represented.[8]

But there is a further step. The vectors in Figure 1 are simply 'hanging in the semantic space', so to speak, without any indication of the basic dimensions of that space. Since the relations between the vectors are invariant no matter where

---

[8] In theory, the correlation between two vectors should be equal to $h_1 h_2 \cos \phi_{12}$, h_1 and h_2 being the lengths of the vectors and ϕ_{12} being the angle between them. It is not always possible to approach this exactly because of error in the data, problems of estimation, etc.

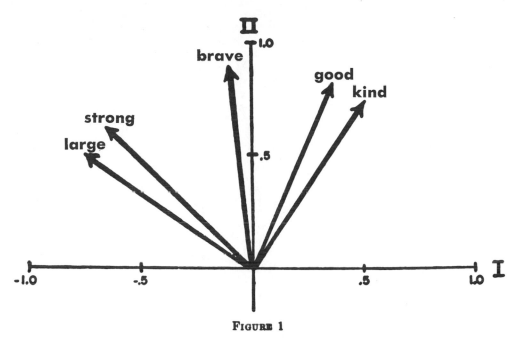

Relative positions of 5 vectors plotted on arbitrary coordinates.
Each vector represents an adjectival scale.

we put the coordinates by which to define the positions of the vectors, it is reasonable to rotate the coordinate frame of reference to a position which will delineate the primary dimensions of that space. Unfortunately, factor analysts have had difficulty in arriving at satisfactory objective criteria for rotating the coordinate frame of reference. Generally, it is regarded as desirable to place the coordinate axes in such a way that the vectors will tend to have a maximum number of near-zero projections. Figure 2 illustrates an orthogonal rotation for the reference frame used in Figure 1; we now have one dimension defined largely by *good* and *kind*, and another dimension defined largely by *large* and *strong*; it now appears that *brave* partakes of both dimensions. We then attempt to 'interpret' or 'identify' the dimensions thus arrived at: what semantic notion do *good*, *kind*, and *brave* have in common, and independent of that, what semantic notion do *large*, *strong*, and *brave* have in common? Osgood's answer would be that *good*, *kind*, and *brave* have a 'positive evaluative' notion, and that *large*, *strong*, and *brave* have in common some sort of notion of 'strength' or 'potency'. (It is remarkable that though we may rather easily intuit the nature of these dimensions our language seems to have no sufficiently generalized cover terms for them.) The meaning of *brave* now falls into place: it is a term which (whatever else it may do) at once characterizes something as 'positively evaluated' and also 'potent'.

The SD semantic space is populated not only by vectors but also by points: these points correspond to the 'concepts' which have been rated, and are located in such a way as to represent the average value of each concept on each semantic dimension. Figure 3 depicts the positions of a number of 'concepts' on the 'evalua-

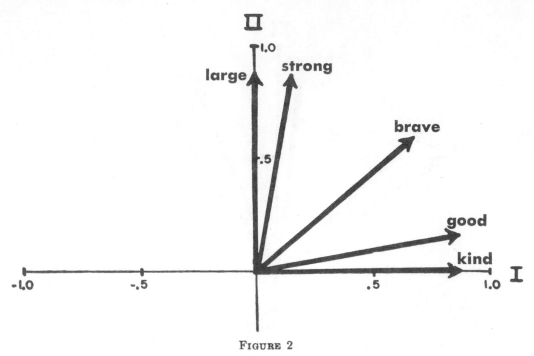

The vectors of Figure 1 'rotated' to a meaningful reference frame.
Factor I is an 'evaluative' factor, and Factor II is a 'potency' factor.

tive' and 'potency' dimensions; the data are from the *Atlas* of Jenkins, Russell, and Suci.

The dimensionality of the semantic space. One of the principal objectives of factor analysis, as I have said, is to determine the minimal number of dimensions which are needed to account for, to a satisfactory degree of precision, all the relationships inherent in a set of data. In most of the studies of semantic space reported in this book, particularly the earlier and simpler ones, three chief 'semantic' dimensions persist in emerging, despite honest efforts on the part of the investigators to avoid bias. We have already mentioned two of these: the 'evaluative' dimension, represented by such scales as *good–bad*, *timely–untimely*, *kind–cruel*, *beautiful–ugly*, *successful–unsuccessful*, *important–unimportant*, *true–false*, and *wise–foolish*, and the 'potency' dimension, represented by *hard–soft*, *masculine–feminine*, *large–small*, and *strong–weak*. The third is usually called an 'activity' dimension; it is represented by such scales as *active–passive*, *fast–slow*, *hot–cold*, *sharp–dull*, and *angular–rounded*. Sometimes the 'activity' and 'potency' dimensions seem to collapse into a single 'dynamism' factor, but as we shall see, this result may be an artifact of the sampling of concepts. In one of their later studies the authors attempted to sample the 'semantic space' more extensively and thus to obtain a larger number of semantic dimensions. In this 'thesaurus' study (47–66), Roget's thesaurus was rather systematically sampled to yield 76 scales (this being the maximum number manageable on the high-speed computing machine available to the authors), on which 100 subjects were to rate

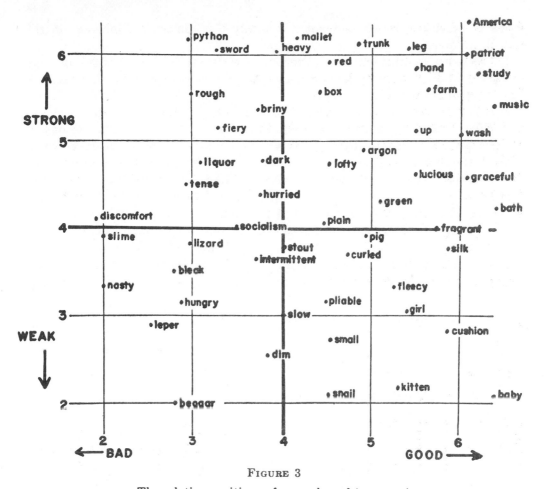

FIGURE 3

The relative positions of a number of 'concepts'
on the 'evaluative' and 'potency' dimensions
as defined, respectively, by the GOOD and STRONG scales.
Data from Jenkins, Russell, and Suci's *Atlas*.

20 'concepts'. This study was not completely successful; the statistical analysis itself is open to certain technical criticisms, but in any event even the authors were not really happy with the results, which entailed various difficulties of interpretation. Nevertheless, eight dimensions were identified and named: (1) evaluation, (2) potency, (3) oriented activity, (4) stability, (5) tautness, (6) novelty, (7) receptivity, and (8) aggressiveness.

It is worthy of comment that the same three prime factors—evaluation, activity, and potency—were also identified in studies where the 'concepts' were not words or anything linguistic, but rather such things as underwater sonar signals (66–8) and representational paintings in an art gallery (68–70). Still, these findings are perhaps not surprising in view of the fact that the adjectival scales utilized in these studies overlapped considerably with those used in the studies of 'concepts', and they suggest that if this is a factor analysis of 'meaning' to any degree whatsoever, it is a factor analysis of the dimensions underlying a series of adjectival scales and not necessarily the dimensions inherent in the stimuli involved.

   Let us pause to consider the requirements for the establishment of two or more independent dimensions in the 'semantic space' (or in any space, for that matter). For any pair of dimensions, the principal requirement is that there be a configuration of points (representing 'concepts', if you will) in the semantic space such as to yield a Pearsonian correlation coefficient of zero between the dimensions. If we ignore the mathematically trivial cases in which there is no variance on one or both of the dimensions, there must be a minimum of four points in order to do this, and they must be symmetrically disposed like the corners of a square, as in Figures 4a–c or some intermediate rotations thereof with the center of the square as a pivot. In the figures, the coordinate axes represent the neutral points of two SD polar adjectival scales, assumed to coincide with two primary dimensions of the semantic space. Figure 4a assumes that all concepts have ratings of 4 or greater (4 being the neutral point of an SD scale), while figures 4b and 4c allow ratings on both sides of the neutral point (a more likely state of affairs). Figure 4a

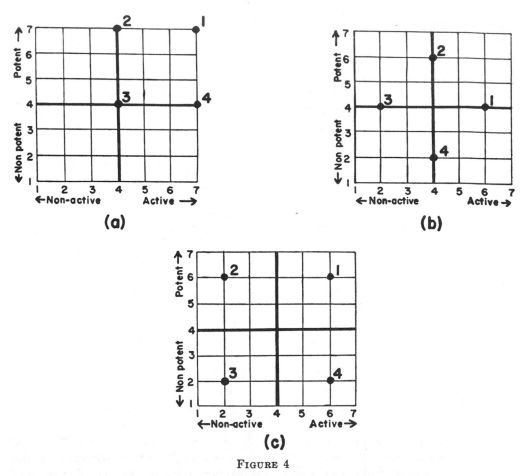

FIGURE 4

Some possible ways of disposing points in the 'semantic space'
so as to demonstrate independence of dimensions.

says, for example, that if we were trying to establish the mutual independence of an 'activity' dimension and a 'potency' dimension, we would have to include in our study four concepts, one with each of the following combinations of characteristics:

1. active and also potent
2. potent, but neither active nor nonactive
3. neither active nor potent
4. active, but neither potent nor nonpotent

Figure 4c says, on the other hand, that we would have to be sure to include four concepts as follows:

1. active and potent
2. nonactive but potent
3. nonpotent and nonactive
4. active but nonpotent

Now, if the situation depicted in Figure 4b is generalized for m factors, there must be at least $2m$ points to establish the mutual independence of all m factors. But for the situations depicted in 4a or 4c, there must be at least 2^m points to establish m independent dimensions. If, for example, the upper left and the lower right points in Figure 4c were eliminated, the remaining points would define a space of one dimension; similarly, elimination of selected points in m dimensions would decrease the dimensionality of the space. It is hard to say what kind of configuration is representative of actual data. Most probably, real data contain points conforming to *both* figures 4b and 4c; hence the minimum number of points is likely to be at least $(2m + 2^m)$; for $m = 10$, this number is 1044—a number much larger than has been employed in any SD research so far. Note that the number of points specified here is only a necessary condition, not a sufficient one, for the points must be disposed in the required manner. Furthermore, we have completely ignored the possibility of errors which are due to the operation of chance and inaccurate measurement.[9]

The essence of all this is that in order to establish the dimensionality of a system, one must adequately sample the total space for which one is seeking dimensions, and this is a very difficult thing to do. It is not really a criticism of Osgood and his associates to say that they have failed to meet the requirements stated above, for up to now the requirements have scarcely been verbalized, much less formulated mathematically; workers who have used factor analysis in other connections (including the present writer) have apparently never become aware of this problem because (for entirely different reasons) they have usually taken

[9] Likewise, we have not considered the effect of intersubject variability in the positioning of 'concepts' in the semantic space; the argument has assumed that the positions of the concepts are either those assigned by a single rater, or those given by the mean or median ratings of groups of raters. Conceivably, intersubject variability might have the effect of reducing the number of 'concepts' required to establish m dimensions, because a given named 'concept' might function as a multiplicity of different 'concepts' in the ratings of a group of subjects. Nevertheless, the evidence thus far available suggests that the amount of intersubject variability is not large enough (except possibly in the case of attitude-objects like STEVENSON, COMMUNIST, GOD) to warrant placing reliance on it as a source of dimensionality.

such large samples of points (seldom less than 100) in the factor space as to create the illusion of adequacy, thus masking the difficulty. None of the studies here reported uses more than 20 concepts (as far as one can tell from the text, for the number of points studied is not always specified). In the light of the foregoing considerations, 20 concepts could yield scarcely more than four factors. *The measurement of meaning* provides little information to enable one to evaluate how well the semantic space has been sampled. Certainly the results of the 'thesaurus study', which utilized 76 scales and 20 concepts, and which yielded 8 somewhat dubious semantic dimensions, must be accepted with much caution.[10]

From a practical standpoint, it might be objected that the use of a larger number of concepts would begin to require fantastic amounts of time from the subjects who are asked to rate them on the SD. Nevertheless, since persons are used solely as measuring instruments rather than as points in the sample space, there is no requirement for every subject to rate every concept. If 'equivalent' groups of subjects are sampled, the data from several such groups, each rating its own set of concepts, could be pooled before analysis; in this way the number of 'concepts' studied could be extended almost indefinitely. (The data for Jenkins, Russell, and Suci's *Atlas* were collected on this plan.)

I will venture the guess that if the semantic space were adequately sampled— both by using an adequate number of adjectival scales and by using an appropriate selection of 'concepts'—a far larger number of dimensions would appear than the three dimensions thus far solidly identified. Indeed, within certain restrictions of which we will speak presently, one could establish dimensions almost at will. It might seem reasonable to suppose, for example, that *redness–greenness* is a basic semantic dimension; according to some varieties of color theory, at least, it is a dimension of sensation. Now, Osgood and his colleagues have included *red–green* as one of the scales on which they ask subjects to rate concepts (37), but they have not included other scales which might sample this dimension, such as *rose–chartreuse, pink–olive, verdant–fiery*. Nor have they sampled 'concepts' which are denotatively near to red or green, such as GRASS, CHEEK, FOREST, LIPS, HOT COALS, etc. If their samples of scales and concepts had been large enough to include these, one can confidently predict that a dimension of 'redness–greenness' would have emerged from the data.

Even in this example, the reader will doubtless have perceived artificiality. In what sense are red and green opposites? Does the ordinary layman know that red and green produce gray or white when mixed on the psychologist's color wheel? Why would it not make more sense to use *gray* as the opposite pole from *red* and indeed from all the colors, at least for the purposes of the SD? Though he speculates on the problem (79, 327), Osgood has not adequately justified his procedures (purely judgmental, apparently) for specifying the 'opposite' ends

[10] The requirements for sampling the space are related to the requirements for what is known as 'minimum rank', but are much more stringent. To define a space of m dimensions, only $m + 1$ points are required, but we are concerned here with the necessity of demonstrating that the dimensions are actually independent, i.e. possessing no mutual intercorrelations significantly greater than zero.

of his polar scales. What is to prevent the use of hybrid scales like *blatant–rational* (to give an ad-hoc example)?

The would-be user of the SD technique, particularly if he is to perform a factor analysis, must face the criticism so often voiced with respect to other uses of factor analysis that 'you get out what you put in', and that consequently nothing is gained by the analysis. Such criticism is nonsense: obviously one cannot possibly 'get out' more than one 'puts in' to any experiment or investigation; the purpose of the experiment is to test the hypotheses on which it was based. Factor analysis, properly used, is a perfectly legitimate technique for confirming or denying certain kinds of hypotheses relating to the association or lack of association between variables, and one cannot predict the outcome with absolute certainty in advance of the investigation. What I am pointing out here, however, is that Osgood's results are limited by his selection of scales and concepts. Osgood has not yet reported research in which he constructs hypotheses concerning what semantic dimensions (beyond the usual ones) might actually be expected to exist and then tests such hypotheses extensively and in detail.

It will be intriguing to see, in future research, precisely how far one can go in establishing dimensions. I spoke above of the restrictions or constraints upon an indefinite proliferation of dimensions of adjectival description. These constraints, one would think, lie in the actualities of human perception and of the phenomenal world. One is unlikely to find a dimension which has no counterpart somewhere in the real world or in the distinctions which the human race has learned to value. The use of 'concepts' which raters must judge as varying in one or more respects, in the SD technique, is one safeguard against spurious dimensions. At the same time, the use of a proper sampling of points in the factor space will help to insure that dimensions do not unduly collapse and merge together. These considerations are at least a partial answer to the possible objection to SD and other factor-analytic research to the effect that the 'factors' or 'dimensions' are 'merely' dimensions of equivalence in meaning. My point is that the dimensions of meaning could not exist without some sort of support in experience. Thus, when a factor-analyst finds that a 'carefreeness' dimension can be demonstrated in a variety of ratings and observations of personality, this does not depend solely upon the existence of adjectives and adjectival phrases; it also depends upon the observed differences among people. The data will not permit the factor-analyst, however, to claim a perfect isomorphism between the factorial dimensions and the genotypic dimensions which might serve to account for the relationships observed in the investigation. For example, the discovery of a 'potency' dimension by no means insures that high-potency objects are all 'potent' for the same reason.

An alternative interpretation of the SD. We are by no means obliged to accept the claim of Osgood, Suci, and Tannenbaum that the SD really measures 'meaning', not even the particular (and somewhat parochial) kind of meaning defined by them. Let us see what kind of alternative (or perhaps supplementary) interpretation we can make for the SD and the results obtained with it.

Notice first that all of the 'scales' customarily employed in the SD are pairs of terms which can be taken to be, in the ordinary terminology, adjectival, and which in some undefined sense can be regarded as 'opposites'. Furthermore, all the 'concepts' are either real stimuli like paintings, samples of ice cream, color chips, or sonar signals, *or* linguistic names for such stimuli, *or* linguistic names for abstractions. If they are linguistic at all, they are always presented as nouns, noun constructions, or pronouns (LADY, BOULDER, MY MOOD TODAY, TAFT, WHITE ROSEBUDS, CONGRESSIONAL INVESTIGATING COMMITTEES, ME). One wonders what sort of results would be obtained if other types of form classes were employed either as scales or as concepts. What would happen if subjects were asked to rate, say, IF, VERY, DEMONSTRATE, AND, IMPETUOUS, and AHA! either on the adjectival scales already studied or on 'scales' formed of other kinds of items like *come–go*, *yes–no*, *mountain–valley*, *ever–never*. If the task proved to be in any measure meaningful to the subjects, or better yet, if the results were of the same order as those obtained with the conventional SD, it would probably be because the subject would interpret the task as one of assigning a truth-value or 'plausibility-value' for possible linguistic utterances formed from such terms. In evaluating IMPETUOUS on the scale *ever–never*, for example, he might be inclined to rate the truth-values of such propositions as *Am I ever impetuous?*, *I am never impetuous*. The same is true of the conventional SD, which invites the subject to place concepts and scales in frames such as *The* (noun) *is* (adj.): *The* LADY *is smooth* (*not rough*); *The* BOULDER *is fast* (*not slow*); etc. If a simple frame doesn't quite fit, almost any reasonable association can be used: *The* LADY'S (*skin*) *is smooth*; *A* LADY'S (*voice*) *is smooth*; etc. Truth-value or plausibility is judged on the basis of experiences—one's own, or those related in the reports of others. Perhaps the SD might better be termed an *experiential* differential, at least to the extent that it is used to provide data about concepts or stimuli.

Furthermore, it will be noted that in its conventional form the SD is always concerned with the particular kind of relationship which is most often encoded in the (modifier)–(thing-modified) construction. What is most characteristically 'semantic' about the SD is its yield of a certain basic set of dimensions by which to describe those linguistic forms which are most frequently used as modifiers. In fact, as we have mentioned, Osgood and his colleagues have investigated a form of the SD in which things-modified (concepts or stimuli) are completely absent (or at least not explicitly present)—the form in which the subject is asked to indicate, in an item like 'SHARP–dull; relaxed–tense', which member of the second pair 'seems closest in meaning to the capitalized member of the first pair' (40). By and large, this form of the SD yields the same dimensions as the conventional one, and it can be argued that this form is the most purely 'classical' in that it is a forced-choice way of asking subjects to specify whether two linguistic forms are equivalent in meaning. It is only in this form that we are able to get at anything like what the linguist or the lexicographer means by 'meaning' in his daily work, i.e. the range of denotation of a certain linguistic item which is accepted in a speech community—or in this case the extent to which the accepted denotative ranges of two terms are likely to overlap. To the extent that representative speakers of a language agree in indicating two linguistic items as equivalent (or close in meaning—mark well the use of the term 'meaning' in the instructions for this form of the SD), we are no longer measuring the transient states of individual speakers, but the highly learned, well-nigh permanent response tendencies built into these users of the language by the process of social reinforcement.[11] But the power of the factor-analytic technique will be lost sight of if one regards this 'pure' form of the SD as nothing more than a series of specifications of close equivalences of meaning. The factor-analysis results make possible a more parsimonious and structured description of the system of equivalences and partial equivalences, and can in time lead to the kind of componential semantic analysis which linguists have been seeking and which would parallel the componential analyses already made in phonology and certain aspects of grammar. To be able to say, for example, that the modifier *brave* contains the notion of positive evaluation plus the notion of potency plus possibly other basic notions, in conjunction with statements about the generality of these basic notions, represents an advance in the description of the denotative meaning of at least one class of linguistic items. Osgood and his associates are to be applauded for their first steps towards identifying a manageable set of dimensions for describing the meanings of certain linguistic forms—those which we customarily call adjectives. It is debatable whether the linguist qua linguist will be interested in how 'concepts' like TAFT, TRUMAN, STEVENSON, and EISENHOWER will be rated on the SD, but at the very least the semantic structuring of the adjectival scales used in the SD deserves his attention.

The psycholinguistic significance of SD dimensions. While the preceding paragraphs may have appeared to trim down to size the importance of the SD research so far performed by Osgood and his associates, I want now to point to some extremely significant implications of it. Despite the technical reservations which have been expressed regarding the semantic-differential dimensions hitherto isolated, there seems to be little reason to doubt that the existence of the three dominant dimensions—evaluation, activity, and potency—will be sustained in further studies. To be sure, there are suggestions of complexity in the evaluative domain (176 ff.) whereby different kinds of evaluation will be measured depending upon the conceptual domain; e.g. *sacred* is positive evaluation in the religious domain whereas *amusing* is positive evaluation in the domain of light entertainment, yet it would verge upon blasphemy to equate *sacred* and *amusing*. Nevertheless, one can hardly deny that evaluation is an important semantic component in a large number of adjectival modifiers.

If evaluation, activity, and potency are such pervasive components of adjectival characterization, they must correspond to fundamental psychological attributes of persons and to the organization of perceptual and conceptual processes. To indulge in some bold speculation perhaps carrying forward the analysis offered by the authors themselves (25–30), let us propose that the three principal SD dimensions represent fundamental dimensions in the adjustment of the individual to the objects in his environment. The first dimension, evaluation, corresponds to the individual's tendency to make an approach to the stimulus or to avoid it; it measures the extent to which the stimulus has positively or nega-

[11] B. F. Skinner, *Verbal behavior* (New York, 1957).

tively reinforced the individual's responses. Reward or reinforcement, of course, is one of the key concepts in contemporary learning theory. SD results thus make it clear that one of the components of the denotative or referential meaning of adjectival forms is an ascription of positive or negative reward value. The second dimension, activity, refers to the necessity or nonnecessity of making movements in adjusting to stimuli. When Osgood finds, in one of his analyses (51), scales like *fast–slow*, *active–passive*, *excitable–calm*, *rash–cautious*, and *heretical–orthodox* loaded on an 'activity' factor, we can agree that each one of these scales refers to the necessity of making a more or less rapid adjustment to stimuli. It is presumably going to be more necessary to change our adjustment to something which is *fast*, *active*, *excitable*, *rash*, or *heretical* than to something which is *slow*, *passive*, *calm*, *cautious*, or *orthodox*. Finally, the third dimension, potency, suggests a measurement of the AMOUNT of adjustment that is made or must be made to a stimulus, or perhaps the amount of effort which is put into the response to a stimulus. Such adjectival scales as *hard–soft*, *masculine–feminine*, *severe–lenient*, *strong–weak*, *tenacious–yielding*, *heavy–light*, and *mature–youthful* (51) refer, it seems, to the amounts of effort which somebody puts into the responses to stimuli characterized by these adjectives; more effort is exerted in adjusting to hard beds than to soft beds, to masculine movements than to feminine movements, to severe punishment than to lenient punishment, and so on.

We have then a sort of theory to account for what happens when an individual is confronted with the task of making a rating of a 'concept' on a series of SD adjectival scales. (Let us suppose, for simplicity, that all the scales and concepts are contained within the three principal dimensions which I have described.) First consider what may happen upon presentation of the 'concept', whether this be a word, a phrase, or a physical stimulus. Presumably the subject makes a series of implicit or explicit responses, some of which he may be only dimly aware of. He perceives it through any appropriate sensory or perceptual system, he reacts to it by implicit motor and autonomic responses (e.g. shuddering, salivating), he may receive kinesthetic and proprioceptive stimulation, he 'holds the concept in mind', he recalls exemplars of the concept, he 'free-associates' with the concept, and he may be aware of some sort of 'image' or memory-trace of the concept. Whatever he does, his responses will depend upon the sum total of the learnings and experiences that are available to him at this moment of his life. Some of these learnings depend upon the reinforcement he has had from other individuals in his speech community—these are the learnings which have made him know what is commonly 'meant' or 'denoted' by the linguistic item which has been presented to him; other learnings depend upon experiences which may be more or less unique to him but which may have common elements with the experiences of others.

Now let the individual be asked to assign a position to the concept (or stimulus) on an adjectival scale like *fast–slow*, *heavy–light*, or *pleasant–unpleasant*. If he acts in accordance with our theory, the position he assigns will be a function of two interrelated things. First, it will be a function of the degree to which he perceives in the stimulus or its referent (1) positive or negative reward value to himself or to individuals with whom he identifies, (2) a necessity for himself (or individuals with whom he identifies) to make more or less rapid adjustments to the referent, and (3) a demand for effort in adjusting to the referent. Second, it will be a function of the degree to which the adjectival scale in question refers to any one or more of these dimensions. Suppose, for example, the individual is presented with the word BOULDER and asked to assign it a position on the scale *brave–cowardly*. Let us suppose the individual perceives in BOULDER a tendency toward a negative reward value (his experiences with boulders have led him to regard them as obstacles and nuisances), a complete lack of necessity to make any rapid adjustments to boulders, but a high degree of demand for effort in making any adjustments to them (if, say, he wanted to move one). Let us suppose further (as seems indicated by SD research data [37]) that *brave* has a component of positive evaluation and a component of high potency, but no component of activity or nonactivity. Under these conditions we might predict that the individual will assign BOULDER to a position about midway between *brave* and *cowardly*, his recognition of high potency being neutralized by his negative evaluation. There is a possibility that his rating might veer slightly toward *brave* on account of the clang association of 'boulder' with 'bolder'; we cannot expect the SD to be uninfluenced by such 'extraneous' factors which contribute to the error variance. In any case, we would predict that the individual might take longer (or in psychological jargon, his response would have a higher latency) to arrive at this assignment than to arrive at a simpler kind of judgment, e.g. to assign HERO to the positive end of *brave–cowardly*.

If this theory, or some variant of it, could be sustained by further study, it would have much to say about the manner in which the individual composes utterances or responds to them. That is, the prelinguistic basis for a certain class of phenomena in verbal behavior is the perception of reward value and of demands for certain kinds of adjustment to stimuli, and the transmission of information about such perceptions. Because such perceptions are so fundamental in human behavior (and also in animal behavior, it would seem) it is not surprising that the cross-cultural or 'cross-linguistic' data thus far collected (170–6) seem to indicate a high degree of generality for the 'semantic dimensions'. Such differences as exist (e.g. the fact that the scale *rich–poor* is found to be more 'evaluative' for Koreans than for Japanese or for Americans) could easily be due to difficulties of translation, differing cultural content of the concepts rated, or other extraneous factors.

Consideration of a theory such as the one presented here also shows how crude the SD is, at least in its conventional form. It may be said that far from making measurements of meaning more precise, the SD capitalizes on ambiguity and vagueness. Both concepts and scales are like the many-armed deities of India: when they are put together they can interlock in a multiplicity of ways. Notice, for example, how the adjective *hard* changes its meaning when linked with such concepts as ABORTION, ANGER, BOULDER, CRIMINAL—to sample a few which according to the *Atlas* have high ratings on *hard–soft*. I am not sure whether there is a good remedy for this characteristic of the SD, or whether in fact there is any need of a remedy. Perhaps a certain degree of ambiguity in the experimental situation is requisite for teasing out semantic dimensions possessing a sufficient degree of generality. Indeed, all the well-known figures of speech—simile, metaphor, personification—feed upon ambiguity, and one may suggest that SD dimensions may be useful in describing and accounting for the uses of metaphor. One must call to mind the fact that the SD was a natural extension of Osgood's prior studies in synesthesia (20–5). On the other hand, one wonders why Osgood and other SD users have generally failed to observe what would appear to be extremely elementary precautions—for example, specifying the intended reading (I will avoid the term *meaning*) of such homonymic 'concepts' as MOLD ('fungus' or 'form'?), RUSSIAN (the national or the language?), VISION (the sensory modality or the imaginative perception?). For another example, note that the instructions customarily employed in SD experiments (82–4) fail to help the subject decide whether he is to rate the abstract concept represented by the linguistic form or an actual referent or exemplar of the concept—is he to rate, for example, the abstract concept of FATHER disembodied from any person, or his own father?

Final evaluation. What can we say, in sum, about the SD technique? That it measures *something*, there can be no doubt, for there is abundant evidence of reasonably high interscale, interconcept, and intersubject consistency of results. I have suggested that when it is indexing 'concepts', it becomes a way of indexing the individual's *experiences* with the objective referents of these concepts, the indexing being with respect to a series of dimensions denoting generalized qualities of experience. When the objective referents themselves are presented as stimuli, it will also index these within the same framework though not necessarily in the same manner. SD results may have important uses in predicting the behavior of individuals insofar as behavior may depend upon the 'mediational processes' which reflect experiences. Osgood, Suci, and Tannenbaum choose to equate such 'mediational processes' with 'meanings', and this is their privilege if it serves their purposes. *The measurement of meaning* is not, however, to be taken as a full scale study of MEANING in the more usual sense of the term (i.e. the relation between symbols and their referents). The SD completely fails to index the referential meaning of the most ordinary nominal concepts. Much less can it express the denotative content of the term MEANING. The authors themselves recognize this when they say, 'It is certain that we are not providing an index of what signs refer to, and if reference or designation is the *sine qua non* of meaning, as some readers will insist, then they will conclude that this book is badly mistitled' (325).

This review, however, suggests that what is most relevant and linguistically interesting in SD research is the system of dimensions it promises to offer for the description of certain kinds of denotation—notably the description of what adjectival modifiers refer to. The factor-analytic results of SD research provide a kind of componential analysis of the denotative meanings of adjectives in terms of a finite number of dimensions: evaluation, activity, potency, and (hopefully) others. The particular dimensions thus far isolated, beyond the first two or three, are still in considerable doubt; in this review I have tried to indicate some of the grounds for caution, but have restrained myself from discussion of a number of mathematical technicalities which can be more appropriately treated in psychometric journals than in LANGUAGE.[12]

It is difficult to give a full impression of the rather extraordinary richness of this book (as such things go) and of the many directions it suggests for further research. To give only one example, consider the exploratory steps that have been made in the study of 'word combination' (275–84): how are the SD locations of concepts affected when they are given adjectival modifiers (AGGRESSIVE LEADER vs. POWERFUL LEADER vs. SYMPATHETIC LEADER)? This is a field for testing Osgood's 'congruity principle' (199 ff.): 'Whenever two signs are related by an assertion, the mediating reaction characteristic of each shifts toward congruence with that characteristic of the other, the magnitude of the shift being inversely proportional to intensities of the interacting reactions.' Thus, 'a lazy athlete is much less active, perhaps less potent, and probably less valuable than he would be otherwise' (200). On the other hand, 'the congruity formula predicts less and less well as the angular displacement of word components in the semantic space increases' (283). To illustrate, 'whereas the meaning of NURSE can easily be devalued by attaching TREACHEROUS to it, attaching SINCERE to PROSTITUTE fails to budge the immoral connotation of the fallen woman' (282) and 'the failure of congruity under these conditions typically appears as dominance of the unfavorably evaluative component' (283).

Alongside the richness of content, there is a certain random, unorganized, incomplete, volatile quality in the book. (Here, perhaps, are more semantic dimensions!) Anyone who wants to use it seriously will be greatly inconvenienced by the lack of any sort of index. There are amusing typographical errors, as in 'meditation reaction' (6) where 'mediation reaction' was obviously intended. Some of Osgood's comments seem to protest too much—as where he takes the psychologist C. E. Noble severely to task for seeming to want to measure 'meaning' by counting subjects' associations to symbols. One can imagine Noble objecting to Osgood's remark, 'Looking into his [Noble's] data we find ... that JELLY, JEWEL, and HEAVEN have approximately the same m-scores and hence, presumably, nearly the same meaning' (16–7). In point of fact, Noble merely wanted to measure the sort of 'meaningfulness' which makes familiar words easy to remember and nonsense syllables hard to remember, and if Noble is to be criticized, it is for persisting in calling this 'meaning'. One might with equal justice turn the tables and remark that because MOTHER, MUSIC, and HOME have highly similar profiles in the *Atlas* they must have the same 'meaning'. Finally, I wish to enter an objection to the jet-black end-papers, most unhandy for jotting notes or writing the owner's signature. After all, *black* has an unfavorable connotation on the SD and the book-designer should have known better.

Nevertheless, the reviewer is inclined to characterize the book by asserting: it is *good*, it is *active*, it is *potent*.

[12] For a particularly good critique by a linguist of some of the logical and technical problems besetting the factor analyst, see Rulon S. Wells, A mathematical approach to meaning, *Cahiers Ferdinand de Saussure* 15.117–36 (1957).

7. Travels through Semantic Space

Uriel Weinreich

1. ATTENTION, LEXICOGRAPHERS

When a linguist turns to lexicography, he becomes a descriptive semanticist, whose purpose is to list the words of a language and to "state their meanings." But it is an open secret that the linguist-lexicographer is a scientist with a bad conscience, for he has not yet found a way of performing his task in a completely reasoned, verifiable manner: separating polysemy from homonymy, breaking down the meaning of a word into "sub-meanings," selecting the terms of the definition, supplying synonyms, etc. Discussions of these problems in recent years, both in introductions to dictionaries compiled by professional linguists and in the journals, have failed to produce a way out of the arbitrariness and subjectivity of lexicography.[1]

Therefore, when the linguist-as-lexicographer learns of a new "experimental semantics" (p. 226 of the book under review [2]) offering prospects of "a quantized Thesaurus" (p. 330), when he hears that in a neighboring discipline procedures have been devised which "objectify expressions of these subjective states [meanings]" (p. 125)

and "completely eliminate the idiosyncrasies of the investigator in arriving at the final index of the meaning" (p. 126), he must sit up and take notice. Has the lexicographic millennium arrived?

This new type of "psycholinguistic" research, entitled "the semantic differential" and heralding revolutionary things for lexicography, was first unveiled in 1952.[3] Charles E. Osgood, professor of psychology and director of the Institute of Communications Research at the University of Illinois, has been chiefly responsible for the new method. In the years since, he has, alone and in collaboration with numerous associates, conducted and published a stream of experiments to follow up his basic theories. The present book is a progress report on this entire family of studies, including materials from many unpublished dissertations by Osgood's students.

There are important aspects of this research which the linguist will not be qualified to judge, such as the details of the statistical design, the applications of the method to personality measurement, to psychotherapy, to advertising, or to mass communications. The integration of the experiments with Osgood's version of general learning theory also lies beyond the linguist's own field. This review thus does not attempt to describe the book in full, nor to give proportionate representation to its several parts.

Reprinted from *Word* (1958), 14: 346–366, by permission.

1. See, for example, Hans Kurath's introduction to the *Middle English Dictionary*, of which he is the editor (Ann Arbor, 1952). Cf. also Alf Sommerfelt, "Sémantique et lexicographie," *Norsk Tidsskrift for Sprogvidenskab* XVII (1956), 485-489; Finngeir Hiorth, "Arrangement of Meanings in Lexicography," *Lingua* IV (1955), 413-424; L. S. Kovtun, "On the Construction of a Lexicographic Article" (in Russian), in *Leksikografičeskij sbornik*, ed. O. S. Axmanova et al., I, Moscow, 1957, 68-97, and other articles in the same volume.

2. Charles E. Osgood, George J. Suci, and Percy H. Tannenbaum: *The Measurement of Meaning*. 342 pp. Urbana: University of Illinois Press, 1957.

3. Charles E. Osgood, "The Nature and Measurement of Meaning," *Psychological Bulletin* XLIX (1952), 197-237. A briefer statement for linguists, by the same author, appeared in *Psycholinguistics* (Osgood and T. A. Sebeok, eds.), Baltimore, 1954, pp. 177-184. Cf. now also Rulon Wells' exegesis for linguists, "A Mathematical Approach to Meaning," *Cahiers F. de Saussure* XV (1957), 117-136.

At the risk of passing over some of the most fascinating investigations recounted in the volume, the review concentrates on the book's relevance to descriptive semantics as the linguist-lexicographer knows it.

In §§ 2-6 of this discussion, the authors' own conception of "meaning" goes unquestioned, and their results are judged on the preliminary assumption that their use of the term "semantic" corresponds to a linguist's expectations. In § 7, this assumption is itself subjected to criticism, resulting in a suggestion that what the "semantic differential" measures is not the "meaning," but chiefly the affect, or the "emotive influence," of words. In § 8, the consequences of this criticism are applied to problems of word combinations. Finally, § 9 broaches the question whether techniques similar to those used by Osgood, Suci and Tannenbaum might be utilized in a type of research whose linguistic-lexicographic validity would be less subject to doubt.

2. IS A KNIFE HUMBLE OR PROUD?

In the typical form of a "semantic differential" study, a subject or group of subjects is presented with a number of pairs of antonymous adjectives, such as *good—bad, kind—cruel, wise—foolish, complex—simple, humble—proud,* etc. The scale between every pair of adjectives has seven places on it. The subject is then given a "concept," e.g. *knife,* and is instructed to place it in one of the seven positions on each scale. Thus, if he considers *knife* very good, he is to put a mark at the *good* end of the *good—bad* scale; if he considers it neither good nor bad, but neutral in this respect, he marks the middle position; and so on for each scale. For a "concept" thus rated on a set of scales, there emerges a ("semantic") profile formed by connecting the checked points of each scale. If the subject then rates another "concept" on the same set of scales,

the two resulting profiles can be compared and the generalized distance between them computed, giving the calculated difference in "semantic" profiles between them. Alternatively, the same "concept" may be rated by another individual, or the same individual may be retested for the same "concept" at another time, and the distance between profiles may be computed in each case, giving measures of interpersonal agreement on profiles and of change of profiles. No standard list of scales or concepts has been fixed; it is the use of such scales, drawn up for a specific problem to elicit differences between profiles, that gives the procedure the name "semantic differential." [4]

Such tests turn out to be surprisingly reliable. This is the case not only when concepts are rated on "appropriate" scales, such as *feather (light—heavy), lady (smooth—rough),* etc. (p. 127), but also when seemingly "inappropriate" scales are added: when 112 subjects were retested as to concepts judged on a set of scales of varying "appropriateness," 66% of the answers deviated by less than half a place, and 87% of the answers deviated by less than a full place (p. 138, Table 20, last column; cf. also *Psychological Bulletin XLIX* [1952], p. 229). To be sure, this is a rather gross measure of reliability; only a DETAILED study of the reliability of particular concept ratings on a specific set of scales could be said to measure the degree of interpersonality of the meaning of that concept. Unfortunately, raw reliability data of this latter type are not published; the nearest equivalent are reliability tests of scores on scales already "factor-analyzed" (cf. § 4). These, as a

4. By now this term has become familiar in many circles, but it was hardly a happy choice to begin with, as one hardly thinks of a "differential" as an instrument for discovering differences. Could it have been suggested by Korzybski's awkward "structural differential"? Misleading, too, is the free alternation of "incongruous" and "incongruent" as technical terms (e.g., p. 213), and the use of "credulity" for "credibility" with reference to statements.

matter of fact, do prove to be very stable, too (pp. 139f.).

3. REPRESENTATIVES OF THE SAMPLE VOCABULARY

Since the linguist-lexicographer's object of description can be nothing less than the entire vocabulary of a language (or, more precisely, some finite stock of "lexemes" and productive derivation and compounding patterns), very small samples of vocabulary are an undecisive test of a new research approach. More important even than the size of samples is their representativeness. If a doubt arises that the words studied by the new technique may be atypically "investigable" items, it becomes uncertain whether the technique can be extended to the whole vocabulary and, consequently, whether its results are realistic approximations of the lexicographer's goals. Osgood, Suci and Tannenbaum nowhere explicitly propose to begin making dictionaries by their method, but lexicographic relevance is clearly implied in such statements as are quoted in § 1, and it is probably not unfair to examine these implications critically.

In this volume, two fundamental investigations are reported on: one, of 20 concepts rated on 50 scales; another, of 20 concepts on 76 scales. The samples were thus, from a lexicographic point of view, almost laughably small in both series. As to representativeness, however, the two investigations differed markedly:

(a) From Roget's Thesaurus, 289 adjective pairs were selected. Since the electronic brain (ILLIAC) which was to perform the computations has a limited "memory," the list of scales had to be trimmed to 76. This was done by sorting the 289 scales into clusters of similar scales, and selecting one representative scale from each cluster (p. 48). This sampling of the polarities expressible by the stock of English adjectives was at least intended by the authors to be fair and "lexicographically realistic," and our

discussion of their results will therefore be concentrated on this, the Thesaurus study. (Most unfortunately from the present point of view, however, only some phases of the factor analysis [cf. § 4], and not the actual profiles, of the concepts rated in this study are published. The "concepts," judged by 100 subjects, included: *foreigner, my mother, me, Adlai Stevenson, knife, boulder, snow, engine, modern art, sin, time, leadership, debate, birth, dawn, symphony, hospital, America, United Nations, family life* [p. 49].)

(b) In an association test, subjects were asked to respond to stimuli (common nouns) with descriptive adjectives. These adjectives, apparently supplemented by their antonyms where these were not automatically forthcoming and by the names of three "sensory continua" (such as *pungent—bland*), were arranged as a list of 50 scales (pp. 33f.), which overlaps only slightly with the Thesaurus list. Here the scales were not even meant to be representative of the language as a whole, and there is reason to suspect the representativeness of responses in a test based on something linguistically so primitive as an association test. The results of this, the lexicographically non-realistic study, turned out to yield themselves to factor analysis (see § 4) much better than those of the Thesaurus study. But because this study (which was conducted first) was presumably unrepresentative, the success of ITS factor analysis at best does nothing to recommend the semantic differential to lexicography; at worst—if a causal link exists between its lexicographic unrepresentativeness and its easy factor-analyzability—it serves as a warning that factor analysis is not pertinent to lexicographic research.

Another feature of the samples studied which will make the lexicographer pause is the compound character of many "concepts." We find not only such items as *modern art* and *family life,* but also more complex phrases, e.g. *flexible price supports* or *recognition of Red China.* Clearly the linguist-lexicographer would face an infinite task if the objects of his description had to be phrases rather than simplex words. The inclusion of deictic components (Jespersen's "shifters") in the concepts, e.g. in *my mother* or *my mood today,* also serves to make the task of description coextensive with the infinity of *I*'s and *today's.* Unless deictic elements can be extracted in a rational way from the "concepts" to be described, and unless the contribution of sub-items to the total meaning of utterances is shown to be finite and computable, there is a serious doubt as to the usefulness of the semantic differential in lexicographic descriptive tasks. (On combinatorial analysis of meanings, see also § 8, toward the end.)

4. FACTOR ANALYSIS

When the rating of concepts on the various scales—76 or 50, as the case may be—was compared, it turned out that some scales showed a fairly high degree of correlation with each other. For example, concepts which are rated "high" on the *good—bad* scale are often also "high" on the following scales: *beautiful—ugly, sweet—sour, kind—cruel, pleasant—unpleasant,* etc.; concepts which are "high" on the *sharp—dull* scale have a tendency also to be "high" on the *fast slow* scale, and so on. To analyze the complex correlations of all scales with all others, a statistical procedure called factor analysis is applied.[5] This procedure assumes that there are certain "factors" which, acting as common causes of the variance of concept ratings on the scales, determine to a certain (varying) extent the placement of these concepts on the several scales. For example, in the Thesaurus study the correlations between ratings on the *optimistic—pessimistic* scale and ratings on the *colorful—colorless* scale are such that we may say that some "factor" which deter-

5. Linguists may find it profitable to consult Wells' article cited in footnote 3 for a description of this technique.

mines, with a weight of 37%, the placement of concepts between *optimistic* . . . and . . . *pessimistic* also determines, with a weight of 20%, the placement of concepts on the *colorful—colorless* scale; with a weight of 16%, on the *stable—changeable* scale; with a weight of 9%, on the *objective—subjective* scale. This "factor" plays virtually no role, however, in determining the placement of concepts of the *fast—slow* or the *ornate—plain* scales, while it alone completely determines judgments as to *good—bad,* and may for that reason be called the *"good—bad"* factor.

The "factors" extracted by this analysis may or may not be identical with any of the scales themselves, i.e. there may be some factors which do not determine 100% the placement of concepts on any particular scale tested. Thus, in the Thesaurus study, that factor which is 92% determining in judgments on the *sober—drunk* scale is not 100% determining on ANY specific scale that has been tested. The analyst tries, by choosing between "realistic" factors (which correspond to real-language scales) and between "abstract" factors (mere constructs), to account for the variance of judgments in the most efficient way. But no matter how he juggles "realistic" against "constructed" factors, there comes a point, in analyzing non-homogeneous material, where each additional factor extracted accounts for a very small proportion of the variance.

Osgood and his colleagues have applied a factor analysis to both sets of data—those based on Thesaurus scales and those based on association scales. The Thesaurus set being the lexicographically more interesting one, let us look at its results. A first factor was found which accounts, to a considerable degree, for judgments on the following tested scales: *good—bad, kind—cruel, grateful—ungrateful, harmonious—dissonant, beautiful—ugly, successful—unsuccessful, true—false, positive—negative, reputable—disreputable, wise—foolish.* It is accordingly dubbed the "evaluative factor." A second factor, displaying high "loadings" on such scales as *hard—soft* (.97 loading), *masculine—feminine, severe—lenient, strong—weak, tenacious—yielding, heavy—light,* and *mature—youthful,* is called a "potency factor." Factor III is identifiable as an "oriented activity factor," with high loadings on such scales as *active—passive* (.98 loading), *fast—slow, excitable—calm, rash—cautious,* and *heretical—orthodox.* Since a similar set of three first factors had also been found in judgments on the association-derived scales (which were studied first), these were considered basic. After a slight switch of procedure, the computer extracted five further factors corresponding very nearly to existing adjective-determined scales: IV, a "stability factor," with high loadings on *sober—drunk* (.92), *stable—changeable,* etc.; V, a "tautness factor," with high loadings on *angular—rounded* (.95), *straight—curved,* etc.; VI, a "novelty factor," with high loadings on *new—old* (.97), *usual—unusual,* etc.; VII, a "receptivity factor," and VIII, an "aggressiveness factor."

5. Evaluation of the Factor Analysis

The effectiveness of a factor analysis can be assessed from the proportion of the total variance of the data that is accounted for by the factors extracted. The closer this proportion is to 100%, the more effective the analysis. In the present case, what proportion of the total variance of concept ratings on the numerous scales is accounted for by the hypothesis that the ratings are determined by the eight factors? Surprisingly and most unfortunately, this figure is not given for the Thesaurus study. We are given only the weights of the factors relative to each other (p. 61): we read that Factor I is twice as weighty as Factor II, 3½ times as weighty as III, nearly five times as weighty as IV, and about seven times as weighty as each of Factors V—VIII. But what their

combined explanatory power is, we do not know.[6] For details, see also (a) below.

Another way of considering the question of effectiveness is by means of the striking geometric metaphor used by the authors. We might imagine all possible concepts to be located in a space of a certain number of dimensions. A pair of antonymous adjectives may be said to define a dimension in such a space. The location of a particular concept may then be specified by its distance from the origin (center) of the space, i.e. the neutral position, either "upwards" or "downwards" along each dimension. For example, on the basis of semantic-differential data, it may be said that the meaning of *quicksand* is a point in the semantic space 3 units from the origin toward *bad,* 3 units from the origin toward *large,* 2 units toward *stale,* 1 unit toward *soft,* 3 units toward *cold,* 2 units toward *relaxed,* etc. (*Psycholinguistics,* p. 179)—for as many dimensions as the space contains. We do not yet know how many independent adjective-defined dimensions the "conceptual" space of English, or any other language, does in fact contain, or whether such a space is even describable. But if the factor analysis of the scales could successfully attribute the variance of judgments to a small number of factors, we would be approaching the definition of a space of relatively FEW independent dimensions (each dimension corresponding to a factor) and a highly economical placement of concepts as points in that space. The value of the venture thus seems to depend on the success achieved in reducing the hundreds of mutually dependent adjective-defined dimensions to a handful of independent factor-defined dimensions. Moreover, under the added requirements of lexicographic realism, the analysis is successful only insofar as it can be thought of

6. We do learn (p. 62) that Factor VIII, which accounts for as much as .624 of the COMMON variance, accounts for only .005 of the TOTAL variance. Proportionately, it would appear that only about .08 of the total variance is accounted for by the factor analysis.

as a sample study of the entire vocabulary.

Taking a linguistically realistic view defined in this way, we again center our attention, for reasons already mentioned, on the "Thesaurus study." We find that the authors' attempt to reduce the semantic space by factor analysis is hardly successful.

(a) Low Proportion of Overall Variance Explained

The eight factors extracted in the Thesaurus study account for an unknown, but small, proportion of the actual variance (less than half, and perhaps as little as one-twelfth). The resulting 8-dimensional "map" is thus only a crude projection of a space of a far higher, and unknown, number of dimensions.

This criticism may perhaps be clarified by an analogy. Suppose we were trying to determine the location of various offices on the island of Manhattan. We find that people describe their locations by phrases such as "nearby," "over there," "near the Battery," "upstairs," "near the George Washington Bridge," "to the west," "three floors down," "used to be right here," "close to the waterfront," "six blocks south," etc. We then perform a factor analysis, which discloses the existence of a factor that has high loadings on such descriptions as "near the Battery," "near the George Washington Bridge," and "six blocks to the south," but not on others; another factor accounts fairly well for such distinctions as "near the George Washington Bridge" and "to the west." We then describe Manhattan as a space of an unknown number of dimensions, in which locations may be at least approximatively specified in two "main," independent dimensions: *uptown—downtown* (Factor I, latitude), and *East—West* (Factor II, longitude). But clearly the omission of other "specific" dimensions, such as altitude, which applies to multistoried buildings, or time, which is crucial for buildings no longer or not yet in existence, is a major defect of the description, an inevitable consequence

of mapping a multi-(four-) dimensional space in fewer (two) dimensions.

(b) Low Proportion of Explained Variance, by Scales

The variance of concept ratings on particular scales is accounted for unevenly, and on the whole quite poorly, by the eight extracted factors, as is evident from the following table (based on Table 5 of the book under review):

TABLE A

Proportion of Variance Extracted of a Scale (h^2)	Number of Such Scales
1.00—	8
.61—.99	0
.41—.60	2
.21—.40	24
0—.20	42
Total	76

The eight scales which are fully (1.00) accounted for by the eight factors are those which were arbitrarily selected for just that purpose as "pivots." Of the remaining 68 scales, two-thirds are exhausted by the eight factors to an extent of 20% or less; and almost none are exhausted more fully than 61%. The average is only about 32%.

(c) Low Proportion of Variance Explained, by Concepts

Still more specifically, we may look at the effectiveness of the first FIVE factors alone in accounting for the total variance of 19 concepts in the Thesaurus study, summing over the several scales. (Here, h^2 is computed as the sum of the squares of the "per cent V" scores given by the authors in their Table 30.)

TABLE B

Proportion of a Concept's Variance Accounted For	Number of Such Concepts
.16 or less	none
.17—.20	2
.21—.30	11
.31—.34	6
.35 or more	none
Total	19

The average variance extracted from a concept by five factors is here about 27%. The proportion of the total variance accounted for by the first factor on the average concept is only 13% (high, 21.7%— *United Nations;* low, 6.0%—*time, engine*). The corresponding proportion for factors I —V together is, in the average concept, only 26.5% (high, 33.5%—*mother;* low, 17.7%—*time*). All these proportions, it is submitted, are quite low.

(d) Unknown Reliability of Some Factors

None but the first three factors have been checked for reliability (p. 74); yet these certainly account for only two-thirds of the common (explained) variance.

(e) Distortion Due to Sampling

At this point we must reconsider the manner in which the Thesaurus scales were sampled (cf. § 3a). The 76 scales tested represent, in a way which was meant to be fair, a larger set of 244 scales. For example, *unusual—usual* is treated as representative of a cluster of scales which also includes *eccentric—conventional, impossible—possible, improbable—probable, uncertain—certain, absurd—axiomatic,* and *infrequent—frequent* (p. 59). But 45 Thesaurus scales (i.e., the difference between 289 and 244) have mysteriously disappeared altogether; one searches in vain for "representative samplings" of such scales as *yellow—green, loud—soft, empty—full,* etc. Now, clearly, if eight factors account for only a certain part (say one-half, or one-fourth, or one-twelfth) of the total variance of judgments on the sample scales, then they would account for a much smaller proportion still on that untrimmed set of scales which the linguist-lexicographer is ultimately interested in. This reduces the success of the analysis even further.

The authors themselves are quite modest in their claims for their instrument; they repeatedly admit that "what we have called the three dominant factors do not exhaust

the dimensions along which meaningful judgments are differentiated" (p. 72) and that "a large portion of the total variance remains unaccounted for" (p. 325).[7] What runs afoul of linguistic-lexicographic skepticism is their far weaker claim that "three factors appear to be DOMINANT, appearing in most of the analyses made" (p. 72) or that "the same three factors . . . have reappeared in a wide variety of judgments," and that the "naïve model" for explaining human semantic judgments "in terms of a relatively small number of orthogonal factors" is surprisingly "close to the truth" (p. 328). To be sure, three reliable factors did appear to be "dominant" in the study based on association-derived scales,[8] but this makes the analysis all the more suspect from a global lexicographic standpoint. Responses in association tests are generally simpler than the stimuli (e.g., they are generally higher-frequency words than the stimuli), and we expect them to have little classificatory power when applied to the universe of "concepts." There is no reason *a priori* to expect that factors appearing in such tests should be effective in accounting for the stock of adjective scales of the full language. The book itself seems to show that they are NOT in fact effective in this sense.

Where then does the authors' enthusiasm

---

7. These judicious statements are, however, contradicted by a more extravagant claim (p. 75) that the existence of dimensions beyond the first seven "is not disastrous as far as measurement is concerned . . . because these added dimensions account for relatively little [!] of the total variance."

8. In the study based on association-derived scales, the proportion of variance of each scale extracted by the first four factors is much higher:

TABLE B

h^2 per Scale	Number of Such Scales
.20 or less	4
.21—.40	14
.41—.60	15
.61—.80	15
.81—1.00	2
Total	50

The average per scale is approximately .55. This is an impressively better showing than in the Thesaurus study.

for their own results come from—an enthusiasm that is so uninfectious to a linguist? We may understand it if we consider that the authors were first impressed with the exhaustiveness of a 3-dimensional description of color; that they were then encouraged by the discovery of "factors" in certain studies of synaesthesia, of social stereotypes, and of political opinion. But although the subsequent exhaustion of 50% of the variance in the first factor analysis, based on association-derived scales, was understandably an exciting discovery, there is little justification for considering the far weaker results of the Thesaurus study, distorted as they are by sampling, as "confirmation" of a general theory of semantic space. On the contrary, it would seem proper to conclude that in the vocabulary of a language as a whole, the "first three factors" account for a not-too-significant part of semantic judgment. And since further analysis, by the authors' own admission, yields no good general factors (pp. 36, 62), it seems fair to conclude that the method of factor analysis does NOT represent a major breakthrough in descriptive semantics. (But see § 9, (a) and (b).)

6. A QUESTION OF VALIDITY

The authors display a great deal of concern with the "validity" of their instrument, i.e. with the ability of the semantic differential to yield measurements that correlate well with scores obtained in some other, independent way. A study is cited in which ten "concepts" *(white rose buds, gentleness, sleep; hero, virility, success; quicksand, fate, death; methodology)* were presented to 160 subjects for rating on a 20-scale version of the semantic differential. When the results were actually mapped in a 3-dimensional model, they turned out to arrange themselves in three clusters of three concepts each, and one cluster of a single concept, as separated by the semicolons in the above listing. This arrangement, the authors argue, has a high

"face validity," since "most people [9] would have clustered these concepts in much the same way without using the differential" (p. 141). But this argument is subject to several important limitations.

(a) The ten concepts can hardly be called a representative sample of our noun vocabulary; they seem definitely "pre-clustered." A more diversified group, such as *knife, gentleness, pepper, methodology, bookbinding,* would hardly lend itself to easy clustering. How would it come out on the differential? Also, the sample is quite small. It is easy to represent four points (corresponding to the four clusters) as equidistant from each other in a 3-dimensional space, but more than four mutually equidistant points could not be accommodated in three dimensions. How would THEY be distributed by the differential?

(b) It is difficult to judge the validity of the representation in detail. The space model makes sense only if the angle formed by the short line within the cluster, e.g. from *death* to *quicksand,* and the long line from that cluster to the *gentleness* cluster, is determinate. From the model (p. 95), they appear to be parallel, yet it is virtually impossible to judge intuitively whether the semantic differences form a proportion, i.e. whether *death* is really to *quicksand* as their common semantic denominator is to *gentleness.*

(c) The semantic differential underlying the model is based on nine scales, selected from the association-derived set because they display atypically high loadings of the first three factors. This is a modification of the instrument in a direction opposite to lexicographic realism.

7. BUT IS IT MEANING?

At this point we are ready to consider the question of what the semantic differential

9. That is, most Americans. As Peter R. Hofstaetter has suggested ("Ueber Aehnlichkeit," *Psyche* I [1955], 54-80), Europeans would probably put *hero* nearer to *tragedy* than to *success.*

really measures. The authors consider it "a psycholinguistic tool, designed . . . to measure the meanings . . . of signs" (p. 275). It measures "meaning" in a particular psychological sense, which they take pains to define.[10] But they are unfortunately rather helpless in placing their position in a historical framework of a general theory of signification. As futile examples of linguists' views on meaning, they cite only a few Americans (Bloomfield, Harris, Joos)—men who are well known to have dogmatically rejected an investigation of semantic problems as such. A reading even of an elementary and relatively conservative presentation, such as Ullmann's *Principles of Semantics,* or of Morris' *Foundations of a Theory of Signs,* would probably have made the authors more fully aware of the conventional forms of the problem of meaning and would have provided them with a more adequate terminology for the discussion of the theoretical questions. They would in any case have found reasons to avoid so crude a dichotomy as "what has variously been called denotative, designative or referential 'meaning' [on the one hand] and . . . connotative, emotive, or metaphorical 'meaning' " (p. 321) on the other, in which terms culled from various writers and from mutually incompatible frames of reference are lumped together.

Osgood, Suci and Tannenbaum claim that "the semantic differential taps the connotative aspects of meaning more immediately than the highly diversified denotative aspects" (p. 290). The authors cannot be using "connotation" in its obsolescent technical sense as developed by J. S. Mill;[11] for on that interpretation, they are investigating NEITHER denotation (i.e. reference, extension, relations between signs and things) NOR connotation (i.e. signification, intension, conditions which must be satisfied if a sign is to denote). What the semantic differential IS equipped to measure seems to be some aspect of the affect of words, their so-called "emotive influence,"[12] their power to produce extra-linguistic emotional reactions. These are perhaps "connotations" in the loose, non-technical sense of the word (of which, incidentally, Bloomfield was also guilty). But by the authors' statement, these "connotations" have (literally!) nothing to do with the referential capabilities or functions of signs.[13] In fact, affective powers can be found, and can be measured by this instrument, in nonsensical phoneme sequences as well as in meaningful ones (p. 287), in pictures as well as in words (p. 68), in non-signs—noises (p. 66) and kitchen smells and decorators' color schemes—as well as in signs. The "psychological states" whose projections the semantic differential is out to capture occur, no doubt, in speech behavior too, but such emotive influence is an

10. "That process or state in the behavior of a sign-using organism which is assumed to be a necessary consequence of the reception of sign-stimuli and a necessary antecedent for the production of sign-responses" (p. 9). This process (a) is "some fractional part of the total behavior elicited by the significate," and (b) it produces "responses which would not occur without the previous contiguity of non-significate and significate patterns of stimulation" (p. 7). However, "the vast majority of signs used in ordinary communication are what we may term *assigns*—their meanings are literally 'assigned' to them via association with other signs" (p. 8).

11. "Connotation: the meaning of a term defined by abstract qualities common to a class of objects or instances designated by that term. . . . The connotation [of "U. S. citizen"] comprises the characteristics of the American citizen and the rights, privileges, and duties conferred by citizenship." H. B. and A. C. English, *A Comprehensive Dictionary of Psychological and Psychoanalytic Terms,* New York, 1958, pp. 111, 144.

12. Cf. Max Black, *Language and Philosophy,* Ithaca, 1949, p. 219, where the internal contradictions of the phrase "emotive meaning" are discussed.

13. "Agreement on the referents of signs," the authors write, "implies nothing whatsoever [!] about similarity of the representation states [i. e. what the semantic differential measures] associated with these signs" (p. 323). "We must admit that distances in our semantic space as between individuals judging the same concepts are *not* indicative of degrees of *referential* agreement" (p. 322). It follows that distances between "concepts" as judged by an individual do not correspond to referential differences, either.

aspect of all experience and all behavior, and is not restricted to language or even to communication in general, in which meaning (signification and reference) are distinctive components.[14]

The intimate relations between meaning and affect deserve systematic investigation, but the first step should be a theoretical distinction between them. Had the authors taken such a step, they would not in their tests have tenaciously retained scales for which factor analysis is manifestly ineffective (e.g., in the study of association-derived scales, *wet—dry,* with an h^2 of .03; *yellow—blue,* with an h^2 of .17; and so on). They would have capitalized on the excellent reliability of the evaluative factor (as a measure of affect or attitude [15]) in contrast with the relatively poor performance of all other factors, which seem to have progressively less and less to do with affect, i.e. with what the semantic differential measures. They would have refrained from pressing subjects for judgments of concepts on demonstrably inappropriate scales.[16] In sum, the reluctance of Osgood and his associates to distinguish meaning from affect makes it difficult, from a linguistic-lexicographic point of view, to sort out their possible successes with respect to affect from their evident or suspected failures with respect to meaning.

14. For an excellent discussion of the irrelevance of (lay or Bloomfieldian) "connotation" to meaning, see now Holger Steen Sørensen, *Word-Classes in Modern English*, Copenhagen, 1958, § 17.

15. On p. 189 the authors appear explicitly to identify "evaluation" with "attitude" by stating that "it has been feasible to identify 'attitude' as one of the major dimensions of meaning-in-general."

16. If *warm* is put at the midpoint of the *hot—cold* scale, this is probably a valid SEMANTIC judgment on an appropriate scale. Similarly, foreigner may occupy an AFFECTIVE midpoint on a *good—bad* scale. But the midpoint location of, say, *boulder* on the *sweet—sour* scale is not due to either semantic or affective judgments, but the inappropriateness of the scale to the concept. An investigation to be productive should include these considerations as axioms; subjects should be free to select and reject scales.

8. THE ALGEBRA OF AFFECT

It is also useful to disentangle meaning proper from affect in discussing the authors' attempt at a combinatorial algebra of "meaning." In one section of the book they concern themselves with "the manner in which meanings interact and are thereby changed" (p. 200). "What happens," they ask, "when two (or more) signs are presented simultaneously, e.g. when the subject sees the phrase *lazy athlete?* Common sense tells us that some interaction takes place—certainly a *lazy* athlete is much less active, perhaps less potent, and probably less valuable than he would be otherwise." Languages, they argue, have devices for bringing signs into a "peculiar evaluative relation to one another that we shall call an assertion" (p. 201). While they have no "precise definition" of this notion and "have not been able to make explicit the criteria on [sic] which [they] operate" (p. 202), they do list, among the forms of assertion, "simple linguistic qualification" of nouns by adjectives and verbs by adverbs, "statements of classification" (e.g. *Tom is an ex-con* or *Cigarettes contain nicotine*) and those "source-object assertions" which are often studied in opinion and attitude research (e.g. *Communists dislike strong labor unions*). Assertions are said to be "either *associative* or *dissociative*, which corresponds to the basic distinction in all languages between affirmation and negation" (p. 201). A "principle of congruity" is developed which states that when two signs are related in an assertion, the "mediating reaction" of each is adjusted to the other, i.e. if *Eisenhower* is favorably viewed, and one is exposed to the assertion *Eisenhower praises new educational policy,* one's evaluation of *new educational policy* shifts in a favorable direction related to that of *Eisenhower.* This is shown to operate in attitude measurement, but no evidence is given that anything except positive-negative evaluation (equivalent to Factor I) is subject to the "principle of congruity." These investigations do not therefore in any proven or promising sense contribute answers to the original question about "the manner in which MEANINGS interact."

A more direct attack on combinations in a linguistically interesting sense may be found in the investigation of Osgood and D. C. Ferguson of "semantic effects of word combination" (pp. 275ff.). Eight adjectives were combined with eight nouns into all possible 64 phrases (rather quaintly called "word mixtures"), e.g. *listless nurse, shy nurse, listless comedian,* etc. Ratings of constituents as well as phrases on a nine-scale differential were obtained, but only the first three factors were considered. The linguistic significance of the study is hard to assess, since the actual data for only one phrase (*shy secretary*) are published. (Yet almost every combination raises interesting separate problems. For example, whatever the semantic profile of *average,* one would expect that this, of all adjectives, is the modifier which would have a null effect on the profile of the noun it modifies. Such information is lost in the summary tabulations.) Still the experiment yielded some interesting and unexpected results, for example: that the adjective exerts a greater affective pull on the phrase than the noun; that derogatory components exert a disproportionately strong pull; that, in general, the scores for the phrases were predicted with remarkable success from the scores of the constituents, the predictions being even better for Factors II and III than for I; and that the less "comparable" two constituents are, i.e. the more disparate their profiles, the more poorly is the profile of the phrase predictable. It would appear, then, that a rough combinatorial formula for calculating the combined AFFECT of some adjective-noun phrases which are affectively harmonious to begin with could be devised; but that for the combinatorial analysis of MEANING proper, the semantic differential is a poor instrument.

Another experiment dealt with the combinatorial properties of "meaning" in the formation of "assigns" (see footnote 10). The study is too crude, from a linguistic point of view, to be considered an approximation of the way in which we understand definitions, for it presupposes only that assigns are "associated" with primary signs (i.e., elements of the definiens), without stating anything about the structure of this association (p. 287), and depending only on the primitive notion of "assertion." That this is an inadequate theory can be seen by examining such assigns as *brother-in-law* and *sister-in-law:* we find them BOTH "associated" with the primary signs *brother, wife,* and "possession" (i.e., =*wife's brother* and =*brother's wife*), yet their meanings are distinct and would probably yield different profiles even on the semantic differential. But if we interpret this experiment more modestly, as showing that some elements of affect are conveyed to a newly learned word by the context in which it was learned, the results are interesting and more specific as to the contributing role of the frequencies of repetition of defining terms, the semantic "polarization" (extremeness) of the defining terms, etc., than what the armchair linguist might expect merely of intuition.

It would be fair also to require this algebra of affect to have been applied in reverse as a demonstration that the profiles of non-simple "concepts" such as *white rose buds* or *my mother* are predictable from those of their constituents. This would have been a test of whether the coverage of an entire language, with its infinity of possible phrases and sentences, by the semantic differential can be reduced to a finite task. This, as was mentioned in § 3 (end), would be an important trial of the relevance of the instrument to linguistic lexicography.

Finally, it may be noted that a clear distinction between signification and affect would have saved the authors from error in their speculations about contextual problems. They ask (p. 323): "How can there be discriminative encoding despite connotative indiscriminability?" That is to say, since concepts like *nurse* and *sincere* "may occupy essentially the same region of our semantic space," why aren't the words in free variation? The answer, according to our authors, is complementary distribution: presumably, we have "habits of usage and association" which provide that when we are in a certain "representational state" *x*, we use *sincere* in the context *she is—* and *nurse* in the context *she is a—*. This argument is demonstrably absurd, since it will be agreed that it is not self-contradictory to say, *She is sincere but not a nurse,* and that *The nurse is a nurse* is tautologous,. but *The nurse is sincere* is not. The absurdity stems from the falsity of the premise. *Nurse* and *sincere* occupy "essentially the same region" NOT in our semantic space, but in a 3-dimensional map of a space of very many dimensions, a map whose order of crudeness is not even known. If this qualification had been constantly in the authors' minds, they would not have ventured the rather preposterous suggestion that affect and linguistic context alone, without signification, are sufficient determinants of the selection and interpretation of signs.

9. VALUE OF NEW TECHNIQUES

What, then, are the contributions of *The Measurement of Meaning* to linguistic lexicography?

(a) The lexicographer must be grateful for the semantic differential, as he must appreciate studies of word association, because of the possibilities it has opened for the systematic description of the "affective" capabilities of words. The day may come when the location of a word in the "affective space" of a language will be included in descriptive dictionaries. This is a promising outlook, because pilot studies already seem to have shown interesting differences between languages. For example, the equivalents of the *rich—poor* and *hot—cold* scales in Korean are apparently more clearly eval-

uative than in (American) English or in Japanese; the *rugged—delicate* scale has a stronger loading on the "dynamism factor" in (American) English than its equivalents in Japanese and Korean (p. 175); and so on.

(b) The insight that the affective powers of words may have a dimensional structure of a certain kind is in itself interesting and valuable. The conclusions of Osgood and his associates are not as clearcut as they might have been with better theoretical underpinnings, and much ground may have to be gone over again with better preparation. But the findings are already challenging.

(c) The traditional lexicographer's way of arriving at a semantic description of a word, *A,* is to ask himself, "What does *A* mean?" Techniques such as those utilized by Osgood and his collaborators make greater objectivity possible in that the describer, instead of asking himself, asks a representative sample of the speech community, and treats the degree of agreement between answers as a significant and measurable variable. In order to keep answers from varying too wildly and to make them suitable for quantitative analysis, the technique prescribes that the subjects make a multiple choice from among a preselected set of possible answers. The resulting quasi-semantic description is then condensed further, by means of statistical manipulation. All these are features which an experimental lexicography may in future want to adopt. The glaring disadvantages of the semantic differential are the lexicological and psychological inappropriateness of some of the preselected answers from which the subject is forced to choose, and the relative ineffectiveness of the condensation achieved by the particular analysis in terms of "factors."

Would it be possible for lexicography to exploit the advantages of objectivity, quantifiability, and condensation while eliminating the disadvantages of inappropriateness and crudeness of mapping? Perhaps it would. One thinks in this connection of the game

"Twenty Questions," to which the authors refer (p. 19) as an implicit analog of the semantic differential. Very little seems to be known about the strategy involved in the game and about the structure of our languages and our conceptual universe as revealed by the game.[17] Yet the game can be played and WON, and it yields recognizable semantic descriptions compared to which the specifications of concepts obtained by the semantic differential seem hopelessly obscure.[18] The game has its limitations as a tool for semantic description: as ordinarily played, its "targets" are restricted to "concrete" noun. But it is worth considering whether a formalized investigation replicating the game would not produce a valid and economical description of a vocabulary from the point of view of signification.

The universe of concepts revealed by "Twenty Questions" seems offhand to be describable by a branching diagram, or tree, corresponding to a sequence of ever finer binary choices. On inspection it turns out that some questions may be asked in any order, whereas the order of other questions is predetermined. Only to the extent that the order of questions is FREE can the tree model economically be converted into an "*n*-dimensional space" model of the type used by Osgood, Suci, and Tannenbaum. The actual breakdown of their space model soon after one passes from affect to signification proper [19] is to be expected from the fact that the order of questions in a lexicologically realistic inquiry like "Twenty Questions" is very largely fixed. On the other hand, it is conceivable that the binary choices of "Twenty Questions" could, in the interests of economy, in certain cases be replaced by multiple choices, some of which may entail scale ratings.[20] Should that turn out to be the case, the scaling procedures developed in connection with the semantic differential may turn out to be useful supplements to the "grading" experience of linguists like Sapir.[21] Also, investigations need not be resricted to noun-by-adjective matching; noun-noun matchings would surely also be productive.

As a result of Columbus' voyage across the Atlantic, the inadequate concept of "India" had to be quite drastically differen-

17. In this game, familiar to American radio and television audiences, Opponent I (the quizmaster) thinks of a "concept" and tells Opponent II (the panel) whether it is animal, vegetable, or mineral, or any combination of these. The panel is entitled to ask twenty questions (e.g., "Is it living?", "Is it human?", "Is it manufactured?", etc.) which are answered by Opponent I by "Yes," "No," or "Sometimes (= Partly)." In some but not in all cases, Opponent II is able to guess the correct concept.—The few available studies, such as D. W. Taylor and W. L. Faust, "Twenty Questions: Efficiency in Problem Solving as a Function of Size of a Group," *Journal of Experimental Psychology* XLIV (1952), 360-367, or A. W. Bendig, "Twenty Questions: an Information Analysis," *ibid.* XLVI (1953), 345-348, display no interest in the lexicological structure of English as such.

18. That is to say, when we specify the meaning of a concept as "animal . . . human . . . living . . . male . . . American . . . political figure . . . federal office holder . . . elective . . ." etc., we are zeroing in on something (let us say, *Eisenhower*); whereas if we specify a concept (in terms of Osgood-type factors) as "somewhat bad, indifferently potent, and quite passive" (p. 88) or even, in terms of actual adjective-determined scales, as "indifferently angular, quite strong, very smooth, rather active, indifferently small, dry, and cold, very good, quite relaxed, and rather fresh (*Psychological Bulletin* XLIX [1952], p. 229), we are hardly zeroing in on anything. (The answers are *fate* and *polite*, respectively.)

19. The quick exhaustion of "general factors" and the need to search for factors specific to particular classes of concepts is the chief manifestation of the breakdown. Note also the splitting up of the evaluative factor into "subfactors" and the mixture of metaphors in describing Factor I as "a sheath with leaves unfolding toward various directions of the total space" (p. 70). The discussion of the possibility of non-Euclidean properties of the "semantic space" (p. 144) seems premature in view of the strictures against the space that is yielded by the factor analysis.

20. The choices in "Twenty Questions" may not seem truly binary, but the third and fourth possible answers "Partly (= Sometimes)" and "Not in the usual sense of the word"—are in reality "meta-answers" which do not affect the basic binarity.

21. Edward Sapir, "Grading: a Study in Semantics," in *Selected Writings of Edward Sapir. . .*, ed. D. G. Mandelbaum, Berkeley and Los Angeles, 1949, pp. 122-149.

tiated into West Indies and East Indies; yet certain positive discoveries of lasting value were achieved. The travels through semantic space by Osgood and his crew of explorers may necessitate an equally radical differen-tiation of their "meaning" into signification and affect. But even if they have not found a new passage to India, their navigational ex-perience may yet be useful in unforeseen ways.

8. Semantic Space Revisited

Charles E. Osgood

Psycholinguistics is a relatively new discipline developing along the border between linguistics and psychology. Both Uriel Weinreich and I are sympathetic to this development, and it is with the view of maintaining harmony along the border that I have written this addendum to his discussion of *The Measurement of Meaning*. Provincialism on either side of the border will hinder progress in interdisciplinary relations.

Weinreich's review is framed on the assumption that the semantic differential was developed as a technique for objectifying linguistic lexicography. He gives a convincing demonstration that the instrument is inadequate for this purpose, and then the authors are roundly criticized for their presumptiveness. But nowhere in the book is such a claim made by Osgood, Suci, and Tannenbaum; in fact, the term "lexicography" never appears on its pages. In the very last chapter, in a single paragraph, and in the context of possible applications of the technique, it is true that we mention the possibility of building "a functional dictionary of connotative meanings—a quantized Thesaurus," but this is a far cry from linguistic lexicography and even this development, as the authors clearly state, would depend upon considerable refinement of the measuring procedures.

The main point is this: The semantic differential was not designed as a linguistic tool but as a psychological one—to assess certain symbolic processes assumed to occur in people when signs are received and produced. It was not designed to classify or evaluate the innumerable correlations between linguistic signs and their referents—which really is not a psychological problem. Weinreich's attempt to make lexicographic distinctions with a version of "Twenty Questions" makes it clear that no standardized and limited set of dimensions could serve this purpose. But we have good evidence that the dimensionality of the *psychological* semantic space—the ways in which implicit, representational reactions can vary—is not so diverse and complex. The repeated appearance of the same general factors

Reprinted from *Word* (1959), 15: 192–200, by permission of the author and the publisher.

* "Travels Through Semantic Space," *Word* XIV (1958), 346–366, a discussion of *The Measurement of Meaning*, by Charles E. Osgood, George J. Suci, and Percy H. Tannenbaum, Urbana, Illinois, 1957.

in replicated factor analyses (not only two, as Weinreich's review seems to imply, but nearer twenty), involving such varied stimuli as linguistic signs, facial expressions and even sonar signals and such varied subject populations as college sophomores, hospitalized schizophrenics, Japanese mono- and bi-linguals, and Navaho Indians, certainly suggests that this aspect, at least, of 'meaning' is capable of measurement.

Since that ugly word, 'meaning', has crept into the discussion, let's come fully to grips with the points raised by Weinreich on our usage of the term. He takes us severely to task for claiming that we are measuring 'meaning' when it is really the 'affect' of words, he thinks, that the semantic differential taps. Had we read even an elementary presentation of semantics, we would have been aware of the conventional statements of the problem of meaning and, at the very least, would have avoided such a crude dichotomy as 'denotative' vs. 'connotative' meaning. And to cap the point, Weinreich says in exasperated good humor, "But by the authors' own statement, these 'connotations' have (literally!) nothing to do with the referential capabilities or functions of signs."

Now, without claiming to be as sophisticated as I probably should be with respect to philosophical and linguistic semantics, I would nevertheless say that there is nothing more confused and confusing than the literature I *have* read bearing on the usage of "connotative meaning." Furthermore, there are several "traditions" in the technical usage of the term 'meaning', one of which, represented by Ogden and Richards' "thought or reference" and Morris' "interpretant," refers to a representational state or process occurring in sign-using organisms when signs are received or produced. Also this is one of the standard usages in the lay language, e.g., when I ask someone to "Tell me what this inkblot *means* to you," he certainly doesn't assume that I want him to tell me what it refers to. In any case, there is nothing sacred about a "conventional" technical usage, particularly when it obfuscates the solution of a theoretical problem—as I think is the case here. Finally, we went to considerable pains (pp. 318–325) to specify how we were using the terms 'denotative' and 'connotative' and to indicate (pp. 2–10) what very limited *meaning* of 'meaning' the semantic differential is assumed to measure. But since our presentation was evidently unclear, and since I feel this is a critical issue, I will repeat the analysis here with some elaboration.

The *denotative meaning* of a linguistic sign I define as a conventional, habitual correlation between: (1) with reference to the speaker, a non-linguistic stimulus pattern, $\dot{S}$, and a linguistic reaction, $\boxed{R}$; or, (2) with reference to the hearer, a linguistic stimulus pattern, $\boxed{S}$, and a non-linguistic stimulus pattern, $\dot{S}$ (or a response, R, appropriate to this non-linguistic stimulus pattern). I use the symbols $\boxed{S}$ and $\boxed{R}$ to refer to *linguistic signs*, as received or produced respectively, the symbol S for the thing signified (significate or referent), and the symbol R for a non-linguistic response. The *connotative meaning* of a linguistic sign I define as that habitual symbolic process, x, which occurs in a sign-user when: (1) a linguistic sign is produced (with reference to speaker); or (2) a linguistic sign is received (with reference to hearer). It is such symbolic, representational processes (x's) that are presumably indexed by the semantic differential. The conditions for learning denotative meanings have been well described by Skinner in his *Verbal Behavior* (1957), and I have tried to describe the conditions for learning connotative meanings in my *Method and Theory in Experimental Psychology* (1953) and elsewhere.

Denotative agreement between two users of the same language exists when they display the same external correlations between linguistic and non-linguistic behaviors. *The crucial thing to note*, as shown by comparison of diagrams A and B below, *is that connotative agreement is not necessary for denotative agreement to occur—indeed, is entirely irrelevant to it*. In other words, as strange as it may seem on first thought, a common, shared psychological state or process between two communicators is not the *sine qua non* of denotative agreement between them.

A. *Denotative Agreement plus Connotative Agreement.*

$$\dot{S}_A \nearrow \begin{array}{l} x_1 \to \boxed{R}\, {}_{A_1} \\[1ex] \searrow x_2 \to \boxed{R}\, {}_{A_2} \end{array}$$

or

$$\dot{S}_{A_1} \to x_1 \to \boxed{R}\, {}_{A_1} \rightsquigarrow \boxed{S}\, {}_{A_2} \to x_2 \to R_{A_2}$$

EXAMPLE 1. When shown an APPLE object ($\dot{S}_A$) and asked to name it, both person 1 and person 2 say *apple* (R_A); when asked to say what they "think" about apples, or to fill out a form of the semantic differential, they give similar reactions, x in person 1 and x in person 2 (e.g., *sweet, tasty,* etc.), but this is irrelevant to the question of denotative agreement.

EXAMPLE 2. Speaker: *Bring me an apple!* Hearer brings this object, and the speaker says, *Thanks.* They both eat it with gusto.

B. *Denotative Agreement without Connotative Agreement.*

$$\dot{S}_A \nearrow \begin{array}{l} x_1 \to \boxed{R}\, {}_{A_1} \\[1ex] \searrow y_2 \to \boxed{R}\, {}_{A_2} \end{array}$$

or

$$\dot{S}_{A_1} \to x_1 \to \boxed{R}\, {}_{A_1} \rightsquigarrow \boxed{S}\, {}_{A_2} \to y_2 \to \boxed{R}\, {}_{A_2}$$

EXAMPLE 1. Imagine a color-blind son, allergic to apples, and a normal father. Although apples don't look the same and certainly don't have the same gratifying consequences to the son as to the father (e.g., x in person 1, y in person 2), both will learn the same rules of usage—saying *apple* when APPLE is pointed to, bringing APPLE when requested with verbal signs, and so on. A machine could be built to do the same thing in a limited semantic area.

EXAMPLE 2. Person 1: *The late Senator McCarthy was an honorable man.* Person 2: *I know what you mean, but I disagree with you completely.* Here we assume that both people agree on the denotative meanings of *McCarthy* and *honorable*—testable by constructing such test frames as "McCarthy was Senator from Wisconsin during the early 1950's" and "You can believe the word of an honorable man." The reciprocally opposed profiles on the semantic differential for the concept THE LATE SENATOR MCCARTHY, but not for HONORABLE, for these two people would provide evidence for the disagreement in connotation. This, incidentally, is the most frequent application of the semantic differential—to index differences between people (patients vs. normals, Democrats vs. Republicans, etc.) in their connotations of signs on which they have denotative agreement.

Connotative agreement between two users of the same language exists when they make the same symbolic reactions, either to the same or to different stimulus patterns (which may be either signs or significates). As will be seen below, in this case *denotative* agreement or disagreement is irrelevant. If I am right, and we do have two independently variable conditions determining agreement in "meaning," then it is not only legitimate, but essential, that we discriminate with two terms—and I have chosen "denotative" and "connotative" as being the traditional terms closest to the distinction I wish to make.

C. *Connotative Agreement with Denotative Disagreement—Same Stimuli or Responses.*

$$\dot{S}_A \overset{x_1 \to \boxed{R}\, B_1}{\underset{x_2 \to \boxed{R}\, A_2}{}} \quad or \quad \begin{array}{l} \dot{S}_{A_1} \to x_1 \to \boxed{R}\, A_1 \\[6pt] \dot{S}_{B_2} \to x_2 \to \boxed{R}\, A_2 \end{array}$$

EXAMPLE 1. Child: *I like this cookie, Mommy.* Mother: *I like it, too, Johnny, but it's an apple, not a cookie.* Note that here we have a microcosmic bit of the learning process where connotative agreement aids in the development of denotative agreement in the usage of signs.

EXAMPLE 2. As is well known to students of international politics, both Soviet and American public speakers are prone to say *Democracy is good, etc.* But despite connotative agreement (x in 1 and x in 2), the *referents* of *democracy* ($\dot{S}_A$ in 1 and $\dot{S}_B$ in 2) are quite different in the two cases, hence there is denotative disagreement.

D. *Connotative Agreement with Denotative Disagreement—Different Stimuli or Responses.*

$$\dot{S}_{A_1} \rightarrow x_1 \rightarrow \boxed{R}_{A_1} \qquad\qquad \dot{S}_{A_1} \rightarrow x_1 \rightarrow \boxed{R}_{B_1}$$
$$or$$
$$\dot{S}_{B_2} \rightarrow x_2 \rightarrow \boxed{R}_{B_2} \qquad\qquad \boxed{S}_{B_2} \rightarrow x_2 \rightarrow R_{A_2}$$

EXAMPLE 1. The left-hand diagram illustrates in learning theory symbols the familiar phrase, "The gourmet approaches his food as a lover approaches his mistress." Both gourmet (person 1) and lover (person 2) have similar connotative states (x in both), but both the significates (food and mistress) and the linguistic labels correlated with them (*lamb chop* and *sweetheart*) are different—although under extremely intense connotative agreement, speakers may confuse the denotative correlations!

EXAMPLE 2. The phenomena of *synesthesia*, as communicated between two people, is a case in point. Person 1 says a loud tone seems *large* (R_B) to him. He presents a pair of tones, one loud and the other soft, to the second person and asks, "Which one of these seems to go best with the word *large*?" The second person indicates the loud one (R_A). We assume that the word *large* and the loud tone elicit similar connotative processes in both people (x in 1 and x in 2), and we can check this with the semantic differential.

If there is neither denotative nor connotative agreement in a communication situation, there is complete communication failure, which may or may not be self-checking with linguistic or non-linguistic means.

$$\dot{S}_{A_1} \rightarrow x_1 \rightarrow \boxed{R}_{A_1} \qquad\qquad x_1 \rightarrow \boxed{R}_{A_1}$$
$$or \qquad \dot{S}$$
$$\dot{S}_{B_2} \rightarrow y_2 \rightarrow \boxed{R}_{A_2} \qquad\qquad y_2 \rightarrow \boxed{R}_{B_2}$$
$$or$$
$$\dot{S}_{A_1} \rightarrow x_1 \rightarrow \boxed{R}_{A_1} \curvearrowright \boxed{S}_{A_2} \rightarrow y_2 \rightarrow R_{B_2}(\dot{S}_{B_2})$$

EXAMPLE 1. The same linguistic slogan, Right-to-Work Bills, refers to different things (freedom from union closed shop for person 1 and union-breaking technique to person 2) and also has entirely different evaluative connotation for the two people. Labor-management discussion using such a term would be difficult, to say the least.

EXAMPLE 2. Both teenager and her father espy a 1940 Ford, all fixed up in hot-rod fashion (S̄); *Cool*, says the daugher; *Junk*, says the father. Here the extra-linguistic knowledge that they are reacting to the same stimulus makes it possible for them to make inferences about each other's denotative and connotative systems.

EXAMPLE 3. Speaker 1: *Bring me a spider!* One is brought by person 2, whereupon the first person shrieks in surprise and fright. The first is a motherly old lady cooking dinner; the second is her young grandson, who is a budding naturalist. Here we have the homonym situation, which can only be clarified by the context. The differences between Uriel Weinreich and myself on the meaning of "meaning" may fit the same category!

The point of all this has been to justify the distinction we made in *The Measurement of Meaning* between "denotative" and "connotative" meaning. It may be true that this distinction comes out of a different tradition than that with which Uriel Weinreich is familiar, and in that case he is entirely justified in disapproving our usage of terms—indeed, he would be justified in saying that from his point of view our book was completely mistitled. But to imply, as he does throughout, that we have failed in our research efforts because we do not provide an index of *his* meaning of "meaning" (one that solves the problems of lexicographers), seems a little unfair to me.

However, Weinreich gives other reasons for being dubious about the success of our research venture. These concern the actual experimental and statistical methods we employed and therefore get into deep waters for the linguist. The reviewer makes a number of errors of interpretation which require correction. But in Weinreich's defense, let me hasten to say that I would certainly make errors of equivalent kind were I to attempt a critical review of a book on technical linguistics.

The first point of this sort concerns the adequacy of our sample, particularly of concepts to be judged. The reviewer refers to our sampling of only 20 concepts in each of two factorial studies as ". . . from a lexicographic point of view, almost laughably small. . . ." Letting pass the fact that we were not operating "from a lexicographic point of view," a linguist who often generates the grammar of a language from two or three informants certainly must realize that the size and nature of one's sample depends upon the variability in the dependent variable across the instances he is sampling. If (as the linguist assumes) there is very little variability across the speakers of a language in phonemics and grammar, then he is justified in using a small sample. Similarly, in the present case, if it can be shown that essentially the same factors emerge from *replicated* factor analyses using sets of different concepts (even if only 20 in each, or even none at all as in one factor analysis Weinreich doesn't mention), then the same argument the linguist applies to himself applies here. However, for quite different reasons—namely, the evidence we have for concept-scale interaction—I am also acutely concerned with sampling concepts as broadly as possible; we made the best compromise we could think of between these purposes and the exigencies of subject effort and computer capacities, but entirely different approaches may be possible.

Yet Weinreich's main concern lies elsewhere. First he says, "The effectiveness of a factor analysis can be assessed from the proportion of the total variance of the data that is accounted for by the factors extracted." He then points out that in the Thesaurus factor analysis, most adequate from the lexicographical point of view, less than half of the total variance (about 40%, actually) is accounted for by 8 factors extracted. Then it is noted that for $\frac{2}{3}$ of the scales in this study less than 20% of total variance is taken out by the factors. Finally, he presents a table purporting to show what proportion of the total variance in judgments of 19 single concepts (based on separate factor analyses of the judgments of these concepts against the same 76 scales) is accounted for by the first five factors—the average value being only 27%.

In the first place, the proportion of total variance accounted for is not the only criterion of effectiveness of an analysis—in fact, this proportion is influenced by a number of subtle things. (A) It must be interpreted in relation to the *error variance*. Any psychological test, involving the judgments of subjects, is subject to some degree of unreliability; given the same items again, a subject will typically shift somewhat (e.g., where FATHER was judged 6 on the *relaxed—tense* scale, he now is judged 5 or 7), and the less relevant or clear the item the more shift can be expected. Even granting an average reliability of .80 to our scales (which is about the value we get on test-retest studies), this means that *the maximum possible reliable variance that could be extracted in an analysis would be 64%* (.80 squared) *of the total*. This means that our eight factors in the Thesaurus study accounted for approximately $\frac{2}{3}$ of all that could be extracted. (B) The proportion of total extractable variance actually taken out also depends upon the intercorrelations among the scales, and hence upon their selection. One factor *could* account for almost all of the reliable variance *if* we deliberately selected scales which were close synonyms of each other. This is what I think tended to happen in the earlier analyses, based on the scales most frequently given as qualifiers of nouns from the Kent-Rosanoff Association Test stimuli: nearly $\frac{2}{3}$ of the scales yielded were clearly evaluative in nature. Now in the Thesaurus study—for precisely this reason (as we stated in the book)—we deliberately *pruned out* close replicates of scales, trying to get as large as possible a number of independent scales. Naturally this reduced the proportion of total variance extracted. This, however, does not deny the validity of Weinreich's general point—that there are presumably a large number of factors still unidentified. Yet I would still claim that their contribution to total variance in human semantic judgments must be relatively small and (for many purposes other than lexicography) unimportant.

Secondly, as far as the variance (h^2) of particular scales is concerned, this depends upon both the sampling of concepts and the sampling of other scales. If there are few if any concepts relevant to a particular scale, say *wet—dry*, then most judgments will be near the midpoint of the scale and correlations with other scales (which determines common or shared variance that can be extracted) will necessarily be low. If the sampling of other scales has failed to include a few of similar meaning, again the correlations will be low and the variance extracted on common factors infinitesimal. Ideally, of course, we should have infinitely large samples of both concepts and scales, but this is practically unfeasible. (Without ILLIAC, a high-speed digital computer, even the 76×20 Thesaurus factor analysis would have taken many months or even years to complete.) This means that many potential dimensions are lost in the effort to demonstrate that a few of the basic, dominant ones are stable and reproducible.

Finally, Weinreich's Table B and the discussion of it implies that five factors were given (in our Table 30) for each of the concepts whose total variances are represented. Actually our table gives the five dominant factors in the total analysis (all concepts combined) and then lists for each concept only those factors of the five which could be clearly identified in the single-concept factor analyses. So we find five factors listed for only four of the nineteen concepts, four factors for nine concepts, only three factors listed for five concepts, and only two factors for one concept. Dividing the variance extracted by the actual number of factors, we find an average per factor of 7%, which for five factors per concept would be 35% of the total variance. Keeping in mind that only *reliable* variance can be extracted by common factors, this means that we are accounting for an average of more than half of the variance that could be accounted for.

If, as is the way with factor analyses, the first factors extracted tend to be the largest ones and subsequent factors decrease in the percentage of total variance according to a negatively accelerated function, then we can envisage a long, long "tail" of minute, specific factors extending toward, but never quite reaching, the limits set by reliability. Solution of the lexicographer's problem may require both the "head" *and* the "tail" of this distribution of semantic factors, but there are many psychological problems and psycholinguistic problems which can be attacked with just what we know about the "head"—the first three or four, most significant and repeatable factors.

I have written this reply to Weinreich's review of *The Measurement of Meaning* in part because I wanted to balance the scales a bit and in part because we represent two disciplines with different traditions and problems (yet which have been interacting fruitfully over the past few years). It may be that our research has no relevance to *linguistics per se*, but I would like to think that it is of some interest to *linguists* as students of language behavior more generally. Uriel Weinreich closes his review with an allusion to Columbus' voyage to what he thought was India but turned out to be a quite different place. I think we know where we're headed, all right —even if the name by which it is called changes with the map one uses— but we've barely set sail, our boat may be leaky, and already the seas are rough.

9. A Rejoinder to Semantic Space Revisited

Uriel Weinreich

1. I do not feel that any grave unfairness was committed by evaluating *The Measurement of Meaning* from the lexicographic point of view. First—and this is to the authors' credit—there is sufficient lexicographic relevance in the theoretical parts of the book to merit a critical discussion of this aspect of the work. Secondly, my discussion was not at all "framed on the assumption that the semantic differential was developed as a technique for objectifying linguistic lexicography." I think that in the last two paragraphs of § 1, I explained the very special nature of my approach to a book which has many other worthy purposes.

2. It would be idle to argue about terms; Osgood has now fully amplified what he means by 'connotation' and 'denotation.' The chief defect of his theory, however, is (to my mind) the absence of a level which is, in some ways, "intermediate" between his 'denotation' and 'connotation.' If the former deals with relations between signs and their referents, and the latter, with relations between signs and their users, there is missing the linguistically crucial domain of relations between signs and other signs such as is expressed in a (non-ostensive) definition. Almost every semantic theorist to date

Reprinted from *Word* (1959), 15: 200–201, by permission.

has distinguished this "ability of signs to refer" from their actual referring; cf. Frege's 'Sinn'/ Bedeutung', Husserl's 'Bedeutung'/ 'Bezeichnung', 'innere Form'/'Bedeutung' in the Humboldtian tradition (especially Marty), Mill's 'connotation'/ 'denotation', Paul's 'Bedeutung'/ 'Benutzung', de Saussure's 'valeur'/'substance', Carnap's 'intension'/ 'extension', Hjelmslev's 'form'/'substance' (of content), Quine's 'meaning'/ 'reference', Morris' 'designation'/'denotation', etc. Osgood's 'denotation' corresponds roughly to the second member of each pair of concepts, but his 'connotation' (which I tried to rename 'affect' or 'emotive influence') does not pertain to this dichotomy at all. It is widely, even though not universally, agreed that it is the first member of each of the above pairs—the one that has no equivalent in Osgood's theory—that is of interest in the description of language.

3. In regard to the effectiveness of the statistical procedures, Osgood's reply serves to demonstrate the divergence in our views. He argues skillfully that his factor analysis is nearly as good as could be *expected* from its design. Be that as it may, I still feel that it is not as good as is *required,* and thus I remain skeptical about its value for semantic analysis as the linguist must practice it.

Part III

METHODOLOGICAL STUDIES OF THE SEMANTIC DIFFERENTIAL TECHNIQUE

10. Adverbs as Multipliers

Norman Cliff

In recent years there has been increasing interest on the part of psychologists in problems relating to language behavior. This interest has found expression in diverse experimental methods, theoretical viewpoints, and areas of emphasis and has resulted in the establishment of the field of psycholinguistics. The older interests and methods of linguistics itself, the study of the physical cues of communication, and the study of what is communicated have all been incorporated to form psycholinguistics as a discipline.

RELATION OF THE PROBLEM TO PSYCHOLINGUISTICS

Of particular interest in psychology has been the study of the communication of emotive or connotative meaning. Osgood (1952) has surveyed theories of meaning and methods of studying it, and also introduces a new method, the Semantic Differential. The Semantic Differential consists of a number of equal-appearing intervals scales, each defined by a pair of polar adjectives—"hot-cold," "good-bad," etc. When words or concepts are rated on this set of scales, it has been found that the variation in the ratings can be accounted for by three common dimensions. This finding indicates

Reprinted from *Psychological Review* (1959), 66: 27–44, by permission of the author and the American Psychological Association.

that variation in connotative meaning is not as complex as might be supposed and that it is amenable to at least a quasi-quantitative analysis. Osgood, in discussing directions for further research (Osgood & Sebeok, 1954, p. 180), talks of "laws of word mixture." Such laws would indeed represent a considerable step forward, for the degree of correspondence between quantitative data and the real number system depends on the operations which can be performed on the data and especially on the manner in which the variables combine (cf. Gulliksen, 1956b; Weitzenhoffer, 1951). In his discussion, Osgood suggests that "laws of word mixture" would follow either something akin to vector addition, i.e., using the Semantic Differential, the coordinates of the combination would be the sum of the coordinates of the components, or there would be an averaging effect, the coordinates of the combination would be the average of the components. This is felt to be too restricted a formulation; there might be several "laws," depending on the words being mixed.

Osgood mainly considered adjective-noun combinations, and it may be that his suggestions are quite relevant to such combinations. However, if connotative communication is to be thought of as the representation of a space in which different words represent projections on some coordinate system, it would seem that words which have no projections of their own but merely serve to stretch or compress the projections of other words would be a useful adjunct. That is, these words would act like the scalar multipliers of vector algebra.

Words which have this stretching property would seem to be the intensive adverbs such as "quite," "very," and "unusually." Subjective analysis of the change in intensity on applying adverbs to adjectives bears this out. Consider "very" applied to "bad" and "pleasant" and judged on the evaluative dimension. "Very bad" is more unfavorable than "bad"; "very pleasant" is more favorable than "pleasant." If "bad" were represented by a negative number, "pleasant" by a positive one, and "very" by a number greater than unity, the combinations would behave in exactly this manner. On the other hand, suppose the same two adjectives were modified by "slightly." Here, the combinations are less extreme than the adjectives alone, but one would still say that "slightly bad" was unfavorable and "slightly pleasant" was favorable. This case can be accounted for by assuming once again that "bad" and "pleasant" are negative and positive numbers, respectively, but that "slightly" is a positive number less than one.

Implicit in the above discussion is the assumption that the number associated with an adjective used alone is the same as that which is multiplied by the adverb number. That is, we are dealing with the same adjective quantity whether the adjective is used alone or in combination.

In a somewhat more formal way, this particular "law of word mixture" may be stated in terms of the following postulates:

1. There is a number associated with each adjective.

2. There is a number associated with each adverb.

3. The intensity of an adverb-adjective combination is *the product of these two numbers*.

4. The intensity of the adjective used alone is *the number associated with it when used in combination*.

5. A set of adjectives can be chosen which may be scaled on a single dimension on which all will have the same zero point.

The last of these postulates is introduced because it will be useful in tying the model to data and also because it is more parsimonious than allowing each adjective to have its own zero point.

The formulation presented here should be reflected by the psychophysical scale values of adverb-adjective combinations of the type described. It is to be remembered, however, that scale values have an arbitrary origin in the sense that any set of scale values, other than one which already constitutes a ratio scale, may have a constant added to each member of the set without distorting the scale.

The scale value of each adverb-adjective combination, then, could be expressed as

$$x_{ij} = c_i s_j + K$$

where

$x_{ij} \equiv$ the obtained scale value of the ith adverb in combination with the jth adjective;

$c_i \equiv$ the multiplying value of the ith adverb;

$s_j \equiv$ the psychological scale position of the jth adjective;

$K \equiv$ the difference between the arbitrary zero point of the obtained scale values and the psychological zero point of the scale.

A matrix X can be formed of the obtained scale values of adverb-adjective combinations with the scale values of the unmodified form of the adjective as the first row, the adverb subscript denoting the row, and the adjective subscript denoting the column. The plot of any row of this matrix, say, i, against any other row I should be linear; its slope is c_i/c_I. Correspondingly, any column j plotted against any other column J should also give a linear relation with slope s_j/s_J. If the scale value of the unmodified adjective is also included, it may be thought of as simply $s_j + K$, and the multiplying value of the adverb in this case may be said to be unity. This additional assumption enables us to find the absolute value of the c_i because the slope then becomes $c_i/1$. It is then possible to work back, substituting the values of the c_i thus obtained to arrive at least-squares estimates of s_j and K. If such a matrix is formed and is found to be of the form indicated, then the model may be said to have been upheld.

EXPERIMENTAL PROCEDURE AND METHOD OF ANALYSIS

Constructing the Questionnaire

The model was to be tested using all combinations of the nine adverbs and fifteen adjectives listed in Table 1 plus the unmodified adjectives. Accordingly, a two-part questionnaire was constructed to secure responses to the stimuli. Part I consisted of these 150 combinations, fifteen of which were repeated, and 39 filler items, which were adjectives preceded by two of the adverbs, e.g., "very slightly admirable." Thus there was a total of 204 stimuli. Table 1 also gives the frequency of usage ratings of the words used. It can be seen that all are quite common.

The careful choice of the experimental definitions of any theoretical construct is felt to be of extreme importance, whether a simple mathematical model such as the present one or some more general theory is being tested. In fact, one may speculate on the possibility

TABLE 1

FREQUENCY RATINGS OF WORDS USED IN COMBINATIONS

Adverb	Frequency[a]	Adjective	Frequency[a]
Slightly	42	Evil	50+
Somewhat	50+	Wicked	36
Rather	100+	Contemptible	4
Pretty[b]	43	Immoral	2
Quite	100+	Disgust (ing)	21
Decidedly	11	Bad	100+
Unusually	11	Inferior	19
Very	100+	Ordinary	50+
Extremely	35	Average	50+
		Nice	100+
		Good	100+
		Pleasant	100+
		Charming	31
		Admirable	10
		Lovable	3

[a] Frequency per million running words as given in Thorndike-Lorge frequency count (1944). Frequency of words occurring 50–99 and 100 or more times per million are given only as 50+ and 100+, respectively.
[b] Frequency of the quantitative adverbial meaning.

of many potentially worthwhile formulations being abandoned because of failure to make the best possible choices at just this point. Consequently, considerable care was used in selecting the words to be included in the study since it was felt that only the true, dimensionless intensive adverbs could be classified with any degree of confidence as multipliers, and it appeared wise at this early stage to limit the adjectives to a single dimension of connotation. There are undoubtedly other adverbs that could have been substituted for those used. "Highly," "moderately," and "fairly" come to mind and there are undoubtedly numerous adjectives that would have served. The adverbs actually chosen were selected because they are essentially "dimensionless," purely quantitative in their usage. "Unusually" is a possible exception to this, but it was the experimenter's belief that the connotation of rarity which this word seems to imply is becoming lost in many contexts and thus would not constitute a complication. "Completely," on the other hand, was rejected because of its implication of fullness, entirety, and conclusiveness.

The adjectives were chosen on the basis of their having little in the way of connotations other than the evaluative. The adjectives used are not completely free of other connotations, but they were felt to be relatively pure in this respect.

The reader who has inspected the list of words may be dismayed at the thought of rating combinations such as "extremely average" or "slightly ordinary." These combinations were only hesitantly included, but the completeness of the experiment won out over good usage. We may anticipate later discussion somewhat and report that these two adjectives turned out to have s_i values very close to zero. This may be the reason for these words sounding so odd when modified, since there is no good reason to try to stretch or multiply anything which is nearly zero.

The stimuli were arranged in random order, subject to the restriction that, except for the filler items, neither the same adjective nor the

---

The most important means of human communication is by means of words, and yet little of a scientific nature is known about how people go about using and interpreting them. This experiment is an attempt to find out about one aspect of this problem.

*   *   *   *   *

SECTION I

To imply favorable or unfavorable opinions about people, many different words and phrases are used, depending not only on the specific context or situation, but also on the degree of the judgment. It is the way in which these different degrees are communicated which interests us in this experiment. Suppose, for example, that someone were described as "Very respectable." How favorable would you feel this was? If you felt that it implied a medium degree of favorableness, you would put a cross in the box labeled 3, as indicated in the following marked sample item.

	Most Unfavorable ↓				Neutral ↓				Most Favorable ↓	

Very respectable □ □ □ □ ■ □ □ ☒ □ □
                  -5 -4 -3 -2 -1 0 1 2 3 4 5

Now imagine that you were to see someone described as "Mediocre." If you thought this indicated a mildly unfavorable description, you would put your cross in the box labeled -1, as indicated in the following example.

Mediocre □ □ □ □ ☒ ■ □ □ □ □ □
          -5 -4 -3 -2 -1 0 1 2 3 4 5

Throughout this booklet you will find words and phrases printed on the left side of the page. You are to imagine that, in your reading, they have been applied to a person and decide how strongly favorable or unfavorable a statement is meant. Then you are to put a cross in one of the boxes to indicate this degree. You will notice that all the words are applicable to a person but not necessarily in the same situations. They all carry, though, implications of favorableness or unfavorableness, and it is on this quality that you are to make your judgments.

FIG. 1.   Directions to the rating scale section.

TABLE 2

STIMULI SCALED BY BOTH PAIRED COMPARI-
SONS AND SUCCESSIVE INTERVALS

Extremely nice	Quite ordinary
Unusually pleasant	Slightly immoral
Pretty good	Rather contemptible
Somewhat admirable	Very inferior
Average	Decidedly bad

same adverb could be used in successive items. The subjects rated the stimuli on an eleven-point scale, from most unfavorable through neutral to most favorable. The subject's task was made more concrete by emphasizing in the directions that the stimuli were all to be rated in terms of how the subject would interpret them on reading and that they were all to be applied to people. The important parts of the directions, including example items, may be seen in Fig. 1.

Two forms of the questionnaire were used. Their only difference was a simple permutation of items, i.e., Items 1 through 102 of Form A were made Items 103 through 204 of Form B, and Items 103 through 204 of Form A were made Items 1 through 102 of Form B.

Part II was a paired comparison schedule using a sample of ten of the combinations, resulting in 45 paired comparison judgments. The combinations used are listed in Table 2.

The questionnaire was pretested on a group of secretaries, clerical assistants, and research assistants at Educational Testing Service and was found to meet satisfactorily the requirements of comprehensibility and time limits.

Subjects and Administration

The subjects used were introductory psychology students at Wayne State University, Princeton University, and Dartmouth College. The administration of the questionnaire took place during a regular class period, and, except for one section of about 40 subjects at Wayne, the experimenter personally administered the questionnaire. Two hundred and eighteen subjects, about half of them men and the other half women, were tested at Wayne; 186, all male, at Princeton; and 133, all male, at Dartmouth.

A few subjects finished the questionnaire in less than 20 minutes, about half in 35 minutes, and only one failed to complete it during the fifty-minute period. There were no evidences of lack of understanding of the task on the part of the subjects during the administration. The completed questionnaires were exam-

ined for evidences of pattern marking and the presence of an appreciable number of unusual responses. If a questionnaire showed an obvious pattern such as all responses in a single category, simple alternation in the paired comparison section, pattern marking in the rating scale section, or multiple responses to a large proportion of items, it was eliminated from further analysis. Also, if a sample page contained more than two unusual responses such as rating "inferior" as highly favorable, the entire questionnaire was examined for consistency. If such responses were consistent throughout for particular adjectives, the questionnaire was included in the analysis. If, on the other hand, the subject was not consistent in this rating, the questionnaire was thrown out on the grounds that this indicated a lack of either understanding or cooperation.

The paired comparison and the rating scale sections were examined separately, so that it was possible for a paired comparison section to be included for analysis but not the rating scale, and contrariwise. At Wayne, nine paired comparison and five rating scale sections were rejected on the basis of one of the criteria; three of each at Princeton and four of each at Dartmouth were also rejected.

The responses to the remaining 525 questionnaires were then punched into IBM cards. An analysis of variance showed that differences in the mean ratings of the same items on the two different forms could be attributed to differences in the individuals given the forms, so responses to Forms A and B were pooled. The data from each school, however, were treated separately throughout the subsequent analysis.

Methods of Deriving Psychophysical Scale Values

The testing of the main hypothesis was to be done using successive intervals scale values derived from the rating scale items since it was felt that, in order to demonstrate a strong quantitative relationship such as multiplication, it would be necessary to have numbers which as nearly as possible fit the axioms of the algebra of real numbers. In the more familiar classification of Stevens' paper (1951, Ch. 1), we are trying to derive a ratio scale.

As discussed by Gulliksen (1946), paired comparison scales derived using the law of comparative judgments are "distance" scales in the sense that the stimuli are ordered along a continuum and the distances between the stimuli are an additive scale. That is to say, given stimuli A, B, C, the stimuli have an order such as $A > B > C$, and the distances between all pairs of stimuli are consistent. In this example, this consistency of distances would imply

$$\overline{AB} + \overline{BC} = \overline{AC}$$

The property of additivity of distances between points is a necessary, although not a sufficient, property of a ratio scale. Accordingly, the use of the law of comparative judgments to arrive at scale values appeared desirable, assuming that subjects will measure distances between magnitudes in the same way they measure the magnitudes themselves. The method of paired comparisons, however, would have involved a completely impractical number of judgments with the number of stimuli necessary for the present study. Fortunately, the method of successive intervals has been found to result in scale values which are linearly related to comparative judgment scale values (Saffir, 1937), so this was decided upon as the scaling method to be used; therefore, the main part of the questionnaire was constructed as a rating scale. It should be noted that some method such as assigning scale values by simply averaging the ratings given by the subjects would not generally be satisfactory in deriving the equivalent of a comparative judgment scale. It would be so only if successive intervals scaling would result in intervals of equal size. This is not usually found to be even approximately true.

The short paired comparison section of the questionnaire was included for the purpose of verifying that the comparative judgment and successive intervals scale values of the stimuli used in this study actually were linearly related.

In deriving the successive intervals scale values, the theory and procedure of Diederich, Messick, and Tucker (1957) were followed, utilizing the punched card procedure described by Messick, Tucker, and Garrison (1955), with slight modifications. The final iteration in the successive intervals solution was performed on the IBM Card Programmed Calculator at Princeton's Forrestal Research Center. The paired comparison scale values were hand calculated using Gulliksen's incomplete data solution (1956a).

The Matrix Solution for the Adverb and Adjective Values

The method of fitting slopes and intercepts suggested by the linear relation of the scale values of the combinations to those of the unmodified adjectives furnishes an adequate test of the model, but it is quite sensitive to errors of measurement of the scale values of the unmodified adjectives. Consequently, a matrix solution which utilizes all the interrelations of the scale values was derived.

Insofar as the formulation is correct, the X matrix described earlier can be represented as the product of two matrices, C and S:

$$X = CS$$

If there are k adverbs, C will be a $k + 1$ by 2 matrix; its first column will contain the "multiplying values" of the adverbs, including a value of unity in the first row as the "multiplying value" of the unmodified form of the adjectives, and its second column will be a constant value of unity. Correspondingly, if there are n adjectives, S will be a 2 by n matrix with the psychological or algebraic scale values of the adjectives as its first row and the constant K as the second. Given a data matrix X, approximations to C and S, $\hat{C}$ and $\hat{S}$, respectively, can be found. The degree to which $\hat{C}$ and $\hat{S}$ reproduce X and have the hypothesized characteristics indicates the degree to which the data support the model.

The determination of $\hat{C}$ and $\hat{S}$ takes place as follows. Utilizing factor analytic techniques, rank-two matrices P and Q are determined such that $X = PQ$ within as close an approximation as possible. Then transformations T and T^{-1} are found which give least-squares approximations to C and S, respectively:

$$PT = \hat{C}$$
$$T^{-1}Q = \hat{S}$$
$$\hat{X} = \hat{C}\hat{S}$$

In order to find T and T^{-1}, T_2, the second column of T, is computed, using the following formula:[5]

$$T_2 = \frac{1}{1 - \phi_c} (P'P)^{-1} P'(1)$$

where

$$\phi_c = \frac{\sum\limits_{i=1}^{k} (c_{i2} - \hat{c}_{i2})^2}{\sum\limits_{i=1} \hat{c}_{i2}^2}$$

and may be computed by the formula

$$1 - \phi_c = \frac{1}{k} [1] P(P'P)^{-1} P'(1)$$

---

[5] In the formulae, the expression (1) means a column vector consisting entirely of 1's and [1] means a row vector of the same type. They act as summators over columns and rows respectively.

The second row of T^{-1}, $(T^{-1})_2$ is computed using the similar expression

$$(T^{-1})_2 = \frac{K}{1 - \phi_s} [1] Q' (QQ')^{-1}$$

in which

$$\phi_s = \frac{\sum\limits_{j=1}^{n} (s_{2j} - \hat{s}_{2j})^2}{\sum\limits_{j=1}^{n} s_{2j}{}^2}$$

and may be computed by means of the formula

$$1 - \phi_s = \frac{1}{n} [1] Q' (QQ')^{-1} Q(1)$$

The remaining elements of T and T^{-1} can be found by utilizing the relationship between the elements of a transformation matrix and those of its inverse and the additional restriction that c_{01}, the "multiplying value" when the adjective is unmodified, is unity. A proof of these formulae and a more detailed discussion of their properties is given in an unpublished manuscript by the present author.[6]

RESULTS

Scale Characteristics of the Data

The first observation to become apparent from the data was the high degree of unanimity of the judgments. The common practice in scaling experiments is to give zero weights to normal deviates based on proportions less than .05 and greater than .95. In the present case this would have resulted in a very drastic reduction in the amount of usable information. Accordingly, proportion limits of .028 and .972 for Wayne, .027 and .973 for Princeton, and .023 and .977 for Dartmouth were set. The variation in these limits is due to the different Ns for the three samples; there was also some small variation in p within schools as N fluctuates slightly due to omissions. These proportions correspond to Muller-Urban weights of

about .13, roughly one-fifth of the maximum.

Even with these somewhat liberalized limits the number of usable proportions was much smaller than the maximum possible. For the 204 items and eleven categories of the successive intervals section, there could be 2040 usable proportions. The numbers which remained after applying the limits described were: Wayne, 845; Princeton, 678; Dartmouth, 760. Since 416 parameters were to be fitted for each school, this leaves 429, 262, and 344 degrees of freedom, respectively.

Similar consistency of judgments was found for the paired comparisons. Upon tabulating the data it was found that the comparison "average-unusually pleasant" had been omitted through a clerical error, so that only 44 different comparisons were made by the subjects. Of these 44, only 22 fell within the proportion limits in the Wayne data, 19 in the Dartmouth data, and 15 in the Princeton data.

Two earlier studies, Mosier's (1941) and that of Jones and Thurstone (1955), had shown that it was possible to scale verbal material by successive intervals provided care was used in selecting unambiguous stimuli. The successive intervals model appeared to be adequate for the present data, but the computational method used does not furnish direct evidence of this. However, successive intervals scaling may be considered a simultaneous normalization of the distribution of responses to each stimulus. Since the first two moments of these response distributions are fitted to the data, the fit must be quite good except in cases where the distributions have more than one mode, have no distinct mode, or have skewnesses opposite in sign to those of other stimuli with about the same mean. Of these, bi-

TABLE 3

SCALE VALUES OF CATEGORY BOUNDARIES

Boundary	1	2	3	4	5	6	7	8	9	10
Sample										
Wayne	.37	.77	1.15	1.46	1.87	2.25	2.58	2.92	3.31	3.72
Princeton	.57	.89	1.18	1.48	1.92	2.29	2.64	2.95	3.28	3.68
Dartmouth	.45	.83	1.16	1.43	1.81	2.24	2.59	2.92	3.32	3.76

modality generally has the most serious effect. The distributions of responses to the stimuli used in the present study did not display any of these defects to any important extent.

The scale values of the category boundaries are given in Table 3, where it can be seen that they were not found to be equally spaced. This indicates that positive verification of our hypothetical model, if observed, could not also have been found using simple averages of the ratings of the stimuli.

Jones and Thurstone, in comparing their results to those of Mosier, observed that the distance between category boundaries may depend in part on the directions given the subjects. It is usually found in successive intervals scaling that the longest intervals are found at the ends of the scale and that they become shorter as the center is approached. In both Mosier's study and the present one, one of the middle categories was also found to be long. Jones and Thurstone, in discussing Mosier's results, contended that this may be due to the directions which call attention to the fact that there are "favorable" and "unfavorable" words and phrases and that these are to be rated on the right and left halves of the scale, respectively. Their own directions did not do this and they did not find a long middle category. This contention seems to be borne out here in that the directions did call attention to the favor-

ableness or unfavorableness of the combinations (see Fig. 1), and, as shown in Table 3, a middle category did turn out to be long, although in the Princeton group the long category was the fifth or −1 category rather than the neutral one.

The fit of scale values to the paired comparison data was also close. Given in Table 4, along with the final scale values of the paired comparison stimuli, are the error terms E for these stimuli, and the number of comparisons falling within the proportion limits is given as W. The E is the standard error of estimating only those obtained normal deviates which fell within the prescribed limits from the derived scale values of the stimuli. The E are reasonably small.

Reproducibility of the Data

As mentioned earlier, fifteen of the combinations were included twice to

TABLE 4

SCALE VALUES OF PAIRED COMPARISON STIMULI

Stimulus	Wayne	Princeton	Dartmouth
Extremely nice	2.739	3.219	3.154
Unusually pleasant	2.087	2.988	2.904
Pretty good	1.458	1.988	1.940
Somewhat admirable	1.495	1.783	2.025
Average	.400	−.037	.278
Quite ordinary	.025	−.761	−.030
Slightly immoral	−1.291	−1.425	−.841
Rather contemptible	−1.687	−2.371	−1.598
Very inferior	−1.767	−2.616	−1.841
Decidedly bad	−2.195	−2.866	−1.937
W	22	15	19
E	.210	.124	.145

TABLE 5

CORRELATIONS BETWEEN SCALE VALUES
OF SETS OF 15 REPEATED ITEMS

	r	Error of Sub-stitution
Wayne	.9991	.039
Princeton	.9987	.055
Dartmouth	.9991	.041

TABLE 7

BETWEEN–GROUP INTERCORRELATIONS OF
PAIRED COMPARISON SCALE VALUES

	Princeton	Dartmouth
Wayne	.989	.991
Princeton		.999

form a basis for estimating the reliability of the ratings. The members of each of these pairs were randomly put into two groups and the scale values correlated. The resulting coefficients are given in Table 5, and, since all three are about .999, the reliability of the judgments is shown to be very high. The 150 scale values from each school which were to be used in subsequent analyses were also correlated among the three schools to get a measure of their comparability across the samples. From Table 6, they can be seen to range from .993 to .998, indicating the high degree of agreement to be expected among quite comparable groups of subjects. These coefficients, however, tend to be somewhat smaller than the reliabilities.

The intercorrelations among schools of the paired comparison scale values are given in Table 7. These are seen to be about .99 and quite comparable to the corresponding coefficients given in Table 6 for the successive intervals. Since the stimuli used for the paired comparisons were also included in the

successive intervals questionnaire, it was possible to compare the values obtained by the two methods. The correlations thus obtained are given in Table 8, and they too are .99 or larger, indicating that similar processes were being used by the subjects by the two means and that there is an almost perfect linear relation between the successive intervals and paired comparison scale values.

Testing the Model

The three sets of successive intervals scale values shown in Table 9 were those to be used to test the model. The reader may be interested to note by inspecting columns of the table that the effect of the adverbs on most of the adjectives is quite marked. The difference between the scale value of an adjective modified by "slightly" and the same adjective modified by "extremely" is usually almost one-fourth of the length of the entire scale. "Ordinary" and "average," on the other hand, remain quite stable, although there is a noticeable tendency for them to move slightly toward the

TABLE 6

INTERCORRELATIONS OF 150 SCALE VALUES
TO BE USED IN TESTING MULTIPLICATIVE
COMBINATION

	Princeton	Dartmouth
Wayne	.993	.996
Princeton		.998

TABLE 8

CORRELATIONS BETWEEN PAIRED
COMPARISON AND SUCCESSIVE
INTERVAL SCALE VALUES

Group	r
Wayne	.998
Princeton	.994
Dartmouth	.998

TABLE 9—x_{ij}: OBTAINED SUCCESSIVE INTERVALS SCALE VALUES OF ADVERB–ADJECTIVE COMBINATIONS

Wayne University

	Evil	Wicked	Contemptible	Immoral	Disgusting	Bad	Inferior	Ordinary	Average	Nice	Good	Pleasant	Charming	Admirable	Lovable
(Unmodified)	.607	.650	.793	.793	.828	1.024	1.323	2.074	2.145[a]	2.636	2.712	2.770	2.912	2.972	3.054
Slightly	1.419	1.328	1.324	1.176[a]	1.327	1.497	1.520	1.980	2.023	2.286	2.417	2.440	2.557	2.542	2.626
Somewhat	1.283	1.124	1.134	1.133	.963	1.323	1.516	2.038	2.080	2.488	2.462	2.505	2.667	2.682[a]	2.705
Rather	1.084	.978	1.047[a]	.954	.990	1.232	1.295	2.034	2.172	2.568	2.755	2.743	2.881	2.853	2.829
Pretty	.914	.964	.867	.884	.753	1.018	1.180	2.026	2.094	2.767	2.622[a]	2.738	2.860	2.867	3.062
Quite	.752	.786	.832	.726	.687	.924	1.127	2.023[a]	2.101	2.738	2.880	2.849	2.955	3.031	3.025
Decidedly	.576	.558	.609	.528	.636	.797[a]	1.013	1.949	2.020	2.969	3.024	3.028	3.153	3.263	3.157
Unusually	.553	.466	.661	.451	.664	.662	.963	1.875	2.062	3.155	3.243	3.107[a]	3.223	3.231	3.250
Very	.465	.446	.633	.465	.502	.639	.927[a]	2.073	2.039	3.016	3.250	3.174	3.182	3.305	3.327
Extremely	.107	.088	.327	−.085	.395	.470	.705	1.936	2.052	3.351[a]	3.449	3.490	3.372	3.561	3.462

Princeton University

	Evil	Wicked	Contemptible	Immoral	Disgusting	Bad	Inferior	Ordinary	Average	Nice	Good	Pleasant	Charming	Admirable	Lovable
(Unmodified)	.739	.771	.858	.956	.836	1.080	1.274	1.869	2.053[a]	2.736	2.910	2.816	2.993	3.095	3.024
Slightly	1.394	1.395	1.342	1.393[a]	1.273	1.546	1.548	1.928	2.008	2.407	2.449	2.457	2.564	2.547	2.604
Somewhat	1.289	1.204	1.217	1.232	1.042	1.365	1.486	1.943	2.050	2.511	2.490	2.572	2.716	2.656[a]	2.689
Rather	1.115	1.112	.995[a]	1.113	.965	1.257	1.396	1.913	2.056	2.685	2.821	2.793	2.939	2.865	2.885
Pretty	1.090	.929	1.046	1.034	.822	1.225	1.183	1.902	2.052	2.711	2.727[a]	2.738	2.869	2.893	2.932
Quite	.892	.882	.884	.893	.736	1.012	.974	1.871[a]	1.951	2.778	2.990	2.920	3.058	3.110	3.059
Decidedly	.764	.756	.742	.791	.718	.889[a]	.986	1.763	1.828	3.009	3.095	3.033	3.178	3.250	3.147
Unusually	.702	.669	.753	.701	.652	.808	.926	1.660	1.877	3.206	3.304	3.240[a]	3.262	3.373	3.287
Very	.698	.632	.744	.765	.593	.834	.899[a]	1.785	1.872	3.042	3.250	3.172	3.244	3.385	3.243
Extremely	.504	.515	.556	.494	.473	.666	.758	1.806	1.800	3.282[a]	3.443	3.437	3.387	3.579	3.431

Dartmouth College

	Evil	Wicked	Contemptible	Immoral	Disgusting	Bad	Inferior	Ordinary	Average	Nice	Good	Pleasant	Charming	Admirable	Lovable
(Unmodified)	.843	.782	.801	1.002	.792	1.125	1.329	2.043	1.984[a]	2.669	2.770	2.830	2.938	2.977	2.991
Slightly	1.420	1.412	1.336	1.328[a]	1.270	1.466	1.487	2.005	2.052	2.366	2.411	2.402	2.468	2.479	2.593
Somewhat	1.305	1.182	1.148	1.227	1.056	1.343	1.452	2.006	2.003	2.483	2.521	2.601	2.681	2.674[a]	2.732
Rather	1.085	1.038	1.032[a]	1.099	.935	1.266	1.347	1.964	2.048	2.594	2.778	2.811	2.874	2.887	2.883
Pretty	1.056	.918	1.015	.974	.749	1.065	1.123	2.025	2.044	2.739	2.686[a]	2.726	2.860	2.874	3.090
Quite	.891	.845	.755	.839	.661	1.004	.985	1.920[a]	1.950	2.760	2.946	2.887	3.042	3.150	3.060
Decidedly	.721	.692	.647	.754	.625	.920[a]	.970	1.969	1.864	2.968	3.052	3.034	3.128	3.292	3.192
Unusually	.713	.611	.663	.653	.571	.837	.893	1.824	1.989	3.170	3.262	3.123[a]	3.244	3.272	3.330
Very	.640	.614	.652	.690	.538	.828	.900[a]	1.903	1.977	3.080	3.228	3.103	3.235	3.339	3.339
Extremely	.450	.375	.465	.372	.325	.725	.703	1.790	1.799	3.326[a]	3.410	3.465	3.372	3.549	3.493

[a] Combination also scaled by paired comparisons.

152

negative with the more extreme adverbs.

A preliminary check on the model was made by plotting x_{0j}, the scale values of the unmodified adjectives, against x_{ij}, those of the adjectives in combination with some particular adverb. These were satisfactorily linear, although there was a tendency for the scale values to bunch at the ends of the scale when the adjectives were paired with extreme adverbs.

The next step in the analysis was the determination of the rank of X and finding the matrices P and Q. This was done by multiplying

$$XX' = R$$

and obtaining the two largest factors of R by an adaptation of the principal components method to obtain P. Q was computed by premultiplying X by the matrix of latent vectors of P'.

The size of the first two latent roots (sum of squares of factor loadings) indicates the degree to which X can be approximated by the product of two rank-two matrices. It is a fundamental theorem of factor analysis (Eckart and Young, 1936) that the sum of the diagonal elements of R, its "trace," which is also the sum of the squares of elements of X, is the sum of the latent roots of R. These roots must all be positive or zero. Therefore, the sum of the first two roots can be compared to the trace to see how nearly the sum of squares of the x_{ij} can be accounted for by the first two orthogonal components. Table 10 lists the two largest roots of each of the three matrices and the percentage of the trace accounted for by them. Since all of the percentages are greater than 99.9, X can be very closely approximated using only two factors in P and Q, as was hypothesized.

The sum of squares of differences between theoretical and obtained x_{ij}

TABLE 10

LATENT ROOTS OF XX'

	Wayne	Princeton	Dartmouth
a_1^2	654.46	668.35	662.21
a_2^2	10.04	7.72	8.24
Residual	.51	.50	.50
Trace	665.01	676.57	670.95
$\dfrac{a_1^2 + a_2^2}{\text{Trace}}$	.9992	.9993	.9993

is equal to the figure given in Table 10 as the residual trace of the R matrices after extracting the two factors. The standard error of substitution of the theoretical for the obtained scale values of the 150 combinations is then

$$\sqrt{\frac{.50}{150}} = .0577$$

for Princeton and Dartmouth, and

$$\sqrt{\frac{.51}{150}} = .0583$$

for Wayne. These values are seen to be only slightly larger than the corresponding figures given in Table 5 as the errors of substitution resulting from substituting the scale values of one set of repeated items for the other. Thus, there seems to be only a small amount of reliable variance which is not accounted for by the two factors.

Next, the transformations T and T^{-1} were determined for each sample and applied to the P and Q matrices to determine $\hat{C}$ and $\hat{S}$. The $\hat{C}$ and $\hat{S}$ matrices for each group are given in Tables 11, 12, and 13.

The goodness of the fit of the data to the model is indicated by the degree of conformity of the obtained $\hat{C}$ and $\hat{S}$ matrices to the hypothesized ones. If the model is to be ideally verified, then not only must there be

TABLE 11

WAYNE ADVERB VALUES MATRIX $\hat{C}$ AND ADJECTIVE VALUES MATRIX $\hat{S}'$

$\hat{C}$			$\hat{S}$		
Adverb	c_i	1	Adjective	s_j	K
(Unmodified)	1.000	.987	Evil	−1.246	2.082
Slightly	.555	1.000	Wicked	−1.158	1.952
Somewhat	.685	.997	Contemptible	−.913	1.746
Rather	.846	1.015	Immoral	−1.177	1.936
Pretty	.935	.995	Disgusting	−.806	1.617
Quite	1.042	.994	Bad	−1.025	2.032
Decidedly	1.216	.997	Inferior	−.813	2.008
Unusually	1.291	1.010	Ordinary	−.078	2.083
Very	1.317	1.008	Average	−.040	2.121
Extremely	1.593	.996	Nice	1.007	1.742
			Good	1.078	1.752
			Pleasant	1.001	1.835
			Charming	.802	2.136
			Admirable	.983	2.001
			Lovable	.836	2.173

only two factors, but the second column of $\hat{C}$ must contain all unities and the second row of $\hat{S}$ must be a constant value K, which is to be remembered to be the difference between the arbitrary zero point of the scale values and the "true" psychological zero point. De-partures from these constant values indicate the degree to which the data do not confirm the model. Examination of the tables shows that the fit was excellent for the adverb matrices, but that for the adjectives, while good, was noticeably less exact. The

TABLE 12

PRINCETON ADVERB VALUES MATRIX $\hat{C}$ AND ADJECTIVE VALUES MATRIX $\hat{S}'$

$\hat{C}$			$\hat{S}'$		
Adverb	c_i	1	Adjective	s_j	K
(Unmodified)	1.000	.991	Evil	−.989	1.918
Slightly	.538	1.003	Wicked	−.951	1.848
Somewhat	.662	.995	Contemptible	−.826	1.749
Rather	.843	1.016	Immoral	−.931	1.878
Pretty	.878	.992	Disgusting	−.801	1.621
Quite	1.047	.991	Bad	−.972	2.051
Decidedly	1.165	.992	Inferior	−.923	2.077
Unusually	1.281	1.010	Ordinary	−.253	2.100
Very	1.254	1.002	Average	−.296	2.254
Extremely	1.446	1.006	Nice	.984	1.842
			Good	1.158	1.777
			Pleasant	1.050	1.856
			Charming	.895	2.116
			Admirable	1.170	1.892
			Lovable	.912	2.108

TABLE 13

DARTMOUTH ADVERB VALUES MATRIX $\hat{C}$ AND ADJECTIVE VALUES MATRIX $\hat{S}'$

$\hat{C}$			$\hat{S}$		
Adverbs	c_i	1	Adjective	s_j	K
(Unmodified)	1.000	.993	Evil	$-.993$	1.972
Slightly	.559	.999	Wicked	$-.997$	1.910
Somewhat	.719	1.001	Contemptible	$-.882$	1.792
Rather	.887	1.014	Immoral	$-.954$	1.910
Pretty	.961	.994	Disgusting	$-.902$	1.715
Quite	1.109	.988	Bad	$-.796$	1.907
Decidedly	1.231	.996	Inferior	$-.861$	2.037
Unusually	1.324	1.001	Ordinary	$-.223$	2.182
Very	1.323	1.007	Average	$-.211$	2.195
Extremely	1.546	.997	Nice	1.011	1.739
			Good	1.075	1.761
			Pleasant	.974	1.860
			Charming	.910	2.013
			Admirable	1.086	1.892
			Lovable	.812	2.207

standard deviation from the theoretically constant values of 1.000 for the second column of $\hat{C}$ are of the order .01, while the standard deviations of the theoretically constant K in the second column of the S' tables are of the order .16 (for convenience, $\hat{S}$ is presented as $\hat{S}'$ in the tables). All three groups gave highly equivalent results.

The multiplying values of the adverbs are given in the first rows of the $\hat{C}$ matrices. They are seen to vary from about .5 to 1.5. The actual values obtained from the three sets of data vary somewhat, but in general are quite comparable. In comparison to the unmodified form of the adjectives, combinations with "slightly" and "somewhat" have the smallest intensities, the multiplying values for these adverbs being considerably less than unity. Combinations with "rather" and "pretty" are also less extreme than the unmodified form but are much nearer to it; "quite" makes adjectives just slightly more extreme, while "decidedly" has a definite effect;

"very" and "unusually" are close together and stronger than "decidedly"; "extremely" is by far the most effective of the intensives included in the list. The values obtained in the experiment seem to agree with subjective impressions of how they are used.

The s_j values derived for the adjectives correspond closely to expectation. Those for the seven adjectives which could be termed definitely unfavorable are relatively large negative numbers, while those for the six favorable adjectives are large positive numbers about equal in absolute value to the s_j of the unfavorable words. "Ordinary" and "average" have s_j near zero but on the negative side. This reflects the stability observed in their scale values and, as observed earlier, perhaps offers an explanation of why these adjectives sound peculiar when modified.

In one respect, however, the results for the adjectives cannot be considered quite as neat as those for the adverbs: the theoretically constant second columns of the $\hat{S}'$ matrices (the K

values) are somewhat variable. The departures from a theoretically constant value might at first thought be dismissed as random errors of measurement, but two things in addition to their magnitude argue against this. First, the entries in the K columns of the $\hat{S}'$ show some consistency across the three groups. Note, for example, that the K for "disgusting" is the smallest in all three cases; also, "ordinary" and "average" have among the highest entries in each of the three groups. The correlations of these values over adjectives among the three groups bear this out. As can be seen from Table 14, they are appreciable. Such high correlations would hardly be expected if the variation in K were a random error of measurement.

The lack of correspondence between data and theory in respect to the K values is also shown in comparing the s_j entries of the $\hat{S}'$ matrices to the scale values of the unmodified adjectives given in the first rows of the X matrices. According to the theory, these scale values should be simply $s_j + K$ within, say, an error comparable to that indicated by the reliability measure. Examination of the two sets of numbers shows that this will not be the case, for, if we subtract the mean of the K from the x_{0j}, the resulting numbers differ somewhat from the corresponding s_j.

The fairly small but consistent variation observed in the K is felt by

the author to be the only important departure from the model and requires some attempt at explanation. The possibility of a computational artifact can be ruled out. The matrix solution fits the data to the model in the least-squares sense, so that the variance of the Ks has been made as small as possible.

Several possible explanations of the variation present themselves. First, it may be that it is an artifact of the scaling task itself or perhaps even of the method of successive intervals. Detailed examination of the data revealed that, for the most part, the lack of fit results from failure of the extreme combinations to be pushed out as far as one would expect from the model. This could result from the subjects rating relatively moderate combinations near the ends of the scale and then not having any means of rating the really extreme ones any farther out. A more flexible means of securing the judgments than using printed questionnaires should remedy this. Alternatively, the successive intervals solution used, while it has many advantages, may be sensitive to the fact that the judgments used here were very consistent over subjects, so that the data were highly "incomplete." If this resulted in underestimating the discriminal dispersions of the extreme combinations, then the result could be the pulling in of the ends of the scale as was observed. The use of the method on artificial data having the required characteristics is required to investigate this possibility, however.

Another possible explanation lies in the fact that the model used here is based on the properties of Euclidean vector spaces. It may be that the properties of the space with which we are dealing here are only approxi-

TABLE 14
INTERCORRELATIONS OF VALUES OF K OBTAINED FOR ADJECTIVES

	Princeton	Dartmouth
Wayne	.890	.846
Princeton		.896

mately those of the Euclidean type. This possibility would introduce many complications, both theoretical and practical, however.

Perhaps the simplest explanation of the variation in the K is that, contrary to assumption, each of the adjectives has its own zero point rather than there being a common one for all the adjectives. In this case the basic formula would become

$$x_{ij} - c_i s_j + K_j$$

Here K_j represents the distance from the arbitrary zero point to the psychological zero point *of the adjective*. This explanation has the advantage of fitting the available data without requiring further experimentation, but the author, at least, is reluctant to settle on it at this point because it detracts from the simplicity of the model.

CONCLUSIONS AND IMPLICATIONS

The data and discussion of the previous section were presented as arguments in favor of the hypothesis that adverbs and adjectives of specifiable types combine according to a multiplicative rule. The consistent discrepancies between data and theory are felt to be small enough to warrant the acceptance of the hypothesis, at least as a good approximation.

Using the results of this study as a base, there are further lines of research which would seem to bear promise of broadening the applicability of the hypothesis. The first of these is the expansion of it to other dimensions. If one were to define an abstract dimension of communicated size, would "very small" be "very" times "small"? The subjective impression of the way the words combine is the same as in the evaluative dimension: "very small" is smaller than "small"

and "very large" is larger than "large," and so on. This particular example is especially interesting because of the implication that there are positive and negative quantities of size whereas, physically, size is a positive quantity. It may be that the intensive adverbs would have the same multiplying value in all dimensions. This is intuitively the most satisfactory way of conceptualizing the relationship, but one might find that they would have different multiplying values in different dimensions even though their action were multiplicative.

Investigation might also be fruitful into the application of the multiplicative rule to combinations other than those containing the common intensive adverbs. Brunot (1922), in his attempt to redefine the grammatical classifications of French, speaks of a general class of expressions of degree. It might be that the English equivalents of most of all of the expressions he includes there would act in this way. It is, of course, very important to extend the findings for English to other languages. While it may be that the rules of combination might be different for languages with a structure other than that of English, some similar type of quantitative abstraction might easily hold.[7]

Combinatory rules other than the one forming the basis of this investigation can perhaps also be found for other types of combinations in Englihs. For instance, adjective-noun combinations usually have characteristics of both the adjective and the noun, so the rule for them might be some form of addition. A combina-

[7] Harold Gulliksen, of Princeton University, is currently gathering data from several European countries to see whether translations of the words used here combine in the same way in other languages.

tion of adjectives might also act in this way.[8]

Extending the search for combinatory rules to various dimensions, languages, and parts of speech, then, seems from the results of this study to hold out a hope for a fairly thorough formal representation of how the emotive aspects of language are communicated. Finding such rules requires fairly exact formulation of them before undertaking experimentation. Also, it is necessary to have measuring instruments which give data accurate enough to show whether or not the theories hold, and the nature of departures from the theory when it is shown to be a good general statement. The method of successive intervals seems from the present results to be such a method.

The results of this study also have relevance to the general problem of psychological measurement. In general, measurement may be said to be the process of relating observables to some ordering system. The field of real numbers is considered the ideal ordering system, since it is possible to perform operations on it and show relations with it which are not possible using other systems. However, it is usually not possible to justify treating measured quantities as completely isomorphic with the real numbers; therefore, various of the real number axioms are relaxed or termed inadmissible in order to prevent the appearance of nonsensical theoretical results in constructing scales. This lack of iso-

morphism has been especially true of psychological data, so types of scales are differentiated on the basis of which of the axioms are altered or relaxed. The distinctions made by Stevens (1951, Ch. I) and elaborated in some respects by Coombs (1951) are examples of the recognition of such disparities. As a result, certain operations such as addition or division are termed inadmissible, weak ordering is substituted for strong, and so on. Weitzenhoffer (1951) presents a cogent discussion of the algebraic axioms in relation to psychological data.

It is felt that the data quantities of this study represent an unusually close approximation to the real numbers, for the operation of multiplication requires both a zero point and a unit of measurement. In a very real sense, "extremely good" may be said to be about one-and-a-half times as good as "good." The multiplication seems to be of the scalar type since the adjectives represent the same kind of meaning whether modified or not. Note that this might not have been found to be the case had more "meaningful" adverbs such as "ridiculously," "sinisterly," or "constantly" been used.

The zero point on the scale seems, for practical purposes, to be slightly above the adjective "average" for these groups. A dimensional unit, analogous to foot or hour, may be set at any convenient point, whereupon all the scale values, representing degrees of favorableness or unfavorableness, are to be expressed as multiples of this point.

This discussion of zero points and units may be premature, especially in view of the possibility that each adjective has its own scale, but the evidence presented here makes it seem not unreasonable. If further experi-

---

[8] Analysis of the filler items in the questionnaire, accomplished since the preparation of this manuscript, indicates strongly that "very, very" is "very-squared." Combinations which contain two different adverbs, e.g., "very slightly admirable," seem to operate by having the two adverbs combine exponentially: "slightly" to the "very" power, but data on the latter rule are not clear-cut.

mental work verifies the present findings in the most important aspects but shows that each adjective does indeed have its own zero point, then the discussion of zero points and scale units would have to be made specific to the adjective. Perhaps the adjective "modified" by the prefix *non-* or *a-* (not the negatives *un-* or *im-*) would then be the zero point and the dimensional units would have to be expressed in terms of good-ness, immoral-ness, and so on.

SUMMARY

This study set out to test the hypothesis that the common adverbs of degree multiply the intensity of the adjectives they modify. That is, there is a number associated with each adjective and with each adverb; the intensity of each combination is the product of the numbers associated with the words. It was assumed that the relationship should be reflected by the psychophysical scale values of adverb-adjective combinations. Accordingly, three groups of subjects rated the combinations of nine intensive adverbs with 15 evaluative adjectives on the favorable-unfavorable dimension. Scale values of the stimuli were determined by the method of successive intervals.

The scale values obtained were found to be highly reliable, highly comparable between groups, and highly correlated with scale values obtained by paired comparisons. A matrix method was employed to test the hypothesis of multiplicative combination and to determine the adverb and adjective values. The degree of correspondence between hypothesis and data was found to be very close in all three groups. This was evidenced by the fact that matrices of scale values could be reproduced with a high degree of precision using only two factors, as was hypothesized, and that certain hypothetically constant values derived from the data were very nearly so. Some consistent discrepancies between hypothesis and data were pointed out.

The relationship discovered is akin to the scalar multiplication of vector algebra. A zero point is implied for the numbers associated with the adverbs and those associated with the adjectives. Scale units analogous to physical units are implied for the adjective numbers, but the adverb numbers are "unitless" scalars. Several extensions of this research are suggested.

REFERENCES

BRUNOT, F. *La pensée et le langue.* Paris: Masson, 1922.

COOMBS, C. H. *A theory of psychological scaling.* Ann Arbor: Engng. Res. Inst., 1951.

DIEDERICH, G. W., MESSICK, S. J., & TUCKER, L. R. A general least squares solution for successive intervals. *Psychometrika,* 1957, **22,** 159–174.

ECKART, C., & YOUNG, G. The approximation of one matrix by another of lower rank. *Psychometrika,* 1936, **1,** 211–218.

GULLIKSEN, H. Paired comparisons and the logic of measurement. *Psychol. Rev.,* 1946, **53,** 199–213.

GULLIKSEN, H. A least squares solution for paried comparisons with incomplete data. *Psychometrika,* 1956, **21,** 125–134. (a)

GULLIKSEN, H. Measurement of subjective values. *Psychometrika,* 1956, **21,** 229–244. (b)

JONES, L. V., & THURSTONE, L. L. The psychophysics of semantics: An experimental investigation. *J. appl. Psychol.,* 1955, **39,** 31–36.

MESSICK, S. J., TUCKER, L. R., & GARRISON, H. W. A punched card procedure for the method of successive intervals. Research Bulletin 55–25. Princeton: Educational Testing Service, 1955. (Multilithed report.)

MOSIER, C. I. A psychometric study of meaning. *J. soc. Psychol.,* 1941, **13,** 123–140.

OSGOOD, C. E.   The nature and measurement of meaning.   *Psychol. Bull.*, 1952, **49**, 197–237.

OSGOOD, C. E., & SEBEOK, T. A. (Eds.)   Psycholinguistics: A sturvey of theory and research problems. Supplement to *J. abnorm. soc. Psychol.*, 1954, **49**, No. 4, Part 2.

SAFFIR, M. A.   A comparative study of scales constructed by three psychophysical methods.   *Psychometrika*, 1937, **2**, 179–198.

STEVENS, S. S.   *Handbook of experimental psychology*.   New York: Wiley, 1951.

THORNDIKE, E. L., & LORGE, I.   *The teacher's word-book of 30,000 words*.   New York: Teachers Coll., Columbia Univer., 1944.

WEITZENHOFFER, A. M.   Mathematical structures and psychological measurements.   *Psychometrika*, 1951, **16**, 387–406.

11. Metric Properties
of the Semantic Differential

Samuel J. Messick

THE use of the Semantic Differential, an instrument designed to measure the meaning of concepts (3), involves several assumptions about metric properties of the individual bipolar scales of which it is composed. For instance, when an integer score is assigned as a concept's scale position on a particular scale, the property of equal intervals within that scale is assumed. Similarly, when a distance measure is taken over several scales (5), equal intervals between scales are assumed. In addition, the application of factor analytic techniques to the assigned scores (6) involves assumptions concerning the location of the scale origins; i.e., it is assumed that the zero-point falls at the same place on each scale, namely at the centroid. If the Semantic Differential scales do not meet these assumptions approximately, a factor analysis of meaning based on such scales may yield a distorted picture of the underlying structure.

In order to investigate these scaling properties, the psychometric method of successive intervals (cf. 2, 7) was applied to nine of the most frequently used scales in the Semantic Differential—*good-bad, clean-dirty, valuable-worthless, large-small, strong-weak, heavy-light, active-passive, fast-slow,* and *hot-cold.* The particular successive interval solution used in this study was a graphical least squares procedure developed by Diederich (1). The analysis was based upon data originally gathered by the method of equal-appearing intervals for a factor analysis of meaning (6). The two methods of equal-appearing intervals and successive intervals are identical with respect to data collection; they differ only in assumptions made to simplify the assignment of scale values. By establishing a subjective metric (8), the method of successive intervals provides an estimate of

Reprinted from *Educational and Psychological Measurement* (1957), 17: 200–206, by permission of the author and the publisher.

interval length and thus permits an evaluation of the equality of intervals along a scale.

In assigning scale values on an assumed equal-interval scale, Osgood used the integers 3, 2, 1, 0, −1, −2, and −3 as successive category mid-points. The six boundary values for these seven response categories are 2.5, 1.5, .5, −.5, −1.5, and −2.5; the assumed boundaries will be designated by a_g. Since the method of successive intervals provides scale values for the boundaries that separate response categories as well as scale values for the stimuli, it is possible to compare the scaled boundary values, designated by t_g, with the assumed boundary values, a_g. Estimates of the size of intervals can also be found by subtracting successive t_g values.

Because of an arbitrary definition of unit and origin, the scale values obtained from successive intervals are determined only within a linear transformation. Thus the scaled boundary values, t_g, can be transformed linearly to be as comparable as possible to the assumed boundaries, a_g. In making this transformation, the origin of the successive intervals scale was placed at the centroid of the t_g values, a position corresponding to the origin of the assumed scale. It was also necessary to multiply the unit of the t-scale by some constant c in order to make the scaled boundaries the same order of magnitude as the assumed boundaries. The linear transformation appropriate for such a change would be:

$$L_g = ct_g, \qquad (g = 1 \cdots 6)$$

where L_g designates the transformed interval boundaries, and t_g values are measured from an origin placed at their centroid.

Since the original definition of a unit was completely arbitrary, it seemed desirable to select the transforming constant according to some least squares criterion. Accordingly, the following function was minimized:

$$\mathcal{Q} = \sum_{g=1}^{6} (a_g - ct_g)^2.$$

The value of c which made this function a minimum was:

$$c = \frac{\sum_g a_g t_g}{\sum_g t_g^2}.$$

It should be noted that this constant is the coefficient for the regression of a on t, so that the computation of the above transformation also yields almost directly an index of the correlation between assumed and scaled boundary values.

Accordingly, the method of successive intervals (1) was applied to nine bipolar scales to obtain six category boundary values, t_g, for each scale. Transformed scores, L_g, were computed using a separate c for each scale. Mid-points were then found for the middle five categories of each scale by interpolation from the boundary values, and estimates of interval size were obtained by subtracting successive boundaries. Table 1 presents the transformed interval boundaries, L_g, along with interpolated category mid-points, m_g, for each of the nine scales. An examination of this table reveals an apparent inequality of intervals within any one of the scales; e.g., the difference $L_5 - L_4$, which is the length of interval five, is generally less than half the size of $L_2 - L_1$, the length of interval two.

However, interval sizes are fairly consistent between scales; i.e., the same categories tend to be too large or too small in similar amounts over all scales. Also, the origin falls in approximately the same place on all scales, the zero point being located so that the midpoint of the center category is always slightly negative.

In order to evaluate scale-to-scale variations in the placement of boundary positions, mean deviations between scales were computed by the following formula:

$$\text{Mean Dev.} = \tfrac{1}{6} \sum_g | Lg_\alpha - Lg_\beta |$$

where α and β designate two different scales. These values are presented in Table 2, along with mean deviations between each bipolar scale and the assumed equal-interval scale. Table 2 indicates that, in general, deviations are less between two bipolar scales than between bipolar and assumed scales. This suggests a greater similarity of intervals between than within scales; i.e., the category boundaries are similarly placed on all nine scales but not exactly in the proper positions for equal intervals.

The question now arises as to whether these deviations can be considered to be only chance fluctuations in the placement of category boundaries. This question can be approached in several ways, but because of the paucity of appropriate statistical tests, none of the approaches are very direct. In the first

TABLE 1

Transformed Interval Boundaries, L_a, Obtained by the Method of Successive Intervals, Along with Interpolated Midpoints

Scale	L_1	m_2	L_2	m_3	L_3	m_4	L_4	m_5	L_5	m_6	L_6
Good-Bad	2.74	2.06	1.38	.84	.30	−.21	−.72	−1.06	−1.40	−1.85	−2.30
Clean-Dirty	2.82	2.02	1.22	.69	.15	−.19	−.53	−.89	−1.25	−1.83	−2.41
Valuable-Worthless	2.81	2.10	1.39	.74	.09	−.33	−.74	−1.02	−1.31	−1.77	−2.23
Large-Small	2.71	2.06	1.40	.81	.21	−.18	−.58	−.95	−1.33	−1.88	−2.42
Strong-Weak	2.84	2.00	1.16	.62	.08	−.20	−.49	−.81	−1.14	−1.80	−2.46
Heavy-Light	2.72	2.06	1.40	.83	.26	−.19	−.64	−1.01	−1.38	−1.87	−2.36
Active-Passive	2.84	2.05	1.26	.65	.03	−.26	−.55	−.88	−1.21	−1.79	−2.37
Fast-Slow	2.67	2.02	1.38	.87	.37	−.11	−.60	−.98	−1.36	−1.91	−2.46
Hot-Cold	2.45	2.01	1.57	1.07	.56	−.10	−.76	−1.04	−1.33	−1.91	−2.50
Assumed Scale	2.50	2.00	1.50	1.00	.50	0	−.50	−1.00	−1.50	−2.00	−2.50

TABLE 2

Mean Deviations Between Scales

$$\tfrac{1}{6}\sum_\sigma | Lg_\alpha - Lg_\beta |$$

Scale	G-B	C-D	V-W	L-S	S-W	H-L	A-P	F-S	H-C	Equal Intervals
Good-Bad............		.14	.08	.08	.20	.04	.15	.08	.18	.18
Clean-Dirty.........	.14		.12	.08	.06	.11	.05	.13	.26	.22
Valuable-Worthless...	.08	.12		.10	.15	.10	.11	.14	.22	.26
Large-Small.........	.08	.08	.10		.14	.04	.11	.05	.17	.16
Strong-Weak.........	.20	.06	.15	.14		.17	.06	.17	.30	.25
Heavy-Light.........	.04	.11	.10	.04	.17		.13	.06	.18	.16
Active-Passive.......	.15	.05	.11	.11	.06	.13		.15	.28	.25
Fast-Slow...........	.08	.13	.14	.05	.17	.06	.15		.14	.12
Hot-Cold...........	.18	.26	.22	.17	.30	.18	.28	.14		.10

place, the mean deviations presented in Table 2 are comparable to error discrepancies reported in reliability studies of the Semantic Differential (4). This certainly indicates a possibility of the intervals actually being equal and the apparent differences being due to chance alone. Indeed, it may be possible that the intervals within a scale seem too large or too small only because of random fluctuations of boundary values in opposite directions, although, on the surface, this possibility seems unlikely because of the consistent placement of category boundaries between scales. Consistency is not a property of random fluctuations, and the fact that the intervals are unequal in approximately the same way on each scale argues against an explanation of inequality within scales solely on the basis of chance. However, this argument must be tempered by the fact that the deviations from equal intervals were small and, as has been pointed out before, within the error of the instrument.

Another factor which might contribute to an apparent inequality of intervals is the distribution of concepts over each scale. Twenty concepts were rated on the Semantic Differential in the study from which the present scaling data was obtained (6), and about three-quarters of these concepts were consistently rated on the positive side of the scale. This means that more estimates of the positive intervals were available in the scaling procedure than estimates of negative ones, but since averages are taken in finding the interval size, the number of different estimates is not as important as their similarity. Since, even on those scales for which as few as four estimates of an end category were available, these estimates were found to be comparatively similar and presumably representative, the resulting distortions of interval size are probably not very marked in this case. There was also a tendency for the extreme categories, both positive and negative, to be large and the center ones small (the so-called "end effect"), which argues against interval distortions solely from concentrations of positive ratings. However, the positive intervals were consistently larger on all scales than symmetric negative ones, so the possibility of such a distortion is at least plausible, if difficult to evaluate.

Instead of trying to decide whether the intervals are "actually" equal, it may be more feasible to consider how far wrong one might go by assuming equality. In other words, how much distortion would be introduced by using the numbers 3, 2, 1, 0, -1, -2, -3 as category labels instead of the mid-points obtained from the scaling procedure? Some indication of this distortion may be obtained from the correlations between assumed and scaled boundary positions. Since the constant, c, used in obtaining the transformed scores, L_g, is the coefficient for the regression of assumed values, a_g, on scaled values, t_g, an index of correlation between a and t for each scale can be readily computed from corresponding constants. These correlations, in an order corresponding to the list of scales in Table 1, are .994, .990, .987, .995, .984, .995, .986, .998, .997.

Due to restrictions on the variation of a and t values, these two scales by their very nature must be highly correlated, but the above correlations are exceedingly high. These correlations indicate that little distortion would be introduced by using successive integers as category mid-points for these nine scales. Considering this and the other indications of the present study, i.e., an approximate equality of corresponding interval lengths from scale to scale and a similar placement of origins across scales, it seems reasonable to conclude that the scaling properties implied by the Semantic Differential procedures have some basis other than mere assumption.

REFERENCES

1. Diederich, G. W., Messick, S. J., and Tucker, L. R. *A General Least Squares Solution for Successive Intervals.* Princeton: Educational Testing Service Research Bulletin, 1955.

2. Gulliksen, H. "A Least Squares Solution for Successive Intervals Assuming Unequal Standard Deviations." *Psychometrika*, XIX (1954), 117–139.

3. Osgood, C. E. "The Nature and Measurement of Meaning." *Psychological Bulletin*, XLIX (1952), 197–237.

4. Osgood, C. E. *A Monograph on the Semantic Differential*. Urbana: University of Illinois Press, (in press).

5. Osgood, C. E., and Suci, G. J. "A Measure of Relation Determined by Both Mean Difference and Profile Information." *Psychological Bulletin*, XLIX (1952), 251–262.

6. Osgood, C. E. and Suci, G. J. "Factor Analysis of Meaning." *Journal of Experimental Psychology*, L (1955), 325–338.

7. Saffir, M. "A Comparative Study of Scales Constructed by Three Psychophysical Methods." *Psychometrika*, II (1937), 179–198.

8. Torgerson, W. S. "A Law of Categorical Judgment." *Consumer Behavior*. New York: New York University Press, (in press).

12. Stability Characteristics
of the Semantic Differential

Warren T. Norman

The semantic differential is a rating procedure introduced by Osgood for the measurement of meaning.[1] It involves a set of 7-point scales terminating in bipolar adjectives, such as *good-bad*. Ss are asked to rate each concept on the entire set of scales, and the rating profile which results is said to indicate the 'meaning' of the concept. Osgood and Suci have proposed that the statistic D may be used as a measure of the degree of meaningful similarity between any two concepts so rated.[2] On the assumption that the scales are mutually orthogonal, with a common unit and zero-point, the scale-values are treated as coördinates of a point representing the concept in the space defined by the scales; the degree of similarity between a pair of concepts is inversely proportional to the distance between them. To facilitate studies of verbal behavior with this technique, an atlas of semantic-differential profiles on a set of 360 concepts has been constructed.[3] Data on interrelationships among the 360 words, including a set of 64,620 D-values, also are available.[4] The present study is concerned with the stability of the semantic differential over time and Ss.

Method. The original set of 360 words for the Atlas had been grouped into sets of 20 for purposes of reducing the amount of time required for each S. Hence, 18 groups of 30 Ss (15 men and 15 women) were used in collecting the data. To study the various kinds of time-lapse stability and the effect of sampling variability, 30 comparable Ss, drawn from the same population, were asked to rate a single set of 20 concepts chosen at random from the 18 original Atlas-sets. Instructions, forms, and scales identical to those used in the Atlas-study were employed. After a period of four weeks. the Ss performed the same task again. The choice of a complete set from the Atlas-study rather than a sampling of individual concepts permitted a determination of S-sampling variability in ratings and D-values with the effects due to concepts and scales held constant.

While the coefficient of correlation is the traditional index of stability, it is not always an appropriate or a meaningful one. For certain purposes, a percentage-index may be more instructive (and sobering). Consider the distribution of the ratings of the first-administration of the set of 20 concepts, on the 20 scales of the semantic

---

Reprinted from *American Journal of Psychology* (1959), 72: 581–584, by permission of the author and the publisher.

[1] C. E. Osgood, The nature and measurement of meaning, *Psychol. Bull.*, 49, 1952, 197-237.

[2] C. E. Osgood and G. J. Suci, Factor analysis of meaning, *J. exp. Psychol.*, 50, 1955, 325-338.

[3] J. J. Jenkins, W. A. Russell, and G. J. Suci, An atlas of semantic differential profiles for 360 words, this JOURNAL, 71, 1958, 688-699.

[4] Jenkins, Russell, and Suci, *Table of Distances for the Semantic Differential Atlas,* Technical Report No. 20, ONR contract N8 onr-66216, University of Minnesota. Available on interlibrary loan.

differential. This distribution consists of $30 \times 20 \times 20 = 12,000$ values between *one* and *seven*. The greatest change that an initial rating of *one* (or *seven*) could show in a second administration would be six, *i.e.* it could move to the other extreme of the scale. Similarly, initial ratings of *two* (or *six*) could show shifts no greater than five points, and so forth. With a change in a given rating of one scale-unit defined as a *unit-discrepancy,* one may compute the maximal number of unit-discrepancies possible in a second administration by multiplying the number of initial ratings at each scale-position by the maximal shift possible and summing these products over all seven categories. The number of unit-discrepancies actually appearing in a second administration may be expressed as a proportion of the maximum (% *MUD*). Such an index provides some information that the coefficient of correlation does not, if indeed the later is at all useful in this setting.

The expected rather then maximal number might, of course, be chosen as a denominator for an index of this kind, on the assumption that, under random marking of the scales on a second administration, a shift of any magnitude is equally likely. The resulting indices would be twice as large numerically as the % *MUD*-values but perfectly correlated with them in a linear manner.

Another easily interpreted stability-metric is the *same-word D-value.*[5] Given the profiles of a concept based on average ratings by two different groups or by the same group on two occasions, the *D*-values that can be computed between these pairs of profiles provide lower bounds on the interpretability of between-word *D*s. In many situations, it is more important to know that *D*s of a given value may be generated by the profiles of the same words rated by the same group of *S*s on two different occasions than to know the correlation between the two series of mean scale-values.

Each major 'factor' or 'dimension of meaning' is represented by two or more scales in the total set of 20. To offset possible effects due to response-position biases, some of the scales within each subset had been reversed systematically (*i.e.* the labels identifying the ends of the scales had been interchanged). To obtain 'factor-scores' (unit-weighted sums of the ratings on scales within each subset), those scales which had been reversed were first complemented.

Results: (1) Consistency of individual ratings. For the two complete sets of ratings, the '% *MUD*' was 23. About 40% of the ratings remained the same; 35% shifted by one unit; and 25% changed by two or more units on these 7-point scales. The average shift was slightly greater than one position ($12,799/12,000 = 1.07$). There was no evidence of a marked sex-difference in over-all consistency.

To determine whether consistency varied markedly from concept to concept, from *S* to *S*, or from scale to scale, separate analyses were performed. Separate analyses also were made for men and women on the concept and scale-consistency breakdowns.

The range of '% *MUD*-values' for concept-consistency for men and women was about the same (18-29). The average shift in ratings from the first to the second test varied from 0.92 (*leper* and *tornado*) to 1.28 (*stars*) scale-units. (The maximum for such an average shift lies between 3.0 and 6.0, depending on the distribution of initial ratings.) The median corresponding *r* was 0.66 and the values ranged from 0.38 to 0.77.[6]

---

[5] This measure was suggested by J. J. Jenkins (personal communication).

[6] All correlations reported are Pearson product-moment coefficients.

The range of the indices for person-consistencies was 17–29% for the men and 18–34% for the women. The average shift in ratings ranged from 0.65–1.76 scale-units. Definite response-tendencies seem to characterize certain of these Ss' ratings. For instance, the one woman with the highest percentage-index had an initial rating distribution in which there were no responses in the middle category. Her rather high general level of inconsistency may have resulted from this flip-flip response-set. What seemed at first to be a tendency by the women to use the extremes more often did not stand up when the ratings of the Atlas-group on the same words were plotted.

The data on scale-consistency also indicate little sex-difference in variability. In the pooled results for men and women, the average shifts in ratings varied from 0.81–1.41 scale-units. The least consistent scale for the set of words used was *curved-straight*. The coefficient of correlation corresponding to this scale's combined percentage-index of 29.7 was 0.44. The most consistent scale was *beautiful-ugly*,

TABLE I

CONSISTENCY-INDICES FOR FACTORS

Factor	No. of scales	Percentage MUD		r	
		Men	Women	Men	Women
Evaluation	8	13.6	14.3	0.79	0.79
Potency	3	16.9	16.1	0.77	0.75
Activity	3	16.7	19.0	0.82	0.78
Tautness	2	22.4	26.6	0.54	0.52
Novelty	2	25.4	23.1	0.37	0.59
Receptivity	2	19.5	20.6	0.69	0.67

which had a stability-coefficient of 0.76 and a percentage-index of 17.1. The scale-consistencies (% MUD) for men and those for women correlated 0.92, as compared to a corresponding coefficient of 0.67 for concept-consistencies.

(2) Consistency of factor-scores. Osgood, taking cognizance of the general in-stability of the ratings on the separate scales, has suggested that factor-scores rather than single-scale values be used in work with a single S.[7] Accordingly, the data from the test-retest study were processed to yield two-scale, three-scale, and eight-scale factor-scores for the various combinations of scales included in the total set of 20 employed. The scales for each factor were chosen on the basis of previous factor-analyses done at Illinois. A factor-score was formed by unit-weighting those scales which had been included to represent the given factor. Percentage-indices and corre-sponding coefficients of correlation are given in Table I.

The moderate increases in consistency reflected by the percentage-indices and coefficients of Table I for two-, three-, and eight-scale factors partly justify Os-good's recommendation. It should be noted, however, that the increases in stability are not very large. The two-scale factors are hardly more stable than are the separate scales. The three-scale factors are about as stable as the best single scales. On the eight-scale factor, we still may expect about 14% MUD over a four-week interval without specific treatments. The picture is much the same when viewed in terms

---

[7] Personal communication.

of the correlational measures. The one factor represented by eight scales has test-retest correlations of less than 0.80. That is, more than 35% of the variance in the second administration is unaccountable in terms of the first set of ratings. It appears, therefore, that the practice of computing factor-scores, especially for factors represented only by a few scales, is not likely to be a fruitful one.

(3) Stability of individual semantic spaces. The low degree of stability of the individual ratings suggests that distance-functions for single Ss based on these ratings also might show low time-lapse stabilities. To avoid excessive computation, only the ratings of the most consistent and the least consistent Ss were analyzed. The complete set of 190 inter-word Ds on each administration plus the 20 same-word Ds across the two testings were computed for each of these Ss. Even for the most consistent S, the test-retest stability of the distance-function ($r = 0.37$) was not within the acceptable range. The r for the second (least consistent) S was 0.16. When same-word Ds range as high as 17.1 with an average of 11.5, as they did for this S, interpretations based on single administrations seem unjustifiable.

(4) Group-mean D-values and group-mean ratings. The correlation between the set of 190 group-Ds from the first administration with those from the second was 0.97; that between the set of Ds based on the Atlas-study with those of the first administration of the present investigation (*i.e.* when a different group of Ss was involved) was 0.92. It would appear, therefore, that a rather high degree of time-lapse and sampling stability exists for the semantic differential for groups of Ss from an undergraduate population. If one correlates the mean scale-values upon which the above Ds were based, similar results are obtained. The two series of 400 pairs (20 scales $\times$ 20 concepts) of mean scale-values yielded coefficients of 0.96 and 0.94, respectively.

(5) Same-word group D-values. When D-values for each word from first to second administrations were computed, the 20 values ranged from 1.07-2.04. The range of values for the first administration vs. the Atlas was 1.28-2.92. Hence if one is interested in interpreting group-Ds (or differences in D) based on multiple testings of the same Ss, values or changes in value less than 2.0 should not be taken very seriously. If the samples change also, then perhaps values of 3.0 or less may represent nothing more than accumulated error over the 20 scales.

The group-mean ratings and Ds therefore show very high stability over time in absence of any systematic intervening treatment. Hence, experiments aimed at restructuring 'semantic spaces' are feasible if a large enough number of Ss is employed.

13. Social Desirability
and the Semantic Differential

LeRoy H. Ford, Jr., and Murray Meisels

THE primary purpose of the present study was to investigate the degree of correspondence between the social desirability variable (Edwards 1957), long viewed as an important factor in personality self-description, and the evaluative dimension (Osgood, Suci, and Tannenbaum, 1957), which consistently emerges as a major factor in semantic differential judgments. The social desirability variable and the evaluative dimension are each receiving considerable attention in the current psychological literature, and each occupies a prominent position in an increasingly large network of empirical data. On the face of it, the two dimensions seem very much alike; each refers to a "good-bad" continuum, and each is regarded as the major source of variation in an important realm of behavior. Yet the two areas of research have developed and continue to flourish quite independently of one another. A few writers (e.g., Feldman and Corah, 1960; Messick, 1960; Zax, Cowen, and Peter, 1963) have indicated an awareness of the similarity between the two dimensions, but their relationship has not been investigated empirically, and no systematic attempt has been made to integrate the data or theoretical formulations associated with them.

The concept of social desirability has been used to refer to: (a) the rated social desirability value of descriptive statements, such as those found in personality and attitude questionnaires; and (b) the differential tendency of individuals or groups to respond to questionnaires or other stimulus situations in a socially desirable manner. The concept of an evaluative dimension has been used to refer to: (a) the evaluative quality or "evaluativeness" of the descriptive bipolar scales of the semantic differential, as indexed by the scales' loadings on the evaluative factor; and (b) the evaluative aspect of "meaningful human judgments," i.e., the use of evaluation, by individuals or groups, in the judgment of stimulus objects and events. Thus both concepts have been used in two senses: to refer to (a) a

Reprinted from *Educational and Psychological Measurement* (1965), 24: 465–475, by permission of the authors and the publisher.

characteristic of items or scales and (b) a characteristic of individual or group behavior. The present investigation is most directly concerned with the relationship between the social desirability value and evaluativeness of descriptive items or scales, but the study also relates to the variables of social desirability and evaluation as characteristics of human behavior.

That the concepts of social desirability value and evaluativeness are qualitatively similar is suggested by a brief comparison of their content. In social desirability research, personality and attitude statements with high social desirability values are those judged to reflect socially accepted or approved, i.e., "good" characteristics, while items with low values are those judged to reflect socially disapproved, negatively sanctioned, or "bad" characteristics. In semantic differential research, highly evaluative scales are those with high loadings on the evaluative factor; examples are *good-bad, kind-cruel,* and *beautiful-ugly.* The social desirability of goodness, kindness, and beauty, and the social undesirability of their opposites seems apparent. Similarly, scales such as *fast-slow* and *thick-thin,* which are evaluatively neutral, also appear to be relatively neutral with respect to social desirability.

For the purposes of this study, the social desirability value of a given bipolar scale was defined as the discrepancy between the mean social desirability ratings of its separate adjectives. The indices of evaluativeness were the evaluative factor loadings and dimension coordinates of the scales (Osgood et al., 1957). It was hypothesized that the concepts of social desirability and evaluativeness are highly similar and that, therefore, high correlations will obtain among the social desirability values, evaluative factor loadings, and evaluative dimension coordinates of the scales. The relationship of social desirability to two other major "dimensions of meaning," potency and activity (Osgood et al., 1957), was also investigated. Since evaluation is largely independent of potency and activity (Osgood et al., 1957), it was predicted that the social desirability values would also be relatively independent of the potency and activity factor loadings and dimension coordinates.

Method

The 50 bipolar scales used by Osgood and his associates in their first two factor analytic studies of the semantic differential (Osgood et al., 1957, pp. 33–46) were chosen as the sample of scales for this study because indices of their evaluativeness were readily available.

Social desirability values were obtained for these scales by two different methods (see below), using two different samples of judges. All judges were undergraduate psychology students at the State University of New York at Buffalo. The first set of social desirability values was obtained from 47 judges, 28 male and 19 female; the second set was obtained from 39 judges, 18 male and 21 female. The two sets of values were then correlated with the evaluative, potency, and activity factor loadings and dimension coordinates of the scales as reported by Osgood and his associates (1957, pp. 37 and 43).

Since there is ample evidence that the factor structure of the semantic differential scales is a function of the concept judged (Osgood, 1962; Osgood et al., 1957), it seemed important to have the social desirability ratings made with respect to a concept which was as representative as possible of the concepts used in obtaining the factor loadings. An inspection of the 20 concepts used by Osgood and his co-workers showed that nine (LADY, FATHER, RUSSIAN, ME, BABY, GOD, PATRIOT, MOTHER, and COP) were person or person-like concepts; no category as large or homogeneous as this was apparent in the remaining eleven concepts (BOULDER, SIN, LAKE, SYMPHONY, FEATHER, FIRE, FRAUD, TORNADO, SWORD, STATUE, AMERICA). Accordingly, the social desirability rating instructions specified the concept "people" as the object of description, and the judges were asked to rate the desirability or undesirability of the adjectives as "human characteristics."

Social Desirability Ratings: Method I

The judges in the first group were each given a mimeographed booklet in which they were to enter their ratings of the adjectives. The instructions and example shown in Table 1 appeared on the first page of the booklet. These were followed by explanations of the example and some repetition of essential points which, to conserve space, are not given here.[3] On the remaining pages of the booklet, the 50 pairs of adjectives were presented, in the manner illustrated in Table 1, with single spacing within pairs and double spacing between pairs. The words designating the nine-point social desirability continuum appeared at the top of each page.

It can be seen that in these social desirability judgments, the two adjectives of each bipolar scale were rated as separate items,

---

[3] A copy of the complete booklet may be obtained from the first author.

TABLE 1

First Part of Social Desirability Rating Instructions: Method I

On the following pages are a number of adjectives that might be used in describing people. The adjectives are grouped in pairs, with the two adjectives in each pair referring to more or less opposite human characteristics. For each adjective, you are asked to rate, on a scale ranging from "extremely undesirable" to "extremely desirable," how *desirable* or *praiseworthy* you think that characteristic would be considered *from the point of view of our society.*

Record your decision for each adjective by putting a mark (X) on the line next to that adjective at the point that best indicates its desirability or undesirability.

An example of how one person rated the adjectives "intelligent" and "stupid" is given below:

	UNDESIRABLE							DESIRABLE
	Extreme	Strong	Moderate	Mild	Neutral	Mild	Moderate	Strong	Extreme
INTELLIGENT								X	
STUPID		X							

Note. The complete instructions may be obtained from the first author.

whereas, in the semantic differential format, the judges respond to the two adjectives as a bipolar unit. It was in order to preserve, as much as possible, the meaning conferred on the separate adjectives by this bipolar context, that the adjectives were grouped in pairs. In order to further emphasize this point, the instructions for the social desirability ratings specified that the adjectives were "grouped in pairs" and that the two members of each pair referred to "more or less opposite" characteristics.

The judges' ratings were scored on a nine-point scale, ranging from one for "extremely undesirable" to nine for "extremely desirable." For each adjective pair (bipolar scale), the mean rating for each member of the pair, and the difference between the two mean ratings, was determined. This latter value, the difference between the mean ratings of the separate adjectives of a given bipolar scale, was taken as the social desirability value of the scale; and the adjective with the higher (more desirable) mean rating was treated as the positive pole of the scale.

Social Desirability Ratings: Method II

Another difference between presenting the paired adjectives as separate items and presenting them as opposite poles of a single scale is in the degree to which the judge can treat the two adjectives of a given bipolar scale as independent of one another if he wishes to do so. In the social desirability rating method described in the pre-

Results

The product-moment correlations among the two sets of social desirability values (Method I and Method II) and the evaluative, potency, and activity factor loadings and dimension coordinates are presented in Table 2. The results are given for the combined sexes ceding section (Method I), a judge's rating of one member of an adjective pair is free to vary independently of his rating of the other member of the pair. In the semantic differential method, however, the judge is forced to treat the two adjectives of a given scale as polar opposites. It seemed possible that this difference between the social desirability and semantic differential rating formats might introduce a source of "method" variance which could function to lower the obtained correlation between the social desirability values and the indices of evaluativeness.

As a check against this possibility, a second rating method was devised which, following the semantic differential format more closely, placed the two adjectives of each pair at opposite ends of a single graphic scale. The nine scale points ranged from "extremely desirable" at the left, through "neither is more desirable" in the middle, to "extremely desirable" at the right. Thus the subject could indicate that neither of the adjectives was the more desirable, or he could assign one of four degrees of desirability (mild, moderate, strong, or extreme) to one adjective or the other. The instructions and procedure were otherwise the same as those of Method I except for minor modifications dictated by the bipolar format.[4]

A new sample of 18 male and 21 female judges rated the 50 bipolar scales using the new method. The ratings were scored on a five-point scale ranging from zero for "neither is more desirable" to four for "extremely desirable." For each pair of adjectives, the sum, across judges, of the ratings assigned to each separate adjective was computed, thus taking into account the number of judges who rated that adjective more desirable than the other member of the pair and also the degree of its rated desirability. The difference between the two sums was then divided by the number of judges to yield a mean social desirability value for the pair of adjectives as a bipolar unit. For each adjective pair, the desirable or evaluatively positive pole was taken to be the adjective with the greater summed rating.

[4] A copy of the complete booklet used in Method II may be obtained from the first author.

TABLE 2

Correlations among Social Desirability Values (SDV) and Evaluative, Potency, and Activity Factor Loadings and Dimension Coordinates

	SDV Method II	Eval. load.	Eval. coord.	Pot. load.	Pot. coord.	Act. load.	Act. coord.
SDV Method I	.99	.92	.88	.15	−.02	.16	.03
SDV Method II		.92	.88	.14	−.04	.17	.06
Eval. load.			.97	.14	−.06	.13	.02
Eval. coord.				.22	.02	.14	.04

Note: $N = 50$, $p < .05$ when $r = .28$, $p < .01$ when $r = .36$.

since the correlations for males and females separately were virtually identical. It will be noted that the social desirability values obtained by the two different methods correlate almost perfectly with one another and show almost identical patterns of correlation with the other variables. It appears, therefore, that the differences in the methods made no appreciable difference in the results. The second method does, however, represent a replication on an independent sample of judges and thus provides evidence for the reliability of the results obtained with the first method. It can be seen from Table 2 that each of the two sets of social desirability values correlates .92 with the evaluative factor loadings and .88 with the evaluative dimension coordinates, and that all four of these indices are very nearly equivalent in their correlations with the potency and activity factor loadings and dimension coordinates. Thus the results lend strong support to the hypotheses under investigation.

An analysis was also made of the social desirability values obtained by Method I for the separate poles of the bipolar scales. The correlation between these two sets of values was −.97 for the combined group of males and females. As might be expected from this finding, the relationship of each of these sets of single-pole values to the evaluative, potency, and activity factor loadings and dimension coordinates was virtually identical to the results obtained with the bipolar values of both Method I and Method II as presented in Table 2.

Discussion

The results of the present study indicate that a large portion of the variance in the evaluative factor loadings and dimension coordinates of the semantic differential scales is predictable from their social desirability scale values, and that the evaluative and social desirability dimensions are both independent of the potency and activity dimensions. Thus the concepts of social desirability value and evaluativeness, as applied to descriptive statements, are highly comparable, if not identical. Although the finding of a substantial degree of correspondence was expected, the magnitude of the relationship was somewhat surprising, at least to the authors, in view of the fact that the evaluative factor loadings represent the result of a complex statistical analysis based on the intercorrelations among judgments on the 50 adjectival scales across 20 diverse concepts, whereas the social desirability values were obtained by a simple and direct rating of the paired adjectives.

Since the several factor loadings and dimension coordinates were based on data obtained from Illinois undergraduates (Osgood et al., 1957), whereas the social desirability values were obtained about eight years later using two independent samples of Buffalo undergraduates, it seems likely that these findings have some generality, at least among college students.

Implications for Theory and Research

In view of the current popularity of both social desirability and semantic differential research, and since even a casual comparison of the two areas would suggest some degree of overlap, it is surprising that the possibility of such overlap has thus far received little attention. Perhaps this is because investigators in the two fields have for the most part addressed themselves to rather different problems. Nevertheless, it should be profitable to examine the research and theory in each of these areas from the vantage point of the other; and the possibility arises that two now relatively discrete but increasingly extensive bodies of knowledge may lend themselves to fruitful integration.

In considering the implications of semantic differential research and theory for the social desirability area, it is pertinent to ask whether the usual interpretation of evaluation as a dimension of "meaning" or "meaningful human judgments" (Osgood et al., 1957) is also applicable to the social desirability variable in personality self-descriptions. A comparison of the instruments most commonly used in assessing these two dimensions, the semantic differential in the case of evaluation, and the personality questionnaire in the case of social desirability, suggests that both instruments tap quite similar behavioral processes. Semantic differential scales and personality questionnaire items are both meaningful verbal stimuli, presented in written form, and used to elicit a set of descriptive or judgmental responses. Just as the semantic differential rater's task is one of making judgments of an explicitly designated concept against a series of descriptive scales, the personality questionnaire respondent's task may be viewed as one of judging an implicit concept such as ME against a series of descriptive statements. Thus, although the two methods differ in format, the responses to both may be regarded as reflecting similar judgmental processes. Therefore, if the semantic differential measures "meaning," so too does the questionnaire; and if evaluation is a dimension of "meaningful human judgments," so too is social desirability.

From this point of view, in spite of the superficial differences between semantic differential scales and questionnaire items, there seems to be no incompatibility in ordering them both to a common evaluative dimension. If, as the combined evidence from social desirability and semantic differential research suggests, evaluation (or, perhaps, "social evaluation") is the major dimension characterizing the realm of descriptive or judgmental statements in general, then the social desirability variable in *self*-descriptive statements may be treated as a special case of this more general dimension. If one wishes to follow Osgood's definition of evaluation as the attitudinal dimension of judgment (Osgood et al., 1957), the social desirability of a questionnaire item or semantic differential scale may be viewed as an index of the cultural "attitude" toward the characteristic referred to by the item or scale; and an individual's endorsement or rejection of a particular characteristic may be taken as one aspect of his "self-attitude."

One implication of the foregoing considerations is that responses to questionnaires and other personality assessment devices may be assumed to tap the same kind of representational mediation process that is hypothesized (Osgood et al., 1957) to underlie semantic differential judgments. A second, related, implication is that the representational model proposed as a link between semantic differential measurement and learning theory (Osgood et al., 1957) may also provide a basis for coordinating personality measurement with learning theory.

Turning attention now to some implications of the social desirability area for work with the semantic differential, it seems likely that many of the results of social desirability research should be applicable to the evaluative variable in semantic differential research.

Much of the research in the social desirability area has been concerned with the extent to which individuals describe themselves in accord with perceived social desirability stereotypes rather than giving a "true" description of their feelings and behaviors. It is now well established that personality questionnaires are sensitive to social desirability response "bias," i.e., the tendency to describe oneself in a socially desirable manner (Edwards, 1957). There is also evidence that the magnitude of this effect increases as the social desirability values of the items increase (Edwards and Walsh, 1963). Mention may also be made of the frequently replicated finding (Edwards, 1957) that the group frequency of endorsement of personality questionnaire items is highly correlated with the social desirability values of the items.

The self-descriptive behavior which has provided the data for the studies referred to above has its most direct semantic differential parallel in subjects' judgments of "self" concepts such as ME, MY ACTUAL SELF, and MY IDEAL SELF. And it is in such semantic differential ratings that the various social desirability phenomena would, presumably, be most likely to appear. Thus, one would expect to find that the tendency to evaluate "self" concepts positively is, in part, a function of the social desirability response tendency as measured by one of the usual social desirability scales (e.g., Crowne and Marlowe, 1960; Edwards, 1957). One would also expect the strength of this relationship to be a function of the social desirability values and evaluative loadings of the bipolar scales against which the judgments are made. And, finally, one would expect both the group frequencies of positive self-evaluation on semantic differential scales, and the mean evaluative scores on the scales, to be highly correlated with the social desirability values and evaluative loadings of the scales.

Although the main body of social desirability research has dealt with personality measurement techniques, there is evidence that the various findings are not confined to trait-descriptive statements or to self-descriptive behavior but extend to attitudinal statements and descriptions of others (Edwards, 1959; Taylor, 1961). Thus there is evidence to suggest that the above hypothesized relationships of social desirability scale values and response bias to semantic differential judgments of "self" concepts may hold for judgments of "other" concepts as well, and the possibility arises that they may also extend to judgments of "non-person" concepts such as, for example, BOULDER, SYMPHONY, or DAWN. In this connection, at least two possibilities seem worth investigating. One is that a highly generalized social desirability tendency, differing among individuals, may be evident across all objects, or a broad class of objects, including the self, other persons, and non-person objects. A second possibility is that an equally general "Pollyanna bias" may occur, i.e., a tendency, differing among individuals, to describe objects favorably or unfavorably, irrespective of the *socially* desirable direction of description. This latter tendency would be confounded with the social desirability tendency when only favorable objects (including the self and desirable others) are judged; but its occurrence can be determined if socially undesirable objects of judgment are also presented. For this reason, the semantic differential lends itself to the investigation of a personality characteristic which may be confounded in most of the studies to date on social desirability as a response style or personality variable.

Summary

The rated social desirability values of 50 semantic differential bipolar scales were found to be highly correlated with the evaluative factor loadings and dimension coordinates of the scales, and to be largely independent of their activity and potency factor loadings and dimension coordinates. The results indicate that the concepts of social desirability value, as applied to personality questionnaire items, and evaluativeness, as applied to semantic differential scales, are highly comparable, if not identical. Although the possibility has not yet received widespread attention, the research and theory relating to each of these concepts should have many implications for the other. A few of these implications were discussed.

REFERENCES

Crowne, D. P. and Marlowe, D. "A New Scale of Social Desirability Independent of Psychopathology." *Journal of Consulting Psychology*, XXIV (1960), 349–354.

Edwards, A. L. *The Social Desirability Variable in Personality Assessment and Research.* New York: Dryden, 1957.

Edwards, A. L. "Social Desirability and the Description of Others." *Journal of Abnormal and Social Psychology*, LIX (1959), 434–436.

Edwards, A. L. and Walsh, J. A. "The Relationship between the Intensity of the Social Desirability Keying of a Scale and the Correlation of the Scale with Edwards' *SD* Scale and the First Factor Loading of the Scale." *Journal of Clinical Psychology*, XIX (1963), 200–203.

Feldman, M. J. and Corah, N. L. "Social Desirability and the Forced Choice Method." *Journal of Consulting Psychology*, XXIV (1960), 480–482.

Messick, S. "Dimensions of Social Desirability." *Journal of Consulting Psychology*, XXIV (1960), 279–287.

Osgood, C. E. "Studies on the Generality of Affective Meaning Systems." *American Psychologist*, XVII (1962), 10–28.

Osgood, C. E., Suci, G. J., and Tannenbaum, P. H. *The Measurement of Meaning*. Urbana: University of Illinois Press, 1957.

Taylor, J. B. "What Do Attitude Scales Measure: The Problem of Social Desirability." *Journal of Abnormal and Social Psychology*, LXII (1961), 386–390.

Zax, M., Cowen, E. L., and Peter, Sister Mary. "A Comparative Study of Novice Nuns and College Females Using the Response Set Approach." *Journal of Abnormal and Social Psychology*, LXVI (1963), 369–375.

14. Dimensions of Semantic Space: A Problem of Individual Differences

Nancy Wiggins and Martin Fishbein

The generality of affective meaning systems, both intra-culturally and cross-culturally, has been attested to by a wide variety of studies utilizing, primarily, the Semantic Differential (Jakobovits, 1966; Osgood, 1960, 1962, 1964; Osgood, Suci, and Tannenbaum, 1957; Tanaka, 1962; Tanaka and Osgood, 1965; Tanaka, Oyama, and Osgood, 1963; Triandis and Osgood, 1958). The three pervasive affective meaning dimensions, *E, P,* and *A* (Evaluation, Potency, and Activity), have emerged across 24 language/culture communities (Jakobovits, 1966) and have tended to be invariant within the American culture with respect to various personological and demographic variables (Block, cited in Osgood *et al.,* 1957, p. 170; Bopp, 1955; McClelland, Whitaker, and First, cited in Osgood, 1962; Osgood and Luria, 1954; Suci, 1960; Ware, 1958).

Recently, the scope and generality of *E, P,* and *A* have been extended beyond language/culture comparisons to include studies involving the dimensions underlying personality trait ratings. In particular, Peterson (1965) has suggested that the consistently recurring two-dimensional structure of verbally defined personality measures (neuroti-

cism and extraversion) may reflect the semantic differential dimensions, Evaluation and Dynamism (Activity and Potency combined), respectively. Hallworth (1965a, 1965b) has partially documented this supposition by showing evaluative scales to mark the first factor underlying personality trait ratings, activity scales the second trait-rating factor, and potency, the fourth factor (the third factor was called "masculinity"). In the realm of self-report inventories, Edwards' sweeping social desirability dimension (1957) might well be conceptualized as a special case of Osgood's evaluative dimension (Ford and Meisels, 1965, Hallworth, 1965b). Although personality theorists might be reluctant at this time to accept a view of personality solely as a linguistic concept, the data do suggest that at least verbally defined tests of personality are heavily saturated with dimensions of meaning.

However, despite the general findings of intra- and inter cultural comparability of semantic dimensions and their extension into the personality realm, a few exceptions to the usual lack of individual differences in meaning structure have been noted (Krieger, 1964; Suci, 1960; Tanaka and Osgood, 1965; Tanaka *et al.,* 1963). The major purpose of this paper is to point out that individual differences in semantic structure do indeed exist. Specifically, we propose that the adjectival scales that serve as valid indicants of a meaning dimension for one individual may be inappropriate as indicants of the same dimension for another individual. We are not here arguing the question of whether there is a common, underlying reference framework, but rather whether

This paper was prepared especially for this volume. The research was supported in part by the University of Illinois Research Board (Grant #41-32-66-392) and by the Institute of Communications Research, University of Illinois. The authors wish to express their appreciation to Professors C. E. Osgood and J. S. Wiggins for their critical reviews of an earlier draft of this manuscript. We are further indebted to Professor Osgood for his continual support and encouragement throughout this project although our views often conflicted with his. We also are grateful to Theresa Spiegel for her help with the extensive data analysis. Portions of this paper were presented at the 39th annual meeting of the Midwestern Psychological Association, 1967.

there is a single universal set of indicants for this underlying framework within or across given population groupings. That the semantic structure of adjectival scales will change as a function of different concept classes has been well documented (Osgood *et al.,* 1957; Tanaka *et al.,* 1963; Tanaka and Osgood, 1965) and is not at issue; what is being questioned is the lack of individual differences in scale structure across concepts.

APPROACHES TO THE PROBLEM OF INDIVIDUAL DIFFERENCES IN SEMANTIC STRUCTURE

One possible approach to the problem of determining the extent of individual differences in semantic structure would be to perform an obverse factor analysis on the intercorrelations among individuals to determine the number of subject factors. Should the number of subject factors be one, the population semantic structure could be said to give an adequate representation of the intra-individual semantic structure. This would not be the case if the number of subject factors were greater than one. This type of approach was taken by Levine (1965), who performed a three-dimensional factor analysis (Tucker, 1966) on a cube of semantic differential data. Although Levine claimed only one subject factor, examination of the distribution of eigenvalues from the subject-mode reveals the distinct possibility of two subject factors (Levine, 1965, p. 446). This interpretation is supported in an unpublished study (Litt, 1966) in which a three-mode factor analysis of the semantic differential cube yielded three subject factors. Similarly, Snyder (1967) re-analyzed Osgood *et al.*'s (1957) original *Thesaurus* data; a three-mode factor analysis revealed the possibility of two subject factors. One major difference among these studies was that Litt's concepts were abstract drawings whereas in the other two studies the concepts were simple nouns, many of which had direct physical referents

(e.g., chair). It may be the case that the number of subject factors obtained is a function of the type of concept judged. Thus, from this limited data it might be inferred that the more abstract the concept class, the greater the number of subject factors.

The general approach taken in the comparison of semantic structure has been that of factor matching across studies involving translation-equivalent scales. Recognizing the methodological difficulties inherent in cross-cultural factor comparisons, Osgood (personal communication) has recently devised a procedure whereby semantic scales from different cultures are embedded in the same factor space. Utilizing 100 translation-equivalent concepts, and 50 culturally indigenous semantic scales, a data cube was generated in each of 24 cultures. After collapsing the subject mode by obtaining subject means for each concept-scale judgment, all scales for all cultures were intercorrelated across the 100 concepts. These intercorrelations were then subjected to a principal components analysis. Thus far, nineteen cultures have been included in this "pan-cultural" factor analysis and the results indicate a large first factor (32 per cent of the total variance) called *E,* with two additional smaller factors, *P* (7 per cent of total variance) and *A* (5 per cent of total variance). Of interest was the fact that each of these factors included defining scales from all of the cultures.

Of more importance is the question as to what this pan-cultural factor structure represents. Since subject means are utilized and since both scale and concept means are removed in standardizing the scores by both scale and concept, what remains is a data matrix whose major sources of variability have been removed. The structure of such a matrix is quite remote from the semantic structure for a given individual or individuals; in fact, the pan-cultural factor structure represents the intra-individual structure for the average, pan-cultural subject. It must be demonstrated that this pan-cultural structure is representative of (a) intra-cultural structure and (b) semantic structure of people within the culture, if such a structure is to measure how people use words.

The major issue here is whether the average semantic structure (either pan-cultural or intra-cultural) is the best representation of the semantic structure for individuals within the culture. One indirect line of reasoning suggests that the semantic structure for Evaluation, at least, would be a function of consistent individual differences. If one accepts the inference that social desirability ratings of self-report questionnaire items is a construct similar to Evaluation (Ford and Meisels, 1965), then lack of inter-individual generality for social desirability would reflect on a possible lack of generality for *E*. Although a number of writers have claimed that social desirability, as operationally defined in terms of Edwards' rating procedure (1957), is invariant with respect to individual differences, recent writers have argued that social desirability itself is a multidimensional construct, with respect both to individuals and to stimuli judged (Messick, 1960; Wiggins, 1966). To the extent that social desirability is similar to *E,* it is argued that the average semantic structure of *E* may not be representative of the individuals comprising the average. This could be demonstrated by showing the existence of systematic individual differences in the perception of Evaluation.

An Empirical Test for Individual Differences in Semantic Structure

To test the major hypothesis that individual differences do exist with respect to the underlying semantic structure of the semantic differential scales, a procedure was developed that was concept-free and allowed (but did not force) the possibility of multidimensionality to emerge with respect both to semantic differential scales and to individuals. The procedure was similar to Osgood *et al.*'s (1957, p. 39), in which sub-

jects matched polar terms from semantic differential *scales* in a paired-comparison judgment. The present procedure differed from Osgood's in that a distance metric between two scales was directly obtained from the subjects. Thus, 105 similarity ratings were obtained between all possible pairs of 15 semantic differential scales. Five of the stimulus scales had previously emerged in a variety of studies as markers of *E* (Osgood *et al.,* 1957); five were markers of *P* and five of *A.* The subjects' (97 male and female college sophomores) task was to indicate the extent of similarity between two bipolar scales on a 7-point similarity rating scale. In addition, the subject indicated which scale poles were similar (where a rating other than zero similarity had been given). Thus, although two scales (good–bad and active–passive) might be judged slightly similar in meaning, good could be conceptualized as related to either active or passive. It is noted that the similarity rating scale was bipolar and as such would allow for both positive as well as negative correlations between the two "positive" poles of the scales. Although for each item, positive poles were presented together, half of the items were reversed so that the "negative" poles appeared first. Two forms of the test were constructed, differing only in that opposite items were reversed for order, thus controlling for an order effect dependent on whether the positive or negative scale poles appeared first. The two sets of tests were randomly distributed to subjects. Since the instructions were complex, subjects were given a page of practice items to insure their understanding of the task and to establish the anchor points of the bipolar similarity rating scale.

The Model

The 105 randomized paired-comparison similarity judgments of scales generated a data matrix consisting of 105 stimulus-pairs $\times$ 97 subjects (the test forms were combined). The Tucker-Messick (1963) multidimensional scaling model was applied to these data in order to allow for multidimensionality with respect to both stimuli (semantic differential scales) and individuals. This model, which has been described in detail elsewhere (Messick and Kogan, 1966; Walters and Jackson, 1966; Wiggins, 1966) involves the following steps: (a) An obverse factor analysis of sums of cross-products among subjects is performed. (Intersubject cross-products are utilized rather than intercorrelations to retain any subject variability on the scale means.) (b) The subject factors are rotated through clusters of response-homogeneous individuals. These rotated factors are called Idealized Individuals. (c) The projections of the 105 stimulus-pairs are obtained on these rotated subject factors. (d) These 105 stimulus-pair projections are interpreted as interstimulus similarities (Pederson, 1962), i.e., "proportional correlations" (Tucker, personal communication). Thus, for each Idealized Individual, his corresponding stimulus-pair projections are assembled into a 15 × 15 interstimulus matrix of correlations. (e) A final factor analysis of this 15 × 15 interstimulus correlation matrix yields the perceived dimensionality of scales for the corresponding Idealized Individual.

In addition to reproducing the perceived dimensionality of the scales for each Idealized Individual, it is also possible to reproduce the dimensionality of these scales based on a "group average" analysis. If the number of subject factors obtained initially was one, it can be concluded that a "group average" analysis would adequately represent the perceptual viewpoints of each of the individuals composing the group. However, if the number of subject factors was greater than one (i.e., more than one Idealized Individual), it would be expected that sufficient inter-individual variability existed such that a "group average" analysis would obscure the perceived dimensionality of the stimuli for many of the real individuals comprising the subject group.

The matrix of cross-products among subjects' similarity judgments was subjected to a principal components analysis. Inspection of the distribution of successive eigenvalues indicated that three factors were sufficient to account for the covariation among subjects. These three subject factors accounted for 73 per cent of the total variance.

Group Average Space

The projections of the 105 stimulus-pairs were obtained on the first of the three unrotated subject factors. These projections were interpreted as "proportional correlations" and were therefore arranged in a 15 × 15 table of interstimulus correlations. The factor analysis of this interstimulus matrix can be directly interpreted as yielding the perceived multidimensional stimulus space for the "group average" (Tucker and Messick, 1963). This 15 × 15 matrix of correlations was subjected to a centroid factor analysis in which communalities were estimated on the basis of the highest correlation in each row of the matrix. Centroid factoring was stopped when the diagonals became negative. Thus the maximum possible variance was extracted. Under this criterion, three factors emerged and were rotated to the varimax (Kaiser, 1958) criterion, an analytic orthogonal solution. Table 1 gives this multidimensional space of the fifteen stimuli for the group average. It should be noted that since the original interstimulus similarities were interpreted as *proportional* to correlations, the resulting factor projections are not correlations between stimuli and factors. Thus, they should be interpreted in terms of their *relative* size. A rigorous criterion for factor naming was adopted. To be called "Evaluative," a factor must have relatively large factor projections on at least four of the five Evaluative scales. In addition, the factor must have essentially zero loadings on all other scales. The same criterion was utilized for *P* and *A*. From Table 1 it is seen that under this criterion, the varimax factors are clearly *E, A,* and

TABLE 1
ROTATED DIMENSIONS OF SEMANTIC
DIFFERENTIAL SCALES FOR GROUP AVERAGE

Scale	Varimax Factor		
	I	II	III
Good–Bad	.49	.05	.01
Fair–Unfair	.37	—.03	.02
Valuable–Worthless	.36	.09	.09
Pleasant–Unpleasant	.43	.01	—.05
Clean–Dirty	.36	.06	—.06
Active–Passive	.09	.43	.15
Fast–Slow	.10	.42	.00
Agitated–Calm	—.23	.44	.02
Hot–Cold	.01	.29	—.03
Sharp–Dull	.18	.27	.04
Strong–Weak	.20	.22	.38
Heavy–Light	—.07	—.13	.44
Large–Small	.03	—.06	.40
Hard–Soft	—.03	.15	.27
Masculine–Feminine	—.03	.10	.43
% Unrotated Total Variance:	40%	31%	23%
% Rotated Common Variance:	37%	32%	31%

P, respectively.

It is clear that this analysis of the group average space yields results that are highly consistent with previous research on the Semantic Differential. When the data are analyzed in a manner that ignores individual differences, strong support is provided for Osgood's three-dimensional view of semantic space. Although *A* emerged as the second factor in the present analysis, whereas in Osgood's data *P* is usually the second factor, this difference may be due, in part, to differences in scale sampling. The clarity of these results indicated that in spite of the complexity of the instructions, the subjects on the average had performed the judgment task demanded of them.

Idealized Individual Viewpoints

Since the number of significant subject factors was three, the results presented above for the group average would not be expected to hold for many of the real subjects in the sample. In order to represent the perceptual viewpoints of response-homogeneous clusters of individuals, the configuration of the subjects in the three-dimensional subject space was examined. The factor plots of the 97 subjects revealed

a circular arrangement of individuals on the second and third principal components (i.e., the second and third unrotated subject factors). To represent this circumplicial arrangement of individuals adequately, ten Idealized Individuals (response-homogeneous subject groups) were located that were related to one another in a circular pattern on the second and third components. These ten vectors were unipolar with respect to the subjects. Thus, in the three-dimensional subject space there were ten vectors circumscribing a cone. For *each* of these ten Idealized Individuals, the 105 stimulus-pair projections were assembled into a 15×15 interstimulus similarity matrix and subjected to a centroid factor analysis and varimax rotation. This procedure was the same as that followed with the group average; centroid factor extraction was stopped when the diagonals became negative. The ten resulting factor matrices were interpreted as representing the multidimensional perceptual viewpoints of the ten Idealized Individuals.

The results indicated that as the Idealized Individuals went around the cone, the number of scale factors went from four to three, to two, back to three, and finally back to four, systematically. For all but one viewpoint, the scale factors explained more than 90 per cent of the total variance. The following rigorous criterion for factor interpretation was adopted: for each Idealized Individual, the "Evaluation" factor was defined as that factor which had the highest factor projections on at least four of the five *E* scales. Then, any other scales that also marked this factor were noted. The same criterion was adopted for Potency and Activity. An exception to this criterion was made for those Idealized Individuals with four scale factors. In these cases *E* or *A* tended to be splintered. Table 2 is a summary of the results for the ten Idealized Individuals in terms of the number of viewpoint dimensions and their substantive characteristics.

A number of conclusions can be drawn

TABLE 2

SOME DIFFERENCES IN AFFECTIVE MEANING FOR TEN IDEALIZED INDIVIDUALS

	Idealized Individuals									
	1	2	3	4	5	6	7	8	9	10
Total Number of Factors:	4	4	3	3	2	3	3	3	4	4
% Total Variance:	95%	98%	90%	96%	76%	97%	99%	96%	97%	95%
Other Markers of E Factor:	Calm	Calm	Calm	Calm Sharp Strong Fast Active	Fast Sharp Active Strong Hot	Strong Active Large Sharp Fast	Sharp Strong	Sharp Strong	Sharp** Strong	Calm**
Other Markers of A Factor:	Hard* Strong Valuable	None*	Small Light	Small Light	No A Factor	Clean Strong	Strong Hard Masculine	Masculine Hard Large	Masculine Hard	Strong Masculine
Splintered or Missing Factors:	Two Activity Factors	Two Activity Factors	None	None	No Activity Factor	None	None	None	Two Eval. Factors	Two Eval. Factors
% Total Variance for Each Factor:	E : 35% P : 32% A_1: 20% A_2: 8%	E : 33% P : 31% A_1: 24% A_2: 10%	E: 32% P: 22% A: 36%	E: 47% P: 18% A: 31%	E: 50% P: 26% No A	E: 57% P: 27% A: 13%	E: 29% P: 14% A: 56%	E: 29% P: 11% A: 55%	E_1: 11% P : 31% A : 32% E_2: 6%	E_1: 39% P : 17% A : 32% E_2: 7%

* Description applies to A_1

** Description applies to E_1

188

on the basis of the data in Table 2. First, it appears that individual differences do exist, both with respect to the number of perceived semantic dimensions and with respect to the substantive interpretation of these dimensions. For example, the usual activity scale, agitated–calm, becomes Evaluation for some of the Idealized Individuals; whereas other activity and potency scales become Evaluation for other Idealized Individuals. It is apparent that the Idealized Individuals vary in the degree to which the evaluative scales dominate the remaining scales. Those Idealized Individuals for whom *E* is predominant may represent real individuals who tend to "over-evaluate" in general. Two of the Idealized Individuals (9 and 10) splintered the evaluative factor. In the case of Idealized Individual 9, the first evaluative factor was defined by Good, Valuable, Pleasant, and Clean, as well as Sharp and Strong. His second *E* factor had high factor projections on Fair, Good, Pleasant, and Calm. Thus, "Fairness" was perceived as being different from "Goodness."

The activity factor also systematically changes in connotation as the circle of Idealized Individuals is traversed. For some Idealized Individuals the connotation of strength ("Strong," "Hard," "Masculine") becomes associated with the activity scales; for other Individuals the activity scales connote agility ("Small," "Light"). One Idealized Individual (5) has no activity factor while two Idealized Individuals (1 and 2) splinter activity into two factors: "Sharp and Fast" *vs.* "Hot and Agitated." As expected, Idealized Individuals who lie close to one another in their circular arrangement also tend to structure semantic scales in a similar fashion.

In addition to substantive differences in semantic structure existing among Idealized Individuals, another important difference emerged: namely, the amount of variance explained by each of the factors in the initial factor extraction. In terms of extracted

variance, the usual ordering of semantic dimensions has been *E, P,* and *A,* respectively. Although some differences in this ordering have been obtained (Tanaka *et al.,* 1963; Tanaka and Osgood, 1965; Tucker, 1955), Osgood and his associates have stressed repeatedly that these differences in factor order are largely a function of the particular concept class. However, the present data which were concept-free suggest that the relative importance of semantic dimensions may also be a function of individual differences.[1]

Not only do the present data suggest individual differences in the perception of semantic structure, but some additional data of the authors indicate that these perceptual differences are themselves related to self-report ratings of personological characteristics. In connection with another project, 82 of the present subjects rated themselves on fifteen 7-point, bipolar rating scales which included personality traits (anxiety, extraversion, affiliation, artistic sensitivity), stylistic dimensions (abstract thinking, creativity), ability dimensions (good *vs.* poor student, mathematical ability), somatic dimensions (tall, heavy, athletic) and some demographic characteristics. In the initial factor analysis of subjects across similarity ratings of semantic differential scales, the three subject

---

1. Osgood (personal communication) has suggested that since no concept class was specified in the present study, Idealized Individuals differed among themselves because they represented real individuals who were utilizing different concept classes. This alternative explanation suggests that the present results only indicate a concept by scale interaction rather than a subject by scale interaction. However, the utilization of a concept free design was based in part on an earlier study by Osgood *et al.* (1957), in which he argued that a concept free method of data collection "eliminates concept differences entirely as a variable" (p. 39). Although at that time he recognized that his technique did not necessarily restrict subjects' concept choice, he reported that "introspectively (and as judged from the comments of subjects) there is usually no particular concept involved" (p. 40). This issue is hardly settled but the means for resolving it are not immediately apparent.

factors (i.e., the projections of individuals on the three subject factors) were treated as independent variables and were utilized to predict each of the above fifteen trait ratings, as well as the speed with which the similarity rating task was performed, a variable calibrated by the experimenter at the time the similarity task was administered. For these outside variables, the following multiple correlations emerged as significant at the .05 level: good *vs.* poor student ratings (R = .33), concrete vs. abstract thinking (R = .30) and speed in completing the rating task (R = .30). At the lowest level of inference these data show that paired-comparison similarity ratings in one verbal task are related to unidimensional self-ratings in another verbally defined task. However, to the extent that the self-ratings are valid, the inference can be made that the manner in which individuals perceive semantic structure is related to other personological variables. Although outside personality variables were not widely sampled and possible method variance contamination was not controlled, the data raise the distinct possibility that perceptions of semantic structure might predict individual differences in personality and stylistic dimensions.

In summary, although an analysis of the group average space provided results that are essentially identical to the findings of Osgood and his associates, subgroups of individuals did perceive semantic space differently, even when these individuals were drawn from a relatively homogeneous population. Not only were individual differences present with respect to the substantive adjective scales defining the obtained semantic dimensions, but, further, the number of dimensions utilized and relative importance placed on these dimensions (in terms of variance accounted for) also varied as a function of individual differences. These data directly supported the major hypothesis that argues against semantic generality across individuals.

DISCUSSION AND IMPLICATIONS

It has been argued that the semantic structure for a group average is not necessarily the best representation of the semantic structure for the individuals comprising the average. Certainly the data here described suggest that scale indicants of *E, P,* and *A* are not substantively similar across individuals. Not only were the particular scales defining semantic dimensions substantively different for individuals, but, even more striking, a scale that served as a factor marker for the group average could mark a totally different factor for a given Idealized Individual. Similarly, in the individual analysis, a scale defining Evaluation for one Idealized Individual could mark Potency for another. Further, while the group average analysis yielded a clear three-factor structure, the analysis of the individuals yielded between two and four factors for which the relative importance placed on these dimensions varied. These results held, although the individuals were relatively homogeneous and the semantic scales utilized in the judgment task were selected as reliable markers of *E, P,* and *A* from numerous previous studies. Thus, if individual differences are found with these purportedly stable, marker scales, it can be inferred that more marked differences would be found for scales whose semantic structure is less clear.

Although the particular task demanded of the subjects departed from the standard semantic differential technique, the instructions were extremely similar to those used by Osgood *et al.* (1957, p. 39) in a validation study of the usual semantic differential methodology. In fact, similar results were obtained in the present study and in Osgood's study when the data were analyzed for the total group of subjects. The differences in results were due to the extension of the present analysis which allowed for the possible emergence of multidimensionality among individuals with regard to their perceptual framework of semantic structure. A simple example can illustrate the importance of a research strategy that maximizes the possibility of obtaining individual differences in this context. When two presumably independent scales are paired, e.g., good–bad and active–passive, the group average correlation between these scales is approximately zero. However, this zero-correlation obscures the fact that some individuals may have judged good and *active* to be slightly related whereas other individuals judged good and *passive* to be related. The present methodology essentially distinguishes these two types of individuals from one another as well as from a third type of individual who does perceive the two scales as independent, or unrelated. To the extent most of the individuals make similar judgments for each of the paired scales, the group average would adequately reflect perceived semantic structure for an individual. However, the present data suggest that this is not the case; subgroups of response-homogeneous judges do differ among themselves in perceived semantic structure as well as differing from the group average result. It should not be inferred that another study of this sort would produce exactly the same Idealized Individuals. What is being generalized here is the emergence of individual differences with respect to both the number and kind of perceived semantic dimensions.

Although the existence of individual differences in perceived semantic structure has been documented here, this result alone does not disprove the theory of semantic generality. At most, what has been established is that different marker scales define E, P, and A for response-homogeneous subgroups of individuals, a result that can be indirectly inferred from the existing literature. On a cultural level, Osgood's, pan-cultural approach suggests that different sets of scales may mark E, P, and A for different cultures. On an individual-difference level, the data

presented here also suggest that different sets of scales are serving as indicants of E, P, and A for different individuals within the same language/culture community.

In comparing the pan-cultural approach and the present individual-difference approach we would argue that the present analysis is more appropriate for the notion of a verbal-mediating response. Thus, if the semantic differential is to serve, in part, as an operational definition of a verbal mediating response, and if, in turn, the verbal mediating response is conceptualized as an intra-individual phenomenon, a research design should be utilized which is representative of individuals, not cultures.

However, it remains to be demonstrated that these different sets of scales are serving as *valid* indicants of the underlying E, P, and A constructs in order to confirm the theory of semantic generality. Thus, for a given dimension, the different sets of marking scales must themselves be correlated (the pan-cultural analysis suggests this to be the case across cultures); in addition, the different sets of scales must have the same pattern of theoretical linkages with outside criteria. For example, Osgood and others (e.g., Fishbein, 1963, 1965, 1967; Fishbein and Raven, 1962; Osgood, 1965; Osgood et al., 1957; Osgood and Tannenbaum, 1955) have identified attitude as "the evaluative dimension of the total semantic space." Thus, one way of establishing the construct validity (Cronbach and Meehl, 1955) of the evaluative dimension would be to demonstrate that the possibly different scales marking evaluation for different individuals nevertheless have *identical* relationships with an independent measure of attitude favorability. In addition, discriminant validation (Campbell and Fiske, 1959) would require these various evaluative scales to be unrelated to activity and potency scales across cultures as well as individuals. If the theory of semantic generality is to hold on an individual level, then it must be the case that the evaluative scales for one group of individuals and the different evaluative scales for another group of individuals have the same pattern of relationships with non-test criteria of Evaluation. If such were the case, a stronger criterion for the generality of semantic structure would be met.

REFERENCES

BOPP, JOAN. 1955. A quantitative semantic analysis of word association in schizophrenia. Unpublished doctoral dissertation, University of Illinois.

CAMPBELL, D., and FISKE, D. 1959. Convergent and discriminant validation by the multitrait-multimethod matrix. *Psychological Bulletin,* 56: 81–105.

CRONBACH, J. J., and MEEHL, P. E. 1955. Construct validity in psychological tests. *Psychological Bulletin,* 52: 281–302.

EDWARDS, A. L. 1957. *The social desirability variable in personality assessment and research.* New York: Dryden Press.

FISHBEIN, M. 1963. An investigation of the relationships between beliefs about an object and the attitude toward that object. *Human Relations,* 16: 233–239.

———. 1965. A consideration of beliefs, attitudes, and their relationships. In I. D. Steiner and M. Fishbein (Eds.), *Current studies in social psychology.* New York: Holt, Rinehart and Winston.

———. 1967. Attitudes and the prediction of behavior. In M. Fishbein (Ed.), *Readings in attitude theory and measurement.* New York: John Wiley and Sons.

———, and RAVEN, B. H. 1962. The AB scales: an operational definition of belief and attitude. *Human Relations,* 15: 35–44.

FORD, L. H., JR., and MEISELS, M. 1965. Social desirability and the semantic differential. *Educational and Psychological Measurement,* 25: 465–475.

HALLWORTH, H. J. 1965a. Dimensions of personality and meaning. *British Journal of Social and Clinical Psychology,* 4: 161–168.

———. 1965b. The dimensions of personality among children of school age. *British Journal of Mathematical and Statistical Psychology,* 18: 45–56.

JAKOBOVITS, L. 1966. Comparative psycholinguistics in the study of cultures. *International Journal of Psychology,* 1: 2–37.

KAISER, H. F. 1958. The varimax criterion for analytic rotation in factor analysis. *Psychometrika,* 23: 187–200.

KRIEGER, MARJORIE H. 1964. A control for social desirability in a semantic differential. *British Journal of Social and Clinical Psychology,* 2: 94–103.

LEVINE, J. 1965. Three-mode factor analysis. *Psychological Bulletin,* 64: 442–452.

LITT, E. N. 1966. A factorial study of responses to abstract paintings. Unpublished master's thesis, University of Illinois.

MESSICK, S. 1960. Dimensions of social desirability. *Journal of Consulting Psychology,* 24: 279–287.

———, and KOGAN, N. 1966. Personality consistencies in judgment: dimensions of role constructs. *Multivariate Behavioral Research,* 1: 165–176.

OSGOOD, C. E. 1960. The cross-cultural generality of visual-verbal synesthetic tendencies. *Behavioral Science,* 5: 146–169.

———. 1962. Studies on the generality of affective meaning systems. *American Psychologist,* 17: 10–28.

———. 1965. Cross-cultural comparability in attitude measurement via multilingual semantic differentials. In I. D. Steiner and M. Fishbein (Eds.) *Current studies in social psychology.* New York: Holt, Rinehart and Winston.

———, and LURIA, Z. A blind analysis of a case of multiple personality using the semantic differential. *Journal of Abnormal and Social Psychology,* 49: 579–591.

———, SUCI, G. H., and TANNENBAUM, P. H. 1957. *The measurement of meaning.* Urbana, Illinois: University of Illinois Press.

———, and TANNENBAUM, P. H. 1955. The principle of congruity in the prediction of attitude change. *Psychological Review,* 62: 42–55.

PEDERSON, D. M. 1962. The measurement of individual differences in perceived personality trait relationships and their relation to certain determinants. Unpublished doctoral dissertation, University of Illinois.

PETERSON, D. R. 1965. Scope and generality of verbally defined personality factors. *Psychological Review,* 72: 48–59.

SNYDER, F. 1967. An investigation of the invariance of the semantic differential across the subject mode. Unpublished master's report, University of Illinois.

SUCI, G. J. 1960. A comparison of semantic structures in American southwest culture groups. *Journal of Abnormal and Social Psychology,* 61: 25–30.

TANAKA, Y. A. 1962. A cross-cultural study of national stereotypes held by American and Japanese college graduate subjects. *Japanese Psychological Research,* 4: 65–78.

———, and OSGOOD, C. E. 1965. Cross-culture, cross-concept, and cross-subject generality of affective meaning systems. *Journal of Personality and Social Psychology,* 2: 143–153.

———, OYAMA, T., and OSGOOD, C. E. A cross-culture and cross-concept study of the generality of semantic spaces. *Journal of Verbal Learning and Verbal Behavior,* 2: 392–405.

TRIANDIS, H. C., and OSGOOD, C. E. 1958. A comparative factorial analysis of semantic structure in monolingual Greek and American college students. *Journal of Abnormal and Social Psychology,* 57: 187–196.

TUCKER, L. R. 1966. Some mathematical notes on three-mode factor analysis. *Psychometrika,* 31: 279–311.

———, and MESSICK, S. 1963. An individual differences model for multi-dimensional scaling. *Psychometrika,* 28: 333–367.

TUCKER, W. T. 1955. Experiments in aesthetic communications. Unpublished doctoral dissertation, University of Illinois.

WALTERS, H. A., and JACKSON, D. N. 1966. Group and individual regularities in trait inference: a multidimensional scaling analysis. *Multivariate Behavioral Research,* 1: 145–164.

WARE, E. E. 1958. Relationships of intelligence and sex to diversity of individual semantic meaning spaces. Unpublished doctoral dissertation, University of Illinois.

WIGGINS, NANCY. 1966. Individual viewpoints of social desirability. *Psychological Bulletin,* 66: 68–77.

Part IV

VALIDITY STUDIES
OF THE SEMANTIC
DIFFERENTIAL TECHNIQUE

15. Meaning and *m*, Correlated but Separate [1]

Arthur W. Staats and Carolyn K. Staats

Noble (1952) has presented a Hullian analysis of meaning and meaningfulness in which meaning is identified as H, the relationship between the stimulus word and the response word. Meaningfulness is determined by the number of different Hs, i.e., a stimulus word is meaningful to the extent that it elicits many response words. In this study, Noble arrived at an index of meaning by measuring the number of word associations made to a given stimulus word in a given period of time. Noble concluded:

Thus, if one were to ask a layman what he intended by saying that "home" to him *means:* "family, spouse, children, friends, love," etc., he would doubtless reply, "I think of these things when 'home' is mentioned." . . . A learning theorist would explain that to the auditory (or visual) *S home*, these various verbal *R*s have become conditioned . . . and under appropriate conditions . . . are elicited. The meaning of *S* subsists in the *H*s developed to it —nothing more (Noble, 1952, p. 429).

Bousfield, Cohen, and Whitmarsh (1958) have recently presented a view of meaning which is consonant with Noble's view. They state that perception of a meaningful word involves the elicitation of two types of implicit response. First, the person says the word subvocally. This is called a verbal representational response, R_{vr}. In addition, however, the subject reacts by making another group of implicit verbal associative responses. For example, to the word BLACK, the subject might respond WHITE, DARK, CAT, etc.

These responses may be said to comprise the associative response composite, R_{va} *comp*. Under appropriate conditions the subject may produce the R_{vr} and the R_{va} *comp* explicitly by saying or writing them. Though a definition of meaning is perhaps gratuitous in this discussion, we believe it is useful to identify meaning with the R_{va} *comp*. This definition appears to be consistent with the Hullian interpretation presented by Noble (Bousfield, Cohen, & Whitmarsh, 1958, p. 1).

This approach contrasts with another concept of word meaning which has been developed by other psychologists, e.g., Cofer and Foley (1942), Mowrer (1954), Osgood (1953), and Staats (1959). This interpretation, put into classical conditioning terms, states that when a word is contiguously presented with a stimulus object, part of the response elicited by the object may be stably conditioned to the word. Staats has elaborated the concept of the classically conditioned meaning response to include a sensory variety (conditioned images), as well as an emotional variety (1959). In the latter case words which elicit an emotional meaning response will also serve as reinforcing stimuli in instrumental conditioning (1968).

The conditioning of a meaning response can also take place through higher-order conditioning, in which case the US, the stimulus object, is replaced by a word which through prior conditioning already elicits a meaning response. Both of these processes are schematized in Fig. 1. In the upper part of the figure the word BAD is paired with a punishing stimulus. The punishment elicits

Reprinted, with minor editorial corrections, from *Psychological Review* (1959), 66: 136–144, by permission of the authors and the publisher.

1. This article is one of a series of studies, formulated by the first author as the principal investigator of a research project supported under Office of Naval Research Contract Nonr-2305 (00), whose general aim is to experimentally verify his integrated learning theory of language. See Staats, 1968, for the more complete account. The junior author made the statistical analysis.

a number of responses which may be called "unpleasant," or of "negative value." After BAD has been paired with punishment a number of times, the conditionable responses (called "detachable" by Osgood) elicited by the punishment are conditioned to BAD. These responses come to constitute the stable meaning of BAD.

Assuming that the conditioning has been sufficiently strong, contiguous presentation of BAD and another word which has no meaning would result in higher-order conditioning. That is, the meaning response elicited by BAD would be conditioned to some extent to the new CS-word. In an actual life situation, a child might be told "Evil means bad." The negative meaning elicited by BAD would be conditioned to EVIL. This is depicted in Part *b* of Fig. 1.

Recently Osgood, Suci, and Tannenbaum (1957) have taken issue with Noble's approach to meaning. They would accept *m* as a measure of the association value of a stimulus word, but vehemently reject the interpretation that the associations may be thought of as word meaning. They state that a basic distinction exists between the meaning of a sign and its associations. They continue as follows:

This point needs to be labored because one recent writer (Noble, 1952), at least, has seriously proposed that the meaning of a sign is nothing more than the number of different associations between it as a stimulus and other signs as responses. According to Noble, "The index of meaning (*m*) of a particular stimulus was defined . . . as the grand mean number of (acceptable) written responses given by all *S*s within a 60 sec. period." . . . It is his basic notion—that meaning and association can be equated—which is wrong. Does BLACK mean *white* because this is the most common associate? Does NEEDLE mean *sew*, BREAD mean *butter*, MAN mean *woman*? Noble's *m* might be identified as meaningfulness rather than meaning, or better, simply the association value of the stimulus, since this is actually what he is measuring (Osgood, Suci, & Tannenbaum, 1957, pp. 16–17).

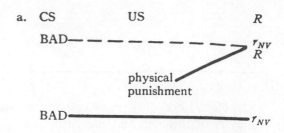

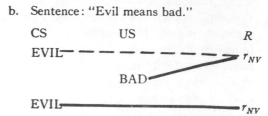

Fig. 1. Diagram a depicts first-order conditioning of word meaning. After a number of pairings of BAD, the CS, with punishment, the US, BAD comes to elicit the conditionable (i.e., "detachable") components of the responses elicited by the punishment (symbolized as r_{NV} because of the negative value). The components of the total response which are not stably conditioned are symbolized as R. Diagram b depicts second-order conditioning of meaning. The negative value meaning responses now elicited by BAD are conditioned to EVIL through contiguous presentation of the two words in the sentence. Although not schematized, it is understood that r_{NV}, as a mediating response, may through the stimuli it produces elicit other overt or implicit responses.

Thus, a rather sharp clash of interpretations is enjoined.

Relationship Between the Two Measures of Meaning

Osgood et al. insist that meaning of a word is not the same as the word's verbal associates, i.e., the meaning of a word involves a psychological process which is separate from word association processes. However, two recently reported experimental results have shown a relationship between *m* and semantic measures. In the first study, reported by Jenkins and Russell

(1956), intensity of meaning, as measured by Osgood's semantic differential, was correlated with Noble's *m*. Intensity of meaning was measured by the extent to which the rating of a word deviated from neutral (4) on a seven-point semantic differential scale.

It was hypothesized here that meaningful words would elicit many extreme ratings on the semantic differential and meaningless words would tend to elicit few such ratings. Accordingly the semantic differential profiles for Noble's concepts were analyzed in terms of their deviations from the neutral scale positions (that is to say, *D*s were calculated for each profile against a hypothetical profile running through the middle of each scale). The hypothesis was in general well substantiated. The correlation between the size of *D* and Noble's "m" was +.71. This represents the first connecting link between what seemed at the outset to be two entirely different ways of talking about psychological meaning (Jenkins & Russell, 1956, p. 7).

In addition, Noble (1958) has recently presented evidence which supports this result. In his experiment, *m* was correlated with what may be called a measure of intensity of evaluative meaning, one of the main factors of meaning found by Osgood and Suci (1955). Instead of using a semantic differential scale, Noble had the *S*s rate each word neutral, pleasant, unpleasant, or mixed. A semantic differential scale of pleasant-unpleasant would allow 7 gradations of evaluative meaning, and has no "mixed" category. Nevertheless, Noble's procedure seems to measure evaluative meaning, and the results should be roughly comparable to scoring words on a pleasant-unpleasant semantic differential scale.

Noble found in his study that this type of evaluative rating (which he calls a measure of emotionality) was correlated with *m* .57 (*p* = .001 level of significance). Thus, in this study and the study of Jenkins and Russell, larger *m* measures were associated with more intense meaning.

The question arises, especially in view of the rejection by Osgood et al. of the relevance of Noble's approach to a conception of meaning, of how to account for the relationship of Noble's measure of meaning and Osgood's semantic measures. As Jenkins and Russell imply, the two studies indicate a relationship which demands explanation—if meaning and word associations are to be separately considered. The present paper, in distinguishing meaning and *m*, must explain the relationship between the two. This explanation will also indicate why a word's meaning may be confused with the word's direct verbal associations.

BASIS OF THE RELATIONSHIP BETWEEN *m* AND MEANING

In the conditioning of word meaning it seems likely that both primary and higher-order conditioning are important, i.e., a word gets its meaning through both of the processes represented in Fig. 1. To some extent word meaning is obtained, and maintained, by contiguous presentation with certain primary stimulus objects. In addition, it is suggested that word meaning is conditioned through contiguous presentations with other words. It is this latter occurrence which accounts for the correlation between intensity of meaning and *m* and which, it is thought, results in confusing the two independent psychological processes. A stimulus word gets its meaning, in part, because each time it is paired with another word the meaning of the response word is conditioned to the stimulus word. This also strengthens the associations between stimulus word and response words. For example, if a nonsense syllable was paired with the word "bad" a number of times, direct associations between the syllable and "bad" would be formed. In addition, the meaning response elicited by "bad" would be conditioned to the syllable. Because of this parallelism in development it is easy to consider direct associations, which underlie *m*, and meaning as the same thing. Thus, although *m* and meaning are not the same, the more often a word is paired with its common associates, the stronger become the direct word-word associates and the word-meaning associates, i.e., the same operation strengthens both types of associations.

The stronger the direct associations, the less the latency of response when the stimulus word is presented. Thus, in a given period of time, stronger associations will result in the occurrence of more response words, i.e., the m measure will be high when word associates are elicited. In addition, strong word-meaning associations will result in semantic differential ratings which are extreme.

However, if a stimulus word obtains its meaning in part from its word associates, the meaning of a stimulus word must be directly related to the meaning of its response words. Thus, a positive correlation between the meaning of stimulus words and the meaning of their word associates would support the preceding interpretation. To verify the point, the following demonstration was conducted.

SIMILARITY OF THE MEANING OF STIMULUS-WORDS AND THE MEANING OF THEIR WORD-ASSOCIATES

Forty-six students in introductory sociology participated in the experiment.

In the experiment words were required on which semantic differential information was available, as well as information concerning the associates of the words. Jenkins, Russell, and Suci (1957) have provided data on the semantic profiles of 360 words, using different semantic differential scales for the semantic measures. Russell and Jenkins (1954) have also provided word association data on 100 words. Some words appear in both of these studies. For the present study 10 words were chosen on which both data were available from these sources. The criteria for choosing the ten words were: (a) that the words be distributed along the "good-bad" evaluative scale,

including words which had extreme positive evaluative meaning (mean rating toward 1) and words which had extreme negative evaluative meaning (mean rating toward 7), as well as words which were in between the extremes; (b) that word association data be available for the ten words selected. The words chosen are as follows: MUSIC, SWEET, TABLE, MOUNTAIN, DEEP, HARD, ROUGH, ANGER, TROUBLE, SICKNESS.

A folder was prepared which included these ten words and 40 additional words of unsystematic meaning, all arranged in random order. Under each word was a semantic differential scale of good-bad. An example is given below.

MUSIC

good   :—:—:—:—:—:—:—:   bad

The Ss were instructed in rating the meaning of the words.

Three weeks later the same Ss rated the meaning of the first twenty word associates of each of the above ten words. The twenty word associates were obtained from Russell and Jenkins (1954). In cases where a word was the associate of more than one of the "evaluative" words it was only listed once. Thus, a folder was used which included the 172 resulting words arranged in random order. The format of this folder was the same as with the first rating task; each word was listed with a "good-bad" scale beneath

TABLE 1

MEAN RATINGS OF STIMULUS WORDS AND TWENTY ASSOCIATED WORDS

Word	Minnesota	Arizona State	20 Associates (AS)
Music	1.60	1.56	2.47
Sweet	1.93	1.98	2.74
Table	2.37	2.85	2.75
Mountain	2.73	2.32	2.96
Deep	3.77	3.85	3.20
Hard	4.13	3.91	3.24
Rough	5.00	4.79	3.11
Anger	5.57	5.88	4.50
Trouble	6.10	6.39	4.28
Sickness	6.30	6.56	3.99

Note.—On the scales, 1 was "good" and 7 "bad."

it. The same instructions were used in administration.

In the analysis of the results the mean meaning scores for the original ten words were computed. In addition, the mean meaning score for the 20 associates of each of the ten words was computed. These means are listed in Table 1. The table also includes the mean meaning scores (on good-bad) on the same ten words obtained by Jenkins, Russell, and Suci using University of Minnesota students.

A rank order correlation coefficient was computed between the mean meaning score obtained in this study and the mean meaning scores obtained by Jenkins, Russell, and Suci. The correlation was .99.

The extent of the relationship between the meaning of the stimulus words and the meaning of their word associates was also measured by rank order correlation of their respective mean evaluative meaning scores. The rank order correlation coefficient was .90, which is significant at better than the .01 level. The results support the hypothesis that the meaning of the associates of a stimulus word tends to be the same as the meaning of the word. This gives credence to the hypothesis that *m* and intensity of meaning are correlated because associating two words conditions the meaning response of one to the other in addition to strengthening associations between the words.

The more often the stimulus word is paired with its associates, the stronger will the direct associations become. At the same time, the meaning of the associates will be more strongly conditioned to the stimulus word, i.e., the stimulus word will acquire more intense meaning. (Studies to be discussed in the next section will give additional support to this interpretation.) Other things equal, contiguous presentations of words will strengthen the associations responsible for high *m* as well as the associations responsible for intense semantic differential meaning. This effect should not necessarily depend on the frequency of use of a word. It depends on the frequency with which a word is paired with a group of associates which has a certain type of meaning. Words such as "the" no doubt occur extremely frequently with few repeats of any particular word associate. Because of this, "the" would have a great many weak word associates, with many different and probably antagonistic meanings. For this reason it would be thought that "the" would not have strong word associates, nor would it elicit strong meaning responses.

ADDITIONAL DISTINCTIONS IN THE CONCEPTS OF MEANING

The foregoing interpretations and empirical results argue that the verbal associates which words elicit do not account for word meaning. The confusion between these two processes may have arisen because the same operation, paired presentations of words, strengthens both types of associations. However, if word associations and word meaning are really independent processes, it should be possible to find independent operations for their development.

In a recent experiment (Staats, *et al.*, 1962), a GSR was conditioned to the word LARGE by pairing the word with noxious stimulation (shock or loud noise—adjusted to be unpleasant for each *S*) as it was presented in a list of words to be learned. After the conditioning the meaning of the word was measured on the semantic differential scale of pleasant-unpleasant. According to the theory of meaning already discussed, part of the "negative" response elicited by the noxious stimuli should be conditioned to LARGE (in the same manner as the GSR) and become, in part, the meaning of the word. This "negative" conditioned meaning response should then mediate the negative rating of LARGE on the semantic differential. The prediction was substantiated —negative evaluative meaning was conditioned to LARGE, without pairing it with other words. In addition, there was a significant correlation between the intensity of the conditioned GSR and the intensity of the conditioned negative evaluative meaning response. There is thus a suggestion that the conditioned GSR and meaning response were part of the same process. Osgood describes an example of the conditioning of negative evaluative meaning which is analogous to this interpretation. In his example, the word SPIDER is paired with the object, a spider, and some of the responses elicited by the spider, including autonomic responses of an aversive nature, are conditioned to the sign. He describes the conditioned autonomic responses as those which "literally confer the unpleasant, connotative meaning of threat upon this word" (Osgood, 1953, p. 696). It may be concluded from the above experimental results that meaning can be conditioned to a word through systematically pairing the word with a nonverbal aspect of the environment.

It might be suggested, however, that nonverbal objects on presentation elicit implicit verbal responses in the individual. Assuming this to be the case in this experimental procedure, if each time shock or sound was presented the S said "shock" or "sound," then word associations to LARGE could be formed. Then it might be said that LARGE had gained negative evaluative meaning because it later elicited the words "shock" and "sound." (This, of course, leaves unanswered the question of how "shock" and "sound" have acquired negative meaning.) However, this interpretation does not account for the significant correlation between the intensity of the conditioned GSR and the intensity of the conditioned meaning response. In addition, it seems questionable whether electric shock and an unfamiliar sound, especially in the experimental procedure, would elicit implicit naming responses.

The above experiment was thought to illustrate first-order conditioning of meaning as depicted in the upper part of Fig. 1. The first author's experimental method has also indicated that meaning may be condi-

tioned through higher-order conditioning (lower part of Fig. 1) independent of strengthening word-word associations. In these experiments a visually presented verbal CS was paired *once each* with 18 *different* auditorily presented words, each word having, however, an identical component of meaning. For example, a nonsense syllable was paired with 18 words like HAPPY, PRETTY, DINNER, and SWEET, which all have what may be called a positive evaluative meaning; and another syllable was paired with words like UGLY, THIEF, AGONY, and DISGUSTING, which have negative evaluative meaning. In addition, four other syllables were each paired in the same manner with 18 different words of no special meaning—yielding a procedure involving six nonsense syllables and 108 different words. Pairing a nonsense syllable only once each with 18 words would yield 18 direct syllable-word associations, all of them weak and mutually inhibitory. On the other hand, the evaluative meaning (either positive or negative) elicited by *each* of the US-words should be strongly conditioned to the syllable with which they were paired. The expected conditioning occurred, even when Ss who were aware of the systematic pairing of a certain type of word with a nonsense syllable were excluded from the analysis. Meaning, as measured by a semantic differential scale, was conditioned to nonsense syllables (Staats, *et al.,* 1959; Staats & Staats, 1957), national and proper names (Staats & Staats, 1958a), and meaningful words (Staats, *et al.,* 1958). In one experiment (Staats & Staats, 1957) the evaluative, potency, and activity factors of meaning found by Osgood and Suci (1955) were conditioned. A further study of "language conditioning" has indicated that the strength, or intensity, of the conditioned meaning increased as did the number of trials, i.e., number of syllable-meaning pairings (Staats & Staats, 1959), again with a syllable paired only once with any particular word.

Conversely, it should be possible to establish strong direct word-word associations without establishing strong word-meaning associations. This would be possible by selecting US-words (or response-words) which elicit antagonistic meaning responses, e.g., some US-words which elicit positive evaluative meaning and an equal number which elicit negative evaluative meaning. In this case the CS-word (or stimulus word) would be paired with each US-word many times. The result would be strong direct associations between the CS- and US-words, but the meaning of the CS-word should remain neutral, as measured on a semantic differential scale. The positive conditioning would cancel the negative. Similarly, a CS-word could be paired many times with words of neutral meaning (or with nonsense syllables) so that strong direct word-word associations would result. The CS-word would then have a high *m,* but it would elicit no meaning response, or the meaning response would be neutral as measured on a semantic differential.[2]

The foregoing illuminates a weakness of the interpretation that word meaning is comprised of the word's verbal associates. The conception that word meaning consists of word associates makes no provision for differentiating words in terms of their relationship to different aspects of the environment. While it seems reasonable to state that a word has meaning because it has certain verbal associates, it *is* reasonable because

2. Staats and associates (1963) have experimentally tested these and others of his expectations regarding the independence of meaning and *m.* The results showed that through paired presentation of words (in a paired-associate learning task) (1) the classically conditioned meaning of a word could be changed while the word's *m* was held constant, (2) meaning and *m* could be varied in a parallel fashion, and (3) a word's *m* could be changed without changing the word's meaning. Moreover, Finley and Staats (1967) have shown that words with negative evaluative meaning will function as positive reinforcers to strengthen instrumental behavior and that negative meaning words will weaken instrumental behavior. Again, these results demonstrate a (meaning) function of language which is independent of word association value.

the associates of the word are *meaningful* themselves. The conception becomes unreasonable if the case is considered where the verbal associates are meaningless words, i.e., nonsense syllables. To state that words gain their meaning by eliciting other words leaves all words in the status of nonsense syllables which have been widely associated with one another. It is unreasonable that this process produces meaningful words. No matter how many meaningless associates a nonsense syllable has it will remain meaningless. An illustration of this can be found by imagining a person learning a foreign language solely by pairing (or defining) the foreign words with each other—without ever pairing a foreign word with aspects of the nonverbal environment, or with meaningful words in a familiar language. With sufficient practice the person could in this manner learn many word associations in the foreign language—but the new language would be meaningless.

A more complete conception of meaning than the theory of word associates must include reference to the systematic pairings of verbal stimuli and various aspects of the environment, and to the properties acquired (emotional and sensory responses) by the verbal stimuli as a result of this process.

VERBAL GENERALIZATION AND MEANING

Since Bousfield *et al.* consider meaning to be the composite of associates of a word, they were able to deduce certain hypotheses concerning semantic generalization. A number of studies, summarized elsewhere (Cofer & Foley, 1942; Osgood, 1953), have shown that a response conditioned to a word will generalize to a word of the same or similar meaning. Bousfield *et al.* conclude that this generalization is mediated, at least in part, by the partial identity of the word associates of two words. They have also provided evidence demonstrating a relationship between the amount of generalization and the degree of identity of word associates. The results of the present study, however, indicate that this relationship may also reflect another variable. Since the word associates in the composites are themselves meaningful words, we may say that they too elicit meaning responses. When two response composites are similar, the meaning responses elicited by the response composites will be similar to one another. Thus, the generalization can also be considered to be due to the mediation of the common meaning responses of the common associates. Including this alternative, semantic generalization may take place on the basis of: (*a*) similarity of meaning responses elicited by two words, (*b*) similarity of the word associates elicited by two words, and (*c*) similarity of the meaning responses elicited by the word associates of the two words. In any situation it may be that each of these factors is contributing to the total generalization.

SUMMARY

Two approaches to meaning were summarized and contrasted. Word meaning may be considered to be the verbal responses made to the word, or word meaning may be a conditioned mediating response, part of the response elicited by the object denoted by the word. The present paper described the latter as meaning and distinguished word meaning from a word's verbal associates. The correlation between intensity of meaning and verbal associate measures which has been reported was seen to be a result of the fact that the same operation strengthens both: the more often a word is paired with its word associates, the stronger the connections between them. In addition, the meaning of the associates is conditioned to the word. This view was supported by showing that the associates of a word tend to have the same meaning as the word.

The two approaches to meaning were discussed further, and it was concluded that words could not gain meaning through verbal associations per se. Originally, it is through systematically pairing words with aspects of the environment that their meaning is gained. The meaning acquired in this process may later be conditioned to other words.

It was also concluded that semantic generalization may be a function of (*a*) similarity of meaning between words, (*b*) similarity of word associates elicited by words, and (*c*) similarity of meaning responses elicited by word associates of words.

REFERENCES

BOUSFIELD, W. A., COHEN, B. A., & WHITMARSH, G. A. Verbal generalization: A theoretical rationale and an experimental technique. *Tech. Rep. No. 23.* Contract No. Nonr—631 (00) between Office of Naval Research and Univer. of Connecticut, 1958.

COFER, C. N., & FOLEY, J. P. Mediated generalization and the interpretation of verbal behavior. I. Prolegomena. *Psychol. Rev.,* 1942, 49, 513–540.

FINLEY, J. R., & STAATS, A. W. Evaluative meaning words as reinforcing stimuli. *J. verb. lg. verb. Behav.,* 1967, 6, 193–197.

JENKINS, J. J., & RUSSELL, W. A. Annual technical report: Basic studies on individual and group behavior. Contract No. N8 onr-66216 between Office of Naval Research and Univer. of Minnesota, 1956.

JENKINS, J. J., RUSSELL, W. A., & SUCI, G. J. An atlas of semantic profiles for 360 words. *Tech. Rep. No. 15.* Contract No. N8 onr-66216 between Office of Naval Research and Univer. of Minnesota, 1957.

MOWRER, O. H. The psychologist looks at language. *Amer. Psychologist,* 1954, 9, 660–694.

NOBLE, C. E. An analysis of meaning. *Psychol. Rev.,* 1952, 59, 421–430.

NOBLE, C. E. Emotionality (e) and meaningfulness (m). *Psychol. Rep.,* 1958, 4, 16.

OSGOOD, C. E. *Method and theory in experimental psychology.* New York: Oxford Univer. Press, 1953.

OSGOOD, C. E., & SUCI, G. J. Factor analysis of meaning. *J. exp. Psychol.,* 1955, 50, 325–338.

OSGOOD, C. E., SUCI, G. J., & TANNENBAUM, P. H. *The measurement of meaning.* Urbana: Univer. Illinois Press, 1957.

RUSSELL, W. A., & JENKINS, J. J. The complete Minnesota norms for responses to 100 words from the Kent-Rosanoff Word Association Test. *Tech. Rep. No. 11.* Contract No. N8 onr-66216 between Office of Naval Research and Univer. of Minnesota, 1954.

STAATS, A. W. Verbal habit—families, concepts, and the operant conditioning of word classes. *Tech Rep. No. 10,* Contract 2794 (02) between the Office of Naval Research and Arizona State University, 1959.

STAATS, A. W. *Learning, language, and cognition.* New York: Holt, Rinehart, and Winston, 1968.

STAATS, A. W., & STAATS, C. K. Attitudes established by classical conditioning. *J. abnorm. soc. Psychol.,* 1958, 57, 37–40. (a)

STAATS, A. W. & STAATS, C. K. Effect of number of trials on the language conditioning of meaning. *J. gen. Psychol.,* 1959, 61, 211–223.

STAATS, A. W., STAATS, C. K., and CRAWFORD, H. L. First-order conditioning of word meaning and the parallel conditioning of a GSR. *J. gen. Psychol.,* 1962, 67, 159–167.

STAATS, A. W., STAATS, C. K., & BIGGS, D. A. Meaning of verbal stimuli changed by conditioning. *Amer. J. Psychol.,* 1958, 71, 429–431.

STAATS, A. W., STAATS, C. K., FINLEY, J. R., and HEARD, W. G. Independent manipulation of meaning and *m. J. gen. Psychol.,* 1963, 69, 253–260.

STAATS, A. W., STAATS, C. K., HEARD, W. G., & NIMS, L. P. Replication report: Meaning established by classical conditioning. *J. exp. Psychol.,* 1959, 57, 64.

STAATS, C. K., & STAATS, A. W. Meaning established by classical conditioning. *J. exp. Psychol.,* 1957, 54, 74–80.

(Received September 11, 1958)

16. Uncertainty and Other Associative Correlates
of Osgood's D4

Edmund S. Howe

This article concerns the question whether Osgood's D_4 measure of the meaning (multi-dimensional distance from the Origin) of verbal stimuli facilitates prediction of several quantitative associative properties of such stimuli. For each of 58 words appearing as stimuli in both the Minnesota and the Connecticut Free Associational Norms Studies as well as in the Semantic Atlas, four associative measures were obtained from each set of norms: H (Uncertainty), N (Number of different associations elicited), f_1 (Frequency of the Primary), and f_I (Number of idiosyncratic associations elicited). Measures of Osgood's D_4 and Noble's m were independently available for each word.

All results are arithmetically congruent over the two "States." The D_4 variable shows borderline r's with H, N, f_I, and f_1 for the 12 evaluatively Bad words, and for evaluatively Good words that are comparatively highly polarized. On the other hand D_4 yields correlations with Noble's m only for Good words of either low Polarization or high Frequency of Occurrence.

Implications of the findings are discussed, and a descriptive hypothesis to account for the differential Bad word/Good word outcomes is presented. It is suggested that Bad word/Good word differences have their psychological roots in a differential affect-arousing potential for Bad versus Good words which are otherwise "equal" in measured polarization. It is shown that both Evaluation factor scores and Activity factor scores independently yield about the same degree of correlation with the associative variables, as does the D_4 measure. But while Evaluation and D_4 are highly correlated, Activity and D_4 are not.

Within the theoretical framework of the semantic differential model of meaning espoused by Osgood (1952; Osgood, Suci, and Tannenbaum, 1957) the meaning of a verbal concept is approximately defined by its coordinates in *n*-dimensional semantic space. When, as is often the case, the data are treated in a three-space, then by simple arithmetic one may derive the distance, D_4, between the concept and the arbitrary origin of the centroid. When the *n*-factor coordinates of a verbal concept thus tend to arbitrary zero (i.e., the neutral points on SD scales) that concept may be said to approach an operational point of connotative meaninglessness. When the coordinates of a verbal concept are large, that concept is said to be richer or more intense in connotative meaningfulness.

It is now known that the degree of verbal generalization, for example, can under some conditions be predicted from the comparative euclidian distances between the D_4-values of verbal stimuli in a three-space (e.g., Dicken, 1961). What is less clear at the moment is whether magnitude of the D_4-value for a verbal concept enables us to predict anything about the quantitative associative stimulus properties of that concept. To make a preliminary survey of this question with extant data is the primary purpose of this article.

Reprinted from *Journal of Verbal Learning and Verbal Behavior* (1965), 4: 498–509, by permission of the author and Academic Press, Inc.

Briefly, 58 stimulus words *in common* were observed in: (a) The Minnesota Free Associational Norms study (Russell and Jenkins, 1954); (b) The Connecticut Free Associational Norms study (Bousfield, Cohen, Whitmarsh, and Kincaid, 1961); and (c) The Semantic Atlas (Jenkins, Russell and Suci, 1959; Jenkins, 1960). This investigation uses the responses obtained to the 58 words in (a) and (b), and the 58 values of D_4 given in the Semantic Atlas Study, in order to show that, given D_4, one can predict several content-free measures of associative behavior. Since the findings were to be replicated over the two "States," a secondary goal can also be achieved at the outset; namely, that of establishing comparability of the Minnesota and Connecticut Norms on these several associative variables.

METHOD

Stimulus Words

The 58 words used as stimuli in both the Minnesota and Connecticut Free Associational Norms studies as well as in the Semantic Atlas are shown in Table 1. Measures were obtained for each stimulus word on the variables described below.

Variables

By use for each stimulus word of the n of 1008 responses appearing in the Minnesota Norms and the n of 150 appearing in the Connecticut Norms, four content-free associative measures were derived from each State.

(1) H: The information-theoretic Uncertainty measure, based on the expression

$$H = \log n - \frac{1}{n} \Sigma n_i \cdot \log n$$

in conjunction with Attneave's (1959) Tables. The value of H in the present case thus increases: (a) the greater the total number of different responses becomes; and (b) the more equiprobable these different responses become.

(2) N: The number of different responses (regardless of Frequency).

(3) f_1: Frequency of the primary (commonest) response.

(4) f_I: Frequency of idiosyncratic (unique) responses.

In addition to these four associative variables two others were used:

(5) Osgood's D_4: These values were taken from the published Semantic Atlas (Jenkins, 1960) which, of course, was independently derived by using Minnesota Ss.

(6) Noble's (1952) m: These values were obtained from 62 contemporary students of introductory psy-

TABLE 1
THE FIFTY-EIGHT STIMULUS WORDS

1. Dark[a]	16. Smooth	30. Hand	44. Health
2. Rough	17. Red	31. Chair	45. Bible
3. Sour	18. High	32. Woman	46. Ocean
4. Hard	19. Sweet	33. River	47. Stove
5. Hungry	20. Light	34. Window	48. Religion
6. Bitter	21. Blue	35. Foot	49. Child
7. Heavy	22. Long	36. Sleep	50. Hammer
8. Afraid	23. Square	37. Girl	51. City
9. Sickness	24. Green	38. Stem	52. Butter
10. Spider	25. Table	39. Lamp	53. Doctor
11. Anger	26. Music	40. Dream	54. Bed
12. Thief	27. Man	41. Bread	55. Street
13. Deep	28. Mountain	42. Justice	56. Baby
14. Soft	29. House	43. Boy	57. Moon
15. Short			58. Bath

[a] The first 12 words are evaluatively "Bad," the remainder evaluatively "Good." See text for explanation of this dichotomy.

chology at the University of Connecticut.[3] It should be remembered that whereas N—the Frequency of the Primary—is based upon the diversity of responses *among* the group of Ss, m is based upon the average diversity of associative responses *within* individual Ss.

Treatment of Data

Step 1. This step involves a comparison of Variables 1 through 4 for Minnesota versus Connecticut data. Since these four between-State product-moment correlations are not uniformly high, Steps 2 and 3 below are performed separately for data derived from *each* State.

Step 2. The matrix of intercorrelations is obtained, for each State, among Variables 1 through 6.

Step 3. Actually, D_4 shows r's with other variables which at best explain only about 10% of the variance. The matrix of r's for each State was therefore broken down for two pairs of subgroups of the 58 words, viz: (a) adjectives versus other words; and (b) "Good" words ($n = 46$) versus "Bad" words ($n = 12$). Good and Bad classifications were made on the basis of mean ratings respectively of less than 4.00 and greater than 4.00 on the singleton Good-Bad bipolar scale used in the Semantic Atlas study.[4] The Good-Bad dichotomy leads to differences in correlations among variables, which differences are reported below. Since the other dichotomous split yields no semblance of such correlational difference, no further reference is made to it.

Two *ex post factum* steps in the analysis will be described later.[5]

---

[3] The booklet used to obtain m values had earlier been filled out by 28 undergraduates at Johns Hopkins University. The over-all r between Hopkins and Connecticut Ss is .93.

[4] A word of explication is in order here concerning our decision to make the Good-Bad breakdown on the basis of mean ratings on the Good-Bad scale, rather than on the basis of factor scores, in which all eight bipolar scales are used, reported by Jenkins (1960) to have comparatively pure evaluative loadings. It was observed that for only one stimulus word—*dark*—was the direction different in the two sources of information listed: *dark* is very slightly Bad on the Good-Bad Scale, but very slightly Good when evaluative factor scores are used. Since we were not seeking an iterative solution for a discrimination between Good and Bad words, the simpler criterion was adopted.

[5] The 58 × 10 rectangle of computed observations upon which most statistics are based will be available on request at a later date.

Distributions of data have been inspected for all variables in all subgroups to be described below; and in a minority of cases the data appear to be skewed and the regressions nonlinear. Consequently, a 7090 program was used to check all contingencies reported in this paper, with Spearman's *rho*-coefficient. Unless otherwise stated during the presentation of results, the reader may safely assume that the values and significances of *rho*-coefficients closely match the values of *r*-coefficients. (Other things equal, of course, *rho* will be slightly lower than *r*.)

RESULTS

Correlations within Variables, between States

The product-moment correlations between the two sets of norms on variables H, N, f_1 and f_I, for which approximate linearity of regression was observed in each case, are shown in Table 2. In the Combined class

TABLE 2
PRODUCT-MOMENT CORRELATIONS BETWEEN MINNESOTA AND CONNECTICUT NORMS ON ASSOCIATIVE VARIABLES
H, N, f_1, AND f_I

Associative variable	Classes of words[a]		
	Bad	Good	Combined
H	.817**	.768***	.753***
N	.687*	.655***	.590***
f_1	.901***	.821***	.825***
f_I	.609*	.598***	.547***

[a] There are 12 "Bad" words, 46 "Good" ones.
* $p < .05$.
** $p < .01$.
*** $p < .001$.

(using all 58 words) the r of .825 for the f_1 variable (Frequency of the primary) is significantly larger ($p < .01$) than the r's for N (Number of different responses) and f_I (Frequency of idiosyncratic responses); and the r of .753 for the H variable (Uncertainty) is significantly larger ($p < .05$) than the r for f_I. These trends, which hold up arithmetically when Good and Bad words are separately considered, indicate moderate comparability of the distributions of associations for the two States. It is noted that while H and f_1 consistently emerge as more ubiquitous variables, still even they fail to account for between 19% and 43% of the "between-States" variance. (About three particular words—of which *table* was the most consistently deviant—regularly fell very much out of line in the scatter plots for each pair of variables.) All further statistics have therefore been replicated over States.

Correlations among Variables, within States

Correlations among associative variables H, N, f_1, and f_I, along with D_4 and m variables, are presented in Table 3. In each cell the r between any pair of variables involving Minnesota data appears above the r for Connecticut data. The unique r between m and D_4 derives, however, from variables which by definition are independent of both sets of associational norms.

Notice first that the entries within each cell (Minnesota *vis-à-vis* Connecticut data) are very similar in magnitude. Considering among others the facts that the Minnesota and Connecticut Norms studies were performed at different points in time, in different geographical regions, with markedly different overall stimulus-word contexts, and that the respective n's were 1008 and 150, the within-

State relationships among all six variables are remarkably consistent. The H, N, f_1, and f_I variables of course yield mutual intercorrelations with each other which are congruent with the definition of H.

Second, observe that D_4 shows no correlation with any variable within the Connecticut data, and but minimal ones with H, N, and f_1 within the Minnesota data. At first blush this result suggests that D_4 ought to be regarded as having no correlate of great import. A seeming exception to this statement is the r of .508 ($p < .001$) between D_4 and m, which result accords with Jenkin's and Russell's (1956) r of .71 (with only 17 df) between similar variables. We shall shortly document, however, that the relationship between D_4 and m is a restricted one: it does not hold up either for both evaluative directionalities, or for all word-frequencies.

Bad versus Good Words

The matrices shown in Table 3 were next obtained separately for the 12 Bad words versus the 16 Good ones. The results are shown in Table 4. In each cell containing four coefficients the two on the left are for Min-

TABLE 3

MATRICES OF PRODUCT-MOMENT CORRELATIONS AMONG ALL VARIABLES, BY STATES

	H	N	f_1	f_I	m	Source of data
D_4	.343**[a]	.250*	— .273*	.181	.508***	Minn.
	.166	.131	— .171	.018		Conn.
H		.766***	— .921***	.586***	.306*	Minn.
		.849***	— .918***	.599***	.307*	Conn.
N			— .537***	.939***	— .029	Minn.
			— .615***	.895***	.113	Conn.
f_1				— .378**	— .375**	Minn.
				— .360**	— .374**	Conn.
f_I					— .205	Minn.
					— .089	Conn.

[a] All $n_j = 58$.
* $p < .05$.
** $p < .01$.
*** $p < .001$.

TABLE 4

MATRICES OF PRODUCT-MOMENT CORRELATIONS AMONG ALL VARIABLES FOR EACH STATE FOR "BAD" VERSUS "GOOD" WORDS

	H	N	f_1	f_I	m	Evaluative class of words
D_4	.682* .537	.571 .775***	−.466 −.600*	.593* .406	.076	Bad
	.246 .090	.040 .855***	−.102 .162	.155 −.047	.520***	Good
H		.607* .896***	−.815*** −.926***	.845*** .565[a]	−.084 .007	Bad
		.199 .764***	−.924*** −.927***	.556*** .617***	.381** .309*	Good
N			−.346 −.720***	.985*** .937***	−.283 −.143	Bad
			−.633*** .557***	.914*** .899***	.134 .108	Good
f_1				−.677* −.131	−.039 −.155	Bad
				−.388** −.393**	−.387** .382**	Good
f_I					−.353 −.183	Bad
					−.038 −.079	Good

Note.—In each cell containing four coefficients, the two on the left were obtained from Minnesota data; the two on the right from the Connecticut data.

* $p < .05$.
** $p < .01$.
*** $p < .001$.

nesota data, the two on the right for Connecticut data. The following remarks apply equally well to the outcomes for both States.

First, the relative values of r's for Bad versus Good words are the same among the H, N, f_1, and f_I variables: that is, the evaluative dichotomy does not generally yield differences in r between any pair of these four valuables. Nor should it. But consider the top row of cells in Table 4. It is seen that (a) the four small r's earlier observed for Minnesota data (*cf.* Table 3) between D_4 on the one hand, and H, N, f_1 and f_I on the other hand, may now be almost entirely ascribed to the *Bad* words rather than to the Good ones; further (*b*) the r of .508 similarly observed (Table 3) between D_4 and m may now be entirely ascribed to the *Good* words ($r = .520$, $p < .001$), not to the Bad ones; and finally (c) that the small r's likewise earlier observed between H and m, and between f_1 and m, are also largely attributable to Good rather than to Bad words.[6]

The results for Connecticut data show arithmetical outcomes congruent with those for Minnesota data. With respect to the r's between D_4 and other variables, however, only that between D_4 and N seriously approaches two-tailed significance ($p = .06$). (For the Minnesota Bad-word data, the *rho* between D_4 and N is .55 [$p = .06$], and between D_4 and f_1, .50 [$p > .05$]. For the Connecticut Bad-word data, the *rho* between D_4 and the four associative variables in the matrix are: .44, .54, —.33, and .30 [$p > .05$]. The discrepancies between the two States can in part be attributed to be consideration that D_4 data were obtained from Minnesota Ss.)

The data presented in this section suggest that D_4 does indeed have associative correlates which are a function of the evaluative

<hr/>

6 Quite aside from our immediate purposes, it is noted that the very small nonsignificant values of r appearing in Table 4, between Noble's m and our N (total number of different responses elicited), forcibly confirm that the two measures are not interchangeable.

directionality of the stimulus words. It is fairly and squarely noted, however, that with only 12 cases in the Bad-word group, this conclusion runs the risk of a Type I error. This risk is partly mitigated, on the other hand, by the fact that it is the group with the *smaller n* (i.e., 12) that yields the correlations, for Minnesota data, in Table 4. Since this sort of question will arise also in the remaining results, it is well to acknowledge that the analysis of extant date inevitably imposes unfortunate constraints on the generality of these findings.

Problems of Comparative Word-Frequency and Polarization

The data marginally indicate correlational differences for Bad *vis-à-vis* Good words. It would be nice were we free to attribute the observed effects simply to evaluative directionality, and to consider the case closed; but on neither statistical nor psychological grounds is the matter so straightforward. Further inquiry shows that, while mean values for Bad versus Good words do not differ on the H, N, f_1, and f_I variables or on the degree of Good-Bad polarization (all $p > .05$), Bad words do yield lower mean values of D_4 ($t = 2.456$, $p < .01$) and of Noble's m ($t = 3.766$, $p < .001$). Means and SDs appear in Table 5. The Bad words also have, as one would expect, an overall lower Frequency of Occurrence than the Good ones. Lower frequency for Bad words was established by reference to Thorndike and Lorge's (1944) General Count: among the 12 Bad words there are eight having frequencies of 99 or less per million, and four of 100 or more per million. For the 46 Good words, on the other hand, these figures are respectively 12 and 34. The value of $\chi^2(1)$ corrected for continuity is 5.571, $p < .05$, in favor of lower Frequency for Bad words. This test is admittedly a coarse one, but the preponderance of high-frequency words among the set of 58 (38 have AA ratings) prohibits a more stringent test of the degree or relationship

TABLE 5

COMPARATIVE DIFFERENCES IN MEANS AND STANDARD DEVIATIONS, ON ALL SIX VARIABLES, FOR BAD VERSUS GOOD WORDS (BY STATES AS APPLICABLE)

Measure	Class of word	Minnesota		Connecticut	
		Mean	SD	Mean	SD
H	Bad	3.433	.980	3.237	.420
	Good	3.672	.926	3.517	.863
N	Bad	106.833	39.729	32.250	5.746
	Good	98.826	23.600	34.500	9.136
f_1	Bad	486.416	167.258	64.333	15.129
	Good	394.673	197.822	55.804	27.956
f_I	Bad	65.500	26.097	20.250	4.985
	Good	54.978	14.332	20.130	6.340
D_4	Bad	4.813	1.066	—	—
	Good	5.690	1.235	—	—
m	Bad	—	—	11.494	.993
	Good	—	—	12.752	1.167

Note.—Compared with Goods words, Bad ones show a lower mean value of D_4 ($p < .01$) and m ($p < .001$). No other within-State differences occur.

between evaluative directionality and Frequency; and the outcome stated is in any case sufficiently clear to demand further explication of the likely consequences of such a difference. Two further arrangements of the data were therefore examined.

First, the 46 *Good words alone* were broken down into two groups: (a) a low-frequency group having Thorndike General Counts of 99 or less per million (of which, fortuitously, there are 12 words, having a distribution of frequencies virtually identical to that for the 12 Bad words); and (b) a high-frequency group of 34 words having counts of 100 or more per million. Correlation matrices—similar to those already presented in Table 4—were obtained for Good words having low frequency, versus Good words having high frequency. If Frequency as measured by the Thorndike General Count is responsible for the differential Bad word/Good word results appearing in Table 4, then one should expect similar differential trends to appear between the two new categories of Good words; i.e., correlations between D_4 and other variables for only the *low*-frequency groups. Table 6 shows the correlations obtained, for these two sets of Good words, between D_4 and the other variables. It is obvious that the predicted differences do not occur for H, N, f_1, or f_I variables derived from either State; and that word-frequency measured via the method described is not a necessary

TABLE 6

PRODUCT-MOMENT CORRELATIONS BETWEEN D_4 AND ALL OTHER VARIABLES, FOR LOW-FREQUENCY VERSUS HIGH-FREQUENCY GOOD WORDS, BY STATES

Frequency	Correlation between D_4 and				
	H	N	f_1	f_I	m
	Minnesota				
Low[a]	.19	.17	— .10	.21	—
High[b]	.26	.25	— .15	.18	—
	Connecticut				
Low	.24	.13	— .34	.09	.44
High	.09	.06	— .07	— .05	.56**

[a] $n_L = 12.$
[b] $n_H = 34.$
** $p < .01.$

determinant of these differences. Here, however, we run the risk of a Type II error which in this case is especially serious since the subgroup predicted to yield r's between D_4 and the four associative variables contains the n of only 12 cases. And one ought be *doubly* suspicious of this particular finding in light of the ubiquitous character of Word Frequency. It should be noted, though, that values of *rho* are in the same direction in all 16 cells of the Table. For example, for Minnesota data, absolute discrepancies between r and *rho* range from .01 to .13. The median difference is .035.

On the other hand the r between D_4 and m does hold up ($r = .56$, $p < .01$) for *high*-frequency Good words ($r = .56$, $p < .01$, with $df = 32$), but not nearly significantly so for low-frequency Good words ($r = .44$, $p > .05$, with $df = 10$). (Consistent with this finding are the observations that the r's appearing [in Table 4] between m and H, and between m and f_1 *for Good words only*, are also found to hold up for the high-frequency but not significantly so the low-frequency Good words.) These results suggest that the differential Bad word/Good word relationships between D_4 and m can perhaps in part be attributed to the word-frequency variable. The interpretive impasse here obviously lies in the fact that high-frequency and evaluative directionality are inseparably confounded with each other because of the very small available sample of Bad words. In any event, a positive correlation between D_4 and m occurs only for high-frequency Good words.

Next, it was established that the graphic plots of D_4 against each associative variable, for all Good words, did not at all yield an impression of *sensible* curvilinearity. Then, for the second rearrangement of data, the 46 Good words were split at the (Good-word) median D_4 value, yielding a Low-D_4 and a High-D_4 group, with n's = 23. The high-D_4 group contains proportionately more nouns and fewer adjectives than the low-D_4 group; the value of $\chi^2(1)$ is 2.82 which falls between the 0.05 and 0.10 levels of significance. (Again tortuously, the Low-D_4 group is observed to have a mean D_4-value practically identical to the mean D_4-value for Bad words.) If the lower mean D_4-value of the Bad-word group is in part responsible for the Bad word/Good word correlational differences appearing in Table 4, then one should expect comparable differences to appear also between the two groups of Good words; i.e., that only the *Low-D_4* group will yield correlations with H, N, f_1, f_I, and m. The correlations between D_4 and other variables, for Low-D_4 versus High-D_4 groups, appear in Table 7.

First, it is observed that, for both States, the High-D_4 (not the Low-D_4) group now yields congruent correlations between D_4 on the one hand, and H, N, f_1, and f_I on the other. In the Minnesota High-D_4 data the *rho*'s for N and f_1 are both .39 ($p = .06$). In the Connecticut High-D_4 data the *rho* for f_1 is $-.61$ ($p < .01$); for f_I it is .35 ($.05 < p < .10$). In all other High-D_4 cells *rho* either equals or exceeds r. Thus the lower overall mean D_4-value of the Bad words cannot be invoked to explain why Bad words yield correlations between D_4, and H, N, f_1 and f_I, while the Good words as a whole do not.

Second, it is seen that the r between D_4 and m now achieves significance ($r = .55$, $df = 21$, $p < .01$) for the low-D_4 words, but not for the high-D_4

TABLE 7
PRODUCT-MOMENT CORRELATIONS BETWEEN D_4 AND ALL OTHER VARIABLES FOR 23 GOOD WORDS ABOVE VERSUS 23 GOOD WORDS BELOW THE D_4 MEDIAN

	Correlation between D_4 and				
	H	N	f_1	f_I	m
	Minnesota				
Low D_4	.20	.05	$-.18$	.01	—
High D_4	.48*	.45*	$-.52*$	.47*	—
	Connecticut				
Low D_4	.17	$-.02$	$-.17$	$-.04$	.55**
High D_4	.50*	.51*	$-.49*$	.42*	.40[a]

Note.—Low D_4 refers to the 23 Good words having D_4 values below the D_4 median for all Good words.

[a] $p = .06$.
* $p < .05$.
** $p < .01$.

words ($r = .40$, $p < .10$). The two correlations do not differ statistically, of course, but the direction of the difference makes sense. Taken in conjunction with the high- and low-frequency data, they suggest the firm hypothesis that the magnitude of the correlation between Osgood's D_4 and Noble's m diminishes, on the one hand, for Good words of either low frequency or high polarization. These two determinants, which are reciprocally related, accord with recent findings (e.g., Koen, 1962). On the other hand, if Koen is correct in his analysis, no correlation should occur between D_4 and Noble's m for Bad words since they are more likely to be "emotional."

Are the D_4 Results Artifactual?

One further question remains to be discussed. The definition of D_4 must often leave an investigator with the disconcerting feeling that, whatever its conceptual and pragmatic value, and however neat and familiar the geometric axioms from which it is derived, still he fails to feel unequivocally sure that a particular empirical correlate of D_4 is not an artifactual result of some third variable which itself happens to be correlated with D_4. Theoretically speaking this is a question of whether—as Osgood would insist—the multi-dimensional nature of meaning requires that specification of its intensity in euclidian space both should and can be given by the unique properties of D_4. Practically, two consecutive issues are involved: (a) do large and significant correlations exist between D_4 scores, and the Evaluation, Potency and Activity scores from which D_4 is computed?: hence (b), if so, do such of these tripartite components scores as yield a correlation with 'D_4 permit the prediction of associational behavior as well as D_4 does? Were this the case then we should not, of course, be justified in concluding that the results reported here are necessarily a genuine function of the unique properties of D_4. Toward this end the following *post hoc* computations were made.

Mean polarization values for each stimulus word were obtained from the mean Good-Bad, Hard-Soft, and Active-Passive scales reported in the Semantic Atlas; these scales had shown high and pure loadings on their respective factors. In addition, the factor scores for each word were obtained from Jenkins' (1960) paper; these scores were derived from eight scales for Evaluation, and three scales each for Potency and Activity. Along with D_4 measures the three singleton variables and three factor-score variables were intercorrelated in two 7×7 matrices— one for Bad words, the other for Good ones.

The results show that: (a) while several small, significant intercorrelations occur (across dimensions) among the six new "dimensional' variables, still these particular correlations account on average for only about 10 or 12% of the variance and can therefore be ignored; but, most importantly, (b) the D_4 variable shows, for both Good and Bad words separately considered, significant correlations both with (singleton) evaluative polarization scores (absolute r's of .61 and .69, $p < .05$) and with evaluative factor scores (r's of .78 and .80, $p < .001$) but no significant correlation with any of the other four dimensional variables. This finding now formally raises the question whether the observed associative distributions can be as well predicted from either the evaluative polarization scores or the evaluative factor scores, as from D_4 scores..

To evaluate this question the computer generated a set of matrices such that we can now report the correlations between the four associative variables and Noble's m on the one hand, and each of our six "dimensional" variables defined above, on the other hand. Matrices were obtained for Bad and for Good words alone, and also separately for high-D_4, low-D_4, high-frequency, and low-frequency Good words separately. Table 8 shows the relationships occurring for evaluation variables.

First notice that the f_1 variable (strength of the primary) is, with few exceptions, predicted almost as well by both evaluative polarization and factor scores, as it is by D_4 (*cf.* Table 7). Second, observe that, for the Connecticut data, the associative variables for high-D_4 Good words are almost as highly correlated with evaluative polarization and factor scores as they are with D_4. This effect is not, however, quite so striking for the Minnesota data. While

TABLE 8

CORRELATIONS BETWEEN ASSOCIATIVE VARIABLES AND e (GOOD-BAD SCORES) AND E (EVALUATIVE FACTOR SCORES), BY STATES AND WORD CLASSES

Items		H	N	D_4	f_1	f_I	m
Conn: Bad	e	.453	.170	.606*	— .678**	— .041	— .001
Conn: Good, Lo D_4	e	.314	.384	— .519**	— .233	.327	— .107
Conn: Good, Hi D_4	e	— .543***	— .503**	— .580***	.498**	— .441*	— .066
Minn: Bad	e	.491	.221	—	— .671**	.227	—
Minn: Good, Lo D_4	e	.076	.311	—	.013	.343	—
Minn: Good, Hi D_4	e	— .432*	— .318	—	.470*	— .214	—
Conn: Bad	E	.439	.235	.777***	— .614*	.053	— .151
Conn: Good, Lo D_4	E	.154	.194	— .667***	— .104	.098	— .201
Conn: Good, Hi D_4	E	— .482**	— .477*	— .625***	.455*	— .490**	.051
Minn: Bad	E	.627*	.473	—	— .671**	.490	—
Minn: Good, Lo D_4	E	— .070	.181	—	.191	— .072	—
Minn: Good, Hi D_4	E	— .361[a]	— .382[a]	—	.391[a]	— .412*	—

[a] $p = .06$.
  * $p < .05$.
 ** $p < .01$.
*** $p < .001$.

we shall not attempt further synthesis of these data (they are uncertain and complex enough as it is), it is evident that both D_4 and evaluative measures contain ingredients which, considered jointly in the form of multiple correlations, would yield stronger and more orderly relationships with our associative variables than now exist. To this extent the independence and uniqueness of the status of D_4 is therefore subject to serious question. Further grist for this charge comes from the following observations.

First, not a single correlation occurs (and only one even approaches significance) between the two Potency measures and the associative variables as defined in Table 8. But, second, the results for the Activity Factor scores (which, it is to be noted, *do not* bear even nearly-significant correlations with D_4) are surprising. Activity Factor scores bear correlations of from .63 to .66 (all two-tailed $p < .05$) with H and N for Bad words only, in both States. These scores also show a correlation of .60 ($p < .05$) with f_1 and one of .55 ($p = .06$) with f_I for Bad words using Minnesota data. For *low-D_4* Good words in both States, the Activity Factor score variable yields correlations with H ($p < .01$), N ($p < .06$), f_1 ($p < .05$), and m ($p < .02$): more "active" words yield higher values of H, etc. These additional outcomes are thoroughly confirmed by the rank-correlation results.

DISCUSSION

The central purpose of this exploratory paper is to inquire whether Osgood's D_4 measure of the connotative meaning of words facilitates prediction of their associative properties. It is documented by means of the Minnesota Norms data that for the Bad words, and only for the Good words having high values of D_4, associative variables H, N, f_1, and f_I occurs as borderline correlates of D_4. When associative data from the Connecticut Norms are used, arithmetically similar outcomes are obtained, although none achieves significance. The results are consistent with Terwilliger's (1962) independent demonstration that a positive relationship between H and polarization holds even when "associative uncertainty" is derived from a novel method presented by Ross and Levy (1960). It follows that within the limits of our results a word which is more polarized— i.e., is further from the Origin in three-di-

mensional semantic space, and hence more meaningful in the terms of the Osgoodian model—will tend to elicit higher associative Uncertainty, a larger number of different associations, a weaker primary, and a larger number of unique responses than will a word lying closer to the arbitrary Origin of the factor space. The findings thus demonstrate limited but real empirical overlap between data derived from the SD model *vis-à-vis* the generic association model of meaning. This communality evidently transcends any question of the literal content of discrete associations and hence stands independent of, and primary to, current discussion—between Bousfield (1961) and Osgood (1961), for example—concerning the nature of mediational processes underlying SD judgments.

At the same time we have presented evidence that both Evaluation and Activity factor scores are on the whole as highly correlated as D_4 is, with the associative variables. This result makes it incumbent upon those who either tacitly believe in the uniqueness of D_4, or use this variable as a measure of stimulus similarity, to be utterly explicit about the psychological and statistical justification for their assumptions.

Since the associative variables yield limited correlations with D_4 for Bad words and for Good words only of high D_4, a descriptive hypothesis is in any case called for to account for this observed difference. While evaluative directionality and degree of polarization (taken over three factors) are partially confounded in the present data, it nevertheless seems reasonable to assume that the basic variable making for the Bad/Good word difference has more to do with evaluative directionality rather than with degree of polarization. Our hypothesis is that "affect arousal" is the crucial, uncontrolled variable in this inquiry; and that D_4 yields associative correlates only for stimuli eliciting stronger degrees of affect. We need simply to recognize the real possibility that Good words are affect-arousing only if highly polarized, whereas

Bad words are affect-arousing even if comparatively less polarized.

Is there any independent evidence suggesting that this hypothesis will be verified under optimal test conditions? There is unfortunately not much: psychologists have historically been much more interested in those emotional stimuli which elicit avoidance and escape behavior than they have in those which elicit approach behavior. In a discussion of the determinants of arousal Berlyne, however, proposes the hypothesis that "pleasant emotional excitement and rewarding stimuli (as well as the unpleasant forms of emotion traditionally studied experimentally) heighten arousal, *although probably less sharply than states of distress and punishing stimuli*" (1960, p. 174, italics added). It is also pertinent here to recall well-established data substantiating that generalization gradients of approach typically show a *more gradual* decrement than do gradients of avoidance; and that Woodworth and Schlosberg (1954) report studies suggesting that on the whole "unpleasant" stimuli evoke larger GSRs than "pleasant" ones. Terwilliger (1964) further concludes that the Bad half of the Good-Bad bipolar scale must cover greater psychological distance than the Good half; and that positive affect *has* an upper limit, while negative affect does not. Previous research in this area has not, however, generally come to grips with the basic problem of separating evaluative directionality from psychological intensity.

What we are in other words proposing is the heuristic assumption that Bad-ness is not, after all, a simple psychometric opposite or reciprocal of Good-ness (no more so, indeed, than Punishment is in any but the most superficial psychological sense the reciprocal of Reward), and that *the inequality involved is obscured within the constraints of the present SD model.* The proposal implies that, given a Bad word and a Good word having equal D_4-values, some imbalance of psychological moments must exist about the arbitrary

Origin for evaluation.[7] If independently substantiated, this hypothesis will carry several poignant implications concerning not only the SD model, but the generic association model of meaning as well.

REFERENCES

ATTNEAVE, F. *Applications of information theory to psychology.* New York: Holt-Dryden, 1959.

BOUSFIELD, W. A. The problem of meaning in verbal learning. In, Cofer, C. N., (Ed.), *Verbal learning and verbal behavior.* New York: McGraw-Hill, 1961.

BOUSFIELD, W. A., COHEN, B. H., WHITMARSH, G. A., AND KINCAID, W. D. The Connecticut free associational norms. *Tech. Rep. No. 35,* University of Connecticut, Contract Nonr-631(00), 1961.

BERLYNE, D. E. *Conflict, arousal, and curiosity.* New York: McGraw-Hill, 1960.

DICKEN, C. F. Connotative meaning as a determinant of stimulus generalization. *Psychol. Monogr.,* 1961, **75**, No. 1 (Whole No. 505).

JENKINS, J. J. Degree of polarization and scores on the principal factors for concepts in the semantic atlas study. *Amer. J. Psychol.,* 1960, **73**, 274-279.

KOEN, F. Polarization, *m,* and emotionality in words. *J. verb. Learn. verb. Behav.,* 1962, **1**, 183-187.

JENKINS, J. J., RUSSELL, W. A, AND SUCI, G. J. An atlas of semantic profiles for 360 words. *Amer. J. Psychol.,* 1958, **71**, 688-699.

NOBLE, C. E. An analysis of meaning. *Psychol. Rev.,* 1952, **59**, 421-430.

OSGOOD, C. E. The nature and measurement of meaning. *Psychol. Bull.,* 1952, **49**, 197-237.

OSGOOD, C. E. Comments on Professor Bousfield's paper. In, Cofer, C. N., (Ed.), *Verbal learning and verbal behavior.* New York: McGraw-Hill, 1961.

OSGOOD, C. E., SUCI, G. J., AND TANNENBAUM, P. H. *The measurement of meaning.* Urbana: Univer. of Illinois Press, 1957.

ROSS, B. M., AND LEVY, N. A comparison of adjectival antonyms by simple card pattern formation. *J. Psychol.,* 1960, **49**, 133-137.

[7] For example, the data of the present inquiry, as well as data reported by Ross and Levy, and by Terwilliger, show that the sorts of pairs of adjectives which are taken to be reliably antonymic to each other (e.g., *beautifully-ugly*)—and typically used to define SD scales—involve different associative Uncertainties as portrayed by *H.*

RUSSELL, W. A., AND JENKINS, J. J. The complete Minnesota norms for responses to 100 words from the Kent-Rosanoff word-association test. *Tech. Rep. No. 11,* University of Minnesota, Contract N8-onr-66216, 1957.

TERWILLIGER, R. F. Free association patterns as a factor relating to semantic differential responses. *J. abnorm. soc. Psychol.,* 1962, **65**, 87-94.

TERWILLIGER, R. F. Familiarity, association value and affective arousal. Unpublished manuscript, 1964.

WOODWORTH, R. S. AND SCHLOSBERG, H. *Experimental psychology.* New York: Holt, 1954.

17. The Associative Structure
of Some Common English Adjectives [1]

James Deese

The associative meaning of any stimulus in free association is defined by the distribution of associations to that stimulus (Deese, 1962a). The intersection or overlap between distributions to various stimuli provides a measure of the similarity or commonality in associative meaning among those stimuli. Analysis of matrices of intersection or overlap coefficients between associative distributions shows that associative meaning is highly structured.

Furthermore, there is a close relation between the distributions of associations and grammatical form-class of words as stimuli (Deese, 1962b). Such a relation implies that associative meaning may be determined by structures which are similar to the conceptual schemes which define form class and which enable English speakers to use words of different classes in appropriate positions in sentences. In other words, it is possible that there is a continuity between grammar and meaning.

Therefore, it is appropriate to study the structure of associative meaning within a grammatical class and to relate the results to the organization of that class. The present paper attempts to accomplish such an analysis for the class of English adjectives.

Reprinted from *Journal of Verbal Learning and Verbal Behavior* (1964), 3: 347–357, by permission of the author and Academic Press, Inc.

[1] The investigation reported here was supported in part by Public Health Service research grants MH-06550-01 and MH-06550-02, from the National Institute of Mental Health.

Earlier work on the distribution of paradigmatic and syntagmatic associations to adjectives (Deese, 1962b) shows that there is a negative correlation between the frequency of syntagmatic associations and frequency of usage. That is to say, uncommon adjectives are likely to elicit words that make ordinary sequences in the language (*administrative decision*), while common adjectives elicit mostly other adjectives (*hot-cold*). Furthermore, the paradigmatic associates to the most common of adjectives are overwhelmingly contrastive or antonymic to the stimulus (as in the above example). These results, it was argued, reflect (a) the relatively unique contexts in ordinary language of rare adjectives, (b) the existence of a fundamental contrast scheme among common adjectives, and (c) the probably intraverbal definition of intermediate adjectives in terms of the fundamental contrasts.

Therefore, such an analysis leads to the view that adjectival meaning can be described by a set of very common adjectives which contrast with one another in meaning. Other, less common adjectives would then have their intraverbal meaning described, in part, by combinations of meaning of the fundamental contrasts. Furthermore, the contrasts themselves might well be correlated, so that the associative meaning of English adjectives could be reduced to a very small number of fundamental contrasts. When we add the possibility that the contrasts have scalar properties, we arrive at the semantic differential. Therefore, one possibility of the analysis of associative meaning of adjectives would be to provide a basis in associative data for the semantic differential.

A complete justification for the semantic differential in associations would be extremely unlikely, however. The authors of the semantic differential (Osgood, Suci, and Tannenbaum, 1957) have argued against such a possibility, and, furthermore, they disclaim any generality to the meaning underlying the 20 scales of the semantic differential by describing the semantic differential as connotative or emotional. In addition, a critical analysis of the semantic differential casts considerable doubt on its generality (Carroll, 1959). Nevertheless, the contrastive property of adjectival meaning seems to be important, and a study of its generality would serve to explain some of the limitations that are imposed on the usual semantic differential technique.

The present paper reports an investigation of (a) the distribution of associations to 278 English adjectives, (b) the intersections of associative distributions among these adjectives, and (c) the general types of structures that described the interrelations in associative meaning among these adjectives and adjectives in general.

METHOD

The basic analysis reported in this study is based upon free associations to 278 adjectives obtained from a sample of 100 Johns Hopkins University undergraduates in the fall of 1962. This section describes the collection of these data and the basic techniques of analysis. In addition to the associative data, various other measures were obtained at other times from other samples of Ss. The particular procedures for these essentially validative studies are described later in the paper.

The Stimuli. The adjectives used as stimuli in this study were either adjectives having a frequency of 50 occurrences per million or greater in the Thorndike-Lorge (1944) G count, or they were adjectives used in the standard form of the semantic differential. The sampling of the higher frequency (A and AA) Thorndike-Lorge adjectives is very nearly complete. Some difficulty was encountered with participles, since the count does not differentiate between use in verbal, adjectival, or nominal (gerundive) position. Therefore, the most serious omission

in the present sample of high-frequency adjectives is in participles commonly used as adjectives.

English is essentially a distributive language, and even adjectives that have formal affixes as markers may be used in nominal or verbal position (*the conceptual is to be avoided; go pretty yourself*). Certain of the adjectives used in the present study are also, in English, used in adverbial positions. Indeed, some of these are probably more often used as adverbs than as adjectives (*inside-outside*). In short, the sample of words can be regarded as representative of the common words that can occupy adjectival position but which, in ordinary English, may also occupy other positions.

The Testing. All 100 Ss produced one association to each of the 278 adjectives in a single session. These words were given with standard free-association instructions in a mimeographed test booklet. Two different random orders of words were used in preparing the mimeograph masters, with the restriction that no two words be adjacent to one another in both orders. Furthermore, the test booklet was assembled in five different orders. There were, therefore, a total of ten different booklets, each administered to ten Ss. Such an arrangement does not eliminate contextual effects in the test, but it severely reduces the effect of unique and particular contexts. A comparison of the distributions obtained in this study with those obtained from earlier studies in which some of the same words were used shows no detectable differences.

The Analysis. The associations were transcribed to IBM cards, and a 7090 program generated an alphabetically arranged frequency distribution to each stimulus. A second program[2] generated the 38,503 intersection coefficients among the associative distributions to these adjectives. The program depends upon the assumption that each S makes a representational response to each stimulus (Deese, 1962a). The intersection coefficients, based upon the total distribution of 100 overt responses per stimulus plus 100 instances of the assumed representational response, were computed as follows:

$$Ic = \frac{\Sigma R_C}{(N_A \cdot N_B)^{1/2}}$$

The numerator of the equation is the distribution of responses in common between two stimuli, A and B, while the denominator is the geometric mean of the two distributions. The equation is identical to

[2] These two programs were developed by Mr. Fred S. Zusman, National Biomedical Research Foundation, Silver Spring, Maryland. Summaries of the programs may be obtained by writing the author of this paper.

that defining the correlation coefficient in terms of common elements.

Validation Techniques. The major analysis reported in this study is aimed at the description of the structure of the internal relationships in associative meaning. Underlying this analysis, however, is the view that *all* intraverbal meaning can be described as subsets of associative meaning. In a word, associative meaning provides the general case of intraverbal meaning. Therefore, associative meaning should describe the ordinary uses of words as well as the results of special techniques for assessing the meaning of individual words (including the semantic differential).

Therefore, a number of special techniques are used in this study, and these techniques are meant to validate various aspects of the structural analysis of associative meaning. Some of the special devices that are used include (a) asking Ss to generate verbal contexts for adjectives ("give me a sentence using the word *hot*"), (b) asking Ss to rate the meaning of particular adjectives, (c) and asking Ss to judge the contextual appropriateness of certain adjective-noun pairs ("Are these words likely to appear together in an ordinary English sentence?"). Various samples of Ss are used in these studies, and both the number of Ss employed and the nature of the particular technique are described in the appropriate place.

RESULTS

The first problem is to reduce the 38,503 individual intersection coefficients to their basic patterns. Perhaps this could be accomplished by the brute-force application of some technique of structural analysis, such as factor analysis. However, it seems to be more efficient and appropriate to make use of some the known properties of adjectives to simplify the analysis.

The contrastive, polar-opposite pattern of adjectives has been widely used (Osgood *et al.*, 1957; Deese, 1962b), but all previous uses have been marred by the necessity of a content or semantic definition (and consequent subjective judgment) of contrast. Yet, if this contrastive property is important in associative meaning, it should be revealed directly by some aspect of the associative distributions themselves. The notion of contrast implies that one member of the pair should have its associative meaning most strongly determined by

the other and that the relationship should be reciprocal.

Therefore, all pairs of words in which the stimulus to one is the most frequently occurring response to the other are contrasting pairs. Table I shows all of the adjectives from the present study that obey this rule. The mutual response frequencies for these pairs are also listed. Two features of this table are (a) the apparent face validity of the associative definition of contrast, and (b) the fact that the pairs which occur in this table account for 29% of the total sample of adjectives used in this study. The sample itself is very nearly exhaustive of common English adjectives, so a very considerable portion of the associative meaning of common English adjectives can be directly described by the contrast or polar-opposite scheme.

These pairs were subjected to a principal-components factor analysis with diagonals of unity and a varimax criterion of rotation (Kaiser, 1959). The results showed that contrasting pairs tended to be defined by factor loadings that were very nearly orthogonal. The discovery of this pattern led to the analysis presented in Table 2.

Table 2 presents correlations between unrotated factor loadings for the first and second factors in pair-by-pair factor analyses. The data presented in Table 2 are only for a sample of the contrasting pairs. The sample is not a random one. The pairs were picked, by inspection, to produce a sample more highly intercorrelated than pairs at random. Therefore, the table exhibits less orthogonality in the pair factor-loadings than does the entire collection of pairs. For example, intuitive judgment as well as the intersection coefficients would suggest that the pairs *big-little* and *large-small* would be related to one another. Therefore, these pairs were included in the sample in Table 2. The sample was not designed to maximize pair intercorrelations (it was more important to represent certain critical pairs) but it shows more intercorrelation than would the entire collection of pairs.

TABLE 1
ALL WORDS THAT FORM CONTRASTING PAIRS BY THE CRITERION OF ELICITING ONE ANOTHER AS PRIMARIES[a]

Words		Response frequencies		Words		Response frequencies	
Above	Below	35	27	Happy	Sad	16	19
Alone	Together	10	6	Hard	Soft	28	15
Active	Passive	17	21	Heavy	Light*	18	5
Alive	Dead	44	22	High	Low	17	31
Back	Front	22	25	Inside	Outside	40	40
Bad	Good	43	29	Large	Small	23	13
Big	Little	14	15	Left	Right*	51	19
Black	White	39	23	Long	Short*	21	11
Bottom	Top	25	28	Married	Single	21	20
Clean	Dirty	15	21	Narrow	Wide	15	12
Cold	Hot	20	41	New	Old	13	20
Dark	Light	16	16	Old*	Young	7	25
Deep	Shallow	10	19	Poor	Rich	19	26
Dry	Wet	19	25	Pretty	Ugly	13	18
Easy	Hard*	17	5	Right	Wrong	39	41
Empty	Full	17	23	Rough	Smooth	10	16
Far	Near	17	35	Short	Tall	14	15
Fast	Slow	19	27	Sour	Sweet	18	12
Few	Many	41	21	Strong	Weak	13	26
First	Last	28	21	Thick	Thin	21	13

[a] For those words marked by an asterisk, the primary has been pre-empted by another contrast. In these cases, the word marked elicits the other member of the pair as its second highest frequency response. The numbers are response frequencies ($N = 100$); the first number is the association from left to right, while the second number is the association from right to left.

TABLE 2
CORRELATIONS BETWEEN FACTOR LOADINGS OF A SELECTED SAMPLE OF PAIR CONTRASTS

	Large-Small	Bad-Good	Pretty-Ugly	Soft-Loud[a]	Soft-Hard	Easy-Hard	Light-Dark	Tall-Short	White-Black	High-Low	Clean-Dirty
Big-Little	0.43	0.09	0.03	0.09	0.06	0.05	0.02	0.09	0.02	0.03	0.03
Large-Small	—	0.06	0.04	0.01	0.05	0.02	0.02	0.08	0.00	0.06	0.02
Bad-Good		—	0.07	0.00	0.03	0.02	0.06	0.02	0.02	0.03	0.06
Pretty-Ugly			—	0.04	0.05	0.00	0.03	0.00	0.04	0.00	0.04
Soft-Loud[a]				—	0.09	0.05	0.03	0.01	0.01	0.04	0.00
Soft-Hard					—	0.14	0.02	0.00	0.04	0.03	0.03
Easy-Hard						—	0.06	0.00	0.03	0.02	0.03
Light-Dark							—	0.00	0.12	0.04	0.08
Tall Short								—	0.00	0.08	0.00
White-Black									—	0.04	0.05
High-Low										—	0.02

[a] Soft-Loud is not a fundamental contrast by the reciprocal primary criterion. It conforms, however, to the general pattern of adjective contrast, and it is included here because of the interest in the series Easy-Hard-Soft-Loud.

The correlations between contrasting pairs were computed from the angles made by the vectors for sets of pairs in two dimensions. Figure 1 shows an example of two factors so plotted. Notice that the loadings for individual members of contrasting pairs are almost precisely the same. Therefore, it was quite easy to determine the angles from single vectors for the pairs. The cosines of the factor-loading vectors are the numbers in Table 2.

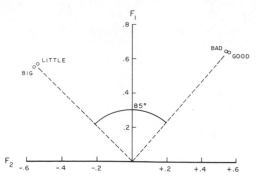

FIG. 1. An example showing the vectors projected by the factor loadings in F_1 and F_2 of fundamental contrasts.

Notice that nearly all of the 66 correlations within this set are very low. Only three exceed .10. The correlation for the *big-little, large-small* pairs is 0.43; that for the *soft-hard, easy-hard* set is 0.14, and that for the *white-black, light-dark* set is 0.12. In other words, most of the vectors defined by the pair factor-loadings are very nearly at right angles. For the present data, a model of completely independent contrasting pairs is not greatly in error. If we remember that the pairs chosen for Table 2 consist of relatively highly related contrasts, the general model of orthogonal contrasting pairs seems to be useful. Therefore, the associative meaning for an appreciable proportion of common adjectives in English can be described as consisting of very nearly independent contrasts. It is very likely that a considerable number of such independent contrasting pairs exists among adjectives not sampled here.

What of the remaining words? Some of them at least owe part of their intraverbal meaning to the fact that scalar properties can be added to certain of the contrasts. That fact is revealed in the analysis below.

Recent work on adverbial qualification of adjectives shows that a certain class of adverbs can scale the intensity of adjectival meaning (Cliff, 1959; Howe, 1963). Furthermore, the inflected series of adjectives (*big, bigger, biggest*) suggests at least an ordering along a single semantic dimension defined by a basic contrast (*big-little*). Finally, intuition suggests ·that adjectives such as *huge* express a position more extreme on the same dimension than such adjectives as *big*. The following analysis is aimed at recovering some examples of such scaled dimensions from the factor analysis of matrices of intersection coefficients.

If different adjectives are to define positions on a scaled dimension given direction by a basic contrast, such adjectives must produce distributions which have appreciable intersections with the basic contrasting pair. Therefore, we can recover a scaled adjectival dimension by considering matrices of intersections in which each word has an arbitrarily large intersection with at least two other words in the set. With the arbitrary cut-off set at 0.10, several sets were so produced, with the two largest (in number of words) presented here.

Table 3 shows unrotated factor loadings for the first three factors for the collection of words centering around *big-little*. The nature of factor analysis permits a simple and straightforward interpretation of the first unrotated factor. The F_1 loadings are proportional to the column sum of the intercorrelations from the original matrix. As such, they reflect the extent to which the words share their associative distributions with other words in the same set. According to the view stated earlier (Deese, 1962a,b) and amplified in this paper, the extent to which words share associative distributions is determined by the extent to which they share contexts in ordinary discourse.

The second column of Table 3 provides a measure of the extent to which each adjective shares the noun contexts of all the other adjectives. The numbers in that column were obtained in the following way. For each of the adjectives, ten Ss were asked to produce ten nouns that might reasonably follow these adjectives in ordinary discourse. The ten most frequently occurring such nouns for a given adjective were combined on a single sheet with the nouns from all the other adjectives. One could say that the sheet reflected the

TABLE 3

FACTOR LOADINGS AND THE APPROPRIATE VALIDATION DATA FOR THE COLLECTION
OF WORDS CENTERING AROUND *Big-Little*[a]

Words	F_1	Context ratings	F_2	L Count	F_3	Size ratings
Tiny	0.460	1.71	—0.301	527	—0.446	0.8
Slight	0.360	1.42	—0.345	419	—0.424	1.5
Little	0.490	3.22	0.413	8659	—0.338	1.8
Small	0.519	3.53	0.382	1818	—0.333	1.9
Big	0.556	3.59	0.335	1773	0.308	4.3
Large	0.544	3.56	0.353	1697	0.323	4.5
Great	0.399	2.15	—0.363	3834	0.342	5.1
Grand	0.372	1.39	—0.330	429	0.347	4.6
Vast	0.406	1.93	—0.380	241	0.365	5.5
Huge	0.473	2.11	—0.315	311	0.381	5.6

[a] The nature of the validation data is explained in text.

"average" nominal context for these ten adjectives. Ten of these sheets were given to each of ten new Ss. At the top of each sheet was listed one of the adjectives. The Ss were asked to judge the appropriateness of adjective-noun combinations by placing a check mark next to those nouns appropriate to the adjective at the top. The measure in column two of Table 3 is the mean number of Ss per noun who judged the adjective-noun combinations to be appropriate. It reflects the extent to which that particular adjective is judged to be appropriate to nouns from all the other adjectives.

Some adjectives are clearly more generally appropriate than others. The adjective *big*, for example, was judged by 3.59 Ss per noun to be appropriate, while the adjective *grand* was judged to be appropriate by only 1.39 Ss per noun. These means produce a rank-difference correlation of 0.903 ($p < 0.01$) with the F_1 loadings. Therefore, the first factor is closely identified with this measure of general context.

The second factor in Table 3 is correlated with word frequency. The numbers in the fourth column are L-count frequencies from the Thorndike-Lorge (1944) count. Again, there is a significant rank-order correlation, 0.612 ($p < 0.05$), between word frequency and F_2 loadings. The single anomalous case

is provided by the adjective *great*, which may be unusual here because perhaps it more often functions as an adverbial qualifier in ordinary speech than as a modifier of nouns.

It is not until we come to F_3 that we come to the principal semantic dimension relating this collection of words. Column five shows that the unrotated F_3 loadings define a bipolar factor which clearly separates the large words from the small words. This factor is highly correlated ($rho = 0.988$, $p < 0.01$) with ratings of these words on a size dimension. The numbers in column six are the mean ratings on a seven-point scale for ten Ss of each adjective according to the size of an object that adjective might describe. The anchors of the scale are the largest thing imaginable and the smallest thing imaginable. It is clear that the factor analysis accomplishes the same sort of ordering of words that is achieved by direct ratings of the words.

The above analysis accomplishes two things: (a) it gives external evidence for the validity of factor analysis of matrices of associative distributions, and (b) it shows that structures underlying the interrelations of associative distributions are partly composed of semantic and partly composed of other linguistic features.

A second analysis of a similar sort is presented in Table 4. This table presents the first two unrotated factors from the inflectional series, *worst, worse, bad, good, better, best.* It so happens that these are among a very few inflected forms found among high-frequency adjectives. As before, the first factor reflects the summed intercorrelations. This time, however, the F_1 loading are almost identical. Taking the viewpoint adopted in the preceding analysis, these words are almost completely interchangeable in context. This

TABLE 4

FACTOR LOADINGS FOR THE FIRST TWO FACTORS IN THE INFLECTED *Good-Bad* SERIES

Words	F_1	F_2
Best	0.524	0.403
Better	0.530	0.374
Good	0.565	0.278
Bad	0.562	—0.279
Worse	0.553	—0.382
Worst	0.559	—0.392

is not entirely true, for the original matrix reveals that the intercorrelations are bunched in three pairs, *good-bad, better-worse,* and *best-worst.* The second factor, in this case, is perfectly ordered with the formal grammatical definition of the inflected series. Therefore, taking the structure of the language itself as a measure, we have further evidence for the validity of the results achieved from a factor analysis of collections of related words.

Finally, one additional factor analysis of

a set of closely related adjectives is presented in Table 5. The first factor is again identified as a contextual one, and such an interpretation is substantiated by the correlation between the context ratings (obtained in the same way as those in Table 3) and F_1 loadings. The *rho* in this case is 0.552, $p \simeq 0.05$. The correlation is lower because the context ratings are less reliable. In this instance, Ss were required, in some cases, to change the nouns from singular to plural and *vice versa.* For example, the sequence *many-times* would have to be changed to *entire-time.* The additional task imposed upon the Ss produced less intersubject agreement.

The F_2 loadings seem to reflect a dimension of amount or numerosity, but some of the details of the loadings in column three of Table 5 are puzzling. For one thing, the F_2 loadings suggest that *many* is a word that is closer to *few* semantically that to *all, total* or *entire.* Also, the adjectives *all, total* and *entire,* which are usually taken to mean the same order of numerosity or amount, differ in F_2 loadings. Nevertheless, a scaling procedure for these adjectives reveals more validity to the analysis than common sense would seem to allow.

The scaling in this case consisted of presenting to 50 Ss a series of statements about (a) an audience of 100 individuals attending

TABLE 5

FACTOR LOADINGS AND THE APPROPRIATE VALIDATION DATA FOR THE COLLECTION OF WORDS DESCRIBING NUMEROSITY[a]

Words	F_1	Context ratings	F_2	Mean numerosity choice
Entire	0.305	4.45	0.511	86.0
Total	0.314	3.89	0.502	71.4
All	0.416	6.13	0.452	85.5
Various	0.451	5.24	0.044	28.9
Numerous	0.525	5.23	—0.042	36.7
Considerable	0.329	3.00	—0.063	34.9
Some	0.483	6.43	—0.159	36.5
Many	0.629	5.84	—0.398	27.5
Several	0.564	5.97	—0.405	13.1
Few	0.581	5.69	—0.434	9.3

[a] The validation data are described in text.

a lecture and (b) an objective examination consisting of 100 questiosn. Each statement contained one of the adjectives in Table 5. The Ss were asked to circle the approximate number described in the statement with the following alternatives: 100, 95, 75, 50, 25, 5, 0. The statements were of the following sort: "A few questions were ambiguous"; "the entire examination consisted of numerical examples"; "some people interrupted the speech with applause"; "many people fell asleep because of the room." The content of the questions was balanced over the adjectives, and all Ss received both series of statements.

The fourth column of Table 5 shows the mean number selected for each adjective. Two features of these data are worth noting: (a) the correlation with the F_2 loadings is high ($rho = 0.903$, $p < 0.01$), and (b) like the factor loadings, the reactions of the Ss to these adjectives when embedded in sentences does not conform to the logical or dictionary definitions for the words. The most remarkable aspect of the latter result is that *many*, on the average, means less than half the total for these two situations, and, furthermore, *many* is very close to *few* and *several* in the mean alternative chosen.

Therefore, not only is some validity established for the factor loadings, but there is the strong implication that such loadings come closer to revealing the actual usage of words in ordinary English than do the formal definitions.

Can scales be established for all contrasting pairs? Because of sampling limitations, we cannot answer that question forthwith; in order to do so, we would need a nearly exhaustive sample of English adjectives. Some indirect evidence may be brought to bear on the question, however, and that evidence suggests that some contrasts are not ordinarily scaled. First of all, there are some contrast pairs that do not ordinarily appear with the class of adverbial qualifiers usually described as intensifiers. Some examples of these are *former-latter, outside-inside, front-back, first-*

last, below-above, and *married-single*. Furthermore, although the formal characteristics would suggest these to be inflected adjectives (Fries, 1952), they are not inflected and would rarely appear with *more* or *most*. Finally, within the limitations of the present sample, none of these words appears to have any appreciable intersection (above 0.10) with any adjective other than its contrasting word. All of this suggests, though does not directly demonstrate, that there is a class of adjectives defined by the contrast scheme for which no scalar properties are usually assigned.

Finally, what of the adjectives that do not appear in any of the contrast schemes? A number of these owe their intraverbal meaning to combinations of underlying contrast schemes. For example, the adjective *great* appears both in the dimension defined F_3 in Table 3 and in an ordered series of adjectives which are based upon *good-bad*. The nature of this multiple dependence on underlying contrasts is not altogether certain, but it is at least very strongly possible that many words, on the average somewhat lower in frequency of usage (Deese, 1962b) have their multiple intraverbal meanings determined by scaled or ordered positions on a number of underlying contrasts.

In addition, however, there are certain adjectives which do not conform to the polar-contrast scheme at all and yet form highly interrelated sets. The most highly organized and numerous set of such adjectives in the present sample is to be found in color names. A large number of these (*black, white, red, gray, yellow, green, blue, pink, orange, brown, purple*) appears in the present sample, but with the single exception of *black-white* they do not meet the criterion of contrast. Nor does a factor analysis of these adjectives suggest any simple semantic organization. It is possible that these organize themselves into a structure resembling color space, but a larger sample would be necessary (to better represent saturation and brightness) before anything definite can be said on that score.

A total of 179 or 64% of the present sample is made up of either basic contrasts or words that appear on one or more scales derived from contrasts. The remaining 81 words (the color words excepted) may appear either as contrasts for which one member of the pair did not appear in the sample or as derived from one or more basic contrasts not present in the sample. It is, at the same time, possible that some of these are from other collections, like the color names, that do not produce basic contrasts. The results analyzed above, however, show that a very large number of common adjectives can be assimilated to the basic contrast scheme. The existence in English of formal affixes (*un, non, im,* etc.) to produce contrast where none exists in the vocabulary itself testifies to the importance of the contrast scheme among adjectives. It is to be noted that the color names, in general, do not appear with these affixes.

DISCUSSION

There are two main topics remaining to be covered in a general discussion. These are (a) the relation of the present data to the semantic differential, and (b) a more general account of possibilities as to how the relations in associative meaning arise. The first question is more specific and may be covered quite directly.

The present data show that an analysis of associative distributions confirms the advisability of using the polar-opposite scheme in the semantic-differential technique. Such a scheme makes the semantic differential a bit more linguistically relevant than, say, the adjective check list. At the same time, both associative and morphological grounds lead to the view that the polar opposite scheme does not apply to all English adjectives.

Furthermore, the present analysis implies severe limitations to the semantic differential (on the assumption, of course, of the validity of the generality of associative meaning). For one thing, the analysis of the present sample

of 278 adjectives shows that, in associative meaning, there are at least 40 nearly orthogonal bipolar dimensions, and it is probable that the present sample comes nowhere near exhausting the possible independent contrasts in the language. From this point of view, the 20 scales of the semantic differential should be regarded as a sample from an appreciably larger set of such contrasts. This is essentially the view advanced by Carroll (1959) in his critical analysis of the semantic differential. In addition, it should be remarked, several of the semantic differential anchors are not fundamental contrasts by the present view.

The associative independence of the contrasting pairs in the present data questions the advisability of trying to reduce the 20 scales of the semantic differential to a smaller number (usually three) of orthogonal factors. Again, Carroll's critique advances the possibility that the usual reduction achieved in a factor analysis of semantic-differential data is a function of sampling limitations in the concepts rated.

In short, while the semantic differential is defensible as a specific technique, the generality of semantic space derived from it can be challenged both on logical grounds (Carroll, 1959) and from the present analysis. Furthermore, the fact that *S*s are required by the semantic differential sometimes to rate bizarre combinations of nouns and adjectives (to decide, for example, whether a *boulder* is *peaceful* or *ferocious*) probably inflates, all out of proportion, what would be very rare linguistic usage. On these grounds, the analysis of associative meaning would more accurately reflect normal linguistic usage.

Finally, while the contrast scheme seems amply justified as a general technique for finding the meaning of adjectives or determining how adjectives are related to the meaning of words of other classes, it is not so certain that a scale, with the contrasts as anchors, is always appropriate. Some adjective pairs do not define scalar dimensions, and, even when they do, they do not always make the best possible anchors (extremes) for those dimensions.

How do the basic structures of associative meaning of adjectives arise? Previous argument (Deese, 1962a,b) as well as the present data point to relations in intraverbal meaning growing out of partial contextual equivalences. Ervin (1961, 1963) and McNeill (1963) have argued for, and presented data in support of, the proposition that paradigmatic (grammatical) equivalences in association grow out of contextual equivalences in ordinary language. McNeill presents data which show that Ss trained on artificial words in identical English contexts increase the frequency with which they will give one paradigmatically equivalent artificial word as an associate to another in free association.

The data showing the correlations between judged contextual appropriateness and F_1 loadings in Tables 3 and 5 strongly imply that the generalized matrices of associative intersection (unrotated first factor-loadings) are very highly related to equivalent matrices of contextual equivalences in ordinary language. There will be associative intersection to the extent that there are contextual equivalences between pairs of words.

Is it possible that the particular general scheme (contrast) that organizes so large a number of adjectives grows out of equivalences in context? Here the issues are more complicated. For one thing, an extra-linguistic psychological hypothesis suggests itself. The strong contrastive property of adjectives may have nothing to do with the contextual equivalences within language, but, instead, may be the result of the correlation between words or morphemes and reinforcement contingencies in nature. The contingencies, of course, are to attributes of objects in the general environment. Such a view would imply that attributes are fundamentally two-fold: things are either *hot* or *cold*, *good* or *bad*, or *big* or *little*. It is to be noted that the most striking exception to the contrastive nature of attributes is color, and color names

are multifold, rather than twofold: *red* can be contrasted with *blue*, with *green* or with *yellow*.

The implication is that pairs themselves are detemined by contextual equivalences but their bipolar contrasts on a semantic dimension by contingencies in the discrimination of attributes and words. Such a view further implies that there is some underlying cause to the two-fold state. There must be a reason why *big* is contrasted with *little* and not, say, with *soft*. Such a cause could be the paradigmatic equivalences in the language, as these have been demonstrated in this and other papers on form-class and association, or it could be the result of some natural perceptual or cognitive property. We cannot decide among these at present; it is, however, worth pointing out the possibilities in order to emphasize the possibility of both intraverbal (linguistic) and external determiners for association and associative meaning. Furthermore, the analysis presented here suggests possibilities for the experimental variation and control of structures of associative meaning by the methods introduced by McNeill (1963).

SUMMARY

This paper presents an analysis of the relations among the associative distributions to 278 English adjectives. These adjectives provide a nearly exhaustive sample of adjectives with Thorndike-Lorge frequencies of 50 occurrences per million or greater. The analysis shows that among these adjectives there are 40 pairs of polar opposites or contrasts. Factor analysis of the intersections of associative distributions among these polar opposites reveals that they are nearly completely orthogonal. There is a sizeable correlation between loadings for the pairs *big-little* and *large-small*; nearly all the remaining pairs produce correlations close to zero.

Some of the pairs define scales on which it is possible to locate parts of the intraverbal meaning of other adjectives. More than 100 adjectives in the present sample are located on one or more scales produced by the basic contrasts. Not all pairs of contrasts, however, have scalar properties; these words define contrasts but not contrasting scales. Finally, not all adjectives are organized by contrast, though it is probable that a very large number, perhaps the majority, are.

Finally evidence is presented for the general linguistic validity of the results of factor analysis of associative meaning. Such evidence points to the determination of intraverbal relations in meaning by partial contextual equivalences plus whatever external contingencies exist between words and the environment at large.

REFERENCES

CARROLL, J. B., Review of OSGOOD, C. E., SUCI, G. J., AND TANNENBAUM, P. H. The measurement of meaning. *Language,* 1959, **35**, 58-77.

CLIFF, N. Adverbs as multipliers. *Psychol. Rev.,* 1959, **66**, 27-44.

DEESE, J. Form class and the determinants of association. *J. verb. Learn. verb. Behav.,* 1962, **1**, 79-84.

DEESE, J. On the structure of associative meaning. *Psychol. Rev.,* 1962, **69**, 161-175.

ERVIN, S. Changes with age in the verbal determinants of word-association. *Amer. J. Psychol.,* 1961, **74**, 361-372.

ERVIN, S. Correlates of associative frequency. *J. verb. Learn. verb. Behav.,* 1963, **1**, 422-431.

FRIES, C. C. *The structure of English.* New York: Harcourt, Brace, 1952.

HOWE, E. S. Probabilistic adverbial qualifications of adjectives. *J. verb. Learn. verb. Behav.,* 1962, **1**, 225-242.

KAISER, H. F. The varimax criterion for analytic rotation in factor analysis. *Psychometrika,* 1958, **23**, 187-200.

MCNEILL, D. The origin of associations within the same grammatical class. *J. verb. Learn verb. Behav.,* 1963, **2**, 250-262.

OSGOOD, C. E., SUCI, G. J., AND TANNENBAUM, P. H. *The measurement of meaning.* Urbana: Univer. of Illinois Press, 1957.

THORNDIKE, E. L., AND LORGE, I. *The teacher's word book of 30,000 words.* New York: Bureau of Publications, Teachers Coll., Columbia Univer., 1944.

18. Probability, Learning,

the Statistical Structure of Concepts,

and the Measurement of Meaning

Charles M. Solley and Samuel J. Messick

Although there have been many discussions about the meaning of
'meaning,' there have been few attempts to measure meaning.[1] This
paucity of measurement stems not only from difficulties as to how to
measure, but also from uncertainty as to what to measure. The possibility should be considered that several different kinds of meaning may
exist for one concept and that various measuring devices may be reflecting
different aspects of meaning. When different aspects of a single concept
exist, they are probably related to the different ways and, in some cases,
to the different situations in which individuals learn that concept. Thus,
a consideration of concept-formation might have important implications
for the systematic description and measurement of various aspects of
meaning.

This experiment is an attempt to relate the measurement of meaning
to certain hypotheses concerning the formation of meaning in a statistical framework. It considers the meaning of a concept to be a reflection
of probability-relationships among and within the referents of the concept. For example, consider one way in which we could learn a concept
such as 'Italians.' First we might experience a large number of referents
to which the label 'Italians' is applied. A specific Italian might be tall,
happy, skinny, and quick; another might be short, happy, fat, and quick.
Whenever *S* experiences a specific Italian, he experiences (or samples) a
combination of perceptual events.[2] Each combination of the potential perceptual events has a certain probability of occurring in the population of
referents to which a common label is being applied. Somehow, as the individual gets more and more experience with more and more referents,
communalities are abstracted, and a concept emerges—a process exempli-

Reprinted from *American Journal of Psychology* (1957), 70: 161–173, by permission of the
authors and the publisher.

[1] C. E. Osgood, The nature and measurement of meaning, *Psychol. Bull.*, 49, 1952,
192-237. For more general discussions see S. I. Hayakawa, *Language in Action*,
1941, 214-261; Charles Morris, *Signs, Language, and Behavior*, 1946, 1-31; C. K.
Ogden and I. A. Richards, *The Meaning of Meaning*, 1938, 185-208.

[2] W. K. Estes, Toward a statistical theory of learning, *Psychol. Rev.*, 57, 1950,
94-107; W. K. Estes and C. J. Burke, A theory of stimulus variability in learning,
Psychol. Rev., 60, 1953, 276-286.

fied by the learning of Hull's Chinese characters.[3] Several abstractions can be made, however, for any given population of referents, and communalities may be combined in different ways for each abstraction. It seems, then, that if we knew more about probability-relationships among the referents of a concept, we could systematically construct what might be called the 'statistical structure' of the concept; *i.e.* we could describe the concept's meaning in terms of the likelihood that certain combinations of the various aspects will occur.

These different combinations of the aspects of a concept may be reflected differentially by various instruments designed to measure meaning. For example, the 'semantic differential' may measure only one statistical aspect of the meaning of a concept; whereas other techniques, such as word association or the method of triads, might reflect different statistical aspects of the same concept.[4] If we knew more about the statistical structure of concepts, then, it might be possible to specify some relationships between that statistical structure and the various devices used to measure meaning.

STATISTICAL STRUCTURE OF CONCEPTS AND PROBABILITY-LEARNING

The following hypothetical example illustrates what is meant here by the statistical structure of the perceptual characteristics of referents. Let us consider an imaginary tribe of 24 South Pacific natives that happens to have the distribution of perceptual characteristics shown in Table I. Fifteen of these tribesmen are tall and nine are short; eighteen are happy and six are sad. All 15 of the tall tribesmen are happy and none is sad, while only three of the short tribesmen are happy and six are sad. If an explorer (*E*) were to land on this island and were to meet these natives one at a time, he would gradually acquire information concerning this combination of characteristics; *i.e.* he would learn that most of the tribesmen are tall and happy, none of the tall tribesmen is sad, and short tribesmen are likely to be sad. If we were to ask *E* to guess what the characteristics would be for the next native he was about to meet, we could gain some information about the way in which he learned these attributes; *i.e.* if *E* were to guess beforehand whether each native in turn was going to be tall or short and happy or sad, we could plot a learning curve for each of the four combinations of attributes. Recent studies on probability-learning suggest the result that, as *E* becomes more and more familiar with these natives, he would begin guessing each combination of characteristics more and more in proportion to their 'true' frequency-distributions.[5]

    [3] C. L. Hull, Quantitative aspects of the evolution of concepts, *Psychol. Monogr.,* 38, 1920 (No. 123), 1-86.
    [4] Osgood, *op. cit.,* 222-232; W. S. Torgerson, Multidimensional scaling: I. Theory and method, *Psychometrika,* 17, 1952, 401-419.
    [5] Egon Brunswik, Probability as a determiner of rat behavior, *J. exp. Psychol.,* 25, 1939, 175-197; R. R. Bush and Frederick Mosteller, A mathematical model for

TABLE I

PERCEPTUAL CHARACTERISTICS OF A HYPOTHETICAL TRIBE

Characteristics	Happy	Sad	Total
Tall	15	0	15
Short	3	6	9
Total	18	6	24

TABLE II

FREQUENCY OF OCCURRENCE OF VARIOUS COMBINATIONS OF CHARACTERISTICS FOR FOUR HYPOTHETICAL TRIBES OF STICKMEN

Characteristics	Tribes			
	A	B	C	D
tall-skinny-happy-white	12	3	0	0
tall-fat-happy-white	0	4	0	0
tall-skinny-sad-white	3	8	0	0
tall-fat-sad-white	0	0	0	0
short-skinny-happy-white	0	5	0	0
short-fat-happy-white	0	0	0	0
short-skinny-sad-white	1	0	0	0
short-fat-sad-white	4	0	0	0
tall-skinny-happy-black	0	0	4	0
tall-fat-happy-black	0	0	1	0
tall-skinny-sad-black	0	0	0	0
tall-fat-sad-black	0	0	0	5
short-skinny-happy-black	0	0	0	0
short-fat-happy-black	0	0	3	8
short-skinny-sad-black	0	0	0	4
short-fat-sad-black	0	0	12	3

This simple example describes how learning increments reflect the proportional occurrences of various combinations of perceived attributes, and it also suggests how this statistical structure might be investigated by an experiment in probability-learning.[6]

To study the probability-learning of combinations of perceptual characteristics, it was decided to construct an artificial concept for which the 'true' frequency-distribution of attributes would be known. The concept chosen was 'Tribe,' and the referents for this concept were a series of drawings of little men whose perceptual characteristics varied with respect to the following bi-polar attributes: *tall-short, happy-sad, fat-skinny,* and *black-white.* Drawings of 20 little men, who came to be known as 'stickmen,' constituted a 'tribe;' four tribes were constructed, each with a different distribution of perceptual characteristics. These distributions are given in Table II.

This table indicates that Tribes A and B are identical with respect to the marginal frequencies of occurrence for the different stimulus-characteristics; *i.e.* there are 15 tall and 5 short stickmen in each tribe, 12 happy and 8 sad, 16 skinny and 4 fat, and 20 white. These two tribes, however, are rather different

simple learning, *Psychol. Rev.,* 58, 1951, 313-323; H. W. Hake and Ray Hyman, Perception of the statistical structure of a random series of binary symbols, *J. exp. Psychol.,* 45, 1953, 64-74.

[6] E. C. Tolman and Egon Brunswik, The organism and the causal texture of the environment, *Psychol. Rev.,* 42, 1935, 43-77.

with respect to the joint occurrence of specific combinations of perceptual characteristics; *e.g.* in Tribe A there are 12 tall, skinny, happy, white stickmen, while only three have that description in Tribe B. Thus, with respect to marginal characteristics, Tribes A and B have identical 'meanings,' but with respect to another statistical aspect of the referents, mainly the joint occurrence of combinations of characteristics, the tribes have somewhat different 'meanings.' Tribes C and D are mirror images of Tribes A and B, respectively; *e.g.* instead of having 12 tall, skinny, happy, white tribesmen as in Tribe A, Tribe C has 12 short, fat, sad, black ones.

So, if a measuring instrument should reflect only the marginal probability-relationships, Tribes A and B should be found to be identical with respect to measured meaning. Tribes C and D should also be identical in this aspect, although their 'meaning' would not be the same as for Tribes A and B. If, however, the measuring instrument reflects the joint occurrence of characteristics or some combination of joint occurrence plus the marginal characteristics, then the meanings of Tribes A, B, C, and D should be differentiated. Since the meanings of concepts, even in terms of only two semantic aspects, involve characteristics varying in more than one way, it seems reasonable to base semantic measurement upon multidimensional models. One such device for measuring meaning multidimensionally is described in the next section, and the adequacy of its measures is evaluated in terms of the statistical theory of concept-referents discussed above.

The Semantic Differential

Mosier made one of the few attempts to measure the meaning of concepts with a unidimensional psychometric scaling procedure, but the complexity and probable multidimensionality of the meaning domain makes a one-dimensional approach seem inadequate for complete coverage.[7] When Osgood and Suci developed the *semantic differential,* a multidimensional analysis of meaning-structure as a basis for more complete measurement became available.[8] By factor analyzing the intercorrelations among 50 scales which had been identified by such bipolar adjectives as *good-bad, strong-weak,* etc., they first obtained some idea of the dimensionality of meaning.[9] Three orthogonal factors were extracted: an evaluative dimension, a potency dimension, and an activity dimension. It was now reasonable to attempt to find some measure that would enable experimenters to locate concepts in such a three-dimensional semantic space. To do this, Osgood required subjects to judge a concept's position along each dimension separately, having selected a small number of relatively pure-factor bipolar scales to represent each of the three semantic dimensions. In other words, a group of subjects (Ss) are asked to judge the position of a concept on a set of bipolar scales representing the evaluative dimension, then on a set representing the potency dimension, and finally on a set representing the activity dimension. The average scale-position of the concept on each of these dimensions locates it as a point in the semantic space.

[7] C. I. Mosier, A psychometric study of meaning, *J. soc. Psychol.,* 13, 1941, 123-140.

[8] C. E. Osgood and G. J. Suci, A measure of relation determined by both mean differences and profile information, *Psychol. Bull.,* 49, 1952, 251-262.

[9] Osgood and Suci, A factor analysis of meaning, *J. exp. Psychol.,* in press.

If, however, the meaning of a concept depends upon probability relationships among characteristics of the concept's referents, the question now arises as to which statistical aspect of meaning is being reflected by the semantic differential. Or, put another way, for what statistical aspects of concepts is the semantic differential 'valid'? In responding to the semantic differential S is asked to check the position of a concept on a bipolar scale (for examples see Fig. 1). For a concept like 'tribe of stickmen' and a scale like *tall-short*, S would have to judge the degree to which stickmen were characterized by tallness or shortness. The judgment process required of S in this case might be conceptualized as the formation of a scale position for the concept in terms of the resultant of the two vectors composing the scale—the 'tall' vector vs. the 'short' vector. That is, S has experienced a number of 'tall' stickmen and a number of 'short' stickmen and he checks at the point describing the average of his experiences. If the scale consists of seven categories running from $+3$ (very tall) through zero to -3 (very short), and if equal intervals are assumed, then the resultant score (an expected value) for the concept 'tribe of stickmen' based *only* on the marginal stimulus-probabilities would be:

$$E_{score} = 3p_{tall} - 3p_{short}$$

where E_{score} is the expected score, p_{tall} refers to the proportion of times tall stickmen occur in the tribe, and p_{short} refers to the proportion of times short stickmen occur in the tribe.

This expected score is based only upon the marginal characteristics of the concept, so Tribes A and B would have identical resultant scores. If this simple two-vector model adequately represents the way in which an individual checks a scale on the semantic differential, then Tribes A and B should both be placed at the same predicted point. If Tribes A and B are both placed at the same point but not at the predicted one, then the semantic differential is still only reflecting the marginal characteristics of the concepts, since these are the only characteristics for which Tribes A and B are identical, but the two-vector score model is not an adequate representation of this. If Tribes A and B are placed at different points on the semantic differential scales, then not only is the two-vector model inadequate, but the instrument is reflecting something more than marginal meaning.

The use of this resultant score to describe an individual's performance on the semantic differential assumes that he has previously learned the perceptual characteristics of the referents. Also, if the measuring device is to have a chance to separate the meanings of Tribes A and B, the Ss must also learn the joint occurrences of combinations as well as the marginal frequencies. So in this experiment the methods used enabled the Ss to become familiar with the referents; the details of the procedure are given in a later section.

Since marginal probabilities for the perceptual characteristics of the artificial concepts of tribe are known, expected values can be computed for each of the scales *tall-short, fat-skinny, black-white, and happy-sad,* thus generating an expected profile of meaning for each of the four concepts of tribe. It must be emphasized here that these expected profiles of meaning are based only upon the marginal characteristics of the concepts, hence Tribes A and B have identical expected profiles, as do Tribes C and D. If, however, the combination frequencies affect the judgment process involved in responding to the semantic differential, some systematic deviation would be expected from the predictions based only on the marginals. Hence, identical profiles for Tribes A and B obtained from the semantic differential would indicate that the judgment process required by that instrument takes only marginal characteristics of concepts into account; whereas different profiles for these two tribes would indicate that the combinations of characteristics are being considered in the procedure. These statements also hold for Tribes C and D.

These predictions, of course, hold only on the assumption that the learned combinations are proportional to the combinations built into the concepts. Even if learning were not complete, however, the above predictions could still be tested by generating expected scores based upon final probabilities of response rather than requiring that the input probabilities be learned exactly.

METHOD

Subjects. Forty undergraduates were used as *S*s. Ten were randomly assigned to each of the four 'tribes' or conditions for learning.

Materials. The materials used in the learning phase of this experiment are described in Table II. Each tribe was composed of 20 cards, upon each of which appeared a schematized figure with a certain combination of characteristics. Two sets of drawings were made for each tribe, and each set was arranged in random order.

The materials used in the measurement phase consisted of a semantic differential composed of 20 scales (as shown in Fig. 1). Four of the scales corresponded specifically to attributes of the stickmen, *i.e. tall-short, fat-skinny, happy-sad,* and *black-white.* The other 16 scales were included to obtain some additional information about possible semantic generalization for the tribes.

Procedure. (1) Learning phase. The procedure for the probability-learning was to have each *S* guess the characteristics of the figure on the top card of the deck, the deck being face down. For example, he would guess whether the drawing on the next card was tall or short, then whether it was happy or sad, then whether it was fat or skinny, and then whether it was black or white. Each *S* thus made one guess for each of the four bipolar attributes on each trial. The card was then turned over, allowing *S* to scan the picture for approximately 5 sec. The card was then removed from view and *S* made his four guesses about the next picture. When guesses had been made for all 20 pictures in this way, another random order of the same deck was presented. This procedure was continued until all the cards in the deck had been seen four times. In pilot work, it had been found that almost all of the learning had occurred by the time *S* had gone through the deck twice.

(2) Measurement phase. The experimenters (*E*s) gave each *S* a copy of a semantic differential composed of 20 scales (as shown in Fig. 1) immediately following the phase of probability-learning. *S* was told to rate on each of the scales the 'tribe of stickmen' he had just seen. The successive intervals were indicated on each scale, but *S* was permitted to check anywhere along the length of the scale rather than being forced to use restricted scale positions.

RESULTS

(1) Learning phase. Summaries of the results of the probability learning are given in Tables III and IV. These tables show that the frequencies

TABLE III

SUMMARY OF LEARNING OF STATISTICAL STRUCTURE OF TRIBES A AND B
(Ten Ss learned each Tribe. Scores are average frequency of guesses for blocks of
20 guesses, a 'trial unit.')

Characteristics	Tribe A, Trial units					Tribe B, Trial units				
	1	2	3	4	Input	1	2	3	4	Input
white-tall-happy-skinny	4.9	10.0	9.7	10.8	12.0	3.6	6.1	5.5	6.8	3.0
white-tall-happy-fat	1.2	.3	.1	.0	.0	2.6	2.1	1.9	2.4	4.0
white-tall-sad-skinny	2.5	3.3	4.8	3.3	3.0	2.6	5.3	5.6	6.5	8.0
white-tall-sad-fat	3.3	.3	.0	.2	.0	1.4	1.5	1.4	.7	.0
white-short-happy-skinny	.9	.3	.5	.4	.0	2.5	1.9	3.5	2.0	5.0
white-short-happy-fat	1.6	1.5	.8	2.2	.0	1.6	1.0	.5	.7	.0
white-short-sad-skinny	.8	.2	.8	.5	1.0	1.2	1.6	1.3	.7	.0
white-short-sad-fat	3.3	3.5	3.1	2.6	4.0	.7	.5	.3	.1	.0
black-tall-happy-skinny	.2	.2	.0	.0	.0	.6	.0	.0	.0	.0
black-tall-happy-fat	.9	.1	.0	.0	.0	.2	.0	.0	.0	.0
black-tall-sad-skinny	.3	.2	.0	.0	.0	.7	.0	.0	.0	.0
black-tall-sad-fat	.5	.0	.0	.0	.0	.2	.0	.0	.0	.0
black-short-happy-skinny	.2	.0	.0	.0	.0	.1	.0	.0	.0	.0
black-short-happy-fat	.4	.0	.0	.0	.0	.9	.0	.0	.0	.0
black-short-sad-skinny	.4	.1	.0	.0	.0	.4	.0	.0	.1	.0
black-short-sad-fat	1.6	.0	.0	.0	.0	.7	.0	.0	.0	.0

TABLE IV

SUMMARY OF LEARNING OF STATISTICAL STRUCTURE OF TRIBES C AND D
(Ten Ss learned each Tribe. Scores are average frequency of guesses for blocks of 20
guesses, a 'Trial unit.')

Characteristics	Tribe C, Trial units					Tribe D, Trial units				
	1	2	3	4	Input	1	2	3	4	Input
white-tall-happy-skinny	1.8	.3	.0	.2	.0	.8	.2	.1	.0	.0
white-tall-happy-fat	1.0	.0	.1	.0	.0	.6	.1	.1	.0	.0
white-tall-sad-skinny	1.9	.4	.2	.1	.0	1.1	.1	.0	.0	.0
white-tall-sad-fat	.6	.0	.1	.0	.0	.3	.1	.0	.0	.0
white-short-happy-skinny	.3	.2	.0	.1	.0	.3	.3	.1	.0	.0
white-short-happy-fat	.8	.0	.0	.1	.0	.3	.2	.2	.0	.0
white-short-sad-skinny	.4	.1	.1	.0	.0	.5	.0	.0	.0	.0
white-short-sad-fat	.5	.0	.0	.2	.0	.4	.1	.3	.0	.0
black-tall-happy-skinny	2.8	.8	1.7	1.8	4.0	.6	.4	.5	.6	.0
black-tall-happy-fat	.8	.5	.6	.9	1.0	2.8	2.8	2.8	1.9	.0
black-tall-sad-skinny	1.9	1.2	.8	.7	.0	1.3	.6	.8	.8	.0
black-tall-sad-fat	.8	1.5	.3	.2	.0	3.3	3.0	1.8	2.2	5.0
black-short-happy-skinny	.6	.4	.2	.1	.0	1.2	1.2	.9	1.1	.0
black-short-happy-fat	1.8	6.1	5.5	3.8	3.0	2.2	5.0	6.9	7.7	8.0
black-short-sad-skinny	.8	.4	.2	.7	.0	1.4	2.7	2.4	1.8	4.0
black-short-sad-fat	3.1	8.0	9.0	11.1	12.0	2.9	3.2	3.1	3.9	3.0

of the Ss' guesses converge, on the average, to the input frequencies for
the combinations of schematized perceptual characteristics. This result
indicates that the Ss learned the joint probabilities for the occurrence of

combinations of characteristics, from which the marginal probabilities could be generated, and not just the marginal aspects of the concepts.

An inspection of Tables III and IV also reveals that the Ss tend to over-guess the frequency of occurrence of *happy*. In only one tribe, Tribe D, were they, however, overguessing *happy* at the end of learning to any marked extent. Although there were more *sad* figures in Tribe D than *happy* ones, the Ss in this group were guessing in almost reversed proportions at the end of learning, *i.e.*, instead of guessing 12 *sad* and 8 *happy*, they were guessing 8.7 *sad* and 11.3 *happy*. This seems to indicate that there might well be perceptual biases existing prior to this kind of experiment and that a design counterbalancing the conditions, such as the one used in the present study, is to be recommended.

TABLE V

EXPECTED SCORES FOR TRIBES BASED ON INPUTS IN LEARNING, E(S), AND ON FINAL RESPONSES IN LEARNING, E(R), WITH EMPIRICALLY OBTAINED MEANS, $\overline{X}$.

Characteristic Scales	Tribe A			Tribe B			Tribe C			Tribe D		
	E(S)	E(R)	$\overline{X}$	E(S)	E(R)	$\overline{X}$	E(S)	E(R)	$\overline{X}$	E(S)	E(R)	$\overline{X}$
tall-short	1.5	1.2	2.2	1.5	1.8	2.0	−1.5	−1.7	−2.1	−1.5	−1.3	−1.6
happy-sad	.6	1.0	1.1	.6	.6	.5	−.6	−.6	−1.5	−.6	.5	.9
black-white	−3.0	−3.0	−3.0	−3.0	−3.0	−3.0	3.0	2.6	2.6	3.0	3.0	3.0
fat-skinny	−1.7	−1.5	−1.7	−1.7	−1.8	−1.6	1.7	1.8	2.2	1.7	1.7	1.6

Since the Ss had now learned certain specifiable aspects of the meaning of these concepts, *i.e.* the joint probabilities for the occurrence of combinations of characteristics as well as the marginal probabilities for the relevant dimensions operating in each case, techniques purported to measure meaning could now be applied to see which semantic aspects are adequately reflected by various measurement devices.

(2)Measurement phase: (a) Comparison of scores. Table V shows the expected scores (concept scale-positions) based on (i) frequencies of marginal input; (ii) frequencies of marginal responses, and (iii) the mean scale-positions empirically obtained. This table shows that the average discrepancy between the mean scores obtained and those predicted is about a third of a scale unit (on the seven-unit scale used by Osgood and Suci). This discrepancy is comparable to average error-discrepancies found in other investigations of the reliability of the semantic differential. Thus, since the predicted scale-positions for the concepts based only upon their marginal relationships were not markedly different from the scale-positions obtained from the semantic differential, it may be concluded that this instrument as it is currently used reflects only the marginal characteristics of a concept's meaning.

Since the predicted scores were based upon a simple two-vector model that assumed equality of intervals along the scales of the semantic differential, the similarity between the scores predicted and obtained can be taken as evidence that the scale-intervals are at least not markedly unequal. The results also show that the semantic differential is valid for at least one statistical aspect of the meaning of concepts, but, on the other hand, they also indicate that the instrument as it is currently used does not adequately reflect all aspects of meaning.

TABLE VI

SUMMARY OF DATA FOR THE SEMANTIC DIFFERENTIAL AND *F*-VALUES AMONG TRIBES
FOR EACH SCALE

Characteristics Scales	Tribes (means)				F-values
	A	B	C	D	
tall-short	2.2	2.0	−2.1	−1.6	153.3‡
happy-sad	1.1	.5	−1.5	.9	11.2‡
black-white	−3.0	−3.0	2.6	3.0	—§
fat-skinny	−1.7	−1.6	2.2	1.6	94.1‡
weak-strong	− .3	− .9	− .4	− .4	.4
large-small	1.2	.7	− .7	− .9	5.1†
sweet-sour	1.2	− .2	− .3	.7	3.6*
good-bad	1.1	.3	.2	1.2	1.6
clean-dirty	1.2	1.4	.3	.5	1.6
honest-dishonest	− .7	− .5	− .5	−1.1	.5
heavy-light	− .5	−1.1	1.1	1.6	8.4‡
rugged-delicate	.0	1.2	.3	.9	1.7
sharp-dull	.6	.8	.2	− .5	1.6
beautiful-ugly	− .2	− .4	− .8	− .3	.4
sick-healthy	−1.2	−1.2	− .7	− .9	.3
relaxed-tense	.7	.5	− .2	1.5	1.7
hard-soft	.8	1.0	− .1	.1	.9
rich-poor	− .5	− .5	− .3	−1.0	.6
rough-smooth	− .9	.7	.3	.0	1.9
fast-slow	1.1	1.0	−1.4	− .8	10.1‡

* 5% significance level.　　† 1% significance level.　　‡ 1/10% significance level.
§ No *F*-value was computable since Tribes A, B, and D had no within-group variance.

(b) Analyses of variance. In addition to the comparison of the scores, simple one by four analyses of variance were made among the concepts for each of the 20 scales. The means obtained for each of the concepts on each of the scales, with corresponding *F*-values, are shown in Table VI. As predicted, significant differences were obtained for each of the four input scales with no significant differences between either Tribes A and B or C and D—with the exception of Tribes C and D on the *happy-sad* scale. Even this deviation, however, is understandable in terms of the final level of learning for Tribe D. The output prediction based upon the final level of learning for Tribe D indicated more 'happy' than 'sad' stickmen,

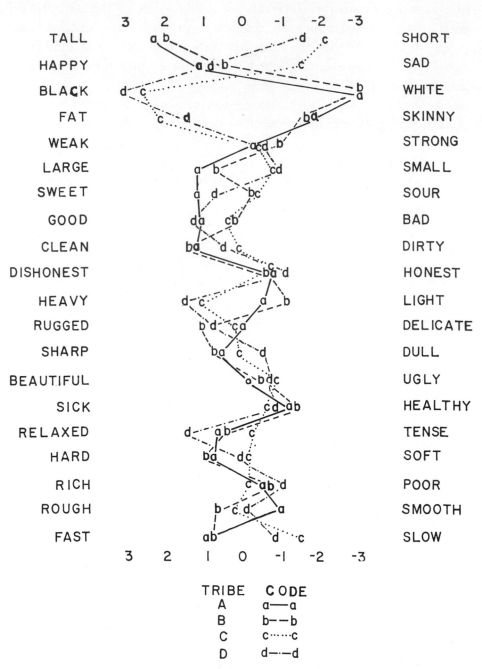

FIG. 1. MEAN PROFILES OF CONCEPTS OF FOUR TRIBES ON 20 SEMANTIC
DIFFERENTIAL SCALES

although the reverse situation was true in terms of the input proportions. In addition, it should be noted that no *F*-value could be computed for the *black-white* scale, since three of the groups, Tribes A, B, and D, showed *no* within-group variance. Every *S* in these three groups checked exactly at the predicted point.

Essentially the same information given in Table VI is shown in Fig. 1. Fig. 1 does, however, have the advantage of showing the form of the semantic differential used in the present study; it also shows more clearly the kind of generalization-pattern obtained, an important consideration to which we will return in a later section on semantic generalization.

If it were desired to obtain some measure of the joint probabilities of occurrence of characteristics, a slight modification of this procedure would probably be adequate. The semantic differential, as it is currently used, requires separate judgments about single characteristics. To measure combinations of characteristics, it would seem reasonable to require judgments about combinations of characteristics directly. A simple procedure might be to include the combination in the task as an adjective modifying the concept to be rated; *i.e.* instead of, or in addition to, rating 'stickmen' on *tall-short, happy-sad,* etc., the *S*s could be asked to rate 'tall' stickmen on *happy-sad, fat-skinny,* etc., scales.

When a person is asked to check the position of a concept like 'tall' stickmen on the *happy-sad* scale, he is in effect being asked to consider the resultant of the two vectors *happy* and *sad* under the restriction that the concept stickmen be limited to only tall-stickmen. In effect, then, we are asking *S* to judge the concept 'stickmen' on the scale *happy-tall* vs. *sad-tall.* In terms of a geometric analogue, this is asking *S* to weight the concept in terms of the resultant of two conditional probability vectors. It should be noted that if *happy* and *sad* are independent of *tall* in the probability sense, one would obtain from *tall* the same effect (resultant) that one would get under no restrictions. If, however, these characteristics are not independent, quite different meaning profiles would be expected.

This procedure was tried out, using the same tribes of stickmen described in the present study, by Sylvan Wiley, a graduate student. In his research the expected scores were calculated using the following equation:

$$E_{\text{score}} = 3p_{\text{tall}} \mid \text{happy} - 3p_{\text{short}} \mid \text{happy}$$

All possible combinations of conditional probability were calculated, and the above is only one specific example. The results of this research will not be reported in full in this paper but Fig. 2 illustrates some of the predictions and empirical results.

Fig. 2 shows that fairly accurate predictions were made for the semantic differential under this modified procedure, using the judgmental model assumed to be the vector of conditional probability. Although these results are encouraging, the procedure must be tested further before generalizing too far. The results do indicate, however, that we may be able with a little manipulation, to reconstruct the joint frequencies of occurrence of stimulus-characteristics for the referents of a concept. That is, since $p(x,y) = [p(x,y)]/[p(y)]$, where $p(y) \neq 0$ and since we can estimate $p(x,y)$ and $p(y)$ from the scores on the semantic differential, we can thus estimate $p(x,y)$ by $p(x,y) = p(x,|y)\ p(y)$.

(3) Semantic generalization. Since little is known about semantic generalization, 16 scales (other than those involved in the above predictions) were included to obtain some preliminary information about it. Although it is a crude test, the *F*-value for each of the other 16 scales was used as

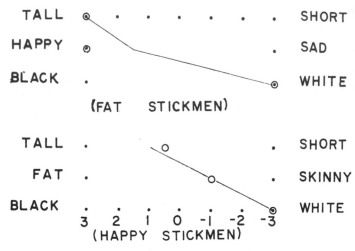

FIG. 2. PREDICTED PROFILES FOR 'FAT' AND 'HAPPY' STICKMEN OF TRIBE B WITH
MEAN RATINGS ON EACH SCALE

an index of a significant amount of generalization. It might be argued that this statistic only indicates significant differentiation between the four groups on the scales for which the *F*-value was significant, but it can be justified as an exploratory technique. It is interesting that significant generalization (or differentiation between concepts) was found for the scales *large-small* and *heavy-light* (which have high factor loadings on Osgood and Suci's *potency* dimension), *sweet-sour* (which has a high factor loading on their *evaluative* dimension), and *fast-slow* (which has a high factor loading on their *activity* dimension). Thus, significant generalization occurred along all three of the semantic dimensions proposed by Osgood and Suci. These results have implications for a systematic, quantitative study of semantic generalization.

If three of the four input characteristics used in the learning phase of the present experiment were held constant at some probability level and the other one varied along a set of probability-values, it would be possible to measure systematic changes in semantic generalization as a function of the statistical structure of the concept involved in learning.

(4) A stereotypic measure. Another way of obtaining information, although admittedly a limited amount, about a set of conceptual referents would be to ask Ss to describe verbally the most typical member of the set. For the concepts used in the present study, this would involve asking each S to describe the 'stickman' which he felt was typical of the tribe he had just reviewed. This description can be considered to be an index of a stereotype of the tribe. When 37 of the Ss in the probability-learning experiment were asked, after having completed the semantic differential, to describe the typical stickman for the tribe they had just seen, 32 of them gave the most frequently occurring combination of characteristics. This occurred in spite of the fact that this combination appeared only 60% of the time in Tribes A and C and only 40% of the time in Tribes B and D, and it did not adequately reflect the marginal characteristics. The combinations given by four of the remaining Ss were such as to maximize the marginal probability relations, with only one S perceiving some other combination as typical.

SUMMARY

An approach to the study of concept formation and the measurement of meaning was suggested which emphasizes the relationships among (a) the statistical structure of the perceptual characteristics of concept-referents, (b) properties of the mathematical models underlying some devices designed to measure meaning, and (c) the psychological judgmental processes involved in the task of measurement. Experimental data were presented relevant to the process of learning the statistical structure of some concepts and to the measurement of their meanings. The *semantic differential* was used as a measure of meaning, and it was shown that this instrument adequately reflects at least one, but not all, of the statistical aspects of a concept's referents.

19. Meaning and Meaning Similarity:

I. A Theoretical Reassessment [1]

John H. Flavell

A. Introduction

The "problem of meaning," for psychology, consists primarily of two problems: (*a*) the general nature of the meaning response and the process by which it is acquired; (*b*) the specific contents or components of this response. As to the first, Mowrer (17), Osgood, Suci, and Tannenbaum (18) and, more recently, Staats and Staats (23, 25) have adopted the position that meanings are acquired by means of a coi•ditioning process and, in fact, constitute conditioned responses. Thus, if stimulus-complex S_1 repeatedly elicits a response-complex R_1 in the presence of some sign s_1, s_1 will tend to become a conditioned stimulus to an implicit response-complex r_1 which is some reduced, covert portion of R_1. This covert response-complex r_1 is thought to be the "meaning" of s_1 and to possess mediating stimulus properties which may elicit other, overt responses "appropriate to the meaning of" s_1. Because r_1 is said both to be a mediating response and to possess stimulus properties, Osgood, Suci, and Tannenbaum (18) call it "$r_m \rightarrow s_m$." The conditioning of meaning is not limited, under this interpretation, to situations in which objects and events constitute UCSs. Many verbal signs (called "assigns" by Osgood) first receive their meanings through a process of being paired with other signs which already have conditioned meanings, i.e., via higher-order conditioning. And probably all signs, however their meanings were established initially, constantly undergo at least some semantic modification by means of such sign-to-sign conditioning.

Although it is certainly not beyond criticism, e.g., (2, Chap. 3), many psychologists would accept a sophisticated conditioning interpretation such as that proposed by Osgood and associates as an at least useful way of thinking about what meanings are, psychologically, and how they are acquired. However, the second problem—the specific components of $r_m \rightarrow s_m$—is a more troublesome one. There are two senses in which the phrase "specific components" may be taken. The first of these concerns the physiological or neurophysiological nature of the covert responses which make up the $r_m \rightarrow s_m$

Reprinted from *Journal of General Psychology* (1961), 64: 307–319, by permission of the author and the Journal Press.

[1] The preparation of this paper was supported in part by a USPHS research grant (M2632A). The author wishes to acknowledge his thanks to a number of people with whom he has discussed the ideas presented here. He wants especially to thank Dr. Charles E. Osgood for a helpful critical reading of an earlier draft of the article, although of course the author assumes sole responsibility for the paper's contents.

complex. As Osgood, Suci, and Tannenbaum rightly point out (18, pp. 7-8), nothing at all is known about this at the present time, and no speculations will be offered here. The other meaning of "specific components" refers to what the $r_m \rightarrow s_m$ response components might be responses *to*, that is, *what* aspects of the total stimulating situation S_1 constitute stimuli for the responses which make up the $r_m \rightarrow s_m$ complex. It is with this question, rather than the first, that the present article is primarily concerned.

B. Osgood's Position

Osgood and his associates (18) have addressed themselves to this second question. Consider the sign "dog" and its referent object *dog* as an example. If for the moment we consider only sign-object rather than sign-sign conditioning, the $r_m \rightarrow s_m$ complex would be presumed to consist of implicit responses of some unspecified kind to similarly undetermined stimuli which the individual has discriminated *in the referent object,* that is, in the various *dogs* with which "dog" has been paired in his past experience. Perhaps the term "attribute" is sufficiently general and indefinite to be an appropriate label here for these "undetermined stimuli," the responses to which make up $r_m \rightarrow s_m$; at least, the polar adjectives which define the end points of Osgood's semantic differential scales *do* seem to refer to what most people would call "attributes," e.g., "good-bad," "active-passive," etc. Thus, it would not be inaccurate to say that, in Osgood's theory, the stimuli for a given $r_m \rightarrow s_m$ complex consist of the discriminated attributes of the referent object; the measured meaning of, say, "dog" will then reflect, to put it most simply, the extent to which semantic differential attributes like "good," "active," etc., have been discriminated in various *dogs* encountered. In the case of assigns, the interpretation is essentially the same, except one step removed. The $r_m \rightarrow s_m$ elicited by the s_1 through past responding to the discriminated attributes of its referent object now becomes, through appropriate pairing of s_1 and s_2, elicitable by s_2 alone.

Since $r_m \rightarrow s_m$ is a mediating process, two signs, s_1 and s_2, ought to tend towards functional equivalence—as measured by positive transfer from s_1 to s_2, by judgments of semantic similarity between s_1 and s_2, or by other appropriate measures—to the extent that their $r_m \rightarrow s_m$'s overlap or are similar (18, pp. 143, 154). As the semantic differential profile is taken as a measure of a single $r_m \rightarrow s_m$, so also is the estimate of profile similarity, the D score, taken to be a measure of similarity between two $r_m \rightarrow s_m$'s. Osgood and his associates have therefore predicted that mediated generalization and other indices of functional equivalence between words ought to be inverse functions of D score. Phrased differently, to the extent that the subject discriminates similar properties or attributes in two referent objects, the $r_m \rightarrow s_m$'s of their signs will tend to be similar and the D score between their semantic differential profile low. In summary, then, the aspect of Osgood's theory with which we are concerned here seems to state: (*a*) the

$r_m \rightarrow s_m$ complex of a sign is in essence composed of covert responses to discriminated attributes of the referent object; (*b*) the functional equivalence between words, as assessed by appropriate independent measures of overt behavior, is mediated by similarity between $r_m \rightarrow s_m$'s which is, in turn, estimated by the semantic differential *D* score.

Although this theoretical account seems to us highly plausible in its main outline, at least one recent study suggests that there may be some problems with it. Dicken (10) compared verbal generalization or transfer among words with low *D* scores between them with generalization among control words. As Osgood's theory would predict, the low-*D* words did show significantly greater generalization. However, although the *D* scores between pairs of words in the low-*D* group were all about equal, fully a third of these words were indistinguishable from controls, i.e., showed no discernible transfer effects at all. Dicken then noticed that the low-*D* words between which the most generalization occurred seemed to be more related, "denotatively," than those low-*D* words between which transfer was low. He therefore obtained from subjects global judgments of "denotative meaning similarity" among the various low-*D* words and found that, within this equal-*D* pool of words, *judged* similarity predicted generalization quite well. He concluded that factors other than those measured by semantic differential *D* scores must be important in semantic generalization phenomena. It may be profitable to reexamine the whole concept of $r_m \rightarrow s_m$ and inter-$r_m \rightarrow s_m$ similarity to see if some of the possible "other factors" might be found.

C. A Reanalysis of Sign and Assign Conditioning

It is our belief that the principal difficulty within Osgood's conception of $r_m \rightarrow s_m$ centers around what components of the stimulating situation—in our terminology, what "attributes"—comprise the stimuli which elicit an $r_m \rightarrow s_m$ complex in the subject. Briefly, the argument that will be developed is this. It seems probable that Osgood's semantic differential measures primarily, if not exclusively, the attributes which the subject discriminates *in the referent object itself,* e.g., the object *dog* itself. However, it can be assumed that *other* attributes in the total stimulus context of which the referent object is a part are also important contributors to $r_m \rightarrow s_m$. To the extent that these other, non-referent attributes are major contributors, it follows that the semantic differential will tend to be an imperfect estimate of $r_m \rightarrow s_m$ and, *a fortiori,* the *D* score an imperfect measure of similarity *between* $r_m \rightarrow s_m$'s. Let us examine this conception in more detail.

Consider once again the sign-object conditioning of the $r_m \rightarrow s_m$ for "dog." The word "dog" is repeatedly spoken in the presence of innumerable stimulus situations or contexts. Common to all these contexts (at least in the simplified conditioning process we are assuming for convenience here) is the presence of some kind of *dog.* Not the *same* dog in all such contexts, of course, but *a* member of the class *dog* occurs as a source of stimulation with a probability

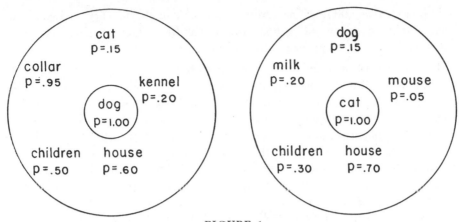

FIGURE 1

<small>HYPOTHETICAL REFERENCE CONTEXTS FOR THE WORDS "DOG" AND "CAT," SHOWING
REFERENT AND NON-REFERENT OBJECTS AND THEIR ASSOCIATED
PROBABILITIES OF OCCURRENCE</small>

of 1.00. But the total reference context inevitably includes other objects and events besides *dog*, and it would seem arbitrary indeed to exclude their stimulus effects from the composition of $r_m \rightarrow s_m$. On the contrary, it seems reasonable to assume that subjects respond to the *whole* stimulus configuration before them, not simply that which lies within the boundaries of the referent object alone. To be sure, unlike the referent object, the other potential stimulus sources tend to co-occur with the word "dog" with probabilities less than 1.00. For example, perhaps the spatial-temporal context of *dog* includes as possible sources of stimuli *children* at $p = .50$ (*children* present in one-half of all *dog* contexts), *house* at $p = .60$, *collar* at $p = .95$, and so on.

The left-hand portion of Figure 1 depicts this situation. The large circle represents the spatial-temporal context within which discriminated stimuli produce the $r_m \rightarrow s_m$ complex for "dog." The principal and most consistent component of the context is *dog* itself, present at $p = 1.00$. A few of the innumerable other potential context members and their hypothetical associated probabilities are also listed. A similar scheme for the word "cat" is shown on the right side of the Figure.

If what has been said so far is correct, two things follow. First, the discriminated attributes of the referent object itself ought to be the most potent *single* contributor to the composition of $r_m \rightarrow s_m$, since the referent object alone is assumed to occur in *all* the stimulus contexts—its probability is 1.00, as the Figure shows. Thus, an index presumed to measure *only* the discriminated attributes of the referent object ought not to be too grossly in error as an estimate of $r_m \rightarrow s_m$. However, and this is the important second point, there has to be *some* error in such an index, since the attributes of other context objects *do* occur, and occur at probabilities dependent upon the probabilities of occurrence of their associated objects (less than 1.00

but greater than .00).[2] The error in question ought to vary in magnitude from sign to sign, depending upon the probability structure of the reference context as regards component objects and their attributes.

It may be asked whether this interpretation can also be applied in the case of assign rather than sign conditioning. If anything, it seems to apply more naturally in the latter case. For example, suppose the word "lion" is the assign whose meaning is to be established by being paired with words rather than physical stimulus contexts which include the object *lion*. There are immediate analogies with the sign-object case. For instance, there is likely to be an approximate synonym involved (e.g., "animal," "cat," etc.) which is analogous to a referent object, and there will be other, contextual words which are the counterparts of non-referent objects. An actual assign context for "lion" might look like this. "A *lion* is a *big cat* which lives in *Africa*, feeds on *zebras*, *gazelles*, etc., tends to congregate near *water holes* . . ." It is easy to see how the $r_m \rightarrow s_m$ for "lion" might in this way come to include not only the already-established meanings of "big cat" (the equivalent of its referent object), but also components from "Africa," "zebras," "gazelles," and so on (the equivalents of its non-referent context objects). Staats and Staats (22, 24, 25) have shown what is probably the experimental analogue of this kind of process.

D. The Nature and Measurement of Meaning Similarity

Any conception about the structure of a single $r_m \rightarrow s_m$ has necessary implications for the assessment of similarity among $r_m \rightarrow s_m$'s. Osgood, Suci, and Tannenbaum (18) are well aware of this and have moved naturally from a conception of how to measure the meaning of isolated signs to one concerning the measurement of meaning similarity. But it is obvious that any inadequacies in the base interpretation of $r_m \rightarrow s_m$ for the individual sign must inevitably distort any measurement of $r_m \rightarrow s_m$ similarity based on this interpretation. We have said we think it likely that the semantic differential measures primarily that portion of $r_m \rightarrow s_m$ which derives from discriminated attributes in the referent object itself, as opposed to those of the other, non-referent objects in the total stimulating context. And we have suggested that a full description of $r_m \rightarrow s_m$ ought to take into account stimulation from *both* referent object *and* non-referent object sources. If this interpretation is correct, it follows that the semantic differential estimate of meaning similarity, i.e., the *D* score, must also be partially inadequate as a measure. One might conceive of the variance among $r_m \rightarrow s_m$'s as being

---

[2] The analysis of the contribution of discriminated attributes from various object sources is of course complicated by the obvious fact that not all instances of a given object class, e.g., *dog, child, house*, etc., have the same attributes. Thus, one *dog* is "big" and "vicious," another "small" and friendly," and so on. Thus, the probability of occurrence of an attribute in a given context is actually the product of two independent probabilities: (*a*) the probability of the attribute, given an instance of the object class; (*b*) the probability of the object class, given the reference context.

partitioned into two sources: that due to attributes discriminated in the referent object, and that due to attributes discriminated in the non-referent objects. The semantic differential D score is probably a good measure of similarity as concerns $r_m \rightarrow s_m$ variance of the first type; some other index is needed to assess variance of the second type. Assuming the availability of such an index, *the two measures taken in combination ought to predict semantic similarity, as estimated from some third, independent measure taken as criterion, better than either one alone.* What is needed, then, is a method of measuring non-referent object variance.

There are several possible measures which might be explored. A somewhat complicated one, which we have so far not yet investigated experimentally, involves subject estimates of how many of the same non-referent objects two signs tend to have in their respective stimulus contexts. One might ask the subjects to write down in a fixed time period all the objects they can think of which are found in immediate contiguity with *each* of two referent objects, A and B. In the case of *cat* and *dog*, for example, subjects might think of *children* and *house* (see Figure 1), plus perhaps *street, yard, pet shop,* and the like. In our formulation, all these objects occur with some probability in the reference contexts of both "cat" and "dog." Presumably, the more context objects the two signs have in common, the more likely that their $r_m \rightarrow s_m$'s will be similar, referent object similarity held constant. A variant of this method could be applied to the verbal context in the case of assign conditioning. Here, one would want to find out how many *words* in the various verbal contexts of "dog" also occur in the various verbal environments in which "cat" is found.

Another, simpler technique, which we *have* recently explored (11, 12, 13) is a somewhat more indirect measure than the first. Let A and B be the signs whose similarity is under investigation. Instruct the subject to imagine some random occasion on which he encounters A's referent object (A). Next, ask him to estimate the probability that B's referent object (B) will also be present in the same, immediate spatial-temporal context. This accomplished, have him then perform the reverse operation: given an instance of B, what is the probability that A would be co-present? The total "co-occurrence score" is the sum (or mean) of these two estimated probabilities. Note that, although the two probabilities will usually be about equal, they need not be. For example, the probability of finding a *telephone* in the immediate context, given a random *phone booth* is, to put it mildly, much greater than the probability of *phone booth*, given a random *telephone*. A less extreme example: the probability of *car*, given *white-walled tires* is greater than the probability of *white-walled tires*, given *car*.

The rationale for this measure is as follows. If two referent objects tend to co-occur frequently in common contexts, the consequence ought to be an increasing similarity between their $r_m \rightarrow s_m$'s. This is true, first of all, because the attributes of each referent object can funnel directly into the $r_m \rightarrow s_m$ of the other. As Figure 1 shows, *cat* is a non-referent object in the context of *dog* and vice-versa; thus, the $r_m \rightarrow s_m$ for each includes components derived from the referent object attributes of the other. Secondly, co-occurrence of referent objects necessarily implies other non-referent objects in common, objects which are non-referent for *both*. *Children* and *house* in Figure 1 are of this type. Although this kind of co-occurrence judgment task is perhaps a more indirect estimate of similarities derived from non-referents than is the first one (a research task for the future would be to correlate the two), it does possess some face validity and is undoubtedly more convenient to administer. And, as with the first measure, the co-occurrence judgment task can of course be modified to fit the assign case.[3]

E. Criterion Measures of Meaning Similarity

The principal hypothesis set forth in this paper is that adequate measurement of both individual $r_m \rightarrow s_m$'s and of similarity between $r_m \rightarrow s_m$'s must take into account the discriminated attributes of non-referent as well as referent objects. Theoretically, one could attempt to test this hypothesis in either of the above domains—either with respect to the measurement of individual $r_m \rightarrow s_m$'s or with respect to the measurement of similarity between $r_m \rightarrow s_m$'s. Although it would be logical to begin with the former, two difficulties intervene. First, although the writer has not yet given serious attention to working out a way of estimating individual $r_m \rightarrow s_m$'s, it is suspected that it might prove a very difficult task. The technique in question ought to be something like a conventional semantic differential, except that it would also measure non-referent object attributes, appropriately weighted for probability of occurrence (with all the difficulties which this weighting implies; see Footnote 2). Second, even if a measure of this kind could be invented, it is difficult to think of a good criterion against which it could be validated. Since it should give a more accurate and complete estimate of $r_m \rightarrow s_m$ than the present semantic differential affords, the latter could hardly serve as a criterion. The fact of the matter is, as Osgood, Suci, and Tannenbaum have pointed out (18, p. 140), there is no readily-available criterion measure of the psychological meaning of a sign.

In the case of similarity among $r_m \rightarrow s_m$'s, the outlook is considerably brighter. In the first place, we have just shown that at least two types of measures are potentially available for measuring the similarity contributed by the non-referent attributes. As to an independent, criterion measure of semantic similarity, there are a number of possible candidates and the only problem is to select among them. In general, any measure of functional equivalence between words is at least worthy of consideration as a potential criterion. The following are some of the indices of functional equivalence

---

[3] Bousfield's *MR* index (6) and the highly similar *Mf*-score of Cofer (9), both based upon commonality of associative responses to two signs, involve a logic very similar to that underlying the two measures of non-referent similarity just described here. The writer was strongly influenced by both conceptions in the development of these measures and the rationale from which they derive.

already extant and some of the studies which have used them: (*a*) global judgments of similarity-of-meaning between words A and B, using either a rating scale or paired-comparison method (1, 12, 15); (*b*) estimates based on the frequency with which the same responses are given to A and B in a word association test (5, 6, 7, 9); (*c*) learn A-X, then study ease-of-learning or similar transfer to B-X (21, 26)—there are many variations on this design; (*d*) learn A-X ($X =$ motor response) and measure the number of B-X "errors" when B is presented (10, 16); (*e*) condition an autonomic response to A, then assess strength of autonomic response elicited by B (19, 20); (*f*) learn A-X, then study the extent to which X is given as a free-associate to B (5, 7); (*g*) learn A, B, C, D, etc., in random order, study the tendency for A and B to "cluster" in recall, i.e., to be recalled together (4). This inventory does not exhaust the variety of techniques which have been used, but it is a fair sample.

On what basis should the choice of one of these techniques as a criterion measure be decided? The matter of selection is important because the various potential criteria may be, and probably are, only imperfectly correlated with each other, e.g., (1, 6, 7, 28). The whole problem of the relationships between the various measures of functional equivalence has received little explicit attention in the literature so far, and it must be admitted that any choice of criterion here is somewhat arbitrary. However, the writer believes that global judgments of similarity constitute *prima facie* as reasonable a criterion measure as any available, and the subsequent papers in this series describe experiments in which such judgments were taken as the standard (11, 13). First of all, there is some precedent for doing so; Osgood, Suci, and Tannenbaum (18, pp. 143-146), in discussing the validity of the semantic differential, cite as evidence a study by Rowan in which similarity judgments were used as the validating criterion. A second reason appeals once more to face validity; a similarity judgment just *seems* intuitively to be a natural and direct way to try to assess similarity between $r_m \rightarrow s_m$'s. And finally, it seems a reasonable first step in an unchartered research area to try to predict one *judgment* from two other *judgments* (semantic differential ratings are, after all, judgments, and of course the co-occurrence task is judgmental); correlations between judgments and other kinds of behavior (recall, autonomic responses, etc.) may be attenuated because of unwanted artifacts arising from fundamental differences between the kinds of behavior correlated.

F. Conclusion

With the decision to use similarity judgments as the criterion measure, the stage is set for an initial, experimental test of the theoretical position developed here. First, obtain data from the following three measures on a suitably-chosen sample of word pairs: (*a*) semantic differential D scores between members of each pair; (*b*) one or the other of our two measures of similarity between non-referent attributes; (*c*) global ratings of judged

semantic similarity. Then, compute the multiple correlation predicting
(c) from (a) and (b). If our hypothesis is correct, the multiple correlation
ought to be significantly higher than *either* of the 0-order correlations
(a)—(c) and (b)—(c); that is, the two measures ought to *combine* to
predict similarity judgments. The following paper in this series (11)
describes an attempt to test the prediction in this manner, using probability
of co-occurrence judgments as measure (b).

Before concluding, it may be worthwhile to examine the differences between
what (a) and (b) are assumed to measure from a non-theoretical, "common
sense" viewpoint. This is perhaps best accomplished by considering two
extreme classes of word pairs. First, there are words whose semantic
differential profiles are very similar, and yet the words themselves appear
to refer to quite distinct and different things, things which seldom share,
in our terminology, common spatial-temporal contexts. Osgood, Suci, and
Tannenbaum have recognized this paradox when they state:

> Given only the profile produced by a subject in judging a particular
> concept, or the point in the space specified by this profile, we are un-
> able to work the system backwards and identify that concept. The force
> of the argument really is this: Many denotatively distinct concepts may
> occupy the same region of our semantic space, i.e., may have highly
> similar profiles—"hero" and "success" and "nurse" and "sincere" would
> be examples. If the state of the speaker which the semantic differential
> presumably indexes were a *sufficient* condition for selective incoding,
> how could we account for discriminative selection of "nurse" rather than
> "sincere," or "hero" rather than "success," when the states in each case
> are essentially the same? (18, p. 323).

Our tentative solution to this paradox—different from the one Osgood
goes on to give—is that the "states in each case" are *not* really "the same,"
because what might loosely be called the "denotative relevance"[4] of one
referent to the other is simply not taken account of in semantic differential
measurement. We believe that "hero" and "success" *are* experienced by
people as possessing bona fide differences—differences in *meaning*—and that
these differences would likely be picked up in a measure, such as our
probability-of-co-occurrence index, which is designed to take into account the
matter of context overlap versus non-overlap. We do not see how the
"habits of usage and association" to which Osgood, Suci, and Tannenbaum
refer (18, pp. 324-325) can bear the full burden of explaining how subjects

---

[4] The writer has up to this point deliberately tried to avoid terms like "denotation"
and "connotation" in discussing what the semantic differential does and does not
measure. The reason is simply that he is inclined to feel that the use of these
rather fuzzy signs tends more to draw one into tangential definitional problems
rather than serve to clarify the issues involved (3, 27). As one example of the
former, what is the denotation of the word "beautiful"? Is it the class of things which
we point at when we use the expression? Is then the Renoir painting *itself* the
denotation of "beautiful," or is it rather an object which "beautiful" may connote?
And the situation seems equally confusing when one turns from adjectives to
verbs, adverbs, and abstract nouns.

differentiate such concepts. And the same issue arises for the second class of word pairs: high D score but considerable "denotative relevance." Once again, one can readily grant the attributive differences between referents indicated by the high D score and still feel convinced that there are real, potentially measurable similarities which have simply been left unmeasured.

One final note—something by way of special pleading. The recent literature reveals two kinds of response to Osgood's theoretical and methodological accomplishments. First of all, there have been the usual book reviews with their expected critical evaluations of theory and method (3, 8, 14, 27). This response could be classed under the "criticism without experimentation" rubric. Second, abundantly illustrated in the Osgood, Suci, and Tannenbaum book itself, there has been a spate of experimental studies —primarily concerned with exploring the possible applications of the semantic differential method to such diverse areas as attitude measurement and psychotherapy changes—which simply accept theory and method as they stand and apply them. These studies fall into the "experimentation without criticism" category. It seems to us that Osgood's achievements deserve something more. Perhaps the time has come to examine critically the theoretical cornerstones of this important system, preserving intact the very considerable portion which seems on present evidence to be of real merit, and proceeding towards a program of reformulation and experimentation on those aspects which appear inadequate or incomplete.

G. Summary

The major purpose of this paper is to propose a modification of Osgood's theory of meaning and meaning similarity. In this revised account, the meaning ($r_m \rightarrow s_m$) of a sign is said to include two classes of response: (*a*) responses to the attributes or properties which the subject discriminates in the sign's referent object itself; (*b*) responses to the discriminated attributes of other, non-referent objects present in the physical context or surround of the referent object. It is believed that the semantic differential measures (*a*) but fails to measure (*b*). Since Osgood's index of meaning similarity between two signs, the D score, is based directly on the semantic differential profiles of the separate signs, it is likewise thought to be an incomplete measure. Two possible techniques are described for measuring that component of meaning similarity between signs which derives from the similarity between their respective non-referent attributes. Finally, an experiment is proposed which tests the hypothesis that judged semantic similarity is best predicted by a combination of two measures: D score and one of the techniques for assessing the non-referent similarity.

References

1. Bastian, J. R. Response chaining in verbal transfer. Minneapolis: Dept. Psychol., Univ. Minnesota, 1956 (Tech. Rep. No. 13, Contract N 8 onr 66216).
2. Brown, R. Words and Things. Glencoe, Ill.: Free Press, 1958. Pp. 398.

3. BROWN, R. W. Review of: "Osgood, Suci, and Tannenbaum, The Measurement of Meaning." *Contemp. Psychol.*, 1958, **3**, 113-115.

4. BOUSFIELD, W. A. The occurrence of clustering in the recall of randomly arranged associates. *J. Gen. Psychol.*, 1953, **49**, 229-240.

5. BOUSFIELD, W. A., COHEN, B. H., & WHITMARSH, G. A. Verbal generalization: a theoretical rationale and an experimental technique. Storrs: Dept. Psychol., Univ. Connecticut, 1958 (Tech. Rep. No. 23, Contract Nonr 631-00).

6. BOUSFIELD, W. A., WHITMARSH, G. A., & BERKOWITZ, H. Partial response identities in associative clustering. Storrs: Dept. Psychol., Univ. Connecticut, 1958 (Tech. Rep. No. 27, Contract Nonr 631-00).

7. BOUSFIELD, W. A., WHITMARSH, G. A., & DANICK, J. J. Partial response identities in verbal generalization. *Psychol., Rep.*, 1958, **4**, 703-713.

8. CARROLL, J. B. Review of: "Osgood, Suci, and Tannenbaum, The Measurement of Meaning." *Language*, 1959, **35**, 58-77.

9. COFER, C. N. Associative commonality and rated similarity of certain words from Haagen's list. *Psychol. Rep.*, 1957, **3**, 603-606.

10. DICKEN, C. F. Connotative meaning as a determinant of stimulus generalization. Unpublished doctoral dissertation, Univ. Minnesota, 1957.

11. FLAVELL, J. H. Meaning and meaning similarity: II. The semantic differential and co-occurrence as predictors of judged similarity in meaning. *J. Gen. Psychol.*, 1961, **64**, 321-335.

12. FLAVELL, J. H., & FLAVELL, E. R. One determinant of judged semantic and associative connection between words. *J. Exp. Psychol.*, 1959, **58**, 159-165.

13. FLAVELL, J. H., & JOHNSON, B. A. Meaning and meaning similarity: III. Latency and number of similarities as predictors of judged similarity in meaning. *J. Gen. Psychol.*, 1961, **64**, 337-348.

14. GULLIKSEN, H. Review of: "Osgood, Suci, and Tannenbaum, The Measurement of Meaning." *Contemp. Psychol.*, 1958, **3**, 115-119.

15. HAAGEN, C. H. Synonymity, vividness, familiarity and association value ratings of 400 pairs of common adjectives. *J. of Psychol.*, 1949, **27**, 453-463.

16. MINK, W. D. Semantic generalization as related to word association. (Unpublished doctoral dissertation, Univ. Minnesota, 1957.)

17. MOWRER, O. H. The psychologist looks at language. *Amer. Psychol.*, 1954, **9**, 660-694.

18. OSGOOD, C. E., SUCI, G. J., & TANNENBAUM, P. H. The Measurement of Meaning. Urbana: Univ. Illinois Press, 1957. Pp. 342.

19. RAZRAN, G. H. S. Experimental semantics. *Trans. N.Y. Acad. Sci.*, 1952, **14**, 171-176.

20. RIESS, B. F. Semantic conditioning involving the galvanic skin reflex. *J. Exp. Psychol.*, 1940, **26**, 238-240.

21. RYAN, J. J. An experimental comparison of response transfer facilitated by meaningfully similar and associated verbal stimuli. Minneapolis: Dept. Psychol., Univ. Minnesota, 1957 (Tech. Rep. No. 21, Contact N 8 onr 66216).

22. STAATS, A. W., & STAATS, C. K. Attitudes established by classical conditioning. *J. Abnorm. & Soc. Psychol.*, 1958, **57**, 37-40.

23. ————. Meaning and *m*: correlated but separate. *Psychol. Rev.*, 1959, **66**, 136-144.

24. STAATS, A. W., STAATS, C. K., HEARD, W. G., & NIMS, L. P. Replication report: Meaning established by classical conditioning. *J. Exp. Psychol.*, 1959, **57**, 64.

25. STAATS, C. K., & STAATS, A. W. Meaning established by classical conditioning. *J. Exp. Psychol.*, 1957, **54**, 74-80.

26. STORMS, L. H. Backward association in verbally mediated learning. Minneapolis: Dept. Psychol., Univ. Minnesota, 1957 (Tech. Rep. No. 18, Contract N 8 onr 66216).

27. WEINREICH, U. Review of: "Osgood, Suci, and Tannenbaum, The Measurement of Meaning." *Word*, 1958, **14**, 346-366.

28. WHITMARSH, G. A., & BOUSFIELD, W. A. The use of free associational responses for the prediction of verbal generalization. (Paper read at East. Psychol. Ass'n, Atlantic City, April, 1959.)

20. Meaning and Meaning Similarity: II. The Semantic Differential and Co-Occurrence as Predictors of Judged Similarity in Meaning [1]

John H. Flavell

A. Introduction

The preceding article in this series (1) presented a theoretical reformulation of the problem of meaning and meaning similarity, using as a point of departure the conceptions of Osgood, Suci, and Tannenbaum (10). The article also described one proposed test of its theoretical position: judged similarity of meaning between pairs of words ought to be better predicted by semantic differential D scores and probability of co-occurrence scores taken in combination than by either measure taken alone.

The present experiment was designed to carry out this test. The general procedure was as follows. Judgments of similarity (S), D scores (D), and co-occurrence judgments (C) were obtained on various kinds or classes of word pairs, i.e., pairs consisting of two concrete nouns, pairs consisting of one concrete noun and one adjective, etc. Then, for each class of pairs separately, 0-order and multiple correlation data were computed on the three measures. The hypothesis was that—within each class of pairs—the multiple correlation between S, taken as the criterion, and C and D, taken as predictors, would be appreciably higher than the 0-order correlations between each predictor and the criterion.

B. Method

1. *Word Pairs*

Jenkins, Russell, and Suci have recently published highly useful tables giving both the semantic differential profiles for each of 360 words (6) and the D scores between all possible pairings of these words (7). The word pairs used in the present research (presented in Table 3 below) were drawn exclusively from this 360 word pool. In all, 120 pairs of words were selected for study, 30 pairs from each of four classes: The first class (CN-CN) consisted of "concrete noun" pairs, words whose referents tended to be perceivable, bounded, thing-like entities. The second class (A-A) consisted of pairs of adjectives. The third class (A-CN) included adjective—concrete

Reprinted from *Journal of General Psychology* (1961), 64: 321–335, by permission of the author and the Journal Press.

[1] The experiment reported here was supported by a USPHS research grant (M2632A). The author wishes to thank Miss Barbara A. Johnson, Dr. Russel F. Green, and especially, Mr. Wilfred Newman for their assistance in the statistical analyses of data.

noun pairs. And the fourth group (AN-AN) consisted of "abstract nouns," nouns whose referents tended to be unbounded, intangible, non-things. As inspection of Table 3 will readily show, not all the words included under CN-CN and AN-AN meet the defining criteria equally well; however, almost without exception, the least abstract AN-AN words appear to be more abstract than the most abstract CN-CN pairs, insofar as one can make discriminations along this rather nebulous continuum. The motive for including word pairs of different types (A-A, A-CN, etc.) in the study was frankly exploratory. So far as the writer is aware, there have been virtually no systematic attempts to use grammatical form class and abstraction level as independent variables in the study of semantic or associational phenomena. We wished to find out if our major hypothesis would be confirmed independent of word pair class and, generally, whether the 0-order and multiple correlations relating the three measures would vary with variation in type of pair.

Two additional criteria were used in the selection of the word pairs. First, an attempt was made to include only words which are relatively unambiguous in meaning; more specifically, we tried to avoid words, such as "light," "strike," etc., which have several different popular or high frequency meanings. Correlatively, the attempt was made to choose, as members of a given form class, words which most people would immediately identify as belonging to that class, e.g., adjectives which most people would perceive as adjectives rather than nouns. The second criterion concerns the semantic-distance characteristics of the word pair samples. The writer tried, on an intuitive, judgmental basis, to select word pairs in each of the four classes which seemed to show fairly wide variation with respect to the criterion measure, judged similarity of meaning. That is, an attempt was made, for each set of 30 pairs, to include: near-synonyms, antonyms (if available), and unrelated words, and other pairs which distribute between these extremes. Note that this selection strategy probably does not produce anything like a random selection of all possible word pairs in the English language; if one were to choose random pairs from a dictionary most of the pairs in the sample would be unrelated or distantly related.

2. Subjects

The subjects in this experiment were drawn from two geographically different populations. All D data were obtained directly from the aforementioned Jenkins, Russell, and Suci tables (7); the scores in these tables were derived from the semantic differential ratings of University of Minnesota students. The S and C judgments were obtained from University of Rochester students. The Minnesota sample consisted of 15 male and 15 female sophomores enrolled in an introductory psychology course.[2] The

---

[2] The same 30 subjects did not rate all 360 words, however. Five hundred and forty subjects were divided into 18 subgroups of 30 each, each subgroup rating a *different* 20 of the 360 words (6).

Rochester sample, also introductory psychology students (and mostly soph-omores), was as follows: for the S group, 8 males and 29 females; for the C group, 9 males and 28 females. All subjects—both Minnesota and Rochester—were obtained on a volunteer basis and were tested in groups.

3. *Procedure*

The testing procedure for the D group is given in detail in Jenkins, Russell, and Suci (6). Briefly, the subjects rated each of the 360 words on 20 scales according to standard semantic differential instructions. The scales were selected to sample six factors: "evaluation" (8 scales); "potency" and "activity" (3 scales each); and "tautness," "novelty," and "receptivity" (2 scales each). The subjects rated a given word on all 20 scales before proceeding to the next word.

The C test was self-administered: each subject in the group was simply given a booklet containing complete test instructions, word pairs, and rating scale and told to follow directions. The instructions were complicated and difficult to summarize. For this reason, and because the technique itself is a novel one, these instructions are given in their entirety here:

> Please read the following instructions slowly and carefully and follow them exactly. First, turn to the last sheet of this test. Now detach this sheet from the rest of the test. This sheet has on it a seven point rating scale which you will be using in judging a series of 90 word pairs.[3] Now the kind of rating you will be doing may seem unusual and strange to you, so be sure to read these instructions *carefully* Think for a moment about the pair of words "car—white-walled tire." These words of course "mean" or designate objects or classes of objects one encounters in everyday life. Suppose you asked yourself the question—if I should see a car coming down the street (or in a garage, or anywhere else one would see a car) what is the likelihood or the probability that I would *also* see a white-walled tire somewhere in the picture? You might judge that the probability is 20 per cent or 30 per cent or some-thing like that; in other words, white-walled tires "co-occur" or tend to be present about 20-30 per cent of the time, given the "occurrence" of the object *car*. How about the other way around? Given some random encounter with a white-walled tire, what is the probability that a car would also be found somewhere in the immediate vicinity? Except for

---

[3] Several items of explanation are in order here. First, the rating scale points were roughly defined for the subject on the scale sheet as follows—given A, probability of B equals: (*a*) 95-100 per cent for scale position 1; (*b*) 0-5 per cent for 7; (*c*) about 50 per cent for 4; (*d*) 50-95 per cent for 2 and 3; (*e*) 5-50 per cent for 5 and 6. Second, the subjects rated only 90 word pairs instead of 120 because it was believed that C judgments could not really apply meaningfully to AN-AN pairs, and thus these pairs were omitted for this group. While it is probable that subjects *could* somehow make C ratings on pairs like "mind—art," it seemed doubtful that the intended meaning of "co-occurrence" could be preserved in the process. This, of course, is an obvious limitation on the usefulness of our co-occurrence measure. It did seem of interest, however, to compare S and D ratings on AN-AN pairs, and therefore the latter were included in the S test. And finally, the 90 word pairs were presented in the test booklet in a fixed random order and the right-left position of each word in a given pair was also randomly assigned.

the case where the white-walled tire is in a warehouse or something like that, the probability is essentially 100 per cent that a car will also be present. We might then say that: given *car, white-walled tire* co-occurs with 20-30 per cent probability; however, given *white-walled tire, car* co-occurs with, say 95 per cent probability (perhaps the tire occurs in a warehouse or something in 5 per cent of the encounters!). This is the kind of judgment you'll be asked to make about the 90 pairs of words in this test. For each pair, you will consider an occurrence, taken at random, of the object, event, or quality which the *left* hand word in the pair refers to. Then you will estimate the probability that the *right* hand object, event or quality will co-occur in the same spatial setting. You will make your estimates in terms of the scale. As it says on the scale, a rating of 1 indicates that the co-occurrence of *B*, given *A* is 95 per cent or better. A scale rating of 4 indicates the 50 per cent probability level and 7 indicates 5 per cent or less. You will simply make your judgment and put the appropriate number on the line to the left of each pair. In each case, remember, the *left* word is your anchor point—it refers to the object which is taken as *occurring*. What you'll be *estimating* is the probability of the *right* word's object being present in the same setting. As you can see from the "car—white-walled tire" example, it may make a lot of difference *which* word you take as the anchor point. In order to keep the direction of your rating clear in your mind, I would suggest that, as you rate each pair, you keep saying to yourself: "Given *A* (left item), what is the probability of *B* (right item)?" After you have rated the 90 pairs in this way, you'll be shown the *same* 90 pairs again in the *reverse* order—B-A instead of A-B—and you will rate them again, but *still* with the *left* word as anchor. In this way, just as in our example of "car—white-walled tire," we well get ratings of co-occurrence of *B*, given *A* and *also* of *A*, given *B*.[4] Thus, you will rate the first 90, then go right on and rate the same 90 in the reverse order. One more thing and then these long-winded instructions will conclude. Before you write down any ratings, read through the first 30 pairs and *mentally* rate them to get the "feel" of how the ratings distribute themselves. Don't be afraid to use the extremes of the scale—1 or 7—where justified. After you've done this, go back to the beginning and start actually putting down numbers for each pair. Go through the first 90 and then the second 90 without skipping any. Make your judgments *carefully*, keeping the scale in front of you, but don't spend too much time on each one. When you've finished, bring your test up to me. If you have any questions at this point about what the instructions have told you to do, raise your hand and I will come to your seat.

The testing procedure for the *S* group was the same as that for the *C* group with the following exceptions. First, the instructions were much less complex: the *S* group subjects were simply asked to rate each pair along a continuum of "similarity-dissimilarity in meaning." Second, the seven-point rating scale was defined at its end points only, i.e., "very similar" for Position 1 and "very dissimilar" for Position 7. Third, since AN-AN

---

[4] The *C* score used in all data analyses was thus the simple sum of the two ratings described here: (*a*) rated probability of *B*, given *A*; (*b*) rated probability of *A*, given *B*.

pairs were included, the test consisted of 120 rather than 90 pairs of words. And finally, two forms of the word pair list were constructed so that 18 subjects (4 male and 14 female) rated a given A-CN pair in one order, e.g., A-CN, and the other 19 subjects (4 male and 15 female) rated it in the opposite order, e.g., CN-A. This was done in order to find out whether one word order leads to greater subjective similarity than the other. It is difficult to find unequivocal theoretical support for either of the two possible predictions here. On the one hand, adjectives are maximally contiguous with nouns in spoken and written language when in the A-CN order, and this proximity may make for subjective similarity. On the other hand, in the CN-A order (e. g., "the *ocean* is *briny*") the two words tend to be connected by similarity-giving copulas like "is," "are," etc. (2).

C. Results

Table 1 shows the 0-order correlations among *S, C,* and *D* for the three classes of word pairs, the multiple correlations ($R_{1.23}$) predicting *S* from *C* and *D*, and the βr expressions showing the per cent of *S* variance accounted for by each predictor, its correlation with the other predictor held constant (3, p. 397). Not shown in the table is the correlation between *S* and *D* for AN-AN pairs: $r = .76$. Let us examine first the individual 0-order

TABLE 1

ZERO-ORDER AND MULTIPLE CORRELATION DATA FOR JUDGED SIMILARITY (S_1), PROBABILITY OF CO-OCCURRENCE (C_2), AND SEMANTIC DIFFERENTIAL (D_3) MEASURES

Word pairs	Zero-order correlations			Multiple correlations		
	$S_1\text{-}C_2$	$S_1\text{-}D_3$	$C_2\text{-}D_3$	$R_{1.23}$	$\beta_{12.3}r_{12}$	$\beta_{13.2}r_{13}$
CN-CN	.84	.79	.71	.88	.47	.31
A-A	.95	.86	.79	.96	.68	.25
A-CN	.94	.40	.33	.94	.85	.04

correlations. In the case of *D* scores, all S-D correlations except that for A-CN pairs are respectably high, this in spite of the fact that the *S* and *D* data were obtained from different subjects in different geographical areas, and the fact that different subject groups in the Minnesota sample contributed to different *D* scores (Footnote 2). In a previous comparison of judged similarity and *D* scores (10, pp. 143-146), high correlations were also reported—correlations even higher than those found here. With the important exception of A-CN pairs, then, the present experiment can in a sense be construed as a second validation study of the *D* score as a measure of semantic distance.

Although moderate to high S-D correlations were expected, the magnitude of the S-C correlations—.84, .95, and .94—were completely unanticipated. As the table shows, the S-C correlations become higher and higher, relative to those between *S* and *D*, as one passes from CN-CN to

A-A to A-CN pairs. This increasing usurpation of the variance in S by C is more clearly seen in the two right-hand columns of the table: There is a progressive increase in the per cent of S variance predicted by C ($\beta_{12.3}r_{12}$) and a corresponding decrease in that predicted by D ($\beta_{13.2}r_{13}$) until, in the case of A-CN, the contribution of D appears to be negligible.

Table 1 also shows that the correlations between C and D are relatively high for CN-CN and A-A pairs but, once again, low in the case of A-CN. Multiple correlational analysis involving the prediction of C from S and D and D from S and C were also carried out, however, with interesting results from the standpoint of the D-C relationship. For CN-CN and A-A as well as A-CN, the prediction of C from D and vice versa—predictor correlation with S held constant—was close to zero. The βr terms in question vary from —.22 to + .11.

The rather surprising findings described thus far make the experimental status of the major hypothesis somewhat ambiguous, at least as stated in its original form: $R_{1.23} > r_{12}$ and r_{13}. $R_{1.23}$ improves very little upon the larger of the two component correlations (S-C in all three cases); the biggest difference is that between .84 and .88 for CN-CN. To be sure, the S-C correlations are so high that even tiny r_{12}-$R_{1.23}$ differences do represent a noticeable increase in S variance predicted: 7 per cent of the remaining variance in the case of CN-CN and 2 per cent in the case of A-A. Nonetheless, it is clear that this is at best very tenuous support for the hypothesis. However, it is possible to rephrase the hypothesis in ways which are still germane to the theoretical position outlined in the previous article (1). For example, there is clear support for the notion that C, as well as—indeed more than D, contributes substantially to the prediction of S in the case of all word pair classes investigated. Moreover, there is evidence that C and D are for all classes of pairs essentially independent and uncorrelated measures, when their common covariance with S is subtracted out. Further, in the case of A-A and especially CN-CN, the right-hand columns of Table 1 suggest that both measures do contribute independently to the prediction of S, C being in both cases much the more potent predictor of the two. Finally, the subsidiary question of whether the interrelationships among the S, C, and D vary with word pair class receives an affirmative answer: whereas the obtained variations in interrelationships from the CN-CN condition to that of A-A may well be due to random error, the striking variations between these and A-CN are probably real.

There are several findings of interest, apart from those concerned specifically with the major hypothesis. First of all, there is no evidence that the right-left order in which A-CN pairs appear on the test sheet has any effect on how similar in meaning the pairs are judged to be. Mean S ratings for each word pair were computed for the two sequences separately and the means and standard deviations of the two distributions of mean ratings were almost identical. It is well-known that word association relationships are usually asymmetrical, i.e., the probability of word A occurring as an associative response to word B will usually not be the same as that of B occurring as a response to A. From the present data, there is no evidence that asymmetry also holds for similarity of meaning judgments.

A second incidental finding concerns the composition of C scores. It will be recalled (Footnote 4) that a C score is the sum of the separate rated probabilities of occurrence of A-given-B and B-given-A. The question arises whether there was any advantage in using the sum score rather than one of the subscores, i.e., whether either subscore predicts S as well as the total score does. Correlations between each estimate of C and S scores were therefore computed with the results shown in Table 2. Although it appears

TABLE 2

CORRELATIONS BETWEEN JUDGED SIMILARITY (S) AND PROBABILITY OF CO-OCCURRENCE (C) MEASURES USING TOTAL COMPONENT C SCORES

Word pairs	C score	r
CN-CN	Total	.84
	A Given B	.73
	B Given A	.73
A-A	Total	.95
	A Given B	.94
	B Given A	.93
A-CN	Total	.94
	A Given B	.84
	B Given A	.78

that the component scores predict almost equally as well in the case of A-A pairs, this is clearly not the case for CN-CN and A-CN pairs. For these latter, as we had anticipated originally, both components do appear necessary for maximum prediction of S.

In a recent study, Flavell and Stedman (2) proposed a theoretical model for judgments of semantic similarity which predicts that distantly related or unrelated pairs of words would tend to be judged as somewhat less dissimilar in meaning than would related words whose relationship is that of contrast or antonymity. Table 3 lists all word pairs, by class, in order of decreasing judged similarity of meaning. The rankings in the Table appear to support this hypothesis for all four classes of pairs. Ordinary antonyms ("beggar—millionaire," "soft—hard," "sickness—health," etc.) and quasi-antonymic, incompatible pairs like "sweet—lemon" and "wet —fire" are both consistently ranked lower than unrelated or distantly related pairs like "flower—mallet," "hungry—round," "leisurely—judgment," etc.

D. DISCUSSION

The results described above provide some support for the major hypothesis of study, although not in the form in which it was originally stated:

TABLE 3

RANKINGS OF SEMANTIC DISTANCES BETWEEN WORD PAIR MEMBERS AS MEASURED
BY JUDGED SIMILARITY (S), PROBABILITY OF CO-OCCURRENCE (C), AND SEMANTIC
DIFFERENTIAL (D) FOR EACH WORD PAIR CLASS

Class CN-CN	Rank S	C	D	Class A-A	Rank S	C	D
child—youngster	1	1	1	rapid—fast	1	3	1
house—home	2	2	2	shiny—gleaming	2	2	2
mother—woman	3	3	3	calm—relaxed	3	1	5
bread—dough	4	7	7	stout—fat	4	4	11
sword—knife	5	17	6	round—curved	5	5	4
stars—sky	6	4	9	clean—nice	6	6	8
food—jelly	7	8	20	harmonious—graceful	7	7	9
lake—boat	8	5	11	sweet—ripe	8	8	3
kittens—puppies	9	19	4	rancid—stagnant	9	11	16
girl—flower	10	15	5	obscure—gloomy	10	9	10
sister—brother	11	6	24	leisurely—refined	11	12	14
feather—stem	12	18	14	narrow—long	12	10	12
dirt—foot	13	14	12	green—blue	13	15	7
liquor—man	14	12	22	dim—slow	14	19	6
lady—cushion	15	16	17	mild—charming	15	13	22
leg—hospital	16	11	16	discordant—bleak	16	14	15
silk—color	17	9	8	hasty—agile	17	20	20
slime—spider	18	22	13	swift—tense	18	16	23
street—water	19	20	15	clumsy—feverish	19	17	17
car—farm	20	10	18	lagging—broken	20	18	21
lizard—pig	21	25	19	coiled—rough	21	21	18
wagon—nail	22	13	10	Russian—flaming	22	27	19
song—money	23	23	23	overcast—fleecy	23	25	26
table—glove	24	21	21	gradual—clumsy	24	22	25
piano—boulder	25	30	27	brave—rich	25	23	13
bread—stench	26	27	28	deformed—red	26	29	28
flower—mallet	27	28	26	loveable—briny	27	30	27
feather—statue	28	29	25	hungry—round	28	28	24
thief—minister	29	26	30	ugly—beautiful	29	26	30
beggar—millionaire	30	24	29	soft—hard	30	24	29

Class A-CN	Rank S	C	D	Class AN-AN	Rank S		D
briny—ocean	1	1	10	music—symphony	1		3
high—mountain	2	3	3	religion—faith	2		2
				peace—United Nations	3		18
rich—millionaire	3	2	1	war—danger	4		7
small—flea	4	6	14	God—Sunday	5		16
hungry—food	5	4	23	discomfort—pain	6		4
rugged—boulder	6	5	19	leadership—courage	7		1
calm—statue	7	11	7	health—joy	8		10
gleaming—stove	8	7	5	art—music	9		6
mild—water	9	10	17	grief—sickness	10		5
dim—barn	10	8	16	joy—dawn	11		12
wise—nurse	11	9	12	mind—art	12		9
fleecy—mother	12	19	13	courage—peace	13		20
curved—knife	13	12	27	comfort—truth	14		22
tall—lady	14	13	26	socialism—justice	15		24
green—feather	15	22	9	grief—rage	16		17
broken—sword	16	23	15	capital punishment—army	17		11
ripe—candy	17	24	2	income—socialism	18		23
pliable—brother	18	18	24	winter—effort	19		15
cold—engine	19	17	20	effort—fear	20		25
elegant—boat	20	14	4	memory—controversy	21		13
heavy—river	21	16	21	time—art	22		8
hasty—beggar	22	21	25	abortion—family	23		30
deformed—puppies	23	28	30	income—winter	24		14
feverish—negro	24	26	8				

TABLE 3 (*continued*)

Class	Rank S	Rank C	Rank D	Class	Rank S	Rank D
A-CN				**AN-AN**		
elevated—jelly	25	29	18	majority opinion —grief	25	19
dreary—lake	26	20	29	memory—army	26	21
leisurely—pigment	27	25	6	justice—sin	27	26
wet—fire	28	15	22	joy—trouble	28	28
hard—silk	29	30	28	fraud—truth	29	29
sweet—lemon	30	27	11	sickness—health	30	27

thus, C has proved an important predictor of S, independent of word pair class; C and D seem to be distinct and different measures which, at least in the case of CN-CN and A-A pairs, appear to make independent contributions to the prediction of S (Table 1). Two immediate questions arise, however. First, how to account for the magnitude of the S-C correlations—both in the absolute sense and relative to the S-D correlations? And second, what is the cause of the variation with word pair class in the size of both S-C and S-D correlations?

As to the first, a general answer would be a restatement of the theoretical formulation given in the previous paper (1): C *ought* to be a good predictor of S since it is supposed to measure an important component of $r_m \rightarrow s_m$ similarity (that stemming from similarity of non-referent, context attributes) not measured by the D score. It may simply be that this component is more dominant than we expected, that C is a better estimate of it than we expected, and so on, and these considerations account for why the S-C correlations are not only substantial but very large.

However, there are other possibilities. First of all, despite the apparent differences in instructions between C and S, subjects may really be making essentially the same judgment in both tasks, and this explains the high correlation. One way this might occur is for the subjects implicitly or explicitly to reduce S judgments to C judgments, that is, simply judge similarity of meaning in terms of co-occurrence of referents. This is the more benign possibility, since it could be considered a translation by the subject, at the here-and-now judgment level, of a long history of $r_m \rightarrow s_m$ conditioning of precisely the type which we have been arguing for in our theoretical conception—non-referent contributions, etc. In other words, the model proposed would perhaps lead one to *expect* that subjects would tend, in part at least, to use co-occurrence as a guide in whatever they do when they make similarity judgments.

However, it may be that, instead, subjects tend to drift into a similarity-of-meaning set when they make co-occurrence judgments. After all, the latter require a certain amount of crude calculation and it may simply be easier to fall back upon a global, unanalyzed intuition of similarity. If this were true, it would mean that both S and C subjects are really making S judgments and the major hypothesis would simply not have been tested in this study. About all one can do to counter this argument is to find word pairs on which the two ratings diverge and see if the divergences appear to "make sense," given the *prima facie* differences between S and C judgments. In Table 3, each word pair is rank-ordered in terms of mean S, D, and C scores. To use CN-CN as an example, word pairs with sizable rank differences between S and C include "sword—knife," "kittens —puppies," "silk—color," and "car—farm." Both the fact of discrepancy and its direction seem intuitively reasonable in most of these cases. For example, it is reasonable to judge *car* and *farm* as objects of relatively high co-occurrence and yet relatively dissimilar along an attributive similarity dimension (note the relatively large D score). Conversely, *kittens* and *puppies* seem not to be frequently encountered in the same immediate context, and yet share the important attributes expressed by the words "animal," "young," "cute," etc. (again, note the small D score). Granted that careful selection of concrete examples can buttress any position, these cases suggest, to us at least, that subjects can and do discriminate S and C judgments when discrimination is called for.

But there is still another possible explanation for the size if not the fact of the S-C correlations. There is what may be an important formal difference between D, on the one hand, and S and C on the other. The latter two derive from a testing situation in which the subject encounters both pair members *together*; D is based on information taken on each word *separately*. Although the study of the effects of verbal context on the semantic or associative properties of a given word is still in its infancy, e.g., (5, 8, 9, 10), there is certainly reason to suspect that the meaning of each word, and therefore the semantic distance between them, may very well change when the words are seen together. If this kind of thing does happen, it may account in part for the magnitude of the S-C correlations, relative to those between S and D. In short, it could be argued that the present experiment favors C as a predictor of S at the expense of D, and we are not inclined to try to counter this argument on the basis of available evidence. Perhaps the only thing to be said at this point is that all three indices are probably limited by the formal conditions—words seen together versus words seen in isolation—intrinsic to the way the measures are taken.

Among the more interesting results of this study is the finding that both S-C and S-D correlations vary in size depending upon the kind of word pairs judged. Consider first the case of the S-C correlations. It is believed that the obtained difference between the CN-CN correlation (.84) and those of A-A and A-CN (.95 and .94) is a genuine one and that there is a good reason why such a difference should obtain. In the case of A-A and A-CN as opposed to CN-CN pairs, it is difficult to see how S and C *can* really oppose each other. Two adjectives whose meanings are judged similar do in fact tend to be applied to the same nouns; stated in terms of referents, similar qualities tend to characterize (co-occur in) the same objects and dissimilar qualities tend to characterize different objects. In a recent article (4), Hays has also conceived of similarity between trait-descriptive adjectives in terms of their tendency to co-occur or "imply" one another, i.e., the extent to which the presence of trait A in a person-object implies the co-presence of B and vice-versa.

The case of A-CN pairs can probably be explained by a variation of the same argument. It is difficult to see how such disparate events as an attribute and an object can be judged along a similarity-dissimilarity continuum except in terms of co-occurrence. Just as two adjectives may be conceived as similar to the extent that they describe the same objects, so also are an adjective and a noun similar to the extent that the adjective describes the noun. The closest thing to "synonymity" between an adjective and a noun is the case where all instances of the noun's referent class must possess the attribute denoted by the adjective (e.g., "ocean—briny"); and conversely, the adjective-noun analogue of "antonymity" must be the case where the referent object cannot and never does possess the attribute in question (e.g., "lemon—sweet"). Where the two words in the pair are both nouns (CN-CN), on the other hand, the situation is quite different. Attributive similarity between *referent* objects (as opposed to *non-referent* objects in the context) is at least theoretically independent of their co-occurrence—although the world of objects *may* in fact show some tendency for similar things to co-occur. The problem in the case of CN-CN pairs is to explain why C predicts S at *all*; the explanation we offer is the one presented above and in the previous article (1).

The variations in the size of the S-D correlation are more striking than those of S-C. Although there is some obtained variation among the S-D correlations for AN-AN, CN-CN, and A-A (.76, .79, and .86, respectively), there is at hand no ready explanation of this variation, an explanation which would incline one to suspect without further evidence that the differences are really non-chance. However, it is certainly unlikely that the sudden drop in correlation in the case of A-CN is a chance affair. As both the S-D correlation and $\beta_{13.2}r_{13}$ show, the D score appears to be almost worthless as a predictor of S where adjective-noun pairs are concerned.

A likely explanation of this appears to be the following. First, there is the fact that co-occurrence of referents—what one might call the "denotative relevance" of the pair members—seems to be the paramount criterion in judging semantic similarity between adjectives and nouns. We have said that this also appears to be true of A-A pairs. However, unlike the case for A-A pairs, the attributive similarity (if one can speak of the "attributes" of an attribute) between an attribute and an object need *not* reflect their level of co-occurrence. Take the case of "briny—ocean," ranked first on both C and S measures but tenth on D. According to the Jenkins, Russell, and Suci semantic differential profiles on these two words (6), "briny" is rated less "kind," "curved," "active," "good," "beautiful," "excitable," "rounded," "important" etc. than is "ocean," despite their obvious denotative relatedness. The reason for the discrepancy probably stems from the fact that *briny* is only *one* of *many* attributes of *ocean*, and these other attributes contribute to the profile of "ocean" but not to that of "briny." Equally illustrative are words which "happen" to have profile similarity but are rated low on both S and C, e.g., "ripe—candy."

One might summarize the whole argument as follows. The semantic differential assesses only the attributive, connotative, or whatever-you-wish-to-call-it semantic characteristics of each sign in isolation. Where attributive similarity is in its own right an important determinant of S (CN-CN and probably AN-AN), and where, important determinant or not, it is highly correlated with C (A-A)—in these two situations D would be expected to predict S quite well. But where attributive similarity and co-occurrence are poorly correlated, with the latter the effective determinant of judged similarity (A-CN), D has to be a very poor predictor of S.

There is one remaining general problem which our findings suggest but unfortunately do not solve. This concerns the relative efficacy of C and D in the prediction of S, especially in the case of individual CN-CN pairs. An examination of Table 3 suggests several distinct prototypes of this kind. First, there are pairs in which C, D, and S tend to converge, so far as rank status is concerned (e.g., "child—youngster," "dirt—foot," and "song—money"); these present no particular problems. Where C and D diverge, there are three possible paradigms: (*a*) S regresses towards D and away from C (e.g., "car—farm" and "sword—knife"); (*b*) S regresses towards C and away from D (e.g., "liquor—man" and "food—jelly"); (*c*) S lies near the midpoint between C and D (e.g., "kittens—puppies" and "girl—flower"). With all due caution and qualification, these paradigms may suggest, respectively: cases in which S is primarily dependent upon attributive similarity, is primarily dependent on co-occurrence, "denotative relevance," etc., and assumes a "compromise" position—about equally dependent on both. Although one can find word pair samples of each prototype *ex post facto*, it would be difficult indeed to predict beforehand which pairs would fall into which prototype. An interesting research endeavor for the future would be to discover the defining characteristics of those classes of pairs, perhaps beginning within the general pool of CN-CN words, for whom subjects tend to use a common "strategy" for assessing similarity. In a sense, the present study is a beginning venture in this direction, insofar as it has suggested how the basis for similarity judgments appears to shift from CN-CN to A-A and A-CN.

E. Summary

The purpose of the present experiment was to make a preliminary test of the following hypothesis, derived from a theoretical position given in a previous paper (1): judgments of meaning similarity between words (S) are better predicted jointly by the semantic differential D score (D) and a recently-devised measure of probability of co-occurrence (C) than by either D or C alone. S, D, and C scores were obtained on three different types of word pairs: concrete noun—concrete noun (CN-CN), adjective—adjective (A-A), and adjective—concrete noun (A-CN). In addition, S and D measures alone were taken on a fourth type of pair: abstract noun—abstract noun (AN-AN). The data did appear to support the general hypothesis, but in a somewhat different way than originally anticipated. The most important findings were the following. The correlations between S and C were much higher than anticipated, especially in the case of A-A and A-CN pairs (.95 and .94, respectively), making it difficult for the multiple prediction of S from C and D to improve substantially upon them. With the notable exception of the A-CN pairs (r = .40), the S-D correlations were also quite high, although always lower than their S-C counterparts. Discussion of results was concerned primarily with possible reasons for the magnitude of the S-C correlations and with the probable causes of the variation, from one type of word pair to another, in the size of both S-C and S-D correlations.

REFERENCES

1. FLAVELL, J. H. Meaning and meaning similarity: I. A theoretical reassessment. *J. Gen. Psychol.*, 1961, **64**, 307-319.

2. FLAVELL, J. H., & STEDMAN, D. J. A developmental study of judgments of semantic similarity. *J. Genet. Psychol.*, (in press).

3. GUILFORD, J. P. Fundamental Statistics in Psychology and Education (Third Ed.). New York: McGraw-Hill, 1956. Pp. 565.

4. HAYS, W. L. An approach to the study of trait implications and trait similarity. *In* R. Tagiuri and L. Petrullo (*Eds.*), *Person Perception and Interpersonal Behavior*. Stanford: Stanford Univ. Press, 1958. Pp. 390. (Chapter 19.)

5. HOWES, D., & OSGOOD, C. E. On the combination of associative probabilities in linguistic contexts. *Amer. J. Psychol.*, 1954, **67**, 241-258.

6. JENKINS, J. J., RUSSELL, W. A., & SUCI, G. J. An atlas of semantic profiles for 360 words. Dept. Psychol., Univ. Minnesota, 1957 (Tech. Rep. No. 15, Contract N 8 onr-66216).

7. ————. A table of distances for the Semantic Atlas. Dept. Psychol., Univ. Minnesota, 1958 (Tech. Rep. No. 20, Contract N 8 onr-66216).

8. JENKINS, P. M., & COFER, C. N. An exploratory study of discrete free association to compound verbal stimuli. *Psychol. Rep.*, 1957, **3**, 599-603.

9. MUSGRAVE, B. S. Context effects on word association using one-word, two-word, and three-word stimuli. Paper read at Eastern Psychol. Ass'n, Philadelphia, April, 1958.

10. OSGOOD, C. E., SUCI, G. J., & TANNENBAUM, P. H. The Measurement of Meaning. Urbana: Univ. Illinois Press, 1957. Pp. 342.

21. Perceived Activity in Semantic Atlas Words as Indicated by a Tapping Response

Andrew K. Solarz

The Semantic Differential has provided a useful method of measuring a cardinal aspect of meaning (Osgood, Suci & Tannenbaum, 1957). Factor analysis of the data has consistently yielded three factors: Factor I, Evaluation; Factor II, Potency; and Factor III, Activity. *S* rates concepts on a 7-point scale bounded by polar adjectives as hot—cold, active—passive. The evaluative factor has been substantially validated by several studies which related Factor I derived hypotheses with independent response measurements (Osgood, *et al.,* 1957, Ch. 4; Solarz, 1960; Solley, Jackson, & Messick, 1957).

The present study was concerned with an independent behavioral measurement of perceived activity in printed words. Perception of activity in a stationary stimulus is undoubtedly a complex process dependent upon the activation of central neural processes with an etiology in past sensory-motor experiences. For the present purpose, the perception of activity or activity as a component of meaning is defined operationally as a mean value obtained from three scales found to have high loading on Factor III as reported in Jenkins (1960). For an interesting discussion of the relationship between perception and meaning, see Solley and Murphy (1960).

Jenkins, Russell, and Suci (1958) presented an atlas of mean profiles for 360 concepts rated by 540 *S*s. Jenkins (1960) later provided mean values for the three salient factors. A sample of these words was used in this study as stimuli to regulate rate of pencil tapping motion, and then the tapping scores were correlated with Factor III activity values.

METHOD

Subjects.—Eighteen female and 10 male volunteers were randomly selected from a pool of 230 introductory psychology students.

Apparatus.—The experiment was conducted in the Foreign Language Laboratory which permitted individual seating of *S*s in semi-soundproofed table cubicles. Following brief orientation *S*s donned headset receivers and all following instructions and time control signals were received from a central tape-recorder located in a control room. The only manipulative equipment provided *S* was a set of pencils and a $2\frac{3}{4} \times 4\frac{1}{4}$-in. pad of paper with numbered pages and a single word printed at the top of each page.

Reprinted from *Perceptual and Motor Skills* (1963), 16: 91–94, by permission of the author and the publisher.

Procedure.—Thirty-seven words were drawn from the Semantic Atlas as presented by Jenkins (1960). A representative random sample was obtained by selecting words whose Factor III scores fell between the calculated Factor III mean and each successive sigma to the right and left. The words were presented in a different random order on each pad; one pad being given to each *S*.

*S*s were divided randomly into two groups, each one meeting for two sessions with a 1-wk. interval. Group I provided a reliability measure of the tapping response by repeating the task at Session two (words were presented in a new random order). Group II gave the tapping response during Session one and took the Semantic Differential for the activity factor during Session two. The polarities of the three scales used (Jenkins, 1960) were counterbalanced and the scales were separated by superfluous scales.

The instructions at the initial session for both groups were (abridged): "The purpose of this experiment is to discover the meaning of certain words by getting your rating of the words in terms of rate of tapping. You will tap with the pencil on each page below the word printed at the top of each page. For example, if you were rating the word 'express train' you would probably consider an express train quite fast and so you would tap quite fast. If, however, you were rating the word 'oxcart' you would probably consider it quite slow and thus tap quite slowly. You must decide just how slow or fast a word seems to you. No two individuals will be working with the same word at the same time so pay strict attention to your own work. You will be told when to turn each page and read the given word. Next, I will say 'motion,' at this time you are to begin, just above the pad, the rate of pencil motion which you feel is appropriate to the word printed. Then on the command 'tap' record your rate of motion by tapping on the page. Continue tapping legibly until I say 'stop.' I will then say 'look up and relax.' The same procedure will be followed for each word on each page."

The time sequence of events was: read the word, 5 sec.; motion, 6 sec.; tap, 8 sec.; relax, 11 sec. The instructions were recorded once and then re-recorded for successive presentation for each word stimulus.

The words "fast" and "slow" were presented at the beginning and again, in reversed order, at the end of the list for each *S*. This provided a check on fatigue effects.

The wearing of the headsets in addition to the sound-proofing and the fact that very few *S*s worked on the same word at the same time, gave ample protection against *S*'s attending to a group determined rate of tapping during the response time.

Scores were obtained by simply totaling the pencil tapping marks on each page for each *S*.

RESULTS

The tapping scores were converted to standard scores for each *S* in order to equalize individual response scales. Of first importance is the Pearson product-moment correlation between the Factor III (activity) values presented by Jenkins (1960) in the Semantic Atlas and the mean standard scores for Groups I and II for the first tapping session. This *r* was .82; however, the relationship was curvilinear following an approximate S-shape with Factor III scores plotted on the *Y* axis. The consequent calculated *eta* for *Y* on *X* was .96, and that for *X* on *Y* .95.

Comparing Group II's mean tapping scores (Session 1) with their obtained mean semantic scale values (Session 2), a similar S-shaped relationship was found, an *r* of .90; the *eta* for *Y* on *X* was .96 and that for *X* on *Y* .94. The

TABLE 1

ATLAS WORDS AND MEAN STANDARD SCORES FOR TAPPING, GROUPS I AND II

Shady	− .69	Abrupt	− .13
Door	− .50	Pig	− .18
Brave	.18	Millionaire	.20
Mad	1.10	Hard	− .36
Relaxed	− .97	Think	.23
Woman	− .02	Hurried	1.39
Sunlight	− .01	Fat	− .57
Soft	− .79	Tense	1.20
Feverish	1.07	River	.09
Harmonious	− .36	Swift	1.20
Fleecy	− .29	Study	− .13
Sweet	− .44	Radiant	.43
Puppies	.57	Lovely	− .31
Sky	− .69	Frigid	− .50
Snail	−1.22	Truth	− .44
Downy	− .73		

correlation between Group II's Semantic Differential values and those reported by Jenkins for the Semantic Atlas was .97.

An indication of reliability of the tapping response was provided by comparing the two tapping sessions of Group I. The resulting *r* was .87.

Fatigue effects were absent. The mean combined tapping standard scores for "fast" and "slow" at the beginning of the task were 1.54 and −1.07, and at the end of the task, respectively, 1.83 and −1.03.

Of special interest are the mean tapping standard scores obtained for the polar adjectives of the three scales reported having high loading for Factor III (Jenkins, 1960; Osgood, Suci, & Tannenbaum, 1957). The scores were: Fast, 1.68—Slow, −1.05; Excitable, 1.17—Calm, −.90; Active, 1.20—Passive, −1.02. "Snail" was perceived as slower than slow, mean tapping rate −1.22 (a mixture effect as "slow snail" would probably be slower). "Fast" had the highest mean tapping rate.

DISCUSSION

The high correlations found in this study provide a behavioral validation correlate for the activity factor of the Semantic Differential. According to Osgood's theory of meaning (1952; 1953; Osgood, *et al.*, 1957) the direction and intensity of motor responses to signs (words) is largely determined by experientially acquired representational mediation processes. Words receiving a similar rate of tapping response, or a similar value on the activity component of the Semantic Differential, presumably would be closely located along some dimension of multidimensional semantic space.

The reliability of the tapping technique appears to be quite high. For a recent discussion of the stability characteristics of the semantic differential, see Norman (1959). It is noteworthy that the Semantic Atlas study, as the present one, used volunteer *S*s from the introductory course in psychology.

It is felt that this restriction in sampling may have accounted partially for the high correlations and *eta*s reported herein.

A study of the raw scores strongly suggested that the relationship of curvilinearity was due to the abrupt cut-off both at the top and bottom of Semantic Differential response values. In contrast, rate of tapping provided a more continuous function as well as a greater range for response.

SUMMARY

A pencil tapping response was related to the Semantic Differential Factor III (activity) values reported in the Semantic Atlas. Two groups of 14 Ss each responded by tapping to a representative sample of words. A curvilinear relationship resulted, with *eta*s equal to .96 and .93. The reliability coefficient of the tapping response, one week interval, was .87. Fatigue effects for tapping were negligible.

REFERENCES

JENKINS, J. J. Degree of polarization and scores on the principal factors for concepts in the Semantic Atlas study. *Amer. J. Psychol.*, 1960, 73, 274-279.

JENKINS, J. J., RUSSELL, W. A., & SUCI, G. J. An atlas of semantic profiles for 360 words. *Amer. J. Psychol.*, 1958, 71, 688-699.

NORMAN, W. T. Stability characteristics of the Semantic Differential. *Amer. J. Psychol.*, 1959, 72, 581-584.

OSGOOD, C. E. The nature and measurement of meaning. *Psychol. Bull.*, 1952, 49, 197-237.

OSGOOD, C. E., SUCI, G. J., & TANNENBAUM, P. H. *The measurement of meaning.* Urbana, Ill.: Univer. of Illinois Press, 1957.

SOLARZ, A. K. Latency of instrumental responses as a function of compatibility with the meaning of eliciting verbal signs. *J. exp. Psychol.*, 1960, 59, 239-245.

SOLLEY, C. M., JACKSON, D. N., & MESSICK, S. J. Guessing behavior and autism. *J. abnorm. soc. Psychol.*, 1957, 54, 32-36.

SOLLEY, C. M., & MURPHY, G. *Development of the perceptual world.* New York: Basic Books, 1960.

Part V

CROSS-CULTURAL STUDIES

Part 1
CROSS-CULTURAL STUDIES

22. A Pilot Study of Cross-Cultural Meaning

Hideya Kumata and Wilbur Schramm

The investigator working in international communications is constantly beset with problems of meaning. In cross-national surveys, for example, it is often the wording and translation of questions which turn out to be the weakest links. In cross-cultural activities, the communicator often is not sure whether he has transmitted a meaningful message to foreign peoples.

It would be extremely helpful if some notion could be obtained of the ingredients which make up the meaningful judgments of peoples in various cultures. Is it possible that the same or near-same dimensions are taken into account by all people in making meaningful judgments? And if not, what are the differences? These are crucial questions. Although popular conception deems otherwise, it has never been demonstrated that semantic frames of reference really differ from culture to culture.

The study reported here is an exploratory investigation of a limited aspect of the problem of meaning cross-culturally. Such a study was made possible by the development of a measurement tool called the *semantic differential*. Using this tool with American subjects, Osgood and associates found that the same three principal factors of meaning recurred when subjects judged various concepts against a sample of bipolar adjectival scales (such as good-bad, strong-weak, etc.) These three factors, labeled evaluation, potency, and activity, seemed to present a description of judgmental dimensions, at least in the area of connotative meaning.[1]

THE PROBLEM

Our concern was to explore the possibilities of using the semantic differential in a translated form in other cultures, in much the same way as it had been used in the American culture. Specifically, we were interested in the following questions:

1. The differential has indicated that a common semantic structure in the area of connotative meaning exists for persons in the American culture (or more correctly,

Reprinted from *Public Opinion Quarterly* (1956), 20: 229–238, by permission of the authors and the publisher.

[1] Osgood, C. E., and Suci, G. J., "Factor Analysis of Meaning," *Journal of Experimental Psychology*, 1955, 50, pp. 325-38.

American college culture, inasmuch as Osgood's reported experiments used college sub-jects). Do the *same semantic factors* operate in the judgments of *different* culture groups?

2. Do the *same or different factors* operate within a bilingual (and bicultural) group when comparisons are made between judgments *in one language* and judgments made *in the second language?* That is, if an individual knows two languages, will he make the same meaning judgments when he is operating in one language as when he is using the other?

3. What *descriptive statements* can we make about the meaning of certain inter-nationally-important concepts by *different culture groups?*

Available space makes it possible to present only a small part of the data and the findings.

Materials. Twenty scales (see Table 1) and 30 concepts (see Table 3)[2] were selected. The scales were picked from the original Osgood study of fifty scales. The scales were selected to include some with high loadings on each of the three factors. The concepts were selected with a view toward obtaining cultural meanings of certain ideological terms, countries, nationali-ties and personalities.

Subjects. Two groups of foreign students were used, 25 Japanese and 22 Koreans. A comparison group of 24 American students was also selected. All three groups were college students at a midwestern university. Length of residence in the United States for the two foreign groups ranged from three months to six years with the median residence four months for the Japanese and two years for the Koreans.

Procedure. All groups received two administrations of the test with three weeks between testings. The Korean and Japanese groups received one form in English and the other form in their native language. The American group received the identical English form on both administrations. Order effect with the two foreign groups was controlled by having half of each foreign group take the English version first and half the native language version first.

All instructions were given in the language appropriate to the version of the test. Instruction cover sheets which accompanied each form were also in the appropriate language. It was thought that conducting the administration in this manner would encourage "thinking" in one language for any one version and minimize any translation attempts on the part of subjects. The administrator for each of the three groups was a member of that group, a Korean tester for the Koreans, a Japanese for the Japanese group, and an American for the American students.[3]

---

[2] Concepts were judged against the set of 20 scales which were presented in the following fashion:

good:_____:_____:_____:_____:_____:_____:_____: bad

[3] The authors wish to thank Raymond Wolfinger and Kyung Won Lee for their help in administering the test. Mr. Lee also served as the coordinator of the Korean translations.

Translation. The translation problem, as has been pointed out, is a crucial one.[4] An advantage of the *differential* is that considerations of syntactics may be omitted since single words are translated. The problem is onerous nevertheless. The scales and concepts were translated by three persons for each language. Unfortunately, no objective check was made on the competency of any of the judges for bilingual facility. All three Korean judges, however, were more facile in Korean than in English. Two of the Japanese judges were superior in Japanese while for the third, English was the dominant language.

These independent translations were compared and an attempt was made by discussion to ameliorate items of disagreement. There was final unanimous agreement for translation of the concepts for both Korean and Japanese. Scales presented some difficulties. When disagreement did crop up the procedure followed was for the investigator to put the adjective to be translated into a simple English sentence. No back translation was done.

RESULTS

A prodigious amount of data is generated when subjects rate concepts on a seven-step scale bounded by polar adjectives. In our study, interesting profiles for each group can be obtained for any particular concept as in Figures 1A and 1B.

In both of these figures, mean judgments on all scales were computed for the native language versions of Japanese and Koreans and the first administration for the Americans. Gross as these profiles may be, they still highlight some interesting differences between groups. For the concept *Atomic Warfare,* the Koreans are less unfavorable than either the Americans or the Japanese. Generally, however, the profiles are quite similar except for the brave-cowardly, good-bad, and belligerent-peaceful scales, where Americans and Japanese rate the concept as more cowardly and more belligerent than the Koreans, and the Koreans think of it as definitely less bad. For the concept *Communism,* the Japanese are generally less unfavorable than the other two groups. Again, on the scale brave-cowardly, the Americans rate Communism as neither brave nor cowardly whereas the two foreign groups rate the concept as somewhat brave.

Space precludes mentioning many other results of these cross-cultural semantic comparisons, which is a pity because they are among the most fascinating products of the experiment. One example only: the Japanese and

---

[4] Ervin, Susan, and R. T. Bower, "Translation Problems in International Surveys," *Public Opinion Quarterly,* Vol. XVI, (1952), No. 4, pp. 595-604; Radyanvi, L. "Problems of International Opinion Surveys," *International Journal of Opinion Research,* 1947, 1, pp. 30-51.

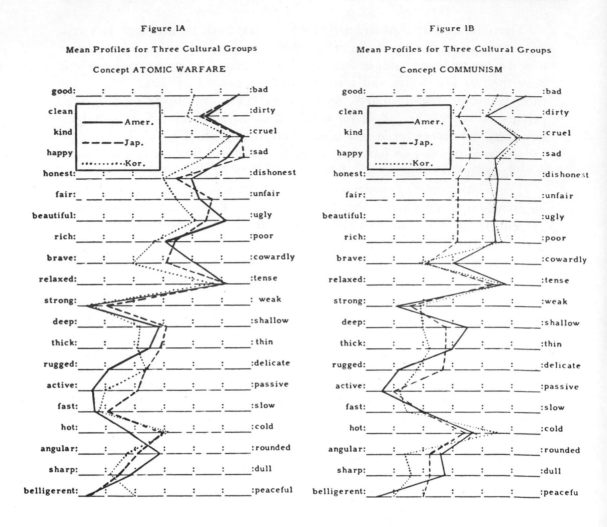

Figure 1A

Mean Profiles for Three Cultural Groups

Concept ATOMIC WARFARE

Figure 1B

Mean Profiles for Three Cultural Groups

Concept COMMUNISM

Koreans, when asked to judge "myself" and "my people", produced profiles that were quite close to each other; that is, the Japanese idea of the Japanese and the Korean idea of the Koreans were not much different. But when the two groups were asked to rate *each other,* the profiles were far apart!

Factor Analysis of Scale Relationships. Scale by scale analysis of profiles, although interesting, is a long and tedious procedure. If some scales are functionally equivalent, that is, if a scale like *good-bad* correlates very highly with a scale like *fair-unfair,* then we can more economically describe the meaning of any concept by a limited number of dimensions. In order to obtain relationships among scales which would be most typical, we summed over both subjects and concepts producing six 20 by 20 intercorrelational matrices of every scale with every other scale for the three groups in two language versions. These six matrices were factor analyzed using the method of principal components and the factors were rotated by the quartimax method.[5]

Eight factors were extracted. The rotated factor matrices for the first two factors for each of the groups appears as Table 1. These first two factors account for from 63 per cent in the case of the Japanese group, Japanese version to 76 per cent of the total variance in the case of the Korean group in both versions. The rest of the factors for all groups and versions yielded no

TABLE 1

ROTATED FACTOR LOADINGS FOR THREE GROUPS*

Scales	Americans				Japanese				Koreans			
	1st Test Factors		2d Test Factors		Eng. Factors		Jap. Factors		Eng. Factors		Kor. Factors	
	I	II	I	II	I	II	I	II	I	II	I	II
good–bad	93	−24	94	00	−93	−12	94	14	93	01	95	05
clean–dirty	86	34	88	33	−85	34	84	−35	90	−28	93	−22
kind–cruel	96	−10	96	12	−97	−08	96	08	94	13	98	00
happy–sad	79	42	86	−34	−87	43	89	−36	85	−42	87	−41
honest–dishonest	94	−03	92	00	−93	01	92	−10	94	−11	94	−13
fair–unfair	94	−08	96	05	−95	04	94	−04	95	−12	93	−19
beautiful–ugly	83	12	83	−02	−66	01	75	05	90	−14	93	01
rich–poor	38	69	49	−62	−38	74	47	−71	68	−62	70	−46
brave–cowardly	36	−09	37	11	−55	42	46	−37	01	−61	53	−62
relaxed–tense	76	10	62	−09	−79	−04	60	10	81	05	80	06
strong–weak	00	94	00	−87	−12	95	26	−83	27	−87	21	−89
deep–shallow	45	12	23	−22	−34	−12	25	00	26	−16	53	−13
thick–thin	−18	25	−22	−28	−31	34	38	01	27	−18	37	−14
rugged–delicate	−30	43	−20	−56	64	29	−44	−25	−85	−12	−76	−12
active–passive	−21	89	−01	−93	−08	91	−07	−94	−03	−96	16	−90
fast–slow	00	83	−12	−84	12	83	−06	−79	14	−93	08	−92
hot–cold	04	−04	17	00	−28	−28	25	29	79	03	69	−10
angular–rounded	−10	20	16	−39	74	08	−55	−17	−91	−23	−92	−11
sharp–dull	00	81	−13	−71	15	61	−11	−56	−09	−64	00	−61
belligerent–peaceful	−87	33	−86	−39	91	11	−84	−22	−94	−14	−91	−32
% total variance	42	24	41	24	47	22	43	20	54	22	56	20

*Due to space limitations, the six 20 by 20 correlational matrices, the unrotated factor matrices and the remainder of the rotated matrices are not included. They may be obtained by writing to the first named author. Decimal points have been omitted in the table.

[5] Thurstone, L. L., *Multiple Factor Analysis*, Chicago: University of Chicago Press, 1947; Neuhaus, J. E., and C. F. Wrigley, "The Quartimax Method: An Approach to Orthogonal Simple Structure," *British Journal of Statistical Psychology*, November, 1954. The intercorrelational matrices and the factor analyses were done on ILLAC, the University of Illinois digital computer. The authors wish to thank Mr. Ray Twery and Mrs. Carol Tucker for their aid in running the problems through the computer.

sensible loading patterns. There was a hint of a third factor in the case of the Japanese and Koreans revolving around the scales deep-shallow and thick-thin. However, the per cent variance accounted for ranged only from 8.5 per cent to 10.5 per cent.

The striking feature of Table 1 is the similarity of factors and factor loadings. Although there is no test for the significance of differences between factors, we ran an approximate measure which gave us the lower limit of agreement among factors. Table 2 gives the figures obtained after comparing the first two factors of each version with the first two factors of every other version. As can be seen, each group produces the highest figure when com-

TABLE 2

INDICES OF FACTORIAL SIMILARITY

THREE GROUPS ON TWO FACTORS

(Upper right part of table is for factor II, lower left for factor I)

	A1	A2	Jj	Je	Kk	Ke
A1		987	929	931	885	904
A2	983		913	905	872	889
Jj	949	934		977	943	961
Je	938	914	989		938	960
Kk	906	881	971	979		983
Ke	892	869	956	957	980	

Note.—Decimals omitted. Lower limit of agreement .782. (See C. F. Wrigley and J. E. Neuhaus, "The Matching of Two Sets of Factors," American Psychologist, 1955, 10, pp. 418-419, abstract, for discussion of indices of similarity.)

parisons are made within the group between two versions. The American first testing (A1) agrees the most with the American second testing (A2). Similarly the agreement is highest between Japanese language version (Jj) with the Japanese group taking the English version (Je). The Korean language version (Kk) shows the highest agreement with the Koreans taking the English language version (Ke). However, for all groups and all versions, the index of factorial similarity is well above the figure computed as a good estimate of the lower limit of agreement.

The first and dominant factor for all six analyses may be identified as an *evaluative* factor. The scales good-bad, kind-cruel, honest-dishonest and fair-unfair have loadings of .80 or better and are relatively "pure" scales in that the extracted variance is almost entirely in this first factor. This first factor is in substantial agreement also with the results obtained in Osgood's study where factor analysis produced a first factor identified as evaluative which accounted for 34 per cent of the variance. Scales beautiful-ugly, relaxed-tense, clean-dirty, and belligerent-peaceful are also highly loaded on this factor but do not restrict their loadings chiefly to this factor.

The second factor might be labeled as *dynamism*. The highest loadings and the most restricted ones are the scales strong-weak, active-passive, fast-slow and sharp-dull. The scale rich-poor has high loadings on this factor but does not restrict its loading to this factor. In effect, this factor combines both the potency and activity factors identified in the Osgood study. It may be that the nature of the concepts judged accounts for this finding.

It would seem that, within the sample of scales and concepts used in this study, the same two factors are utilized by these three language groups. Further, it would seem that the same factors are utilized by bilinguals regardless of language used. The implications of these statements will be taken up in the discussion section.

Description of concepts. Given the correspondence of factors across groups, we can specify the meanings of concepts in two dimensions. We have some confidence, also, that comparisons of concepts either within a group or between groups are feasible—insofar as comparisons are restricted to these two factors. Stated conversely, unless knowledge of the common factors shared by different groups is available, no comparisons could be validly made.

Figures 2A and 2B are examples of the plotting of various concepts in two dimensional space.[6] Factor I (the horizontal axis) in both figures is the evaluative dimension and factor II (the vertical axis) is the dynamism factor. These plots were obtained by summing across the high and "purely" loaded scales for the two factors. These figures may be viewed in two ways. First, between group comparisons may be made for the same concept. Thus in Figure 2A, the concept United States is considered quite good and quite dynamic by the Americans and Koreans. The same concept is considered somewhat dynamic and somewhat less good by the Japanese. In Figure 2B both Americans and Koreans rate Mao Tse Tung as somewhat bad and somewhat dynamic. The Japanese on the other hand rate Mao as somewhat dynamic but slightly good. Second, comparisons of several concepts for the same group may be made. Thus for the Americans in Figure 2A, the United States is rated quite good and somewhat dynamic, South Korea is rated somewhat good and somewhat passive, Japan is rated slightly good and indifferent as to dynamism, and the Soviet Union is rated quite bad and quite dynamic.

Differences between concepts. Given the orthogonality of factors and equal representation in the set of scales, we can note differences between the concepts either within a group or between groups by the use of the D statistic[7] which takes into account both profile and mean difference information. Table 3 gives D scores of comparison of concepts between the three

[6] Space limitations preclude the inclusion of all the plots. These plus mean profile data for each concept may be obtained by writing the first named author.

[7] Osgood, C. E. and G. J. Suci, "A Measure of Relation Determined by Both Mean Difference and Profile Information," *Psychological Bulletin,* 1952, 49, pp. 251-262.

Two Dimensional Plot of Selected Concepts
FIGURE 2A (Nationality)

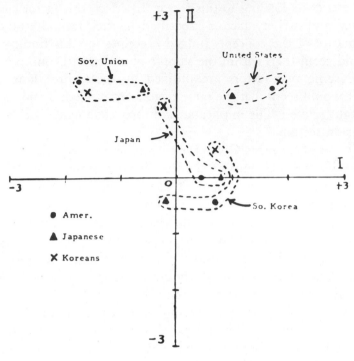

FIGURE 2B (Country)

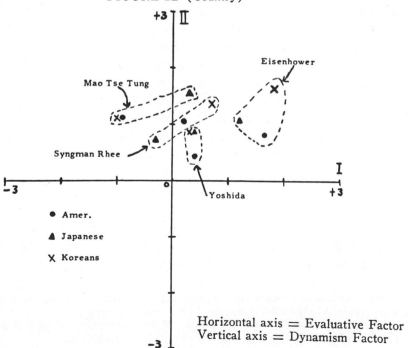

Horizontal axis = Evaluative Factor
Vertical axis = Dynamism Factor

groups; in other words what we hope is a rough approximation to their close-ness or farness in semantic space. There is no adequate method for determin-ing the significances of differences between distances.[8] We can make some rough comparisons, however. For example: note that in Table 3 for the concept India, the D between Americans (A) and Koreans (K) is the small-est and the distance between the Americans and the Japanese (J) is the largest.

TABLE 3

D MEASURES BETWEEN THREE CULTURAL GROUPS

	A–J	A–K	J–K		A–J	A–K	J–K
India	1.27	.27	.41	Chiang	1.12	.57	.19
U. S.	.51	.02	.76	Nehru	.37	.08	.50
Sov. Union	1.13	.04	1.09	Yoshida*	.38	.30	.02
China	.57	.31	.24	Rhee	.24	.33	1.44
Japan	.19	1.98	2.74	Communism	2.10	.08	1.43
S. Korea	.41	.85	1.62	Police	.08	.52	.67
U. N.	.44	.84	.40	Atomic War	.44	.85	.92
Americans	.02	.13	.16	Labor Union	.20	.04	.07
Japanese	.08	1.12	1.16	Colonialism	.93	.74	.14
S. Koreans	.61	1.36	1.81	Christianity	.02	.34	.25
Chinese	.06	.06	.18	Majority Rule	.29	.14	.47
Eisenhower	.23	.02	.62	Father	.33	.70	.77
Truman	.07	1.09	.63	Myself	.44	.09	.28
MacArthur	.45	1.98	.98	Male	.14	.18	.14
Mao Tse Tung	1.58	.01	1.89	Waterfall	.63	.03	.86

*Premier of Japan at the time of the study.

We ranked the D measures from smallest to largest for each concept and ran a Friedman's X_r^2 test[9] to test the hypothesis that the two foreign groups would be closer in distance for all concepts than either group in compari-son with the Americans. The hypothesis was not borne out. The figure for X_r^2 was 5.06 which at 2 d.f. reached the 8 per cent level. But, the sum of ranks between the Japanese and the Koreans was the largest, meaning that the two groups had the greatest distance in the three comparisons. Interest-ingly, when concepts referring to one's own group were eliminated from the analysis, (i.e. concepts such as U. S., Japan, South Korea, American people, Japanese people, South Korean people, Eisenhower, Truman, MacArthur, Yoshida, and Rhee), the probability level obtained was .24 indicating that distances were greater between groups when judging concepts referring to one's own group. In other words, the three nationalities differed most in their mutual opinions of each other.

[8] See the treatment of this problem by Eric Lenneberg in the forthcoming monograph, "The Language of Experience," which will appear as a supplement to the *International Journal of American Linguistics.*

[9] Friedman, J., "The Use of Ranks to Avoid the Assumption of Normality," *Journal of the American Statistical Association,* 1937, 32, pp. 675-701.

DISCUSSION

The results of the factor analyses of scale relationships raise an intriguing question. The remarkable correspondence across cultures tempts one to say that perhaps there is a pervasive semantic frame of references used by humans. Of course, with such a small sample of subjects no such definite statement can be made. Furthermore, it must be remembered that all subjects were tested in the American culture. The mere presence of the foreign students in the United States may make them atypical with respect to their native cultures. We cannot refute such a possibility. However, we feel that the results are encouraging enough to warrant a larger scale study using subjects within their own cultures excluding bilinguals. This is now in preparation.

A better sampling of scales in a larger study may bring out other factors not adequately tapped by our scales. The scales we used were developed by Osgood through free association by subjects to a list of stimulus words taken from the Kent-Rosanoff list. If, as Osgood suggests, a sample of scales was derived on a logically exhaustive basis, such as using Roget's *Thesaurus* as a source, additional factors may be brought out.

The use of the semantic differential in studies of comparative meanings cross-culturally has proved in this experiment to be promising and hopeful. It might give additional dimension to studies of stereotypes such as that of Katz and Braly[10] and Buchanan and Cantril.[11] Unquestionably we have here a tool which can give us a better basis for formulating hypotheses on the sources of differences between groups.

[10] Katz, D., and K. W. Braly, "Verbal Stereotypes and Racial Prejudice," in T. M. Newcomb and E. L. Hartley (Ed.), *Readings in Social Psychology*. New York: Holt, 1947, pp. 204-10.

[11] Buchanan, W., and H. Cantril, *How Nations See Each Other*. Urbana, Illinois: University of Illinois Press, 1953.

23. A Comparison of Semantic Structures in American Southwest Culture Groups [1]

George J. Suci [2]

A<small>N</small> OBJECT is perceived, or a concept described, in terms of a set of attributes, and most attributes, but not necessarily all, have linguistic equivalents that permit their communication. This assumption is, in part, the basis for an operational definition of meaning—the semantic differential, extensively described elsewhere (Osgood, Suci, & Tannenbaum; 1957). Briefly, concepts or objects are judged on rating scales defined with adjective opposites (e.g., *good–bad*). In English, adjectives appear to be related such that only a few dimensions are needed to account for most variation in such judgments. These dimensions define a semantic space and the meaning of a concept is given by the coordinates of its location in this space.

A concept has the same meaning for two individuals or two culture groups when the concept is located in the same position of the respective semantic spaces. That such an equivalence between concepts can be said to exist depends on the equivalence of the semantic spaces; i.e., the dimensions, and therefore attributes, must mean the same for the two

Reprinted from *Journal of Abnormal and Social Psychology* (1960), 61: 25–30, by permission of the author and the American Psychological Association.

[1] This study was conducted as a part of the Southwest Project in Comparative Psycholinguistics, sponsored by the Committee on Linguistics and Psychology of the Social Science Research Council under a grant from the Carnegie Corporation of New York. The data were analyzed at the University of Illinois Computer Laboratories. For a more complete description of the entire project, see Casagrande (1956). The author wishes to express his appreciation to the following members of the project who were kind enough to collect the data used in this study: Susan Ervin for Navaho; J. B. Carroll, Lois Elliott, and H. S. Maclay for Hopi; J. R. Bastian, Sally Bastian, E. H. Lenneberg, and S. S. Newman for Zuni; and S. Saporta for Spanish.

[2] This study was carried out when the author was at the University of Illinois.

individuals. To avoid circularity, the meaning of attributes cannot be inferred from the meanings, or locations, of the concepts; instead, such meaning is inferred from the totality of relations among the attributes themselves. If the same relations exist between a set of attributes for two different individuals, their semantic spaces are equivalent and their meanings of a concept may be compared. Obviously without such equivalence of space, communication between individuals regarding the meanings of their concepts is seriously impeded.

Extremely different subjects have shown highly similar semantic structures. Suci (1952) found that a group of high and a group of low scorers on the California F Scale judged ethnic concepts in similar semantic frames of reference. The meanings of the ethnic concepts, however, differed significantly between the groups. The same kind of results were demonstrated when Republican and Democratic subjects rated politically relevant concepts (Osgood et al., 1957, pp. 104–124). Meanings of concepts like FDR, MCCARTHY, POLICY IN CHINA differed significantly while the attribute relations remained constant. Similar results are reported by Bopp (1955) for normal and schizophrenic subjects.

Does semantic constancy occur across subjects selected from different cultural and linguistic backgrounds? Kumata and Schramm (1956) showed equivalent semantic structures for Korean bilingual exchange students, Japanese bilingual exchange students, and American natives when the semantic judgments were made in the respective languages. Later Kumata (1957) showed the same kind of equivalence for Japanese and American monolinguals, thus extending the generality of the Kumata and Schramm findings. Triandis and Osgood (1958), aiming more directly at a test of Whorf's hypothesis (1956) that language determines cognition, found that Greek and American monolinguals used similar semantic spaces. Thus, Triandis and Osgood, as well as Kumata, have produced evidence against the Whorfian hypothesis, at least with respect to meaning as measured by the semantic differential. The present study extends the comparison of semantic structures to subjects from the American Southwest—Spanish, Hopi, Zuni, and Navaho subjects.

Method

In general, the design consisted of constructing a semantic differential and administering it to subjects (*S*s) from each culture group, intercorrelating the semantic scales for each group, factoring each of these sets of relationships, and comparing the obtained factor structures. The Southwest groups will be designated as "experimental" groups to differentiate them from an English-speaking "control" group which is described below.

The Semantic Differential

A first selection of bipolar adjective scales was made as follows. Each of 42 nouns was translated into the native language by an informant from each experimental group. The nouns were read one at a time as stimuli to each informant who was instructed to respond with as many appropriate adjective forms as he could. Each "adjective" obtained in this fashion was read back to the informant who was instructed to respond with a proper opposite. Of the total number of bipolar opposites obtained in this fashion, 25 were common to three of the experimental groups. These were retained as items in the semantic differentials given to the *S*s. In the field it was necessary for each investigator to adjust his list because of poor translations, or *S*s' refusals to respond to some of the items. This resulted in the use of different polar terms by different investigators, and, in the final analysis, only 15 scales were common to all groups.

Ten concepts were selected to be rated on the scales. As with the scales, many of the concepts were found unsatisfactory because of translation difficulties or because they touched on sensitive areas and threatened rapport with the *S*s; therefore, new concepts had to be substituted in some cases and different sets of concepts resulted for some groups. *S*s of all groups rated: MEXICAN, CORN, MAN, WOMAN, HORSE, and RAIN. The Zuni group also rated COYOTE, RED, YELLOW, and BLUE-GREEN. The Hopi and Navaho also rated NAVAHO, WHITE PEOPLE, COYOTE, and SELF, and the Spanish group rated RELIGION, DEATH, ARMY, and GODFATHER.

Control for Concept Differences

Semantic structures may vary with different concepts (Osgood et al., 1957, pp. 176–188); therefore, it was necessary to estimate the extent of semantic space variation due to differences in concepts rated by each group. All the different concepts were presented to a "control" group of English speakers, monolingual college students at the University of Illinois. Three semantic spaces were factored out, each one based on a subset of concepts rated by an experimental group. The three semantic spaces were compared. Since each English speaking *S* was his own control, differences between these structures could be attributed only to differences in concepts, not to differences in language or culture; therefore, factor differences between the control semantic structures implied that comparisons between experimental groups were not valid for those factors. In the analysis, no comparisons between experimental groups were made when such differences occurred.

Subjects

The experimental *S*s were 26 Zuni, 28 Hopi, and 27 Navaho Indians, and 32 Spanish speakers from the Albuquerque, New Mexico area. All *S*s were fluent speakers of their native language, but English was spoken with varying degrees of competence. The Spanish, Hopi, and Zuni *S*s were bilingual but dominant in their own language as judged by the linguists working with these groups. The extent of bilingualism in the Navaho *S*s was judged on the basis of a bilingualism test.[3] Of the 27 Navaho, 14 were English dominants, 6 were Navaho dominants, and 7 were Navaho monolinguals. The median age and age-range for each group was as follows: Zuni, 35, 12–70; Hopi, 24, 12–64; Navaho, 45, 17–75; Spanish, 26, 18–34; English speakers, 21, 19–26. The sex distribution, male and female respectively, in each group was as follows: Zuni, 15, 11; Hopi, 12, 16; Navaho, 8, 19; Spanish, 21, 11; American, 18, 15.

Instructions and Procedure

The literate Spanish and control groups received standard instructions (Osgood et al., 1957, pp. 82–84). Administration was in a group using paper-and-pencil forms printed in the respective native languages.

Since the Indian people are nonliterate in their native languages, *S*s from these groups could not respond to the standard rating procedure and a modified technique had to be devised. Twenty-five lines, one for each scale, with the ends and the middle of each line marked, were mimeographed on legal size paper. The lines were six inches long. The instructions, given below, will explain the procedure employed in the administration of the items to the Indian *S*s.

We would like to know how you describe or talk about certain things. For example, you may think of something being very fast or very slow, or a little bit strong or a little bit weak. Suppose we wanted

---

[3] The bilingualism test was developed by Susan Ervin.

TABLE 1
First Three Factors after Biquartimin Rotation

Scales	Navaho			Hopi			Zuni			Spanish			A-N-H[a]			A-Z[b]			A-S[c]		
	1	2	3	1	2	3	1	2	3	1	2	3	1	2	3	1	2	3	1	2	3
heavy–light	07	47	−01	09	45	−29	11	10	53	−35	34	07	−04	47	33	01	12	02	−21	49	−12
hard–soft	−26	26	−05	−01	30	−25	−08	23	−08	−28	22	26	−29	28	−10	−38	45	−05	−07	30	−18
pretty–ugly	51	07	−02	72	01	−14	64	−06	00	79	00	−01	61	−06	10	66	01	06	41	−03	27
hot–cold	−40	40	08	20	−01	−39	20	−16	42	42	14	38	01	00	54	−05	02	59	−08	05	65
clean–dirty	34	26	00	58	−07	14	65	03	10	61	08	−12	75	−05	−12	72	03	−12	67	−06	−10
dry–wet	−12	−15	28	−05	−22	−43	12	−18	−15	−13	−11	23	−20	01	15	−29	22	37	−09	−01	17
industrious–lazy	41	01	24	48	05	07	16	67	−02	15	62	−06	34	32	−04	17	66	07	29	46	17
happy–sad	24	42	−13	53	07	02	59	08	−02	53	11	08	39	−06	31	37	00	46	19	03	53
rich–poor	00	49	−06	54	03	07	60	11	15	33	11	−43	61	24	−15	59	26	−07	61	16	−18
sweet–sour	32	02	02	21	−08	47	33	24	17	78	−03	06	58	−20	15	63	−16	10	44	−22	29
long–short	05	48	03	13	33	08	23	31	21	−04	51	−01	13	54	−10	14	36	24	07	43	−30
fast–slow	03	−03	65	−02	53	01	−10	71	12	08	45	−10	08	60	−10	−03	63	−07	09	48	08
strong–weak	12	46	−07	01	64	05	02	72	−04	−03	64	00	01	58	16	−04	54	11	02	64	10
straight–crooked	05	05	00	06	−19	05	50	05	−05	38	20	−05	53	17	21	55	12	09	48	08	04
good–bad	53	18	01	42	05	34	31	46	−26	77	02	−01	69	02	12	71	−02	00	52	06	25
% Common Variance	14.9	17.3	7.1	25.1	15.4	11.4	28.8	26.4	8.9	41.6	19.9	6.4	35.9	19.6	8.7	36.1	20.3	10.1	22.1	17.2	13.8

Note.—Decimal points are omitted.

[a] American control for Navaho and Hopi concepts.

[b] American control for Zuni concepts.

[c] American control for Spanish concepts.

to know how strong or weak something like MOUN-TAIN is. You could think of this end (experimenter [E] points to one end of a line) as being something very, very strong and this end as something very, very weak. Now since MOUNTAIN is very, very strong, it would be very much like the very, very strong thing on this end and you would show me, by pointing (or pencil mark), that this is where MOUNTAIN belongs.

On the other hand, something like GRASS is not strong, but quite weak, and you would show me this by placing it close to this thing which is very, very weak. A TREE is quite strong but certainly not as strong as MOUNTAIN, so you might put TREE here, on the strong side, but not as close to the very, very strong end as MOUNTAIN. A BUSH is not as strong as a TREE, but neither as weak as GRASS, you may put it between GRASS and the TREE, here, but a little on the strong side. (The E repeats the above with BREAD, BLANKET, SPIDER, and SNAKE, in that order form good to bad, on scale *good–bad*.)

Now think of this end as very, very active and this other end as very, very passive. Now where do you think MOUNTAIN should go? COW? DEER? BEE?

Now here are a number of lines. I will tell you for each line what each end is. Then I will ask you to

put something like RAIN where you think it belongs on the line. There is only one place on the line where you cannot put the thing you are to describe, and that is on this point (E points to center). You may put it close to this point, but not on it (this is to help force the S to make a discrimination).

The above instructions were followed as closely as possible by each investigator. One concept was presented with each sheet of scales. The ends of the scale and the concept were read to the S for each judgment. The items were given in the native language to all Ss. English instructions were used except with the Navaho who were instructed in Navaho.

Results

Digits 1 through 7 were assigned in left to right order to the seven points on the scales of the English and Spanish semantic differentials. A score was the digit corresponding to the check-mark representing the S's rating. The Indian differentials were scored by measuring the distance, in one-tenth inches, from the left side of the scale to the check-mark locating the concept. Each S's rating formed a scale by concept matrix of order 15 × 10. Since

TABLE 2

COEFFICIENTS OF FACTORIAL SIMILARITY

| Factor 1 | | | | | | | | Factor 2 | | | | | | |
N	H	Z	S	N-Hᵃ	Zᵇ	Sᶜ		N	H	Z	S	N-Hᵃ	Zᵇ	Sᶜ
1.00	.72	.61	.69	.79	.79	.72	Navaho	1.00	.60	.42	.65	.60	.45	.63
	1.00	.91	.81	.87	.83	.82	Hopi		1.00	.74	.79	.87	.70	.88
		1.00	.83	.91	.88	.86	Zuni			1.00	.84	.76	.80	.79
			1.00	.90	.90	.86	Spanish				1.00	.92	.89	.95
				1.00	.99	.96	American–Navaho–Hopi					1.00	.88	.97
					1.00	.94	American–Zuni						1.00	.90
						1.00	American–Spanish							1.00

| Factor 3 | | | | | | | | Factor 4 | | | | | | |
N	H	Z	S	N-Hᵃ	Zᵇ	Sᶜ		N	H	Z	S	N-Hᵃ	Zᵇ	Sᶜ
1.00	−.15	.11	.03	−.05	.08	.15	Navaho	1.00	.64	.02	−.23	−.15	.18	−.13
	1.00	−.27	−.55	−.32	−.42	−.09	Hopi		1.00	−.24	−.32	−.50	.25	−.28
		1.00	.12	.45	.17	.08	Zuni			1.00	.71	.59	−.17	.66
			1.00	.61	.60	.47	Spanish				1.00	.60	.09	.78
				1.00	.80	.73	American–Navaho–Hopi					1.00	−.16	.86
					1.00	.88	American–Zuni						1.00	−.04
						1.00	American–Spanish							1.00

ᵃ American control for Navaho and Hopi concepts.

ᵇ American control for Zuni concepts.

ᶜ American control for Spanish concepts.

there were N such matrices, a $15 \times 10N$ matrix was formed for each group.

Product-moment correlation coefficients were calculated between scales for each group by summing the cross-products over both Ss and concepts so that the number of pairs entering into each coefficient was $10N$. The 15×15 correlation matrix for each group was factored using the principal-axis technique with a communality estimate in the main diagonal, and extracting all 15 factors.[4] The first four principal components were rotated into simple structure using a modification of Carroll's method (1953).[5] Finally, to measure

[4] The tables of intercorrelations and the first four principal components for each group have been deposited with the American Documentation Institute. Order Document No. 6238, from ADI Auxiliary Publications Project, Photoduplication Service, Library of Congress, Washington 25, D. C., remitting in advance $1.25 for microfilm or $1.25 for photocopies. Make checks payable to Chief, Photoduplication Service, Library of Congress.

[5] The rotations were performed by J. B. Carroll using an IBM Type 650 program developed by J. B. Carroll, F. Weinfeld, and A. Beaton.

the similarity between the factors, indices of similarity (Wrigley & Neuhaus, 1955) were calculated between related factors.

As shown in Table 2, the first three factors for the control groups were highly similar, but the fourth factors were quite dissimilar. Such dissimilarity implied that differences on Factor 4 could be attributed to concept differences, and that inferences regarding language or culture differences on this meaning dimension could not be made.

The coefficients of similarity for Factors 1 and 2 were consistently positive for all the groups. Factor 3, however, produced some extremely low, and even negative, similarity coefficients. Triandis and Osgood (1958) accepted a value of .75 as the lower limit for statistically significant factorial similarity. Not all coefficients exceeded this value for Factors 1 and 2. The Navaho group consistently produced coefficients less than .75. The other groups, with the exception of Zuni and Hopi whose coefficient for Factor 2 had a border line value of .74, were above this value for Factors 1 and

2. None of the experimental groups showed relations above .75 for Factor 3.

From the loadings in Table 1, the first factor was readily interpretable as evaluative with scales like *pretty–ugly, clean–dirty* (with the exception of Navaho) and *good–bad* (with the exception of Zuni) producing some of the higher loadings for all the groups. This factor explained the most variance for every group except the Navaho where it accounted for only 14.9%, slightly less than the 17.3% shown by the Navaho second factor. The second factor appeared as a combination of potency (*strong–weak*) and activity (*fast–slow*) for all groups except Navaho who displayed mostly potency scales on this factor with *fast–slow* appearing independently on the third factor. This combination of activity and potency has been termed "dynamism" (Osgood et al., 1957, p. 74) and commonly appears with English speakers. The third factor was not readily interpretable for any group.

DISCUSSION

With the exception of the Navaho group, a high degree of similarity in the semantic structures of Ss from different cultural backgrounds was found. Since most Ss were bilinguals, the results do not have the generality of those from the Triandis and Osgood (1958) or the Kumata (1957) studies based on monolingual subjects.

Conclusions are further limited in that only a small amount of the judgmental variance is explained in some cases, especially the Navaho. The first three Navaho factors accounted for only 39% of the reliable variance. In contrast, the three Spanish factors accounted for 68% which concurs with the 70% accounted for by the Greek and English factors (Triandis & Osgood, 1958). In other words, a vast amount of reliable attribute space remains undefined for the Navaho group. To a lesser extent this is also true for the Hopi, whose first three factors account for about 52%. Thus, for the Navaho especially, only a narrow base for comparison with other groups was available. Only further research can tell if this lack of accountable variance explains the Navaho deviation from the other groups. Such limita-

tions, although important and suggestive for further research, should not be permitted to hide the significance of the high degree of similarity. Despite differences in culture, concepts, method of administration and education, similarity between groups was high. Further, the main two dimensions were interpretable as evaluative, and activity-potency, or dynamism, the same factors found with all the other culture groups studied. Thus, taking into account other studies in this series, a high degree of similarity may be assumed to exist in the semantic frames of reference used by subjects of different cultural background.

SUMMARY

The present study is one of a series investigating the similarity of semantic structures for different groups of subjects—in this case Ss from different American Southwest cultures. The factor structures of a sample of semantic scales indicated that Zuni, Hopi, Spanish, and English-speaking Ss define a semantic space with similar evaluative and dynamism dimensions. Although the semantic space for a group of Navaho could be defined with the same dimensions, the similarity measures were consistently lower for this group. A third factor for each group could not be interpreted and was highly dissimilar for all groups. Since most Ss were bilinguals, the generality of the findings was limited in comparison to findings from studies using only monolinguals. Only a small amount of variance is accounted for by the first three factors for some groups, especially the Navaho, suggesting that a large amount of attribute space needs to be defined with further research.

REFERENCES

Bopp, Joan. A quantitative semantic analysis of word association in schizophrenia. Unpublished doctoral dissertation, Univer. Illinois, 1955.

Carroll, J. B. An analytic solution for approximating simple structure in factor analysis. *Psychometrika*, 1953, **18**, 23–38.

Casagrande, J. B. The Southwest project in comparative psycholinguistics: A progress report. Soc. Sci. Res. Council, *Items*, 1956, **10**, 41–45.

Kumata, H. A factor analytic investigation of the generality of semantic structure across two selected cultures. Unpublished doctoral dissertation, Univer. Illinois, 1957.

KUMATA, H., & SCHRAMM, W. A pilot study of cross-cultural methodology. *Publ. opin. Quart.*, 1956, **20**, 229–237.

OSGOOD, C. E., SUCI, G. J., & TANNENBAUM, P. H. *The measurement of meaning.* Urbana: Univer. Illinois Press, 1957.

SUCI, G. J. A multidimensional analysis of social attitudes with special reference to ethnocentrism. Unpublished doctoral dissertation, Univer. Illinois, 1952.

TRIANDIS, H. C., & OSGOOD, C. E. A comparative factorial analysis of semantic structures in monolingual Greek and American college students. *J. abnorm. soc. Psychol.*, 1958, **57**, 187–196.

WHORF, B. L. *Language, thought and reality: Selected writings of Benjamin Lee Whorf.* New York: Wiley, 1956.

WRIGLEY, C. F., & NEUHAUS, J. O. The matching of two sets of factors. *Amer. Psychologist* 1955, **10**, 418–419.

24. A Cross-Cultural and Cross-Concept Study
of the Generality of Semantic Space

Yasumasa Tanaka, Tadasu Oyama, and Charles E. Osgood

A series of recent experiments has attempted to determine the generality of the
affective semantic space. Osgood and associates (1957) have reported the three dominant factors of meaning, which they regard
as the primary dimensions that appear to
organize this space. These most salient factors of meaning, labeled Evaluation, Potency,
and Activity, have been found in many population samples with different linguistic and
cultural backgrounds (Kumata and Schramm,
1956; Kumata, 1958; Miron, 1961; Osgood,
1962, Oyama *et al.*, 1962; Sagara *et al.*,
1961; Tanaka, 1962; Triandis and Osgood,
1958; Watanbe *et al.*, 1959). These previous
studies offer empirical evidence that human
beings utilize a similar semantic frame of
reference irrespective of their linguistic and
cultural background.

There have been a number of studies that
originated in Japan. Watanbe and associates
(1959) reported in their study of the public

attitude toward the Japan National Railways
that the semantic space used by native Japanese *S*s appears similar to what had been
reported in American studies. Still another
study was carried out by Sagara and associates (1961). This study, dealing with the
structure of Japanese language, also has
shown that approximately 100 Japanese college students utilized the same three most
salient semantic factors in their judgment of
120 Japanese words rated on a semantic-
differential form.

In every analysis the same three factors
appear most salient. However, it is also made
evident that the scale composition of semantic spaces can be to some extent modified in
terms of the objects of judgment. It has been
noted that the relative importance of, and
relationship among, factors may vary with
the concept class being judged. First, some
scales may change their meaning in the sense
of factorial composition or orientation in the
semantic space. Examples of this kind are
found in Tucker's (1955) study of the aesthetic judgment and in the "Thesaurus
study" by Osgood and associates (1957).
Some of the more recent cross-cultural studies
also report such a result (Miron, 1961;
Tanaka, 1962). Second, the ordering of the
three most salient factors differs in terms of
the variance extracted. In the Tucker
study, for example, the Activity factor was
demonstrated to be the most salient in terms
of the variance extracted when *S*s judged
paintings, whereas studies using verbal

Reprinted from *Journal of Verbal Learning and Verbal
Behavior* (1963), 2: 392–405, by permission of the
authors and Academic Press, Inc.

[1] This study is part of a research project on the
Cross-Cultural Generality of Meaning Systems, supported by the Human Ecology Fund, New York,
N. Y., of which C. E. Osgood, Director, Institute of
Communications Research, University of Illinois,
is principal investigator. The writers wish to express
their gratitude to a number of colleagues, both in
Japan and in the United States, for their cooperation, and to the University of Illinois Statistical
Service Unit and Digital Computer Laboratory for
the use of their facilities.

stimuli usually find the Evaluative factor to be first in salience. Recently, in their study of color components in interior designing, Ogiso and Inui (1961) in Japan obtained a result similar to Tucker's finding. Miron (1961) finds the Potency factor most salient across both Japanese and American *S*s, using auditory stimuli in a cross-cultural investigation of phonetic symbolism. Somewhat less clearly, Solomon (1954) demonstrated that some Potency scales rotated toward the Evaluative factor when subjects rate sonar signals.

Judging from these previous results, it appears reasonable to hypothesize that the semantic space determined by one class of concepts, such as words, may have a significantly different factorial composition than one determined by some other class of concepts, such as sounds or colors. To test this hypothesis, three concept classes, Colors, Abstract Words, and Line Forms, were selected. Factor analytic results obtained separately for each concept class and compared across concept classes should test cross-concept factorial uniqueness. Second, two groups of *S*s who differ in their culture and language—Japanese and Americans—should enable us to test cross-cultural and cross-linguistic generality under these conditions. Third, we will also investigate cross-cultural and cross-conceptual uniqueness of scales used in the semantic judgments.

METHOD

Measuring Instrument. In order to index the connotative meaning of the three classes of stimulus materials, a 35-scale form of semantic differential was constructed. The scales were selected partly to represent the three dominant factors of Evaluation, Potency, and Activity, previously discovered in factor analyses of verbal stimuli (Osgood *et al.,* 1957), and partly to reflect the meaningful aspects of judging the Colors, Abstract Words, and Forms used in this study. The same 35 translation-equivalent scales were used for the Japanese and American *S*s in their native language, translation being done from Japanese to English in this case, first using a Japanese-English Dictionary and then

having the results rechecked by a bilingual Japanese.[2]

Stimulus Materials. The stimuli used as concepts in this study consisted of 16 Colors, 14 Abstract Words, and 14 Line Forms.[3] The Colors were represented by color cards. They included 3 achromatic colors (BLACK, NEUTRAL GRAY, and WHITE), 12 well-saturated colors (RED, ORANGE, YELLOW-ORANGE, YELLOW, YELLOW-GREEN, GREEN, BLUE-GREEN, GREENISH BLUE, BLUE, BLUE-PURPLE, PURPLE, and RED-PURPLE), and one unsaturated color (PINK). The same color cards were used in Japan and in America.

The 14 Abstract Words were ETERNITY, VIRGINITY, DREAM, HAPPINESS, HOME, LOVE, QUIETNESS, NOSTALGIA, JEALOUSY, ANXIETY, LONELINESS, SIN, FEAR, and ANGER. Most of these were chosen from the color-symbolism personality test devices by Obonai and Matsuoka (1956). Translation of the Words was also done from Japanese to English, using the same method as used in translating the scales.

The Line Forms were mostly selected from previous studies on visual symbolism (Azuma, 1953; Fox, 1935; Kohler, 1930). Each Form was drawn in black ink on white construction paper. Both Japanese and American *S*s were shown the same set of visual stimuli.

Subjects. A total of 108 Japanese and 67 American college girls served as *S*s. Forty-three Japanese and 21 American *S*s judged the Colors; 25 Japanese and 23 Americans rated the Abstract Words; and 40 Japanese and 23 American girls judged the Line Forms. The Japanese *S*s were Home Economics and Literature majors, while all the American *S*s were Home Economics majors.

Procedure. Tests were performed in Sapporo, Japan, and in Urbana, Illinois. All testing was in groups. In administering the tests, somewhat different procedures were followed by the Japanese and the American *E*s. In the first place, the Japanese girls were divided into six sub groups: a group of 25 rated eight Colors and another group of 18 judged the remaining eight; 13 *S*s rated seven Abstract Words while 12 rated the other seven; a group of 20 *S*s judged the first seven forms and another group of 20 rated the other seven. American *S*s were divided into the Color, Abstract Word, and

---

[2] For the translation-equivalent Japanese scales, see Oyama *et al.* (1962, 1963).

[3] The Munsell notations of the 16 Colors and the 14 Line Form stimuli are displayed in Oyama and Haga (1963) and Oyama *et al.* (1962, 1963).

Line Form groups, each total group judging all Colors, Words, or Forms, respectively. Second, the order and direction of the 35 scales were both randomized among the Japanese Ss, whereas they were initially randomized by the E and then administered uniformly for all American Ss. Third, for the Japanese, in the Word groups, each stimulus word, consisting of Chinese ideographs or a combination of an ideograph and Japanese *kana,* was written in black ink on thick white construction paper, and they were shown to the Ss one by one; for the Americans, each Word was mimeographed on a separate page of the semantic-differential form.

RESULTS

Scale Intercorrelations and Factor Analyses

Only the intercorrelation matrices for scales were factored in this study. A total of six

TABLE 1

FIRST THREE VARIMAX-ROTATED FACTORS OBTAINED IN JUDGING 16 COLORS

	Factor					
	Evaluation		Potency		Activity	
American scale	J(II)	A(III)	J(III)	A(II)	J(I)	A(I)
stable-unstable	— 0.03	0.20	0.46	*0.81*	*— 0.82*	— 0.49
hard-soft	0.24	— 0.21	*0.70*	*0.94*	— 0.44	0.21
near-far	— 0.14	0.03	0.08	— 0.35	*0.88*	*0.66*
excitable-calm	0.01	— 0.19	— 0.05	0.03	*0.96*	*0.95*
womanly-manly	— 0.26	0.16	— 0.36	*— 0.83*	*0.66*	0.36
happy-sad	0.17	0.38	— 0.15	— 0.46	*0.85*	*0.78*
hot-cold	— 0.39	— 0.17	0.07	— 0.24	*0.85*	*0.78*
deep-shallow	— 0.21	— 0.04	*0.82*	*0.94*	— 0.49	— 0.23
heavy-light	— 0.44	— 0.22	*0.76*	*0.94*	— 0.42	— 0.12
strong-weak	0.05	0.09	*0.95*	*0.95*	0.17	0.19
full-empty	— 0.11	0.12	*0.80*	*0.72*	— 0.53	0.50
wet-dry	— 0.43	0.36	0.25	0.04	*— 0.68*	— 0.19
large-small	*0.50*	0.09	0.25	*0.86*	0.02	— 0.04
light-dark	**0.52**	0.24	— 0.29	*— 0.90*	*0.79*	0.18
new-old	*0.92*	0.52	0.03	*— 0.61*	0.27	0.57
distinct-vague	0.46	0.35	*0.77*	0.13	0.28	*0.88*
fast-slow	*0.67*	0.20	— 0.13	— 0.04	*0.61*	*0.97*
sharp-blunt	*0.68*	0.26	0.46	— 0.02	0.10	*0.92*
healthy-unhealthy	*0.84*	*0.83*	0.05	— 0.30	0.30	0.41
tense-relaxed	0.20	— 0.32	*0.82*	0.20	0.32	*0.84*
smooth-rough	0.31	*0.68*	— 0.11	*— 0.54*	— 0.21	— 0.21
beautiful-ugly	*0.71*	*0.92*	0.38	— 0.04	— 0.18	0.13
intellectual-unintellectual	*0.45*	*0.68*	*0.58*	*0.52*	*— 0.51*	— 0.15
good-bad	*0.87*	*0.87*	0.05	— 0.29	— 0.24	0.17
ordered-chaotic	— 0.11	*0.68*	0.47	— 0.02	*— 0.81*	*— 0.59*
unreal-real	0.21	*— 0.86*	— 0.41	— 0.24	0.08	— 0.10
dynamic-static	0.39	0.28	0.04	0.13	*0.87*	*0.90*
fresh-stale	*0.93*	*0.74*	— 0.10	— 0.30	— 0.04	0.50
dangerous-safe	— 0.14	*— 0.60*	— 0.06	0.48	*0.90*	0.32
clear-muddy	*0.94*	*0.75*	0.10	— 0.36	— 0.12	0.49
gay-sober	0.25	0.41	0.10	— 0.45	*0.94*	*0.77*
rounded-angular	— 0.47	0.38	— 0.42	*— 0.62*	*0.63*	— 0.26
characteristic-common	0.29	— 0.11	*0.63*	— 0.06	0.49	*0.79*
interesting-boring	0.51	0.45	*0.73*	— 0.02	0.29	*0.82*
positive-negative	0.37	*0.74*	0.48	— 0.30	*0.75*	0.54
% TV	24	24	22	28	34	32

matrices were factor-analyzed, two for the Japanese and American Color groups (J_c and A_c), two for the Japanese and American Word groups (J_w and A_w), and two for the Form groups (J_f and A_f).[4] Thurstone's (1947) centroid factor analysis routine with fixed

[4] For the Color groups, each of the scale cor-

communalities was applied to each of the six 35 $\times$ 35 intercorrelation matrices.

relations is based on an N of 16 Colors for which the basic entry was the mean scale value of each of the two subject groups. Likewise, for the Word groups, each scale correlation was obtained on an N of 14 Abstract Words, and for the Form group, on an N of 14 Line Forms.

TABLE 2

FIRST THREE VARIMAX-ROTATED FACTORS IN JUDGING 14 ABSTRACT WORDS

	Factor					
	Evaluation		Potency		Activity	
American scale	J(I)	A(I)	J(II)	A(II)	J(III)	A(III)
stable-unstable	0.94	0.72	0.02	0.61	0.14	0.28
hard-soft	− 0.77	− 0.91	0.53	− 0.13	0.11	− 0.26
near-far	0.10	0.20	0.68	0.83	− 0.43	− 0.07
excitable-calm	− 0.66	− 0.55	0.33	− 0.25	− 0.62	− 0.71
womanly-manly	0.36	0.33	− 0.51	0.18	0.13	0.51
happy-sad	0.93	0.89	0.04	0.42	− 0.21	0.03
hot-cold	0.76	0.52	− 0.32	0.43	− 0.43	− 0.54
deep-shallow	0.51	0.42	− 0.27	0.65	0.33	0.08
heavy-light	− 0.86	− 0.92	0.35	− 0.28	0.15	− 0.11
strong-weak	0.24	0.50	0.82	0.70	− 0.30	− 0.41
full-empty	0.91	0.83	0.13	0.47	0.16	− 0.27
wet-dry	− 0.51	− 0.05	− 0.65	0.05	0.15	− 0.75
large-small	0.48	0.45	− 0.17	0.51	− 0.34	− 0.48
light-dark	0.97	0.93	− 0.03	0.31	− 0.05	0.05
new-old	0.78	0.91	0.23	0.12	0.04	− 0.05
distinct-vague	0.22	0.23	0.86	0.90	− 0.09	− 0.11
fast-slow	− 0.36	− 0.12	0.66	− 0.11	− 0.59	− 0.91
sharp-blunt	− 0.24	− 0.55	0.62	0.20	− 0.15	− 0.72
healthy-unhealthy	0.97	0.92	0.04	0.38	0.01	0.04
tense-relaxed	− 0.26	− 0.90	0.79	− 0.26	0.17	− 0.27
smooth-rough	0.87	0.97	− 0.42	0.24	0.21	0.25
beautiful-ugly	0.90	0.93	− 0.25	0.28	0.25	0.19
intellectual-unintellectual	0.87	0.82	0.10	0.42	0.44	0.29
good-bad	0.92	0.93	− 0.06	0.31	0.25	0.12
ordered-chaotic	0.90	0.68	0.10	0.51	0.19	0.49
unreal-real	0.26	− 0.34	− 0.73	− 0.88	0.00	− 0.08
dynamic-static	− 0.09	0.14	0.13	0.22	− 0.84	− 0.92
fresh-stale	0.94	0.90	0.08	0.38	0.11	− 0.07
dangerous-safe	− 0.91	− 0.90	0.21	− 0.29	− 0.05	− 0.28
clear-muddy	0.90	0.74	− 0.14	0.58	0.27	0.16
gay-sober	− 0.47	0.86	0.07	0.45	− 0.77	− 0.05
rounded-angular	0.89	0.86	− 0.39	0.41	0.09	0.28
characteristic-common	− 0.53	0.81	0.26	0.23	− 0.38	0.04
interesting-boring	0.83	0.85	− 0.29	0.30	− 0.08	− 0.34
positive-negative	0.20	0.88	0.35	0.47	− 0.69	0.05
% TV	49	53	18	20	12	15

The factors thus derived within each group were rotated by using Kaiser's (1958) Varimax simple structure criterion. Four factors for the Japanese and American Color groups, three factors for the two Word groups, and four factors for both Form groups were rotated. If a cross culturally stable semantic frame of reference were operating within each concept class, the same factors in the same order of salience should appear across subject groups, Japanese and American, when judging the same concepts; if the same semantic frame of reference were operating for all concept classes, the same factors in the same order should appear across concept classes. In brief, generality is found across

TABLE 3
FIRST THREE VARIMAX-ROTATED FACTORS IN JUDGING 14 FORMS

	Factor					
	Evaluation		Potency		Activity	
American scale	J(II)	A(III)	J(I)	A(II)	J(III)	A(I)
stable-unstable	0.87	0.65	0.25	0.30	— 0.02	— 0.56
hard-soft	0.17	0.31	0.96	0.91	— 0.07	— 0.09
near-far	0.36	0.15	— 0.24	— 0.52	— 0.02	— 0.73
excitable-calm	— 0.71	— 0.61	— 0.29	0.17	0.53	0.75
womanly-manly	— 0.20	— 0.01	— 0.92	— 0.90	0.08	0.22
happy-sad	0.08	— 0.23	— 0.78	0.36	— 0.12	0.80
hot-cold	— 0.20	— 0.47	— 0.93	— 0.68	0.02	0.37
deep-shallow	— 0.16	0.06	0.55	0.26	0.04	— 0.00
heavy-light	— 0.02	0.25	— 0.14	0.49	— 0.28	— 0.52
strong-weak	0.51	0.59	0.69	0.61	0.16	— 0.28
full-empty	0.93	0.24	0.13	0.02	0.09	— 0.32
wet-dry	— 0.42	— 0.27	— 0.80	— 0.83	0.14	0.43
large-small	0.44	0.05	— 0.60	— 0.06	— 0.11	— 0.37
light-dark	0.88	0.07	— 0.15	— 0.68	0.02	0.40
new-old	0.34	— 0.45	0.12	— 0.17	0.75	0.85
distinct-vague	0.59	0.66	0.68	0.72	0.00	— 0.12
fast-slow	0.26	0.04	0.45	0.31	0.36	0.74
sharp-blunt	0.25	0.07	0.89	0.95	0.05	0.19
healthy-unhealthy	0.88	0.84	0.21	0.10	— 0.17	— 0.16
tense-relaxed	0.39	0.03	0.86	0.89	— 0.08	0.25
smooth-rough	0.13	0.32	— 0.90	— 0.79	0.07	— 0.25
beautiful-ugly	0.77	0.10	0.44	— 0.43	0.07	0.82
intellectual-unintellectual	0.57	— 0.12	0.66	0.19	0.25	0.92
good-bad	0.92	0.82	0.24	— 0.39	— 0.02	0.13
ordered-chaotic	0.80	0.84	0.22	0.33	— 0.49	— 0.35
unreal-real	— 0.47	— 0.74	— 0.84	— 0.30	0.12	0.58
dynamic-static	— 0.46	— 0.35	— 0.53	0.21	0.53	0.79
fresh-stale	0.63	— 0.38	0.60	— 0.18	0.11	0.86
dangerous-safe	— 0.82	— 0.62	0.11	— 0.45	0.22	0.53
clear-muddy	0.65	0.89	0.62	0.25	— 0.05	— 0.23
gay-sober	— 0.54	0.20	— 0.46	0.21	0.50	0.78
rounded-angular	— 0.04	— 0.13	— 0.98	— 0.94	— 0.01	0.03
characteristic-common	— 0.48	— 0.62	0.02	— 0.07	0.82	0.72
interesting-boring	— 0.15	— 0.54	0.05	— 0.11	0.88	0.80
positive-negative	0.36	0.38	0.75	— 0.42	0.44	0.68
% TV	30	21	36	27	11	30

subject samples but not across concept samples.

Evidence of Cross-Cultural Generality

The results of the factor analyses are shown in Tables 1, 2, and 3. Our first interest lay in ascertaining the extent to which the Ss in different language-culture groups can be shown to use the same semantic factors in making their meaningful judgments. It is clear in these tables, first, that the three most salient factors in all analyses are identifiable as Evaluation, Potency, and Activity, although the orderings of variance extracted across concept classes are definitely different and the scale composition of the factors varies somewhat.

Second, it should be noted that the shift in relative salience in terms of the variance extracted tend to be the same for both groups as the concept class is changed. An Activity factor is most salient for both Japanese and American groups when judging the Colors. For Abstract Words an Evaluative factor is most salient for both groups, and Potency tends to become most salient for both when judging Forms although this is not so clear for the Americans as the Japanese.

Third, it can be seen by inspection that the shifts in scale loadings on the three factors tend to be similar across the subject groups. For instance, Potency characteristics of each concept class are indexed in both Japanese and American groups by such scales as *strong-weak* or *deep-shallow* when judging Colors; by *Angular-rounded, sharp-blunt,* or *hard-soft* when judging Forms; and *distinct-vague, real-unreal,* or *strong-weak* when judging Words.

In connection with these results, it appears pertinent to question whether the judgment variation among the subject groups in terms of using individual scales is more stable than the variation resulting from concept-scale interaction. To get at this problem, two separate measures were taken.

TABLE 4
CROSS-CULTURE AND CROSS-CONCEPT CORRELATIONS AMONG CORRELATION MATRICES BY CORRESPONDING CELLS

	A_c	A_w	A_f	J_c	J_w	J_f
A_c	—	0.41	0.43	*0.62*	0.36	0.32
A_w		—	0.24	0.21	*0.65*	0.25
A_f			—	0.43	0.28	*0.52*
J_c				—	0.33	0.51
J_w					—	0.41
J_f						—

First, the six original correlation matrices for scales were correllated with each other across corresponding cells as a measure of over-all similarity (Table 4). As expected, the critical values (J_c/T_c; J_w/A_w; and J_f/A_f) for the two groups judging the same concept class are clearly higher than any other values in the same rows or columns. These higher correlations offer evidence that the use of judgment scales is more consistent across the subject groups judging the same concepts than across the concept classes judged by the same language-culture groups.

Second, in an approach to the question of cross-culture and cross-concept factor-structural similarity, the first three Varimax-rotated factors for each of six concept-subject groups were correlated utilizing the Wrigley-Neuhaus (1955) indices of factorial similarity. The results shown in Table 5 display a definitely closer factorial composition for the same concept class and factors *as a group* considered interculturally than for intracultural concept-class comparisons. The only exception to this rule was observed where the American Potency factor for Words (P_{Aw}) is more similar to the Japanese Evaluative factor for Words (E_{Jw}) than to the Japanese Potency factor for Words (P_{Jw}).

Evidence for Cross-Concept and Cross-Culture Uniqueness

From the results demonstrated in Tables 4 and 5, it is clear that the factorial structure of a semantic space varies as concept class

TABLE 5

INDICES OF CROSS-CULTURE AND CROSS-CONCEPT FACTORIAL SIMILARITY

	E_{Ac}	P_{Ac}	A_{Ac}	E_{Aw}	P_{Aw}	A_{Aw}	E_{Af}	P_{Af}	A_{Af}	E_{Jc}	P_{Jc}	A_{Jc}	E_{Jw}	P_{Jw}	A_{Jw}	E_{Jf}	P_{Jf}	A_{Jf}
E_{Ac}	—	0.31	0.27	0.79	0.68	0.13	0.44	0.26	0.30	0.65	0.22	0.01	0.69	0.00	0.04	0.64	0.17	0.18
P_{Ac}		—	0.18	0.34	0.02	0.26	0.16	0.65	0.30	0.20	0.63	0.48	0.27	0.31	0.13	0.05	0.40	0.14
A_{Ac}			—	0.22	0.35	0.59	0.19	0.11	0.58	0.54	0.32	0.65	0.07	0.49	0.62	0.06	0.14	0.58
E_{Aw}				—	0.75	0.23	0.23	0.50	0.30	0.50	0.16	0.16	0.85	0.19	0.06	0.54	0.09	0.30
P_{Aw}					—	0.01	0.46	0.11	0.02	0.36	0.50	0.16	0.63	0.24	0.16	0.59	0.16	0.10
A_{Aw}						—	0.32	0.26	0.33	0.18	0.24	0.33	0.30	0.34	0.59	0.20	0.02	0.40
E_{Af}							—	0.24	0.57	0.20	0.31	0.39	0.33	0.26	0.29	0.72	0.42	0.52
P_{Af}								—	0.19	0.12	0.50	0.29	0.39	0.68	0.03	0.09	0.72	0.09
A_{Af}									—	0.47	0.03	0.48	0.12	0.03	0.35	0.16	0.02	0.76
E_{Jc}										—	0.21	0.15	0.46	0.25	0.11	0.55	0.42	0.40
P_{Jc}											—	0.26	0.11	0.55	0.01	0.38	0.55	0.19
A_{Jc}												—	0.04	0.17	0.76	0.30	0.33	0.48
E_{Jw}													—	0.21	0.16	0.70	0.04	0.02
P_{Jw}														—	0.26	0.28	0.64	0.07
A_{Jw}															—	0.29	0.19	0.49
E_{Jf}																—	0.47	0.28
P_{Jf}																	—	0.00
A_{Jf}																		—

295

is changed. In other words, each concept class appears to possess its own unique factorial composition. Although the three most salient factors are common to all three concept classes, the factors definitely differ in their relative importance as concept-class changes.

These results not only offer clear evidence for concept-scale interaction, but they also indicate that human beings in general may utilize a unique factor space for each concept class being judged. If this interpretation holds, each judgment scale should change its meaning in conformity with its relation to the dominant attributes of the concept class it is used to judge.

From the factor-analytic results, three general categories of scales can be established. It is clear that some scales, such as *good-bad*, *strong-weak*, or *dynamic-static*, are stable both across concept classes and across cultural groups. They appear to be least susceptible to concept-class or subject-group change, and, therefore, they can be regarded as "stereotypic" in the semantic frame of reference. Some other scales, such as *hot-cold* and *hard-soft*, clearly shift their factorial "nuance" from concept class to concept class, presumably on the basis of denotative relevance, the shift nonetheless being parallel for the subject groups. The remaining scales appear to be not only factorially unstable across concept classes but they also interact with the subject groups doing the judging.

On the basis of cross-concept and cross-culture stability of scales in the semantic space, the following scale interaction effects may be examined. If one scale is found to be more highly correlated, for instance, with *good-bad* for one concept class than with *strong-weak* or *dynamic-static*, but with *strong-weak* for another concept class, both conditions occurring similarly across the subject groups, then the change should be taken as evidence of concept-scale interaction. However, if the same scale is found to be more highly associated with *good-bad* than with

the other two scales for one class of concepts in one subject group, but with *strong-weak* for the same class of concepts but in another subject group, then the change can be taken as evidence for subject scale interaction.

To examine these scale interaction effects the three most "stereotypic" scales, *good-bad*, *strong-weak*, and *dynamic-static*, were chosen, each representing one of the three most salient semantic factor dimensions. From the six separate, original intercorrelation matrices for scales, the correlations between these three and the remaining scales were then examined.[5]

The results of this analysis are shown in Table 6, the 35 scales being classified into three general categories discussed above, Category *A* consisting of stable scales, Category *B* of conceptually unstable scales, and Category *C* of both conceptually and culturally unstable scales.[6] In the table, *E* denotes a high association of the scale with *good-bad* relative to the other two scales, *P* with *strong-weak*, and *A* with *dynamic-static*, parenthesized figures representing correlations with either of the three marker scales. Dashes indicate no significant correlation with any of the three scales. These results were found to be in general agreement with the results of the previously obtained factor analyses.

Several things became clear in this analysis in connection with concept-scale and subject-scale in-

[5] In fact, the stereotypic uniqueness of these three scales is demonstrated by consistently low intercorrelations among them in all the concept classes in both cultural groups. The only exception was found in the American group judging Abstract Words, where *strong-weak* was correlated with *good-bad* (0.64) and with *dynamic-static* (0.60).

[6] Theoretically, we can posit the presence of another category of scales which are cross conceptually stable but cross culturally unstable. No scales of this category were found in the present analysis, although a few scales marked (a) in Table 6 display such tendency. The general absence of this category of scales in our data may further support the argument that the scales tend to be more stable in cross-cultural than in cross-conceptual comparisons.

teractions. Let us first find evidence of *concept-scale interaction*. First, it is obvious that the Category *B* scales change their factorial nuance from concept class to concept class but similarly across the subject groups, indicating both cross-conceptual uniqueness and cross-cultural stability. Second, some Categories *B* and *C* scales exhibit what might be called "intracultural factorial nuance reversal." For instance, the scales, *hot-cold* for the Americans (Category *B*) and *wet-dry* for the Japanese (Category *C*) are highly associated with *strong-weak* for Words and Forms, but they reverse the direction of association within the given subject group as concept class is changed; for Words, *wet* is *strong* for the Japanese and *hot* is *strong* for the Americans, whereas for Forms *wet* becomes *weak* for the Japanese just as *hot* becomes *weak* for the Americans. Such factorial nuance reversal within the same subject group can be taken as clear evidence of concept-scale interaction, presumably affected by denotative relevance of the given concept class.

Next, there is also evidence of *subject-scale interaction*. First, we found one particular case of what might be called "intercultural factorial nuance reversal," displayed by a Category *B* scale, *gay-sober*. Although this scale, as shown in Table 6, is highly associated with *good-bad* for both subject groups judging Words, the direction of association is entirely opposite cross culturally, that is, for the Japanese *gay* is associated with *bad,* whereas for the Americans it is associated with *good*. This appears to be a unique case of subject-scale interaction, especially because for both Colors and Forms the same scale displays a perfect cross-cultural and cross-conceptual stability. Although no direct diachronic explanation is possible to this point, it is generally agreed that the Japanese are more introverted than Americans and the former are more reserved than the latter. Presumably, this specific scale happens to tap the differences in the *S*s' temperament and their criterion of values related to the abstract words. Second, less extreme cases of subject-scale interaction are shown by some Category *C* scales which demonstrate what we shall call "intracultural factorial stability." They are examplified by scales, such as *distinct-vague* for the Japanese and *fast-slow* for the Americans, that are factorially stable only within the same subject group. They seem not to be susceptible to concept-scale interaction within the same subject group, but obviously susceptible to subject-scale interaction. It is suggested that such scales may have a stable factorial association in one culture but not in the other. In this connection, it is interesting to note that the Japanese scale for *fast-slow* is in homophonous relation to *early-late* when written in

kana. Since in this study the scale was given the Japanese *S*s in *kana,* it is quite likely that the scale was interpreted by the *S*s both as *fast-slow* and as *early-late*.[7] We can expect that the factorial association of the scale should become less clear under such conditions. Third, a different pattern of factorial association was found cross culturally on many Category *C* scales when the two subject groups judged the same class of concepts. For instance, the scale, *light-dark,* for Colors, displays the higher association with *dynamic-static* for the Japanese, but with *strong-weak* for the Americans, while the same scale is higly related to *good-bad* for the Japanese and *strong-weak* for the Americans when both judge Forms. Now that the instances of subject-scale interaction are most often found for the Form class, let us examine which scales are least susceptible to subject-scale interaction for the Forms. In theory, it is expected that scales, such as *distinct-vague, rounded-angular,* and *sharp-blunt,* which have denotative relevance to Forms, should display cross culturally stable interaction with the Forms which they are used to judge. In fact, these scales are found to show no subject-scale interaction for the Forms: although as concept class is changed, and as the scales no longer tap the "denotative" meaning of stimulus concepts—either Colors or Words—they are found to interact with the subject groups. Subject-scale interaction appears more likely to occur where scales are irrelevant to the concepts being judged and, consequently, associative strength is weak in the interacting concept and scale.

Irrespective of these complex interactions from concept class to concept class, and from subject group to subject group, the assumption that each concept class utilizes a unique factor domain as a major judgment criterion appears to be justified. As stated before, the semantic factor nuance rotation of individual scales should tend toward the

---

[7] Japanese orthography normally combines an alteration between *kana* and *kanji* forms. The *kana* forms are based on a phonetic rendition of modern spoken Japanese. *Kanji,* on the other hand, are Chinese ideographs for which *kana* orthographical forms may alternate. Most modern Japanese orthography is rendered in *kana*. There is a tendency in modern colloquial Japanese to minimize the use of Chinese ideographs, or *kanji,* and, as a consequence, many native, young users of Japanese prefer, and in cases as cited above, indeed may only recognize *kana,* i.e., phonetic spellings. Hence, the homophonous *kana* qualifier pair, *hayai-osoi,* was chosen as being most familiar despite the inherent semantic ambiguity.

TABLE 6

SCALE TYPES UNDER CONDITIONS OF CONCEPT-SCALE INTERACTION

(r's with reference scales *good-bad*, *strong-weak*, and *dynamic-static*)

	J_c	A_c	J_w	A_w	J_f	A_f
Category A: Stable scales						
good-bad	E (1.00)	E (1.00)	E (1.00)	E (1.00)	E (1.00)	E (1.00)
healthy-unhealthy	E (0.77)	E (0.92)	E (0.89)	E (0.99)	E (0.86)	E (0.69)
clear-muddy	E (0.82)	E (0.85)	E (0.96)	E (0.92)	E (0.76)	P (0.76)
beautiful-ugly	E (0.75)	E (0.88)	E (0.93)	E (0.98)	E (0.86)	A (0.62)
strong-weak	P (1.00)	P (1.00)	P (1.00)	P (1.00)	P (1.00)	P (1.00)
dynamic-static	A (1.00)	A (1.00)	A (1.00)	A (1.00)	A (1.00)	A (1.00)
Category B: Conceptually unstable scales						
hard-soft	P (0.67)	P (0.96)	E (−0.71)	E (−0.91)	P (0.77)	P (0.78)
excitable-calm	A (0.86)	A (0.83)	E (−0.82)	E (−0.66)	A (0.76)	A (0.91)
gay-sober	A (0.91)	A (0.74)	E (−0.66)[b]	E (0.94)[b]	A (0.89)	A (0.80)
near-far	A (0.65)	A (0.64)	P (0.61)	P (0.65)[c]	—	A (−0.73)[c]
happy-sad	A (0.81)	A (0.76)	E (0.79)	E (0.96)	—	A (0.68)
hot-cold	A (0.57)	A (0.65)	E (0.62)	P (0.82)[c]	P (−0.74)	P (−0.91)[c]
deep-shallow	P (0.68)	P (0.85)	E (0.55)	E (0.56)	P (0.43)	P (0.85)
heavy-light	P (0.64)	P (0.89)	E (−0.80)	E (−0.95)	—	A (−0.53)
full-empty	P (0.64)	P (0.83)	E (0.87)	E (0.89)	E (0.85)	A (0.79)
new-old	E (0.69)	E (0.74)	E (0.69)	E (0.88)	P (0.41)	A (0.79)
distinct-vague	P (0.84)[a]	A (0.96)	P (0.78)[a]	P (0.80)	P (0.79)[a]	P (0.89)
intellectual-unintellectual	E (0.56)	E (0.52)	E (0.93)	E (0.94)	P (0.76)	A (0.79)
fresh-stale	E (0.79)	E (0.83)	E (0.90)	E (0.97)	P (0.78)	A (0.77)
rounded-angular	E (−0.44)	P (−0.59)	E (0.86)	E (0.96)	P (−0.70)	P (−0.59)
interesting-boring	P (0.72)	A (0.79)	E (0.74)	E (0.83)	A (0.47)	A (0.85)

TABLE 6 (*Continued*)

	J_c	A_c	J_w	A_w	J_f	A_f
Category C: Both conceptually and culturally unstable scales						
unreal-real	P (−0.53)[a]	E (−0.65)	P (−0.53)[a]	P (−0.75)	P (−0.81)[a]	A (0.68)
stable-unstable	A (−0.70)	P (0.63)	E (0.87)	E (0.90)	E (0.84)	P (0.81)
womanly-manly	E (−0.45)	P (−0.71)	E (0.45)	E (0.50)	A (−0.78)	P (−0.59)
wet-dry	A (−0.79)	—	P (0.50)[c]	A (0.80)	P (−0.79)[c]	P (−0.76)
large-small	E (0.43)	P (0.82)	—	P (0.81)	—	A (−0.45)
light-dark	A (0.89)	P (0.83)[c]	E (0.88)	E (0.97)	E (0.76)	P (−0.63)[c]
fast-slow	A (0.84)	A (0.92)[a]	P (0.65)	A (0.75)[a]	P (0.49)	A (0.83)[a]
sharp-blunt	P (0.49)[a]	A (0.93)	P (0.61)[a]	A (0.69)	P (0.77)[a]	P (0.50)
tense-relaxed	P (0.78)[c]	A (0.73)	P (0.50)[a]	E (0.93)	P (0.83)[a]	A (0.45)
smooth-rough	—	E (0.64)[a]	E (0.38)	E (0.96)[a]	A (0.57)	E (0.43)[a]
ordered-chaotic	A (−0.77)	E (0.49)	E (0.83)	E (0.85)	E (0.81)	P (0.80)
dangerous-safe	A (0.72)	E (−0.68)	E (−0.83)	E (−0.98)	E (−0.73)	A (0.85)
characteristic-common	P (0.69)	A (0.62)	A (0.56)	E (0.86)	A (0.64)	A (0.74)
positive-negative	A (0.83)	E (0.88)[a]	P (0.74)	E (0.97)[a]	P (0.77)	E (0.47)[a]

[a] Scales representing *intraculture factorial stability.*
[b] Scale representing *intercultural factorial nuance reversal.*
[c] Scales representing *intracultural factorial nuance reversal.*

most salient factor in the semantic space. Here Category A scales must be considered as exceptions, for they display powerful, stereotypic stability, both cross culturally and cross conceptually. However, Category B scales perfectly conform to the salience of Evaluation for Words, since the factorial shift is toward Evaluation from either Potency or Activity. For the Category C scales, the following standard was established: If a concept class utilizes one unique factor as a major criterion of judgment, and scales tend to rotate toward that factor, then the scales which are not associated with that factor for that concept class should *not* be associated with that factor for other concept classes. That is, for example, if a particular scale is *not* associated with Evaluation for Words, the most salient factor for this concept class, then it should not be associated with Evaluation for other concept classes where Evaluation is less salient. In this analysis, the factor salience was ranked on the basis of variance accounted for in the factor analyses, and so Activity, rather than Potency, was taken as most salient for Forms for the Americans. Of the 14 Category C scales, the rule worked out quite well with only one exception: *characteristic-common,* which is associated by the Japanese with Potency for Colors and with Activity for Forms. This rule obviously is not applicable to the Category A scales, but it is perfectly applicable to the Category B scales with only one exception, *interesting-boring,* which is associated by the Japanese with Potency for Colors and with Activity for Forms.

Speculation on the Source of Concept-Scale and Subject-Scale Interaction

Having evidence for both over-all cross-culture generality and cross-concept and cross-culture uniqueness, we now suggest two likely variables affecting the emergence of concept-scale and subject-scale interaction.

First, let us consider some interesting evidence previously reported elsewhere. Analyzing the same data used in this paper, Oyama and associates (1962) found that there is a high correlation between the semantic factors and the psychophysical correlates of Colors: they report that the most salient factor for Colors, Activity, is highly correlated with Munsell hue for both the Japanese and the Americans. A similar relation between semantic factors and the physical correlates of auditory stimuli was reported by Miron

(1961). He found that the Potency factor, first in salience in his study, tends to follow the second vowel format and tends to be related to high and low frequencies, when both Japanese and American Ss rate recorded nonsense syllables. Still another study reported by Solomon (1959) demonstrates that scales which obviously contribute to the Potency factor discriminate sonar signals with low frequencies from those having high frequencies. All these studies show that many scales tend to converge toward the most salient factor of the given stimulus class. It thus appears that some specific influence is exerted by the dominant semantic attribute of the stimulus input, this influencing judgments within the semantic space. Our evidence to date indicates that there is a high degree of cross-cultural generality in this regard, semantic-factor salience influencing the pattern of concept-scale interaction similarly in different cultures.

Second, with respect to the cultural uniqueness of scale meaning, it appears that a second source of interaction may also be operating in the semantic space. It seems apparent from the results of this and other studies to date that there are some specific scales that seem to be susceptible to interaction with the Ss judging the concepts, despite the over-all generality of factor-scale compositions of the semantic space. For instance, Miron (1961) reported that the scale, *colorful-colorless,* was associated with *good-bad* by the Americans judging the auditory stimuli, whereas it was related to *small-large* by the Japanese judging the same stimuli; similarly, Tanaka (1962) reported that, in judging national stereotypic concepts, the Japanese Ss associated *democratic-undemocratic* with the Activity factor, whereas the American Ss related the same scale to an Evaluative factor. In the present study, *gay-sober* was found to reverse the direction of its Evaluative meaning for Words between the two subject groups, while Category C scales displayed such subject-scale interactions to varying degrees. It was further noted that some scales exhibited the cross-concept stability of meaning clearly for one culture group but not for the other.

These instances of cultural uniqueness lead us to the further consideration that translation equivalence of scales may be sometimes imperfect across languages. We have already pointed out earlier that a Japanese scale, *fast-slow*, is in *homophonous* relation with *early-late*, both being mutually indistinguishable when given in *kana*. This being the case with our present study, we have no way of knowing whether the scale meaning to the Japanese was *fast-slow* or *early-late*. Presumably, for some Japanese it meant *fast-slow* and for others, *early-late*. Had the scale been written in *kanji* or Chinese ideographs, the lexical redundancy would have been considerably reduced, and then the scale might have become "Activity" rather than "Potency" in all the concept classes. Furthermore, another Japanese scale, *positive-negative*, has two different synonymous scales in English, that is, it can be translated either as *positive-negative* or as *active-passive* in English. If the Japanese scale had been translated as *active-passive* instead of *positive-negative*, the English translation equivalence would have become more "Activity" than "Evaluation." These are a few examples in which it is clear that some linguistic phenomena like homophones or synonyms in one language can affect the results of cross-cultural comparison through lack of translation equivalence.

SUMMARY AND CONCLUSIONS

Results obtained both in the United States and Japan over the past 10 years suggest that scale-factor structure may vary from concept class to concept class. To test this hypothesis, three concept classes, Colors, Abstract Words, and Line Forms, were used as concepts to be rated on a translation-equivalent, 35-scale, semantic-differential form. Two

groups of *S*s, differing in both culture and language—Japanese and Americans—were chosen to test cross-cultural and cross-concept generality or uniqueness.

The over-all results clearly demonstrate cross-cultural generality along with cross-concept uniqueness. First, with respect to cross-cultural generality, it was found that the first three most salient factors as a group are identifiable as Evaluative, Potency, and Activity in all the culture-concept class combinations, although the relative importance of these three factors differed as concept class was changed; yet even these shifts tend to be parallel for both subject groups. Second, a definitely closer factorial composition was displayed by the Wrigley-Neuhaus indices of factorial similarity for the same concept class and factors considered interculturally than for intracultural concept-class comparisons. Third, it was shown that the shifts of scales within the three-factor space tend to be similar across the subject groups.

Cross-concept uniqueness was demonstrated both by different orderings of factor salience for the three concept classes and by the different scale compositions of the factors for different concept classes. The 35 scales used in this study could be classified into three general categories: (1) scales that are factorially stable across concept classes, (2) scales that are factorially unstable across concept classes but stable across subject groups, and (3) scales that are both factorially unstable and susceptible to interaction with subject groups. Scales of the first category are "stereotypic" in that they are least susceptible to either concept-class or subject-group change. Scales of the second category shift meaning from concept class to concept class, but do so similarly across the subject groups. Scales of the third category seem to vary both with concept class and subject groups, displaying apparent cultural uniqueness.

The results of the foregoing analyses lead

to the conclusion that the characteristic attribute of a concept or a concept class exerts a selective influence upon semantic judgments by causing rotation of scales within the semantic space, although a few exceptional scales nonetheless display specific cultural uniqueness.

REFERENCES

AZUMA, Y. An experiment on physiognomic perception in phonetic symbolism. *Tokyo Joshidai Ronshu,* 1953, **4**, 109-114 (in Japanese).

FOX, C. W. An experimental study of naming. *Amer. J. Psychol.,* 1935, **47**, 545-579.

KAISER, H. F. The varimax criterion for analytic rotations in factor analysis. *Psychometrika,* 1958, **23**, 187-200.

KOHLER, W. *Gestalt psychology.* New York: Horace Liveright, 1930.

KUMATA, H. A factor analytic investigation of the generality of semantic structures across selected cultures. Unpublished Ph.D. dissertation, Univer. of Illinois, 1958.

KUMATA, H., AND SCHRAMM, W. A pilot study of cross-cultural meaning. *Publ. Opin. Quart.,* 1956, **20**, 229-238.

MIRON, M. S. A cross-linguistic investigation of phonetic symbolism. *J. abnorm. soc. Psychol.,* 1961, **62**, 623-630.

OBONAI, T., AND MATSUOKA, T. Color-symbolism personality test. *J. gen. Psychol.,* 1956, **55**, 229-239.

OGISO, S., AND INUI, M. Measurement of the effect of colors in architecture by the semantic differential. *Nihon Kenchikugakkai Ronbunshu,* 1961, **67**, 105-113 (in Japanese).

OSGOOD, C. E. Studies on the generality of affective meaning systems. *Amer. Psychologist,* 1962, **10**, 10-28.

OSGOOD, C. E., SUCI, G. J., AND TANNENBAUM, P. H. *The measurement of meaning.* Urbana: Univer. of Illinois Press, 1957.

OYAMA, T., AND HAGA, J. A study on figural and phonetic symbolism. *Psychologia,* 1963. In press (in Japanese).

OYAMA, T., TANAKA, Y., AND CHIBA, Y. Affective dimensions of colors: A cross-cultural study. *Jap. psychol. Res.,* 1962, **4**, 78-91.

OYAMA, T., TANAKA, Y., AND HAGA, J. Color-affection and color-symbolism in Japanese and American students. *Jap. J. Psychol.,* 1963. In press (in Japanese with English summary).

SAGARA, M., YAMAMOTO, K., NISHIMURA, H., AND AKUTO, H. A study on the semantic structure of Japanese language by the semantic differential method. *Jap. psychol. Res.,* 1961, **3**, 146-156.

SOLOMON, L. N. A factorial study of complex auditory stimuli (passive sonar sounds). Unpublished Ph.D. dissertation, Univer. of Illinois, 1954.

SOLOMON, L. N. Search of physical correlates to psychological dimensions of sounds. *J. acoust. Soc. Amer.,* 1959, **31**, 492-497.

TANAKA, Y. A cross-cultural study of national stereotypes held by American and Japanese college graduate subjects. *Jap. psychol. Res.,* 1962, **4**, 65-78.

THURSTONE, L. L. *Multiple factor analysis.* Chicago: Univer. of Chicago Press, 1947.

TRIANDIS, H., AND OSGOOD, C. E. A comparative factorial analysis of semantic structures of monolingual Greek and American college students. *J. abnorm. soc. Psychol.,* 1958, **57**, 187-196.

TUCKER, W. T. Experiments in aesthetic communications. Unpublished Ph.D. dissertation, Univer. of Illinois, 1955.

WATANBE, H., ISHIGE, N., KASHIWAGI, S., OCHIAI, H., AND TANAKA, T. The study of cognitive structure in human relations—A trial by semantic differential techniques. Labor Science Research Office, Japan National Railways, 1959. (Mimeograph report in Japanese.)

WRIGLEY, C., AND NEUHAUS, J. O. The matching of the two sets of factors. Contract Memorandum Rep. A-22, Urbana: Univer. of Illinois, 1955.

25. Semantic Differential Technique in the Comparative Study of Cultures[1]

Charles E. Osgood

MOST comparisons across cultures are extremely difficult when they concern nonmaterial traits. In part, this is an obvious consequence of the subjective nature of comparisons; in part also, however, this difficulty is attributable to the fact that nonmaterial traits must often be assessed through the medium of language. Indeed, if the Sapir-Whorf psycholinguistic relativity hypothesis were taken literally and considered completely general to all aspects of human cognition, such comparisons would be impossible. The essential point is this: to note differences within any phenomenal domain and order them in any rigorous fashion, one must have certain similarities underlying the phenomena as a frame of reference against which to compare them. Only to the extent that physical objects share such attributes as length, weight, and volume, and to the extent that these attributes can be abstracted and quantified, can comparison be made on anything other than an intuitive basis.

The denotative or referential uses of terms—the way the lexicon carves up the world—appear largely arbitrary and unique to particular languages until the ethnolinguist discovers a framework of semantic components that can be imposed comparably on these phenomena. In closely analogous fashion, our own researches over the past few years provide evidence for a universal framework underlying certain affective or connotative aspects of language. These findings enliven the possibility of constructing instruments for measuring these aspects of "subjective culture" comparably in diverse societies—in effect, circumventing the language barrier. Since the affective reactions people make to symbols and events are important determiners of their overt behaviors with respect to these symbols and events, having comparable means of measuring affective meanings assumes some importance in a world that is rapidly shrinking psychologically, socially, and politically.

A SEMANTIC SPACE

In order to understand the research procedures we have followed and the kinds of cultural data they can provide, it will be useful to begin with a brief presentation of our theoretical model and its measurement implications. Imagine a space of some unknown number of dimensions. This will be our hypothetical semantic space, and we can explore it by analogy with the more familiar color space. Like all self-respecting spaces, this one has an origin,

Reprinted from *American Anthropologist* (1964), 66: 171–200, by permission of the author and the publisher.

which we define as complete "meaninglessness" (analogous to the neutral grey center of the color space). The meaning of a sign can be conceived as some point in this n-dimensional space, and can thus be represented by a vector from the origin to that point: the length of this vector would index the "degree of meaningfulness" of this sign (like saturation in the color space) and its direction would index the "semantic quality" of this sign (analogous to both hue and brightness in the color space).

To talk about "direction" in any space requires that we have some reference coordinates. Again the analogy with the color space will serve: Just as complementary colors are defined as points equidistant and in opposite directions from the origin in the color space, which when mixed together in equal proportions cancel each other out to neutral grey, so may we conceive of verbal opposites as defining straight lines through the origin of the semantic space. Lexicographers assure us that true verbal opposites do cancel each other out semantically, component for component, when "mixed." Imagine now a whole set of different straight-line "cuts" through the semantic space, each passing through the origin and each defined by a pair of opposites. In order to discover the location of concept x in this space, we might play a game of "Twenty Questions" with our subject: it is *beautiful*, not *ugly* (cut no. 1), it is *soft*, not *hard* (cut no. 2), it is *quick*, not *slow* (cut no. 3), and so forth. If these "cuts" were at right angles to each other, and hence independent, then each such binary decision would reduce uncertainty about the location of x by half. Or, if each straight-line "cut" were scaled into seven discriminable steps, as we have done in our work, then each decision would reduce uncertainty of location by 6/7ths, and only three "cuts" would yield a space of 343 discrete regions.

But the assumption of independence (orthogonality) of dimensions demands justification, of course, and we still have the problem of reference coordinates.

Is the up-down, north-south, and east-west of the semantic space to be completely arbitrary, or is there some "natural" built-in structuring of this space analogous to the gravitational and magnetic determinants of geophysical space? These are empirical questions, and the logical tool is some variant of factor analysis. We need to take a large and representative sample of qualitative dimensions defined by verbal opposites, determine their intercorrelations when used by subjects in differentiating a representative sample of concepts, and then see if they do fall into "natural" clusters or factors which can serve as reference coordinates. And one factor analysis is not enough—it is too liable to the happenstances of sampling. Factor analysis becomes a hypothesis, confirming procedure only when analyses of the same domain are replicated, when the rules of sampling this domain are independent of the factors previously discovered, and when, nevertheless, the same factors keep reappearing.

Now let us look at the measurement model. In the typical semantic differentiation task, a subject judges a series of concepts (e.g., *my mother, Chinese, modern art*, etc.) against a series of bipolar, seven-step scales defined by verbal opposites (e.g., *good-bad*, *strong-weak*, *fast-slow*, *hot-cold*, *fair-unfair*, etc.). The concept is given at the top of each sheet, and the subject judges it against each successive scale by putting his checkmark in the appropriate position, e.g., $+3$ *extremely good*, $+2$ *quite good*, $+1$ *slightly good*, 0 *equally good and bad or neither*, -1 *slightly bad*, -2 *quite bad*, and -3 *extremely bad*. These particular quantifiers have been shown by Norman Cliff (1959) to yield approximately equal degrees of intensity.

When a group of people judge a set of concepts against a set of adjectival scales, representing what we call a "semantic differential," a cube of data is generated. The rows in this cube are defined by the scales, the columns by the concepts being judged, and the "slices" from front to back by the subjects. Each cell represents with a single value how a particular subject rated a particular concept against a particular scale. In analyzing these data we are usually —but not necessarily—interested in the correlations among the scales. We may correlate them across subjects or across concepts; we may collapse the subject dimension of the cube when we are interested in "cultural meanings"; we may run separate analyses for single subjects or classes of subjects (correlating scales across the concepts judged) to determine their individual semantic spaces; or, we may do this for single concepts or classes of concepts (correlating scales across the people judging) to determine the uniqueness of judgmental spaces for concept classes, if such exist. In other words, there are many ways one can slice this semantic space, each appropriate for answering a different kind of question. For the most part, we have employed Pearson product-moment correlation procedures to generate a scale-by-scale matrix of intercorrelations and then subjected this matrix to principal axes factor analysis and varimax rotation.

In the past decade or more, we have made many such factor analyses of data cubes obtained from American speakers of English. Much of this work is summarized by Osgood, Suci, and Tannenbaum (1957). Despite deliberate and independent variations in the sampling of scales, of concepts, and of subjects, three dominant and independent (orthogonal) factors have kept reappearing: an Evaluative Factor (represented by scales such as *good-bad*, *pleasant-unpleasant*, and *positive-negative*), a Potency Factor (represented by scales such as *strong-weak*, *heavy-light*, and *hard-soft*), and an Activity Factor (represented by scales such as *fast-slow*, *active-passive*, and *excitable-calm*). What this means is that there are at least three "directions" in the semantic space which are regions of relatively high density, in the sense of many closely related modes of qualifying, and that these "directions" tend to be orthogonal to each other, in the sense of being independently variable dimensions of meaning. It is also apparent that, contrary to my early expectations, these factors are more reactive in nature than sensory, more broadly affective than discriminatively cognitive, and thus closer to connotative than to denotative aspects of meaning.

In the course of this early work we made many comparisons between groups of people within the English-speaking American culture—between old people and young, between males and females, between students exposed to a new kind of course in international relations and those given the traditional course, between Republicans and Democrats, and even between schizophrenics and normals. The results of all these comparisons can be summarized very simply: in no case have we found significant differences in the underlying dominant factors. Note carefully that this does *not* indicate that the meanings of particular concepts were necessarily the same. Females have a different meaning of the self than do males. Republicans have a very different meaning for *Harry Truman* than do Democrats, and so forth. What this does indicate is that the semantic framework within which these affective judgments are made is constant; the modes of qualifying concepts display the same correlational structure, despite real differences in location of particular concepts within the common framework. Indeed, it is only by virtue of this common frame of reference that differences between people for the same concept and between concepts for the same people can be specified.

THE SEARCH FOR CROSS-LINGUISTIC AND CROSS-CULTURAL GENERALITY

The research described so far has been limited to English-speaking participants in American culture. Although considerable generality of semantic factor structure has been demonstrated for various groups within this particular language/culture composite, the most critical test of generality remains: does the same semantic framework hold for people who speak different languages and enjoy different cultures? Demonstration of such generality would be of considerable scientific interest in and of itself, but, more than this, the existence of such a shared framework would permit us to devise comparable "yardsticks" for measuring similarities and differences in certain aspects of subjective culture—the affective or emotive aspects.

Prior to the major research effort to be reported here, a number of studies had been carried out designed to assess the generality of affective meaning systems across selected language and culture groups. These included a study by Kumata (1957), comparing Korean bilinguals and Japanese bilinguals and monolinguals with American monolinguals, a study by Triandis and Osgood (1958), comparing Greek and American college students, and one by Suci (1960), comparing several Southwest Indian cultures with Spanish-speaking Americans and Anglos. Even though the details of methods varied, as did the selection of semantic scales and concepts judged—and the same factors nevertheless kept appearing—one dubious aspect of methodology ran through all of these early studies: the samples of scales used were selected either partly or wholly on the basis of results obtained in prior American investigations. Such scales were often simply translated into the languages of the other groups under study. Despite the care with which these translations were carried out (cf. Kumata 1957), the fact that translation served as the vehicle for demonstrating structural similarities in all cases seemed to be the most likely source of bias, if indeed the similarities were artifactual. It was out of this background that we began, in 1960,[2] to apply a design which we hoped would rigorously test the limits of possible generality. To avoid the potential bias of translation, and resultant ethnocentrism, the procedures for selecting modes of qualifying were to be entirely intracultural; each language/culture group must determine its own scales. However, in order to make possible the intercultural comparisons essential for testing the generality hypothesis, the over-all methodology of these intracultural samplings had to be carefully standardized. Additionally, it was clear that our design required as heterogeneous a sample of both languages and cultures as could be obtained practically.

The term "practically" here implied several things for us: first, we would work only with literate, "high" cultures in the beginning, since data could be collected more efficiently from groups of subjects in written form; second, we

TABLE I. SUMMARY OF LANGUAGE/CULTURE GROUPS COMPRISING TOTAL SAMPLE

Country	Language	Language family	Field center	Field staff
*U.S.A.	English	Indo-European	Urbana	Miron, May, Tanaka, Shanmugam
*Finland	Finnish	Finno-Urgic	Helsinki	Allardt, Haavio
*Japan	Japanese	Japanese	Tokyo	Obonai, Asai
*India	Kannada	Dravidian	Mysore	Kuppuswamy Vatsala, Nikam
Netherlands	Dutch	Indo-European	Amsterdam	Jansen, Duijker
Belgium	Flemish	Indo-European	Brussels	Jansen, Nuttin
France	French	Indo-European	Paris	Jansen, Sutter
*Lebanon	Arabic	Semitic	Beirut	Prothro, Diab
Sweden	Swedish	Indo-European	Uppsala	Himmelstrand, Asplund
*Hong Kong	Cantonese	Sino-Tibetan	Hong Kong	Li
*Iran	Farsi	Indo-European	Tehran	Siassi, Minou
Afghanistan	Farsi	Indo-European	Kabul	Majrouh, Sarwari
Yugoslavia	Serbo-Croatian	Indo-European	Belgrade	Tomekovic, Georgievich
India	Hindi	Indo-European	Delhi	Rastogi, Shukla
Poland	Polish	Indo-European	Warsaw	Schaff, Sarapata
Afghanistan	Pashto	Indo-European	Kabul	Majrouh, Ayeen

would work with relatively homogeneous samples of young males (12–16 years of age) rather than strive for representative samples of populations, since what is "representative" is very obscure cross-culturally and would, in any case, not be comparable; third, our original sample of six sites, along with the United States as control, would include as many different language families and as gross cultural differences as possible—efficiencies of our data-processing later made it possible to extend our sample to some 16 sites. Table I gives the research sites (original set indicated by asterisks), the languages involved, and the names of field staff.

Phase I. Qualifier Selection

Data collection and analysis falls rather naturally into two phases. Phase I involves collection of a large and representative sample of modes of qualifying experience in each language/culture community, on the basis of which to construct a set of bipolar descriptive scales characteristic of each such community.[3]

A standard list of substantives. It was decided to use a modified word-association procedure to elicit qualifiers in each site—a procedure in which subjects give the first qualifier (adjective, in English) that occurs to them when presented with each substantive (noun, in English). But the requirement of standardization demanded that a common list of substantives be used, ideally involving completely culture-common and culture-fair terms. A pool of 200 substantives was finally drawn from items used in glottochronological studies and purported to be of wide linguistic applicability (Swadesh, 1950; Lees, 1953), from the Kent-Rosanoff list, and from category headings in the Human Relations Area Files Index. Reduction of this pool was accomplished by means of two criteria: *Translation fidelity* was estimated by having the total list translated into Arabic, Cantonese, Finnish, Hindi, Kannada, Japanese, and Persian by panels of approximately 10 English/mother-tongue bilinguals, along with informal back-translation checks; wherever difficulty was encountered in any language, that item was dropped for all languages. *Substantive productivity* was estimated by having the 200 item set administered in Finland and the United States; items yielding relatively few qualifier types were eliminated (e.g., the item *blood* was found to yield predominantly a single response, *red*, in both languages, and so was dropped). These procedures enabled us to reduce the substantive list to the 100 items given in Table II. It should be noted that this list includes a good number of abstract terms, as well as the concrete terms that might be expected. It should also be noted that this is the only point at which translation could in any way affect our results.

Eliciting qualifiers. For a variety of reasons, it is not possible simply to translate English instructions into other languages and expect to get comparable results. For one thing, cultural differences in implicit assumptions about the task exist (e.g., "to say what most people would say" vs. "to give unusual responses"), and we are not sure but what some of these effects are still embodied in our data. For another thing, the linguistic frames which define qualifiers vary with the grammatical structure of each language. Therefore, our ethnolinguist, William Kay Archer, working with field personnel, devised frames in each language presumably as appropriate for that language as the test frames "The —————— *Butterfly*" and "The *Butterfly* is ——————" are for English. Given practice with such frames in their own language, 100 young males supplied one qualifier each for each of the items in Table II. In collating these data, the field workers were instructed to use the same frames for testing dubious items. To facilitate analysis on IBM and ILLIAC computers (and to eliminate the need for translation), orthographic schemes were devised for languages whose alphabetization practices made this necessary. The total "basketful" of approximately 10,000 qualifiers (100 subjects×100 substantives) obtained in each site, organized in "alphabetized" lists under each substantive, were shipped to Illinois for analysis.

TABLE II. THE 100 SUBSTANTIVE STIMULI AS USED IN QUALIFIER ELICITATIONS

1. House	35. Work	68. Thunder
2. Girl	36. Story	69. Truth
3. Picture	37. Punishment	70. Author
4. Meat	38. Wealth	71. Music
5. Trust	39. Woman	72. Sleep
6. Pain	40. Cloud	73. Future
7. Defeat	41. Cat	74. Egg
8. Book	42. Poison	75. Root
9. Lake	43. Crime	76. Sun
10. Star	44. Hunger	77. Dog
11. Battle	45. Choice	78. Money
12. Danger	46. Noise	79. Smoke
13. Sympathy	47. Need	80. Fish
14. Progress	48. Hope	81. Man
15. Cup	49. Anger	82. Wednesday
16. Courage	50. Tongue	83. Chair
17. Thief	51. Horse	84. Guilt
18. Bread	52. Marriage	85. Luck
19. Love	53. Game	86. Peace
20. Fruit	54. Color	87. Hair
21. Bird	55. Heart	88. Food
22. Snake	56. Friend	89. Seed
23. Heat	57. Death	90. Policeman
24. Map	58. Knowledge	91. Father
25. Husband	59. Freedom	92. Fear
26. Rain	60. Belief	93. Pleasure
27. Tree	61. Success	94. Purpose
28. Stone	62. Rope	95. Fire
29. Tooth	63. Hand	96. Doctor
30. Ear	64. Mother	97. Power
31. Respect	65. Knot	98. Window
32. Laughter	66. Life	99. River
33. Moon	67. Head	100. Water
34. Wind		

Qualifier selection. After punching onto IBM cards, completely computerized procedures were applied to the qualifier data. These procedures were designed to order qualifier-types in terms of three criteria: (a) maximum overall frequency of usage (salience), (b) maximum diversity of usage (productivity), and (c) minimum correlation in usage (independence). In other words, working "blindly" with standardized computer procedures, we wanted to derive uniquely for each language/culture community a set of terms that would comprise its most characteristic and representative modes of qualifying experience. The first two criteria, frequency and diversity of usage, could be combined into a single index—the *H*-statistic of information theory; if a qualifier-type (e.g., *good*) should be given by all subjects to all items, it would have the maximum value of H, whereas a qualifier-type that occurred to only one substantive would have an H-value of 0.

When the qualifier-types for each language/culture sample are ranked according to the H-statistic, rather striking similarities are revealed even at this level. Table III gives the correlations in rank (here, separately for frequency and diversity indices) of the 40 highest ranking qualifiers, as translated into English in each case. Despite the difficulties of "mapping" one language onto another in translation, these correlations are all positive and highly significant. In other words, the relative importance (frequency and diversity) of various modes of qualifying experience appear to be shared despite differences in both language and culture.

Finally, the distribution of usage across the set of substantives of each qualifier lower in the H-ranked list was correlated with the distribution of every higher-ranked qualifier, using the *phi* coefficient. Where correlations were above a rather stringent criterion, the lower-ranking qualifier was discarded. An illustration will clarify this procedure: suppose that *nice* has a usage profile across the 100 nouns that is highly correlated with *good;* if *good* has a higher H-rank, it is kept and *nice* is discarded. Our purpose here is to eliminate semantically redundant scales and thus maximize the opportunity for independent dimensions to appear in the sample.

Opposite elicitation and scale production. A final list of about 60 qualifiers, ranked according to H (frequency and diversity) and pruned according to semantic redundancy (*phi*-coefficients), is returned to the field staff in each site. They are instructed to use these items as stimuli in eliciting verbal opposites according to a standardized procedure (no difficulties have yet been encountered in this procedure—the notion of, and utilization of, "oppositeness" seems to be a common characteristic of languages). Where certain terms have no agreed upon opposite, or where the opposites are multiple (e.g., homonyms such as *light-dark* and *light-heavy*), rules of procedure are given for either elimination of the term as a scale or further probing. The end result is a list of 50 bipolar scales, representing the highest ranking items remaining after the process. These scales provide the dimensions for concept differentiation in Phase II.

Phase II. Concept-on-scale Factorizations

In this phase the original 100 substantives (Table II) are judged as concepts against the set of 50 bipolar qualifier scales derived from Phase I by a different, but equivalent, group of young males in each country. These data are factored, both uniquely for each group and pan-culturally. On the basis of the common factors derived, short (15 to 18 scales) semantic differentials are selected for each language/culture group for subsequent applied research.

Collection of concept-on-scale data. Since rating 100 concepts on 50 scales is an extremely time-consuming task, the concepts were divided into 10 subsets and each subset of 10 concepts was judged against the total scales by a group of 20 subjects (we have found that the means for groups of this size

TABLE III. TRANSLATION ANALYSIS ELICITED QUALIFIER INTERCORRELATIONS

	Frequency								Diversity							
	English	Arabic	Dutch	Finnish	Kannada	Japanese	French	Flemish	English	Arabic	Dutch	Finnish	Kannada	Japanese	French	Flemish
English	1.00	.53	.66	.78	.76	.43	.58	.65	1.00	.64	.56	.68	.70	.60	.53	.56
Arabic		1.00	.29	.35	.31	.39	.37	.34		1.00	.37	.53	.49	.46	.50	.40
Dutch			1.00	.73	.59	.29	.53	.95			1.00	.49	.48	.33	.41	.89
Finnish				1.00	.66	.39	.62	.71				1.00	.54	.56	.64	.55
Kannada					1.00	.33	.45	.56					1.00	.39	.46	.52
Japanese						1.00	.33	.34						1.00	.47	.36
French							1.00	.55							1.00	.42
Flemish								1.00								1.00

311

are highly stable, within about ⅓ of a scale unit). This task thus involved 200 subjects. A 50 (scale)×100 (concept)×20 (subject) cube of data was thus generated in each language/culture community. Since we were here interested in cultural meaning systems, not individual, these data cubes were collapsed along the subject dimension by summing and averaging over the 20 subjects for each concept-scale judgment. These data were shipped back to Illinois for analysis.

Analysis of concept-on-scale data. Following the usual transfer of data to IBM cards, the first step was to generate a 50×50 scale-by-scale correlation matrix by correlating across the mean judgments for the 100 concepts. This matrix was then factored by the principal component method and usually rotated by the varimax method. This procedure yields a unique solution for each language/culture community, and comparisons can only be made intuitively by inspection of the scales (as translated into English) having high loadings on the factors. Table IV gives the six highest loading scales for each of the first three factors for six language/culture communities. The first factor in order of magnitude (% variance extracted) is clearly interpretable as *Evaluation* in every case, without any intuitive strain. The second factor in order of magnitude is interpretable either as *Potency* or *Activity*, the former with less intuitive strain than the latter, and the remaining factor is always Potency where the second is Activity, or vice versa. In other words, on such an interpretive basis, the first three factors in every case resemble the Evaluation-Potency-Activity pattern repeatedly found for American English speakers.

To eliminate the problem of intuitive interpretation in comparing two (or more) factorizations, it is necessary to put the variables being compared into the same mathematical space. In the usual two-way factor problem (people against tests), this means that either the subjects must be the same or the tests the same. In our three-way problem (people against concepts against scales) this would mean that one of these sources of variance would have to be the same; this is clearly not the case for our people (different language/culture communities), for our scales (some are translation-equivalent, but many are unique), nor for our concepts (translation equivalent, but no guarantee of semantic identity). However, whereas there exist no possibilities of ordering the data according to people or scales (there is no rationale for pairing), this can be done for the concepts; that is, we can correlate scale *x* for Americans with scale *y* for Finns directly, using the means for Americans on *x* and Finns on *y* across the 100 pairable translation-equivalent concepts. To the extent that our assumption of common concept meanings is *not* justified, all this can do is reduce the possible magnitude of correlations (by introducing random "noise") and hence work against the hypothesis of factorial similarity.

We have made two types of such "pan-cultural" factor comparisons. The first type involves all of the scales in two language/culture groups (i.e., 100 scales) intercorrelated across the common 100 concepts. So far we have only done this against American English as a common base. Tables V and VI illustrate these results for Finnish and Japanese against English, respectively. Note, first, that the common factors of Evaluation, Potency, and Activity

TABLE IV. PRINCIPAL COMPONENT FACTORS OF FULL-SCALE INSTRUMENT
AS USED IN CONCEPT-SCALE TASK*

American	Factor I (45.5%)		Factor II (12.0%)		Factor III (5.6%)	
	nice-awful	.96	big-little	.81	fast-slow	.64
	sweet-sour	.94	powerful-powerless	.75	noisy-quiet	.56
	heavenly-hellish	.93	deep-shallow	.69	young-old	.55
	good-bad	.93	strong-weak	.68	alive-dead	.55
	mild-harsh	.92	high-low	.64	known-unknown	.48
	happy-sad	.91	long-short	.64	burning-freezing	.36

Dutch	Factor I (27.8%)		Factor II (17.8%)		Factor III (5.9%)	
	pleasant-unpleasant	.95	absorbing-boring	.81	big-little	.70
	cozy-cheerless	.93	changeable-constant	.74	long-short	.66
	pretty-not pretty	.93	active-passive	.72	heavy-light	.63
	happy-unhappy	.92	wild-tame	.71	thick-thin	.57
	good-bad	.91	impressive-not impressive	.70	strong-weak	.56
	beautiful-ugly	.88	exchanging-even	.69	hard-soft	.41

Finnish	Factor I (30.8%)		Factor II (9.2%)		Factor III (7.8%)	
	nice-not nice	.88	agile-clumsy	.68	long-short	.56
	light-gloomy	.88	delicate-sturdy	.63	sharp-dull	.52
	pleasant-unpleasant	.85	capricious-steady	.60	energetic-unenergetic	.50
	sweet-sour	.81	flexible-rigid	.58	large-small	.49
	good-bad	.80	fast-slow	.53	strong-weak	.48
	happy-unhappy	.80	young-old	.53	sturdy-delicate	.47

Flemish	Factor I (27.2%)		Factor II (8.0%)		Factor III (7.8%)	
	agreeable-disagreeable	.90	bloody-not bloody	.69	long-short	.79
	cozy-cheerless	.89	shrewd-naive	.69	big-small	.77
	pleasant-boring	.89	quick-slow	.68	strong-weak	.64
	magnificent-horrible	.89	sharp-blunt	.64	deep-shallow	.60
	beautiful-ugly	.88	active-passive	.61	old-new	.54
	good-bad	.84	violent-calm	.44	old-young	.51

Japanese	Factor I (41.0%)		Factor II (13.0%)		Factor III (8.5%)	
	pleasant-unpleasant	.96	heavy-light	.76	cheerful-lonely	.76
	comfortable-uncomfortable	.95	difficult-easy	.71	colorful-plain	.68
	good-bad	.94	strong-weak	.65	noisy-quiet	.68
	happy-sad	.93	brave-cowardly	.63	active-inactive	.61
	elegant-vulgar	.92	sturdy-fragile	.62	fast-slow	.60
	troublesome-thankful	.93	thick-thin	.60	early-late	.58

Kannada	Factor I (30.8%)		Factor II (7.2%)		Factor III (4.8%)	
	merciful-cruel	.89	many-few	.68	fast-slow	.53
	good-bad	.86	big-small	.68	active-dull	.45
	calm-frightful	.84	huge-small	.68	fatty-slim	.42
	beautiful-ugly	.83	great-little	.54	unstable-stable	.42
	delicate-rough	.82	plenty-little	.54	noisy-quiet	.36
	soft-rough	.79	strong-weak	.44	hasty-considered	.34

* Excluding Flemish; factor coefficients reported for that language were obtained by Varimax rotation.

are clearly identified in both comparisons; note, second, that rather than a
factor being defined by scales in one language (high loadings) and only faintly
supported by semantically related scales in the other language (lower loading),
here the factors clearly run through scale clusters simultaneously defined by
both languages (high loadings tend to alternate across languages). Needless

TABLE V. PRINCIPAL COMPONENT FACTORIZATION OF COMBINED ENGLISH AND FINNISH PHASE II TASK

Factor I (36.5%)		Factor II (9.1%)		Factor III (6.7%)		Factor IV (3.7%)		Factor V (3.3%)	
American English		*American English*		*American English*		*American English*		*American English*	
nice-awful	.94	big-little	.83	fast-slow	.65	burning-freezing	.44	dry-wet	.62
sweet-sour	.93	powerful-powerless	.70	noisy-quiet	.51	unknown-known	.42	burning-freezing	.51
heavenly-hellish	.91	deep-shallow	.67	alive-dead	.48	hot-cold	.41	hot-cold	.50
happy-sad	.91	strong-weak	.66	burning-freezing	.36	high-low	.40	known-unknown	.32
good-bad	.91	high-low	.64	young-old	.34	weak-strong	.34	short-long	.31
mild-harsh	.90	long-short	.61	sharp-dull	.32				
beautiful-ugly	.90	heavy-light	.59	hot-cold	.32				
faithful-unfaithful	.88	hard-soft	.46						
clean-dirty	.88	old-young	.45						
helpful-unhelpful	.88	sharp-dull	.44						
useful-useless	.87								
sane-mad	.87								
needed-unneeded	.86								
fine-coarse	.86								
honest-dishonest	.84								
Finnish		*Finnish*		*Finnish*		*Finnish*		*Finnish*	
nice-not nice	.89	sturdy-delicate	.71	agile-clumsy	.70	light-dark	.40	red-blue	.54
light-gloomy	.87	large-small	.65	flexible-rigid	.68	distant-near	.39	hot-cold	.44
pleasant-unpleasant	.87	heavy-light	.54	fast-slow	.67	high-low	.35	steady-capricious	.39
good-bad	.84	strong-weak	.52	lively-subdued	.56	weak-strong	.35	short-long	.35
reassuring-frightening	.79	thick-thin	.46	lively-tired	.50	deep-shallow	.34	shallow-deep	.32
valuable-worthless	.78	long-short	.45	sharp-dull	.49				
ripe-raw	.78	old-young	.42	multicolored-unicolor	.47				
clean-dirty	.78	high-low	.41						
white-black	.77	steady-capricious	.34						
happy-unhappy	.77	brave-timid	.33						
honorable-despicable	.76								
flourishing-barren	.76								
sweet-sour	.76								
right-wrong	.75								
smooth-rough	.70								

TABLE VI. PRINCIPAL COMPONENT FACTORIZATION OF COMBINED ENGLISH AND JAPANESE PHASE II TASK

Factor I (40.9%)		Factor II (10.9%)		Factor III (6.3%)		Factor IV (3.9%)		Factor V (3.9%)	
American English		*American English*		*American English*		*American English*		*American English*	
nice-awful	.96	powerless-powerful	.76	fast-slow	.65	low-high	.53	serious-funny	.44
good-bad	.93	little-big	.70	noisy-quiet	.56	little-big	.47	burning-freezing	.44
sweet-sour	.93	weak-strong	.68	young-old	.46	short-long	.39	hot-cold	.44
heavenly-hellish	.92	shallow-deep	.56	alive-dead	.41	known-unknown	.36	few-many	.42
happy-sad	.91	short-long	.56	burning-freezing	.38	shallow-deep	.35	weak-strong	.32
mild-harsh	.90	light-heavy	.54	known-unknown	.37	unbroken-broken	.32		
beautiful-ugly	.90	low-high	.51	hot-cold	.36				
helpful-unhelpful	.90	soft-hard	.50						
needed-unneeded	.88	smooth-rough	.48						
clean-dirty	.88	funny-serious	.48						
useful-useless	.88								
faithful-unfaithful	.87								
honest-dishonest	.87								
sane-mad	.86								
safe-dangerous	.86								
Japanese		*Japanese*		*Japanese*		*Japanese*		*Japanese*	
pleasant-unpleasant	.93	light-heavy	.72	cheerful-lonely	.73	plain-colorful	.44	few-many	.56
good-bad	.92	small-big	.67	noisy-quiet	.68	near-far	.40	rare-common	.40
comfortable-uncomfortable	.92	weak-strong	.65	colorful-plain	.65	narrow-wide	.35	late-early	.38
happy-sad	.91	cowardly-brave	.63	active-inactive	.55	sturdy-fragile	.32	slow-fast	.38
elegant-vulgar	.90	fragile-sturdy	.62	red-blue	.53	small-big	.32	difficult-easy	.36
thankful-troublesome	.90	easy-difficult	.61	fast-slow	.53	low-high	.31		
beautiful-ugly	.88	thin-thick	.59	early-late	.50				
necessary-unnecessary	.87	soft-hard	.53						
great-unimportant	.86	simple-complex	.48						
interesting-boring	.86	loose-tight	.47						
wise-foolish	.86								
optimistic-pessimistic	.85								
skillful-unskillful	.80								
great-not great	.80								
tasty-untasty	.80								

to state, these are most encouraging and convincing results. Limitations on the capacities of our computers make it impossible to throw all scales for all of our 15 or more language/culture communities into a single pan-cultural factor analysis. However, it is possible to take the highest loading scales on each of the major factors derived in single community factor analyses and combine them in a single analysis for all communities. Table VII shows the results ob-

TABLE VII. PAN-CULTURAL FACTOR SCALE ANALYSIS (18 highest loading scales for each pan-cultural factor arranged by culture)

	Factor I (27.7%)		Factor II (14.9%)		Factor III (10.5%)	
American-English	nice-not nice	86	powerful-powerless	69	fast-slow	55
	sweet-sour	81	big-little	62	noisy-quiet	48
	heavenly-hellish	80			young-old	44
					little-big	39
Dutch	pleasant-unpleasant	86	big-little	63	active-passive	61
	pretty-not pretty	83	absorbing-boring	55	absorbing-boring	44
	cozy-cheerless	80	long-short	46		
			changeable-constant	45		
			active-passive	45		
Finnish	nice-not nice	83	energetic-unenergetic	60	agile-clumsy	67
	pleasant-unpleasant	81	dull-sharp	44	capricious-steady	48
	light-gloomy	78	sturdy-delicate	41	delicate-sturdy	42
French	pleasant-unpleasant	83	large-little	75	fast-slow	58
	good-bad	80	strong-weak	66	lively-indolent	55
	likable-repugnant	78	huge-tiny	61	living-dead	44
			indolent-lively	55		
			dead-living	42		
Japanese	comfortable-uncomfortable	83	strong-weak	56	colorful-plain	52
	pleasant-unpleasant	83	heavy-light	40	noisy-quiet	52
	good-bad	82			light-heavy	42
					cheerful-lonely	37
Kannada	calm-frightful	73	big-small	46	fast-slow	37
	merciful-cruel	73			active-passive	36
	good-bad	68				

tained when this is done for seven of our communities where data analysis has proceeded to this stage. Again, there is clear and convincing confluence of semantically similar (in translation to English) scales upon common factors of Evaluation, Potency, and Activity. It is from data such as these that final selection of specific scales for comparable differentials in each language/culture community will be made.

Cross-linguistic and Cross-cultural Similarities: Summary

Before turning attention to cultural differences we will summarize the major cross-cultural similarities found in the "tool-making" Phases I and II. (a) *Salience and productivity of modes of qualifying.* It is evident in our data that, even on the basis of crude and "noisy" translation into English, the modes of qualifying experience that have high H-ranks (frequency and diversity of usage) in English also tend to have high rank in other languages. (b) *Qualifier frequency-of-usage functions.* When the total sample of qualifiers for each language are plotted as lognormal functions (cf., Zipf-type functions), they are found to have very similar slopes, albeit some interesting differences in mean. (c) *Oppositeness.* The functional use of oppositeness in the qualifier realm was clearly present for all languages studied—it did not need to be forced. (d) *Affective factors.* The major hypothesis of this research—that human beings share a common framework for differentiating the affective meanings of signs—is clearly borne out in the data. The dominant factors in the affective meaning system are Evaluation, Potency, and Activity, usually in that order. Whether this system will be found to hold up for non-literate groups remains to be tested in future research, but pilot studies suggest that it will.

EVIDENCE FOR DIFFERENCES IN SUBJECTIVE CULTURE

Differences between language/culture communities that can be drawn from data we are collecting fall into three general categories. First, there are differences that fall out more or less incidentally from the "tool-making" procedures just described. Despite the over-all similarities stressed above, certain differences between groups are also evident in each phase, and the standardization of procedures enhances the significance of such differences. However, no attempt will be made here to give cultural interpretations of these "incidental" differences; this would require more intimate knowledge of the cultures than the present writer possesses. Second, in our future work we plan to apply the short-form differentials derived from the pan-cultural factor analyses to the development of what might be called a "World Atlas of Affective Meanings." This will involve a greatly expanded set of concepts, deliberately selected for their intercultural discriminating power. Third, we plan to undertake a number of pan-cultural comparative studies in particular concept areas, e.g., the self-concept and kin-concepts more generally.

Differences in Existing Data

(1) *H-ranks of qualifiers.* The fact that there are correlations in the .50 to .70 range across the various language-culture communities in modes of qualifying has already been demonstrated (cf., Table III). Although there is the general semantic correspondence among the top 10 H-ranked qualifiers (as translated into English) for the eight groups shown in Table VIII, there are also some apparent uniquenesses. Some of these are suggested by italics (e.g., *white* and *red* for Arabic; *firm, spoiled*, and *difficult* for Finnish; *tall, white, black*, and *violent* for French; *merry* and *glad* for Japanese; *dark* and *fair* for Kannada).

Color terms vary in their occurrence and ordering among the first 40 H-ranks as shown in Table IX. All seven color terms occur for American English; no color terms occur among the top 40 for Japanese. *White* and *black* are very salient "colors" semantically, both in occurrence and H-rank, and among the hues *red* is clearly the most salient; relative emphasis on *white* and *black*

TABLE VIII. THE 10 HIGHEST *H*-RANKED QUALIFIERS FOR EIGHT LANGUAGE/CULTURE GROUPS

American English		Lebanese Arabic		Dutch		Finnish		Flemish		French		Japanese		Indian Kannada	
Q	*H*	*Q*	*H*	*Q*	*H*	*Q*	*H*	*Q*	*H*	*Q*	*H*	*Q*	*H*	*Q*	*H*
good	228	large	324	large	519	good	393	big	425	tall	132	big	347	good	336
big	140	beautiful	241	good	255	big	374	good	203	good	083	pretty	325	big	172
great	091	great	168	beautiful	137	firm	185	beautiful	166	deep	048	beautiful	311	slight	115
small	082	severe	122	small	093	small	158	little	078	white	045	merry	303	much	093
large	076	small	121	much	084	beautiful	119	hard	066	hard	044	fearful	190	dark	083
bad	072	long	104	hard	063	long	097	long	061	black	037	small	141	fair	074
little	067	strong	088	heavy	059	bad	087	strong	060	fine	036	glad	131	severe	072
long	063	plentiful	085	long	041	pleasant	067	thick	058	violent	031	strong	123	bad	068
hard	053	white	065	bad	040	spoiled	060	intense	058	pleasant	031	wonderful	116	dreadful	067
strong	043	red	058	thick	033	difficult	043	bad	053	soft	030	good	110	small	067

is shared by Lebanese, French, and Kannada-speaking Indians, as against the other groups. Similar comparisons could be made for other qualifier classes.

(2) *Orientation of translation-equivalent scales.* It had been apparent in our earlier studies that semantic differential scales may meet the usual criteria for

TABLE IX. *H*-RANKS FOR COLOR TERMS OCCURRING AMONG TOP 40 IN RANK

	American	Lebanese	Dutch	Finnish	Flemish	French	Japanese	Kannada
white	15	9	34	37	13	4	—	6 (fair)
black	11	11	14	23	19	6	—	5 (dark)
red	12	10	15	21	16	11	—	14
yellow	36	34	—	33	—	—	—	—
green	40	32	—	—	—	—	—	—
blue	21	—	—	38	—	31	—	36
brown	25	—	—	—	—	—	—	—

translation equivalence and yet have quite different affective connotations as evidenced in their factorial orientation. An example from Kumata's (1957) Japanese study was the scale, *rugged-delicate;* this was clearly a Potency scale for Americans, but equally clearly an Evaluative scale (*delicate/good—rugged /bad*) for the Japanese. The implications for international communication, or lack thereof, of such unintended qualifier connotation is obvious. Similar uniquenesses in what qualities connote Evaluation, Potency, or Activity can be found in the present data, despite over-all factorial similarities. The reader is referred back to Table IV. Evaluation is connoted by *elegant-vulgar* (cf., *delicate-rugged* in earlier study) for the Japanese and by *merciful-cruel, delicate-rough*, and *soft-rough* for the Kannada-speaking Indians. Potency is connoted by *high-low* for Americans, by *old-new* and *old-young* for the Flemish-speaking Belgians, by *difficult-easy* for the Japanese, and by *many-few* and *plenty-little* for the Kannada-speaking Indians. Activity is connoted by *noisy-quiet* for Americans, Japanese, and Indians, by *delicate-sturdy* for Finns, by *bloody-not bloody* and *shrewd-naive* for Belgians, and by *fatty slim* for Indians (note the reversal in direction here from what Americans would predict, e.g., *slim* should be associated with *active*, not *fatty!*). This type of analysis could be extended over the entire data to yield inferences as to what general modes of qualifying have what affective implications in different cultures.

(3) *H-ranks of substantives.* In each language/culture community 100 qualifiers were elicited for each substantive, and one can thereby inquire into the entropy characteristics of the substantives themselves. A substantive to which many subjects gave the same response (e.g., *star*-bright) would have a low *H*-rank and could be called a *culturally stereotyped concept*, whereas one to which subjects tended to give many idiosyncratic responses would have a high *H*-rank and could be called a *culturally amorphous concept*. When the *H*-ranks for substantives were computed for five groups available at that time, and the rank orderings were correlated as had been done with the qualifier-

types, it was clear that here there was great diversity: the obtained correlations were .22, .28, .21, and .09 for comparisons of English with Dutch, Afghan Farsi, Iranian Farsi, and Kannada respectively. These values should be contrasted with the .50 to .70 correlations for analogous qualifier ranks.

We may ask which concepts tend to be stereotyped to the same degree across language/culture communities and which tend to display unique culture dependencies in this respect. Table X orders the 100 substantives according to the standard deviation in *H*-ranks across five groups (eventually this will be done across our much larger, total sample). Concepts toward the top of the list display similar degrees of stereotopy across cultures; concepts low in this ranking display marked differences in stereotypy. The actual level of stereotopy is indicated by the *H*-ranks in the table, large ranks indicating high degrees of stereotyping and small ranks, low degrees. Concepts such as *star, luck, cloud, wealth, sun, danger, poison,* and *heat* tend to be stereotyped everywhere; conversely, concepts such as *man, fish, policeman, woman, love, hand, horse, thief,* and *dog* tend to be amorphous (diversely qualified) everywhere.

At the other end of the list in Table X we find some very interesting differences: *work* is highly stereotyped in mode of qualifying by Americans (rank 97), but highly amorphous for Indians (rank 2); similarly, the concept *friend* is stereotyped for Americans (rank 92) but amorphous for Indians (rank 6); *belief* is quite stereotyped for all except the Dutch (rank 2); the concepts *mother* and *father* are highly stereotyped for both Farsi-speaking groups, Afghan (ranks 92 and 83) and Iranian (ranks 92 and 94); *house* is a stereotyped notion for the Farsi-speaking groups again (ranks 95 and 99) and the Dutch (rank 98), but clearly amorphous for the Kannada-speaking Indians (rank 9).

It is also suggestive to look comparatively at certain clusters of concepts in terms of degrees of sterotyping. For all groups except Indian, abstract *wealth* is more stereotyped than concrete *money;* for Americans, Dutch, and Indians, the concept *hope* is more stereotyped than the concept *future*, but the reverse holds true for the two Farsi-speaking groups, and to an extreme degree (Afghan from rank 20 for *hope* to rank 97 for *future* and Iranian from rank 26 to rank 90); for all groups except Americans *man* is more diversely qualified than *woman*, while for all groups except Indians *woman* is more diversely qualified than *girl;* if we look at the spread in masculine roles, we find marked differences culturally—with Americans having the smallest spread (*man* 19, *husband* 14, *father* 9), the Dutch fairly small (*husband* 37, *father* 19, *man* 5), the Indians having a much larger spread (*father* 63, *husband* 41, *man* 1) and the two Farsi groups extremely large, Afghans (*father* 83, *husband* 9, *man* 3) and Iranians (*father* 94, *husband* 70, *man* 1)—and note that for the latter three groups with large spreads it is always *father* that is most stereotyped and *man* least; finally, we note that for all groups except Afghan Farsi, *cats* are more stereotyped than *dogs!*

(4) *Polarization of substantives.* The polarization (or affective intensity) of a concept, it will be recalled, is indexed by its distance from the origin of

TABLE X. 100 NOUNS RANKED BY STANDARD DEVIATION OF H-RANK

	American English	Dutch	Afghan Farsi	Iranian Farsi	Kannada	Mean Rank*		Rank S. D.
				H-rank				
1. Star	84	79	85	73	74	79.0	(4)	5.4
2. Man	19	5	3	1	1	5.8	(1)	
3. Fish	27	14	7	22	13	16.6	(1)	
4. Policeman	12	21	1	4	15	10.6	(1)	
5. Luck	96	75	84	95	100	87.8	(4)	
6. Chair	38	23	29	45	21	31.2		
7. Woman	3	29	10	11	29	16.4	(1)	
8. Love	8	7	37	14	14	16.0	(1)	
9. Trust	45	68	75	71	54	62.6		
10. Cloud	76	74	100	100	96	89.2	(4)	13.05
11. Cup	48	34	11	37	30	32.0		
12. Punishment	21	56	45	52	43	43.4		
13. Doctor	49	15	32	17	37	30.0		
14. Wealth	70	96	77	93	62	79.6	(4)	
15. Hand	17	6	25	10	44	20.4	(1)	
16. Sleep	41	42	21	40	65	41.8		
17. Success	73	59	48	31	45	51.2		
18. Money	55	72	46	87	68	65.6		
19. Horse	11	1	41	19	5	15.4	(1)	
20. Knowledge	53	69	28	42	34	45.2		16.5
21. Rope	54	84	88	74	53	70.6		
22. Thief	1	13	26	6	42	17.6	(1)	
23. Laughter	56	32	36	8	35	33.4		
24. Snake	57	61	42	58	20	47.6		
25. Sun	95	55	96	79	70	79.0	(4)	
26. Map	36	19	15	29	59	31.6		
27. Meat	46	85	43	56	72	60.4		
28. Bread	62	65	19	43	40	45.8		
29. Respect	42	93	69	75	61	68.0		
30. Danger	100	100	53	82	84	83.8	(4)	19.3
31. Poison	86	88	64	96	49	76.6	(4)	
32. Cat	78	80	31	57	50	59.2		
33. Bird	22	35	10	72	22	38.2		
34. Lake	31	58	52	89	57	57.4		
35. Heat	60	49	72	97	95	74.6	(4)	
36. Head	44	62	58	28	85	55.4		
37. Egg	29	39	71	59	80	55.6		
38. Tongue	6	17	34	12	60	25.8		
39. Smoke	82	41	91	88	94	79.2	(4)	
40. Story	52	30	61	21	8	34.4		21.9
41. Dog	7	28	49	50	4	27.6		
42. Fruit	68	78	89	55	31	64.2		
43. Anger	51	11	67	20	38	37.4		
44. Music	58	44	12	9	51	34.8		
45. Death	34	10	8	3	58	22.6	(1)	
46. Heart	33	60	2	7	19	24.2	(1)	
47. Battle	23	26	4	67	39	31.8		
48. Freedom	64	4	57	38	36	39.8		
49. Crime	32	25	78	65	69	53.8		
50. Pain	18	67	62	69	79	59.0		23.7

* Numbers in parentheses indicate mean rank of first or fourth quartile.

TABLE X—(Continued)

	American English	Dutch	Afghan Farsi	Iranian Farsi	Kannada	Mean Rank*	Rank S. D.
				H-rank			
51. Sympathy	24	66	80	54	83	61.4	
52. Color	20	50	70	18	17	35.0	
53. Rain	72	47	59	91	28	59.4	
54. Ear	40	52	98	47	78	63.0	
55. Choice	39	94	76	39	52	60.0	
56. Husband	14	37	9	70	41	34.2	
57. Wind	71	90	63	63	23	62.0	
58. Wednesday	43	64	94	41	88	66.0	
59. River	25	36	27	84	27	39.8	
60. Need	85	97	33	81	87	76.6 (4)	25.1
61. Hunger	28	46	68	78	91	62.2	
62. Marriage	61	82	24	24	64	51.0	
63. Hair	81	45	99	35	71	66.2	
64. Author	83	71	30	34	24	48.4	
65. Fire	79	27	82	27	47	52.4	
66. Power	93	70	23	86	67	67.8	
67. Moon	35	99	51	36	75	59.2	
68. Pleasure	77	95	50	32	32	57.2	
69. Water	13	20	6	15	76	26.0	
70. Tree	69	53	74	61	3	52.0	28.5
71. Life	65	3	39	2	56	33.0	
72. Peace	37	8	54	25	81	40.2	
73. Truth	59	31	18	68	92	53.6	
74. Girl	80	86	90	85	18	71.8	
75. Tooth	74	33	93	23	33	51.2	
76. Guilt	2	51	73	64	77	53.4	
77. Future	50	22	97	90	73	66.4	
78. Window	87	77	17	48	25	50.8	
79. Seed	94	38	35	62	11	48.0	
80. Picture	10	91	66	77	46	58.0	30.1
81. Stone	47	24	79	76	7	46.6	
82. Courage	4	76	47	83	66	55.2	
83. Defeat	26	54	5	51	90	45.2	
84. Hope	67	40	20	26	98	50.2	
85. Book	16	92	13	49	26	39.2	
86. Knot	75	12	86	44	89	61.2	
87. Food	90	16	87	33	48	54.8	
88. Purpose	63	87	22	30	97	59.8	
89. Progress	5	83	65	46	12	42.2	
90. Root	88	48	38	5	82	52.2	34.0
91. Work	97	43	44	60	2	49.2	
92. Friend	92	81	60	80	6	63.8	
93. Noise	99	63	56	92	10	64.0	
94. Game	91	9	55	13	16	36.8	
95. Belief	89	2	81	53	86	62.2	
96. Mother	30	73	92	98	55	64.2	
97. Father	9	18	83	94	63	53.4	
98. House	66	98	95	99	9	73.4	
99. Fear	15	89	14	66	93	55.4	
100. Thunder	98	57	16	16	99	57.2	41.2

* Numbers in parentheses indicate mean rank of first or fourth quartile.

the semantic space. This can be computed either as an average of the *absolute* deviations of judgments of individual subjects from the midpoints of scales, or by the *algebraic* average of the deviations for individual subjects—in which case concepts for which different members of the culture have antagonistic meanings will suffer cancellation in polarization toward zero. The polarization rank data given in Table XI utilized the second method since we were interested in what might be termed "cultural polarization." Table XI is analogous to Table X, in that the concepts are ranked according to the standard deviations among the polarization ranks across five language/culture communities (here, American, Finnish, Flemish, Japanese, and Kannada). Within the body of the table, the most polarized concepts have low ranks and the least polarized, high ranks.

Again, we look first at those concepts for which there seems to be agreement across groups in polarization: the concepts *mother, thief, battle, truth, courage, marriage, love, freedom, fruit, bread*, and *heart* have high affective intensities everywhere; the concepts *hand, wednesday, chair, rope, choice, heat, fish, wealth*, and *future* have relatively low affective intensities everywhere. Turning to the lower end of the table, we again find some intriguing differences: *respect* has high affective intensity for the Kannada-speaking Indians (rank 1), but relatively little for the Finns (rank 71); *luck* is very polarized in affect for the Japanese (rank 8), but clearly not so for Americans (rank 93); *noise* is polar affectively for Japanese (rank 18), but obviously not so for either Americans (rank 96) or Indians (rank 100); *hope* is a polarized concept for Americans (rank 17), but clearly not so for either Finns (rank 93) or Belgians (rank 96); *crime* is an extremely affective notion for all groups except the Kannada-speaking Indians, where it has a rank of 98; yet *guilt* is not emotionally polarized for Americans along with Indians (ranks 97 and 95), as compared with the Finns (rank 28), the Flemish-speaking Belgians (rank 19) and the Japanese (rank 4).

(5) *Octant allocations of substantives.* The three dominant, orthogonal factors in the common semantic space can be used to define eight octants, e.g., *good, strong*, and *active* (E+, P+, A+), *good, strong*, and *passive* (E+, P+, A−), etc. In a crude anticipation of the profiles that would be presented in a semantic atlas (cf. below), we may inspect the similarities and differences in allocation of concepts to these eight octants across four of our language/culture communities (here, American, Finnish, Flemish, and Japanese). Table XII shows concept distributions to octants regardless of concept identifications. We note first that there is general agreement cross-culturally in octant densities: evaluatively positive regions (E+) are more densely occupied by concepts than evaluatively negative regions (E−), to an average ratio of 79 per cent to 21 per cent; similarly, positive potency (P+) is more characteristic than negative potency (P−), to an average ratio of 72 per cent to 28 per cent; on the other hand, positive and negative activity are about equally prominent, 46 to 54 per cent. Furthermore, Belgian-Flemish is more similar in concept distribution to American English than are either Finnish or Japanese. The

TABLE XI. THE 100 CONCEPTS RANKED BY STANDARD DEVIATION OF POLARITY

								Polarity Rank
	American English	Finnish	Flemish	Japanese	Kannada	Mean Rank*	Rank S. D.	
1. Mother	12	14	8	17	9	12.0	(1)	3.7
2. Hand	70	63	71	60	70	66.8		
3. Thief	6	4	13	1	12	7.2	(1)	
4. River	57	62	56	48	49	54.4		
5. Wednesday	100	99	91	100	84	94.8	(4)	
6. Chair	80	73	58	75	69	71.0		
7. Battle	19	3	20	5	19	13.2	(1)	
8. Truth	35	47	26	25	25	31.6		
9. Rope	91	70	75	84	66	77.2	(4)	
10. Courage	38	58	40	27	39	40.4		11.1
11. Anger	28	40	30	54	51	40.6		
12. Choice	69	98	74	82	91	82.8	(4)	
13. Marriage	2	7	10	21	32	14.4	(1)	
14. Love	4	8	4	33	14	12.6	(1)	
15. Pleasure	32	52	18	32	35	33.8		
16. Freedom	1	2	31	9	6	9.8	(1)	
17. Fruit	36	36	11	35	11	25.8		
18. Heat	86	61	78	72	99	79.2	(4)	
19. Moon	26	31	14	49	12	26.4		
20. Bread	20	15	12	41	44	26.4		15.0
21. Tooth	40	34	36	65	63	47.6		
22. Fish	92	55	89	90	83	81.8	(4)	
23. Smoke	68	37	79	67	58	61.8		
24. Bird	43	24	53	43	67	46.0		
25. Hair	77	94	65	85	53	74.8	(4)	
26. Picture	63	42	88	66	61	64.0		
27. Star	18	38	34	45	64	39.8		
28. Head	81	51	46	61	37	55.2		
29. Cup	72	50	70	36	76	60.8		
30. Father	16	22	52	14	8	22.4	(1)	17.3
31. Seed	67	43	47	87	62	61.2		
32. Window	60	44	60	74	28	53.2		
33. Cloud	31	67	68	69	41	55.2		
34. Rain	48	72	69	94	88	74.2		
35. Knot	99	56	85	99	94	86.6	(4)	
36. Map	79	49	72	37	73	62.0		
37. Laughter	30	68	43	58	75	54.8		
38. Food	39	83	50	40	43	51.0		
39. Power	56	77	92	93	54	74.4		
40. Book	62	64	63	71	23	56.6		19.1
41. Heart	8	5	49	30	7	19.8	(1)	
42. Man	64	60	66	24	74	57.6		
43. Death	73	29	32	31	56	44.2		
44. Cat	85	45	44	81	78	66.6		
45. Life	52	91	35	62	52	58.4		
46. Wealth	59	95	55	98	60	73.4		
47. Danger	66	17	39	15	47	36.8		
48. Future	55	88	97	50	89	75.8	(4)	
49. Music	49	21	57	46	5	35.6		
50. Peace	23	59	6	11	46	29.0		22.8

* Numbers in parentheses indicate mean rank of first or fourth quartile.

TABLE XI—(*Continued*)

Polarity Rank

	American English	Finnish	Flemish	Japanese	Kanhada	Mean Rank*	Rank S. D.
51. Egg	33	21	61	73	26	42.8		22.9
52. Poison	53	39	48	6	68	42.8	
53. Horse	24	13	51	57	4	29.8	
54. Lake	22	48	54	16	72	42.4	
55. Trust	21	46	64	38	82	50.2	
56. Thunder	78	74	80	23	57	62.4	
57. Purpose	80	92	100	39	71	77.0	(4)
58. Water	41	31	3	63	10	29.6	
59. Friend	11	10	27	64	3	23.0	(1)
60. Sun	5	1	1	7	59	14.6	(1)	25.0
61. Root	90	84	82	53	31	68.0	
62. Color	45	69	76	77	18	57.0	
63. Fire	54	32	7	76	33	40.4	
64. Work	74	79	94	52	27	65.2	
65. Progress	37	41	62	10	79	45.8	
66. Defeat	47	26	87	55	86	60.2	
67. Game	65	80	33	47	13	47.6	
68. Punishment	75	16	9	51	34	37.0	
69. Fear	87	33	81	42	90	66.6	
70. Sympathy	58	27	25	92	45	49.4		27.4
71. Money	29	54	93	91	81	69.6	
72. Husband	50	96	45	22	36	49.8	
73. Stone	74	23	16	78	48	47.8	
74. Dog	61	9	86	59	44	51.4	
75. Policeman	46	86	77	70	15	58.8	
76. Hunger	82	75	21	68	97	68.6	
77. House	51	87	23	19	21	40.2	
78. Need	94	100	28	80	92	78.8	(4)
79. Belief	13	65	42	44	93	61.4	
80. Sleep	25	18	17	20	87	33.4		30.0
81. Ear	34	89	37	95	38	58.6	
82. Author	89	97	83	83	20	74.2	
83. Success	44	82	59	2	22	41.8	
84. Story	89	78	38	79	16	60.0	
85. Tongue	27	57	95	96	40	63.0	
86. Woman	14	12	29	89	24	33.6	
87. Respect	15	71	67	56	1	42.0	
88. Pain	84	53	24	29	96	57.2	
89. Snake	95	76	22	28	77	59.6	
90. Luck	93	66	84	8	65	63.2		33.1
91. Tree	71	25	90	12	30	45.6	
92. Noise	96	85	73	18	100	74.4	
93. Doctor	10	35	98	26	50	43.8	
94. Meat	42	91	15	86	85	63.8	
95. Wind	98	81	41	91	17	65.6	
96. Hope	17	93	96	34	81	64.2	
97. Girl	7	11	5	88	55	33.2	
98. Knowledge	3	19	99	13	29	32.6	
99. Crime	9	6	2	3	98	23.6	(1)
100. Guilt	97	28	19	4	95	48.6		44.1

* Numbers in parentheses indicate mean rank of first or fourth quartile.

lower portion of Table XII lists the concepts which fall into the same octants for all four or at least three of this small sample of groups; it should be noted that there are three octants in which no common concepts are found. Whether this unequal utilization of the affective space is characteristic of the human

TABLE XII. CONCEPT DISTRIBUTIONS BY OCTANTS IN FOUR CULTURES

Culture	Octant							
	E+ P+ A+	E+ P+ A−	E+ P− A−	E+ P− A+	E− P+ A+	E− P+ A−	E− P− A−	E− P− A+
American	20	48	10	3	14	4	1	0
	16	37	12	3	18	8		
Flemish	16	37	12	3	18	8	3	1
	23	25	9	24	9	2		
Finnish	23	25	9	24	9	2	3	1
Japanese	31	27	8	13	3	0	11	4
Total*	90	137	39	43	44	14	18	6

* Total adds to 391 rather than 400 because a few concepts fell precisely at the midpoints of a factor.

CONCEPTS COMMONLY ASSIGNED TO THE OCTANTS BY THREE OR FOUR OF THE FOUR CULTURES EXAMINED

	E+, P+, A+ good strong active	E+, P+, A− good strong passive	E+, P−, A− good weak passive	E+, P−, A+ good weak active	E−, P+, A+ bad strong active
Four	Courage Dog Success	Meat Tree Lake Author Symphony Truth Belief Moon Rope Knowledge			Anger Thunder
Three	Progress Husband Laughter Wealth Work Horse Luck Future	House Book Star Sleep Chair Food Window Story	Tooth Seed Tongue Cup Egg	Bird Woman	Defeat Battle Thief Noise Crime Danger Fear

species (e.g., a general "pollyanna" tendency we have noted consistently in our earlier work) or is a happenstance of our particular sample of 100 concepts remains to be determined.

Some of the differences in concept allocation are suggestive of real culture differences; for example: *progress* is *good-strong-active* for all except Finnish, where it is *passive*; similarly, *future* is *good-strong-active* for all except Finnish, where it is *good*, but *weak* and *passive; work* is *good-strong-active* for all but Flemish, where it is *bad-strong-passive*, for some reason; both *friend* and *man* are *good-strong-active* for Americans and Japanese, but *passive* for the Flemish and *weak* for Finns; only for Americans is *policeman good-strong-active*, being *bad-strong-passive* for the Flemish and *bad-strong-active* for the Japanese (unassigned for Finns); *mother* and *father* are both *good-strong-passive* for Americans and Flemish and are both *good-strong-active* for Japanese, but *father* is *good-strong-active* and *mother good-weak-active* for the Finns; the concept of *power* is *good-strong-active* for both Americans and Flemish speakers; but it becomes *passive* for Finns and turns both *bad* and *weak* (but still *active*) for Japanese; and one last set of comparisons—concepts like *defeat, battle, thief, crime,* and *danger* are all *bad-strong-active* for Americans, Belgians, and Finns, but for the Japanese *defeat, thief, crime,* and *danger* are *bad-weak-passive* and *battle* is *good-weak-active*.

All of these comparisons, and those that have preceded, should be taken *cum grano salis* for the present and treated merely as illustrations of the types of differences that might be determined. There are several reasons for this: For one thing, although we exercised care in the translations of the list of 100 substantives and the obtained qualifiers, rather slight shifts in denotative mapping could produce marked effects here. For another thing, the samples of language/culture communities upon which these substantive comparisons are being made are still quite small and in no case represent even half of our present total group. Even further, we have not as yet introduced appropriate statistical tests for the significances of the various differences that have been alluded to, since we are waiting for a large sample of our data. Given these caveats, the types of differentiations of subjective culture illustrated seem potentially valuable.

An Atlas of Affective Meanings

The various steps in Phases I and II of the general project provide a great deal of quantitative psycholinguistic information obtained in standardized fashion from subjects in various language/culture groups. For example, we obtain lognormal functions characterizing the over-all distributions of modes of qualifying, entropy indices, reflecting both frequency and diversity of usage, for both qualifiers and substantives, factors and resultant vectors for all scales utilized, locations and polarizations of individual concept meanings for the basic list of 100 substantives, and so forth. Such data derive automatically from the necessary operations of the "tool-making" phases. To this information we plan to add, particularly, affective meaning profiles (against the final pan-cultural factors) for additional concepts so as to bring the total in the concept-meaning sections of the Atlas to 1,000 translation-equivalent terms.

Comparable information of this sort about languages should have a wide variety of uses. Linguists, psycholinguists, anthropologists and others will be able to make lexical and semantic analyses of such data, e.g., on the compa-rability of "semantic fields" of the translation-equivalent "nouns" as deter-mined by the overlap in the qualifiers they produce. There is a present trend of interest among linguists in "language universals," and these data should contribute to study of universals in the lexico-semantic aspects of language. The Atlas should also serve as a sorce of verbal materials having known affec-tive properties for use in many types of cross-cultural psycholinguistic experi-ments—experiments on human cognition, perception, learning, and so forth. On the more practical side, such an Atlas of Affective Meanings should con-tribute to more effective international communication. For example, we al-ready know from our Greek study (Triandis and Osgood 1958) that the con-cept *hospital* has very different affective connotations for Greeks as compared with Americans—for the former it has connotations of warmth and sociability, whereas for the latter it conveys the connotation of cold efficiency (and these differences correlate with cultural customs associated with this institution).

Sampling

In order to make the subject-sample for the new Atlas material (the addi-tional concepts to yield a 1,000 total) comparable with that already obtained in Phases I and II, the subjects will also be young males of junior high school equivalence. Because of the large number of concepts to be included in the Atlas, relatively small subsets of subjects (25–30 in a group) will be used for subsets of the concepts (probably about 50, handled in two sessions). For comparison purposes, and for only a subset of the total 1,000 concepts, a mature adult "elite" sample will also be taken. As the Atlas is extended to nonliterate subject groups, it is anticipated that again the subject and concept sample will have to be somewhat modified. The *concept-sample* will include: (a) the basic set of 100 substantives used in Phases I and II, these being "nouns" selected as culture-fair and readily translatable; (b) an additional 500 lexical items (Fries Types I–IV words, e.g., nouns, adjectives, verbs, and adverbs and their functional equivalents in other languages) selected on the basis of frequency-of-usage across language/culture groups (using Thorndike-Lorge type lists for printed material where available, or collecting such data ourselves); and (c) 400 additional concepts selected by the local and foreign staff to tap basic abstractions (life, death, past, present, future, freedom, deity, privacy, law, nation, marriage, disease, health, etc.), occupational stereotypes (farmer, doctor, teacher, soldier, policeman, student, cook, politician, and so forth), national stereotypes (a representative and large sam-ple of nation-names), and various symbols for racial, religious, and other human groupings. The *scale-sample* for Atlas purposes will be the final 15–18 scale form for each language/culture group resulting from the pan-cultural factor analyses of Phase II.

General procedure

The Atlas of Affective Meanings will be organized as sections of tables, each section introduced by some text describing the nature of the tables, how the data were obtained, and some of their possible uses. In order to facilitate expansion as new language/culture groups are added, we plan to make the Atlas loose-leaf in format. Whether this should be printed and published, or simply mimeographed for private distribution, will be decided later when we have a better idea of what the demand for it might be. As presently planned, the sections of the Atlas will be:

(1) tables of qualifiers given to each of the 100 substantives with frequency greater than one, listed in order of frequency;

(2) the over-all qualifier distribution characteristics for each group—log-normal functions, means, and sigmas;

(3) H-indices and H-ranks for the 200 highest H qualifiers;

(4) H-indices and H-ranks for the 100 substantives used as elicitors;

(5) scale vectors (loadings) in the three-factor space, based on unique factorization (not pan-cultural) for each group;

(6) scale vectors in the three-space defined by pan-cultural factors;

(7) the generalized Semantic Differential (15–18 scale) recommended for use in each language, based on pan-cultural factorizations;

(8) localizations (factor scores), polarizations (distances from origin) and clustering (all other concepts falling within a sphere of constant radial distance, e.g., $D = 2.00$, centered on each concept) of all 1,000 concepts;

(9) distributions of concepts in octants of the space, as derived from above;

(10) other psycholinguistic indices, e.g., Noble's, 1952 m values, tables of associative overlap based on Noble's sequential association procedure).

THE NEED FOR AN ADEQUATE MEASURE OF DENOTATIVE MEANING

The research reported above all involves what has been termed the "semantic differential" technique in one form or another. It is now abundantly clear that this method taps only one, restricted (albeit pragmatically important) aspect of meaning. Another important aspect of meaning—indeed, that with which linguists, lexicographers and philosophers have been most concerned—is what I shall call *denotative meaning*. By "denotative" I refer to the descriptive use of signs as contrasted with their emotive or affective use, which appears to be tapped by the semantic differential technique. It is this denotative aspect which leads one to conclude intuitively that *"nail* is more similar to *pebble* than it is to *mouse*," the aspect which presumably underlies the labelling confusions that we regularly observe in anomic aphasics ("That is a . . . *pipe*—no; a . . . *match*—no; it's a . . . *cigarette*—yes, a *cigarette!*") and also the semantic slips of normals ("Patty, where are the pliers—no, I mean nailclippers!").

The problem comes out clearly in the verbal-behavior laboratory when we try to account fully for the phenomena of mediated (or semantic) generalization; associative bonds between training and test words account for a part of the variance and affective or connotative similarity as indexed by the semantic differential for another part, but there is still a large chunk of variance unaccounted for, and it presumably is that due to what we are calling denotative similarity. An adequate measure should reflect the multidimensional nature of meaning, should yield a quantitative measure of degrees of denotative similarity, should be completely general for all pairs of terms measured, and should meet the usual criteria of reliability, validity, and comparability across subjects and concepts.

Linguistic componential analysis, as applied to restricted semantic domains like kin-terms, provides only a partial answer—precisely because the components appropriate to one area (e.g., male-female, older-younger, blood-marital relation, etc., as applied to kinship) prove to be completely irrelevant to another (e.g., utensils or foodstuffs or modes of transportation). The semantic differential, as usually applied, reflects affective or connotative similarities, but clearly fails to reflect denotative similarities in any consistent fashion (e.g., pairs of terms like *nurse* and *sincerity* or *rabbit* and *melody* or *fate* and *quicksand* may have almost identical locations in affective space).

However, one recent direction of our methodological research holds out some promise. To the question, "Is a *baby large* or *small?*" most people respond *small*. To the question, "Is a railroad *spike large* or *small?*" most people say *large*. Within the class of human organisms, a baby *is* a *small* one, and within the class of nails, a spike *is* a *large* one. The usual semantic differential technique, in which a single stimulus is judged successively on a series of scales, tends to draw out these within-class connotations of signs. In all other psychophysical methods, including the so-called absolute judgment methods, a series of different stimuli (e.g., weights, tones, brightnesses, etc.) are judged against a single scale at a time. Note that if the question becomes, "Is a *baby larger or smaller* than a *spike?*" everyone says *larger*. The general hypothesis, then, is that if a series of concepts, falling into different implicit classes, is judged comparatively on single semantic differential scales one at a time, the scales will tend to be used denotatively to the extent that they have denotative properties. By assessing the dimensionality of the scale-space under these conditions we may be able to generate a denotative semantic space. Such a space will certainly contain many more factors than the affective semantic space. Furthermore, the distances between concepts within this space may provide a usable quantitative index of denotative similarity. The development of a satisfactory quantitative measure of denotative meaning appears to me to be one of the most important problems for contemporary psycholinguistics.

SPECULATIONS CONCERNING GENERALITY

When this research was begun over a decade ago, I had expected that the dimensions of the semantic space would correspond to the ways in which the sensory nervous system divides up the world, e.g., there would be visual brightness, hue and saturation factors, auditory loudness and pitch factors, olfactory factors, and so on. (This result would have been in flat contradiction to my own mediation theory of meaning—according to which meanings are anticipatory portions of the *reactions* we make to signs—although this did not occur to me at the time.) However, the Evaluation, Potency, and Activity dimensions which have reappeared in analysis after analysis are clearly responsive-like in character rather than sensory.

But these factors are more than simply reactive; they have an *affective* character. The similarity of these factors to Wundt's three dimensions of feeling—pleasantness, strain, and excitement—has been suggested by others.

The highly generalized nature of the affective reaction system—the fact that it is independent of any particular sensory modality and yet participates with all of them—appears to be the psychological basis for the universality of three factors of Evaluation, Potency, and Activity, as well as the basis for synesthesia and metaphor. That is, it appears to be *because* such diverse sensory experiences as a *white* circle (rather than black), a *straight* line (rather than crooked), a *rising* melody (rather than a falling one), a *sweet* taste (rather than a sour one), a *caressing* touch (rather than an irritating scratch) can all share a common affective meaning that one can easily and lawfully translate from one modality into another in synesthesia and metaphor. The labelling of this shared affective response is apparently uncovered in the factor analysis of adjectives.

Speculating still further, I would suggest that this affective meaning system is intimately related to the nonspecific projection mechanisms from the hypothalamic, reticular, or limbic systems and their cortical connections in the frontal lobes. Both are gross, nondiscriminative, but highly generalized systems, and both are associated with the emotional purposive and motivational dynamics of the organism. As yet, only some incidental and entirely inadequate evidence on aphasics supports this last speculation. In a study of a small sample of aphasiac patients, it was found that despite gross disturbances in labelling, sequencing, and other denotative and grammatical tasks, these patients seemed to have no impairment in appropriate affect and made synesthetic judgments essentially like normals on a pictorial (nonverbal) form of the semantic differential.

NOTES

[1] I wish to express my thanks for the contributions of many colleagues, both at Illinois and in many countries around the world, to this cooperative research.

[2] From January, 1960, to the present writing, April, 1963, this research has been supported entirely by the Human Ecology Fund, and we here express our gratitude for this assistance.

[3] Phase I actually terminated with a correlational and factorial analysis of the interrelationships among these scales when they are judged against each other (rather than used in differentiating concepts), but since these analyses merely confirm later, more rigorous, tests of the generality hypothesis they will be omitted from this report.

REFERENCES CITED

CLIFF, N.
    1959   Adverbs as multipliers. Psychological Review 66:27–44.
GOODENOUGH, W.
    1956   Componential analysis and the study of meaning. Language 32:155–216.
KUMATA, H.
    1957   A factor analytic investigation of the generality of semantic structure across two
            selected cultures. Unpublished Ph.D. dissertation, University of Illinois.
LEES, R. B.
    1953   The basis of glottochronology. Language 29:113–127.
LOUNSBURY, F. G.
    1956   A semantic analysis of the Pawnee kinship usage. Language 32:158–194.
MURDOCK, G. P.
    1949   Social structure. New York, Macmillan.
NOBLE, C. E.
    1952   An analysis of meaning. Psychological Review 59:421–430.
OSGOOD, C. E.
    1960   The cross-cultural generality of visual-verbal synesthetic tendencies. Behavioral
            Science 5:146–169.
OSGOOD, C. E., S. SAPORTA, and J. C. NUNNALLY
    1956   Evaluative assertion analysis. Litera 3:47–102.
OSGOOD, C. E., G. J. SUCI, and P. H. TANNENBAUM.
    1957   The measurement of meaning. Urbana, Illinois, University of Illinois Press.
SUCI, G. J.
    1960   A comparison of semantic structures in American Southwest culture groups. Journal
            of Abnormal and Social Psychology 61:25–30.
SWADESH, M.
    1950   Salish internal relationships. International Journal of American Linguistics 16:157–
            167.
TRIANDIS, H. C. and C. E. OSGOOD.
    1958   A comparative factorial analysis of semantic structures in monolingual Greek and
            American college students. Journal of Abnormal and Social Psychology 57:187–196.

Part VI

DEVELOPMENTAL STUDIES

26. The Development of Children's Terms

Susan M. Ervin and Garrett Foster

CHILDREN frequently confuse the names for physical dimensions. If two objects differ in size, they may say one is STRONGER than the other. If they differ in weight, one may be called BIGGER than the other. This is, of course, just what one would expect in the early stages of learning if size, weight, and strength are empirically correlated.

Osgood, Suci, and Tannenbaum (1957) have found correlations of a similar sort in examining the structure of meanings measured by semantic differential scales. Three factors have been found repeatedly—Evaluation, Potency, and Activity. Little attention has been given to the development or origin of these factors. Inspection of the scales defining each factor suggests that two conditions would create correlations. One is verbal conjunction; if whatever is said to be GOOD is also said to be FAIR the scales will be correlated through verbal associations. Secondly, "ecological co-variation" (Brunswik, 1947) exists for certain sensory dimensions. We would thus expect BIG, HEAVY, and STRONG to be correlated for all cultural groups.

It is clear that adults can discriminate the sensory dimensions that children confuse verbally. On the semantic differential, however, they are normally asked to extend terms metaphorically, as in judging the size and weight of FREE PRESS or EDUCATION. Even on the semantic differential, the correlation of size and weight scales can be destroyed by inclusion of items like DIAMOND and MIST where a check with sense experience is possible and the usual trait correlation is reversed. To the extent that the semantic differential reflects covariation in experience of traits that are logically independent, we would expect that there would be an increase with age in denotative discrimination of the terms that are

Reprinted from *Journal of Abnormal and Social Psychology* (1960), 61: 271–275, by permission of the authors and the American Psychological Association.

correlated on the differential. In the following study, age changes in children's verbal confusions are examined.

The more highly correlated two attributes are, the less probable are encounters with discrepant instances. It is useful to note three different variants on this situation. One category may constitute a subclass of a larger category. Thus, if 98% of a child's encounters with men, in which there is direct address or verbal reference to a man, involve his father, we would expect that the child might at first call all adult males DADDY. Discrepant instances would at first be too few for a differentiation to take place. If there were two adult males in the family such an extension would be unlikely. Thus Leopold (1939) noted that while his daughter called all men PAPA, women had individual names and there was no word for FRAU.

The subclass of a hierarchy of classes is actually an extreme instance of the second variant of correlation, a partial overlap of two classes. The degree of correlation or overlap should predict the probability of two terms being confused. Thus, communism and atheism might be confused by those unaware of discrepancies such as religious communist settlements. From a matrix showing the probability of being right in applying the term COMMUNIST to an atheist, we can see that the higher the correlation of the two terms, the greater the probability of being right, and the greater the likelihood that the two ideologies are called by one term. There are other features that enter into the failure to differentiate terms. One is the relative size of the two categories. If there are more atheists than communists, one is more likely to be wrong in calling an atheist a COMMUNIST than calling a communist an ATHEIST. The extreme case would be that in which the whole size of the class of communists is equal to the overlapping class. That is, for example, all communists are atheists but the reverse is not true. This case is identical with the one cited earlier of hierarchical classes.

Other relevant factors are the perceptibility of an attribute or class, the consequences of correct and incorrect class discrimination (which may not be the same for the classes involved), the frequency of the terms in usage, and degree of logical independence.

If the dimensions of reference are continuous attributes rather than classes, then the relation may be described by a scatterplot rather than a matrix of frequencies. The same observations apply; the probability of being correct in saying that a bigger object is HEAVIER is a function of the attribute correlations.

In adult speakers of English, the differentiation of the attributes weight, size, and strength is such that if speakers can make appropriate tests, they are unlikely to say that the heavier of two like-sized objects is BIGGER. There are, however, situations in which the attribute extension in this simple physical case is appropriate. One is in the situation of prediction, where a value on one attribute only is known. Then it becomes useful to be able to predict the probable value on the other attribute. The second situation is one in which metaphor is exploited in verbal or pictorial communication, and one attribute may be used to suggest another.

Thus, we would expect that correlated attributes would appear in experienced speakers' usage, in situations of prediction and metaphorical extension, but not in denotation where the evidence for attribute discrimination is available.

In new learners, however, one term may apply to both attributes, which are not in fact discriminated, or both terms may appear as interchangeable synonyms for the two undiscriminated attributes.

In the following study two semantic differential factors, Evaluation and Potency, are presented as far as possible in conditions requiring denotative discrimination of three attribute expressions of each. A reduction with age is predicted with respect to the use of the wrong terms when a difference in only one attribute of the correlated set is present.

METHOD

Subjects. There were two groups of Ss, a group of 16 male and 17 female first grade children, and a group of 18 male and 18 female sixth graders. Both groups were from the same school in a lower socioeconomic Negro

district. To reduce variability, the extremely bright and extremely dull children were excluded, the criterion being the teacher's rating in the first grade, and deviations of 20 points from the norm on available IQ tests in the sixth grade.

Materials. In Part I of the experiment, materials were selected to vary successively three of the dimensions on Osgood's potency factor. These three dimensions—weight, strength, and size—had been found to have loadings of .62 with the rotated factor analysis, involving concepts rated against scales, and coordinates of 1.68, 1.81, and 1.76, respectively, on another analysis of scales judged against scales. These were the largest components of the factor in each case.

The objects used were: (*a*) opaque salt shakers identical but for weight, (*b*) opaque jars identical but for weight, (*c*) cork balls differing in size, (*d*) sterofoam balls differing in size, (*e*) a pair of insulated wires with the wire removed from the middle third of one, leaving it flexible, and (*f*) a dry sponge and a damp one matched in size.

In Part II drawings of a girl's face were used to represent three of four dimensions representing Osgood's evaluative factor. The pictured dimensions were CLEAN-DIRTY, HAPPY-SAD, and PRETTY-UGLY. A fourth was included in the questioning: GOOD-BAD. These had loadings, respectively, of .82, .76, .86 (BEAUTIFUL-UGLY), and .88, and coordinates of 2.38, 2.09, 2.40, 2.29 on the first factor.

Procedure. All of the Ss were individually tested with the following questions:

I would like to ask you some questions and you can give me the correct answers... OK? [For first graders:] It's kind of a game and lots of fun. First I'm going to ask about these objects. [2 objects contrasting in weight put in subject's hands.] Is one of these heavier and one lighter or are they both the same weight? [If says different] Which is heavier? Is one black and one white or are they both the same color? Is one bigger and one smaller or are they both the same size? [If says different] Which is bigger? Is one stronger and one weaker or are they both the same strength? [If says different] Which is stronger?

If the child failed to indicate the item that was heavier on the first question, he was eliminated from the rest of Part I. The second question, to which the answer was "the same" was to control set. A similar series of questions was asked about all the items, starting with the actual contrast as a screening question. One of the six possible key questions was omitted, concerning perception of weight in objects differing in size. If weight in the objects were controlled, the smaller object might be called heavier on the grounds of its scale weight. Because of the ambiguity of the term HEAVY applied to objects differing in size, the question was omitted.

In the analysis the percentages were computed over the whole set of responses, which included two for each question for each child because of the double set of materials. The Ns used in the significance tests were for the actual number of children tested.

In Part II a similar procedure was followed, with the control question "Does one picture have red hair and one black hair or are they both the same?" The questions and pictures were rotated, with every fourth question a control question.

RESULTS

In Table 1 it can be seen that between 39 and 66% of the first-grade children offered contaminated responses for the various dimensions of the physical materials. In the sixth grade the proportion was reduced to a range between 20 and 44%. While none of the individual changes in percentage was significant, there was a reduction for every comparison, including the subgroups by sex. A sign test is significant at the .01 level. The dimension that changes the least is the response that the heavier object is STRONGER; this is also the statement of highest frequency at both ages for both sexes. Since strength is less evident than weight, it is possible that this particular inference would continue in adult *S*s. The inference that a bigger object is STRONGER is next in probability, supporting the notion that it is the inferred character of strength that is involved. Size is least often presented as a contaminated response, and it is also the most obvious.

It might be thought that the reduction in the sixth grade is due to a tendency to be more careful about differentiating at all, and thus to an increase in *same* responses. This was not the case. While the percentage of reversals was relatively low, it increased in the sixth grade. This increase occurred in stating that the heavier was SMALLER, that the stronger was SMALLER and LIGHTER. In the latter case these frequencies probably arise because a wet sponge is usually larger, and contains water.

Only boys gave the last reversal, 22% of the boys in the sixth grade saying the stronger was LIGHTER, and no girls. Nine percent of the boys and 28% of the girls said the stronger was SMALLER. In the last case this was a larger proportion than those saying it was larger. It might be argued, then, that the reduction in the last two cases was due to sophistication with respect to one of the objects used.

On the study of the evaluative dimension using faces, almost no reversals occurred at either age. The age differences on Table 2 are striking. It may be noted that they do not occur markedly on three cases. Two of these refer to CLEAN. The frequency of children saying one child was CLEANER than the other for the other attributes was small at both ages. Clean may be said to be the most visible of the attributes. In fact it could be argued that it is the only one with a clear-cut physical criterion.

The third instance of lack of marked change was one in which the proportions were very high at both ages. The smiling face was said to be PRETTIER.

With the CLEANER dimension excluded, the range in the first grade is between 42 and 97% offering a contaminated response. The highest are those offering the smiling face as more GOOD and the cleaner face as PRETTIER. All of the first grade boys gave these responses. In the sixth grade the range is between 14 and 75% with the highest now being the smiling face which is seen as PRETTIER about as often as it was in the first grade. Thus, there is a shift in responses as with the physical attributes, but it is markedly different for the different attributes.

TABLE 1
PROPORTION ASCRIBING CORRELATED ATTRIBUTE DIFFERENCES TO OBJECTS

Stimulus Differences	Response	First Grade			Sixth Grade			
		Boys	Girls	Total	Boys	Girls	Total	Differences
Heavy	BIG	40.6	36.0[a]	38.6[a]	16.7	25.0	20.8	17.8
Strong	BIG	31.2	52.0	39.7	30.6	25.0	27.8	11.9
Strong	HEAVY	37.5	46.2	41.4	33.3	33.3	33.3	8.0
Big	STRONG	50.0	53.8	51.7	36.1	38.9	37.5	14.2
Heavy	STRONG	56.2	76.9	65.5	41.7	47.2	44.4	21.1
	N[b]	16	13	28	18	18	36	

[a] The number of cases in this cell is reduced by one due to loss of data.

[b] The *S*s reported were those who correctly differentiated the stimulus attribute for all three attributes on all materials.

TABLE 2
<small>PROPORTION ASCRIBING CORRELATED ATTRIBUTE DIFFERENCES TO FACES</small>

Stimulus Differences	Response	First Grade			Sixth Grade			Differ-ences
		Boys	Girls	Total	Boys	Girls	Total	
Happy	CLEAN	12.5	5.9	9.1	0.0	11.1	5.6	3.5
Pretty	CLEAN	28.6	7.7	18.5	5.6	5.6	5.6	12.9
Clean	HAPPY	37.5	47.0	42.4	5.6	22.2	13.9	28.5*
Pretty	HAPPY	85.7	91.7	88.5	67.1	38.9	50.0	38.5*
Clean	PRETTY	100.0	82.4	90.9	50.0	50.0	50.0	40.9*
Happy	PRETTY	81.2	82.4	81.8	83.3	66.7	75.0	6.8
Clean	GOOD	50.0	70.6	60.6	27.8	33.3	30.6	30.0*
Happy	GOOD	100.0	94.1	97.0	77.8	55.6	66.7	30.3*
Pretty	GOOD	78.6	50.0	65.4	44.4	22.2	33.3	32.0*
	N^a	16	17	33	18	18	36	

^a Changes in N due to failure to name stimulus difference correctly: first-grade boys for PRETTY stimulus 14, girls 12; sixth-grade boys, 17, and girls, 16.
* Significant at the .01 level.

DISCUSSION

The slight rate of change with respect to discrimination of physical dimensions suggests the kind of learning to be expected where the criteria are most obvious.

With the personal attributes the findings are both more extreme and more uneven. It is clear that the only term of those used which designates a simple visible trait—CLEAN—is the one seldom offered to describe any other attribute. This finding agrees with the fact that BIG, the most obvious physical attribute, was less often used with the physical materials to describe other differences.

The other evaluative dimensions refer to more complex traits that are not entirely logically independent. PRETTY may also be said to designate a physical characteristic, but one that adults use both as a constant and a temporary trait, so that a clean smiling face might be deemed prettier than a dirty or frowning one. Thus, while the traits are discriminable they are not independent in the sense that the physical traits are.

HAPPY was used to designate a smiling face, but as children learn the use of the term they may find that it refers to a state of feeling only partially correlated with external evidence. Thus even the smiling–nonsmiling distinction might bear only an imperfect relation to the term HAPPY. One of the largest changes was in the use of HAPPY in describing the prettier girl, and the drop was most extreme in girls—a drop of 53%. The children were from the start, especially the boys, only moderately likely to describe the cleaner girl as HAPPIER.

One possible reason for a drop in the ascription of terms to a correlated difference is a change in metaphorical treatment of pictures. Occasionally children would refuse to say that both children were the same in hair color, but said that one had red and one black hair. The hair in the drawing was white, that is, not filled in in the black-and-white outline picture. Younger children, used to story-book imagination, may be less literal about what is on the page. While this might account for the increase in *same* responses with age, it does not predict the direction of the ascription, by the first graders, which was in no case in the opposite direction from that predicted.

Does the failure to differentiate on this test imply that the children use the terms as virtual synonyms for an undifferentiated referent? With respect to the physical dimensions, only one child was so extreme as to use the same terms interchangeably for all three attributes on all the materials. But if we examine the faces test and omit CLEAN which seems to fall out of the pattern, it appears that 62% of the children used HAPPY-GOOD-PRETTY synonymously, in the first grade.

We would like to argue that the factors that appear as clusters of correlated terms in the semantic differential studies of adults derive from empirical correlations of attributes. They could, of course, be linked purely by verbal associations, as in "He's a good clean player."

If this were the case, differentiation of reference might still be accompanied by semantic differential correlations, since many of the terms on the semantic differential can be applied to the "concept" only metaphorically. DEMOCRACY is clean, fragrant, and sweet only in the poetic sense.

While verbal associations may be one source of such dimensions, we are proposing that the history of concept development in the child provides another source. What remains as a connotative, metaphorical relationship in adults may in many cases start as denotative nondifferentiation. In a sense, the child might be said to acquire first a concept, for instance, of "big-strong-heavy . . ." in other words, a potency referent. The terms he applies to this referent may variously be BIG, STRONG, HEAVY. He may prefer one of these terms for people, another for boats, another for baseballs. Presumably he will only come to differentiate the terms and apply them appropriately to different stimulus dimensions when uncorrelated instances occur and he is corrected, or hears others differentiate the terms. By chance, the sample he selects may have a 100% correlation and he may not encounter errors immediately.

SUMMARY

The physical dimensions of size, weight, and strength are empirically correlated. If the correlation delays discrimination of these attributes as referents for descriptive terms, then younger children should more often use incorrect terms to describe differences between objects. The terms GOOD, PRETTY, CLEAN, and HAPPY should also be used as synonyms prior to differentiation.

A set of materials was prepared in which size, weight, and strength were independently varied in pairs of objects. First-grade children more often than sixth graders said that the pairs of objects differed on other dimensions in addition to the attribute actually contrasted. In a set of pictures of faces, over half of the youngest children treated GOOD, PRETTY, and HAPPY as interchangeable synonyms. The proportion dropped markedly with age. The more easily identified traits, such as the referents of BIG and CLEAN, were least often confused with other attributes.

The results are interpreted as showing that attributes which have metaphorical and connotative links in adult usage, may be denotatively confused at first. The factors found by Osgood on the semantic differential studies of verbal meaning may actually be the referents for several terms used as synonyms, prior to differentiation of finer distinctions between attributes.

REFERENCES

BRUNSWIK, E. *Systematic and representative design of psychological experiments.* Berkeley: Univer. California Press, 1947.

LEOPOLD, W. F. *The speech development of a bilingual child.* Evanston, Ill.: Northwestern Univer. Press, 1939–50.

OSGOOD, C. E., SUCI, G. J., & TANNENBAUM, P. H. *The measurement of meaning.* Urbana: Univer. Illinois Press, 1957.

27. Ontogenetic Change in the Meaning of Concepts as Measured by the Semantic Differential

Howard E. Maltz

An area of extremely high promise in the study of cognitive functioning of children is semantics. A tool which has had widespread use in this field recently is Osgood's semantic differential. The application of this instrument to the investigation of the meaning of concepts to children, however, has been neglected (1).

The semantic differential was developed in concordance with the theory of a conceptual space delimited by a set number of axes representing dimensions along which meaning can be said to vary. With respect to these axes, any given concept can be placed. Empirical evidence indicates that semantic space is defined by three axes, evaluative, potency, and activity (4).

The meaning of concepts as represented by their position in semantic space has been shown to differ from individual to individual and from culture to culture (2). Taking into account the vast amount of work done on the developmental change of cognitive functioning in children (e.g., Piaget [5]), it seems highly probable that a similar systematic variation should be found between age levels. The primary purpose of the present study is to determine whether the connotative meanings of concepts, as measured by the semantic differential, change as the child gets older.

It is important in a study of this type to take into consideration the relative novelty and lack of refinement characteristic of semantic differential and the untried context in which it is being used. With respect to the first consideration, this instrument is, and will be for some time, in a constant state of modification and redefinition of applicability (3). Accordingly, the experimenter runs the risk of having his results limited by some newly formulated modification. With respect to the second consideration, semantic differential was developed from research with adults in an English speaking society. There is little evidence to allow one to presuppose conclusively that a model measuring the meaning of concepts in adults is also applicable to children. Hence, the present study takes on a second, and perhaps even more important, purpose than the original one. It is a pilot study attempting to establish whether semantic differential can be used as a true measure of meaning for a wide range of age groups.

Reprinted from *Child Development* (1963), 34: 667–674, by permission of the author and the publisher. Copyright © 1963 by The Society for Research in Child Development, Inc.

METHOD

Instrument

In practical application, the semantic space generated by the semantic differential is arrived at by having individuals rate the concepts along graded scales, each having polar (opposite in meaning) adjectives as end points. Three orthogonal cuts through semantic space are generated by using scales which are representative of the three independent factors: evaluative (k'_1), potency (k'_2), activity (k'_3). These axes all meet at one point, the origin, designated here as "meaninglessness" and represented by the midpoints of the scales.

The scales used in this study are: good-bad (k_1), clean-dirty (k_2), pretty-ugly (k_3), hard-soft (k_4), strong-weak (k_5), large-small (k_6), fast-slow (k_7), hot-cold (k_8), sharp-dull (k_9). In choosing the scales, consideration was given to their weighting on the three factors, their relevancy to the concepts being tested, and their likelihood of being understood by young children. With respect to the first criterion, scales k_1, k_2, k_3 are weighted heavily on the evaluative factor; scales k_4, k_5, k_6 are weighted heavily on the potency factor; scales k_7, k_8, k_9 are weighted heavily on the activity factor. These weightings were determined in previous research (4).

The concepts that were rated are: candy (m_1), sun (m_2), friend (m_3), school (m_4), fire (m_5), kitten (m_6), ghost (m_7). Insofar as could be anticipated, each concept has a unitary meaning for any one individual and all seven were familiar to the youngest children tested. The latter was ascertained by noting the presence of the concepts in a widely used second-grade reader.

To apply semantic differential to grade school children, several modifications of Osgood's original scale had to be effected. The major change made was the use of a five-step scale as opposed to a seven-step scale. A young child may be expected to experience difficulty with something as complex as seven alternatives against which to judge a concept (4). In addition, the adverbs, "very," "somewhat," and "not," were used to define the five alternatives. These appear synonymous with those originally used by Osgood, yet are more easily understood by young children. Finally, the definitive adjectives were printed directly below the appropriate alternatives to make the format of the scales clear to the young children. A model scale is shown below:

:	:	:	:	:	:
VERY	SOMEWHAT	NOT +	SOMEWHAT	VERY	
+	+	NOT −	−	−	

In scoring the differential, the values, +2, +1, 0, −1, and −2, were assigned to the respective gradients going from positive pole to negative pole.

Subjects

Samples from four school grades were tested: second grade, fourth grade, sixth grade, college. The second-, fourth-, and sixth-grade *S*s attended a grammar school in Burlington, Vermont, considered to be representative of the population. The college *S*s were enrolled in a General Psychology class at the University of Vermont.

The number of *S*s in each grade level respectively was 17, 25, 26, and 23.

Procedure

The *S*s in the grade school were tested one at a time; those in college were tested five at a time. *S* was told that he was going to play a word game in which he would be rating a set of words on scales according to what the words meant to him. He was told to go as fast or as slow as he wished and to ask questions at any time. All second-graders and some fourth-graders were made to read the scales aloud as they proceeded. The *S*s appeared to understand the task very well. An occasional difficulty came up with some of the younger *S*s but these were easily cleared up by further explanation.

In the presentation of the semantic differential, each of the seven concepts in turn was rated along the nine scales. For the grade school children, the concepts were printed on separate index cards and the scales on separate sheets of paper. The scales were handed to *S* one at a time and were turned over after each judgment was made. This was done to reduce what Osgood considers "halo effect" or the influencing of subsequent judgments by *S* having before him choices which he had made previously. The technique with college students differed in that the concepts were printed on a blackboard one at a time and the scales were presented on separate pages in booklets.

The polarity of the scales was randomized so that the positive pole did not always appear on *S*'s left and the negative pole on *S*'s right. The order of scales was also randomized so that it differed for all concepts. The form of the test was the same from subject to subject, however.

In an attempt to support some of the results of semantic differential, another test was administered to each age group a week or more after completion of the semantic differential. This was Rowan's method of triads (4). The seven concepts tested on semantic differential were arranged in all possible combinations of three, forming 35 triads in all. *S* was given a booklet consisting of 35 pages with one triad printed on each. His task was to draw a circle around the two most similar words. Osgood suggests that the probability of two words not being chosen together may be expected to be highly related to the distance, in semantic space, between concepts as measured by the semantic differential. This suggestion was made on the basis of studies by Rowan and Wilson (4).

TABLE I

SEMANTIC DIFFERENTIAL FACTOR MEANS AND STANDARD DEVIATIONS FOR EACH CONCEPT

	k'_1 Evaluative		k'_2 Potency		k'_3 Activity	
Concepts	Mean	SD	Mean	SD	Mean	SD
m_1 Candy						
2nd grade	.88	1.76	— .06	1.33	— .73	.93
4th grade	.97	1.07	— .03	.94	— .23	.75
6th grade	.99	.93	— .05	.73	— .06	.69
College	.78	1.13	— .20	.69	.10	.51
m_2 Sun						
2nd grade	1.00	1.07	1.16	1.14	.35	1.61
4th grade	1.24	.85	1.19	1.04	.43	1.35
6th grade	1.27	.81	.94	1.29	.73	1.18
College	1.71	.62	1.00	1.14	.86	1.08
m_3 Friend						
2nd grade	1.00	1.03	.04	1.04	— .10	.97
4th grade	1.17	.81	.31	.84	.19	.73
6th grade	1.12	.83	.29	.75	.28	.66
College	1.29	.83	.61	.94	.64	.77
m_4 School						
2nd grade	1.08	1.15	1.41	.94	— .29	1.09
4th grade	1.33	.85	.97	.89	.13	.75
6th grade	1.01	1.08	.81	.80	.08	.83
College	1.13	.72	.88	.73	.41	.77
m_5 Fire						
2nd grade	— .61	1.30	.51	1.15	.88	1.40
4th grade	— .51	1.11	.60	1.04	1.07	1.06
6th grade	.09	1.19	.36	1.01	1.10	.98
College	.12	1.14	.77	1.03	1.46	.77
m_6 Kitten						
2nd grade	1.02	1.16	.98	1.20	— .06	1.22
4th grade	1.29	.69	— .77	1.14	.32	.64
6th grade	1.21	.88	—1.10	.90	.56	.95
College	1.04	.87	—1.28	.66	.46	.91
m_7 Ghost						
2nd grade	— .96	1.30	— .20	1.30	.02	1.28
4th grade	— .37	.99	— .05	.97	.15	.82
6th grade	— .41	1.19	— .14	1.10	.01	1.11
College	— .19	.89	— .23	.95	— .10	.96

RESULTS

In original form, the semantic differential generates a three-dimensional matrix of scores: subjects (n) by concepts (m) by scales (k). When the individual scores are averaged over subjects and the scale scores are averaged over factors (k'), an m by k' matrix is obtained. This was done for each grade level. Table 1 represents the means and standard deviations of such a matrix for the various grades.

To test the significance of difference in the meanings of the concepts between any two grades for each of the factors, chi square tests were employed. Table 2 presents the chi square values of those tests that were significant beyond the .05 level of confidence. Table 3 presents the total number of significant differences between each combination of two grades.

By comparing the second grade with each of the remaining grades, or by comparing the college group with each of the remaining grades, it may be seen that the greater the age difference the greater the number of significant values. The change in the meaning of concepts thus appears to be a function of age difference.

It can be seen from Table 1 that the standard deviations of the second-grade judgments are quite a bit higher than those of the other groups. An analysis of variance test of the standard deviations was done for each factor. This was treated as a mixed model analysis with concepts as the random variable, and grade levels fixed. The F values reported apply to grade levels. For the evaluative factor F is 11.76; for the potency factor F is 5.42; for the activity factor F is 9.00. In each instance, the results are significant beyond the .01 level of confidence.

On applying Tukey's gap test for each factor, it was found that the relatively high standard deviations of the second grade are the primary cause for each of the significant values obtained in the analysis of variance. It can be concluded from this that, on the average, factor-concept standard deviations of the youngest Ss are significantly higher than those for the older Ss.

The above analyses were done taking for granted the assumptions underlying the semantic differential. To ascertain whether the three dimensions of semantic space are independent of each other for the data of the present study, a matrix of correlation coefficients relating scale scores with scale scores was computed for each grade. If the factors are truly independent, the correlation coefficients between scales of the same factor should be significantly higher than those between scales of different factors. One-tailed median tests were applied. In each instance, results significant at the .05 level of confidence were obtained. This demonstrates the measuring of a common factor by scales purporting to measure that factor and the independence of those scales within one factor from the others outside it.

A comparison was made between the semantic differential data and the

TABLE 2

CHI SQUARE VALUES* OF THE DIFFERENCES BETWEEN GRADE PAIRS FOR EACH CONCEPT-FACTOR COMBINATION

	GRADE		PAIRS			
Concept-Factor[†]	2nd–4th	2nd–6th	2nd–Coll.	4th–6th	4th–Coll.	6th–Coll.
m_1 *Candy*						
k'_1	....	....	....	....	....	....
k'_2	....	....	....	....	....	....
k'_3	14.82	20.62	20.33	....	....	....
m_2 *Sun*						
k'_1	....	....	17.06	....	15.54	14.02
k'_2	....	....	....	....	....	....
k'_3	....	....	....	....	7.09	....
m_3 *Friend*						
k'_1	....	....	....	....	....	....
k'_2	....	....	4.13	....	....	....
k'_3	....	....	10.76	....	6.96	6.89
m_4 *School*						
k'_1	....	....	....	....	5.84	....
k'_2	16.23	34.50	32.77	....	....	....
k'_3	9.88	5.56	5.24	....	5.44	9.34
m_5 *Fire*						
k'_1	....	8.63	8.85	4.89	5.20	....
k'_2	....	....	....	....	....	....
k'_3	....	....	....	....	....	....
m_6 *Kitten*						
k'_1	....	....	....	....	....	....
k'_2	....	....	....	....	10.95	....
k'_3	....	5.37	4.14	....	....	....
m_7 *Ghost*						
k'_1	6.26	8.11	9.86	....	....	....
k'_2	....	....	....	....	....	....
k'_3	....	....	....	....	....	....

* Only those values significant beyond the .05 level are given.

† k'_1 evaluative factor, k'_2 potency factor, k'_3 activity factor.

data from the triad method. For each grade level, empirical distances between concepts (D) were calculated from the former, and the probabilities of each pair of concepts not being chosen as most similar with respect to the other five ($1 - p$) were calculated from the latter.

TABLE 3

NUMBER OF SIGNIFICANT FACTOR-CONCEPT
CHI SQUARE VALUES FOR EACH GRADE PAIR

	Second	Fourth	Sixth	College
Second	—			
Fourth	4	—		
Sixth	6	1	—	
College ...	9	7	3	—

Reliability coefficients for both of these measures were determined at each grade level by dividing Ss into two groups. For the D measure the coefficients are $+.86$, $+.94$, $+.87$, and $+.96$ for the second, fourth, sixth, and college grades, respectively; for the $(1 - p)$ measure the coefficients are $+.90$, $+.96$, $+.90$, and $+.91$.

The correlation coefficients between D^2 and $(1 - p)$ are $+.03$, $+.30$, $+.11$, and $+.38$ for the second, fourth, sixth, and college grades, respectively. These are extremely low values to arrive at in comparing two groups of data which should be related to each other quite highly. A rationale for this discrepancy is suggested by close inspection of the data. In a great number of instances where D^2 is low and $(1 - p)$ is high, it is found that the two concepts are similar along two factors in semantic space but differ along the third. Conversely, where D^2 is high and $(1 - p)$ is low, it is found that the two concepts differ along two factors but are relatively equivalent with respect to the third. This gives weight to the hypothesis that different categories of concepts have, as a basis of their meaning, a dominant characteristic. Perhaps the three dimensions of semantic space do not always contribute equally under practical circumstances.

DISCUSSION

It is shown in this study that the semantic differential measures a change in the meaning of concepts to the child as he grows older. This change is a progressive one in that it becomes more apparent the greater the difference in age between the two groups compared. An interesting fact to consider here is that of all the concepts tested, "school" underwent the greatest quantitative change between age levels, especially for Ss in grades 2, 4, and 6. This could be due to the fact that the child's perception of school is continually changing as a result of new experiences with that stimulus situation.

It is also demonstrated that the standard deviations of concept judgments within factors are significantly higher for the youngest children tested than they are for any of the older groups. These results imply that the meaning of concepts to younger children is not as consistent as it is to older ones.

The age at which the meaning of concepts takes on this consistency seems to be reached sometime before the fourth grade level is attained in school. It would be interesting to attempt a more precise definition of the time at which this conceptual consistency becomes apparent and investigate the causes of this phenomenon.

The fact that the results are what would logically be expected gives the semantic differential, as used in this study, an aura of validity. However, the attempt to support this instrument by use of the triad method met with little success. As was implied earlier, further work must be done to refine the semantic differential in this "child development" context before more conclusive results can be obtained. In a recent article (3), it was shown that a single semantic differential model is not universally applicable to all classes of concepts. Perhaps this is the major source of error in this study.

The investigation of conceptual development of children is an area of extremely high potential. The results of this study show the ease with which semantic differential can be made structurally applicable to children and indicate a high degree of sensitivity of semantic differential to the ontogenetic changes in the meaning of concepts. It is foreseeable in the near future, with the use of an experimentally modified and refined semantic differential, that the question of how conceptual processes develop will be studied in a more quantitative and objective light than is possible at the present time.

SUMMARY

A modified form of semantic differential was given to Ss from four age levels: second grade, fourth grade, sixth grade, college. The task consisted of seven concepts being rated along nine scales.

It is shown that the connotative meaning of the concepts, as measured by the semantic differential, changes with age in such a way that the change becomes more apparent as the age difference becomes greater. It is also concluded that the meaning of concepts is less consistent in the youngest children than in the others.

It is suggested that, although it may need further modification, semantic differential is a useful and valid instrument for measuring the meaning of concepts to children.

REFERENCES

1. CHURCH, J. *Language and the discovery of reality.* Random House, 1961.
2. MACLAY, H., & WARE, E. E. Cross cultural use of the semantic differential. *Behavioral Sci.,* 1961, 6, 185-190.
3. OSGOOD, C. E. Generality of affective meaning systems. *Amer. Psychologist,* 1962, 17, 10-28.
4. OSGOOD, C. E., SUCI, G. J., & TANNENBAUM, P. H. *The measurement of meaning.* Univer. of Illinois Press, 1957.
5. PIAGET, J. *The language and thought of the child.* Meridian Books, 1955.

28. Developmental Patterns
in the Use of Modifiers
as Modes of Conceptualization

Francis J. Di Vesta

As the first phase of a systematic investigation of the development of affective meaning systems, modifiers were elicited from 100 Ss in each of grades 2–6. The standardized procedure was a restricted word-association task requiring S to respond with a single modifier for each of 100 substantives. The frequency and diversity of each modifier were summarized. Each substantive and modifier was described by an index combining frequency and diversity. A list of modifiers, for applications in semantic differential scales, was selected according to the criteria of frequency of occurrence, diversity of usage, and independence from other modifiers. Essential agreement in the usage of modifiers across grade levels was found. Differences among age groups existed in the manner in which substantives were qualified. Modifiers having higher values on the frequency-diversity index were those representing the evaluative and potency dimensions, followed by those representing the color and activity dimensions. Developmental trends in the characteristics of modifiers and substantives were described.

The representational processes functioning in meaningful behavior account for much of the variety in the child's behavior. Self-evoked verbalizations can result in the control of his own behavior or that of others, whether control is consciously intended or not, for good or for ill. Communications from others in his environment can be used to control the child's behavior by associations of whatever meanings have already been acquired for the language symbols. The symbolic processes predispose the child to respond in accordance with the semantic link between verbal sign and meaning. New words with mediating properties may be acquired by transferring meanings from signs to signs or from things to signs through predication (Mowrer, 1960) or assertion (Osgood, Suci, & Tannenbaum, 1957). The impressions the child gains of others, his reactions of approach or avoidance, his acquisitions of generalizations or distinctiveness among stimuli, and a multitudinous variety of usually adaptive responses to the environment are economically facilitated without the necessity of direct experience.

An understanding of this process requires the definition of the operations to be used in identifying idiosyncratic definitions of meanings. In this

Reprinted from *Child Development* (1965), 36: 185–213, by permission of the author and the publisher. Copyright © 1965 by The Society for Research in Child Development, Inc.

regard, Osgood et al. (1957) have noted that responses to the question, "What are some of the things that (concept or event) makes you think of?" are quite different from those to the question, "What does that (concept or event) mean to you?" Associates elicited by the first question may be substantives, opposites, adjectives, or other grammatical forms. The latter question results in the evocation of a statement usually containing modifiers. For example, when a person is asked to describe the meaning of an event or concept he typically employs modifiers like "large," "smooth," "active," and "repulsive." Since the child's language fluency is limited and since the data obtained in introspective reports are not easily quantified, the desirability of objective measurement procedures is evident.

The semantic differential permits one solution in the use of linguistic encoding as an index of meaning. The child is provided with a number of pairs of verbal opposites representing the meaning dimensions. If each pair encloses a seven-point scale, the child indicates not only whether the adjective applies to a concept being judged but also the intensity of the judgment made.

The theoretical framework of semantic differentiation and consequent research in the measurement of meaning have been reported in detail elsewhere (e.g., Osgood et al., 1957; Osgood, 1962). The productivity and utility of the rationale for research on the learning process and psycholinguistics require little elaboration. It is noteworthy that the majority of the investigations, however, have used adult and adolescent subjects.

In the study of meaningful behavior, the highly developed verbal skills of the person at adolescence and maturity may make it potentially difficult to isolate variables involved in the experimental study of the associative processes. The investigator soon becomes aware of the complex, and often uncontrolled, interrelationships in symbolic mediation that may confound the effects of the variables being studied. These are illustrated, in part, by the familiar learning-how-to-learn and warm-up effects described by Spiker (1956). (While these two variables can be controlled adequately by appropriate experimental design, regardless of whether the experiment is conducted with children or with adults, the nature of the development of these two processes is in itself a legitimate area of investigation.)

As serious in its consequences in research with children is the fact that the associative strengths of the verbal stimuli and their arrangement in an hierarchical order, with but few expections, are based on normative data for college sophomores. It is unlikely that these norms are directly applicable to adult populations outside of the college population and much less likely that they are applicable to children.

Other complicating variables include the nature of the effective mediating processes used by children compared to those used by adults. The effective mediators may be cued differentially for the two groups by the nature of the associative norms used, for examples, those norms based on pronunciability ratings, associative meaning, associative relatedness, or connotative meaning; and by the nature of the formal stimulus attributes of the verbal unit. Other effective mediators are based on the previous experience of the subject concerning the nature of the task and the intent of the experimenter. These include the more or less sophisticated hypotheses related to modes of learning.

The efficacy of the study of verbal learning in children is well documented. The utility of normative data on the language habits of children in a variety of situations has been aptly summarized by Palermo (1963). There is, at present, sufficient evidence indicating need for, and potential usefulness of, normative data regarding the affective meaning systems at various stages of development in conducting experiments on the verbal behavior of children. Representative of such research is that conducted by Ervin (1960), Eisman (1955), Di Vesta (1962), Osipow (1960), Di Vesta and Stover (1962), Kagan, Hosken, and Watson (1961), Castaneda, Fahel, and Odom (1961), Downing, Moed, and Wight (1961), Small (1957), Sievers (1956), and McCullers (1963).

Small (1957) has studied the factorial composition of meaning in children by borrowing scales from the study of meaning by Osgood et al. (1957). However, as these investigators indicate, the factor analysis is limited both by the scales used for ratings and by the concepts rated. If scales for the semantic differential are deliberately selected to represent the evaluative, potency, and activity factors there is a possibility that these same factors will emerge from ratings performed on these scales. A systematic study of the generality of affective meaning systems at the earlier (childhood) developmental levels requires, initially, a study of children's use of qualifiers. The employment of adult norms of semantic meaning in studies of the verbal behavior of children would appear, on the surface, to be of limited value. The variables affecting the verbal behavior of the adult population presumably would be reflected in the studies of children. Similarly, the selection of the scales based on the judgments of adult investigators or subjects has the potential of forcing factorial equivalence, where none existed, between the structure of the adult's and the child's language habits.

Accordingly, the purpose of the present study was to conduct a systematic investigation of the modes of qualifying used by children at five age levels. A restricted word-association task was used to elicit a sample of modifiers from children in each of grades 2–6. However, even the smallest number of modifiers from any one grade would be too large to use in the construction of semantic differential scales. The primary need was to select a relatively small number of unique qualifiers that simultaneously represented the major affective dimensions. The criteria employed for selecting words from this pool of responses were as follows: (a) the adjective should occur frequently in word associations; (b) the adjective should apply to a diversity of substantives; and (c) the use of the adjective should be relatively independent of other adjectives. The results of the analyses related to the data for modifiers and for substantives, where appropriate, are presented below. The statistical characteristics of the adjectives provide an objective basis for selecting adjectives to be used in measuring the development of the semantic aspects of the affective domain. In addition, they may be used to suggest the course of development of language skills in the use of modifiers (see Carroll, 1939).

METHOD

Subjects

There were 633 Ss used in the study. They came from two suburban elementary schools in a predominantly middle-class district. To facilitate the analysis, Ss were rejected to achieve an N of 100 in each age group about equally divided between the two schools. Rejection was accomplished as follows: 15 Ss from the second grade; 4 from the third grade; 8 from the fourth grade; and 6 from the sixth grade. The extra fourth-grade Ss were rejected at random. The Ss in the remaining grades were rejected as indicated below. The number of Ss in each grade with the means and standard deviations of their chronological ages are presented in Table 1. While Ss were sampled according to grade level, groups will be described interchangeably either by grade *or* by their average age.

The Stimulus List

The elicitation of adjectives was conducted by using a stimulus list of 100 familiar nouns compiled by Osgood, Archer, and Miron (1962) for use in the cross-cultural study of affective meaning systems. The list of words had been selected by these investigators from an original list of 200 substantives. The screening was accomplished by eliminating terms that were diffuse, vague, ambiguous, or culture bound. Further screening was based on variability, productiveness, and degree to which the words could be translated into other languages. The terminal list of 100 nouns was intended to contain items that would have a high yield of diverse modifiers in the elicitation procedure. The list of substantives is reproduced in Tables 9 and 10 of this report.

Procedure for Elicitation of Adjectives

A standardized word-association procedure restricted to the elicitation of modifiers was conducted on an individual basis for all Ss in the second, third, and fourth grades and for 50 Ss in the fifth grade. The remaining 50 Ss in the fifth grade and all Ss in the sixth grade were administered the stimulus list in groups.

The instructions, in brief, to all Ss were as follows:

TABLE 1

MEANS AND STANDARD DEVIATIONS OF Ss' CHRONOLOGICAL AGES
IN EACH OF THE GRADES 2–6

| | SCHOOL A | | | SCHOOL B | | |
GRADE	N	Mean[a]	SD[b]	N	Mean[a]	SD[b]
2.....	47	7–9	3.78	53	7–9	5.16
3.....	55	8–6	3.60	45	8–8	4.87
4.....	56	9–5	3.61	44	9–6	6.90
5.....	62	10–6	4.92	38	10–6	4.80
6.....	43	11–7	2.95	57	11–6	4.08

[a]Means are in years and months.
[b]Standard deviations are in months.

We are going to play a word game that I am sure you are going to like. This is the way the game is played. I am going to say a word and I want you to say another word that tells something about my word; that is, I want you to tell me a word that goes along with mine. Sometimes these words are called adjectives. Let's practice with a few words. The first word is "butterfly." Tell me a word that describes "butterfly," a word that explains or tells something about "butterfly." If you can't think of a word right away try putting it into a sentence like this: [S is shown a card] "A(n) _____ butterfly"; or "A butterfly is _____." You could say, for example, "The *beautiful* butterfly," or "The butterfly is *beautiful*," "The *small* butterfly," or "The butterfly is *small*." Are there other words you can use to tell about a butterfly? Let us try some other words. [The same procedure is followed for other words including racing car, face, bang, stove, bug, and so on until the S appeared familiar and at ease with the procedure.]

Remember, I want only *one* word. Sometimes you will not know the meaning of my word or may never have heard the word I give you. If this happens, tell me whatever word seems to you to fit the sound of my word. In every case give the first word that you can think of that can be used to explain or tell something about my word. Don't think too much about the word. I want you to give me the word that *you* think goes along best with my word, *not* one that you think I want. It makes no difference what word you answer with as long as it is the word you feel is the best one you know for my word.

The instructions were the same for both individual and group administrations. To restrict associations to the modifier form, each substantive was placed in a frame, thus, "The _____ (noun)." In the individual administrations E read the frame while S read his copy and then E recorded the response. If S did not answer with a legitimate modifier E asked for another response. No more than two responses were required in such circumstances. The first adjective was the one used in the analysis. If more than 10 per cent of an S's responses to the nouns required two responses, his paper was rejected from the analysis.

In the group administrations one E read the instructions and then read each frame individually. The Ss responded to the stimulus by writing their answers. Two other Es circulated among the Ss to answer questions and to ascertain whether adjectives were being used. In each class where group administrations were conducted a few Ss did not understand the directions, were unable to write, or were unable to use adjectives. The aim of efficiency in the procedure prevented giving these Ss more than nominal attention during the gathering of data; accordingly their papers were eliminated in the analysis.

All modifiers were carefully screened, and unclear modifiers and clear non-modifiers were eliminated. The general rule used was that the modifier should fit the frame, "A _____ house is a house that is _____." All unique modifiers were tabulated. Grammatical inflections of modifiers with the same root were combined in tabulating the results. While it is recognized that participles are legitimate members of the class of modifiers, they were eliminated since it was not clear whether children were using them as verbs or as modifiers. Furthermore, in pilot studies conducted concurrently with the present one it was noted that the children were unable to provide opposites to the participles.

Analysis

The raw data consisted of the number of times each unique modifier was associated with each substantive. For each modifier three indices were calculated to describe the modifier and later to be the basis for the selection of modifiers for semantic differential scales. These indices were: (a) the over-all frequency of occurrence of each modifier; (b) the number of substantives modified (diversity) by an adjective; and (c) a joint index of diversity and frequency, the entropy index H. Only the H ranks of the substantives are to be presented. The calculation of these indices and other analyses used will be described in more detail below.

The selection of qualifiers meeting the criterion of independence of usage was handled via the uncorrected ϕ-coefficient. The procedure was employed by first ranking all modifiers within a grade from high to low H rank. This ranking (see Tables 2–6) provided the order of priority for the calculations. The distributional overlap of a modifier with each modifier of higher rank was compared by using a fourfold table. The table was divided as follows: number of substantives qualified by modifier A but not by modifier B; number of substantives qualified by both A and B; number of substantives qualified by B but not by A; and number of substantives qualified by neither A nor B. If the modifier was *not* significantly correlated with any of those with larger H values, it was retained. Any modifier significantly correlated with any one of those above it was eliminated in favor of that with the higher H-value. The critical ϕ-coefficient was 0.29, which represents the value required for significance at the .005 level. Osgood et al. (1962) indicate that the limiting features of the ϕ-coefficient under ordinary usage becomes an attribute when used in the manner described. That is, the marginal totals become considerably smaller as one proceeds further into the ranks of modifiers with lower H values. Accordingly, the marginals for many of the calculations are disparate. Under these conditions the maximum ϕ progressively decreases. This is a desirable characteristic here since it places a more conservative estimate on the degree of correlation, minimizing the chance factor.

RESULTS

Characteristics of Modifiers

The characteristics of the unique modifiers as described in the subsections immediately below are based on the data in Tables 2–6. These tables summarize the frequency of occurrence, the diversity, and the H values for the top 100 modifiers, in each age level, ordered[1] according to the magnitude of H.

Frequency of occurrence.[2]—This is a basic descriptive index of the modifiers elicited. It is simply a straightforward count of the number of times a specific word appeared in the total of 10,000 responses elicited at each age level. The obviously discernible trend from these data is that the same modifiers appear as those most frequently used at all age levels. Among these are modifiers representative of all dimensions comprising the factorial structure of meaning discovered with adult groups. However, differences among age groups are to be found in frequency data for the more popular modifiers; thus, for example, the general use of *good* or *bad* is inversely related to the developmental level of the group. Conversely, modifiers that are less popular within the 7-year-old group are used progressively more often by children in the older age groups, as illustrated by the data for the modifiers "tiny," "delicious," "sharp," and "faithful." In no instance are the latter trends as striking as the former. The data for the less popular adjectives represent the effects of numerous individual-differences variables affecting vocabulary growth, such as training, intellectual growth rates, socioeconomic class, and other environmental and personality factors, including chance factors.

[1] In Tables 2–6 the words within grades are ranked according to the values of H. However, the reader will note that there are a number of words with the same H value but with different ranks. Where the diversity and frequency of two or more words are identical, they should, indeed, be ranked the same since their H values would be the same. However, this is a relatively infrequent occurrence. To conserve space, our original data, which were carried out to eight decimal places, are rounded off to three decimal places. The number before each qualifier represents its rank in 100 based upon the H value before rounding. It was decided not to assign tied ranks to those few words that had exactly the same H value, although these can be easily determined by the reader and adjustments made if desired. All correlations and means involving the use of H are based on the original data.

[2] The occurrence frequencies of every qualifier made to each substantive are summarized, by grade, in another report (Di Vesta, 1964c). It is available from the author or may be obtained on loan by addressing the Interlibrary Loan Librarian, Pattee Library, The Pennsylvania State University, University Park, Pa. 16802.

Diversity.—The second basic index used in describing the elicited modifiers is the measure of diversity. This measure is obtained by a count of the number of nouns to which an adjective was applied. Since 100 substantives were used, the diversity is never more than 100. Frequency of occurrence has been ignored in deriving this measure. Thus, both *sad* and *tan*, each with a diversity of 10 (see Table 2), were elicited to ten different nouns, but "sad" was used 3.1 times on the average for each noun while "tan" was used 1.2 times. The trends for diversity are much like those for frequency. The diversity of the modifiers most popular in the early grades tends to decrease over developmental levels while that for the less popular modifiers tends to increase. The number of modifiers used to define the list of substantives appears to be extended at the upper-age levels when compared to the lower-age range.

Index of diversity-frequency.—The entropy (*H*) score, used as a basis for ordering the modifiers, combines into a single index the characteristics of diversity and frequency.[3] The formula for partial *H*, employed in this analysis, is derived from the formula for conditional *H* (see, e.g., Attneave, 1959) and is interpreted in terms of uncertainty, as is the basic entropy measure. The derivation of the measure as used here and its computation are given in Osgood et al. (1962). An informal illustration may be helpful in interpreting the meaning of *H*. A high value indicates that the modifier is associated with many different substantives, that these associations are relatively equiprobable and/or that the modifier has a high frequency of occurrence. A low *H* value indicates that a modifier is associated with substantially fewer substantives, has differing probabilities of association with these substantives, and/or occurs less frequently in the responses to the substantive. For the purpose of the present study, *H* describes the extent to which a modifier is used by a sample of Ss and the application of the modifier to a wide range of substantives. Both characteristics are considered to be desirable in selecting adjectives for a generalized scale such as the semantic differential. A major assumption in selecting modifiers for this purpose is that they should be common to the vocabulary usage of the children to be employed as Ss (high frequency), and the adjectives should be applicable in the definition of a variety of concepts (wide diversity). Since *H* is an index based on the combination of diversity and frequency, the data in Tables 2–6 should be useful in experimental investigation where these properties must be controlled. They should also be useful in suggesting levels of materials for teaching language fundamentals and for reading materials appropriate to learners at given developmental levels.

[3] The index for each individual qualifier, in terms of frequency notation, is: $H = 1/N_i(n_i \log_2 n_i - \Sigma_j n_{ij} \log_2 \Sigma n_{ij})$; where N_i = the total number of all responses to all stimuli; n_{ij} = the number of Ss responding with a given qualifier to each of the stimuli; and n_i = the total frequency of a given qualifier taken over all stimuli (Osgood et al., 1962, p. 14).

TABLE 2

MODIFIER ELICITATION SUMMARY: CA 7

H Rank	Modifier	Frequency	Diversity	H	H Rank	Modifier	Frequency	Diversity	H
1.....	good[a]	1687	90	.981	51.....	noisy	29	6	.005
2.....	bad[a]	852	71	.417	52.....	short	16	10	.005
3.....	nice	717	78	.392	53.....	deep	24	6	.005
4.....	big[a]	618	86	.361	54.....	purple	15	11	.005
5.....	pretty[a]	248	46	.109	55.....	right[a]	22	8	.005
6.....	white[a]	255	37	.108	56.....	dark[a]	24	7	.005
7.....	little[a]	183	62	.097	57.....	gold (en)[a]	25	6	.005
8.....	hard[a]	224	41	.092	58.....	pink	17	9	.004
9.....	red[a]	213	26	.075	59.....	dirty[a]	13	9	.004
10.....	long[a]	185	33	.075	60.....	tan	12	10	.004
11.....	brown	177	32	.073	61.....	sad[a]	12	10	.004
12.....	blue[a]	157	22	.055	62.....	dead	12	9	.004
13.....	small	110	36	.052	63.....	lovely[a]	13	8	.003
14.....	black[a]	144	23	.052	64.....	tight	35	2	.003
15.....	round[a]	137	22	.049	65.....	brave[a]	19	6	.003
16.....	yellow	102	22	.040	66.....	shiny[a]	12	6	.003
17.....	old[a]	76	41	.036	67.....	true[a]	12	6	.003
18.....	hot[a]	151	13	.034	68.....	sweet	12	6	.003
19.....	new[a]	62	46	.033	69.....	kind[a]	11	6	.003
20.....	awful	74	28	.033	70.....	tiny[a]	8	8	.003
21.....	green	93	21	.031	71.....	helpful	9	7	.002
22.....	tall[a]	95	14	.030	72.....	rotten[a]	9	6	.002
23.....	strong[a]	83	21	.029	73.....	thick	10	6	.002
24.....	wonderful[a]	57	35	.028	74.....	scary[a]	10	5	.002
25.....	wet[a]	107	17	.026	75.....	thin[a]	7	7	.002

356

Table 2 – *Continued*

No.	Modifier			
26.....	beautiful	57	26	.024
27.....	funny[a]	77	20	.022
28.....	cold	81	14	.022
29.....	soft	52	21	.020
30.....	happy[a]	42	24	.018
31.....	gray	62	14	.018
32.....	terrible	45	19	.018
33.....	bright	72	8	.016
34.....	great	33	30	.016
35.....	loud[a]	97	7	.015
36.....	fat	30	17	.012
37.....	fast[a]	34	13	.010
38.....	orange	26	16	.010
39.....	fine[a]	24	18	.010
40.....	heavy[a]	29	13	.010
41.....	high	26	14	.009
42.....	horrible[a]	24	15	.009
43.....	dangerous	30	9	.008
44.....	warm	36	11	.008
45.....	mean[a]	21	13	.007
46.....	light	21	11	.007
47.....	mad	31	10	.006
48.....	colorful	19	12	.006
49.....	bright	21	10	.006
50.....	large	16	13	.006
76.....	naughty[a]	7	7	.002
77.....	gentle	7	7	.002
78.....	clear	12	4	.002
79.....	easy	9	5	.002
80.....	painful	8	5	.002
81.....	useful	7	5	.002
82.....	delicious[a]	7	6	.002
83.....	healthy	6	3	.002
84.....	handsome	10	3	.001
85.....	clean[a]	10	3	.001
86.....	loose	13	5	.001
87.....	smart[a]	6	3	.001
88.....	free	14	4	.001
89.....	busy	7	3	.001
90.....	first[a]	13	3	.001
91.....	quiet	22	5	.001
92.....	powerful	5	5	.001
93.....	young[a]	6	4	.001
94.....	out	6	4	.001
95.....	juicy[a]	8	3	.001
96.....	scarlet	5	4	.001
97.....	hungry[a]	10	3	.001
98.....	ugly	6	3	.001
99.....	guilty[a]	6	3	.001
100.....	poison (ous)	7	3	.001

[a] Modifiers selected according to the criterion of independence of meaning.

357

TABLE 3

MODIFIER ELICITATION SUMMARY: CA 8

H Rank	Modifier	Frequency	Diversity	H	H Rank	Modifier	Frequency	Diversity	H
1	good[a]	1600	85	.922	51	soft	25	9	.007
2	big[a]	888	93	.547	52	dark[a]	31	8	.007
3	bad[a]	993	77	.522	53	kind	26	8	.007
4	nice	580	73	.317	54	high	22	10	.007
5	little	244	81	.141	55	true	23	7	.006
6	pretty[a]	298	40	.131	56	orange[a]	23	10	.005
7	long[a]	257	37	.111	57	mad	24	8	.005
8	hard[a]	210	45	.086	58	dangerous	21	8	.005
9	small[a]	143	55	.075	59	shiny	20	7	.005
10	red	193	27	.071	60	tasty[a]	16	9	.005
11	white[a]	147	32	.063	61	wrong[a]	14	10	.004
12	blue	166	24	.060	62	rotten	15	8	.004
13	awful	108	35	.052	63	wide	14	9	.004
14	black[a]	128	30	.049	64	angry[a]	13	9	.004
15	wonderful[a]	103	37	.049	65	helpful	12	10	.004
16	funny[a]	121	37	.047	66	noisy[a]	15	7	.004
17	yellow	100	28	.038	67	light[a]	11	10	.004
18	brown	92	20	.035	68	clean	16	6	.003
19	beautiful	71	34	.032	69	easy[a]	12	7	.003
20	green	75	22	.028	70	warm[a]	24	6	.003
21	large[a]	48	36	.024	71	giant	10	8	.003
22	round	64	20	.023	72	thick[a]	10	7	.003
23	tall[a]	82	14	.023	73	gold (en)[a]	10	7	.003
24	strong[a]	73	21	.023	74	same	8	8	.002
25	hot[a]	127	9	.023	75	excellent	8	8	.002

TABLE 3—Continued

Rank	Modifier			Prop.	Rank	Modifier			Prop.
26	great[a]	52	26	.023	76	tiny	9	7	.002
27	bright[a]	87	11	.022	77	pink[a]	11	5	.002
28	happy	51	23	.021	78	delicious[a]	9	6	.002
29	right	53	26	.021	79	ugly	8	6	.002
30	horrible	42	25	.019	80	clear[a]	9	5	.002
31	old	43	25	.018	81	thin[a]	7	6	.002
32	new[a]	40	26	.018	82	different	7	5	.002
33	terrible	41	21	.017	83	full	8	4	.002
34	short	37	24	.016	84	quiet[a]	18	4	.002
35	gray	53	12	.015	85	scarlet[a]	8	6	.002
36	fast[a]	40	15	.014	86	skinny[a]	6	6	.002
37	mean[a]	33	14	.012	87	lovely	6	6	.002
38	sad[a]	29	17	.011	88	merry	6	4	.002
39	fat	30	14	.011	89	silver (y)[a]	13	5	.002
40	smart	27	16	.010	90	dead	6	4	.001
41	dirty	31	13	.010	91	wiggly	7	4	.001
42	loud[a]	76	6	.010	92	brave[a]	22	3	.001
43	wet[a]	53	8	.010	93	sick	5	5	.001
44	real[a]	32	15	.010	94	whole	6	4	.001
45	deep[a]	35	9	.009	95	weak	6	4	.001
46	cold	36	7	.008	96	honest[a]	6	4	.001
47	purple	20	16	.008	97	poison (ous)	6	4	.001
48	first	35	11	.008	98	silly	5	4	.001
49	colorful (ed)	24	12	.007	99	tan	5	4	.001
50	heavy[a]	22	11	.007	100	lovable[a]	5	4	.001

[a] Modifiers selected according to the criterion of independence of meaning.

TABLE 4
MODIFIER ELICITATION SUMMARY: CA 9

H Rank	Modifier	Frequency	Diversity	H	H Rank	Modifier	Frequency	Diversity	H
1	good[a]	1263	73	.700	51	cold[a]	27	8	.007
2	big[a]	988	96	.614	52	delicious	33	5	.007
3	bad	679	67	.336	53	wet[a]	45	6	.007
4	nice	426	61	.217	54	gold	22	7	.005
5	small	258	77	.148	55	colorful	18	9	.005
6	long[a]	323	45	.142	56	first[a]	28	9	.005
7	little[a]	176	70	.100	57	true[a]	19	8	.005
8	great[a]	186	53	.097	58	giant[a]	16	10	.005
9	pretty[a]	238	35	.096	59	right[a]	21	8	.005
10	large[a]	171	65	.096	60	terrific[a]	14	11	.005
11	hard[a]	223	42	.089	61	brave	29	7	.004
12	wonderful	146	37	.069	62	clean[a]	14	10	.004
13	strong[a]	155	32	.060	63	sweet[a]	15	8	.004
14	red[a]	146	28	.058	64	clear	23	5	.004
15	awful[a]	123	34	.056	65	dark	19	5	.004
16	beautiful	116	31	.050	66	orange	21	7	.004
17	white	120	24	.048	67	fast[a]	13	8	.004
18	blue	108	22	.040	68	wrong[a]	13	8	.004
19	funny[a]	92	32	.034	69	helpful[a]	12	9	.004
20	terrible	73	27	.033	70	bloody[a]	21	7	.004
21	round[a]	83	19	.029	71	warm[a]	31	5	.004
22	black[a]	100	14	.027	72	deep	14	7	.004
23	hot	121	11	.027	73	tiny	15	6	.003
24	old[a]	53	35	.025	74	rotten[a]	18	4	.003
25	loud[a]	132	7	.024	75	fresh	14	6	.003

TABLE 4—*Continued*

No.	Modifier				No.	Modifier			
26	brown	65	20	.024	76	lucky	10	9	.003
27	yellow[a]	58	20	.023	77	strange	10	9	.003
28	new[a]	45	33	.022	78	honest	17	5	.003
29	happy	60	18	.021	79	easy	11	7	.003
30	bright	90	8	.020	80	silver	17	6	.003
31	short[a]	42	27	.019	81	high[a]	9	6	.002
32	tall[a]	73	11	.018	82	different[a]	8	7	.002
33	soft[a]	41	19	.015	83	light	8	7	.002
34	green	46	15	.015	84	wide	16	4	.002
35	sad	39	20	.015	85	purple	10	5	.002
36	mean	38	16	.014	86	shiny	10	5	.002
37	heavy[a]	41	15	.014	87	tasty	12	4	.002
38	horrible	32	19	.013	88	handsome	10	5	.002
39	dirty	33	16	.012	89	tight[a]	30	2	.002
40	huge[a]	30	17	.012	90	painful	7	6	.002
41	gray	44	9	.011	91	poor	7	6	.002
42	fat	23	18	.009	92	full[a]	15	3	.002
43	kind	31	11	.008	93	gay	9	4	.002
44	smart	23	13	.008	94	thin	7	5	.002
45	dangerous	29	10	.008	95	quiet	15	4	.002
46	mad	39	8	.007	96	noisy	13	3	.002
47	real	31	12	.007	97	slippery[a]	12	3	.002
48	ugly[a]	21	14	.007	98	young	6	3	.001
49	lovely	22	11	.007	99	cute[a]	7	5	.001
50	thick	30	7	.007	100	sore	7	4	.001

[a] Modifiers selected according to the criterion of independence of meaning.

TABLE 5
MODIFIER ELICITATION SUMMARY: CA 10

H Rank	Modifier	Frequency	Diversity	H	H Rank	Modifier	Frequency	Diversity	H
1....	good[a]	811	73	.450	51....	tiny[a]	23	14	.008
2....	big[a]	455	86	.272	52....	colorful	25	10	.007
3....	bad[a]	387	61	.194	53....	orange	24	11	.007
4....	nice	257	41	.120	54....	lovely	24	12	.007
5....	small	185	57	.098	55....	thick	22	9	.006
6....	long[a]	217	39	.096	56....	fat	18	12	.006
7....	red[a]	202	30	.078	57....	clean	24	8	.006
8....	hard[a]	203	40	.077	58....	noisy	20	10	.006
9....	pretty[a]	180	34	.071	59....	mad	28	9	.005
10....	awful	146	46	.070	60....	sad[a]	20	9	.005
11....	great[a]	140	44	.069	61....	warm	28	9	.005
12....	wonderful	134	40	.065	62....	wide[a]	23	8	.005
13....	little[a]	110	58	.061	63....	deep[a]	20	6	.005
14....	strong[a]	130	33	.051	64....	dangerous[a]	18	8	.005
15....	blue	131	23	.047	65....	fine[a]	13	12	.005
16....	large[a]	93	42	.046	66....	dreadful[a]	15	9	.005
17....	beautiful	96	29	.041	67....	silver (y)[a]	18	8	.004
18....	white	103	23	.038	68....	wrong	16	8	.004
19....	brown[a]	103	21	.036	69....	true	17	7	.004
20....	terrible	82	25	.035	70....	honest	19	7	.004
21....	black	122	18	.035	71....	tremendous	12	12	.004
22....	green	88	20	.032	72....	tough	14	9	.004
23....	new	58	34	.028	73....	rich[a]	27	6	.004
24....	tall[a]	91	14	.026	74....	ugly	13	9	.004
25....	round	76	16	.024	75....	dark[a]	22	6	.004

TABLE 5—*Continued*

No.	Word			
26	loud[a]	142	6	.024
27	yellow[a]	64	19	.023
28	bright[a]	92	11	.023
29	funny[a]	78	20	.023
30	hot[a]	115	8	.022
31	short[a]	52	21	.021
32	heavy	45	29	.021
33	happy[a]	51	20	.019
34	horrible	50	20	.019
35	gray	61	13	.017
36	old	38	22	.016
37	soft[a]	39	20	.016
38	mean	38	17	.014
39	smart	40	11	.012
40	huge	28	19	.011
41	right[a]	33	15	.011
42	real	37	14	.010
43	delicious[a]	46	6	.010
44	first[a]	43	11	.010
45	helpful	30	15	.010
46	dirty[a]	26	15	.010
47	wet	50	7	.009
48	kind	31	10	.009
49	cold	35	10	.009
50	fast[a]	29	12	.009

No.	Word			
76	bloody[a]	25	5	.004
77	high[a]	15	8	.004
78	shiny	11	8	.003
79	gold (en)	12	7	.003
80	unbearable	11	8	.003
81	stupid[a]	10	9	.003
82	sweet[a]	12	7	.003
83	rotten	15	6	.003
84	purple	10	8	.003
85	easy	11	6	.003
86	enormous[a]	9	8	.003
87	hopeful[a]	9	8	.003
88	friendly[a]	10	7	.003
89	gay	11	6	.003
90	poor	12	6	.003
91	rough[a]	9	7	.002
92	dead	10	6	.002
93	swift	10	6	.002
94	sharp	11	6	.002
95	lonely	8	8	.002
96	brave[a]	28	4	.002
97	handsome	15	4	.002
98	light[a]	8	7	.002
99	tight[a]	29	2	.002
100	oval	14	4	.002

[a] Modifiers selected according to the criterion of independence of meaning.

363

TABLE 6
MODIFIER ELICITATION SUMMARY: CA 11

H Rank	Modifier	Frequency	Diversity	H	H Rank	Modifier	Frequency	Diversity	H
1....	good[a]	507	59	.269	51....	fast[a]	36	12	.009
2....	big[a]	302	77	.177	52....	rough[a]	31	12	.009
3....	bad[a]	277	55	.131	53....	tremendous[a]	24	16	.009
4....	great	258	47	.124	54....	helpful	24	15	.009
5....	small[a]	216	70	.123	55....	dark	31	12	.009
6....	large	142	48	.072	56....	cold[a]	79	8	.009
7....	wonderful	153	41	.072	57....	sad	29	12	.008
8....	long[a]	179	27	.071	58....	real	31	10	.007
9....	hard[a]	185	33	.069	59....	strange[a]	18	16	.007
10....	strong	152	38	.068	60....	wet[a]	42	6	.007
11....	nice	143	36	.067	61....	easy	22	13	.006
12....	terrible	125	30	.055	62....	tasty	29	6	.006
13....	little[a]	91	45	.046	63....	sly	20	13	.006
14....	pretty[a]	133	23	.044	64....	rotten[a]	34	6	.006
15....	red	109	24	.040	65....	dead	20	10	.006
16....	beautiful	92	27	.037	66....	faithful	20	10	.006
17....	black[a]	89	24	.033	67....	sharp[a]	23	8	.006
18....	kind	80	16	.028	68....	weak[a]	17	12	.006
19....	awful	69	24	.028	69....	smooth	23	10	.006
20....	bright[a]	115	11	.028	70....	thin	18	11	.006
21....	blue (ish)	87	19	.026	71....	clean	21	10	.006
22....	brown	72	19	.026	72....	right[a]	21	9	.006
23....	white	76	18	.024	73....	gay[a]	22	8	.006
24....	loud[a]	140	6	.024	74....	shiny[a]	20	9	.005
25....	soft	64	17	.023	75....	dangerous[a]	21	8	.005

TABLE 6—Continued

No.	Freq.	Modifier			No.	Freq.	Modifier		
26....	.023	huge	48	31	76....	.005	bloody	51	5
27....	.020	green	68	17	77....	.005	wide	17	10
28....	.019	tall[a]	68	13	78....	.005	ugly[a]	18	8
29....	.018	mean	50	16	79....	.005	painful[a]	15	11
30....	.018	happy	51	16	80....	.005	fresh	17	8
31....	.017	old	40	16	81....	.005	smart[a]	16	9
32....	.017	yellow	44	22	82....	.005	first[a]	21	6
33....	.016	true[a]	47	19	83....	.004	silver (y)	21	7
34....	.015	round[a]	43	18	84....	.004	clear[a]	23	5
35....	.014	hot[a]	69	16	85....	.004	pink[a]	19	7
36....	.014	funny[a]	57	8	86....	.004	poor	12	11
37....	.014	horrible[a]	41	10	87....	.004	hopeful[a]	14	8
38....	.014	dirty[a]	38	16	88....	.004	tough	13	9
39....	.013	deep[a]	44	16	89....	.004	unhappy	13	9
40....	.013	colorful (ed)	42	12	90....	.004	slimy	21	6
41....	.013	warm[a]	44	15	91....	.004	enormous[a]	12	9
42....	.012	heavy[a]	32	13	92....	.004	cool	16	6
43....	.011	fat[a]	30	16	93....	.004	false	13	9
44....	.011	delicious[a]	51	18	94....	.004	harsh	15	7
45....	.011	short[a]	31	7	95....	.003	sorrowful	12	8
46....	.011	lovely	29	16	96....	.003	orange[a]	13	7
47....	.011	tiny	35	17	97....	.003	gentle	13	7
48....	.010	thick[a]	39	14	98....	.003	horrid	11	9
49....	.010	gray	39	10	99....	.003	stupid[a]	10	10
50....	.010	new	24	10	100....	.003	quiet[a]	12	8

[a] Modifiers selected according to the criterion of independence of meaning.

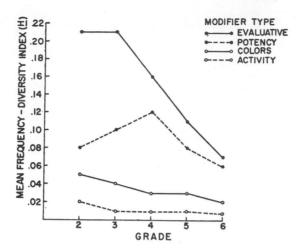

FIG. 1.—Mean *H* values for four types of modifiers at grades 2–6.

Trends in the average magnitude of the *H* value for words representing the three major factors of meaning and for words representing colors are summarized in Figure 1. The display indicates that the major changes are in the *H* values for the evaluative words and, to a lesser degree, in the words representing the potency factor.

Selection of independent modifiers.—The ϕ coefficient was selected on the assumption that the extent to which two qualifiers were applied to the same 100 substantives was an index of meaning overlap. Thus, the meaning of a word is defined by the total number of syntactical contexts in which it appears. This approach seems reasonable if the list of words used as stimuli can be considered a sampling of all possible contexts. The general procedures for the present study, in which the frame approach was employed, appear adequately to sample (i.e., within the above limitation) the syntactical environments of qualifiers (see Osgood et al., 1962, for further elaboration of this point). The uncorrelated adjectives, that is, those with relatively small amount of meaning overlap, are identified in Tables 2–6 by the superscript "a."

Summary of all modifiers.—The total number of elicited modifiers, grouped according to their diversity characteristics, is summarized in Table 7. There it may be seen that twice as many modifiers were elicited from the 11-year-old group as from the 7-year-old group. It is interesting to note that modifiers with a diversity of one (modifiers applied to only a single substantive) account for a major part of the total number of modifier-associates and include as many items at all age levels as modifiers with a diversity of 4 or over (modifiers applied to four or more substantives). All categories of diversity types progressively increase to the point where at 11 years of age the number is double that at 7 years.

Relationship between diversity and frequency.—An incidental analysis

TABLE 7

FREQUENCY OF MODIFIERS GROUPED BY DIVERSITY TYPE

| | DIVERSITY TYPE | | | | TOTAL No. |
AGE GROUP	4 and Over	3	2	1	OF WORDS
7......	118	17	44	85	264
8......	130	23	47	86	286
9......	146	24	33	103	306
10......	187	25	49	159	420
11......	245	46	104	214	609

TABLE 8

CORRELATIONS BETWEEN FREQUENCY AND DIVERSITY[a]

CA	Correlation
7........................	.81
8........................	.81
9........................	.78
10........................	.82
11........................	.84

[a] Based on responses to the top 100 H-ranked modifiers within each CA group.

was made of the correlations between diversity and frequency. This relationship for the top 100 modifiers according to H rank is summarized in Table 8. The correlations are essentially the same at all age levels and account for 65–70 per cent of the common variance. Thus, diversity covaries regularly, though not perfectly, with frequency for all groups.

Characteristics of Substantives

Analyses similar to those made for the modifiers were also made of the substantives in an effort to identify developmental trends in word complexity. A total of 100 substantives was used, as indicated above. The same substantives were used for all groups of Ss.

The frequency of associates to the substantives varies only to the degree that non-clear modifiers and clear non-modifiers were eliminated from the responses. Since the median frequency ranged from 78 to 93, the frequencies may be considered to be high and relatively homogeneous. The H value, while affected to some extent by these differences in frequencies, is, thus, primarily a reflection of diversity.

The substantives ranked according to the magnitude of H are presented in Table 9. The first rank (rank of 1) indicates the largest H (greatest number of different associates) and the last rank (rank of 100) indicates the substantive with the lowest H (least number of different associates) within an age group. Most apparent in this summary is the trend from concrete

TABLE 9

H-RANKED SUBSTANTIVES

	CA				
RANK	7	8	9	10	11
1...	hand	head	woman	woman	woman
2...	cup	cup	chair	policeman	man
3...	fish	hand	sympathy	hand	defeat
4...	chair	fish	hand	stone	fruit
5...	ear	cat	fish	father	house
6...	snake	woman	future	head	picture
7...	river	smoke	lake	fish	death
8...	cat	chair	policeman	water	meat
9...	seed	water	stone	log	horse
10...	book	root	belief	bird	anger
11...	bird	man	water	man	choice
12...	woman	moon	man	laughter	purpose
13...	rope	stone	color	sympathy	future
14...	smoke	picture	moon	lake	policeman
15...	money	power	life	hair	marriage
16...	star	book	marriage	fruit	log
17...	root	policeman	cat	color	fish
18...	window	snake	snake	music	lake
19...	lake	color	bird	ear	love
20...	egg	defeat	log	moon	father
21...	wind	husband	smoke	guilt	cat
22...	tongue	sympathy	cup	future	color
23...	log	log	horse	chair	trust
24...	color	hair	peace	death	cup
25...	girl	belief	meat	mother	truth
26...	map	life	guilt	anger	friend
27...	moon	cloud	tongue	husband	bread
28...	power	horse	courage	root	sympathy
29...	stone	love	book	house	stone
30...	cloud	lake	fruit	horse	root
31...	man	author	river	punishment	punishment
32...	policeman	house	freedom	picture	success
33...	tooth	knot	purpose	marriage	hand
34...	hair	tongue	tree	snake	bird
35...	horse	girl	love	rain	smoke
36...	water	seed	bread	meat	laughter
37...	tree	fire	need	wind	water
38...	head	money	picture	truth	hair
39...	picture	progress	music	tree	pleasure
40...	pain	egg	mother	cloud	life
41...	fire	river	fear	cup	hope
42...	thunder	peace	defeat	life	head
43...	father	purpose	death	freedom	courage
44...	fruit	star	egg	crime	story
45...	poison	map	anger	courage	husband
46...	house	tree	hair	danger	moon
47...	mother	marriage	cloud	bread	tree
48...	fear	music	rain	rope	progress
49...	purpose	freedom	root	fear	respect
50...	marriage	bread	danger	battle	ear

TABLE 9—*Continued*

H-RANKED SUBSTANTIVES

			CA		
RANK	7	8	9	10	11
51...	sun	ear	story	peace	tongue
52...	meat	courage	wind	poison	egg
53...	life	wind	ear	love	snake
54...	battle	meat	father	purpose	danger
55...	bread	story	truth	success	crime
56...	love	future	poison	pleasure	food
57...	choice	battle	husband	cat	wealth
58...	husband	rain	tooth	tongue	book
59...	music	need	head	need	freedom
60...	rain	bird	heart	doctor	money
61...	danger	hope	hunger	river	knowledge
62...	knot	tooth	seed	belief	belief
63...	author	father	star	knowledge	thief
64...	hope	fruit	money	pain	cloud
65...	need	fear	author	book	heat
66...	anger	pleasure	battle	tooth	power
67...	story	truth	trust	girl	pain
68...	death	sleep	girl	knot	battle
69...	freedom	trust	success	wealth	mother
70...	peace	choice	rope	egg	poison
71...	noise	guilt	house	progress	doctor
72...	sleep	success	knowledge	story	girl
73...	doctor	Wednesday	doctor	sleep	guilt
74...	friend	mother	knot	fire	luck
75...	heart	doctor	power	choice	peace
76...	courage	hunger	wealth	hope	rain
77...	Wednesday	laughter	sleep	smoke	need
78...	future	rope	sun	food	fear
79...	hunger	window	hope	star	sun
80...	truth	respect	pleasure	author	Wednesday
81...	pleasure	poison	noise	defeat	rope
82...	crime	anger	fire	respect	wind
83...	trust	death	progress	friend	music
84...	luck	knowledge	laughter	heart	river
85...	work	noise	choice	trust	chair
86...	heat	game	respect	money	hunger
87...	laughter	heart	heat	power	author
88...	game	danger	crime	hunger	knot
89...	thief	sun	window	heat	tooth
90...	food	friend	punishment	thief	window
91...	success	wealth	thunder	game	star
92...	punishment	crime	game	seed	fire
93...	belief	punishment	pain	map	heart
94...	progress	pain	friend	sun	map
95...	guilt	luck	food	thunder	game
96...	respect	thief	map	luck	work
97...	defeat	work	luck	window	thunder
98...	wealth	food	Wednesday	noise	noise
99...	knowledge	heat	work	Wednesday	seed
100...	sympathy	thunder	thief	work	sleep

to abstract in the ordering of the words. In the 7-year-old group, for example, 47 of the top 50 H-ranked substantives are representative of concrete concepts in the sense that they have some identifiable and tangible physical referent. In the 11-year-old group 30 of the top 50 words have clearly identifiable physical referents, whereas the remainder are mainly abstract concepts.

Another summary of these data is presented in Table 10. In that display the substantives are ranked in terms of homogeneity, based on the standard deviation of the ranks, across all grades. The substantive with a rank of 1 indicates that it appeared in about the same position for all grades, and the substantive with a rank of 100 indicates that its position varied the most across all grades. It should be noted that, in Table 10, high or low H-ranked substantives may appear at any position. For example, "game" appears in the first rank and "woman" appears in the third rank. The former, however, was ranked uniformly low ($\bar{X} = 90.4$) on the basis of its relative H value for all age groups, while the latter was ranked uniformly high ($\bar{X} = 4.2$) for all age groups. The data for substantives with rankings above 50 reflect distinct trends with age for which antecedents causing the changes may be hypothesized. Illustrations of clear-cut trends in rank among the substantives may be noted in the data for "snake" and "egg" where meanings become more common with increase in age whereas "success," "truth," and "punishment" become more idiosyncratic with an increase in age.

DISCUSSION

The present study was directed toward the application of a standard procedure in which samples of children at different age levels were used to determine their own modes of modifying substantives. The modifiers are subsequently to be used in the construction of semantic-differential scales appropriate to the range of ages in the elementary school, or, if necessary, in the construction of scales that are specific to each age group. The decision to use a restricted word-association task in the elicitation of the modifiers was based on evidence (Underwood and Schulz, 1960) that the frequency of emission of a word associate is clearly related to frequency of experience with that word.

The frequency of occurrence and diversity were jointly described by the entropy index, H, for each substantive and modifier. The magnitude of this index increases as both frequency and diversity increase and as the distribution of frequencies for each associate becomes more equal. Although H is a measure of the degree of "sameness" or stereotypy of the stimuli (substantives) or responses (modifiers) it should be noted that this measure does not directly reflect the same kind of similarity (or differences) in meaning found in the factorial composition of language based on semantic-differential ratings. Diversity, as reflected in the index, however, is a characteristic (Noble, 1952) of word associates which is highly correlated with meaning as measured by the semantic differential (Staats & Staats, 1959). While this relationship should, perhaps, not be regarded as a firm and general one, it does appear to hold for "neutral" if not for "emotional" words (Koen, 1962).

The final selection of modifiers was made from the pool of obtained modifiers, according to the characteristics of frequency, diversity, and independence. This selection has the advantage of yielding adjectives, for bipolar scales, free of the bias ordinarily imposed when adjectives are borrowed from the investigations in which adult subjects are used. These lists can be used to compile a basic set of semantic-differential scales representative of the modifiers used by children at each age level or across age levels. By inspection it can be seen that the selected modifiers provide representation of the major dimensions of meaning as reported in studies with adults. There are sufficient modifiers, common to all age groups, to provide for the construction of uniform scales across all age levels, if desired. Consistency in the use of specific modifiers is especially apparent in the adjectives occupying the upper H ranks. In other applications it may be desirable to collate scales common to all age levels plus another group of scales specific to each age level. In our initial studies using these adjectives the antonyms for constructing bipolar scales were determined by asking groups of children in each grade to provide opposites for the modifier. Our general finding was that the opposites elicited were similar to those used by adults for the word in question.

The intercorrelations (not presented here) on both frequency and diversity characteristics of the modifiers among age groups were sufficiently high to reflect considerable agreement. The resulting correlation matrices conformed reasonably to the requirements of a perfect simplex. Thus, while the data indicate an underlying structure of increasing complexity, they permit considerable confidence in the high degree of similarity of both the order and type of qualifiers appearing at each age level. Since the distributional characteristics of the associates and the underlying simplex structure representing changes in maturation are special theoretical problems, they have been discussed in separate papers (Di Vesta, 1964a, 1964b).

Although agreement in modes of qualifying is an essential requirement if one is to develop scales appropriate across grades, the converse is required of the substantive characteristics. The expectation is that considerably less agreement would exist, across grades, with regard to the manner in which the modifiers are applied to the substantives. Obviously, if all substantives were regarded (qualified) in the same way there would be little necessity in attempting to measure developmental differences in meaning. That such differences do exist is documented by the intercorrelations of the H-ranked nouns. These correlations were found to be of decreasing magnitude as the spacing of grades increased. In addition, the decrease was orderly, reflecting systematic changes again conforming to the simplex model in the application of modifiers to the substantives (Di Vesta, 1964b).

The characteristics of the H index for the substantives should be noted.

TABLE 10

The 100 Substantives Ranked by Standard Deviation of *H* Rank

RANK	NOUN	AGE GROUP					MEAN RANK	RANK SD
		7	8	9	10	11		
1...	game	88	86	92	91	95	90.4	3.14
2...	color	24	19	13	17	22	19.0	
3...	woman	12	6	1	7	1	4.2	
4...	fish	3	4	5	7	17	7.2	
5...	tree	37	46	34	39	47	40.6	
6...	log	23	23	20	9	16	18.2	
7...	doctor	73	75	73	60	71	70.4	
8...	work	85	97	99	100	96	95.4	
9...	battle	54	57	66	50	68	59.0	
10...	lake	19	30	7	14	18	17.6	7.50
11...	horse	35	28	23	30	9	25.0	
12...	luck	84	95	97	96	74	89.2	
13...	man	31	11	12	11	2	13.4	
14...	hunger	79	76	61	88	86	78.0	
15...	policeman	32	17	8	2	14	14.6	
16...	bread	55	50	36	47	27	43.0	
17...	story	67	55	51	72	44	57.8	
18...	stone	29	13	9	4	29	16.8	
19...	noise	71	85	81	98	98	86.6	
20...	hair	34	24	46	15	38	31.4	10.84
21...	Wednesday	77	73	98	99	80	85.4	
22...	heat	86	99	87	89	65	85.2	
23...	sleep	72	68	77	73	100	78.0	
24...	heart	75	87	60	84	93	79.8	
25...	hand	1	3	4	3	33	8.8	

RANK	NOUN	AGE GROUP					MEAN RANK	RANK SD
		7	8	9	10	11		
51...	pleasure	81	66	80	56	39	64.4	
52...	respect	96	80	86	82	49	78.6	
53...	snake	6	18	18	34	53	25.8	
54...	egg	20	40	44	70	52	45.2	
55...	meat	52	54	25	36	8	35.0	
56...	tooth	33	62	58	66	89	61.6	
57...	knot	62	33	74	68	88	65.0	
58...	mother	47	74	40	25	69	51.0	
59...	cat	8	5	17	57	21	21.6	
60...	peace	70	42	24	51	75	52.4	18.64
61...	bird	11	60	19	10	34	26.8	
62...	crime	82	92	88	44	55	72.2	
63...	author	63	31	65	80	87	65.2	
64...	girl	25	35	68	67	72	53.4	
65...	success	91	72	69	55	32	63.8	
66...	truth	80	67	55	38	25	53.0	
67...	ear	5	51	53	19	50	35.6	
68...	pain	40	94	93	64	67	71.6	
69...	wind	21	53	52	37	82	49.0	
70...	progress	94	39	83	71	48	67.0	20.72
71...	fruit	44	64	30	16	4	31.6	
72...	father	43	63	54	5	20	37.0	
73...	music	59	48	39	18	83	49.4	
74...	house	46	32	71	29	5	36.6	
75...	thunder	42	100	91	95	97	85.0	

TABLE 10—Continued

No.	Word						Mean	Group
26	moon	27	12	14	20	46	23.8	
27	freedom	69	49	32	43	59	50.4	
28	thief	89	96	100	90	63	87.6	
29	poison	45	81	56	52	70	60.8	
30	need	65	59	37	59	77	59.4	12.99
31	life	53	26	15	42	40	35.2	
32	cloud	30	27	47	40	64	41.6	
33	root	17	10	49	28	30	26.8	
34	water	36	9	11	8	37	20.2	
35	picture	39	14	38	32	6	25.8	
36	fear	48	65	41	49	78	56.2	
37	hope	64	61	79	76	41	64.2	
38	rain	60	53	48	35	76	55.4	
39	love	56	29	35	53	19	38.4	
40	knowledge	99	84	72	63	61	75.8	14.16
41	tongue	22	34	27	58	51	38.4	
42	cup	2	2	22	41	24	18.2	
43	marriage	50	47	16	33	15	32.2	
44	wealth	98	91	76	69	57	78.2	
45	purpose	49	43	33	54	12	38.2	
46	sun	51	89	78	94	79	78.2	
47	danger	61	83	50	46	54	59.8	
48	husband	58	21	57	27	45	41.6	
49	food	90	93	95	78	56	83.4	
50	courage	76	52	28	45	43	48.8	15.69
76	book	10	16	29	65	58	35.6	
77	fire	41	37	82	74	92	65.2	
78	head	38	1	59	6	42	29.2	
79	trust	83	69	67	85	23	65.4	
80	money	15	38	64	86	60	52.6	24.20
81	friend	74	90	94	83	26	73.4	
82	smoke	14	7	21	77	35	30.8	
83	rope	13	78	70	48	81	58.0	
84	choice	57	70	85	75	11	59.6	
85	anger	66	82	45	26	10	45.8	
86	river	7	41	31	61	84	44.8	
87	star	16	44	63	79	91	58.6	
88	future	78	56	6	22	12	34.8	
89	death	68	83	43	24	7	45.0	
90	power	28	15	75	87	66	54.2	27.82
91	guilt	95	71	26	21	73	57.2	
92	window	18	79	89	97	90	74.6	
93	map	26	45	96	93	94	70.8	
94	belief	95	25	10	62	62	50.4	
95	punishment	92	93	90	31	31	67.4	
96	laughter	87	77	84	12	36	59.2	
97	chair	4	8	2	23	85	24.4	
98	seed	9	36	62	92	99	59.6	
99	sympathy	100	22	3	13	28	33.2	—
100	defeat	97	20	42	81	3	48.6	35.59

373

A high degree of diversity may be a reflection of a relatively large number of associates resulting from breadth of experience and contextual arrangement as, for example, in the use of the word "woman." Conversely, a low degree of diversity may reflect limited or stereotyped experience with a particular concept as, for example, with the words "thief" or "poison." Regarding those concepts where there is little variation in H rank among age groups it appears to be a reasonable assumption that such concepts are formed early and probably as a result of direct, primary experience (Di Vesta, 1964b).

Other support for the validity of the H index as a basis for determining those modifiers most frequently experienced is to be found in the ordering of words with high H values. One expectation is that the simpler and more concrete substantives should possess higher H values than would the more abstract substantives. Further, this ordering of substantives should be more clear-cut in the earlier grades than in the later grades. This is found to be the case by inspection of the data in Tables 2–6. The simplest, concrete words in the second grade occupy the highest H ranks, almost without exception. In addition, intercorrelations, based on the H ranks of the 100 substantives between grade levels, as with the modifiers, form a perfect simplex. These data clearly indicate that the underlying factor of the increasing complexity of language growth is tapped by the results of the association procedure.

The change in the major dimensions represented by the modifiers at each grade level are of interest. Those modifiers having higher H values are clearly those representing the evaluative dimension, followed by potency, colors, and activity dimensions, respectively. It appears that the use of the restricted word-association task may be a more sensitive instrument for measuring changes in meaning and have more potential for this purpose than had heretofore been supposed. There is a clear-cut preponderance of the use of evaluative words in the 7- and 8-year-old subjects and a rapid (linear) decline in the use of evaluative words in the intermediate ages 9–11, inclusive. Furthermore, the H values of these words are, at all ages represented, ordered according to the magnitude of the variances accounted for by each of the factors found in adult studies, that is, the familiar evaluation, potency, and activity order.

These findings point to the expectation that we may not find differences between adult groups and the age groups studied here in the factorial structure of the meaning systems typically investigated by use of the semantic differential, that is, the affective-meaning systems. It also appears reasonable to suppose that whatever is tapped by the semantic-differential scales is likely to be developed at an age earlier than that represented here. On the other hand, we would clearly expect to find differences in the development of meanings of specific concepts or classes of concepts among age groups. The data and conclusions drawn in this study are, of course, descriptive. The hypotheses suggested or implied regarding the development of language behavior must be subjected to experimental investigation if the direct antecedents are to be identified.

REFERENCES

Attneave, F. *Application of information theory to psychology.* New York: Holt, 1959.

Castaneda, A., Fahel, Leila Snyder, and Odom, R. Associative characteristics of sixty-three adjectives and their relation to verbal paired-associate learning in children. *Child Develpm.*, 1961, **32**, 297–304.

Carroll, J. B. Determining and numerating adjectives in children's speech. *Child Develpm.*, 1939, **10**, 215–229.

Di Vesta, F. J. The effects of mediated generalization on the development of children's preferences for figures. *Child Develpm.*, 1962, **33**, 309–322.

Di Vesta, F. J., and Stover, D. O. The semantic mediation of evaluative meaning. *J. exp. Psychol.*, 1962, **64**, 467–475.

Di Vesta, F. J. The distribution of modifiers used by children in a word association task. *J. verb. Learn. verb. Behav.*, 1964, **3**, 421–427. (a)

Di Vesta, F. J. A simplex analysis of changes with age in responses to a restricted word association task. *J. verb. Learn. verb. Behav.*, 1964, **3**, 505–510. (b)

Di Vesta, F. J. Norms for modifiers used by children in a restricted word-association task. Tech. Rep. No. 9, Research Grant No. HD-00872, National Institute of Child Health and Human Development, 1964. (c)

Downing, R. W., Moed, G., and Wight, B. W. Studies of disability: a technique for measurement of psychological effects. *Child Develpm.*, 1961, **32**, 561–575.

Eisman, Bernice S. Attitude formation: the development of a color-preference response through mediated generalization. *J. abnorm. soc. Psychol.*, 1955, **50**, 321–328.

Ervin, Susan. The development of meaning in children's descriptive terms. *J. abnorm. soc. Psychol.*, 1960, **61**, 271–275.

Kagan, J., Hosken, B., and Watson, S. Child's symbolic conceptualization of parents. *Child Develpm.*, 1961, **32**, 625–636.

Koen, F. Polarization, *m*, and emotionality of words. *J. verb. Learn. verb. Behav.*, 1962, **1**, 183–187.

McCullers, J. C. An analysis of some factors underlying intralist associative transfer in paired-associate learning. *J. exp. Psychol.*, 1963, **65**, 163–168.

Mowrer, O. H. *Learning theory and the symbolic processes.* New York: Wiley, 1960.

Noble, C. E. An analysis of meaning. *Psychol. Rev.*, 1952, **59**, 421–430.

Osgood, C. E. Studies of the generality of affective meaning systems. *Amer. Psychologist*, 1962, **17**, 10–28.

Osgood, C. E., Archer, W. K., and Miron, M. S. *The cross-cultural generality of meaning systems.* Urbana: Institute of Communication Research, Univer. of Illinois, 1962. (mimeographed report.)

Osgood, C. E., Suci, G. J., and Tannenbaum, P. *The measurement of meaning.* Urbana: Univer. of Illinois Press, 1957.

Osipow, S. The effects of verbal mediation on the modification of children's attitudes. *J. educ. Psychol.*, 1960, **51**, 199–207.

Palermo, D. S. Word associations and children's verbal behavior. *Advanc. child Develpm. and Behav.*, 1963, **1**, 31–68.

Sievers, Dorothy J. Development and standardization of a test of psycholinguistic growth in preschool children. Unpublished doctoral dissertation, Univer. of Illinois, 1956.

Small, Edna R. Age and sex differences in the semantic structure of children. Unpublished doctoral dissertation, Univer. of Michigan, 1957.

Spiker, C. E. Experiments with children on the hypotheses of acquired distinctiveness and equivalence of cues. *Child Develpm.*, 1956, 27, 253–263.

Staats, A. W., and Staats, C. K. Meaning and *m*: correlated but separate. *Psychol. Rev.*, 1959, **66**, 136–144.

Underwood, B. J., and Schulz, R. W. *Meaningfulness and verbal learning.* New York: Lippincott, 1960.

29. A Developmental Study of the Semantic Structures of Children [1]

Francis J. Di Vesta

Three separate studies were conducted to investigate the development of children's affective meaning systems. Semantic differential ratings were made of 20 concepts in one study and 100 concepts in each of the other two studies by Ss in grades 2 through 7. The data were analyzed by the principal-factor solution to factor analysis and rotated by varimax and equamax routines. There was evidence for the stability of the Evaluation—Potency—Activity framework even down to the second-grade level. Progressive refinement and differentiation were evident in the unrotated principal-axes factors as reflected in the shift from a predominantly two-factor system, comprised of the Evaluation and Dynamism factors, to the three-factor EPA system.

Previous applications of the semantic differential (SD) with adults are numerous and diverse. Considerably fewer applications have been made with children as Ss. These studies are briefly reviewed here.

In one experiment (Di Vesta, 1962) it was found that positive Evaluative words used as reinforcers for a previously neutral color in a discrimination task increased the child's preference for that color. In another study (Di Vesta and Stover, 1962), it was demonstrated that positive, neutral, or negative Evaluative words associated with nonsense figures produced corresponding changes in the evaluative ratings of, and preference for,

the figures. Kagan, Hosken, and Watson (1961) found that six- and seven-year old children's SD rating of mother, father, and self verified some of the classical hypotheses regarding symbolic manifestation of the sex roles and that the Evaluative dimension is one of the primary structuring principles used in classification. Ervin and Foster (1960) had first- and sixth-grade children discriminate among materials varying on three of the scales in the Potency dimension, and among pictures of faces rated on the Evaluative dimension. The results implied that attributes which have metaphorical and connotative links in adult usage may be denotatively confused at first. Maltz (1963), compared second-, fourth-, sixth- and college-grade Ss' ratings of seven concepts on nine SD scales representing the three salient factors. Changes in ratings became more apparent as the age differences became greater. The meanings of concepts were less consistent in the youngest children than in the other groups. Downing, Moed, and Wight (1961) investigated the use of the SD for studying psychological effects of disability and institutionalization on the growth and development of children 7 to 19 years of age. Pollio (1964) found the correlation between SD ratings of a word and its primary associate

Reprinted from *Journal of Verbal Learning and Verbal Behavior* (1966), 5: 249–259, by permission of the author and Academic Press, Inc.

[1] The studies reported here were supported by grant MH2900 from the National Institute of Mental Health and grant HD00872 from the National Institute of Child Health and Human Development, United States Public Health Service. The data were collected and analyzed at Syracuse University. Certain of the analyses were made on the Iliac by the University of Illinois Statistical Service Unit and Digital Computer Laboratory. The author wishes especially to express his gratitude to Charles E. Osgood and Murray Miron for their consultation at various stages of this project.

to be significantly higher for children than for adults on the Potency factor, although no differences were found in correlations based on Evaluative and Activity ratings. Small's (1957) study[2] is the only one known to the present investigator in which a factorial study was made of children's semantic structures.

The experimental and descriptive studies mentioned above consistently support the hypothesis of generality of the major dimensions that organize the affective meaning space. Despite the variety of conditions under which the studies were conducted, the samples of scales were selected from *The Measurement of Meaning* (Osgood, Suci, and Tannenbaum, 1957) in which adult *S*s were used, or were selected on a subjective basis by the investigator, thus incorporating potential methodological artifacts in the designs. In some of the studies, other methodological weaknesses may have resulted from the use of an insufficient number of concepts, thereby failing to permit the emergence of more than three factors.

The present report summarizes the second phase of a systematic study designed to investigate the feasibility of measuring children's semantic meanings, and of the developmental emergence of children's affective meaning systems as measured by the SD. It was assumed that among the first experiences of the child within the American culture were those related to affective expression learned through the *effects* of experiences on him. The expectation was that the dominant dimension affecting the ratings of concepts would be that of Evaluation in the earlier grades, with decreasing emphasis on that dimension in the later grades. The test of this hypothesis appeared to require an approach employing adjectives actually used by children for the

construction of bipolar rating scales. Thus, a detailed analysis was made of adjectives elicited by children in response to a restricted word-association task (Di Vesta, 1964a, 1964b, 1965) in preparation for the present investigation. In addition, if developmental change in semantic differentiation was to be demonstrated, it was evident that a representative sample of concepts with a relatively wide range of difficulty should be rated by the *S*s.

A secondary hypothesis was that a simple-factor structure comprised of dimensions indexing primary sensory experiences, for example, colors, pain, and brightness, might be observed. Scales were included in the present studies which would tap a general "sensation" factor if this was as important as the attitudinal, Evaluation, dimension. However, a direct test of the existence of specific dimensions was not made, since the inclusion of a number of scales sampling each of the new hypothesized dimensions, as well as the sampling of a number of concepts denotatively related to these dimensions would be required.

In order to test the generality of the main hypothesis, factor analyses were made of data collected under three separate conditions. These studies varied from one another in the number of scales used, the specific adjectives employed in the bipolar scales, and in the number and kind of concepts rated. The three studies were conducted with different groups of children.

STUDY I

Method

Subjects. The *S*s were 100 children from each of the grades 2-6 inclusive. One half of the sample was from a city school in a lower-middle socioeconomic area. The other half of the sample was from the campus school of a state college and was representative of a middle socioeconomic area. All children within each class were administered the semantic differential scales. Data were excluded for those identified by the teacher as nonreaders (primarily in the second grade); those who marked their scales in a pattern (e.g., marking papers

---

[2] The excellent study performed by Small (1957) was brought to our attention sometime after the present study was proposed. However, as indicated in this report some features of this investigation were changed as a result.

diagonally from left to right, then right to left);
and those who omitted items on more than three
concepts. These procedures never resulted in more
than 10 Ss being excluded from a grade. In order to
facilitate analysis, other Ss were eliminated at
random in order to achieve $N = 100$ within a grade-
group. The mean ages, in months, for the grade-
groups 2 through 6 were 97.84, 111.21, 123.24,
134.68, and 144.88, respectively.

Selection of Scales. In an earlier phase of this
study, adjectives had been elicited from children in
each of the above five grade-levels but from different schools. The adjectives in this pool for each
grade were ranked according to their *H*-score, an
entropy index combining frequency and diversity
(Di Vesta, 1965). From the top 100 adjectives in
these rankings, 37 were selected that appeared to
be relatively independent of each other, were representative of several different meaning dimensions,
and were commonly used by the five grade-groups.
The opposite used in a given bipolar scale was the
one most frequently elicited, in other samples of
children, to each of the adjectives. A seven-point
scale was used for rating purposes. The important
scales in the final set of bipolar adjectives are discussed in the Results section for Study I.

Concepts. The concepts represented the major
meaning dimensions and were familiar to the younger
as well as the older Ss. Words related to the self-
image were included. The 20 concepts were *Teacher,
America, Lamb, Brave, Science, Freedom, Me, De-
sert, Angry, Mother, Music, Eagle, My best friend,
God, Spider, War, Losing, Russia, Father* and
Enemy.

Procedure. The scales were administered to entire classes by the teacher, who was trained in the
procedures and was given periodic supervision by
E. The large number of scales made it necessary
to obtain ratings on only two or three concepts at
a time depending on the Ss' apparent fatigue rate.

The instructions given by Osgood *et al.* (1957,
pp. 82-84) were simplified and adapted for the age
range of the Ss. Children in the second and third
grade were given an individual instruction period
of 15 to 20 min during which the purpose of the
study and the method of making ratings were explained and practiced until the child felt at ease
with the procedure. Essentially the same instructions,
with similar practice opportunities, were administered
to entire classes of children in the fourth, fifth, and
sixth grades.

In administering the SD, the teacher read the concept-name and all scales for each concept orally to
the group in order to pace the Ss. Reminders were
frequently interjected of the concept being rated and
of the fact that any point on the scale might be

used. Emphasis was placed on the phrase "check
the box that best tells what the word you are rating
means to *you*." Some teachers completed this phase
in 10 school days; the longest period taken was
18 school days. Ratings were collected at regular
intervals and checked immediately. In the event of
absences, or of an S's failure to mark one or two
scales, the concept was again administered to that
S by an assistant in order to assure complete data.

Results[3]

The procedures used in the factor analysis
of the data followed closely those used in
previous studies to permit comparison of results. The second-grade data were the first
to be analyzed. If the semantic structure
emerging from this analysis corroborated the
findings of investigations with adults, it was
assumed that other analyses would be more
profitable than that of repeating the analyses
for each age level.

The raw data were coded into scores from 1 to
7. The basic data for the factor analysis consisted
of the correlation matrix comprised of the product-
moment correlations of the mean concept rating on
each scale with that on every other scale. The
37×37 interscale correlation matrix served as the
input for the factor analysis. The principal-axes
solution, employing the least-squares principle, was
used for the initial factorization. Units were incorporated in the principal diagonal of the correlation matrix. Each successive factor extracted by
this procedure accounts for the maximum possible
variance of the total variance in all scales. The
use of fixed communalities, as described, tends to
maximize the amount of variance accounted for by
each factor; that is, some of the unique variance in
the intercorrelation matrix will be imposed on the
factor matrix. After factorization the solutions were
rotated by the varimax (Kaiser, 1958) routine to
identify meaningful configurations of scales. This
routine is designed to distribute the variance of the
factors in more equal fashion than the quartimax
rotation.

[3] A 31-page set of tables giving the intercorrelation matrices for Studies I and III, the unrotated
principal components solution, and the complete
rotated matrices for all analyses described in this
report has been deposited with the American Documentation Institute. Order Document No. 8853, remitting $2.25 for 35-mm microfilm or $5.00 for
6 by 8-inch photocopies.

The varimax rotation of five principal axes factors accounted for 85.58% of the total variance. An arbitrary criterion of loadings greater than .90 for Factor I and those larger than .60 for the remaining factors was used as a basis for the discussion that follows.

The most salient factor, accounting for the largest part (40.62%) of the total variance, is Factor I, the familiar Evaluation factor. It is defined in the second-grade data, by the scales of *sweet-sour, awful-nice, smooth-rough, unfriendly-friendly, pretty-ugly, wonderful-terrible, bad-good, clean-dirty, cruel-kind,* and *helpful-harmful.* Factor II accounts for less than half the variance (15.60%) found for the first factor. It parallels that factor commonly designated as Potency. The important scales ordinarily associated with this factor are *small-big, light-heavy,* and *weak-strong.* These same scales are also to be found among those with the highest loadings in this analysis. (The one exception is the *weak-strong* scale which has a loading of .56 on Factor II and of .69 on Factor III.) The scales *thin-thick, narrow-wide, long-short,* and *full-empty* also have loadings greater than .68 on the Potency factor. Factor III accounts for 11.54% of the total variance and corresponds to the Activity factor found in previous studies. The dominant scales associated with this factor are *last-first, weak-strong, fast-slow, down-up,* and *dull-sharp,* with all loadings greater than .66. It should be noted that the *still-moving* and the *small-big* scales have loadings of .32 and .40 on this factor. The configuration of scales on Factor III is similar to the Dynamism factor found by Small (1957). Factor IV accounts for 9.74% of the total variance and is comprised of the *red-green, quiet-noisy, loud-soft,* and *curved-straight* scales. These scales appear to relate to differentiations of Pointedness. Factor V, while accounting for only 8.1% of the total variance, is listed here because it was consistently identified in the three studies. The most dominant scales associated with Factor V

are *wet-dry* (loading of .86) and *cold-hot* (loading of .76), apparently involving discriminations of Warmth. The *blue-yellow* and *moving-still* scales have loadings of .64 and .67, respectively on this factor. The unique characteristic of Factors IV and V is that they define dimensions involving sensory discriminations.

These results correspond to the findings in other investigations. Osgood, Archer, and Miron (1962), for example, found that the three salient factors of Evaluation, Potency, and Activity extracted from ratings of 100 concepts on 50 scales by American high school Ss accounted for 45.46, 12.02, and 5.56%, respectively, of the total variance. Small (1957) reports median percentages of 37.5, 19.0, and 8.0, respectively, of the variance accounted for by the three most important factors, of which the second factor was Dynamism. Her results were based on third, sixth, and ninth grade children's ratings of 20 concepts on 16 scales. The total variance accounted for, and the similarity in the factors extracted, implies that comparable results are obtained under quite independent conditions when the same methods of analysis are employed.

As a result of this analysis it was reasonably established that the results replicate those of earlier studies. The need for further factor analyses at each grade-level was considered to be unnecessary for Study I. An inspection of the main factors, however, suggested the hypothesis that they were syncretic factors and might be further analyzed into primary factors.

In order to determine whether such primary factors could be extracted, the scale intercorrelations were obtained by using data from the total sample of grades 2, 4, and 6 inclusive. An important variation in this procedure, from that given above, was the computation of the intercorrelations based on individual ($N = 6000$) ratings in order to take into account this source of variability. The principal-axes solution, with fitted communalities rather than units was employed in the factor analysis. The resulting factors were then rotated by the normal equamax routine (Saunders, 1962). The factoring procedure used in this routine accounts for correlation rather than variance; that is, it accounts for the reliable portion of the ratings rather than the total rating. The rotation functions to achieve simple structure.

The factors emerging from the analysis of the data for the three grades may be described as: I—Abstract Evaluation, II—Concrete Evaluation, III—Softness, IV—Noise, V—Quantity-Size, VI—Primacy, VII—Quantity-Weight, VIII—Activity, IX—Warmth, and X—Dryness. It is immediately apparent, from these labels, that the objective of achieving simple structure was attained. These factors reflect the differentiated composition of the syncretic factors. Thus, the Equamax Factors I, II, III, and VI comprise the Evaluation dimension; Factors V and VII comprise the Potency dimension; Factors IV and VIII are related to Activity; and Factors IX and X make up the Warmth factor. Lower scale loadings were obtained in these analyses, probably as a result of substituting communality estimates for the unit diagonal and of substituting individual ratings for the more stable means of ratings.

STUDY II

While the method of selecting adjectives in Study I was subject to a certain amount of bias, since the independence criterion was not employed, it was assumed that the use of 37 scales was sufficiently large to overcome errors in judgment. An advantage of the first study was the use of a large number of Ss at each grade level to rate each concept. The principal weakness of that study was in the use of only 20 concepts. The selection was not necessarily a representative sample of concepts despite an attempt to make it so. Most of the words dealt with concepts related to personality or to tangible objects. Thus, in addition to the manner in which the

scales were selected, the sampling of the semantic space may have been biased. Both factors were considered in the design of Study II.

Method

The procedure used in Study I was modified by selecting adjectives for use in the bipolar scales on a completely objective basis, and by obtaining ratings on 100 rather than 20 concepts.

Subjects. There were 100 Ss in each of the grades 2 through 7. The children, different from those in Study I, were from schools in a predominantly middle-middle socioeconomic area. The mean ages, in months, for the grade-groups 2 through 7 were 94.30, 104.00, 119.30, 128.96 and 151.99, respectively. The means and standard deviations of IQ scores from the California Test of Mental Maturity for the grade-groups 2 through 6 were 107.36 ($SD =$ 14.86), 106.24 ($SD = 14.08$), 110.04 ($SD = 19.80$), 111.69 ($SD = 12.01$) and 112.06 ($SD = 16.49$), respectively. The IQ scores were not available for the seventh-grade Ss.

Scales. The adjectives were selected from the same pool as in Study I. After they were ordered according to H-values, by grade, the phi-coefficient was used to compare the distributions of two adjectives at a time within each grade. A detailed description of this analysis is provided in another report (Di Vesta, 1965). The phi-coefficient, used in this way, is an index of meaning overlap. Each adjective, screened by these procedures, was characterized by high frequency of usage, being applicable to a diversity of concepts, and independence of meaning. The selected adjectives were made into the following bipolar scales: *wrong-right, round-square, sweet-sour, dark-light, little-big, first-last, wet-dry, ugly-pretty, light-heavy, sad-funny, good-bad, quiet-loud, cold-hot, strong-weak, red-blue* (*blue* was the popular opposite elicited to *red*), *tight-loose, new-old, fast-slow, long-short, soft-hard,* and *brave-not brave.* Six other scales were added, although the adjectives involved occurred below the top 100 H-ranks in some of the grades. These were: *still-moving, friendly-unfriendly, dull-sharp, smooth-rough, make believe-real,* and *same-different.* The above 27 scales were used for all grades 2 through 7. An additional six scales for grades 4 through 7 were included as follows: *wonderful-terrible, strange-usual, powerless-powerful, useful-useless, narrow-wide,* and *painless-painful.*

Concepts. The concepts rated by the Ss in Study II included 95 of those used in the Adjective Elicitation Study. These, in turn, were identically the same as those used in the Illinois Cross-Cultural

Study of Affective Meaning Systems (Osgood *et al.,* 1962). Five adjectives used as marker-concepts were added to bring the total number of words rated to 100.

Procedure. The general procedure described for Study I was followed in the present study. The one modification was in the number of children rating each concept. It would have been impractical to have each *S* rate all 100 concepts from the standpoint of the time involved and the maintenance of interest. However, ". . . since *S*s are used as measuring instruments rather than points in the sample space there is no requirement for every *S* to rate every concept" (Carroll, 1959, p. 70). The groups of *S*s rating each concept were assumed to be equivalent. Each group was required to rate a separate set of concepts following the procedures used by Jenkins, Russell and Suci (1958).

The 100 concepts were divided equally into 10 sets subjectively judged to be equivalent in difficulty. A group of 20 *S*s rated one set of 10 concepts (Series A) and then rated another set (Series B) of 10 concepts. The five Series A sets were selected to represent each of the octants comprising the Evaluation, Potency and Activity dimensions as judged by adolescents' ratings of the original list of 100 words (Osgood *et al.,* 1962). An entire second- or third-grade class was administered an entire set from among those in either series. Thus, five classes were used in each of the latter two grades. This procedure was followed, since it was believed necessary to read the specific concept-name aloud and to remind the *S*s at frequent intervals of the concept being rated. In the remaining grades, the five sets in each series were first ordered in random fashion according to a table of random numbers and then passed out to *S*s in each row of seats. The time required for completing all ratings varied from 2 to 6 weeks.

The procedure described above was also used in the seventh grade with the exception that the scales were administered by a graduate student in three sessions, of 30 to 40 min each, on consecutive days.

Analysis. The ratings of concepts in Series A and B were separately analyzed for each of the grades 2 and 3. In addition, separate analyses of the data based on 27 scales was made for each of the grades 4 through 7. The principal-components analysis based on intercorrelations of mean ratings and the unit diagonals were used with the varimax routine for these data. As in the previous study, another analysis was made based on intercorrelations of individual ratings of all *S*s in all grades. With fitted communalities, the principal-components factors were identified and rotated with the normal equamax routine for the factor analysis over all grades based on 27 scales, and another analysis over grades 4 through 7 based on 33 scales.

Results

The important scales associated with each of six varimax factors for grades 2 through 7 are summarized by grade in Table 1. The analyses were comparable with regard to the number of scales ($N = 27$), the number of concepts, and the number of principal axes factors ($N = 6$) rotated. In order to determine whether the number of scales had a limiting effect on the nature or number of dimensions extracted or on the amount of variance accounted for by each factor, the same procedure was followed for the 33-scale form of the semantic differential used in grades 4 through 7.

In both analyses there was little difference among grades in the factors identified, in the variance accounted for by each factor, or in the scales associated with a specific factor. The Evaluation, Potency, Activity, Warmth, Tautness and Novelty-Reality factors appeared with considerable stability in each grade when the 27 scales were used. Similar results were obtained with the factor analysis based on 33 scales. The principal difference, in the latter analysis, was that the Potency and Activity factors appear as the Dynamism and Quantity factors. The results of the other analyses were so similar they will not be discussed further.

An inspection of the unrotated principal-axes factors revealed two important changes over grade levels for Study II data. One change was the gradual increase in loadings of the *first-last* scale on the Evaluation factor, from a loading of .13 in the second grade to a loading of .63 in the seventh grade. The second change was the dominance of the Dynamism factor in the second through fourth grades reflected in the shift in loading on the *fast-slow* scale from the dimension that might otherwise be labeled Potency to the Activity dimension. However, in the fifth

TABLE 1

SUMMARY OF LOADINGS FOR MAJOR SCALES ASSOCIATED WITH SIX VARIMAX FACTORS BASED
ON THE MEAN RATINGS OF 100 CONCEPTS ON 27 SCALES

Factors-scales		Grade					
		2	3	4	5	6	7
Evaluation							
good-bad		93	95	96	95	95	93
friendly-unfriendly		92	95	94	92	92	93
pretty-ugly		83	90	84	86	87	87
right-wrong		80	87	92	93	90	91
sweet-sour		70	85	81	84	89	88
funny-sad		74	80	74	78	78	80
	Percent of TV	18.58	22.04	21.50	22.67	24.26	24.24
Potency							
little-big		86	90	86	84	87	83
light-heavy		76	70	68	69	74	65
weak-strong		67	75	47	43	50	59
short-long		66	78	75	81	79	72
smooth-rough		37	30	56	45	36	37
	Percent of TV	11.51	12.90	10.27	9.60	11.06	10.41
Activity							
quiet-loud		69	69	62	65	69	73
slow-fast		69	64	82	79	81	79
still-moving		67	40	70	70	81	78
last-first		53	20	34	37	18	16
dull-sharp		33	65	57	65	41	55
not brave-brave		44	24	64	70	53	56
	Percent of TV	9.75	8.31	11.13	11.70	10.29	10.80
Warmth							
cold-hot		80	88	89	89	86	85
wet-dry		68	75	74	68	63	81
blue-red		65	78	75	72	77	63
	Percent of TV	7.80	8.32	7.54	7.48	7.02	7.11
Tautness							
loose-tight		82	77	84	81	82	75
soft-hard		64	83	81	81	80	81
	Percent of TV	7.64	9.29	8.18	9.19	8.68	8.59
Novelty-reality							
round-square		63	75	75	67	58	72
same-different		61	36	74	53	68	66
real-make believe		10	67	61	67	68	58
new-old		39	38	60	45	66	37
	Percent of TV	5.81	7.28	9.37	7.44	7.65	7.24

grade through seventh grade the breakdown of the Dynamism factor clearly emerges in the form of its two components, the Potency and Activity factors.

These results should be viewed in the context that the scales were selected according to completely objective criteria and were representative of those used by elementary-school children. Furthermore, ratings were made of a representative sampling of concepts including abstract and concrete concepts as well as some which were undoubtedly outside the speaking vocabulary of the majority of the younger children. This latter point explains, in some measure, the lowered degree of total variance accounted for by the first factor compared to that accounted for in Study I.

STUDY III

The third study was conducted primarily for the purpose of obtaining ratings on 100 additional concepts. These ratings, together with those in the earlier studies, were to provide an atlas of semantic profiles for a number of words that might be used for experimental purposes. The factor analysis of these data is presented here, since certain variations permit further examination of the stability of the factorial composition of the semantic structure in children and of the extent to which the results can be generalized to other groups.

Method

Subjects. A total of 504 Ss were used from the third ($N = 194$), fifth ($N = 129$), and seventh ($N = 181$) grades. All Ss came from the same school system, but were in a school district different from either of those represented in the first two studies. The mean ages, in months, of the grade groups 3, 5, and 7 were 107.42, 128.64, and 153.12, respectively. The means and standard deviations of the California Test of Mental Maturity intelligence quotients based on total scores were 111.18 ($SD = 12.89$), 114.72 ($SD = 15.79$), and 111.69 ($SD = 13.73$).

Procedure. The general procedure used in Study II was followed. The scales were selected to represent those factors which were common to Studies I and II. The 21 scales are described in the presentation of results.

The 100 concepts rated on these scales were selected to include words from the Kent-Rosanoff (1910) list and a number of words from the Jenkins *et al.* (1958) list that were not rated in the first two studies. As in Study II, this list was divided into ten sets of ten words. Each S rated 20 concepts. All concepts were rated within a 1-week period.

Results

The means of the scale ratings by the total sample were employed in the basic intercorrelation matrix for the analysis of these data. The results of the principal-components analysis with fitted communalities were rotated by the equamax routine. An analysis of the third-grade data was also made by means of the varimax routine to check the results of previous analyses.

The equamax results are summarized in Table 2. The salient factors were again extracted. It should be noted that these results were obtained without attempting to select concepts that would sample the semantic space in a representative fashion and with disregard for level of concept-difficulty. On the basis of scales with the highest loadings, the factors are defined as follows: Factor I—Evaluation (*terrible-wonderful, unfriendly-friendly, good-bad*); Factor II—Potency (*powerless-powerful, strong-weak*); Factor III—Activity (*quiet-noisy, fast-slow, still-moving*); Factor IV—Quantity-Size (*little-big, long-short*); Factor V—Quantity-Weight (*heavy-light, quiet-noisy, smooth-rough, soft-hard*); and Factor VI—Novelty-Reality (*make-believe-real, usual-strange*). Of the remaining two factors, Factor VIII is the Warmth factor with the high loadings on the *dry-wet* and *hot-cold* scales. No interpretation was made of factor VII (*smooth-rough, soft-hard, dark-light*), since two of the critical scales are also weighted on Factor V. These eight factors account for 42.3% of the variance and 93.1% of the correlation. Two characteristics of the factors are readily identifiable. The first is that the salient factors are defined precisely as in the forerunners to the present study without the collapsing of the Potency and Activity dimension into the Dynamism factor. The Dynamism factor may not have been extracted in this analysis because of the large proportion of Ss in the fifth and seventh grades. The second characteristic of this analysis is that, with the exception of Factor VII, all factors were repeatedly identified in the previous studies.

DISCUSSION

The results of the studies summarized here indicate that the dimensions of the child's affective semantic space correspond closely to those of the adolescent (Osgood *et al.,*

TABLE 2
TABLE 2

EQUAMAX MATRIX OF FACTOR LOADINGS FOR THE 21 SCALES IN STUDY III BASED ON THE MEAN RATINGS OF *Ss* IN GRADES 3, 5, AND 7 OF 100 CONCEPTS

Scales	Factor							
	I	II	III	IV	V	VI	VII	VIII
heavy-light	—02	18	05	35	—59	05	—13	04
quiet-noisy	—11	—15	—41	—03	48	04	—02	15
dry-wet	—03	—02	—12	—03	08	06	05	61
hot-cold	—03	05	11	04	—06	—01	02	23
make believe-real	10	—06	—04	00	03	—57	05	00
terrible-wonderful	78	—02	04	—02	—07	—21	—13	—05
smooth-rough	—23	—06	—05	—03	35	08	49	08
powerless-powerful	00	—65	—21	—14	16	—04	14	—03
usual-strange	—15	—03	—03	01	05	63	06	06
unfriendly-friendly	67	—03	03	01	—09	—15	—17	—03
moving-still	04	14	73	—04	—01	02	—06	—03
strong-weak	—01	64	17	28	—26	06	—07	09
good-bad	—80	—01	—05	05	06	20	14	10
fast-slow	05	31	54	06	—03	—01	02	06
old-new	10	11	—05	15	—02	10	—27	00
soft-hard	—10	—15	12	—09	46	03	33	—13
little-big	04	—20	02	—65	26	—02	09	—04
straight-curved	—01	02	—08	09	02	03	31	21
dark-light	21	01	03	11	—19	—04	—21	—04
long-short	—01	12	04	66	—04	00	00	06
brave-not brave	05	48	30	17	—04	00	00	03

1962) and adult (in addition to other studies mentioned earlier see Tanaka, Oyama, and Osgood, 1963). The mode of experiencing the environment and the way in which the experiences are encoded, with regard to the development of connotative meaning, appear to be securely fashioned by the time the child is in the second grade. For all practical purposes Evaluation, Potency, Activity, Tautness, Warmth, and Novelty-Reality may be considered as reliable dimensions of the child's use of language.

In Study I the percentages of variance accounted for by the three most salient factors in the second grade data were essentially the same as those found in all previous investigations with American adults and adolescents. The percentages of variance accounted for by these factors in Studies II and III were considerably lower than those for parallel factors in Study I, particularly for the Evaluation factor, although the *proportions* of variance accounted for appear substantially the same. Thus, the hypothesis that the Evaluation factor, which accounts for the greatest proportion of variance in adults, would progressively change with age was not supported.

One is tempted to attribute the apparent change in variance accounted for by the Evaluation factor in Study II to developmental variables. However, pending further comparisons with data from preschool children and perhaps adolescents, the more cautious interpretation would be to attribute these changes to procedural variation, instability of the ratings, and error of measurement rather than to developmental processes. Factor analytic procedures provide an indication of the contribution of the various scales to the overall variability among *Ss* and are used to determine possible interrelationships among variables. However, as in all factor analytic studies, there is the possibility of error in the weightings of each scale on a given factor. These errors in loadings are due to the number of degrees of freedom available and·the computations which compound initial errors.

An interesting outcome of this study is the emergence of the Warmth factor which appears to be unique to children. While there was a hint of this dimension in the Small (1957) investigation, it does not appear elsewhere. Since the *hot-cold* scale is generally associated with Activity in studies with adults, its emergence as a separate factor here suggests a lack of metaphorical extension in the child's linguistic structure. (It should also be noted that a recent article by Tanaka and Osgood (1965) reports the extraction of the warmth factor in a pancultural factorization of scales employed by adults in rating 16 color/form stimulus combinations.)

The two Quantity dimensions are of interest because they too appear to be unique to children and also had not been identified in earlier studies. It is apparent from the present study that separate discriminations of both size and weight *are* made by the child at a maximum age of 12 years (the approximate age of the oldest group in the analysis). Since these are orthogonal factors, the implication is that judgments of size and weight are independent. A more accurate test of this aspect of the development of language usage, however, can perhaps be best obtained through an analysis of the ratings of specific concepts. Discriminations based on the Quantity dimension may be related to the denotative qualities of the concept being rated. Will young children, for example, find it equally easy to apply the *light-heavy* scale to *symphony* and to *stone?*

Progressive refinement and differentiation of the effective meaning systems of children are also indicated by these data. When the results of Small's (1957) study are coupled with those of the present study there is sufficient evidence to imply that the two-factor system, comprised of the Evaluation and Dynamism factors, emerges before the three-factor EPA system. This observation suggests that the hypothesized initial emergence of the

one-factor Evaluation system must be tested at the preschool level. In addition, the progressive changes of the loadings of the *first-last* scale on the Evaluation factor provides intriguing evidence for the introception of social values.

The explication of more specific developmental trends is dependent on the use of designs other than those used here. With a sufficiently large number of scales and a number of concepts denotatively related to these dimensions each factor identified here would, with a reasonable degree of certainty, emerge more clearly and consistently. The latter approach appears to be a logically and potentially productive "next step" in further studies of the development of meaning.

The results of the three studies reported here clearly indicate the generality of the EPA system in children's use of language. Although the scales were selected on an objective basis, the results are similar to those of Small (1957) whose scales were adopted from earlier studies with adults. The number and kind of scales used apparently do not make a major difference in the end result, provided the major dimensions are represented. Even the sampling of concepts (assuming a representative sampling) does not appear to change radically the factors emerging from the analyses. However, our data perhaps suggest that factorial uniqueness may be identified across age groups by ratings of specific classes of concepts (Tanaka *et al.*, 1963). A practical implication of the present study is that the use of the SD technique is applicable at the age at which children first learn to read, thereby providing the opportunity to trace changes in the *manner* in which stimulus patterns are encoded. As suggested earlier (Di Vesta, 1964b), it appears the child's *use* of modifiers corresponds closely with those of the adult. On the other hand, the variety of experiences with signs and assigns in a rich assortment of environmental contexts makes for a difference in the *way* in which these modifiers are used in differentiating the environment. Thus the SD provides an excellent basis for comparing the location of concepts in semantic space among wide ranges of age groups.

REFERENCES

CARROLL, J. B. *Review* of 'The measurement of meaning,' by C. E. Osgood, G. J. Suci, and P. H. Tannenbaum. *Language,* 1959, **35**, 58-77.

DI VESTA, F. J. Mediated generalization in children's learning of preferences for figures. *Child Develpm.,* 1962, **33**, 209-220.

DI VESTA, F. J. The distribution of modifiers used by children in a word-association task. *J. verb. Learn. verb. Behav.,* 1964, **3**, 421-427. (a)

DI VESTA, F. J. A simplex analysis of changes with age in responses to a restricted word-association task. *J. verb. Learn. verb. Behav.,* 1964, **3**, 505-510. (b)

DI VESTA, F. J. Developmental patterns in the use of modifiers as modes of conceptualization. *Child Developm.,* 1965, **36**, 185-214.

DI VESTA, F. J., AND STOVER, D. O. Semantic mediation of evaluative meaning. *J. exp. Psychol.,* 1962, **64**, 467-475.

DOWNING, R. W., MOED, G., AND WIGHT, B. W. Studies of disability: A technique for measurement of psychological effects. *Child Develpm.,* 1961, **32**, 561-575.

ERVIN, S. M., AND FOSTER, G. The development of meaning in children's descriptive terms. *J. abnorm. soc. Psychol.,* 1960, **61**, 271-275.

JENKINS, J. J., RUSSELL, W. A., AND SUCI, G. J. An atlas of semantic profiles for 360 words. *Amer. J. Psychol.,* 1958, **71**, 688-699.

KAGAN, J., HOSKEN, B., AND WATSON, S. Child's symbolic conceptualization of parents. *Child Develpm.,* 1961, **32**, 625-636.

KAISER, H. F. The varimax criterion for analytic rotation in factor analyses. *Psychometrika,* 1958, **23**, 187-200.

KENT, G. H., AND ROSANOFF, A. J. A study of association in insanity. *Amer. J. Insanity,* 1910, **67**, 37-96, 317-390.

MALTZ, H. E. Ontogenetic change in the meaning of concepts as measured by the semantic differential. *Child Develpm.,* 1963, **34**, 667-674.

OSGOOD, C. E., ARCHER, W. K., AND MIRON, M. S. The cross-cultural generality of meaning systems. Progress report: January, 1960-September, 1962. Urbana, Ill.: Institute of Communications Research, Univ. of Illinois, 1962. (Mimeo.)

OSGOOD, C. E., SUCI, G., AND TANNENBAUM, P. *The measurement of meaning.* Urbana, Ill.: Univ. of Illinois Press, 1957.

POLLIO, H. R. Some semantic relations among word associates. *Amer. J. Psychol.,* 1964, **77**, 249-256.

SAUNDERS, D. R. Trans-varimax: Some properties of the ratiomax and equamax criteria for blind orthogonal rotation. Paper read at the meetings of the American Psychological Association in St. Louis, September 5, 1962.

SMALL, E. R. Age and sex differences in the semantic structure of children. Unpublished Ph.D. dissertation, Univ. of Michigan, 1957.

TANAKA, Y. AND OSGOOD, C. E. Cross-culture, cross-concept, and cross-subject generality of affective meaning systems. *J. Pers. Soc. Psychol.,* 1965, **2**, 143-153.

TANAKA, Y., OYAMA, T., AND OSGOOD, C. E. A cross-culture and cross-concept study of the generality of semantic spaces. *J. verb. Learn. verb. Behav.,* 1963, **2**, 392-405.

Part VII

SEMANTIC DIFFERENTIAL TECHNIQUE IN EXPERIMENTAL PSYCHOLOGY

30. Factor-Structure of Semantic Differential Responses to Visual Forms and Prediction of Factor-Scores from Structural Characteristics of the Stimulus Shapes

Lois L. Elliott and Percy H. Tannenbaum

The work presented in this paper combines two previously unrelated approaches to psychological phenomena. It utilizes stimulus-materials and certain theoretical concepts from the psychophysics of visual form-perception as well as techniques and hypotheses concerning meaning and language which are pertinent to the semantic differential.

Previous investigators, hypothesizing that perceptual responses are determined by physical characteristics of the stimulus which are theoretically amenable to exact specification, have attempted to develop a psychophysics of form-perception.[1] For example, Attneave demonstrated that a large proportion (90%) of the variance of scaled judgments of stimulus-complexity could be related to certain physical characteristics by multiple correlation techniques.[2] Arnoult, in turn, showed that not only 'complexity,' but also judgments of size, familiarity, and meaningfulness could be related to physical characteristics of the stimuli although not always with as much success.[3] Recently, Edelman, Karas, and Cohen, in exploring judged complexity and latency of free association for randomly generated symmetrical and asymmetrical shapes, obtained higher association-latencies for more complex shapes and lower latencies for symmetrical shapes (when total number of sides was equated).[4]

The other aspect of this study, the semantic differential, which was originated at the University of Illinois by Osgood, has been directed at determining the underlying dimensions of meaning.[5] Although experimental results have varied, particu-

Reprinted from *American Journal of Psychology* (1963), 76: 589–587, by permission of the authors and the publisher.

[1] Among others, see J. J. Gibson, *The Perception of the Visual World*, 1950, 59-76.

[2] Fred Attneave, Physical determinants of the judged complexity of shapes, *J. exp. Psychol.*, 53, 1957, 221-227.

[3] M. D. Arnoult, Prediction of perceptual responses from structural characteristics of the stimulus, *Percept. mot. Skills*, 11, 1960, 261-268.

[4] S. K. Edelman, G. G. Karas, and B. J. Cohen, The relative contributions of complexity and symmetry to the perception of form, Paper presented at Midwestern Psychological Association, May 1961.

[5] C. E. Osgood, The nature and measurement of meaning, *Psychol. Bull.*, 49, 1952, 197-237.

larly as new concepts and new cultures have been investigated, the dimensions most frequently recurring have been those of evaluation, potency, and activity.[6]

Hochberg, using a modified version of the semantic differential to evaluate responses to the words *takete* and *uloomu* as well as to the graphic figures which are usually matched with these words, obtained evidence of greater similarity in semantic differential response to matching pairs of word and figure.[7]

Research in audition has investigated semantic dimensions of complex sounds and their associated physical correlates. Solomon applied this approach using both Sonar signals and systematically varied sounds. His results showed that semantic judgments were most strongly related to frequency spectra although rhythm of amplitude modulations was also important.[8]

The present study was designed first, to locate the major semantic dimensions applicable to a population of randomly generated, nonsense-shapes. The second purpose was to determine the relationship of these dimensions or factors to physical characteristics of the stimuli by multiple correlation techniques.

Method: (1) Stimuli. The shapes used in this study (70 in number) were selected from the 72 shapes employed by Arnoult and Elliott[9] Thirty-six of the shapes were constructed by Method 1 as outlined by Attneave and Arnoult, while the remaining 34 were constructed by Method 2.[10] Since Arnoult has recently demonstrated that the shapes constructed by Method 1 and those prepared by Method 2 are responded to by *S*s as partially different sets,[11] the stimuli in the present study were divided for analytical purposes into two groups and designated Sample 1 and Sample 2.[12]

Photographs of the shapes, measuring $3\frac{1}{2} \times 5$ in., were prepared and assembled in random order in individual test-booklets equipped with hard covers. Since there was inadequate time for each *S* to judge all shapes, the total stimulus-series was divided into three parts: (a) three groups of 20 shapes with physical parameters distributed across the three groups; (b) a pair of two very dissimilar shapes (practice shapes); and (c) a residual set of 10 shapes. Each *S* judged 32 shapes: (a) the pair of practice shapes for which judgments were discarded; (b) 20 shapes from 1 of the 3 groups; and (c) the 10 shapes of the residual group.

Measurable physical characteristics of the shapes included the following variables: Perimeter (P), Area (A), Perimeter squared divided by Area (P^2/A),

---

[6] C. E. Osgood, G. J. Suci, and P. H. Tannenbaum, *The Measurement of Meaning,* 1957, 1-75; esp. 72f.

[7] J. E. Hochberg, Psychophysics and stereotype in social perception, in Muzafer Sherif and M. O. Wilson, (eds.), *Emerging Problems in Social Psychology,* 1957, 134.

[8] L. N. Solomon, Semantic approach to the perception of complex sounds, *J. acoust. Soc. Amer.,* 30, 1958, 421-425; Search for physical correlates to psychological dimensions of sounds, *ibid.,* 31, 1959, 492-497; Semantic reactions to systematically varied sounds, *ibid.,* 31, 1959, 986-990; In another modality Tannenbaum has used a similar approach in the study of color stimuli (unpublished research).

[9] Arnoult, *op. cit.,* 262; L. L. Elliott. Reliability of judgments of figural complexity. *J. exp. Psychol.,* 56, 1958, 335-338.

[10] Fred Attneave and M. D. Arnoult, The quantitative study of shape and pattern perception, *Psychol. Bull.,* 53, 1956, 452-471.

[11] Arnoult, *op. cit.* 264.

[12] Sample 1 includes Symmetry and Curvature as variables, while Sample 2 does not (see footnote 11).

Angular Variability (AV), Total Sides (TS), Independent Sides (IS), Symmetry (Sy) and Curvature (C).[13] These measures were defined in the same manner reported by Attneave.[14]

(2) Subjects. Participating in the experiment were 300 basic trainees from the Air Force, screened to possess aptitudes roughly equivalent to those of a college population. Previous work had shown that ratings of shape-complexity made by basic airmen are highly consistent with paired-comparisons made by college graduates.[15] The Ss were tested in groups of 15. One hundred Ss judged each subset of 20 stimuli, while all 300 Ss judged the remaining 10 shapes.

(3) Scales. Twenty bi-polar adjective-scales representing factors obtained in other research with the semantic differential were selected as being appropriate to the stimulus-series under study. A seven-point rating-form was used.

(4) Procedure. Booklets were prepared containing separate pages for judgments of each shape. Instructions introduced the experiment as a research designed to improve terminology with which Air Force navigators might discuss radar displays. The Ss were required to examine each photograph in their booklet before starting to rate the practice-shapes.

Results. Analysis of results consisted of two phases: obtaining the factor structure of the semantic judgments and determining the relationship of factor scores to the physical measurements.

The 20 × 20 intercorrelation based on standardized mean rating-scores for each of the shapes (each correlation coefficient based on 70 pairs of standardized mean ratings) was factored by the centroid method and rotated by the quartimax technique.[16] This was repeated three times: independently for the shapes in Samples 1 and 2 and finally for the total sample. Extraction of factors in each sample was halted at four factors, since approximately all of the estimated common variance had been extracted. Results of the three analyses are shown in Table I.

Since, with few exceptions, the three resulting sets of factors are in excellent agreement, they will be discussed jointly.

The first, Factor I, represents a complexity-activity dimension with *fancy-plain,*

[13] Total Sides refers to the number of lines joining separate points in the original plotting of the figure. The measure of Independent Sides differs from this (a) when the shape is symmetric or (b) when, for example, three plotted points fall on a straight line so that only one line is required to connect them instead of two. Angular variability refers to the mean of the difference between size of external angles of the shape measured consecutively. For example, a regular figure such as a star would have 0.0 Angular Variability, while a highly irregular figure would have a considerable larger AV score. Area and Perimeter are self-explanatory. The measures of Symmetry and Curvature apply only to Sample 1 and are dichotomous measures.

[14] Attneave, *op. cit.*, 222-223

[15] Elliott, *op. cit.*, 336.

[16] Factoring was initiated prior to general availability of the varimax technique.

TABLE I

QUARTIMAX ROTATIONS OF FACTOR MATRICES FOR SAMPLE 1, SAMPLE 2, AND THE TOTAL SAMPLE

Factor loadings

Scale	Factor I			Factor II			Factor III			Factor IV			Communalities		
	Sample 1	Sample 2	Total	Sample 1	Sample 2	Total	Sample 1	Sample 2	Total	Sample 1	Sample 2	Total	Sample 1	Sample 2	Total
Pleasant —unpleasant	19	00	41	−94	−90	−86	07	13	17	−19	−07	14	97	84	97
hard —soft	−42	−01	−61	17	67	33	−34	−38	−42	79	41	−55	96	78	98
active —passive	−94	−95	−97	02	−08	00	21	14	15	16	03	−12	97	95	99
careful —careless	21	31	45	−90	−90	−83	−09	−02	−03	15	02	−14	90	92	93
warm —cool	59	09	67	−41	−30	−40	−02	16	16	−61	−54	47	90	43	88
usual —unusual	79	88	89	−48	−17	−31	11	26	12	10	−02	−11	89	89	92
ugly —beautiful	09	58	12	95	75	89	−06	−16	−19	09	−01	−08	93	94	86
light —heavy	−17	−60	−37	−08	−24	−15	93	76	88	−08	00	−03	91	99	95
slow —fast	79	89	90	16	10	09	−39	−36	−30	−29	−06	21	91	96	97
sober —drunk	47	61	61	−74	−52	−59	12	00	02	30	16	−35	89	69	86
fancy —plain	−97	−98	−98	03	−01	−02	−14	−06	−04	04	−07	08	97	99	99
large —small	−07	41	00	02	28	14	−93	−79	−90	10	−02	00	88	89	84
good —bad	16	00	38	−94	−88	−88	04	08	12	−15	02	11	96	80	95
masculine —feminine	−14	57	−08	11	42	30	−61	−61	−74	63	15	−45	82	91	86
excitable —calm	−96	−98	−98	20	07	11	07	06	08	07	12	00	98	99	99
stable —unstable	73	90	86	−51	−09	−30	−30	−29	−32	25	01	−16	97	92	97
colorful —colorless	−93	−98	−94	−21	−07	−19	−15	03	01	01	−05	11	94	99	95
horizontal —vertical	58	39	59	−04	−23	−10	−24	−11	−10	−34	−09	23	52	23	43
simple —complex	89	92	95	−27	−09	−14	23	26	18	−12	07	−03	95	94	97
rounded —angular	49	70	70	10	−18	−09	03	−05	18	−79	−60	62	86	91	92
% of variance accounted for	51	56	61	23	32	24	19	7	11	7	5	4			

(Decimal points have been omitted.)

excitable-calm, active-passive, simple-complex, and *colorful-colorless* having highest loadings. Scales having substantial loadings include *slow-fast, usual-unusual, stable-unstable, horizontal-vertical, sober-drunk,* and *rounded-angular. Warm-cool* has moderate loadings for Sample 1 and for the total group but fails to load for Sample 2. In contrast *heavy-light* has a moderate loading in Sample 2 but fails to contribute appreciably in either Sample 1 or the total group.

Factor II represents an esthetic-evaluative dimension with *ugly-beautiful, good-bad, pleasant-unpleasant,* and *careful-careless* having highest loadings. In addition, *hard-soft* has a moderate loading for Sample 2.

Factor III refers to size or potency with *light-heavy* and *large-small* having high loadings. In addition, *masculine-feminine* has moderately high loadings in all three analyses. Considering the association of *light, small,* and *feminine,* this might also be interpreted as a dimension of femininity.

Factor IV, less clearly defined, denotes a 'hardness-angularity' dimension. Defining scales were *hard-soft, rounded-angular, warm-cool,* and for Sample 1, *masculine-feminine.* Another interpretation might contrast this with Factor III and call it a masculinity factor with *hardness, angularity,* and *coolness* mutually associated. Supporting this suggestion is the fact that four of the six scales involved have high loadings for one factor and essentially zero loadings for the other. Intercorrelations of Factors III and IV are —0.16 for Sample 1 and —0.28 for Sample 2 which are not significantly different from zero.

These factors agree fairly well with those found in semantic differential analyses of other materials. Factor I is roughly an 'activity' factor; Factor II an 'evaluation' dimension, while Factor III and perhaps IV could be considered as 'potency' factors.

In exploring the relationship between the factors and the physical measures, it was first necessary to obtain factor-scores for the stimuli. This was accomplished separately for the two samples by regressing semantic differential scores (standardized within each subsample) on factor-loadings according to the formula $P = S^1F(F^1F)^{-1}$ where 'S' contains mean rating-scores standardized over 70 shapes, 'F' contains rotated factor loadings, and 'P' contains estimated factor scores. (Shapes with high and low factor scores are shown in Figs. 1 and 2.) Regression coefficients and multiple correlations were computed within each sample by regressing factor scores on the physical measurements. (Since both scores and physical measurements were standardized within each group, the regression coefficients are actually beta coefficients.) Results are shown in Tables II and III.

Multiple correlations for three factors of Sample 1 are higher than the corresponding ones for Sample 2. This result could be due to the different methods of constructing the shapes, to the presence of symmetry and curvature variables in Sample 1 but not in Sample 2, or to both possibilities. Multiple correlation coefficients for Factor I (complexity-activity) are roughly equivalent and reasonably substantial in both groups. Factor III (size-potency) also has fairly good prediction from the physical variables, although the multiple correlation is higher in Sample 1. Examination of Tables II and III shows that for the two factors (Factors II and IV), which

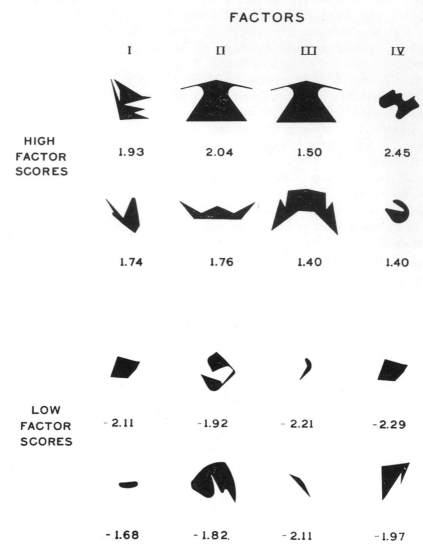

FIG. 1. REPRESENTATIVE SHAPES WITH HIGH AND LOW FACTOR SCORES: SAMPLE 1.

have very low multiple correlations in Sample 2 as compared to Sample 1, the variables of symmetry and curvature have relatively large beta co-efficients in Sample 1. Results in Table III indicate that the relative magnitudes of beta coefficients for all factors differ considerably between Samples 1 and 2. Presumably this also is attributable to the symmetry and curvature variables in Sample 1. Other investigators have found that shapes possessing symmetry constitute a distinct group.[17]

Comparisons of these multiple correlations with those obtained by Arnoult are shown in Table IV.[18] Factor I of this study corresponds to

FACTORS

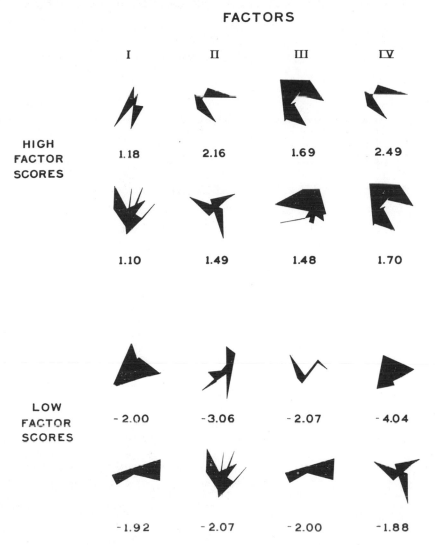

FIG. 2. REPRESENTATIVE SHAPES WITH HIGH AND LOW FACTOR SCORES: SAMPLE 2.

Arnoult's complexity judgments, while Factor III is related to his judgments of size. There are two major differences between the two studies. In Arnoult's work, the multiple correlations involve a single perceptual judg-

[17] Edelman, Karas, and Cohen, *op. cit.*
[18] Arnoult, *op. cit.*, 265.

ment while in the present study the factor scores are obtained by compounding judgments on 20 adjectival scales. Secondly, Arnoult selected the best predictor variables while in the present study all available physical measurements entered the analyses. In view of these differences it is remarkable that nearly identical multiple correlations were obtained. While

TABLE II

MULTIPLE CORRELATIONS FOR EACH FACTOR REGRESSED ON PHYSICAL MEASUREMENTS

	R_{mult}	
	Sample I	Sample II
Factor I	.87	.89
Factor II	.84	.35
Factor III	.93	.83
Factor IV	.95	.42

TABLE III

BETA COEFFICIENTS FOR EACH FACTOR REGRESSED ON PHYSICAL MEASUREMENTS

	Factor I		Factor II		Factor III		Factor IV	
	Sample 1	Sample 2	Sample 1	Sample 2	Sample 1	Sample 2	Sample 1	Sample 2
P	−1.01	.24	−1.32	.45	.87	.07	−1.09	.54
A	.31	−.31	.51	−.67	−.05	.49	.21	−.22
P^2/A	.77	.18	.59	−.59	−.56	−.37	.53	−.33
AV	.49	.30	.43	.12	.04	.26	.34	.14
TS	−.32	.28	−.09	−.12	.00	.03	−.17	−.26
IS	1.08	.04	.02	−.04	.21	.41	.83	.29
Sy	.70		.97		.30		.87	
C	−.20		−.20		−.01		.82	

TABLE IV

COMPARISON BETWEEN MULTIPLE CORRELATIONS OBTAINED BY ARNOULT AND OBTAINED IN THE PRESENT STUDY

	R_{mult}			
	Sample I		Sample II	
	Present study	Arnoult	Present study	Arnoult
Complexity-Activity	.87	.93	.89	.91
Size	.93	.96	.83	.86

Arnoult's coefficients are slightly larger than ours, he, too, found poorer prediction for Sample 2.

Discussion. Factor analysis in this study appears to have two major implications. The factors resulting from programmed rotational procedures correspond reasonably well to those obtained in semantic differential analyses of other materials. This contributes additional support to the thesis that the same meaningful dimensions underly a large portion of human behavior. The second finding, that of very similar factor structures in separate analyses for the two stimulus-samples, provides strong evidence that the results obtained are not chance occurrences. When viewed in the context of the multiple correlations, the results imply that the semantic dimensions may be generalized to other populations of visual stimuli more readily than can the predictive equations based on physical measurements.

The findings of the multiple correlations suggest the possibility that in judgments of nonsense-shapes the portion of semantic space enveloped by the set of complexity judgments (Arnoult's) roughly coincides with that denoted by the complexity-activity factor—and similarly for the size-judgments and the factor of size-potency. It should be stressed that this hypothesis would pertain to nonsense-shapes and would not necessarily apply to more meaningful stimuli.

SUMMARY

Two samples of nonsense-shapes, containing 36 and 34 stimulus-shapes, respectively, were judged on 20 semantic differential scales. Separate factor analyses and rotations produced highly similar factor structures for the two samples and the total group. Four factors were obtained, representing dimensions of complexity-activity, esthetic-evaluation, size-potency and hardness-angularity. Multiple regression solutions, predicting factor-scores from physical measurements, indicated better prediction for the sample in which symmetry and curvature were varied.

31. Word Values, Word Frequency, and Duration Threshold

Ronald C. Johnson, Calvin W. Thomson, and Gerald Frincke

A number of studies have shown a relation to exist between word frequency, word value, and visual duration thresholds. Certain issues have developed concerning the interpretation of the observed relations. Two types of interpretation of results can be distinguished:

1. Those interpretations that claim word frequency to be the major determinant of visual duration threshold. This point of view contends that the responses made to the tachistoscopic presentation of words are learned in the same manner that other responses are learned. Differences in the visual duration thresholds of words can then be accounted for in terms of word frequency so that the introduction of such tenuous and "unanchored" variables as perceptual selectivity and perceptual defense is a violation of the law of parsimony. Thus, the problems that exist with regard to the differential visual duration thresholds of words are problems in learning, not problems in perception.

2. Those interpretations that attempt to show that differences in the visual duration thresholds of words are due, all or in part, to differences in the affective qualities (values, goodness–badness, affective tone, emotional valence) attached to words. These affective qualities affect visual duration thresholds directly, through perceptual selectivity and/or perceptual defense. Visual duration thresholds of words are determined by variables that can be called perceptual variables instead of or

Reprinted from *Psychological Review* (1960), 67: 332–342, by permission of the authors and the American Psychological Association.

along with those variables that usually bear upon learning.

We wish to center our introductory discussion around those few studies which, for us, best exemplify the two positions described above. Solomon and Howes (1951) take the position that differences between words can be accounted for on the basis of word frequency. The perceptual process does not differ in any fundamental way from the learning process. They say:

> Emotional factors undoubtedly operate to an important extent in the building of word frequencies in a given life history. In this way they would be related to word frequency and, indirectly, to the duration thresholds. . . . But to date we can find no evidence to suggest that emotional factors operate in the tachistoscopic situation independently of their effect on word frequency (p. 267).

According to Solomon and Howes (1951, p. 258) visual duration threshold can be accurately predicted from a knowledge of population-wide word frequency as given in the Thorndike-Lorge tables (1944). There is no need to bring in concepts such as perceptual selectivity or perceptual defense in order to explain differences in visual duration thresholds of words. To Solomon and Howes emotional factors operate only in producing idiosyncratic variation in word frequency. These differences in frequency account for differences in the visual duration thresholds of words such as those found between the visual duration threshold of a value-oriented word for subjects (*S*s) who score high as opposed to low on specific scales of the Allport-Vernon Study of Values. They do not have any other influence on visual duration threshold.

The second position concerning the relation between word frequency, word value and visual duration threshold is clearly expressed by Postman and Schneider (1951). Faced with the problem of salvaging value as a variable influencing visual duration threshold, they say that

It may . . . be more profitable theoretically to regard both frequency of word usage and duration thresholds as dependent variables, both manifestations of more fundamental psychological properties attributed to the organism, such as "habits," hypotheses, or even, perhaps, "personal values" (p. 277).

While not denying that word frequency can account for a considerable proportion of the variance in visual duration thresholds of words, they claim that values (called directive factors in this paper) directly influence the visual duration thresholds of infrequent words.

Postman, in a later article (1953), suggests that the frequency of usage of a specific word is determined by its reinforcing qualities. He suggests that frequent as opposed to infrequent words differ systematically in affective tone. He presents evidence to show that the sheer number of pleasant words is much greater than that of unpleasant words. Postman says, "Social control over environmental stimuli will, then, tend to create a correlation between frequency and positive value" (p. 68). Whether called values, directive states, or affective qualities, certain emotive or affective aspects of words influence their general (e.g., Thorndike-Lorge) frequency. Affective quality determines frequency, not merely in an idiosyncratic way as Solomon and Howes (1951) suggest, but also in a very general sense for all words used by all individuals.

It has been hypothesized from this second position that values can influence visual duration threshold in two ways. The affective qualities of words influence visual duration threshold *directly* as in the case of an *S*'s Allport-Vernon score influencing his thresholds for infrequent value oriented words (Postman & Schneider, 1951). (It has been shown that the *S* who values an area such as aesthetics highly reports infrequent "aesthetic" words at lower thresholds than an individual who does not value aesthetics highly. However, as Solomon and Howes point out, this may be due to "idiosyncratic" differences in frequency of exposure.) The affective qualities of words influence visual duration threshold *indirectly*, since the frequency of general usage of any word is determined to a considerable extent by the affective tone of that word, with this frequency then acting as a determiner of visual duration threshold (Postman, 1953).

A third position might also be taken concerning the relations between word frequency, word value, and visual duration threshold. Postman (1953) touches upon this last possible interpretation. He says, "Finally, we cannot entirely discount the possibility that familiarity resulting from frequency may be in itself a source of positive value" (p. 68).

It appears, historically, as if the first point of view—that emphasizing word frequency, playing down the influence of value except as it produces idiosyncratic differences in word frequency—has won out. None of the three positions described above have been proven to be untenable, however. Indeed, we have all of the original questions left, plus a few new ones as well. The questions that we see as being testable and requiring further investigation are these:

1. Is word value related, in a general sense, to word frequency? All of the three positions described above would admit the existence of a relation between value and

frequency—they would diverge in opinion with regard to the generality of the relationship. It is true that a knowledge of word frequency allows us to predict visual duration threshold. But why is the frequent word frequent? Perhaps we should go one step beyond frequency to determine whether other attributes of words vary systematically with frequency.

2. If a general relation between value and frequency exists, does it exist because more positively valued words are used more frequently or because one increases positive affect merely by increasing frequency? Or does the dependent–independent relationship depend on the experimental procedure used?

3. If value and frequency are related in a general, not merely an idiosyncratic sense, then one would have to separate out the influences of each on visual duration threshold. Are there significant differences in visual duration threshold between "good" and "bad" words of equal population-wide frequency? Are there significant differences between frequent and infrequent words equal in affective tone?

These are the three problems that we have attempted to deal with in the series of experiments reported below.

Our first concern was to determine whether a general relation exists between word value and word frequency. As we noted above, there is reason to suspect that emotional factors do operate in the building of word frequency. In a large sample of words for which we have actual measures of goodness, the words in the semantic atlas prepared by Jenkins, Russell, and Suci (1958), one finds better than a two to one preponderance of good over bad words. While the words in this atlas are not a random selection of words in the English language, the sources from which the words were selected seem unlikely to be systematically biased in frequency of pleasant as opposed to unpleasant words. One is led to believe that this ratio is characteristic of the entire English language when examining proportions of pleasant to unpleasant words in a sample of 150 words selected at random from the Thorndike-

Lorge tables for use in the experiments in Series I, discussed below. Of these 150 words, 95 were on the good end (4.00 or less) of the semantic differential, a ratio of approximately 2:1. It seems highly probable that the sheer number of pleasant words in the English language is far greater than the number of unpleasant words.

It seems equally likely that the frequency with which any specific word is used also depends to a considerable extent on its goodness or badness: hence on its reinforcing qualities. This question is amenable to determination. As Solomon and Howes (1951) state, "In the absence of further data it seems best merely to define word frequency for English words as the frequency of words in the Thorndike-Lorge tables" (pp. 264–265). If affective factors operate in the building of word frequency, then pleasantly toned words should have higher frequencies in the Thorndike-Lorge word count than unpleasantly toned words. Experiment I was designed to determine whether this was the case.

EXPERIMENT I

In the first of this series of experiments we attempted to determine whether the pleasantness of words—in this case measured by the good–bad scale of the semantic differential—was related to word frequency as measured by the Thorndike-Lorge tables.

We selected a sample of words from the Thorndike-Lorge tables. This sample of words consisted of two words selected at random from within every alphabetic category (except X) in the tables. These words were rated on the good–bad dimension of the semantic differential by 24 Ss, all freshmen taking an introductory psychology course. The rank order correlation between the goodness and the L count frequency of these words was +.63. Another random sample of 50 words was taken from the Thorndike-Lorge word list in the manner described above. These words were rated by 28 Ss, a different group than those who made the first set of ratings. The rank order correlation between goodness and L count frequency in this list was +.40, again significant to the .01 level of confidence. A third random sample of 50 words was drawn from the Thorndike-Lorge tables. These words were rated by 24 Ss, none of whom had taken part in previous experiments. The correlation between L count frequency and goodness for this set of words was +.38. All of these three correlations are significant to the .01 level. The results of these experiments, regardless of differences in the magnitude of the correlations, indicate that there is a positive and significant correlation between word frequency and goodness. Value attributes of words are related to word frequency and not merely in an idiosyncratic way, but in a far more general sense as well.

EXPERIMENT II

Solomon and Howes (1951) list 30 frequent and 30 infrequent words that they used in a study of the relation of word frequency to visual duration threshold. Five frequent and 5 infrequent words had to do with each of the six value areas of the Allport-Vernon Study of Values. Frequent and infrequent words were sometimes, but not always, synonymous. We paired these words, matching the first frequent with the first infrequent word, and so on, through the two lists. Position of presentation within pairs was determined by coin flip. These 30 pairs of words were presented to 34 freshman introductory psychology students, none of whom had taken part in any previous psychological experiments. Ss were told to "encircle the most pleasantly

toned word of each pair." In 26 of the word pairs, the more frequent word was chosen by the majority of the Ss as the most pleasantly toned. (The 4 exceptions, in which the least frequent word was chosen as the more pleasantly toned, were the word pairs limousine-automobile, economics-assets, orchestra-ensemble, and celestial-heavenly.) A sign test (Guilford, 1956, p. 248) indicates that this preference for the more frequent word in each pair could occur by chance less than one time in a hundred. Again, the more frequent word is rated as the better word.

In the experiment discussed below we attempted to determine whether frequency and goodness were related when nonsense syllables were used as stimulus materials.

EXPERIMENT III

Twenty-two Ss rated two separate visually represented lists of nonsense syllables for goodness, as measured by the semantic differential. An interval of one week separated the ratings of the two lists. Each list consisted of eight 100%, eight 47–53%, and eight 0% association value (Glaze, 1928) nonsense syllables in random order. Syllables were selected at random from within each block of ten Glaze syllables as listed in the *Handbook of Experimental Psychology* (Stevens, 1951, pp. 540–546) at each of the association values used. Then the eight syllables used in each list at each association level were drawn from this pool of randomly selected syllables. We believed that if frequency of exposure was related to goodness, then the higher the association value of the syllable, the better the syllable should be rated. This seemed likely, since the association value of nonsense syllables appears to be determined largely by the frequency of occurrence of the letter combinations in meaningful words (Underwood

1959). Table 1, showing two sets of syllables and their mean ratings of goodness, indicates this to be the case.

A Mann-Whitney (1947) test of the significance of differences between syllables of 100% and 47–53% association values in List 1 indicates that the 100% list is rated as somewhat better (*P* < .10). The difference in goodness between 47–53% and 0% syllables is significant (*P* < .01); Mann-Whitney tests of List 2 show the 100% and the 47–53% list to differ in goodness (*P* < .01); and the 47–53% list and the 0% list to differ significantly (*P* < .05) as well.

Just as the goodness and the frequency of meaningful words in the English language are related to one another, so also is goodness related to the association value of nonsense syllables; the higher the association value, the better the syllable.

Our data indicate that value and frequency are related. We have moved at

TABLE 1
RATINGS OF NONSENSE SYLLABLES OF DIFFERING ASSOCIATION VALUES ON THE GOOD–BAD DIMENSION OF THE SEMANTIC DIFFERENTIAL

100% Syllables	Rating	47–53% Syllables	Rating	0% Syllables	Rating
List 1					
BUL	4.72	WOB	4.59	ZEQ	4.91
FES	3.41	KAW	4.33	WUH	4.48
HON	2.11	DUX	4.33	XIW	5.36
JIN	2.98	BOZ	4.00	WUQ	5.26
RAC	3.98	VOK	3.46	QIH	4.87
ROV	3.74	GEY	2.93	GUV	4.39
SUR	2.72	TIZ	3.52	VEC	3.91
WIL	2.46	VOZ	4.30	XUR	5.28
List 2					
DUL	4.27	BEK	3.46	YUF	4.46
BAL	2.35	PIJ	5.17	QIF	4.44
LOV	1.44	WEP	4.71	ZUK	5.04
SAR	3.23	RIQ	4.46	ZIF	4.06
LIK	2.50	YAF	3.96	XAD	4.85
HAV	2.35	LUB	4.15	XUC	5.35
WAT	3.46	GOW	3.75	QUJ	5.00
ROV	3.54	RUV	3.83	GUQ	5.98

least somewhat beyond the empirical fact that word frequency is related to visual duration threshold. We know something else about the stimulus qualities of frequent as opposed to infrequent words; frequent words are not only more frequent but are better as well. Our second question then becomes relevant. Does a manipulation of frequency cause systematic variation in value or do differences in value produce differences in word frequency, or does the independent–dependent status of each of these variables vary depending on the experimental procedures used? Experiment IV bears upon this question.

EXPERIMENT IV

Fourteen *S*s rated the goodness of twenty nonsense words. These words were from the list of words used by Solomon and Postman (1952) in their study of the effect of "built in" frequency on visual duration threshold. The words used were: JANDARA, AFWORBU, BIWOJNI, NANSOMA, ENANWAL, IKTITAK, SARICIK, ZABULON, CIVADRA, LOKANTA, KADIRGA, ADAFNAW, BORULCE, NIJARON, ENSHIMI, INDULAM, TAVHANE, UDIBNON, DILIKLI, and MECBURI. Mean goodness scores were obtained. One week later each *S* was tested individually. When the *S* entered the experimental room he was given the following instructions (from Solomon & Postman, 1952):

This is an experiment concerning the effectiveness of repetition in learning to pronounce strange words correctly. It has a direct bearing on the problem of reading words in a foreign language, as compared to hearing the words spoken. In addition, we are interested in knowing whether the relative effectiveness of the two kinds of learning methods depends on general reading ability.

We are going to give you a deck of cards On each card is printed a strange word. We would like you to look at each card carefully and then pronounce the word in the way it would be pronounced if it were a word in the

English language. Proceed steadily from card to card, turning over each one after you have finished with it. Go right through the deck and then stop unless you have serious doubts about your pronunciations.

The experimenter (*E*) handed the *S* a pack of 90 3″ × 5″ cards. In this pack were the words listed above. The first five words above were presented 10 times apiece, the next five, 5 times apiece, the next five, 2 times apiece, and the last five, once each. The cards were shuffled thoroughly after each *S* completed this task, so that they were in a relatively random order.

All responses were taped in order to lend realism to the expressed purpose of this new situation. Since *S*s had participated in another experiment on the pronounceability of words, it seems likely that (although the *S*s had seen the words before while rating them on the semantic differential) they were misled as to the purpose of this experiment. Each *S* rated the nonsense words a second time following this pronounceability test.

Figure 1 indicates the mean pre-exposure and postexposure ratings for words of each frequency of exposure. While the differences between ratings prior to exposure were not significant, a Kruskal and Wallis *H* test (1952) shows that words of differing frequencies of exposure do differ significantly in the postexposure test ($P < .01$, $H = 7.83$).

In this experimental situation a manipulation of word frequency alters *S*s' evaluations of word goodness. One can, however, think of instances where the reverse might well occur. The most obvious example of this is in verbal conditioning, where the differential reinforcement of a class of words produces systematic variation in the frequency with which this class of words is emitted. We would suspect that in this case frequency of emission (and

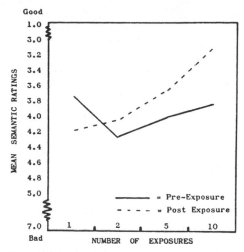

FIG. 1. Ratings of nonsense words before and after word frequency was manipulated.

hence of reinforcement) alters the affective quality of the words. Reinforcement might then produce further variation of frequency.

No matter whether frequency of exposure alters value or vice versa, or both, one thing is evident—there is a relation between word frequency and *S*s' ratings of word goodness. Since this is so, our third question also becomes relevant. Since value and frequency are generally related, it became necessary to experiment with samples of words matched in frequency, varying in goodness, plus samples of words varying in frequency, matched in goodness, in order to separate out the influence of value and of frequency on visual duration threshold. This was attempted in Experiment V.

EXPERIMENT V

We had various groups of *S*s rate the goodness of a large number of words on the semantic differential. These groups rated 60 words of a Thorndike-Lorge G count of 12, 13, or 14, three random samples of 50 words each (described in Experiment I), and 39 words, one sample of 30 words plus

TABLE 2

WORDS USED IN THE TACHISTOSCOPIC EXPERIMENT

Words of Matched Goodness						Words of Matched Frequency					
Frequent			Infrequent			Good			Bad		
Word	SD Rating	Thresh-old	Word	SD Rating	Thresh-old	Word	G Count	Thresh-old	Word	G Count	Thresh-old
Sample 1											
Think	2.34	.0373	Income	2.52	.0500	Rally	12	.1092	Stammer	12	.1538
Butter	1.97	.0692	Caress	1.97	.1085	Glisten	13	.0777	Corrupt	12	.0985
Doctor	1.60	.0369	Ivory	1.68	.0262	Prosper	13	.1046	Defect	14	.0815
Health	1.97	.0492	Piano	1.97	.0546	Ivory	13	.0262	Hinder	13	.0969
Sleep	2.22	.0362	Radiant	2.08	.0662	Ginger	13	.0446	Wretch	12	.1285
Sweet	1.93	.0631	Patriot	1.90	.0992	Alert	14	.0392	Sneer	12	.0785
Mother	1.73	.0315	Vision	1.57	.0546	Deputy	13	.0446	Scandal	13	.1123
House	2.46	.0323	Agile	2.74	.0623	Vehicle	13	.0492	Dismal	13	.1162
Flower	1.87	.0369	Bible	1.87	.0462	Caress	12	.1085	Penalty	13	.0469
Sample 2											
Mountain	2.73	.0687	Bodice	2.74	.0965	Bodice	2	.0965	Slime	4	.0713
Water	2.43	.0217	Dough	2.47	.0757	Candy	32	.0409	Beggar	29	.1087
Window	2.68	.0400	Gradual	2.63	.0965	Engine	A	.0565	Bitter	A	.1704
Green	2.93	.0296	Elegant	3.00	.0852	Brave	A	.0739	Anger	A	.0417
Smooth	2.57	.0522	Zenith	2.62	.0330	Statue	32	.0748	Divorce	29	.0948
Father	2.36	.0800	Jelly	2.49	.0800	Cushion	21	.0900	Inferior	19	.1948
Pretty	2.13	.0661	Refresh	2.09	.0661	Garment	40	.1043	Grief	45	.0687
Street	2.77	.0496	Lenient	2.77	.1522	Church	AA	.0530	Danger	AA	.0583

9 words which happened to appear on the other lists, from Jenkins' semantic atlas. From these words, and from Jenkins' atlas, we selected 17 pairs of words matched in frequency, varying in goodness, and 17 pairs of words matched in goodness, varying in frequency. (Some words among those matched in goodness were rated by Jenkins' Ss and by our own. Although the rank order correlation of goodness ratings between our own and Jenkins' sample of Ss was +.98, for a group of 30 of these words, there was some variation in ratings between the two samples. Whenever this occurred, we used the mean goodness rating assigned by our Ss.) The first 9 words from each list were presented to the first group of 26 Ss; the last 8 to a second group of 23 Ss. The four lists of words, divided as they were presented to two sample populations, are presented in Table 2.

The words were put on slides in the form of bold faced capital letters. The words were presented to Ss by means of a Revere 888 tachistoscope. Each S

sat 18 feet from the screen on which the words were projected. The testing room was fully illuminated while the tachistoscope was used at the smallest possible lens opening. The ratio of room illumination to screen illumination was 1:1.08. The words were presented in random order with the order remaining constant in all presentations to any specific S but with the order varying between Ss. A modified method of limits was used in which each of the 36 words was presented once at each of the following speeds: 1/100, 1/50, 1/25, 1/5, 1/2, and 1 second. Under the conditions of presentation used in this experiment, only one word was recognized at 1/100 of a second while all words were recognized at 1 second.

Each S's mean visual duration threshold for frequent as opposed to infrequent and good as opposed to bad words was obtained. The Ss in the first sample ($N = 26$), exposed to the first group of words, differed significantly in mean thresholds for good vs.

bad words ($t = 3.56$, $P < .01$, using the formula for correlated data), with good words reported at lower thresholds. These Ss also differed in mean thresholds for frequent vs. infrequent words ($t = 2.33$, $P < .05$), with frequent words reported at lower thresholds. The Ss in the second sample ($N = 23$), exposed to the second group of words, differed significantly in mean thresholds for good vs. bad words ($t = 3.25$, $P < .01$), with good words reported at lower thresholds, and in threshold for frequent vs. infrequent words ($t = 3.82$, $P < .01$), with frequent words reported at lower thresholds.

DISCUSSION

We attempted to obtain data relevant to three specific questions. Let us look at these questions, along with the relevant data.

1. Is value related, in a general sense, to word frequency? Our data is unequivocally affirmative. Whether dealing with samples of words in the English language, with frequent vs. infrequent words in various Allport-Vernon value areas, or with nonsense syllables, frequency, as measured by the Thorndike-Lorge tables and by association value, and positive value, as measured by the good–bad scale of the semantic differential, are significantly related in a general sense.

2. If this general relation exists, does it exist because more positively valued words are used more frequently or because one increases positive value merely by increasing frequency? We found that a manipulation of frequency produces systematic variation in Ss' ratings of the goodness of words. It seems highly probable, however, that the reverse may also be true—that by increasing the goodness of words, one also increases frequency. At this point it seems likely that the independent-dependent relation between goodness and frequency would depend on the experimental situation. We would not hazard a guess as to the effect of each on the other in general speech, although a relation between frequency and goodness has been shown to exist.

The data gathered in the first three experiments suggest that other attributes of the stimulus vary systematically as one varies frequency. Perhaps this is true for other forms of learning also. The fourth experiment would suggest the possibility that a manipulation of the frequency of occurrence of a stimulus and a contiguous response, in itself and without any regard to drive reduction, changes the reinforcing qualities of the stimulus. Perhaps we should look beyond the influence of frequency on response probability and ask *why* frequency changes response probability. Is it the difference in association value (and hence, in frequency of occurrence) that causes 100% association value syllables to be learned more rapidly than 0% syllables? Or is it the variation in affective quality accompanying differing frequencies of occurrence? Since the relation between goodness and frequency is not perfect, one can obtain syllables that vary from 0 to 100% in association value, yet are equal in semantic rating—this should provide a test for our question.

These results seem to have considerable social consequence. If word frequency and word goodness are related, and if a manipulation of the frequency of occurrence of a word produces systematic variation in word value, then one wonders whether ideas and personal values are manipulable in the same fashion. If so, then perhaps those elements of society that believe in censorship would find support in these experiments for one of their major assumptions, viz., that frequent exposure to an idea or a set of behaviors—violence, drinking alcoholic beverages, or what have you—lessens the "evil" associated with the idea of behavior. The validity of their second major assumption—that if we make a thing evil enough, people won't do this thing—is, of course, a very different problem.

If the more frequent becomes demonstrably better merely because it is more frequent, one can well understand the values of advertising. If it is generally true that the most frequent words in the English language are also the most good, the logical conclusion that this would lead to is that ads would be more effective if written at an even lower vocabulary level than is currently used. "Oh, brave new world. . . ."

3. If value and frequency are related, what are the influences of each on visual duration threshold when the other variable is held constant? Words equal in frequency, varying in value, are correctly reported by Ss at different mean thresholds, with good words being correctly identified at significantly lower thresholds than are bad words. Words equal in goodness, varying in frequency, are reported by Ss at different mean thresholds, with frequent words being correctly identified at significantly lower thresholds.

While it has been generally accepted that values have some secondary effect on visual duration thresholds, it is also generally accepted that the influence of values on threshold is small, producing idiosyncratic variations in frequency and hence influencing thresholds in this way. Our results indicate that values influence threshold even when frequency of exposure is held constant, and that this influence is approximately equal to that of frequency with value held constant, using these lists of words.

Since word goodness, independent from frequency, does significantly influence visual duration threshold, we are left with the problem of "Why?" The terms "perceptual selectivity" and "perceptual defense" are descriptive, not explanatory. We have no answers here, although we would like to discuss several possible explanations.

One interpretation of the fact that good words are perceived at lower threshold than bad words of the same frequency might be called the "simple" guess theory. Good words appear to be about twice as common as bad words

in the English language. Specific good words are likely to be more frequently used than specific bad words. It seems, then, that good words occur between three and four times as frequently as bad words in terms of usage. Even though the frequency of occurrence of the stimuli are equaled, by matching good and bad words for Thorndike-Lorge frequency, response probabilities probably are still not equal. If an S sees a word in a tachistoscope but identifies only a "g—— d——" he is probably three or four times more likely, on the basis of responses made in the past, to fill in the gaps with a good word, such as "gradual," rather than a bad word, such as "goudge." This simple guess explanation may be partially correct but is not too satisfying to us, since an examination of our Ss' responses to words on the good–bad lists indicates that there seems to be a rather strong likelihood that when Ss guess at but miss a bad word, they respond with another bad word—incorrect but still bad, while when they respond incorrectly to the tachistoscope presentation of a good word, the incorrect response is usually another good word. This finding runs contrary to the idea that perceptual defense is a significant variable but also suggests that something more systematic than mere guessing is involved in errors and in correct responses to tachistoscopically presented words.

A second explanation for the differences in Ss' mean visual duration thresholds might be called the "complex" guess theory. This explanation is derived from Bruner and Postman's (1949) hypothesis theory of perception and cognition. According to Postman (1951) hypotheses are, "in the most general sense, expectancies or predispositions of the organism' which serve to select, organize, and transform the stimulus information that comes from the environment" (p. 249). The strength or availability of certain hypotheses is stronger than that of others. This strength is a function of the following factors: frequency of past confirmation of the hypothesis, number of alternative hypotheses, motivational relevance, and cognitive support. The first two factors—frequency of past confirmation and number of alternative hypotheses—fit well into the simple guess theory, while the last factor, that of cognitive support, may not be relevant to this discussion. The factor of motivational relevance might possibly, however, produce differential predictions between the two explanatory devices that we have labeled simple and complex guessing. As Postman (1951) puts it: "The stronger the motivational support for a given hypothesis, the less of appropriate information is required to confirm it" (p. 255). We would limit this statement somewhat by tying it only to the effect of reward or reinforcement on the number of cues required for the confirmation of a hypothesis. It may be that the differential reinforcement of various stimuli causes those stimuli (as well as those responses) that have most frequently led to reinforcement in the past to be more readily observable or available in the present. The availability of a specific response may well depend on the frequency that this response has been rewarded in the past—but perhaps because that aspect of the stimulus situation that has called forth the rewarded response in the past has become more salient—has become more of a "figure" as opposed to the other stimuli becoming more like the "ground." To paraphrase our quotation from Postman given above: The more reinforcing or rewarding a word is, the less cues are needed for the recognition of this word. We are advancing the proposition that reinforcement not only influences the probability that a given response will be emitted, but also that reinforcement causes that aspect of the stimulus situation that is salient at the time that the rewarded response is made to become more likely to be salient at the next presentation of the stimulus. If this is true, then even if word frequencies of good and bad words are equal and even if habitual modes of response (such as guessing good words) are controlled, the stimulus qualities of rewarding or reinforcing words would be such that less information is needed before the word is correctly recognized than would be the case for words which were presented with equal frequency but were not equally reinforcing. Something that might be called perceptual sensitivity might then be said to exist. This sensitivity would not, however, be a unique perceptual process, but would instead depend on those old standbys in all forms of learning: frequency and reinforcement, a little intermingled to be sure, but still observably present.

We have no way of testing out the "why" question with these data, although the types of wrong guesses made in our study incline us away from the simple guess theory. We believe that the data presented in this study are valuable chiefly in reviving the concept of perceptual selectivity, not in solving the problem of why what is called perceptual selectivity exists. By systematically varying frequency of exposure and frequency of reinforcement and nonreinforcement of nonsense syllables in future experiments, we hope to eventually be able to deal with the question of why good words are perceived at lower mean thresholds than are bad words.

SUMMARY

Three positions may be taken concerning the relation between word value and word frequency, and the relation of each of these to visual duration threshold. Two of these points of view would suggest a general relation to exist between word frequency and word value. Three experiments demonstrate the existence of this relationship. The more frequent a word or a nonsense syllable occurs in the English language, the better it is likely to be rated on the good–bad scale of the semantic differential. Since this relation does exist, we attempted to test out, in Experiment IV, one possible explanation of *why* the relation exists. A manipulation of the frequency of nonsense words produces systematic variation in the rated goodness of these nonsense words. Words that are frequent are also very likely to be rated as good. Hence, to separate out the influence of word value and of word frequency on visual duration threshold, we tachistoscopically presented lists of words matched in frequency, varying in goodness; matched in goodness, varying in frequency. Subjects reported the good words at significantly lower thresholds than the matched bad words; the frequent words at significantly lower thresholds than matched infrequent words. Both frequency and value appear to operate in producing differential visual duration thresholds for words. Possible explanations and certain implications of these findings were discussed.

REFERENCES

BRUNER, J. S., & POSTMAN, L. Perception, cognition, and behavior. *J. Pers.,* 1949, **18,** 12–31.

GLAZE, J. A. The association value of nonsense syllables. *J. genet. Psychol.,* 1928, **35,** 255–267.

GUILFORD, J. P. *Fundamental statistics in psychology and education.* (3rd ed.) New York: McGraw-Hill, 1956.

JENKINS, J. J., RUSSELL, W. A., & SUCI, G. J. An atlas of semantic profiles of 360 words. *Amer. J. Psychol.,* 1958, **71,** 688–699.

KRUSKAL, W. H., & WALLIS, W. A. Use of ranks in one criterion variance analysis. *J. Amer. Statist. Ass.,* 1952, **47,** 583–621.

MANN, H. B., & WHITNEY, D R. On a test of whether one of two random variables is stochastically larger than the other. *Ann. math. Statist.,* 1947, **18,** 50–60.

POSTMAN, L. Towards a general theory of cognition. In J. H. Rohrer & M. Sherif (Eds.), *Social psychology at the crossroads.* New York: Harper, 1951. Pp. 242–272.

POSTMAN, L. The experimental analyses of motivational factors in perception. In J. S. Brown (Ed.), *Current theory and research in motivation.* Lincoln: Univer. Nebraska Press, 1953. Pp. 59–108.

POSTMAN, L., & SCHNEIDER, B. H. Personal values, visual recognition, and recall. *Psychol. Rev.,* 1951, **58,** 271–284.

SOLOMON, R. L., & HOWES, D. H. Word frequency, word value, and visual duration thresholds. *Psychol. Rev.,* 1951, **58,** 256–270.

SOLOMON, R. L., & POSTMAN, L. Usage as a determinant of visual duration thresholds of words. *J. exp. Psychol.,* 1952, **43,** 195–201.

STEVENS, S. S. (Ed.) *Handbook of experimental psychology.* New York: Wiley, 1951.

THORNDIKE, E. L., & LORGE, I. *The teacher's word book of 30,000 words.* New York: Bureau of Publications, Teachers College, 1944.

UNDERWOOD, B. J. Verbal learning and the educative process. *Harvard educ. Rev.,* 1959, **29,** 107–117.

32. Mediated Generalization as a Function of Semantic Differential Performance

James C. Baxter

This study was designed to test two implications of Osgood's theory of meaning.[1] According to this position, the meaning of a sign is contained in the manifold of representational, mediative reactions associated with it and hence is aroused in the subject (*S*) upon its subsequent presentation. The mediators associated with most signs are thought to be multidimensional, as a result of diverse associative experiences; and the pairs of polar reactions defining each of the several dimensions are presumed to be reciprocally antagonistic in function.[2] At the level of linguistic behavior, Osgood has proposed the semantic differential as a measure relevant to these processes. This instrument allows *S*s to describe the meaning of a variety of signs by means of patterns of scaled judgments made to pairs of contrasting adjectives. Factor analyses of these scales across a broad range of signs have indicated that their structure can be meaningfully described by a relatively small number of orthogonal coördinates in a semantic space.

In an effort to draw this position into closer alignment, Osgood has recently proposed additional relationships between theory and test. He has assumed that "there is some finite number of representational mediation reactions available to the organism, [and] that the number of these alternative reactions . . . corresponds to the number of dimensions or factors in semantic space. Corresponding to each of the major dimensions of the semantic space, defined by a pair of polar terms, is a pair of reciprocally antagonistic mediating reactions, which we may symbolize as r_{MI} and $\bar{r}_{MI}$ for the first dimension, r_{MII} and $\bar{r}_{MII}$ for the second dimension, and so forth."[3] Accordingly, point locations in semantic space are taken to reflect the composition and intensity of the mediators aroused, and multidimensional distance between points is adopted as a measure of meaning similarity.

Although experimental verification of this relationship between theory and test would seem to be of central importance to Osgood's position, a recent review of

Reprinted from *American Journal of Psychology* (1962), 75: 66–76, by permission of the authors and the publisher.

[1] C. E. Osgood, The nature and measurement of meaning, *Psychol. Bull.*, 49, 1952, 197-237; *Method and Theory in Experimental Psychology*, 1953, 690-699. C. E. Osgood, G. J. Suci, and P. H. Tannenbaum, *The Measurement of Meaning*, 1957, 5-30.
[2] Osgood, Meaningful similarity and interference in learning, *J. exp. Psychol.*, 36, 1946, 277-301; An investigation into the causes of retroactive interference, *J. exp. Psychol.*, 38, 1948, 132-154; The similarity paradox in human learning, *Psychol. Rev.*, 56, 1949, 132-143.
[3] Osgood, Suci, and Tannenbaum, *op. cit.*, 1957, 27.

the literature has revealed only two lines of evidence presently available. The first, representing several studies demonstrating conditioning and interaction-effects between mediators, is somewhat indirect;[4] whereas the second, a series of studies investigating mediated generalization, is of doubtful confirmatory value.[5] Although Dicken was able to show significant differences in generalization between clusters of words varying in semantic profiles, he also found anomalous differences in generalization between theoretically equivalent words within clusters. Moreover, Staats *et al.* were unable to demonstrate generalization between signs as a function of semantic similarity.

The present study employed a paradigm of mediated generalization in which the galvanic skin-response (GSR) was conditioned to one of a sample of experimental signs (words) by means of contiguous pairing with a noxious significate (electric shock). Under these conditions, two hypotheses were advanced: (I) It was expected that the amplitude of the GSR generalizing to noncritcial test-words should bear an inverse relationship to the multidimensional distance (D) in semantic space between these words and the critical word employed in response-acquisition; (II) The second hypothesis was aimed at evaluating Osgood's principle of reciprocal inhibition. Since noxious stimulation was used as a significate during training, it was expected that the mediational part (r_M) of the observable behavior (GSR) associated with this stimulation should correspond primarily to the negative pole of the evaluative dimension. If Osgood's position is sound, acquisition of the GSR should be facilitated in association with negatively evaluated words, whereas generalization to positively evaluated words should be antagonized. On the other hand, acquisition of the response in association with positive words should be antagonized, with facilitated generalization to negative words. Differences in the slopes of generalization gradients were expected to occur, then, as a function of the evaluative meaning of the critical word used during training.

METHOD

Semantic differential. A sample of 6 words was selected from the atlas of 360

---

[4] D. C. Ferguson, Unpublished manuscript, University of Illinois, 1956; C. K. Staats and A. W. Staats, Meaning established by classical conditioning, *J. exp. Psychol.,* 54, 1957, 74-80; Attitudes established by classical conditioning, *J. abn. soc. Psychol.,* 57, 1958, 37-40; A. W. Staats, C. K. Staats, and D. A. Biggs, Meaning of verbal stimuli changed by conditioning, this JOURNAL, 71, 1958, 429-431; A. W. Staats, C. K. Staats, W. G. Heard, and L. P. Nims, Replication report: meaning established by classical conditioning, *J. exp. Psychol.,* 57, 1959, 64.

[5] C. F. Dicken, Connotative meaning as a determinant of stimulus generalization, Unpublished doctoral dissertation, University of Illinois, 1958; A. W. Staats, C. K. Staats, and H. L. Crawford, First-order conditioning of meaning and the parallel conditioning of a G.S.R., Unpublished manuscript, Arizona State College, 1958.

words whose semantic differential profiles have been described by Jenkins.[6] Words were chosen on the basis of four specific criteria: (1) diverse representation on the evaluative dimension; (2) lack of readily detectable physical similarity; (3) absence of obvious denotative similarity; and (4) lack of obvious, disorganizing emotional connotations. The words selected were *home, nurse, money, bleak, fraud,* and *starve*. Evaluative weightings (estimated from *good-bad*) were 6.53, 6.40, 5.63, 2.73, 1.63, and 1.50 respectively; activity weightings (estimated from *active-passive*) were 5.23, 6.07, 5.80, 2.83, 4.97, and 4.10 respectively; and potency weightings (estimated by *hard-soft*) were 2.77, 2.43, 5.87, 4.53, 5:67, and 6.53 respectively.[7]

Twelve adjectival scales were chosen, with four scales representing each of the three major factors in semantic space. Criteria for selection were: (a) high, relatively specific loadings on the dimension of interest; and (b) relatively direct application to the experimental words. These scales and the six words were presented in a graphic form of the semantic differential. Three different test-forms were devised, each with scale-order and adjective-position randomized. Instructions were adapted from Osgood.[8]

Apparatus. An exposure apparatus, developed in the Texas laboratory, was used to present the experimental words to *S*.[9] By means of this apparatus the stimulus-cards could be exposed consecutively in any desired order and for variable lengths of time. The experimental words were printed in India ink on white cards in letters approximately $\frac{1}{4}$-in. high. Blank filler cards were also prepared, which were similar to the others in every respect except that no words were printed on them.

A Fels dermohmmeter, connected to an Easterline Angus graphic recorder, provided a continuous record of *S*'s *GSR*. Electrodes from the dermohmmeter were attached to *S*'s palms, and were taped on to insure uniform contact. A microswitch on the back of the exposure-shutter activated a Hunter timer, which in turn activated a Bird inductorium. This instrument, connected to *S*'s left wrist, constituted the shocking circuit. The timer also signaled the occurrence of exposures on the recorder.

Experimental series. Twenty separate cards were made for every word, along with five blank cards (total = 125). In this way it was possible to 'stack' the entire series for an individual *S*. Word orders were prearranged for every *S*, except for the choice of his critical word. These series were arranged by the following plan (randomized for each *S*). At the outset of the series, a succession of 18 pre-training trials was given in order to familiarize *S* with the apparatus and to extinguish existing GSRs. This block of trials consisted of three presentations of each of the six words, arranged in random orders within blocks of six words. Immediately following the pre-training trials, a block of 17 training trials was presented, consisting of 12 reinforced (shock) exposures of the critical word, along with five non-reinforced, randomly interspersed blank cards (a constant order for blank cards was used for all *S*s). The blank cards were employed in an effort to extinguish re-

[6] J. J. Jenkins, W A.. Russell, and G. J. Suci, An atlas of semantic profiles for 360 words, this JOURNAL, 71, 1958, 688-699.

[7] Judgments inclining toward 7.00 represent the positive, active, or potent poles of the three dimensions (from Jenkins *et al.*).

[8] Osgood, Suci, and Tannenbaum, *op. cit.,* 1957, 82.

[9] K. M. Dallenbach, A simple and inexpensive card-changer, this JOURNAL, 73, 1960, 139-141.

spones to cues from the apparatus. A block of generalization-trials immediately followed the training block. This block was composed of one randomly ordered presentation of each of the non-critical words. Three non-reinforced repetitions of the critical word followed the generalization-block, providing data for the presence of conditioning.

Subjects and procedure. The Ss (60 men and women), from undergraduate courses in psychology, were randomly subdivided into 3 groups of 20 each.

Individual sessions were conducted with each S according to the following plan. Upon entering the experimental room, S was seated in a comfortable chair in front of the apparatus and given general instructions to the task. Stress was placed upon the task as a study of the relationship between thought and physiological processes. Following the standardized introductory set, S was presented the semantic differential with attached instructions, and asked to complete it. Any questions raised were answered in general terms. After S had begun working, the experimenter (E) casually checked to insure that instructions were being followed appropriately. A few Ss failed to understand, and required additional instructions at this point.

Following completion of the semantic differential, the GSR- and shock-electrodes were attached to S's palms and wrist respectively. He was asked to assume a comfortable position and to hold it with arms relaxed and his fingers resting on the table in front of him. He was instructed to focus his eyes on the shutter of the apparatus, where a series of words would be presented. He was further instructed to pronounce each word subvocally when it was exposed but to keep his mind as blank as possible between exposures. After this, the inductorium was adjusted to S to a degree that the shock was definitely unpleasant but not painful. He was then given a 3-min. rest before the experimental series was begun.

During this interval, the evaluative dimension of S's semantic differential was key-scored, and a critical word was assigned according to S's group-membership. Ss of Group I were assigned one of the six experimental words at random; whereas members of Groups II and III were assigned words judged extreme on the evaluative dimension. The critical word for the Ss of Group II was the one he judged most positive. The Ss of Group III, on the other hand, received the word they had judged to be most negative. Choice was random in cases of ties.

Following the choice of S's critical word, the experimental words were organized in their predetermined order and placed in the apparatus. At the completion of the rest-interval, the dermohmmeter was calibrated, and the experimental series was begun. Exposure-time for each word was approximately 2 sec., with an inter-trial interval of approximately 20 sec. Shock was associated with the critical word only during the training phase of the experimental series. The shock occurred 0.5 sec. after the appearance of the word and continued until the word was obscured by the shutter.

Results. Logarithmic transformations of micromho conductance units were used since these measures seem to approximate best the assumptions of parametric analysis.[10] Conductance change was determined by subtract-

---

[10] E. A. Haggard, On the application of analysis of variance to G.S.R. data: I. The selection of an appropriate measure, *J. exp. Psychol.*, 39, 1949, 378-392; III. Some effects of the use of inappropriate measures, *ibid.*, 39, 1949, 861-867.

ing the reciprocal of *S*'s resistance at the point of presentation from the reciprocal of his resistance at the point of maximal deflection occurring within an interval of 5 sec. after presentation. These measures were then converted to micromho conductance units, *i.e.* conductance $\times 10^6$, a constant was added, and log values were determined from a four-place table.

Training. The present design permitted evaluation of the adequacy of training on two counts. First, by comparing the mean *GSR* deflection of the three pretraining exposures of the critical word with that of the three post-training exposures, a measure of conditioning was derived. Further, an index of differential conditioning was provided by comparing the mean

TABLE I

MEAN DIFFERENCES IN *GSR* BETWEEN PRE- AND POST-TRAINING AND BETWEEN
CARDS WITH CRITICAL WORDS, AND THOSE THAT ARE BLANK
(N = 20 for each group)

Comparison	Group	Mean diff.	SE	t
Pre- vs. post-training	I	.238	.024	9.90*
	II	.246	.033	7.45*
	III	.129	.042	3.07*
Critical word vs. blank card	I	.196	.024	8.21*
	II	.224	.029	7.69*
	III	.100	.025	4.00*

* Significant at or beyond the 5% point (one-tailed).

GSR deflection of the last three training exposures of the critical word with that of the last three blank card exposures.

The results of these two comparisons are summarized in Table I. Response-levels between pre- and post-training exposures of the critical word and between critical word and blank card exposures were significantly different in all three groups (p < 0.05).[11] Accordingly, it was assumed that an acceptable degree of differential conditioning was achieved in each group during training.

Generalization. Hypothesis I was that the amplitude of *GSR* generalization to non-critical test-words should bear an inverse relationship to their multidimensional distance from the critical word. Accordingly, Ss of Group I were assigned critical words at random from among the six words. *GSR* results for the remaining five words constituted generalized responses.

Difference-measures were found for each generalization-word for every *S* by subtracting its response-amplitude on the last pre-training trial from

[11] The 5% level of confidence (one-tailed) is accepted as significant throughout this report.

that of its test, or generalization-trial; hence, variation in the amplitude of the response to these words was independent of S's habituation to the situation, and presumably a function of the training itself. The test-words were then ranked in terms of their multidimensional distance from the critical word for each individual S. Corresponding measures of response were then entered in a treatment by S-analysis of variance table, with the five treatments defined as increasing multidimensional distances from the critical word. It was expected that treatment-means would reflect a decreasing monotonic trend as a function of multidimensional distance. An analysis of the variance of these means failed to reach significance at the 5% level of confidence ($F < 1.00$). The comparison indicated a lack of systematic variation in response-means as a function of multidimensional distance, and thus failed to support the hypothesis.

Hypothesis II predicted interaction of generalization-gradients as a function of the location of the critical word on the evaluative dimension of the semantic differential. Accordingly, Ss in Group II were assigned the words they judged most positive, while those in Group III were assigned the words they judged negative. Generalization-words were adjusted for pre-training level in the same manner as was done for the Ss of Group I. The distance of each word was then ranked from the critical word (evaluative dimension only), and corresponding GSR-values were entered in an analysis of variance table. The design employed to test this hypothesis was that which Lindquist designates a Type I trend analysis design.[12] Interaction of the several means (unidimensional distance) between groups was of principal interest by way of reflecting an interaction in generalization trends.

Before conducting the analysis for over-all trend, it was necessary to consider first the comparability of the group-trends involved. The problem involved demonstrating the comparability of distance-intervals between groups. A test of this condition was provided by computing the median distance associated with each treatment (across both groups). Median tests were then conducted for each distance treatment in turn, to determine whether distances within both groups could be regarded as having come from the same populations, each possessing these over-all medians. In no case did the Chi-square reach significance at the 5% level of confidence. It was concluded, therefore, that the distances could be regarded as comparable between groups. These medians were adopted as intervals for both groups.

[12] E. F. Lindquist, *Design and Analysis of Experiments in Psychology and Education,* 1953, 267-273.

A summary analysis of the generalization data of Hypothesis II is presented in Table II. This analysis indicates that the comparison of principal interest, *i.e.* trend-interaction, reached statistical significance at the 5% level of confidence. It is also evident from the table that the

TABLE II

ANALYSIS OF THE VARIANCE OF *GSR* GENERALIZATION AS A FUNCTION
OF UNIDIMENSIONAL DISTANCE
(Groups II and III)

Source	df	Mean square	F
Independent			
Subjects	39	.091	
Groups	1	.004	.05
Error	38	.094	
Dependent			
Within Subjects	160	.024	
Distance	4	.021	
Distance×Group	4	.058	2.52*
(Trend interaction)			
Error	152	.023	
Total	199		

* Significant at the 5% point.

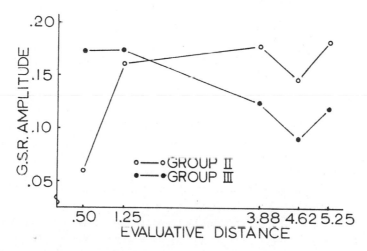

FIG. 1. THE EFFECT OF EVALUATING MEANING OF THE CRITICAL
WORD ON *GSR* GENERALIZATION

over-all response-level between groups (trend-level) does not differ significantly ($p > 0.05$). The mean *GSR*-amplitude for each evaluative distance is presented graphically in Fig. 1. It can be seen that the two trends did interact as expected, and that an intersection of the gradients occurred somewhere between Distance-points 2 and 3.

Following completion of this analysis, differences in response-means between groups were computed to evaluate their individual significance. These differences were found to be 0.11, 0.01, −0.05, −0.06, and −0.07 for treatments 1 through 5 respectively. Tukey's Wholly Significant Difference Test (*WSD*) was employed in evaluating the several differences.[13] Differences associated with Treatments 1 and 5 exceeded the *WSD*-value at the 5% level (*WSD* = 0.06). It was, therefore, concluded that the present data confirmed Hypothesis II.

Replication. It was thought advisable to replicate the test of Hypothesis I to assess the reliability of the result found in the main experiment. In addition, the new group of Ss also provided an opportunity to evaluate the predicted relationship with an alternative response which was simultaneously recorded. Since electric shock was again employed as the significate during training, it was possible to record the mild

TABLE III

MEAN DIFFERENCES IN RESPONSE AMPLITUDE BETWEEN PRE- AND POST-TRAINING AND BETWEEN CARDS WITH CRITICAL WORDS AND THOSE THAT ARE BLANK

Response	Comparison	Mean diff.	SE	t
GSR	Pre- vs. Post-Training	.228	.032	7.14*
(N=20)	Critical Word-Blank Card	.253	.027	9.36*
Tonic flexion	Pre- vs. Post-Training	4.53	2.31	1.96*
(N=14)	Critical Word-Blank Card	15.46	3.30	4.70*

* Significant at or beyond the 5% point (one-tailed).

tonic flexion response which reliably accompanies this stimulation, and then observe its generalization in addition to that of the *GSR*.

To record this flexion-response, a stabilometer was devised by making appropriate modifications on a standard Keeler polygraph. The stabilometer was fashioned by enclosing the rubber bulb of the sphygmomanometer (inflated to 10 mm. Hg) in a small wooden container with a 'floating' top. Thus, slight variations in pressure on this bulb were continuously recorded on the polygraph. Word-exposures were also recorded on this apparatus by triggering the pneumograph harness with the shutter of the exposure-apparatus. This tonic flexion-response was recorded simultaneously with the *GSR*.

Twenty men and women Ss (Group IV) were recruited from introductory courses in psychology. Individual experimental sessions were conducted according to the same procedure used with Group I, with one exception; the Ss were asked to rest their hands on the 'platform' on the table, rather than on the table itself.

GSR-responses were recorded, transformed, and analyzed by the method described above. Our prediction was the same as in Hypothesis I of the main experiment. The results of the differential training, *i.e.* differences in amplitude of the responses to critical words between pre- and post-training and between cards with critical words and those that are blank, are presented in Table III. Both of these differences were reliable at the 5% point of confidence. It was concluded, there-

[13] T. A. Ryan, Multiple comparisons in psychological research, *Psychol. Bull.,* 56, 1959, 26-47.

fore, that satisfactory differential training had again occurred. An analysis of the trend of the means of the responses as a function of multidimensional distance was conducted as explained above. The variance of these means failed to reach significance ($F < 1.00$).

The data obtained from the stabilometer were analyzed by a procedure analogous to that used with the *GSR*-data. Tonic flexion-response was defined as the maximal stabilometer deviation, in either recorded direction, which occurred within a period of 5 sec. after the stimulus-word was exposed. Deviations were measured to the nearest 0.25 mm. Six Ss were excluded from this group as a result of instrument failure, reducing the sample to 14.

The results of differential training are presented in Table III. These comparisons were reliable at the 5% level of confidence. Results of generalization were determined by subtracting the pre-training levels of response for each test-word from its test-level for each *S*, and entering these values in a table of analysis of variance. It was expected that these means would reflect a decreasing trend. The variability in these means did not, however, reach statistical significance at the 5% level of confidence ($F < 1.00$). The hypothesis also failed to find support with this alternate method of measuring responses.

Discussion. The results of this study provide only limited support for the position of Osgood *et al.* While confirmation of the predicted interaction of generalization-gradients is congruent with Osgood's proposed antagonistic relationship between mediators of the evaluative dimension, the failure of multidimensional distance to predict successfully the order of magnitude of a generalizing response is in contradiction. Further, replication of this test, using both the *GSR* and a simultaneously recorded tonic flexion-response, provided comparable results. In view of these data, it seems clear that multidimensional distance is unable to provide a measure of similarity capable of predicting generalization under these conditions.

Several questions are raised by the results of the experiments testing Hypothesis I. Since a relatively small sample of signs was used, which was selected on the basis of broad evaluative representation, it could be argued that adequate sampling of the semantic space was not achieved. Repeated evidence of the orthogonality of these dimensions[14] suggests, however, that this procedure should not drastically interfere with representation on other dimensions. Furthermore, data from Jenkins substantiate this expectation with respect to these signs on the three dimensions used.[15] A related possibility is that the signs used were representative of some unknown class of signs whose semantic composition is poorly reflected by the differential. While theoretical statements relative to this question are lacking,

[14] Osgood, Suci, and Tannenbaum, *op. cit.*, 31-75.
[15] Jenkins, Russell, and Suci, *op. cit.*, 688-699.

Osgood has identified some signs which seem to possess special properties, viz. political candidates and election issues.[16] Similarly, Dicken has found that semantic differential-defined synonymity corresponds poorly to a mediated generalization definition for some signs.[17]

These data also raise the question of the class of responses which should be expected to provide mediators corresponding to the semantic dimensions. While this study assumed that the mediators associated with the significate behavior (*GSR*) elicited by shock should correspond *primarily* to the evaluative dimension, no assumption of its *unique* correspondence to this dimension is warranted. Certainly mediators from this behavior as well as those from other associated behaviors (*e.g.* tonic flexion) could be expected to relate to a number of dimensions. The present data do not, however, clarify this point.

Multidimensional distance (*D*) as an index of similarity may also possess some characteristics of significance to this study. One property of this measure is that of weighting equally each of the factors contributing to the measure. Since previous evidence has shown that the evaluative dimension accounts for approximately twice the scale variance attributable to the other two major dimensions, it is possible that some bias is inherent in the index.[18] For example, Osgood has speculated that evaluative meaning may be of more "cognitive importance" than the other dimensions presently known. If this should be the case, it is reasonable to expect that differential weighting of this dimension would improve prediction of semantic similarity. While these questions may be raised by the results of this study, no data are available which bear upon their answer.

SUMMARY

The order of magnitude of *GSR*-generalization among a sample of six words was predicted on the basis of semantic differential performance. It was hypothesized that (I) the amplitude of the *GSR* generalizing to non-critical test-words would bear an inverse relationship to the multidimensional distance of these words from the critical word; and (II) differences in the slopes of generalization would occur as a function of the evaluative meaning of the critical word. Sixty men and women were assigned to three groups of 20 *S*s each. Critical words were randomly chosen for Group I, while the *S*s of Groups II and III were assigned words judged

[16] Osgood, Suci, and Tannenbaum, *op. cit.*, 1957, 104-124.
[17] Dicken, *op. cit.*
[18] Osgood and Suci, Factor analysis of meaning, *J. exp. Psychol.*, 50, 1950, 325-338; Osgood, Suci, and Tannenbaum, *op. cit.*, 31-75.

to be extreme on the evaluative dimension. Generalization of the response to non-critical words was analyzed.

Hypothesis I was not supported in the present study. No orderly variation in response-amplitude was found as a function of multidimensional distance. Replication of this part of the study, using both the *GSR* and a tonic flexion response, also failed to support the hypothesis. Hypothesis II was supported by the data ($p < 0.05$). The slopes of generalization between words interacted as predicted.

Results of the study were interpreted as offering limited support for Osgood's position. Support of Hypothesis II was taken as confirmation of Osgood's principle of reciprocal inhibition with respect to the evaluative dimension. The data obtained in testing Hypothesis I were interpreted as indicating a failure of multidimensional distance to provide an effective measure of meaning similarity. Some possible reasons for this failure were discussed.

33. Relationships between the Meanings of Verbal Stimuli and Their Associative Responses [1]

Robert A. DeBurger and John W. Donahoe

The similarity between the meaning of verbal stimuli (S) and the meaning of their associative responses (R) was investigated in the present study by means of the semantic differential. In previous work on the nature of the S-R relationship, Karwoski and Berthold (1945) employed an a priori classification system and found that approximately 75% of the associative responses were either "essentially similar" to the stimulus (e.g., large-big) or "identified" with the stimulus in some manner (e.g., cabbage-vegetable). While the classification procedure establishes the existence of a logical relationship between S and R, the psychological relevance of the response classes is open to question, particularly as classification was performed by judges rather than by the Ss who produced the responses. A second procedure for investigating the S-R relationship was used by Staats and Staats (1959). Ten stimulus words and their 20 most frequent associates as determined from normative data (Russell and Jenkins, 1954) were each rated on one evaluative scale (*good-bad*) of the semantic differential. The rank-order correlation coefficient between the mean rating of the stimulus and the mean rating of all 20 associates to the stimulus was .90. This finding was interpreted

as indicating that association strength, as measured by m (Noble, 1952), and representational meaning, as measured by the semantic differential, are correlated because the contiguous presentation of verbal stimuli facilitates both processes. However, procedural questions can again be raised, for although the Ss produced the ratings upon which the inference of similarity was based, the Ss did not produce the associative responses.

In the present experiment, the same Ss were employed both for the production of the associates and the rating of the semantic differential scales. Scales measuring all three major semantic factors—evaluation, potency, and activity—were used. Additionally, the covariation of associational and representational processes was assessed through the use of two association conditions: repeated association and chain association. In repeated association a number of associates are given to the same S; in chain association each associate serves as S for the following R. To the extent that repeated association results in more associates to the orignal S than chain association, the similarity between the meaning of S and R words should be greater in the repeated association condition.

METHOD

Subjects

Thirty-two volunteer Ss from laboratory sections of the introductory psychology course were used in the experiment. The sample, which included males and females in approximately equal number, was

Reprinted from *Journal of Verbal Learning and Verbal Behavior* (1965), 4: 25–31, by permission of the authors and Academic Press, Inc.

[1] This research was supported by a grant from the Faculty Research Fund, University of Kentucky, to the second author. The authors wish to express their appreciation to the Computing Center for making its facilities available to this project.

randomly subdivided into two groups of 16 Ss to form a Repeated Association Group and a Chain Association Group.

Experimental Materials

Association-Task Stimuli. The stimulus words had the following properties: (a) all were nouns, (b) all tended to elicit nouns as associates, (c) as a group, they sampled a wide range of intensity of the three major semantic dimensions, (d) no S elicited any other S as a primary associate, and (e) no S elicited opposites as a frequent response. The last restriction was imposed, as it is Osgood's position that "the directly opposite response is not . . . attributed to semantic mediation but rather to the overlearning of purely verbal habits in the culture" (Osgood, 1953, p. 709). Stimuli having the above properties were selected from the re-standardized Kent-Rosanoff norms (Russell and Jenkins, 1954), an atlas of semantic profiles (Jenkins, Russell, and Suci, 1957), and data from preliminary investigations by the present authors. The 15 stimulus words were *table, butter, lamp, man, music, house, child, doctor, trouble, window, hammer, thief, tornado, snail,* and *butterfly.*

Semantic Differential. Nine scales (three for each semantic factor) were chosen from among those studied in the original factor analysis of meaning (Osgood, Suci, and Tannenbaum, 1957, p. 37). Scales were selected which had an appreciable loading on only one factor. The scales were evaluation (*good-bad, nice-awful,* and *clean-dirty*); potency (*strong-weak, heavy-light,* and *large-small*); and activity (*active-passive, fast-slow,* and *hot-cold*). Each scale was divided into seven rating classes with a score of 1 assigned to the *good, strong,* and *active* ends of the scale and a score of 7 to the *bad, weak,* and *passive* ends of the scale.

Procedure

Association Task. The experiment required two sessions which were spaced 1 week apart. In the first session, the association task, Ss produced 10 responses to each of the 15 stimulus words. Each S in the Repeated Association Group was given fifteen 10-page booklets. The stimulus word was repeated on each page of the booklet and a space was left in which S could write his association. The stimulus word was repeated to reduce the possibility of previous responses influencing succeeding associations. For the Chain Association Group, fifteen 11-page booklets were constructed. A stimulus word was printed on the first page of the booklet and each of the following 10 pages contained a single space in which S could write his association. The Ss were given detailed oral instructions. Essen-

tially, the Chain Association Group was told to write "the first word that comes to mind upon reading the stimulus word" and, for the following responses, to write "the first word that comes to mind when you think of the word you have just written." For the Repeated Association Group, the instructions were modified so that responses were given to the original stimulus word only. The order of stimulus words was independently randomized for each S and each booklet was completed before a new one was begun. All Ss were further instructed to produce only noun associates and to use a response only once as an associate to each stimulus word. Although no time limit was imposed, Ss were encouraged to proceed quickly. When the association task was completed, Ss were asked to return 1 week later. The purpose of the second session was not explained.

Rating Task. In the rating task, each S was given a set of booklets containing a word at the top of the page followed by the nine semantic differential scales. All 15 stimulus words and 105 of the 150 associations from each S were included. The order of words and scales was randomized. Responses 1, 2, 3, 4, 6, 8, and 10 were selected for rating since the greatest changes in meaning were expected in the early associates. Standard semantic differential scaling instructions were used. This procedure yielded nine scale ratings on 120 words for each S.

RESULTS

S-R Meaning Relationship

To determine the initial comparability of the rating behavior of the Repeated and Chain Association Groups, the similarity of the ratings given the stimulus words was assessed. The product-moment correlation coefficient between the mean ratings of the 15 stimuli was .99 ($p < .01$) for each of the three semantic factors and indicated a high degree of agreement between the two groups of Ss.

The relationship between the meaning of S and R words was obtained by examining the ratings of the associates as a function of the rating class of the stimulus. A stimulus word was assigned to a particular rating class (1–7) on the basis of its mean rating on the three scales measuring each semantic factor. The rating class was independently determined for each semantic factor and for each S. Thus, the same stimulus word might be placed in different rating classes for different

TABLE 1

MEAN RATINGS OF THE ASSOCIATIVE RESPONSES ON THE THREE MAJOR SEMANTIC FACTORS FOR THE REPEATED AND CHAIN ASSOCIATION GROUPS

Rating class of the stimulus	Evaluation			Potency			Activity		
	First associate	Total associates		First associate	Total associates		First associate	Total associates	
		Repeated	Chain		Repeated	Chain		Repeated	Chain
1	2.23	2.49	2.68	2.92	3.15	3.14	2.96	3.44	3.10
2	2.64	2.71	2.64	3.29	2.99	3.57	3.05	3.32	3.33
3	2.73	2.89	2.67	3.45	3.70	3.48	3.40	3.45	3.45
4	3.19	3.34	2.84	3.56	3.57	3.42	3.76	3.71	3.71
5	3.94	3.11	3.12	3.91	3.80	3.49	3.82	3.65	3.65
6	4.50	3.82	3.33	4.34	3.99	3.82	4.38	3.99	3.95
7	4.72	4.10	3.42	4.40	3.98	3.79	5.38	4.49	4.49
rho^a	1.00**	.96**	.89**	1.00**	.89**	.72*	1.00**	.93**	.96**
F^b		19.19**	7.89**		11.86**	4.49**		14.12**	11.32**

* $p < .05$.
** $p < .01$.
[a] The rank-order correlation coefficients between the rating class of the stimulus and the mean rating of the associates.
[b] The F ratios associated with the effect of the rating class of the stimulus on the mean rating of the associates. Each ratio is referred to a distribution having 6, 90 df.

424

Ss. The mean scale rating of the associates to all stimuli of the same rating class was then calculated. The scale ratings for the first associate and for the total seven associates (1, 2, 3, 4, 6, 8, and 10) are presented in Table 1. The ratings of the first associate were averaged across the association groups because the first associate in both the Repeated and Chain Association Groups was given to stimuli of the same rating class. The meaning of the first associate was related to the meaning of S in perfect monotonic fashion for all three semantic factors (*rho* = 1.00). The mean rating of the total associates was also positively related to the meaning of S for both association conditions (*rho* varied from .72 to .96). These statements received additional support from repeated-measurement analyses of variance.[2] For each of the six combinations of semantic factors with association groups, the rating class of S exerted a statistically reliable effect on the meaning of the associates (see Table 1, row *F*).

The tendency of stimuli to elicit associates of similar meaning decreased with continued association. Figure 1 in which the evaluative meaning of the associates is plotted for both association groups illustrates this finding. Comparable results were obtained with the potency and activity factors. In the Repeated Association Group, the meaning of the associates was affected by the rating class of the stimulus throughout much of the response

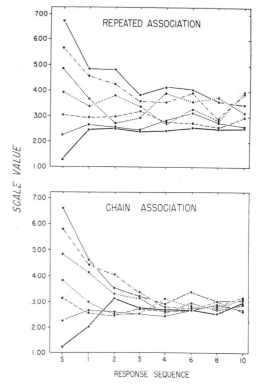

FIG. 1. The evaluative ratings of the associates as a function of the ordinal number of the response sequence. The mean ratings of the stimuli are included to identify the appropriate rating class for each curve.

sequence, whereas little effect of the stimulus was present in the Chain Association Group beyond the first few responses. The more rapid decrease in similarity of S-R meaning in the Chain Association Group is reflected in the analyses of variance by a significant interaction between the rating class of the stimulus and the ordinal number of the response sequence. The *F* ratios for the evaluation, potency, and activity factors were 3.08 (36, 400 *df*), *p* < .01; 2.10 (36, 407 *df*), *p* < .05; and 8.04 (36, 295 *df*), *p* < .01, respectively. The interaction was nonsignificant for all semantic factors in the Repeated Association Group. Table 2 provides a direct comparison between the Repeated and Chain Association Groups in the rate of change of

---

[2] When *S* failed to rate the stimuli so that all rating classes were represented, the missing entries were estimated and the *df* for error was reduced appropriately. Missing entries occurred infrequently with the evaluation and potency factors (85% of the cells contained experimental observations), but this was a cause of concern with the activity factor. Under repeated association with the activity factor, 80% of the observations were present but, under chain association, only 67% were present. The results with the activity factor must therefore be considered as tentative although the findings were comparable to those obtained with the evaluation and potency factors (see Tables 1 and 2).

TABLE 2

RATE OF CHANGE IN MEANING OF THE ASSOCIATIVE RESPONSES

Rating class of S	Evaluation		Potency		Activity	
	Repeated	Chain	Repeated	Chain	Repeated	Chain
1	.428	.479	.481	.564	.500	.400
2	.089	.067	.094	.149	.130	.148
3	—.032	—.019	.065	.031	.035	.386
4	—.092	—.099	—.024	—.054	—.023	—.034
5	—.130	—.189	—.064	—.115	—.056	—.085
6	—.130	—.179	—.111	—.099	—.095	—.130
7	—.142	—.255	—.126	—.167	—.086	—.242

the meaning of associative responses. The larger the value of the slope,[3] the more rapidly does the meaning of the associate diverge from that of the stimulus. Of the 21 pairs of slopes from the combination of seven rating classes with three semantic factors, the larger slope (greater change in meaning per associative response) was found in the Chain Association Group in 16 instances. This outcome is significant by a two-tailed sign test ($p = .027$) and indicates that the similarity between the meaning of S and R words declined more rapidly with chain association.

The one systematic difference between semantic factors in the meaning of successive associates is indicated by a further inspection of Table 2. Whereas the change in sign of slope uniformly occurred between rating classes 3 and 4 with the potency and activity factors, the sign change occurred between rating classes 2 and 3 with the evaluative

[3] The application of curve-fitting procedures to these data requires some comment. Although the number of the associative response within the response sequence is an ordinal variable, a comparison of the slopes from corresponding rating classes of S is interpretable since the relative magnitudes of the slopes are invariant under any monotonic transformation. Thus, while the numerical values of the slopes are without significance, the ordinal relationship between corresponding slopes is meaningful. The use of a hyperbolic function, $Y = X/(a + bX)$, produced a median standard error of estimate of 0.03 scale unit and a median index of correlation of .95 for the extreme rating classes (1 and 7).

factor. This finding implies that the asymptotic evaluative rating of the associates differed from the asymptotic potency and activity ratings. A comparison among the meanings of the 10th associates supports this interpretation. The semantic factors differed reliably; $F (2, 60) = 22.01$, $p < .01$; with the mean ratings of the associates being 3.08, 3.59, and 3.68 for the evaluation, potency, and activity factors, respectively. The tendency of a relatively unselected group of words (the 10th associates) to obtain a *good* rating suggests that, unlike potency and activity meaning, the evaluative meaning of a random set of words is not at the scale midpoint.

S-R Association Relationship

The associative proximity of the response words to the stimulus words was determined through an association index. This index was obtained by assigning a number from 1 to 7 to each response dependent upon its frequency of occurrence among the first six associates in the Russell-Jenkins norms. All responses not occurring among the first six noun associates were given a value of 7. The mean association index is plotted as a function of the ordinal position of successive associates in Fig. 2. The first response under both association procedures received a highly similar value since the stimuli were the same for both procedures. Thereafter, the association index was consistently higher (more

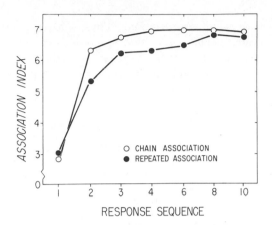

FIG. 2. The association index of the responses as a function of the ordinal number of the response sequence.

remote associations) for the Chain Association Group.[4] As with the semantic differential data, only the first two or three response words in the Chain Association Group were related to the stimulus. Thus, while the remoteness of the associates increased with successive responses in both association conditions, the increase occurred more rapidly with chain association than with repeated association.

DISCUSSION

In the present study, stimulus words elicited associative responses of similar meaning, the similarity tending to decrease with continued association. The decrease in similarity was more pronounced with chain association than with repeated association. The changes in meaning, as measured by the semantic differential, were paralleled by changes in the remoteness of associates. That is, continued association resulted in responses

[4] The association index, while it is adequate for present purposes, tends to overestimate the associative strength of those responses occurring beyond the first six associates to a stimulus. This deficiency causes the curves for the Chain and Repeated Association Group to converge more rapidly than if the sheer frequency of association were used as a measure of associative strength.

which were increasingly remote associates of the stimulus with the increase in remoteness being greatest in the Chain Association Group. Taken together, the above results not only indicate that semantic differential meaning and associative strength are grossly related (Staats and Staats, 1959) but also demonstrate that this relationship is preserved throughout the association process. The conclusions, it will be remembered, are based upon stimulus words that do not elicit opposites as their most probable response. Typically, the first associate to stimuli that elicit opposites has a semantically opposite meaning with later associates possessing meanings which are similar to those of the stimulus. For example, although Staats and Staats used some stimulus words which elicited opposites with appreciable regularity (e.g., *rough, hard,* and *sweet*), the total meaning of all 20 associates to the stimulus was similar to the meaning of the stimulus. Within the framework of representational mediation theory (Osgood *et al.*, 1957), the opposite relationship is viewed as having an associational basis in the contiguity of verbal stimuli (e.g., *rough-smooth*) but as lacking a representational basis because the pairing of the stimulus word with many other words whose meanings are inconsistent with that of the opposite results in counter-conditioning (e.g., *rough-hard, uneven, coarse, rugged,* etc.).

The finding that continued association to a stimulus results in the emission of responses which are increasingly remotely associated with the stimulus is of considerable interest in itself. First, it is consistent with the frequently held implicit assumption that the frequency of a particular associative response based upon single responses from a large number of Ss is a measure of the associative strength of a large number of responses from a single S. The tenability of this assumption is particularly encouraging in view of the restricted set of stimuli (stimuli which elicit opposites were excluded) and possible responses (responses other than nouns were not permitted). Second, the finding suggests an associative basis for the phenomenon of "verbal satiation" as an alternative to the more commonly advanced representational interpretation (Lambert and Jakobovits, 1960; Jakobovits and Lambert, 1961). The associative interpretation stems from an elaboration of the hypothesis that the implicit response to a brief presentation of a verbal stimulus is the stimulus itself (Jenkins and Cofer, 1957; Bousfield, Cohen, and Whitmarsh, 1958; Deese, 1962). If the hypothesis is extended such that a prolonged presentation of the stimulus is assumed to produce implicit *associative* responses, much of the verbal satiation data may be successfully rationalized. The finding that a satiated stimulus elicits infrequent associates (Smith and Raygor, 1956) and neutral ratings on the semantic differential (Lambert and Jakobovits, 1960) is consistent with the present hypothesis. Moreover, the associative approach indicates that variables known to be relevant to the association process—e.g., the frequency of the stimulus—should also play a role in verbal satiation (Yelen and Schulz, 1962).

SUMMARY

This study investigated the relationship between verbal stimuli and successive associative responses using both a measure of meaning (the semantic differential) and an index of association strength. Two methods of response production were employed: repeated association and chain association. The meaning of the response became progressively less similar to the stimulus with succeeding associates, the effect being more pronounced with chain association. The index of association strength indicated that the later associates were less strongly linked to the stimulus, the effect again being more pronounced with chain association. Thus, changes in meaning and associative strength were similarly affected by the association method, this covariation being maintained throughout the association process.

REFERENCES

BOUSFIELD, W. A., COHEN, B. H., AND WHITMARSH, G. A. Verbal generalization: A theoretical rationale and an experimental technique. Tech. Rep. No. 23, Contract NONr onr 631 (00), 1958.

DEESE, J. On the structure of associative meaning. *Psychol. Rev.*, 1962, **69**, 161-175.

JAKOBOVITS, L. A., AND LAMBERT, W. E. Semantic satiation among bilinguals. *J. exp. Psychol.*, 1961, **62**, 576-582.

JENKINS, J. J., RUSSELL, W. A., AND SUCI, G. J. An atlas of semantic profiles for 360 words. *Amer. J. Psychol.*, 1958, **71**, 688-699.

JENKINS, P. M., AND COFER, C. N. An exploratory study of discrete free associations to compound verbal stimuli. *Psychol. Rep.*, 1957, **3**, 599-602.

KARWOSKI, T. F., AND BERTHOLD, F., JR. Psychological studies in semantics. II. Reliability of the free-association tests. *J. soc. Psychol.*, 1945, **22**, 87-102.

LAMBERT, W. E., AND JAKOBOVITS, L. A. Verbal satiation and changes in the intensity of meaning. *J. exp. Psychol.*, 1960, **60**, 376-383.

NOBLE, C. E. An analysis of meaning. *Psychol. Rev.*, 1952, **59**, 421-430.

OSGOOD, C. E. *Method and theory in experimental psychology.* New York: Oxford Univer. Press, 1953.

OSGOOD, C. E., SUCI, G. J., AND TANNENBAUM, P. H. *The measurement of meaning.* Urbana: Univer. Illinois Press, 1957.

RUSSELL, W. A., AND JENKINS, J. J. The complete Minnesota norms for responses to 100 words from the Kent-Rosanoff test. Tech. Rep. No. 11, Univer. Minnesota, 1954.

SMITH, D. E. P., AND RAYGOR, A. L. Verbal satiation and personality. *J. abnorm. soc. Psychol.*, 1956, **52**, 323-326.

STAATS, A. W., AND STAATS, C. K. Meaning and *m*: Correlated but separate. *Psychol. Rev.*, 1959, **66**, 136-144.

YELEN, D. R., AND SCHULZ, R. W. Verbal satiation? *J. verb. Learn. verb. Behav.*, 1962, **1**, 372-377.

34. Semantic Satiation of Words and Numbers

S. Messer, L. A. Jakobovits, R. Kanungo, and W. E. Lambert

One purpose of the study reported is to compare the effect of continuous verbal repetition on the semantic ratings of words and numbers. A second is to examine the effectiveness of the semantic differential to index distinctive features of numbers as well as words. The procedure used is parallel to an earlier study on semantic satiation with words with the notable difference that, in the present case, a completely mechanized method is developed to present stimuli and record rating responses and their latencies. The following main findings are reported: (1) Regular semantic differential scales reflect significant satiation effects with words, but not with numbers, while a 'Meaningful-Meaningless' scale indexes significant shifts toward the 'Meaningless' pole with numbers, but not with words. (2) Certain differences are observed between words and numbers in the manner in which these are rated on standard semantic differential scales. (3) The M-shaped relationship between response latency and scale position reported earlier by Osgood is confirmed in the present paper. The implications of these findings in relation to the earlier study and with respect to the applicability of the semantic differential to numbers are discussed.

INTRODUCTION

The semantic differential is particularly useful as a method of determining distinctive characteristics of various types of stimuli. It has not only been frequently used as an indirect measure of the connotative meaning of words and word combinations (Osgood, Suci & Tannenbaum, 1957), but has also served as a convenient means of assessing the associational value of nonsense syllables (Fichman, 1959) and the distinctive aspects of non-verbal stimuli, including colour patches, pictures of objects (Osgood *et al.* 1957) and actual objects (Wimer & Lambert, 1959). Its versatility is evident, too, in its use as an index of changes in meaning resulting from the continuous verbal repetition of words (Lambert & Jakobovits, 1960) and the continuous observation of objects (Jakobovits & Lambert, 1964).

The commonly used form of the semantic differential was developed through factor analyses of subjects' ratings of common word stimuli on a wide range of semantic scales. One purpose of the present study was to examine its effectiveness as a method of differentiating the distinctive features of numbers as well as words. In a recent study, Jakobovits & Lambert (1962) argued that the meaning of numbers could be reduced through their continuous use, much as the meaning of words can be satiated (Lambert & Jakobovits, 1960). It was demonstrated that continuous verbal repetition of a number such as '7' prior to its occurrence in a simple addition problem $(7 + 4 = ?)$ increased the time taken to add. Because the design called for rapid switching from repetition of a number to adding, no attempt was made to measure meaning changes of numbers with the semantic differential. The second purpose of the present experiment was to compare the effect of continuous verbal repetition on the semantic ratings of both words and numbers.

Reprinted from *British Journal of Psychology* (1964), **55**: 155–163, by permission of the authors and Cambridge University Press.

METHOD

Subjects

Eighty McGill undergraduate students, none of whom had participated in an experiment of this nature, were tested invididually. The subjects were second-, third- and fourth-year undergraduates.

Material and apparatus

The symbols presented were six commonly used words and three numbers. The six words were divided into two sets of three each (Set X: *bus, city, smoke*; Set Y: *water, sky, key*). The numbers were either in digit form (1, 4, 9) or in word form (*one, four, nine*). Six control words (*lake hammer, tree, castle, car, bank*) and three control numbers both in digit form (2, 3, 8) and in word form (*two, three, eight*) were employed in the Different Word Control procedure, described below.

Each word and number was typed in capital letters on a slide to be projected on a ground-glass screen by means of a Kodak automatic slide projector. The seven points of the semantic differential scales were represented by seven electric keys (numbered 1 to 7 from left to right). These were connected in series to seven writing pens of an Esterline-Angus Operation Recorder (Model AW). The keys were ½ in. wide and arranged in a straight line separated from each other by 1½ in. intervals. They were placed on the table in front of the screen where the subject could comfortably reach them from his sitting position. Four semantic differential scales representing the three major factors were used in this experiment (*Good–Bad*; *Unpleasant–Pleasant*; *Hard–Soft*; *Passive–Active*). A fifth scale, *Meaningful–Meaningless*, similar to that used by Lambert & Jakobovits (1960), was added. The bipolar adjectives of each of the five scales were printed on slides in such a manner that the two adjectives appeared one under the other, with an arrow above the first adjective pointing left and an arrow below the second pointing right. The subjects were trained to use the keys on the left and right of centre to indicate how appropriate each adjective was for the stimulus under consideration.

The subject was instructed to put his index finger on a button placed near the centre of the bank of keys. After pressing one of the seven keys, he was to return his finger to the 'ready' button in preparation for his next response. The slide projector and the operation recorder, located out of view behind the ground glass screen, were connected to a time circuit in such a manner that each change of slide and each key pressing response were recorded on the chart of the Esterline-Angus apparatus. The time circuit was made to change a series of slides at certain fixed pre-arranged intervals. Since the projector was automatic, all the experimenter had to do was change the trays containing the slides. A two-minute rest period was given between the initial series and the final series while the experimenter changed the tape on the time circuit.

Procedure

Subjects were randomly assigned to one of four different groups, each composed of 20 subjects. One group performed under the experimental satiation condition and the other groups under three control conditions: *silence control, different-word control*, and *retest control*. In each group 10 subjects were assigned the words of set X and the numbers in digit form. To counterbalance the effect of order of presentation, five of these 10 subjects received the words before the numbers and the remaining 5 received them after the numbers. The other 10 subjects were assigned the words of set Y and the numbers in word form. The effect of order of presentation was controlled in the same manner as above.

All subjects were shown how to indicate their semantic ratings of words and numbers by means of the keys in front of them. Key positions were defined in terms of the scale positions of the semantic differential. They were given practice in making semantic ratings of figures, words, nonsense words, and numbers. They were frequently asked to report verbally what they meant by their responses, to ensure that they understood the instructions. No instruction about speed of responding was given. Subjects were simply told to act on their 'first impression' of the stimulus.

The first phase of the experiment proper was to obtain normal semantic profile ratings of the stimuli and latencies for making the ratings. Since there were three words and three numbers, each rated on five scales, 30 initial responses were recorded for each subject.

Satiation condition. After obtaining the initial response measures for the 20 subjects in this group, a word (or number) was exposed on the screen for 15 sec. and the subject was asked to repeat it aloud at a rate of two to three repetitions per sec. while looking at the word (or number) on the screen. After 15 sec. a scale was exposed and this subject made his rating by pressing one of the seven keys. The order of presentation maximized the separation of the recurrence of each word (or number) and each scale.

Silence control condition. The same procedure, with one exception, was used with 20 other subjects: they did not repeat aloud the words or numbers during the 15 sec. interval between the exposures of the stimulus symbol and the semantic scale. They were instructed to wait until a scale was presented before responding. Thus, a word (or number) was briefly exposed, then a 15 sec. interval elapsed before the semantic scale was shown, at which time the subject gave his rating.

Different word control condition. Using the same general procedure, another 20 subjects repeated aloud a particular control word or number during the time interval, and were then presented with a different word or number to rate. For example, the number '8' was exposed and the subject repeated it aloud for 15 sec. Then the number '1' was immediately exposed, and the subject was asked to pronounce and rate the number '1' on a semantic differential scale. This control condition was introduced to determine what effect the act of repeating aloud had upon the stability of the ratings. Whereas the previous condition is an 'unfilled-interval' control, the present is a 'filled-interval' control.

Retest control condition. The 20 subjects in this group merely repeated the initial series, i.e. they rated the same words and numbers twice with a rest interval of 2 min. between initial and final ratings.

Scoring

The semantic differential scores were transferred from the record chart. For latencies, each subject's record chart was analysed by means of a calibrated ruler which allowed for a maximum error of 0·08 sec. for individual measurements. Scoring reliability was checked by having a second judge, who was not aware of direction or meaning of differences, analyse a sample of 25 responses. The product-moment correlation coefficient between the two judges was found to be 0·99.

RESULTS

Three different response measures were analysed in the present experiment: the ratings on the four regular semantic differential scales; the ratings on the 'Meaningful–Meaningless' scale; and the latencies of rating responses. Each measure will be dealt with separately.

Regular semantic differential ratings

Semantic ratings for words. The means of the initial and final semantic scores for the three words on four scales were calculated for each of the four groups. These means represent polarity or extremity scores as used earlier by Lambert & Jakobovits (1960). The mean differences between these two scores, representing change of extremity of meaning, were also calculated and their significance levels determined. These are presented in Table 1. The Satiation and Different Word Control groups show significant amounts of meaning decrement following the repetition treatment and the other two control groups show no semantic change. A $4 \times 2 \times 2$ analysis of variance was performed on the mean difference scores to isolate the effects of the four different treatment conditions, the two sets of words (X and Y) used in each condition, and the order of presentation. The results reveal that there is a significant treatment-conditions effect with respect to meaning change ($F = 3\cdot45$, $P < 0\cdot05$). Neither of the two other main effects is significant ($F = 2\cdot49$ and $F = 1\cdot64$, respectively). The triple order interaction was similarly insignificant ($F = 1\cdot12$). The Satiation group is significantly different from the Silence Control group at the 0·01 level and from the Retest Control group at the 0·05 level, while the difference between the Satiation and the Different Word Control groups is not reliable. Furthermore, the three control groups do not differ significantly from each other.

Table 1. *Average change in polarity for three words or three numbers, summed over four scales*

		Change in polarity scores for									
		Words					Numbers				
Condition	No.	Initial mean	Final mean	Mean diff.	s.d. diff.	t	Initial mean	Final mean	Mean diff.	s.d. diff.	t
Satiation	20	21·20	17·05	−4·15	4·60	3·92**	10·65	9·35	−1·20	4·71	1·20
Silence control	20	21·80	22·00	+0·20	4·17	0·21	13·75	12·40	−1·35	4·05	1·45
Different word control	20	20·10	17·75	−2·35	4·26	2·40*	10·85	11·95	+1·10	3·01	1·59
Retest control	20	19·60	18·70	−0·90	4·15	0·95	13·50	12·25	−1·25	4·64	1·18

* $P < 0.05$.   ** $P < 0.001$.

The entries are group means representing the sums of 12 ratings per subject, the maximum possible score being 36.

Semantic ratings for numbers. The mean difference between the initial and the final extremity ratings, representing change of intensity of meaning, was calculated for each group and none of these mean differences was found to be significantly different from zero (Table 1). A $4 \times 2 \times 2$ analysis of variance was performed for the numbers. Of the three main effects, only 'order of presentation' was significant ($F = 4.99$, $P < 0.05$). None of the interaction effects reached significance (the largest F value being 1·61). In order to examine the nature of the significant order effect, the means of the initial ratings were computed for the 40 subjects who were presented the numbers first, i.e. before the words, and for the other 40 subjects who were presented the numbers last, i.e. after the words. The means were 14·25 and 12·55, respectively, and these are significantly different ($t = 2.25$, $P < 0.05$).

Ratings on the Meaningful–Meaningless scale

The mean differences between the initial and final ratings on this scale were calculated for words and numbers and their significance levels were determined. These results are presented in Table 2. The continuously repeated numbers became significantly more meaningless whereas the change in the expected direction for repeated words did not reach acceptable significance levels (Table 2).

Latencies of semantic rating responses

An analysis of variance was performed for differences between the initial and the final latencies for both words and numbers. None of the main effects or interactions was significant, indicating that the Satiation group did not differ from the control groups with regard to response latencies. However, latencies generally decreased from the initial to the final ratings for most subjects. A correlated t test between the initial and final latency measures for all 80 subjects reveals a decrease significant at the 0·01 level (mean = -1.66, $t = 2.77$) in the case of the words, and at the 0·05

Table 2. *Average change in polarity for three words or three numbers on the Meaningful–Meaningless scale*

| | | Change in polarity | | | |
| | | Words | | Numbers | |
Condition	No.	Mean diff.	s.d. diff.	Mean diff.	s.d. diff.
Satiation	20	−1·20	4·72	−2·45*	5·24
Silence control	20	−0·30	2·09	+0·10	3·19
Different word control	20	−0·50	2·73	−1·25	3·03
Retest control	20	+0·25	1·84	+0·25	3·33

* $P < 0.05$.

A negative sign indicates a shift of subjects' rating response away from the 'meaningful' and towards the 'meaningless' end of the scale. A shift in the opposite direction is indicated by a plus sign.

level (mean $= -1·55$, $t = 2·25$) in the case of the numbers. This decrease in latency is presumed to be due to accumulated practice in responding to the scales.

Comparison of modes of rating words and numbers

In order to determine whether the standard scales of the semantic differential are appropriate for rating both numbers and words, detailed analyses of the ratings of both types of stimuli were made.

Fig. 1 presents the distribution of ratings of both words and numbers over the 7-point scale of the semantic differential. The ratings for all subjects ($N = 80$) were summed over all stimuli and all regular scales. The maximum possible frequency of usage of a point is 960 (80 subjects × 3 stimuli × 4 scales) and would occur if all subjects used that position for all their ratings. Fig. 1 reveals certain differences and similarities in the manner of rating words and numbers. First, the 'positive' half of the scales (that defined by *extremely, quite* or *slightly good, pleasant, hard* or *active*) is used more often than the opposite half (*bad, unpleasant, soft, passive*) both with numbers and words (using a sign test, $P < 0·01$ in all four cases, i.e. initial and final ratings for both numbers and words). Secondly, the middle position, defined as 'neutral, irrelevant or meaningless', is used more often with numbers than with words ($P < 0·01$ with sign test). This last observation is in agreement with the data given in Table 1 indicating that the means of initial extremity scores for words are markedly larger than the corresponding means for numbers. Thirdly, the positive points on the scales are used more often for words than for numbers ($P < 0·01$ with sign test). However, there is no significant difference between words and numbers in the frequency of using negative scale positions, this being relatively low for both types of stimuli.

Fig. 2 presents the distribution of ratings over the 7-point Meaningful–Meaningless scale for both words and numbers. The ratings for all subjects ($N = 80$) were summed over all words or numbers. The maximum possible frequency of usage of a point is 240 (80 subjects × 3 stimuli) and would occur if all subjects used that position for all of their ratings. It will be noted: (1) that the positive points on the scale (Meaningful) are used more often than the negative positions (Meaningless); (2) the middle position

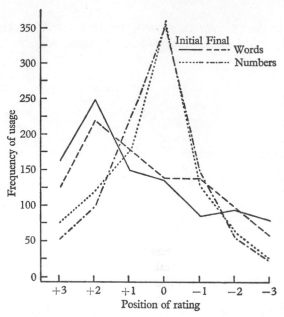

Fig. 1. Distribution of ratings of both words and numbers over the 7-point scale of the semantic differential. Each point represents the sum of ratings of 80 subjects over three stimuli and four scales.

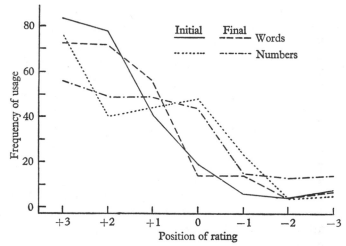

Fig. 2. Distribution of ratings of both words and numbers over the 7-point Meaningful–Meaningless scale. Each point represents the sum of ratings of 80 subjects over three stimuli.

is used more often with numbers than with words; (3) the positive points are used more frequently with words than with numbers. These three comparisons are in the same direction as those noted in Fig. 1 with regular semantic differential scales. However, the negative positions on this scale (Meaningless) are used significantly more often with numbers than with words. On this scale, too, as on the regular scales, the mean initial extremity of rating for the three words is significantly greater than for the numbers (for all four groups combined, the mean initial extremity of rating is 4·90 and 3·84 respectively, $t = 2·29, P < 0·05$).

Osgood (1941; also reported in Osgood *et al.* 1957, pp. 228–9) found shortest latencies for extreme judgements, longest latencies for intermediate judgements, with ratings in the middle position falling between these levels. Fig. 3 presents the distribution of latencies over the 7 points of regular semantic differential scales for both words and numbers. Fig. 3 and that presented by Osgood (1941) are very similar, even though different methods for measuring latencies were used (a voice key in the case of Osgood's data). Inspection of Fig. 3 reveals no systematic difference between words and numbers. It is interesting to note that the M-shaped relationship between response latencies and scale position holds for both initial and final ratings, irrespective of treatment and of the significant improvement effect noted earlier. It seems, then, that scale position is the determining factor of latency of response on the semantic differential for both numbers and words.

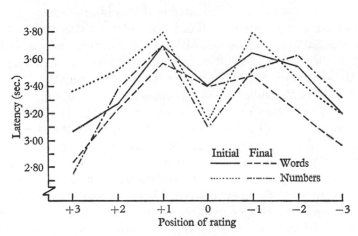

Fig. 3. Latency of response of standard semantic differential ratings as a function of their scale position. Each point represents the average latency per rating for 80 subjects.

Discussion

The effects of continuous repetition on intensity of meaning. Continuous verbal repetition seems to have different effects on words and numbers when indexed with regular semantic differential scales. With words as stimuli, massed repetition induces a significant decrease in the intensity of semantic ratings made on standard semantic-differential scales. This finding is of special interest because it supports earlier work on satiation with an important change in procedure—the use of a fully mechanized method for presenting stimuli and recording both the position and latencies of ratings.

Two findings differ from those obtained in the earlier study of Lambert & Jakobovits (1960). In the 1960 study, words given satiation treatment moved towards the 'meaningless' and 'incomprehensible' poles of the scales 'meaningful–meaningless' and 'comprehensible–incomprehensible', and when the ratings for both scales were combined, the change was significant. The insignificant change toward the 'meaningless' pole in the present study may be due either to the failure to include the 'comprehensible' scale (making for less reliability) or to the fact that subjects in this case rated both numbers and words. A closer examination of such a possible interaction suggests that it may have a differential effect upon the reliability with which the Meaningful–Meaningless scale indexes satiation of words as compared to the regular semantic differential scales. Thus, the mean initial–final difference score on this scale for the 10 subjects in the Satiation condition who received order A (words first, numbers second) was −3·00, indicating a change toward the Meaningless point, while the corresponding mean for the 10 subjects receiving order B (numbers first, words second) was 0·60, indicating a slight change toward the Meaningful point. However, this difference does not reach statistical significance ($t = 1·75$, $0·10 > P > 0·05$). On the other hand, no such trend is apparent when the satiation effect is indexed by means of the regular semantic differential scales (the corresponding means are −3·50 and −4·10 respectively, $t = 0·31$). Without the benefit of additional data, it is difficult to speculate on the nature of this interaction.

In the second place, the Different Word Control condition was not significantly different from the Satiation condition, although the difference was in the direction expected. In the 1960 study, the Different Word Control also yielded a large negative mean, as was the case here, but in the earlier study it was reliably different from the Satiation condition. Both studies are in agreement with the finding that the Different Word control condition does not differ significantly from the Silence and Retest control conditions. It is to be noted that in the Different Word control condition the subject was asked to repeat one word for 15 sec., then to repeat a different word one time, and finally to rate the second word on a semantic scale. This switch of attention from one word to another may be difficult to understand or manage even after full instructions and practice are given. There are two potential sources of error that can occur when using this procedure: the subject could inadvertently rate the first word—the one he has seen and repeated for 15 sec.—rather than the second, or he could rate some combination of the first and second words, and in either case he would be rating at least a partially satiated stimulus. Errors of this sort could account for the relatively large negative means noted for the Different Word Control condition, in both the present and the earlier study. It would seem, therefore, that it is not an appropriate control in comparison with the Satiation condition and other controls, none of which involves a rapid switch in stimuli to be rated. In cases where one is mainly interested in the effect of such a switch on encoding and decoding processes (as was the case in the bilingual study of Jakobovits & Lambert, 1962), the procedure is appropriate and particularly valuable.

In summary, the results indicate: (1) That continuous repetition of words significantly reduces the intensity of their meanings, as measured by the standard scales of the semantic differential. This change in meaning is attributable neither to the unreliability of ratings nor to the delay period before rating the second time, since both Retest and Silence controls showed no reliable changes. However, the meaning change is not reliably reflected on the Meaningful–Meaningless scale. (2) Because there were no differences between conditions in latency of rating, it appears that the satiation effect on words does not involve indecision about how to rate the word. Instead, subjects in the Satiation condition show no hesitation in making less extreme ratings following the repetition treatment when compared with controls whose ratings do not become less extreme. In fact, latencies in rating are determined more by the scale position being used than by variations in satiation or control procedures. (3) In the case of numbers, the satiation treatment did not affect the intensity of ratings on standard scales of the semantic differential but did induce a reliable shift in ratings toward the Meaningless pole of the Meaningful–Meaningless dimension. (4) The M-shaped relationship between response latencies and scale position, noted earlier by Osgood, holds for both numbers and words.

Semantic differential ratings of words and numbers. Words are rated much more frequently than numbers in the extreme positions (positive) of the semantic differential scales. Since extremity of rating is positively correlated with meaningfulness (Staats & Staats, 1959), numbers are judged as less meaningful than words by our subjects, a conclusion that is supported by the finding that words are rated as significantly more meaningful than numbers on the Meaningful–Meaningless scale. Furthermore, the middle scale position is used significantly more frequently for rating numbers than for rating words. These contrasting results suggest that the standard scales of the semantic differential, at least those used here, are not sensitive to the distinctive characteristics of numbers. This does not mean that other scales could not be chosen which would be more appropriate for numbers. In fact, the similarities noted in modes of rating words and numbers (apparent in both the latency data, Fig. 3, and in the tendency to use the positive scale positions more frequently than the negative, Fig. 1) suggest that a different form of the semantic differential would reveal the essential characteristics of numbers. The satiation treatment apparently does affect the connotative meaning of numbers since subjects indicated that numbers became reliably less meaningful after continuous verbal repetition. This finding lends support to the argument presented by Jakobovits & Lambert (1962) that the meaning of numbers is reduced by continuous verbal repetition making it more difficult to use them in addition problems.

REFERENCES

FICHMAN, S. H. (1959). The relation between association value of nonsense syllables and their meaning. *Undergraduate Research Projects in Psychology*, Vol. 1, Department of Psychology, McGill University. (Mimeo).

JAKOBOVITS, L. A. & LAMBERT, W. E. (1962). Semantic satiation in an addition task. *Canad. J. Psychol.* **16**, 112–19.

JAKOBOVITS, L. A. & LAMBERT, W. E. (1964). Stimulus-characteristics as determinants of semantic changes with repetition. *Amer. J. Psychol.* (in the Press).

LAMBERT, W. E. & JAKOBOVITS, L. A. (1960). Verbal satiation and changes in the intensity of meaning. *J. Exp. Psychol.* **60**, 376–83.

OSGOOD, C. E. (1941). Ease of individual judgement process in relation to polarization of attitudes in the culture. *J. Soc. Psychol.* **14**, 403–18.

OSGOOD, C. E., SUCI, G. J. & TANNENBAUM, P. H. (1957). *The Measurement of Meaning.* Urbana: University of Illinois Press.

STAATS, A. W. & STAATS, C. K. (1959). Meaning and *m*: separate but correlated. *Psychol. Rev.* **66**, 136–44.

WIMER, C. C. & LAMBERT, W. E. (1959). The differential effects of words and object stimuli on the learning of paired associates. *J. Exp. Psychol.* **57**, 31–6.

Part VIII

SEMANTIC DIFFERENTIAL TECHNIQUE IN SOCIAL PSYCHOLOGY

35. Stereotypes and Semantic Space

E. Terry Prothro and J. D. Keehn

A. INTRODUCTION

The work on the factor analysis of meaning which has been carried out by Osgood and his collaborators (7, 8) seems to have provided social psychology with a useful new technique for the study of opinions which individuals hold about members of national or racial groups. These investigators have argued that "any description or judgment can be conceived as the allocation of a concept to an experiential continuum," that many continua are "essentially equivalent and hence may be represented by a single dimension," and that a limited number of such dimensions will define "a semantic space within which the meaning of any concept can be specified" (8, p. 326; 7, p. 227). In several analyses (8) they have found three independent dimensions of connotative meaning: evaluation, potency, and activity.

From this point of view, an individual's judgment or description of members of some national group could be specified to a considerable degree by having the individual locate the group members on each of the three dimensions of semantic space. Thus a person's image or stereotype of Turks could be ascertained by having him locate the concept *Turk* on an evaluative scale, a potency scale, and an activity scale. Such a procedure would have obvious advantages over a study which merely elicited "attitudes" toward Turks, for the "attitude" is judgment on only one (evaluative) dimension. The "semantic scale" would likewise be more efficient than the usual study of stereotypes, for many of the adjectives ascribed in a study of stereotypes are essentially equivalent. Moreover, studies of stereotypes ordinarily elicit only those adjectives on which a group rates very high, and do not describe a group with respect to other continua.

The analyses of Osgood and collaborators were based on studies which involve judgments of many concepts, such as *lady, fraud, America, feather,*

Reprinted from *Journal of Social Psychology* (1957), 45: 197–209, by permission of the authors and the Journal Press.

on 50 bipolar descriptive scales, such as *good-bad, red-green, fresh-stale,* and *wide-narrow*. Because of the wide range of concepts and descriptive scales used in the analyses, they conclude tentatively that the connotative aspect of meaningful judgments can be described in three dimensions, and that this aspect accounts for a large portion of the total variance in human judgment or in the meaning of adjectives.

Can judgments of national groups be reduced to these three dimensions of evaluation, potency, and activity? This study was designed as a step toward answering that question. As a test of the generality of Osgood's findings, we have factor analyzed the ratings which English-speaking Arab students gave three national groups on 41 descriptive scales.

B. Procedure

Subjects were 100 bilingual Arab students in this university. It was assumed that the students had had adequate experience with the English language because all of them had passed English-language entrance examinations before entering the university and were pursuing courses in which the classroom lectures and discussions and the course readings were in English. Of the 100 subjects, 59 were male. Median age was 20.5. Of those who indicated religion, 35 were Moslem and 58 were Christian. There were 45 Lebanese in the sample, and the remainder were from neighboring Arab states.

At regular class sessions, subjects were asked to participate anonymously in a study of language behavior. Each subject was presented with a mimeographed booklet on which he indicated sex, nationality, age, and religion. The subjects were then asked to read with care the instructions on the cover of the booklet. The instructions began as follows:

> We are interested in making a study of rating scales. In order to do this we want to ask your coöperation in filling out the attached scales. Please follow the directions as carefully as possible. Our work depends on your serious coöperation.
>
> On the next sheet you will be asked to describe an average or typical person of some nationality. We realize that there are differences between different individuals of one nationality. We also recognize that you may not be acquainted with many persons of that national group. Therefore we are only asking for your impressions. In general, what seem to be the characteristics of an *average* person of that group?
>
> You are asked to rate on a 7-point scale. A score of 7 represents a very high score, a score of 4 is average, and a score of 1 is very low. You are to encircle the score you feel is most appropriate. Here is an example:

The example specified *Lebanese* as the group to be rated on several traits, and demonstrated how various judgments were to be indicated on the answer sheets. A seven-point scale was used, with "very much" written above the "7," "average" above the "4," and "very little" above the "1." "Don't know" could be encircled by anyone uncertain about an adjective.

As soon as all subjects had completed the sample, the class was instructed to turn to the next page and work through the following nine pages to the end of the booklet. Each page contained a list of 30 adjectives alphabetically arranged. At the top of each page was the name of the concept to be rated: "Italian," "German," or "Turk." The order of presentation of the national groups was varied to minimize positional effects. Each nationality was rated on 90 adjective-scales. The adjectives were chosen from studies of national stereotypes (6, 9) and from the list used by Ogood (8). The selection of nationalities to be rated was determined by two considerations. First, previous studies had shown that local students had fairly clear stereotypes of Italians, Turks, and Germans, so they could be expected to respond readily to those names. In the second place, the content of the stereotypes for the three groups was quite different, so the students could be expected to respond differently to each name.

Before the data were examined, 30 of the adjective-scales were selected for the factor analysis. The only principle of selection was the judgment of the experimenters that they covered a wide range of "meaning." After the first analysis was completed for each concept (nationality) separately, nine scales from the first analysis and 11 new scales were submitted to factor analysis. The new scales were introduced because conventional studies of stereotypes here (9, 10) had shown that those 11 adjectives were often ascribed to Germans, Turks, or Italians. The second analysis was also conducted separately for each of the three concepts.

There were, then, 41 scales analyzed. The first analyses were of adjectives selected by the experimenters as representing a wide range of meaning and the second were of additional adjectives which had emerged from studies of stereotypes, together with nine adjectives which had emerged as significant in the first analyses.

C. Results

1. *The Factors*

Rotated factor loadings obtained in the two analyses are shown in Tables 1 and 2 . Thurstone's centroid method was employed. In the first analyses, rotation was carried out blindly toward "orthogonal simple structure." In the second analyses, rotation was carried out with attention to the factors which emerged in first analyses.

Factor I corresponds to Osgood's evaluative factor. Substantial loadings are found for the following adjectives: *dishonest, treacherous, cruel, un-*

TABLE 1
ROTATED FACTOR LOADINGS—FIRST ANALYSES

Concept rated Adjectives	Italians			Turks			Germans		
	FI	FII	FIII	FI	FII	FIII	FI	FII	FIII
Dishonest	67	—22	29	—78	—15	12	59	—02	07
Treacherous	66	00	14	—60	—12	40	66	02	05
Bad	54	—04	27	—69	—12	18	58	—14	—25
Untruthful	50	—16	16	—72	—12	35	55	17	11
Cruel	64	08	—12	—66	02	—07	40	07	—29
Aggressive	43	25	—30	—67	—01	—22	47	08	—32
Materialistic	42	23	26	—26	13	18	55	—01	—11
Superficial	46	00	18	—23	—24	19	53	—30	—03
Good	—43	47	05	50	40	20	—18	15	05
Self-confident	00	66	—28	12	66	—17	—12	59	—16
Strong-willed	—05	54	—40	—09	70	—17	13	47	—11
Energetic	00	46	—38	07	68	—05	—19	38	—12
Strong	—06	60	—11	—17	62	—25	—03	35	—25
Quick	—05	59	04	—02	64	06	01	31	—19
Progressive	08	54	—12	09	60	07	—15	38	—24
Intellectual	18	59	—08	16	65	20	05	26	—36
Courageous	—20	59	—29	01	64	—34	02	22	—52
Rich	19	57	—40	—03	50	—13	25	—12	—21
Scientific	14	63	—11	11	—68	24	—11	14	—59
Clean	—05	40	—22	21	45	27	—05	35	04
Artistic	02	35	00	27	55	21	05	30	—12
Emotional	04	42	55	04	35	—07	06	10	15
Pleasant	—20	23	47	35	53	11	07	25	28
Nervous	08	39	46	—15	24	—07	36	28	—20
Easy-going	—11	09	19	05	—03	42	39	08	21
Poor	01	—15	39	—20	—18	27	—01	32	02
Militaristic	10	43	—40	—21	58	—23	01	19	—72
Passive	05	—21	47	—06	—33	61	18	—04	50
Peaceful	—31	05	47	46	17	29	—08	06	52
Weak	47	—27	53	—18	—32	50	48	—12	26
Per cent of total variance	10.4	15.9	9.8	13.1	19.9	6.7	10.5	6.4	8.6

truthful, bad, aggressive, unstable, humanistic (negative), *materialistic, good* (negative), and *superficial*. The interpretation of these adjectives as "evaluative" or as reflecting the "attitude" of like-dislike or as lying along a dimension of *good-bad* could be made from a study of the list alone. Such an interpretation is strongly supported by the fact that Osgood found *good-bad, kind-cruel,* and *honest-dishonest* to have loadings of more than .80 on the evaluative factor.

Factor II is similar to Osgood's potency factor. Adjectives with substantial loadings, roughly in order of size of loading, are: *self-confident, strong-willed, ambitious, strong, energetic, quick, intellectual, courageous, progressive, nationalistic.* Almost all of these terms would be used in describing a powerful personality, and when they are taken together the picture is clearly one of "potency." The strength here is not merely one of mass, as the terms *energetic, quick,* and *progressive* emphasize. Osgood found that such

TABLE 2

ROTATED FACTOR LOADINGS—SECOND ANALYSES

Concept rated	Italians			Turks			Germans		
Adjectives	FI	FII	FIII	FI	FII	FIII	FI	FII	FIII
Dishonest	—62	09	43	75	16	14	—54	—02	33
Treacherous	—58	27	29	48	—14	40	—60	09	38
Unstable	—45	15	42	52	—28	17	—43	06	29
Humanistic	49	08	31	—50	24	27	27	18	19
Sociable	44	18	06	—29	57	25	25	16	24
Democratic	54	19	16	—14	49	24	19	24	16
Self-confident	19	66	—30	—12	67	—20	—04	67	—21
Strong-willed	33	59	—33	19	71	—18	—05	56	—14
Ambitious	20	52	—21	07	64	—15	03	47	—17
Strong	31	47	—18	15	61	—20	—08	26	—14
Stubborn	—02	51	—07	30	31	08	—15	34	—37
Nationalistic	13	45	—23	24	40	—30	—22	32	—22
Athletic	31	53	—16	—18	53	08	—03	14	—43
Artistic	38	23	24	—25	50	30	31	38	24
Musical	27	32	36	—45	48	12	14	19	45
Militaristic	10	33	—40	19	60	—31	—26	43	—51
Passive	01	—16	56	00	34	55	—03	—12	41
Weak	—49	—03	54	34	—35	51	—42	—07	40
Imaginative	13	20	55	—19	24	29	—11	00	48
Lazy	—20	03	45	29	—38	38	—37	—04	35
Per cent of total variance	12.8	12.6	11.9	11.0	21.5	8.2	8.0	9.0	10.7

scales as *large-small, strong-weak,* and *heavy-light* were most heavily loaded on his Factor II. The *strong-weak* loading corresponds to our finding, and the other choices were not given our subjects. When judging Italian and Turks, our subjects responded to *rich* in terms of *potency* whereas Osgood's subjects treated the *rich-poor* dimension as one of *evaluation.* The fact that Americans respond similarly to *rich* and *good* whereas Arabs, sometimes at least, respond similarly to *rich* and *strong* raises interesting questions regarding cross-cultural differences in the reinforcement of verbal responses.

Factor III is less clear than the other factors in our analyses. The adjective *passive* seems to typify the factor best, for it had consistently high loadings on Factor III and low loadings on other factors. Other terms which are loaded on this factor are: *weak, peaceful, imaginative*. Osgood called his third factor an *activity* factor because of the importance of the *active-passive* scale in his results. He also found that his *ferocious-peaceful* scale was loaded on this factor. In both these respects our results agree with his. His *fast-slow* scale was also heavily loaded on this factor. In our data *quick* was related to Factor II and not to Factor III. Whether this difference testifies to a difference between the "meaning" of *fast* and *quick* cannot be determined from our data, but Osgood's work on differences between such near synonyms as *good* and *nice* raises this possibility (7, p. 230).

2. *The Stereotypes*

Information on the stereotypes of our subjects can be derived from Table 3. In the classical techniques for the study of stereotypes, developed by Katz and Braly (6) one asks subjects to check adjectives which seem best to characterize a national group. In this way a list of adjectives is obtained on which the nationality under study rates high. From our data we might obtain a somewhat similar list by taking all adjectives on which the median rating is above 5.0. If we adopt this criterion, then the following stereotypes emerge:

Italians are: artistic, musical, emotional, imaginative, pleasant, sociable.

Turks are: aggressive, cruel, nationalistic.

Germans are: nationalistic, militaristic, energetic, ambitious, self-confident, strong-willed, scientific, courageous, progressive, strong, intellectual, musical, stubborn, quick, artistic, athletic, clean, cruel.

It might also be argued that adjectives on which a group is rated very *low* should also be included as a part of the stereotype. And what of the traits on which a nationality is thought of as average? If the subjects are in agreement that the people of a certain nationality are about average with respect to self-confidence, then "average on self-confidence" is also a part of the stereotype. From this point of view, the variability in ratings rather than the mean rating is the criterion for the selection of adjectives which belong to the stereotype. The stereotype of a group of raters consists of all ratings on which there is consensus, whether the rating is extremely high, extremely low, or just average.

The study of consensus requires that we use some measure of dispersion. The use of Q as a measure of spread of ratings was precluded by two considerations. First, we wished to include those choosing "Don't Know" with those who did not rate the group near the median. Second, for many adjectives, the proportion of persons choosing Category 1 or 7 was greater than 25 per cent (3, p. 229).

We have indicated the agreement among the subjects on ratings assigned by listing in Table 3 the number of subjects who chose the two categories

TABLE 3

MEDIAN RATINGS ASSIGNED AND NUMBER OF PERSONS CHOOSING THE TWO CATEGORIES
AT THE MEDIAN

Adjectives	Italians		Turks		Germans	
	Mdn	No. choosing	Mdn	No. choosing	Mdn	No. choosing
Aggressive	3.9	38	5.8	44	3.1	24
Athletic	4.0	61	4.2	51	5.4	59
Clean	3.6	46	3.0	53	5.3	48
Energetic	4.3	42	4.3	55	6.6	86
Humanistic	4.7	47	2.6	46	3.7	47
Militaristic	3.4	42	4.8	46	6.7	89
Nationalistic	4.7	53	5.3	54	6.7	86
Passive	3.8	48	3.1	39	1.5	76
Poor	4.2	53	4.2	45	3.6	65
Progressive	4.2	60	3.4	54	6.0	65
Rich	3.3	58	3.2	56	4.0	66
Self-confident	4.1	56	3.9	51	6.2	77
Sociable	5.2	59	3.6	57	4.6	59
Strong-willed	4.1	47	4.2	47	6.2	82
Ambitious	4.5	63	4.7	55	6.4	87
Bad	2.7	51	3.9	37	2.3	41
Courageous	3.8	49	4.7	47	6.2	71
Dishonest	3.0	46	3.9	29	2.1	43
Easy-going	4.2	55	3.2	45	2.2	40
Good	4.2	64	3.2	52	4.7	62
Lazy	3.1	33	3.5	39	1.3	91
Nervous	4.8	44	4.6	51	4.5	47
Quick	4.5	56	4.0	59	5.5	72
Scientific	4.1	56	3.3	51	6.2	79
Stubborn	4.0	46	4.9	51	5.6	58
Treacherous	2.8	39	4.3	32	1.6	58
Untruthful	3.2	37	4.2	37	2.0	58
Artistic	6.5	80	3.2	49	5.4	59
Cruel	3.0	50	5.6	41	5.2	47
Democratic	4.1	49	3.6	44	3.8	47
Emotional	6.0	69	4.2	54	4.1	38
Imaginative	5.7	58	3.8	56	4.1	34
Intellectual	4.4	65	3.4	58	5.7	66
Materialistic	4.4	54	4.9	54	4.8	54
Musical	6.3	72	4.2	46	5.7	36
Peaceful	4.6	58	2.8	49	3.0	51
Pleasant	5.3	61	3.3	58	4.0	56
Strong	3.9	59	4.6	52	5.9	54
Superficial	3.8	41	4.2	42	2.3	47
Unstable	4.1	49	4.3	44	2.6	41
Weak	3.7	54	3.3	43	1.6	82

"adjacent to the median." That is, when the median was between 3.0 and 4.0, we indicated the frequency choosing Categories 3 and 4. Thus there were 38 persons who rated the Italians as either 3 or 4 on *aggressive*, and there were 44 persons who rated the Turks as either 5 or 6 on *aggressive*. When the median was at the mid-point of an interval, we arbitrarily chose that interval and the adjacent one with the largest frequency. For example, on *athletic*, for which Italians had a median of 4.0, 41 subjects gave them a rating of 4, 20 gave them a rating of 3, and only 14 gave them a rating of 5, so we entered the frequency of 61 in the table.

If we arbitrarily adopt a 50 per cent frequency in the two categories at the median as our criterion of whether an adjective is a part of our subjects' stereotype, then the stereotypes of the three national groups are as follows:

Italians

High on: artistic, musical, emotional, pleasant, sociable, imaginative.
Above average on: ambitious, peaceful, quick, nationalistic.
About average on: intellectual, good, athletic, progressive, strong, self-confident, scientific, easy-going, materialistic, weak, poor.
Below average on: rich, cruel.
Low on: bad.

Turks

High on: nationalistic.
Above average on: ambitious, materialistic, strong, nervous, stubborn.
About average on: quick, sociable, imaginative, energetic, emotional, athletic, self-confident.
Below average on: intellectual, pleasant, rich, progressive, clean, good, scientific.
Low on: none of these 41 adjectives.

Germans

High on: militaristic, ambitious, energetic, nationalistic, strong-willed, scientific, self-confident, quick, courageous, intellectual, progressive, athletic, artistic, stubborn, strong.
Above average on: good, sociable, materialistic.
About average on: rich, poor, pleasant.
Below average on: peaceful.
Low on: lazy, weak, passive, treacherous, untruthful.

In Figure 1 we have tried to describe the stereotypes of our subjects in terms of a three-dimensional semantic space. The dimensions are the three orthogonal factors. For the purpose of this graph we have defined each factor in terms of the three adjectives which seemed best to represent it. For Factor I, we chose *dishonest, treacherous, cruel.* For Factor II, we chose *self-confident, strong-willed,* and *ambitious.* For Factor III, we chose *passive, weak,* and *peaceful.* The coördinates of the location of each national group were determined by the median values assigned those adjectives as shown in Table 3. For each dimension, we took the median of the values

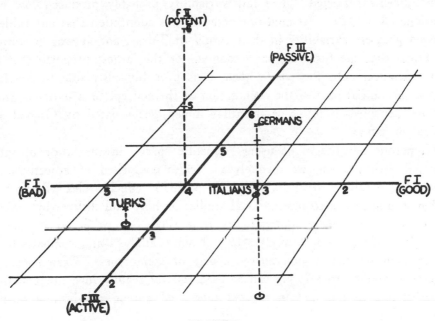

FIGURE 1
THREE-DIMENSIONAL REPRESENTATION OF THE STEREOTYPES OF ITALIANS, TURKS, AND
GERMANS

assigned the three adjectives. For example, our subjects gave the Italians median ratings of 3.0 on *dishonest,* 2.8 on *treacherous,* and 3.0 on *cruel,* so we assigned the Italians a rating of 3.0 on Factor I.

D. Discussion

Our analyses yielded three factors which seem to be the three factors which Osgood found in his more general study of meaning. To what extent, then, can we describe the concept of a national group in terms of a three-dimensional semantic space? In Osgood's study he was able to account for about half the total variance of ratings on 50 scales. From the totals shown in Tables 1 and 2 it can be seen that the amount of the total variance on the 41 adjective-scales which can be accounted for by our three factors varies from 26 to 41 per cent. There are probably two explanations for the lower factor loadings in our study. Osgood's technique involved summing over both concepts rated and subjects rating, so his correlations included variance attributable to differences between concepts (8, p. 322). We treated concepts (national groups) separately. In the second place, our subjects rated concepts on which there was considerable agreement. Indeed the concepts were selected because previous studies have shown that such agreement existed. The low variability probably produced low correlations (8, p. 329). It might be noted in this connection that our subjects showed greatest variability in their rating of Turks, and it was on ratings of Turks that the three factors accounted for the largest proportion of the total variance. On the whole, then, it is probably justifiable to conclude that a substantial part of the connotation of the concept of a national group can be identified in terms of the three dimensions isolated by Osgood and his collaborators.

Numerous advantages of using "semantic space" in the study of international attitudes suggest themselves. Scales comprised of adjectives can serve as generalized attitudes scales (7, p. 231). Such scales will literally add new dimensions to international studies of likes and dislikes by separating opinions on potency and passivity from those on evaluation as good or bad. The scales lend themselves to systematic analysis and comparison far better than do purely descriptive reports of stereotypes. Examination of adjectives applied to a group can be used equally readily in content analysis of written materials and in surveys conducted among non-literate or preliterate people.

The factorial approach to meaning also sheds new light on some of the studies of patterning in the attribution of adjectives. As an example, we might choose one part of the well-known study of Asch (1 and 2, pp. 208-213) on how impressions of personality are formed. To each of two groups, he read a list of "character-terms." The list was identical for the two groups except that the term *warm* was in the list presented to Group *A* and *cold* was in the list presented to Group *B*. Such terms as *intelligent, industrious,* and *determined* were in both lists. Next he presented a list of other adjectives to each group, and asked whether those new adjectives did or did not characterize the fictitious person. He found that Group *A* and Group *B* agreed in calling the person *strong*, but disagreed on whether he was *humane* and *generous*. From these and other similar data he concluded (2, p. 210) that "a change of one quality produces a fundamental change in the entire impression. Also, the differentiating quality does not give an undiscriminating . . . 'halo effect' . . . the 'warm' person was not more favorably viewed in all respects . . . not all traits are equally central."

A non-Gestalt, though not necessarily anti-Gestalt, explanation of these data could be presented by analyzing the dimensions of the adjectives used by Asch. Although we do not have data on the adjectives employed by him, it is possible that the adjectives presented to both groups (*intelligent, industrious, determined*) specified that the person described was high on the potency factor, whereas the adjectives *warm* and *cold* described him as at opposite poles on the evaluative factor. If this were true, then Group *A* and Group *B* would be expected to rate the person similarly on adjectives with high loadings on the potency factor and low loadings on the evaluative factor, but to rate him differently on adjectives with high evaluative loadings and low potency loadings. Thus *strong* may have been chosen by both groups because of its heavy loading on potency. *Humane* and *generous* may have been chosen by one group and rejected by the other group because of the loading of these adjectives on the evaluative factor.

Instead, then, of drawing the broad conclusion that a change of one quality forces a reformulation of a Gestalt, we might conclude that in certain selected situations a change in one adjective can change the quadrant in semantic space in which a concept is located. Such a special situation exists when the adjective being manipulated is the only one with a heavy loading on one of the major dimensions of connotative meaning. Similarly, instead of concluding that not all traits are equally central, we might conclude that not all traits are significantly loaded on the factor defined by the trait being manipulated. We do not wish to minimize the importance of Asch's pioneering work, but we do believe that the factor analysis of meaning offers a technique for systematic attack on the problems which he has raised.

We have followed Osgood in treating correlations among scales as revealing common meaning in the scales. Yet, in psychological studies involving the use of rating scales, correlations among scales have often been treated as errors on the part of raters. In such cases there has been the unstated premise that various traits are uncorrelated, so that any correlations found are evidence of a "halo effect." Johnson (4, p. 203; 5, p. 130) has pointed out that correlations among traits do not demonstrate the halo effect, because such correlations may be objective facts rather than errors of judgments. Guilford also notes (3, p. 279) that correlations are not sufficient evidence for a halo effect because correlations among traits are produced whenever there is "semantic overlapping." Although his remarks were apparently addressed to cases in which the rater was in error in assuming there was overlap, his observation would hold equally well for cases in which the rater was using the overlapping terms properly.

The work on factor analysis of meaning could be thought of as study of "semantic overlap." Apparently large groups of adjectives have some meaning in common, and these commonalities are found even under conditions (8, p. 327) which Guilford (3), and Johnson (5) describe as ideal for minimizing halo. If various adjectives in one such a group are given the status of trait names by an experimenter, then we would expect ratings on those traits to show some intercorrelations. Such intercorrelations cannot always be dismissed as rater errors. If an "error" exists, it may be on the part of the experimenter who overlooks the fact that a large portion of the variance in human judgment can be accounted for in terms of a small number of basic variables.

E. Summary

Studies by Osgood and others have shown that a large part of the connotative aspect of judgment can be described in terms of the three orthogonal factors of evaluation, potency, and activity-passivity. We applied the factorial approach to the study of the ratings which English-speaking Arab students gave to Italians, Turks, and Germans on 41 adjective-scales. From ratings obtained it was possible to describe the stereotypes of our subjects in considerably greater detail than could have been done by using the classical technique for the ascertaining of stereotypes. Factor analysis of the ratings revealed three factors which seemed to be those found by Osgood. It was possible to describe the stereotypes of our subjects in terms of these factors. Such a description added depth to the usual report of attitudes although it accounted for less than half of the total variance on the 41 scales. Some implications for social psychology of the factorial approach to meaning were discussed.

References

1. Asch, S. E. Forming impressions of personality. *J. Abn. & Soc. Psychol.*, 1946, **41**, 258-290.

2. ———. Social Psychology. New York: Prentice-Hall, 1952.

3. Guilford, J. P. Psychometric Methods (2nd ed.) New York: McGraw-Hill, 1954.

4. Johnson, D. M. A systematic treatment of judgment. *Psychol. Bull.*, 1945, **42**, 193-224.

5. Johnson, D. M., & Vidulich, R. N. Experimental manipulation of the halo effect. *J. Appl. Psychol.*, 1956, **40**, 130-134.

6. Katz, D., & Braly, K. W. Verbal stereotypes and racial prejudice. *In:* T. M. Newcomb and E. L. Hartley (*Eds.*), *Readings in Social Psychology*. New York: Holt, 1947. (Pp. 204-209.)

7. Osgood, C. E. The nature and measurement of meaning. *Psychol. Bull.*, 1952, **49**, 197-237.

8. Osgood, C. E., & Suci, G. J. Factor analysis of meaning. *J. Exp. Psychol.*, 1955, **50**, 325-338.

9. Prothro, E. T., & Melikian, L. H. Studies in stereotypes: III. Arab students in the Near East. *J. Soc. Psychol.*, 1954, **40**, 237-243.

10. Prothro, E. T., & Melikian, L. H. Studies in stereotypes: V. Familiarity and the kernel of truth hypothesis. *J. Soc. Psychol.*, 1955, **41**, 3-10.

36. Initial Attitude toward Source and Concept as Factors in Attitude Change through Communication

Percy H. Tannenbaum

Though there have been many studies of attitude change through communication, but little experimentation has been done on the variables controlling the attitude change of a given communication. In the study reported here, the author investigated the effects on the amount of change of the original attitudes of the audience. He demonstrates that the attitudes toward source and concept affect the amount of change, and describes the nature of the functions of these factors in the communication situaiton.

Perhaps the simplest and most typical communication message is one in which an identifiable source (*S*) makes a favorable or unfavorable assertion about a particular object or concept (*C*). In most cases, a person exposed to such a message brings into the communication situation his original (i.e., pre-exposure) attitudes toward both *S* and *C*. A problem for research may then be: What effect is exercised by these original attitudes of the *recipient* of the communication on determining the attitude change toward *C* and toward *S*?

As a general field of study, this is not novel. Many investigators have studied segments of the overall problem, particularly with respect to the influence of the source on attitude shift toward the concept. Typical of such studies have been those in "prestige suggestion"[1] or source "credibility."[2] The majority of such investigations have demonstrated a significant source effect in terms of change in judgment of the concept. Thus, when the source—if we may use that blanket term—is held in high regard (the most common experimental situation), subjects tend to change their judgments of the concept in the direction of the source's assertion.[3] When *S* is held in low esteem, the effect is less than that for the favorable *S*, or in the direction opposite

Reprinted from *Public Opinion Quarterly* (1956), 20: 413–425, by permission of the author and the publisher.

[1] Cf. S. E. Asch, "The Doctrine of Suggestion, Prestige and Imitation in Social Psychology," *Psychological Review*, 1948, Vol. 55, pp. 250-276.

[2] Cf. C. I. Hovland, I. L. Janis, and H. H. Kelley, *Communication and Persuasion*. New Haven: Yale University Press, 1953.

[3] E.g., H. E. Burtt, and D. R. Falkenburg, Jr., "The Influence of Majority and Expert Opinion on Religious Attitudes," *Journal of Social Psychology*, 1941, Vol. 14, pp. 269-278.

from his assertion.[4] In the few instances where a "neutral" S was employed, the effect was an intermediate.[5]

Another factor that has been studied is the susceptibility to change of the original attitudes. Birch,[6] for example, attributed the failure of his subjects to change their judgments to the fact that he was dealing with "well-structured beliefs." In effect, what we have here is a special case of one of communication theory's few general "laws"—that weakly held (or, less intense) attitudes are more susceptible to change than strongly-held (more intense) ones. But even this general principle has never been studied systematically; it appears to have been distilled from a number of separate studies rather than from a direct approach.[7]

Most of the experimentation in this general area has been focused on the problem of change in the judgment of the concept. However, a possible by-product of a communication event in which S makes an assertion about C is that there will occur a shift in judgement of S as well as—or, perhaps, instead of—the intended shift toward C. Such a view has been advanced, but it has been a most unexploited area of investigation.[8] Despite the relative paucity of experimentation, it is apparent that attitude toward the communicator is not independent of what he says or does. Indeed, this is probably one of the main avenues through which attitudes toward persons and groups are developed, altered, and maintained.

The present study was undertaken to provide a systematic study of attitude shift toward both the concept and the source of a communication as a function of the original attitudes of the recipient of the communication toward both these elements. In so doing, specific hypotheses, relating mainly the amount of shift, were put to experimental test.[9]

Susceptibility Hypothesis. The amount of attitude change toward an object is inversely proportional to the intensity of the original attitude toward that object. This is merely a more generalized re-statement of the susceptibility principle mentioned earlier. The purpose here is to provide a direct test of the principle. Moreover, as a general principle, it should apply to both attitude change toward C and toward S.

[4] E.g., F. Hoppe, "Erfolg und Misserfolg."

[5] E.g., H. C. Kelman, and C. I. Hovland, " 'Reinstatement' of the Communicator in Delayed Measurement of Opinion Change," *Journal of Abnormal and Social Psychology*, 1953, Vol. 48, pp. 327-335.

[6] Birch, H. G., "The Effect of Socially Disapproved Labeling Upon a Well-Structured Attitude," *Journal of Abnormal and Social Psychology*, 1945, Vol. 40, pp. 301-310.

[7] Cf. W. Schramm, "The Effect of Mass Communications: A Review," *Journalism Quarterly*, 1949, Vol. 26, pp. 397-409.

[8] Heider, F., "Attitudes and Cognitive Organization," *Journal of Psychology*, 1946, Vol. 21, pp. 107-112.

[9] A general theoretical statement to account principally for the direction of change is presented in a separate report. Cf. C. E. Osgood and P. H. Tannenbaum, "The Principle of Congruity and Prediction of Attitude Change," *Psychology Review*, In press.

Relationship Hypothesis. (a) The amount of attitude change toward the concept in direction of the assertion is directly proportional to the degree of favorableness of the original attitude toward the source. (b) The amount of attitude change toward the source in a favorable direction is directly proportional to the degree of favorableness of the original attitude toward the concept when the assertion is favorable, but is inversely proportional when the assertion is unfavorable.

The two forms of this hypothesis attempt to define the functional relationships between attitude change toward one element as a function of attitude toward the other element. In terms of *C*-shift, the present study attempts to provide a more comprehensive test of what has been demonstrated earlier on a gross basis. In terms of *S*-shift, the experiment will concern itself with something that has never been experimentally studied.

The present investigation will also attempt to measure the significance of the interaction between the two variables under consideration. Often alluded to, this interaction has never been demonstrated.[10]

METHOD

Test Material. On the basis of a pretest of 36 potential sources and concepts, three source-concept combinations were selected which most closely met the criteria of (a) approximately equal numbers of subjects holding favorable, neutral, and unfavorable original attitudes toward each source and concept, and (b) lack of correlation between attitude toward the particular source and concept in each pair. The three source-concept pairs thus selected were:

Material	Source	Concept
X	Labor Leaders	Legalized Gambling
Y	*Chicago Tribune*	Abstract Art
Z	Sen. Robert Taft	Accelerated College Programs

Two versions of each set of material were written—a *favorable version* in which the source made a favorable assertion about the concept, and an *unfavorable version* in which the assertion was unfavorable toward the concept. Two additional stories were written to serve as filler material, but were not included in the analysis.

These eight stories, two versions of each of the three experimental stories and one each of the filler stories, were reproduced in standard newspaper type along with appropriate headlines. For material Y, which took the form

---

[10] E.g., W. A. Lurie, "Measurement of Prestige and Prestige-suggestibility," *Journal of Social Psychology*, 1938, Vol. 9, 219-225; Hovland, Janis and Kelley, *op. cit.*

of an editorial, the precise masthead and type used on the *Chicago Tribune* editorial page were employed.

Measuring Instrument. A feature of the present study was the use of a novel technique to measure attitude. The technique is an outgrowth of research under the direction of Charles E. Osgood on the measurement of meaning.[11] The meaning of a concept is regarded as its location in a multidimensional space, and attitude toward that concept is its projection on one of the dimensions of meaning—the evaluative dimension.

In one factor analytic study, in which 20 diversified concepts were each judged by 100 subjects against 50 scales selected on a frequency-of-usage criterion, it was found that the first factor to appear and the one accounting for the most variance is clearly identifiable as an evaluative one. Six scales which had high loadings on this factor and minimal, negligible loadings on the other factors were taken as measures of attitude in the present study. These scales consist of seven-step continua, each defined by a pair of polar adjectives. The six scales used in this experiment were: *fair-unfair, dirty-clean, tasty-distasteful, good-bad, pleasant-unpleasant* and *worthless-valuable.* In addition, four filler scales representing the other factors were included, but they did not enter into the analysis.

These scales are scored by assigning unit weights, ranging from one to seven, to the seven steps of each scale. In the present study, the unfavorable end (e.g., *unfair, dirty, bad,* etc.) was assigned the lowest score of one, and the favorable end (e.g., *fair, clean, good,* etc.) was assigned the score of seven. The attitude score of an object (i.e., either S or C) was the sum of ratings over all six scales. The range of attitude score for a single object, then, is from 6 (most unfavorable) to 42 (most favorable).[12]

Subjects. Subjects were undergraduate psychology students. The data for 405 subjects were employed in the analysis. The subjects participated in the experiment in two sessions, both of which took place during the regular discussion section meetings of the course. There were 26 such sections.

Procedure. The testing procedure was quite standard. All subjects were given a *before-test* in which each of the sources and concepts were rated on the selected scales. Subjects were instructed on the use of the semantic differential (the name given to Osgood's scales) and were told the purpose of the study was "to try to find out how college students . . . feel about certain issues and personalities in the news today, and to try out a new instrument . . . to get at these feelings."

[11] Osgood, C. E., "The Nature and Measurement of Meaning," *Psychological Bulletin,* 1952, Vol. 49, pp. 197-237.

[12] Cf. P. H. Tannenbaum, "Measurement and Prediction of Attitude Change," paper presented at Midwestern Psychological Association meetings, Columbus, Ohio, April, 1954, for a more thorough presentation of the rationale for the use of this technique, including evidence of reliability and validity; an article on this subject is presently in preparation.

Five weeks later, subjects were exposed to the communication material, immediately followed by the *after-test*. In terms of the exposure, there were three versions of each story—the favorable and unfavorable versions mentioned earlier, and a third neutral version which consisted of no story at all. Exposure was randomized so that each group was exposed to each of the three experimental stories once and only once, and to each of the three versions once and only once. Thus, one group may have had story X in a favorable version, story Y in an unfavorable version, and story Z in a neutral version; for another group it was story X unfavorable, story Y neutral, and story Z favorable, and so on.

Subjects were told that the before-test had shown the instrument to be a useful one and that "we were now interested in seeing how it stacked up against a standard reliable method of widespread use, the 'Johnson technique.'" They were told this latter technique consisted of reading a story and then reproducing its "essence" in 25 words or less.[18] Subjects then read each of the experimental stories, along with the filler material, applied the "Johnson technique," and then took the after-test, which was identical with the before-test. They were told it was necessary to repeat the ratings "since a gap of five weeks is too much to allow for valid comparison."

Design. The basic design was a 3x3x3 factorial design where the rows represent original attitude toward the concept, the columns represent original attitude toward the source, and the blocks represent the stories. Thus, there were three levels of original attitude toward the concept: favorable (C+), neutral (C0), and unfavorable (C—). Similarly, there were three levels of original attitude toward the source: S+, So, and S—. And there were three stories or material: X, Y, and Z, as previously indicated. This design was the same for each of the three versions of the stories—favorable, neutral and unfavorable. Thus, for each version there was a 27-cell (N = 15 for each cell[14]) factorial design, with no replication of subjects within each version. There was replication between versions and consequently a separate analysis was conducted for each version.

Subjects were assigned to their respective groups for analysis according to their ratings on the before-test on attitude toward both the source and concept of a particular combination. Thus, on story X, for example, a particular subject may have had favorable attitudes toward both the *S* and *C* and was allocated to the S+C+ group; on story Y, he may have been neutral

---

[18] There is good reason to assume that this attempt to "cloak" the aim of the study was successful. There were no cases of suspicion noted among the subjects, and even the class instructors seemed convinced.

[14] After the data were gathered, the smallest number of subjects that fell in any cell was 15. The number of subjects in each of the other cells was reduced by random selection to this number, as an aid in the computational analysis.

toward S and unfavorable toward C, and thus fell into the S0C— group, and so on.

Since the design necessitated the separation of attitude scores into three distinct categories, the following breakdown was arbitrarily adopted: favorable (+) included scores from 6-17, inclusive; neutral (0) from 16-30, inclusive, and unfavorable (—) from 31-42.

RESULTS

Stability of the attitude. The inclusion of a neutral version of the stories in the form of no story at all was to provide a measure of the stability of the attitudinal objects dealt with and to serve as a control for the experimental stories. Table 1 presents the test-retest change scores (after-test score *minus* before-test score) for both change in attitude toward the concept (C-shift), and for change in attitude toward the source (S-shift). Each interior cell represents the sum of change scores for 45 subjects (15 subjects on each of

TABLE 1

CONCEPT-SHIFT (UPPER CELL VALUES) AND SOURCE-SHIFT (LOWER VALUES) FOR
NEUTRAL VERSION

Original Attitude toward Concept	Original Attitude toward Source			Totals
	$S+$	So	$S-$	
C+	-7	0	+3	-4
	-6	+8	-1	+1
Co	-7	+2	+1	-4
	+6	+1	-1	+6
C-	+6	0	-4	+2
	+5	-9	-1	-5
Totals	-8	+2	0	-6
	+5	0	-3	+2

three stories).[15] It is readily apparent that we are dealing with highly stable attitudinal objects, and that this stability holds for all combinations of attitude toward C and S.

Concept-shift. Table 2 presents the amount of C-shift for the favorable and unfavorable assertions, according to different levels of original attitude toward C and S. Again, the interior cells represent the sum of scores for 45 subjects. Comparing the *net* shift with the control (neutral version), there is a significant difference beyond the 2 per cent level for both the favorable

---

[15] Because analysis of variance showed very *insignificant* differences between the three stories, the data for all three was combined. The same applies to subsequent tables of results.

and unfavorable versions. The difference between the two experimental versions is significant well beyond the 1 per cent level.

TABLE 2
CONCEPT-SHIFT FOR FAVORABLE (UPPER VALUES) AND UNFAVORABLE (LOWER VALUES)
ASSERTIONS

Original Attitude toward Concept	Original Attitude toward Scource			Totals
	S+	So	S−	
C+	+ 51	+ 39	− 24	+ 66
	− 88	− 72	+ 19	−141
Co	−245	+ 80	− 52	+273
	−180	− 79	+ 22	−237
C−	+107	+ 48	− 10	+145
	− 39	− 34	+ 16	− 57
Totals	+403	+167	− 86	+484
	−307	−185	+ 57	−435

Source-shift. Table 3 shows the *S*-shift for both favorable and unfavorable assertions. In this case, none of the differences in *net* change are significant

TABLE 3
SOURCE-SHIFT FOR FAVORABLE (UPPER VALUES) AND UNFAVORABLE (LOWER VALUES)
ASSERTIONS

Original Attitude toward Concept	Original Attitude toward Source			Totals
	S+	So	S−	
C+	+ 25	+150	+ 49	+224
	− 45	− 68	− 33	−146
Co	+ 16	+ 25	+ 13	+ 54
	+ 1	+ 17	− 3	+ 15
C−	− 42	− 94	− 7	−143
	+ 34	+ 96	+ 34	+164
Totals	− 1	+ 81	+ 55	+135
	− 10	+ 45	− 2	+ 33

at the 5 per cent level. This is not too surprising since the stories were directed at changing attitude toward the concept and not specifically toward the source. However, it will be noted that these net *S*-shifts result from a "cancelling out" of some very substantial changes between the different levels or original attitude toward *C* and toward *S*.

Susceptibility Hypothesis. Figure 1 presents the results of plotting the mean amount of change against original attitude, for both *C-* and *S*-shift.

The curves have been "smoothed" by taking the mean of three adjacent values as the value for the second of the three. Each curve includes change on both favorable and unfavorable versions, the mean change being determined regardless of direction. Assuming intensity being least for neutral attitudes and increasing progressively as the attitude becomes more favorable or unfavorable, the data in Figure 1 generally confirm the hypothesis.[16]

An unexpected finding, however, occurs at the point of extreme neutrality —a score of 24. Insead of the expected peak, there is a pronounced dip in the curves. One explanation is that the semantic differential does not provide an adequate measure of intensity, although available evidence tends to eliminate this possibility.[17] Another explanation is that people can be *intensely neutral*. This tends to contradict earlier evidence but deserves consideration. Osgood, using latency as a measure of intensity of verbal judgements of the seven-step continua, found exactly this relationship—intensity was highest at the extreme points, next highest at the mid-point (neutrality) and least at the intermediate points.[18] A third possibility which merits consideration is that many subjects may have been unmotivated and disinterested in the task and checked down the middle of the scales as "an easy way out." The present evidence does not allow us to decide among these alternatives, but if the second of those offered proves to be the case, it may have some important implications for attitude measurement—e.g., Guttman and Suchman's procedure for deciding on the zero-point of a scale as the point of least intensity.[19]

A direct statistical test of the general trend in Figure 1 is contained in comparing three levels of attitude used in the study with respect to amount of change—i.e., compare the change scores between C+, C0, and C— groups with respect to *C*-shift, and the S+, So, and S— groups with respect to *S*-shift. A non-parametric[20] analysis of variance[21] to test this demonstrated significant differences in every instance (p. < .02 to p < .001).

Relationship Hypothesis. Figure 2 presents the results of plotting the mean *C*-shift against original attitude toward *S* and includes both the favorable

[16] Cf. H. Cantril, "The Intensity of an Attitude," *Journal of Abnormal and Social Psychology,* 1946, V. 41, pp. 129-136; D. Katz, "The Measurement of Intensity," in H. Cantril (Ed.), *Gauging Public Opinion.* Princeton, New Jersey: Princeton University Press, 1944.

[17] Cf. C. E. Osgood, *Report on Development and Application of the Semantic Differential.* Urbana, Illinois: Institute of Communications Research, University of Illinois, 1953.

[18] Osgood, C. E., "Ease of Individual Judgement-processes in Relation to Polarization of Attitudes in the Culture," *Journal of Social Psychology,* 1941, Vol. 14, pp. 403-418.

[19] Guttman, L. and E. A. Suchman, "Intensity and Zero-point for Attitude Analysis," *American Sociological Review,* 1947, Vol. 12, pp. 57-67.

[20] Because of a high degree of heterogeneity of variance in the data, the standard analysis of variance was prohibited. Rather than attempt data transformations, the advice of an expert (Dr. C. R. Blyth, Department of Mathematics, University of Illinois) was followed and the non-parametric techniques were employed.

[21] Cf. L. E. Moses, "Non-parametric Statistics for Psychological Research," *Psychology Bulletin,* 1952, Vol. 49, pp. 122-143.

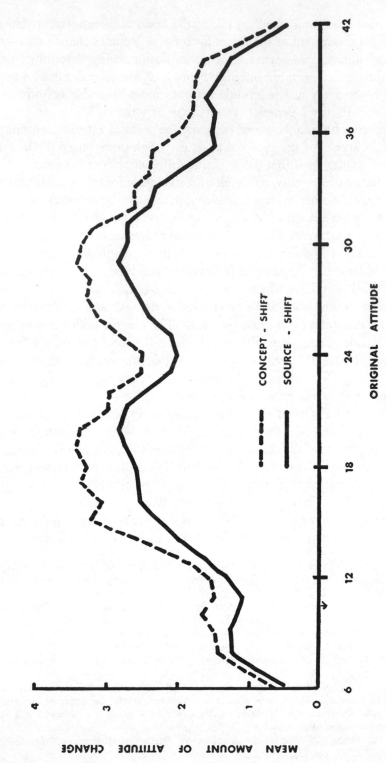

ORIGINAL ATTITUDE

FIGURE 1

Amount of Attitude Change as a Function of Original Attitude Toward the Object.

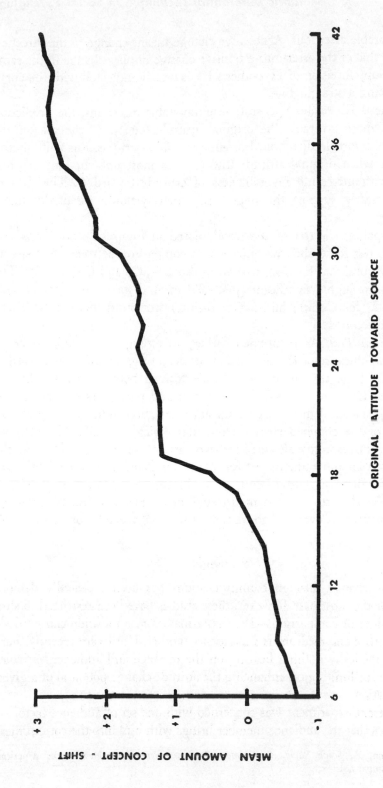

ORIGINAL ATTITUDE TOWARD SOURCE

FIGURE 2

AMOUNT OF CONCEPT-SHIFT AS A FUNCTION OF ORIGINAL ATTITUDE TOWARD THE SOURCE.

and unfavorable assertions. A negative change means change in the direction opposite to that of the assertion; a positive change implies change in the same direction. Substantiation of Hypothesis IIa is clearly indicated with the curve approximating a straight line.

Hypothesis IIb relates to S-shift. For favorable assertions, the prediction is that the more favorable the original attitude toward C, the greater the S-shift in a favorable direction. For unfavorable assertions, this shift should be greatest when original attitude toward C is most unfavorable and then decrease with increasing favorableness of attitude toward C. The data in Figure 3 clearly support the hypothesis, again yielding essentially linear functions.

A non-parametric test of the trends noted in Figures 2 and 3 was also made. The test for C-shift was based on a comparison between the S+, So and S— groups, that for S-shift between the C+, Co and C— groups. The differences are highly significant (p < .001 in all cases), and referring back to Tables 2 (for C-shift) and 3 (for S-shift) we found them to be in the predicted directions.

Interaction Test. As mentioned earlier, an attempt was made to determine the significance of the interaction between original attitudes toward C and toward S on the amount of change toward both elements. The test rests in the isolation of the SxC interaction and testing its significance by appropriate statistical means. A significant interaction indicates a significant departure of the obtained change from that which is predictable solely on the basis of the respective effects of the two variables operating independently.

Wilcoxon's non-parametric test for interaction based on ranked data [22] was applied. For both S- and C-shift, a significant interaction was indicated (p < .02 in all cases), and demonstrated an interactive effect between the two variables that is over and above that of the two variables operating independently.

DISCUSSION

Attitude change through communications has been repeatedly demonstrated. For the most part, however, these studies have been restricted to simple evaluations or comparisons—i.e., that a mass communication can produce change, or that one medium is superior to another. Until very recently there has been practically nothing bearing on the message and audience variables responsible for limiting on enhancing the attitude change potential of a given communication.

The present experiment was concerned with one set of audience factors— the attitudes that the audience member brings with him into the communica-

[22] Wilcoxon, F., *Some Rapid Approximate Statistical Procedures.* New York: American Cyanamid Company, 1949.

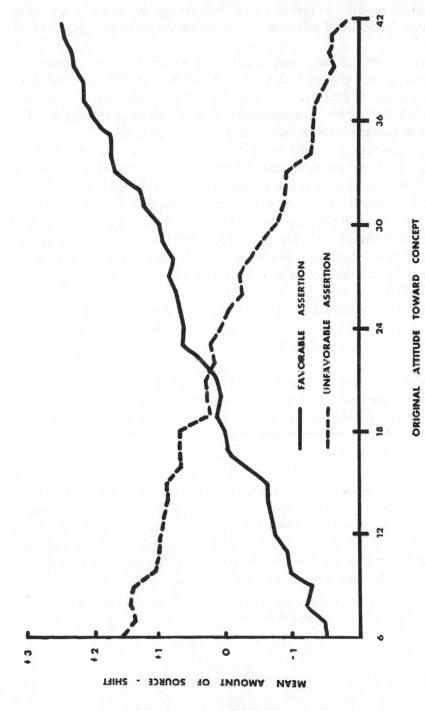

ORIGINAL ATTITUDE TOWARD CONCEPT

FIGURE 3

AMOUNT OF SOURCE-SHIFT AS A FUNCTION OF ORIGINAL ATTITUDE TOWARD THE CONCEPT.

tion situation toward the source and concept of a message. As such, these variables are regarded as part of a set of intervening variables which serve to determine the frame of reference within which the message is perceived or *decoded*.

It was shown that both these variables are significant in determining the amount of attitude change, both with respect to concept-shift, the usual focus of inquiry, and to source-shift, which until recently has been a subject for speculation but not for experimentation. It was also demonstrated that the interaction between these two variables is a significant factor.

This study also attempted to go beyond the mere demonstration of the significance of the variables; the nature of their functions was also explored.[23] A major finding is that the susceptibility to change is inversely proportional to the intensity of initial attitude. One suggestion of this finding is that the occasional discrepancy between results of experiments in this field may be a function of the types of attitudes dealt with. On several occasions it has been reported that no attitude change took place as a result of the introduction of communication material. It may well be that examination of these studies will reveal that they were dealing with highly-structured, intense attitudes to begin with. Indeed, initial attitude should be controlled in all studies dealing with attitude change. Birch has made this point with respect to prestige suggestion studies; it may apply equally to other investigations of attitude change.[24]

Another implication of the results of this study is that the mere measurement of attitude before and after communication exposure on a gross basis, without regard for the intervening variables, may often be misleading. With respect to S-shift on an unfavorable assertion, for example, the results of such an approach would show no significant change—in the present study, the net shift was only $+33$ over 405 subjects. However, this net shift is something of an artifact. Looking more closely into the results in terms of original attitude toward C and S, we find this net change to be a result of a "cancelling-out" of some very substantial changes—e.g., the $C+$ group shows an S-shift of -146 and the $C-$ group $+164$, both over 135 subjects. These are both significant changes. It cannot be said, then, that no appreciable change takes place following exposure to such communication material.

---

[23] A discussion of the nature of the interactive effect was considered beyond the scope of this paper. It is contained in Osgood and Tannenbaum, *op. cit.*

[24] Birch, *op. cit.*

37. Deriving an Attitude Scale from Semantic Differential Data

James E. Brinton

This paper presents a method for selecting adjective pairs, from semantic differential data, for use in an attitude scale. The selected adjectives are submitted to Guttman scale analysis, producing a scale with high reproducibility and scalability.

THE semantic differential, which has found a variety of uses in recent years since its development by Osgood,[1] is known to contain a strong evaluative factor. A number of factor analyses by the Illinois group found evaluation to be the strongest dimension measured by the differential, followed generally by two other dimensions, activity and potency.

In the semantic differential, which is made up of seven-step scales bounded on either end by polar adjectives, certain of the adjectives were found to have high evaluative loadings when applied to many objects or concepts. It was possible to score a large number of adjectives on their loadings on the evaluative factor. Tannenbaum used a number of these adjectives to form a scale in measuring attitude toward certain concepts.[2] Others have since used the differential in a variety of ways in the field of attitude measurement. Validity of the differential attitude scales appears to be high, based on high correlations with scores gathered by the traditional Thurston, Likert, and Guttman types of scales.

This paper outlines a method of selecting specific adjectives to be used in an attitude scale based on semantic differential data. The selection of adjectives was submitted to Guttman-scale analysis as a check on dimensionality. The method can be used either with a small sample of subjects in the pre-test phase of a study or on data that have already been gathered.

Reprinted from *Public Opinion Quarterly* (1961), 25: 289–295, by permission of the author and the publisher.

[1] Charles E. Osgood, George J. Suci, Percy H. Tannenbaum, *The Measurement of Meaning*, Urbana, Ill., University of Illinois Press, 1957.

[2] Percy H. Tannenbaum, "Initial Attitude toward Source and Concept as Factors in Attitude Change through Communication," *Public Opinion Quarterly*, Vol. 20, 1956, pp. 413-425.

For an example, let us take a study of attitude toward capital punishment. Here it was desirable to have an attitude test that would be somewhat concealed and would yield a numerical score for correlational and other statistical purposes.

PROCEDURE

Among a list of sixteen adjective pairs used in the capital punishment study were a number of pairs that were reported to have generally high evaluative loadings.[3] Scales were made up, bounded on either end by the polar adjectives. Following the semantic scale, another single scale was added:

How would you rate your over-all feeling about capital punishment?

Strongly in
favor of it _____:_____:_____:_____:_____:_____:_____ against it
Strongly

The purpose of this single scale was to establish an attitudinal ranking for the subjects so that they could be divided into pro– and anti–capital punishment groups. Other methods could be used to get pro– and anti–capital punishment groups. Subjects for the two groups could be selected on the basis of some known behavioral activity or from their scores on a verbal attitude test. However, the single scale, rating over-all feeling, seemed to be an extremely simple method of dividing the subjects into two groups. The test, using the sixteen adjective pairs and the final over-all scale, was administered to 160 students at three universities—55 at North Carolina, 56 at Stanford, and 49 at Washington.[4]

Distribution of scores on the single scale is shown in Table 1. Subjects checking the first, second, or third intervals on the scale were placed in a pro–capital punishment group. Subjects checking the fifth, sixth, or seventh intervals were placed in an anti–capital punishment group. Those scoring 4 were regarded as being in a neutral position.

Means for each group on each of the sixteen polar adjective scales were then computed. The group means and the differences between them are in Table 2. On five of the adjective-pair scales, differences between means for the pro and anti groups were 2.00 or greater. The largest difference, 3.87, occurred on the just-unjust scale. Other differences of 2.00 or greater were: good-bad (3.51), valuable-worthless (3.17), honest-dishonest (2.00), and fair-unfair (3.38).

Evaluative factor loadings for these adjectives, as reported by Osgood,

---

3 Osgood *et al., op.cit.,* p. 37.

4 The author is grateful to Professor Merritt E. Benson, University of Washington, and Professor Wayne A. Danielson, University of North Carolina, for administration of the tests to students at those universities.

TABLE 1

DISTRIBUTION OF SCORES ON CAPITAL
PUNISHMENT RATING SCALE

Score	Number
1	(17)
2	(19)
3	(20)
4	(22)
5	(14)
6	(36)
7	(32)
	(160)

Suci, and Tannenbaum, were: good-bad (.88), valuable-worthless (.79), honest-dishonest (.85), and fair-unfair (.83). No loading was reported for the just-unjust pair. With these high loadings on the evaluative factor, these adjective pairs should be expected to be the ones that would show large mean differences between two groups formed on

TABLE 2

MEANS AND DIFFERENCES ON SIXTEEN ADJECTIVE PAIRS FOR
PRO– AND ANTI–CAPITAL PUNISHMENT GROUPS

Adjective Pair	Pro Group Mean	Anti Group Mean	Difference in Means
*Just-unjust	2.19	6.06	3.87
Fast-slow	2.59	3.38	.79
Peaceful-ferocious	3.81	5.22	1.41
Active-passive	2.47	3.44	.97
*Good-bad	2.66	6.17	3.51
White-black	3.79	5.05	1.26
Nice-awful	4.34	6.00	1.66
Kind-cruel	4.07	5.91	1.84
*Valuable-worthless	2.21	5.38	3.17
Clean-dirty	3.26	4.60	1.34
Soft-hard	5.17	5.35	.18
*Honest-dishonest	2.45	4.45	2.00
*Fair-unfair	2.24	5.62	3.38
Delicate-rugged	5.17	4.96	.21
Beautiful-ugly	5.19	5.95	.76
Brave-cowardly	3.74	4.95	1.21

* Five adjective pairs with largest differences between means.

an attitudinal basis. However, some other adjectives which have high evaluative loadings did not produce much in the way of differences between the means of the two groups. For instance, the adjective pair, beautiful-ugly, which has a reported evaluative loading of .86, pro-

duced a mean difference of only .76 between the groups. The evaluative
factor loadings, which represent an average over many concepts, may
not be the best criterion for selecting adjectives for use on one specific
concept. The meanings and evaluative strengths of adjectives can
change from one concept to another.

When applied to the concept of capital punishment, the beautiful-
ugly adjective pair appears to lose much of its evaluative strength. It
is probable that this loss is due to a shift in meaning from connotative
to denotative when applied to this particular concept. In other cases
loss of evaluative strength might be caused by ambiguity when applied
to a given concept or to irrelevance to the concept.

It appears that the five adjective pairs with high mean differences
between the two groups are the adjectives in this set of sixteen pairs
that have the highest evaluative strength when applied to the concept
of capital punishment.

In order to check whether this selection method is consistent over
several samples of subjects, the procedure was followed for each of the
subsamples—Stanford, North Carolina, and Washington. Each subsample was divided into pro and anti groups, and then separate group
means were compared for each adjective. The results are shown in
Table 3. Asterisks mark those pairs of adjectives which have the greatest
mean differences between pro and anti groups. Four of the pairs—just-
unjust, good-bad, valuable-worthless, and fair-unfair—show the greatest

TABLE 3

DIFFERENCES IN MEANS ON SIXTEEN ADJECTIVE PAIRS
FROM THREE INDEPENDENT SAMPLES

Adjective Pair	Differences between Pro and Anti Groups		
	North Carolina	Stanford	Washington
Just-unjust	3.97*	3.80*	3.82*
Fast-slow	.58	.88	.60
Peaceful-ferocious	1.39	1.82	.67
Active-passive	.41	.97	1.92
Good-bad	3.55*	3.08*	3.79*
White-black	1.25	.94	1.71
Nice-awful	1.66	1.58	1.76
Kind-cruel	1.78	2.06*	1.44
Valuable-worthless	2.95*	3.08*	3.37*
Clean-dirty	1.44	.80	1.56
Soft-hard	.13	.06	.28
Honest-dishonest	1.86*	1.75	2.44*
Fair-unfair	3.41*	3.25*	3.28*
Delicate-rugged	.12	.63	.23
Beautiful-ugly	.96	.55	.90
Brave-cowardly	.61	1.53	1.45

* Five adjective pairs with largest differences between means.

difference on the full sample and also on the three subsamples. The other adjective pair, honest-dishonest, has the fifth greatest difference on the full sample and on the North Carolina and Washington samples. However, it is displaced in fifth position by the pair, kind-cruel, on the Stanford sample. With this one exception, the method selected identical adjective pairs from the full sample and the three subsamples.

SCALING SELECTED ADJECTIVES

Five adjective pairs for which the means for the pro and anti groups showed the greatest differences were selected as the five items to form the scale. On each adjective pair, each subject received a score of 1, 2, 3, 4, 5, 6, or 7, the low scores being in favor of capital punishment and the high scores against it. Individual scores were summed over the five scales, resulting in total scores ranging from 5 to 35. This set of scores produced a product moment correlation of .823 with the single seven-step attitude scale.

The usual Guttman scaling procedure was followed. Subjects' item scores were arranged in order of the total score for all items. In this case, with scores of 35 at the top and descending to scores of 5 on the bottom, the individual item scores formed gradients running from 7 down to 1. Objective cutting points in the item columns were located to minimize error, and new item scores were given on the basis of the cutting points. Subjects were re-ordered on the basis of new total scores, and the columns were re-ordered to place those with higher cutting points at the left and those with lower cutting points at the right. The data, with all items reduced to dichotomies, reduce to the form shown in Table 4.

The scale, which orders the individuals into six scale types from 0 to 6, has an over-all coefficient of reproducibility of .975 and coefficients of scalability of .915 for items and .892 for individuals.[5] These coefficients are extremely high and indicate the selected adjective pairs are in a single dimension.

CONCLUSIONS

This paper demonstrates a relatively simple method of extracting a Guttman scale from semantic differential data. Adjective pairs for use in the scale were selected on the basis of differences between mean scores for pro– and anti–capital punishment groups. Five pairs of adjectives—just-unjust, good-bad, valuable-worthless, honest-dishonest, and fair-unfair—were selected. Individual scores on these five pairs were summed to produce an initial score for ranking in the scaling

[5] Herbert Menzel, "A New Coefficient for Scalogram Analysis," *Public Opinion Quarterly*, Vol. 17, 1953, pp. 268-280.

TABLE 4

FINAL ARRANGEMENT OF CASES ON COMPLETED SCALE

Scale Type	Unfair Fair	Bad Good	Worthless Valuable	Unjust Just	Dishonest Honest	Number of Cases	Errors
5	1	1	1	1	1	(18)	0
4	0	1	1	1	1	(37)	0
4	0	1	1	1	0	(4)	4
4	0	1	0	1	1	(6)	6
3	0	0	1	1	1	(26)	0
3	0	0	1	1	0	(2)	2
3	0	0	1	0	1	(3)	3
2	0	0	0	1	1	(24)	0
2	0	0	0	1	0	(3)	3
1	0	0	0	0	1	(13)	0
0	0	0	1	0	0	(2)	2
0	0	0	0	0	0	(22)	0
Errors	0	0	8	3	9	(160)	20

Coefficient of reproducibility:
$$\frac{800 - 20}{800} = .975$$

Coefficient of scalability (by items):
$$\frac{234 - 20}{234} = .915$$

Coefficient of scalability (by individuals):
$$\frac{185 - 20}{185} = .892$$

process. Routine Guttman scaling resulted in a scale with high reproducibility and high scalability. As a result, individuals may be ranked in types according to their attitude toward capital punishment.

The method can produce some economy in research. Many times semantic differential data are used to produce profiles, for distance analysis, or for some other purpose. An attitude score, because of its close relationship with the evaluative factor in the semantic differential, is almost always present in the data. If data have already been gathered, the method illustrated in this paper could be used to determine the set of adjectives to be used in an attitude scale. If the study were in its development stages, analysis of pre-test data could help determine which adjectives would be most useful as an attitude scale in the final study.

A scale developed by the method outlined in this paper will naturally be specific to the concept or attitudinal dimension around which it was developed. Such a scale might not work well when applied to another attitudinal dimension. If one wanted a scale that would be effective in measuring attitudes in a number of areas, then a more general approach would be needed—such as the use of adjective pairs chosen for their high evaluative loadings over a number of concepts. We do not propose to enter a controversy of long standing on the relative merits of specific and generalized attitude scales.[6] We merely wish to point out a basic difference between the type of scale developed here and one that would result from use of general evaluative loadings as a basis of selecting adjectives. In either case, we believe the Guttman-scale method can be useful in testing dimensionality of the selected adjectives and in ordering individuals on the dimension.

[6] An excellent discussion of generalized attitude scales appears in Osgood *et al.*, *op.cit.*, pp. 195 f.

38. Connotations of Racial Concepts and Color Names [1]

John E. Williams

Language custom designates racial groups by the color names white, black, red, yellow, and brown, a practice which may condition the connotative meanings of color names to concepts representing racial groups. This study compared the connotative meanings of triads of color-linked concepts consisting of: color names (e.g., black), color-person concepts (e.g., black person), and ethnic concepts (e.g., Negro). For Caucasian Ss from both South and Midwest, color-linked concepts were substantially more similar in meaning than were non-color-linked concepts. The evaluative (good-bad) connotations of ethnic concepts were predictable from their associated color names. Different results were obtained for Negro Ss. The findings were interpreted as indicating that the color-coding of racial groups is related to the perception of these groups and the favorability of attitudes toward them.

Language custom designates racial groups according to a "color code" in which Caucasians are called white, Negroes are referred to as black, and Orientals, American Indians, and Southwest Asians are designated, respectively, as yellow, red, and brown. On reflection, it is obvious that this color code has little descriptive accuracy with regard to skin color; Caucasians are not literally "white," nor is the modal American Negro "black," and yet, applications of this color nomenclature are encountered daily, for example, in popular press accounts of racial problems or incidents. Although admittedly convenient, and seemingly innocuous, the practice of color coding may have hidden and, perhaps, undesirable effects since color names such as white and black are regularly used in other contexts as general cultural symbols to convey different connotative meanings such as goodness and badness (Williams, 1964). The present study was concerned with the question of whether the color-coding practice is related to the way in which different racial groups are perceived.

In an earlier investigation, Williams (1964) studied the connotative meanings of

Reprinted from *Journal of Personality and Social Psychology* (1966), 3: 531–540, by permission of the author and the American Psychological Association.

[1] This research was supported, in part, by a grant from the Wake Forest College Graduate Council. The author is grateful to Lafayette Parker and Jefferson Humphrey of Winston-Salem State College, to Bertram Spiller of Washburn University, and to Jack Hicks, formerly of Washburn University, for their assistance in data collection.

color names presented in a nonracial context. It was demonstrated that there are striking differences in the connotative meanings of color names and that these meanings are relatively stable across both regional and racial lines. For example, the connotative meaning of the color name *white* was found to be "good," "active," and "weak," while the color name *black* was "bad," "passive," and "strong." Since it is known that the connotative meanings of words can be classically conditioned to other words (Staats & Staats, 1957, 1958), it seemed likely that the consistent association of a color name, such as *black*, with a racial concept, such as *Negro*, would tend to condition the connotations of the former to the latter. In this way, the practice of color coding might operate as a background factor in the development and/or maintenance of attitudes toward racial groups.

One way to observe the effects of using color names to designate groups of persons would be to study the meaning similarity between color names, as such, and color names used as adjectives to describe people. For example, is there a similarity in the connotative meanings of the concepts *black* and *black person?* One might also study color-person concepts in relation to color-code related ethnic concepts (e.g., *black person* and *Negro*) and observe the degree of connotative meaning similarity. In a third type of comparison, one might study the meaning similarity of ethnic names (e.g., *Negro, Caucasian*) to the color names with which the color code associates them.

The general hypothesis for this study was that similarities in connotative meaning will be found to be greater among concepts which are linked by the color code than among concepts not so related. Although no specific predictions were made, it was anticipated that Caucasian subjects and Negro subjects might differ in their ratings of the racially significant concepts of the present study, in spite of their generally similar performance in rating color names in the earlier study (Williams, 1964).

METHOD

This study was an extension of Williams' (1964) earlier study of the connotative meanings of color names, with the same subject populations and data gathering procedures being employed. The reader is referred to the earlier study for a more detailed description of materials and procedures.

Subjects

Subjects were introductory psychology students from three institutions: Caucasian [2] students from Wake Forest College, a liberal arts college in North Carolina; Caucasian students from Washburn University, a municipal university in Kansas; and Negro students from Winston-Salem State College, a liberal arts college in North Carolina. The numbers of subjects from each institution rating the color-person concepts were, respectively, 86, 88, and 106. The numbers rating the ethnic-national concepts were 110, 70, and 60. In the two Caucasian groups, no subject rated both groups of concepts. In the Negro group, approximately one quarter of the subjects rating the ethnic-national concepts had rated the color-person concepts approximately 1 month earlier. All research groups were composed of equal numbers of men and women.

Semantic Differential

Other than the concepts rated, the rating procedure used was identical to that employed by Williams (1964) which was based on the work of Osgood, Suci, and Tannenbaum (1957).

Color-person concepts. The 10 color-person concepts were formed by pairing the word person with each of the 10 color names studied by Williams (1964), that is, black person, white person, brown person, yellow person, red person, blue person, green person, purple person, orange person, and gray person. The concepts were presented to the subject in random order and rated on 12 scales, 6 of which had been chosen to reflect the evaluation (E) factor,

[2] The term Caucasian is used throughout this paper in its popular meaning of "white person" rather than in any technical ethnological sense.

3 the potency (P) factor, and 3 the activity (A) factor.

Ethnic-national concepts. This group of 14 concepts included 5 concepts selected because of their relevance to color and color-person concepts—Negro, Caucasian, Indian (Asiatic), Oriental, Indian (American); 4 other ethnic-national concepts—American, African, Chinese, Japanese; and 5 general reference concepts—citizen, foreigner, friend, enemy, and person. Using the same 12-scale rating sheet the subjects rated person first; then the other 4 reference concepts in random order; and, finally the 9 ethnic-national concepts in random order.

Procedure

The procedure was administered to groups of subjects by an experimenter of the same race using conventional semantic differential rating instructions. The concepts to be rated were presented to the subject in a mimeographed booklet with a single concept name heading each page and with the 12 rating scales presented below. Subjects recorded their sex but no other identifying information was requested.

RESULTS

The basic data for study consisted of the E, P, and A scores for the five race-related color-person concepts—black person, white person, brown person, yellow person, and red person; and for five corresponding ethnic concepts—Negro, Caucasian, Indian (Asiatic), Oriental, and Indian (American).

Each rating sheet was scored by assigning the digits 1–7 to the 7 positions on each rating scale and summing the ratings on the appropriate scales for the E, P, and A factors. Low scores represented the "good" end of the E dimension, the "weak" end of the P dimension, and the "passive" end of the A dimension. Separate analyses by sex were not made after inspection of the data indicated that men and women subjects were responding to the task in essentially the same manner. Table 1 displays the three mean factor scores for each concept, separately for each of the three groups of subjects. Included in Table 1 are the scores for the five race-related color names from the Williams (1964) study.

Intercorrelations of E, P, and A Scores

In the earlier study of color names, it was found that the E, P, and A scores were characterized by a high degree of statistical independence, thus supporting the notion that the

TABLE 1

MEAN SEMANTIC DIFFERENTIAL SCORES FOR CONCEPTS RATED BY CAUCASIANS FROM THE SOUTH,
CAUCASIANS FROM THE MIDWEST, AND NEGROES FROM THE SOUTH

	Evaluation			Potency			Activity		
	Caucasian		Negro	Caucasian		Negro	Caucasian		Negro
	South	Midwest		South	Midwest		South	Midwest	
White	1.79	1.85	2.05	3.60	3.49	3.52	4.75	4.90	5.10
Black	5.09	4.98	4.11	5.98	6.29	5.70	3.31	3.69	3.63
Brown	4.45	4.25	3.82	4.95	5.20	4.92	2.74	2.95	3.51
Yellow	2.82	2.64	2.52	3.21	3.10	3.24	4.99	4.77	5.00
Red	3.18	3.18	3.08	5.58	5.96	5.19	6.23	6.32	5.77
White person	2.63	2.45	3.75	4.24	4.26	3.53	5.24	5.06	4.48
Black person	4.52	4.76	3.89	5.79	5.22	5.23	3.53	3.73	4.45
Brown person	4.02	4.14	3.22	5.01	4.86	4.72	3.61	3.77	4.58
Yellow person	3.61	3.81	3.47	2.69	2.69	3.54	4.31	4.27	4.49
Red person	3.69	3.72	3.83	5.15	5.21	4.69	5.51	5.52	4.96
Caucasian	2.69	2.98	3.89	4.86	4.66	4.14	5.17	5.06	4.42
Negro	4.08	3.92	2.89	5.10	4.72	4.93	3.52	3.99	4.72
Indian (Asiatic)	3.65	3.84	3.68	3.83	3.79	4.26	3.85	3.84	4.27
Oriental	3.20	3.53	3.63	3.01	3.10	3.85	4.35	4.24	4.37
Indian (American)	3.24	3.46	3.53	4.91	4.64	4.47	4.66	4.41	4.72
Person	2.56	2.88	2.69	4.47	4.30	4.40	5.10	4.70	4.93
Friend	1.91	1.85	2.40	4.94	4.77	4.70	5.55	5.75	5.28
Enemy	5.68	5.67	5.41	4.74	4.53	4.07	4.73	4.22	4.18
Citizen	2.74	2.69	2.81	4.71	4.60	4.64	5.00	5.00	4.92
Foreigner	3.18	3.18	3.41	4.09	3.98	4.00	4.45	4.45	4.22

Note.—Scores shown are mean factor scores divided by number of scales. Color-name data are from Williams (1964).

different scores reflected different aspects of connotative meaning. In order to assess the degree of independence of the three scores in the present study, correlation coefficients were computed for each pair of the three scores, for each of the five race-related color-person concepts and for each of the five corresponding ethnic concepts, separately for each of the three groups of subjects. For the color-person concepts, the median coefficients were as follows: E versus P, $r = +.03$; E versus A, $r = -.40$; P versus A, $r = +.29$. For the ethnic concepts the median coefficients were: E versus P, $r = -.28$; E versus A, $r = -.46$; P versus A, $r = +.40$. While these correlations indicated that the E, P, and A scores were not statistically independent, the amount of common variance was not high (0–20%) and it was judged useful to analyze and report the scores separately.

Comparison of Caucasian Groups

The E, P, and A scores of the two Caucasian groups were analyzed to determine whether the connotative meanings of the concepts under study were rated differently by Southern and Midwestern college students.

Color-person concepts. For each of the three scores (E, P, and A), separately, a Lindquist (1953) Type I analysis of variance was performed with the five color-person concepts comprising the within-subjects dimension and the two groups of Caucasian subjects as the between-subjects dimension. In each analysis, the between-groups and interaction effects were not significant while the between-concepts effect was highly significant ($p < .001$).

Ethnic concepts. The analyses of the E, P, and A scores for the five ethnic concepts paralleled the color-person analyses just described with similar findings: nonsignificant between-groups and interaction effects, and highly significant ($p < .001$) between-concepts effects.

On the basis of the foregoing analyses, it was judged appropriate to pool the data of the Southern and Midwestern Caucasian groups in subsequent analyses.

Comparison of Caucasian and Negro Groups

This analysis was to determine whether the Negro subjects were responding to the race-related color-person and ethnic concepts in a manner similar to that of the Caucasian subjects. For each of the two groups of five concepts, three Lindquist (1953) Type I analyses of variance were run, one each for the scores E, P, and A. In these analyses the five concepts represented the within-subjects dimension and the Causasian-Negro classification was the between-subjects dimension. In each of the six analyses, the interaction effect was highly significant ($p < .001$) indicating that the two groups of subjects were responding quite differently to the concepts and, hence, that the subsequent analyses should be made separately for Caucasian and Negro subjects.

Caucasian Subjects: Comparison of Related Color, Color-Person, and Ethnic Concepts

In the top portion of Figure 1 are displayed the scores for related triads of color, color-person, and ethnic concepts along the E dimension. The vertical lines connect color-code related triads of concepts, that is, white-white person-Caucasian; black-black person-Negro; brown-brown person-Indian (Asiatic); yellow-yellow person-Oriental; red-red person-Indian (American). The general similarity of rank orders along the E dimension is quite apparent with the concepts white, white person, and Caucasian rated most "good," the concepts black, black person, and Negro rated most "bad," and the other three triads occupying intermediate positions. Thus, one can predict the rank position of color-person and ethnic concepts on the E dimension quite accurately on the basis of the rank position of the color concept with which they are conventionally associated.

The middle and lower thirds of Figure 1 indicate a substantial degree of rank-order similarity for related triads along the P and A dimensions but not as high a degree of consistency as that found for the E dimension. On the P dimension, the color-person con-

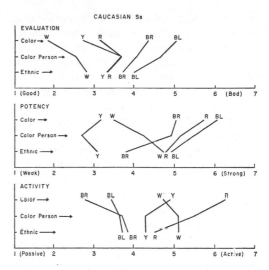

FIG. 1. Semantic differential scores of Caucasian subjects for color-linked triads of color, color-person, and ethnic concepts. (Vertical lines connect triads, as follows: W = white, white person, Caucasian; Y = yellow, yellow person, Oriental; R = red, red person, Indian (American); BR = brown, brown person, Indian (Asiatic); BL = black, black person, Negro.)

cepts maintain the same rank order as the color concepts, but a shift out of rank order is seen for the ethnic concepts Caucasian and Indian (Asiatic). On the A dimension, there is some shifting of rank order both from color to color-person concepts, and from color-person concepts to ethnic concepts.

D scores. The similarities in meaning seen in Figure 1 may be conveniently summarized by the use of the *D* index developed by Osgood and his associates (1957, pp. 89 f.). Based on the generalized distance formula of solid geometry, *D* provides an index of the distance between pairs of concepts in three-dimensional semantic space. Osgood et al. (p. 93), note that the use of *D* to indicate absolute semantic distances requires the assumption that the three variables employed are statistically independent, a condition not met in the current instance (see above). It was judged, however, that in the present situation where interest was in the *relative* magnitude of different *D* scores, the partial violation of this assumption was not critical.

Applying the formula of Osgood et al. (1957, p. 91), *D* scores were computed between: each color and each color-person concept, each color and each ethnic concept, and each color-person and each ethnic concept. To illustrate, the D score for any two concepts was obtained by: computing the difference between the two mean E scale scores, the two mean P scale scores, and the two mean A scale scores; squaring each of these differences; summing the squares and taking the square root of the sum. From this, it can be seen that low D scores indicate high similarity in overall meaning while high scores reflect low similarity. It should also be noted that the D procedure weights all three difference scores equally, ignoring the greater pervasiveness of the E factor (in a factor analysis sense) and also its greater relationship to positive and negative attitudes as traditionally measured (Osgood et al., 1957, p. 193).

Table 2 lists the 75 D scores obtained when each concept in one class was compared with each concept in the other two classes. These D scores provide a convenient place for a formal testing of the hypothesis that similarities in connotative meaning will be found to be greater among concepts linked by the color code than among concepts not so related. To test this hypothesis, a Mann-Whitney U test (Peatman, 1963) was computed for each third of Table 2 separately. For the comparison of color and color-person concepts at the upper left, the D score for the five related concepts (along the diagonal) were found to be significantly ($p < .001$) smaller than the 20 D scores for unrelated

concepts. For the comparison of color and ethnic concepts at the upper right, the related D scores were again significantly ($p < .025$) smaller, as were the related D scores for the comparison of color-person and ethnic concepts at the lower right ($p < .001$). The consistency of the predicted effect may also be observed by comparing any one of the D scores for related concepts with the mean of the other four D scores in its particular row or column. *In every instance,* the D for related concepts is smaller than the mean of the other four unrelated D scores. These findings were taken to indicate that the general hypothesis was confirmed for Caucasian subjects.

The relative similarity of color-linked and non-color-linked concepts for Caucasian subjects is summarized in the upper portion of Figure 2. In the triangle on the left, the distance between any two vertices represents the mean of the five D scores for color-related pairs of concepts. For example, the distance between the points designated C and CP was obtained by averaging the five D scores for related color and color-person concepts (i.e., white versus white person, black versus black person, etc.). The distance between the vertices labeled CP and E represents the average of the five D scores for related color-person and ethnic concepts (i.e., white person versus Caucasian, black person versus Negro, etc.). The distance between the C and E vertices represents the average of the five D scores for white versus Caucasian, black versus Negro, etc. Thus, the distances shown in the small

TABLE 2

SEMANTIC DISTANCES (D SCORES) FOR CAUCASIAN SUBJECTS BETWEEN THREE GROUPS OF CONCEPTS:
COLOR VERSUS COLOR PERSON, COLOR VERSUS ETHNIC, AND COLOR PERSON VERSUS ETHNIC

	White person	Black person	Brown person	Yellow person	Red person	Caucasian	Negro	Indian (Asiatic)	Oriental	Indian (American)
White	**1.10**	3.63	2.88	2.11	2.62	**1.65**	2.82	2.13	1.64	2.00
Black	3.54	**0.79**	1.51	3.74	2.63	3.08	**1.56**	2.66	3.58	2.41
Brown	3.08	0.98	**0.94**	2.86	2.80	2.82	0.98	**1.74**	2.71	2.29
Yellow	2.92	2.72	2.44	**1.25**	2.60	1.62	2.48	1.57	**0.85**	1.76
Red	1.95	3.02	2.84	3.66	**1.06**	1.52	2.80	3.13	3.32	**1.94**
White person						**0.59**	2.17	1.81	1.66	1.13
Black person						2.47	**0.85**	1.94	2.86	1.75
Brown person						1.93	0.04	**1.12**	2.13	1.16
Yellow person						2.42	2.32	1.20	**0.52**	2.16
Red person						1.05	1.84	2.15	2.47	**1.09**

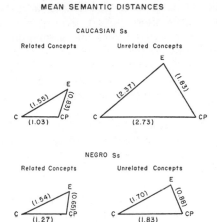

FIG. 2. Mean semantic distances (*D* scores) for color-related triads of color (C), color-person (CP), and ethnic (E) concepts; and for non-color-related triads of C, CP, and E concepts.

triangle represent the average distances among the various pairs of color-related concepts.

The distances between the vertices of the right-hand triangle were computed in analogous fashion. The distance between any two vertices is the mean distance between the concepts in a particular group and the four unrelated concepts in the second group. Thus, the C to CP distance is the mean distance between each of the five color concepts and all of the unrelated color-person concepts, for example, the distance between white and all color-person concepts except white person, the distance between black and all color-person concepts except black person, etc. The relative size of the two triangles again reflects the great similarity of connotative meaning found for color-related concepts.

Some relationships of particular interest may be seen in Table 2. In the color versus color-person comparison, these Caucasian subjects rated the concept white person as most similar to white and most different from black; while black person was most similar to black and most different from white. In the color-person versus ethnic comparison, the concept Negro was well differentiated from white person while the concept Caucasian was most similar to white person and least similar to black person. In the color versus ethnic comparison, the concept Caucasian ap-

peared about equally similar in meaning to red, yellow, and white, and most differentiated from black. The concept Negro was most similar to brown, next most similar to black, and most differentiated from white and red.

Negro Subjects: Comparison of Related-Color, Color-Person, and Ethnic Concepts

An examination of the mean color-person and ethnic scores for the Negro subjects (see Table 1) indicated that there was much less interconcept variability for these subjects than for the Caucasian subjects. The first step, then, was to determine whether there were statistically significant interconcept differences for the Negro subjects. Treatments by subjects analyses of variance (Lindquist, 1953) were employed for this purpose with an individual analysis made for each of the three scores (E, P, and A), separately for the five color-person concepts and the five ethnic concepts. For the color-person concepts, the between-concepts effect was significant at the .01 level for all three scores. For the ethnic concepts, the between-concepts effect was significant at the .01 level for the E and P scores and of borderline significance ($p < .10$) for the A scores. On the basis of these findings it was concluded that, although the observed differences were much smaller for Negro subjects, there were significant differences in interconcept meaning.

Figure 3 displays the mean scale scores for the related triads of color–color-person–ethnic concepts for Negro subjects. The contrast between Figure 3 and Figure 1 is rather striking. While the color-concept data from the earlier study (Williams, 1964) shows virtually identical rank orders along the E, P, and A dimensions for Negro and Caucasian subjects, it is clear that the similarity of the color-linked triads found with Caucasian was not present to the same degree in the data of the Negro subjects. On the E dimension, the Negro subjects agreed that black person was "least good" but did not agree that white person was "most good," rating this concept not differently from black person. The most positive evaluative rating was given to brown person which was rated significantly more positive than either white person or black person. For the ethnic concepts on the

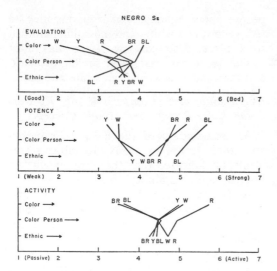

NEGRO Ss

FIG. 3. Semantic differential scores of Negro subjects for color-linked triads of color, color-person, and ethnic concepts. (Vertical lines connect triads, as follows: W = white, white person, Caucasian; Y = yellow, yellow person, Oriental; R = red, red person, Indian (American); BR = brown, brown person, Indian (Asiatic); BL = black, black person, Negro.)

E dimension, the Negro subjects rated the concept Negro significantly more positive and Caucasian significantly more negative than the other three ethnic concepts.

The Negro subjects P scores, displayed in the middle of Figure 3, indicate a substantial degree of consistency among the color-linked triads with the general rank order of the color scores being repeated for the color-person and ethnic concepts. In particular,

black, black person, and Negro were rated substantially more potent than were white, white person, and Caucasian. Comparatively, it can be noted that this finding is consistent with the P ratings given by the Caucasian subjects, except that Caucasian subjects did not rate the concepts Negro and Caucasian differently.

In the bottom portion of Figure 3, it can be seen that the dispersion of mean A scores of the Negro subjects decreased sharply in moving from the color concepts to the color-person and ethnic concepts. The color-person concepts appear to be undifferentiated on the A dimension with the exception of red person which was rated significantly more active than the other four. The small observed differences among the ethnic concepts were not statistically significant.

D scores. The data of the Negro subjects was subjected to the same *D*-score analysis as that described above for the Caucasian subjects. These scores are given in Table 3. As would be expected from the foregoing discussion, the *D* scores of these Negro subjects showed less differentiation among concepts, generally. Mann-Whitney *U* tests were again employed to determine whether color-linked concepts were more similar in connotative meaning than were non-color-linked concepts. For the color versus color-person comparison, the *D* scores for the color-related concepts were significantly ($p < .01$) smaller than the *D* scores for unrelated concepts. For the other two comparisons, the *D* scores for re-

TABLE 3

SEMANTIC DISTANCES (*D* SCORES) FOR NEGRO SUBJECTS BETWEEN THREE GROUPS OF CONCEPTS:
COLOR VERSUS COLOR PERSON, COLOR VERSUS ETHNIC, AND COLOR PERSON VERSUS ETHNIC

	White person	Black person	Brown person	Yellow person	Red person	Caucasian	Negro	Indian (Asiatic)	Oriental	Indian (American)
White	**1.81**	2.59	1.76	1.55	2.14	**2.06**	1.69	1.97	1.77	1.80
Black	2.36	**0.97**	1.63	2.41	1.70	1.76	**1.80**	1.63	2.05	1.74
Brown	1.70	0.99	**1.24**	1.73	1.47	1.20	1.53	**1.05**	1.39	1.32
Yellow	1.37	2.48	1.69	**1.12**	1.95	1.51	1.75	2.35	**1.41**	1.62
Red	2.21	1.55	1.29	2.12	**1.21**	1.89	1.10	1.86	2.01	**1.35**
White person						**0.62**	1.66	0.76	0.36	1.00
Black person						1.09	**1.08**	1.01	1.41	0.88
Brown person						0.90	0.41	**0.72**	0.21	0.42
Yellow person						0.73	1.41	0.78	**0.37**	0.96
Red person						0.77	1.00	0.82	1.04	**0.45**

lated concepts were generally smaller but in neither case significantly so. Thus, the data of the Negro subjects provided only slight support for the hypothesis under investigation.

The relative similarity of color-linked, and non-color-linked concepts for Negro subjects is summarized in the lower portion of Figure 2. As would be expected from the statistical tests discussed above, the related concepts triangle is somewhat smaller than the unrelated concepts triangle. It seems clear, however, that classification of concepts as "color-related" and "color-unrelated" has much less significance for the Negro subjects than for the Caucasian subjects. The relative size of the two right-hand triangles illustrates, again, the lesser degree of concept differentiation by the Negro subjects.

Certain of the D scores in Table 3 are of particular interest. These Negro subjects rated the concept Caucasian as most similar to the concept white person and most different from the concepts black person and brown person; while Negro was most similar to brown person and least similar to white person. It is noteworthy that the largest D score among the ethnic versus color-person comparisons was that between Negro and white person. In the color versus ethnic comparison, it is of interest that these subjects rated Caucasian as least like white and Negro as least like black.

Comparisons with Reference Concepts

It will be recalled that certain reference concepts had been rated along with the ethnic concepts. Included were the concept person and two sets of logically contrasted concepts, namely, friend and enemy and citizen and foreigner. It was considered of interest to study the connotative similarity of the concepts Caucasian and Negro to these reference concepts. (Mean scores for the reference concepts are given in Table 1.)

D scores computed for the data of the Caucasian subjects revealed that the concept Caucasian had a higher similarity to citizen (.20) than to foreigner (1.01) and a higher similarity to friend (1.06) than to enemy (2.94). On the other hand, the concept Negro was seen as more similar to foreigner (1.48) than to citizen (1.84) and more similar to

enemy (1.88) than to friend (2.87). For these Caucasian subjects, the similarity of the concept person to the five ethnic concepts was, in decreasing order, Caucasian (.45), Indian (American) (.84), Indian (Asiatic) (1.60), Oriental (1.62), and Negro (1.88). The similarity of the concept person to the five color-person concepts was, in decreasing order, white person (.31), red person (1.40), brown person (1.94), black person (1.95), and yellow person (2.09). The mean of the D scores between person and the color-person concepts was 1.54. This figure may be compared with the mean D score of 1.03 between color and color-person concepts, noted above.

Turning to the data of the Negro subjects, the concept Negro was found to be more similar to citizen (.36), than to foreigner (1.18) and more similar to friend (.78) than to enemy (2.72). On the other hand, Negro subjects saw the concept Caucasian as more similar to foreigner (.54) than to citizen (1.29) and more similar to enemy (1.54) than to friend (1.81). For the Negro subjects, the similarity of the concept person to the five ethnic concepts was, in decreasing order, Negro (.63), Indian (American) (.63), Oriental (.76), Indian (Asiatic) (.83), and Caucasian (1.00). The similarity of the concept person to the five color-person concepts was, in decreasing order, brown person (.50), yellow person (.57), red person (1.03), white person (1.15), and black person (1.33).

DISCUSSION

The data of the Caucasian subjects provided evidence in strong support of the hypothesis under investigation; namely, that racial concepts have connotative meanings similar to the color names with which they are linked by the color-coding custom. Although similarities in meaning were found for the A and P dimensions, the most consistent similarity was seen on the E dimension. This is perhaps the most important finding of the study since it is known that score variation along the E dimension covaries closely with score variation on conventional attitude tests (Osgood et al., 1957, p. 193). Using this interpretation, we can note that the attitudes of Caucasian subjects would appear to be most favorable toward Caucasians, somewhat less favorable toward American Indians and Orientals, and least favorable toward Asiatic Indians and Negroes. This is to be compared with their favorable evaluative rating of white and progressively less favorable ratings of yellow, red, brown, and black. While the direction of cause and effect cannot be demonstrated here, these data are consistent with the notion that the evaluative connotations of color names applied to racial groups are one determinant of the favorability of attitudes toward the racial groups. A hypothesis under current investigation is that evaluative color connotations—particularly white as good and black as bad—are learned early in childhood and influence the subsequent development of racial attitudes.

It was interesting to observe how the meaning of the word person was modified by the use of color adjectives. In the data of the Caucasian subjects, it was seen that the meanings of the color-person concepts were generally more similar to their associated color names than to the concept person. Apparently, the color adjective takes precedence over the noun and the connotative meaning communicated by the concept black person is *black*-person rather than black-*person*.

The high consistency in the data of the two Caucasian groups is worthy of note. As in the earlier study of color names (Williams, 1964), Caucasian students in North Carolina and in Kansas were found to rate the connotative meanings of racial concepts in a highly similar fashion indicating that the hypothesized effects of color coding may have some geographical generality. It would be interesting to know whether the same effects would be found among Caucasian subjects from other geographical regions with differing histories and customs in racial matters.

While it was clear that the Caucasian subjects saw each triad of color-code related concepts as belonging to the same "meaning family," this was not the case for the Negro subjects. While generally agreeing with Caucasians on the meanings of color names presented in a nonracial context, Negro subjects responded to the racial concepts in a quite different fashion, particularly along the evaluative (attitude) dimension. Examples of the different ratings of the Negro subjects were

their rating of Negro as good and Caucasian as relatively bad, and their rating of brown person as more good than white person and black person. It is not surprising, of course, to find that the responses of Negro subjects to racial concepts differ from Caucasian responses since the groups obviously have had differential experiences with the concepts. In addition, there appears to be developing resistance among Negroes to the color-coding practice with its connotative significance. This is seen in extreme form in the efforts of the Black Muslims and others to arbitrarily reverse the conventional symbolism by associating black with goodness and white with badness. It would seem doubtful that such deliberate efforts at reversal can generally succeed in a culture where the symbolism of white as good and black as bad is so thoroughly entrenched in literature, religion, the mass media, etc.

A simpler way of dealing with the unfortunate effects of color coding would be an attempt to bypass the problem by a deliberate effort to reshape language habits so that groups of persons are not designated by color names. For example, if the popular press would forego the convenience of discussing racial problems in terms of white persons and black persons, one important avenue of reinforcement would be removed. As noted elsewhere (Williams, 1964), such a proposal would probably encounter resistance from many Caucasians who, while perhaps willing to part with the designation of Negroes as black or brown, would be reluctant to give up the designation of their own group as white, with its positive evaluative connotations. And, of course, the abolition of the custom of color coding would not fully solve the color problem since there are average differences in skin color between Caucasian and Negro persons and lighter skin would no doubt continue to be positively valued. However, one might say that white Americans and black Americans will continue to find it very difficult to solve their problems, while Americans (with differing shades of skin color) would have a better chance of doing so. Indications of the problems remaining to be solved were seen in the comparisons of ethnic concepts and reference concepts where it was shown that each racial group saw its own racial designation as most similar to the concepts person, friend, and citizen and the designation of the other racial group as most similar to enemy and foreigner.

REFERENCES

LINDQUIST, E. F. *Design and analysis of experiments in psychology and education.* New York: Houghton Mifflin, 1953.

OSGOOD, C. E., SUCI, G. J., & TANNENBAUM, P. H. *The measurement of meaning.* Urbana: University of Illinois Press, 1957.

PEATMAN, J. G. *Introduction to applied statistics.* New York: Harper & Row, 1963.

STAATS, A. W., & STAATS, C. K. Attitudes established by classical conditioning. *Journal of Abnormal and Social Psychology,* 1958, **57,** 37–40.

STAATS, C. K., & STAATS, A. W. Meaning established by classical conditioning. *Journal of Experimental Psychology,* 1957, **54,** 74–80.

WILLIAMS, J. E. Connotations of color names among Negroes and Caucasians. *Perceptual & Motor Skills,* 1964, **18,** 721–731.

39. Objective Measurement of Social Role Concepts via the Semantic Differential

C. Jack Friedman and John W. Gladden

Summary.—A methodological study for quantifying the construct of role on three dimensions of a Semantic Differential: Evaluative, Potency, Activity. Male and female university students rated 8 social roles on a standard 25-item Semantic Differential under two instructional procedures. Support was obtained for a central assumption embraced by role theorists, that there is consensual agreement as to characteristics associated with certain roles. Ratings of the roles for the two instructional conditions, actual and ideal, closely paralleled the concepts "role" and "position," respectively. Each of the three semantic dimensions significantly differentiated the 8 roles, indicating that three semantic dimensions provided greater precision in measurement than only an attitudinal dimension.

The present research[3] attempted to develop an approach for objectively measuring the construct of "role" along several dimensions provided by a scaling instrument known as the *semantic differential*. Despite the widespread use of the construct of role, there have been relatively few attempts to quantify this construct along dimensions other than attitudinal or evaluative. This has, perhaps, contributed to the ambiguity of role definitions and to the equivocal status of experimental attempts to relate role theory constructs to one another (Newcomb, 1950; Argyle, 1952; Sarbin, 1954, pp. 222-258; Bates, 1956). Objectivity in this area seems necessary for removing existing barriers to communication and the surplus meanings attached to role concepts which so frequently have obscured genuine controversial issues.

The measuring instrument, the semantic differential, consists of a series of bipolar, descriptive adjectives, e.g., good-bad, honest-dishonest, etc., which are employed in the rating of selected stimuli or concepts. Past factor analytic studies provide information regarding the factor composition of a large number of descriptive, bipolar adjectives. These studies further suggest that judgments on the semantic differential can be described in terms of three major dimensions or factors (Osgood, Tannenbaum, & Suci, 1958). These include: (1) an Evaluative factor on which positive loading reflects "goodness" or

Reprinted from *Psychological Reports* (1964), 14: 239–247, by permission of the authors and the publisher.

[3]The authors are indebted to Dr. Robert Scofield and Dr. Leonard Worell for their supervisory assistance and helpful suggestions.

"favorableness," e.g., good-bad, optimistic-pessimistic; (2) a Potency factor, on which positive loading indicates "toughness," e.g., strong-weak, dominant-submissive; and (3) an Activity factor on which positive loading is descriptive of "movement," e.g., active-passive, dynamic-static.

More specifically, the purposes of this study were (1) to test the assumption embraced by most role theorists that certain identifiable behaviors or characteristics are associated with certain roles, (2) to determine possible sex differences in the rating of selected role concepts, and (3) to test the effects of two different instructional procedures.

METHOD

Construction of a semantic differential.—The semantic differential used in this study consisted of a standard form of 25 bipolar adjectives which appeared at the extremes of a 10-point scale. The use of a 10-point scale was intended to increase precision of measurement (Gulliksen, 1950) and provide a forced choice for dichotomizing Ss' responses as reflecting greater preference for one or the other bipolar adjective. Scales, representing the three major factors and several "sub-evaluative" modes and clusters, were selected on the basis of past factor analytic investigations, and for their particular relevance to the role concepts.[4] In Table 1 is a listing of the 25 scales and identification according to their factor composition.

The term "role concept" was used to designate the stimuli rated by Ss on this scaling instrument. For this initial investigation, 8 role concepts were selected: SELF (the only concept with specific reference to Ss), FATHER, MOTHER, ADULT, COLLEGE STUDENT, JUVENILE DELINQUENT, ADOLESCENT, and CHILD. It was assumed these roles were familiar to Ss. Some attempt was made to provide role concepts which varied as to age, sex, and social desirability. A sample "concept" and scale are presented below.

COLLEGE STUDENT

conforming :—:—:—:—:—:—:—:—:—: nonconforming

Subjects.—Ss were 19 male and 20 female undergraduate university students enrolled in an introductory psychology course. Ss were approximately homogeneous with respect to age, socio-economic background, general intelligence, etc., although the specific relevance of these factors to "consensuality" among Ss in their ratings of the role concepts was assumed.

Procedure.—The 8 role concepts were successively printed at the top of the standard scale forms and stapled into booklets. A brief description of the

---

[4] These scales were not here subjected to factor analysis to determine factorial composition. The scales labeled "meek goodness, dynamic goodness, and dependable goodness" were determined from a factor analysis employing a Quartimax rotation and are tentative sub-evaluative factors. The remaining "morally, socially, and emotionally evaluative" scales were obtained from a cluster analysis based on correlations of scales within the evaluative factor, and are tentative. Readers may refer to Osgood, *et al.* (1957, pp. 62-63, 70-71).

TABLE 1

FACTOR COMPOSITION OF 25 DESCRIPTIVE ADJECTIVES

Evaluative	"emotionally evaluative"
good-bad	tense-relaxed
optimistic-pessimistic	*Potency*
friendly-unfriendly	strong-weak
"meek goodness"	dominant-submissive
altruistic-egotistic	mature-youthful
graceful-awkward	masculine-feminine
"dynamic goodness"	free-constrained
successful-unsuccessful	cooperative-resistive
important-unimportant	*Activity*
"dependable goodness"	active-passive
skeptical-believing	dynamic-static
wise-foolish	changeable-stable
"morally evaluative"	
moral-immoral	
fair-unfair	
"socially evaluative"	
honest-dishonest	
rich-poor	
brave-cowardly	

nature of the study along with directions for using the scales were printed on a cover sheet. *S*s were told that the purpose of the study was to measure the *meanings* of certain words and that they were being asked to participate as judges. It was emphasized that this was not a test and hence there were no "right" or "wrong" answers.

In the first administration, *S*s were instructed to rate the words at the top of each page of scales "as you actually think they are, in terms of the meanings they have for you." *S*s were further told, "The first word at the top of the first page refers specifically to you. You may think of the others as 'in general,' that is, not referring to any specific person."

After all *S*s had completed their ratings of the 8 role concepts, the booklets were collected, and another set of booklets containing the same role concepts in the same sequence were handed out. For this second administration, *S*s were told, "You have rated this first series of words on the basis of what they mean to you, in the sense of how you actually feel they are. On this next series, which includes the same words in the same order, and the same scales, you are to rate each word on the basis of how it should *ideally* be, the way it is supposed to be as opposed to how it actually is."[5]

---

[5] These directions were especially confusing for rating "juvenile delinquent." Following inquiry of one *S*, the group was told to think of and rate the stereotype of juvenile delinquent.

RESULTS

Analyses were separate for the male and female groups, and for the first (Actual) and second (Ideal) instructional procedures. There were thus four component groups: Males-Actual, Males-Ideal, Females-Actual, and Females-Ideal.

The assumption of consensuality or agreement among Ss in their ratings of role concepts on the semantic differential was tested by dichotomizing responses in terms of their proximity toward one or the other bipolar adjective. For each of the component groups there were 8 role concepts $\times$ 25 scales, or 200 items. These frequency data were tested for significance by χ^2, two-tailed test. The tallied frequencies are presented in Tables 2 and 3.

For the male group (Table 2) 93 out of 200 scales were significant ($p \le .05$) for the first instructional procedure and 124 for the second instructional procedure. For the female group (Table 3) 92 and 139 out of 200 scales were significant, respectively, for the first and second instructional sets.

To determine whether each of the three dimensions significantly distinguished or differentiated the 8 roles, two scales were chosen to represent each factor: *evaluative,* good-bad, optimistic-pessimistic; *potency,* strong-weak, dominant-submissive; and *activity,* active-passive, dynamic-static. These scales were scored from 1, i.e., most favorable, tough, active, to 10, i.e., least favorable, tough, active. A sum was then computed for each dimension, separately for each S. For each S, the sums representing each dimension were ranked across the 8 roles and subjected to analysis by a Friedman Two-way Analysis of Variance. These results are presented in Table 4.

TABLE 4

DIFFERENCES AMONG 8 ROLE CONCEPTS OF THREE SEMANTIC DIMENSIONS

Dimensions	Male		Female	
	Actual	Ideal	Actual	Ideal
Evaluative	59.02*	31.28*	55.50*	35.63*
Potency	44.14*	59.77*	78.19*	76.27*
Activity	30.46*	25.21*	15.01**	17.66†

$*p < .001.$ $**p < .02.$ $†p < .05.$

As shown in Table 4, Ss' ratings on all three dimensions for both the first and second instructional procedures were significant beyond the .05 level. Furthermore, only the female group's ratings on the Activity dimension failed to reach significance at the .001 level.

The final analysis attempted to determine the relative location of roles on all three semantic dimensions. This particular procedure operationally de-

TABLE 2

FREQUENCIES OF RESPONSES FOR EACH CONCEPT BY MALES

	Actual								Ideal							
	Self	Fa.	Mo.	Adult	Coll. Stu.	Juv. Delin.	Ado-les.	Child	Self	Fa.	Mo.	Adult	Coll. Stu.	Juv. Delin.	Ado-les.	Child
optimistic	5*	6	6	12	4	16	9	5	2	4	17	3	4	13	2	2
weak	17	19	8	17	17	3	8	1	19	19	16	19	19	8	11	8
dishonest	19	18	18	16	14	1	16	15	19	19	19	19	19	8	18	17
active	1	2	8	9	1	8	3	2	0	0	0	0	0	6	0	0
moral	1	1	0	9	7	17	5	2	0	0	0	0	0	11	0	0
free	16	3	5	10	3	10	10	8	0	12	16	1	0	8	5	5
egotistic	8	13	14	11	9	4	10	6	16	16	16	16	15	8	12	12
tense	8	11	8	8	4	0	12	14	18	17	17	18	15	8	14	17
successful	2	3	1	4	4	19	10	8	0	0	0	0	0	11	4	5
submissive	18	14	7	12	8	7	4	7	16	18	8	16	15	7	8	4
wise	1	2	2	5	5	19	15	15	0	0	0	0	0	11	7	8
dynamic	5	1	6	10	4	15	7	7	1	1	3	4	2	8	5	7
cowardly	19	19	13	16	17	3	11	8	19	19	18	19	19	8	14	15
youthful	16	19	17	17	11	0	0	0	17	19	18	19	17	4	4	0
good	0	18	1	1	2	18	3	3	0	0	0	0	0	10	1	0
changeable	5	12	12	12	2	1	1	1	12	16	14	16	10	4	4	3
poor	15	15	16	14	13	0	12	12	18	19	19	19	17	7	17	17
resistive	15	14	17	15	16	0	8	9	16	18	17	16	14	7	14	14
skeptical	13	13	12	13	9	1	12	16	13	15	16	14	9	7	14	15
masculine	0	1	19	10	7	1	6	7	1	0	19	8	6	4	5	8
unfriendly	17	19	18	16	18	0	17	17	19	19	18	19	18	7	19	18
awkward	19	5	17	16	16	4	5	5	19	19	19	18	19	10	10	12
fair	0	1	2	5	3	18	5	5	0	0	0	0	0	10	3	3
nonconforming	12	12	17	14	13	2	14	14	13	11	14	13	10	5	9	9
important	3		16	4	1	11	5	3	1	0	0	0	0	8	1	0

*$f \leq 3$, $p = .05$, two-tail test; $f \geq 16$, $p = .05$ for bipolar adjective to one presented.

488

TABLE 3

FREQUENCIES OF RESPONSES FOR EACH CONCEPT BY FEMALES

	Actual								Ideal							
	Self	Fa.	Mo.	Adult	Coll. Stu.	Juv. Delin.	Ado-les.	Child	Self	Fa.	Mo.	Adult	Coll. Stu.	Juv. Delin.	Ado-les.	Child
optimistic	7*	7	8	12	8	19	8	5	0	1	1	0	1	7	2	2
weak	16	19	16	19	17	1	6	7	20	20	20	20	20	10	14	12
dishonest	20	20	20	17	15	2	19	17	20	20	20	20	20	11	19	19
active	4	3	5	4	1	8	0	2	0	0	0	0	0	3	1	2
moral	0	0	0	5	9	18	0	1	0	0	0	0	0	7	0	0
free	6	4	11	10	9	14	11	7	2	3	4	2	4	10	5	9
egotistic	15	16	19	14	10	1	11	5	20	20	20	20	17	11	15	11
tense	12	14	6	10	8	1	11	16	20	20	19	20	20	10	19	17
successful	5	1	1	9	6	19	10	8	0	0	1	0	0	14	3	4
submissive	16	16	13	16	14	11	5	4	16	19	11	19	19	9	9	2
wise	6	1	1	5	10	19	15	18	0	0	0	0	1	9	5	9
dynamic	7	5	7	7	6	10	6	8	2	3	5	4	2	12	4	7
cowardly	19	20	17	18	18	9	16	9	20	20	20	20	20	12	15	15
youthful	17	19	16	15	9	1	1	0	17	19	17	19	17	5	5	1
good	1	1	0	5	3	18	3	1	0	0	0	0	0	9	1	0
changeable	9	18	11	12	3	1	0	2	16	19	17	18	16	4	6	4
poor	14	15	16	16	14	1	13	15	20	20	20	20	19	7	19	18
resistive	19	17	19	18	17	1	12	12	19	19	20	18	18	9	19	15
skeptical	18	13	18	10	8	1	15	17	18	19	19	15	18	10	19	19
masculine	19	0	20	10	10	4	13	16	19	1	20	11	11	7	12	16
unfriendly	20	19	20	19	19	3	16	18	20	20	20	20	20	11	19	19
awkward	17	16	19	15	17	2	7	5	20	19	20	20	20	10	12	12
fair	1	1	0	5	3	18	5	8	0	0	0	0	0	9	1	2
nonconforming	17	14	16	17	12	18	17	15	4	14	16	18	14	11	18	18
important	3	0	1	4	3	12	7	7	1	0	0	0	2	10	3	2

*$f \leq 3$, $p = .05$, two-tail test; $f \geq 17$, $p = .05$, for bipolar adjective opposite to one presented.

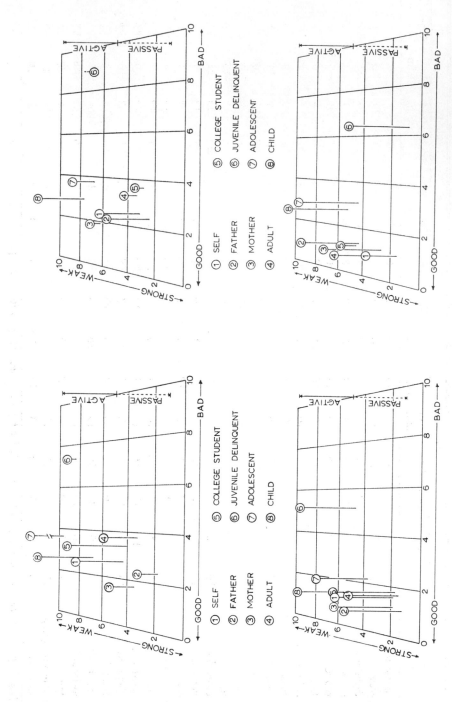

Fig. 1. Actual (top) and Ideal (bottom) locations of 8 role concepts on three semantic dimensions for males (left) and females (right)

490

fines "meaning" for semantic differential ratings of these role concepts. The scale good-bad was chosen to represent *evaluation,* active-passive to represent the *activity* factor, and strong-weak to represent the *potency* factor. The scales were again scored from 1 to 10 and an average factor score obtained for each component group. Their coordinates were then located relative to the three factors and are presented in Fig. 1. The reader may note the differences in spatial relationships among roles for the two instructional procedures, and their similarity in patterning for different sex groups under the same instructional set.

Conclusions.—The results of this methodological study offer support for a central assumption made by role theorists, namely, that there is generally high agreement among persons as to characteristics associated with various roles, and further that these characteristics reflect learned expectancies in relation to persons occupying these roles, or as some would maintain, these positions. Differences between Actual and Ideal ratings suggest some justification for two notions, *role* which may vary according to the individual occupying it, and *position,* a standard or ideal series of behaviors which the role player may approximate in varying degrees.

The combined use of an attitudinal, i.e., evaluative, potency, and activity dimension points up a potentially useful technique for investigating different kinds of characteristics associated with roles. Complete reliance upon attitudinal criteria would have revealed no difference between Father and Child in the present study. However, the addition of a potency dimension permits making the rather obvious distinction. Relevant to this, the potency dimension was in almost all cases statistically more sensitive in differentiating the 8 roles than either the evaluative or activity dimensions. It may therefore be concluded that all three dimensions have something to offer in measuring or describing roles or positions.

The measurement of "meaning" offers an operational method for defining role conflict, in much the same manner that Rogerians have described maladjustments as discrepancy between Self and Ideal Self. Simply stated, conflict could be described in terms of the spatial distance between two roles or positions on the three dimensions.

One indirect finding of the present investigation was suggested by the obtained differences between Actual and Ideal instructions. The semantic differential seems a particularly sensitive instrument to what might be termed "situational factors." Thus, the effects of various treatments could be assessed in a post-administration of the measurement, as could successive treatments over time. In short, the semantic differential appears to have numerous possible applications to an area in which objectivity in measurement has often been neglected in favor of gross subjective appraisals.

REFERENCES

ARGYLE, M. The concepts of role and status. *Sociol. Rev.*, 1952, 44, 39-52.

BATES, F. L. Position, role and status: a reformulation of concepts. *Soc. Forces*, 1956, 34, 313-321.

GULLIKSEN, H. How to make meaning more meaningful. *J. contemp. Psychol.*, 1958, 3, 115-119.

NEWCOMB, T. M. *Social psychology.* New York: Holt, Reinhart, & Winston, 1950.

OSGOOD, C. E., SUCI, G. J., & TANNENBAUM, P. H. *The measurement of meaning.* Illinois: Univer. of Illinois Press, 1957.

SARBIN, T. R. Role theory. In G. Lindzey (Ed.), *Handbook of social psychology.* Vol. 1. Reading, Mass.: Addison-Wesley, 1954. Pp. 223-258.

40. Profiles of Some Stereotypes
Held by Ninth-Grade Pupils

James G. Snider

Stereotyping, defined (8, p. 107) as "a tendency to attribute generalized and simplified characteristics to a group of people in the form of a verbal label," is probably one of the major correlates of tensions in intergroup relations. In recognition of this probability, the Third Session of the General Conference of UNESCO (1, p. 1) designated "the ideas which the people of one nation hold concerning their own and other nations," as one of the areas of "Tensions Affecting International Understanding." Young states (2, VII) that "the understanding of international tensions is beclouded with stereotyped thinking," and Klineberg submits (2, p. 124) that "our educational attack must be against all forms of stereotyped thinking." Granting the validity of these views, it would seem especially important for teachers, and others concerned with education, to have some knowledge of the stereotypes held by their pupils.

The Purpose of the Study

The purpose of this study is to provide information about the stereotypes of Canadians, French Canadians, Englishmen, Americans, Indians, and Russians, as they are perceived by ninth-grade Alberta pupils. It is felt that such information would be helpful to teachers in general, and especially those concerned with teaching against stereotyping and toward intergroup and international understanding.

The Instrument Used

As a measure of stereotyping, a test devised by Stautland (7) was used.* Constructed after the manner of Osgood's semantics differential (4), and as revised for this study,‡ the test places the respondent in the situation of judging various concepts: Canadians, French Canadians, Americans, Englishmen, Indians and Russians, in regard to pairs of polar terms: practical-impractical, kind-cruel, intelligent-dumb, superior-inferior, happy-sad, clean-dirty, brave-cowardly, peaceloving-warlike, honest-dishonest, hardworking-lazy. These polar terms were chosen from terms reported by UNESCO to be

Reprinted from *Alberta Journal of Educational Research* (1962), 8(3): 147–156, by permission of the author and the publisher.

*Permission of the author was obtained both to use and revise the test.

‡The only change made was to substitute the concepts Canadians, French Canadians, and Indians for the concepts Chinese, Mexicans, and Norwegians. Stautland had included Americans, Englishmen, and Russians in the original test.

most often used by the peoples of the world to describe each other (2).

The respondent judges the concepts in relation to a seven-point scale, where the directions are that marking the middle of the scale indicates the respondent thinks the concept is neutral in relation to the ends of the scale, and marking outward from the middle indicates the respondent thinks the concept has a progressively stronger relation to either end of the scale, as follows:

Concept
(Canadian, French Canadian, etc.)

Polar
Term
(Kind,
etc.)   (3) (2) (1) (0) (1) (2) (3)   Polar
Term
(Cruel,
etc.)

For testing purposes, the polar terms were arranged by random procedures, the arrangement being different for each concept. For purposes of statistical treatment, the scale was weighted from one to seven, starting with one at the positive side each time, the polar terms being arranged with the positive terms on the left, the negative on the right. This was done to make clear the position of each group concept on each positive-negative continuum,* Since there are 10 pairs of polar terms for each group concept, and since the smallest value possible for any pair is one, the lowest score obtainable for any group is 10, the highest 70. For the total test the range is from 60 to 420.

As evidence of the reliability of the test, Stautland presents test-retest total score reliabilities of over .90 for groups of high school pupils. As evidence of validity, Stautland obtained a validity co-efficient of .39 with a test of stereotyping reported by Siegel (5). However, it is also evident that the test has a certain "face" validity, or logical validity, for with it we are able to ascertain the strength of a respondent's "tendency to attribute a verbal label to a group of people." We can also ascertain some specific characteristics of the verbal label.

The Sample

Two considerations provide the rationale for choosing the ninth-grade level for the investigation of stereotypes: (a) pupils are old enough at this level to have developed somewhat definite intense stereotypes, and (b) pupils at this level still have some years of schooling before them, so that such implications for curriculum change as information about pupil stereotyping behavior might provide may still be implemented.

In selecting a sample of ninth-grade pupils for the study, in-

---

*This is equivalent to adding a constant of 4 to the original weights of 3210123. Such an addition does not change the shape of a distribution. It was made in this case simply for convenience and does not in any way alter the results of the study.

dividuals were sought of approximately similar socio-economic background, educational level and age. Accordingly, the stereotyping test was administered to five typical ninth-grade classes in a Calgary junior high school, comprising 70 boys and 62 girls chosen for their homogeneity in respect to the aforementioned variables.

Results

The stereotyping test was given to the sample on April 18, and, in order to obtain test-retest reliability coefficients, again on May 9, 1961. Table I shows the test-retest coefficients for the total test and for each group by boys, girls, and total sample. It is not surprising that these coefficients are rather low, given the age range of the sample, the brevity of the subscales, and the fact that, in testing for stereotypes, we are dealing with attitudes which are often none too stable. It will be noticed that in terms of absolute differences in reliability coefficients and except for the Indian group, it seems at first glance that girls might be more reliable in their stereotyping responses than boys. However, for each subscale a t value was calculated for the difference in reliability coefficients of boys and girls, using Fisher's r to z transformation (3, p. 147), and no difference in test-retest reliability coefficients for boys and girls was found to be statistically significant. Apparently the boys and girls did not differ in reliability of stereotyping responses.

TABLE I

TEST-RETEST RELIABILITY COEFFICIENTS FOR THE STEREOTYPING TEST BY BOYS, GIRLS, TOTAL SAMPLE*

	Boys	Girls	Total Sample
Canadian	.49	.64	.56
French Canadian	.64	.65	.64
American	.47	.56	.52
English	.50	.58	.55
Indian	.53	.49	.52
Russian	.41	.53	.46
Total Test	.50	.70	.60

*1st Administration, April 18, 1961.
2nd Administration, May 9, 1961.

Still another question may be asked: Are there significant differences in reliability of response as between the six groups? We may answer this by again applying the r to z transformation. Since there were no statistically significant differences between boys and girls, the technique was applied only to differences for the total sample. Of the possible fifteen significant differences in reliability coefficients, just one was statistically significant, that being the difference between French Canadians and Russians, which was significant at the 5% level of confidence. This is not a very meaningful finding, however, for one significant difference in fifteen possibilities may easily occur by chance. We must conclude that the sample did not show any particular tendency to vary in its reliability of response as between groups.

The means and standard deviations for the groups, by boys, girls, and total sample, are shown in Table II. These statistics were obtained by using the system previously described: the means for each group were derived by assigning values from one to seven along the continuums, starting with one at the positive side each time. Thus, the lower the mean, the more positive the stereotype. This procedure enables us to put the groups in a rank order. In terms of absolute scores for the total sample, and from the most positive stereotype to the most negative, the rank order is: Canadians, French Canadians, Americans, Englishmen, Indians and Russians. That is, Canadians are seen as being closest to the positive end of the scale, French Canadians next, and so on. In view of the proximity of Canadians, French Canadians, and Americans, and in view of Canada's historical ties with England, this ranking of stereotypes is what we might have reasonably expected, as are the more negative stereotypes held for Indians and Russians.

TABLE II
MEANS AND STANDARD DEVIATIONS FOR STEREOTYPING TEST FOR BOYS, GIRLS, AND TOTAL SAMPLE*

	Boys M (N=70) SD		Girls M (N=62) SD		Total Sample M (N=132) SD	
Canadian	24.5	7.4	25.2	6.7	24.9	7.0
French Canadian	27.2	8.1	29.3	7.5	28.3	7.8
American	28.3	8.0	29.6	6.7	29.1	7.4
English	28.8	6.4	29.5	6.5	29.2	6.5
Indian	34.8	7.3	36.8	7.7	35.9	7.6
Russian	36.2	6.9	35.9	7.5	36.0	7.2
Total Test	180.3	30.0	186.8	29.6	183.9	30.0

*1st administration.

To examine for differences between groups, a Friedman two-way analysis of variance by ranks (6, p. 166) was run and the resulting X^2r of 45.1 found to be significant at beyond the .001 level. From this, we may assume that there were significant differences between groups. To examine for specific differences, t tests were calculated for differences between means. Taking the 5% level of confidence as significant, there were no statistically significant differences for boys and girls for either mean or standard deviations for the groups, or for the total test. Because of this similarity of response of boys and girls, only the total sample means were used for t tests of the significance of differences as between groups. Table III summarizes the results of these tests.

TABLE III
SIGNIFICANCE OF MEAN DIFFERENCES BETWEEN GROUPS FOR TOTAL SAMPLE*

	F. Can.	Amn.	Eng.	Ind.	Russ.
Canadian	0.5%	0.5%	0.5%	0.5%	0.5%
French Canadian		NSD	NSD	0.5%	0.5%
American			NSD	0.5%	0.5%
English				0.5%	0.5%
Indian					NSD

*1st administration.

Perhaps the most noticeable finding presented in Table III is that Canadians was the only group concept perceived significantly different from all other group concepts. The term Canadians was apparently seen as significantly more positive than any others. The Indian and Russian group concepts were apparently perceived as significantly less positive in comparison with the other groups, although there was not a significant difference in the two. French Canadians, Americans, and Englishmen were seen as somewhat similar, for the means of these groups do not differ significantly from one another, yet these group concepts are seen as different from the others.

Tables II and III suggest that the six groups are in three "clusters" along the positive-negative continuum: Canadians being seen most positively and as different from the other groups; French Canadians, Americans and Englishmen being seen next most positively and as like one another but different from the other groups;

and Indians and Russians being seen least positively and as like one another but different from the other groups.

TABLE IV

INTERCORRELATIONS FOR THE STEREOTYPING TEST
BY TOTAL SAMPLE*

	F. Can.	Amn.	Eng.	Ind.	Russ.
Canadian	.55	.62	.58	.31	.04
French Canadian		.45	.53	.43	.25
American			.53	.35	.07
English				.25	.24
Indian					.27

*1st administration.

The intercorrelations presented in Table IV lend general support to the observation of three "clusters" within the six stereotypes. The concept Canadians is most highly correlated with the cluster already observed to be most like it, the French Canadians, Americans, Englishmen stereotypes. It has its lowest correlations with Indians and Russians. The lowest correlation between any two groups is that between Russians and Canadians, as we might expect, since these stereotypes are the greatest distance apart on the continuum. However, the intercorrelations do not present a picture completely consistent with the previously presented findings. The discrepancies observed (e.g., that Indians and Russians are not very highly correlated, even though they occupy nearly the same position on the continuum) may be better understood through an examination of the specific profiles of the various groups. Figures 1, 2, and 3 present the profiles of the six groups by total sample, the profiles being obtained by taking the means for various pairs of polar terms and plotting them. It should be noted, again, that the arrangements of the polar terms in the Figures is only for convenience in presenting the profiles. On the test itself, the polar terms were arranged randomly, there being a different arrangement for each group concept.

The profiles are presented in the three figures so as to correspond with the clustering tendency already pointed out. Perhaps the first point of significance concerning the profiles has to do with the similarities and differences in their shapes. Even though the overall Canadians mean is significantly different from the overall means of

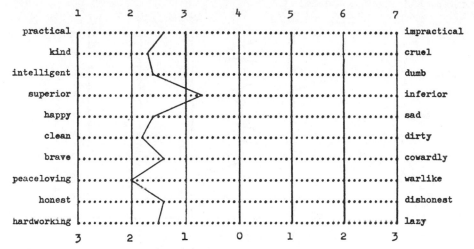

Figure 1. Profile for <u>Canadians</u> for the total sample of 132 boys and girls. This profile was derived by plotting the means of the categories for the first administration of the test.

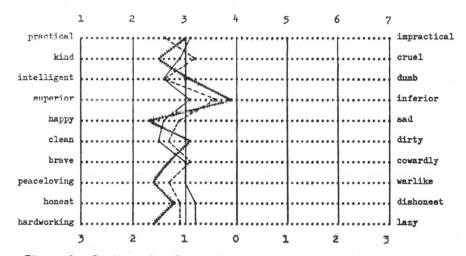

Figure 2. Profiles for <u>French Canadians</u> ⚬⚬⚬⚬ , <u>Americans</u> ——— and <u>Englishmen</u> ———— for the total sample of 132 boys and girls. These profiles were derived by plotting the means of the categories for the first administration of the test.

French Canadians, Americans and Englishmen, the shape of the Canadians profile is strikingly similar to the profiles of these groups. The similarity is particularly apparent as between Canadians, Americans, and Englishmen. Undoubtedly the most closely fitting profiles are those of the Americans and Englishmen. All four of these profiles have a sharp peak toward *inferior* on the superior-inferior category. At first, this makes little sense, considering that these groups are perceived as more intelligent, more kind, more practical, etc., than the other groups. Why then should there be such a peak

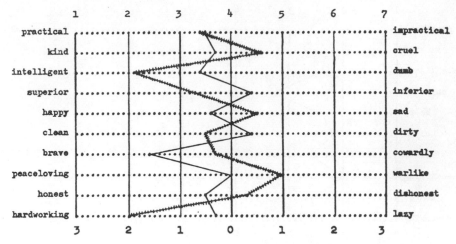

Figure 3. Profiles for Indians —— and Russians ⚊⚊⚊ for the total sample of 132 boys and girls. These profiles were derived by plotting the means of the categories for the first administration of the test.

on inferior? It appears that this can be explained if we think again of the directions under which the test is taken. It will be recalled that in marking the test the middle of the scale indicates neutrality. It seems reasonable to suppose that while respondents are willing to mark terms such as clean, dirty, sad, etc., which describe rather specific characteristics, toward the ends of the scales, they are less willing to make sweeping judgments of groups, such as their being superior or inferior. The peaks on inferior probably really indicate a neutral feeling. It may be that the superior-inferior category is a different kind of dimension from the other categories, and is measuring something different from them.

An examination of the Indians and Russians profiles shows that even though these groups have almost identical overall means they have very different profiles from each other and from the other groups. The most variable profile of all the groups is that of the Russians, while the Indains profile is next most variable. The high peaks of these profiles seem particularly significant. We note that the Russians are perceived as the most extremely intelligent, hardworking, warlike, and cruel of the groups. The Indians are seen as the bravest. Thus, despite the fact that the perceptions of Indians and Russians are generally less positive than the perceptions of the other groups, these groups still have some quite positive attributes. Even though these groups occupy nearly the same mean position on the scales, they are perceived by pupils as distinctly different groups.

There is another interpretation possible for the Indians and Russians profiles, however, other than that they are generally more negative than the other four. The overall means for Indians and Russians are 35.9 and 36.0 respectively, which indicates, from the directions for taking the test, that these overall means are nearly at the neutral position of the scale. It would seem that, from one point of view, the subjects of the study were less willing to judge these groups as positive or negative, the exceptions being where we find high peaks on the profiles.

The boys and girls of the sample can be said, in one sense, not to have made up their minds about the Indians and Russians concepts, except that these concepts are definitely not seen in as positive a light as the other four.

Conclusions

The sample used in the study was composed of urban, middle class, ninth-grade pupils from a junior high school in Calgary, Alberta, and while this limits the generalizations we may make about pupil stereotyping behavior, as regards the population concerned, the following conclusions seem justified: —

1. There is probably no sex differential in relation to reliability of tendencies to stereotype: boys and girls at the age range of the ninth-grade appear to be equal in reliability over time and as between groups.

2. The stereotypes held by ninth-grade pupils in this study were rather unstable, indicating that they may fairly easily change or be changed. This seemed to hold true even for group concepts such as Canadians, where we might have expected a relatively stable stereotype.

3. There are probably no sex differences relative to the degree to which different groups are stereotyped.

4. Statistically significant differences were found between groups, but these differences tended to be in "clusters": Canadians had a mean stereotype score significantly more positive than any other group; French Canadians, Americans, and Englishmen were seen next most positively and more like each other than like other groups; and Indians and Russians were seen least positively and more like one another than like other groups. There were statistically significant differences between all of these "clusters".

5. Although different groups were perceived as having different stereotypes, there were some very regular similarities between stereotypes. It was found that the shapes of the profiles for the stereotypes of Canadians, Americans, and Englishmen matched closely. French Canadians, Indians and Russians had uniquely shaped profiles.

6. The study yielded one very positive finding. Even though the Indians and Russians concepts were seen as definitely less positive than the other concepts, they were not seen as extremely negative concepts. Actually, these concepts were rated as near the neutral position on the scales. This would seem to indicate that ninth-grade Alberta pupils do not feel negative toward any of the group concepts presented in the study. All of the stereotypes obtained are either neutral or positive.

REFERENCES

1. Committee on International Relations of the National Education Association, *Education for International Understanding in our Schools,* Washington: National Education Association for the United States, 1948.
2. Klineberg, O., *Tensions Affecting International Understanding,* New York: Social Science Research Council, 1950.
3. McNemar, Q., *Psychological Statistics,* New York: Wiley, 1955.
4. Osgood, C. E., Suci, G. J., and Tannenbaum, P. H., *The Measurement of Meaning,* Urbana, Illinois: University of Illinois Press, 1947.
5. Siegel, S., "Certain Determinants and Correlates of Authoritarianism," *Genetic Psychology Monographs,* 1954, *49*, 187-229.
6. Siegel, S., *Nonparametric Statistics for the Behavioral Sciences,* New York, McGraw Hill, 1956.
7. Stautland, S., "Some Correlates and Determinants of National Stereotyping," Unpublished Doctoral Dissertation, Stanford University, 1959.
8. Vinacke, W. E., "Explorations in the Dynamic Processes of Stereotyping," *Journal of Social Psychology,* 1956, *43*, 105-32.

Part IX

SEMANTIC DIFFERENTIAL TECHNIQUE IN PERSONALITY AND CLINICAL PSYCHOLOGY

41. A Blind Analysis of a Case of Multiple Personality Using the Semantic Differential

Charles E. Osgood and Zella Luria

FOR MORE than a year the writers have been collecting semantic data from patients undergoing psychotherapy. This has been feasible through the cooperation of psychotherapists in various parts of the country. When the manuscript of "A Case of Multiple Personality" (3) arrived, the editor of this journal, without our knowledge, suggested to Thigpen and Cleckley that it would be interesting to have semantic data from each of the "personalities" in their patient. Thigpen and Cleckley accepted the suggestion and administered a form of the differential we have been using for this purpose to their patient in each of her three personalities. The editor also suggested that we might see how much these semantic data would allow us to infer about the patient without our having any knowledge of the case history, protocol, or prognosis.[1] This appeared to be a useful and rather intriguing way to estimate the validity and sensitivity of this instrument. If we could infer descriptions of the three personalities which correspond with clinical observations, and if we could make reasonably accurate interpretations and predictions, we would be encouraged to continue our efforts to improve the semantic differential as a clinical tool.

THE SEMANTIC DIFFERENTIAL

The semantic differential is a combination of association and scaling procedures designed to give an objective measure of the connotative meaning of concepts. The under-

Reprinted from *Journal of Abnormal and Social Psychology* (1954), 49: 579–591, by permission of the authors and the American Psychological Association.

[1] We wish to thank Dr. J. McV. Hunt, editor of this journal, for utilizing the opportunity presented by the work of Thigpen and Cleckley to arrange for the data in this study, for suggesting the blind analysis, and for his general encouragement. We are also very grateful to Drs. Thigpen and Cleckley for giving the semantic differential to their patient and for their interest in the Instrument.

lying logic (1) can be summarized as follows: (*a*) The process of description or judgment can be conceived as the allocation of a concept to a set of experiential continua defined by pairs of polar terms. Thus the connotative meaning of a linguistically complex assertion, such as "My father has always been a rather submissive person," can be at least partially represented as

MY FATHER active__:__:__:__:$\times$:__:__passive
MY FATHER soft__:$\times$:__:__:__:__:__hard

The greater the strength of association, e.g., "... extremely submissive, a regular doormat," the more polarized, toward 1 or 7, the allocation (2). Since many scales of judgment are highly intercorrelated (e.g., *good-bad, fair-unfair, honest-dishonest, kind-cruel*, and so forth all reflect mainly the single "evaluative" factor in judgments), a limited number of such continua can be used to define a semantic space within which the connotative meaning of any concept can be specified. This clearly indicates some variant of factor analysis as the basic methodology in developing such an instrument. Two such analyses have been completed, both providing evidence for three general factors, "evaluation," "potency," and "activity," and some unknown number of specific factors that are probably denotative in nature.

The form of semantic differential we have been using in studying psychotherapy is based on this factor analytic work. In the 10 scales used, it gives approximately equal weight to the first three factors isolated. These scales and their factor loadings are given in Table 1. The 15 concepts used in this form of the differential were selected after consultation with clinicians and pretesting for their differentiating power. Ideally, they should sample the major persons and problems involved in therapy-in-general; we are not entirely satisfied with the present set, however, and more work should be done here. The concepts used are also shown in Table 1. In the test form itself, concepts are rotated against scales in such a way that each concept appears once with each scale, but with a maximum interval between successive appearances of both. The subject is instructed to do his checking rapidly, without struggling over particular items, to give his "immediate impressions." A 150-item form such as this usually takes less than 10 minutes to complete.

Reordering the raw data for a single subject on a single testing yields a matrix of N columns (here, 15 concepts) and i rows (here, 10 scales). The *meaning* of a particular concept to the subject, as defined by the operations of measurement here, is the profile of numbers in its column (or, more efficiently, the position in the n-dimensional space defined by the projection of these numbers onto the factors). *Difference in meaning* for two concepts is defined by the distance between their positions in this space, as computed by the generalized distance formula, $D = \sqrt{\Sigma d^2}$, in which d is the difference in allocation of the two concepts on a single scale (2). The more similar any two concepts are in connotative meaning, the smaller will be the value of D.

TABLE 1
CONCEPTS AND SCALES USED IN THIS ANALYSIS

Concepts

LOVE	MENTAL	SELF-CON-
CHILD	SICKNESS	TROL
MY DOCTOR	MY MOTHER	HATRED
ME	PEACE OF	MY FATHER
MY JOB	MIND	CONFUSION
	FRAUD	SEX
	MY SPOUSE	

Scales and Their Factor Loadings

Scales	Evaluation	Activity	Potency
valuable-worthless	.79	.13	.04
clean-dirty	.82	.03	−.05
tasty-distasteful	.77	−.11	.05
fast-slow	.01	.70	.00
active-passive	.14	.59	.04
hot-cold	−.04	.46	−.06
large-small	.06	.34	.62
strong-weak	.19	.20	.62
deep-shallow	.27	.14	.46
tense-relaxed	−.55	.37	−.12

Change in meaning (of the same concept at different times during therapy, or in different "personalities") can be defined by the same operation, except that d here refers to the differences in allocation of the same concept on the same scale at different testings. The mathematical properties of this formula also allow us to represent the *semantic structure* of an individual in a concise form; computation of the distance, D, of every concept from every other concept yields an N/N matrix (here, 15/15) of distances which have the property of plotting within a space having dimensionality equal to the number of factors. To the extent that the individual subject being studied uses the same three factors isolated in our general factor work, his data will plot accurately in three dimensions.

THE SEMANTIC DATA

At this point we should state exactly what information we have about this case. We know that we are dealing with a case of triple personality, and these have been labeled for us (presumably by the therapists who collected the semantic data) "Eve White," "Eve Black," and "Jane." We suppose that the "White" and "Black" have some connotative significance—certainly, as will be seen, the quantitative semantic data distinguish sharply between them. We also know, of course, that the patient is a woman, presumably participating in some kind of therapy; we do not know the stage of therapy or whether or not she is hospitalized. We considered it also fair to ask (from J. McV. Hunt) about the following items of sociological status, because they contribute to the meaningful interpretation of certain concepts: Concept CHILD—does this woman have a child? Yes, she does. Concept SPOUSE—is this woman married? Yes, she is. Concepts FATHER and MOTHER—are her parents alive? The mother is, but Hunt doesn't know about the father. Concept MY JOB—has this woman had a job outside of homekeeping? Yes, she has. This is the sum total of our external information about the case.

The semantic differential was given to this woman twice while "in" each of her three personalities; a period of about 2 months intervened between the two testings. The raw semantic data for each of the three personalities are given in Tables 2–4. The roman numerals I and II refer to first and second testings respectively.[2] We take the space to give these raw data in full so that anyone who is interested may study them and test any particular "hypotheses" about the case he wishes. Low values in these tables indicate judgments toward the polar term on the left and high values judgments toward the polar term on the right. The data in these tables show the semantic profiles, or meanings, of each concept at each testing and while "in" each personality. Since the form given at each testing was actually a double form (each item repeated once), we were able to estimate the reliability of these data. The immediate test-retest reliability coefficients for each of the testings are as follows: Eve White I, .82; Eve White II, .90; Eve Black I, .65; Eve Black II, .89; Jane I, .89; Jane II, .94. These coefficients indicate (*a*) a generally satisfactory level of reliability, (*b*) a consistent trend in all three personalities toward greater stability through time, and (*c*) that Jane is the most consistent or stable personality over short intervals of time and Eve Black is the least.

To obtain measures of semantic similarity and structure, we computed the matrices of *D* for each concept with every other concept, for each personality and testing. With an ordinary desk calculator and a table of square roots, these operations are very simple and rapid. In order to conserve space, the six matrices of *D* are not given here. These "distances" are based on application of the formula given earlier across all 10 scales. For convenience in plotting the models which appear as Fig. 1–6, the data for scales contributing to each of the three factors were averaged and new *D*'s computed. This, in effect, forces those data into three dimensions and, hence, into solid models that have no error. The very slight amount of distortion, or loss of information, resulting from this averaging process and restriction to three dimensions can be seen from the following correlations between original (10 scale) and "factor" *D* matrices (3 average scales): Eve White I, .91; Eve White II, .93; Eve Black I, .96; Eve Black II, .98; Jane I, .86; Jane II, .92. In other words, nearly all of the variance

in this woman's judgments can be accounted for in terms of three factors. Figures 1–6, then, provide quite accurate representations of the ways various concepts are related in each of the personalities; the smaller the distance between any two concepts the more similar in connotative meaning they are.

THE THREE PERSONALITIES AND THEIR CHANGES THROUGH TIME

The general assumption we are following is that "mental illness" is essentially a disordering of meanings or ways of perceiving from those characteristic of people judged "normal" in our society, and that the process of psychotherapy from the patient's point of view is essentially a reordering and changing of these meanings. Within the limitations of our type of measurement and our sampling of concepts, the locations and relations among concepts shown in Fig. 1–6 can be thought of as pictures of how this woman perceives herself, the significant people about her, and certain modes of action—when functioning "in" her several personalities.[3] We assume that this woman is receiving some kind of treatment through the period covered by our two samplings, I and II, and therefore look particularly for the types of changes in meaning that are taking place in the three personalities, as well as at the general nature of their organization. For purposes of ready comparison, all of the models are oriented in respect to the concept MY DOCTOR, which stays practically constant in meaning (*good, strong,* and *quite active*) through both time and personalities; spatially, in the figures, *good* is up and *bad* down, *active* to the left and *passive* to the right, and *strong* is away from the viewer while *weak* is near to or toward the viewer; the solid ball represents the origin of the space, e.g., a hypothetical "meaningless" concept that would result from checking all 4's.

Eve White

Semantic structures for Eve White I and II are shown in Fig. 1 and 2. The most general characterization would be that *Eve White perceives "the world" in an essentially normal fashion, is well socialized, but has an unsatis-*

<hr />

[2] These values are actually averages of two checkmarks, a double form of the semantic differential having been used for reliability purposes. In this double form, each item appears twice.

[3] The authors wish to thank Professor Jozef Cohen for his help in preparing these figures.

TABLE 2

Raw Data for Eve White

	LOVE		CHILD		MY DOCTOR		ME		MY JOB		MENTAL SICKNESS		MY MOTHER		PEACE OF MIND		FRAUD		MY SPOUSE		SELF-CONTROL		HATRED		MY FATHER		CON-FUSION		SEX		
	I	II	I	II	I	II	I	II	I	II	I	II	I	II	I	II	I	II	I	II	I	II	I	II	I	II	I	II	I	II	
cold	5.0	5.5	4.0	6.0	6.0	5.0	4.0	3.5	5.0	4.0	4.0	5.0	1.5	6.0	5.0	5.4	01.0	1.0	4.0	2.5	4.0	5.0	01.0	1.0	6.0	5.0	1.0	04.0	3.5	2.0	hot
valuable	1.0	1.0	1.0	1.0	1.0	1.0	1.0	4.0	6.0	1.0	4.0	5.0	1.0	1.0	1.0	1.0	07.0	7.0	3.0	3.5	1.0	1.0	07.0	7.0	01.0	1.0	03.0	05.0	52.0	54.5	worthless
tense	4.0	2.5	4.0	7.0	7.0	7.0	1.0	1.0	2.0	2.0	1.0	1.0	1.5	3.5	7.0	7.0	01.0	1.0	4.0	5.0	5.5	5.0	01.0	1.0	51.5	6.0	01.0	1.0	52.5	54.5	relaxed
small	7.0	6.0	1.0	7.0	7.0	7.0	1.0	1.0	2.0	2.0	1.0	1.0	57.0	7.0	7.0	01.0	1.0	4.0	5.5	5.0	5.0	03.0	4.0	2.0	01.0	1.0	04.0	52.5	hot		large
fast	7.0	4.5	5.0	2.5	2.0	3.0	2.0	5.5	6.0	5.7	6.0	5.5	5.7	7.0	7.0	01.0	1.0	5.0	5.0	5.6	5.6	51.0	07.0	05.0	06.0	02.5	06.0	02.5			slow
dirty	7.0	7.0	7.0	7.0	7.0	5.0	5.6	5.4	5.4	07.0	07.0	57.0	57.0	7.0	7.0	01.0	1.0	5.0	4.0	5.0	5.6	51.0	07.0	05.0	03.0	04.0	05.0	04.0			clean
weak	7.0	5.0	1.0	1.0	7.0	7.0	01.0	1.0	05.0	5.6	01.0	1.0	6.5	7.0	7.0	7.0	01.0	1.0	05.0	4.0	06.0	5.1	01.0	1.0	07.0	7.0	01.0	56.0	53.0	02.5	strong
tasty	1.0	2.0	1.0	1.0	1.0	01.0	1.0	03.0	05.0	1.0	05.6	01.0	1.0	57.0	06.5	7.0	7.0	01.0	1.0	04.0	3.5	57.0	06.0	01.0	07.0	7.0	01.0	54.0	02.5	distasteful
deep	1.0	2.0	1.0	1.0	1.0	03.0	05.0	51.0	1.5	7.5	7.0	05.0	1.0	01.0	1.0	07.0	7.0	01.0	1.0	02.5	3.5	1.5	57.0	07.0	01.0	1.0	02.0	01.0	51.5	53.5	shallow
active	1.0	2.5	1.0	1.0	1.0	04.0	05.0	02.5	4.0	01.0	1.0	01.0	1.0	1.0	07.0	03.5	4.0	02.0	4.5	4.5	51.0	2.0	01.0	02.5	51.0	01.0	1.0	54.0	05.0		passive

TABLE 3

Raw Data for Eve Black

	LOVE		CHILD		MY DOCTOR		ME		MY JOB		MENTAL SICKNESS		MY MOTHER		PEACE OF MIND		FRAUD		MY SPOUSE		SELF-CONTROL		HATRED		MY FATHER		CON-FUSION		SEX		
	I	II	I	II	I	II	I	II	I	II	I	II	I	II	I	II	I	II	I	II	I	II	I	II	I	II	I	II	I	II	
cold	4.0	1.0	1.0	1.0	07.0	7.0	01.0	1.0	01.0	1.0	01.0	1.0	1.0	1.0	1.57	05.0	5.56	56.0	02.51	03.5	2.06	06.0	6.07	06.54	01.07	07.07	07.0	01.01	01.0		hot
valuable	7.0	7.0	7.0	6.0	01.0	1.0	1.0	07.0	07.0	07.07	07.04	52.51	03.0	02.0	7.07	04.54	51.52	01.07	07.07	07.0	07.07	07.07	07.0	07.0	worthless
tense	1.0	1.0	1.0	1.57	07.0	7.07	07.0	01.0	07.07	04.01	02.51	04.57	05.56	06.06	04.02	02.06	06.55	01.02	01.51	01.01	01.0	02.01	01.51	01.0	relaxed
small	1.0	1.07	7.0	1.07	7.0	7.07	04.01	02.51	04.01	04.57	05.56	52.51	06.04	56.56	01.04	04.01	01.01	01.0	large
fast	7.0	1.04	03.51	01.02	07.07	07.0	1.01	01.01	1.01	05.56	52.51	57.06	06.52	01.51	01.51	54.51	54.05	5.5	slow
dirty	2.0	2.01	03.07	07.07	04.01	01.51	07.04	01.51	07.04	07.06	05.06	04.01	04.54	56.06	57.07	01.51	04.01	01.0	clean
weak	1.0	1.07	01.57	07.07	01.01	04.01	01.04	04.07	07.06	06.06	04.01	05.05	06.56	01.01	51.04	01.01	01.0	strong
tasty	7.0	7.07	06.01	01.01	07.07	07.04	07.07	05.1	51.52	01.52	04.57	03.54	52.02	01.01	01.52	07.02	04.07	07.0	distasteful
deep	7.0	7.02	51.01	01.07	07.04	07.07	07.01	01.51	02.51	01.52	04.07	02.01	51.52	07.02	04.04	07.07	shallow
active	7.0	7.07	07.07	01.01	01.07	07.07	07.01	01.01	1.51	57.07	07.04	51.51	57.07	04.01	51.51	01.04	07.07	07.0	passive

508

TABLE 4
RAW DATA FOR JANE

	LOVE I	LOVE II	CHILD I	CHILD II	MY DOCTOR I	MY DOCTOR II	ME I	ME II	MY JOB I	MY JOB II	MENTAL SICKNESS I	MENTAL SICKNESS II	MY MOTHER I	MY MOTHER II	PEACE OF MIND I	PEACE OF MIND II	FRAUD I	FRAUD II	MY SPOUSE I	MY SPOUSE II	SELF-CONTROL I	SELF-CONTROL II	SELF-HATRED I	SELF-HATRED II	MY FATHER I	MY FATHER II	CON-FUSION I	CON-FUSION II	SEX I	SEX II	
cold	4.0	6.0	4.0	6.5	4.0	5.5	4.0	6.0	4.0	4.5	4.0	4.5	4.0	6.5	1.0	2.0	4.0	6.0	4.0	6.0	4.0	6.0	1.0	1.5	6.0	6.5	4.0	4.5	4.0	6.5	hot
valuable	1.0	1.0	1.0	1.0	4.0	2.0	1.0	1.0	2.0	2.0	1.0	1.0	1.0	1.0	2.0	6.5	1.0	1.0	7.0	7.0	4.0	1.0	1.0	6.0	7.0	1.0	1.0	2.5	4.0	1.0	worthless
tense	7.0	7.0	5.0	5.0	7.0	7.0	2.0	1.0	1.5	2.0	1.0	1.5	2.0	7.0	7.0	1.0	7.0	7.0	4.5	2.0	7.0	7.0	6.0	4.0	1.0	1.5	1.5	7.0	7.0	7.0	relaxed
small	7.0	7.0	6.5	7.0	7.0	4.0	4.5	7.0	6.5	7.0	6.5	5.5	6.5	7.0	7.0	4.5	1.5	7.0	7.0	7.0	7.0	6.5	7.0	6.0	7.0	6.5	7.0	6.0	4.0	6.5	large
fast	7.0	6.5	3.0	1.5	1.0	2.0	4.5	2.0	7.0	7.0	7.0	6.0	3.5	2.0	7.0	6.0	1.5	2.0	3.0	2.5	7.0	6.0	4.0	2.0	1.5	2.0	4.0	4.0	6.5	7.0	slow
dirty	7.0	7.0	7.0	7.0	7.0	7.0	7.0	7.0	6.0	1.5	2.0	7.0	7.0	7.0	1.0	2.0	7.0	1.0	2.0	7.0	7.0	2.0	2.0	7.0	4.0	7.0	7.0	4.0	4.0	4.0	clean
weak	7.0	7.0	4.0	6.0	7.0	7.0	4.5	4.0	6.5	6.5	4.0	5.0	2.0	6.0	7.0	2.0	6.0	7.0	7.0	1.0	2.0	7.0	1.0	1.0	7.0	4.0	4.0	7.0	6.5	7.0	strong
tasty	1.0	1.0	1.0	1.0	3.5	2.0	5.0	4.5	2.0	5.0	4.0	2.0	1.0	1.0	1.0	7.0	7.0	1.0	1.0	1.0	7.0	1.0	1.0	2.0	1.0	7.0	5.5	1.0	1.0	7.0	distasteful
deep	1.0	1.0	2.0	1.0	1.5	2.0	3.0	1.0	1.5	1.0	2.0	2.0	1.5	1.0	1.5	1.0	1.0	2.0	2.0	1.5	1.5	1.0	2.0	2.0	1.0	1.5	1.0	1.5	4.0	1.0	shallow
active	2.5	1.5	1.0	1.0	1.0	2.0	1.5	4.5	2.0	1.0	1.0	1.0	5.5	2.5	6.0	4.5	4.0	1.0	2.5	2.0	2.5	2.0	1.0	1.5	2.5	4.0	1.5	1.0	4.0	1.5	passive

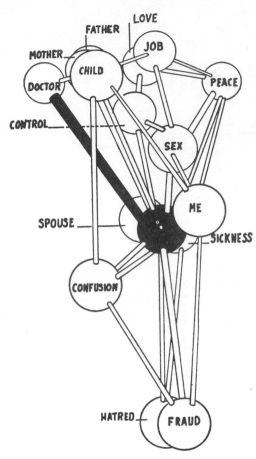

FIG. 1. EVE WHITE I

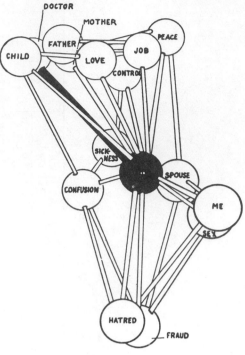

FIG. 2. EVE WHITE II

(a bad, weak thing like herself) have moved still further apart.

Eve Black

Semantic structures for Eve Black I and II are shown in Fig. 3 and 4. The most general characterization here would be that *Eve Black has achieved a violent kind of adjustment in which she perceives herself as literally perfect, but, to accomplish this break, her way of perceiving "the world" becomes completely disoriented from the norm.* The only exceptions to this dictum are MY DOCTOR and PEACE OF MIND, which maintain their *good* and *strong* characteristics, the latter, interestingly enough, also becoming *active* on II. But if Eve Black perceives herself as being *good*, then she also has to accept HATRED and FRAUD as positive values, since (we assume) she has strong hatreds and is socially fraudulent. So we find a tight, but very un-normal, favorable cluster of ME, MY DOCTOR, PEACE OF MIND, HATRED, and FRAUD. What are positive values for most people—CHILD, MY SPOUSE, MY JOB, LOVE, and SEX—are com-

factory attitude toward herself. Here the usual societal "goods" are seen favorably—MY DOCTOR, MY FATHER, LOVE, SELF-CONTROL, PEACE OF MIND, and MY MOTHER are all *good* and *strong* whereas FRAUD, HATRED, and to some extent CONFUSION are *bad*. The chief evidence of disturbance in the personality is the fact that ME (the self concept) is considered a little *bad*, a little *passive*, and definitely *weak*. Substantiating evidence is the *weakness* of her CHILD, as she sees him (or her), and the essential meaninglessness to her of MY SPOUSE and SEX. Note also the wide evaluative separation between LOVE and SEX. In the interval between testings I and II ME and SEX become more *bad* and *passive* and simultaneously become almost identical in meaning to her—and note that her conceptions of LOVE (a good, strong thing) and SEX

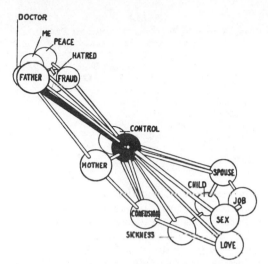

FIG. 3. EVE BLACK I

pletely rejected as *bad* and *passive*, and all of these except CHILD are also *weak* (this may be because CHILD was weak in Eve White and much of the change here is a simple "flip-flop" of meanings). Note that it is MOTHER in this personality that becomes relatively meaningless; FATHER, on the other hand, stays *good* but shifts completely from *strong* (in Eve White) to *weak*—possible implications of these familial identifications will be considered later. Note also that in this personality LOVE and SEX are closely identified, both as *bad*, *weak*, *passive* things.

Jane

Semantic structures for Jane I and II are shown in Fig. 5 and 6. The general charac-

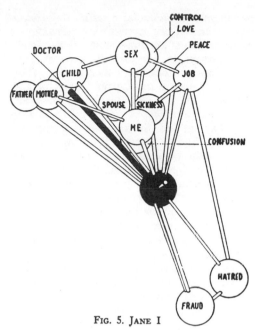

FIG. 5. JANE I

terization is that *Jane displays the most "healthy" meaning pattern, in which she accepts the usual evaluations of concepts by her*

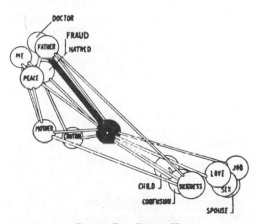

FIG. 4. EVE BLACK II

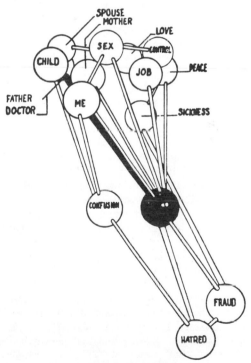

FIG. 6. JANE II

society yet still maintains a satisfactory evaluation of herself. MY FATHER, MY MOTHER, MY CHILD, and MY DOCTOR—most of the significant persons in her life—are seen as good, strong, and active. The major modes of behavior, PEACE OF MIND, LOVE, SELF-CONTROL, and MY JOB, are seen as equally good and strong, but somewhat passive—as if these ways of behaving and thinking were simply accepted without stress. The two socially agreed-upon evils, HATRED and FRAUD, are put in their proper places. The most significant characteristics of Jane's meaning system, however, are these: The self concept, ME, while still not strong (but not weak, either) is nearer the good and active directions of the semantic space; note also the close identification of ME and MENTAL SICKNESS, which here is not an unfavorable concept to her. Her attitude toward her husband, MY SPOUSE, is for the first time meaningful (unlike Eve White) and tending toward the good, strong, active directions, like the other significant persons (unlike Eve Black). And LOVE and SEX (quite unlike Eve White) are both favorable and quite closely identified. The changes from testings I to II are simply such as to strengthen the "healthy" pattern evident in the first view. ME becomes considerably more good and active; MY SPOUSE for the first time becomes completely identified connotatively with MY DOCTOR and MY FATHER (and loses its tie with CONFUSION); and LOVE and SEX become intimately identified with each other and close in meaning to SELF-CONTROL and PEACE OF MIND.

The thumbnail semantic sketches of each personality just given make it intuitively evident that the semantic differential does draw sharp distinctions between the three personalities inhabiting one nervous system. It is possible to demonstrate these distinctions quantitatively by intercorrelating D matrices between personalities and over time. If two of our models are generally similar in structure, such that large and small distances between concepts in one are reflected also in the other, then the r will be high. Table 5 gives these correlations. The first thing to note is that the correlation of each personality with itself (e.g., testings I and II) is regularly much higher than the correlation of that personality with any other personality (with the single exception of Eve White I and Jane I). This

TABLE 5
CORRELATIONS OF D-MATRICES BETWEEN PERSONALITIES AND OVER TIME

	White I	White II	Black I	Black II	Jane I	Jane II
White I	—					
White II	.73	—				
Black I	−.06		—			
Black II		−.02	.86	—		
Jane I	.73		−.26		—	
Jane II		.53		−.08	.92	—

is quantitative justification for the statement that the semantic differential does differentiate between the several personalities of this woman. Whether it differentiates in a valid way is a matter that can be judged only by relating our analysis to the detailed case history material available elsewhere (3).

Another important thing to note about these correlations is that Eve White and Jane (the two "socialized" personalities) are fairly highly correlated whereas the correlations of Eve Black with the other two are definitely low, even negative. In other words, Eve Black is clearly the most deviant and disordered personality. Finally, it should be noted that these three personalities differ somewhat in their stability, as indexed by the I/II correlations, Eve White being the least stable and Jane the most.

CHANGES IN MEANING OF SPECIFIC CONCEPTS

As noted earlier, the meaning of a specific concept is operationally defined as its profile against the differential (e.g., its position in semantic space). Change in meaning between testings I and II can be measured directly by the D between I and II profiles for the same concept (e.g., between the paired columns in Tables 2–4). These D values are given under "Within Personalities, Between Testings" in Table 6. Changes in meaning between personalities for the same concepts can be measured directly by the D between profiles for the same concept but as judged in two different personalities; these D values are given under "Between Personalities, Within Testings" in Table 6.

Semantic Stability Through Time

In general, although the differences are not great, Eve Black is the least stable personality

TABLE 6

CHANGES IN MEANING OF SPECIFIC CONCEPTS

Concept	Within Personalities, Between Testings			Between Personalities, Within Testings					
	$D_{I\text{-}II}$ Eve White	$D_{I\text{-}II}$ Eve Black	$D_{I\text{-}II}$ Jane	$D_{W\text{-}B}$		$D_{W\text{-}J}$		$D_{B\text{-}J}$	
				I	II	I	II	I	II
LOVE	.42	.67	.23	1.58	1.44	.35	.57	1.62	1.81
CHILD	.71	.96	.37	1.65	1.40	.68	.54	1.47	1.41
MY DOCTOR	.15	.05	.27	.23	.23	.28	.25	.30	.12
ME	.36	.32	.42	1.21	1.40	.60	.88	.83	.77
MY JOB	.27	.62	.42	1.30	1.43	.49	.43	1.19	1.54
MENTAL SICKNESS	.45	.45	.19	1.24	1.38	.40	.32	1.30	1.47
MY MOTHER	.54	.78	.46	.71	.78	.66	.23	1.02	.68
PEACE OF MIND	.40	.35	.41	.86	.66	.21	.28	.81	.61
FRAUD	.64	.17	.40	1.46	1.35	.73	.34	1.29	1.22
MY SPOUSE	.30	.62	.47	.62	.96	.89	1.04	.92	1.75
SELF-CONTROL	.32	.25	.24	.78	.80	.34	.39	.92	1.01
HATRED	.51	.19	.44	1.54	1.31	.51	.23	1.37	1.19
MY FATHER	.53	.71	.09	1.06	.60	.25	.43	1.06	.43
CONFUSION	.64	.67	.44	.86	.96	.71	.42	.98	.88
SEX	.62	.34	.47	1.10	.62	.63	1.20	1.45	1.76

Note.—Numbers in italics indicate concepts that serve best to characterize differences between Eve White and Jane.

through time and Jane the most stable (cf., columns 2–4 in Table 6). The concept-by-concept data thus confirm the stability of Jane as shown in the structural data given above. For Eve White the most unstable or labile concepts are CHILD, MY MOTHER, FRAUD, HATRED, MY FATHER, CONFUSION, and SEX. For Eve Black the most labile concepts are LOVE, CHILD, MY JOB, MY MOTHER, MY SPOUSE, MY FATHER, and CONFUSION. For Jane the most unstable notions are ME, MY JOB, MY MOTHER, MY SPOUSE, HATRED, CONFUSION, and SEX. We note that the family constellation—mother, father, spouse, child—tend to be more susceptible to change through time within these personalities, but that the self concept stays relatively constant within personalities (e.g., the location of the self concept, in a sense, defines these three personalities). HATRED, SEX, and CONFUSION also seem to be points of stress.

Semantic Stability Between Personalities

The data given in columns 5–10 in Table 6 make it clear that concept meanings in general shift more between Eve Black and the other two than between Jane and Eve White, this again substantiating the over-all correlations between total structures. The only concept that remains strictly constant in meaning

through the personality changes in this woman is MY DOCTOR, although PEACE OF MIND and CONFUSION show greater stability than most others. It is interesting to note which concepts serve best to characterize the differences between Eve White and Jane (Eve Black shows gross differences on almost all concepts). These two "socialized" personalities differ from one another chiefly on ME, MY SPOUSE, and SEX, and these differences are increasing in magnitude through time. This clearly suggests this woman's sexual life as a core problem, Eve White being highly critical of all three concepts and Jane accepting them as positive values. It is also interesting to note in this connection that semantic differences between Eve White and Jane on CHILD, MY MOTHER, FRAUD, HATRED, and CONFUSION are decreasing through time.

INTERPRETATIONS OF THESE SEMANTIC DATA

The analyses of these personalities and their changes given so far have been descriptive rather than interpretive for the most part. In a sense, we have merely put into words what this woman herself, in her several personalities, has indicated by her check marks. The treatment of semantic differential data, from the patterns of check marks to construction of the models shown in Fig. 1–6, is completely objective, and any investigator starting from the same data and following the rules would have to end up with the same pictures we have.

Making interpretations and predictions about this case on a "blind" basis is another matter entirely. In this section we go far beyond the objective data, and we are consequently much less confident about our statements. For one thing, neither of the writers is an experienced clinician—certainly not experienced with respect to the dynamics and characteristics of multiple personality. For another thing, we do not know at what stage in therapy our two testings were made, and interpretation would certainly vary greatly in terms of such information. It should also be pointed out that in the ordinary use of the semantic differential as a clinical tool (as compared with a blind analysis) many other sources of information would be available to support certain alternative interpretations and render others farcical. Let it be understood, then, that what follows is a flight into conjecture, in contrast with the preceding, factual reporting of semantic data.

Interpretive Descriptions of the Three Personalities

Eve White is the woman who is simultaneously most in contact with social reality and under the greatest emotional stress. She is aware of both the demands of society and her own inadequacies in meeting them. She sees herself as a passive weakling and is also consciously aware of the discord in her sexual life, drawing increasingly sharp distinctions between LOVE as an idealized notion and SEX as a crude reality. She maintains the greatest diversity among the meanings of various concepts. She is concerned and ambivalent about her CHILD, but apparently is *not* aware of her own ambivalent attitudes toward her MOTHER—and seems to become more resistant to this by testing II. Those psychoanalytically inclined may wish to identify Eve White with dominance of the *superego*: certainly, the superego seems to view the world through the eyes of Eve White, accepting the mores or values of others (particularly her mother) but continuously criticizing and punishing herself. If this case came to the psychotherapists with a voluntary, self-initiated plea for help, then it seems likely that Eve White was dominant at the time.

Eve Black is clearly the most out of contact with social reality and simultaneously the most self-assured. To rhapsodize, Eve Black finds PEACE OF MIND through close identification with a God-like therapist (MY DOCTOR, probably a father symbol for her), accepting her HATRED and FRAUD as perfectly legitimate aspects of the God-like role. Naturally, she sees herself as a dominant, active wonderwoman and is in no way self-critical. She is probably unaware of her family situation. Those psychoanalytically inclined could say that the *id* looks out at the world through the eyes of Eve Black. Like a completely selfish infant, this personality is entirely oriented around the assumption of its own perfection. Actually, Eve Black seems to be more harmonious with the Adlerian than with the Freudian model, since personal perfection is apparently the demand acceded to rather than sexuality. If the case was committed to an institution, it seems likely that this personality was the reason for commitment.

Jane is the most puzzling of the three personalities, and our interpretation will have to depend upon assumptions about the stage of treatment (see below). Superficially, Jane is a very healthy personality: "all's well with the world, and day by day I'm getting better and better." Thus we find all the people in her life perceived as *good* and *strong* and *active* and all the socially approved modes of action perceived as *good* and *strong* and *passive*; SEX is LOVE-ly, her SPOUSE is becoming more like the noble DOCTOR all the time, and she is coming to perceive herself even, as a pleasant and reasonably active (if somewhat weak and submissive) person. But all this is a little too rosy, a little too pat. We note that Jane is becoming more and more "simple-minded"— all of her judgments tending to fall along a single factor of *good-strong* vs. *bad-weak*— which makes the Jane II model the most restricted and undiversified of all. Those psychoanalytically inclined may wish to view this personality as representing dominance of a self-deceptive *ego* which has woven a web of repression as to the state of reality; or, they may wish to view Jane as an essentially strong, healthy, and improving ego-dominated personality. In any case, we doubt if Jane would have either come for therapy or have been institutionalized—as such.

Possible Dynamisms Operating in the Case

Identification mechanisms. We say the patient "identifies" with some other person when her meaning of herself, ME, is semantically close to her meaning of the other person; e.g., if she sees her father as a kind, active, relaxed, etc. person and describes herself in the same terms, we infer identification. However, the pattern of identifications displayed by this patient seems unusual. Only in Eve Black, the obviously disoriented personality in terms of her values, is there clear differential identification—with her FATHER (and this may reflect the semantic tie-up between FATHER and MY DOCTOR). Jane shows some slight tendency toward closer identification with MOTHER, but it is not close. Eve White shows none with either parent. The fact that identification with FATHER (and MY DOCTOR) in Eve Black is accompanied by rejection of MOTHER to meaninglessness is suggestive of an underlying conflict in identifications. Note also, in this connection, that in Eve Black I the ascendancy of ME to the *good, strong, active* position is accompanied by making FATHER *weak*—as if she were taking over her father's role and putting her mother in her own previous place. And, interestingly enough, the concept SELF-CONTROL suffers the same fate as MOTHER. This picture of Eve Black is certainly suggestive of an *Electra complex* as the underlying dynamism. In "real" life, her MOTHER is or was the dominant, threatening figure—moralizing, demanding standards and SELF-CONTROL—and in Eve Black this woman escapes the pressure by rendering both MOTHER and SELF-CONTROL meaningless and simultaneously identifying with and taking her FATHER'S place (via the therapist). Suggestive evidence may be found in Tables 2–4: MOTHER is consistently *colder* than FATHER and usually more *tense* and *fast* (e.g., Factor 3). Identification of the self with the therapist in Eve Black is perfect, of course. The concept MY DOCTOR is the only personal concept to show perfect stability both between personalities and through time. The patient thus displays what might be called maximal *positive transference* in all three personalities; there is no sign of any negative transference at either testing, which may be indicative of the stage of therapy (e.g., early).

Significance of the patient's sexual life. Although Jane shows a rosy acceptance of normal sexual patterning—with LOVE and SEX linked and passively favorable, Eve White clearly displays awareness of a basic conflict in this area—SEX is early somewhat more distasteful than LOVE and becomes distinctly distasteful and dirty by testing II. In Eve White also we find ME and MY SPOUSE becoming linked with SEX in this unpleasant location. Eve Black, on the other hand, rejects both SEX and LOVE—but closely links them in her thinking. If we were to relate these facts with the Electra situation described above, the interpretation would be that her persisting conflict with her mother and attempts to identify with her father make it impossible for her to experience normal sexual satisfactions with her husband and to carry out the normal mother-wife-home role. Eve White is aware of this, in a sense, but Jane clearly is not. The concept MY JOB is interesting in this connection: its persistent linkages with LOVE, PEACE OF MIND, and SELF-CONTROL in the two "socialized" personalities, coupled with its linkage with SEX

and MY SPOUSE in Eve Black, clearly suggests to us that this woman is interpreting MY JOB in the sense of "my job as a mother, wife, and homebuilder" rather than in terms of her outside work (which we understand she has). In any case, there is clear evidence of involvement with her sex life as a major problem, and this may have been the presenting problem when she began therapy.

Repression and amnesia. Knowing that we are dealing with a case of multiple personality—usually characterized by complete dissociation between states—it is interesting to speculate on what meanings are repressed in the several personalities. It will be recalled that, operationally, meaninglessness of a concept is defined by its closeness to the origin (the solid balls in the models). This is probably to be interpreted as "connotative deadness" or "damping of affect" with respect to the concept involved. Within the matrix of our instrument, however, there is another way in which repression or amnesia may show up, and that is via a complete shift in meaning of the concept being judged (e.g., CHILD may shift from the personal reference of "my own youngster" to "children-in-general"). Looking back at the semantic data with these points in mind, we hazard the following guesses: Eve White probably has the best contact with reality and may not be amnesic at all (except for the other personalities); Eve Black may be amnesic for her mother and her own role as a mother and wife; Jane in Pollyanna fashion may be amnesic for her own problems, e.g., MENTAL SICKNESS and CONFUSION, and the indiscriminate way in which she lumps all socially favorable concepts at least suggests that she is judging CHILD, MOTHER, etc. in the abstract rather than as MY CHILD, MY MOTHER, and so forth.

Interpretation I—Assumed Early Stage of Therapy

The "original" personality, in the sense of being most characteristic of the woman her friends and relations knew, was Jane. The first testing of this personality shows a relatively weak ME that is associated with MENTAL SICKNESS; i.e., she was dimly aware of her own inadequacies but was striving to maintain a rigid acceptance of the real world and maintain an adequate home life. The people about her, with the exception of her husband, were seen as strong and active (perhaps threatening) in relation to herself, and her love life was regarded as a sort of deliberate, controlled duty. She was completely unaware of her (repressed) emotional ambivalence toward her mother, husband, and child. The things being hidden in this personality, and providing the force behind the eventual split, were (*a*) her Electra complex, (*b*) her repugnance for sexual relations with her husband, and (*c*) her ambivalent attitude toward herself. We suspect that she had a position in society that demanded "good front."

We must assume strong and about equal pressures toward solving the Electra complex, (*a*) by identifying with FATHER and asserting the self (id?), and (*b*) toward solving it by identifying with MOTHER and devaluing herself (superego?). This produces a two-way split away from the Jane pattern, one into Eve Black where selfish needs for superiority and playing the father role are achieved and another into Eve White where societal needs for submission and playing the mother role are achieved. This split, and the subsequent availability of the other roles, allows Jane to shift toward the "sweetness and light" view of the world, and this is clearly demonstrated by the changes between Jane I and Jane II. Eve White continues to become more simply and rigidly self-critical and Eve Black continues to become more simply and rigidly self-satisfied.

Assuming successful therapy is possible—which seems questionable—it will involve less and less time being spent in being Jane and Eve Black and a consequent shift into Eve White, where better contact and differentiation seems to be maintained. But here it will be necessary to bring Eve White to understand the reason for her depression, the role of her ambivalence toward her mother in her problem—which shows no signs of happening yet—and thence a gradual restructuring in which ME becomes more favorable, along with SPOUSE and SEX, and identifications with FATHER and MOTHER are reassigned. This will probably involve a period of negative transference, with MY DOCTOR and MOTHER becoming closely identified and being temporarily shifted to *bad*, *strong*, and *active* directions of the semantic space. In other words, successful treatment will mean increasing time spent in,

and a gradual restructuring of, Eve White to the point where it incorporates what is now Jane, but with a realignment of significant persons. On the other hand, if this woman is in a mental institution and remains there, it seems likely that Eve Black will become the dominant house she lives in. In either case, it is probable that Jane will appear less and less.

Interpretation II—Assumed Late Stage of Therapy

If we assume that we are seeing the terminal stages of therapy with a case of this sort, then a quite different interpretation is necessary. The difference in interpretations hinges upon Jane, either as a deceptive and vanishing original personality (interpretation I) or as an increasingly healthy and augmenting personality (interpretation II). In the latter case we would assume that Eve White had been the "original" personality as people knew her—a socially acceptable wife and mother, but one laden with conflicts, anxieties, and self-criticism. The split in this case—into one personality in which the self-criticism completely disappears via irrationality (Eve Black) and another in which self-criticism vanishes via rationality (Jane)—seems less sensible, however. Jane seems unnecessary at this stage and really should have developed out of Eve White rather than being contemporaneous. If we assume there was a split in any case, Jane is clearly the most healthy personality, since LOVE and SEX are identified, the world is viewed in acceptable fashion, and the self concept is becoming more favorable all the time. The prediction here would be increasing time spent in Jane and less in the others. The stumbling blocks in the way of this interpretation are (*a*) the lack of any realignment of the system of parental identifications, and (*b*) the fact that Jane is becoming *less* diversified semantically (more "simple-minded") rather than the reverse. This second interpretation was actually the one we first adopted—because of the superficial "healthiness" of Jane—but consideration of all the evidence seems to favor the first interpretation. However, it should be noted that *if* this case is near the end of successful therapy, Jane is the only personality that combines both a normal view of the world and reasonable (increasing) acceptance of the self.

Interpretation III—Combination of I and II

It is possible to combine interpretations I and II by assuming that Jane is both the original personality which broke apart and the terminal personality which is being developed out of therapy. In this case, the early development of the case, probably in childhood, would be the same as that given under interpretation I the conflicting parental identifications (id and superego determined respectively) were of about equal strength and finally became too intense to be contained within the self-deceptive personality organization of Jane. During the middle course of the case, when therapy was undertaken, we thus find all three personalities oscillating, temporary dominance of the mother and wife role being represented by Eve White, temporary dominance of the self-gratifying father role being represented by Eve Black, and temporary dominance of the face-saving, problem-solving ego being represented by Jane. Intentionally or unintentionally, the effect of therapy may be to strengthen the self-deceptive organization of Jane without resolving the underlying conflicts dramatized by Eve White and Eve Black. The oversimplified, Pollyanna-like ways of perceiving herself as *good* along with all the other significant persons in her life yields a superficially happy person who views the world in an acceptable, if rigidly stereotyped, fashion. If the present combined interpretation approximates the actual situation, then we feel compelled to predict another breakdown at some later period in this person's life. In other words, the effect of therapy (whatever type it may have been) seems to have been further to strengthen the self-deceptive original organization of Jane, while making this personality even more rigid and insensitive to subtle differences in meaning and without resolving the underlying conflicts which created the original disturbance.

What Price Therapy?

It is impossible to tell from our semantic data whether the increasing simplification in structure characteristic of all three personalities is due to therapy itself or is happening despite therapy. However, a number of specialists in psychotherapy have from time to time expressed concern over the "hidden" effects of therapy even in so-called successful cases—particularly reduction in initiative, creativeness, and flexibility of the patient. Certainly in the present case we are witnessing an over-all reduction in differentiation of meanings. If overt behavior is in considerable part determined by meanings, as we believe it is, then we must expect Jane (if she is the terminal personality) to be now even less capable of behaving differentially to her mother, father, spouse, and child—they are all essentially undifferentiated "strong-active-goodness" to her. This would also be true, but to a lesser extent, of Eve White, although here we would assume an earlier stage of therapy and hence a possibility of secondary elaboration of semantic diversity under sensitive therapy.

Is rigidity of this sort a necessary price of therapy? In striving to achieve the goals of societal acceptability and invididual happiness, does the therapist have to sacrifice the richness, individuality, and subtler adjustiveness of the patient? These are serious questions raised by the data of this single case—but not answered by them, of course. From the larger sample of cases we are presently working on, better answers may be forthcoming, but the cases are generally less severe. One other interesting phenomenon in the present cases should be mentioned: Despite the gross changes in meaning of concepts in the several personalities, and the over-all reduction in diversity, the semantic judgmental frame of reference remains constant. In other words, all three of the personalities in this woman utilize semantic scales in the same ways—the correlations between scales are the same for all three personalities and reduction in diversity in all of them is accomplished by a coalescence of *good*, *strong*, and *active* into a single evaluative dimension. Thus it would appear that the level of scale meanings is below that at which concepts vary, and common to all three personalities.

REFERENCES

1. Osgood, C. E. The nature and measurement of meaning. *Psychol. Bull.*, 1952, **49**, 192–237.
2. Osgood, C. E., & Suci, G. J. A measure of relation determined by both mean difference and profile information. *Psychol. Bull.*, 1952, **49**, 251–262.
3. Thigpen, C. H., & Cleckley, H. A case of multiple personality. *J. abnorm. soc. Psychol.*, 1954, **49**, 135–151.

42. Changes in Meaning during Psychotherapy as Measured by the Semantic Differential

Norman S. Endler

Personality theorists and psychotherapists maintain that certain perceptual and behavioral changes occur during psychotherapy. Snygg and Combs (1949) claim that one of the criteria for effective therapy is a change in a client's meanings, especially with respect to the phenomenal self. Other theorists (Freud, 1933; Mowrer, 1953; and Sullivan, 1953) add the importance of changes in the meaning of the father and mother figures that occur during therapy. Previous studies (Rogers, 1954; Dymond, 1953; Sheerer, 1949; Ewing, 1954; and others) of perceptual change, or changes in meaning during therapy, utilized unidimensional measuring instruments which were susceptible to bias, and which measured constructs that were not clearly defined.

The present study uses Osgood's (1952) Semantic Differential technique as an index of changes in meaning during therapy. This technique measures meaning, an intervening variable, explicitly defined as *a representational mediation process,* a learned state, that is elicited by *signs* (stimuli) and constitutes their *significance,* and that initiates overt responses (linguistic and nonlinguistic) and constitutes their *intention* (Osgood, Suci, & Tannenbaum, 1957). The Ss' overt responses to the Semantic Differential serve as an operational index of the *representational mediation process* or meaning. The construct of meaning is derived from a general conceptual scheme presented by Osgood, et al. (1957).

Reprinted from *Journal of Counseling Psychology* (1961), 8: 105–111, by permission of the author and the American Psychological Association.

The Semantic Differential technique employs a multidimensional approach and is considered to be relatively free of response biases. Furthermore, previous factor analytic studies of the Semantic Differential have yielded relatively pure factors of the construct of meaning Osgood, (et. al., 1957).

Osgood, et al. (1957) consider meaning an important personality dimension. They state that "the significance of meaning as a critical variable in personality is most apparent perhaps in the process of therapy itself, where the principal changes that occur appear to be changes in significance or meaning that various persons, events, and situations have for the patient and changes in the inter-relationships between these significances" (Osgood, et al., 1957, p. 273). The most important concepts seem to be the self, father, and mother concepts. Modifications that occur during therapy should be reflected in changes in the meanings of the relevant concepts. Furthermore, modifications in identification patterns during therapy should be reflected by changes in the semantic distance between self and father or self and mother. Lazowick (1955) and Osgood (1952) state that the degree of similarity of meaning (i.e., mediating processes) between a subject (self) and a model (father or mother) is an index of identification.

Present Study

The present study is concerned with changes in meaning of the self, father, and mother concepts in the client's semantic space during therapy and the relationship of these changes to estimated improvements. The relationship of changes in the semantic distance (i.e., identification) between self and father or self and mother, to movement in therapy is also considered.

Specifically, the hypotheses to be tested are:

1A. There will be changes in the meaning of the client's self, father, and mother figures during therapy. These changes will occur on the evaluative, potency and activity factors of meaning.

1B. The changes in the meaning of the self, father, and mother figures will be related to estimated improvement. Direction of change is not predicted because some clients initially misperceive themselves and their parents as valuable, strong, and active; while others misperceive these figures as worthless, weak, and passive.

2A. After therapy male subjects will perceive themselves as closer to both their mothers and their fathers than before therapy.

2B. This increased identification to both parents is related to estimated improvement in therapy.

2C. After therapy male subjects will identify more with their fathers than their mothers.

2D. This discrepancy in parental identification after therapy is related to estimated improvement.

All the hypotheses about changes in meaning are with respect to the evaluative, potency, and activity factors of meaning.

Method

Tests

The Semantic Differential. The Semantic Differential is an objective, reliable, valid, and general method for measuring the connotative meaning of concepts. Osgood (1952, p. 227) summarizes the logic of this method as follows:

1. The process of description or judgment can be conceived as the allocation of a concept to an experiential continuum definable by a pair of polar items.

2. Many different experiential continua or ways in which meanings vary are equivalent and hence may be represented by a single dimension.

3. A limited number of such continua can be used to define a semantic space within which the meaning of any concept can be specified.

The three major continua represent the evaluative, potency, and activity factors, and the construct of attitude can be identified with the evaluative dimension of the total semantic space.

The particular form of the Semantic Differential used in this study consisted of 15 concepts which were rated on ten polar scales. The intensity of a rating was indicated by the position of a subject's check mark on a seven-step scale, where four is the neutral position. Of the 15 concepts and ten scales, only the results of three concepts (me, father, and mother) and nine scales, were analyzed for this study. The nine scales were taken as representative of three connotative factors of meaning isolated in factor analytic studies by Osgood (1952).

The factors and the scales are as follows: 1. an evaluative factor represented by the valuable-worthless, clean-dirty, and tasty-distasteful scales; 2. a potency factor represented by the strong-weak, deep-shallow, large-small scales; and 3. an activity factor represented by the active-passive, fast-slow, and hot-cold scales.

Each scale has maximal loading on the factor it represents and minimal loading on the other two factors. In general, the test-retest reliability is .85. The three factors account for about 60 per cent of the total variance, and about 70 per cent of the common variance is due to the evaluative factor.

When subjects rate the "me," "father," and "mother" concepts on the nine scales, profiles can be generated for each subject on every concept. Since there are three factors of meaning it is possible to generate three profiles for every concept. If subjects are administered the Semantic Differential before and after therapy, it is possible to index the changes in the "me" (self), "mother," and "father" concepts. The distance or change between the pre and post profiles for each concept, and each factor, can be determined by the D measure of profile similarity, where D is the square root of the sum of the squared distances between co-ordinate items on the two profiles (Cronbach & Gleser, 1953; Osgood, 1952). Similarly, the distance, D, between the me and father or me and mother profiles can serve as an inverse index of identification; the smaller the D, the greater the identification.

The Movement Scale. The Hunt-Kogan Movement Scale (1952) is an equal interval scale which estimates improvement during therapy. It has a range from minus 20 (maximum deterioration) to plus 40 (maximum improvement) and it has been standardized and validated. The criteria used to make judgments of movement or improvement are definite and explicit.

Counselors

Eight counselors, with amount of experience varying from two to over twenty years, were used in this study. The schools of psychotherapy in which they were trained include the Adlerian (one), the neo-Freudian (one), the Rogerian (two), and eclectic. Two of the younger counselors received their training in clinical and counseling psychology at the University of Illinois where this study was conducted. Clients were randomly assigned to the various counselors.

Subjects

Twenty-two college students, 17 males and 5 females, who were in psychotherapy for some type of personal or emotional problem served as subjects. Each client completed a minimum of 5 interviews, and 1 client completed as many as 65 interviews. The median number of interviews for the group was 19.

Procedure

The 22 subjects were administered the Osgood Semantic Differential both before entering psychotherapy and immediately after psychotherapy.

At the end of therapy, the therapist estimated the client's improvement on the Hunt-Kogan Movement Scale.

Analysis of Data

Both the D statistic and the rank order correlation coefficient, *rho*, can be used as methods of assessing profile similarities. The D statistic takes into account both the

absolute discrepancy and the profile similarities (shape, scatter, and elevation) between sets of measurement, whereas the *rho* correlation coefficient, which is a special case of D, reflects only profile similarities (shape) (Cronbach & Gleser, 1953; Osgood, 1952). For this study the D statistic was used where the aim was to determine the significant differences between profiles, while *rho* was used where the aim was to determine significant congruence between profiles.

Results

Changes in Meaning Data

To test the hypothesis of changes in the "me," "father," and "mother" concepts during therapy, difference scores were computed between the pre and post profiles of these concepts, on each of the factors; and the ranks of the differences were subjected to the Wilcoxon paired replicates test (1949). The only significant change that resulted was for the meaning of the "me" concept on the evaluative factor ($N = 22$).

To test the hypothesis that changes in the "me," "father," and "mother" concepts are related to estimated improvement in therapy, the distances, D, between pre and post profiles on each of these concepts and for each factor were rank order correlated with movement ratings. The results of these correlations are shown in Table 1. A multiple correlation was calculated between the changes on the three factors of the "me" concept and movement (or improvement), with a result of .646 which is significant at the 5 per cent level ($N = 18$).

Changes in Identification Data

The identification data were analyzed for the 17 male subjects only, because there were not enough female subjects to warrant a statistical analysis.

To test the hypothesis that there is increased identification with both parents after therapy, the pretherapy "me-father" and pretherapy "me-mother" D values were computed for all factors and compared with the posttherapy "me-father" and "me-

Table 1

Rho Correlations Between Movement in Therapy and Changes in Meanings of Me, Father, and Mother Concepts (N = 18)

Concepts	Factors of Meaning		
	Evaluative	Potency	Activity
Me	.627	.370	.470
	$p<.01$	N.S.	$p<.05$
Father	.349	.161	.531
	N.S.	N.S.	$p<.05$
Mother	—.438	.523	—.297
	N.S.	$p<.05$	N.S.

mother" *D* values, respectively. The Wilcoxon paired replicates test was used to determine whether the post *D* values were significantly smaller than the pre *D* values. The results were not significant for either parent (N = 17).

To test the hypothesis that male subjects identify more with their fathers than with their mothers after therapy, the posttherapy *D* values between "me" and "father" concepts on all factors were compared with the posttherapy *D* values between "me" and "mother" concepts on all factors, by means of the Wilcoxon paired replicates test. There was no significant difference (N = 17).

To test the hypothesis that changes in parental identification during therapy, and discrepancies between father and mother identification after therapy are related to improvement, *rho* correlations were calculated between the appropriate *D* values and the movement ratings. There were no significant relationships (N = 17).

Since there were no changes in identification, using *D* as the index, it would be important to determine whether there was any parental identification either before or after therapy. The *rho* statistic which only measures similarity of profile shapes can be used as a crude approximation of identification or some sort of self-parent relationship.

Rho correlations were computed between "me" and "father" profiles and between "me" and "mother" profiles, for all meaning factors, both before and after therapy. There were no significant correlations between "me" and "mother" profiles either

before or after therapy and no significant correlations between "me" and "father" profiles before therapy. The correlations between "me" and "father" profiles after therapy are indicated in Table 2 (N = 17). Converting the *rho* scores to Z scores and calculating the differences between pre and post Z scores indicate that there were no significant shifts in the relationship of the "me" and "mother" profiles but that there was a significant shift (at the 5 per cent level) in the relationship of the "me" and "father" concepts on the evaluative factor during therapy (N = 17).

Table 2

Rho Correlations Between Clients' Meanings of Me and Father Concepts After Therapy (N = 17)

	Factors of Meaning		
	Evaluative	Potency	Activity
Me-Father *Rho*	.818	.491	.168
p	<.01	<.05	N.S.

Discussion

Changes in Meaning

The results of this study indicate that the evaluative meaning of the self (me) concept is significantly modified during psychotherapy in the direction of greater self-valuation. Although changes occur in the meanings of the "father" and "mother" concepts, none of these changes are significant. This corroborates the contention (Rogers, 1951; Snygg & Combs, 1949) that the phenomenal self is the key personality concept, and psychological adjustment is greatly determined by its significance or meaning. The "father" and "mother" concepts appear to be important but secondary. The greatest changes occur on the evaluative factor of the "me" concept, primarily because it accounts for most of the variance of the meaning construct and is especially important in the context of personality adjustment. Even the most sophisticated members of our society perceive behavior disorders in an evaluative manner.

The results also indicate that changes in (a) the evaluative and activity meanings of the "me" (self) concept; (b) the activity meaning of the "father" concept; and (c) the potency meaning of the "mother" concept, regardless of direction of change, are significantly related to estimated improvement during therapy. Furthermore, it is possible to predict improvement from a knowledge of changes of the three meaning factors of the me (self) concept. This corroborates Snygg and Combs' (1949) notion that one of the criteria of effective therapy is a change in the client's meaning system, or a perceptual reorganization of the phenomenal field. There is a communality of importance, of the relationship between movement and changes in the activity factor, for the "father" and self concepts (for this male predominant sample), and a lack of communality with the "mother" concept. For the "mother" concept, however, changes in meaning of the potency factor are significantly related to movement in therapy (see Table 1). Perhaps in our society the active-passive factor is more important for perceiving father figures, while the potency-weak factor is more important for perceiving mother figures. This may be because mothers spend more time at home and play a more significant role in rearing children during the formative years, and hence are perceived most clearly along a potent-weak continuum, whereas fathers are away from home, working and thus may be perceived most clearly along an active-passive continuum. The direction of change of parental figures was disregarded, because some clients may initially misperceive their parents as potent or active while others may misperceive them as weak or passive. Possibly a differential diagnosis of the type of neurotic disorder might permit the prediction of the direction of changes in the perception of the parental figures.

Identification Changes

The results, using the D statistic, indicate that there were no significant changes in identification with parents for male subjects during therapy. Furthermore, identification changes or differences that did occur were not significantly related to estimated improvement.

Since the data were not collected by a Q-sort (Rogers & Dymond, 1954) it was not possible to ascertain significant *identification* either before or after therapy. Using *rho,* it was possible to determine whether there were any significant perceived relationships between the male subjects and parental figures either before or after therapy. There were no significant self-mother or self-father relationships before therapy, and no significant self-mother relationships after therapy. However, the relationships between the "me" and the "father" concepts after therapy were significant for the evaluative and potency factors; and the changes in the relationship during therapy were significant for the evaluative factor.

From the above, we can conclude that prior to therapy there is no relationship between the perception of self and perception of father, but after therapy the client's perceptual field becomes more differentiated (Snygg & Combs, 1949). Although the client does not necessarily *identify* with his father after therapy, his perceptual field is more highly differentiated, and he perceives some relationship between himself and his father. Thus, the ability to *relate* to the same sexed parent, rather than the ability to *identify* with the same sexed parent, appears to be a crucial variable. However, there are two limitations to this conclusion: (1) the changes in the perceived relationship between self and father during therapy are not necessarily related to estimated improvement; and (2) since the same data were subjected to two statistical analyses, D and *rho,* the confidence levels are slightly above 1 per cent and 5 per cent. Nevertheless, there still appears to be some perceived relationship between male subjects and the father figure after therapy which does not exist before therapy. This perceived relationship does not exist with respect to the mother figure either before or after therapy. Since the evaluative and potency factors each account for more of the variance than the activity factor, they are more sensitive to **the posttherapy self-father relationship.**

Summary and Conclusions

Twenty-two clients rated the meaning of their self (me), their "father," and their "mother" concepts on the Semantic Differential before and after therapy. Changes in the evaluative, potency, and activity factors of the "me," "father," and "mother" concepts, as well as changes in the perceived relationships between self and parental figures (identification changes) were correlated with the therapists' estimation of improvement in personal adjustment during therapy.

The results indicated that there were significant changes in the evaluative meaning of the self (me) concept, and that changes in the evaluative and activity meanings of the self concept were significantly related to estimated improvement. Changes in the potency meaning of the mother concept and the activity meaning of the father concept were significantly related to estimated improvement.

There were no significant changes in *identification* for male subjects. Changes that did occur were not related to estimated improvement. There was a significant *relationship* in the perception of self and the perception of father, for male subjects, after therapy.

In view of the results, it can be concluded that changes in the meaning of the self concept is a promising criterion of improvement during therapy. The evaluative factor of meaning is the most sensitive to change, and seems to be an important determinant of psychological adjustment. *Identification* between males and their fathers does not seem crucial for adjustment; however, a *perceived relationship* between the two appears to be rather important.

This experiment has value as a pilot study and its findings are suggestive rather than conclusive. Two noteworthy limitations of this study are: (1) a small sample was used, and (2) the same clients were used to test the hypotheses for the two sections of this study. Better controls are needed and these might be accomplished by: (1) comparing a clinical group to a normative group to determine which changes occur independent of therapy; and (2) determining via differential diagnosis the direction of change of different types of clients.

In conclusion it can be stated that meaning, as measured by the Semantic Differential, is an important personality construct and one which can serve as an index of adjustment, maladjustment, and therapeutic improvement.

References

Cronbach, L. J., & Gleser, G. C. Assessing similarity between profiles. *Psychol. Bull.*, 1953, **50**, 456-473.

Dymond, Rosalind F. An adjustment score for Q-sorts. *J. consult. Psychol.*, 1953, **17**, 339-342.

Ewing, T. N. Changes in attitude during counseling. *J. counsel. Psychol.*, 1954, **1**, 232-239.

Freud, S. *New introductory lectures of psychoanalysis.* London: Hogarth, 1933.

Hunt, J. McV., & Kogan, L. S. *Measuring results in social casework.* (Rev.). New York: Family Service Assoc., 1952.

Lazowick, L. M. On the nature of identification. *J. abnorm. soc. Psychol.*, 1955, **51**, 175-183.

Mowrer, O. H. *Learning theory and personality dynamics.* New York: Ronald, 1950.

Mowrer, O. H. Changes in verbal behavior during psychotherapy. In O. H. Mowrer (Ed.), *Psychotherapy and research.* New York: Ronald, 1953, 463-545.

Osgood, C. E. The nature and measurement of meaning. *Psychol. Bull.*, 1952, **49**, 197-237.

Osgood, C. E., & Suci, G. J. A measure of relation determined by both mean differences and profile information. *Psychol. Bull.*, 1952, **49**, 251-262.

Osgood, C. E., Suci, G. J., & Tannenbaum, P. H. *The measurement of meaning.* Urbana: Univer. of Ill. Press, 1957.

Rogers, C. R. *Client centered therapy.* New York: Houghton Mifflin, 1951.

Rogers, C. R., & Dymond, Rosalind F. *Psychotherapy and personality change.* Chicago: Univer. of Chicago Press, 1954.

Scheerer, E. T. An analysis of the relationship between acceptance of and respect for self and acceptance of and respect for others in ten counseling cases. *J. consult. Psychol.*, 1949, **13**, 169-175.

Snygg, D., & Combs, A. W. *Individual behavior.* New York: Harper, 1949.

Sullivan, H. S. *The interpersonal theory of psychiatry.* New York: Norton, 1953.

Wilcoxon, F. *Some rapid approximate statistical procedures.* American Cyanamid Co., 1949.

43. Anxiety and Semantic Differential Responses

Diane Brod, Phyllis Kernoff, and Robert F. Terwilliger

50 words were rated on a 9-scale form of the semantic differential by 50 Ss. For each S the following scores were obtained: (a) response bias on the differential defined as the use of "very" and "neutral" categories, (b) discrimination on the differential defined as the tendency to use all categories equally often, (c) Scholastic Aptitude Test scores, and (d) Manifest Anxiety and Lie scores. It was hypothesized that there would be a positive correlation between anxiety and discrimination and 0 correlation between aptitude and discrimination. The results supported these hypotheses. In addition, a positive correlation between Lie score and response bias was found. It was argued that the nature of a high Lie score would tend to produce this type of correlation.

An investigation by Kerrick (1956) on the relationship between intelligence, anxiety as measured by the Taylor (1953) Manifest Anxiety (*MA*) scale, and discrimination among concepts on the semantic differential (Osgood, Suci, & Tannenbaum, 1957) reports the following relationships: a positive relationship between IQ and discrimination, a zero relationship between anxiety and discrimination, and an interaction between IQ, anxiety, and discrimination. In view of more recent results (Ware, as reported by Osgood, 1962) which suggest that there is no relationship between intelligence and responses on the semantic differential and in view of several inadequacies in the Kerrick study, it appears that this problem requires further investigation.

Two basic faults exist in the Kerrick study. The first is methodological. Having run 20 subjects, each of whom rated 10 concepts on 10 semantic differential scales, Kerrick used $20 \times 10 \times 10 = 2,000$ as the *N* for statistical analysis. It would appear that an *N* of 20 would have been more appropriate. Kerrick wished to make generalizations about subjects and so would require 20 independent scores, 1 per subject, rather than 2,000 dependent scores. It is not clear what generalizations may be made from the latter. This inflation of *N*, therefore, may invalidate all of the statistical conclusions of the study. The second problem is theoretical and centers about Kerrick's definition of a discriminating response. Kerrick assumes that discrimination is shown when the subject uses the "quite" and "slightly" (± 2 and ± 1) positions on the semantic differential rather than the extreme, "very" and "no meaning" (± 3 and 0) positions. This appears to the authors to be a rather debatable assumption for the following reason.

The most extreme example of discriminating behavior occurs when an individual makes a different response to each different stimulus presented to him. Thus, on the semantic differential, discrimination among concepts will be shown if each concept receives a different rating on the differential scales. Since there are only seven different responses which can be made on a given semantic differential scale, discrimination will appear, in this situation, as the use of all positions on the differential equally often. Only in this way can the maximum discrimination, the maximum number of different responses for different concepts be obtained. Discrimination, then, does not consist in restricting one's responses to only four out of the possible seven which can be made, as Kerrick assumes, but consists in making all seven, and making them equally often.

What Kerrick appears to have been measuring, rather than discrimination, was a form of response bias. This in itself is a phenomenon of interest but certainly does not qualify as discrimination. In previous work with the semantic differential, Terwilliger (1962) noticed that there seemed to be two rather distinct sub-

Reprinted from *Journal of Abnormal and Social Psychology* (1964), 68: 570–574, by permission of the authors and the American Psychological Association.

groups of subjects: those who restricted their responses primarily to the extreme categories (± 3 and 0) and those whose responses were restricted to the middle positions on the scale (± 2 and ± 1). These groupings correspond to Kerrick's nondiscriminating and discriminating responses, respectively. It is conceivable that certain variables may be predictive of a tendency to bias one's responses on the semantic differential in one of these two ways.

The purpose of this study is to test the following hypotheses:

1. Following the conclusions of Ware (see Osgood, 1962) but in contradiction to those of Kerrick there will be no correlation between intelligence and either discrimination or response bias on the semantic differential.

2. Following the results of Spence and Beercroft (1954), it is hypothesized that there will be a positive correlation between manifest anxiety and discrimination in semantic differential responses. Discrimination will be indicated by a tendency to use all positions on the semantic differential scales and to use them equally often.

3. It is predicted that a positive correlation will be found between response-bias tendencies on a standard personality inventory and response biases on the semantic differential. Specifically it is assumed that a high Lie (L) scale score on the MMPI indicates a tendency toward response biases. If this is the case then it follows that there will be a negative correlation between L scores and discrimination on the semantic differential, since response bias is the opposite of discrimination.

METHOD

Fifty volunteer female undergraduates were administered a form of the semantic differential. They were to rate 50 words [4] on each of nine scales, three scales representing each of the three dimensions of meaning (evaluation, activity, and potency) reported by Osgood et al. (1957). From 1 day to 1 week later, at the convenience of the subjects,

[4] Words: SHORT, BABY, OCEAN, LION, WOMAN, JUSTICE, HUNGRY, MEDICINE, BLUE, DEEP, ANGER, SOUR, MUSIC, MAN, RED, NUDE, LIGHT, EARTH, YELLOW, QUIET, EYES, CABBAGE, PRAYER, SWIFT, ROUGH, WHITE, CITY, GREEN, HEAVY, SWEET, RIVER, DOCTOR, BOY, COTTAGE, WHISKEY, LOVE, LOUD, RIGHT, SMOOTH, HELL, SOFT, BEAUTIFUL, DARK, BUTTERFLY, LONG, CHILD, STEM, BITTER, BLACK, MOON.

Scales: Evaluative—good-bad, wise-foolish, true-false; Potency—hard-soft, heavy-light, masculine-feminine; Activity—excitable-calm, active-passive, fast-slow.

TABLE 1

CORRELATIONS BETWEEN DISCRIMINATION AND INDIVIDUAL DIFFERENCES

	Discrimination index (H)		
	Evaluation	Potency	Activity
SAT	.07	$-.08$	$-.15$
MA scale	.31*	.27*	.27*
L scale	$-.33$*	$-.33$*	$-.32$*
MA and L scales Multiple R	.42*	.39*	.38*

* $p = .05$, one-tailed test.

the Taylor Manifest Anxiety (MA) scale and a form of the L scale were administered. For each subject a measure of intelligence was obtained by summing the verbal and numerical scores which they obtained on the Scholastic Aptitude Test (SAT) prior to their admission to college.

The discrimination index for each subject was computed in the following manner: Each subject made a total of 150 responses on each of the three dimensions of meaning measured by the semantic differential. A separate discrimination index was computed for each of these three dimensions. The proportion of the subject's responses falling into each of the seven scale categories was calculated. These proportions were entered into the entropy equation [5] derived by Shannon (Shannon & Weaver, 1949). The quantity thus obtained (which will be referred to as H) will increase under two conditions: as the number of response categories used increases, and as the proportions of responses in each category become more equal. Hence an increase in H will indicate an increase in discrimination as defined above.

RESULTS

Table 1 shows the product-moment correlations obtained between the three individual difference variables measured, intelligence, MA scale, and L scale, and the discrimination indices on each of the three dimensions of meaning. As can be seen, the correlations between SAT scores and discrimination are in no case significant. Correlations between the MA scale and discrimination are significantly positive, as was predicted, in all cases while, again according to prediction, all correlations between the L score and discrimination are significantly negative. Multiple correlations are also reported which indicate that the prediction of discriminative responses can be increased by taking into account both MA scale and L scale scores at once. Since an r of $-.19$ was obtained between the MA scale and

[5] $H = -\Sigma p \log_2 p$.

TABLE 2

CORRELATIONS BETWEEN RESPONSE BIAS AND INDIVIDUAL DIFFERENCES

	Frequency of 0 responses			Frequency of ±3 responses			Total frequency of 0 and ±3 responses		
	Evaluation	Potency	Activity	Evaluation	Potency	Activity	Evaluation	Potency	Activity
SAT	−.33*	−.01	−.07	.04	−.13	−.10	−.19	−.12	−.14
MA scale	−.16	−.22	−.24	−.04	.15	.09	−.11	−.06	−.06
L scale	.16	.09	.24	.16	.27	.37*	.43*	.38*	.41*

* $p = .05$, two-tailed test.

the L scale score it is apparent that these two variables are not measuring the same thing, an assumption which was made in making the predictions for this study.

Data relevant to the nature of the response biases observed in this study are presented in Table 2. Extreme responses (±3 and 0) were selected for analysis for reasons which will be discussed shortly. It should be noted that there will be a perfect negative correlation between the frequency of responses in this category and the frequency of responses in the other category which is the second type of response bias (±2 and ±1). This must be, of course, because the total of these two biases must always equal 150, the total number of responses made by a subject on the dimension in question. Hence only one type of response bias need be analyzed. The results for the other type will be of identical magnitude but opposite in direction.

It can be seen that all correlations between the MA scale and the response-bias indices are nonsignificant as are all but one of the correlations between response bias and SAT score. All three correlations between the L scale score and the total of 0 and ±3 responses are significant as is one of the six correlations between the separate 0 and 3 response frequencies.

DISCUSSION

In general it can be said with reasonable assurance that there is no effect of intelligence on either discrimination or response bias on the semantic differential. The one significant correlation obtained, a negative one between SAT and frequency of 0 responses, can be safely attributed to chance. (The probability of 1 statistical test out of 12 being significant at the .05 level, assuming the null hypothesis, is approximately .34.) There are, of course, certain reservations which might be advanced about this conclusion. The SAT is certainly not as "pure" a measure

of intelligence as would be one of the individual IQ tests. Moreover, there is no doubt that using a sample of college students restricted the available IQs to a rather narrow range at the upper end of the population distribution. Both of these restrictions might tend to conceal any potential effects of intelligence. Nevertheless, it should be noted that the SAT is an instrument which is specifically designed to discriminate among members of this upper range of intelligence. And thus if any instrument was going to show an effect on this sample it would be the SAT or some similar instrument. But no effect of intelligence was shown, and since this is consonant with other current results, such as those of Ware (see Osgood, 1962), the conclusions must stand at that.

Regarding the effects of anxiety, it is equally apparent that there is a positive relationship between anxiety, as measured by the Taylor MA scale and discrimination. This result is contradictory to that of Kerrick (1956) but can be easily explained by the methods which were used to measure discrimination. The conclusions of this study are based on a method which assumed that discriminatory behavior involves using all response categories as equally as possible. The fact that anxiety is positively related to discrimination as so measured and that this fact would be predicted by Spence and Beercroft (1954) serves to validate the measure.

Since it has been assumed that discrimination is somewhat the opposite of response bias, some comment should be made on why there is not a significant negative correlation between anxiety and the response-bias indices. First, it should be noted that the correlation between the MA and L scales indicates that these two are largely independent dimensions. Therefore it is not necessary to assume that the MA and L scales will predict equally nor that they will predict oppositely. Or, to approach it from another direction, it is true that a high anxiety score subject cannot make an extremely high 0, ±3 score and be discriminating. However, his 0, ±3 score may still be higher than a low anxious, nondiscriminating subject whose response falls only into the ±1, ±2 categories. Anxiety, in other words may either increase or decrease the frequency of 0, ±3 responses. Hence the nonsignificant correlations between the *MA* scale and the response bias indices are not surprising and in no way serve to invalidate the general conclusion that anxiety and discrimination are positively related.

The results also serve to indicate that there is a positive correlation between the *L* scale score, which is itself a response-bias measure, and the use of 0 and ±3 categories on the semantic differential. The use of these categories predominantly constitutes a response bias as well. The correlations between the *L* scale and either 0 or ±3 alone are not as high as are correlations between the *L* scale and the total of 0 and ±3. To the authors this indicates that the proper response unit for the analysis of response biases on the semantic differential is the total and not either 0 or ± 3 alone.

Now the question may be raised concerning why this particular type of response bias is positively related to the *L* scale score rather than the alternate type, that is, the use of ±1 and ±2 responses predominately. To illustrate this, take as an example the *L* scale item "I get angry sometimes." A response of false to this item is counted as one point in the *L* score. A subject who gives such a response to such an item is likely to be motivated by two considerations: a general tendency to fake responses by giving the more socially desirable response, and by an inability to react to qualifications such as "sometimes." A person who answers false to this item can be one who only reacts to "always" and "never" but not to the shades of gray between these blacks and whites. It is obvious that both of these tendencies would lead to response bias on the semantic differential. The social desirability motive would lead to the continuous production of the response which the

subject felt was desired and none of the other possibilities. The "black-white" dichotomy would lead to the production of a few rather than many different responses, to lack of discrimination, in other words.

It is the black-white response tendency which accounts for the use of extreme semantic differential responses in the view of the authors of this study. Such a person who is unable or unwilling to qualify responses may well react to the semantic differential as follows: A word is to be rated on the good-bad scale. To this subject the word is either good or bad or irrelevant. If it is good, it is definitely good, very good, and if bad, it is definitely bad, very bad. There are no shades of gray on this dimension or any other. Thus the ratings produced will be 3's except for those words which are seen to be irrelevant to the dimension, in which case zero responses will be used. It is the conclusion of this study that the positive correlation obtained between the *L* scale score and the use of ±3 and 0 responses on the semantic differential occurs for the above reasons.

REFERENCES

KERRICK, J. The effects of manifest anxiety and IQ on discrimination. *J. abnorm. soc. Psychol.*, 1956, 52, 136–138.

OSGOOD, C. E. Studies on the generality of affective meaning systems. *Amer. Psychologist*, 1962, 17, 10–28.

OSGOOD, C. E., SUCI, G. J., & TANNEBAUM, P. H. *The measurement of meaning.* Urbana: Univer. Illinois Press, 1957.

SHANNON, C. E., & WEAVER, W. *The mathematical theory of communication.* Urbana: Univer. Illinois Press, 1949.

SPENCE, K. W., & BEERCROFT, R. Differential conditioning and level of anxiety. *J. exp. Psychol.*, 1954, 48, 399–403.

TAYLOR, JANET A. A personality scale of manfest anxiety. *J. abnorm. soc. Psychol.*, 1953, 48, 285–290.

TERWILLIGER, R. F. Free association patterns as a factor relating to semantic differential responses. *J. abnorm. soc. Psychol.*, 1962, 65, 87–94.

44. A Comparison of Set "A" of the Holtzman Inkblots with the Rorschach by Means of the Semantic Differential

Mark W. Otten and R. L. Van de Castle

The semantic differential technique (Osgood, Suci & Tannenbaum, 1957) has found application in a wide variety of research settings (Moss, 1960). One of the interesting approaches has been the attempt to clarify the meanings attributable to inkblot stimuli. Several investigators (Kamano, 1960; Levy & Kurz, 1957; Little, 1959; Rabin, 1959; Rosen, 1960; Sines, 1960; Zax & Benham, 1961; Zax & Loiselle, 1960a, 1960b; Zax, Loiselle & Karras, 1960) have utilized the semantic differential in studies of the traditional Rorschach cards. Since the Rorschach has frequently been criticized because of its well known psychometric limitations, (Block, 1962) Holtzman (Holtzman, Thorpe, Swartz & Herron, 1961) recently constructed a new testing format and set of inkblots which he felt would overcome such shortcomings. Due to its apparent success in achieving its goals of adequate normative data and desirable statistical properties, the Holtzman Inkblot Test will undoubtedly receive widespread usage. One of the aspects of this new test which will need to be better understood is that of the "meaning" of the individual Holtzman cards and how these cards compare with the Rorschach cards. The present study was therefore undertaken to investigate these aspects.

METHOD

Subjects

A total of 52 subjects comprised of 26 male and 26 female students from the University of Denver was employed in this study.

Stimulus Materials

The 45 cards from Set "A" of the Holtzman Inkblot Test and the 10 Rorschach cards were rated by all *Ss*. An individual rating sheet for each of the 55 cards was prepared and stapled into a booklet. Each rating sheet contained 14 bipolar adjectives which were checked on a 7 point continuum. Three pairs of adjectives were selected for each of the three factors of evaluation, potency, and activity. The remaining five adjective pairs were selected because it was thought they would have particular relevance for inkblot stimuli. The 14 adjective pairs were:

1. pleasant (P) ....unpleasant (U)
2. clean (C) ....dirty (D)
3. beautiful (B) ....ugly (U)
4. rugged (R) ....delicate (D)
5. heavy (H) ....light (L)
6. masculine (M) ....feminine (F)
7. active (A) ....passive (P)
8. fast (F) ....slow (S)
9. excitable (E) ....calm (C)
10. meaningful (M)
                    meaningless (ML)
11. formed (F) ....formless (FL)
12. paternal (P) ....maternal (M)
13. relaxing (R) ....disturbing (D)
14. interesting (I) ....boring (B)

The above numbers will be used subsequently throughout this paper to refer to the 14 scales and the letters will be used to identify the specific member of the adjective pair for each scale. The actual serial order of the scales on each rating sheet in the test booklet was: 10ML, 1P, 4R, 11F, 12P, 13R, 7A, 2C, 5H, 8F, 14I, 3U, 6F, 9C.

Reprinted from *Journal of Projective Techniques and Personality Assessment* (1963), 27: 452–460, by permission of the authors and the publisher.

The letter following each number indicates which member of the adjective pair appeared on the left hand side of the rating continuum.

Procedure

A group testing procedure was utilized. The stimulus cards were shown on a screen by means of an opaque projector. Trial card Y was shown first and questions about the task were encouraged and answered before proceeding with the regular cards. Two minutes per card were allowed for Ss to make their semantic differential ratings. A total of 28 Holtzman cards were rated during the initial testing session, and the remaining 17 Holtzman cards followed by the Rorschach cards were rated during the second testing session. The interval between testing sessions was one day for the majority of Ss, but for some Ss in an evening class it was approximately fifteen minutes.

RESULTS

In order to determine which adjectives could be considered relevant for any specific card, it was decided to employ the criterion that the mean value obtained for any scale must deviate at least one scale unit from the midpoint value of 4.00. Thus any mean scale value of 3.00 or less, or mean value of 5.00 or larger was considered as representing one end of the continuum, and the polar adjective associated with that end was considered descriptive of that particular card. The results of this analysis are shown in Table I.

TABLE I—Adjectives Descriptive of Form A Holtzman and Rorschach Inkblots

Holtzman

Card	Descriptive Adjectives
1	ugly, rugged, heavy
2	active, meaningful, formed, interesting
4	masculine, active, fast, meaningful, formed, interesting
5	interesting
6	interesting
7	delicate, light, formed, interesting
8	rugged, heavy
9	active, interesting
10	pleasant, clean, delicate, light
11	heavy, formed
12	pleasant, clean, beautiful, active, meaningful, formed, interesting
13	pleasant, clean, light, formless
14	active
15	interesting
16	active, excitable, interesting
18	heavy, interesting
19	active, meaningful, formed, interesting
22	formed
23	ugly
25	pleasant, rugged, masculine, active, fast, excitable, meaningful, formed, interesting
26	ugly, rugged, heavy
27	pleasant, clean, beautiful, active, meaningful, formed, interesting
28	pleasant, clean, beautiful, delicate, light, interesting
29	unpleasant, ugly
31	unpleasant, ugly, rugged, heavy, active, excitable, formed, disturbing
33	pleasant, interesting
34	masculine, active, fast, meaningful, formed, interesting
39	meaningful, formed, interesting
40	ugly, rugged, heavy
41	beautiful, meaningful, formed, interesting
42	pleasant, clean, beautiful, delicate, light, feminine, relaxing
43	light, active, interesting
44	meaningful
45	pleasant, clean, beautiful, light, formed, interesting

Rorschach

Card	
1	rugged
2	pleasant, meaningful, formed, interesting
3	feminine, active, meaningful, formed, interesting
4	ugly, rugged, heavy, masculine, slow
5	formed
7	pleasant, clean, delicate, light, meaningful, formed, relaxing, interesting
9	interesting
10	delicate, active, interesting

No attempt was made to apply direct tests of statistical significance to all of the results of Table I. However, every adjective that had been included in the table which had a mean score close to a value of 3 or 5 was tested by the Chi square method. This was done by dichotomizing the scores at the midpoint of 4.0, equally dividing scores of 4.0 between the two groups and comparing the number of persons above and below the midpoint. In every case, the resulting p value was less than .01. Thus every adjective listed in Table I that possessed more extreme mean values can also be considered statistically significant beyond the .01 level. Since 630 (45 cards x 14 scales) possible Holtzman comparisons exist, the number of adjectives significant at the .01 level that should occur by chance would be approximately six or seven, and 123 such values were actually obtained. Similarly, of the 140 possible Rorschach comparisons, 28 significant values were obtained, whereas only one or two should have been expected on a chance basis.

As shown in Table I, 11 Holtzman and 2 Rorschach cards had no descriptive adjectives associated with them, while other cards had as many as nine descriptive adjectives. The frequency with which certain adjectives are checked also varied considerably. The paternal-maternal scale did not apply to a single Holtzman or Rorschach card, while the excitable-calm and relaxing-disturbing scales were employed on only three cards. On the other hand, the interesting-boring scale was considered appropriate for 24 cards and the formed-formless scale appropriate for 18 cards.

For five of the scales, only a single end of the continuum was considered relevant in making ratings. These preferred adjectives and their frequency of usage were: interesting, 24; active, 14; meaningful, 13; clean, 8; excitable, 3. As might be expected, some adjectives were generally associated together. Every one of the 8 cards rated as clean was also rated pleasant, while out of the 6 cards rated both rugged and heavy 5 were labelled ugly. Similarly, the 13 cards termed meaningful were, with one exception, also judged both formed and interesting.

TABLE II—Group Mean Factor Scores for the Two Sets of Inkblots

Holtzman Card	Factors I. Evaluative (Scales 1,2,3)	II. Potency (Scales 4,5,6)	III. Activity (Scales 7,8,9)
1	3.30	5.17	3.68
2	4.01	3.98	4.86
3	4.11	3.86	4.34
4	4.25	4.81	5.24
5	4.25	3.90	3.92
6	4.53	4.07	3.76
7	4.63	2.87	4.30
8	4.00	4.91	4.25
9	3.72	4.56	4.74
10	5.10	2.76	3.67
11	3.65	4.64	4.02
12	5.10	3.48	4.88
13	5.15	3.15	4.39
14	4.06	3.75	4.72
15	4.67	3.91	3.91
16	3.55	3.75	5.06
17	4.62	3.81	3.85
18	3.46	4.74	4.37
19	4.40	4.09	5.11
20	3.78	4.17	4.32
21	4.31	4.20	4.27
22	4.14	4.18	3.58
23	3.32	4.53	3.47
24	4.12	3.70	4.08
25	4.82	5.10	5.51
26	3.22	5.21	4.18
27	5.17	3.79	4.39
28	5.26	2.99	4.04
29	3.10	4.49	4.12
30	3.86	4.46	3.57
31	3.15	5.17	4.85
32	4.06	3.64	4.23
33	4.98	4.19	3.85
34	4.39	4.99	5.44
35	3.73	4.38	3.62
36	3.94	4.59	3.55
37	3.89	3.83	4.36
38	3.94	3.90	4.14
39	4.29	4.01	3.92
40	3.10	4.94	4.25
41	4.91	3.26	4.30
42	5.57	2.56	3.33
43	4.30	3.53	4.81
44	4.55	3.47	3.81
45	5.14	3.33	4.32
Rorschach Card			
I	3.57	4.88	4.01
II	4.70	4.50	3.96
III	4.66	3.13	5.03
IV	3.02	5.42	3.51
V	3.55	3.83	4.31
VI	3.91	4.38	3.65
VII	5.33	2.81	4.15
VIII	4.47	3.57	4.04
IX	4.58	3.59	4.58
X	4.63	3.19	4.83

In Table II are shown the factor scores for the various cards. Inspection of Table II reveals considerable variability among the cards on their patterning of factor scores. Some cards, such as 38, had all factor scores close to a neutral value of 4.0 while card 42 had the highest evaluative and lowest potency and activity scores of any of the 55 cards. No card had all three factor scores below a value of 4.0, but five Holtzman cards (4, 19, 21, 25, 34) had all three factor scores above the midpoint. No Rorschach card was rated as jointly high on evaluation, potency and activity.

To ascertain whether any sex differences were present for the types of adjectives checked for the various cards, two types of comparisons were made. One method was designed to determine what might be termed "sex unique" adjectives. In order to qualify for this distinction, an adjec-tive had to have a mean scale value of 3.00 or lower or a value of 5.00 or higher for the one sex, without having received such an extreme rating by the other sex. A listing of the cards containing "sex unique" adjectives is provided in Table III.

Examination of Table III reveals that a total of 54 card listings for males and 66 for females appears when the above criteria for uniqueness are employed. Males were found to be more prone to describe cards as unpleasant, ugly, rugged, masculine, excitable, meaningless, maternal and disturbing. The total number of cards rated as possessing these somewhat socially undesirable qualities was 25 for males but only 1 for females. The number of cards described in such generally more positive and socially acceptable terms as pleasant, clean, beautiful, delicate, heavy or light, fast, relaxing and interesting was 49

TABLE III—Adjectives Considered Descriptive of the Two Sets of Inkblots Unique to One of the Sexes

Scale	Adjective	Male Cards	Female Cards
1	pleasant	10, R3	13, 25, 41, 45
	unpleasant	29, 40	
2	clean		7, 12, 13, 25, 27, 33, 41, 45, R8, R9
	dirty		
3	beautiful	10, R7	12, 13, 41, 45
	ugly	11, 16, 18, 26, 31	
4	rugged	4, 34, 40	18
	delicate	R10	5, 7, 13, 28, 41, 43, 45, R3
5	heavy	8	11, 18, 23, R1
	light		5, 12, 28, 45
6	masculine	5, R4	
	feminine	R3, R7	7
7	active	14, 43, R9	16, 27, R10
	passive	30	
8	fast	43	4, 12, 13, 16, R3
	slow	1	
9	excitable	4, 19, 25, 31, 34, R9	
	calm		
10	meaningful	7, 16, 18, 29, 31, R5, R9	11, 17, 33, 39, 41, 42, 43, 45
	meaningless	13, 30	
11	formed	16, 18, 29	17, 22, 45
	formless	30	24
12	paternal		
	maternal	42, R7	
13	relaxing		13, 28
	disturbing	26, 31, 40	
14	interesting	1, 21, 29, 31	3, 5, 10, 13, 17, 33, 43, 44
	boring		

for females and 11 for males. For some scales no overlapping of adjectives occurred, *e.g.* all ten cards rated as clean were done so by females and all six cards rated as exciting were done so by males. Males were more likely to assign sex characteristics to the cards as shown by giving four masculine-feminine and two maternal ratings while only one card was rated as feminine by women.

Although the preceding analysis brings to light those adjectives checked in a more extreme fashion by one sex, it doesn't follow that the differences in ratings were necessarily very large between sexes. When a comparison was made of the number of adjective pairs in which the mean values assigned by males and females differed by· more than one scale unit, 27 such differences were found on the Holtzman but only 2 were found on the Rorschach cards.

In order to evaluate the sex differences of one unit's difference statistically, the number of male and female *S*s scoring above and below the midpoint value of 4.00 was tallied and differences evaluated by the Chi square technique. In Table IV are recorded those differences which reached the .05 level of significance. More significant sex differences (14) occur on the Holtzman than on the Rorschach (2). Some attention should probably be drawn to card 2 because males checked this card on the masculine and paternal ends of those scales (mean values of 3.15 and 3.04 respectively) while females felt this card was more feminine and maternal (mean values of 4.42 and 4.50). It is also interesting to note that almost all of these significant sex differences occurred on completely achromatic

cards or on cards where achromatic colors clearly predominated. Only one significant difference occurred to chromatic stimuli (card 44).

Another frequently investigated variable in Rorschach studies has been that of the "meaning" of color. Work in this area has been hampered because of the limited range of chromatic stimuli available in the Rorschach. There are only three totally chromatic Rorschach cards and two cards (II and III) which are a combination of chromatic and achromatic stimuli. Since the Holtzman has a much larger number of stimuli to choose from, it should be possible to more adequately evaluate what sort of adjectival description would be applied to inkblots that are more homogeneous in their chromatic and achromatic characteristics.

Six "pure" achromatic and six chromatic cards from the Holtzman were selected in such a way that the two series would be closely matched with regard to their presumed degree of form structure. This was accomplished by using the ratings on the formed-formless scale that had been obtained in this study. This control was thought to be important because otherwise any differences that might be obtained could possibly be attributed to the contaminating influence of form. The results of this analysis are shown in Table V. It can be seen that there are quite consistent differences between the two types of stimuli that are statistically signifi cant. The chromatic stimuli are seen as more pleasant, clean, beautiful and feminine, while the achromatic cards are more rugged, slow, heavy and disturbing. Statistical significance was computed by means of the Chi square

TABLE IV—Differences in Scale Values Which are Statistically
Significant Between Sexes

	Card Numbers										
	2	5	18	24	29	30	31	43	44	45	R1	R7
Scales	6	4	10	11	11	3	10	14	12	9	9	6
	12	13	11			14						

technique. The mean score for each S was added for all six achromatic cards and a tally was made of the number of Ss scoring above and below the neutral midpoint value of 24 with midpoint values being equally divided. This same method of tallying was repeated for the chromatic cards and Chi square was applied to the resulting 2 x 2 table.

A comparison between achromatic-chromatic differences was also made with the Rorschach cards. These results appear in Table V. Every scale showing significant differences on the Holtzman was also significant on the Rorschach with the exception of scale 12. Except for scales 9 and 11, the direction of the scale differences between achromatic-chromatic ratings was the same for the Holtzman and the Rorschach. There were three scales (7, 9, 14) that revealed significant achromatic-chromatic differences on the Rorschach that were not significant on the Holtzman. The significant difference on scale 7 can be attributed to the extremely high activity scores assigned to card III. This is a good example of how an erroneous impression might be conveyed about the possible effect of color when cards are used which contain other important determinants in addition to color.

In order to assess the similarity between the ratings of individual Holtzman cards and individual Rorschach cards, a comparison by means of D scores was made. The D score is obtained by squaring the difference between each scale value for any two cards, summing these differences and then taking the square root. Since D actually refers to "assumed dissimilarity" the lower the D score, the greater is the similarity between any two cards.

Examination of the D scores indicated that if one wished to choose the Holtzman cards most resembling the Rorschach cards in semantic space the following list would be selected (D scores appear in parentheses) : I-11 or 18 (1.16) ; II-15 (1.20) ; III-12 (1.35) ; IV-1 (1.31) ; V-37 (1.47) ; VI-36 (.68) ; VII-41, (1.42) ; VIII-32 (.96) ; IX-32 (1.31) ; X-41 (1.45). If the criterion were used that no D scores below a value of 1.95 appear for any of the ten Rorschach card comparisons, then cards 2, 4, 5, 10, 13, 16, 19, 25, 34, and 42 of the Holtzman represent rather original patterns of card meaning not tapped by the Rorschach stimuli.

DISCUSSION

If the individuality of any S's reaction to an inkblot is to be correctly identified and properly interpreted, the common stimulus meaning of that inkblot should be known. There is a rich heritage of studies relating to the stimulus aspects of the Rorschach, but because of its recent arrival on the projective scene, the Holtzman cannot lay claim to the same form of actuarial data. The use of the semantic differential technique has recently helped to clarify the "meaning" of

TABLE V—Mean Scale Scores for Achromatic and Chromatic Holtzman and Rorschach Inkblots

Scales	1	2	3	4	5	6	7	8	9	10	11	12	13	14
H Achromatic [a]	4.26	4.12	4.61	3.52	3.47	3.61	3.96	4.40	3.76	3.87	3.50	3.90	4.22	3.31
H Chromatic [b]	3.35	3.23	3.58	4.52	4.47	4.44	3.86	3.89	4.05	3.51	3.54	4.26	3.66	3.06
H p values	.001	.001	.001	.001	.001	.001	N.S.	.01	N.S.	N.S.	N.S.	.05	.01	N.S.
R Achromatic [c]	3.90	3.92	4.54	3.72	3.64	3.84	3.98	4.28	3.96	3.36	3.18	4.02	3.98	3.56
R Chromatic [d]	3.26	3.22	3.69	4.46	4.41	4.34	3.08	3.62	3.72	3.15	3.02	4.16	3.66	2.81
R p values	.001	.001	.001	.001	.001	.001	.001	.001	.05	N.S.	N.S.	N.S.	N.S.	.01

Note — Scores below the midpoint (4.00) refer to the left adjective of the scale
[a] Cards 1, 5, 18, 29, 36, and 38.
[b] Cards 16, 20, 28, 33, 42, and 44.
[c] Cards I, IV, V, VI, VII.
[d] Cards II, III, VIII, IX, X.

the various Rorschach cards and should be able to serve a similar role for the Holtzman.

It has been well accepted that individual Rorschach cards do possess some common intra-card connotations and that these connotative meanings vary from card to card. The practice of assigning populars to certain cards and interpreting particular cards as "father" or "mother" cards attests to the widespread belief that such consistencies in responses to inkblots do occur. The question arises as to whether such response tendencies would be evoked equally well to a new set of inkblot stimuli or whether there might be something special about the "Big Ten". The results of this study indicate that the Holtzman cards elicit almost exactly the same proportion of descriptive adjectives as does the Rorschach. When college students were asked to judge both sets of cards on the same list of 14 bipolar adjectives, they checked as relevant approximately twenty times as many adjectives for each set as would have been expected to occur on a chance basis.

The adjectives elicited to the Rorschach are not evenly divided among the various cards. Some cards produce no adjectives while others produce as many as eight. As was shown in Table I, a similar pattern is evident for the adjectives associated with the Holtzman. There is a high degree of agreement about the impact of some of the Holtzman cards while others possess no consensually shared meaning. If a more specific comparison is made, 20% of the Rorschach cards and 24% of the Holtzman cards had no adjectives associated with them, while 10% of the Rorschach cards and 9% of the Holtzman cards had seven or more adjectives checked as relevant. Thus, in terms of semantic differential ratings, Set A of the Holtzman appears to possess equally as much "meaning" and approximately the same pattern of intra-card consistency and inter-card variability of

meaning as does the Rorschach. In addition, as was found with the *D* scores, there are several Holtzman cards containing high factor scores that tap patterns of meaning that are not embodied in the Rorschach cards.

If popular responses are by definition those frequently given, and if we assume that attributed meaning is some function of recognizing the popular, then it would follow that there should be greater agreement about the meaning of cards containing populars than cards not containing them. This expectation is borne out by the results as an average of 3.60 adjectives appear to the 25 cards listed as popular for Holtzman Set A as opposed to an average of 1.65 adjectives for non-popular cards. This finding thus provides some indirect support for the validity of the listed populars. However, the failure to find a single adjective as applicable for cards 17, 21, 24 and 30 raises a question as to whether these cards do convey enough similarity of meaning to be considered as containing populars. It is possible that the failure of card 21 to lead to generally agreed-upon ratings may have been due to the fact that either duck or person is considered popular and differential associations could be expected depending upon which form was recognized. The only adjective frequently checked for card 5 was "interesting" which also raises some doubts about its popular status. Reversing the same logic, it seems plausible that card 31, which has no popular listed, should be reconsidered as perhaps possessing some common meaning since eight adjectives (unpleasant, ugly, rugged, heavy, active, exciting, formed and disturbing) were consistently applied to it. On the basis of the preceding adjectives, if no specific popular percept is found for this card it would still seem plausible to expect some general form of "shock" response as popular for this card.

One aspect in which the Holtzman differs from the Rorschach is that of being more sensitive to sex differences. Several previous investigators (Little, 1959; Rabin, 1959; Zax & Loiselle, 1960a) utilizing the semantic differential with the Rorschach were consistent in their failure to find any noticeable sex differences in the ratings obtained. Similarly, in this study, only two instances of a scale unit's difference and two statistically significant differences were found between males and females on the Rorschach. By way of contrast, 27 instances of a scale unit's difference and 14 statistically significant differences were found between the sexes on the Holtzman. The types of adjectives preferred by the two sexes were found to be quite different with women more generally classifying the cards as beautiful, clean and delicate while males had a greater tendency to accept the cards as ugly, disturbing and exciting. It might be possible to capitalize on such differences in adjective preference by constructing a masculinity-feminity scale that would possess some interesting research possibilities. The results of this study strongly suggest that the lack of sex differences noted in earlier studies was more a function of the particular Rorschach stimuli rather than of inkblots in general. Of course, whether the apparently greater sensitivity of the Holtzman to sex differences would be considered as a desirable feature or not is clearly dependent upon the individual clinician's theoretical orientation. The reader should perhaps be reminded that all of the above statements are based upon semantic differential results and are not intended to imply that sex differences in location choices or determinant variables would be found on the Holtzman.

A point of agreement between the present study and earlier Rorschach studies resides in the similarity of the findings about the impact of chromatic stimuli. Previous investigators (Levy & Kurz, 1957; Little, 1959; Rabin, 1959; Rosen, 1960) reported that the chromatic stimuli were rated as more generally pleasant and positive than were the achromatic stimuli. However, an inherent methodological difficulty in making such comparisons with Rorschach cards rests with the marked dissimilarity of their form structuredness and the mixture of chromatic and achromatic stimuli on the same cards (cards II & III). These sources of contamination were overcome in the present study where comparisons were based upon six totally chromatic and six totally achromatic cards closely matched for ratings of form definiteness. Since under these more stringent controls, chromatic stimuli still emerged as more pleasant, clean, beautiful, delicate and relaxing, the interpretation of color as having a positive connotation for college students takes on a more substantial weight. Further research is needed to establish whether a reversal of this pattern in the direction of finding color more disturbing would hold true for anxious or neurotic patients.

SUMMARY AND CONCLUSIONS

Fifty-two college students, 26 males and 26 females rated the Rorschach and Set A of the Holtzman cards on the same list of 14 semantic differential scales. Adjectives were considered descriptive if they were checked as one unit or more away from the midpoint of the seven point scale. A listing of descriptive adjectives was presented for the group and the two sexes separately. Group results were presented on the three factors of evaluation, potency and activity. Each factor represented a combination of three scales. By means of D scores, group comparisons were made for each Holtzman card with every individual Rorschach card. A group comparison of assigned meanings was also made between six chromatic and six achromatic Holtzman cards matched for degree of form structure. The latter results were compared to Rorschach chromatic-achromatic differences. The following conclusions were drawn:

1. The connotations of the Holtzman and the Rorschach inkblots vary markedly among the different cards.

2. The number of adjectives considered descriptive was proportionately equivalent between the Holtzman and Rorschach cards.

3. The number of cards showing a high degree of meaning (seven or more descriptive adjectives) and a lack of consensual meaning (no descriptive adjectives) were proportionately similar between the two sets of cards.

4. Holtzman cards containing a popular response produced a greater number of descriptive adjectives than cards not containing a popular response.

5. Some Holtzman cards, particularly those with high factor scores, tap patterns of meaning not found in the Rorschach cards.

6. Sex differences in the attribution of meaning were much more pronounced on the Holtzman than on the Rorschach cards.

7. Differences in the types of adjectives checked by the two sexes were relatively consistent among the various cards.

8. Pronounced differences in the ratings assigned to chromatic and achromatic cards were found in the same direction on both the Holtzman and Rorschach cards. In general, chromatic stimuli were judged as more positive and pleasant.

REFERENCES

Block, W. E. Psychometric aspects of the Rorschach technique. *J. proj. Tech.*, 1962, *26*, 162-172.

Holtzman, W. H., Thorpe, J. S., Swartz, J. D., & Herron, E. W. *Inkblot perception and personality.* Austin: Univer. of Texas Press, 1961.

Kamano, D. K. Symbolic significance of Rorschach cards IV and VII. *J. clin. Psychol.*, 1960, *16*, 50-52.

Levy, L. H., & Kurz, R. B. The connotative impact of color on the Rorschach and its relation to manifest anxiety. *J. Pers.*, 1957, *25*, 617-625.

Little, K. B. Connotations of the Rorschach inkblots. *J. Pers.*, 1959, *27*, 397-406.

Moss, C. S. Current and projected status of semantic differential research. *Psychol. Rev.*, 1960, *10*, 47-54.

Osgood, C. E., Suci, J., & Tannenbaum, P. H. *The measurement of meaning.* Urbana: Univer. of Illinois Press, 1957.

Rabin, A. I. A contribution to the "meaning" of Rorschach's inkblots via the semantic differential. *J. consult. Psychol.*, 1959, *23*, 368-372.

Rosen, E. Connotative meanings of Rorschach inkblots, responses, and determinants. *J. Pers.*, 1960, *28*, 413-426.

Sines, J. O. An approach to the study of the stimulus significance of the Rorschach inkblots. *J. proj. Tech.*, 1960, *24*, 64-66.

Zax, M., & Benham, F. G. The stimulus value of the Rorschach inkblots as perceived by children. *J. proj. Tech.*, 1961, *25*, 233-237.

Zax, M., & Loiselle, R. H. Stimulus value of Rorschach inkblots as measured by the semantic differential. *J. clin. Psychol.*, 1960a, *16*, 160-163.

Zax, M., & Loiselle, R. H. The influence of card order on the stimulus value of the Rorschach inkblots. *J. proj. Tech.*, 1960b, *24*, 218-221.

Zax, M., & Loiselle, R. H., & Karras, A. Stimulus characteristics of Rorschach inkblots as perceived by a schizophrenic sample. *J. proj. Tech.*, 1960, *24*, 439-443.

45. Subjects' Descriptions of Selected TAT Cards
via the Semantic Differential

C. Jack Friedman, Carleton A. Johnson, and Kermit Fode

A 30-scale form of a semantic differential was used to obtain data on the stimulus properties of 10 TAT cards. Ss were university students divided into 4 groups according to sex and geographical location. Degree of intragroup consistency in judgments of the stimulus cards was unimpressive when averaged for the 30 scales. But consensual agreement was statistically significant for about ⅓ of the 300 scales, independent of sex and geographical location. Inferences from significantly rated adjectives were generally in agreement with descriptions of the TAT cards (i.e., Murray, Henry, and Bellak), although there were also divergences. The results indicate that clinical interpretation of the TAT could be improved by attaching greater importance to significant adjective descriptions. This method was recommended for exploring new stimulus dimensions and for establishing base-line data for the TAT.

Clinical interpretation of the Thematic Apperception Test (TAT) involves the assumption that the subject, while responding to certain stimulus qualities in the cards reveals his own needs, desires, conflicts, hopes, and fears. The stimulus elements in the cards are assumed to elicit fantasy material and to provide a core or matrix around which a story is woven. The definition and delineation of the test stimuli, therefore, are necessary first steps for determining the degree to which TAT themes are influenced by factors other than those inherent in the test materials.

Murray's description of the TAT cards (1943), along with others (e.g., Bellak, 1954; Henry, 1956; Stein, 1955; Tomkins, 1947) have provided a basis for interpreting TAT fantasy material. On the weight of primarily clinical evidence interpretive significance has been attatched to omissions, perceptual distortions, misidentification of persons and objects, and to the avoidance of strong affective qualities in the cards, which are assumed to represent departures from the *known* stimulus attributes of the test materials. Bellak (1954) stated that the omission of the seminude on

Reprinted from *Journal of Consulting Psychology* (1964), 28: 317–325, by permission of the authors and the American Psychological Association.

Card 4 from the story was possibly indicative of a sexual problem; perceptual distortion of the "gun" on Card 3BM as a cigarette case or hole in the floor signified repressed latent aggression; misidentification of the figure on Card 3BM as a female by males offered a potential clue to latent homosexuality; and, the avoidance of aggressive qualities in Card 18GF by females characterized how hostility was handled. The more extreme the departure from the stimulus, the more significant and revealing the particular response.

In addition to interpretive methods based on subjective appraisals of the TAT cards, studies have reported on mood and emotional tone (Coleman, 1947; Eron, 1948; Eron, Terry, & Callahan, 1950; Garfield & Eron, 1948; Lebo, 1955) frequency of themes (Eron, 1948; Rosenzweig & Flemming, 1949) and identification of persons and objects in the cards (Eron, 1950; Rosenzweig & Flemming, 1949). While some support has been obtained for clinically derived assumptions regarding the stimulus properties of the cards, there have also been frequent contradictions. Eron (1950), for example, noted a greater frequency of sexual confusions among nonhospitalized subjects than among hospitalized mental patients. Rosenzweig and Flemming (1949) found that 50% of their male group described the figure on Card 3BM as a female,

TABLE 1

COMPARISON OF UNIVERSITY OF NORTH DAKOTA AND OKLAHOMA STATE UNIVERSITY SUBJECTS

	N	Mean age	Age range	Single	Married	Divorced
University of North Dakota						
Males	37	21.18	19–29	32	5	0
Females	63	20.33	18–45	57	5	1
Oklahoma State University						
Males	56	20.46	17–35	46	10	0
Females	60	19.38	17–36	50	9	1

whereas Murray (1943) described this figure as a young boy. At the present time there is no sound basis for determining whether a response for the TAT is *really* or only *apparently* deviant. It is recognized that numerous factors in the test situation (e.g., instructions, examiner-subject relationship, and method of TAT administration) may influence thematic productions. But more extensive and representative normative information, systematically obtained, is needed if the TAT is to reach clinical maturity.

The purposes of this research were (*a*) to develop a flexible and economical method for obtaining objective base-line data for the TAT against which to compare responses, (*b*) to determine the degree of consistency of data obtained from similar male and female subject populations from different geographical regions of the country, (*c*) to test some of the hypotheses regarding the stimulus properties of selected TAT cards, and (*d*) to explore new stimulus dimensions of the test materials.

METHOD

Subjects

Male and female students attending the University of North Dakota (UND) and Oklahoma State University (OSU) who were enrolled in introductory psychology courses served as subjects. A comparison of subject populations according to sex and geographical location is presented in Table 1.

Criterion

The semantic differential was used as the criterion. The semantic differential consisted of a series of bipolar adjectives (e.g., good-bad, hostile-friendly, active-passive) each appearing at the extremes of a 10-point scale. The 10-point scale, a departure from the 7-point scale recommended by Osgood, Suci, and Tannenbaum (1957) was employed to increase the

precision in measurement and to provide a forced-choice situation for dichotomizing subjects' responses. Thus, subjects' ratings could be scored for both direction and intensity. Factor-analytic studies of semantic differential scales by Osgood et al. (1957) indicated that particular adjectives could be grouped according to factor composition. This information was used to select scales heavily loaded on the Evaluative, Potency, and Activity factors. The choice of scales was also influenced by a consideration of their general applicability to the selected TAT cards and their relevance to specific clinical assumptions regarding the stimuli. A standard form of 30 scales, randomly ordered as to polarity and sequence, was constructed.[4] A sample scale is presented below.

good :—:—:—:—:—:—:—:—:—: bad

TAT Cards

Six of the TAT cards selected for presentation to subjects (e.g., 1, 2, 3BM, 4, 11, 13MF) were among

---

[4] The assumption that scale order and polarity do not effect ratings on the semantic differential was tested in a subinvestigation within the framework of the present research. Three different forms of the semantic differential were constructed by randomly varying polarity and order of the same 30 scales. These were administered in three sequence patterns to 10, 9, and 9 male subjects, respectively, in the OSU group. Analysis of the data took into account both direction and intensity of scale ratings for the 9 picture cards. For each subject, a sum was computed for three scales heavily loaded on the Evaluative factor. Each scale was scored from 1 (most favorable) to 10 (least favorable). These sums were ranked from 1 through 28 for each card excluding 16, and a Kruskal-Wallis test was applied to the ranked data. The same procedure was followed for 3 scales heavily loaded on Potency and on Activity. Of 27 such analyses (9 TAT cards × 3 factor scores), two were significant at the .05 level. However, two analyses were also nonsignificant at the .98 and .99 levels thus indicating that scale order and polarity do not significantly effect semantic differential ratings. These findings are consistent with those reported by Osgood et al. (1957).

TABLE 2

Significant Adjective Descriptions of 10 Selected TAT Cards for University of North Dakota and Oklahoma State University Female Groups

	1	2	3BM	4	7BM	8BM	11	13MF	18GF	16
pessimistic	*		*		*					
successful		u	*	u	*		*	*	*	
rugged		o		x	*				u	
controlled	u	*		*	u	*		u		
sad	*	*	*	*	*	o		*		o
clear							*			
hostile	*		*	*	o			*		*
submissive			*							
pleasing		u	*	*	*		*	*	*	*
strong	*		*	*	u	*	u	u		
cruel				o	o					
usual	u									
simple		o	o							o
masculine	*		*		*	*	*	u	n	*
cowardly							*	*		
sociable			*	*	*	*	*	*		*
aggressive	*		*	u		u	u	u	u	*
graceful						*				
tense	*		*	*	*	*	u	*	*	o
mature			o	u	o	o		u	*	
subtle	*		*	*	o			*	u	*
present		*			o	o	o	o	o	*
unrealistic		*	*	*	u	*	*	*	*	*
meaningful	*				*					
unimportant	*	*	*	*	*	u	u	*	*	u
moral	*	*	u	u	u	*	u	*		*
chaotic									o	o
good	u	*	u	u	u	u		*		*
passive	*		o	*	o	o		o	o	
beautiful			*	*				o	*	*

	1	2	3BM	4	7BM	8BM	11	13MF	18GF	16
optimistic	o	u								o
unsuccessful	u	u	*	*				*	*	
delicate									u	
impulsive			*							o
happy	u						*	*	*	*
hazy		*		*						
friendly										
dominant				*						
annoying	o		*		*	o	u	*		*
weak	u		*			o	*	*		
kind	u					*			u	
unusual			o							
complex			*		u	o	*	u	u	
feminine	u	*				*			*	
brave	*	*	*	*		*	*	*		*
unsociable	+		*	*			u			
defensive				u	o	o		u		o
awkward			o	o						
relaxed	*									
youthful										
obvious			*					o	o	
past	o	o		*	*	u		o	o	*
realistic	o	*	x	*	*	*	u	o	*	*
meaningless										
important	o	*	x	u	u	u		u	o	*
immoral						*		*	*	*
calm	*	*								o
bad				u	u			*		u
active	o		o	*		o		o		
ugly					o	o		o	*	

^u *p* .05 level, University of North Dakota females only.
^o *p* .05 level, Oklahoma State University females only.
[*] *p* .05 level for both University of North Dakota and Oklahoma State University female groups in independent analyses.

those recommended by Bellak (1954) for administration of the TAT to both males and females. Three cards (e.g., 7BM, 8BM, 18GF) were included because of their frequent clinical use. Card 16, the blank card, was selected to test the hypothesis that, in the absence of a picture or scene, subjects' ratings on the standard form of scales would be random. Since there was no way to determine the effect of card order of presentation on semantic differential ratings, the TAT cards were presented to all subjects in the same sequence (e.g., 1, 2, 3BM, 4, 7BM, 8BM, 11, 13MF, 18GF, 16).

Procedure

The task was introduced to subjects as an attempt to measure the *meanings* of a series of pictures to be projected onto a screen in the dimly lit auditorium. Subjects were informed that they were participating as judges, that this was not a test, and there were no right or wrong answers. It was emphasized that the subjects give honest impressions in rating the pictures but work rapidly. In addition to this information, specific instructions for using the scales were printed on a cover sheet of the answer booklets. The directions were read aloud by a proctor who permitted a brief period for questions in order to clarify any misunderstandings in using the scales.

The TAT cards were displayed on a large screen by means of an opaque projector.[5] Upon presentation of the first card, the subjects were told they would have approximately 3 minutes to complete their ratings on all 30 scales of the standard form. This was intended to permit administration of the selected cards within a single class period. In actuality the cards remained on the screen until the entire group of subjects had completed their ratings. For Card 16, the blank card, the subjects were instructed to think

---

[5] Lebo and Sherry (1959) have suggested that distance from a screen and angle of viewing weaken the effectiveness of group administration procedures. In order to test for the effects of these factors on semantic differential ratings, all subjects in the UND group were directed to record their row and seat numbers, thereby permitting analysis of the data according to distance from the screen and angle of viewing. Inspection of the data indicated negligible effects on semantic differential ratings due to these variables. Such effects were further contraindicated by the high consensual agreement obtained. Two other factors were also assumed to have negligible effects upon semantic differential ratings, these being intensity of the TAT cards and time of exposure. Weisskopf (1950) photographically varied the brightness of TAT cards but found no significant effect upon transcendence index scores. Bradley and Lysaker (1957) report a study in which illumination of TAT cards was varied and found no differences in productivity of responses attributable to this variable. Kenny (1954) determined that beyond several seconds, continued exposure of TAT cards did not affect fantasy production. A similar finding is also reported by Weisskopf (1950) using transcendence index scores.

of a picture or scene, and then to rate the imagined picture on the standard form of scales. When the subjects completed their ratings for Card 16, they were directed to write a title which would describe the picture they had imagined.

RESULTS

Data were analyzed separately for UND males, UND females, OSU males, and OSU females. The subjects' ratings of 30 scales on the semantic differential for each of 10 TAT cards yielded a total of 300 ratings. No more than two subjects in any component group failed to contribute a rating for the 10 cards. In those instances, the statistical analyses were based upon the total number of ratings contributed.

The first analysis of the data was intended to measure the *frequency* of intragroup agreement among subjects in their judgments of the stimulus cards. Each of the 300 scales was scored for direction of the rating. The frequency with which one or the other bipolar adjective was checked was tested for significance by chi square. The .05 level for a two-tailed test was chosen for rejection of the Null Hypothesis. From this analysis, 133 scales were significant for UND males, 181 for UND females, 141 for OSU males, and 171 for OSU females. These results are presented in Tables 2 and 3. The two columns of adjectives in Tables 2 and 3 appeared in the same sequence and polarity on the standard form of scales. It should be noted that the two adjectives in each row are bipolar and on the standard scale forms appear at the extremes of the scale (e.g., pessimistic-optimistic; successful-unsuccessful; rugged-delicate; etc.). Entries in the left-hand side of these tables indicate that a significant number of subjects in a given group favored the left pole of the continuum, and entries on the right-hand side mean that the other pole was favored. Thus, the columns identify the scales and TAT cards, the rows identify the attribute continuums, and the halves of the tables indicate the direction favored by a significant number of subjects.

In comparisons between like sex groups from different geographical regions, 101 scales reached significance in independent analyses for the two male groups, and 138 scales reached significance in independent analyses

TABLE 3

SIGNIFICANT ADJECTIVE DESCRIPTIONS OF 10 SELECTED TAT CARDS FOR UNIVERSITY OF NORTH DAKOTA AND OKLAHOMA STATE UNIVERSITY MALE GROUPS

	1	2	3BM	4	7BM	8BM	11	13MF	18GF	16		1	2	3BM	4	7BM	8BM	11	13MF	18GF	16
pessimistic		o		u	u					o	optimistic			*						o	o
successful		*	*	*							unsuccessful			*	*						o
rugged		*		o	o						delicate			u						u	
controlled				*	u					o	impulsive										o
sad	*		*	*	*	o	*	*	*		happy			*				*	*		*
clear		o	o	o	o			u			hazy		*								
hostile	*	*	*	*							friendly			*	*	u					
submissive						u			u	o	dominant			*	u	u					
pleasing		*	*		o	*				*	annoying			*							
strong		*	*	u	u				u		weak			*							
cruel											kind										
usual			o		o	o		*			unusual		u	u			u	u	u		
simple	o			u	*			*		*	complex	u	*	*	u		*		*	o	*
masculine			*	*	*	*	*	u			feminine	*	*	*	u	u	*	*		o	
cowardly										*	brave				u	u				*	
sociable					*					*	unsociable										*
aggressive		o	*	u	u	u				o	defensive		u	o				o			o
graceful				*	*	*				o	awkward	u								*	o
tense		*	*	*	*	*	*	*	*		relaxed		*						*		
mature		o							o		youthful		o								o
subtle					*						obvious	*	*	*	*	*	*	*	*	*	*
present		*	*	*	*	*	*	o		*	past	*	*	*		*					
unrealistic		*	*	*	*			*			realistic	*	u	*	u	u		*	*	u	
meaningful						*				o	meaningless	r	*	*							
unimportant	*	*	*	*	*			u		o	important	u	*	*	u	u	u		u	u	
moral			*	*	*	*		u		o	immoral										
chaotic		*		u							calm	o	o		u						
good	*	*	*	*	*					o	bad		c	o	*	u			u	o	
passive		*	*							o	active			o				o			
beautiful			*							o	ugly			*					*	o	o

---

u p .05 level, University of North Dakota males only.
o p .05 level, Oklahoma State University males only.
* p .05 level for both University of North Dakota and Oklahoma State University male groups in independent analyses.

for the two female groups. Thus, in what might be considered a replication of the results obtained with the male and female UND groups, approximately 75% of the number of significant scales reached significance for the male and female OSU groups, respectively. These findings, along with those from the independent analyses of the component groups are presented in Table 4.

TABLE 4

FREQUENCIES OF SIGNIFICANT ADJECTIVES FOR SELECTED TAT CARDS

Card number	University of North Dakota males	Oklahoma State University males	Frequency of agreement
1	10	10	8
2	16	20	14
3BM	19	21	17
4	24	18	17
7BM	16	10	9
8BM	8	8	6
11	8	8	7
13MF	16	11	10
18GF	8	11	5
16	8	24	8
Total	133	141	101

Card number	University of North Dakota females	Oklahoma State University females	Frequency of agreement
1	19	16	12
2	20	19	15
3BM	18	21	17
4	27	23	22
7BM	15	15	10
8BM	12	14	9
11	15	9	9
13MF	23	19	17
18GF	16	14	12
16	16	21	15
Total	181	171	138

The next analysis was intended to provide an estimate of the amount of intragroup agreement for each of the 10 TAT cards. A contingency coefficient (Siegel, 1956) was computed for each scale, and an average contingency coefficient was computed for each card. For dichotomized data C has an upper

TABLE 5

INTRAGROUP AGREEMENT FOR FOUR SUBJECT GROUPS BASED ON AVERAGE CONTINGENCY COEFFICIENTS FOR 10 TAT CARDS

Card number	University of North Dakota males	Oklahoma State University males	University of North Dakota females	Oklahoma State University females
1	.24	.22	.30*	.26*
2	.29	.30*	.28*	.28*
3BM	.32	.32*	.30*	.32*
4	.38*	.29*	.38*	.33*
7BM	.26	.20	.21	.28*
8BM	.19	.16	.18	.21
11	.17	.19	.21	.17
13MF	.29	.20	.34*	.32*
18GF	.20	.21	.22	.22
16	.21	.36*	.22	.29*

* $p \leq .05$ for a two-tailed test.

limit of .58. The confidence level for C is derived from the confidence level of the chi square from which it was computed. These results are presented in Table 5.

In the final analyses of the data, intercorrelations (e.g., rhos) were computed among the four groups from the distributions of ratings on the standard form of scales. A frequency count was made of the ratings favoring only those bipolar adjectives which appeared on the left-hand side of the standard

TABLE 6

INTERGROUP AGREEMENT ON SEMANTIC DIFFERENTIAL RATINGS FOR SELECTED TAT CARDS (Rhos)

Card number	University of North Dakota males and females	Oklahoma State University males and females	University of North Dakota and Oklahoma State University males	University of North Dakota and Oklahoma State University females
1	.83	.86	.74	.85
2	.90	.90	.81	.85
3BM	.93	.93	.90	.92
4	.97	.94	.92	.96
7BM	.83	.80	.85	.86
8BM	.87	.90	.67	.71
11	.90	.80	.79	.83
13MF	.83	.87	.87	.93
18GF	.84	.76	.93	.88
16	.10	.92	.73	.10

scale forms. This procedure was followed for each of the 10 TAT cards. The frequency data was then ranked for the 30 scales included in the standard form. Spearman Rank Order Correlations were then computed between like sex groups from different geographical regions, and unlike sex groups from the same geographical locations, respectively, for each of the 10 TAT cards. The results of this analysis are presented in Table 6. Only two rhos for Card 16 failed to reach significance at the .01 level.

Discussion

The results of the present investigation indicate that subjects' ratings of selected TAT cards follow an orderly and seemingly lawful pattern. However, there was sufficient variation in consensual adjective descriptions of the cards to suggest that relatively fine distinctions can reliably be obtained by this method. With the exception of Card 16, the predominant tendency was to rate the cards as "sad." Yet, there were uniform variations from card to card on other adjectives. Card 1, it may be noted from Tables 2 and 3, was significantly rated "passive," "submissive," and "youthful," in sharp contrast to Card 4 which was rated "active," "dominant," and "mature." Thus, it was empirically determined that significant agreement on specific indices can be obtained for selected TAT cards. Moreover, the obtained agreement was logically related to the stimulus materials (e.g., the figure on Card 1 is described as a young boy, whereas the figures on Card 4 are described as adults).

The intragroup consistency in card ratings, as determined by the average contingency coefficients, was not impressive, although degree of agreement was significant for 17 out of 40 analyses. This means that not all of the 30 scales in the standard forms elicited uniform judgments. Inspection of the data indicates that greater agreement could have been obtained by selecting specific and therefore different scales for each TAT card. It had been assumed that the 30 scales comprising the standard form of the semantic differential were generally applicable to all of the selected TAT cards. However, subjects were frequently faced with arbitrary choices and con-

flictual stimulus elements in the cards which required a compromise solution. Card 13MF, for example, was neither significantly "masculine" nor "feminine" for the OSU groups, presumably because the subjects differed in their preferences for attributing greater precedence to the male and female figures pictured in this card. For Card 11 there was a slight incidence of significant adjectives which typically describe human attributes. However, adjectives more relevant to describing inanimate objects elicited uniform judgments. Thus, "sociable," "interested," and "good" were not statistically significant but "rugged," "hazy," and "strong" were. It therefore appears that the degree of intragroup agreement would have been enhanced by eliminating those adjectives which were minimally related to certain cards. This is not to imply that all instances of nonuniformity in judgments could be eliminated by this procedure. Rather, certain of those adjectives which did not elicit consensual agreement might reflect personal differences or the indirect expression of feelings and needs which the subjects imposed upon the stimulus cards. The identification of such scales, however, awaits further research with less homogeneous groups than were used in this study.

The outcome of the ratings for Card 16 was particularly surprising and poses a problem for interpretation. Assuming that the obtained ratings were in fact random, approximately 2 out of the 30 scales would be expected to be statistically significant. However, two unexpected findings emerged. First, a greater than chance number of scales reached significance. Second, all groups used evaluatively favorable adjectives to describe the imagined picture or scene. The use of positively toned adjectives to describe this card may have represented a reaction against the use of negatively toned adjectives on the previous 9 cards. An alternative explanation is offered by Murstein (1958) who found a relationship between TAT card ambiguity and pleasantness of the stimulus. With regard to structural elements, Card 16 is certainly the most ambiguous card in the set. This is supported by the finding that no two titles used to describe this card, or the imagined scene, were the same. Hence, the uniformity in ratings would be the result of the precedence given to affectively pleasing adjectives.

Comparisons between groups differing as to sex and geographical location revealed a striking similarity in their ratings of the selected TAT cards. The relative frequencies of ratings on the standard scale forms was highly consistent from group to group. In other words, the ranked frequency data on 30 scales for any given card revealed similar patterns of agreement and dissension among subject populations. The percentage of significant scales replicated in the second phase of the study with the OSU groups and determined from independent analyses suggests that uniformities in judgments were a function of readily discernible stimulus qualities in the test materials.

Generally, the inferences that could be drawn from the significant adjective descriptions of the cards were consistent with Murray's (1943) descriptions. In several instances, as with earlier normative research, there were divergences. The figure in Card 3BM was rated as "feminine" by both males and females indicating that this figure was perceived as a girl rather than a boy. Another discrepancy was noted between Murray's (1943) description of Card 18GF and the present findings. According to Murray, this scene depicts a woman who has her hands squeezed around the throat of another woman whom she appears to be pushing backwards across the banister of a stairway. Although consensual agreement consistent with a murder theme would have been expected to elicit significant ratings on adjectives such as "hostile," "aggressive," and "immoral," such ratings were conspicuously absent. It could be argued that the subjects used in this study denied the aggressive overtones of this card, but this does not explain why the same adjectives were so unanimously checked for certain other cards (e.g., Card 4). The reader may note similar discrepancies by reference to Tables 2 and 3.

There were no marked differences between Henry's classification of the cards and the present findings. Card 4, in accordance with Henry (1956) was rated "clear" by a majority of subjects in both sex groups, but failed to reach significance. In other instances hypotheses received experimental support, as for example, the consistency between Henry's description of Card 11, and significant ratings on "hazy" and "unusual."

The most crucial issue raised by the present research findings revolves around the question of what constitutes a deviant response on the TAT with respect to interpretive significance. In spite of the general quality of Murray's card descriptions (i.e., limited as to structural and emotional details) there are evidences of inaccuracies. The originators of the TAT made no attempt to test systematically the assumptions underlying these interpretive procedures. As a result, interpretation of the TAT evolved in a traditional manner, and alternative ways of conceptualizing the test materials were in effect discouraged. The trend has been to extend the original card descriptions, and in certain instances (Bellak, 1954; Henry, 1956; Murstein, 1959) to exercise caution in assuming what is *given* and hence what might be assumed to have particular interpretive significance for a given individual. In clinical practice, the tendency has been to rely on a few cliched interpretations. Almost invariably these deal with sexual identification, hostility, and dependency. In contrast, the present investigation indicates that there are equally important qualities inherent in the test materials which are highly relevant to the interpretation of TAT themes but which have not received attention. Thus, 56 out of 56 males and 60 out of 60 females in the OSU groups rated Card 3BM as "sad." What then might be the meaning or significance of a happy theme in response to this card, and how deviant would such a story be? Card 4 elicited adjective ratings that were heavily loaded on the Potency factor (i.e., "masculine," "rugged," "strong"). Perhaps the use of adjectives negatively loaded on the Potency factor in the writing of a theme for Card 4 would be as important an interpretive finding as failure to mention the "seminude." The findings generally suggest that interpretation of the TAT could be further improved by attaching greater significance to the subjects' descriptions of the cards.

The data question the procedure of administering a separate set of TAT cards to males and females. It was found that different cards elicit different responses, but there was high consensuality in judgments on specific adjective scales between the sexes. One alternative to using a separate set of cards for males and females would be to administer TAT cards according to their stimulus qualities and the themes they tend to elicit, and to do this on an empirical rather than a priori basis.

There is much to be learned about the stimulus properties of the TAT cards, and caution should be used in generalizing from the present findings. However, there are advantages to avoiding what Murstein (1959) has labeled a "wholly subject oriented" approach to the test stimuli, and as a result improve the accuracy and adequacy of clinical interpretations of thematic material. It seems evident that consensual descriptions of the cards offer a flexible and economical means to establish base-line data for the TAT. Rather than restricting the usefulness of this instrument, this kind of approach could contribute additional dimensions for the analysis and interpretation of TAT stories.

REFERENCES

BELLAK, L. *The Thematic Apperception Test and the Children's Apperception Test in clinical use.* New York: Grune & Stratton, 1954.

BRADLEY, J. E., & LYSAKER, R. E. Ambiguity in the use of projective techniques. Minneapolis, Minn.: Pillsbury Mills, 1957. (Mimeo)

COLEMAN, W. Thematic Apperception Test II: Some quantitative observations. *J. clin. Psychol.,* 1947, **3**, 257–264.

ERON, L. D. Frequencies of themes and identifications in the stories of schizophrenic patients and non-hospitalized college students. *J. consult. Psychol.,* 1948, **12**, 387–395.

ERON, L. D., TERRY, D., & CALLAHAN, R. The use of rating scales for emotional tone of TAT stories. *J. consult. Psychol.,* 1950, **14**, 473–478.

GARFIELD, S. L., & ERON, L. D. Interpreting mood and activity in thematic test stories. *J. abnorm. soc. Psychol.,* 1948, **43**, 338–345.

HENRY, W. E. *Analysis of fantasy: The Thematic Apperception Technique in the study of personality.* New York: Wiley, 1956.

KENNY, D. T. Transcendence indices, extent of personality factors in fantasy responses, and ambiguity of TAT cards. *J. consult. Psychol.,* 1954, **18**, 345–348.

LEBO, D. Immediate affective reaction to TAT cards. *J. clin. Psychol.,* 1955, **11**, 279–299.

LEBO, D., & SHERRY, J. P. The visual and verbal TAT. *J. proj. Tech.,* 1959, **23**, 59–63.

MURRAY, H. A. *Thematic Apperception Test (manual).* Cambridge, Mass.: Harvard Univer. Press, 1943.

MURSTEIN, B. I. Nonprojective determinants of perception on the TAT. *J. consult. Psychol.,* 1958, **22**, 195–198.

MURSTEIN, B. I. A conceptual model of projective techniques applied to stimulus variations with thematic techniques. *J. consult. Psychol.,* 1959, **23**, 3–14.

OSGOOD, C. E., SUCI, G. J., & TANNENBAUM, P. H. *The measurement of meaning.* Urbana, Ill.: Univer. Illinois Press. 1957.

ROSENZWEIG, S., & FLEMMING, E. E. Apperceptive norms for the thematic apperception test, I.: The problem of norms in projective method. *J. Pers.,* 1949, **17**, 475–482.

ROSENZWEIG, S., & FLEMMING, E. E. Apperceptive norms for the thematic apperception test, II: An empirical investigation. *J. Pers.,* 1949, **17**, 483–503.

SIEGEL, S. *Nonparametric statistics.* New York: McGraw-Hill, 1956.

STEIN, M. L. *The Thematic Apperception Test: An introductory manual for its clinical use with adults.* Cambridge, Mass.: Addison-Wesley, 1955.

TOMKINS, S. S. *The Thematic Apperception Test: The theory and technique of interpretation.* New York: Grune & Stratton, 1947.

WEISSKOPF, E. Experimental study of the effect of brightness and ambiguity on projection in the Thematic Apperception Test. *J. Psychol.,* 1950, **29**, 407–416.

46. Experimental Paradigms for the Hypnotic Investigation of Dream Symbolism [1]

C. Scott Moss

The process of symbolization has been both the most intriguing and controversial aspect of the rich fabric of theory advanced by psychoanalysis and unfortunately, the most resistant to scientific exploration. This paper will outline a variety of experimental approaches to the investigation of dream symbolism through innovations in hypnotic technique. The value of hypnosis in dream research is that it seemingly provides access to the symbol-translating mechanism. For instance, recall of forgotten dream elements can be facilitated, some subjects are able to "dream" upon command, and others demonstrate an increased capacity to interpret symbolic materials (Erickson and Kubie, 1938, 1940; Farber & Fisher, 1943; Rapaport, 1952; Moss, 1957a). The principal measuring instrument employed throughout these studies was the semantic differential, a method specifically designed to provide an objective measurement of the connotative (feeling) aspects of meaning.[2]

Reprinted from *International Journal of Clinical and Experimental Hypnosis* (1961), 9: 105–117, by permission of the author and the publisher.

[1] Presented at the XVI International Congress of Psychology, Bonn Germany, August, 1960.

[2] The semantic differential is not a particular test but rather a highly generalizable operation of measurement which can be adapted to specific research problems. Its originators postulate a geometrical model in the form of a semantic space defined by logical opposites. Factor analysis was used to identify the independent dimensions of this space, representing the ways human beings make meaning judgments. The generality of this factor structure was further tested by varying subject populations, concepts judged, type of judgmental situation and the factoring method used in analyzing data.

The measuring operation or semantic differential can be described as follows: Adjectives were identified as representative of the major dimensions along with meaningful processes vary; these have a high coverage of meaning on one factor and a negligible amount on the others. These logical opposites are used to define the ends of seven point scales. In practice, an individual judges a particular concept against a set of these scales. Judgments result in the successive allocation of a concept to a point in multidimensional space. In this manner, change in the meaning of a concept over time, the subtle differences between two or more concepts, and individual differences in the meaning of a single concept may be quantitatively represented. (Refer to Moss, 1960, for a resume of current research with the semantic differential.)

In an early experiment (Moss, 1957b), an attempt was made to test the psychoanalytic idea of dream symbol disguise, by translating it into the operationally defined concept of *semantic distance*. Ordinarily choice of a symbol should be determined by the similarity of mediational processes between a potential symbol and the latent content to be represented. However, according to Freud, anxiety-stimulating latent content results in the choice of symbols that are semantically distant; a symbol that is semantically distant from the latent content becomes unintelligible and may be said to be disguised.

Seventy-six dreams of a single patient in psychotherapy over a year period were intensively studied. A form of the semantic differential was used to measure the distance between symbol and latent content when the covert content was anxiety-arousing and when it was not. In operational terms, disguise would be indicated by a relative increase in semantic distance coincident with anxiety.

Identification of the meaning of dream symbols used by the patient-subject was a primary problem, and reliance upon conventional methods of interpretation was supplemented by training the patient to interpret his own dreams under hypnosis. The patient free-associated to the dream elements, first in the waking and then in the hypnotic state, in order to identify the latent content. Associative material obtained in hypnosis was invariably centrally-related to the meaning of the dream.

The following dream demonstrates the highly meaningful nature of the patient's dreams and his facility in dream interpretation.

The patient and his wife are going on an ocean voyage. They find the gangplank steep and lined with girls. On deck the captain inquires whether the patient has a newspaper. When the patient replies that he does not, the captain assures him that he'll find one in his cabin. The patient next travels slowly down a spiral slide and finds himself seated in the dining room. There he refuses an offer of hamburgers. He is suddenly ashore again, standing beside a convertible. A voice says, "Tell your uncle he is holding up the works."

Waking associations. The dream was essentially without meaning to the patient. The predominate emotion was apprehension. The significant associations were as follows. *Water:* the patient had long suffered a mild aquaphobia. *Voyage:* his only sea voyage was in military service. *Hamburgers:* the patient was surprised at his refusal since he liked hamburgers. *Uncle:* a favorite with the patient.

Hypnotic reconstruction. The patient's first association was to *ocean voyage.* "The phrase 'going from the old to the new' enters my mind." He then drew the analogy that therapy was a means of exchanging an old, unsatisfactory adjustment for a new mode, and in this sense is like a journey. "I also find myself thinking of the voyage I took in service and how frightened I was." Therapy is therefore initially perceived as "a voyage on dangerous waters." (Later it became apparent that the patient unconsciously associated the awesome, cruel, overpowering quality of water with intense hostile impulses threatening his control and self-esteem.) The next association was to *gangplank:* "I remember how very steep it seemed—it was hard getting aboard. My *wife* being with me meant that this is *our* problem—she's the main reason I'm here." The *line of girls* momentarily thwarted recognition, but the patient then stated quite positively they represented different aspects of the relationship with his wife. To *ship captain* he associated, "Men who are strong and strict, but just—it makes me think of in here, of you, that you will help channel my thoughts into the right direction, also that it will not be an easy job, either." The *newspaper* was explained as a reference to the dreams he had been told to report, i.e., "both are a chronical of events." "I remember telling you I didn't dream very often and you said 'don't worry about it.' 'Below decks,' makes me think of 'below the surface'—dreams come from below the surface when one sleeps, in the cabin or bedroom." The patient interpreted the *slide* as, "a roundabout way of reaching a goal," meaning his old inadequate mode of adjustment. "I'm afraid that when the going gets tough, I'll slide back into the old way of thinking." "*Hamburgers* make me think of 'food for thought'—they represent the things we're talking about here, things that are distasteful and I don't want to face or swallow." The *return to shore,* was interpreted by the patient as another expression of ambivalence towards therapy, that is, his fear that the content discussed would be unpleasant and he would want to escape. The *convertible,* like the slide, was translated as an old and established but "unsafe" (neurotic) mode of goal attainment. The verbal reference to the *uncle* stimulated recall of a recent statement by the uncle to the effect that the primary defect of the patient was a lack of self-confidence. This remark sensitized the patient to his tendency to be withdrawn from problem situations and made it difficult for him to retreat from therapy, i.e., "This remark keeps me from using the convertible." The three component parts of the dream are thus: ambivalence towards therapy, rejection of the situation, but inability to return to the old adjustment.

When the patient presented such a dream, one or more symbols were selected, and he was asked to rate these in-the-dream context on the differential. The patient would associate to the dream, first in the waking and then in the hypnotic state, in order to establish the latent meaning. Subsequently, in the waking state with complete recall for his dream analysis, the patient rated the identified latent content.

No adequate measure of the anxiety associated with a specific dream symbol was available; however, independent measures (psychological tests and staff ratings) indicated progressive patient improvement over a year's time. In addition, five clinicians agreed in classifying 13 of the patient's dreams as highly anxious ("nightmares"), 11 of which occurred in the first half of therapy. Contrary to psychoanalytic theory, the semantic distances between the mediational processes of dream symbols and things symbolized, as reflected on the differential, were not significantly greater for the first half as compared with the second half of therapy. Thus the hypothesis that dream symbols acquire a disguise function under the impetus of anxiety was not substantiated.

Mature consideration, however, led to the recognition that the semantic differential had definite limitations in detecting the effect of a dream censorship process. While many competent therapists seem agreed that the affective qualities of the dream are usually not subject to distortion, this is the aspect of meaning primarily measured by the differential. Needed was the development of a denotative differential.[3] Since the relationship between symbol and latent content is typically quite tenuous, such a measuring instrument would also have to be extremely sensitive to relatively minute and highly individual aspects of meaning, rather than measuring the common variance among groups of subjects.

A second study used a form of the differential composed of scales designed to measure physical qualities (e.g., large-small, wet-dry, long-short, angular-rounded, etc.); subjects were also instructed to respond to the "physical" rather than the "feeling" characteristics of symbols and things symbolized. Instead of spontaneous night dreams, data this time consisted of hypnotically induced "dreams."

Three normal, psychologically naive subjects were first intensively studied through interview and projective techniques in order to identify areas of personal conflict. They were then induced to "dream" under hypnosis about both pleasant and unpleasant, or anxiety-arousing, personal content. The hypnotic products were typically similar to the autosymbolic phenomena experienced in the transitional hypnagogic state between waking and sleep; while symbols were employed, they appeared relatively poor in multiple meaning.

A female subject's concern regarding a dependency conflict is depicted in this brief, representative "dream."

I am hit by a big truck which comes to rest on me. It is very heavy. I appeal to my parents to remove it but they ignore me. I struggle very hard and finally succeed in pushing it off.

In every instance the subject was instructed to be amnesic for the dream suggestion. At the conclusion of a dream the subject rated selected dream symbols on the differential (e.g.: *truck*). She was next asked to associate to the dream in the waking and hypnotic states in order to clarify and confirm the meaning of the latent content, and to rate this

---

[3] Dreams reported during psychotherapy reveal many examples of denotative distortion. One illustration is that of a 34-year-old female patient who reported that at age 8, she had experienced a particularly vivid, recurring dream of being terrified at the pursuit of a tiny white dog. Hypnosis facilitated understanding that the dog had represented her recent discovery of death. As a child she had conceived of death as large, black, cold, ugly and threatening, and had attempted to neutralize this fear by representing it in her dream as a small, white, warm, cuddly puppy. Thus the denotative qualities were distorted to the extreme, that is, representation by a diametrically opposite symbol, but the affect remained appropriate to the latent content of the dream. The resistances which maintain repression are nicely illustrated through employment of hypno-projective dream analysis: Cf., Moss (1957c).

content on the differential (e.g.: *guilt related to my struggle for independence*).

Ratings of 42 symbols and the corresponding latent content were obtained from 31 anxiety provoking dreams, while 34 such measurements were obtained from 22 dreams with pleasant content. The average semantic distance under the two conditions for each of the three subjects, did not differ significantly. These investigations again failed to support the hypothesized effect of a censorship mechanism; the results of both studies suggest that the dream work is simply a translation, representing what a person thinks while asleep. An unanswered question was the exact nature of the relationship between spontaneous and hypnotic dreams, and whether censorship could be expected to manifest itself in the latter.[4]

Hypnosis provides a unique opportunity of studying the dynamic interaction involved in the acquisition and modification of the significance of signs and symbols, and a third study focused attention on the mode of symbolic transformation per se.

Four hospitalized, neurotic patients were again trained to produce hypnotic dreams, a procedure providing the opportunity to observe the transformation of a suggested content into its symbolic equivalent. An important innovation was the training of subjects to project *static* symbolic images on an imagined movie screen, such that a single symbol would depict a suggested content. Freud recognized that dream symbols are typically overdetermined, and this mechanism of condensation (in combination with displacement) was accorded primary responsibility for the unintelligibility of dreams. It is also a factor which greatly complicates precise semantic measurement. The present approach was

---

[4] Authorities are not agreed as to the exact relationship between hypnotic and spontaneous night dreams. M. Brenman (1949) states, "It is curious that investigators appear to have taken it for granted that the hypnotic suggestion to 'dream' issues in a dream." She argues that hypnotic dreams are relatively oversimplified, less influenced by unconscious thought processes, and are basically motivated by the desire to preserve the relationship with the hypnotist, rather than preservation of sleep. However, this argument is greatly weakened by her admission that spontaneous night dreams are by no means homogeneous in their expressive form and like the hypnotically induced dream, may range from an embellished reminiscence to a highly elaborated, symbolized product. In contrast, M. Mazer (1951) states that a dream should be defined by the nature of the production not by the circumstances of its occurrence, and that the hypnotic dream possesses all of the distortions characteristic of the regular night dream. It seems agreed that the hypnotically induced dream varies greatly, but that a general, unstructured posthypnotic suggestion to be carried out during regular sleep results in a product very similar to a spontaneous night dream. Present experiments are based on the assumption that hypnotic and spontaneous dreams are sufficiently similar in the employment of symbolism to allow cross-generalization.

an attempt to partially control the effect of condensation while studying displacement or symbolization. In addition, suggestions were restricted to the symbolization of simple, concrete sexual anatomy and
activities. Abstract latent content is often difficult to rate against a
denotative differential (just as a connotative differential was not applicable to many varieties of concrete manifest content). It was hoped
to tailor both content levels for use with the denotative differential.
This emphasis on sexual content was consistent with the psychoanalytic penchant for assigning sexual significance to dream symbols.[5]

Sometimes subjects responded with a single symbolization; they also
responded with series of symbols, each representing the suggested content. For instance, one female subject was unhappily married, and
possessed an intense fear, dislike and envy of men. When asked to
symbolize the male organ, she perceived in rapid succession: "A knife,
a bull with tremendous horns, an enema bulb." Her hypnotic associations revealed that she thought of men as aggressively assaulting
women. She also produced a vivid memory of impotent rage towards
her mother who frequently "violated me" with enemas as a child. Her
symbolizations of the female organ were also revealing of highly personal attitudes: "An outhouse, a pedestrian traffic-tunnel (where men
urinate), a door on which hung a sign 'No Peddlers or Agents,' and a
new green car parked beside a pile of breadcrusts." The last represented her envy of male prerogatives. This approach allowed objective
measurement, and identification of the elements of meaning common
to a variety of symbolizations of a single latent content.

The possible methodological variations provided by hypnosis in
the study of the symbolic process in action are practically unlimited,
and several additional approaches are suggested in the following examples. Subjects were instructed to project a series of static symbols,
each of which would become increasingly transparent in meaning,
until the latent content was directly represented (a desymbolizing
process). For example, when a second single, female subject was given
a suggestion to symbolize the male genitalia, she responded:

"I see a couple of small peanuts. They are moving about, they won't stand
still. Now they have spots like potatoes. Sprouts are growing out of the spots—
they are changing, curving. It looks like a unicorn with a horn on its nose. I

[5] A characteristic suggestion given subjects was as follows: "In a moment you
will fall deeply asleep. When you do, a dream will form. You will find yourself
seated in a movie theater looking at a blank screen. You will then clearly see (a
suggested sexual content) followed immediately by a second picture or series of
pictures which represent or stand for the same thing; just as you might have experienced it in a dream."

just see the head. There are circular lines around the horn. The head is changing again, into a sac—it is wrinkled. Oh! testicles and penis!"

A second type, detailed experiment with the same subject will demonstrate the potentialities inherent in another variation, that of directly suggesting the symbols a subject should use to depict a specified content.

1. The subject rated three sexual concepts on the differential, *penis, vagina, intercourse,* interspersed among a dozen irrelevant (nonsexual) concepts. Hypnosis was then induced and she was instructed to fall deeply asleep and to have a dream of being seated in a movie theater looking at a blank screen. She was instructed to perceive the male sex organ on the screen, and that it would be followed immediately by a second picture which represented or stood for the same thing, "just as you might experience it in your dreams."

2. The patient signaled the beginning and termination of a dream. Still under hypnosis she reported having seen "a man with no clothes on—the lower part of his body. *It* looked big and hard and bony. It gave me a funny feeling in my stomach." She reported that this image was then replaced by a "necktie with a tight knot in the end of it." The patient was told that when she awakened she would be amnesic for this episode until a given signal, whereupon she would remember *only* the necktie (not its covert meaning).

3. The patient awoke, smiled, and apologized, saying that she must have dozed off. Questioning elicited no apparent memory for what had transpired. She was then asked to rate the general concept "necktie" on the differential. Next she was asked her associations to the concept. "An article of men's wearing apparel. I think of them as being attractive. They are so versatile and come in so many different shapes, colors, sizes, and designs. I also think of them as reflecting the personalities of the men who wear them."

4. At the pre-arranged signal she instantly and with seeming surprise, recalled the necktie she perceived on the screen (but not its association with the male organ). She was asked to visualize the scene as vividly as possible, and then to rate this specific necktie on the differential (Refer to Fig. 1).

5. The patient entered a second hypnotic trance, and was again told to perceive the movie screen and upon it the now familiar necktie, but that this time the necktie would depict the female genitalia.[6] She

[6] Another test of a prevalent psychoanalytic belief suggests itself here. To paraphrase Jones (1950, p. 98), an individual is free to choose his dream symbols or to make new ones, what he cannot do is to give a regular (universal) symbol a different meaning.

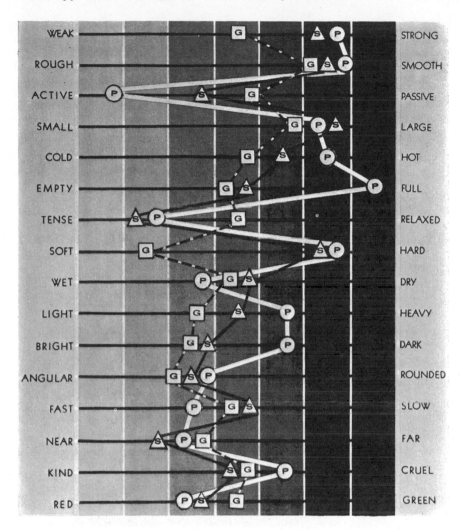

FIG. 1. Comparison of three concepts: *Penis* (P), rated prior to experiment; *Necktie* △S, as an unconscious symbol for penis, rated in dream context; *Necktie* ☐G, general or nonsymbol rated later out of the dream context. Quantitative relationship (D statistic): Penis vs. Necktie-nonsymbol = 7.68; Penis vs. Necktie-symbol = 4.80; Necktie-nonsymbol vs. Necktie-symbol = 5.48. (The smaller the number, the closer the relationship).

was again requested to be amnesic for the suggestion. Upon indication that the "dream" had ceased, she awoke and stated that she had again seen the necktie but that this time it was a "red necktie, just about the reddest necktie you can imagine; it had a crease down the center of it and seemed quite curved."

6. She rated this new necktie on the differential. Asked to associate to the new tie, she replied, "The red makes me think of something

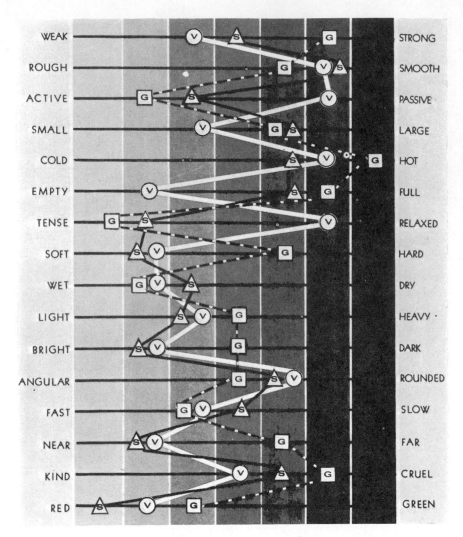

Fig. 2. Comparison of three concepts: *Vagina* Ⓥ rated prior to experiment; *Necktie* △S, a male symbol which subject was required to use as a female symbol, rated in the dream context; *Necktie* ☐G, nonsymbol, rated out of the dream context. (Quantitative relationships: Vagina vs. Necktie-female symbol = 7.28; Vagina vs. Penis = 11.22; Intercourse vs. Necktie-female symbol = 6.56; Vagina vs. Necktie-nonsymbol = 6.40; Intercourse vs. Necktie-nonsymbol = 7.81.)

that is very bright and active, something which is very stimulating, it is definitely more feminine than most colors than men will wear." (Refer to Figure 2).

7. The subject was placed in a third hypnotic state and was instructed that this time she would briefly witness herself having intercourse, and that this scene would then be replaced by another picture

representing the same thing to her; she was told to remember only the latter scene.

After signalling completion of the dream," the subject reported that she had seen, "A hotdog between two slices of bun. It was an extremely large hotdog, pointing straight upwards, and also there was a large slice of onion between it and the bun." She was instructed to be amnesic for the entire experience.

8. Upon awakening the subject was asked to rate "hotdog" on the differential. By a pre-arranged signal she next remembered the hotdog seen on the screen (but not the immediately preceding scene or latent content) and was asked to rate it.

9. The patient was returned to a hypnotic state, and was asked to associate to each of the symbols she had used and to attempt an interpretation of their meaning.

First Necktie—"As I said before, an article of men's clothing, something intimately related to a man, something definitely masculine. The straightness of it makes me think maybe it is starched or stiff. The knot in the end looks like, well, like a man's organ."

Second Necktie—"That reminds me of a man's organ, too, but it's different somehow. The curve reminds me of the curve of a woman's body. The red makes me think of something that is very much alive; it makes me think of the vagina. I connect the idea of redness with the act of menstruation. I feel afraid of the penis though I know it would not really hurt me, but I am afraid it would make me pregnant. The vagina is not pregnant when it menstruates. The crease down the front of the tie is actually the opening of the woman's organ, and the curve is the shape of the vagina, too. Actually, this necktie is both male and female, but the female seems to predominate. The first necktie was only the penis. Both of them are stimulating, but the second is more so. It sort of makes me think of a penis being in a vagina, that is, of sexual intercourse."

Hotdog—"Well, the hotdog is the penis, too. It is very pointed and it is slanted—it is slanting away from me. This causes the thought that I mustn't touch it because it would make me pregnant. The bun is the vagina, and the fact that it is holding the weiner indicates that sexual intercourse is taking place. The whiteness of the onion indicates purity to me—the need to avoid having intercourse so that pregnancy will not occur. It, and the slant of the hotdog, and the redness of the necktie all represent the same thing—the need to avoid sexual contact."

10. The patient was obviously rather distressed at this point and was to talk further about her feelings. She responded that the hotdog had brought up a "forgotten" subject to her, "Something that I had put out of my mind and refused to even think about anymore." She then related that six months previous she had gone on a picnic with her boy friend and they had experienced intercourse for the first time. She spontaneously recalled a specific memory of lying wrapped in the blanket with him after having completed the act, and glancing

up over his shoulder and seeing a half-eaten, shriveled hotdog. She laughed and commented that it looked like his "hotdog." Thus, the choice of the symbol produced in the experimental situation was apparently determined by this repressed but dynamically active experience. She further volunteered that later she had experienced several nightmares in which she was choking on a hotdog, and that in the past six months for reasons until now unknown to her, hotdogs had become completely unappetizing.

It is of considerable interest to note that the subject is not merely a symbolizing automaton, but responds with symbolic productions which graphically depict personal needs and problems. Rich potentialities for the clinical employment of this technique as a projective method for personality exploration have only recently been explored (Watkins, 1956). Here the suggestion activated a very real conflict situation for the subject, reflecting both sensitivity of the method and the precautions that must be observed in its experimental application.

The remainder of the paper will deal with one specific application of the demonstrated methods, the study of the process of cognitive interaction involved in meaning formation and change which Osgood et al, refer to as the principle of congruity (Osgood, 1957, p. 200). Briefly, this principle states that whenever two signs having different meanings (different mediation processes and different profiles against the semantic differential) are related, the meaning of each shifts toward agreement with the other, the magnitude of the shift being *inversely proportional* to the *intensity* (degree of polarization, as reflected on the differential) of the interacting reactions. Two signs are said to be congruent to the extent that their mediating reactions are equally intense, either in the same (compatible) direction, or in the opposite direction. Results obtained in the reported investigations suggest several features concerning the process of dream symbol acquisition and modification.

1) At the moment of symbol selection a situation exists in which the latent impulse "scans" a pool of potential symbols which share one or more physionomic qualities with the content to be represented (e.g., the similarity in shape between hotdog and penis). Logically, the analogy may be quite tenuous, of course. Differences are largely disregarded, with two important exceptions: (a) Each dream has a general theme or setting [e.g., psychotherapy = a dangerous ocean voyage], determined by the predominant affect and the selection of one or two key symbols. The remaining symbols will tend to be consistent [e.g., gangplank = resistance, ship captain = therapist, cabin = sleep, etc.]. This gives the dream its theatrical quality. (b) The *preinter-*

action location of the potential symbol in relation to the latent content cannot be highly incongruent with respect to the emotional aspects of meaning. This would appear to account for seeming preference for symbols which, in their own right (independent of the dream context), are often innocuous or affectively neutral.

2) The fact that the latent content has, typically, powerful associated affective and cognitive processes, which in combination with the affectivity neutral (or possibly congruent) potential symbol, determines the flow of significance from the primary sign (A) to the secondary idea or symbol (B). These observations are completely predictable from the principle of congruity. The more polarized one sign is, relative to the other, the less change it undergoes. Where one member of an assertion is neutral, *all* the shift in meaning is concentrated on this concept.

3) Insofar as B receives its meaning from identification with A, it functions as its symbolic equivalent. In the dream a momentary situation obtains in which the interaction is maximized, that is, the meaning of each sign is shifted totally to the point of mutual congruence. At this moment the dreamer is completely credulous: He accepts the symbol as reality! However, the tendency is, after such cognitive interaction, for the meanings of related signs to "bounce" back to their original locus, and the whole phenomena has a mercurial quality which defies direct measurement, although the employment of hypnotic techniques allows almost immediate access to and reproducibility of this symbol-making process. When the dreamer awakens, there will be a reduction in the congruity effect both as a function of time and an altered state of consciousness (the semantic distance between latent and manifest content increases to the point where dream symbols become largely unintelligible).

It should be noted that when the affect associated with the primary idea is too intense (as in the last case example), an individual continues to experience a continuing, disturbing, logically incomprehensible identity of signs (hotdog = intercourse) resulting in a phobic reaction, or in the extreme case, a psychotic delusion or hallucination.

Summary

Several forms of Osgood's Semantic Differential were employed in the study of spontaneous and hypnotically induced dreams. While the use of hypnosis to investigate symbolization is not original with these studies, the feasibility of objectification of this elusive psychological phenomenon has been demonstrated, including a step towards identification of the psychological laws underlying the acquisition, and modification of sign significance. The primary intent of the paper is to stimulate and provoke experimentation in an important area of human behavior long resistant (resisted) to scientific investigation.

REFERENCES

BRENMAN, M. Dreams and hypnosis. *Psychoanal. Quart.*, 1949, 18, 455–465.

ERICKSON, H. M. AND KUBIE, L. The use of automatic drawing in the interpretation and relief of a state of acute obsessional depression. *Psychoanal. Quart.*, 1938, 7, 95–133.

ERICKSON, H. M. AND KUBIE, L. The translation of cryptic automatic writing of one hypnotic subject by another in a trance-like dissociated state. *Psychoanal. Quart.*, 1940, 9, 51–63.

FARBER, L. AND FISHER, C. An experimental approach to dream psychology through the use of hypnosis. *Psychoanal. Quart.*, 1943, 12, 202–216.

JONES, E. *Papers on Psychoanalysis.* Baillière, Tindall & Cox, London, 1950, Fifth Edition.

MAZER, M. An experimental study of the hypnotic dream. *Psychiat.*, 1951, 14, 265–277.

Moss, C. S. Use of the schizophrenic in Rorschach content analysis. *J. Proj. Tech.*, 1957, 21, 384–390. (a)

Moss, C. S. Dream symbols as disguises. *Etc.: J. Gen. Sem.*, 1957, 14, 267–273. (b)

Moss, C. S. A forced hypnoprojective fantasy used in the resolution of pseudo-epileptic seizures. *J. Clin. Exp. Hyp.*, 1957, 5, 59–66. (c)

Moss, C. S. Current and projected status of semantic differential research. *Psychol. Record*, 1960, 10, 47–54. (d)

OSGOOD, C. E., SUCI, G. J., AND TANNENBAUM, P. H. *The Measurement of Meaning.* Univ. Ill. Press, Urbana, 1957.

RAPAPORT, D. *Organization and Pathology of Thought* (Section III: symbolism). New York: Univ. Columbia Press, 1952.

WATKINS, J. G. Projective hypnoanalysis. In *Experimental Hypnosis,* (Ed: L. M. LeCron), Macmillan Co., New York, 1956, 442–462.

Part X

*SEMANTIC DIFFERENTIAL
TECHNIQUE IN
ESTHETICS AND
COMMUNICATION
RESEARCH*

47. The Cross-Cultural Generality
of Visual-Verbal Synesthetic Tendencies *

Charles E. Osgood

The Sapir-Whorf hypothesis that the structure of a language influences cognitive behavior is questioned in this study of comparability of experience in different sense modalities. Do the Navajo, like ourselves, see HAPPY as more up and SAD as more down? Do the Japanese, like ourselves, conceive of EXCITEMENT as colorful and CALM as colorless? Do the Navajos and Anglos differ widely in their connotative meanings of the words "blue" and its correlate in Navajo, yet agree closely on their meanings for a specific BLUE color chip? Here is a first attempt to demonstrate that the visual-verbal synesthetic relationships characteristic of our own language/culture community are shared by peoples who speak different languages and enjoy different cultures. Perhaps there is a "world view" that is relatively stable despite differences in both language and culture.

THIS study was planned as part of the Southwest Project in Comparative Psycholinguistics (Casagrande, 1956) during the summer of 1955. This project as a whole was concerned with the ways in which language or culture, or both, may produce differences in cognitive processes; *or*, conversely, the degree to which certain cognitive processes may be independent of differences in language or culture, and hence general across language/culture groups. One area of cognition studied was that of *connotative meaning*; specifically, translation-equivalent forms of the semantic differential (Osgood, Suci, & Tannenbaum, 1957) were given to subjects in several Southwest Indian communities, as well as to Mexican-Spanish and Anglo subjects. Suci (1957) has reported the results of this work elsewhere.

Reprinted from *Behavioral Science* (1959), 5: 146–169, by permission of the author and the publisher.

* The author designed this experiment, ran the Anglo control subjects, interpreted the results, and wrote them up. Dr. Susan Ervin collected data from the Navajo subjects; Dr. Sol Saporta administered the experiment to the Mexican-Spanish subjects; Mr. Hiroshi Azuma obtained data from Japanese subjects and analysed them. Mr. Murray Miron handled the analysis of the data (except for the Japanese) on IBM and ILLIAC. Without the help of these people, for which I am very grateful, this paper could not have been written.

The usual form of the semantic differential requires the subject to judge verbal concepts (e.g., HORSE, CORN, MAN) against verbally defined scales (e.g., *strong-weak*, *active-passive*, *good-bad*). Problems of translation equivalence therefore enter at two places. In the present experiment the concepts to be judged are verbal, but the 'scales' are visual—binary pictorial alternatives with which the subject must selectively associate the verbal concept being judged. Thus, instead of the bipolar words *thin-thick*, the subject sees a *thin* line paired with a *thick* line, and he simply points to whichever drawing seems to 'go best' with the concept being judged; instead of the bipolar adjectives *angular-rounded*, he sees a jagged, *angular* line-drawing paired with a *rounded* line-drawing. The difference between the drawings in each pair is restricted to a single dimension, e.g., angularity, size, nearness, etc. The verbal concepts judged against these pictorial alternatives included both concept-terms (e.g., MAN, YELLOW) and scale terms (e.g., STRONG, BAD, LIGHT, GOOD, WEAK) taken from the standard semantic differential used in the Southwest Project by Suci.

One purpose of the present study, then, was to check the generality of semantic factors in a situation where at least the 'scales' of judgment were non-linguistic. Another purpose was to study the cross-cultural generality of visual synesthesia itself (and, indirectly, of metaphors based on visual analogies). Do the Navajo, like ourselves, see HAPPY as more *up* and SAD as more *down*? Do the Japanese, like ourselves, conceive of EXCITEMENT as *colorful* and CALM as *colorless*? And if certain differences in visual metaphor do appear, can these be related to what we know about the differences in culture? A third purpose was to see if those terms in Navajo, Mexican-Spanish, and Japanese selected as translation-equivalent to verbal opposites in English actually function as opposites in the meaningful judgments of non-Anglo subjects. Treating our paired visual alternatives as a sort of projective device, can the choices for GOOD be shown to be the mirror-image of those for BAD, for example? A final, and somewhat supplementary, purpose was to study similarities and differences in the connotations of both color terms and actual color samples. Can it be shown, for example, that Navajos and Anglos may differ widely in their connotative meanings of the words "blue" and its correlate in Navajo, yet agree closely on their meanings for a specific BLUE color chip? This analysis was restricted to the Navajo/Anglo comparison.

METHOD

Subjects

The synesthesia experiment was run on four groups of subjects, each representing a different language/culture base. Two of these groups, 40 Navajos and 10 Mexican-Spanish subjects, were included in the Southwest Project on Comparative Psycholinguistics (SWPCP), and the data were collected during the summer of 1956. Dr. Susan Ervin obtained the Navajo data and Dr. Sol Saporta obtained the Mexican-Spanish data. These subjects were, for the most part, rural people with little formal education. During the following year, the writer collected control data from a group of 27 Anglos, graduate and undergraduate students in psychology at the University of Illinois. The 20 Japanese subjects were either staff or students at the University of Illinois, but had been in this country less than two years; Mr. Hiroshi Azuma collected these data, as a research project in the author's course in psycholinguistics. It should be noted, first, that all but the Anglo subjects were bilingual to some degree with respect to English, and, second, that there are marked differences in education (and perhaps intelligence) between the Anglo and Japanese groups on the one hand and the Navajo and Mexican-Spanish on the other. The phenomena of visual synesthesia with which we are dealing here may be largely independent of these variables, but nevertheless they should be kept in mind in interpreting the results.

Materials

The verbal concepts used in this study are listed in Table 1. They include some of both the polar terms and the concepts used in the completely verbal semantic differential developed by Suci for SWPCP. They also include some color terms, for purposes of comparison with other experiments in the Southwest Project in which actual color chips were judged. Although the concepts are given here only in English, in administering the experiment the translation-equiv-

TABLE 1

VERBAL CONCEPTS USED IN SYNESTHESIA EXPERIMENT

1. HEAVY	*10. QUIET	*20. NOISY
2. GOOD	11. BLUE	*21. GREY
3. FAST	12. BAD	22. SLOW
4. HAPPY	13. LIGHT	23. WHITE
*5. UP	*14. DOWN	24. CALM
*6. ENERGETIC	15. BLACK	25. MAN
*7. LOOSE	16. WOMAN	26. YELLOW
8. STRONG	*17. LAZY	27. WEAK
9. EXCITEMENT	*18. TIGHT	28. SAD
	19. GREEN	

Pictorial Alternatives Used in Synesthesia Experiment
(see Figure 1)

1. up-down	5. thick-thin	10. rounded-angular
2. vertical-horizontal	6. dark-light	*11. diffuse-concentrated
3. homogeneous-heterogeneous	7. crooked-straight	12. large-small
4. colorless-colorful	8. hazy-clear	*13. near-far
	*9. blunt-sharp	

* These concepts and visual alternatives were omitted in the materials given to Mexican-Spanish subjects.

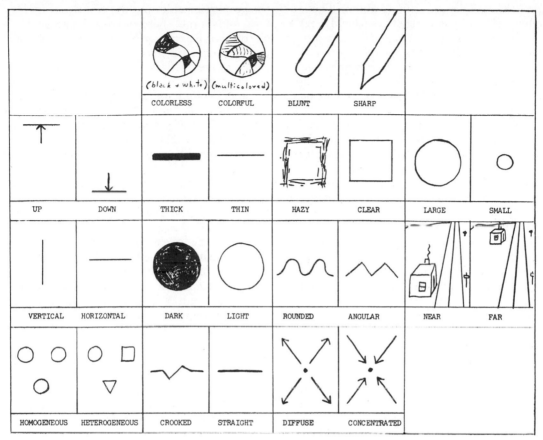

FIG. 1

alent terms in the subject's native language were given by the experimenter or interpreter. The equivalents for Japanese were determined by the back-translation technique (using different bilinguals in the two stages). Despite the extreme care exercised by the SWPCP linguists and by Mr. Azuma in achieving close translation-equivalence, perfect equivalence is probably impossible, and this is therefore another possible source of apparent differences in visual synesthetic tendencies across language groups.[1]

[1] Mr. Azuma, for example, reports several cases of only partial equivalence: the Japanese "karu-i," the equivalent of LIGHT, is used only with respect to weight, not also with respect to illumination, as in English; "reisei-na" (CALM) refers exclusively to emotional states, not being extended to weather, etc., as in English; "otoko" means male human and is not extended to human beings in general as is MAN in English; "haya-i," on the other hand, includes the notion of *early* as well as FAST.

The visual alternatives, or 'scales,' used in this study are displayed in Figure 1 and listed *verbally* in Table 1. The labelling of these visual alternatives is somewhat arbitrary and is done only to facilitate talking about them. The subjects were given no verbal characterizations, although they may well have done some spontaneous labelling. Each pair of visual alternatives was drawn on a single card, so that the order of presentation could be varied if desired; the left-right orientation on each card was as shown in Figure 1.

Procedure

The general procedure was to name one of the concepts to be judged and then run through the series of cards, having the subject point to or otherwise indicate which of the two visual alternatives on each card seemed most appropriate to that concept. Then the next concept would be named and run through in the same fashion. Thus, in effect, the subject judged whether HEAVY (in his own language) seemed more *up* or *down, vertical* or *horizontal, homogeneous* or *heterogeneous,* and so forth through the 13 alternatives; then he did the same thing for the concept GOOD, and so on through the test.

There were some minor variations in procedure that may be noted, even though it is doubtful that they would have much effect on such a simple judgment process. For Navajo, Japanese, and Anglo subjects, the order of presenting the concepts was as given in Table 1; the order for the Mexican-Spanish subjects was different. Also, for the Mexican-Spanish group, certain concepts and 'scales' were omitted (those shown by asterisks in Table 1). The Navajo, Mexican-Spanish, and Japanese subjects were tested individually, each concept being spoken aloud before its series of judgments (and repeated whenever necessary). The Anglos were tested in two groups, the visual alternative cards being handed around from subject to subject in regular, repeating sequence; they indicated their judgments by marking "L" (left) or "R" (right) in the appropriate row, defined by printed concepts, and appropriate column, defined by number 1 to 13 for the 'scales.' For the Navajo and Japanese subjects the order of presenting 'scales' was randomized within subjects; for the Mexican-Spanish subjects the order of 'scales' was simply reversed on alternate concepts; for the Anglos the order was constant for all concepts. The direction, left to right, for each visual alternative card was constant for all subjects and groups.

RESULTS

Intra-cultural synesthetic tendencies

The first step in the treatment of the data was to compute the percentages of subjects in each group choosing each of the visual alternatives for each verbal concept. In other words, before comparing *across* language/culture groups, we want to determine the consistencies of synesthetic tendencies *within* each group. Table 2 presents these data. Since there were only two alternatives for each judgment, the proportion choosing one is always the reciprocal of

the proportion choosing the other, and therefore only the percentage choosing the alternative listed at the top of each column is given, e.g., the fact that only .07 Anglos chose *up* means that .93 of them chose *down* as appropriate to HEAVY. To conserve space, the data for all four groups are included in this table, the first per cent in each quadruplet giving the Anglo data (A), the second the Navajo data (N), the third the Mexican-Spanish (S), and the last the Japanese data (J).

If we are to conclude that a particular synesthetic tendency is shared by the members of a cultural group, then we must show that a significant proportion of that group made the same choice. Accepting the 1% level of confidence as a conservative criterion of significant agreement within a group (except for the Mexican-Spanish, where the small *N* makes the 5% level seem more appropriate), then approximately 20/27 Anglo subjects (percentage values greater than .74 or less than .26 in Table 2), 28/40 Navajo subjects (percentages greater than .68 or less than .32), 8/10 Mexican-Spanish subjects (percentages greater than .79 or less than .21) and 16/20 Japanese subjects (percentages greater than .80 or less than .20) must choose the same way for the relationship to be considered non-chance.

Inspecting Table 2 with such criteria in mind, we find, for example, that Anglos agree among themselves that HEAVY is *down, colorless, thick, dark, concentrated,* and *near;* Navajos see HEAVY as *thick, dark, crooked, blunt, large* and *near;* Mexican-Spanish see it as *down, horizontal, heterogeneous, thick, dark, crooked, hazy,* and *large;* Japanese agree among themselves that HEAVY is *down, colorless, thick, dark, crooked, hazy, concentrated, large, near,* and *blunt.* The synesthetic associations for other concepts in Table 2 can be explored by the reader.

If these intra-cultural synesthetic tendencies were chance-like in their occurrence, we would expect about as many items to reach significance as the level of confidence we select, i.e., 1% of them. The fact of the matter is that 52% of all items for Anglos, 30% of all items for Navajos, 50% of all

TABLE 2

PERCENTAGES OF ANGLOS (A), NAVAJOS (N), MEXICAN-SPANISH (S) AND JAPANESE (J) CHOOSING THE VISUAL ALTERNATIVES DEFINING EACH COLUMN AS BEING APPROPRIATE TO THE VERBAL CONCEPT DEFINING EACH ROW.

	up	vert	homo	color-less	thick	dark	crooked	hazy	blunt	rounded	diffuse	large	near
HEAVY													
(A)	7*	37	37	78	93*	96*	30†	52	52	59	15	70	81*
(N)	33	65	48	50	95	85	73	63	75	45	35	87	80
(S)	10	20	20	40	90	100	100	90		70		100	
(J)	20	40	65	85	100	100	80	00	90	55	15	85	95
GOOD													
(A)	74	37	81*	11	15	26*	37	30	56	59	74	78	52
(N)	60	45	75	28	33	23	23	33	35	28	45	70	45
(S)	50	60	70	30	70	10	00	00		30		90	
(J)	45	25	90	35	25	5	00	10	45	40	50	70	95
FAST													
(A)	81	41	44	52	7*	22*	37	33	19	30	78*	22	22
(N)	50	38	50	60	30	23	40	25	43	40	70	58	58
(S)	60	60	90	80	00	20	00	40		30		10	
(J)	55	00	50	70	00	20	15	40	00	15	95	00	5
HAPPY													
(A)	89	70	63	7*	22	11*	41	41	56	78†	85	93	59
(N)	48	50	68	28	25	10	25	33	38	28	68	62	43
(S)	90	70	50	10	10	00	50	20		30		90	
(J)	60	25	95	10	45	5	00	25	95	15	45	70	80
UP													
(A)	96*	100	63	30	59	26	89	63	59	15	96*	52†	4
(N)	90	55	55	35	43	40	68	48	60	35	73	70	20
(S)													
(J)	100	95	65	20	15	10	00	00	50	40	100	15	00
ENERGETIC													
(A)	93	89	15†	22*	48†	37†	81	56	4	26	70	52	48
(N)	63	48	70	30	33	33	38	33	30	45	50	73	68
(S)													
(J)	85	75	65	10	95	85	70	25	55	55	85	100	80
LOOSE													
(A)	56	52	33	56	22	15	70	93*	81*	81*	93	70	70
(N)	35	45	38	58	45	35	75	68	83	75	28	43	55
(S)													
(J)	50	20	75	15	50	25	30	95	95	95	70	90	65
STRONG													
(A)	41	74	74	81	100	100	22	4	44	22	15	37	59
(N)	58	65	63	48	55	53	43	48	33	35	48	38	80
(S)	30	80	80	60	100	80	30	40		40		70	
(J)	25	55	65	90	90	90	65	5	65	15	35	70	85
EXCITE-MENT													
(A)	89	89	7	7*	52	52	96	81	15	22	67	67	56
(N)	44	53	51	26	51	36	53	51	36	47	44	75	56
(S)	80	80	20	10	70	70	90	90		40		100	
(J)	95	95	25	5	65	70	90	65	00	15	70	75	50
QUIET													
(A)	30	4*	93	81	22	41	00	37	100	96	41	37	26
(N)	30	33	58	55	40	35	35	53	45	40	58	23	50
(S)													
(J)	20	10	90	70	50	35	00	40	90	55	15	40	10
BLUE													
(A)	44	33	70	52	70†	93†	30†	59	78	70	44	63	26
(N)	53	50	41	15	47	29	73	70	44	44	44	50	56
(S)	90	60	60	60	70	60	60	50		70		30	
(J)	45	50	65	25	20	35	45	55	30	45	50	50	25

TABLE 2—*Continued*

	up	vert	homo	color-less	thick	dark	crooked	hazy	blunt	rounded	diffuse	large	near
BAD													
(A)	4	52	26*	89*	93*	96*	89*	67	41†	22†	15	26	48
(N)	43	58	28	83	80	83	85	88	73	73	43	33	38
(S)	10	40	10	90	100	100	100	100		50		60	
(J)	35	75	10	75	95	95	100	90	20	40	55	30	60
LIGHT													
(A)	100	67	52	15	00*	00*	41	70†	52	44	96	63	37
(N)	50	25	58	52	13	13	28	30	58	68	63	20	28
(S)	80	50	70	20	00	00	20	10		60		20	
(J)	80	55	55	25	5	5	25	95	15	70	85	25	5
DOWN													
(A)	00*	52	15	89	89†	93	89*	48†	33	44	19	33	63
(N)	13	45	45	65	38	40	70	63	48	63	35	38	85
(S)													
(J)	00	80	30	75	85	95	90	15	30	30	25	50	90
BLACK													
(A)	4	89	41	96*	100*	96*	52	37	19	48	00*	15	48
(N)	34	71	64	94	89	94	53	61	18	58	31	58	68
(S)	20	70	40	100	100	100	90	70		60		30	
(J)	25	70	40	100	100	100	80	5	45	45	5	35	80
WOMAN													
(A)	74	41	81	4*	26*	19*	56	67	89	93	48	44	48
(N)	50	50	58	35	30	8	50	58	58	55	35	35	38
(S)	80	30	60	10	50	40	70	40		70		50	
(J)	65	55	65	5	15	15	30	100	65	80	65	30	35
LAZY													
(A)	15	15	70	67	44	48	19†	59	100*	89	41	70	48
(N)	40	43	38	75	55	68	70	65	73	55	43	38	55
(S)													
(J)	25	35	65	40	60	65	60	95	95	90	70	80	45
TIGHT													
(A)	44	48	44	74	56	74†	33	7*	4	7*	7	7†	22
(N)	60	53	60	53	25	28	10	30	35	23	55	83	43
(S)													
(J)	30	80	25	85	65	85	85	5	00	00	15	5	45
GREEN													
(A)	48	48	59	4*	33†	33	44	56	59	56	78†	70	41
(N)	47	53	50	25	62	43	58	50	36	43	32	53	66
(S)	60	50	90	20	20	30	60	20		40		50	
(J)	40	40	80	5	15	5	30	55	60	90	75	50	50
NOISY													
(A)	74	89	15	19	70	56	93*	81	7	15	85	78	70
(N)	58	63	43	55	65	50	73	63	55	48	50	75	50
(S)													
(J)	70	70	15	15	70	65	90	70	5	30	75	65	85
GREY													
(A)	44	11	85	89	37†	37	48	93	81	74	52	67	41
(N)	37	27	63	48	27	31	69	69	73	63	63	37	51
(S)													
(J)	25	50	35	75	75	70	70	75	60	45	35	55	35
SLOW													
(A)	15*	26*	81	63	74†	67†	44	70	85*	93	44	78	44
(N)	35	35	53	53	28	13	38	45	73	53	43	45	58
(S)	10	20	30	50	80	80	70	80		80		70	
(J)	20	10	70	40	90	60	55	85	100	95	25	90	80
WHITE													
(A)	93	37	74	63	4*	4*	30	44	74	52	96	96	48
(N)	52	14	79	65	9	3	24	11	65	35	65	59	43
(S)	90	20	80	60	00	00	10	00		30		70	
(J)	65	40	75	90	00	5	15	45	45	60	85	85	35

TABLE 2—*Continued*

	up	vert	homo	color-less	thick	dark	crooked	hazy	blunt	rounded	diffuse	large	near
CALM													
(A)	41	7	100	59	26	15*	7	37	96	93	59	70†	30
(N)	29	29	64	42	39	31	39	51	72	51	53	34	47
(S)	50	10	80	60	30	20	10	30		60		70	
(J)	25	30	80	95	25	20	5	5	45	45	15	40	35
MAN													
(A)	63†	96	30	85	89*	89	48	22	26	22	52	67	67
(N)	64	71	56	58	68	56	61	44	41	44	50	71	71
(S)	60	90	20	90	70	80	30	60		20		90	
(J)	25	75	25	100	100	75	55	00	35	20	50	85	80
YELLOW													
(A)	74	56	37	15*	15	11*	59	78*	59	56	74	56	37
(N)	48	34	66	10	31	17	59	66	59	51	63	59	63
(S)	60	40	70	00	20	20	60	30		60		50	
(J)	65	40	60	5	30	20	45	80	50	65	80	50	50
WEAK													
(A)	52	19	48	56†	19*	26*	81	93	67	70	74	52	48
(N)	34	36	34	66	20	36	71	56	64	66	49	31	36
(S)	30	70	60	30	10	10	80	50		60		30	
(J)	60	70	15	00	10	10	50	100	65	75	80	30	20
SAD													
(A)	7	11	59	93*	70	85	41	85	78†	74	11	33	33
(N)	47	36	33	69	69	47	60	63	63	58	50	31	47
(S)	00	30	00	100	90	100	70	100		60		10	
(J)	25	70	5	100	55	65	65	90	25	40	55	5	25

* Items where all three groups (Mexican-Spanish excluded) make the same choices at the 1% level of significance.

† Items where one of the three groups (Mexican-Spanish excluded) makes a significant (1% level) deviant choice.

items for Mexican-Spanish, and 44% of all items for Japanese reach this conservative criterion. In other words, when 28 verbal concepts are judged against 13 different visual alternatives in all possible combinations (364 items), approximately half of the items yield evidence for consistent intra-cultural synesthesia.

Cross-cultural synesthetic tendencies

The principal purpose of this research was to explore similarities and differences in synesthetic tendencies across language/culture groups. To the extent that peoples in two cultures share a common basis for synesthesia, the deviations from a 50/50 selection of alternatives should be in the same direction. Thus if more Anglos judge EXCITEMENT to be *large* rather than *small*, more Navajos should make this choice rather than the reverse, and similarly throughout all items and all group compari-

sons. Our first test of shared synesthetic tendencies, then, is to compute, for each pair of groups, the percentage of items yielding the same direction of choice. For Ango vs. Navajo groups we find 65% of 364 items agreeing in direction; for Anglos vs. Mexican-Spanish 72% of 190 items agree; for Anglos vs. Japanese 78% of 364 items agree; for Navajo vs. Mexican-Spanish 61% of 190 items agree; for Navajo vs. Japanese 71% of 364 items agree; and for Mexican-Spanish vs. Japanese 69% of 190 items agree in direction. Although these percentages may not appear impressive in size, they are nevertheless significant at beyond the .005 level of confidence. The most conservative test of significance was used here, counting items where choices were 50/50 with the disagree proportion and using a two-tail test.

The preceding test includes many items where the synesthetic tendency in one or both groups is essentially chance, and gives all items equal weight (e.g., a 19/21 split counts as much as a 2/38 split). A more meaningful test, therefore, is to count only those items for which *both* groups being compared yield significant within-group agreement. In other words, if the subjects in each of two different language/culture groups agree among themselves as to the direction of synesthetic association, is the direction favored the same for both groups?

For Anglos *vs.* Navajos there were 73

items where both groups yielded significant within-group agreement; of these 86% were in the same direction of synesthetic association. For Anglo *vs.* Mexican-Spanish, 67 items met these criteria and 100% of them were in the same direction of association. For Anglos *vs.* Japanese, 98 items were significant for both and 99% (all but one) were in the same direction. For Navajos *vs.* Mexican-Spanish, we have 49 common significant items yielding 96% agreement. For Navajos *vs.* Japanese 90% of 71 shared

TABLE 3

SIGNIFICANT (APPROX. .01 LEVEL) SYNESTHETIC AGREEMENTS AND DISAGREEMENTS AMONG ANGLO, NAVAJO AND JAPANESE GROUPS

ANGLOS, NAVAJOS AND JAPANESE AGREE THAT:		ANGLOS, NAVAJOS AND JAPANESE DISAGREE ON WHETHER:	
HEAVY	is down, thick, dark and near.	HEAVY	is crooked (A) or straight (N, J)
GOOD	is homogeneous and bright.		
FAST	is thin, bright, and diffuse.		
HAPPY	is colorful and bright.	HAPPY	is rounded (A) or angular (N, J).
UP	is up and diffuse.	UP	is large (N) or small (J).
ENER-GETIC	is colorful.	ENER-GETIC	is heterogeneous (A) or homogeneous (N); is thin and light (N) or thick and dark (J).
LOOSE	is hazy, rounded and blunt.		
STRONG			
EXCITE-MENT	is colorful.		
QUIET	is horizontal.		
BLUE		BLUE	is thick, dark and straight (A) or thin (J), or light and crooked (N).
BAD	is heterogeneous, colorless, thick, dark and crooked.	BAD	is angular (A) or rounded (N); is blunt (N) or sharp (J).
LIGHT (weight)	is thin and bright.	LIGHT	is clear (N) or hazy (J).
DOWN	is down and crooked.	DOWN	is thick (A, J) or thin (N); is hazy (N) or clear (J).
BLACK	is colorless, dark, thick, and concentrated.		
WOMAN	is colorful, thin and bright.		
LAZY	is blunt.	LAZY	is straight (A) or crooked (N).
TIGHT	is clear and angular	TIGHT	is dark and small (A, J) or bright and large (N).
GREEN	is colorful.	GREEN	is thin and diffuse (A, J) or thick and concentrated (N).
NOISY	is crooked.		
GREY		GREY	is thin (N) or thick (J).
SLOW	is down, horizontal and blunt.	SLOW	is thick (A, J) and dark (A) or thin and bright (N).
WHITE	is thin and bright.		
CALM	is bright.	CALM	is large (A) or small (N).
MAN	is thick.		
YELLOW	is colorless, bright and hazy.		
WEAK	is thin and bright.	WEAK	is colorless (N) or colorful (J).
SAD	is colorless.	SAD	is blunt (A, N) or sharp (J).

significant items show the same direction of choice. For the Mexican-Spanish/Japanese comparison, 97% of 58 common significant items agreed in direction. It is clear that when we count only those items for which the groups being compared both show *intra*-cultural consistency, the *cross*-cultural agreement becomes very impressive indeed. Although the Navajo group shows slightly lower agreement with the other groups, all of these percentages are significant at well beyond the .001 level of confidence.

Having demonstrated over-all generality of synesthetic relationships, we may now consider specific agreements and—particularly—disagreements. Table 3 summarizes this information. It is restricted to comparisons among Anglos, Navajos, and Japanese; not only does the small *N* for Mexican-Spanish limit the possible significance of comparisons, but the other three groups represent extreme variations in both language families and culture. While inspecting Table 3 it should be kept in mind that *thick, near, homogeneous,* etc., refer to the visual alternatives shown in Figure 1.

A few of the significant agreements are artifactual, e.g., that UP is *up* and that BLACK is *colorless*. But most of the significant agreements across the Anglo, Navajo, and Japanese groups bring out what we feel intuitively to be appropriate synesthetic relations in our own languages of aesthetics and metaphor. Thus FAST is *thin, bright,* and *diffuse*; LOOSE is *hazy, rounded* and *blunt*; ENERGETIC and EXCITEMENT are *colorful*; BAD is *heterogeneous, colorless, thick, dark,* and *crooked*; NOISY is *crooked*; SLOW is *down, horizontal,* and *blunt*; and so forth.[2] The visual alternatives selected here are not denoted by the verbal concepts and their translation equivalents; rather, they are connoted on a synesthetic (or metaphoric) basis.

The significant disagreements are open to a number of different interpretations: (1) Differences in the metaphorical extensions of the visual dimensions themselves. This may be the case as between Anglos and

[2] The one case of cross-cultural agreement that goes against the writer's intuitive grain is that of CALM being seen as *bright*, but in this he must be idiosyncratic.

Japanese, on the one hand, and Navajo on the other, for the scales *thick-thin, dark-light* and *straight-crooked*. (2) Differences in the denotative meanings of verbal concepts, and hence unsuccessful translation. This is certainly the case for Anglo *vs.* Navajo meanings of BLUE (cf., results for color study below). (3) Differences in the connotative implications of translation-equivalent verbal concepts. This may be the case for Anglo *vs.* Navajo meanings of ENERGETIC, LAZY, FAST, SLOW, and TIGHT. It is obviously impossible to choose among these alternative interpretations on the basis of these data alone. In passing it may be noted that there were almost four times as many significant disagreements between Navajo and the other two groups as between Anglo and Japanese.

Correlation matrices

The percentage table for each group, combined as Table 2, can be used to generate two correlation matrices: (A) *Concept correlation matrix*. Here we correlate each concept with every other concept (rows of Table 2) across the *n* visual dimensions (columns), *n* being 13 for Anglo, Navajo, and Japanese correlations and 10 for the Mexican-Spanish correlations. This generates a 28/28 matrix of intercorrelations for the three main groups and a 19/19 matrix for the Mexican-Spanish. Here we are using the visual alternatives as a set of 'ink blots' and we want to know how the various verbal concepts relate to each other. Do GOOD and ENERGETIC, for example, 'mean' more nearly the same thing to the Navajo than to American Whites, in the sense that the pattern of choices by the Navajo for these concepts is more similar? (B) *Visual-alternative correlation matrix*. Here we correlate each visual dimension with every other (columns) across the set of *N* concepts (rows), *N* being 28 for the three main groups and 19 for Mexican-Spanish. This generates a 13/13 (or 10/10 for Mexican-Spanish) matrix of intercorrelations. Here we are interested in relationships among the visual dimensions themselves. Does the selection of *dark* vs. *light* tend to correlate with the selection of *thick* vs. *thin*, for example, across the set of verbal concepts for all four groups? Due to the magnitude of these

TABLE 4

CORRELATIONS BETWEEN STANDARD VERBAL OPPOSITES (IN ENGLISH) ACROSS VISUAL ALTERNATIVES FOR ANGLO, NAVAJO, MEXICAN-SPANISH AND JAPANESE SUBJECTS

	ANGLO	NAVAJO	MEXI-CAN-SPAN-ISH	JAPA-NESE
HEAVY-LIGHT	−.87	−.82	−.81	−.96
GOOD-BAD	−.92	−.91	−.55	−.75
FAST-SLOW	−.61	.47	−.73	−.52
HAPPY-SAD	−.73	−.66	−.89	−.85
UP-DOWN	−.39	−.72		−.58
ENERGETIC-LAZY	−.91	−.82		−.16
LOOSE-TIGHT	−.84	−.58		−.96
STRONG-WEAK	−.89	−.71	−.45	−.90
EXCITEMENT-CALM	−.75	−.21	−.54	−.72
BLACK-WHITE	−.82	−.47	−.75	−.55
MAN-WOMAN	−.86	−.35	−.70	−.91
QUIET-NOISY	−.95	−.62		−.92

correlation tables, they are not reproduced here,[3] but the results are summarized in the factor analyses to be reported in a later section.

(A) Concept matrices. One specific question that can be answered from the concept correlation matrices is this: do terms that are translation-equivalent to standard verbal opposites in English function as semantic opposites in Navajo, Mexican-Spanish, and Japanese? If they do function in this fashion, then the profile of choices for GOOD, say, should be reciprocal to that for BAD and hence yield a high negative correlation across the visual alternatives. Table 4 summarizes the data on this question, i.e., the correlations between concepts that are standard opposites in English for the various language/culture groups. The consistent negative *r*'s in this table permit us to conclude with confidence that Navajo, Mexican-Spanish, and Japanese groups do treat these concepts functionally as opposites. If one visual alternative is chosen as appropriate to

[3] These data have been deposited as Document number 6240 with the ADI Auxiliary Publications Project, Photoduplication Service, Library of Congress, Washington, 25, D.C. For a copy, cite document number and remit $2.50 for photoprints, or $1.75 for 35 mm. microfilm. Advance payment is required. Make checks or money orders payable to: Chief, Photoduplication Service, Library of Congress.

HAPPY (say, the *light* circle), we can predict that the other alternative will be chosen as appropriate to its opposite, SAD (the *dark* circle). Since the alternatives associated with the verbal concepts are not themselves verbal, and further, since the verbal opposites appeared independently and widely separated in the test, this seems to be an adequate demonstration of functional opposition. The oppositions are not as polar for the Navajo as for the other groups, but whether this is due to lower reliability, to inaccurate translation, or to a less clear conception of opposition cannot be told from these data. Several exceptions to the rule may be noted in Table 4: The glaring exception is the *positive* correlation between FAST and SLOW for the Navajo; we will consider this in discussion. It can also be seen that UP-DOWN functions less clearly as an opposition for Anglos than for the other groups, that ENERGETIC-LAZY is hardly a functional opposition for the Japanese, and that EXCITEMENT-CALM and MAN-WOMAN are less clear oppositions for the Navajo than for the other groups.

Highly significant agreements across all language/culture groups for other than direct opposite relations are shown in Table 5 (A). Again, because of the small sample and missing items, the Mexican-Spanish data are not included (but inspection indicates that with no exceptions the relations shown here also apply to this group). To facilitate visual inspection, relations are repeated in clusters for each verbal concept (e.g., the GOOD/HAPPY correlations appear both in the GOOD cluster and in the HAPPY cluster). Some of these consistent relations seem to reflect nothing more than we would expect from the commonness of human beings and their physical environments: it is GOOD to be HAPPY and BAD to be SAD; LIGHT (weight) things tend to be FAST and EXCITEMENT tends to be NOISY; TIGHT musculature is associated with STRONG and LOOSE musculature with WEAK; MAN tends to be STRONGer than WOMAN, and WOMAN is LIGHTer (weight). Other consistent relations across these cultures suggest 'true' shared metaphors: subjects tend to make the same synesthetic choices for WHITE as they do for GOOD, CALM, and FAST; opposed synesthetic choices are made for LIGHT (weight) vs. BLACK (i.e., BLACK has a "heavy" connotation); the choices for WOMAN are similar to those for YELLOW, but opposed to those for BLACK.

Table 5 (B) lists the most extreme cases

of disagreement among these three language/culture groups in concept correlations. Since the disagreements clearly cluster in terms of certain key verbal concepts, the table is organized on the basis of such clusters. The Navajo use ENERGETIC in the same visual metaphors as they do GOOD, STRONG, HAPPY, and TIGHT (and the

TABLE 5

A. Concept Correlations for Which Anglos, Navajos and Japanese Display *Agreement* in Direction (r > ±.50)

	A	N	J		A	N	J
GOOD/HAPPY	.88	.86	.81	BAD/HAPPY	− 93	− 87	− 87
GOOD/SAD	− .56	− .77	− .74	BAD/SAD	.57	.80	.80
GOOD/WHITE	.78	.59	.52	BAD/WHITE	− .82	− .63	− .64
HAPPY/GOOD	.88	.86	.81	SAD/GOOD	− .56	− .77	− .74
HAPPY/BAD	− .93	− .87	− .87	SAD/BAD	.57	.80	.80
				SAD/ENERGETIC	− .73	− .81	− .60
LIGHT (wt.)/FAST	.70	.50	.57				
LIGHT (wt.)/BLACK	− .82	− .55	− .81				
LIGHT (wt.)/WOMAN	.53	.53	.81				
FAST/LIGHT (wt.)	.70	.50	.57				
FAST/WHITE	.60	.82	.60				
ENERGETIC/ EXCITEMENT	.94	.65	.56				
ENERGETIC/SAD	− .73	− .81	− .60				
EXCITEMENT/ ENERGETIC	.94	.65	.56	CALM/QUIET	.90	.68	.61
EXCITEMENT/NOISY	.95	.52	.88	CALM/WHITE	.62	.52	.55
TIGHT/STRONG	.83	.66	.62	LOOSE/STRONG	− .91	− .53	− .51
				LOOSE/WEAK	.83	.75	.51
STRONG/TIGHT	.83	.66	.62	WEAK/LOOSE	.83	.75	.51
STRONG/LOOSE	− .91	− .53	− .51				
STRONG/MAN	.71	.80	.83	WEAK/MAN	− .79	− .65	− .82
MAN/STRONG	.71	.80	.83	WOMAN/LIGHT (wt.)	.53	.53	.81
MAN/WEAK	− .79	− .65	− .82	WOMAN/YELLOW	.65	.61	.87
				WOMAN/BLACK	− .66	− .57	− .84
NOISY/EXCITEMENT	.95	.52	.88	QUIET/CALM	.90	.68	.61
WHITE/GOOD	.78	.59	.52	BLACK/LIGHT (wt.)	− .82	− .55	− .81
WHITE/FAST	.60	.82	.60	BLACK/WOMAN	− .66	− .57	− .84
WHITE/CALM	.62	.52	.55	BLACK/YELLOW	− .80	− .70	− .81
WHITE/BAD	− .82	− .03	− .64				
YELLOW/BLACK	− .80	− .70	− .81				
YELLOW/WOMAN	.65	.61	.87				

TABLE 5—*Continued*

B. Some Extreme *Disagreements* in Concept Correlations Between Anglos, Navajos and Japanese

	A	N	J		A	N	J
ENERGETIC/GOOD	.05	.87	.30	LAZY/GOOD	.14	−.84	−.10
ENERGETIC/STRONG	−.26	.76	.28	LAZY/BAD	−.14	.84	−.13
ENERGETIC/TIGHT	.02	.69	.06	LAZY/HAPPY	−.04	−.80	.27
				LAZY/SAD	.65	.77	−.10
ENERGETIC/NOISY	.89	−.08	.48	LAZY/NOISY	−.80	.04	−.27
TIGHT/HAPPY	−.66	.78	−.73	LOOSE/HAPPY	.49	−.44	.72
TIGHT/BAD	.58	−.78	.69	LOOSE/BAD	−.44	.55	−.59
TIGHT/DOWN	.52	−.44	.81	LOOSE/DOWN	−.39	.64	−.66
TIGHT/GOOD	−.56	.83	−.44	LOOSE/SAD	−.19	.57	−.53
TIGHT/BLACK	.76	−.14	.82				
TIGHT/WHITE	−.49	.62	−.48				
TIGHT/SAD	.21	−.67	.53				
MAN/BAD	.44	−.39	.37				
MAN/DOWN	.49	−.10	.79	WOMAN/DOWN	−.68	.16	−.80
MAN/CALM	−.64	−.69	.20				
FAST/ENERGETIC	.46	.54	−.46	SLOW/CALM	.64	.67	.06
FAST/HAPPY	.39	.68	−.16	SLOW/LIGHT (wt.)	−.45	.62	−.35
				SLOW/WHITE	−.10	.67	−.21
STRONG/GOOD	−.44	.66	.12				
STRONG/BAD	.48	−.68	.21				
STRONG/HAPPY	−.56	.47	−.14	EXCITEMENT/	−.63	−.56	.08
STRONG/SAD	.25	−.71	−.03	SAD			
STRONG/EXCITE-MENT	−.34	.69	−.13				
BLUE/EXCITEMENT	−.55	.60	.26	GREEN/HAPPY	.80	−.02	.70
BLUE/QUIET	.58	−.22	−.04	GREEN/LIGHT (wt.)	.70	−.64	.57
BLUE/NOISY	−.56	.50	.02	GREEN/WHITE	.53	−.45	.46
BLUE/SAD	.67	−.05	−.22	GREEN/BLACK	−.78	.18	−.74
BLUE/ENERGETIC	−.67	.18	−.02	GREEN/DOWN	−.73	.20	−.66
BLUE/LAZY	.62	−.14	.15	GREEN/HEAVY	−.53	.55	−.45
BLUE/YELLOW	−.38	.70	.64	GREEN/STRONG	−.63	.52	−.64
BLUE/GREEN	.01	.66	.59	GREEN/MAN	−.55	.60	−.68
GREY/CALM	.73	.80	−.08	YELLOW/STRONG	−.89	.11	−.83
GREY/MAN	−.69	−.74	.32	YELLOW/TIGHT	−.75	.10	−.77
GREY/WOMAN	.34	.61	−.40				
GREY/WEAK	.65	.74	−.28				

reverse for LAZY); for Anglos and Japanese these concepts are essentially unrelated, except that ENERGETIC goes with NOISY (and LAZY the reverse), which is not the case for Navajos. Similarly we find the Navajo using TIGHT and LOOSE in clearly different metaphorical relations than do Anglos and Japanese, TIGHT being used like HAPPY, GOOD, and WHITE (and the reverse for LOOSE); the other two cultures reverse these relations systematically. MAN behaves like DOWN, and WOMAN more like UP, for Anglos and Japanese, but there is no relation for the Navajo; yet Anglos and Navajos agree, in contradistinction to the Japanese, in seeing MAN as unlike CALM. The FAST/SLOW relations are confused—the Japanese are

TABLE 6

A. Visual-Alternative Correlations for Which Anglos, Navajos, Japanese and Mexican-Spanish Display *Agreement* in Direction (r > ±.35)

	A	N	J	MS
up/colorful	.75	.36	.68	.51
up/diffuse	.83	.44	.75	—
vertical/sharp	.73	.44	.51	—
homogen./straight	.74	.73	.78	.66
colorless/dark	.64	.54	.51	.57
thick/dark	.94	.90	.92	.91
thick/concent.	.73	.54	.59	—
dark/concent.	.84	.47	.55	—
blunt/rounded	.87	.54	.73	.00*
large/near	.36	.37	.65	—

* M-S data not used as criterion.

B. Some Extreme *Disagreements* in Visual-Alternative Correlations Between Anglos, Navajos, Japanese and Mexican-Spanish Groups

	A	N	J	MS
N and MS vs. A and J				
homogeneous/angular	−.65	.58	−.54	.22
colorless/hazy	−.21	.16	−.52	.44
thick/hazy	−.20	.58	−.31	.70
dark/hazy	−.27	.56	−.32	.88
dark/rounded	−.29	.26	−.45	.30
crooked/rounded	−.48	.61	−.38	.53
angular/large	−.33	.67	−.31	.31
N vs. A, J, and MS				
vertical/large	−.04	.59	−.18	.05
heterogeneous/blunt	−.77	.41	−.66	—
crooked/blunt	−.49	.43	−.33	—
clear/diffuse	−.33	.49	−.56	—
sharp/large	−.35	.45	−.49	—
A vs. N, J, and MS				
dark/crooked	.04	.56	.82	.63
diffuse/large	.63	.03	−.09	—
diffuse/far	.08	.48	.43	—
J vs. A, N, and MS				
hazy/far	−.08	−.16	.46	—
hazy/crooked	.52	.85	.04	.76
N vs. J (others neutral)				
colorful/rounded	−.04	−.43	.49	.09

the divergent group in FAST/ENERGETIC, FAST/HAPPY, and SLOW/CALM correlations, but the Navajo diverge from the other two groups for the SLOW/LIGHT (weight) and SLOW/WHITE correlations. The Navajo see STRONG as most like the positive evaluators, GOOD and HAPPY, and like EXCITEMENT; the Anglos, surprisingly, see STRONG as more like negative evaluators; the Japanese treat STRONG as essentially independent of (uncorrelated with) evaluative concepts. On the color terms we find very systematic differences: the concept BLUE is clearly used differently by the Anglos than by the Navajos and Japanese; by the former it is used like QUIET, SAD, and LAZY and is uncorrelated with YELLOW or GREEN; by the latter it is used like the other color terms. The concepts GREEN and YELLOW, on the other hand, are handled similarly by the Anglos and Japanese, but 'deviantly' by the Navajo, who see GREEN as related to HEAVY, STRONG, and MAN and who see YELLOW as independent of STRONG and TIGHT (this color being significantly NOT-STRONG and NOT-TIGHT for the other two groups). Finally, the Japanese are 'deviant' in the use of GREY, failing to use it like CALM, WEAK, and WOMAN, as do the Anglos and Navajo.

(B) Visual-alternative matrices. These correlation matrices indicate which visual dimensions tend to be used the same or different ways in differentiating the 28 verbal concepts. Table 6 (A) lists the *agreements* across groups in use of visual dimensions and Table 6 (B) gives the most notable *disagreements*. Since the data for the Mexican-Spanish seem particularly relevant here, and were based on correlations over 19 concepts, they are also included. The clearest relationships within the visual frame of reference for all groups are that *up* goes with *colorful* and *diffuse*; *dark* goes with *colorless*, *thick*, and *concentrated*; and *thick* goes with *dark* and *concentrated* (and the opposites of these terms, of course, showing the reverse relations). Other specific agreements: *vertical* functions like *sharp*; *homogeneous* is seen as being like *straight* (not *crooked*); while *blunt* is seen to be like *rounded* (not *angular*); and, quite reasonably, *large* goes with *near*. These relationships within the visual framework will be found (below) to contribute heavily to the major factors extracted from the visual-alternative matrices.

The disagreements among language/

culture groups shown in Table 6 (B) are interesting. The largest number of disagreements separate the Navajo and Mexican-Spanish, on the one hand, from the Anglos and Japanese on the other—which could be due to either geographical (visual locale) or education-literacy differences. Navajos and Mexicans in the Southwest agree (in contradistinction to Anglos and Japanese): in seeing *homogeneous* as like *angular*; *colorless, thick*, and *dark* as being like *hazy*; *dark* and *crooked* as being like *rounded*; and *angular* as being *large*. Navajos 'deviate' from the other groups: in relating *vertical* with *large*; *heterogeneous* (rather than *homogeneous*) and *crooked* (rather than *straight*) with *blunt*; *clear* with *diffuse*; and *sharp* with *large*. It is possible that the Mexican-Spanish would have agreed with the Navajo on most of these relations also, but they were not tested on most of these terms. Anglos 'deviate' from the other groups on three items: they do not see *dark* as being liked *crooked*, or *diffuse* as being like *far*, but rather they see *diffuse* as like *large*, which the other groups do not. Japanese 'deviations' are restricted to the *hazy* dimension, this visual polarity being associated with *far* but not with *crooked* as in other groups (non-evaluative for Japanese?). Japanese and Navajo differ in seeing *colorful* as *rounded* (J) or *angular* (N). In interpreting these similarities and differences in the visual frame of reference, the reader should refer back to the diagrams in Figure 1 and keep in mind that it was these drawings, not words, to which the subjects were reacting.

Correlations between matrices

One way of getting an over-all picture of the similarities between groups in synesthetic tendencies is to correlate their intercorrelation matrices cell by cell. To the extent that the matched coefficients covary throughout the two matrices being compared, we have evidence that common variables are operating. This estimate of similarity has the advantage of being independent of the absolute magnitudes of the *r*'s in the two matrices; it has the disadvantage that lack of independence between the rows and

TABLE 7

CORRELATIONS BETWEEN INTERCORRELATION MATRICES FÓR ANGLO, NAVAJO, MEXICAN-SPANISH AND JAPANESE GROUPS

	CONCEPT MATRICES		
	Navajo	Mexican-Spanish	Japanese
Anglo	.43	.75	.67
Navajo		.41	.24
Mexican-Spanish			.68

	VISUAL-ALTERNATIVE MATRICES		
	Navajo	Mexican-Spanish	Japanese
Anglo	.37	.43	.76
Navajo		.81	.39
Mexican-Spanish			.42

columns makes it impossible to estimate significance levels of the *r*'s. However, gross differences in the similarities of groups can be indicated in this manner. Table 7 gives such over-all correlations for both concept matrices and visual-alternative matrices. The first thing to note is that all of these correlations are positive and, for the most part, of reasonable size. This supports the conclusion reached earlier on the basis of item analyses that there are considerable similarities in synesthetic tendencies across language/culture groups. The second thing to note is that whereas Navajo is the one deviant group for correlations of *concept* matrices (markedly lower *r*'s with all other groups), both the Navajo and Mexican-Spanish groups separate sharply from the Anglo and Japanese groups in the correlations of *visual-alternative* matrices. Another way of expressing this finding is to say that the Mexican-Spanish shift their 'allegiance' from the Anglo on concept relations to the Navajo on scale relations. This is a rather remarkable contrast.

Factor analyses

Our final interest in these data lay in the structure or system among both verbal concepts and visual dimensions, as displayed in this synesthesia task. To what extent can

TABLE 8
ROTATED FACTOR LOADINGS FOR CONCEPT MATRICES

	Factor I			Factor II			Factor III			Factor IV		
	A	N	MS	A	N	MS	A	N	MS	A	N	MS
HEAVY	−78	−25	−55	23	42	−11	−34	−31	−10	*−35	−63	−81
GOOD	*92	94	66	05	−09	40	−11	17	−49	−27	−05	−07
FAST	64	60	36	02	−30	16	26	−12	04	*65	39	83
HAPPY	*90	88	90	−06	−34	09	15	17	27	−32	07	−19
UP	45	34		−04	−13		*57	86		29	−04	
ENERGETIC	22	93		−04	−06		95	−08		07	−18	
LOOSE	44	−67		*−81	−55		−01	−09		00	−26	
STRONG	−51	74	−10	*83	11	58	−11	−25	−47	07	−35	−05
EXCITEMENT	10	52	07	−20	04	14	93	03	42	*−15	−76	−75
QUIET	19	−01		−02	−50		*−96	−47		14	45	
BLUE	−20	02	00	23	−34	−41	−68	21	−05	−28	−83	60
BAD	*−96	−98	−89	−02	13	10	11	05	03	15	−01	−38
LIGHT	89	11	77	*−27	−71	−33	29	12	10	09	64	50
DOWN	−96	−37		01	−31		12	−74		06	−23	
BLACK	*−86	−21	−91	*36	73	12	04	−49	05	14	06	07
WOMAN	62	06	47	*−39	−78	−75	−27	27	−03	−25	−16	−26
LAZY	01	−90		−20	−09		*−94	−25		−23	08	
TIGHT	−53	82		66	12		11	16		47	25	
GREEN	74	22	82	−27	18	−28	04	−23	16	−49	−86	04
NOISY	−00	−15		−13	25		*93	44		−18	−63	
GREY	10	−22		*−49	−92		−77	−08		21	02	
SLOW	−24	09	−68	−17	−81	−23	*−82	−23	−25	−37	12	−59
WHITE	*87	53	81	−09	−52	05	−21	00	−28	18	48	32
CALM	50	−04	53	−07	−83	−11	*−84	−23	−64	−04	17	19
MAN	−11	47	−18	*68	63	93	45	−12	−02	12	−34	−07
YELLOW	71	40	75	*−60	−75	−58	29	04	19	−05	−47	−18
WEAK	28	−62	28	*−90	−59	−40	−16	04	71	17	21	08
SAD	*−65	−81	−99	−19	−18	01	−69	−05	−01	06	15	−01

* Concepts tending to load in same way on a factor for all groups.

the subjects in different language/culture groups be shown to be using the same underlying factors in making their synesthetic judgments, and do these factors correspond in any identifiable way with those obtained by Suci with the usual semantic differential? Both concept and visual-alternative matrices (separately) for Anglos, Navajos, and Mexican-Spanish were factored by Thurstone's Centroid Method (with communalities fixed at 1.00), rotated by the Quartimax Method, and related across groups by the Wrigley-Neuhaus Coefficient of Factorial Similarity.[4] The Japanese data, collected later, were not submitted to factor analysis; however, both the high over-all correlations of Japanese with Anglo matrices

[4] More detailed description of these methods and references to the original descriptions are given in Osgood et al. (1957).

(Table 7) and inspection of the Japanese correlations (knowing the Anglo factors— see below) indicate that the Japanese factors would correspond closely to the Anglo factors. All correlational and factorial work was done on ILLIAC.

Concept matrices. It will be recalled that many of the polar scale terms used by Suci (e.g., *heavy-light, good-bad, happy-sad, fast-slow, strong-weak*) were included *as verbal concepts* in the present synesthesia study. If a stable semantic frame of reference is operating, one would expect the same or highly similar factors to appear in both cases. The first four factors in the unrotated Centroid Analysis accounted for 89% of the total variance for Anglos, 82% for Navajos, and 84% for Mexican-Spanish. Table 8 gives the rotated factor loadings obtained by Quartimax. Table 9 gives the indices of factorial similarity across groups for these rotated factors; the italicized values in the diagonals index the similarity among 'corresponding' factors for the several groups.

The first factor is quite well defined as *evaluative* by the concepts which load highly on it for all three language/culture groups: GOOD, HAPPY, and WHITE on the positive pole *vs.* BAD, SAD, and BLACK on the negative pole. The difference between Anglos and Navajos in what is "evaluatively relevant" is also well defined: STRONG, TIGHT, ENERGETIC, and MAN are also positively evaluated by the Navajos (conversely for WEAK, LOOSE, and LAZY), whereas the reverse evaluation, with the exception of ENERGETIC, is given these concepts by the Anglos. The first factor for Mexican-Spanish corresponds almost perfectly with that for Anglos. The indices of factorial similarity for Factor I (A/N .60, A/MS .95, N/MS .64) are consistent with these interpretations. Inspection of the Japanese correlation matrix shows that the same concepts (with the exception of WHITE and BLACK) tend to cluster together. Suci interpreted the first factor in his analysis (of Navajo, Hopi, Zuni, and Mexican-Spanish groups) as being evaluative, the clearest scales across all groups being *good-bad*, *clean-dirty*, and *pretty-ugly*.

The second factor in our study is fairly well defined across all groups as a *potency* factor: STRONG and MAN have sizeable positive loadings for all groups and LIGHT (weight), WOMAN, YELLOW, and WEAK have sizeable negative loadings. The Japanese would probably add TIGHT *vs.* LOOSE, HEAVY *vs.* LIGHT, and BLACK *vs.* WHITE to the potency factor, this being merely suggested in Table 8. The indices of factorial similarity (A/N .69, A/MS .75, N/MS .66) confirm the above picture. Suci's second factor included *strong-weak*, *heavy-light*, *hard-soft*, and *long-short* for all groups, but also *fast-slow* and *industrious-lazy* for some groups, and he dubbed it a *dynamism* factor.

Factor III is the least generalized across groups. For Anglos it is clearly an *activity* factor: UP, ENERGETIC, EXCITEMENT, and NOISY in contrast to QUIET, LAZY, SLOW, and CALM. But this pattern does not hold up satisfactorily across the other groups, as the low indices of factorial similarity (A/N .18, A/MS .52, N/MS .25) show. Inspection of the Japanese correlation data suggests that we would have ENERGETIC, EXCITEMENT, and NOISY in contrast with SLOW, LAZY, CALM, and QUIET—which is pretty close to the Anglo pattern. Suci also had difficulty

TABLE 9

INDICES OF FACTORIAL SIMILARITY FOR CONCEPT MATRICES

	Factor I			Factor II			Factor III			Factor IV		
	A	N	MS	A	N	MS	A	N	MS	A	N	MS
FACTOR I												
A		.60	.95	−.50	−.63	−.32	.13	.43	.04	−.11	.19	.34
N			.64	.25	−.09	.31	.30	.07	−.24	−.15	−.16	.09
MS				−.37	−.50	−.25	.20	.40	.04	−.14	.03	.34
FACTOR II												
A					.69	.75	.04	.38	−.53	.11	.17	.04
N						.66	.39	−.37	.02	.12	−.27	−.17
MS							.32	.29	−.30	.32	.05	−.03
FACTOR III												
A								.18	.52	.29	−.09	.08
N									.25	−.07	.11	.15
MS										.09	−.10	−.08
FACTOR IV												
A											.60	.54
N												.42

TABLE 10

ROTATED FACTOR LOADINGS FOR VISUAL-ALTERNATIVE MATRICES

	Factor I			Factor II			Factor III			Factor IV		
	A	N	MS	A	N	MS	A	N	MS	A	N	MS
up	−30	−80	−30	−91	−28	−42	−15	−34	−68	01	16	07
vertical	−86	−08	−88	−16	−08	−13	−21	00	03	24	92	−37
homogeneous	85	08	−01	−13	−25	10	−41	−80	−87	−10	−18	−25
colorless	17	15	01	82	89	74	01	23	46	−18	15	−22
thick	−34	07	−17	83	15	26	−10	34	87	26	87	07
dark	−24	08	−06	91	34	19	−12	36	95	13	81	−03
crooked	−67	−06	16	−08	−09	−51	60	88	78	10	37	−08
hazy	15	17	11	−22	−16	−08	89	86	94	13	32	−04
blunt	94	−16		−08	23		10	67		11	−37	
rounded	90	33	75	−03	19	−28	16	81	36	18	−18	−20
diffuse	−04	−61		−93	02		14	−34		15	−48	
large	28	−28	−39	−52	−20	−13	08	−55	10	72	63	85
near	−26	61		22	−12		20	−09		78	56	

demonstrating any consistent third (or further) factor in his study. Our Factor IV displays somewhat higher indices of factorial similarity (A/N .60, A/MS .54, N/MS .42), but it is difficult to come to grips with semantically. Its positive pole is best defined by FAST, LIGHT, TIGHT, WHITE and its negative pole by HEAVY, EXCITEMENT, WOMAN. There is perhaps a Freudian flavor to this factor— something which touches on many shared myths—but the quantitative data won't bear much weight.

Visual-alternative matrices. In the unrotated factor matrices for visual dimensions, the first four factors extracted accounted for about the same proportions of total variance as in the concept factor analyses— 87% for Anglos, 82% for Navajos, and 86% for Mexican-Spanish. However, the factors are not so readily interpreted (perhaps because all the variables are from a small domain). Table 10 gives the rotated loadings and Table 11 the indices of factorial similarity.

For Factor I the indices of factorial similarity only permit us to compare Anglos and Mexican-Spanish, where we seem to be dealing with a kind of *flatness* factor: *rounded* and *horizontal* best reflect the nature of the factor, with the Anglos including *homogeneous, straight,* and *blunt.* Inspection of the Japanese correlation matrix

suggests that it would duplicate the Anglo factor closely. The Navajo Factor I is actually closer to Anglo II, as the indices of similarity show.[5]

Factor II for the visual alternatives displays the highest factorial similarities (A/N .80, A/MS .75, N/MS .75) found anywhere in this study. Perhaps surprising, since this is a visual domain, it seems to be essentially an *evaluative* factor connotatively. The defining characteristics are *colorless, dark, thick, down,* and *small* (vs. the opposite, favorable pole, *colorful, light thin, up,* and *large*). An interesting difference is that Anglos would include *concentrated* in the definition of the negative pole, but not Navajo. Inspection of the Japanese data confirms this picture, *concentrated* being included with *dark, down,* etc. as with the Anglos.

Factor III for these visual dimensions also displays a high degree of cross-cultural correspondence (A/N .75, A/MS .62, N/MS .84), but one is hard put to label it. For all groups the positive pole of the factor is characterized by *hazy, crooked, rounded, heterogeneous,* and *down,* and the negative pole by their opposites, *clear, straight,*

[5] Factors were grouped so as to maximize the sizes of the indices. In this case, Navajo Factor II has a higher similarity to Anglo II (.75) than does Navajo I (.62), and hence the apparently anomalous fact that Navajo I is assigned with Anglo I where its index is only .38.

TABLE 11

INDICES OF FACTORIAL SIMILARITY FOR VISUAL-ALTERNATIVE MATRICES

	Factor I			Factor II			Factor III			Factor IV		
	A	N	MS	A	N	MS	A	N	MS	A	N	MS
FACTOR I												
A		.38	.62	−.07	.05	.19	−.08	−.19	−.27	−.09	−.54	.07
N			.54	.62	.46	.44	.20	.45	.42	.20	−.16	−.40
MS				.16	.22	−.04	.35	.45	.16	−.35	−.60	−.16
FACTOR II												
A					.80	.75	−.11	.35	.59	−.17	.28	−.29
N						.75	−.05	.35	.46	−.23	.12	−.29
MS							−.32	−.14	.15	−.30	.02	−.15
FACTOR III												
A								.75	.62	.19	.10	.09
N									.84	.06	.25	−.31
MS										.35	.60	.00
FACTOR IV												
A											.69	.62
N												.14

angular, homogeneous, and *up*. One possible interpretation would be that this is a *figure vs. ground* factor. Aspects of the visual environment that stand out as figures are *clear, straight, angular, homogeoneous,* and *up* in perceptual experience. But whereas *thickness* and *darkness* is attributed to what we have called the "background" character by the Mexican-Spanish, this is not so for the Anglos.

Factor IV seems to be what might be called a *distance* factor, but the evidence is not very impressive—particularly since there is no correspondence between the Navajo and Mexican-Spanish factors. Common to all three groups we have *large* vs. *small*; Anglos and Navajos would include *near* vs. *far*—and so would the Japanese—hence the "distance" notion; but Navajos would include *vertical-horizontal, thick-thin, dark-light,* and to some extent *concentrated-diffuse*.

Addendum: Some data on color meanings

In the course of the Southwest Project on Comparative Psycholinguistics, Dr. Susan Ervin collected semantic differential data from 21 Navajo subjects when they were judging actual samples of colored paper. These were 2¼″ by 1¾″ rectangles of dime store colored papers: red, yellow, light green, blue, purple, brown, black, and white. The red was intensely saturated and bright, the green was very pale, and the blue was about the color of the non-carbon part of carbon paper, i.e., quite deep in hue but not too heavily saturated. These color chips were rated against the 27 scales given in Table 12. These scales were *verbally* defined and they were *6-step* scales, the middle position being eliminated to force the subjects to indicate some directional choice in each case. Subsequently, Mr. Murray Miron collected equivalent data from 24 Anglos (students at the University of Illinois), using the same color chips and the same 6-step scales. Table 12 gives the mean scale positions for each color chip on each scale, Anglo (A) and Navajo (N) results being directly compared.

Non-differentiating scales and scales used differently by Anglos and Navajos. Inspecting Table 12 we can see that there are a few scales which, either for Anglos or Navajos or both, do not differentiate among the color chips—that is, are irrelevant with respect to this stimulus domain. The scale *long-short* fails to differentiate for both Anglos and Navajos. The scales *sharp-dull, up-down,* and *rich-poor* fail to differentiate for the Navajos. Asterisks between Anglo and Navajo values indicate

TABLE 12

MEAN SEMANTIC PROFILES FOR COLOR CHIPS FOR ANGLOS (A) AND NAVAJOS (N)

	Red		Yellow		Green		Blue		Purple		Brown		Black		White		
	A	N	A	N	A	N	A	N	A	N	A	N	A	N	A	N	
**good	3.9	4.2	3.0	3.0	3.0	3.5	3.3	3.5	3.8	3.5	4.4	3.8	4.8	4.4	1.8*	2.9	bad
happy	2.3	3.2	2.4	2.3	2.5	2.4	4.3*	3.2	4.0*	2.6	4.6*	3.3	5.1*	3.7	2.5	2.0	sad
pretty	2.3*	4.2	2.5	2.8	2.5	3.1	3.2	3.5	3.5	3.5	4.8	3.9	4.8	4.7	2.7	2.8	ugly
sweet	2.8	3.6	2.8*	1.8	3.7	2.9	3.9*	2.7	4.3*	3.0	4.3*	2.9	4.4*	3.4	2.5	2.2	sour
clean	2.7	3.4	2.3	2.2	2.0	2.2	3.6	3.4	3.8	2.9	4.8*	3.7	5.1*	3.5	1.4	1.5	dirty
strong	1.6	2.0	4.5	4.1	4.3*	3.2	2.0	2.3	2.3	2.8	2.7	2.7	1.8	2.1	4.0	3.3	weak
hard	2.4	2.6	4.1	3.2	4.0	3.5	2.8	3.1	3.5	3.0	2.8	2.8	2.2	2.0	4.6	4.1	soft
heavy	3.3	3.5	5.3*	3.7	5.4*	3.7	2.0	2.1	2.7	2.6	1.8	2.2	1.2	1.7	5.8*	4.1	light
large	2.5	1.9	4.3*	2.9	4.0	3.7	2.8	2.4	3.0	2.7	2.4	2.4	2.3	2.0	2.7	3.6	small
thick	2.6*	1.3	5.0	1.3	1.8	1.0	2.1*	3.0	2.6*	3.0	2.0*	3.2	2.1	2.7	1.1	1.2	thin
long	3.3	2.9	3.9	3.3	3.2	3.0	3.4*	2.4	3.0	2.5	3.2	2.5	2.8	2.7	2.6	2.7	short
fast	2.0*	3.4	2.7*	4.1	2.6*	4.3	3.8	3.3	3.9	4.1	5.0	4.1	4.5	4.4	2.8*	4.1	slow
sharp	2.0	2.7	2.6	3.4	2.7	2.7	3.9	3.1	3.3	2.8	5.0*	3.3	4.5*	3.3	2.8	3.4	dull
energetic	2.1*	4.0	3.0	3.6	3.0	3.7	3.7	3.3	3.5	3.5	4.9	4.1	4.8	4.8	3.4*	2.4	lazy
hot	1.5	2.4	2.9	3.0	4.5	3.9	3.8*	2.6	3.2	2.4	3.5	3.2	3.5	2.8	4.3	4.2	cold
young	2.1*	4.0	2.5	3.4	2.0*	3.4	3.8	3.6	4.0	4.1	4.7	4.4	5.4*	4.3	2.2	2.6	old
up	3.1	2.6	2.0*	3.1	2.7	3.5	3.3	2.6	4.0*	3.0	4.6*	3.5	5.6*	2.5	1.6*	2.6	down
smooth	4.0	3.9	2.3*	3.7	2.1*	4.0	4.0	4.3	3.5	4.4	4.9*	3.9	4.4	4.2	1.7	2.5	rough
happy	4.8	5.0	2.1	2.9	2.1	2.4	4.0	3.9	4.0	4.1	4.2	3.7	5.1	5.1	2.2	2.9	angry
ripe	1.4	1.7	2.5	2.9	4.6	3.9	3.4	3.4	2.9	2.8	3.5	2.6	3.3	2.4	3.5	3.0	unripe
rich	2.7	3.0	2.5	2.9	3.0	3.4	2.9	2.6	2.1	2.9	4.3	3.4	4.0*	2.7	2.4	2.6	poor
taut	2.7	2.2	3.8	3.3	3.2	3.8	3.3	2.4	3.3	2.7	3.8	3.5	3.3	2.5	3.7	3.1	loose
straight	3.0*	4.2	3.0	3.2	3.1	3.6	2.7*	3.8	3.7	3.8	4.1	4.3	3.9	4.0	2.9	2.8	crooked
noisy	1.5*	3.2	4.0	4.0	3.9	4.8	4.3	4.1	3.7	4.0	3.9	4.0	3.7	4.3	5.1*	4.0	quiet
male	3.3	2.5	4.7*	3.6	4.7*	3.6	2.5	2.7	3.6	2.8	2.7	2.8	2.2	2.3	4.6	3.9	female
white	3.8	3.4	2.2	2.9	2.5	2.0	4.4*	3.3	4.4*	3.3	4.7*	3.5	5.9*	4.8	1.1	1.4	black
dry	3.2	4.1	3.4	3.5	3.8	4.0	4.0	4.4	3.5*	4.5	2.7	3.4	3.6	4.0	3.2	3.5	wet

* Asterisk between Anglo and Navajo values indicates a difference ≧ 1.00 scale units.

** Means were computed so that low values are toward left-hand scale term (e.g., good) and high toward right-hand term (e.g., bad).

that the difference in means is equal to or greater than 1.00 scale unit—an arbitrary unit that probably approximates a reliable difference (Osgood et al., 1957). Looking along the rows defined by scales, it can be seen that a few scales yield four or more (out of 8 possible) differences at this level: *happy-sad, sweet-sour, fast-slow, thick-thin, up-down,* and *white-black.* Whether these represent the dimensions along which Anglo/Navajo differences in color symbolism are most marked, or merely scales for which translation equivalence was not obtained, cannot be determined from these data.

Over-all similarities in color connotations. Despite the occasional differences in connotation, indicated by asterisks in Table 12, the over-all similarities between Anglos and Navajos are quite striking, as inspection reveals. A rough way of estimating the significance of this connotative agreement is as follows: In each color column in Table 12 we note each scale for which the mean deviates 1.00 units from the midpoint (3.50) *for either group*—in other words, we count only those items where at least one of our two groups shows a probably significant connotation. Then we ask: on what proportion of such items do both groups deviate in the same direction from the midpoint? For RED we find that 12/15 go the same way, for YELLOW 14/15 the same, for GREEN 12/13, for

BLUE 6/7, for PURPLE 4/5, for BROWN 11/14, for BLACK 16/19, and for WHITE 15/15 deviate in the same way from the midpoints. Since all of these proportions approximate or exceed the 5% level of significance (by a one-tail test, appropriate because we are predicting "same" rather than "different" directions), we can conclude that in general Anglos and Navajos have similar connotative profiles for these color chips. But is there anything systematic about these shared color connotations?

Connotations of brightness (WHITE vs. BLACK). Table 12 is arranged to facilitate analysis in terms of semantic factors. From inspection of the WHITE and BLACK columns, it is clear that these chips differ sharply in evaluation for both groups, WHITE being *good, happy, pretty, sweet,* and *clean* as compared with BLACK. Other unclassified scales reflect the same tendency, BLACK being judged *rougher, angrier,* and *more crooked.* Brightness also connotes potency and activity, but less consistently; BLACK tends to be the more potent and masculine but WHITE the more active and feminine. Note that *hot-cold* reverses this trend in both groups, perhaps because of the specific association of WHITE with snow and ice.

Connotations of saturation (YELLOW and GREEN vs. RED, BLUE, PURPLE, and BROWN). Yellow is the least saturated region of the spectrum and, as noted earlier, the green used in this study was a pale, pastel shade; the other colors were quite saturated. The scales which differentiate among these two sets of colors for both groups are mainly along the potency dimensions. Thus we find the more saturated colors judged to be much *stronger, harder, heavier, larger,* and *thicker.* The same factor is reflected in the unclassified scales which differentiate these two sets: saturated colors are *angrier, dirtier,* and *more masculine,* as well as being judged *rougher* by the Anglos.

Connotations of hue (following the spectrum, from RED through PURPLE). Here we get evidence of differences between Anglos and Navajos. Anglos yield a number of activity scales which follow the spectrum (*fast-slow, sharp-dull, energetic-lazy,* and *young-old*), with RED being the most active

and BLUE or PURPLE being the most passive. The Navajos have *noisy-quiet, taut-loose, hot-cold,* and *ripe-unripe* follow the spectrum, but with GREEN at the peak of *cold, quiet, loose,* and *unripe.* The Anglos show the same trend for *hot-cold* and *ripe-unripe;* Anglos also include some evaluative scales as following the spectrum, *happy-sad, pretty-ugly,* and *sweet-sour,* RED being on the favorable sides—but this may be an effect of the particular color samples used.

Some salient differences in color connotations. In the following summary, only Anglo/Navajo differences equal to or greater than 1.00 scale unit *and* with means falling on opposite sides of the midpoint (3.50) are counted. RED is *pretty, young, energetic, straight,* and *thick* for the Anglos, but not for the Navajo (who characterize it particularly as *taut, angry,* and *masculine*).[6] YELLOW is *small, fast,* and *smooth* and GREEN is *weak, fast,* and *smooth* for Anglos, but not for Navajo (who do, however, see these pastel shades as favorable evaluatively like the Anglos). Anglos and Navajos agree perfectly on the connotative directions of WHITE, with the single exception of *fast-slow*—Anglos seeing WHITE as quite fast and the Navajos as quite slow. The remaining colors, all dark hues, are judged less favorably by the Anglos: thus, for them, BLUE is the more *sad, sour, thick, cold, straight,* and *black;* PURPLE is more *sad, sour, thick, down,* and *black;* BROWN is more *sad, sour,* and *dull;* and BLACK is more *sour, dull, down,* and *poor* than for Navajos.

DISCUSSION

This paper began with a set of questions. The first was: *can the factors obtained by Suci (1957) for Anglo controls and for the*

---

[6] In a personal communication, Professor Clyde Kluckhohn has pointed out that "color enters very prominently into Navaho ceremonialism, and therefore the reaction to such a color as red is culturally influenced in a very special way." Such ceremonial usages of color undoubtedly account for some of the differences found in this study. The fact that great similarities in color connotation are found despite such ceremonial usage may mean that the significances attached to colors in ceremonies themselves tend to follow the same rules of synesthetic translation.

Navajo (and other Southwest Indian cultures) *with verbally defined concepts and scales of a semantic differential be confirmed when his scales serve as concepts judged against 'scales' defined by purely visual alternatives?* Suci obtained two clearly identifiable factors: an evaluative factor (*pretty, sweet, good*) and a potency factor (*heavy, rich, long,* and *strong*). Our own factor analyses of the concept matrices produced two clearly defined factors also— evaluation (GOOD, HAPPY, WHITE) and potency (STRONG, TIGHT, MAN). In both cases, the third and further factors did not yield satisfactory correspondence. To this extent, then, we have confirmed the factorial generality described by Suci, in a situation where the problem of translation equivalence of scale terms is minimized.

The second question was: *can cross-language and cross-culture generality of visual-verbal synesthesia be demonstrated?* There is ample evidence for visual-verbal synesthesia within our own culture. As early as 1921, Lundholm (1921) reported data on the "feeling tones" of lines: that SAD was represented by large, downward-directed curves; that MERRY was represented by small, upward-directed lines; that GENTLE was represented by large, horizontally-directed curves, and so on. Poffenberger and Barrows (1924) confirmed and extended the relationships reported by Lundholm. Karowski, Odbert and Osgood (1942) were able to demonstrate similar relationships between word meanings and the synesthetic drawings of photistic visualizers. More recently, Scheerer and Lyons (1957), Hochberg and Brooks (1956), and McMurray (1958) have reported Western intracultural consistencies in relating line drawings and/or verbally defined visual dimensions to connotative meanings or feeling-tones. As far as I am aware, the present study is the first attempt to demonstrate that the visual-verbal synesthetic relationships characteristic of our own language/culture community are shared by peoples who speak different languages and enjoy different cultures—the Navajo, the Japanese, and the Mexican-Spanish living in the American Southwest. The over-all similarities in synesthetic tendencies across

these groups are impressive—when the synesthetic relationships that are significant (.01 level) intraculturally are tested for cross-cultural agreement, approximately 90% of the relationships prove to be in the same direction. We can conclude with confidence, then, that the determinants of these synesthetic relations are shared by humans everywhere—to the extent that our sample of "everywhere" is representative.

A third question in which we were interested was: *are terms which are translation-equivalent to functional opposites in our language also functionally opposed in other language/culture groups?* The answer to this question is important for several reasons: For one thing, the semantic differential as a measuring instrument is based on the assumption that 'true' opposites do 'slice up' the semantic space into meaningfully opposed regions; for another thing, the notion of logical opposition has always had a fundamental and primitive status in Western philosophical thought—is this merely a figment of our Western language structure, or is it really fundamental to human thinking wherever it may occur? Again, to the extent that our sample of human languages and cultures is representative, the answer is clear and compelling: peoples who use different languages and have grown up in different cultural settings also utilize meaningful opposition as a pillar of their logical constructions. This conclusion was obtained under conditions in which the verbal opposites were separated in time of judgment and were determined by association with purely visual alternatives. This over-all conclusion (see Table 4) is not countered by the occasional negative instances which were found: Landar's (1957) analysis of four Navajo folk tales implies that for the Navajo the logical opposition is between *moving-stationary*, the Anglo *fast-slow* as translated being degrees of moving; the failure of *energetic-lazy* to function as an opposition for the Japanese is also tagged as a translation problem.[7] For 11 of the 12 Anglo

[7] Both Professor Seizo Ohe (at the Center for Advanced Study in the Behavioral Sciences, Stanford, 1958) and a Japanese friend agreed that the terms we used for "energetic" and "lazy" were not really opposites in their language.

oppositions described in Table 4, functional opposition is demonstrated for the other language/culture groups as well.

The fourth question concerned the connotative meanings of colors: *do colors have similar connotations for Navajos as for Anglos, and is agreement greater for actual color chips than for color words?* A separate study of the connotations of colored papers, using verbally defined 6-step scales, revealed considerable agreement in connotation. For both Anglo and Navajo groups, the brightness dimension was shown to correspond to *evaluation* (WHITE favorable, BLACK unfavorable), the saturation dimension to *potency* (saturated colors being the more potent), and, with somewhat less agreement across cultures, the hue dimension to *activity* (RED being the most active and BLUE-PURPLE the most passive). These results agree generally with those of Ross (1938) on the effects of stage lighting on moods of the audience; of Odbert, Karwoski, and Eckerson (1942) on the relations of colors to verbally defined moods; and of Wexner (1954) on similar relations. The specific correlates between color dimensions and semantic factors found in our study agree with results obtained by Tannebaum on the use of color in both abstract art and advertising (cf., Chapter 7 in Osgood et al., 1957). Our results extend these relations to at least one group differing in language and culture.[8] Because of lack of correspondence in the yardsticks used (verbally defined scales for color chips and visual alternatives for color words), direct comparisons of the connotations of actual colors with the connotations of color words were not possible. However, my own impression, based on the frequencies of disagreements on the meanings of color words [cf., Table 5 (B)] and on comparisons between word-meanings and chip-meanings where the scales were roughly similar, is that Anglos and Navajos agree more on the connotations of color chips than on the connotations of color words. For example, whereas Anglo "blue" refers to a relatively dark color close to Navy, Navajo "blue" refers to a region of the color space close to turquoise.[9]

Despite impressive over-all similarities across the language/culture groups studied in visual synesthetic tendencies, there are some clear-cut differences on particular relations [cf., Tables 3, 5 (B), 6 (B), and 12]. Such differences are open to a variety of interpretations—with no clear guideposts as to which applies in any single case. The Navajo data are somewhat less reliable throughout (which is understandable given the difficulties of communicating instructions under field conditions). This by itself could be the reason that Navajos display a smaller number of significant synesthetic tendencies (cf., Table 2), but this finding could also indicate a greater concreteness of cognitive processes in the Navajo. It may be that pre-literate peoples—peoples without a written literature—generalize less broadly through metaphor. Differences in the denotative reference of some of the verbally defined concepts (and hence, in a sense, inadequate translation) undoubtedly contribute to some of the differences described here also.

Nevertheless, there are probably some "real" cultural differences in visual synesthesia that cannot be explained away as artifactual on any of the above grounds. For one thing, it seems possible that the Navajo do not utilize an activity factor in connotative meaning to the same extent that Anglos do; in both the factor analyses of verbal concepts (Table 8) and the correlates of color dimensions (brightness, saturation, and hue), the Anglos clearly display a third, activity factor which is only suggested in the Navajo data. For another thing, we noted that both in terms of significant differences in correlations among the visual

[8] A paper by Kimura (1950) indicates that Japanese subjects relate the hue dimension to a warm-cool scale (activity), red being the most warm; and saturation to a heavy-light scale (potency), black, blue, and red being the heaviest and green, yellow, and white the lightest. These observations are consistent with our findings for Anglos and Navajos.

[9] Dr. Susan Ervin, who collected the Navajo color data says: "The two terms that are most different in reference are the words for blue and for grey. Blue refers to any color within the range we would call green-blue-purple. The best Navajo blue is a bright aqua, about the shade of the turquoise popsicles they have in the Southwest (I think expressly for Indians!)."

alternatives (Table 6) and in the over-all correlations of the visual-alternative matrices (Table 7), the Southwest-living Navajo and Mexican-Spanish agreed with each other as against the Anglos and Japanese. The shift of the Mexican-Spanish, from "allegiance" with the Anglos on concept meanings to "allegiance" with the Navajo on visual scale meanings, was particularly striking. Does this mean that growing up in the visual environment provided by the Southwest helps to organize the dimensions of the visual frame of reference in a somewhat different way than elsewhere?

This research obviously has bearing on the Sapir-Whorf "Weltanschauung" hypothesis—but in support of the converse. Most of the discussion and research relating to this hypothesis has been designed to demonstrate that differences in language do produce differences in "world view," and certainly there is both observational (Carroll, 1956) and experimental (Brown & Lenneberg, 1954; Lenneberg & Roberts, 1956) evidence for this view. The present study and others along the same line (Kumata, 1957; Kumata & Schramm, 1956; Suci, 1957; Triandis & Osgood, 1958) strongly support the position that, for certain aspects of cognitive behavior at least, "world view" may remain relatively stable despite differences in both language and culture. The apparent conflict between these two sets of findings disappears if one makes a distinction between two general classes of cognition—which, for lack of better terms, I shall call *denotative* and *connotative*. The phenomena which seem to display generality across human groups regardless of language or culture are essentially connotative—the affective "feeling tones" of meaning which contribute to synesthesia, metaphor and the like. The phenomena which display dependence upon the structure and lexical categorizing of language seem to be essentially denotative— the multitudinous and arbitrary sets of correlations between perceptual events and linguistic events (i.e., the "rules of usage" of any language code). The distinction I am making has the status of an hypothesis, not a conclusion, but the meager evidence available seems to be consistent with it.

Finally, we may inquire into the reasons behind similarities in connotative systems despite language/culture differences. First, by virtue of being members of the human species, people are equipped biologically to react to situations in certain similar ways— with autonomic, emotional reactions to rewarding and punishing situations (evaluation), with strong or weak muscular tension to things offering great or little resistances (potency), and so on—and hence they can form connotative significances for perceived objects and their linguistic signs varying along the same basic dimensions. Such connotative reactions enter into a wide variety of meaningful situations, are therefore broadly generalized, and provide a basis for synesthetic and metaphorical transpositions. Beyond this shared connotative framework, there are many specific relations between human organisms and their generally similar environments whose stability can be the basis for synesthetic and metaphorical translations. These may be either innate to the species or developed by learning under similar conditions. An example of the former (innate) basis may be the common association of the red end of the spectrum with warmth and activity and the blue end with coldness and passivity. An example of the latter (acquired) basis may be the common association of visually large with auditorily loud—it is simply a characteristic of the physical world that as any noise-producing object approaches or is approached, increases in visual angle are correlated with increases in loudness. These "homotropisms" and experiential contingencies may be expressed in language but are independent of the structure of any particular language.

REFERENCES

Brown, R. W. & Lenneberg, E. H. A study in language and cognition. *J. abnorm. soc. Psychol.*, 1954, 49, 454–462.

Carroll, J. B. (Ed.). *Language, thought and reality: Selected writings of Benjamin Lee Whorf.* New York: Wiley, 1956.

Casagrande, J. B. The Southwest Project in Comparative Psycholinguistics: A progress report. Social Science Research Council, 1956, Item 10, 41–45.

Hochberg, J. & Brooks, V. An item analysis of physiognomic connotation. Unpublished study, privately distributed, 1956.

Karwoski, T. F., Odbert, H. S., & Osgood, C. E. Studies in synesthetic thinking: II. The role of form in visual responses to music. *J. gen. Psychol.*, 1942, 26, 199–222.

Kimura, T. Apparent warmth and heaviness of colours. *Japanese J. Psychol.*, 1950, 20, 33–36.

Kumata, H. A factor analytic investigation of the generality of semantic structure across two selected cultures. Unpublished doctoral dissertation, University of Illinois, 1957.

Kumata, H. & Schramm, W. A pilot study of cross-cultural methodology. *Publ. Opin. Quart.*, 1956, 20, 229–237.

Landar, H. J. Four Navajo summer tales. Report of the Southwest Project in Comparative Psycholinguistics, 1957.

Lenneberg, E. H. & Roberts, J. M. The language of experience. *Suppl. int. J. Amer. Linguistics*, 1956, 22, 33.

Lundholm, H. The affective tone of lines: Experimental researches. *Psychol. Rev.*, 1921, 28, 43–60.

McMurray, G. A. A study of "fittingness" of signs to words by means of the semantic differential. *J. exp. Psychol.*, 1958, 56, 310–312.

Odbert, H. S., Karwoski, T. F., & Eckerson, A. B. Studies in synesthetic thinking: I. Musical and verbal association of color and mood. *J. gen. Psychol.*, 1942, 26, 153–173.

Osgood, C. E., Suci, G. J. & Tannenbaum, P. H. *The measurement of meaning.* Urbana: The Univ. of Illinois Press, 1957.

Poffenberger, A. T. & Barrows, B. E. The feeling value of lines. *J. appl. Psychol.*, 1924, 8, 187–205.

Ross, R. T. Studies in the psychology of the theatre. *Psychol. Record*, 1938, 2, 127–190.

Scheerer, M. & Lyons, J. Line drawings and matching responses to words. *J. Pers.*, 1957, 25, 251–273.

Suci, G. J. An investigation of the similarity between the semantic spaces of five different cultures. Report for the Southwest Project in Comparative Psycholinguistics, 1957.

Triandis, H. C. & Osgood, C. E. A comparative factorial analysis of semantic structures in monolingual Greek and American college students. *J. abnorm. soc. Psychol.*, 1958, 57, 187–196.

Wexner, L. B. The degree to which colors (hues) are associated with mood-tones. *J. appl. Psychol.*, 1954, 38, 432–435.

48. A Cross-Linguistic Investigation of Phonetic Symbolism [1]

Murray S. Miron [2]

A series of recent experiments have attempted to determine the universality of phonetic symbolism in languages. In a study by Brown, Black, and Horowitz (1955), subjects were given the task of choosing from a pair of antonyms, in a language familiar to them, that word which represented a translation equivalent from a second pair of antonyms in a language unfamiliar to them. A study by Maltzman, Morrisett, and Brooks (1956), in which a single stimulus word was to be matched with one of a pair of response words, also employed materials in languages unfamiliar to the subjects in both the stimulus and response positions. Still another variant procedure was employed by Brackbill and Little (1957). In this study subjects were required to make same-different judgments for pairs of single words; the members of the pairs being from different languages, one or both of which were unfamiliar to the subjects. All procedures, however, have aimed at demonstrating greater than chance accuracy in the choice of the unknown translation equivalent. This is not the place for a lengthy statement of the difficulties inherent in attempting to establish a workable criterion of translation equivalence, except to point out that linguists have generally despaired of any really satisfactory, analytic criterion. Brackbill and Little (1957) have pointed out that the selection procedures for the items used by these investigators have not been sufficiently rigorous. It is doubtful whether any selection procedure, no matter how analytic, can avoid the possibility of bias. A translator faced with the problem of choosing a translation equivalent from among several alternative words of varying meaning

overlap might well condition his choice on the basis of a similarity in sound or form. If the translations are as dissimilar as possible, no phonetic symbolism effect would be expected. It is also clear that not all words in any given language are faithful examples of phonetic symbolism. It seems apparent, therefore, that the demonstration of any such effect may be crucially conditioned in a biased fashion by precisely the same variables that are under investigation.

Perhaps a better beginning point for demonstration of universality of phonetic symbolism would be one which attempts to determine the actual meanings *assigned* to various phonetic elements in nonsense combinations by subjects from diverse linguistic communities. Similarity of assigned meanings for subjects using different languages, although not directly attacking the problem of phonetic symbolism in natural languages, at least would assure us that some basis for a linguistic symbolic communality is tenable. Accordingly, the purpose of this study is to determine: (*a*) if systematically sampled speech sounds arranged in nonsense combinations display consistently different meanings when judged on certain descriptive (affective) dimensions; (*b*) if the changes in meaning bear any consistent, lawful relation to the phonetic properties of the sounds; and (*c*) if the meaningful differentiations of speech sounds and their relations to phonetic properties correspond across two contrasting linguistic communities, American English versus Japanese.

METHOD

Subjects

The American English-speaking subjects were 79 undergraduate and graduate students of both sexes in residence at the University of Illinois. All subjects in this group spoke English as a native language and did not have any knowledge of Japanese. The Japanese-speaking subjects were 41 Japanese foreign students and staff members with varying competence in English, employed by or attending the University of Illinois. All subjects in this group spoke the Tokyo dialect of Japanese and had resided in this country an average of 13.9 months at the time of testing. Although all Japanese subjects were familiar with English, a total of 17

Reprinted from *Journal of Abnormal and Social Psychology* (1961), 62: 623–630, by permission of the author and the American Psychological Association.

[1] This paper is based on a doctoral dissertation presented to the University of Illinois.

[2] The writer gratefully acknowledges the supervision and guidance of Charles E. Osgood.

of the 41 subjects in this group had entered the country less than 3 months before testing. A single subject had resided in the United States for a total of 54 months and represented the maximum length of time in the country for this group.

Stimulus Materials

After a careful search of several languages historically unrelated to English for correspondence in the phonemic inventory, Japanese was finally selected. The phones selected are displayed in Table 1 with the specific combinations employed in the experiment. The choice of these combinations was conditioned by three criteria: meaninglessness of the stimulus in both English and Japanese, equal representation of each of the sound elements in the total list with equal number of occurrences of each consonant element before and after each of the five vowel elements, and adherence to the phonemic distribution laws of each of the languages. Preliminary work with Japanese bilingual informants uncovered six stimulus items that were identified as real words in Japanese. An identical number were found to be listed in English source books. Exclusion of these real words found in English and Japanese was made impossible by the second and third criteria listed above.

The final stimulus list was recorded on high quality equipment as spoken by a trained phonetician.[3] Because of the presence of minor differences between the articulation of the vowel and consonant phones in the two languages, a series of compromises in the production of the sounds was attempted by the speaker. These compromises were designed to favor neither of the groups with respect to the articulations. After recording the items the experimenter and the phonetician selected the one item of several attempts on each item which best approximated the desired effect both with respect to articulation and technical recording criteria. These items were then cut out of the original tape and spliced end-to-end to form a continuous loop that could be played repetitively.

Measuring Instrument

In order to index the symbolic meaning of the stimulus materials, a 15-scale form of the semantic differential was constructed. The scales were chosen to represent, in part, the factors of evaluation, potency, and activity previously found in factor analyses of various stimuli (see Osgood, Suci, & Tannenbaum, 1957) and in part to reflect various sorts of physical dimensions deemed appropriate to the evaluation of sounds.

The scales so chosen were combined, for purposes of analysis, into three composite scales identified as an evaluative composite (E), a potency composite (P), and an activity composite (A). The scales chosen to comprise the evaluative composite were: good-bad, beautiful-ugly, pleasant-unpleasant, high-low, and colorful-colorless. Those comprising the potency composite were: heavy-light, powerful-powerless, thick-thin, large-small, hard-soft, and strong-weak. The activ-

[3] Grateful acknowledgment is extended to Elizabeth T. Uldall of Edinburgh University for her expert assistance in the recording of the stimuli.

TABLE 1

MATRIX OF CONSONANT AND VOWEL COMBINATIONS EMPLOYED IN THE EXPERIMENT

	p	n	č	š	g	
p		pin		piš		i
n	nip	nin				
č			čič		čig	
š			šič		šig	
g	gip			giš		

	p	n	č	š	g	
p	pep		peč			e
n		nen			neg	
č	čep			češ		
š		šen		šeš		
g			geč		geg	

	p	n	č	š	g	
p		pan			pag	a
n	nap			naš		
č			čač	čaš		
š		šan	šač			
g	gap				gag	

	p	n	č	š	g	
p				poš	pog	o
n			noč		nog	
č	čop	čon				
š			šoč	šoš		
g	gop	gon				

	p	n	č	š	g	
p		pun			pug	u
n			nuč	nuš		
č	čup				čug	
š	šup	šun				
g			guč	guš		

Note.—The 10 phonemic elements displayed in the table have the following orthographic equivalents: /p/ as in pat, /n/ as in nap, /č/ as in chap, /š/ as in shop, /g/ as in gap, /i/ as in cheap, /e/ as in gape, /a/ as in pot, /o/ as in note, /u/ as in shoot.

ity composite was derived from the scales: quiet-noisy, slow-fast, passive-active, and cold-hot. One additional scale was included, a familiar sounding-unfamiliar sounding scale, which did not enter into any of the composite scores. This scale was included to assess the relative familiarity of each of the stimulus items and always appeared at the bottom of the judgment forms.

All scales were translated into Japanese by a panel of five Japanese-English bilingual informants; subsequent to this first translation, a second panel of three bilinguals independently translated the scales from Japanese into English. The scales previously listed were all back-translated by the second set of informants into exactly the same form as given to the first panel of translators.

The seven-point scales were randomized as to order

and position of the adjectival opposites. Booklets of 28 pages were assembled, each page duplicating the 16 scales, one page for each of 25 stimulus items plus three practice items used in the first of two testing sessions or three repeated items used in the second session.

Procedure

Instructions for the experiment were read to the subjects in the language appropriate to each language group. In the Japanese groups this was accomplished by a native Japanese experimenter, the author ostensibly present only to handle the tape recorder. The instructions essentially paralleled those suggested by Osgood, Suci, and Tannenbaum (1957, p. 82ff.).

Each subject served a total of 2 hours, each of the hours separated by at least a week's interval. Twenty-eight stimuli were presented at each session. The first three stimuli of the first session were practice items and were not analyzed. The first three stimuli of the second session were repeated items, chosen at random (the tape loops were shuffled in a large box) from the 25 experimental items presented in the previous testing. Subjects were tested in subgroups ranging in size from 5 to 20 members. The order of the 25 stimuli was randomized for each of the groups before presentation. The two sets of 25 items were obtained by dividing the 50 stimuli at random into two sets of 25 items each. This initial division of the items remained constant for both language groups, the randomization before each subgroup presentation within the two major language groups being used only on the two separate subsets of 25 items.

Each of the stimuli was repeated until all members of the subgroup had completed checking all 16 scales for that item. In those subgroups containing a few much slower subjects, a certain amount of speeded pacing was performed. No stimulus item, however, was repeated fewer than 15 times.

RESULTS AND DISCUSSION

Scale Intercorrelations and Factor Analyses

It will be recalled that the choice of particular scales to be grouped into composites for the purposes of later analysis was made quite independently of the data collected in this experiment. The present data were analyzed, however, to determine the adequacy of these a priori decisions. This analysis took the form of two sets of factor analyses and ancillary intercorrelations of the scale means for each of the language groups taken across all of the stimulus items. That is, each of the correlations is based on an N of 50 stimulus items for which the basic entry was the mean scale position of each of the subject groups as a whole. These intercorrelations were then factor analyzed using Thurstone's centroid procedure. A total of 12 factors was extracted

from each of the language group scale intercorrelation matrices. Three of these factors were chosen for subsequent orthogonal rotation by means of the varimax criterion devised by Kaiser (1958). These factors were found to have approximate latent roots greater than 1.00 and were thus considered the major factors present in the correlation data. No other factors displayed approximate latent roots greater than one in either analysis.[4] The rotated factor structures for the two language groups are displayed in Tables 2 and 3.

It is strikingly clear that, despite some shuffled scales in the two analyses (the greater number occurring in the analyses of the Japanese data), these factors are easily identifiable as the well-established first three factors obtained from analyses of meaningful verbal material by Osgood et al. (1957). Although the choice of scales was deliberately dictated by the expectation that the same basic factors would appear in the present situation, the fact that they do maintain this structure when nonsense materials are being judged suggests that the same system of affective meaning can be extended to the new type of stimulus materials. In any case, these data justify the a priori decisions concerning the groupings of scales into composite scales. It remains to be seen whether some more extensive sampling of scales would have resulted in the factor structure identified here.

A comparison of the factor loading profiles for the two groups, using rank order correlations, was carried out to determine the degree of similarity of the two groups as to factor structure. Since the first two Japanese factors appeared to correspond most nearly to a reversal of those factors for the American analysis, these correlations were computed between Factor 1 of the American analysis, identified as the evaluative factor, with Factor 2 of the Japanese data, similarly identified; Factor 2 of the American data, the potency

[4] Raw factor analyses and analyses of variance tables have been deposited with the American Documentation Institute. Order Document No. 6767 from ADI Auxiliary Publications Project, Photoduplication Service, Library of Congress; Washington 25, D. C., remitting in advance $1.25 for microfilm or $1.25 for photocopies. Make checks payable to: Chief, Photoduplication Service, Library of Congress.

TABLE 2

AMERICAN GROUP ROTATED SCALE
CENTROID FACTOR LOADINGS

Scale	Factors		
	1	2	3
Good-bad	.82	−.08	−.04
Beautiful-ugly	.84	−.35	.11
Pleasant-unpleasant	.89	−.31	.16
Colorful-colorless	.78	.01	.45
High-low	.30	−.44	.75
Strong-weak	.12	.93	.16
Heavy-light	−.54	.68	−.40
Hard-soft	−.41	.54	.49
Powerful-powerless	.14	.90	.21
Thick-thin	−.37	.79	−.37
Large-small	−.13	.87	−.20
Passive-active	−.01	−.36	−.80
Quiet-noisy	.54	−.47	−.48
Slow-fast	−.23	.21	−.91
Cold-hot	−.60	−.09	.00
Familiar-unfamiliar	.70	.07	.16
Percentage variance	29.5	28.9	19.8

TABLE 3

JAPANESE GROUP ROTATED SCALE
CENTROID FACTOR LOADINGS

Scale	Factors		
	1	2	3
Good-bad	.27	−.88	.22
Beautiful-ugly	.45	−.82	.26
Pleasant-unpleasant	.42	−.84	.18
Colorful-colorless	.84	−.26	−.32
High-low	.70	−.23	−.55
Strong-weak	−.46	.21	−.78
Heavy-light	−.90	.32	−.10
Hard-soft	.20	.46	−.72
Powerful-powerless	−.74	.24	−.52
Thick-thin	−.95	.14	−.14
Large-small	−.90	.05	−.27
Passive-active	.14	.14	.84
Quiet-noisy	−.11	−.47	.77
Slow-fast	−.87	.15	.33
Cold-hot	.81	.03	.21
Familiar-unfamiliar	−.04	−.80	−.12
Percentage variance	40.1	22.6	22.1

factor, was compared with its counterpart, Factor 1 of the Japanese; and the third or activity factors in each group were compared with one another. Loadings on the evaluative factors of the American and Japanese data correlated .89, the potency factor of the two groups correlated .74, and the activity factor in each group correlated .64. All correlations are significant at the .01 level. Thus it may be concluded, at least with respect to the profiles of factor loadings, that the two language groups use similar semantic dimensions.

Analyses of Variance

In view of the foregoing findings of reasonable independence of the three composite measures, the original decision to carry out independent significance tests on each of these composite measures appeared to be justified.

Assessment of the significance of the differences obtained in this experiment took the form of six separate four-variable classification analyses of variance, one for each of the three composite measures in each of the two language groups. The experimental classifications were those for consonant, vowel, position, and subject effects. The position variable represents the grand means for each of two equal subsets of the 50 stimulus items, each subset conforming to the experimental requirement of equal representation of all consonant elements before and after each of the vowel elements exercised for the stimulus list as a whole. Thus we have two miniature subsets of 25 stimulus items, each duplicating the experimental conditions imposed upon the original 50-item list. All variables with the exception of the subject effect were assumed to be fixed. The over-all model for the analysis is therefore of the mixed type. It was assumed that the interaction effects of the observations in which fixed and random effects enter are to be treated as random sampling variables. Tests of the random variable interactions and the subjects main effect were made utilizing the highest order interaction, or residual, in this analysis.

A summary of the significance levels found in all analyses is presented in Table 4. Only the .01 and .05 levels are reported, even though in most instances the F ratios were significant far beyond the .01 level.[5]

Inspection of the analyses for American subjects, displayed in Table 4, reveals that all main effects for all composite scores with the exception of the position effect are significant at the .01 level. The position effect reaches significance at the .05 level in the activity score analysis. Since all phoneme elements, as well as all consonant-vowel transitions, are

[5] See Footnote 4.

TABLE 4

Summary of Significance Levels for Analysis of Variance of American and Japanese Group Composite Scores

Source	American Group			Japanese Group		
	E	P	A	E	P	A
Consonant	.01	.01	.01	.01	.01	.01
Vowel	.01	.01	.01	.01	ns	.01
Position	ns	ns	.05	ns	ns	ns
Subject	.01	.01	.01	.01	.01	.01
V × C	.01	.01	.01	.01	.01	.01
V × P	.01	ns	.05	ns	ns	.05
V × S	.01	.01	.01	.01	.01	.01
C × P	.01	.01	ns	.01	.01	ns
C × S	.01	.01	.01	.01	.01	.01
P × S	ns	ns	ns	ns	ns	ns
V × C × P	.01	.01	.01	.01	.01	.01
V × C × S	ns	ns	ns	ns	.05	ns
V × P × S	ns	ns	ns	ns	ns	ns
C × P × S	ns	ns	ns	.01	.01	ns
V × C × P × S	—	—	—	—	—	—

represented an equal number of times in both sublists, the position effect provides a test of the adequacy of the experimental controls in randomizing the individual bias effects accruing to specific phoneme combinations. The activity composite score analysis indicates that this division was not adequate and represents a caveat that must be borne in mind in interpreting the effects of consonant position with regard to that score. The vowel × position and subject × position interactions provided a similar check on the adequacy of counterbalancing with respect to the vowel and subject determinations, respectively. The P × S interactions are all nonsignificant in these analyses. Two of the V × P interactions reached significance at or beyond the .05 level in the American data analysis. The bias reflected by these significant interactions is undoubtedly due to disproportionate effects of specific vowel-consonant combinations, the total effect of which is made more apparent because of the smaller number of items in the shortened sublists.

The higher order interactions were, as can be seen, uniformly nonsignificant in the American analyses, with the exception of the V × C × P effects. This latter interaction provided a test equivalent to a simple subjects by items analysis of variance and indicates that the stimulus items were reliably differentiated in the aggregate.

Inspection of the Japanese data analyses

reveals that these results are in almost all regards parallel to those found for the American group. The most notable exception is the C × P × S interaction. The CVC pattern is relatively uncommon in Japanese. This fact could well account for the idiosyncratic subject judgments of the consonant-position combinations and hence for the significant variance contribution of this interaction. Notice should also be taken of the nonsignificant vowel effect for the potency composite measure in this group.

With the specific exceptions apparent in the table, the two sets of analyses indicate reliable differentiation of the phoneme elements, consonant positions and unique stimulus items. In addition, even though subjects were reliably differentiated with respect to judgments of these phoneme elements, such differences were not great enough to obscure the obtained differences between the elements themselves. Further, the absence of significant highest order interactions and stimulus-list subset biases, with several notable exceptions, lends credence to the utility of the experimental design.

Familiarity Judgments

In order to assess the extent of the influence of the subjects' judgments of the familiarity of the stimulus items upon the composite measure judgments, the familiarity scale scores were correlated with each of the composites. These correlations took the form of Pearson product-moment coefficients, for which the N was the 50 stimuli. The correlations for the American data between familiarity judgments and the evaluative, potency, and activity composites were: .59, −.15, and −.12, respectively. In the Japanese data, correlation coefficients between familiarity judgments and evaluative, potency, and activity composites were: .50, −.15, and −.02, respectively. In addition, the mean familiarity judgments indicated that the stimuli were in truth relatively unfamiliar, although significant internal variation in this regard was present. If the subjects' judgments of these nonsense stimuli had been conditioned by some generalization from close real-word associates, the covariation of the familiarity and composite measures should have been much more extensive. The data, however, support a conclusion that attributes the meanings assigned to these stimuli on the basis of inherent symbolic content other than, or at least beyond, that which might accrue to generalization from real words more familiar to the subjects.

Composite Scale Means

The preceding results indicate that we are justified in examining the stimulus configurations and phoneme element means in some detail in order to determine the precise nature of the symbolic content obtained. The individual phoneme element trends are displayed in Figures 1, 2, and 3. These displays are ordered so that the stimulus elements follow the organogenetic descriptions of the elements with regard to articulatory position from "front" to "back," in the classical sense of these terms.

Inspection of Figures 1 and 2 indicates, in general, that the more anterior consonant or vowel elements are judged to be more positive in evaluation and more negative in potency than the more posterior elements. The functions are hardly monotonic in character, although the direction of the change as a function of the stimulus dimension is surprisingly regular in character for the evaluative and potency composites. The activity composite means are much more erratic in terms of the dimension employed. This composite measure, on the other hand, accounted for the least amount of total judgment variance of the three composites as determined by means of the factor analyses.

Of the alternative orderings of the phoneme elements in terms of physical correlates, the organogenetic basis is probably not the most desirable. Instead, since the acoustic end-product of the articulatory modifications corresponds more closely to the proximal stimulus giving rise to the perception of these stimuli, it might seem reasonable to turn to this type of description as a basis for the stimulus ordering. Fairbanks (1960) has dramatically demonstrated that the organogenetic description, however, is almost perfectly correlated with the acoustic description in terms of formant locations. His vowel plots using Formant 1 and 2 coordinates indicate that the two descriptive systems are highly redundant. Although the stimuli were not actually submitted to any harmonic analysis, it is possible to use data collected by Fairbanks and others

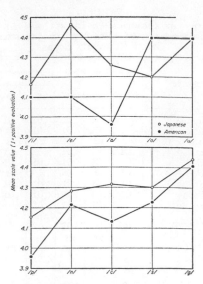

FIG. 1. American and Japanese group mean evaluative composite scores for vowels (upper) and consonants (lower).

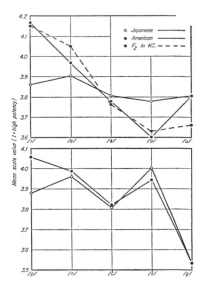

FIG. 2. American and Japanese group mean potency composite scores for vowels (upper) and consonants (lower).

in assessing the degree of covariation of these judgments with other acoustical analyses of the phonemes selected. The upper display of Figure 2 shows the relative values of Formant 2, after rescaling, as taken from data collected by Holbrook (1958). The most striking difference between the two descriptive systems in terms of the judgmental data collected in

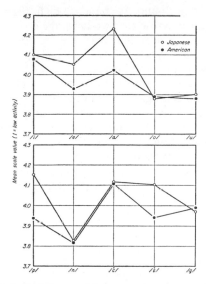

FIG. 3. American and Japanese group mean activity composite scores for vowels (upper) and consonants (lower).

this experiment involves the return of the potency judgments for the vowel /u/ to a higher level, ("weaker" judgments) giving the function a J-shaped character. The F_2 formant values follow this function at all points for the American data. (It will be recalled that the Japanese data did not disclose a significant vowel effect for this composite measure.)

At least one reasonable interpretation for the obtained effect on this composite measure derives from the nearly universal correlation between high pitches and small objects to be found in nature. Thus by metaphorical extension, to a correspondence between small objects and weakness. A previous experiment reported by Solomon (1959), in which passive sonar signals were evaluated on a set of semantic differential scales similar to those used in this study, obtained almost identical results. Scales that were classified as contributing to a potency composite were found to distinguish between sonar signals having a preponderance of energy in the lower octave bands from those with energy concentrated in the higher bands. The direction of the correspondence was as reported in this study, i.e., the greater the low frequency energy in the signal, the "heavier" and "stronger" the judgments, and vice versa.

Cross-Linguistic Correspondences

In order to assess the over-all correspondence of the two language groups in phonetic symbolism tendencies, product-moment correlations were computed for each of the composite scores utilizing all determinations available within each group, i.e., the individual mean judgments for each of the stimulus items. These correlations were found to be .46, .53, and .54 for the evaluative, potency, and activity composites, respectively. All correlations are significant at the .01 level with 49 df. The summary measures for each of the composite scores for each of the five vowel and consonant phoneme elements, as displayed in the foregoing exhibits, were also compared across the two language groups. The evaluative composite correlation coefficient for the vowel elements was computed to be .23 and that for consonants .95. The coefficient computed for the vowel elements is not significant while the consonant correlation reaches significance at the .01 level. The comparable correlations for the potency composite were found to be .57 and .91 for the vowel and consonant elements, respectively. The activity composite correlations were .61 for the vowels and .64 for the consonants. All correlations for these second two composites are significant at the .05 level or beyond. As can be seen, the coefficients for the consonant correlations are uniformly higher than those for the vowels. If we assume for a moment that phoneme element judgments may be conditioned in part by some imaged articulatory posture characteristic of the sound elements, the foregoing result suggests an interesting conclusion: Since the consonants are more easily discriminated with respect to articulatory production, i.e., they are characterized by more easily identifiable muscle features of more diverse kinds, it is possible that the higher degree of correspondence obtained for these elements reflects the presence of this greater number of discriminable cues.

In conclusion, it seems clear that, although this study does not afford direct evidence regarding the existence of phonetic symbolism in natural languages—evidence difficult to obtain in any study—the magnitude of the differences in meanings assigned to these stimuli and the similarity of these meanings across the two language groups provides at least indirect evidence of its presence and generality.

SUMMARY

An experiment is reported in which a set of 50 nonsense stimulus items of CVC shape were judged on a set of 16 semantic differential scales by two groups of subjects with contrasting linguistic backgrounds. The subject languages used were Japanese and English. Experimental stimulus controls took the form of an incomplete latin square design in which each of five consonant elements preceded and followed each of five vowel elements an equal number of times with all elements represented and equally frequent in the final matrix.

The mean judgments for all subjects in both groups indicated a general trend toward evaluating the front vowels and consonants as "pleasant" and "weak" and the back vowels and consonants as more "unpleasant" and "strong."

Four-way analyses of variance indicated that, in the main, the phoneme elements, the consonant positions, and the phoneme combinations were reliably differentiated in the aggregate by the subjects of both groups.

Data collected on the familiarity of the stimulus items showed significant internal variation but was shown to covary with evaluative scores only.

Centroid factor analysis of the scale intercorrelations revealed the presence of three factors that accounted for a high percentage of the total judgment variance for both groups. These factors were easily identifiable as corresponding to previously observed dimensions and were found to have a high degree of similarity across the two language groups.

It was concluded that the materials had expressive symbolic value accruing to their inherent phonetic content and not to any meanings via real-word associates. These affective meanings were found to bear consistent, lawful relations to the phonetic properties of the sounds. The fact that these meaningful differentiations and their relations to phonetic properties proved to be highly similar across two contrasting linguistic groups suggests that the laws governing phonetic symbolism may have a universal character.

REFERENCES

BRACKBILL, YVONNE, & LITTLE, K. Factors determining the guessing of meanings of foreign words. *J abnorm. soc. Psychol.*, 1957, **54,** 312–318.

BROWN, R., BLACK, A., & HOROWITZ, A. Phonetic symbolism in natural languages. *J. abnorm. soc. Psychol.*, 1955, **50,** 388–393.

FAIRBANKS, G. *Voice and articulation drillbook.* New York: Harper, 1960.

HOLBROOK, A. An exploratory study of diphthong formants. Unpublished doctoral dissertation, University of Illinois, 1958.

KAISER, H. The varimax criterion for analytic rotation in factor analysis. *Psychometrika*, 1958, **23,** 187–200.

MALTZMAN, I., MORRISETT, L., JR., & BROOKS, L. O. An investigation of phonetic symbolism. *J. abnorm. soc. Psychol.*, 1956, **53,** 249–251.

OSGOOD, C. E., SUCI, G., & TANNENBAUM, P. *The measurement of meaning.* Urbana: Univer. Illinois Press, 1957.

SOLOMON, L. N. Search for physical correlates to psychological dimensions of sounds. *J. Acoust. Soc. Amer.*, 1959, **31,** 492–497.

49. Vectors of Prose Style

John B. Carroll

The very concept of style implies variation. It takes little argument or evidence to secure agreement that there are different manners of writing, and that these differ among themselves not only by virtue of the content or the subject matter treated but also by virtue of a host of "stylistic" elements which are present in varying degree in samples of prose. But what, exactly, are these stylistic elements? Ever since man discovered the pleasure of commenting upon his own and others' oral and written compositions, he has been seeking a useful set of pigeonholes for classifying style. The tendency has been for the classifications to proliferate without design or system. Literary criticism today does not have any well and sharply defined set of elements by which a sample of prose may readily be characterized.

In 1935, the renowned psychologist L. L. Thurstone published a book (**414**) in which he presented the technique of what is generally known as *factor analysis*—a statistical procedure for identifying and measuring the fundamental dimensions ("vectors") that account for the variation to be observed in any set of phenomena. Since then factor analysis has·been a tool widely used by psychologists in studying intelligence, personality, interests, emotions, rates of learning, and even word meanings, but the technique has never heretofore been applied to the study of literary style. If we can study the "personalities" of people by factor analysis, we should be able to study the "personalities" of samples of prose. In the simplest possible terms, factor analysis enables the investigator to apply a large number of measurement procedures to a sample of objects and find out to what extent these measures overlap with each other.

Although the objective study of literary style by means of statistical analysis is not a completely novel endeavor, none of the scholars who have engaged in such study has ventured to ask the question raised here: what are the basic dimensions in which style varies? In contrast to previous statistical studies of style, each of which has fixed attention on one or a

Reprinted from Thomas A. Sebeok (Ed.), *Style in Language* (New York: John Wiley & Sons, 1960), by permission of the author and the publisher.

small number of the possible ways of measuring style, this investigation[1] examines the relations among a large number of indices of style and attempts to identify the most salient ways of describing stylistic variation in prose.

The notion of attempting to quantify aspects of literary style will be repulsive to many literary critics and outright ridiculous to others. The writer must confess that even he, after completing the study, remains skeptical whether the dimensions identified here adequately represent the aspects of style that truly make the difference between great literature and the not so great, or even the aspects that serve to differentiate some of the recognized styles of writing. Nevertheless, some of the hopes in which the study was undertaken seem to have been realized: the study points to some of the more obvious characteristics of prose which have to be observed, mentioned, and duly noted before the literary critic can really go to work. It injects a semblance of order into the study of "readability" and suggests certain bases for guiding the teaching of English composition in schools. Further, it provides leads toward the psycholinguistic study of the "encoding" processes by which the individual translates nonverbal prelinguistic states of behavior into linguistically encoded output. It lends some support to the notion that certain factors of literary style correspond to predispositional "sets" which govern the emission of large classes of verbal responses—personal pronouns, for example.

PROCEDURES

There are two distinct kinds of problems to be faced in designing any study that seeks to identify the major dimensions of a set of phenomena: (1) how can we obtain a sufficiently heterogeneous sample of the things we want to study, and (2) what measurements shall we take in order to sample

[1] The research reported herein was performed pursuant to a contract with the United States Office of Education, Department of Health, Education, and Welfare. Reproduction in whole or in part is permitted for any purpose of the United States Government. I am indebted to the eight raters used in the study, Zita Gray, Grace Kestenman, Don McCaull, R. Dale Painter, Mrs. Newton Press, Dr. E. H. Sauer, Mrs. Mary G. Seifel, and Mary Alice Tomkins, and to Marilyn Brachman, Mrs. Mary S. Carroll, Arthur S. Couch, Marjorie Morse, Frederic Weinfeld, and Mrs. Marcia Wideman for their help in various aspects of analysis. The statistical computations were performed by means of facilities made available at the Littauer Statistical Laboratory of Harvard University, the Computation Center of Massachusetts Institute of Technology, and the John Hancock Life Insurance Company, and thanks are hereby tendered to each of these organizations. A longer and more detailed report of the study is being submitted for publication elsewhere.

all the significant ways in which the phenomena vary? Practical considerations set certain limits in both of these problems.

The sample of objects studied here consisted of 150 passages from various sources and styles of English prose. Each passage was chosen so as to be more or less self-contained within a little more than 300 words. By selecting passages according to categories—novels (both British and American, both nineteenth and twentieth centuries), essays, newspaper features and editorials, biographies, scientific papers, textbooks, speeches, legal documents, personal letters, and sermons were among the categories used—we hoped to include the widest possible assortment of subject matters and styles. The sample even included several relatively low-grade high-school English compositions.

The measures taken on these 150 passages fell into two classes: subjective and objective. The objective measures involved various counts, indices, and ratios based on the enumeration of certain classes of words, clauses, sentences, and other linguistic entities and included some of the measures used in previous statistical studies of style. Subjective measures were secured partly to help in the interpretation of results for the objective measures, partly to provide bench marks for certain characteristics of style which the objective measures could hardly be expected to describe. It was of intrinsic interest, also, to study the extent to which a group of competent judges could agree in assigning ratings, and to determine the totality of ways they could find for characterizing the passages. In order to make the rating task as simple as possible, 29 adjectival scales were chosen with a view to covering the major qualities and traits of style as far as they could be determined a priori, and 8 expert judges—all with interest and training in English literature—were secured to rate each of the 150 passages on each of the 29 scales, the form of which may be illustrated as follows:

meaningless ___ : ___ : ___ : ___ : ___ : ___ : ___ meaningful

The 8 judgments obtained for each passage on each scale were then averaged.

In all, 68 scores were obtained for each of the 150 passages: the 29 averaged ratings of the 8 judges, and 39 objective measures. The names of the measures are listed in the first column of Table 1; unfortunately, space does not permit a full description of the procedures for obtaining the objective measures. The resulting 68 × 150 scores formed the basis for the ensuing statistical analysis. The correlation of each measure with each other measure was determined—the results being exhibited in a very large table with 68 rows and 68 columns. This *correlation matrix* was then subjected to a factor analysis in order to determine how many fundamental

Table 1. Results for 68 Measures of Prose Style; Reliability Coefficients and Loadings on Six Dimensions (Factors) of Prose Style

Variable	Variable Number	Reliability	General Stylistic Evaluation A	Personal Affect B	Ornamentation C	Abstractness D	Seriousness E	Characterization F
*Subjective Ratings**								
Profound-superficial	1	.84	.43	−.11	.06	.53	.41	.15
Subtle-obvious	2	.81	.20	−.17	.09	.72	−.09	.15
Abstract-concrete	3	.90	.02	−.01	.18	.64	.11	.16
Meaningful-meaningless	4	.70	.70	−.11	−.04	.04	.41	.03
Succinct-wordy	5	.78	.51	−.15	−.65	−.15	.14	−.01
Graceful-awkward	6	.73	.84	−.01	.07	.17	−.08	.12
Vigorous-placid	7	.80	.26	.63	.17	−.06	.21	−.10
Lush-austere	8	.80	−.01	.43	.55	.07	−.29	.17
Earnest-flippant	9	.87	.06	−.05	−.01	.05	.71	.13
Intimate-remote	10	.87	.10	.82	.02	−.33	.03	−.01
Elegant-uncouth	11	.82	.33	.29	.44	.40	−.11	.02
Natural-affected	12	.80	.49	.06	−.51	−.26	.29	.08
Clear-hazy	13	.78	.72	.16	−.09	−.45	.10	−.17
Interesting-boring	14	.78	.84	.25	−.04	.12	.01	.06
Strong-weak	15	.64	.88	.21	.13	.00	.11	−.07
Opinionated-impartial	16	.89	−.01	.53	.36	.01	.07	.02
Original-trite	17	.77	.54	−.08	.04	.44	−.20	.15
Ordered-chaotic	18	.69	.65	−.29	−.04	−.15	.06	−.09
Vivid-pale	19	.80	.61	.54	.07	−.09	−.05	−.01
Personal-impersonal	20	.86	.03	.83	.14	−.26	.00	.01
Precise-vague	21	.71	.64	.00	−.10	−.47	.03	−.17
Masculine-feminine	22	.85	.22	.06	.08	−.08	.58	−.09
Varied-monotonous	23	.75	.75	.22	.04	.20	−.10	.15
Emotional-rational	24	.90	−.05	.77	.22	−.12	−.02	.09
Complex-simple	25	.82	−.09	−.18	.48	.51	−.07	.04
Pleasant-unpleasant	26	.75	.88	.15	−.03	.07	−.11	.08
Serious-humorous	27	.92	.01	−.12	.00	.13	.70	.08
Florid-plain	28	.82	−.08	.33	.66	.16	−.28	.11
Good-bad	29	.74	.95	.01	−.02	.12	−.05	.02

Objective Measures (All based on 300 words)

	No.						
No. paragraphs	30	—	−.09	−.13	−.50	−.02	−.23	−.03
No. syllables	31	.86	−.10	−.58	.30	.05	.09	−.23
No. sentences	32	.85	.05	−.03	−.61	.13	−.18	.05
Standard deviation sentence length	33	.17	.11	.25	.54	.00	.12	−.01
No. clauses	34	.78	.01	.28	−.60	.25	−.22	.04
Clause complexity index	35	.60	−.08	.18	.39	.02	.18	−.15
% noun clauses	36	—	−.02	.01	−.22	.45	.13	−.25
% adjectival clauses	37	—	−.13	−.07	.19	−.21	.05	.34
% adverbial clauses	38	—	.11	.09	.04	−.20	−.17	.06
% parenthetical clauses	39	—	−.01	.04	.08	−.01	−.02	−.29
% "action" verbs	40	.76	.06	.11	−.40	−.17	−.23	−.01
% "cognitive" verbs	41	.58	.06	.46	.07	.12	.05	−.06
% transitive verbs	42	.33	.01	−.06	.03	−.15	−.03	−.63
% intransitive verbs	43	.26	−.14	.14	−.09	−.05	−.17	.32
% copulative verbs	44	.44	.04	−.04	.06	.18	.12	.43
% Latin-derived verbs	45	.57	−.06	−.33	.20	.12	.10	−.25
% passive verbs	46	.49	−.06	−.45	.15	−.07	.16	.12
Mean tense	47	.88	−.12	−.15	.11	−.02	−.01	.04
Entropy of tense	48	.42	−.16	.07	−.02	.06	−.04	−.29
No. infinitives	49	—	.04	.16	−.14	−.01	.05	−.02
No. participles	50	—	.08	−.08	.17	−.31	−.07	−.15
No. gerunds	51	—	.13	−.20	−.03	.08	−.04	−.15
No. proper nouns	52	.83	−.04	.01	−.03	.01	−.01	−.38
No. common nouns	53	.74	.01	−.49	.18	−.22	−.11	.13
% unmodified common nouns preceded by "the"	54	.45	.07	.07	−.50	.10	.03	.18
% nouns with Latin suffixes	55	.69	−.06	−.22	.42	.22	.20	−.22
No. articles	56	.52	.18	−.28	−.11	.01	.04	.20
% indefinite articles	57	.48	.07	−.09	−.10	−.01	−.48	.01
No. personal pronouns	58	.84	.11	.60	−.23	.20	−.10	−.09
No. possessive pronouns	59	.64	−.07	.30	.09	.08	−.21	−.14
No. indefinite pronouns	60	.43	.01	.28	−.18	.14	.21	.27
No. indefinite and quantitative determiners	61	.27	−.13	−.09	.11	−.24	.35	.20
No. demonstrative pronouns	62	.44	−.13	.11	−.05	.05	.22	.13
No. numerical expressions	63	.67	−.01	−.07	−.09	.49	−.06	−.02
No. prepositions	64	.58	.01	−.34	.35	−.01	.09	−.01
No. pronouns	65	.83	−.01	.58	−.26	.18	−.14	−.13
No. determiners	66	.52	−.19	.01	.00	−.45	.34	.25
No. descriptive adjectives	67	.66	.11	−.18	.38	.09	−.10	.20
No. participial modifiers	68	.38	.09	−.05	.33	.01	−.13	−.01

* The positive pole of the adjectival scales is represented by the *first* of the two adjectives specified.

dimensions would be needed, at a minimum, to account for all the inter-relations among the 68 measures.[2]

RESULTS

The formidable appearance and size of Table 1 are due simply to the desire to compress a maximum of the essential results of the study into a single table; the reader is invited to examine it carefully. It contains information bearing on two kinds of questions about the 68 measures. (1) How "reliable" are the measurements? In the case of the 29 subjective measures, this question relates to the extent to which the judges agreed in their ratings. A reliability coefficient of 1.00 would denote perfect agreement, and a coefficient of .00 would denote purely random agreement. In the case of the 39 objective measures, the coefficients given in Table 1 (where they are present at all) refer to the extent to which each measure gives consistent results from the first half of a 300-word sample to the second half. (2) What general trait or traits does each variable measure and to what extent? The data relevant to this question are the coefficients found in the last six columns of the table. All coefficients larger than about .25 in absolute magnitude may be regarded as significant for purposes of interpretation.

The reliability coefficients (in the first data column of Table 1) for the 29 averaged subjective ratings range from .64 for the scale *weak-strong*, to .92 for the scale *humorous-serious*, with a median at .80. Although the figures are high enough to suggest that each measure is sufficiently reliable to give meaningful results, the lack of perfect agreement is particularly noticeable for some scales. Some scales, such as *meaningful-meaningless* and *ordered-chaotic*, have low reliability because, we may guess, judges differ in their conceptions of how these terms apply to prose passages. It is of more than passing interest that scales which (as will be seen later) denote general stylistic evaluation, such as *good-bad*, *pleasant-unpleasant*, *strong-weak*, *interesting-boring*, *graceful-awkward*, *varied-monotonous*, *clear-hazy*, have uniformly low reliabilities, whereas such scales as *serious-humorous*, *abstract-concrete*, *emotional-rational*, *opinionated-impartial*, *earnest-flippant*, *intimate-remote*, and *personal-impersonal*, all of which refer to specific and relatively nonevaluative qualities of style, have high reliabilities. Judges can often agree in making descriptive classifications

[2] Of possible technical interest to some readers is the fact that the initial factor analysis was performed by means of Thurstone's centroid method, after which the factors were "rotated" to oblique simple structure by the writer's so-called *normal biquartimin* criterion (57). All these computations were performed with the aid of high-speed electronic computing machines.

of prose passages but they agree less often in making general evaluations of style. Perhaps this is what makes literary criticism exciting.

Concerning the reliabilities of the objective measures, we shall only comment that the figures indicate the extent to which a writer is likely to hold certain formal characteristics of his style constant within relatively short stretches.

We come now to the main findings of the study, the findings that give a provisional answer to the question of what are the dimensions of literary style. Although *seven* dimensions were indicated by the factor analysis technique, it appeared that only six of these could be given meaningful interpretation, and thus the data for the seventh are omitted from Table 1. The order in which the six remaining factors are discussed is actually immaterial, but they are listed in Table 1 as factors *A, B, C, D, E,* and *F,* in order of their apparent interest, importance, and relevance in connection with the study of literary style.

The variables having high coefficients in column *A* of Table 1 are in every case subjective ratings. In order of the magnitude of their "loadings" (as the coefficients are often called) they are the scales *good-bad* (29), *pleasant-unpleasant* (26), *strong-weak* (15), *interesting-boring* (14), *graceful-awkward* (6), *varied-monotonous* (23), *clear-hazy* (13), *meaningful-meaningless* (4), *ordered-chaotic* (18), *precise-vague* (21), *vivid-pale* (19), *original-trite* (17), *succinct-wordy* (5), *natural-affected* (12), *profound-superficial* (1), *elegant-uncouth* (11), and *vigorous-placid* (7). All these scales, in differing degrees, denote over-all positive or negative evaluation of a prose passage. We are therefore inclined to identify this factor by the name General Stylistic Evaluation. Notice, however, that some of the scales have significant loadings on certain other factors. Only the first six scales mentioned are unequivocal measures of stylistic evaluation alone. It is cheering to note that not a single objective measure shows any significant loading on factor *A*, General Stylistic Evaluation. Although the style of literary passages can be indexed in certain ways mechanically, it cannot be *evaluated* mechanically!

The key to the interpretation of factor *B* seems to be the presence of the subjective scales *personal-impersonal* (20), *intimate-remote* (10), *emotional-rational* (24), *vigorous-placid* (7), and to a lesser extent *vivid-pale* (19) and *opinionated-impartial* (16). Let us call this dimension Personal Affect. It is also indexed by a number of objective measures, such as number of personal pronouns (58), number of pronouns (65), and (negatively) number of syllables (31). (The negative loading of number of syllables is to be interpreted as indicating that passages with high Personal Affect have a relatively small number of syllables in 300 words, that is, the words tend to be short.) The dimension of Personal Affect is unrelated to General

Stylistic Evaluation: it refers simply to the extent to which a passage uses personal references, emotive terms, and similar devices, without necessarily making for "good" style or for "bad" style, either, for that matter.

Let us proceed to column *C* in Table 1. If the reader will run his finger down this column he will find high loadings for the following subjective scales: *florid-plain* (28), *wordy-succinct* (5) [reversing the polarity of the scale makes the loading positive], *lush-austere* (8), *affected-natural* (12), *complex-simple* (25), and *elegant-uncouth* (11). The factor is also indexed by long sentences (measure 32), long clauses (34), wide variation in sentence length (33), a relatively high proportion of common nouns which are preceded by adjectival or participial modifiers (54), long paragraphs (30), a high proportion of nouns with Latin suffixes (55), a low proportion of verbs denoting physical action (40), a high degree of use of dependent clauses of various orders (35), and a high number of descriptive adjectives (67). "Ornamentation" (as opposed to "plainness") is clearly a suitable name for this dimension.

The subjective scales having high loadings on factor *D* are *subtle-obvious* (2), *abstract-concrete* (3), *profound-superficial* (1), *complex-simple* (25), *hazy-clear* (13), *original-trite* (17), *elegant-uncouth* (11), and *remote-intimate* (10). The common element in these scales seems to be a generalized notion of abstractness and obscurity as opposed to concreteness, precision, and perspicuity; for convenience let us call this dimension Abstractness. Like factors *B* (Personal Affect) and *C* (Ornamentation), it is independent of factor *A* (General Stylistic Evaluation); that is, abstractness versus concreteness, the use of personal references versus the failure to use them, and ornamentation versus plainness have nothing to do with whether a prose passage is favorably thought of or with each other. Factor *D* (Abstractness) can be fairly well measured by several objective indicators: by a low proportion of numerical expressions (63), a low number of determining adjectives and pronouns like "this," "each," etc. (66), a high proportion of noun clauses (36), and a low number of participles (50).

Factor *E* we call Seriousness. The two subjective scales measuring this factor best are *earnest-flippant* (9) and *serious-humorous* (27). We are somewhat surprised to find, however, that the scale *masculine-feminine* (22) also relates to this factor. Evidently the term "masculine" as applied to literary style connotes earnestness and seriousness, whereas flippancy and humor are associated with femininity. Other scales measuring seriousness are *meaningful-meaningless* (4) and *profound-superficial* (1), and the factor can be indexed objectively by a low proportion of indefinite articles (57), a high proportion of indefinite and quantifying determining adjectives (61), and a high number of determiners (66). Whether these objective measures are intrinsically related to seriousness, or whether the findings are simply a reflection of the particular sample of literary passages used, we do not know.

Factor *F* in Table 1 is measured exclusively by objective measures: a low proportion of transitive verbs (42), a high proportion of copulative verbs relative to all verbs (44), a low number of proper nouns (52), a high

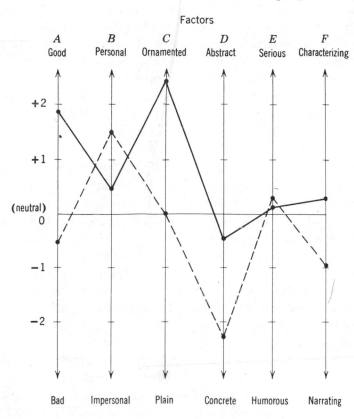

Figure 1. Style profiles of two prose passages: (———) a selection from F. Scott Fitz-gerald's *A Diamond as Big as the Ritz*; (– – – –) a selection from Mickey Spillane's *Vengeance is Mine*.

proportion of adjective clauses (37), and a high proportion of intransitive verbs (43). We can make only a tentative interpretation of the underlying significance of this dimension; the evidence seems to point to a dimension of Characterization versus Narration. We would expect passages with high scores on this factor to be those that are more concerned with the "characterization" of entities—either by equating them with other entities through the use of copulative verbs or by describing them through the use of adjective clauses. Passages with low scores on this factor are more likely to be concerned with the reporting of action, most frequently the action of persons; they would thus be found to have a high proportion of transitive verbs and proper nouns.

These, then, are the six independent dimensions of "style" which have been identified in this study: General Stylistic Evaluation, Personal Affect, Ornamentation, Abstractness, Seriousness, and Characterization versus Narration. Just to intimate the possibility of using these dimensions as the basis for a typology of style, we present in Figure 1 the "profiles" of two of the passages measured in the study. One was a selection from F. Scott Fitzgerald's short story *A Diamond as Big as the Ritz*, in which the author paints a vivid picture of the impressions of the hero and his companion as they wander through the diamond palace. The other is a passage from a very different sort of writing, that of Mickey Spillane.

Two questions may have harassed the reader: are all these dimensions really of "style"—are not some of them rather a matter of the content of a passage? And are not some of these "dimensions" merely dimensions of the *meaning* of adjectives, not necessarily dimensions truly inherent in samples of prose? With respect to the first question, we must reply that there is no hard and fast distinction between style and content. Try as we may to define style as the *manner* of treating subject matter, the type of subject matter will in general impose constraints upon the possible kinds of stylistic treatment. In the present study a vain attempt was made to have judges differentiate between content and style: *content* was to be rated with scales 1 through 4, and *style* was to be rated with scales 5 through 29. The results make it abundantly clear that the judges did not differentiate content and style, at least not in their ratings.

With respect to the second question, it must be insisted that even though somewhat comparable results might be obtained by asking raters simply to judge adjectives for similarity of meaning in the abstract, the dimensions of meaning themselves cannot exist without some support in the real world to which the adjectives presumably refer. The reality and substantiality of these dimensions is further attested to by the abundant instances of correlation between subjective ratings and completely objective, quantitative indices which derive meaning only when applied to actual samples of prose.

57. Carroll, J.B. "Biquartimin criterion for rotation to oblique simple structure in factor analysis," Science 126.1114-1115 (1957).

414. Thurstone, L.L. The vectors of mind: multiple-factor analysis for the isolation of primary traits. Chicago, 1935.

50. Cognitive Similarity and Interpersonal Communication in Industry

Harry C. Triandis

The present paper reports a test of the hypothesis that cognitive similarity affects the process of interpersonal communication. It presents methods for the measurement of cognitive similarity and shows that the measures obtained are related to perceived effectiveness of communication and liking between two people. Since permanent, long-standing relationships were necessary for purposes of the study, supervisors and subordinates in industry were used as Ss. Other pairs, such as child-parent, therapist-patient, or student-teacher, could have been used, though each presents special difficulties. A laboratory replication of the study has been reported elsewhere (Triandis, 1959a).

Two kinds of cognitive similarity are considered. The first, *categoric similarity*, is obtained by comparing the categorizations of two Ss, through an adaptation of Kelly's (1955) Role Repertory Test. The second, *syndetic similarity*, is obtained by comparing the ways concepts are associated with other concepts, and uses Osgood's (1952) semantic differential.

Recent studies of perception (Hayek, 1952) and thinking (Bruner, Goodnow, & Austin, 1956) have emphasized the importance of categorization. If categorization is central to these processes it should also be important in interpersonal communication. That is, if two people categorize events, objects and concepts in similar ways they should be able to communicate more effectively.

The work of Osgood and his associates (Osgood, Suci, & Tannenbaum, 1957) stresses the importance of the "semantic space" in phenomena related to attitudes and communication. It seems a reasonable hypothesis that if two people have similar "semantic spaces"

Reprinted from *Journal of Applied Psychology* (1959), 43: 321–326, by permission of the author and the American Psychological Association.

they should be able to communicate more effectively.

Cognitive similarity is related to additional variables. Newcomb (1953, 1956, 1958) suggests the following model: If A and B are cognitively similar and there is an opportunity for communication (propinquity), the communication will be more effective, the relationship between A and B will be more rewarding, and A and B will therefore like each other more than if A and B are not cognitively similar. Cognitive similarity implies a similar orientation towards X, in Newcomb's A-B-X model. Increased liking leads to higher rates of interaction between A and B and this, in turn, permits greater cognitive similarity thus starting the cycle all over again.

This paper relates categoric similarity and syndetic similarity to perceived communication effectiveness and liking of the supervisor by the subordinate. The hypotheses that are tested may be stated as follows: (*a*) The higher the communication effectiveness between supervisor and subordinate, the more the liking of the subordinate for the supervisor. (*b*) The higher the categoric similarity between the supervisor and subordinate the greater the communication effectiveness and the more the liking of the subordinate for the supervisor. (*c*) The higher the syndetic similarity between the subordinate and the supervisor, the greater the communication effectiveness and the liking of one for the other.

Method

The study was conducted in an industry employing 300 people. Approximately one half of the employees participated in the study. Details on the company and the Ss can be found in Triandis (1958 or 1959b).

Procedure. (*a*) *Categoric similarity:* Twelve triads of jobs and 12 triads of people were presented to the Ss (see Triandis 1958 or 1959b for exact jobs and

Table 1

Intercorrelations between the Main Variables

	K_p	O_j	O_p	C_e	L
K_j	.48**	.15	.20	.14	.04
K_p	—	.14	.27	.29	.35
O_j		—	.50**	.45**	.49**
O_p			—	.34	.41*
C_e				—	.54**
L					—

* $p < .10$.
** $p < .05$.

people). The Ss were asked: "Which one of these three jobs (people) is more different from the other two?" "Why?" and "What is the logical opposite of the characteristic that makes it different?" Thus, we obtained lists of characteristics of jobs and people and their logical opposites. These lists were then subjected to a content analysis and rated as to their similarity by the two judges. The corrected inter-rater reliability was .92 for people and .87 for jobs. The instructions to the raters and the rating scale can be found in Triandis (1958 or 1959a). (b) *Syndetic similarity:* A semantic differential was constructed for jobs and another one for people. Most of the scales of these differentials were relevant to the concepts that were to be rated on them. Twenty-eight of the scales of the differentials were obtained from a stratified random sample of the lists of characteristics obtained from the categoric similarity procedure described under (a) above. Ten additional scales were selected so as to represent the seven factors of Osgood et al. (1957, pp. 62–64). Eleven concepts were judged against these scales. They were: a welder's job, a teacher's job, a personnel director's job, a vice president's job, and a clerk's job. The sequence of these jobs was counterbalanced, for every group of Ss. The people-concepts used were: Dick T. (the personnel director of the company), your supervisor, the boss of your supervisor, the vice president of your division, a fellow at work whom you like, and an effective manager you have known well and who is not the same as any of the men already rated. The instructions as well as the exact

semantic differentials used may be found in Triandis (1958, pp. 296–298). The test-retest reliability of the differentials for 20 workers was .83 and .92. The syndetic similarity was computed from

$$0 = 1 - \frac{D^2}{36\,n} = 1 - \frac{\sum_1^n d^2}{36\,n}$$

where n is the number of scales over which the difference d between the ratings of the two Ss is being summed. The constant $36 = 6^2$ is due to our use of a seven-point scale. Five jobs and three people were used in the computation of the syndetic similarity coefficients. (c) *Communication effectiveness and liking scales.* Two scales were constructed, one for each variable. The Thurstone method of successive intervals (Edwards, 1957) was used. The items and scale values can be found in Triandis (1958, pp. 110–112). The parallel form reliability of these attitude scales, using 45 college student Ss, was .88. The scales were subjected to a scalogram analysis and yielded Guttman coefficients of reproducibility of .85 and .88, respectively. The two scales were highly intercorrelated. For 31 female clerks $r = .76$; for 31 male clerks $r = .84$; for 42 managers $r = .83$ and for 51 workers $r = .92$.

Results

Correlational analysis. Since we considered independent pairs of supervisors and subordinates we could only use 20 such pairs for this analysis. Table 1 shows the matrix of intercorrelations.

Factor analysis of the matrix of intercorrelations. The matrix of intercorrelations which consists of the correlation coefficients of variables K_j, K_p, O_j, and O_p as well as C_e and L was factored by means of Thurstone's (1947) centroid method. Three factors were extracted and rotated for simple structure. The unrotated and rotated matrices are shown in Tables 2 and 3.

The first factor, which accounts for 31.3%

Table 2

Unrotated Factor Matrix, of Matrix of Intercorrelations between Our Main Variables

Variable	a_1	a_2	a_3	a_1^2	a_2^2	a_3^2
Categoric similarity—jobs (K_j)	.419	−.510	−.222	−.176	.260	.049
Categoric similarity—people (K_p)	.566	−.439	−.145	.320	.192	.021
Syndetic similarity—jobs (O_j)	.628	.379	−.203	.394	.143	.041
Syndetic similarity—people (O_p)	.625	.143	.232	.391	.021	.054
Communication effectiveness (C_e)	.647	.211	.212	.419	.045	.045
Liking for supervisor (L)	.667	.335	.248	.445	.112	.062

Table 3

Rotated Factor Matrix of Matrix of Intercorrelations between Our Main Variables

Variable	a_1	a_2	a_3	$a_1{}^2$	$a_2{}^2$	$a_3{}^2$	h^2
K_j	.670	.204	−.006	.458	.041	.000	.491
K_p	.690	.186	.113	.485	.035	.013	.533
O_j	.096	.405	.605	.009	.164	.364	.537
O_p	.276	.394	.456	.076	.154	.210	.400
C_e	.237	.001	.654	.056	.000	.430	.486
L	.143	−.003	.747	.020	.000	.560	.580
Percentage of total variance				31.3	13.7	55.0	100.0

of the variance accounted for is a *categoric similarity* factor. The second factor accounts for 13.7% of the variance and may be called a *syndetic similarity* factor. The third factor accounts for 55% of the variance and is saturated with L, C_e, O_j, and O_p. It may be called an *evaluative factor*.

The regression equations. The means and standard deviations of the six main variables are presented in Table 4.

Using the standard methods for the determination of regression equation (McNemar, 1949, Chap. 9), including Doolittle's method, we obtained the following equations, expressed in standard form.

$$z'_{C_e} = .0001\ z_{K_j} + .289\ z_{K_p} \quad [1]$$

$$z'_{C_e} = .373\ z_{O_j} + .153\ z_{O_p} \quad [2]$$

$$z'_L = .168\ z_{K_j} + .428\ z_{K_p} \quad [3]$$

$$z'_L = .380\ z_{O_j} + .221\ z_{O_p} \quad [4]$$

$$C_e = -1.6\ K_j + 9.4\ K_p + 38.5\ O_j$$
$$+ 5.2\ O_p - 33.6 \quad [5]$$

with an error of 2.2.

$$L = -1.9\ K_j + 3.2\ K_p + 9.3\ O_j$$
$$+ 1.9\ O_p - 2.48 \quad [6]$$

with an error of .45.

If we multiply both sides of Equation [6] with 4.15, to equalize the coefficient of O_j, we can compare [5] and [7] more conveniently.

$$4.15\ L = -.79\ K_j + 13.2\ K_p + 38.5\ O_j$$
$$+ 7.9\ O_p - 10.2 \quad [7]$$

Thus, the communication effectiveness and liking for supervisor scores can be predicted from the knowledge of the categoric simi-

larity, and syndetic similarity coefficients. The multiple r for the liking for supervisor scores is .61 ($p < .003$), and the one for the communication effectiveness scores is .51 ($p < .02$). The most effective predictor of either communication effectiveness or liking for supervisor is the syndetic similarity for jobs. The second most effective predictor is the categoric similarity about people. The other two cognitive similarity coefficients are ineffective.

The analysis of variance. The correlation procedures that gave the results reported above have one great deficiency; they waste data. Each correlation is based on only a few supervisor-subordinate pairs because of the requirements for independence. Since results based on small samples are less convincing, and significant relationships are not easily obtained with such samples, it is desirable to use other statistical procedures. Analysis of variance is the appropriate technique. If each supervisor is considered a different "treatment," then it is possible to use many more Ss in our computations. We have, then, two classifications of the data; one according to

Table 4

Means and Standard Deviations of Variables

Variable	M	SD
Categoric similarity—jobs (K_j)	.128	.078
Categoric similarity—people (K_p)	.097	.064
Syndetic similarity—jobs (O_j)	.920	.024
Syndetic similarity—people (O_p)	.926	.049
Communication effectiveness (C_e)	7.38	2.55
Liking for supervisor (L)	5.77	.58

Table 5

The Results of the Analyses of Variance—Summary

Independent Variables	Dependent Variables	Level of Significance (One-tail)	Percentage of Total Variance	N used in Analysis
Double Classification Analyses				
$S + K_p$	C_e	$p < .02$	6.0	70
$S + K_p$	L	$p < .01$	6.6	70
$S + K_j$	C_e	N.S.	0	60
$S + K_j$	L	N.S.	0	60
$S + K_{p+j}$	C_e	$p < .10$	5.7	60
$S + K_{p+j}$	L	N.S.	2.3	60
$S + O_j$	C_e	$p < .001$	6.6	148
$S + O_j$	L	$p < .01$	4.9	148
$S + O_p$	C_e	N.S.	2.3	103
$S + O_p$	L	N.S.	1.5	103
$S + O_{p+j}$	C_e	$p < .025$	5.9	103
$S + O_{p+j}$		$p < .03$	4.9	103
Triple Classification Analyses				
$S + O_{p+j} + K_p C_e$		$p < .125$ (for O)	2.6	53
		.200 (for K)	2.2	
$S + O_{p+j} + K_j C_e$		$p < .30$	0	53
$S + O_j + K_p L$		$p < .001$ (for O)	7.1	53
		N.S. (for K)	.3	

Note.—S = supervisor; K = categoric similarity; O = syndetic similarity; p = people; j = jobs; $j + p$ = average of $j + p$ scores; C_e = communication effectiveness; L = liking for supervisor; and N.S. = nonsignificant.

cognitive similarity, the other according to supervisor. Since there is a variable number of subordinates reporting to each supervisor, however, we have unequal subclass n's. Also, in some cases we have had missing cells (*all* subordinates of a given supervisor were either very similar, or very dissimilar). We avoided a large number of missing cells by excluding from our analyses supervisors who had only one subordinate for whom we had complete data. Even with this restriction, however, we had a number of missing cells—in other words, we did not have the standard type of analysis of variance. Analyses of variance with missing cells and unequal n's are described in Snedecor (1956, pp. 382–385). About twenty such analyses were undertaken. The most interesting will be discussed below.

A triple classification analysis of variance is particularly suitable for our data (effect of categoric similarity, syndetic similarity, and supervisor). Such analyses were not available for unequal n's and missing subclasses when the analyses were first undertaken. Professor C. R. Henderson, of Cornell's De-

partment of Animal Husbandry, a mathematical geneticist, solved the problem after a request from this writer.

Table 5 presents a summary of all the analyses of variance. The results of these analyses are as follows:

1. Categoric similarity based on people is significantly related to both communication effectiveness and liking for supervisor. It takes care of 6.0 and 6.6% respectively of the variance of scores.

2. Categoric similarity based on jobs is not significantly related to either communication effectiveness or liking for supervisor.

3. If we average the categoric similarity scores we can predict communication effectiveness, accounting for 5.7% of the variance, but not liking for supervisor.

4. Syndetic similarity about jobs is highly related to both communication effectiveness and liking and accounts for 6.6 and 4.9% of the variance.

5. The results of the triple classification indicate that syndetic similarity is a much more important variable than categoric similarity.

Table 6

Analysis of Variance of Communication Effectiveness
Scores Classified According to Supervisor and
Levels of Syndetic Similarity About Jobs

(Management Group Only)

Source	SS	df	Variance	F	Percentage of Variance
Supervisor	646.45	17	48.0	4.45**	60
O_j	91.44	1	91.0	8.40*	9
$S \times O_j$	70.35	11	6.4		7
Individual Differences	—	—	10.8		24
Total	1070.00	76	156.2		100

* $p < .01$.
** $p < .001$.

In addition to these analyses, in the case of syndetic similarity on jobs (O_j) we have enough cases to make separate analyses for workers, clerks, and managers.

Table 6 presents the analysis of variance results for the management group; Table 7 for the clerks, Table 8 for the workers, and Table 9 for all groups combined.

Discussion

Examination of Tables 6, 7, 8, and 9 shows that both differences in level of syndetic similarity about jobs and differences in supervisor determine portions of the variance of communication affectiveness scores. This phenomenon is most clear with the management

Table 7

Analysis of Variance of Communication Effectiveness
Scores Classified According to Supervisor and
Levels of Syndetic Similarity About Jobs

(Clerks Only)

Source	SS	df	Variance	F	Percentage of Variance
S	58.55	8	7.31	—	30
O_j	29.61	1	29.61	1.43	15
$S \times O_j$	33.52	4	8.38		18
Individual Differences	—	—	19.98		37
Total	192.59	21	65.28		100

Table 8

Analysis of Variance of Communication Effectiveness
Scores Classified According to Supervisor and
Levels of Syndetic Similarity About Jobs

(Workers)

Source	SS	df	Variance	F	Percentage of Variance
S	45.72	3	15.24	2.57*	14
O_j	10.91	1	10.91	1.84	3
$S \times O_j$	25.26	3	8.42		8
Individual Differences	—	41	5.92		75

* $p < .05$.

group, less clear with the clerks and least clear with the workers. One is tempted to generalize that the extent to which the job held by the Ss is "intellectual" determines the influence of syndetic similarity about jobs on the communication scores. It may be that when a S has a manual job, his perception of that job and other jobs is not very important in terms of communication with his supervisor. Very often the worker takes a job that pays X dollars per hour and is not very concerned with the nature of the job. The supervisor tells him what the job is and he does it. With professional jobs, however, such as with engineers or managers, differences in the perception of jobs between supervisor and subordinate appear to be crucial.

Table 9

Analysis of Variance of Communication Effectiveness
Scores Classified According to Supervisor and
Levels of Syndetic Similarity About Jobs

(All Groups)

Source	SS	df	Variance	F	Percentage of Variance
S	868.69	17	51.44	7.55**	52
O_j	110.65	1	110.65	16.24**	7
$S \times O_j$	150.44	7	21.49	3.15*	9
Individual Differences	—	112	6.81		32

* $p < .01$.
** $p < .001$.

Explanation of the relative effectiveness of the four indices of cognitive similarity. Syndetic similarity based on jobs and categoric similarity based on people were the only indices that were related to communication effectiveness and liking. This requires an explanation.

C. E. Osgood, in a private communication, suggested that the difference in the effectiveness of the two syndetic similarity indices is due to differences in the representativeness of the concepts rated. He argued that the jobs used in the computation of the syndetic similarity coefficients for jobs were more diverse and representative. They were welder, teacher, vice president, clerk, and personnel director. The people used in the syndetic similarity coefficients for people, on the other hand, were more homogeneous. They were the personnel director, a supervisor, and the vice president of the employee's division—all "supervisory." This seems a reasonable explanation. It suggests further research to establish whether in fact one would get an even higher correlation between liking and syndetic similarity when extremely diverse concepts are rated by two Ss. One might conceivably extend this explanation to explain also the greater effectiveness of categoric similarity based on people as compared to the categoric similarity based on jobs.

There is then, some evidence that certain kinds of cognitive similarity are related to communication effectiveness and liking between two Ss. Whether this is a specific or a general phenomenon is subject for further research. A laboratory test of the hypothesis tested in the present paper (Triandis, 1959a) suggests that it is a sufficiently stable phenomenon to deserve further study.

Summary

One hundred and fifty-five Ss responded to 12 triads of jobs and 12 triads of people. The Ss were asked to state "Which job (person) is more different from the other two?" and "Why?" The responses of subordinates and supervisors to these triads were compared by two judges. If the responses were judged to be similar the index of *categoric similarity* of the pair was high. The same Ss were asked to rate five jobs and six people on specially constructed semantic differentials. Similarity of the "semantic profiles" obtained indicated high *syndetic similarity* between a boss and a subordinate. Successive interval scales on perceived communication effectiveness and liking within the boss-subordinate pair were also constructed. Correlational analyses and analyses of variance showed an association between categoric similarity based on people and syndetic similarity based on jobs and communication effectiveness and liking within the pair. This is considered evidence supporting the hypothesis that cognitive similarity is a significant variable in interpersonal communication and liking.

REFERENCES

BRUNER, J. S., GOODNOW, J. J., & AUSTIN, G. A. *A study of thinking.* New York: Wiley, 1956.

EDWARDS, A. L. *Techniques of attitude scale construction.* New York: Appleton-Century-Crofts, 1957.

HAYEK, F. A. *The sensory order: An inquiry into the foundations of theoretical psychology.* Chicago: Univer. of Chicago Press, 1952.

JENKINS, W. L. A quick graphic method for the product moment *"r." Educ. Psychol. Measur.,* 1945, **5**, 437–443.

McNEMAR, Q. *Psychological Statistics.* New York: Wiley, 1949.

NEWCOMB, T. M. An approach to the study of communicative acts. *Psychol. Rev.,* 1953, **60**, 393–404.

NEWCOMB, T. M. The prediction of interpersonal attraction. *Amer. Psychologist,* 1956, **11**, 575–586.

NEWCOMB, T. M. The cognition of persons as cognizers. In R. Tagiuri & L. Petrullo (Eds.), *Person perception and personal behavior.* Stanford: Stanford Univer. Press, 1958.

OSGOOD, C. E. The nature and measurement of meaning. *Psychol. Bull.,* 1952, **49**, 197–237.

OSGOOD, C. E., SUCI, G. J., & TANNENBAUM, P. H. *The measurement of meaning.* Urbana: Univer. of Illinois Press, 1957.

SNEDECOR, G. W. *Statistical methods.* Ames, Iowa: Iowa State Coll. Press, 1956.

THURSTONE, L. L. *Multifactor analysis.* Chicago: Univer. of Chicago Press, 1947.

TRIANDIS, H. C. Some cognitive factors affecting communication. Unpublished doctoral dissertation, Cornell Univer., 1958.

TRIANDIS, H. C. Categoric similarity and the communication of the dyad. *Sociometry* (in press), 1959. (a)

TRIANDIS, H. C. Categories of thought of managers, clerks and workers about jobs and people in industry. *J. appl. Psychol.,* 1959, **43**, 338–344. (b)

51. Connotations of Twenty Psychological Journals
to Their Professional Readers

Leon A. Jakobovits and Charles E. Osgood

I N 1958, following the suggestion of Roger F. Brightbill, a student of George A. Miller at Harvard at the time, a pilot study on the "images" of 20 psychological journals was run by Murray S. Miron of the Institute of Communications Research staff. Judgments of these 20 journals against 20 semantic differential scales were collected from approximately 50 students and staff at Harvard, Stanford, and Illinois. Factor analysis of the scales yielded three main factors, identified as seriousness, value, and interestingness. By assigning factor scores to the journals, it was possible to display their clustering in the three-factor space as well as their connotative differences. The face validity of the results of this pilot study encouraged us to extend the method of analysis to a larger and more representative number of psychologists, as part of the American Psychological Association's National Science Foundation Project on Scientific Information Exchange in Psychology.

SELECTION OF MATERIALS

Concepts

Twenty professional journals of interest to psychologists were included in the sample. These included all of the journals published by the APA, except two (*Psychological Abstracts* and *Psychological Monographs*), as well as 10 non-APA journals. These journal concepts, along with the abbreviations that will be used throughout this report, are given in Table 1.

Scales

The semantic differential scales used in this study were selected, in part, from the results of the pilot study—those having high and relatively pure loadings in that factor analysis. These were supplemented with scales gleaned from the spontaneous descriptions of various journals by several psychologists at the University of Illinois. The final form consisted of 20 scales. These are also listed in Table 1 (no relation between journals and the scales which happen to parallel them in this table is implied).

Questionnaire

In addition to the 20 concept × 20 scale semantic differential form, a number of questions were included in the booklet. These questions were designed to get at the following information: (*a*) *subscription* (to which of the 20 journals does the subject subscribe); (*b*) *familiarity* (scaled from "read it cover to cover" to "glance at the titles"); (*c*) *publication preferences* (scaled from "I would definitely consider publishing in X" to "I would refuse to publish in X under any circumstances"); (*d*) *division affiliation* (checklist of divisions to which subject belongs); (*e*) *seniority* (subject's latest degree and year it was obtained); (*f*) *area of degree* (11 categories, like experimental, social, clinical, were used); (*g*) *area of present interest* (organized into 15 areas); (*h*) *type of employment* (percentage of time devoted to teaching, administration, research, scholarly writing, counselling, other).

SELECTION OF SUBJECTS

The latest available membership list was obtained from the Central Office of the APA and was used to select a representative sample of the membership. The list was arranged by members in states, in alphabetical order. Foreign addresses were excluded from the sample. Every nineteenth name on the list was selected. This procedure yielded an original sample of 979 members. Of these, 535 had no divisional affiliation, 282 belonged to a single division only, and the remaining 162 were members of two or more divisions. It was decided to reduce the group with no divisional

Reprinted from *American Psychologist* (1967), 22: 792–800, by permission of the authors and the American Psychological Association.

TABLE 1

JOURNALS (CONCEPTS), THEIR ABBREVIATIONS, AND
SCALES USED IN THIS STUDY

Journals	Abbreviations	Scales
APA journals		
American Psychologist	AP	Active-passive
Contemporary Psychology	CP	Unimportant-important
Journal of Abnormal and Social Psychology	JASP	Earnest-flippant
Journal of Applied Psychology	JAP	Broad-narrow
Journal of Comparative and Physiological Psychology	JCPhP	Humorous-serious
Journal of Consulting Psychology	JCP	Theoretical-empirical
Journal of Educational Psychology	JEdP	Impersonal-personal
Journal of Experimental Psychology	JExP	Dull-interesting
Psychological Bulletin	PB	Easy-difficult
Psychological Review	PR	Positive-negative
Non-APA journals		
American Journal of Psychology	AJP	Valuable-worthless
Behavioral Science	BS	Applied-basic
Educational and Psychological Measurement	EPM	Disreputable-reputable
Journal of Clinical Psychology	JClP	Useless-useful
Journal of Genetic Psychology	JGtP	Varied-monotonous
Journal of Personality	JPl	Unscientific-scientific
Journal of Social Psychology	JSP	Strong-weak
Psychiatry	P	Good-bad
Psychoanalytic Review	PaR	Partial-impartial
Psychometrika	PmK	Loose-rigorous

affiliation; therefore, every fifth name in this group was chosen to remain in the sample, while the rest were discarded. The final sample thus was made up of 107 nondivision members, 282 single-division members, and 162 multiple-division members—a total of 551 potential subjects.

A test booklet, together with a covering letter from John G. Darley, then Executive Officer of APA, and a self-stamped return envelope, was sent to each subject. About 8 weeks later, a follow-up letter signed by the second author was sent to all subjects as a reminder to send the test booklet back. When the analysis of the data was begun, 287 booklets (51%) had been returned. Of these, 20 were not filled out, so that the analysis of the data is based on 267 returns (46%). Even some of these subjects failed to rate some of the journals (often because of complete lack of familiarity, as stated by the subjects), so the *N* varies somewhat from concept to concept. The maximum response was made to *AP* (*American Psychologist*), 257 total—47 nondivision, 85 multiple division, and 135 single division. Responses were highest for APA journals, as might be expected; low responses relatively were made to *BS*, *PaR*, *JSP* and one APA journal, *JCPhP* (see Table 4, Column 1).

RESULTS

Factor Analysis of Scales

Two different ways of factoring the raw data were used. The first analysis involved factoring of individual ratings, such that N = subjects × concepts × scales. The second approach involved factoring of mean ratings for all subjects, such that N = concepts × scales. In both cases, the principal axis solution was used with the varimax rotation. The two approaches yielded slightly different factor structures.

Table 2 presents the factor analysis *based on individual ratings* (subjects × concepts × scales) for the total sample of subjects. Four factors emerge and account for 74% of the total variance. Factor I loads highest on good-bad, valuable-worthless, and positive-negative; these seem to reflect valuableness. Factor II loads highest on scientific-unscientific, rigorous-loose, and reputable-disreputable, which seem to reflect scientific rigor. Factor III loads highest on personal-impersonal and interesting-dull and thus seems to reflect what we shall call interestingness. Factor IV loads highest on theoretical-empirical and basic-applied and we will call it orientation. It should be noted that the first three factors here are essentially the same as those obtained in the pilot study (except for one reversal in the order of variance accounted for—seriousness, valuableness, interestingness) in which fewer than 50 subjects were used.

Factor analysis of the means (concept × scales)

TABLE 2

Varimax Rotation of Principal Axis Solution:
Scales × Concepts × Subjects

Variables	Factors				
	I	II	III	IV	h²
Active-passive	.80	.12	.02	.03	.66
Unimportant-important	−.28	.74	.35	.07	.76
Earnest-flippant	.68	.03	.55	.03	.76
Broad-narrow	.71	.12	−.31	−.12	.62
Humorous-serious	.21	.63	.41	−.20	.65
IVᵃ Theoretical-empirical	.34	.13	.18	−.80	.81
III Impersonal-personal	.34	−.10	.78	−.11	.75
III Dull-interesting	−.21	.44	.73	−.11	.78
Easy-difficult	.31	.69	−.19	.26	.68
Positive-negative	.88	−.00	.08	−.01	.78
I Valuable-worthless	.91	−.15	.06	−.07	.86
IV Applied-basic	.28	.60	.04	.57	.78
Disreputable-reputable	−.20	.82	.12	−.04	.72
Useless-useful	−.30	.74	.39	−.12	.82
Varied-monotonous	.81	.11	−.27	−.03	.74
II Unscientific-scientific	−.06	.88	−.05	.08	.79
Strong-weak	.85	−.21	.19	−.13	.82
I Good-bad	.91	−.12	.10	−.07	.86
Partial-impartial	.06	.68	.08	−.10	.49
II Loose-rigorous	.02	.87	−.10	.10	.78

Note.—% Total Variance: Value, 30.63; Rigor, 26.81; Interest, 11.18; Orientation, 5.98. % Total Variance, 74.60.
ᵃ Scales used subsequently for factor scores.

yielded only three major factors, accounting for 90% of the variance. Factor I loaded highest on valuable-worthless, good-bad, useful-useless, important-unimportant, and positive-negative (reflecting primarily valuableness); this factor also seemed to absorb scientific rigorousness (high loadings on reputable-disreputable, rigorous-loose, scientific-unscientific, and impartial-partial). In other words, the first two *independent* factors, when subject variance is included, in the analysis above, merge into one when subject variance is eliminated. Factor II loaded highest on interesting-dull, personal-impersonal, humorous-serious, varied-monotonous, flippant-earnest and easy difficult, and seems to reflect interestingness. Factor III loaded highest on theoretical-empirical and basic-applied and seems to reflect orientation. Since the subject × concept × scale analysis indicated independence beween valuableness and scientific rigor, we shall maintain this distinction and refer to the first scale factor analysis henceforth.

Factor Analysis of Journals

Using a transpose of the raw data on mean ratings for the total sample of subjects, a principal axis solution and varimax rotation was carried out for concepts as variables, and the results are presented in Table 3. As can be seen, four factors are extracted which account for 98% of the total variance. Factor I loads highest on *Pmk, JExP, JCPhP, PR, JGtP,* and *BS;* thus it seems to select those journals with a tradition of high scientific rigor. Factor II loads highest on *JAP, JEdP, JClP, EPM,* and *JCP,* and thus rather obviously reflects orientation toward the applied aspect of information in the psychological network. Factor III loads highest on *AP* and *CP;* it appears to represent what could be termed the service (or interest) function of some journals in the network. Finally, Factor IV loads highest on *PaR* and *P,* but with subsidiary loadings also on *JPl* and *JClP;* it therefore seems to reflect the clinical side of the journal network.

Journal Profiles

As a way of summarizing a large mass of data, Table 4 presents the scale factor scores of the 20 journals, based on data for the total subject sample. The two highest loading scales for each factor in the first (subject × concepts × scales) analysis are used for deriving factor scores. Factor I, value, is the average of scores on valuable-

TABLE 3

Varimax Rotation of Principal Axis Solution:
Concepts (Means) × Scales

Journal	Factors				
	I	II	III	IV	h²
AP	.22	.32	.89	.16	.97
CP	.35	.25	.89	.08	.99
JASP	.73	.42	.49	.17	.99
JAP	.31	.92	.20	.06	.99
JCPhP	.94	.24	.18	.02	.98
JCP	.38	.77	.46	.18	.99
JEdP	.28	.88	.13	.31	.97
JExP	.96	.23	.05	.02	.98
PB	.83	.23	.49	.05	.99
PR	.88	.10	.45	.08	.99
AJP	.82	.32	.45	.01	.99
BS	.86	.24	.40	.15	.99
EPM	.59	.77	.20	.10	1.00
JClP	.26	.76	.39	.41	.98
JGtP	.87	.39	.21	.11	.98
JPl	.64	.42	.46	.38	.95
JSP	.59	.56	.52	.22	.97
P	.11	.56	.44	.68	.99
PaR	.02	.23	.07	.96	.99
Pmk	.95	.21	−.05	.08	.96
	Rigor	Orientation	Service	Clinical	
% Total Variance	42.92	25.79	19.36	10.03	

Note.—% Total Variance 98.10.

TABLE 4

FACTOR SCORES AND RANKS FOR 20 PSYCHOLOGICAL JOURNALS (TOTAL SAMPLE)

Journals	N members responding	Factors			
		I[a]	II	III	IV
AP	267	5.74 (2)	4.12 (16)	5.58 (1)	3.62 (14)
CP	244	5.66 (3)	4.63 (11).	5.30 (2)	3.98 (11)
JASP	248	5.33 (6)	4.98 (7)	4.04 (8)	3.92 (12)
JAP	233	4.74 (16)	4.54 (12)	3.62 (15)	2.09 (20)
JCPhP	204	5.38 (5)	5.86 (3)	3.28 (18)	4.64 (5)
JCP	232	4.88 (10.5)	4.33 (13)	4.14 (6.5)	2.84 (17)
JEdP	222	4.52 (19)	4.00 (17)	3.76 (12)	2.94 (18)
JExP	225	5.28 (8)	6.20 (1)	2.78 (19)	4.79 (2)
PB	242	5.79 (1)	5.63 (4)	3.82 (10)	4.78 (3.5)
PR	227	5.55 (4)	5.51 (5)	3.70 (13.5)	5.36 (1)
AJP	218	5.10 (9)	5.15 (6)	3.70 (13.5)	4.29 (7)
BS	202	4.88 (10.5)	4.94 (8)	3.81 (11)	4.52 (6)
EPM	225	4.86 (12)	4.69 (10)	3.52 (16.5)	2.98 (17)
JClP	223	4.68 (17)	3.99 (18)	4.32 (5)	3.00 (16)
JGtP	193	4.83 (13)	4.86 (9)	3.52 (16.5)	4.24 (8)
JPl	227	4.76 (15)	4.30 (14)	4.14 (6.5)	4.15 (9)
JSP	203	4.78 (14)	4.28 (15)	3.95 (9)	3.79 (13)
P	215	4.58 (18)	3.26 (19)	4.58 (4)	3.39 (15)
PaR	207	4.21 (20)	2.80 (20)	4.61 (3)	4.00 (10)
Pmk	216	5.32 (7)	5.98 (2)	2.70 (20)	4.78 (3.5)
		Value	Rigor	Interest	Orientation

[a] The larger the score, the more Valuable, more Rigorous, more Interesting, and more theoretical in Orientation, respectively, the journal in question.

worthless and good-bad; Factor II, rigor, is the average of scores on scientific-unscientific and rigorous-loose; Factor III, interestingness, is the average of personal-impersonal and interesting-dull; and Factor IV, orientation, is the average of scores on theoretical-empirical and basic-applied. The location of a particular journal in the four-space above is defined by its scores on the four factors, as given in Table 4. The ranks of journals on factors are also given to facilitate interpretation. The following is a summary of these data.

Value. The most valuable (5.5–6.0) journals to the profession as a whole are *PB, AP, PR,* and *CP*—which may be, in part, a function of their eclecticism. Also judged valuable (5.0–5.5) are *JASP, PmK, AJP, JExP,* and *JCPhP,* the hard core of experimental journals. Least valuable (< 4.5) in the eyes of the profession as a whole, are *PaR* and *JEdP,* which seems to indicate professional focusing.

Rigor. The most rigorous (scientific) journals according to the profession as a whole (5.0–4.0) are *PmK, PB, JExP, PR,* and *JCPhP,* with *AJP* falling just outside the limit. The least rigorous

journals in our sample (< 4.0) are *JPl, P, AP, PaR, JEdP,* and *JClP.* All other journals fell between 4.0 and 5.0 on this factor.

Interestingness. The journals judged most interesting in our sample (> 5.0) are *CP* and *AP,* which certainly fits their intended functions. Also interesting (4.5–5.0) are *JASP, PB, P, PaR,* and *PR,* which also seems to fit expectations. Not interesting (4.0–3.5) are *EPM, JGtP, JAP, JEdP,* and *JCPhP*—for the psychology profession generally. And flatly dull (< 3.5) in the judgment of the total sample were *Pmk* and *JExP!*

Orientation. Most basic (theoretical) in the judgment of members of APA (> 4.5) are *PmK, PB, JExP, PR,* and *JCPhP;* also quite basic (certainly not applied) are *AJP* and *JGtP* (4.0–4.5). Going toward the applied direction (3.0–3.5) are *AP, PaR,* and *JSP,* while the most applied journals in the judgment of the profession are *EPM, P, JCP, JAP, JEdP,* and *JClP* (< 3.0).

Table 5 gives some idea of the range of mean judgments on the 20 scales by listing the *most* and *least* journals for each scale. *PB* is judged most important, valuable, reputable, useful, strong, good,

TABLE 5

THE MOST POLAR JOURNALS: MEANS OF JOURNALS ON SCALES

Scales	Most	Least
1. Active (passive)	AP (5.99)	JGtP (4.45)
2. Important (unimportant)	PB (5.88)	PaR (4.32)
3. Earnest (flippant)	JExP (6.12)	AP (4.72)
4. Narrow (broad)	Pmk (5.44)	CP (2.13)
5. Serious (humorous)	JExP (6.20)	AP (3.83)
6. Theoretical (empirical)	PR (5.56)	JAP (2.49)
7. Personal (impersonal)	AP (5.12)	Pmk (2.13)
8. Interesting (dull)	AP (5.84)	Pmk (3.28)
9. Difficult (easy)	Pmk (5.96)	AP (2.30)
10. Positive (negative)	AP (5.72)	PaR (4.40)
11. Valuable (worthless)	PB (5.88)	PaR (4.20)
12. Basic (applied)	JExP (5.42)	JAP (1.70)
13. Reputable (disreputable)	PB (6.27)	PaR (4.47)
14. Useful (useless)	PB (5.92)	PaR (4.26)
15. Varied (monotonous)	CP (5.82)	Pmk (3.34)
16. Scientific (unscientific)	JExP (6.24)	PaR (2.92)
17. Strong (weak)	PB (5.54)	PaR (4.00)
18. Good (bad)	PB (5.70)	PaR (4.20)
19. Impartial (partial)	PB (5.06)	PaR (2.90)
20. Rigorous (loose)	JExP (6.16)	PaR (2.68)

and impartial. *JExP* is most earnest, serious, basic, scientific, and rigorous. *AP* is the most active, personal, interesting, and positive—but also the least earnest, serious, or difficult. *PaR*, for members of the psychological profession, at least, is clearly the least respected journal in our sample (but this, of course, is the essence of professional focusing). Other characterizations can be made by the reader himself from Tables 4 and 5.

Effects of Divisional Membership

The total sample was divided into three categories according to membership in divisions of APA: nondivision, which includes the largest proportion of membership in APA; single membership, which has the next largest proportion of membership in APA; and multiple division, which covers the smallest proportion of members of APA. Differences on this basis were analyzed, but tables will not be presented. It should be pointed out that our assignment of psychologists to these three categories in no way reflects their actual divisional affiliations and it completely obscures the pattern of membership of the multiple-division people.

In general, type of membership in APA has little effect upon the connotations of journals—the means by types were only occasionally significantly different. However, certain significant ($\frac{1}{3}$ of a

scale division or more, cf. Osgood, Suci, & Tannenbaum, 1957) differences should be noted: Particularly on the value factor, 11 of the 20 journals (*AP, PCPhP, JEdP, JCP, JExP, AJP, BS, CP, EPM, JGtP,* and *JPl*) display the same pattern—multidivision members giving highest evaluation, single-division members giving next highest evaluation, and nondivisional members giving least evaluation. This suggests a general "involvement" factor, multidivision members being most involved and nondivision members least. Actually, the only journals to which nondivision members give highest evaluation (compared with other members) are *JClP* and *PaR*. Single-division members give highest evaluation to *JAP* and *JSP*. *JASP* is evaluated almost identically by all three groups. Multiple-division members give significantly higher evaluations to *PB, PR, BS,* and *EPM* than do nondivisional members.

Rigor and interest factors yield no clear distinctions among members having different types of affiliation with APA. However, there were some interesting differences on the orientation factor: Multiple-division members see *PB* and *PR* as relatively more basic or theoretical, but *JCP, JClP,* and *JSP* as more applied, as compared with other members. Single-division members see *JExP* as more theoretical but *JAP* as even more applied than do other members. Nondivision members see *JAP, JCP,* and *JSP* as more theoretical in orientation than do members who belong to one or more divisions. Relativity of judgment to the location of the observer is evident in these data.

Effects of Other Variables

Analyses of differences based upon other questionnaire items (such as area of degree, area of present interest, subscription (or lack thereof), familiarity with journals, and publication preferences) were carried out, but they do not merit detailed report. When our sample was fractionated so finely, the Ns in cells often became less than 20. Generally, as might be expected, psychologists give preference to, are willing to publish in, and usually subscribe to those journals which are close contentwise to their areas of interest, as indicated by their areas of degree and present interest. Thus, *PaR* is alien to most psychologists with degrees in general experimental, but intriguing and certainly more familiar to those with degrees in clinical; *Pmk* is judged less valuable by clinical

TABLE 6

Interjournal Distances in Terms of Connotation Profiles

Journal	JCPhP	JExP	AJP	PR	PB	JGIP	EPM	JEdP	JAP	JASP	JSP	JPl	JCP	JCIP	P	PaR	CP	Pmk	BS	AP
JCPhP	.00	.63	.94	.92	.73	1.23	2.11	2.42	3.58	1.37	2.01	1.95	2.56	2.79	3.26	3.59	2.47	.61	1.18	3.08
JExP	.63	.00	1.49	1.31	1.29	1.69	2.51	2.86	3.97	1.96	2.51	2.48	3.05	3.29	3.79	4.08	3.10	.24	1.70	3.71
AJP	.94	1.49	.00	1.25	.98	.44	1.42	1.54	2.80	.58	1.08	1.03	1.74	1.89	2.33	2.69	1.80	1.41	.40	2.34
PR	.92	1.31	1.25	.00	.65	1.49	2.62	2.65	3.94	1.59	2.15	1.94	2.90	3.00	3.26	3.44	2.29	1.27	1.22	2.92
PB	.73	1.29	.98	.65	.00	1.38	2.25	2.46	3.62	1.19	1.96	1.82	2.53	2.71	3.10	3.43	1.96	1.26	1.17	2.59
JGIP	1.23	1.69	.44	1.49	1.38	.00	1.27	1.24	2.57	.80	.85	.84	1.62	1.72	2.11	2.42	1.99	1.57	.41	2.45
EPM	2.11	2.51	1.42	2.62	2.25	1.27	.00	.93	1.53	1.21	1.01	1.38	.71	1.08	1.85	2.49	2.19	2.41	1.59	2.40
JEdP	2.42	2.86	1.54	2.65	2.46	1.24	.93	.00	1.48	1.39	.55	.89	.86	.73	1.11	1.60	2.09	2.73	1.48	2.20
JAP	3.58	3.97	2.80	3.94	3.62	2.57	1.53	1.48	.00	2.49	1.92	2.28	1.27	1.27	1.64	2.31	2.93	3.83	2.86	2.76
JASP	1.37	1.96	.58	1.59	1.19	.80	1.21	1.39	2.49	.00	.90	.92	1.34	1.53	2.02	2.52	1.35	1.88	.78	1.84
JSP	2.01	2.51	1.08	2.15	1.96	.85	1.01	.55	1.92	.90	.00	.41	.98	.92	1.28	1.73	1.66	2.39	1.00	1.91
JPl	1.92	2.48	1.03	1.94	1.82	.84	1.38	.89	2.28	.92	.41	.00	1.32	1.21	1.37	1.67	1.51	2.37	.82	1.83
JCP	2.56	3.05	1.74	2.90	2.53	1.62	.71	.86	1.27	1.34	.98	1.32	.00	.46	1.32	2.09	1.83	2.96	1.82	1.86
JCIP	2.79	3.29	1.89	3.00	2.71	1.72	1.08	.73	1.27	1.53	.92	1.21	.46	.00	.87	1.65	1.81	3.19	1.87	1.76
P	3.26	3.79	2.33	3.26	3.10	2.11	1.85	1.11	1.64	2.02	1.28	1.37	1.32	.87	.00	.85	1.98	3.67	2.19	1.77
PaR	3.59	4.08	2.69	3.44	3.43	2.42	2.49	1.60	2.31	2.52	1.73	1.67	2.09	1.65	.85	.00	2.43	3.95	2.44	2.27
CP	2.47	3.10	1.80	2.29	1.96	1.99	2.19	2.09	2.93	1.35	1.66	1.51	1.83	1.81	1.98	2.43	.00	3.06	1.79	.69
Pmk	.61	.24	1.41	1.27	1.26	1.57	2.41	2.73	3.83	1.88	2.39	2.37	2.96	3.19	3.67	3.95	3.06	.00	1.60	3.64
BS	1.18	1.70	.40	1.22	1.17	.41	1.59	1.48	2.86	.78	1.00	.82	1.82	1.87	2.19	2.44	1.79	1.60	.00	2.31
AP	3.08	3.71	2.34	2.92	2.59	2.45	2.40	2.20	2.76	1.84	1.91	1.83	1.86	1.76	1.77	2.27	.69	3.64	2.31	.00

and social psychologists, but more valuable by experimental and measurement people. The data display such overall face validity throughout.

Connotative Distances and Clustering among Journals

Interpoint distances from each journal to every other were computed by Shepard's (1962) procedure. This method yields that set of distances which best satisfies the rankings of the journals on all four scale factors simultaneously. Table 6 presents this distance matrix. A visual representation of these distances (necessarily somewhat approximate since four dimensions had to be compressed into three) is shown as Figure 1. In this model, the rigor factor runs roughly from upper left (*Pmk* and *JExP*) to lower right (*PaR*), the orientation factor runs from upper right (*PR*, theoretical) to lower left (*JAP*, applied), and the interest factor is represented in the third dimension by circle sizes, most interesting (*CP* and *AP*)

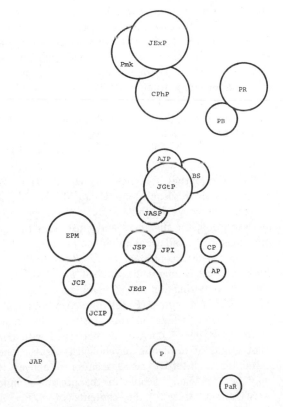

Fig. 1. Distances between journals in terms of connotative meanings.

being far and least interesting (*Pmk* and *JExP*) being near; the general value factor, which yielded the smallest range of journal scores (cf. Table 4), does not have definite representation in the model.

The journals were ordered in Table 6 for convenience in comparing distances in connotation with distances based on reciprocal bibliographical citation (see Table 5 in Xhighnesse & Osgood, 1967), the first 16 journals given being common to both studies. To test the hypothesis that journals having similar "feeling tones" to psychologists will tend to cite each other reciprocally and frequently, the two distance matrices were correlated with each other, cell by corresponding cell. The correlation is .53. This lends some support to the notion that the journals authors read and cite tend to have similar connotation to the journals in which they publish.

The clusterings of journals shown by inspection of Table 6 and Figure 1 seem to be intuitively reasonable. Using distances less than 1.00 as a criterion, we find, for example, that *JExP*, *Pmk*, and *JCPhP* form one tight cluster; they are simultaneously considered the most rigorous scientifically and the least interesting or personal. *PB* and *PR* form another cluster, being simultaneously high in value and in theoretical orientation. *CP* and *AP* are off by themselves connotatively, being simultaneously highly valued and highly interesting and personal. *JAP* is isolated by virtue of its extreme applied nature (as judged) as are both *PaR* and *P* by virtue of being judged low in both rigor and value. *JASP* falls in the middle of an interesting cluster which includes *AJP*, *BS*, *JGtP*, *JSP*, and *JPl*. But why should *AJP* fall in this group? It may be that many people in our sample were not familiar with the contents of *AJP* (the smaller sample of academic psychologists in the pilot study did cluster *AJP* with *JExP* and *JCPhP*). *JCP* and *JClP* are appropriately close in connotation, and they have bordering neighbor relations with *JEdP*, *EPM*, *JSP*, and *P*.

INTERPRETIVE SUMMARY

The sample of journals used in this image study cannot be considered representative of the entire psychological network. It overrepresents journals published by the American Psychological Association and underrepresents the rapidly proliferating, usually more specialized, journals published outside the Association. On the other hand, it probably does represent actual readership fairly well, since the journals included are, for the most part, those most heavily subscribed to by members of the profession.

The factors derived for the 20 scales by two methods, one based on individual ratings and the other based on group means, correspond reasonably well. Valuableness, scientific rigor, interestingness, and orientation ("pure" vs. "applied") appear in the first method as independent dimensions and account for 75% of total variance; the only difference in the results of the second method (using group means) is that valuableness and scientific rigor collapse into a single factor. Since one method demonstrated that value and rigor can be independent dimensions, the results of the first method were used to derive four factor scores for each journal for use in subsequent analyses. We may conclude, then, that the "feeling tones" psychologists have about their journals can be described in terms of four major dimensions of variation—their value, their rigorousness, their interestingness, and their orientation toward theory or toward application. The first three factors in this journal domain seem to parallel those regularly found for the affective meanings of concepts in general (Osgood, Suci, & Tannenbaum, 1957)—evaluation (here valuableness), potency (here scientific rigor), and activity (here interestingness).

The ways the journals distribute themselves within the space defined by the four factors are entirely sensible. For the profession as a whole, the most valuable journals are *PB*, *AP*, *PR*, and *CP;* the most scientifically rigorous journals are *Pmk*, *PB*, *JExP*, *PR*, and *JCPhP;* the most interesting journals are *CP* and *AP;* and the most basic (or theoretical) in orientation are *Pmk*, *PB*, *JExP*, *PR*, and *JCPhP*. Although judged scientific rigor and judged theoretical orientation are independent as factors, the same set of journals are highest on both. Extreme scale judgments serve to characterize individual journals in ways that have high face validity. *CP* is judged simultaneously as the *most varied* and *most broad* in content of the 20 journals. *PB* stands out as the most generally respected journal of the sample. *AP* is the most personal.

When the total sample of respondents is broken down into nondivision members, members belonging to only one division, and multiple-division members, some consistent trends appear—although the differences are not large in magnitude. For one thing, multiple-division members attribute the highest valuation to journals generally (highest on 15 of the 20 journals) and nondivision members give the lowest valuations generally (lowest on 13 of the 20). For another, whereas multiple-division members see *PB* and *PR* relatively more theoretical in orientation and *JCP*, *JClP*, and *JSP* as even more applied than other members, nondivision members show a reverse trend, with *JAP*, *JCP*, and *JSP* being viewed as relatively more theoretical and *JExP*, *PB*, and *PR* as relatively less so. One implication here is that those members having the greatest involvement with the Association (multiple-division members) tend to be academic in orientation and also place the greatest general value on the journals. Nondivision members seem to be more clinical and applied in orientation.

Relationships found between journal connotations and the educational backgrounds and professional habits of APA members are those one would expect. Psychologists have relatively more respect for journals reflecting their own areas of training and present interest, for journals they subscribe to, are more familiar with, and would publish in. PhDs, as compared with MAs, are more favorably disposed toward journals like *Pmk* and less favorably disposed toward journals like *JAP* and *PaR*. Interestingly enough, senior psychologists (in terms of year of degree) are simultaneously more favorable toward both *JAP* and *Pmk* than are their younger colleagues.

The interjournal distances, given as Table 6 and represented visually as Figure 1, provide a general summary of this study. With perhaps one exception, the distances and clusterings fit our intuitions. We find what might be dubbed a "Division 3 cluster" composed of *JExP*, *JCPhP*, and *Pmk*, and what might be dubbed a "Division 8 cluster" centering on *JASP* and including *BS*, *JGtP*, *JSP*, *JPl*, and *AJP* (all non-APA journals). The inclusion of *AJP* in this cluster, rather than in the "Division 3 cluster" as happened with our pilot group of academic psychologists, is the one exception to intuitive sense mentioned above; it may be that many people in the present sample were unfamiliar with the contents of *AJP*. A somewhat looser "Division 12 cluster" is also suggested in the data, composed of *JCP* and *JClP* at its core and *EPM, JEdP, JSP, JPl,* and *P* on its periphery.

The fact that connotative distances between journals do generally fit the expectations of those familiar with their contents testifies to overall agreement among psychologists on journal images, regardless of their personal preferences as determined by divisional, occupational, educational, or other differences.

REFERENCES

OSGOOD, C. E., SUCI, G. J., & TANNENBAUM, P. H. *The measurement of meaning.* Urbana: University of Illinois Press, 1957.

SHEPARD, R. N. The analysis of proximities: Multidimensional scaling with an unknown distance function. I & II. *Psychometrika,* 1962, *27,* 125–140, 219–246.

XHIGNESSE, L. V., & OSGOOD, C. E. Bibliographical citation characteristics of the psychological journal network in 1950 and 1960. *American Psychologist,* 1967, *22,* 778–791.

52. Fitting the Semantic Differential
to the Marketing Problem

William A. Mindak

ADVERTISING and marketing men frequently are faced with the problem of quantifying highly subjective data, representing difficult-to-verbalize reactions of people to the "image" of a brand, product, or company.

Consistent with this attempt to define an "image" is the technique originated by Charles E. Osgood and his associates, called the semantic differential.[1] This technique attempts to measure what meaning a concept might have for people in terms of dimensions which have been empirically defined and factor-analyzed. Since this concept can indeed be something as abstract or nebulous as a company image, the semantic differential has seen increasing use in various ways.[2]

Osgood's semantic differential involved repeated judgments of a concept against a series of descriptive polar-adjectival scales on a 7-point equal-interval ordinal scale. These scales were usually selected from 50 pairs of polar adjectives, with heavy factor loadings labeled "evaluative" (on which are based the attitudinal measures), "activity," and "potency."

An example would be:

good__:__:__:__:__:__:__:bad

Progressing from left to right on the scale, the positions are described to the subjects participating in the experiment as representing "extremely good," "very good," "slightly good," "being both good and bad," "slightly bad," "very bad," and "extremely bad." Subjects are encouraged to use the scales as quickly and as honestly as possible and not to puzzle over any particular concept.

In scoring the differential, weights can be assigned to each position; and these in turn can be converted to individual or group mean scores and presented in "profile" form. Reliability of the differential is reasonably high, and the measure has a high degree of face validity.

Reprinted from *Journal of Marketing* (1961), 25: 28–33, by permission of the author and the American Marketing Association.

[1] Charles E. Osgood, George J. Suci, and Percy H. Tannenbaum, *The Measurement of Meaning* (Urbana, Illinois: University of Illinois Free Press, 1957).

[2] William A. Mindak, "A New Technique for Measuring Advertising Effectiveness," JOURNAL OF MARKETING, Vol. 20 (April, 1956), pp. 367-378. Mogul, Lewin, Williams & Saylor, Inc., "Product Semantic Indices," (private publication) (New York, 1958). John F. Bolger, Jr., "How to Evaluate Your Company Image," JOURNAL OF MARKETING, Vol. 24 (October, 1959), pp. 7-10.

SEMANTIC DIFFERENTIAL IN MEASURING "IMAGES"

The semantic differential has a number of specific advantages for marketing researchers interested in measuring brand, product, or company images:

1. It is a quick, efficient means of getting in readily quantifiable form and for large samples not only the *direction* but *intensity* of opinions and attitudes toward a concept . . . be it brand, product, or company. If desired, these "profiles" can be used as a guide to indicate areas for more intensive research or interviewing.

2. It provides a comprehensive picture of the "image" or meaning of a product or personality. Duncan Hines and Betty Crocker as corporate personalities might both be looked upon favorably, but reacted to differently in terms of "activity," "strength," "warmth," "helpfulness," etc.

3. It represents a standardized technique for getting at the multitude of factors which go to make up a brand or product "image." Comparison of one brand with another must take into consideration *specific brand attributes* (size, shape, price, ingredients, etc.) as well as *general product class characteristics* (including competition); the *sources* of the impressions (merchandising, packaging, advertising, media, etc.); the *company* that makes the product; and *types of consumers* associated with the product.

4. It is easily repeatable and quite reliable. Therefore, it can be used as a continuing measure sensitive enough to note changes in consumer reactions from year to year.

5. It avoids sterotyped responses and allows for individual frames of reference. The sheer number of scales and concepts and the speed of administration (both with groups and individuals), encourage quick "top-of-mind" responses. For this reason it has sometimes been called a "semantic projection" test.

6. It eliminates some of the problems of question phrasing, such as ambiguity and overlapping of statements. In addition, it facilitates the interviewing of respondents who may not be too articulate in describing their reactions to such abstruse factors as a brand, product, or company image.

MODIFICATIONS FOR ADVERTISING RESEARCH

To make the differential even more sensitive in evoking subtle distinctions in the images of physically similar products, researchers have suggested many modifications. The most important of these are:

1. *Descriptive nouns and phrases.* These are in addition to (and sometimes as a substitute for) simple one-word adjectives. The original differential dealt primarily with single-word adjectives such as "good-bad," "weak-strong," "pleasant-unpleasant," etc. The "evaluation," "activity," and "po-tency" factors are still retained, but with increased shades of meaning provided by these longer, more involved scales.

Here is an example for a beer:

Happy-go-lucky—kind of serious
Something special—just another drink
Little after-taste—lots of after-taste
Really refreshing—not really refreshing
American flavor—foreign flavor

Here is an example for people who drink beer:

Live in average homes—live in expensive homes
Take life easy—always on the go
Drink just to be sociable—really enjoy it
Really know beer—can't tell one from another
Snobs—regular guys
Housewife—career girl

Edmund W. J. Faison, President of Visual Research Inc., in an attempt to match personality types with package designs, labels, colors, etc., has used these phrases as one end of a scale:

Stands out in a crowd
Self-made man
Likes to hunt and fish
Factory worker making $400 a month
Belongs to a higher social class than his parents

2. *Tailor-made scales.* In attempting to set up standardized scales, certain researchers have concentrated on the classic list of 50 word-pairs, factor-analyzed by Osgood. This direction offers comparative possibilities and a hope of generalized attitude scales. In rating TV commericals, Burleigh Gardner of Social Research, Inc., consistently uses 30 word pairs, with heavy factor loadings on evaluation, activity, strength, etc.

But for many researchers such a standardized list lacks flexibility and appropriateness to the specific problems at hand. They find it necessary to construct tailor-made word and phrase lists. Sources for these lists are content analyses of their own and competitive advertising, word association tests with consumers, individual or group interviews, and factor analyses.

In such exploratory or pretests, simple opposites are used, often without the 7-

point scale. Once it is agreed that these adjectives and phrases cover the factors best delimiting the image, they are then scaled to permit profile comparisons.

3. *"Connotative" and "non-polar" opposites.* Although in theory every adjective or phrase should have a denotative opposite (true-untrue, good-bad, bright-dull), researchers have found that in practice respondents often refuse to "play the game," as it were. In an advertising context or in rating large well-known companies, subjects often balk at using negative sides of scales or to gradate a concept negatively.

Respondents can, and do, make sharp distinctions as to the level of believability of a company's advertising or of a particular claim. But they either hesitate to rate a concept as unbelievable (feeling that "if it is advertised, it must be true") or they are unable to gradate their feelings of unbelievability.

This failure frequently results in indiscrimate clustering about the middle of the scales, thus making it difficult to differentiate among concept profiles. Some researchers have attempted to circumvent this tendency either by "heightening" the level of the dimensions or by using phrases which, although not necessarily *denotatively* opposite, still seem to fit more logically and naturally into people's frame of reference. Scales such as these are used:

> Really modern—sort of old-fashioned
> High-quality product—so-so quality product
> Heavy beer drinker—a "sometimes" beer drinker
> Really peps you up—somehow doesn't pep you up

4. *Built-in control concepts.* As a realistic control, it is helpful to get ratings on such concepts as, "the ideal company," or "my favorite brand," or "brand I would never use." These control profiles can be compared with test concepts or competitive concepts. Although one might expect respondents simply to use the extremes on all scales to represent their "ideal" or their "least-liked," such is not really the case.

5. *Personal interviews and mail questionnaires.* Early experiments with the differential usually were conducted with "cap-

tive" audiences, often students in class. In the main, though, the advertising researcher prefers to do field studies and depends on individual personal interviews. The differential has been used in these situations, and respondents show little reluctance in performing the task of checking several concepts on a variety of scales. The need for tailor-made scales is often quite apparent, however, in that certain age groups and certain socio-economic groups find it relatively difficult to think in terms of various continua and to deal with such abstractions as "concepts."

Other researchers have even experimented with the differential in mail questionnaires, although this means of delivery obviates most of the projective qualities of this test. Respondents have too much time to deliberate over their judgments and have too much control over their ratings. Personal supervision is necessary to assure speed and "top-of-mind" responses.

A BRAND-IMAGE STUDY

The following case study demonstrates the use of the differential, as well as some of the modifications discussed. This particular study's purpose was to determine beer drinkers' reactions to the personalities of three local brands of beer (and specifically Brand Y), compared with three competitive national brands in a large midwest city. Various facets of this image were to be explored, such as specific characteristics of each brand, the attitudes toward advertising, the image of the company, and feelings about various consumers who might be associated or not associated with each brand of beer.

Respondents were asked to rate these six beers on several dimensions. Scales were selected from content analyses of depth-interview responses, as well as from advertisements for the various brands. The mean ratings were converted into profiles for comparison purposes. Figures 1 through 4 illustrate certain critical scales for three local brands of beer.

Results

1. Looking at the profiles of products, company, and advertising image, (Figures

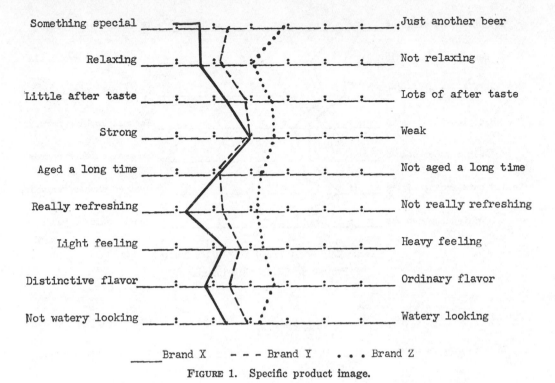

FIGURE 1.   Specific product image.

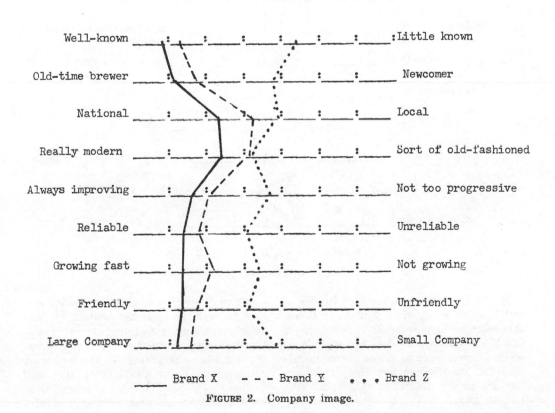

FIGURE 2.   Company image.

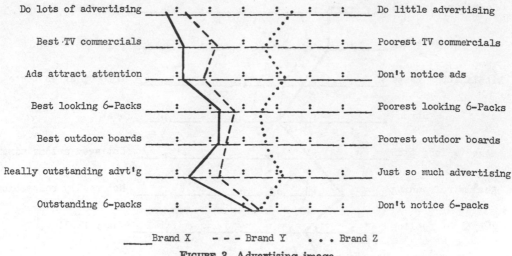

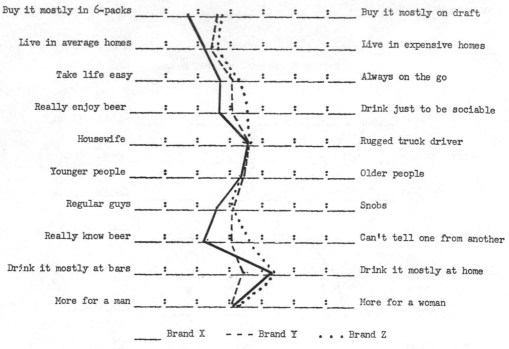

FIGURE 3. Advertising image.

FIGURE 4. Consumer profile.

1, 2, and 3) it is apparent that Brands X and Y enjoy many more positive or favorable ratings than Brand Z. This reflects X and Y's domination of sales and their large market share. None of X's or Y's mean ratings fall on the negative side; and very few are in the neutral or indifferent area (3.5 to 4.5).

Brand X received essentially positive ratings in regard to specific <u>product</u> (it was quite refreshing, something special, relaxing, and had a distinctive flavor); <u>advertising</u> (it was outstanding, it was attention getting, and there was lots of it); and <u>company</u> (it was friendly, large, well-known, and an old-time brewer who still manages to grow fast and always improve).

Although Brand Y's ratings usually were favorable, they were not as extreme as Brand X. The only two exceptions occurred in ratings of the specific products. Beer drinkers rated Y about the same as X on the "weak-strong" scale and the "aged-a-long-time" dimension. *Brand Z*, a relative newcomer to the city, was reacted to quite neutrally—in this case, an indication of little consumer experience with, or knowledge of, the beer. In addition to its "militant indifference," Brand Z was thought to be less well-known than the other two brands, to do less advertising, and to be more of a local beer.

2. In products such as beer, advertising researchers are interested in determining the "types" of consumer most often associated with a particular brand. Social Research, Inc., the Psychological Corporation, the Institute for Motivational Research, Inc., and other organizations increasingly emphasize psychological typologies rather than conventional demographic characteristics.

In this case, Figure 4 shows that the consumer profile ratings, that is, the types of people considered likely to buy each of these beers, tend to cluster much more than for the other three factors. It might be advantageous for a beer *not* to be inordinately connected or identified with a particular type of consumer.

Beer drinkers thought Brands X and Y more "universal" than Z. They were "all things to all beer drinkers." Brand X was thought of as being consumed more at home and by average people who really enjoy and know beer. Brand Y was considered to be drunk more in bars. Brand Z's image tended toward home drinking and use by less discriminating beer drinkers.

The results of this study were interpreted by the management of Y company to be quite favorable, particularly when the ad-

vertising budgets of X and Y were compared. Management was pleased with reactions to the company which a few years back had not enjoyed the best of reputations. Possible weak areas which might need strengthening were Brand Y's dealer displays (6-packs); the feeling that the company was not as modern as it could be; and the need of upgrading the image of the beer among "higher-class," sophisticated, home beer drinkers.

Implications

A great deal of controversy (some genuine, some "strawman") exists between the "quantifier" and the "qualifier" in attempting to delineate the image of a product, brand, or company. The semantic differential and techniques similar to it help to quantify what too often has been considered abstract, mysterious, and qualitative material regarding consumers' opinions, feeling tones, and emotional reactions. In addition, the modifications suggested by advertising researchers (phrases and nouns in addition to single adjectives, connotative as well as denotative opposites, tailor-made scales) add more scope and direction to what may be superficial quantitative information.

The differential serves as a two-edged tool: (1) It is a simple, large sample, nose-counting device which can be repeated from time to time to detect trends in consumer reactions, and to measure interaction between advertising and consumer attitudes. (2) In addition, the differential "profiles" serve as useful directional indicators for further and more intensive probing, using many of the qualitative projective techniques.

In either case, this knowledge can be quite useful in deciding on a possible advertising or marketing plan, in spotting weak areas which might need to be strengthened or strong areas which might need to be emphasized.

Appendix: Semantic Atlas for 550 Concepts *

The eleven measures in order and by column heading are:

COMPOSITE FACTOR SCORES: The mean score for each dimension (E, P, A) using the four scales derived from the pan-cultural analysis for each dimension.

STANDARDIZED COMPOSITE SCORES: Each composite score is standardized by the dimension mean and standard deviation.

FAM: The mean score on the *familiar-unfamiliar* scale.

D-ORG: The distance of the Concept from the origin of a three-dimensional space. The co-ordinates of the point/Concept are taken as the three composite factor scores.

$$0.0 \leq \text{D-ORG} = \sqrt{E^2 + P^2 + A^2} \leq 5.196$$

Example: AUTOMOBILE E = 1.9, P = 2.0,

A = 1.2, D-ORG = 2.84

P-IND: Polarity or meaningfulness based on every *individual* subject's absolute deviation from the midpoint of the scale. The midpoint is assumed to be the origin of the scale and in this sense is defined as meaningless. Here subjects checking on opposite sides of a scale *add* to the total sum of absolutes.

* A description of the cross-cultural project within which these data were collected may be found in C. E. Osgood, Semantic Differential Technique in the Comparative Study of Cultures, in Part V.

$$0.0 \leq \text{P-IND} = \frac{\sum\limits_{sc} \sum\limits_{ss} |(X-4)|}{\text{Nsc} \times \text{Nss}} \leq 3.0$$

Where, Nsc = Number of scales
and Nss = Number of subjects

P-GRP: Polarity or meaningfulness based on the absolute deviation of the *group* means from the midpoint of the scales. Note that subjects checking opposite sides of a scale will *cancel out* in the mean and *lower* the value.

$$0.0 \leq \text{P-GRP} = \frac{\sum\limits_{sc} \left| \frac{\sum\limits_{ss} (X-4)}{\text{Nss}} \right|}{\text{Nsc}} =$$

$$\frac{\sum\limits_{sc} |X|}{\text{Nsc}} \leq 3.0$$

CI: Cultural instability of the Concept. This is the simple difference.

$$\text{CI} = (\text{P-IND}) - (\text{P-GRP})$$

A high CI is the result of a high P-IND (subjects checking extremes) minus a low P-GRP (little agreement on which end of the scale applies to the Concept) and is often interpretable as conflict or lack of stereotypy in the culture for that concept.

MEAN AND STANDARD DEVIATION OF COMPOSITE SCORES AND FAMILIAR SCALE OVER ALL CONCEPTS

E		P		A		FAM	
MEAN	S	MEAN	S	MEAN	S	MEAN	S
.883	1.044	.902	.758	.062	.613	1.387	.782

	COMPOSITE FACTOR SCORES			STANDARDIZED COMPOSITE SCORES - Z			FAM	D-ORG	P-IND	P-GRP	CI
	E	P	A	E	P	A					
ACCEPT THINGS	.637	.544	-.144	-.235	-.473	-.336	1.100	.850	1.400	.596	.804
ACCIDENT	-1.750	.744	.256	-2.522	-.209	-.316	1.075	1.919	1.558	1.162	.396
ADOLESCENCE	.381	.344	.787	-.480	-.736	1.182	1.175	.940	1.479	.508	.971
ADULTERY	-1.412	1.206	.187	-2.199	.401	.204	.200	1.867	1.723	1.056	.667
AFRICA	.088	1.412	-.203	-.762	.673	-.432	.432	1.429	1.667	1.149	.518
AGGRESSIVE	.781	1.381	.525	-.097	.632	.754	1.250	1.671	1.504	.992	.513
AIR	2.112	1.750	.431	1.178	1.118	.602	2.325	2.777	1.952	1.610	.342
AIRPLANE	1.725	1.675	1.250	.807	1.020	1.937	1.900	2.710	1.912	1.550	.362
ANGER	-1.169	.946	.473	-1.966	-.058	.670	1.189	1.576	1.583	.984	.599
ANIMAL	1.277	.723	.892	.378	-.236	1.353	1.892	1.717	1.473	.964	.509
ANSWER	.294	1.031	.050	.394	-.170	-.020	1.300	1.655	1.479	.904	.575
APPLE	.892	.534	.716	.967	-.486	1.066	1.946	2.092	1.619	1.074	.545
APRIL	1.225	.481	.137	-.328	-.555	.123	1.825	1.323	1.277	.710	.567
ARGUMENT	-.974	.763	.382	-1.779	-.183	.521	1.789	1.295	1.360	.917	.443
ARM	1.844	1.662	1.119	.921	1.003	1.723	2.200	2.723	1.758	1.625	.133
ARMY	1.408	2.250	1.059	.503	1.778	1.625	1.447	2.858	1.958	1.708	.250
ARTIST	-.662	.050	-.431	-.211	-1.124	-.805	.500	.792	1.294	.573	.721
ASIA	-.212	1.381	-.325	-1.049	.632	-.631	.700	1.435	1.631	.965	.667
ASTROLOGY	1.169	1.325	-.437	.274	.558	-.815	.325	1.820	1.548	1.110	.437
ATHEISTS	-.925	-.525	-.119	-1.732	-1.882	-.295	-.575	1.070	1.673	.585	1.088
ATOMIC BOMB	-1.306	2.462	1.531	-2.097	2.058	2.395	-.000	3.180	2.329	1.850	.479
AUGUST	1.075	.606	.119	.184	-.390	.092	2.050	1.240	1.283	.704	.579
AUNT	1.439	.068	-.101	.533	-1.101	-.267	1.892	1.444	1.509	.968	.541
AUTHOR	.912	.775	-.200	-.029	-.168	-.428	.825	1.214	1.425	.829	.596
AUTHORITY	.625	.400	.087	-.247	.657	.041	1.800	1.536	1.596	.950	.646
AUTOMATION	.850	1.337	1.169	-.031	.574	1.804	.400	1.969	1.615	1.119	.496
AUTOMOBILE	1.894	1.919	1.200	.969	1.341	1.855	2.175	2.951	1.950	1.671	.279
BABY	1.534	-2.074	1.216	-.624	-3.926	1.881	1.730	2.852	2.414	1.973	.441
BALDNESS	-.937	-.037	-.837	-1.744	-1.239	-1.467	.425	1.258	1.329	.825	.504
BALL	1.244	.631	.619	.346	-.357	.907	2.325	1.526	1.494	.835	.658
BANKER	1.056	.987	-.219	.166	.113	-.458	1.125	1.462	1.512	1.012	.500
BARBER	1.462	.669	-.369	.556	-.308	-.500	1.725	1.650	1.387	.958	.429
BATH	1.912	1.000	.256	.987	.129	-.519	2.125	2.173	1.827	1.265	.562
BATTLE	-1.562	1.556	.325	-2.343	.863	.428	.475	2.229	1.852	1.352	.500
BEAR	-.075	1.919	-.575	-.918	1.341	-.836	.900	2.004	1.694	1.152	.542
BEARD	-.319	-.600	-.819	-1.151	-.398	-1.437	1.100	1.064	1.500	.800	.700
BED	1.962	1.344	-.250	1.035	.583	-.509	2.600	2.392	1.927	1.269	.658
BEGGAR	-1.437	-1.469	-.825	-2.223	-3.127	-1.447	-.550	2.215	1.598	1.244	.354
BELIEF	1.513	1.632	-.059	.604	.962	-.198	1.947	2.226	1.629	1.371	.259
BICYCLE	1.369	.337	-.137	.466	-.745	-.123	1.975	1.416	1.302	.694	.608
BIRD	1.480	-.717	1.171	.573	-2.136	1.808	2.211	2.019	1.522	1.123	.399
BIRTH	1.527	.264	.730	.617	-.842	1.088	1.541	1.713	1.822	1.002	.820
BIRTH CONTROL	-.200	.750	.306	-.654	-.200	.398	-.200	.834	1.519	.552	.967
BLACK RACE	-.062	.837	.312	-.906	-.085	.408	1.075	.896	1.496	.700	.796
BLANKET	1.612	.944	-.475	-.699	.055	-.876	2.250	1.928	1.435	1.044	.392
BLIND	-1.881	-.331	-.887	-2.648	-1.627	-1.549	-.275	2.106	1.775	1.258	.517
BLOOD	1.756	1.181	-.481	.837	.368	-.683	1.725	2.171	1.852	1.406	.446
BLUE	1.225	.812	-.375	.328	-.118	-.713	1.950	1.517	1.329	.921	.408
BODY	2.075	1.487	1.225	1.143	.772	1.896	2.350	2.832	1.912	1.596	.317
BOOK	1.544	1.081	-.375	.634	.236	-.713	1.850	1.922	1.529	1.158	.371

AMERICAN ENGLISH

	COMPOSITE FACTOR SCORES			STANDARDIZED COMPOSITE SCORES - Z							
	E	P	A	E	P	A	FAM	D-ORG	P-IND	P-GRP	CI
BORROWING MONE	.550	.656	-.169	-.319	-.324	-.377	1.025	.873	1.387	.592	.796
BOTTLE	.919	.769	-.162	.035	-.176	-.367	1.425	1.209	1.279	.621	.658
BOX	1.081	.987	-.212	.190	-.113	-.448	1.700	1.480	1.240	.760	.479
BOY	1.175	1.052	1.656	.280	.212	2.599	1.900	2.292	1.594	1.298	.296
BRAIN	2.106	1.794	.750	1.172	1.176	1.121	2.000	2.866	2.187	1.767	.421
BREAD	1.950	.319	-.325	1.023	-.769	-.631	2.275	2.002	1.431	.965	.467
BRIDE	2.125	-.031	.550	1.190	-1.231	.795	1.500	2.195	1.794	1.185	.608
BRIDEGROOM	1.800	1.094	1.000	.879	.253	1.529	1.100	2.332	1.769	1.398	.371
BRIDGE	1.601	1.545	.027	.689	.584	-.057	1.405	2.091	1.613	1.108	.505
BROTHER	1.007	.432	1.115	.119	-.619	1.716	1.865	1.563	1.586	.851	.734
BROWN RACE	.350	.662	.644	-.510	-.316	-.948	1.250	.988	1.381	.706	.675
BUDDHISTS	-.362	.194	-.656	-1.193	-.934	-1.172	-.475	.774	1.096	.446	.650
BUS	1.300	1.287	.194	.400	.508	.214	1.275	1.840	1.506	1.010	.496
BUSINESS	1.387	1.706	.694	.484	1.061	1.030	1.450	2.306	1.775	1.454	.321
BUTTER	1.519	-.450	-.544	.610	-1.783	-.988	2.125	1.675	1.325	.842	.483
CAKE	1.856	.587	.094	.933	-.415	.051	1.925	1.749	1.558	1.025	.533
CANCER	-2.547	1.642	-.635	-3.286	.976	-1.137	.676	3.096	2.320	1.761	.559
CANDY	1.462	.087	-.187	.556	-1.074	-.407	2.350	1.477	1.600	.637	.962
CANNED FOODS	1.325	.131	-.062	.424	-1.017	-.020	1.600	1.333	1.348	.719	.629
CAPITALISM	-.723	1.034	.074	-1.538	.174	.693	.676	1.264	1.628	.750	.878
CAT	-.219	-.662	.487	-.636	-2.063	-.540	1.625	.851	1.506	.698	.808
CENSORSHIP	.012	.944	-.269	-.834	-.055	-1.314	1.175	.981	1.404	.487	.917
CENTURY	.769	1.362	-.744	-.109	.607	-1.865	1.000	1.732	1.379	1.067	.312
CHAIR	1.456	.719	-1.081	.550	-.242	-1.865	2.175	1.351	1.419	1.085	.333
CHAMPION	1.587	1.881	1.256	.675	1.292	1.947	1.575	2.764	1.833	1.575	.258
CHARACTER	1.225	1.325	-.406	.328	.558	-.601	.875	1.350	1.394	1.073	.321
CHARITY	1.637	1.287	-.306	-.723	.508	-1.651	1.175	2.105	1.531	1.252	.279
CHEATING	-2.069	-.819	-.950	-2.828	-2.270	-.477	.675	2.419	2.000	1.279	.721
CHEESE	1.000	.506	-.844	-.113	-.113	-2.041	1.725	1.403	1.475	.946	.529
CHESS	.723	.291	-1.189	-.153	-.522	-.989	1.351	1.422	1.468	.793	.676
CHILD	1.337	-1.337	1.406	-.436	-.806	2.191	2.250	2.357	1.940	1.477	.463
CHILD, ILLEGIT	-.581	-.588	.669	-1.504	-2.954	-.203	-.162	1.053	1.545	.694	.851
CHOICE	1.419	1.056	-.062	.514	-1.965	-.459	1.750	2.857	1.258	1.029	.229
CHRISTIANS	1.056	1.900	.344	1.172	-.203	.968	2.075	1.695	2.017	1.733	.283
CINEMA	1.900	.912	-.656	-.370	1.316	1.835	1.675	1.002	1.287	.946	.321
CIRCLE	1.269	.480	-.426	-.108	.014	.632	1.405	1.951	1.225	.586	.342
CITY	.770	1.387	-.187	-.187	-.557	-.153	1.600	2.715	1.600	1.208	.640
CIVILIZATION	.687	2.119	.450	-.723	.640	.408	1.950	2.636	1.969	1.698	.392
CLEANLINESS	1.637	1.325	.156	1.388	1.605	-1.263	2.400	1.873	1.883	1.525	.271
CLERGYMAN	2.331	1.050	.312	.610	.558	-.570	1.275	1.680	1.427	1.115	.358
CLOTH	1.519	.444	-.712	-.610	.195	-.595	1.950	1.474	1.446	.925	.312
CLOTHES	1.619	.344	-.287	-.705	-.604	-1.477	2.450	1.735	1.512	.837	.521
CLOUD	1.007	1.033	-.303	.119	-.736	-1.335	1.789	1.418	1.404	.855	.675
COFFEE	-.231	.234	-.844	-.624	-.173	-.498	1.700	.923	1.410	.573	.548
COLD	-.612	1.031	-.756	-1.433	-.802	.826	1.675	1.418	1.467	.800	.837
COLOR	1.474	.858	-.243	.566	-.170	.622	2.237	1.728	1.419	.989	.667
COMPETITION	.975	1.537	.569	.089	-.044	-.112	1.850	1.948	1.635	1.144	.430
COMPULSORY SER	-.344	1.159	.444	-.516	.904	-.443	.200	1.297	1.585	.877	.492
CONFLICT	-1.106	1.237	-.131	-1.906	.352	-.622	.450	1.665	1.592	1.054	.708
CONTEMPLATION	.291	.453	-.209	-.567	-.593	-.443	.351	.577	1.016	.408	.608

	COMPOSITE FACTOR SCORES			STANDARDIZED COMPOSITE SCORES – Z			FAM	D-ORG	P-IND	P-GRP	CI
	E	P	A	E	P	A					
COOPERATION	1.572	1.467	.441	.661	.745	.617	1.658	2.195	1.529	1.208	.320
COTTON	1.681	.031	-.612	.765	-1.148	-1.100	1.550	1.790	1.575	.917	.658
COUNTRY	1.962	2.062	.725	1.035	1.531	1.081	2.450	2.938	2.004	1.658	.346
COURAGE	1.894	1.962	.694	.969	1.399	1.030	1.525	2.814	1.862	1.579	.283
COW	1.619	1.181	.025	.705	.368	-.061	2.025	2.004	1.750	1.308	.442
CREATURE	-.944	1.494	.431	-1.750	.780	.602	-.400	1.819	1.506	1.106	.400
CREDIT	1.158	.954	-.092	.264	.069	-.252	1.789	1.503	1.375	.840	.535
CRIME	-2.075	1.287	.119	-2.834	-.508	-.092	.300	2.445	1.998	1.502	.496
CROW	-.900	-.131	.825	-1.708	-1.363	1.244	1.750	.958	1.444	.765	.679
CUBE, A	.581	-.212	-.731	-.289	-.909	-1.294	1.525	.958	.950	.587	.362
CUP	1.200	.012	-.656	.304	-1.173	-.928	2.025	1.368	1.335	.719	.617
DAM	1.844	2.456	.631	.921	2.050	.928	2.050	3.135	2.210	1.677	.533
DANCING	1.337	.550	-.631	-.436	-.464	-.928	1.675	1.578	1.590	.919	.671
DANGER	-1.337	1.462	.231	-2.127	.739	.276	.750	1.995	1.640	1.152	.487
DAY	1.512	1.062	.569	-.604	.212	.826	1.550	1.934	1.548	1.048	.500
DEAF	-1.925	-.106	-1.381	-2.690	-.330	-2.354	-.450	2.372	1.825	1.296	.529
DEATH	-1.131	.544	-1.700	-1.930	-.473	-2.873	.550	2.113	1.879	1.208	.671
DEBT	-1.606	.644	-.762	-2.385	-.341	-1.345	.850	1.891	1.629	1.025	.604
DECEMBER	1.050	.950	-.375	-.160	-.063	-.713	2.400	1.604	1.604	.958	.646
DEFEAT	-.804	.676	-.176	-1.616	-.299	-.388	1.297	1.065	1.637	.628	.009
DEFENSE	1.650	2.094	.719	.735	1.572	1.070	1.300	2.761	2.075	1.737	.337
DEMOCRACY	1.625	2.019	.656	.711	1.473	.968	1.675	2.673	1.767	1.517	.250
DEVIL	-2.037	1.725	-.350	-2.798	1.085	-.672	-.925	2.475	1.690	1.496	.667
DEVOTION	1.775	.669	-.037	.855	.459	-.051	1.575	1.235	1.348	1.435	.254
DIALECT	.494	.962	-1.112	.148	-.308	-1.915	1.075	1.552	1.635	.748	.600
DIRT	-.944	.362	.031	-.373	-.080	-.163	1.775	1.706	1.375	.965	.671
DISCIPLINE	1.294	1.062	.406	.059	.607	.561	1.425	1.688	1.456	.958	.417
DISCUSSION	1.062	1.387	.212	.394	.212	.245	1.175	2.641	1.933	1.056	.400
DISEASE	-2.162	-.612	-.612	-2.918	-.640	-1.100	1.625	1.259	1.175	.517	.417
DISH	1.194	-.031	-.400	.298	-1.231	-.754	-.375	1.768	1.698	.600	.575
DIVORCE	-1.694	.506	-.031	-2.469	-.522	-.153	1.811	2.191	1.779	.965	.733
DOCTOR	1.797	1.230	.243	.876	.432	.295	1.700	1.979	1.673	1.441	.338
DOG	1.062	1.106	1.250	.172	-.269	1.937	.500	.364	1.002	1.140	.533
DOWN	-.125	-.219	-.262	-.726	-.901	-.530	1.500	.948	1.483	.260	.742
DREAM	.744	.575	-.119	-.133	-.431	-.295	1.324	1.191	1.450	.600	.883
DRESS	-1.142	-.223	-.257	-.248	-.896	-.520	.825	1.492	1.931	.649	.802
DRUNKENNESS	-1.369	-.556	-.206	-2.157	-.456	-.438	1.925	1.821	1.525	.898	1.033
DUTY	1.087	1.431	-.287	-.196	.698	.377	-.400	.884	1.119	1.046	.479
DYSENTERY	-.750	.369	-.287	-1.564	-.703	-.570	-.725	2.229	1.921	.469	.650
EAR	1.925	.831	.756	.999	-.093	1.132	2.500	3.359	2.421	1.462	.458
EARTHQUAKE	-2.094	2.506	-.787	-2.852	2.116	-.611	-.825	1.166	1.415	2.129	.292
EAST	.712	.869	-.312	-.163	-.044	-.194	2.400	2.209	1.644	.777	.637
EATING	1.931	1.056	.181	1.005	.203	.194	2.475	3.127	2.110	1.215	.429
EDUCATION	2.112	2.256	.475	1.178	1.786	.673	1.850	3.068	1.490	1.719	.392
EGG	1.606	-.281	-.781	.693	-.561	-1.561	2.350	3.068	2.200	.894	.596
ELECTRICITY	2.031	2.162	-.181	1.101	1.663	1.172	.750	2.358	1.935	1.800	.400
ELEPHANT	.894	2.181	-.056	-.011	1.687	-.193	.950	1.472	1.385	1.702	.233
ENVY	-1.319	.644	-.033	-2.109	-.341	-.155	.895	1.970	1.627	.773	.612
EUROPE	1.178	.579	-.119	-.283	.022	-.341	.125	1.238	1.433	1.276	.351
EVOLUTION	.356	-.919	-.750	-.504	-1.324	-.750				.829	.604

AMERICAN ENGLISH — STANDARDIZED

	COMPOSITE FACTOR SCORES			COMPOSITE SCORES – Z							
	E	P	A	E	P	A	FAM	D-ORG	P-IND	P-GRP	CI
EXAMINATION	.181	1.256	-.481	-.672	.467	-.886	1.400	1.357	1.640	.890	.750
EXCREMENT	-.131	.231	-.156	-.720	-.885	-.356	-.325	.308	1.044	.269	.775
EYES	2.075	1.562	.719	1.143	.607	1.070	2.075	2.584	1.944	1.740	.204
FACE	1.406	.675	.837	.502	-.299	1.264	2.225	1.770	1.385	.994	.392
FACTORY WORKER	1.101	1.250	.655	-.210	.459	.967	1.054	1.790	1.601	1.106	.495
FAILURE	-1.487	.569	-.337	-2.271	-.703	-.652	.475	1.569	1.323	.790	.533
FALL	1.081	.731	-.106	.190	-.225	-.275	2.325	1.310	1.648	.773	.875
FAMILY	1.700	1.419	.750	.783	.682	1.121	2.125	2.338	1.756	1.298	.458
FAMILY, BIG	.544	1.094	.519	-.325	.253	.775	.525	1.334	1.404	.842	.562
FARMER	1.375	1.244	.319	.472	.451	.418	1.850	1.881	1.787	1.167	.621
FAT	-1.400	.406	-.837	-2.187	-.654	-1.467	-.300	1.681	1.635	1.123	.513
FATALISM	-.800	.294	-.381	-1.612	-.802	-.723	-.100	.934	1.042	.504	.537
FATHER	1.944	1.875	.469	1.017	1.283	-.061	2.550	2.741	1.825	1.629	.196
FEAR	-.800	1.150	.025	-1.612	-.327	-.703	.425	1.401	1.533	.817	.717
FEBRUARY	.294	-.012	-.369	-.564	-1.206	-.703	1.875	.472	1.371	.429	.942
FEET	1.431	1.119	.656	.526	.286	.968	2.350	1.932	1.669	1.223	.446
FEMALE	2.276	-.568	.914	1.335	-1.676	1.389	2.368	2.481	1.739	1.410	.329
FEMININITY	1.642	.264	.574	.728	-.842	.835	1.486	1.759	1.682	1.016	.667
FESTIVALS	1.437	1.156	.719	.532	.335	1.070	1.275	1.980	1.692	1.267	.425
FIELD	1.294	1.169	-.275	.394	.352	-.550	1.500	1.765	1.508	1.046	.463
FIGHTING	-1.000	1.081	.506	-1.804	.236	.724	1.200	1.557	1.575	1.137	.437
FIRE	-1.137	1.831	.887	-1.936	1.226	1.346	1.675	2.331	1.823	1.419	.404
FISH	.162	1.056	.687	-.268	.203	1.019	1.350	1.715	1.565	1.090	.475
FIVE	.369	-.575	-.131	-.492	-1.948	-.316	1.925	.696	1.058	.454	.604
FLAG	1.969	1.919	-.019	1.041	1.341	-.132	2.550	2.749	1.915	1.669	.246
FLOOR	1.250	1.094	-.581	.352	.253	-1.049	1.775	1.760	1.425	.975	.450
FLOWER	1.223	-.628	-.034	-.326	-2.018	-.157	1.459	1.375	1.610	1.016	.595
FOG	-1.094	.394	-1.537	-1.894	-.670	-2.608	1.450	1.927	1.800	1.071	.729
FOOD	2.131	1.500	.125	1.196	.789	-.102	2.250	2.609	1.756	1.444	.312
FOREIGNER	-.838	.196	.446	-.043	-.931	.626	.838	.969	1.354	.633	.721
FOREST	1.934	2.158	-.441	1.008	1.656	-.820	1.684	2.931	2.107	1.853	.254
FORGIVENESS	1.816	1.230	-.191	.894	.433	-.413	1.474	2.202	1.605	1.259	.346
FOUR	.819	-.156	.006	-.061	-1.396	-.091	1.625	.834	1.210	.452	.758
FREE WILL	1.737	1.562	.608	1.071	.871	.890	1.300	2.381	1.623	1.394	.229
FREEDOM	2.000	1.791	.594	1.029	1.172	.642	1.892	2.752	2.056	1.484	.572
FRIDAY	1.956	1.087	.456	.734	.245	.867	2.125	2.316	1.879	1.267	.612
FRIEND	1.649	1.155	1.250	.214	.334	1.937	2.216	2.370	1.649	1.351	.297
FRIENDSHIP	2.150	2.087	.475	1.214	1.564	.673	2.300	3.034	1.967	1.779	.187
FRUG, THE	-.219	.294	.681	-.636	-.802	1.009	-.225	.773	1.065	.406	.658
FRUIT	1.756	.606	.362	.837	-.390	.490	2.150	1.893	1.575	1.021	.554
FUNERAL	-.387	-.669	-2.050	-1.217	-.308	-3.444	1.425	2.191	1.815	1.169	.646
FUTURE	1.544	1.725	.925	.634	1.085	1.407	-.025	2.493	1.744	1.398	.346
GAME	-1.462	.512	-.500	-.556	-.514	.714	2.000	1.628	1.512	.921	.592
GHOSTS	-1.312	-.694	-.919	-2.103	-1.841	-1.600	-.250	1.676	1.729	.971	.758
GIRL	2.394	.250	1.075	1.448	-.860	1.651	2.425	2.636	1.906	1.356	.550
GLASS	1.519	.131	-.700	.610	-1.017	-1.243	2.000	1.677	1.387	.833	.554
GOD	2.425	2.406	.431	1.478	1.984	.602	2.075	3.443	2.321	2.121	.200
GUVERN CLERK	.856	.462	.187	-.025	-.580	-.204	.475	.991	1.369	.681	.687
GRAFT	.369	.537	-.206	-.492	-.481	-.438	.050	.684	1.233	.487	.746
GRAMOPHONE	1.506	.619	.387	.598	-.374	.530	2.050	1.674	1.375	.871	.504

AMERICAN ENGLISH

	COMPOSITE FACTOR SCORES			STANDARDIZED COMPOSITE SCORES - Z							
	E	P	A	E	P	A	FAM	D-ORG	P-IND	P-GRP	CI
GRANDFATHER	1.811	.824	-.655	.889	-.102	-1.170	1.811	2.095	1.827	1.412	.414
GRANDMOTHER	1.612	.025	-.869	.699	-1.157	-1.518	1.700	1.832	1.794	1.202	.592
GRASS	1.575	-.087	.037	.663	-1.305	-.040	2.475	1.578	1.771	.958	.812
GREED	-1.606	.369	-.406	-2.385	-.703	-.764	.075	1.697	1.431	.865	.567
GREEN	-.969	.706	-.619	.083	-.258	-1.110	1.775	1.349	1.577	.910	.667
GREY	-.200	-.394	-1.362	-1.037	-1.709	-2.323	1.175	1.432	1.369	.756	.612
GROUP	.770	1.074	.730	-.108	.227	1.088	.811	1.510	1.426	.858	.568
GROWING	1.862	1.224	.447	.938	.424	.628	2.158	2.272	1.708	1.414	.294
GUILT	-.987	.344	-.344	-1.792	.583	-.662	1.075	1.703	1.633	.892	.742
GYPSY	-.350	.137	-.187	-1.181	-.008	.204	-.300	.420	1.181	.379	.804
HAIR	1.419	.675	.000	.514	-.299	-.102	2.500	1.571	1.594	.990	.604
HAND	1.631	1.256	.894	.717	.467	1.356	2.125	2.245	1.806	1.435	.371
HAPPINESS	2.162	1.831	.519	1.226	1.226	.744	2.175	2.881	2.017	1.592	.425
HAT	.919	-.225	-.687	.035	-1.486	-1.223	1.875	1.169	1.335	.627	.708
HEAD	1.622	1.264	.757	.708	.477	1.132	2.108	2.191	1.624	1.282	.342
HEART	1.994	1.800	.950	1.065	1.184	1.447	2.150	2.849	1.977	1.581	.396
HEAT	1.137	1.406	-.131	.244	.665	-.316	2.025	1.813	1.442	1.150	.292
HEAVEN	2.550	2.469	-.644	1.598	2.066	-1.151	-.100	3.607	2.375	2.108	.267
HELL	-2.087	1.925	-.912	-2.846	1.349	-1.589	-.750	2.983	2.429	1.908	.521
HERBS	.494	-.425	-.381	-.373	-.629	-.723	-.400	.755	1.292	.692	.600
HERO	1.800	1.850	1.087	.879	1.250	1.672	1.150	2.801	1.875	1.579	.296
HIGH SCHOOL	1.262	1.144	-.731	.364	.319	1.091	2.125	1.854	1.683	1.046	.638
HINDUS	-.081	.344	-.456	-.924	-.736	-.845	-.225	.577	.977	.348	.629
HISTORY	1.069	1.262	-.819	.178	.475	-1.437	1.375	1.846	1.583	1.050	.533
HOMOSEXUAL	-1.318	-.223	-.068	-2.108	-1.484	.009	-.297	1.338	1.635	.802	.833
HOPE	1.500	1.406	-.156	.592	.665	-.356	1.850	2.062	1.550	1.237	.312
HORSE	1.581	1.781	1.150	.669	1.160	1.774	1.850	2.645	1.825	1.504	.321
HOSPITAL	1.644	1.750	-.056	.729	1.118	-.193	1.725	2.402	2.008	1.479	.529
HOTEL	1.419	1.119	-.031	.514	-.286	-.153	1.150	1.807	1.410	1.119	.292
HOUR	.700	.419	-.450	-.175	-.637	-.835	1.475	.932	1.194	.635	.558
HOUSE	1.825	1.256	-.312	.903	.467	-.611	2.000	2.238	1.502	1.165	.338
HUNGER	-1.461	.678	-.671	-2.245	-.296	-1.196	.632	1.744	1.625	.936	.689
HUSBAND	1.725	1.625	.956	.807	.954	1.458	1.500	2.556	1.690	1.435	.254
ICE	.550	.731	-.437	-.319	-.225	-.815	1.825	1.014	1.431	.573	.858
IDEA	1.556	1.544	.375	.645	.846	.510	2.000	2.224	1.746	1.329	.417
ILLITERATE	-1.230	-.322	-.500	-2.024	-1.615	-.917	.368	1.367	1.421	.732	.689
IMMIGRANT	.175	.244	.031	-.678	-.868	-.051	-.300	.302	1.154	.458	.696
IMMORTALITY	.469	1.006	-.369	-.397	-.137	-.703	-.700	1.170	1.481	.727	.754
INDEPENDENT	1.625	1.441	.507	.711	.711	.724	2.184	2.230	1.603	1.200	.404
INFINITY	-.539	1.289	-.664	-.329	.511	-1.185	-.158	1.548	1.362	.879	.482
INITIATIVE,TAK	-.588	-.439	.277	-.282	-.610	.350	-.243	.784	1.133	.448	.685
INSANE	-1.906	-.494	-.319	-2.672	-1.841	-.621	-.400	1.995	1.931	1.277	.654
INSURANCE	1.606	1.437	-.200	.693	.706	-.428	1.150	2.165	1.569	1.194	.375
INTESTINES	-.819	1.081	-.181	-.061	.236	-.397	.975	1.368	1.515	.981	.533
IRON	1.162	1.387	-.394	-.268	.640	-.744	1.625	1.852	1.531	1.027	.504
I(MYSELF)	1.406	1.206	1.387	.502	.401	2.161	2.325	2.315	1.650	1.358	.292
JANUARY	.650	.900	-.175	-.223	-.003	-.387	1.800	1.124	1.342	.642	.700
JAZZ MUSIC	1.025	1.112	1.275	.136	.278	1.977	1.350	1.978	1.462	1.137	.325
JEWELRY	1.137	.300	-.450	.244	-.794	-.835	1.325	1.260	1.454	.629	.825
JEWS	.050	-.119	-.250	-.798	-1.346	-.509	-.275	.281	1.198	.402	.796

AMERICAN ENGLISH

	COMPOSITE FACTOR SCORES			STANDARDIZED COMPOSITE SCORES - Z			FAM	D-ORG	P-IND	P-GRP	CI
	E	P	A	E	P	A					
JOKE	.881	.281	.712	-.001	-.819	1.060	1.900	1.168	1.354	.625	.729
JULY	1.731	.862	.481	.813	-.052	.683	2.200	1.993	1.537	1.100	.437
JUNE	2.094	1.369	.594	1.161	.616	.867	2.150	2.571	1.906	1.352	.554
JUNGLE	-.475	1.869	.137	-1.301	1.275	.123	-.725	1.933	1.648	1.194	.454
JUSTICE	1.544	1.812	-.125	.634	1.201	-.305	1.100	2.384	1.781	1.394	.388
KINDNESS	2.250	1.800	.106	1.310	1.184	.072	1.950	2.883	1.869	1.669	.200
KING	-.387	1.287	.031	-.474	.508	-.051	.225	1.345	1.531	.877	.654
KISSING	2.275	1.887	-.019	1.334	1.300	-.132	1.700	2.956	2.140	1.844	.296
KNIFE	-.776	.903	-.520	-.102	-.008	-.949	2.132	1.303	1.388	.923	.465
KNOT	-.487	.644	-.394	-.379	-.341	-.744	1.550	.898	1.208	.608	.600
KNOWLEDGE	2.100	2.075	-.100	1.166	1.547	-.265	1.925	2.954	2.129	1.712	.417
LABOR UNIONS	1.125	1.794	.619	.232	1.176	-.907	1.550	2.206	1.562	1.296	.267
LABORATORY	1.625	1.681	.262	.711	1.028	.326	.150	2.353	1.660	1.269	.392
LADY	1.556	-.275	.737	.645	1.552	1.101	1.450	1.744	1.602	.944	.658
LAKE	1.412	1.637	-.250	.508	.970	-.509	1.925	2.177	1.762	1.229	.533
LAMP	1.487	.219	-.400	.580	-.901	-.754	2.225	1.556	1.452	.852	.600
LAND	1.831	1.994	-.525	.909	1.440	-.958	1.800	2.758	1.817	1.646	.171
LANGUAGE	1.625	1.562	.300	.711	.871	.388	1.750	2.274	1.654	1.333	.321
LAUGHTER	1.762	1.219	.931	.843	.418	1.417	1.700	2.336	1.654	1.304	.350
LAW	1.469	1.112	-.337	.562	.597	.449	1.100	2.595	1.844	1.544	.300
LAWYER	1.385	1.873	.743	.490	.467	.938	1.325	1.982	1.554	1.133	.421
LEADER	1.319	1.256	.637	.482	1.288	1.110	1.541	2.449	1.858	1.408	.450
LEFT HAND	1.837	1.312	.531	.418	-.102	.765	2.025	1.644	1.533	1.058	.475
LEG	1.506	.375	-.294	.915	.541	-.695	2.075	2.394	1.835	1.506	.329
LEISURE	1.669	1.444	-.625	.598	-.695	-.581	1.900	1.580	1.767	.842	.925
LIBRARY	2.125	1.750	-.175	.753	-.715	-1.121	2.375	2.293	1.792	1.375	.417
LIFE	2.044	1.937	1.037	1.190	1.366	1.590	2.200	3.057	2.025	1.700	.325
LIGHT	-.825	1.750	-.175	1.113	1.118	-.387	2.125	2.695	2.006	1.752	.254
LINE	-.150	-.337	-.319	-.055	-.745	-.621	2.000	.947	1.165	.544	.621
LION	1.784	2.119	1.062	-.989	1.605	1.631	.500	2.375	1.673	1.290	.383
LIPS	1.169	.203	.581	.864	-.922	.846	1.811	1.887	1.802	1.086	.716
LIPSTICK	-.437	.169	.319	.274	-.967	.418	1.900	1.223	1.385	.794	.592
LOTTERIES		-.006	-.106	-1.265	-1.181	-.275	-.150	.450	1.204	.404	.800
LOVE		.087	-.606	1.382	1.935	-.887	1.725	3.374	2.246	1.908	.337
LUCK	2.325	-.300	-.012	-1.678	-1.074	-.122	1.375	1.423	1.387	.725	.662
LYING	-.869	1.819	-.294	-.520	-.794	-.581	1.975	.965	1.517	.529	.988
MACHINE	1.506	-.283	1.144	-.598	-.209	1.763	.526	2.624	1.769	1.490	.279
MAGIC	-.026	1.512	-.493	-.820	-1.563	-.906	2.275	.569	1.272	.452	.820
MALE	1.494	1.78	-.637	-.586	.805	1.733	1.800	2.583	1.658	1.467	.192
MAN	1.337	1.512	-.556	.436	.805	.938	2.075	2.117	1.562	1.225	.338
MAP	1.494	.28	-.119	-.586	-.819	-1.009	1.800	1.619	1.410	.869	.542
MARCH	.931	.812	.544	-.047	-.118	.092	.475	1.242	1.379	.792	.587
MARRIAGE	1.862	1.487	1.025	.939	.772	.785	1.525	2.445	1.931	1.298	.633
MASCULINITY	1.756	1.925	.250	.837	1.349	1.570	2.800	2.800	1.790	1.569	.221
MATURITY	1.837	1.669	-.250	.915	1.011	-.061	1.725	2.482	1.902	1.490	.412
MAY	1.546	.592	-.262	.636	-.409	.306	2.395	1.674	1.458	.888	.570
MEAT	1.950	.950	-.164	1.023	.063	-.530	2.250	2.185	1.579	1.137	.442
MEDICINE	1.921	2.007	-.145	.995	1.457	.167	1.947	2.783	1.969	1.728	.241
MEMORY	1.434	1.434	-.256	.529	.702	-.338	1.737	2.033	1.618	1.316	.303
MENSTRUATION	.231	.756		-.624	-.192	-.519	.075	.831	1.160	.615	.546

	COMPOSITE FACTOR SCORES			STANDARDIZED COMPOSITE SCORES - Z							
	E	P	A	E	P	A	FAM	D-ORG	P-IND	P-GRP	CI
MIDDLE AGE	.425	.512	-.187	-.438	-.514	-.407	.525	.692	1.162	.533	.629
MIDDLE CLASS	1.012	.850	-.444	.124	-.069	.622	1.325	1.394	1.390	.802	.587
MILK	2.225	1.162	.162	1.286	.344	-.163	2.575	2.516	1.896	1.367	.529
MIND	1.987	1.969	.937	1.059	1.407	1.427	1.675	2.950	2.073	1.794	.279
MISSIONARY	1.925	1.344	.031	-.999	.583	-.051	1.300	2.348	1.846	1.375	.471
MOMENT	.842	.112	.099	-.039	-1.042	.059	1.526	.855	1.110	.645	.465
MONDAY	-.206	-.187	-.437	-1.043	-.942	-.815	2.050	.519	1.252	.277	.975
MONEY	1.819	1.325	-.144	.897	.558	-.336	1.625	2.255	1.687	1.308	.379
MONKEY	.219	-.294	1.412	-.636	-1.577	2.202	.600	1.459	1.358	.708	.650
MOON	1.125	1.156	-1.362	-.232	.335	-2.323	.525	2.112	1.802	1.215	.588
MOSLEMS	-.131	.469	-.350	-.971	-.571	-.672	-.200	.600	1.325	.471	.854
MOTHER	2.162	2.125	-.719	1.226	.294	1.070	2.350	2.541	1.756	1.440	.317
MOUNTAINS	1.250	2.169	-1.262	.352	1.671	-2.160	1.475	2.804	1.952	1.565	.387
MUSIC	1.425	.925	-.256	.520	.030	-.316	1.650	1.718	1.531	1.115	.417
MUSTACHE	-.494	-.519	-.694	-1.319	-1.874	-1.233	-.400	.997	1.315	.615	.700
MY OWN TONGUE	1.794	2.000	-.300	.873	.448	.388	2.050	2.703	1.923	1.610	.312
NAACP, THE	.369	.862	.712	-.492	-.052	1.060	-.200	1.178	1.194	.694	.500
NAIL	1.187	.956	.181	.292	.072	.194	1.750	1.535	1.608	1.008	.600
NAKEDNESS	.973	.615	-.446	.087	-.379	.626	1.189	1.234	1.507	.827	.680
NAME	1.656	.912	-.162	.741	.014	-.367	2.350	1.898	1.556	1.115	.442
NATIONALISM	.519	1.437	.181	-.349	-.706	.194	.750	1.539	1.450	.912	.537
NECKTIE	.882	-.493	-.836	-.001	-1.840	-1.464	2.500	1.311	1.224	.746	.478
NEED	.757	.892	.047	-.121	-.013	-.024	.865	1.171	1.462	.723	.739
NEGRO	.281	.600	.406	-.576	-.398	.561	1.025	.777	1.162	.546	.617
NEUROTIC PERSON	-1.225	-.619	-.281	-2.019	-2.006	-.560	-.425	1.401	1.387	.887	.500
NEUTRALITY	.669	.262	-.337	-.205	-.843	-.652	.725	.794	1.131	.523	.608
NEWS	1.294	1.550	-.487	.394	.855	.693	1.225	2.077	1.640	1.319	.321
NEWSPAPERS	1.587	1.606	-.287	.675	.929	.367	1.900	2.277	1.640	1.327	.312
NIGHT	1.467	1.118	-.546	-.560	.285	-.992	2.632	1.924	1.614	1.193	.421
NOISE	-.757	1.236	-.709	-1.571	.441	1.055	1.324	1.614	1.455	1.005	.450
NON-BELIEVER	-1.006	-.694	-.094	-1.810	-2.105	-.254	-.250	1.226	1.352	.690	.662
NORTH	.595	1.041	-.203	-.276	.183	-.432	1.135	1.215	1.261	.703	.559
NORTH AMERICA	2.033	2.086	.770	1.102	1.561	1.154	2.395	3.012	2.029	1.682	.346
NOSE	1.294	.431	.294	.394	-.621	.377	1.725	1.395	1.310	.775	.504
NOVEMBER	.806	.925	-.231	-.073	-.030	-.479	1.700	1.249	1.271	.775	.496
NUMBER	1.181	.875	-.112	.286	-.036	-.285	1.450	1.474	1.240	.906	.333
NYLON	1.750	.456	-.250	.831	-.588	.306	1.550	1.826	1.598	1.002	.596
OCTOBER	.894	.744	-.200	.011	-.209	-.428	1.575	1.180	1.171	.737	.433
OLD AGE	-.395	-.329	-1.079	-1.224	-1.624	-1.861	.974	1.195	1.434	.882	.553
OLD PEOPLE	.862	-.612	-1.100	-.019	-1.998	-1.895	1.100	1.526	1.612	1.112	.500
ONE	-.387	-1.106	-.369	-.474	-2.649	-.703	1.725	1.229	1.387	.637	.750
ORPHAN	-.131	-.775	.319	-.971	-2.212	.418	-.125	.848	1.367	.671	.696
PAIN	-1.562	.650	-.125	-2.343	-.332	-.305	1.575	1.697	1.762	.896	.867
PAINT	1.600	.650	-.187	.687	-.332	-.407	1.950	1.737	1.637	.937	.700
PAPER	1.365	-.020	-.108	.462	-1.216	-.278	1.541	1.369	1.516	.705	.811
PARENTHOOD	1.704	1.428	.520	.787	.693	.746	1.053	2.283	1.647	1.283	.364
PARENTS, MY	1.887	1.319	.406	.963	.550	.561	2.350	2.338	1.929	1.375	.554
PASSION	1.275	1.656	.162	.376	.995	.163	1.225	2.096	1.798	1.206	.592
PAST, THE	.868	.809	-.553	-.014	-.122	-1.003	1.368	1.309	1.463	.814	.649
PATIENT	.669	.062	-.406	-.205	-1.107	-.764	1.125	.785	1.325	.512	.812

AMERICAN ENGLISH

	COMPOSITE FACTOR SCORES			STANDARDIZED COMPOSITE SCORES - Z							
	E	P	A	E	P	A	FAM	D-ORG	P-IND	P-GRP	CI
PEACE	2.387	1.469	-.012	1.442	.747	-.122	1.525	2.803	2.081	1.623	.458
PEACE CORPS	2.131	1.875	1.331	1.196	1.283	2.069	.950	3.135	2.167	1.779	.388
PEASANTS	.400	-.225	-.112	-.462	-1.486	-.285	.125	.473	1.262	.558	.704
PEN	1.069	.381	-.056	.178	-.687	-.193	1.900	1.136	1.385	.785	.600
PENCIL	1.169	-.262	-.656	-.274	-1.536	-1.172	2.125	1.366	1.383	.779	.604
PEOPLE, MOST	.875	.331	.900	-.007	-.753	1.366	1.175	1.298	1.173	.702	.471
PERFUME	1.806	.875	.019	.885	-.036	-.071	1.625	2.007	1.821	1.142	.679
PERSON	1.112	.831	.550	.220	-.093	.795	2.100	1.494	1.335	.831	.504
PERSPIRATION	-.487	-.606	-.250	-1.313	-.390	-.509	1.100	.817	1.373	.594	.779
PHILOSOPHY	1.075	1.606	-.306	-.184	-.929	-.601	.425	.957	1.471	1.171	.300
PICTURE	1.356	.644	-.419	.454	-.341	-.784	1.250	1.559	1.385	.894	.492
PIG	1.287	1.169	.687	.388	.352	1.019	2.050	1.870	1.781	1.269	.513
PILLOW	1.769	.194	-.800	-.849	-.934	-1.406	2.175	1.951	1.492	1.092	.400
PLACE	.812	.637	.075	-.067	-.283	.021	.900	1.067	1.054	.650	.404
PLANK	-.439	-.676	-.520	-.425	-.299	-.950	1.297	.959	1.333	.613	.721
PLAY	1.494	.837	1.181	.586	-.085	1.824	1.725	2.080	1.621	1.171	.450
PLAYING CARDS	.612	.419	.444	.259	-.637	-.825	1.525	.865	1.404	.592	.812
PLAYING TENNIS	1.381	.681	1.237	.478	-.291	1.916	1.125	1.976	1.529	1.100	.429
PLEASURE	1.806	1.281	-.531	.885	.500	.765	2.050	2.277	1.719	1.294	.425
POETRY	-.550	-.450	-.769	-.319	-.596	-1.355	-.675	1.047	1.519	.665	.854
POISON	-1.356	1.569	-.450	-2.145	.879	-.835	.375	2.122	1.896	1.354	.542
POLICEMAN	1.105	1.053	.829	.213	.199	1.250	1.789	1.737	1.627	1.009	.618
POLITICS	-.678	1.658	.368	-.196	-.997	-.499	1.105	1.829	1.586	1.217	.368
POOR PEOPLE	-.319	-.825	-.400	-1.151	-2.278	-.754	.125	.971	1.385	.681	.704
PORNOGRAPHY	-.149	-.189	.182	-.703	-.940	-.196	-1.108	.302	.849	.218	.631
POT	.625	.819	-.556	-.247	-.110	-1.009	1.225	1.171	1.283	.717	.567
POWER	1.644	2.275	.662	.729	1.811	.979	1.325	2.884	1.906	1.652	.254
PRAYER	2.394	2.212	-.381	1.448	1.728	-.723	2.300	3.282	2.237	2.004	.233
PREGNANCY	1.675	1.519	.700	.759	.813	1.040	1.025	2.367	1.815	1.381	.433
PRESENT, THE	1.144	1.212	1.062	.250	.410	1.631	1.450	1.977	1.465	1.140	.325
PRISON	-.675	1.700	-.687	-1.492	1.053	-1.223	-.650	1.954	1.700	1.117	.583
PRIVACY	1.881	.756	-.312	.957	-.192	-.611	1.900	2.052	1.696	1.162	.533
PROBLEM	-.697	.704	-.322	-1.514	-.261	-.627	1.763	1.042	1.136	.645	.491
PROFESSOR	1.074	.689	-.135	.184	-.281	-.119	.378	1.284	1.633	1.007	.626
PROGRESS	1.717	1.836	.842	.800	1.231	-.119	1.974	2.651	1.829	1.465	.364
PROPHET	1.044	1.006	-.325	-.154	-.137	-.631	.600	1.486	1.408	.979	.429
PROSTITUTE	-.770	.039	.533	-1.583	-1.138	-.767	-.184	.937	1.671	.583	1.088
PSYCHOLOGY	-.900	1.262	-.325	.017	.475	-.631	.275	1.584	1.279	.917	.362
PUNISHMENT	-.437	.775	-.119	-1.265	-.168	-.295	1.175	.898	1.477	.702	.775
PURPOSE	1.444	1.219	-.037	.538	.418	-.163	1.225	1.890	1.504	1.062	.442
PYRAMID, A	.514	1.581	-1.385	-.354	.896	-2.360	-.135	2.164	1.709	1.196	.514
QUESTION	.862	1.012	.200	-.019	.146	-.225	1.225	1.345	1.354	.837	.517
QUESTIONTHINGS	-.600	1.069	.250	-.271	.220	.306	.475	1.251	1.190	.731	.458
RABBIT	1.289	-.513	.730	-.390	-1.867	1.089	2.421	1.558	1.529	1.134	.395
RACE CONFLICT	-.770	.132	.283	-2.541	-.303	.360	1.632	2.120	1.829	1.355	.474
RADIOS,POCKET	1.456	.006	1.181	.550	-1.181	1.824	1.850	1.875	1.698	1.110	.587
RAILROADS	1.725	1.744	.800	.807	1.110	1.203	1.975	2.530	1.981	1.690	.292
RAIN	1.287	1.200	.537	.388	.393	.775	2.025	1.840	1.646	1.112	.533
REALITY	1.031	1.362	-.069	.142	-.607	-.214	1.200	1.710	1.492	.958	.533
RED	1.256	1.012	-.050	.358	.146	-.183	1.950	1.614	1.540	.956	.583

AMERICAN ENGLISH	COMPOSITE FACTOR SCORES			STANDARDIZED COMPOSITE SCORES – Z			FAM	D-ORG	P-IND	P-GRP	CI
	E	P	A	E	P	A					
RED RACE	.059	.296	-.000	-.789	-.799	-.102	-.000	.302	1.154	.408	.746
REFUGEE	.469	.131	.125	-.397	-1.017	-.102	.250	.503	1.000	.454	.546
REINCARNATION	.250	.344	-.644	-.606	-.736	-1.151	.125	.771	1.458	.442	1.017
RELATIVES	1.306	.719	-.437	-.406	-.242	-.612	2.200	1.554	1.392	.946	.446
RESPECT	1.925	.931	-.237	-.999	1.358	-.489	2.150	2.737	1.860	1.648	.213
RESTAURANT	1.850	.850	.637	-.927	-.069	.938	1.725	2.133	1.525	1.112	.412
RESURRECTION	1.494	1.637	-.231	.586	.970	-.479	-.300	2.228	1.637	1.342	.296
REVOLUTION	-.356	1.231	.319	-1.187	.434	-.418	-.125	1.321	1.606	.840	.767
RICE	1.525	-.012	-.437	-.616	-1.206	-.815	1.550	1.587	1.408	.908	.500
RICH PEOPLE	.469	1.037	-.137	-.397	-.179	-.123	-.275	1.147	1.452	.777	.675
RIGHT HAND	1.844	1.637	1.050	.921	.970	1.610	2.325	2.680	1.827	1.594	.233
RIVER	1.031	1.875	.244	.142	1.283	.296	1.425	2.154	1.742	1.358	.383
ROADS	1.750	1.270	-.441	.831	.485	-.617	2.289	2.207	1.702	1.272	.430
ROCK	.031	1.462	-1.281	-.816	-.739	-2.191	1.700	1.945	1.433	1.033	.400
ROMANCE	2.137	1.869	.425	1.202	1.275	.591	1.600	2.871	2.060	1.706	.354
ROOF	1.637	1.394	-.812	.723	.649	-1.426	1.900	2.299	1.565	1.281	.283
ROOM	1.337	.744	-.319	-.436	-.209	-.621	2.000	1.563	1.171	.804	.367
ROOT	.594	1.344	-.506	-.277	.583	-.927	1.650	1.554	1.631	1.160	.471
ROPE	1.312	1.412	-.419	.412	.673	-.784	1.650	1.973	1.531	1.123	.408
ROSE	1.744	-.237	.275	.825	-1.503	.347	1.875	1.781	1.681	1.169	.513
RUG	1.431	-.706	-.881	-.526	-.258	-1.538	1.550	1.823	1.356	1.006	.350
SALARY	2.171	-.934	.191	1.235	.042	.210	1.947	2.371	1.603	1.191	.412
SALT	.875	.331	-.912	-.007	-.753	-1.589	2.150	1.307	1.456	.998	.458
SATURDAY	1.944	.775	1.519	1.017	-.168	2.375	2.425	2.586	1.725	1.412	.312
SAVING MONEY	1.769	1.631	-.281	.849	.962	-.560	1.650	2.423	1.819	1.315	.504
SCENE	.925	.431	.087	.041	-.621	.041	1.350	1.024	1.319	.640	.679
SCHOOL	1.256	1.550	-.144	.358	.855	.133	2.100	2.000	1.629	1.087	.542
SCIENTIST	1.619	1.731	.231	-.705	1.094	-.276	.900	2.381	1.815	1.373	.442
SEA	1.450	2.594	.331	.544	2.231	.439	1.625	2.990	2.225	1.837	.388
SECOND, A	-.287	-.975	.156	-.570	-2.476	-.153	1.700	1.028	1.473	.669	.804
SEED	1.787	.031	-.056	.867	-1.148	-.010	2.250	1.789	2.017	1.321	.696
SENTENCE	.719	.887	-.381	-.157	-.019	-.723	1.825	1.204	1.283	.762	.521
SEPTEMBER	.547	.642	-.419	-.321	-.343	-.785	1.459	.942	1.284	.595	.689
SERVANT	1.444	.325	-.287	-.538	-.761	.367	.700	1.508	1.473	.902	.571
SEX	-1.950	2.069	.731	1.023	-1.539	1.091	1.700	2.935	2.046	1.708	.337
SHAME	-1.094	.662	-.444	-1.894	-.316	-.825	.550	1.354	1.296	.754	.542
SHIP	1.456	1.906	.125	.550	1.325	-.102	1.050	2.402	1.717	1.300	.417
SHOES	1.456	.700	-.587	.550	-.266	-1.059	2.000	1.719	1.431	.935	.496
SHOP	1.081	.681	.094	.190	-.291	.051	1.150	1.281	1.223	.760	.462
SIGHT	2.094	1.762	.444	1.161	1.135	.622	2.200	2.773	2.100	1.787	.312
SILENCE	1.525	.700	-1.112	-.616	-.266	-1.915	1.900	2.013	1.596	1.112	.483
SIN	-1.656	.806	-.512	-2.433	-.126	-.937	1.025	1.912	1.812	1.029	.783
SINGING	1.349	.382	.308	-.447	-.686	.531	2.000	1.454	1.360	.873	.487
SISTERS	.800	-.106	.837	-.079	-1.330	1.264	2.025	1.163	1.306	.685	.621
SIT-INS	-.462	-.200	-.225	-1.289	-1.453	.265	.375	.552	1.308	.396	.912
SKIN	1.719	.644	-.031	.801	-.341	-.153	2.025	1.836	1.810	1.235	.575
SLEEP	1.987	1.012	-.731	1.059	-.146	-1.294	2.150	2.347	1.931	1.306	.625
SMOKE	-1.514	.426	-.926	-2.296	-.628	-1.611	1.027	1.824	1.811	.955	.856
SNAKE	-.325	1.162	-.012	-1.157	-.344	-.122	.875	1.207	1.537	.892	.646
SNOW	.094	.862	-.906	-.756	-.052	-1.579	2.375	1.255	1.558	.683	.875

AMERICAN ENGLISH

	COMPOSITE FACTOR SCORES			STANDARDIZED COMPOSITE SCORES - Z							
	E	P	A	E	P	A	FAM	D-ORG	P-IND	P-GRP	CI
SOCIALISM	-.000	1.081	.006	-.846	.236	-.091	.550	1.081	1.575	.633	.942
SOIL, THE	1.744	2.181	-1.056	.825	1.687	-1.824	2.425	2.986	2.073	1.815	.258
SOLDIER	1.401	1.270	1.118	.497	.485	1.722	1.632	2.197	1.509	1.263	.246
SOLITUDE	-.069	.406	-.925	-.912	-.654	-1.610	.050	1.013	1.542	.483	1.058
SONG	1.369	.544	.087	.466	-.473	.041	2.025	1.475	1.387	.321	.567
SOUND	1.100	1.000	.650	.208	.129	.958	1.900	1.622	1.412	1.000	.412
SOUTH	.312	.912	-.112	-.546	.014	-.285	.450	.971	1.617	.750	.867
SOUTH AMERICA	.955	1.287	-.294	.071	.508	-.581	.625	1.630	1.758	1.137	.621
SPACE TRAVEL	1.594	1.812	1.237	.681	1.201	1.916	.375	2.712	2.048	1.548	.500
SPHERE, A	.919	1.025	-.462	.035	-.162	-.856	1.200	1.452	1.315	.856	.458
SPIT	-1.612	-1.019	-.469	-2.391	-2.533	-.866	.875	1.964	1.712	1.050	.662
SPRING	2.050	1.625	.769	1.119	.954	1.152	2.450	2.727	2.169	1.506	.662
SQUARE, A	-.406	-.006	-.687	-.456	-1.198	-1.223	1.450	.799	.971	.412	.558
STAR	1.312	1.537	-.825	.412	.838	-1.447	1.850	2.183	1.967	1.346	.621
STEEL	1.455	2.000	-.387	-.550	1.448	-.733	1.750	2.504	1.927	1.348	.579
STICK	.312	.475	-.112	-.546	-.563	-.285	1.300	.580	1.175	.442	.733
STOMACH	1.431	1.406	.381	-.526	.665	.520	1.675	2.042	1.777	1.215	.562
STONE	.044	1.300	-1.462	-.804	.525	-2.486	1.900	1.957	1.506	1.023	.483
STOREKEEPER	1.312	.312	.262	.412	-.778	.326	1.825	1.374	1.342	.775	.567
STORY	1.394	.862	-.206	.490	-.052	-.438	1.700	1.552	1.458	.937	.521
STOVE	1.687	1.156	-.581	.771	-.335	-1.049	2.075	2.127	1.554	1.162	.392
STREET	1.250	.601	-.250	.352	-.397	-.306	1.730	1.409	1.493	.872	.622
STREET CLEANER	1.269	.625	-.125	.370	-.365	-.305	.725	1.420	1.623	.969	.654
STUDENT	1.375	.944	1.000	.472	-.055	1.529	2.025	1.945	1.527	1.169	.358
STUFF	-.125	-.100	-.494	-.726	-1.322	-.907	.800	.519	1.015	.269	.746
SUBMARINE, NUCL	1.719	2.550	1.025	.801	2.174	1.570	.475	3.241	2.131	1.844	.287
SUCCESS	1.981	1.637	-.119	1.053	.970	.092	1.275	2.573	1.812	1.442	.371
SUICIDE	-2.012	-.162	-.719	-2.774	-.975	-1.273	-.375	2.143	1.781	1.240	.542
SUMMER	2.244	1.425	-.700	1.304	.690	-1.040	2.600	2.749	1.952	1.456	.496
SUN	2.069	2.656	-.537	1.137	2.314	-.978	2.500	3.409	2.387	2.071	.317
SUNDAY	1.569	.986	-.338	.656	.111	-.652	2.324	1.383	1.689	1.122	.568
SWEATER	1.744	.556	-.394	.825	-.456	-.744	2.100	1.372	1.431	.948	.483
SYMPATHY	1.006	.681	-.400	.118	-.291	-.754	1.075	1.279	1.383	.733	.650
TABLE	1.325	.531	-.794	-.424	-.489	-1.396	2.275	1.533	1.417	.921	.496
TALK	1.237	1.050	-.587	.340	-.195	.856	1.600	1.726	1.583	1.075	.508
TEA	-.914	-.303	-.783	.031	-1.589	-1.378	1.947	1.241	1.294	.667	.627
TEACHER	1.075	.694	.375	.184	-.275	.510	1.625	1.333	1.260	.785	.475
TELEPHONE	1.831	.615	.932	.909	-.379	1.419	2.189	2.145	1.716	1.225	.491
TELEVISION	1.755	1.394	1.237	-.837	-.649	1.916	1.925	2.561	1.858	1.462	.396
THIEF	-1.824	-.088	.041	-2.594	-1.074	-.035	.486	1.327	1.858	.980	.878
THIN	-.119	-1.262	-.087	-.959	-.909	-.041	.900	1.271	1.306	.656	.650
THING	-.175	-.269	-.031	-.678	-.835	-.153	.550	.322	1.100	.296	.804
THOUGHT	1.694	1.481	-.494	.777	.764	-.907	2.250	2.304	1.869	1.435	.433
THREAD	1.169	-.725	-.494	-.274	-2.146	-.907	1.500	1.461	1.404	.804	.600
THREE	-.534	-.223	-.122	-.334	-1.484	-.097	1.162	.591	1.284	.419	.865
THUNDER	-.975	1.537	.700	-1.780	.838	1.040	2.000	1.351	1.983	1.275	.708
THURSDAY	-.487	-.212	-.256	-.379	-.909	-.519	1.650	.590	1.181	.423	.758
TIME	-.937	1.056	-.087	.053	-.203	-.244	1.725	1.415	1.619	1.010	.608
TONGUE	1.230	.461	.500	.333	-.582	.714	2.211	1.406	1.467	.958	.509
TOOTH	1.534	.959	.595	.624	.076	.868	2.189	1.304	1.696	1.137	.559

AMERICAN ENGLISH

	COMPOSITE FACTOR SCORES			STANDARDIZED COMPOSITE SCORES – Z							
	E	P	A	E	P	A	FAM	D-ORG	P-IND	P-GRP	CI
TRADITION	.941	1.099	-.342	.056	.259	-.659	1.816	1.486	1.346	.969	.377
TRAGEDY	-1.987	1.150	-.106	-2.750	.327	-.275	.550	2.299	1.985	1.356	.629
TRAIN	1.800	2.075	1.112	.879	1.547	1.712	1.925	2.964	2.150	1.850	.300
TRAVEL	1.437	1.019	.400	.532	.154	.551	1.425	1.807	1.448	1.135	.312
TREE	1.456	1.625	-.450	.550	.954	-.835	1.750	2.228	1.765	1.498	.267
TRIANGLE, A	.656	.325	-.431	-.217	-.761	-.805	1.175	.850	1.042	.517	.525
TRUST	1.750	1.600	-.012	.831	.921	-.122	1.975	2.371	1.629	1.387	.242
TRUTH	1.381	2.056	-.206	.478	1.522	.235	1.550	2.486	1.702	1.331	.371
TUESDAY	.789	-.125	-.033	-.089	-1.025	-.155	2.237	.800	.978	.447	.531
TWO	.862	-.400	.044	-.019	-1.717	-.030	1.675	.952	1.340	.619	.721
UNCLE	1.493	.901	.289	.585	-.001	.370	2.500	1.768	1.443	1.136	.307
UNIVERSITY	1.706	1.987	.319	.789	1.432	.418	.925	2.639	2.029	1.517	.512
UP	.919	.919	-.156	.035	.022	-.356	1.275	1.309	1.377	.852	.525
VALLEYS	1.079	1.099	-.632	.188	.259	-1.131	1.316	1.664	1.379	.976	.404
VEGETABLES	1.362	.081	.219	.460	-.819	.255	2.125	1.408	1.446	.908	.537
VIET NAM	-1.487	-.081	.362	-2.271	-1.083	.490	-.050	1.533	1.769	.910	.858
VILLAGE	1.230	-.554	-.203	.333	-1.920	-.432	.459	1.364	1.459	.865	.595
VOICE	1.487	1.287	.687	.580	.508	1.019	1.725	2.084	1.550	1.262	.288
WALK	1.525	.875	.125	.616	-.036	-.102	1.900	1.763	1.587	1.033	.554
WALL	.812	1.112	-.894	-.067	.278	-1.559	1.950	1.642	1.319	.940	.379
WAR	-2.020	1.855	-.145	-2.781	1.257	-.134	.921	2.746	2.055	1.669	.386
WARMTH	1.675	1.212	-.275	.771	.410	-.550	1.850	2.096	1.671	1.200	.471
WATER	1.987	.375	-.312	.759	1.432	.510	2.075	2.626	1.837	1.587	.250
WAY	.594	.325	-.312	-.277	-.761	-.611	.500	.746	.852	.423	.429
WEALTH	1.731	1.744	-.019	.813	1.110	-.132	.250	2.457	1.752	1.340	.413
WEDDING	1.587	1.281	.487	.675	.500	-.693	1.125	2.097	1.623	1.227	.396
WEDNESDAY	-.787	.456	-.156	-.091	-.588	-.356	1.700	.923	1.119	.579	.537
WEIGHT	-.025	.950	-.394	-.870	.063	-.744	1.100	1.029	1.767	.602	.517
WEST	1.256	1.906	.362	.358	1.325	.490	.725	2.312	1.767	1.417	.350
WHITE	1.125	-1.225	-.500	.232	-1.486	-.917	1.900	1.251	1.521	.700	.821
WHITE RACE	1.406	1.844	.644	.502	1.242	.948	2.300	2.407	1.885	1.615	.271
WIDOW	.675	-.550	-.769	-.199	-1.915	-1.355	.550	1.162	1.498	.810	.687
WIDOWER	-.181	-.156	-.475	-.672	-1.396	-.876	.325	.532	1.204	.637	.567
WIND	-.337	1.619	.125	-.522	-.945	.102	1.700	1.658	1.331	.998	.333
WINDOW	1.119	-.419	-.856	-.226	-1.742	-1.498	1.975	1.470	1.535	.931	.604
WINE	-.569	1.219	-.331	-.301	-.418	-.642	1.175	1.385	1.906	.865	1.042
WINTER	-.619	1.450	-.575	-1.439	-.723	-1.039	2.000	1.678	1.494	.890	.604
WOMAN	1.912	.362	1.087	.987	-.712	-1.672	1.875	2.230	1.637	1.121	.517
WOOD	1.559	1.349	-.605	.648	.589	-1.088	2.079	2.149	1.583	1.184	.399
WORD	1.162	1.014	-.020	-.043	-.147	-.135	1.649	1.542	1.394	.840	.554
WORK	-.837	1.437	-.169	-.762	.706	.174	2.175	1.672	1.448	1.035	.412
WORKER	1.414	1.105	.993	.510	.268	1.518	1.500	2.052	1.478	1.171	.307
WORLD	1.144	2.125	.444	.250	1.613	-.622	1.775	2.454	1.950	1.612	.337
WRITING	1.562	.762	-.781	.651	-.184	-1.375	2.000	1.906	1.669	1.065	.604
YEAR, A	1.281	1.362	-.019	.382	-.607	-.132	1.950	1.870	1.617	1.133	.483
YELLOW	.544	-.212	-.637	-.325	-1.470	-1.141	1.550	.864	1.194	.560	.633
YELLOW RACE	.087	.294	.006	-.762	-.802	-.091	-.700	.307	1.267	.487	.779
YOUTH	1.887	1.137	1.844	.963	.311	-2.905	2.450	2.873	2.110	1.623	.487
ZERO	-.050	-.694	-.950	-.894	-2.105	-1.651	1.450	1.177	1.556	.631	.925

A Bibliography of Literature Relevant to
the Semantic Differential Technique

ABAN-ALLEN, R. M. 1966. Personality correlates of the movement of concepts in the semantic space: an investigation of the effect of some personality variables on the magnitude of association between initially meaningless assigns and previously meaningful signs. *Dissert. Abstr.*, 27(2-A): 382-383.

ABELSON, R. P. 1960. Scales derived by consideration of variance components in multi-way tables. In H. Gulliksen and S. J. Messick (Eds.), *Psychological scaling: theory and applications.* New York: John Wiley.

————, and ROSENBERG, M. J. 1958. Symbolic psychologic: a model and H-itudinal cognition. *Behavioral Science*, 3: 1-13.

ACCURSO, R. 1967. Development of a music differential. Unpublished master's thesis, University of Illinois.

ACKER, L. E., and EDWARDS, A. E. 1964. Transfer of vasoconstriction over a bipolar meaning dimension. *J. exp. Psychol.*, 67: 1-6.

ADLERSTEIN, A. M. 1959. The relationship between religious belief and death effect. *Dissert. Abstr.*, 19. 3016-3017.

AGARIE, N. 1964. Effects of verbal contexts on meaning: a study of the connotative meaning of words in isolation and combination. *Dissert. Abstr.*, 25: 3673.

AGRAWAL, K. G. 1965. Influence of age on meaningfulness. *Journal of Psychological Researches*, 9: 74-76.

AIKEN, E. G. 1965. Alternate forms of a semantic differential for measurement of changes in self-description. *Psychol. Reps.*, 16: 177-178.

ALEXANDER, S., and HUSEK, T. R. 1959. The development of a measure of situational anxiety. Urbana: University of Illinois, Institute of Communications Research.

————, . 1962. The anxiety differential: initial steps in the development of a measure of situational anxiety. *Educ. psychol. Measmt.*, 22: 325-348.

ALLISON, R. B. 1963a. A two-dimensional semantic differential. *J. consult. Psychol.*, 27: 18-23.

————. 1963b. Using adverbs as multipliers in semantic differentials. *J. Psychol.*, 56: 115-117.

ALLPORT, G. W., and ODBERT, H. S. 1936. Trait-names: a psycho-lexical study. *Psychol. Monog.*, No. 211.

AL-MANIEY, N. T. 1964. A cross-cultural study of freedom of expression through written communication. Master's thesis, Indiana University. *Journ. Abstr.*, 2: 45.

AMES, M. C. 1963. An experiment to determine the correlation of the semantic differential and paired comparisons techniques of measuring brand image. Master's thesis, Northwestern University. *Journ. Abstr.*, 1: 20.

AMMERMAN, H. L. 1958. Stability of word meanings over various employee evaluation contests. Unpublished master's thesis, Purdue University.

AMSFELD, ELIZABETH, and LAMBERT, W. E. 1964. Evaluational reactions of bilingual and monolingual children to spoken languages. *J. abnorm. soc. Psychol.*, 69: 89-97.

AMSTER, HARRIET. 1964. Evaluative judgment and recall in incidental learning. *J. verb. Learn. verb. Behav.*, 3: 466-473.

ANISFELD, M. 1962. The role of affective tone in verbal learning. Unpublished Ph.D. thesis, McGill University.

————, BOGO, N., and LAMBERT, W. E. 1962. Evaluation reactions to accented English speech. *J. abnorm. soc. Psychol.*, 65: 223-231.

————, and LAMBERT, W. E. 1966. When are pleasant words learned faster than unpleasant words? *J. verb. Learn. verb. Behav.*, 5: 132-141.

————, MUNOZ, S. R., and LAMBERT, W. E. 1963. The structure and dynamics of the ethnic attitudes of Jewish adolescents. *J. abnorm. soc. Psychol.*, 66(1): 31-36.

ANONYMOUS. 1958. Mogul semantic differential aims to provide qualitative research data. *Advertising Age*, 29(36): 3.

ANTHONY, J. P. 1967. Do-it-yourself pretesting helps build better ads. *Indust. Market.*, 68-69.

ARNOLD, J. B. 1964. A test of some unifying assumptions for meaningfulness and meaning. *Dissert. Abstr.*, 24: 3830.

ARNOULT, M. D. 1960. Prediction of perceptual responses from structural characteristics of the stimulus. *Percept. mot. Skills*, 11: 261-268.

ARTHUR, A. Z. 1965. Clinical use of the semantic differential. *J. clin. Psychol.*, 21: 337-338.

————. 1966. Response bias in the semantic differential. *Brit. J. soc. clin. Psychol.*, 5: 103-107.

ASHER, J. J., and EVANS, R. I. 1959. An investigation of some aspects of the social psychological impact of an educational television program. *J. appl. Psychol.*, 43: 166-169.

ATKIN, K. L. 1960. Measurement of supermarket images. Paper read at Association for Education in Journalism convention. Pennsylvania State University, August.

ATKINSON, J. W. 1960. Personality dynamics. *Ann. Rev. of Psychol.*, 11: 276-277.

ATTNEAVE, F., and ARNOULT, M. D. 1956. The quantitative study of shape and pattern perception. *Psychol. Bull.*, 53: 452-471.

AZUMA, Y. 1953. An experiment on physiognomic perception in phonetic symbolism. *Tokoyo Joshidai Ronshu*, 4: 109-114.

BARAFF, A., and CUNNINGHAM, ANN P. 1965. Asthmatic and normal children. *JAMA*, 192(1): 13-15.

BARATZ, S. S. 1961. A semantic analysis of the Second Test. Unpublished master's thesis, University of Kansas.

BARBAN, A. M. 1963. Measurement of the differences in the social meanings attached to advertising by white and Negro consumers through the use of the semantic differential. Unpublished Ph.D. dissertation, University of Texas.

BARBER, W. H. 1964. Parental attitudes toward institutionalization. *Psychol. Reps.*, 14: 375-379.

BARCLAY, A. 1965. Parental attitudes toward children's hospitalization experiences. *Psychol. Reps.*, 17: 761-762.

————, and THUMIN, F. J. 1963. A modified semantic differential approach to attitudinal assessment. *J. clin. Psychol.*, 19: 376.

BARCLAY, W. D. 1964. The semantic differential as an index to brand attitude. *J. Ad. Res.*, 4: 30-33.

BARKER, D. G. 1964. Concepts of disabilities. *Personnel Guid. J.*, 43: 371-374.

BARLOW, JUDITH. 1967. Semantic satiation and the semantic differential. *Cornell J. soc. Relations*, 1(2): 111-117.

BARNARD, J. W. 1966. The effects of anxiety on connotative meaning. *Child Develpm.*, 37(2): 461-472.

BARNETT, S. 1962. Persuasion and prejudice. An experimental study of the effects upon listener attitudes of the addition of extreme and moderate ideas to persuasive speeches. Unpublished Ph.D. dissertation, Indiana University.

BARRETT, G. V., and OTIS, J. L. 1967. The semantic differential as a measure of changes in meaning in education and vocational counseling. *Psychol. Reps.*, 20(1): 335-338.

BASS, A. A. and FIEDLER, F. E. 1959. Interpersonal perception scores: a comparison of D scores and their components. Technical Report No. 5, Group Effectiveness Research Laboratory, University of Illinois, U.S. Public Health Project M-1774.

BASTIAN, J. R. 1961. Associative factors in verbal transfer. *J. exp. Psychol.*, 62: 70-79.

BAUMGOLD, J., TEMERLIN, M. K., and RAGLAND, R. 1965. Experience of freedom to choose in mental heath, neurosis and psychosis. *Psychol. Reps.*, 16: 957-962.

BAXTER, J. C. 1959. Mediated generalization as a function of a semantic differential. *Dissertation Abstr.*, 20: 1857.

————. 1962. Mediated generalization as a function of semantic differential performance. *Amer. J. Psychol.*, 75: 66.

BEACH, L. R. 1964a. Recognition, assimilation, and identification of objects. *Psychol. Monogr.*, 78(6), Whole No. 683.

————. 1964b. Cue probabilism and inference behavior. *Psychol. Monogr.*, 78(5), Whole No. 582.

BEAN, R. W. 1964. Public relations ethics: the effects of group sanction on the cognitive and affective components of attitude. Master's thesis, University of Florida. *Journ. Abstr.*, 2: 53.

BEARDSLEE, D. C., and O'DOWD, D. D. 1961. The college-student image of the scientist. *Science*, 133: 997-1001.

BECKER, R. W., and PARKER, E. B. 1963. A model for simulation of attitude change within an individual. In W. Danielson (Ed.), *Paul J. Deutschmann memorial papers in communications research*. Cincinnati: Scripps-Howard Research.

BEIR, E. G. 1964. A comparison of differential ratings on three different semantic scales. Unpublished paper. Ref: *Amer. Psychol.*, 19(9): 709.

BEITNER, M. S. 1961. Word meaning and sexual identification in paranoid schizophrenics and anxiety neurotics. *J. abnorm. soc. Psychol.*, 63: 289-293.

BENNIS, W. G., BURKE, R. L., CUTTER, H., HARINGTON, H, and HOFFMAN, JOYCE. 1957. A note on some problems of measurement and prediction in a training group. *Group Psychother.*, 10: 328-341.

BERKOWITZ, L. 1961. Anti-semitism, judgmental processes, and displacement of hostility. *J. abnorm. soc. Psychol.*, 62: 210-215.

BERLO, D. K. 1960. *The process of communication*. New York: Holt, Rinehart and Winston.

————, and KUMATA, HIDEYA. 1956. The investigator: the impact of a satirical radio drama. *Journ. Quart.*, 33: 287-298.

BERLYNE, D. E. 1954a. A theory of human curiosity. *Brit. J. Psychol.*, 45a: 180-191.

————. 1954b. Knowledge and stimulus-response psychology. *Psychol. Rev.*, 61: 248.

————. 1966. Mediating responses: a note of Fodor's criticisms. *J. verb. Learn. verb. Behav.*, 5: 408-411.

————, and PECKHAM, S. 1966. The semantic differential and other measures of reaction to visual complexity. *Canad. J. Psychol.*, 20(2): 125-135.

BETTINGHAUS, E. P. 1963. Cognitive balance and the development of meaning. *J. Comm.*, 8(2): 94-105.

BIERI, J. 1955. Cognitive complexity-simplicity and predictive behavior. *J. abnorm. soc. Psychol.*, 50: 263-268.

————, LOBECK, R., and GALINSKY, M. D. 1959. A comparison of direct, indirect, and fantasy measures of identification. *J. abnorm. soc. Psychol.*, 58: 253-258.

BINGHAM, W. E. 1943. A study of the relations which the galvanic skin response and sensory reference bear to judgments of the meaningfulness, significance, and importance of 72 words. *J. Psychol.*, 16: 21-34.

BIRCH, D., and ERICKSON, M. 1958. Phonetic symbolism with respect to three dimensions from the semantic differential. *J. gen. Psychol.*, 58: 291-297.

BIRDWELL, A. E. 1964. Influence of image congruence on consumer choice. *American Marketing Association Proceedings*, Educators Conference, 290-303.

BJERSTEDT, A. 1966. Symbols of interaction potentialities: I. Movement patterns. *Educ. Psychol. Interactions*, 14: 24.

BLANDFORD, D. H., and SAMPSON, E. E. 1964. Induction of prestige suggestion through classical conditioning. *J. abnorm. soc. Psychol.*, 69: 332-337.

BLOCK, J. 1957. Studies in the phenomenology of emotions. *J. Abnorm. soc. Psychol.*, 54: 358-363.

————. 1958. An unprofitable application of the semantic differential. *J. consult. Psychol.*, 22: 235-236.

BLOCK, W. E. 1962. A study of meaning set in the judgment of clinical test data. *J. clin. Psychol.*, 18: 511-512.

BOBREN, H. M. 1960. Student attitudes toward instructional television: Additional evidence. *AV Comm. Rev.*, 8: 6.

————, and SIEGEL, S. L. 1959. Student attitudes toward instructional television. *AV Comm. Rev.*, 8: 3.

BOKANDER, I. 1964. Semantic description of complex and meaningful stimulus material. *Psychol. res. Bull.*, 4(2): 10 pages.

————. 1966. Semantic description of complex and meaningful stimulus material. *Percept. mot. Skills*, 22: 201-202.

BOLGER, F. J., JR. 1959. How to evaluate your company image. *J. Marketing*, 24: 7-10.

BONDLY, W. H. 1962. Some effects of abstractness of concept on psychological meaning as measured by the semantic differential technique. *Dissertation Abstr.*, 23: 2198.

BOPP, JOAN A. 1955. A quantitative semantic analysis of word association in schizophrenia. Unpublished Ph.D. dissertation, University of Illinois.

BORELLI, G. L. 1961. A study of the meanings of Rorschach cards through use of the semantic differential technique. *Dissertation Abstr.*, 21: 3161.

BOSSART, P. 1963. The effects of context, frequency and order of presentation on impression formation. Ph.D. dissertation, Syracuse University, submitted for publication.

————, and DIVESTA, F. J. 1966. Effects of context, frequency, and order of presentation of evaluative assertions on impression formation. *J. pers. soc. Psychol.*, 4(5): 538-544.

BOUSFIELD, W. A. 1944. An empirical study of the production of affectively toned items. *J. gen. Psychol.*, 30: 205-215.

————. 1950. The relationship between mood and the production of affectively toned associates. *J. gen. Psychol.*, 42: 67-85.

————. 1953. The occurrence of clustering in the recall of randomly arranged associates. *J. gen. Psychol.*, 49: 229-240.

————. 1961. The problem of meaning in verbal learning. In C. N. Cofer (Ed.), *Verbal learning and verbal behavior*. New York: McGraw-Hill.

————, and COHEN, B. H. 1953. The effects of reinforcement on the occurrence of clustering in the recall of randomly arranged associates. *J. Psychol.*, 36: 67-81.

————, and PUFF, C. R. 1965. Relationship between free associational and judgmental measures of word relatedness. *Psychol. Reps.*, 16: 279-282.

————, WHITMARSH, G. A., and BERKOWITZ, H. 1958. Partial response identities in associative clustering. Storrs: Department of Psychology, University of Connecticut. Technical Report No. 27, Contract N-onr 631-00.

————, ————, and DANICK, J. J. 1958. Partial response identities in verbal generalization. *Psychol. Reps.*, 4:703-713.

BRANCA, A. A. 1957. Semantic generalization at the level of the conditioning experiment. *Amer. J. Psychol.*, 70: 541-549.

BRANDWIN, M. A. 1965. Levels of reference in connotative meaning: a developmental study. *Papers of the Michigan Academy of Science, Arts, and Letters*, 50(2): 343-353.

————. 1966. Levels of mediation in connotative meaning. A developmental study. *Dissert. Abstr.*, 27(2-B): 597.

BRINTON, J. E. 1961. Deriving an attitude scale from semantic differential data. *Pub. Opin. Quart.*, 25: 289-295.

BROD, DIANE, KERNOFF, PHYLLIS, and TERWILLIGER, R. F. 1964. Anxiety and semantic differential responses. *J. abnorm. soc. Psychol.* 68(5): 570-574.

Brody, N. 1965. Psychology of the Scientist: XIII scientific and religious experiences distinguished by their "affect." *Psychol. Reps.*, 16: 737-744.

Bronson, G. W. 1959. Identify diffusion in late adolescents. *J. abnorm. soc. Psychol.*, 59: 414-417.

Brown, R. W. 1957. *Words and Things*. Glencoe, Ill: The Free Press.

———. 1958a. How shall a thing be called? *Psychol. Rev.*, 65(1): 14-21.

———. 1958b. The measurement of meaning. *Contemp. Psychol.*, 3: 113-115. (Book review.)

———. 1962. Models of attitude change. In *New Directions in Psychology*. New York: Holt, Rinehart and Winston.

———, Black, A., and Horowitz, A. 1955. Phonetic symbolism in natural languages. *J. abnorm. soc. Psychol.*, 50: 388-393.

———, Leiter, R. A., and Hildum, D. C. 1957. Metaphors from music criticism. *J. abnorm. soc. Psychol.*, 54: 347-352.

———, and Lenneberg, E. H. 1954. A study in language and cognition. *J. abnorm. soc. Psychol.*, 49: 454-462.

Brown, S. W., Guilford, J. P., and Hoepfner, R. 1966. A factor analysis of semantic memory abilities: studies of aptitudes of high-level personnel. *Reports from the Psychological Laboratory*, July, 37. University of Southern California.

Brown, W. P. 1964. The titles of paperback books. *Brit. J. Psychol.*, 55(3): 365-368.

Bruner, J. S., and Goodman, C. C. 1947. Value and need as organizing factors in perception. *J. abnorm. soc. Psychol.*, 42: 33-44.

Buchwald, A. M. 1957. The generality of the norms. *Amer. J. Psychol.*, 70(2): 233-238.

Bulatao, J. C. 1961. The direction of aggression in clinically depressed women. *Dissertation Abstr.*, 22: 1249-1250.

Burdick, H., Green, E., and Lovelace, J. 1959. Predicting trademark effectiveness. *J. appl. Psychol.*, 43: 285-286.

Burke, R. L., and Bennis, W. G. 1961. Changes in perception of self and others during human relations training. *Human Relations*, 14: 165-182.

Burt, C. 1948. The factorial study of temperamental traits. *Brit. J. Psychol. Statist. Sect.*, 1: 178-203.

Campbell, D. J. 1957. A typology of tests, projective and otherwise. *J. consult. Psychol.*, 21: 207-210.

Campbell, D. T. 1953. Generalized attitude scales. In O. K. Buros (Ed.), *The fourth mental measurements yearbook*. Highland Park, N.J.: Gryphen Press. pp. 90-91.

Cantril, H. 1946. The intensity of an attitude. *J. abnorm. soc. Psychol.*, 41: 129-136.

Capell, M. D., and Wohl, J. 1959. An approach to the factor structure of clinical judgments. *J. consult. Psychol.*, 23: 51-53.

Caputo, D. V. 1961. Characteristics of the parents of schizophrenics. *Dissertation Abstr.*, 22: 1713-1714.

Carlson, E. R. 1956. Attitude change through modification of attitude structure. *J. abnorm. soc. Psychol.*, 52: 256-261.

Carmichael, L., Hogan, H. P., and Walter, A. A. 1932. An experimental study of the effect of language on the reproduction of visual perceived form. *J. exp. Psychol.*, 15: 73-86.

Carroll, J. B. 1959a. *The measurement of meaning*, by C. E. Osgood, G. J. Suci, and P. H. Tannenbaum. *Language*, 35: 58-77. (Book review.)

———. 1959b. Some cautionary notes on the semantic differential. Paper presented to the American Psychological Association. Cincinnati, September.

———. 1960. Vectors of prose style. In Thomas A. Sebeok (Ed.), *Style in language*, New York.

Carter, R. F. 1965. Communication and affective relations. *Journ. Quart.*, 42(2).

Cartwright, D. 1957. Social psychology and group processes. *Annual Review of Psychol.*, 8: 230.

CATTELL, R. B., HORN, J., and BUTCHER, H. J. 1962. The dynamic structure of attitudes in adults: a description of some established factors and of their measurement by the motivational analysis test. *Brit. J. Psychol.*, 53: 57-69.

CHAFFEE, S. H. 1965. Two sources of value change: salience and pertinence. Unpublished Ph.D. dissertation, Stanford University.

CHANCE, ERIKA, ARNOLD, J., and TYRELL, S. 1962. Communality and stability of meaning in clinical case description. *J. abnorm. soc. Psychol.*, 64: 389-406.

CHESKIN, L. 1959. *Why people buy.* New York: Liveright.

CHIEN CHU, G. 1964. Culture, personality, and persuasibility. *Journ. Abstr.*, 2: 5-6.

CHOYNOWSKI, MIECZYSLAW. 1967. Dimensions of Painting. Psychometrical Lab. Polish Academy of Sciences, Warsaw, Poland, 25, 128 Southern Universities Press.

CHRISTIANSEN, H. 1959. The relationship of several self-other indices to claimed and measured interests of vocational high school seniors. Unpublished Ph.D. thesis, University of Minnesota.

CHURCH, J. 1961. *Language and the discovery of reality.* New York: Random House.

CLARK, E. K. 1953. Generalized attitude scales. In O. K. Buros (Ed.), *The fourth mental measurements yearbook.* Highland Park, N.J.: Gryphen Press.

CLAYSON, M. D. 1964. Therapeutic progress in terms of semantic variability. *Dissert. Abstr.*, 25(1): 623.

CLEVENGER, T., JR. 1962. Relationship of certain semantic properties of words to occurrence of the GSR, Report No. PR-001, University of Wisconsin Communication and Public Address Experimental Laboratory.

———, LAZIER, G. A. and CLARK, MARGARET L. 1966. Measurement of corporate images by the semantic differential. *J. market. Res.*, 2(1): 80-82.

CLIFF, N. 1956. The relation of adverb-adjective combinations to their components. Unpublished Ph.D. dissertation, Princeton University.

———. 1959. Adverbs as multipliers. *Psychol. Rev.*, 66: 27-44.

COFER, C. H. 1957a. Associative commonality and rated similarity of certain words from Haagen's list. *Psychol. Reps.*, 3: 603-606.

———. 1957b. Reasoning as an associative process: III. the role of verbal responses in problem solving. *J. gen. Psychol.*, 57: 58-68.

COFER, C. N., and FOLEY, J. P. 1942. Mediated generalization and the interpretation of verbal behavior. I. prolegomena. *Psychol. Rev.*, 49: 513-540.

———, JANIS, M. G., and ROWELL, M. M. 1943. Mediated generalization and the interpretation of verbal behavior. III. experiments. *J. exp. Psychol.*, 32: 266-269.

COFFIN, T. E. 1941. Some conditions of suggestion and suggestibility: a study of certain attitudinal and situational factors influencing the process of suggestion. *Psychol. Monogr.*, 53(4). (Whole No. 241.)

COHEN, R. 1959. Eine Untersuchung des Wartegg-Zeichentestes, Rorschachtestes unde z-Testes mit dem Polaritaets-profil. *Diagnistica*, 5: 155-172.

COLE, S., and WILLIAMS, R. L. 1966. Semantic generalization as a function of associative value of stimuli. *Psychon. Sci.*, 6: 173-174.

COLEMAN, E. B. 1964. Supplementary report: on the combination of associative probabilities in linguistic contexts. *J. Psychol.*, 57: 95-99.

COOK, D. R. 1959. A study of the relationship of the meaning of selected concepts to achievement and ability. Unpublished Ed.D. dissertation, Indiana University.

COOPERSMITH, S. 1964. Relationship between self-esteem and sensory (perceptual) constancy. *J. abnorm. soc. Psychol.*, 68: 217-221.

COWAN, T. M. 1965. The semantic differential as a basis for obtaining clustering. *Dissert. Abstr.*, 25(8): 4824-4825.

COWEN, E. L., BOBROVE, P. H., ROCKWAY, A. M., and STEVENSON, J. 1967. Development and evaluation of an attitude to deafness scale. *J. pers. soc. Psychol.*, 6(2): 183-191.

COYNE, L., and HOLZMAN, P. S. 1966. Three equivalent forms of a semantic differential inventory. *Ed. psychol. measmt*, 26: 665-674.

COZENS, W. R., and JACOBS, A. 1961. Empirically derived distributions similar to those used in computing the semantic differential. *J. psychol. stud.*, 12(4): 143-149.

CRANE, E. L. 1962. A comparison of the immunization effects of implicit and explicit presentation of counter-arguments. *Dissert. Abstr.*, 22: 3745.

CRAWFORD, J. L., and VANDERPLAS, J. M. 1959. An experiment on the mediation of transfer in paired-associate learning. *J. Psychol.*, 47: 87-98.

CREELMAN, MARJORIE B. 1966. *The experimental investigation of meaning: a review of the literature*. New York: Springer.

CRESPI, I. 1961. Use of a scaling technique in surveys. *J. Market.*, 26: 69-72.

CRITES, J. O. 1962. Parental identification in relation to vocational interest development. *J. educ. Psychol.*, 53: 262.

CRONBACH, L. J. 1946. Response sets and test validity. *Educ. psychol. Measmt*, 6: 475-494.

————. 1960. *Essentials of psychological testing*. New York: Harper.

———— and GLESER, GOLDINE C. 1953. Assessing similarity between profiles. *Psychol. Bull.*, 50: 456-473.

CROWNE, D. P., STEPHENS, M. W., and KELLY, R. 1961. The validity and equivalence of self-acceptance. *J. Psychol.*, 51: 101-112.

DANIELSON, W. A., NELSON, H. L., FLORES, T., GARDELS, K., LEFTUS, BEVERLY, LYNCH, M., and NELSON, RUTH. 1958. *Sensationalism and the life history of magazines: a preliminary study*. School of Journalism, University of Wisconsin. (Dittoed report.)

DARNELL, D. K. 1964. A technique for determining the evaluative discrimination capacity and polarity of semantic differential scales for specific concepts. *Journ. Abstr.*, 2: 7-8.

————. 1966. Concept-scale interaction in the semantic differential. *J. Comm.*, 16(2): 104-115.

DAS, J. P. 1964. Hypnosis, verbal satiation, vigilance, and personality factors. *J. abnorm. soc. Psychol.*, 68: 72-78.

————. 1966. Relation between semantic and verbal conditioning. *Brit. J. Psychol.*, 57 (1-2): 87-91.

————, and NANDA, D. C. 1963. Mediated transfer of attitudes. *J. abnorm. soc. Psychol.*, 66: 12-16.

DAS, RHEA S. 1965. An application of factor and canonical analysis to multivariate data. *British J. math. Stat. Psychol.*, 18: 57-67.

DAVIS, H. B. 1962. Some symbolic meanings of the Rorschach inkblots. *Dissertation Abstr.*, 22(pt. 1): 4405-4406.

DAVIS R. 1961. The fitness of names to drawings. A cross-cultural study in Tanganyika. *Brit. J. Psychol.*, 52: 259-268.

DAVIS, R. C. 1948. Responses to "meaningful" and "meaningless" sounds. *J. exp. Psychol.*, 38(6): 744-756.

DAVITZ, J. R. 1964. *The communication of emotional meaning*. New York: McGraw-Hill.

DAW, R. P. 1965. An assessment of the Holtzman and the Rorschach inkblots using the semantic differential. *Dissertation Abstr.*, 26(1): 448-489.

DE BURGER, R. A., and DONAHOE, J. W. 1965. Relationship between the meanings of verbal stimuli and their associative responses. *J. verb. Learn. verb. Behav.*, 4: 25-31.

DEESE, J. 1960. Frequency of usage and number of words in free recall: the role of association. *Psychol. Reps.*, 7: 337-344.

————. 1962. On the structure of associative meaning. *Psychol. Rev.*, 69(3): 161-175.

————. 1964. The associative structure of some common English adjectives. *J. verb. Learn. verb. Behav.*, 3: 347-357.

————. 1965. *The structure of associations in language and thought*. Baltimore: Johns Hopkins Press.

DeMontollin, G.., and Le Ny, J. F. 1962. Conditionement d'attitude et conditione-ment verbal, *Psychol. Fran.*, 7: 67-74.

Denmark, F. L., and Guttentag, Marcia. 1967. Dissonance in the self-concepts of college and non-college oriented women. *J. counsel. Psychol.*, 14(2): 113-115.

Derbyshire, R. L. 1966. United States Negro identity conflict. *Sociol. soc. Res.*, 51(1): 63-77.

Deutschmann., P. J. 1959. The semantic differential and public opinion research. *Pub. opin. Quart.*, 23(3): 435.

Diar, L. N. 1965. Studies in social attitudes. III: attitude assessement through SD. *J. soc. Psychol.*, 67(2): 303-314.

Dick, R. N. 1964. Information diffusion and decision making regarding adult education opportunities in two small Wisconsin communities. Master's thesis, University of Wisconsin. *Journ. Abstr.*, 2: 72.

Dicken, C. F. 1958. Connotative meaning as a determinant of stimulus generalization. Unpublished Ph.D. dissertation, University of Minnesota.

————. 1961. Connotative meaning as a determinant of stimulus generalization. *Psychol. Monogr.*, 75 (No. 1). (Whole No. 505).

Diebold, A. R., Jr. 1965. A survey of psycholinguistic research, 1954-64. In C. E. Osgood and T. A. Sebeok (Eds.), *Psycholinguistics: a survey of theory and research problems*. Bloomington: Indiana University Press.

Diedrich, G. W., Messick, S. J., and Tucker, L. R. 1955. *A general least squares solution for successive intervals*. Princeton, N. J.: Educational Testing Service. (Mimeographed.)

Dilts, Martha, and Taylor, R. E. 1964. The semantic differential of color pyramid test instructions. *Percept. mot. Skills*, 19(3): 968-970.

Dirkzwager, A. 1961. "Onaangename Situaties" in de Betekenis-Ruimte van Osgood. *Nederlands Tijdschrift voor de Psychologie*, 16(6): 433-443.

DiVesta, F. 1961. Contrast effects in the verbal conditioning of meaning. *J. exp. Psychol.*, 62(6): 535-544.

————. 1964a. The distribution of modifiers used by children in a word-association task. *J. verb. Learn. verb. Behav.*, 3: 421-427.

————. 1964b. A simplex analysis of changes with age in responses to a restricted word-association task. *J. verb. Learn. verb. Behav.*, 3: 505-510.

————. 1965a. Developmental patterns in the use of modifiers as modes of conceptualization. *Child. Develpm.* 36(1): 186-213.

————. 1965b. Semantic differential ratings of 220 concepts by grade school children. Technical Report No. 11, National Institute of Child Health and Human Development Research Grant HD-00872.

————. 1966a. A developmental study of the semantic structures of children. *J. verb. Learn. verb. Behav.*, 5: 249-259.

————. 1966b. A normative study of 220 concepts rated on the semantic differential by children in grades 2 through 7. *J. gen. Psychol.*, 109: 205-229.

————. 1966c. Norms for modifiers used by children in a restricted word-association task: grades 2 through 6. *Psychol. Reps.*, 18: 65-66.

————, and Blake, K. 1959. The effects of instructional "sets" on learning and transfer. *Amer. J. Psychol.*, 72(1): 57-67.

————, and Dick, W. 1966. The test-retest reliability of children's ratings on the semantic differential. *Educ. psychol. Measmt*, 26: 605-616.

————, and Stover, D. O. 1962. The semantic mediation of evaluative meaning. *J. exp. Psychol.*, 64: 467-475.

Dixon, Joan F., and Simmons, Carolyn H. 1966. The impression value of verbs for children. *Child Developm.*, 37(4): 861-866.

Dixon, T. R. 1965a. The effect of pre-experimentally acquired verbal habits upon verbal conditioning. *J. Psychol.*, 59: 335-347.

————. 1965b. Neutral-impression verbs and the conditioning of pronouns. *J. Psychol.*, 61: 3-11.

————, and DIXON, J. F. 1964. The impression value of verbs. *J. verb. Learn. verb. Behav.*, 3: 161-165.

DODGE, JOAN. 1955. A quantitative investigation of the relation between meaning development and context. Unpublished Ph.D. dissertation, University of Illinois.

DOLEYS, E. J. and KREGARMAN, J. 1959. Construct validity of the Chicago Q-sort: frustration tolerance. *J. clin. Psychol.*, 15: 177-179.

DOLLARD, J.., and MILLER, N. E. 1950. *Personality and psychotherapy.* New York: McGraw-Hill.

DONAHOE, J. W. 1961. Changes in meaning as a function of age. *J. gen. Psychol.*, 99: 23-28.

DONNAHOE, A. S. 1960. The public image of advertising media. *Bus. Econ. Rev.* 1(1). University of Missouri.

DORCUS, R. M. 1932. Habitual word associations to colors as a possible factor in advertising. *J. appl. Psychol.*, 16: 277-287.

DOVRING, KARIN. 1965. Troubles with mass communications and semantic differentials in 1774 and today. *Amer. Behav. Scientist*, 9(1): 9-14.

DOWLING, R. M., and BRAUN, H. W. 1957. Retention and meaningfulness of material. *J. exp. Psychol.*, 54: 213-217.

DOWNING, R. W., and RICKELS, K. 1962. Personality and attitudinal correlates of response to drug treatment in psychiatric outpatients: II. preliminary investigation and implications for further research. *J. Psychol.*, 54: 345-361.

DREVER, J. 1960. Perceptual learning. *Ann. Rev. Psychol.*, 11: 136.

DUKES, W. F. 1955. Psychological studies of values. *Psychol. Bull.*, 52: 24-50.

DUNLAP, J. W., and KROLL, A. 1939. Observations on the methodology of attitude scales. *J. soc. Psychol.*, 10: 475-487.

DUSTIN, D. S., and BALDWIN, PATRICIA M. 1966. Redundancy in impression formation. *J. pers. soc. Psychol.*, 3(5): 500-506.

EARLE, MARGARET J. 1967. Bilingual semantic merging and an aspect of acculturation. *J. pers. soc. Psychol.*, 6(3): 304-312.

EASTLACK, J. O., Jr. 1964. Consumer flavor preference factors in food product design. *J. Market. Res.*, February.

EATON, TREVOR. 1966. *The semantics of literature.* Paris, The Hague: Mouton and Co.

EBNER, G. H. 1964. Some factors influential in audience selection of early evening news programs. Master's thesis, Pennsylvania State University. *Journ. Abstr.*, 2: 73.

EDELMAN, S. K., KARAS, G. G., and COHEN, B. J. 1961. The relative contributions of complexity and symmetry to the perception of form. Paper presented at Midwestern Psychological Association, May.

EDWARDS, A. L. 1946. A critique of "neutral" items in attitude scales constructed by the method of equal appearing intervals. *Psychol. Rev.*, 53: 159-169.

————. 1957. *Techniques of attitude scale construction.* New York: Appleton-Century-Crofts.

————, and WALSH, J. A. 1963. The relationship between the intensity of the social desirability keying of a scale and the correlation of the scale with Edwards' SD Scale and the first factor loading of the scale. *J. clin. Psychol.*, 14: 200-203.

EISDORFER, C., and ALTROCCHI, J. 1961. A comparison of attitudes toward old age and mental illness. *J. Gerontol.*, 16: 340-343.

EISENMAN, R., BERNARD, J. L. and HANNON, J. E. 1966. Benevolence, potency, and God: a semantic differential study of the Rorschach. *Percept. mot. Skills*, 22(1): 75-78.

————, and RAPPAPORT, JOAN. 1967. Complexity preference and semantic differential ratings of complexity-simplicity and symmetry-asymmetry. *Psychon. Sci.*, 7(4): 147-148.

EKMAN, G. 1954. Similarity analysis of olfaction: A preliminary investigation. *Reports from the Psychological Laboratory*, 10. Stockholm: The Psychological Laboratory, University of Stockholm.

————. 1955. Dimensions of emotion. *Nordisk Psykologi*, 7: 103-112.

————. 1965. Two methods for the analysis of perceptual dimensionality. *Percept. Mot. Skills*, 20: 557-572. Monograph Supplement 2-V20.

————, and BRATFISCH, O. 1965. Subjective geographic distance and emotional involvement. *Reports from the Psychological Laboratory*, 189. Stockholm: The Psychological Laboratory, University of Stockholm.

————, ENGEN, T., KUNNAPAS, T., and LINDMAN, R. 1964. A quantitative principle of qualitative similarity. *J. exp. Psychol.*, 68(6): 530-536.

————, and HOSMAN, BRITA. 1965. Note on subjective scales of number. *Percept. Mot. Skills*, 21: 101-102.

EKMAN, P., TUFTE, E. R., ARCHIBALD, K., and BRODY, R. A. 1966. Coping with Cuba: divergent policy preferences of state political leaders. *J. Conflict Resolution*, 10(2): 180-197.

ELLING, K. A. 1966. Meaning and the influence of emotionally elated or depressed states. *Dissert. Abstr.*, 27: 623.

ELLIOT, LOIS L. 1958. Reliability of judgments of figural complexity. *J. exp. Psychol.*, 56: 335-338.

————, and TANNENBAUM, P. H. 1963. Factor structure of semantic differential responses to visual forms and prediction of factor scores from structural characteristics of the stimulus-shapes. *Amer. J. Psychol.*, 76: 589-597.

ENDLER, N. S. 1961. Changes in meaning during psychotherapy as measured by the semantic differential. *J. counsel. Psychol.*, 8: 105-111.

ENGBRETSON, R. O. 1964. Cognitive adjustment of perceived self credibility, perceived source credibility, and perceived task difficulty as a result of feedback in task oriented dyads. *Journ. Abstr.*, 2: 9-10.

ENGEN, T., and LEVY, N. 1955. The influence of standards on psychophysical judgments. *Percept. Mot. Skills*, 5: 193-197.

————, ————. 1956. Constant-sum judgments of facial expressions. *J. exp. Psychol.*, 51: 396-398.

EPSTEIN, W., ROCK, I., and ZUCKERMAN, C. B. 1960. Meaning and familiarity in associative learning. *Psychol. Monogr.*, 74, No. 4. (Whole No. 491.)

ERICKSEN, S. C. 1962. Studies in the abstraction process. *Psychol. Monogr.*, 76, No. 18. (Whole No. 537.)

ERTEL, S. 1965a. Further investigation of the standardizing of a set of SD, Z *exp., angew. Psychol.*, 12(2): 177-208.

————. 1965b. Der Lautcharakter kunstlicher Lautgebilde. *Psychologischen Forschung*, 28: 491-518.

————. 1965c. Neue soziometrische perspektiven. *Psychologichen Forschung*, 28: 329-362.

————. 1965d. Standardisierung eines Eindrucksdifferentials. *Z. exp. angew. Psychol.*, 12(1): 22-58.

————. 1965e. Weitere Untersuchungen zur Standardisierung eines Eindrucksdifferentials. *Z. exp. angew. Psychol.*, 8(2): 177-208.

————. 1966a. Ein differentialmethodischer Versuch zum Intelligenzproblem. *Psychologische Forschung*, 30: 151-199.

————. 1966b. Ist Lautcharakter Sprachspezifisch oder universell? *Studia Psychologica*, 8(3): 216-230.

————, and DORST, R. 1965. Expressive Lautsymbolik. *Z. exp. angew. Psychol.*, 4: 557-569.

————, and THEOPHILE I. 1966. Ein Versuch zur Messung richtungspezifischer Aktivierung. *Psychologischen Forschung*, 29: 241-263.

ERVIN, SUSAN M. 1962. The connotations of gender. *Word*, 18(3): 249-261.

————, and FOSTER, G. 1960. The development of meaning in children's descriptive terms. *J. abnorm. soc. Psychol.*, 61: 271-275.

ERVIN-TRIPP SUSAN M., and SLOBIN, D. I. 1966. Psycholinguistics. *Ann. Rev. Psychol.*, 17· 450-462.

EVANS, R. I., WIELAND, B. A., and MOORE, C. W. 1961. The effect of experience in telecourses on attitudes toward instruction by television and impact of a controversial television program. *J. appl. Psychol.*, 45:11-15.

FEINTUCH, A. 1955. Improving the employability and attitudes of "difficult-to-place" persons. *Psychol. Monogr.*, 69, No. 7. (Whole No. 392.)

FELDMAN, S., and ABELSON, R. P. 1962. Test of a model for predicting ratings of word combinations. Institute of Communications Research, University of Illinois; Yale University. (Manuscript.)

FELSTEHAUSEN, H. H. 1964. Economic knowledge and comprehension in a Netherlands farming community. *Journ. Abstr.*, 2: 12.

FERNALD, L. D. 1962. Client distortion of psychological test data in the test-interpretation interview. *Dissert. Abstr.*, 22: 2457.

FIEDLER, F. E., DODGE, JOAN S., and HUTCHENS, E. B. 1958. Interrelations among measures of personality adjustment in nonclinical populations. *J. abnorm. soc. Psychol.*, 56: 345-351.

———, HUTCHINS, E. B., and DODGE, J. S. 1959. Quasi-therapeutic relations in small college and military groups. *Psychol. Monogr.*, 73, No. 3. (Whole No. 473.)

FILLENBAUM, S. 1963. Verbal satiation and changes in meaning of related items. *J. verb. Learn. verb. Behav.*, 2: 263-271.

FINGELD, T. E. 1953. An experimental study of the ability to select words to convey intended meaning. Unpublished Ph.D. dissertation, University of Illinois.

———. 1966. The ability to select words to convey intended meanings. *Quart. J. Speech*, 52: 255-258.

FINK, C. F. 1962. The strength of perceived relations as a factor in cognitive-affective consistency: an experimental study. *Dissert. Abstr.*, 23: 336.

FINLEY, J. R., and STAATS, A. W. 1967. Evaluative meaning words as reinforcing stimuli. *J. verb. Learn. verb. Behav.*, 6(2): 193-197.

FISCHER, H. 1961. Ce que la methode des "semantic differentials" apporte au probleme des images des peuples. *Rev. Psychol. Peuples*, 16: 306-318.

FISHBEIN, M., and HUNTER, RONDA. 1964. Summation versus balance in attitude organization and change. *J. abnorm. soc. Psychol.*, 69: 505-510.

———, and RAVEN, B. H. 1962. The AB scales: an operational definition of belief and attitude. *Hum. Relat.*, 15: 35.

FISHER, A., and SKURNIK, L. 1961. The effects of level of saturation of color upon black and white advertisements. Unpublished manuscript, Purdue University.

FISKE, D. W. 1957. The constraints on intra-individual variability in test responses. *Educ. psychol. Measmt*, 17: 317-337.

FITZGERALD, D., and ROBERTS, KARLENE. 1966. Semantic profiles and psychosexual interests or indicators or identification, *Pers. guid. J.*, 44(8): 802-806.

FLAVELL, J. H. 1961a. Meaning and meaning similarity: I. a theoretical reassessment. *J. gen. Psychol.*, 64: 307-319.

———. 1961b. Meaning and meaning similarity: II. the semantic differential and co-occurrence as predictors of judged similarity in meaning. *J. gen. Psychol.*, 64: 321.

———, and FLAVELL, ELEANOR R. 1959. One determinant of judged semantic and associative connection between words. *J. exp. Psychol.*, 58: 159-165.

———, and JOHNSON, ANN. 1961. Meaning and meaning similarity: III. latency and number of similarities as predictors of judged similarity in meaning. *J. gen. Psychol.*, 64: 337-348.

FLOYD, R. L. 1962. Semantic satiation: replication and test of further implications. *Psychol. Reps.*, 11: 274.

FLUCKIGER, F. A. 1962. The interaction of verbal mediators following the acquisition of new meanings, an investigation of changes in meaning of stimulus signs occurring with the acquisition of meaning for an initially meaningless assign, as reflected by a form of the semantic differential. *Dissert. Abstr.*, 23: 2215.

FOA, U. G. 1963. A facet approach to the prediction of communalities. *Behav. Sci.*, 8(3): 220-226.

———. 1965. New developments in facet design and analysis. *Psychol. Rev.*, 262-273.

FODOR, J. A. 1965. Could meaning be an r_m? *J. verb. Learn. verb. Behav.*, 4: 73-81.

———. 1966. More about mediators: a reply to Berlyne and Osgood. *J. verb. Learn. verb. Behav.*, 5: 412-415.

FOLEY, J. P. and MACMILLAN, Z. L. 1943. Mediated generalization and the interpretation of verbal behavior: V. "free association" as related to differences in professional training. *J. Exp. Psychol.*, 33: 299-310.

FOLKINS, C., and LONROW, P. B. 1966. An investigation of the expressive value of graphemes. *Psychol. Rec.*, 16(2): 193-200.

FORD, L. H. Jr., and MEISELS, M. 1965. Social desirability and the semantic differential. *Educ. psychol. Measmt*, 25(2): 465-475.

FORSTER, K. I., TRIANDIS, H. C., and OSGOOD, C. E. 1964. An analysis of the method of triads in research on the measurement of meaning. Urbana: Department of Psychology, Technical Report No. 17, University of Illinois.

FOSDICK, J. A. 1963. Stylistic correlates of prescribed intent in a photographic encoding task. Unpublished Ph.D. dissertation, University of Wisconsin.

FOX, C. W. 1935. An experimental study of naming. *Amer. J. Psychol.*, 47: 545-579.

FRANCIONI, M. 1966. La semantica esistenziale di Eugene Minkowski. *Rivista di Psicologia Sociale e Archivis Italiano di Pricologia General e del Lavoro*, 33(2-3): 179-196.

FRASE, L. T. 1965. Syllogistic reasoning behavior as a function of the evaluative ratings of terms used. Unpublished Ph.D. dissertation, University of Illinois.

———. 1966. Belief, incongruity, and syllogistic reasoning. *Psychol. Reps.*, 18: 982.

FRIEDMAN, C. J., and GLADDEN, J. W. 1964. Objective measurement of social role concepts via the semantic differential. *Psychol. Reps.*, 14: 239-247.

———, JOHNSON, C. A., and FODE, K. 1964. Subjects descriptions of selected TAT cards via the semantic differential. *J. consult. Psychol.*, 28: 317.

FRIJDA, N. H., and PHILIPSZOON, ELS. 1963. Dimensions of recognition of expression. *J. abnorm. soc. Psychol.*, 66: 45-51.

FUCHS, D. A. 1964. Two source effects in magazine advertising. *Journ. Abstr.*, 2: 13-14.

GAMPEL, DOROTHY H. 1966. Temporal factors in verbal satiation. *J. exp. Psychol.*, 72: 201-206.

GARDNER, R. A. 1957. Probality-learning with two and three choices. *J. Amer. Psychol.*, 70: 171-185.

GARMEZY, N., and RODNICK, E. H. 1959. Premorbid adjustment and performance in schizophrenia: implications for interpreting heterogeneity in schizophrenia. *J. Nervous Mental Disease*, 129: 450-465.

GARSKOF, B. E., and HOUSTON, J. P. 1963. Measurement of verbal relateness: an idiographic approach. *Psychol. Rev.*, 70: 277-288.

GATTY, R., and ALLAIS, C. 1960. The semantic differential applied to image research. *Tech. A. E. No. 2, Dept. of Agric. Econ.*, Rutgers University.

GEBELS, G. 1966. An investigation of phonetic symbolism in different cultures. University of New South Wales. (Manuscript.)

GELFAND, DONNA M., GELFAND, S., and RARDIN, M. W. 1965. Some personality factors associated with placebo responsivity. *Psychol. Reps.*, 17: 555-562.

———, and SINGER, R.D. 1964. Generalization of children's verbally conditioned personality judgments. Unpublished paper, ref: *Amer. Psychol.*, 19(9): 713.

GEORGE, JANE. 1965. Interpretative significance of animal responses in Rorschach: a comparative study. *Transactions of All-India Instiiute of Mental Health*, 5: 75-85.

GERBNER, G. 1958. The social anatomy of the romance-confession cover girl. *Journ. Quart.*, 35: 299-306.

GEROW, J. R., and POLLIO, H. R. Word association, frequency of occurrence, and semantic differential norms for 360 stimulus words. Technical Report No. 1, Department of Psychology, University of Tennessee.

GHISELIN, M. T. 1966. On semantic pitfalls of biological adaptation. *Phil. Sci.*, 33: 147-153.

GIFFIN, K. 1966. The contribution of studies of source credibility to a theory of interpersonal trust in the communication process. The Communication Research Center, University of Kansas, Lawrence.

GINSBERG, A. 1954. Does Hullian theory provide the adequate foundations for a comprehensive theory of human behavior? *J. gen. Psychol.*, 51: 301-329.

GLATTER, A. N. and REECE, M. M. 1962. Tactility and sexual symbolism. *Percept. Mot. Skills*, 14: 302.

GOLDING, S. L., ATWOOD, G. E., and GOODMAN, R. A. 1966. Anxiety and two cognitive forms of resistance to the idea of death. *Psychol. Reps.*, 18: 359-364.

GOLDFRIED, M. R. 1962. On differences in meaning between normals and neurotics. *Psychol. Reps.*, 11: 183.

————, 1963. The connotative meaning of some animal symbols for college students. *J. proj. Tech.*, 27: 60-67.

————, and KISSEL, S. 1963. Age as a variable in the connotative perceptions of some animal symbols. *J. proj. tech. pers. assess.*, 27: 171-180.

GOMBRICH, E. H. 1965. The use of art for the study of symbols. *Amer. Psychol.* 20: 34-50.

GOODALE, R. A. 1964. Meaningfulness: the correlation between M and some aspects of D. Unpublished paper, ref: *Amer. Psychol.*, 19(9): 732.

GOODENOUGH, W. 1956. Componential analysis and the study of meaning. *Language*, 32: 155-216.

GORDON, H. L., and GROTH, C. 1961. Mental patients wanting to stay in hospitals: attitudes. *Arch. gen. Psychiat.*, 4: 124-130.

GORMAN, A. M. 1961. Recognition memory for nouns as a function of abstractness and frequency. *J. exp. Psychol.*, 61: 23-29.

GORSUCH, R. L. 1966. A fortran item analysis program for items scored on a categorical or interval basis. *Educ. Psychol. Measmt*, 26: 179-183.

GREEN, L. 1964. Relationship between semantic differential measurement of concept meanings and parent-sex identification phenomenon: a study of the construct validity of the semantic differential. *Disser. Abstr.*, 25: 3100.

GREEN, P. E., and TULL, D. S. 1961. *Research for marketing decisions*. Englewood Cliffs, N. J.: Prentice Hall.

GREEN, R. F., and GOLDFRIED, M. R. 1965. On the bipolarity of semantic space. *Psychol. Monogr.*, 79, No. 6. (Whole No. 599.)

————, and NOWLIS, V. 1958. Experimental analysis of verbal report of mood. Technical Report, Research Project #NR171-342, Contract N6-onr-241, University of Rochester.

GREENBERG, B. S. 1964. On relating attitude change and information gain. *J. Comm.*, 14(3): 157-171.

————. 1965. Television for children: dimensions of communicator and audience perceptions. *Comm. Rev.*, 13(4): 385-396.

GREGORY, J. R. 1961. Some psychological aspects of motion picture montage. *Disser. Abstr.*, 22: 317.

GREGSON, R. A. 1964. Aspects of the theoretical status of aesthetic response typologies. *Psychol. Reps.*, 15: 395-398.

GRIGG, A. E. 1959a. Validity study of the semantic differential technique. *J. clin. Psychol.*, 15: 179-181.

————. 1959b. A validity test of self-ideal discrepancy. *J. clin. Psychol.*, 15: 311-313.

CRISELL, J. 1964. The role of meaning in the mediated generalization of avoidance behavior. *Dissert. Abstr.*, 24: 4795.

GROSS, C. F. 1960. Intrajudge consistency in ratings of heterogeneous persons. *Dissert. Abstr.*, 21: 952.

GROSSER, G. S., and WALSH, A. A. 1966. Sex differences in the differential recall of taboo and neutral words. *J. Psychol.*, 63: 219-227.

GRUEN, W. 1960. Preference for new products and its relationship to different measures of conformity. *J. appl. Psychol.*, 44: 361-364.

GULLIKSEN, H. 1954. A least squares solution for successive intervals assuming unequal standard deviations. *Psychometrika*, 19: 117-139.

————. 1956. Measurement of subjective values. *Psychometrika*, 21: 229-244.

————. 1958. How to make meaning more meaningful. *Contemp. Psychol.*, 3: 115-118.

————, and MESSICK, S. J. 1960. *Psychological scaling: theory and applications*. New York: John Wiley.

GWALTNEY, H. O. 1959. Reference identification as a variable in convalescence and chronicity of mental hospital patients. Unpublished Ed.D. dissertation, University of Missouri.

GYNTHER, M. D., MILLER, I. T., and DAVIS, H. T. 1962. Relations between needs and behavior as measured by the Edwards PPS and interpersonal check list. *J. soc. Psychol.*, 57(2): 445-451.

HAAGEN, C. H. 1949. Synonymity, vividness, familiarity, and association value ratings of 400 pairs of common adjectives. *J. Psychol.*, 27: 453-463.

HAFNER, A., and ROSEN, E. 1964. The meaning of Rorschach inkblots, responses and determinants as perceived by children. *J. proj. tech. per. Assess.*, 28(2): 192-200.

HALLWORTH, H. J. 1965. Dimensions of personality and meaning. *Brit. J. soc. clin. Psychol.*, 4: 161-168.

————, and ABIRI, J. 1966. A comparative factorial analysis of some Nigerian adolescent attitudes. *Brit. J. educ. Psychol.*, (in press.)

————, and WAITE, G. 1963. A factorial study of value judgments among adolescent girls. *Brit. J. stat. Psychol.*, 16: 37-46.

————, ————. 1965. The semantic differential and adolescent value judgments: a comparative study of the affective meaning systems of boys and girls. *Bull. Brit. Psychol. Soc.*, 59: 3.

————, ————. 1966. A comparative study of the value judgments of adolescents. *Brit. J. educ. Psychol.*, 36: 202-209.

HAMMOND, K. R. 1948. Measuring attitudes by error-choice: an indirect method. *J. abnorm. soc. Psychol.*, 43: 38-48.

HANSSON, G. 1964. *Diktiprofil*. Goteborg: Scandinavian University Books.

HARBIN, SUSAN P. and WILLIAM, J. E. 1966. Conditioning and color connotation. *Percept. mot. Skills*, 22(1): 217-218.

HASLAM, W. B., and PEDERSON, D. M. 1966. Points of view in the perception of facial expressions of emotion. *Percept. mot. Skills*, 22(2): 645-646.

HASTORF, A. H., OSGOOD, C. E., and ONO, H. 1966. The semantics of facial expressions and the prediction of the meanings of stereoscopically fused facial expressions. *Scand. J. Psychol.*, 7(3): 179-188.

HAVE, R. D. 1964. Cognitive factors in transfer of meaning. *Psychol. Reps.*, 15: 199-206.

HAYGOOD, R. C. 1966. Use of semantic differential dimensions in concept learning. *Psychon. Sci.*, 5(8): 305-306.

HEATH, E. H. 1966. A semantic differential study of attitudes relating to recreation as applied to a bicultural setting. *Dissert. Abstr.*, 27(3-A): 657-658.

HEIDER, F. 1946. Attitudes and cognitive organization. *J. Psychol.*, 21: 107-112.

HEISE, D. R. 1965. Semantic differential profiles for 1,000 most-frequent words. *Psychol. Monogr.*, 79, No. 8.

————. 1966. Sensitization of verbal response-dispositions by n Affiliation and n Achievement. *J. verb. Learn, verb. Behav.*, 5: 522-525.

————. 1966. Social status, attitudes, and word connotations. Sociological Inquiry, 36: 227-239.

HELFANT, K. 1952. Parents' attitudes vs. adolescent hostility in the determination of adolescents' sociopolitical attitudes. *Psychol. Monogr.*, 66, No. 13 (Whole No. 345.)

HELPER, M. M. 1955. Learning theory and the self concept. *J. abnorm soc. Psychol.*, 50: 184-194.

————. 1958. Parental evaluations of children and children's self-evaluation. *J. abnorm. soc. Psychol.*, 56: 190-193.

————, and GARFIELD, S. 1965. Use of SD to study co-culturation of American Indian adolescents. *J. pers. soc. Psychol.*, 2(6): 817-822.

HEPLER, H. W. 1966. The ability of English speakers to respond to the structural cues of written language: measuring instruments. *Dissert. Abstr.*, 27(4-A): 1045-1046.

HERR, V. V. 1966. Further research in the Loyola language study. *J. clin. Psychol.*, 22: 281-287.

HERRMANN, T. 1964. Urteilsnuanciertheit und Fraktionierung des Bezugssystems. Eine Zweifaktorentheorie des semantischen Differenzierens. *Psychol. Beitr.*,7:539-557.

HERTWECK, E. R. 1966. Semantic differential ratings of counselor nonverbal and verbal communications. *Dissert. Abstr.*, 27(4-A): 954.

HEVNER, KATE. 1936. Experimental studies of the elements of expression in music. *Amer. J. Psychol.*, 48: 246-268.

HILL, C. R. 1964. Mood, self derogation and anomia as factors in response unreliability. Unpublished Ph.D. dissertation, University of Iowa.

HILL, E. W. 1962. Corporate images are not stereotypes. *J. Marketing*, 26: 72-75.

HINCKLEY, E. D. 1932. The influence of individual opinion on construction of an attitude scale. *J. soc. Psychol.*, 3: 283-296.

HOAR, J. R., and MEEK, E. E. 1965. The semantic differential as a measure of subliminal message effects. *J. Psychol.*, 60: 165-169.

HOFSTATTER, P. R., 1956a. Farbsymbolik und Ambivalenz. *Psychologische Beitrage*, 2(4): 526-540.

――――. 1956b. Mannlich und weiblich. *Wiener Archiv fur Psychologie, Psychiatrie und Neurologie.* 6(Heft 3/4): 3-16.

――――. 1959a. *Einfuhrung in die Sozialpsychologie.* Stuttgart: Kroner.

――――. 1959b. Zur Problematik der Profilmethode. *Diagnostica.*, 5: 19-25.

――――. 1963. Uber sprachliche Bestimmungsleistungen: Das Problem des grammatikalischen Geschlects von Somme und Mond. *Z. Exp. angew. Psychol.*, 10: 91-108.

――――, and PRIMAC, D. W. 1957. Colors and color-blind. *J. gen. Psychol.*, 57: 229-240.

HOGENRAAD, R. 1966. L'évolution de la contraine du contexte sur le processue de signification dans deux cas d'analyse de groupe. *J. de Psychologie*, 4: 437-462.

HOLLAND, M. K., and WERTHEIMER, M. 1964. Some psysiognomic aspects of naming or Maluma and Takete revisited. *Percept. mot. Skills*, 19(1): 11-117.

HOLTZMAN, P. S., and ROUSEY, C. 1966. The voice as a percept. *J. pers. soc. Psychol.*, 4(1): 79-86.

HOMZIE, M. J., and WEIMER, J. 1967. Connotative similarity and paired-associate learning. *J. verb. Learn. verb. Behav.*, 6: 136-138.

HOPPER, D., and PADDEN, D. 1965. Psychiatric roles and their meaning. *Brit. J. soc. clin. Psychol.*, 4: 35 38.

HORMAN, M. 1960. Implicit personality theories of clinicians as defined by semantic structures. *J. consult. Psychol.*, 24: 180-186.

HORTON, D. L., and KJELDERGAARD, P. M. 1961. An experimental analysis of associative factors in mediated generalization. *Psychol. Monogr.*, 75, No. 11. (Whole No. 515.)

HOVLAND, C. I., JANIS, I., and KELLEY, H. H. 1953. *Communications and persuasion.* New Haven: Yale University Press.

――――, and SHERIF, M. 1952. Judgemental phenomena and scales of attitude measurement: item displacement in Thurstone scale. *J. abnorm. soc. Psychol.*, 47: 822-832.

HOWARD, J. A. 1965. *Marketing theory.* Boston: Allyn and Bacon.

HOWE, E. S. 1962. Probablistic adverbial qualifications of adjectives. *J. verb. Learn. verb. Behav.*, 1: 225-242.

――――. 1964. Three-dimensional structure of ratings of exploratory responses shown by a semantic differential. *Psychol. Reps.*, 14: 187-196.

――――. 1965a. Further data concerning the dimensionality of ratings of the therapists' verbal exploratory behavior. *J. consult. Psychol.*, 29(1): 73-76.

———. 1965b. Uncertainty and other associative correlates of Osgood's D4. *J. verb. Learn. verb. Behav.*, 4: 498-509.

———. 1966a. Associative structure of quantifiers. *J. verb Learn. verb. Behav.*, 5: 156-162.

———. 1966b. Verb tense, negatives, and other determinants of the intensity of evaluative meaning. *J. verb. Learn. verb. Behav.*, 5: 147-155.

———, and POPE, B. 1960. Multiple scaling of therapists' responses with a semantic differential. *Amer. Psychol.*, 15: 415.

———. ———. 1961. The dimensionality of ratings of therapist verbal responses. *J. consult. Psychol.*, 25: 296-303.

HOWES, D. H., and OSGOOD, C. E. 1954. On the combination of associative probabilities in linguistic contexts. *Amer. J. Psychol.*, 67: 241-258.

HUFF, V. E. 1967. The effect of interview replay on client movement toward psychological health. *Dissert. Abstr.*, 27(7-A): 2069.

HULL, C. L. 1933. The meaningfulness of 320 selected nonsense syllables. *Amer. J. Psychol.*, 45: 730-734.

HUNT, R. G. 1961. Conceptual congruity among psychiatric patients and staff. *Psychol. Reps.*, 9: 53-54.

HUSEK, T. R. 1961. Acquiescence as a response set and as a personality characteristic. *Educ. Psychol. Measmt.*, 21: 295-307.

———. 1964. Correlated or uncorrelated measures of related or unrelated constructs. *Psychol. Reps.*, 14: 463-466.

———, and WITTROCK, M. C. 1962. The dimensions of attitudes toward teachers as measured by the semantic differential. *J. ed. Psychol.*, 53: 209.

IRWIN, F. W. 1961. On desire, aversion, and the affective zero, *Psychol. Rev.*, 68: 293-300.

JACOBSON, E. 1932. Electrophysiology of mental activities. *Amer. J. Psychol.*, 44: 677-694.

JAKOBOVITS, L. A. 1962. Effects of repeated stimulation on cognitive aspects of behavior: some experiments on the phenomenon of semantic satiation. Unpublished Ph.D. dissertation, McGill University.

———. 1965a. Evaluational reactions to erotic literature. *Psychol. Reps.*, 16: 985-994.

———. 1965b. Semantic satiation in concept formation. *Psychol. Rep.*, 17:113-114.

———. 1966a. Comparative psycholinguistics in the study of cultures. *Int. J. Psychol.*, 1(1): 15-37.

———. 1966b. Mediation theory and the "single-stage" S-R model: different? *Psychol Rev.*, 73: 376-381.

———. 1966c. Studies of fads: I. the hit parade. *Psychol. Reps.*, 18: 443-450.

———. 1966d. Utilization of semantic satiation in stuttering: a theoretical analysis. *J. Speech and Hearing Disorders*, 31(2)

———, and LAMBERT, W. E. 1961. Semantic statiation among bilinguals. *J. exp. Psychol.*, 62: 576-582.

———, ———. 1962. Semantic satiation in an addition task. *Canad. J. Psychol.*, 16(2): 112-119.

———, ———. 1964. Stimulus-characteristics as determinants of semantic changes with repeated presentation. *J. Amer. Psychol.*, 77: 84-92.

———, and OSGOOD, C. E. 1963. Connotations of twenty psychological journals to their professional readers. Urbana: Institute of Communications Research, University of Illinois.

———, and RICE, U. M. 1966. Semantic satiation as a function of initial polarity and scale relevance. University of Illinois. (Manuscript.)

JANSEN, MATHILDA J., and SMOLENNARS, A. J. 1966. A brief report concerning a cross-culturally standardized semantic differential. *Niederlands Tijdschrift Voor de Psychologie en harr Grensgebieden.* 21(3): 211-216.

JASPERS, J. M. 1966. On social perception. Unpublished Ph.D. dissertation. Leiden, The Netherlands: Leiden University.

JEFFREY, W. E., and KAPLAN, R. J. 1957. Semantic generalization with experimentally induced associations. *J. exp. Psychol.*, 54: 336-338.

JENKINS, C. D. 1966. Group feelings in perception: a study of community feelings about tuberculosis. *Amer. J. Soc.*, 71(4): 417-429.

JENKINS, J. J. 1960. Degree of polarization and scores on the principal factors for concepts in the semantic atlas study. *Amer. J. Psychol.*, 73: 274-279.

————, RUSSELL, W. A., and SUCI, C. J. 1958a. An atlas of semantic profiles for 360 words. *Amer. J. Psycol.*, 71: 688-699.

————, ————, ————. 1958b. Studies in the role of language in behavior. N8-onr-66216, Technical Report No. 20, University of Minnesota.

————, ————, ————. 1959. A table of distances for the semantic atlas. *Amer. J. Psychol.*, 72: 623-625.

JENKINS, P. M., and COFER, C. N. 1957. An exploratory study of discrete free associations to compound verbal stimuli. *Psychol. Rep.*, 3: 599-602.

JOHNSON, K. G. 1962. Differential judgments of science news stories and their structural correlates. *Journ. Abstr.*, 2,

JOHNSON, M. G. 1967. Syntactic position and rated meaning. *J. verb. Learn. verb. Behav.*, 6(2): 240-246.

JOHNSON, R. B. 1966. The pragmatic meaning of interpersonal terms: an investigation of the relations among the measures of selected interpersonal terms as determined by selected scales of the SD and by components of the multilevel measurement of interpersonal behavior. *Dissert. Abstr.*, 27(4-A): 958-959.

JOHNSON, R. C., FRINCKE, G., and MARTIN, LEA. 1961. Meaningfulness, frequency and affective character of words as related to visual duration threshold. *Canad. J. Psychol.*, 15(4): 199-204.

————, and MANN, CAROL E. 1967. An attempt to explain both correct and incorrect matches in tests of phonetic symbolism. University of Colorado. (Manuscript.)

————, THOMSON, C. W. and FRINCKE, G. Words values, word frequency and visual duration thresholds. *Psychol. Rev.*, 67: 332-342.

————, WEISS, R. T., and ZELHORT, P. F. 1964. Similarities and differences between normal and psychotic subjects in responses to verbal stimuli. *J. abnorm. soc. Psychol.*, 68: 221-226.

JOLLIFFE, H. R. 1956. A semantic slant on objectivity vs. interpretation. *Journ. Quart.*, 33: 189-193.

JONES, E. E., GERGEN, K. J., and DAVIS, K. E. 1962. Some determinants of reactions to being approved or disapproved as a person. *Psychol. Monogr.*, 76, No. 2. (Whole No. 521.)

JONES, L. V., and THURSTONE, L. L. 1955. The psychophysics of semantics: an experimental investigation. *J. appl. Psychol.*, 39: 31-36.

JONES, W. S. 1962. Some correlatives of the authoritarian personality in a quasi-therapeutic situation. *Dissertation Abstr.*, 23: 691.

KAGAN, J., and LEMKIN, JUDITH. 1960. The child's differential perception of parental attributes. *J. abnorm. soc. Psychol.*, 61: 440-447.

KAHNEMAN, D. 1963. The semantic differential and the structure of inferences among attributes. *Amer. J. Psychol.*, 76: 554-567.

KAISER, H. F. 1958. The varimax criterion for analytic rotations in factor analysis. *Psychometrika*, 23: 187-200.

KAMANO, D. K. 1960a. Investigation on the meaning of human figure drawing. *J. clin. Psychol.*, 16: 429-430.

————. 1960b. Symbolic significance of Rorschach cards IV and VII. *J. clin. Psychol.*, 16: 50-52.

————. 1961. Self-satisfaction and psychological adjustment in schizophrenics. *J. consult. Psychol.*, 25: 492-496.

KAMENETZKY, J., BURGESS, C. G., and ROWAN, T. 1956. The relative effectiveness of four attitude assessment techniques in predicting a criterion. *Educ. Psychol. Measmt.*, 16: 187-194.

KANFER, F. H. 1961. Comments on learning in psychotherapy. *Psychol. Reps.*, 9: 681-699.

KANSAKER, J. 1963. The analytical study of affective values of color-combinations. *Japanese J. Psychol.*, 34: 1-12.

KANUNGO, R. N. and LAMBERT. W. E. 1963. Sematic satiation and meaningfulness. *J. Amer. Psychol.*, 76: 421-428.

———, ———. 1964. Effects of variations in amount of verbal repetition on meaning and paired-associate learning. *J. verb. Learn. verb. Behav.*, 3: 358-361.

———, ———, and MAUER, S. M. 1962. Semantic satiation and paired-associate learning. *J. exp. Psychol.*, 64: 600-607.

KAO, Y. L. 1958. A comparison of semantic structure in Chinese and English. *Dissert. Abstr.*, 19: 1437-1438.

KARWOSKI, T. F., GRAMLICH, F. W., and ARNOTT, P. 1944. Psychological studies in semantics: I. free association reactions to words, drawings, and objects *J. soc. Pychol.*, 20: 233-247.

———, and ODBERT, H. S. 1938. Color-music. *Psychol. Monogr.*, 50, No. 2, (Whole No. 222.)

———, ———, and OSGOOD, C. E. 1942. Studies in synesthetic thinking: II. the roles of form in visual responses to music. *J. gen. Psychol.*, 26: 199-222.

KASHIWAGI, S. 1965. Geometric vector orthogonal solution for the semantic differential scales of Sagara *et al. Psychol. Reps.*, 16: 914.

KATZ, D. 1944. The measurement of intensity. In H. Cantril (Ed.), *Gauging public opinion.* Princeton: Princeton University Press.

———, McCLINTOCK, C., and SARNOFF, I. 1957. Measurement of ego-defense related to attitude change. *J. Pers.*, 25: 465-474.

KATZ, M. 1959. Meaning as a correlate of marital success. Unpublished Ph.D. dissertation, Columbia University.

———. 1965. Agreement on connotative meaning in marriage. *Family Process*, 4: 64-75.

KAUFMANN, HELEN J. 1959. The semantic differential: a critical appraisal. *Pub. opin. Quart.*, 23(3): 437-438.

KEIL, C., and KEIL, ANGELIKI. 1966. Musical meaning: a preliminary report. *Ethnomusicology,* 10(2): 153-173.

KELLER, M. 1943. Mediated generalization: the generalization of a conditioned galvanic skin response established to a pictured object. *Amer. J. Psychol.*, 56: 438-448.

KELLY, G. A. 1955. *The psychology of personal constructs.* New York: W. W. Norton.

KELLY, JANE A., and LEVY, L. H. 1961. The discriminability of concepts differentiated by means of the semantic differential. *Educ. psychol. Measmt.*, 21: 53-58.

KELMAN, H. C. and HOVLAND, C. I. 1953. Reinstatement of the communication in delayed measurement of opinion change. *J. abnorm. soc. Psychol.*, 48: 327-335.

KENDLER, H. H. 1959. Learning. *Ann. Rev. Psychol.*, 10: 54-55.

KENDLER, T. S. 1961. Concept formation. *Ann. Rev. Psychol.*, 12: 459-460.

KENNEDY, J. L., KOSLIN, B. L., SCHRODER, H. M., BLACKMAN, S., RAMSEY, J. O., and HELM, C. E. 1966. Cognitive patterning of complex stimuli: a symposium. *J. gen. Psychol.*, 74: 25-49.

KENT, GRACE H., and ROSANOFF, A. J. 1910. A study of association in insanity. *Amer. J. Insanity*, 67: 37-96, 317-390.

KENTLER, H. 1959. Zur Problematic der Profilmethode. *Diagnostica*, 5: 5-18.

KEPPEL, G. 1963. Word value and verbal learning. *J. verb. Learn. verb. Behav.*, 1: 353-356.

KERLINGER, F. N. 1964. *Foundation of behavioral research.* New York: Holt, Rinehart.

KERRICK, JEAN S. 1954. The effects of intelligence and manifest anxiety on attitude change through communications. Unpublished Ph.D. dissertation, University of Illinois.

———. 1955. The influence of captions in picture interpretation. *Journ. Quart.*, 32: 177-182.

———. 1958. The effect of relevant and non-relevant sources on attitude change. *J. soc. Psychol.*, 47: 15-20.

———. 1959. New pictures, captions, and the point of resolution. *Journ. Quart.*, 36: 183-188.

———, and McMILLAN, D., III. 1961. The effects of instructional set on the measurement of attitude change through communications. *J. soc. Psychol.*, 53: 113-120.

KESWICH, G. 1958. *Public utilities opinion survey.* Chicago: Needham, Louis, and Brorby.

KING-FUN LI, ANITA. 1966. The Cantonese semantic differential scales. *J. Educ.*, 23.

KITAO, N. 1965. An analysis of semantic mediative factors in paired-associate learning. *Jap. J. Psychol.*, 36: 133-138.

KJELDERGAARD, P. M. 1961. Attitudes toward newscasters as measured by the semantic differential: a descriptive case. *J. appl. Psychol.*, 45: 35-40.

———, and MASANORI, H. 1962. Degree of polarization and the recognition value of words selected from the semantic atlas. *Psychol. Reps.*, 11: 629-630.

KLAPPER, J. T. 1959. The semantic differential: its use and abuse. *Pub. Opin. Quart.*, 23: 435-438.

KLEIN, E. B. 1960. Stylistic components of response as related to attitude change. *Dissert. Abstr.*, 21: 1275-1276.

———, and SOLMAN, L. 1966. Agreement, response tendency, and behavioral submission in schizophrenia. *Psychol. Reps.*, 18: 499-509.

KLEIN, G. S. 1964. Semantic power measured through the inference of words with color-naming. *J. Amer. Psychol.*, 77: 576-588.

KLEINMUNTZ, B. 1960. Two types of paranoid schizophrenia. *J. clin. Psychol.*, 16: 310-312.

KOCH, H. L. 1956. Attitudes of young children toward their peers as related to certain characteristics of their siblings. *Psychol. Monogr*, 70, No. 16. (Whole No. 426.)

KOEN, F. 1962. Polarization, *m*, and emotionality in words. *J. verb. Learn. verb. Behav.*, 1: 183-187.

KOGAN, N., and WALLACH, M. A. 1960. Certainty at judgment and the evaluation of risk. *Psychol. Reps.*, 6: 207-213.

KOLTUV, B. B. 1062. Some characteristics of intrajudge trait intercorrelations. *Psycho. Monogr.*, 76, No. 33. (Whole No. 552.)

KOMORITA, S. S., and BASS, A. R. 1967. Attitude differentiation and evaluative scales of the semantic differential. *J. pers. soc. Psychol.*, 6(2): 241-244.

KORMANN, M. 1960. Implicit personality theories of clinicians as defined by semantic structures. *J. consult. Psychol.*, 24: 180-186.

KORN, H. A., and GIDDON, N. S. 1964. Scoring methods and construct validity of the dogmatism scale. *Educ. Psychol. Measmt.*, 24: 867-874.

KORN, S. J. 1966. Relatedness and semantic generalization. *Dissert. Abstr.*, 27: 1305-1306.

KORSTUEDT, S. S. 1962. The acquisition of meaning in children with neurotic inhibition of learning. *Dissert. Abstr.*, 62: 6462.

KOUWER, B. J. 1958. Ein berekining van de polariteitsprofeilenmethode van Osgood. *Nederlands tijdschrift v. d. Psychologie*, 12: 1-4.

——— 1961. Onaagename situaties. *Ned. Tijdschr. Psychol.*, 16: 117-125.

KRIEGER, MARGERY H. 1964. A control for social desirability in a semantic differential. *Brit. J. soc. clin. Psychol.*, 3(2): 94-103.

KUMATA, HIDEYA. 1957. A factor analytic investigation of the generality of semantic structures across two selected cultures. Unpublished Ph.D. dissertation, University of Illinois.

———. 1960. Teaching advertising by television: a report on two experiments. Attitude change and learning as a function of instructor and mode of presentation. In W. Schramm (Ed.), *The impact of educational television.* Urbana: University of Illinois Press.

———, and SCHRAMM, W. 1956. A pilot study of cross-cultural methodology. *Pub. Opin. Quart.*, 20: 229-238.

KÜNNAPAS, T., and WIKSTRÄM, I. 1963. Measurement of occupational preferences: a comparison of scaling methods. *Reports from the Psychological Laboratory*, 156. Stockholm: The Psychological Laboratory, University of Stockholm.

Kuppuswamy, B., and Agrawal, K. G. 1966a. The meaning of work: I. a factorial study. II. attitude and meaning. III. urbanization. New Delhi: India International Center. (Mimeo.)

———, ———. 1966b. Noble's *m* and the meaning of work. *J. psychol. Res.*

Kuusinen, J. 1966a. Change in the structure of personality ratings according to the relevance of objects. Jyvaskyla, Finland: Center for Educational Research, University of Jyvaskyla. (Mimeo.)

———. 1966b. The stability of the individual structure of personality ratings. Jyvaskyla, Finland: Center for Education Research, University of Jyvaskyla. (Mimeo.)

Kyriazis, C. 1963. A comparison of semantic structures of ideal and actual concepts of the self and certain important socializing agents in male prisoner mental patients who have expressed aggressive behavior in the form of criminal assault, homicide, or rape. Unpublished Ph.D. dissertation, George Washington University.

Kyriazis, P. W. 1965. The relation between measured hypochondriasis and semantic differential profiles (among college students). *George Washington Univ. Bull.* Summaries of doctoral dissertations, 65(2): 34-35.

Laffal, J. 1964. Linguistic field theory and studies of word association. *J. gen. Psychol.*, 71: 145-155.

———. 1965. *Pathological and normal language.* New York: Atherton Press.

Lambert, W. E., Gardner, R. C., Bank, H. C., and Turnstall, K. 1963. Attitudinal and cognitive aspects of intensive study of a second language. *J. abnorm. soc. Psychol.*, 66: 358-368.

———, Havelka, J., and Crosby, C. 1958. The influence of language-acquisition contexts on bilingualism. *J. abnorm. soc. Psychol.*, 56: 239-244.

———, and Jakobovits, L. A. 1960. Verbal satiation and changes in the intensity of meaning. *J. exp. Psychol.*, 60: 376-383.

———, ———. 1963. The case for semantic satiation. McGill University. (Manuscript.)

Lana, R. E. and Pauling, F. J. 1965. Opinion change when the semantic differential is a pretest. *Psychol. Reps.*, 17: 730.

Landins, R., Kuroda, Y., and Kuroda, Alice. 1963. Peace Corps trainees as measured by the semantic differential. *Proceedings of the Montana Academy of Sciences*, 23: 203-207.

La Porte, M. S. 1965. Communication and pseudo-communication: the differential connotations of nouns. *Word*, 21(2): 257-264.

Larkin, E. F. 1964. The role of the weekly newspaper publisher in the community power structure. Master's thesis. *Journ. Abstr.*, 2: 102-103.

Lazier, G. A., Clevenger, T., Jr., and Clark, Margaret L. 1964. Stability of the factor structure of Smith's semantic differential for theatre concepts. Unpublished paper, Department of Speech and Theatre Arts, University of Pittsburgh.

Lazowick, L. M. 1955. On the nature of identification. *J. abnorm. soc. Psychol.*, 51: 175-183.

Le Ny, Jean-Francois. 1966. Conditioning of meaning, semantic generalization and evaluative ratings in a complex situation. *J. Verb. Learn. verb. Behav.*, 5: 268-274.

Levin, J. 1963. Three mode factor analysis. Unpublished Ph.D. dissertation, University of Michigan.

Lévi-Strauss, C. 1962. *The savage mind.* London: Weidenfield and Nicolson.

Levy, L. H. 1956. A factorial study of personal constructs. *J. consult. Psychol.*, 20: 53-57.

Levy, S. G. 1963. Multidimensional content analysis: an extension of the semantic differential. Unpublished Ph.D. dissertation, University of Michigan.

Lewis, W. A., and Wigel, W. 1964. Interpersonal understanding and assumed similarity. *Pers. Guid. J.*, 43: 155-158.

LEWIT, D. W. 1960. Attitudes in discrimination learning. *J. soc. Psychol.*, 52: 315-327

LIEBERMAN, A. J. 1961. Discrimination of some dimensions of connotative meaning. *Dissert. Abstr.*, 21: 2014-2015.

LIGHT, C. S., ZAX, M., and GARDINER, D. H. 1965. The relationship of age, sex, and intelligence level to extreme response style. *J. pers. soc. Psychol.*, 2: 907-909.

LILLY, R. S. 1966. A developmental study of the semantic differential. *Dissert. Abstr.*, 26(7): 4063-4064.

LIN, S. J. 1961. On anxiety indices in Rorschach tests. *Acta Psychologica Taiwanica*, 115-124.

LIPTON, L., and BLANTON, R. L. 1954. The semantic differential and mediated generalization as measures of meaning. *J. exp. Psychol.*, 6: 431.

LIVANT, W. P. 1963. A comparison of noun and verb forms on the semantic differential. *J. verb. Learn. verb. Behav.*, 1: 357-360.

LOEHLIN, J. C. 1961. Word meanings and self-descriptions. *J. abnorm. soc. Psychol.*, 62: 28-34.

LONG, BARBARA, HENDERSON, E. H. and ZILLER, R. C. Childrens self-ratings on the semantic differential: content vs. response set. Goucher College; University of Delaware; University of Oregon. (Manuscript.)

LOUISELLE, R. H., and KLEINSCHMIDT, A. 1963. A comparison of the stimulus value of Rorschach inkblots and their precepts. *J. proj. Tech. Pers. Assess.*, 27(2): 191-194.

LOUNSBURY, F. G. 1956. A semantic analysis of the Pawnee kinship usage. *Language*, 32: 158-194.

LOW, J. H. 1963. Some effects of various group communication networks on concept meaning as measured by Osgood's semantic differential technique. *Dissert. Abstr.*, 23: 3030.

LURIA, ZELLA. 1959. A semantic analysis of a normal and a neurotic therapy group. *J. abnorm. soc. Psychol.*, 58: 216-220.

LYLE, J. 1960. Semantic differential scales for newspaper research. *Journ. Quart.*, 37: 559-562, 646.

LYNCH, M. L. 1960. Development of an index for measuring sensational news. Unpublished M.S. thesis, University of Wisconsin.

LYNN, J. R. 1963. Advertising and the teacher: a study of attitudes in an Illinois school system. Master's thesis. *Journ. Abstr.*, 1: 61.

MACLAY, H., and WARE, E. E. 1961. Cross-cultural use of the semantic differential. *Behav. Sci.*, 6: 185-190.

MACLEAN, M. S., JR., CRANE, E., and KIEL, D. F. 1960. What makes an ETV program interesting? In W. Schramm (Ed.), *The impact of educational television*. Urbana: University of Illinois Press.

MADDEN, J. E. 1961. Semantic differential rating of self and of self-reported personal characteristics. *J. consult. Psychol.*, 25: 183.

MALMSTROM, E. J. and FRENCH, G. M. 1963. Scale-symmetry and the semantic differential. *Amer. J. Psychol.*, 76: 446-451.

MALTZ, H. E. 1963. Ontogenetic change in the meaning of concepts as measured by the semantic differential. *Child Develmt*, 34: 667-674.

MALTZMAN, I., and BROOKS, L. O. 1956. A failure to find second-order semantic generalization. *J. exp. Psychol.*, 51: 413-417.

———, MORRISETT, L., JR., and BROOKS, L. O. 1956. An investigation of phonetic symbolism. *J. abnorm. soc. Psychol.*, 53: 249-251.

MANIS, M. 1958. Personal adjustment, assumed similarity to parents, and inferred parental-evaluations of the self. *J. consult. Psychol.*, 22: 481-485.

———. 1959. Assessing communication with the semantic differential. *Amer. J. Psychol.*, 72: 111-113.

———. 1960. The interpretation of opinion statements as a function of recipient attitude. *J. abnorm. soc. Psychol.*, 60: 340-344.

———. 1961a. The interpretation of opinion statements as a function of message ambiguity and recipient attitude. *J. abnorm. soc. Psychol.*, 63: 71-81.

————. 1961b. The interpretation of opinion statements as a function of recipient attitude and source prestige. *J. abnorm. soc. Psychol.*, 63: 82-86.

————. 1965. Immunization, delay and the interpretation of persuasive messages. *J. pers. soc. Psychol.*, 6(1): 541-550.

————, and DAWES, ROBYN M. 1961. Cloze score as a function of attitude. *Psychol. Reps.*, 9: 79-84.

————, GLEASON, T. C., and DAWES, ROBYN M. The evaluation of complex social stimuli. University of Michigan and Ann Arbor VA Hospital. *J. pers. soc. Psychol.*, in press.

MARKEL, N. N. 1966. The validity of the semantic differential for psycholinguistic analysis. *J. verb. Learn. verb. Behav.*, 5: 348-350.

————, EISLER, R. M., and REESE, H. W. 1967. Judging personality from dialect. *J. verb. Learn. verb. Behav.*, 6: 33-35.

————, and HAMP, E. P. 1960. Connotative meanings of certain phoneme sequences. *Stud. Linguis.*, 15: (3-4).

————, and MEISELS, M. 1964. Judging personality from voice quality. *J. abnorm. soc. Psychol.*, 69: 458-463.

————, and ROBLIN, G. L. 1965. The effect of content and sex-of-judge on judgments of personality from voice. *Int. J. soc. Psychiat.*, 11(4): 295-300.

MARKS, I. 1965. *Patterns of meaning in psychiatric patients: semantic differential responses in obsessives and psychopaths.* London: Oxford University Press.

MARLOWE, L. 1962. Perceptions of a culture hero. *Dissert. Abstr.*, 23: 1104.

MARSHAL, G. R., and COFER, C. N. 1962. Associative indices as measures of word relatedness: a summary and comparison of ten methods. Technical Report No. 10, Department of Psychology, New York University.

MASON, M. 1941. Changes in the galvanic skin response accompanying reports of changes in meaning during oral repetition. *J. gen. Psychol.*, 25: 353-401.

MAURER, L. L. 1963. The effects of verb choice on connotative meaning and retention of material presented in four newspaper articles. Master's thesis. *Journ. Abstr.*, 1: 63-64.

MAX, L. W. 1935. An experimental study of the motor theory of consciousness. III. action-current responses in deaf-mutes during sleep, sensory stimulation, and dreams. *J. comp. Psychol.*, 19: 469-486.

————. 1937. An experimental study of the motor theory of consciousness. IV. action-current responses in the deaf during awakening, kinaesthetic imagery, and abstract thinking. *J. comp. Psychol.*, 24: 301-344.

McCARTIN, ROSE A., and MEYERS, C. E. 1966. An explanation of six semantic factors at first grade. *Multiv. behav. Res.*, 1(1): 74-94.

McDIARMID, C. G. 1957. The components contributing to the variance of semantic differential ratings. Unpublished paper, University of Illinois.

McGEHEE, N. E. 1963. Stimulus meaningfulness, inter-stimulus similarity and associative learning. *Dissert. Abstr.*, 63: 1320.

McGINLEY, W. H. 1964. Interaction of denotative and connotative meanings. Unpublished paper, Long Beach State College.

McGOVERN, J. B. 1964. Extinction of associations in four transfer paradigms. *Psychol. Monogr.*, 78, No. 16. (Whole No. 593.)

McGRATH, J. E., and McGRATH, MARION F. 1962. Effects of partisanship on perceptions of political figures. *Pub. Opin. Quart.*, 26: 236-248.

McMURRAY, G. A. 1958. A study of fittingness of signs to words by means of the semantic differential. *J. exp. Psychol.*, 56: 310-312.

————. 1960. Meaning associated with the phonetic structure of unfamiliar foreign words. *Canad. J. Psychol.*, 14: 166-174.

————. 1964. The background of thought and language. *Canad. Psychol.*, 5: 3-16.

McNAMARA, J. J., and FISCH, R. I. 1965. Attributed meaning of an unstructured stimulus. *Percept. mot. Skills*, 20(3, pt. 1): 853-857.

McNELLY, J. T. 1961a. Mass communication and people's interests. *Search*, 6(1).

————. 1961b. Meaning intensity as related to readership of foreign news. *Dissert. Abstr.*, 22: 347-348.

————. 1962. Meaning intensity as related to readership of foreign news. *Journ. Abstr.*, 2.

McNemar, Q. 1946. Opinion-attitude methodology. *Psychol. bull.*, 43: 289-374.

Mehling, R. 1959a. Attitude changing effect of news and photo combinations. *Journ. Quart.*, 36: 189-198.

————. 1959b. A simple test for measuring intensity of attitudes. *Pub. Opin. Quart.*, 23: 576-578.

Meredith, G. M. 1964. Personality correlates of pidgin English usage among Japanese-American college students in Hawaii. *Jap. Psychol. Res.*, 6(4): 176-183.

Messer, S., Jakobovits, L. A., Kanungo, R., and Lambert, W. E. 1964. Semantic satiation of words and numbers. *Brit. J. Psychol.*, 55: 155-163.

Messick, S. J. 1956. Some recent theoretical developments in multidimensional scaling. *Educ. Psychol. Measmt.*, 16(1): 82-100

————. 1957. Metric properties of the semantic differential. *Educ. Psychol. Measmt.*, 17: 200-206.

————. 1960. Dimensions of social desirability. *J. consult. Psychol.*, 24: 279-287.

————. 1961. Separate set and content scores for personality and attitude scales. *Educ. Psychol. Measmt.*, 21: 915-924.

————, and Abelson, R. P. 1956. The additive constant problem in multidimensional scaling. *Psychometrika*, 21(1): 1-15.

————, and Solley, C. M. 1957. Word association and semantic differentiation. *Amer. J. Psychol.*, 70: 586-593.

Michon, J. A. 1960. An application of Osgood's "semantic differential" technique. *Acta Psychol. Amst.*, 17: 377-391.

Micko, H. D. 1962. Die Bestimmung Subjektiver Ähnlichkeiten mit dem Semantischen Differential. *Z. err. Angew. Psychol.*, 9: 242.

Miller, A. W., Jr. 1966. Conditioning connotative meaning. *J. gen. Psychol.*, 75(2): 319-328.

Miller, G. A. 1954. Communication. *Ann. Rev. Psychol.*, 5: 412-413.

Mindak, W. A. 1955. Measuring advertising effectiveness from a communications point of view. Unpublished Ph.D. dissertation, University of Illinois.

————. 1956. A new technique for measuring advertising effectiveness. *J. Marketing*, 20: 367-369.

————. 1961. Fitting the semantic differential to the marketing problem. *J. Marketing*, 25: 28-33.

Mink, W. D. 1957. Semantic generalization as related to word association. *Disser. Abstr.*, 17: 2072-2073.

Minkowich, A., Weingarten, Linda L., and Blum, G. S. 1966. Empirical contributions to a theory of ambivalence. *J. abnorm. Psychol.*, 71: 30-41.

Miron, M. S. 1961a. A cross-linguistic investigation of phonetic symbolism. *J. abnorm. soc. Psychol.*, 62: 623-630.

————. 1961b. The influence of instruction modification upon test-retest reliabilities of the semantic differential. *Educ. psychol. Measmt.*, 21: 883-893.

————, and Osgood, C. E. 1966. The multivariate structure of qualification. In R. B. Cattell (Ed.), *Handbook of multivariate experimental psychology*. Chicago: Rand McNally.

————, and Wolfe, Sharon. 1964. A cross-linguistic analysis of the response distributions of restricted word associations. *J. verb. Learn. verb. Behav.*, 3: 376-384.

Mischel, T. 1966. Pragmatic aspects of explanation. *Phi. Sci.*, 33(1-2): 40-60.

Mitsos, S. B. 1959. Semantic aspects of prognosis. *J. abnorm. soc. Psychol.*, 58: 137-140

————. 1961. Personal constructs and the semantic differential. *J. abnorm. soc. Psychol.*, 62: 433-434.

Mogar, R. E. 1960. Three versions of the F scale and performance on the semantic differential. *J. abnorm. soc. Psychol.*, 60: 262-265.

Mogul, Lewin, William, and Saylor, Inc. 1958. Product semantic indices. (A private publication.) New York: The author.

MORDKOFF, A. M. 1963. An empirical test of the functional antonymy of semantic differential scales. *J. verb Learn. verb. Behav.*, 2: 504-508.

———. 1965. Functional vs. nominal antonymy in semantic differential scales. *Psychol. Reps.*, 16: 691-692

MORIMATO, H. 1957. A study of semantic relation by association method and the semantic differential. *Jap. J. educ. Psychol.*, 4: 131-137.

MORRIS, C. W. 1946. *Signs, language, and behavior.* New York: Prentice-Hall.

———. 1964. *Signification and significance.* Cambridge: M.I.T. Press.

MORRISON, A., and McINTYRE, D. 1966. The attitudes of students towards international affairs. *Brit. J. soc. clin. Psychol.*, 5: 17-23.

MOSCOVI, S. 1963. Attitudes and opinions. *Ann. Rev. Psychol.*, 4: 247.

MOSEL, J. N., and ROBERTS, JUNE B. 1954. The comparability of measures of profile similarity: an empirical study. *J. consult. Psychol.*, 18: 61-66.

MOSIER, C. I. 1941. A psychometric study of meaning. *J. soc. Psychol.*, 13: 123-140.

MOSS, C. S. 1953. An experimental investigation of symbolic processes. Unpublished Ph.D. dissertation, University of Illinois.

———. 1957. Dream symbols as disguises. *Etc.: Rev. Gen. Sem. (Summer)*, 14: 267-273.

———. 1958. Therapeutic suggestion and autosuggestion. *J. clin. exp. Hypnosis.* 6(2): 109-115

———. 1960a. Current and projected status of semantic differential research. *Psychol. Rec.*, 10: 47-54.

———. 1960b. Dream symbols as disguises: a further investigation. *Etc.: Rev. Gen. Sem.*, 17(2): 257-266.

———. 1961. Experimental paradigms for the hypnotic investigation of dream symbolism. *Int. J. clin. exp. Hypnosis*, 9: 105-117.

———. 1962a. A mediation theory of symbolism as an aid to the experimental investigation of symbolic behavior. *Psychol. Rec.*, 12(1): 75-84.

———. 1962b. Objective assessment of the psychology internship experience. *J. counseling Psychol.*, 9: 158-163.

MOWRER, O. H. 1953. *Psychotherapy: theory and research.* New York: Ronald Press.

———. 1954. A psychologist looks at language. *Amer. Psychol.* 9: 660-694.

MUELLER, W. S. 1966. Anxiety level, inferred identification and response tendencies on a semantic differential. *J. consult. Psychol.*, 13(2): 144-152.

MULIAK, S. A. 1963. A factor analytic investigation of the equivalence of personality factors with semantic factors. *Dissert. Abstr.*, 24: 1687-1688.

———. 1965. Reliability as the upper limit of a test's communality. *Percept. Mot. Skills*, 20: 646-648.

MUNSINGER, H. L. 1962. Secondary reinforcement: the effect of variations in amount of meaningfulness. *Dissert. Abstr.*, 62: 3525.

MUSGRAVE, B. S. 1957. Context effects on word association using one-word, two-word, and three-word stimuli. *Psychol. Reps.*, 3: 599-603.

NATHANSON, I.A. 1964. A semantic differential analysis of parent-son relationship in schizophrenics. *Dissert. Abstr.*, 25(1): 623.

NEBERGALL, R. C. 1958. An experimental investigation of rhetorical clarity. *Speech Monogr.*, 25: 243-254.

NELSON, C., ROSENBERG, S., and VIVEKANANTHAN, P. S. 1967. A multidimensional approach to the structure of personality impressions. Unpublished manuscript.

NEUHAUS, J. O., and WRIGLEY, C. F. 1954. The quartimax method, an analytic approach to orthogonal simple structure. *Brit. J. Statist. Psychol.*, 7: 81-91.

NEURINGER, C. 1961. Dichotomous evaluations in suicidal individuals. *J. consult. Psychol.*, 25: 445-449.

———. 1963. Effect of intellectual level and neuropsychiatric status on the diversity of intensity of semantic differential ratings. *J. consult. Psychol.*, 27: 280.

NEWBIGGING, P. L. 1961. The perceptual redintegration of words which differ in connotative meaning. *Canad. J. Psychol.*, 15: 133-141.

NEWCOMB, T. M. 1941. Attitude scales. In O. K. Buros (Ed.), *The 1940 mental measurements yearbook.* Highland Park, N.J.: Gryphen Press.

——. 1953. An approach to the study of communicative acts. *Psychol. Rev.,* 60: 393-404.

NICHOLS, R. C., and STRUMPFER, D. J. 1962. A factor analysis of draw-a-person test scores. *J. consult. Psychol..,* 26(2): 156-161.

NOBLE, C. E. 1952. An analysis of meaning. *Psychol Rev.,* 59: 421-430.

——. 1957. Psychology and the logic of similarity. *J. gen. Psychol.,* 57: 23-43.

——. 1958. Emotionality (*e*) and meaningfulness (*m*). *Psychol. Reps.,* 4: 16.

NORDENSTRENG, K. 1966a. Psychological measurement of complex sounds I: Semantic differential dimensions of speech and music. Submitted to *J. Acoustical Society of America.*

——. 1966b. Psychological measurement of complex sounds II: A comparison between the semantic differential and the similarity analysis. Submitted to *Scand. J. Psychol.*

NORMAN, W. T. 1959. Stability-characteristics of the semantic differential. *Amer. J. Psychol.,* 72: 581-584.

NOWLIS, V. 1960. Some studies of the influence of films on mood and attitude. Technical Report No. 7, January, University of Rochester.

——. 1963. The concept of mood. In Farber and Wilson (Eds.) *Conflict and creativity.* New York: McGraw-Hill.

——. 1966. Final report on the development of a mood adjective check list (MACL). Report No. 12, January, University of Rochester.

——, and GREEN, R. F. 1965. Factor analytic studies of the mood adjective checklist. Technical Report No. 11, January, University of Rochester.

NUNNALLY, J. C., and BOBREN, H. M. 1959. Attitude change with false information. *Pub. Opin. Quart.,* 23: 260-266.

——, FLAUGHER, R. L., and HODGES, W. F. 1963. Measurement of semantic habit. *Educ. Psychol. Measmt.,* 23: 419-434.

——, and HODGES, W. F. 1965. Some dimensions of individual differences in word association. *J. verb. Learn. verb. Behav.,* 4: 82-88.

——, and KITTROSS, J. M. 1958. Public attitudes towards mental health professors. *Amer. Psychol.,* 13: 589-594.

NURNBERGER, J. I., SPRAGUE, H. G., VANDIVEER, J. M., BARRETT, BEATRICE H., and BREEIJEN, A. 1963. Psychological correlates of somatic complaints in pregnancy and difficulty in childbirth. *J. consult Psychol.,* 27: 324-329.

OBONAI, T., and MATSUOKA, T. 1956. Color-symbolism personality test. *J. gen. Psychol.,* 55: 229-239.

ODBERT, H. S. 1948. An approach to language behavior through a test of word meanings. *Amer. Psychol.,* 3: 274-275.

——, KARWOSKI, T. F., and ECKERSON, A. B. 1942. Studies in synesthetic thinking: I. musical and verbal associations of color and mood. *J. gen. Psychol.,* 26: 153-173.

OETTING, E. R. 1964. Cross-cultural communication and the semantic differential: research note. *J. counsel. Psychol.,* 3: 292-293.

OGDEN, C. K. and RICHARDS, I. A. 1923. *The meaning of meaning.* New York: Harcourt, Brace.

OGISO, S., and INUR, M. 1961. Measurement of the effect of colors in architecture by semantic differential. *Nihon Kenchikugakkai Ronbunshu,* 67: 105-113. (In Japanese).

OHNMACHT, F. W. 1966. Some dimensions of meaning of the concept televised instruction. *Educ. psychol. Measmt.,* 26: 395-401.

O'NEILL, H. W. 1963. Pretesting advertising with the differential attitude technique. *J. Market.,* 27(1): 20-24.

ONO, H., HASTORF, A. H., and OSGOOD, C. E. 1966. Binocular rivalry as a function of incongruity in meaning. *Scand. J. Psychol.,* 7: 225-233.

ORLIK, P. 1965. Eine Modelstudie sur Psychophysick des Polaritaetsprofils (A prototype study of the polarity profile and its relation to psychophysics). *Zeitschrift fuer Experimentelle und Angewandte Psychologie*, 12(4): 614-647.

OSGOOD, C. E. 1941. Ease of individual judgment-processes in relation to polarization of attitudes in the culture. *J. soc. Psychol.*, 49: 403-418.

————. 1946. Meaningful similarity and interference in learning. *J. exp. Psychol.*, 36: 277-301

————. 1948. An investigation into the causes of retroactive interference. *J. exp. Psychol.*, 38: 132-154.

————. 1952. The nature and measurement of meaning. *Psychol. Bull.*, 49: 197-237.

————. 1953. *Method and theory in experimental psychology.* New York: Oxford University Press.

————. 1956. Fidelity and reliability. In H. Quastler (Ed.), *Information theory in psychology.* Glencoe, Ill.: Free Press.

————. 1957a. A behavioristic analysis of perception and meaning as cognitive phenomena. In J. Bruner (Ed.), *Contemporary approaches to cognition.* Cambridge, Mass.: Harvard University Press

————. 1957b. Motivational dynamics of language behavior. (Nebraska Symposium on Motivation.) In M. R. Jones (Ed.), *Current theory and research in motivation.* Lincoln: University of Nebraska Press.

————. 1958. A question of sufficiency. *Contemp. Psychol.*, 3: 209-212.

————. 1959a. The cross-cultural generality of visual-verbal synesthetic tendencies. *Behav. Sci.*, 5: 146-169.

————. 1959b. The representational model and relevant research methods. In I. Pool (Ed.), *Trends in content analysis.* Urbana: University of Illinois Press.

————. 1959c. Semantic space revisited. *Word*, 15: 192-200.

————. 1960a. Cognitive dynamics in the conduct of human affairs. *Pub. Opin. Quart.*, 24: 341-365.

———— 1960b. Some effects of motivation on style of encoding. In T. A. Sebeok (Ed.), *Style in language*, New York: John Wiley.

————. 1962. Studies of the generality of affective meaning systems. *Amer. Psychol.*, 17: 10-28.

————. 1963a. Cross-cultural comparability in attitude measurement via multilingual semantic differentials. Paper presented at the International Congress of Psychology, August.

————. 1963b. Cross-cultural studies of affect and symbolism. Paper presented at American Psychiatric Association, May.

————. 1963c. An exploration into semantic space. In W. Schramm (Ed.), *The science of human communication.* New York: Basic Books.

————. 1963d. On understanding and creating sentences. *Amer. Psychol.*, 18: 735-751.

————. 1964. Semantic differential technique in the comparative study of cultures. *Amer. Anthro.*, 66(3): 171-200.

————. 1966a. Meaning cannot be r_m? *J. verb. Learn. verb. Behav.*, 5: 402-407.

————. 1966b. Speculations on the structure of interpersonal intentions. Technical Report No. 39. Urbana: Department of Psychology and Institute of Communications Research, University of Illinois.

————, ARCHER, W. K., and MIRON, M. S. 1963. The cross-cultural generality of meaning systems. Urbana: Institute of Communications Research, University of Illinois. (Mimeo.)

————, and HOWES, D. 1954. On the combination of associative probabilities in linguistic contexts. *Amer. J. Psychol.*, 67: 241-258.

————, and LURIA, ZELLA. 1954. A blind analysis of a case of triple personality using the semantic differential. *J. abnorm. soc. Psychol.*, 49: 579-591.

————, SAPORTA, S., and NUNNALLY, J. C. 1956. *Evaluative assertion analysis.* Urbana: Institute of Communications Research, University of Illinois. (Mimeo.)

————, and SEBEOK, T. A. 1954. Psycholinguistics: a survey of theory and research problems. *J. abnorm. soc. Psychol.* (Suppl.), 49, Part 2.

————, and STAGNER, R.. 1941. Ease of individual judgment-processes in relation to polarization of attitudes in the culture. *J. soc. Psychol.*, 14: 403-418.

————, ————. 1946. Impact of war on a nationalistic frame of reference: I. changes in general approval and qualitative patterning of certain stereotypes. *J. soc. Psychol.*, 24: 187-215.

————, and SUCI, G. 1952. A measure of relation determined by both mean difference and profile information. *Psychol. Bull.*, 49: 251-262.

————, ————. 1955. Factor analysis of meaning. *J. exp. Psychol.*, 50: 325-338.

————, ————, and TANNENBAUM, P. 1957. *The measurement of meaning*. Urbana: University of Illinois Press.

————, and TANNENBAUM, P. 1955. The principle of congruity and the prediction of attitude change. *Psychol. Rev.*, 62: 42-55.

————, WARE, E. E., and MORRIS, C. 1961. Analysis of the connotative meanings of a variety of human values as expressed by American college students. *J. abnorm soc. Psychol.*, 62: 62-73.

OSIPOW, S., and GROOMS, R. R. 1962. On semantic differential resistance to response bias based on stimulus word position. *Psychol. Reps.*, 10: 634.

OSKAMP, S. 1965. Attitudes toward U.S. and Russian actions: a double standard. *Psychol. Bull.*, 16: 43-46.

OTTEN, M. W., and VAN DE CASTLE, R. L. 1963. A comparison of set "A" of the Holtzman inkblots with the Rorschach by means of the semantic differential. *J. Proj. Tech. Pers. Asses.*, 27: 452-460.

OYAMA, T., and HAGA, J. 1963a. Common factors between figural and phonetic symbolism. *Psychologia*, Kyoto, 6: 131-143.

————, ————. 1963b. A study on figural and phonetic symbolism. *Psychologia*, in press.

————, TANAKA, Y., and CHIBA, Y. 1962. Affective dimensions of colors: a cross-cultural study. *Jap. psychol. Res.*, 4: 78-91.

————, ————, and HAGA, J. 1963. Color-affection and color-symbolism in Japanese and American students. *Jap. J. Psychol.*, in press.

PAIVIO, A. 1966. A factor analytic study of word attributes and verbal learning. Research Bulletin No. 22. London, Ontario: Department of Psychology, University of Western Ontario.

PARKER, G. V., and NOBLE, C. E. 1963. Experimentally produced meaningfulness (m) in paired-associate learning. *Amer. J. Psychol.*, 76(4): 579-588.

PEABODY, D. 1962. Two components in bipolar scales: direction and extremeness. *Psychol. Rev.*, 69: 65-73.

PEAK, H. 1958. Generalization of attitude change within an opposite structure. II. USN Tech. Rep., ONR, Nonr 1224 (10)NR 171-039, No. 4 (c), June.

———— 1959a. Attitudes, opposites structuring and F scores. USN Tech. Rep., ONR, Nonr 1224 (10)NR 171-039, No. 5 (a), May.

————. 1959b. Some correlations of opposites structure. USN Tech. Rep., ONR, Nonr 1224 (10)NR 171-039, No. 7 (b), June.

————, MUNEY, B., and CLAY, M. 1960. Opposite structures, defenses, and attitudes. *Psychol. Monogr.*, 74, No. 8. (Whole No. 495.)

PESESTKY, F. J. 1961. Variability in the meaning of deviant behavior. *Dissert. Abstr.*, 22: 1259.

PETERS, J. S. 1957. Social economic egocentricism in delinquents and non-delinquents. Studies in Higher Education (Study #85). Division of Educational Reference, Purdue University, February.

PETERSON, D. R. 1960. The age generality of personality factors derived from ratings. *Educ. psychol. Measmt.*, 20: 461-474.

————. 1965. Scope and generality of verbally defined personality factors. *Psychol. Rev.*, 72: 48-59.

PETTIGREW, T. F. 1958. The measurement and correlates of category width as a cognitive variable. *J. Pers.*, 26: 532-544.

PHILLIPS, L. W. 1958. Mediated verbal similarity as a determinant of the generalization of a conditioned GSR. *J. exp. Psychol.*, 55: 56-62.

PIC'L, M. E. 1966. On "intentional-adequacy." *Quart. J. Speech*, 52: 385-388.

PLUTCHIK, R. 1967. The affective differential: emotion profiles implied by diagnostic concepts. *Psychol. Repos.*, 20: 19-25

PODELL, HARRIET A., and PODELL, J. E. 1963. Quantitive connotation of a concept. *J. abnorm. soc. Psychol.*, 67: 509-513.

PODELL, J. E. 1961. A comparison of generalization and adaptation-level as theories of connotation. *J. abnorm. soc. Psychol.*, 62: 593-597.

POLLIO, H. R. 1962. Word association as a function of semantic structure. Unpublished Ph.D. dissertation, University of Michigan.

———. 1964a. Composition of associative clusters. *J. exp. Psychol.*, 67(3): 199-208.

———. 1964b. Some semantic relations among word-associates. *Amer. J. Psychol.*, 77: 249-256.

———, and LORE, R. K. 1965. The effect of a semantically congruent context on word association behavior. *J. Psychol.*, 61: 17-26.

POPE, B., and BARE, CAROLE E. 1963. Rorschach percepts and personal concepts as semantically equivalent members. *Percept. mot. Skills*, 17: 15-22.

PORTNOG, STEPHANIE, and SALZINGER, K. 1964. The conditionability of different verbal response classes: positive, negative and non-affect statements. *J. gen. Psychol.*, 70: 311-323.

PORTNOY, M. 1962. Conditioning of verbal behavior and its effect upon meaning: an experimental study of positive and negative reinforcement applied to word associations of varying strengths and its consequent effects upon meaning. *Dissert. Abstr.*, 22(1): 4411.

POSTMAN, L. and BRUNER, J. S. 1948. Perception under stress. *Psychol. Rev.*, 55: 314-324.

———, ———, and McGINNIES, E. 1948. Personal values as selective factors in perception. *J. abnorm. soc. Psychol.*, 43: 142-154.

———, and MURPHY, G. 1943. The factor of attitude in associative memory. *J. exp. Psychol.*, 33: 228-238.

POWELL, F. A. 1962. Open-and-closed-mindedness and the ability to differentiate source and message. *J. abnorm. soc. Psychol.*, 65: 61-64.

———, 1964. Source credibility, dissonance theory, and attitude change. *Journ. Abstr.*, 2: 26-27.

PRATT, C. C. 1961. Aesthetics. *Ann. Rev. Psychol.*, 12: 83.

PROTHRO, E. T., and KEEHN, J. D. 1957. Stereotypes and semantic space. *J. soc. Psychol.*, 45: 197-209.

PYRON, B. 1966. Rejection of avant-garde art and need for simple order. *J. Psychol.*, 63: 159-178.

QUEVILLON, NAOMI M. 1960. Semantic behavior of three different personality groups. *Dissert. Abstr.*, 21: 242.

RABIN, A. L. 1959. Contributions to the "meaning" of Rorschach's inkblots via the semantic differential. *J. consult. Psychol.*, 23: 368-372.

RAO, C. R. 1948. The utilization of multiple measurements in problems of biological classification. *J. royal stat. Soc.*, Sec. B., 10: 159-203.

RASHAP, B. L. 1961. An exploratory study of mediational processes in verbal behavior: an investigation of verbal mediator interaction reflected by changes in the form of the semantic differential as applied to a thematic projective technique. *Dissert. Abstr.* 22: 653.

RAU, LUCY. 1958. Variability in response to words: an investigation of stimulus ambiguity. *J. Amer Psychol.*, 71: 338-349.

RAY, W. S. 1958. Generalization among meaningful relations in problem solving. *J. Amer. Psychol.*, 71: 737-741

RAZRAN, G. H. 1935-36. Salivating and thinking in different languages. *J. Psychol.*, 1: 145-151.

———. 1939. A quantitative study of meaning by a conditioned salivary technique (semantic conditioning). *Science*, 90: 89-90.

———. 1952. Experimental semantics. *Trans. N.Y. Acad. Sci.*, 14: 171-176.

REECE, M. W. 1964. Masculinity and femininity: a factor analytic study. *Psychol. Reps.*, 14: 123-139.

REES, R. D. and PEDERSON, DARHL. 1965. A factorial determination of points of view in poetic evaluation and their relationship to various determinants. *Psychol. Reps.*, 16: 31-39.

REEVES, JOAN W. 1967. *Thinking about thinking.* New York: Delta.
REEVES, MARGARET P. 1954. An application of the semantic differential to the Thematic Apperception Test material. Unpublished Ph.D. dissertation, University of Illinois.
REMMERS, H. H. 1934. Studies in attitudes. *Bull. Purdue Univ. Stud. higher Educ.,* 35, No. 4.
———. 1954. *Introduction to opinion and attitude measurement.* New York: Harper.
———, and SILANCE, ELLA B. 1934. Generalized attitude scales, *J. soc. Psychol.,* 5: 298-312.
REYNIERSE, J. H. and BARCH, A. M. 1963. Semantic satiation and generalization. *Psychol. Reps.,* 13: 790.
RHINE, R. J. 1958. A concept-formation approach to attitude acquisition. *Psychol. Rev.,* 65: 362-369.
RICHARDSON, A. 1965. The place of subjective experience in contemporary psychology. *Brit J Psychol.,* 56: 223-232.
RICHMOND *Times Dispatch.* 1959. The climate of persuasion: a study of the public image of advertising media. Unpublished report to the Richmond Times Dispatch, Virginia.
RICKELS, K., and DOWNING, R. W. 1962. Personality and attitudinal correlates of response to drug treatment in psychiatric outpatients: 1. theoretical orientation and measuring instruments to be employed. *J. Psychol.,* 54: 331-344.
RIDDERHEIM, D., and LEVY, N. 1958. A developmental study of the concept of symmetry. Paper read at Eastern Psychological Association, Philadelphia, April.
RIEGEL, K. F. and RIEGEL, R. M. 1963. An investigation into denotative aspects of word-meaning. *Lang. Speech,* 6(1): 5-21.
RIESS, B. F. 1940. Semantic conditioning involving the galvanic skin reflex. *J. exp. Psychol.,* 26: 238-240.
———. 1946. Genetic changes in semantic conditioning. *J. exp. Psychol.,* 36: 143-152.
ROBLIN, G. L. 1964. A comparative analysis of translation equivalence of connotative meaning for Tagalog and English speaking subjects. *Dissert Abstr.,* 24: 4286.
ROGERS, C. R. 1964. Toward a science of the person. In T. W. Wann (Ed.), *Behaviorism and phenomenology.* Chicago: University of Chicago Press.
ROMMETVEIT, R. 1960. Stages in concept formation and levels of cognitive functioning. *Scand. J. Psychol.,* 1: 115-124.
ROOT, R. T. A multidimensional scaling analysis of meaning. *Dissert. Abstr.,* 63: 1149.
ROSEN, E. 1959. A cross-cultural study of semantic profiles and attitude differences (Italy). *J. soc. Psychol.,* 49: 137-144.
———. 1960. Connotative meanings of Rorschach inkblots, responses and determinants. *J. Pers.,* 28: 413-426.
ROSENZWEIG, S. 1960. The effects of failure and success on evaluation of self and others: a study of depressed patients and normal. *Dissert. Abst.,* 21:675.
ROSLWALB, I. 1958. *The Measurement of meaning,* by C. E. Osgood, G. J. Suci, and P. H. Tannenbaum (Urbana: University of Illinois Press). *Media/scope,* March. (Book review.)
ROSS, B. M., and LEVY, N. 1960. A comparison of adjectival antonyms by simple card-pattern formation. *J. Psychol.,* 49: 133-137.
ROSS, J. 1965. Change in the use of semantic differential with a change in context. *J. verb. Learn. verb. Behav.,* 4: 148-151.
ROUBICZEK, P. 1956. *Thinking in opposites.* London: Routledge and Kegan Paul.
ROUSE, R. O., and VERINIS, J. S. 1962. The effect of associative connotations on the recognition of flashed words. *J. verb. Learn. verb. Behav.,* 1: 300-303.
ROWAN, T. C. 1954. Some developments in multidimensional scaling applied to semantic relationships. Unpublished Ph.D. dissertation, University of Illinois.
RUBINSTEIN, H., and ABORN, M. 1960. Measures of meaning. *Ann. Rev. Psychol.,* 11: 304-306.
RUDIN, S. A. 1959. Application of the methods of bisection and equal appearing intervals to the perception of persons. *Psychol. Reps.,* 5: 99-106.
———, and STAGNER, R. 1958. Figure-ground phenomena in the perception of physical and social stimuli. *J. Psychol.,* 45: 213-225.
RUESCH, J. 1961. *Therapeutic communication.* New York: W. W. Norton.

————, and BATESON, G. 1951. *Communication: the social matrix.* New York: W. W. Norton.

RUSSEL, W. A., and JENKINS, J. J. 1954. The complete Minnesota Norms for responses to 100 words from the Kent-Rosanoff word-association test. Contract N8-onr-66216, Technical Report No. 11, University of Minnesota.

RUSSEL, W. A., and STORMS, L. H. 1955. Implicit verbal chaining in paired-associate learning. *J. exp. Psychol.*, 49: 287-293.

RYCHLAK, J. F. 1959. Forced associations, symbolism, and Rorschach constructs. *J. consult. Psychol.*, 23: 455-460.

RYDELL, SUSAN T., and ROSEN, E. 1966. Measurement and some correlates of need-cognition. *Psychol. Reps.*, 19: 139-165.

SACKS, J. M., HOFFMAN, JOYCE M., CUTTER, H. S., and HAEFNER, D. P. Changes in perception and interaction in group therapy. *Group Psychother.*, 13: 101-109.

SAFFIR, M. 1937. A comparative study of scales constructed by three psychophysical methods. *Psychometrika*, 2: 179-198.

SAGARA, M., YAMAMOTO, K., NISHIMURA, H., and AKUTO, H. 1961. A study on the semantic structure of Japanese language by the semantic differential method. *Jap. psychol. Res.*, 3: 146-156.

SAGINUR, R. 1962. The effect of repeated typing on the semantic rating of a word. Undergraduate Research Projects in Psychology. Department of Psychology, McGill University.

SALTZ, E., and WICKEY J. 1965. Resolutions of the liberal dilemma in the assassination of President Kennedy. *J. Pers.*, 33(4): 636-648.

SALZINGER, K. 1959. Experimental manipulation of verbal behavior: a review. *J. gen. Psychol.*, 61: 65-94.

SAMPSON, E. E., and JUSKO, C. A. 1964. Cognitive consistency and performance in the autokinetic situation. *J. abnorm. soc. Psychol.*, 68: 184-192.

SANSON, W. E. 1964. A study of the relationship between personality and connotative meaning. *Dissert. Abstr.*, 25: 252.

SAPPENFIELD, B. R., KAPLAN, B. B. and BALOGH, BELA. 1966. Perceptual correlates of stereotypical masculinity-femininity. *J. pers. soc. Psychol.*, 4(5): 585-595.

SATTLER, J. M. 1963. The relative meaning of embarrassment. *Psychol. Reps.*, 12: 263-269.

SCHAEFER, E. S., and PLUTCHIK, R. 1966. Interrelationships of emotions, traits, and diagnostic constructs. *Psychol. Reps.*, 18: 399-410.

SCHEERER, M., and LYONS, J. 1957. Line drawings and matching responses to words. *J. Pers.*, 25: 239-273.

SCHOLSBERG, H. 1952. The description of facial expression in terms of two dimensions. *J. exp. Psychol.*, 44: 229-237.

————. 1954. Three dimensions of emotion. *Psychol. Rev.*, 61: 81-88.

SCHRAMM, W. 1953. What we know about attitude change through mass communication. Institute of Communications Research, University of Illinois. Unpublished manuscript, privately distributed.

————. 1962. Mass communications. *Ann. Rev. Psychol.*, 13: 261.

SCHUH, A. J. 1966. Use of the semantic differential in a test of Super's vocational adjustment theory. *J. appl. Psychol.*, 50(6): 516-522.

SCHULBERG, H. C., and TOLOR, A. 1962. The meaning of the Bender-Gestalt test designs to psychiatric patients. *J. proj. Tech.*, 2: 455-461.

SCHULTZ, R. E., and NAUMOFF, H. 1963. An application of Mowrer's sentence conditioning paradigms in developing evaluative meaning. *J. verb. Learn. verb. Behav.*, 1: 459-462.

SCHWARTZ, F., and ROUSE, R. O. 1961. The activation and recovery of associations. *Psychol. Issues*, 3, No. 1, Monogr. 9.

SEBEOK, T. A. (Ed.). 1960. *Style in language.* New York: John Wiley.

SELLTIZ, CLAIRE, JAHODA, MARIE, DEUTSCH, M., and COOK, S. W. 1959. *Research methods in social relations.* New York: Holt Dryden. (rev. ed.)

SEMANS, CATHERINE B. 1957. Use of the semantic differential with lobotomized psychotics. *J. consult. Psychol.*, 21: 264.

SHAPIRO, M. B. 1966. The single case in clinical-psychological research. *J. gen. Psychol.*, 74: 3-23.

SHAW, D. R. 1955. Variation in inter-scale correlation on the semantic differential as a function of the concept judged. Unpublished master's thesis, University of Illinois.

SHELL, S. A., JR., O'MALLY, J. M., and JOHNSGARD, K. W. 1964. The semantic differential and inferred identification. *Psychol. Reps.*, 14: 547-558.

SHERIF, M., and HOVLAND, C. I. 1953. Judgmental phenomena and scales of attitude measurement: placement of items with individual choice of number of categories. *J. abnorm. soc. Psychol.*, 48: 135-141.

SHONTZ, F. C., and FINK, S. L. 1957. The significance of patient-staff rapport in rehabilitation of individuals with chronic physical illness. *J. consult. Psychol.*, 21: 327-334.

SINES, J. O. 1961. An approach to the study of the stimulus significance of the Rorschach inkblots. *J. proj. Tech.*, 25: 233-237.

————. 1962. An indication of specificity of denotative meaning based on the semantic differential. *J. gen. Psychol.*, 67: 113-115.

SINGER, R. D. 1961. A note on the use of the semantic differential as a predictive device in milieu therapy. *J. clin. Psychol.*, 17: 376-378.

SKINNER, B. F. 1936. The verbal summator and a method for the study of latent speech. *J. Psychol.*, 2: 71-107.

SLAMECKA, N. J. 1963. Choice reaction-time as a function of meaningful similarity. *J. Amer. Psychol.*, 76: 274-280.

SMALL, EDNA RUTH. 1959. Age and sex differences in the semantic structure of children. *Dissert. Abstr.*, 19: 872-873.

SMITH, D. E., and RAYGOR, A. L. 1956. Verbal satiation and personality. *J. abnorm. soc. Psychol.*, 52: 323-326.

SMITH, G. 1958. Six measures of self-concept discrepancy and instability: their interrelations, reliability, and relations to other personality measures. *J. consult. Psychol.*, 22: 101-112.

SMITH, P. A. 1962. A comparison of three sets of rotated factor analytic solutions of self-concept data. *J. abnorm. soc. Psychol.*, 64: 326-333.

SMITH, P. A. Factor analysis studies of the self concept. Unpublished paper. VA Hospital, Ann Arbor, Michigan.

————, BARROWS, H. S., and WHITNEY, J. N. Psychological attributes of occupational therapy crafts. Unpublished paper. VA Hospital and Department of Psychology, University of Michigan, Ann Arbor.

SMITH, R. G. 1959. Development of a semantic differential for use with speech-related concepts. *Speech Mongr.*, 26: 263-272.

————. 1961. A semantic differential for theatre concepts. *Speech Monogr.*, 28: 1-8.

————. 1962. A semantic differential for speech correction concepts. *Speech Monogr.*, 29: 32.

————. 1963. Validation of a semantic differential. *Speech Monogr.*, 3(1): 50-55.

————. 1966. Semantic differential dimensions and form. *Speech Monogr.*, 33(1): 17-22.

SMYKAL, A. 1962. A comparative investigation of home environmental variables related to the achieving and underachieving behavior of academically able high school students. *Dissert. Abstr.*, 23: 315.

SNIDER, J. G. 1962. Profiles of some stereotypes held by ninth-grade pupils. *Alberta J. educ. Res.*, 8: 147-156.

————. 1964. Stereotyping and the use of all-inclusive terms. *Alberta J. educ. Res.*, 10: 170-174.

————. 1966. All-inclusive conceptualization and intensity of meaningfulness. *Alberta J. educ. Res.*, 12: 281-284.

————. In press. The D4*m* measure. *Psychol. Reps.*

————. In press. The D4*m* measure: intensity of response to degrees of meaningful-ness. *Alberta Psychol.*

————, Cole, C. W., and Oetting, E. R. 1968. The D4*m* and D4*m*F measures. American Institutes for Research, Pittsburgh. Unpublished.

Solarz, A. K. 1960. Latency of instrumental responses as a function of compatibility with the meaning of eliciting verbal signs. *J. exp. Psychol.*, 59: 239-245.

————. 1963a. Perceived activity in semantic atlas words as indicated by a tapping response. *Percept. mot. Skills*, 16: 91-94.

————. 1963b. Reliability of affective arrangement of word-cards on a plane. *Percept. mot. Skills*, 16: 111-118.

Solley, C. M., Jackson, D. N., and Messick, S. J. 1957. Guessing behavior and autism. *J. abnorm. soc. Psychol.*, 54: 32-35.

————, and Messick, S. J. 1957. Probability-learning, the statistical structure of concepts, and the measurement of meaning. *Amer. J. Psychol.*, 70: 161-173.

————, and Stagner, R. 1956. Effects of magnitude of temporal barriers, type of goal, and perception of self. *J. exp. Psychol.*, 51: 62-70.

Solomon, L. N. 1954. A factorial study of complex auditory stimuli (passive sonar sounds). Unpublished Ph.D. dissertation, University of Illinois.

————. 1958. Semantic approach to the perception of complex sounds. *J. acoust. soc. Amer.*, 30: 421-425.

————. 1959a. Search of physical correlates to psychological dimensions of sounds. *J. acoust. soc. Amer.*, 31: 492-497.

————. 1959b. Semantic reactions to systematically varied sounds. *J. acoust. soc. Amer.*, 31: 986-990.

————. 1960. The influence of some types of power relationships and game strategies upon the development of interpersonal trust.

————. 1961. *The semantic differential—past, present and future.* LaJolla, Calif.: Western Behavioral Science Institute.

————. 1962. A semantic approach to psychological nosology. *J. clin. Psychol.*, 18: 18-22.

Soma, K. 1962. Semantic measurement of interpersonal relationships of juvenile delinquents with some word concepts. *Family Court Probation*, 2: 63-70.

Somer, R. 1965. Anchor-effects and the semantic differential. *Amer. J. Psychol.*, 78(2): 317-318.

Spence, D. P. 1961. An experimental list of schema interaction. *J. abnorm. Psychol.*, 62: 611-615.

Sperber, Z., and Spanner, M. 1962. Social desirability, psycho-pathology, and item endorsement. *J. gen. Psychol.*, 67: 105-112.

Spilka, B., Horn, J., and Rangenderfer, L. 1966. Social desirabilities among measures of social desirability. *Educ. Psychol. Measmt.*, 26: 111-120.

Springbett, B. M. 1960. The semantic differential and meaning in non-objective art. *Percept. mot. Skills*, 10: 231-240.

Staats, A. W., and Staats, Carolyn K. 1957. Meaning established by classical conditioning. *J. exp. Psychol.*, 54: 74-80.

————, ————. 1958. Attitudes established by classical conditioning. *J. abnorm. soc. Psychol.*, 57: 37-40.

————, ————. 1959a. Effect of number of trials on the language conditioning of meaning. *J. gen. Psychol.*, 61: 211-223.

————, ————. 1959b. Meaning and *m*: Correlated but separate. *Psychol. Rev.*, 66: 136-144.

————, ————, and Biggs, D. A. 1958. Meaning of verbal stimuli changed by conditioning. *J. Amer. Psychol.*, 71: 429-431.

————, ————, and Crawford, H. 1962. First order conditioning of meaning and the parallel conditioning of a GSR. *J. gen. Psychol.*, 67: 159-167.

————, ————, Finley, J. R., and Heard, W. G. 1963. Independent manipulation of meaning and *m*. *J. gen. Psychol.*, 69: 253-260.

———, ———, ———, and MINKE, K. A. 1961. Meaning established by classical conditioning controlling associates to the UCS. Technical Report No. 17, Contract N-onr-2794 (02), Arizona State University.

———, ——— and HEARD, W. G. 1959. Language conditioning of meaning to meaning using a semantic generalization paradigm. *J. exp. Psychol.*, 57: 187-192.

———, ———, ———. 1960. Attitude development and ratio of reinforcement. *Sociometry*, 23: 338-349.

———, ———, ———. 1961. Denotative meaning established by classical conditioning. *J. exp. Psychol.* 61: 300-303.

———, ———, ———, and NIMS, L. P. 1959. Replication report: Meaning established by classical conditioning. *J. exp. Psychol.*, 57: 64.

———, ———, MINKE, A., and FINLEY, J. R. 1961. Operant conditioning of a class of negative evaluative meaning words. Technical Report No. 20, N-onr-2794 (02), Arizona State University.

STACHOWIAK, J. G. 1962. Hypnosis, the principle of congruity, and attitude change. *Dissert. Abstr.*, 22: 4107.

STAGNER, R., and OSGOOD, C. E. 1941. An experimental analysis of a nationalistic frame of reference. *J. soc. Psychol.*, 14: 389-401.

———, ———. 1946. Impact of war on a nationalistic frame of reference: I. changes in general approval and qualitative patterning of certain stereotypes. *J. soc. Psychol.*, 24: 187-215.

STAYTON, S. E., and WIENER, M. 1961. Value, magnitude, and accentuation. *J. abnorm. soc. Psychol.*, 62: 145-147.

STEINBERG, D. D., and OAKES, W. F. 1964. Conditioning semantic response classes. *Psychol. Reps.*, 15: 802.

STEINER, G. A. 1963. *The people who look at television*. New York: Alfred A. Knopf.

STEINER, I. D., and FIELD, W. L. 1960. Role assignment and interpersonal influence. *J. abnorm. soc. Psychol.*, 61: 239 245.

STELLWAGEN, W. T. 1966. Metaphoric transfer: generalization between alternative meanings of the same word. *J. verb. Learn. verb. Behav.*, 2: 375-378.

STRICKER, G. 1961. Word values, word frequency and visual duration thresholds. *Psychol. Rev.*, 68: 420-422.

———. 1963. The use of the semantic differential to predict voting behavior. *J. soc. Psychol.*, 59: 159-167.

———. 1964a. The operation of cognitive dissonance on pre- and post-election attitudes. *J. soc. Psychol.*, 63(1): 111-119.

——— 1964b. Stimulus properties of the Rorschach to a sample of pedophiles. *J. proj. tech. pers. Asses.*, 28(2): 241-244.

———, TAKAHASHI, S., and ZAX, M. 1967. Semantic differential discriminability: a comparison of Japanese and American students. *J. soc. Psychol.*, 71(1): 23-25.

———, and ZAX, M. 1966. Intelligence and semantic differential discriminability. *Psychol. Reps.*, 18: 775-778.

STROMBERG, C. E. 1963. Semantic differentiation of social behavior of valued persons by female college groups. *Dissert. Abstr.*, 63: 1689.

STRUPP, H. H. 1962. Psychotherapy. *Ann. Rev. Psychol.*, 13: 453.

SUCI, G. J. 1952. A multidimensional analysis of social attitudes with special reference to ethnocentrism. Unpublished Ph.D. dissertation, University of Illinois.

———. 1957. An investigation of the similarity between the semantic spaces of five different cultures. Report for the Southwest Project in Comparative Psycholinguistics.

———. 1960. A comparison of semantic structures in American Southwest culture groups. *J. abnorm. soc. Psychol.*, 61: 25-30.

———, and TANNENBAUM, P. H. 1955. On the relationship between the generalized distance measure D^2 and the intraclass correlation coefficient. Institute of Communications Research, University of Illinois. (Mimeo.)

SUNDBERG, N. D. 1966. A method for studying sensitivity to implied meanings. *Gawein*, 15(1): 1-8.

SWEIGERT, R. L., JR. 1964. Information seeking as a function of cognitive imbalance in a decision situation. *Journ. Abstr.*, 2: 33-34.

SYDIAHA, D. 1962. Interviewer consistency in the use of empathic models in personnel selection. *J. appl. Psychol.*, 46: 344-349.

TAKAHASHI, S. 1965. A comparative factorial analysis of semantic structures of Rorschach inkblots in university students and juvenile delinquents. *Jap. Psychol. Res.*, 7(2): 69-74.

TALBOT, E., MILLER, S. C., and WHITE, R. B. 1961. Some aspects of self-conceptions and role demands in a therapeutic community. *J. abnorm. soc. Psychol.*, 63: 338-345.

TANAKA, Y. 1961. A cross-cultural investigation of the cross-subject stability of affective meaning systems in the judging of national stereotypes. Unpublished manuscript, Institute of Communications Research, University of Illinois.

———. 1962. A cross-cultural study of national stereotypes held by American and Japanese college graduate subjects. *Jap. Psychol. Res.*, 4(2): 65-78.

———. 1964. Studies on the measurement of-meaning and the generality of affective meaning systems: a review. *Jap. psychol. Res.*, 8: 27-69.

———. 1965a. SD-ho Mochi-ita Kikkakan Taibutsunichisekutei no Hikaku Kenkyu (A cross-cultural study of the measurement of international objects of cognition through the use of the semantic differential). *Nempo Shakai Shirigaku (Ann. soc. Psychol)*, No. 6: 100-124.

———. 1965b. Kokkakan Taibutsu Ninchi-Moderu: SD-ho no Seiji Shinrigakutekioyo ni Kansuru Kchishiren (An international objects cognition model: an attempt at the application of the semantic differential in political psychology), *Kagaku Kiseren Kenkyu (Basic Studies of Science)*, 7(3): 125-133.

———. 1966. An exploratory cross-cultural study of behavioral components of social attitudes by the behavioral differential methods. *Jap. J. Psychol.*, 37: 104-108.

———. 1967. Cross-cultural compatibility of the affective meaning systems measured by means of multilingual semantic space. *J. soc. Issues*, in press.

———, and IWAMATSU Y. Is Japan's nuclear-weapon ownership thinkable? An exploratory study of the affective and the cognitive components of the attitudes held by Japanese college Ss toward nuclear testings and proliferation. Annenberg School of Communications, University of Pennsylvania, and Department of Politcal Science, Gakushuin University, Tokyo.

———, and OSGOOD, C. E. 1965. Cross-culture, cross-concept, and cross-subject generality of affective meaning systems. *J. pers. soc. Psychol.*, 2: 143-153.

———, OYAMA, T., and OSGOOD, C. E. 1963. A cross-culture and cross-concept study of the generality of semantic spaces. *J. verb. Learn. verb. Behav.*, 2: 392-405.

TANNENBAUM, P. H. 1953. Attitudes toward source and concept as factors in attitude change through communications. Unpublished Ph.D. dissertation, University of Illinois.

———. 1955. What effect when TV covers a congressional hearing? *Journ. Quart.*, 32: 434-440.

———. 1956a. The effect of background music on interpretation of stage and television drama. *Audio-Visual Comm. Rev.*, in press.

———. 1956b. The indexing process in communication. *Pub. Opin. Quart.*, 20: 413-425.

———. 1956c. Initial attitudes toward source and concept as factors in attitude change through communication. *Pub. Opin. Quart.*, 20: 413-425.

———. 1959. Selected applications of the semantic differential. *Pub. opin. Quart.*, 23(3): 435-439.

———. 1966. Mediated generalization of attitude change via the principle of congruity. *J. pers. soc. Psychol.*, 3(5): 493-499.

————, GREENBERG, B. S. and SILVERMAN, F. S. 1961. The great debate: influence on candidates' images. Mass Communication Research Center, University of Wisconsin. (Unpublished study.)

————, and LYNCH, M. D. 1960a. Sensationalism in newspaper and radio wire copy. *Journ. Quart.*, 37: 590-591, 622.

————, ————. 1960b. Sensationalism: the concept and its measurement. *Journ. Quart.*, 37: 381-392.

TATOSSIAN, A., and BLUMEN, G. 1965. Trial application of Osgood's SD to understanding suicidal tendencies. *Cahiers de Psychol.*, 8(2-4): 189-198.

TAYLOR, J. B. 1961. What do attitude scales measure: the problem of social desirability. *J. abnorm. soc. Psychol.*, 62: 386-390.

TAYLOR, J. R., and MANGAN, G. L. 1962. Perceptual learning and verbal meaning. *Percept. mot. Skills*, 14: 223-229.

TAYLOR, R. E. 1961. Extinction following qualitative change in the reinforcing stimulus. *Dissert. Abstr.*, 22(3): 929.

TERWILLIGER, R. F. 1962a. Free association patterns as a factor relating to semantic differential responses. *J. abnorm. soc. Psychol.*, 65: 87-94.

————. 1962b. Social desirability of self-reference statements as a function of free association patterns. *J. abnorm. soc. Psychol.*, 65: 162-169.

THIGPEN, C. H. and CLECKLEY, H. 1954. A case of multiple personality. *J. abnorm. soc. Psychol.*, 49: 135-151.

THOMAS, G. L., and DAVID, R. C. 1959. A study of the effect of audience proximity on persuasion. *Speech Monogr.*, 26: 300-307.

THOMPSON, J. W. 1962. Language, thinking, and electronic machines. *Estratto Rivista Methodes*, 14: 147-152.

————. 1963. Bi-polar and unidirectional scales. *Brit. J. Psychol.*, 54: 15-24.

THURSTONE, L. L. 1931. *Scales for the measurement of social attitudes.* Chicago: University of Chicago Press.

————. 1947. *Multiple-factor analysis.* Chicago: University of Chicago Press.

TOGROL, BEGLAN. 1963. 13-17 Yaslarindaki 100 erkek cocugunum belirli deney sartlarinda kullandiklari sifatlarin Istatiksel alalizi (A statistical analysis of qualifiers used by Turkish male adolescents). *Klinik Symposium*, 6: 418-429.

————. 1967. *Duygusal Anlam sistemleri.* Edebiyat Fakultesi Matbaasi, No. 1220. Istanbul, Turkey: University of Istanbul Publications.

TOLMAN, E. C., and JOHNSON, ISABELLE. 1958. A note on association time feeling. *Amer. J. Psychol.*, 71: 187-195.

TOLOR, A. 1960. The "meaning" of the Bender-Gestalt Test designs: a study in the use of the semantic differential. *J. proj. Tech.*, 24: 433-438.

————, and KISSINGER, R .D. 1965. "The role of the therapist." Interventions in a simulated therapy situation. *J. clin. Psychol.*, 21: 442-445.

TOGERSON, W. S. 1952. Multidimensional scaling: I. theory and method. *Psychometrika*, 17: 401-419.

————. 1961. Scaling and test theory. *Ann. Rev. Psychol.*, 12: 60.

TORRANCE, E., and HARMON, J. A. 1961. Effects of memory evaluative and creative reading sets on test performance. *J. educ. Psychol.*, 52: 207-214.

TRANEL, N. N. 1962. The effects of perceptual isolation of introverts and extraverts. *Dissert. Abstr.*, 23: 726.

TRAUGOTT, N. N., and FADEYEVA, V. K. 1934. The effect of difficult extinction of food-procuring conditioned reflexes upon the general and speech behavior of children [trans. from Russian title]. *Psychol. Abstracts*, 9, No. 1167.

TRIANDIS, H. C. 1958. Some cognitive factors affecting communication. Unpublished Ph.D. dissertation, Cornell University.

————. 1959a. Categories of thought of managers, clerks, and workers about jobs and people in industry. *J. appl. Psychol.*, 43: 338-344.

————. 1959b. Cognitive similarity and interpersonal communication in industry. *J. appl. Psychol.*, 43: 321-326.

————. 1959c. Differential perception of certain jobs and people by managers, clerks, and workers in industry. *J. appl. Psychol.*, 43: 221-225.

————. 1959d. Similarity in thought processes and boss-employee communication. In Peter Holis (Ed.), *Communication in organizations: some new research findings.* Ann Arbor: Foundation for Research in Human Behavior.

————. 1960a. Cognitive similarity and the communication of the dyad. *Human Relations,* 13: 175-183.

————. 1960b. A comparative factorial analysis of job semantic structures of managers and workers. *J. appl. Psychol.*, 44: 297-302.

————. 1960c. Some determinants of interpersonal communication. *Hum. Relat.*, 13: 279-286.

————. 1964a. Cultural influences upon cognitive processes. In L. Berkowitz (Ed.), *Advances in experimental social psychology.* New York: Academic Press.

————. 1964b. Exploratory factor analysis of the behavioral component of social attitude. *J. abnorm. soc. Psychol.*, 68: 420-430.

————, and FISHBEIN, M. 1963. Cognitive interaction in person perception. *J. abnorm. soc. Psychol.*, 67: 446-453.

————, and OSGOOD, C. E. 1958. A comparative factorial analysis of semantic structures in monolingual Greek and American college students. *J. abnorm. soc. Psychol.*, 57: 187-196.

————, and TRIANDIS, L. M. 1962. A cross-culture study of social distance. *Psychol. Monogr.*, 76, No. 21. (Whole No. 540.)

TUCKER, L. R. Some mathematical notes on three-mode factor analysis. *Psychometrika,* 31(3): 279-311.

————, and MESSICK, S. J. 1960. Individual differences in multidimensional scaling. Princeton, N.J.: Educational Testing Service. (Mimeo.)

TUCKER, W. T. 1955. Experiments in aesthetic communications. Unpublished Ph.D. dissertation, University of Illinois.

————. 1961. How much of the corporate image is stereotype? *J. Marketing,* 25: 61-65.

ULDALL, ELIZABETH. 1960. Attitudinal meanings conveyed by intonal contours. *Lang. Speech,* 3: 223-234.

UMEMOTO, T. 1962. Paired-associate learning as a function of similarity: semantic similarity between stimulus-and response-items. *J. Amer. Psychol.*, 75: 85-93.

VAN DE GEER, J. P., and JASPARS, J. M. 1966. Cognitive functions. *Ann. Rev. Psychol.*, 17: 154-155.

————, LEVELT, W. J., and PLOMP, R. 1962. The connotation of musical consonance. Report IZF No. 4, Institute for perception RVO-TNO, Soesterberg, The Netherlands.

VASTENHOUW, J. 1961. *Relationships between meanings.* The Hauge: Mouton.

VIELHALER, D. P., and GOTTHEIL, E. 1965. First impressions and subsequent ratings of performance. *Psychol. Reps.*, 17: 916.

VOIERS, W. D. 1964. Perceptual bases of speaker identity. *J. acoustical soc. Amer.*, 36(6).

VORYS, KARL VON. 1959. The legislator in underdeveloped countries. *PROD.* 3(3): 22-26.

VOSS, J. F., THOMPSON, C. D., and KEEGAN, J. H. 1959. Acquisition of probabilistic paired associates as a function of S-R, S-R probability. *J. exp. Psychol.*, 58: 390-399.

WAGNER, C. 1966. Expectation and attractiveness of group membership as functions of task difficulty and magnitude of reward. *Psychol. Reps.*, 18: 471-482.

WALKER, L. 1962. A concept formation analogue of attitude development. *Dissert. Abstr.*, 22: 2482-2483.

WARE, E. E. 1959. Relationships of intelligence and sex to diversity of individual semantic meaning spaces. *Dissert. Abstr.*, 19: 3016.

WARR, P. B., and KNAPPER, C. 1965. Some factors affecting the reliability and validity of semantic differential scales. Based on paper read to British Psychological Society, Aberdeen, Scotland, April.

———, ———. 1966. The relative importance of verbal and visual information in indirect person perception. *Brit. J. soc. clin. Psychol.*, 5: 118-127.

WARREN, W. B., MATHENY, A., and LARSON, G. 1963. Eye movements as a paradigm of approach and avoidance behavior. *Percept. mot. Skills*, 16: 341-347.

WATANHE, H., ISHIGE, N., KASHIWAGI, S., OCHIAI, H., and TANAKA, T. 1959. The study to cognitive structure in human relations—a trial by semantic differential techniques. Labor Science Research Office, Japan National Railways. (Mimeo., Japanese.)

WATT, N. F., and FISHER, H. The assessment of semantic meaning: a tentative rationale. Zurich. Forschungsstelle fur Arbulspsychologie (Swiss Federal Institute of Technology).

WEAVER, C. H. 1957. Measuring the point of view as a barrier to communication. *J. comm.*, 7: 5-9.

———. 1958. The quantification of the frame of reference in labor management communication. *J. appl. Psychol.*, 42: 1-9.

WEAVER, C. J. 1959. Semantic distance between students and teachers and its effects upon learning. *Speech Monogr.*, 26: 273-281.

WEBB, A. P., and HARRIS, J. T. 1963. A semantic differential study of counselors in an NDEA Institute. *Personnel guid.* J. 42: 260-263.

WEBB, W. W. 1963. Premorbid adjustment and the perception of meaning. *Percept. mot. Skills*, 17: 762.

WEBSTER, H. 1952. A note on profile similarity. *Psychol. Bull.*, 49: 538-539.

WEED, CAROL L. 1967. A cross-linguistic and developmental study of the connotations of gender. Berkeley: University of California Press.

WEIMA, J. 1966. About the independence of a "religious" factor in the application of the semantic differential technique. *Soc. Compass*, 8(2): 151-157.

WEINREICH, U. 1958. Travel through semantic space. *Word*, 14: 346-366.

———. 1959. A rejoinder (Osgood, C. E., Semantic space revisited [*Word*, 1959, 15: 192-200]). *Word*, 15: 200-201.

WEISS, EDWARD A., and COMPANY. 1955. A manual on the semantic differential. Chicago: The authors.

WEISS, J. H.. 1963. Role of "meaningfulness" versus meaning dimensions in guessing the meanings of foreign words. *J. abnorm. soc. Psychol.*, 66: 541-546.

———. 1966. A study of the ability of English speakers to guess the meanings of nonantonym foreign words. *J. gen. Psychol.*, 74(1): 97-106.

———, GOLDFRIED, M. R., and BAYROFF, I. 1965. The level of hypothesis and the study of stimulus value of projective test items. *J. proj. tech. pers. Asses.*, 29(4): 445-453.

WEISS, W., and LIEBERMAN, B. 1959. The effects of "emotional" language on the induction and change of opinions. *J. soc. Psychol.*, 50: 129-141.

———, and MARGOLIUS, G. 1954. The effect of context stimuli on learning and retention. *J. exp. Psychol.*, 48: 318-322.

WEITZENHOFFER, A. M. 1951. Mathematical structures and psychological measurements. *Psychometrika*, 16: 387-406.

WEKSEL, W., and HENNES, J. D. 1965. Attitude intensity and the semantic differential. *J. pers. soc. Psychol.*, 2(1): 91-94.

WELLMAN, C. 1961. *Language and ethics.* Cambridge, Mass.: Harvard University Press.

WELLS, R. 1957. A mathematical approach to meaning. *Cahiers Ferdinand de Saussuve*, 15: 117-136.

WELLS, W. D. 1958. A change in a product image. *J. appl. Psychol.*, 42(2): 120-121.

———, and SMITH, GEORGIANNA. 1960. Four semantic rating scales compared. *J. appl. Psychol.*, 44: 393-397.

WERNER, H. 1954. Change of meaning: a study of semantic processes through the experimental method. *J. gen. Psychol.*, 50: 181-208.

————, and KAPLAN, EDITH. 1950. Development of word meaning through verbal context: an experimental study. *J. Psychol.*, 29: 251-257.

WERTHEIMER, M. 1958. The relation between the sound of a word and its meaning. *Amer. J. Psychol.*, 71: 412-415.

WETZEL, R. J. The effect of a marriage course on the personality characteristics of students. *Dissert. Abstr.*, 63: 1833.

WHELAN, R. J. 1966. Semantic differential behavior of normal and emotionally disturbed school age males. *Dissert. Abstr.*, 27(6-A): 1677-1678. (*Psych. Abstracts,* June 1967, p. 7868.)

WHISLER, L. D. 1957. A study of the descriptive validity of activity vector analysis. *J. Psychol.*, 43: 205-225.

WHITE, W. F., and ANDERSON, H. E., JR. 1967. A study of scaled dimensions of teacher behavior as perceived by students. *J. Psychol.*, 65(2): 223-232.

WHITMARSH, G. A. 1962. A comparative study of two theories of verbal generalization. *Dissert. Abstr,.* 22: 2890-2891.

WIENER, D. N., and EHRLICH, D. 1960. Goals and values. *Amer. J. Psychol.*, 73: 615-617.

WIEST, W. M. 1965. A quantitative extension of Heider's theory of cognitive balance applied to interpersonal perception and self-esteem. *Psychol. Monogr.*, 79, No. 14. (Whole No. 607.)

WIGGINS, NANCY, and FISHBEIN, M. 1967. Dimensions of semantic space: a problem of individual differences. Paper presented at the Midwest Psychological Association, Chicago, May. Urbana: Institute of Communications Research, University of Illinois. (Submitted for publication.)

WILCOX, R. C. 1966. Effects of context on semantic differential ratings. *Psychol. Reps.*, 18: 873-874.

WILLIAMS, J. E 1964. Connotations of color names among Negros and Caucasians. *Percept. mot. Skills*, 18: 721-731.

————. 1966. Connotations of racial concepts and color names. *J. pers. soc. Psychol.*, 3: 531-540.

WILLIS, F. N. 1961. The movement interpretation of threat and level of self-acceptance. *Dissert. Abst.*, 22: 1719.

WILLIS, R. H. 1962. East and West as seen from Finland. Washington University. Paper presented at the American Psychological Association Convention, St. Louis, August.

WILLOUGHBY, P. V. 1964. Viewer evaluation of ten randomly selected colors according to six pairs of bipolar adjectives. Master's thesis. *Journ. abstr.*, 2: 142-143.

WILSON, K. 1954. Multidimensional scaling of data obtained by method of triads. Urbana: Control Systems Laboratory, University of Illinois. (Mimeo.)

WIMER, CYNTHIA C. 1961. Meaningfulness, similarity, and paired-associate learning. *Dissert. Abstr.*, 22: 1728.

————. 1963. An analysis of semantic stimulus factors in paired associate learning. *J. verb. Learn. verb. Behav.*, 1: 397-407.

————, and LAMBERT, W. E. 1959. The differential effects of word and object stimuli on the learning of paired associates. *J. exp. Psychol.*, 57: 31-36.

WINOGRAD, E. 1966. Recognition memory and recall as a function of degree of polarization on the semantic differential. *J. verb. Learn. verb. Behav.*, 5: 566-571.

WINTER, D. G., ALPERT, R., and McCLELLAND, D. C. 1963. The classic personal style. *J. abnorm. soc. Psychol.*, 67: 254-265.

WINTER, W. D. 1961. Values and achievement in a freshman psychology course. *J. educ. Res.*, 54: 183-186.

WIRT, R. D., and WIRT, A. L. 1961. Discussion of Howes and Pope study on therapists ratings of other therapists. *Ann. Rev. Psychol.*, 14: 376.

WISHNER, J. 1960. Reanalysis of "impressions of personality." *Psychol. Rev.*, 67(2): 96-112.

WITT, E. L. 1966. The connotative meaning of selected "forced" Rorschach percepts as measured by the semantic differential technique. Master's thesis, University of Houston. *Dissert. Abstr.*, 27(7): 4083-4084.

WITTROCK, M. C. 1964. The connotative meaning of concepts, teachers and children. *Calif. J. Ed. Res.*, 15: 60-67.

WODTKE, KOHO, et. al. 1963. Patterns of needs as predictors of classroom behavior of teachers. *Educ. psychol. Measmt.*, 23: 569-577.

WOHL, J. 1957. A note on the generality of constriction. *J. proj. Tech.*, 21: 410-413.

WOLFINGER, R. E. 1955. Attitude change toward source and issue resulting from one-sided and two-sided communication. Unpublished master's thesis, University of Illinois.

WORTH, S. Cognitive aspects of sequence in visual communication. Annenberg School of Communications, University of Pennsylvania. (Manuscript)

WOZNIAK, D. F. 1964. A factor analytic study of semantic structure of closed, open, and medium belief-disbelief systems. *Journ. Abstr.*, 2: 40-41.

WRIGHT, B. 1958. A semantic differential and how to use it. Chicago: Social Research, Inc.

―――, and RAINWATER, L. 1962. The meanings of color. *J. gen. Psychol.*, 67: 89-99.

WRIGHTSMAN, L. S., JR. 1962. Dimensionalism of attitudes toward the Negro. *Psychol. Reps.*, 11: 439-448.

WRIGLEY, C., and McQUITTY, L. L. 1953. The square root method of factor analysis. Department of Psychology, University of Illinois. (Mimeo.)

―――, and NEUHAUS, J. O. 1955. The matching of the two sets of factors. Contract Memorandum Report A-22. University of Illinois.

WYLIE, RUTH. *The self concept.* Lincoln: University of Nebraska Press.

YAVUZ, H. S. 1963. The retention of incidentally learned connotative responses. *J. Psychol.*, 55: 409-418.

―――, and BOUSFIELD, W. A. 1959. Recall of connotative meaning. *Psychol. Reps.*, 5: 319-320.

YELEN, D. R., and SCHULZ, R. W. 1963. Verbal satiation? *J. verb. Learn. verb. Behav.*, 1: 372-377.

YOSHIDA, M. 1962. Psychometric analysis of fabric handle. *Hiushitsu Kauri* (*Quality Control*), 13(10): 106-111.

―――. 1963a. Dimensions of tactual impressions. *J. Jap. Women's Univer.*, 13: 47-68.

―――. 1963b. Psychometric analysis of fabric handle (II). *Hiushitsu Kauri* (*Quality Control*), 14(10): 68-74.

―――. 1963c. Similarity among different kinds of taste near the threshold concentration. *Jap. J. Psychol.*, 34: 25-35, (Abstract in English)

―――. 1964a. Structure of preference. *Hiushitsu Kauri* (*Quality Control*), 15(10): 80-86.

―――. 1964b. Studies in psychometric classification of odors (4). *Jap. Psychol. Res.*, 6(3): 115-124.

―――. 1964c. Studies of psychometric classification of odors (5). *Jap. Psychol. Res.*, 6(4): 145-154.

YOUNG, R. K., and UNDERWOOD, B. J. 1954. Transfer in verbal materials with dissimilar stimuli and response similarity varied. *J. exp. Psychol.*, 47: 153-159.

YOUSSEF, Z. I., and SALTZ, E. 1963. The semantic differential as a measure of individual differences in mediated generalization. *J. verb. Learn. verb. Behav.*, 1: 397-407.

ZAKHOUR, I. Y., and SALTZ, E. 1964. The semantic differential as a measure of individual differences in mediated generalization. *J. verb. Learn. verb. Behav.*, 3: 226-230.

ZALTMAN, G. 1965. *Marketing: contributions from the behavioral sciences.* New York: Harcourt, Brace.

ZAMANSKY, H. S., and BRIGHTBILL, R. F. 1965. Attitude differences of volunteers and non-volunteers and of susceptible and non-susceptible hypnotic subjects. *Int. J. clin. exp. Hypnosis*, 13(4): 279-290.

Zax, M., Gardiner, D. H., and Lowy, D. G. 1964. Extreme response tendency as a function of emotional adjustment. *J. abnorm. soc. Psychol.*, 69: 654-657.

———, and Louiselle, R. M. 1960a. The influence of card order on the stimulus value of the Rorschach inkblots. *J. proj. Tech.*, 24: 218-221.

———, ———. 1960b. Stimulus values of Rorschach inkblots as measured by the semantic differential. *J. clin. Psychol.*, 16: 160-63.

———, ———, and Karras, A. 1960. Stimulus characteristics of Rorschach inkblots as perceived by a schizophrenic sample. *J. proj. Tech.*, 24: 439-443.

———, and Takahashi, S. 1967. Cultural influences on response style: comparisons of Japanese and American college students. *J. soc. Psychol.*, 71(1): 3-10.

Zippel, B. 1967. Semantic differential measures of meaningfulness and agreement of meaning. *J. verb. Learn. verb. Behav.*, 6(2): 222-225.

Ziskin, J. H. 1964. An effect of verbal conditioning on nonverbal behavior. *Dissert. Abstr.*, 25: 2039.

Zukerman, M., and Eisen, B. 1962. Relationship of acquiescence response set to authoritarianism and dependency. *Psychol. Reps.*, 10(1): 94-102.

Index